The Little,
Brown Reader

Eighth Edition

The Little, Brown Reader

Marcia Stubbs
Wellesley College

Sylvan Barnet
Tufts University

 LONGMAN

An Imprint of Addison Wesley Longman, Inc.

New York • Reading, Massachusetts • Menlo Park, California • Harlow, England
Don Mills, Ontario • Sydney • Mexico City • Madrid • Amsterdam

Acquisitions Editor: Lynn Huddon
Supplements Editor: Donna Campion
Marketing Manager: Renee Ortbals
Project Manager: Dora Rizzuto
Design Manager and Cover Designer: Rubina Yeh
Electronic Production Specialist: Sarah Johnson
Senior Print Buyer: Hugh Crawford
Electronic Page Makeup: Allentown Digital Services
Printer and Binder: Quebecor
Cover Printer: Coral Graphics
Cover Photos: front (left to right): *Amy Tan:* Reed Schumann/Reuters/Corbis;
  Martin Luther King, Jr.: Globe Photos Inc.; *Virginia Woolf:* AP/Wide World Photos;
  John Updike: AP/Wide World Photos; back (left to right): *Robert Frost:* AP/Wide World
  Photos; *Eudora Welty:* AP/Wide World Photos; *Maya Angelou:* AP/Wide World Photos;
  Richard Rodriguez: Brit Thurston/Georges Borchardt, Inc.

For permission to use copyrighted material, grateful acknowledgment is made to the
copyright holders on pages 879–885, which are hereby made part of this copyright page.

Library of Congress Cataloging-in-Publication Data

The Little, Brown reader / edited by Marcia Stubbs, Sylvan Barnet. —
    8th ed.
        p.   cm.
    Includes index.
    ISBN 0-321-02401-X
    1. College readers.   2. English language—Rhetoric Problems,
exercises, etc.   3. Report writing Problems, exercises, etc.
I. Stubbs, Marcia.   II. Barnet, Sylvan.
PE1417.L644   1999   99-36899
808'.0427—dc21   CIP

Please visit our Web site at
http://www.awlonline.com/littlebrown

ISBN 0-321-02401-X

12345678910—ARF—02010099

BRIEF CONTENTS

CONTENTS

3 Academic Writing 43

4 Writing an Argument 63

5 Reading and Writing about Pictures   91

6 Memoirs: Discovering the Past   111

7 All in the Family   173

*Fiction

*Fiction
**Poetry

8 Identities   259

*Fiction
**Poetry

9 Teaching and Learning   353

10 Work and Play   465

Illustrations

*Fiction

11 Messages   549

**Poetry

12 Art and Life   621

Illustrations

**Poetry

Short Views   626

Théophile Gautier, Samuel Butler, George Sand, Holbrook Jackson, Lady Murasaki, Lillian Hellman, Willa Cather, Grace Paley, Ezra Pound, Flannery O'Connor, Anonymous, Miles Davis, Mahalia Jackson, George Eliot, Ansel Adams, Leonardo da Vinci, Grandma Moses, Agnes de Mille, Twyla Tharp

*Fiction
**Poetry

13 Law and Order   677

**Poetry

*Fiction

15 Classic Essays   807

**Poetry

RHETORICAL TABLE
OF CONTENTS

Analogy

Analysis

Argument

Description

Diction

Evaluation

Exposition

Irony

Narration

Style

PREFACE

Books have been put to all sorts of unexpected uses. Tolstoy used Tatishef's dictionaries as a test of physical endurance, holding them in his outstretched hand for five minutes, enduring "terrible pain." Books (especially pocket-sized Bibles) have served as armor by deflecting bullets. And they have served as weapons: two hundred years ago the formidable Dr. Johnson knocked a man down with a large book.

In a course in writing, what is the proper use of the book in hand? This anthology contains some one hundred and thirty essays, together with a few poems, stories, and fables, and numerous "Short Views," that is, paragraphs and aphorisms. But these readings are not the subject matter of the course; the subject matter of a writing course is writing, particularly the writing the students themselves produce. The responsibilities we felt as editors, then, were to include selections that encourage and enable students to write well, and to exclude selections that do not.

To talk of "enabling" first: Students, like all other writers, write best when they write on fairly specific topics that can come within their experience and within their command in the time that they have available to write. A glance at our table of contents will reveal the general areas within which, we believe, students can find topics they have already given some thought to and are likely to be encountering in other courses as well: family relationships, love and courtship; schools; work, sports, and play.

Although other sections ("Messages" and "Art and Life") are also on familiar subjects—language, art, and popular culture—the selections themselves offer ways of thinking about these subjects that may be less familiar. Television commercials and films, for example, can be thought of as networks that articulate and transmit values implicit in a culture.

Other sections are about areas of experience that, while hardly remote from students' interest, are perhaps more difficult for all of us to grasp concretely: the tension between civil rights and liberties and the need for law and order; matters of gender and ethnic identity; prophecies about the future. In these sections, therefore, we have taken particular care to exclude writing that is, for our purposes, too abstract, or too technical, or too elaborate. Finally, we conclude with "Classic Essays," ranging from Jonathan Swift to Martin Luther King, Jr.

As editors we have tried to think carefully about whether selections we were inclined to use—because they were beautifully written or on a stimulating topic—would encourage students to write. Such encouragement does not come, we feel, solely from the subject of an essay or from its excellence; it comes when the essay engenders in the reader a confidence in the writing process itself. No one quality in essays automatically teaches such confidence: not length or brevity, not difficulty or simplicity, not necessarily clarity, and almost certainly not brilliance. But essays that teach writing demonstrate, in some way, that the writers had some stake in what they were saying, took some pains to say what they meant, and took pleasure in having said it. The selections we include vary in length, complexity, subtlety, tone, and purpose. Most were written by our contemporaries, but not all. The authors include historians, sociologists, scientists, saints, philosophers, and undergraduates, as well as journalists and other professional writers. And we have included some pictures in each section. The pictures (beautiful things in themselves, we think) provide immediate or nearly immediate experiences for students to write about. But we hope that everything here will allow students to establish helpful connections between the activities that produced the words (and pictures) in these pages and their own work in putting critical responses to them on paper.

Although any arrangement of the selections—thematic, rhetorical, alphabetical, chronological, or random—would have suited our purposes, we prefer the thematic arrangement. For one thing, by narrowing our choices it helped us to make decisions. But more important, we know that in the real world what people write about is subjects, and we don't want to miss any opportunity to suggest that what goes on in writing courses is something like what goes on outside. The thematic categories are not intended to be rigid, however, and they do not pretend to be comprehensive; some of the questions following the selections suggest that leaping across boundaries is permitted, even encouraged. And, for instructors who prefer to organize their writing course rhetorically, we have added a selective table of contents organized rhetorically. Finally, we append a glossary of terms for students of writing.

What's New in the Eighth Edition?

William Hazlitt said that he always read an old book when a new one was published. We hope that this new edition allows instructors to read both at once. We have of course retained those essays and the special features (for example the head notes and the Topics for Critical Thinking and Writing at the end of each essay) that in our experience and the experience of many colleagues have consistently been of value to instructors and to students. But guided by suggestions from users of the seventh edition we have made many changes and additions. In the first five chapters devoted to reading and writing, users will find additional sections on

- Critical Thinking
- Tone and Persona
- Summarizing and Outlining
- Academic Writing
- Interviewing
- Negotiating Agreements (Rogerian Argument)

and several new essays by students. The increased emphasis on argument has led us to include several letters responding to published essays. The reader will also find a new checklist, so that we now provide

✓ A Checklist for Analyzing and Evaluating an Essay That You Are Writing About

✓ A Checklist for Editing: Thirteen Questions to Ask Yourself

✓ A Checklist for Rogerian Argument

✓ A Checklist for Revising Drafts of Arguments

We have also added two new sections of readings:

- Memoirs: Discovering the Past
- The Millennium

and there are new essays in every section. Some of the additions are in casebooks:

- A Casebook on Divorce
- A Casebook on Race
- A Casebook on Computers in the Schools
- A Casebook on Crime
- A Casebook on Cloning

Acknowledgments

As usual, we are indebted to readers-in-residence. Morton Berman, William Burto, and Judith Stubbs have often read our material and then told us what we wanted to hear.

We are grateful also to colleagues at other institutions who offered suggestions for the eighth edition:

Dr. James Barcus, Baylor University; Linda Bensel-Meyers, The University of Tennessee; David Daniel, Newbury College; Theresa Enos, University of Arizona; Carol Franks, Portland State University; Susan Halter, Delgado Community College; Karen Hattaway, San Jacinto College North; Michael Hennessy, Southwestern Texas University; Kathleen Nulton Kemmerer,

Pennsylvania State University, Hazleton; David Magill, University of Kentucky; Marjorie Peoples-McDonald, University of Maryland, Eastern Shore; Sarah Quirk, Northern Illinois University; Gerald Richman, Suffolk University; Catherine Smith, Syracuse University.

We thank those instructors who generously offered suggestions based on their classroom experience with the first seven editions: Bonnie Alexander, Kenneth Alrutz, Marianne Antczack, Norman Sidney Ashbridge, Andrew Aung, Donald Babcock, Betty Bamberg, James Barcus, Lloyd Becker, Frank Bidart, Joseph Blimm, Frank Bliss, Beverly Boone, Grant Boswell, George Branam, Peggy F. Broder, Eric D. Brown, Lillian Broderick, Ruth Brown, Jean Young Brunk, Beth Burch, Debra L. Burgauet, Anne Burley, Carol Burns, D. G. Campbell, Domenick Caruso, J. V. Chambers, Benjamin A. L. Click III, John Clifford, Ann Connor, Anne Cooney, Kenneth Cooney, Marion Copeland, Robert Cosgrove, Helene Davis, Geraldine DeLuca, Donald DeSulis, William Devlin, John A. R. Dick, Fiona Emde, Robert Erickson, Richard Fahey, Evelyn Farbman, Michael Feehan, Linda Feldmeier, Gretchen Fillmore, Sister Jeremy Finnegan, Kathleen P. Flint, Martha Flint, William Ford, Joseph S. Frany, James French, Charles Frey, Yvonne Frey, David Gadziola, Joanna Gibson, Shelby Grantham, George Griffith, George D. Haich, Steve Hamelman, Bettina Hanlon, Brian O. Hannon, Douglas Hesse, Hymen H. Hart, Pat Hart, Steven Harvey, Mal Haslett, Stephen Hathaway, Mark Hawkins, George Hayhoe, Zelda Hedden-Sellman, Ruth C. Hage, Kathryn Hellerstein, Dr. Elbert R. Hill, Maureen Hoal, David Hoddeson, Kathryn Holms, John Howe, William Howrath, Morris Husted, Lois B. Janzer, Johanna Jung, F. A. Kachur, Michael Kalter, Cynthia Lee Katona, Robert D. Keohan, Richard Kirchoffer, Walt Klarner, Robert Knox, Karl Kumm, Sandra M. Lee, Dorinda Lemaire, Claudia Limbert, Joyce D. Lipkis, William E. Lucas, Robert F. Lucid, William Lutz, Celia Martin, Cecelia Martyn, Marie M. McAllister, Anne McCormich, Charles McLaughlin, Garry Meritt, George Miller, Lori Ann Miller, John Milstead, Mary F. Minton, Michael G. Moran, Chris M. Mott, Abigail Mulcahy, John Nesselhof, Robert Ohafson, Terry Otten, Jewyl Pallette, Linda Pelzer, Richard Prince, Richard Priebe, Thomas E. Recchio, Phyllis Reed, Karyn Riedell, William E. Rivers, Leo Rockas, Duncan Rollo, Harriet Rosenblum, Ronald Ruland, Ralph St. Louis, Jack Selzer, Don Share, Mary Shesgreen, Emerson Shuck, Carol Sicherman, James Smith, Larry Smith, Mark Smith, Ronald E. Smith, Harry Solomon, John Stahl, Judith Stanford, Carol Starikoff, Petra Steele, William B. Stone, Mary Lee Strode, William L. Stull, Tereatha Taylor, David Templeman, Elizabeth Tentarelli, Robert Thompson, Leatrice Timmons, Pamela Topping, Marilyn Valention, Carla J. Valley, J. Keith Veizer, Harvey Vetstein, Brother Roland Vigeant, Lorraine Viscardi, Anthony Vital, Carolyn Wall, Don Wall, Doug Watson, Mary Weinkauf, Mark Wenz,

Michael West, Richard Whitworth, Lyn Yonack, Lee Yosha, Thomas Young, and Richard J. Zbaracki.

We owe a special debt to Professor John Harwood and other teachers in the composition program at Pennsylvania State University for suggesting ways in which *The Little, Brown Reader* can be used in a course that emphasizes persuasive writing.

People at Longman have been unfailingly helpful; we would especially like to thank Lynn Huddon, Dora Rizzuto, Rubina Yeh, Sarah Johnson, and Thomas Farrell.

We are indebted to Caroline Gloodt, who effectively handled the difficult job of obtaining permission for copyrighted material.

MARCIA STUBBS
SYLVAN BARNET

SELECTED RESOURCES FOR TEACHERS AND STUDENTS

- An updated Instructor's Manual, *Teaching The Little Brown Reader*, is available to adopters of this edition.
- In conjunction with Penguin Putnam, Inc., Longman is proud to introduce "The Penguin Program." This program allows us to offer a wide variety of Penguin titles at a significant discount when they're packaged with any Longman title. Popular titles include Mike Rose's *Lives on the Boundary* and *Possible Lives*, and Neil Postman's *Amusing Ourselves to Death*.
- *Researching Online, 3/e,* by David Munger, gives students detailed, step-by-step instructions for performing electronic searches, using e-mail, listservs, Usenet newsgroups, IRCs, and MU*s to do research, and assessing the validity of electronic sources.
- *The Essential Research Guide* is a two-page, handy laminated card, featuring guidelines for evaluating different kinds of print and on-line sources, a list of editing and proofreading symbols, and a list of cross-curricular web site resources.
- *Daedalus Online* is the next generation of the highly awarded Daedalus Integrated Writing Environment (DIWE). This web-based writing environment allows students to explore online resources, employ pre-writing strategies, share ideas in real-time conferences, and post feedback to an asynchronous discussion board. *Daedalus Online* also offers instructors a suite of interactive management tools to guide and facilitate their students' interaction. Specifically, instructors can:
    - Effortlessly create and post assignments;
    - Link these assignments to online educational resources;
    - Tie these lessons to selected Longman textbooks;
    - Customize materials to fit with any instructional preference.
- *The English Pages* website at ⟨http://www.awlonline.com/englishpages⟩ provides instructors and students with continuously updated resources for reading, writing, and research practice in four areas: Composition, Literature, Technical Writing, and Basic Skills.

1
A WRITER READS

One reads well only when one reads with some personal goal in mind. It may be to acquire some power. It may be out of hatred for the author.

Paul Valéry

Good writers are also good readers—of the works of other writers and of their own notes and drafts. The habits they develop as readers of others—for instance evaluating assumptions, scrutinizing arguments, and perceiving irony—empower them when they write, read, and revise their own notes and drafts. Because they themselves are readers, when they write they have a built-in awareness of how their readers might respond. They can imagine an audience, and they write almost as if in dialogue with it.

Active reading (which is what we are describing) involves writing at the outset: annotating a text by highlighting or underlining key terms, putting question marks or brief responses in the margin, writing notes in a journal. Such reading, as you already may have experienced, helps you first of all to understand a text, to get clear what the writer seems to intend. Later, skimming your own notes will help you to recall what you have read.

But active reading also gives you confidence as a writer. It helps you to treat your own drafts with the same respect and disrespect with which you read the work of others. To annotate a text or a draft is to respect it enough to give it serious attention, but it is also to question it, to assume that the text or draft is not the last word on the topic.

But let's start at the beginning.

Previewing

By *previewing* we mean getting a tentative fix on a text before reading it closely.

If you know something about the **author,** you probably already know something about a work even before you read the first paragraph. An essay by Martin Luther King Jr. will almost surely be a deeply serious discussion centering on civil rights, and, since King was a Baptist clergyman, it is likely to draw on traditional religious values. An essay by Woody Allen or one by Annie Dillard will almost surely differ from King's in topic and tone. Allen usually writes about the arts, especially the art of film, and Dillard writes highly personal meditations, often on the sacredness of nature. All three writers are serious (though Allen also writes comic pieces), but they are serious about different things and serious in different ways. We can read all three with interest, but when we begin with any one of them, we know we will get something very different from the other two.

King, Allen, and Dillard are exceptionally well known, but you can learn something about all of the authors represented in *The Little, Brown Reader* because they are introduced by means of biographical notes. Make it a practice to read these notes. They will give you some sense of what to expect. You may never have heard, for example, of J. H. Plumb—we include one of his essays later in this chapter—but when you learn from the note that he was a professor of history at the University of Cambridge and that he also taught in U. S. universities, you can tentatively assume that the essay will have an historical dimension. Of course, you may have to revise this assumption—the essay may be about the joys of trout fishing or the sorrows of being orphaned at an early age—but in all probability the biographical note will have given you some preparation for reading the essay.

The **original organ of publication** may also give you some sense of what the piece will be about. The essays in *The Little, Brown Reader* originally were published in books, magazines, or newspapers, and these sources (specified, when relevant, in the biographical notes) may in themselves provide a reader with clues. For instance, since *The American Scholar* is published by Phi Beta Kappa and is read chiefly by college and university teachers or by persons with comparable education, articles in *The American Scholar* usually offer somewhat academic treatments of serious matters. They assume that the readers are serious and capable of sustained intellectual effort. Whereas a newspaper editorial runs about one thousand words, articles in *The American Scholar* may be fifteen or so pages long.

Some journals have an obvious political slant, and the articles they publish are to some degree predictable in content and attitude. For instance, William Buckley's *National Review* is politically conservative. Its subscribers want to hear certain things, and *National Review* tells them what they want to hear. Its readers know, too, that the essays will be lively and can be read fairly rapidly. Similarly, subscribers to *Ms.* expect highly readable essays with a strong feminist slant.

The **form,** or **genre** (a literary term for type or kind of literature), may provide another clue as to what will follow. For instance, you can expect a letter to the editor to amplify or contradict an editorial or to comment approvingly or disapprovingly on some published news item. It will almost surely be concerned with a current issue. Martin Luther King Jr.'s "Letter from Birmingham Jail," a response to a letter from eight clergymen, is a famous example of a letter arguing on behalf of what was then a current action.

The **title,** as we have already noted, may provide a clue. Again, King provides an example; even before studying "I Have a Dream," a reader can assume that the essay will be about King's vision of the future. Another example of a title that announces its topic is "We Have No 'Right to Happiness.'" This title is straightforward and informative, but suppose you pick up an essay called "Do-It-Yourself Brain Surgery." What do you already know about the essay?

Skimming

"Some books are to be tasted, others to be swallowed, and some few to be chewed and digested." You may already have encountered this wise remark by Francis Bacon, a very good reader (and a good writer, too—though he did not write Shakespeare's plays). The art of reading includes the art of skimming, that is, the art of gliding rapidly over a piece of writing and getting its gist.

Skimming has three important uses: to get through junk mail and other lightweight stuff; to locate what is relevant to your purpose in a mass of material, as, for instance, when you are working on a research paper; and (our topic now) to get an overview of an essay, especially to get the gist of its argument. Having discovered what you can from the name of the author, the title of the work, and the place of publication, you may want to skim the essay before reading it closely.

The **opening paragraph** will often give you a good idea of the **topic** or general area of the essay (for instance, the family). And if the essay is essentially an argument, it may announce the writer's **thesis,** the point that the writer will argue (for instance, that despite the high divorce rate, the family is still in good shape). Here is an example from J. H. Plumb's "The Dying Family." (The entire essay is printed later in this chapter.)

> I was rather astonished when a minibus drove up to my house and out poured ten children. They had with them two parents, but not one child had them both in common as mother and father, and two of them belonged to neither parent, but to a former husband of the wife who had died. Both parents, well into middle ages, had just embarked, one on his fourth, the other on her third marriage. The children, who came in all sizes, and ranged from blonde nordic to jet-haired Greek, bounded around the garden, young and old as happy as any children that I have ever seen. To them, as Californians, their situation was not particularly odd; most of their friends had multiple parents. Indeed to them perhaps the odd family was the one which Western culture has held up as am model for two thousand years or more—the life-long union of man and wife. But it took me a very long time to believe that they could be either happy or adjusted. And yet, were they a sign of the future, a way the world was going?

Taking into account the author's profession (an historian), the title ("The Dying Family"), and the first paragraph, a reader assumes that the essay probably will examine the new the new family in relation to the tradition Western model. A reader probably also assumes, on the basis of the first paragraph, that Plumb will not go on to scold this California family; we can't of course be certain of his position, but thus far he seems willing to grant that the family may really be happy.

If the title and first paragraph do not seem especially informative (the first paragraph may be a sort of warmup, akin to the speech maker's "A funny thing happened to me on my way here"), look closely at the second. Then, as you scan subsequent paragraphs, look especially for **topic sentences** (often the first sentence in a paragraph), which summarize the paragraph, and look for passages that follow **key phrases** such as "the important point to remember," "these two arguments can be briefly put thus," "in short," "it is essential to recall," and so on. Plumb's third paragraph, for instance, begins thus:

> Basically the family has fulfilled three social functions—to provide a basic labor force, to transmit property and to educate and train children not only into an accepted social pattern, but also in the work skills upon which their future subsistence would depend.

Not surprisingly, Plumb goes on to amplify—to support with details—these assertions, and you won't be wrong if you guess that later in the essay he will indicate that a change in historical conditions has changed the role of the family.

In skimming an essay, pay special attention to the **final paragraph,** which usually reformulates the writer's thesis. Plumb's final paragraph is fairly long, and we need not quote it in full here, but it ends thus:

> Like any other human institution the family has always been molded by the changing needs of society, sometimes slowly, sometimes fast. And that bus load of children does no more than symbolize the failure not of marriage, but of the role of the old-fashioned family unit in a modern, urbanized, scientific and affluent society.

Later, when you reread his essay carefully, you'll be on the lookout for the evidence that supports this view.

As you scan an essay, you'll find it useful to highlight phrases or sentences, or to draw vertical lines in the margin next to passages that seem to be especially concise bearers of meaning. In short, even while you are skimming you are using your pen.

If the essay is divided into sections, **headings** may give you an idea of the range of coverage. You probably won't need to highlight them—they already stand out—but there's no harm in doing so.

When you skim, you are seeking to get the gist of the author's **thesis** or **point.** But you are also getting an idea of the author's **methods** and the author's **purpose.** For instance, skimming may reveal that the author is using statistics (or an appeal to common sense, or whatever) to set forth an unusual view. When Plumb begins by confessing he was "astonished" by the children in the minibus, he is using a bit of personal history to assure us that he is not a dry-as-dust historian whose understanding of life is based entirely on research in libraries. We immediately see that Plumb is writing for all of us, not just for professional historians, and we see that his purpose is to inform us in an engaging way. He will do a little preaching along the way, but even in skimming we can see that his chief purpose is to educate us, not (for instance) to censure us for our high divorce rate. Another author might take the minibus as a symbol of what is wrong with the American family today, but such an author probably would, from the outset, let us sense what was coming, perhaps by depicting the children as quarreling or sulking.

During this preliminary trip through a piece of writing, you may get a pretty good ideas of the writer's personality. More precisely, since you are not encountering the writer in the flesh but only the image that the writer presents in the essay, you may form an impression of the **voice,** or **persona,** that speaks in the essay. Something of Plumb's persona is evident in passages such as "I was rather astonished," "to them, as Californians, their situation was not particularly odd" (clearly the writer is *not* a Californian), and "it took me a very long time to believe that they could be either happy or adjusted." We will return to this important matter of persona later, on page 16–17.

Let's now look at Plumb's essay. We suggest that in your first reading you skim it—perhaps highlighting, underlining, or drawing vertical lines next to passages that strike you as containing the chief ideas. To this extent, you are reading for information. But because you have ideas of your own and because you do not accept something as true simply because it appears in print, you may also want to put question marks or expressions of doubt ("Really?" "Check this") in the margin next to any passages that strike you as puzzling. Further, you may want to circle any words that you are not familiar with, but at this stage don't bother to look them up. In short, run through the essay, seeking to get the gist and briefly indicating your responses, but don't worry about getting every detail of the argument.

J. H. Plumb

The Dying Family

I was rather astonished when a minibus drove up to my house and out poured ten children. They had with them two parents, but not one child had them both in common as mother and father, and two of them belonged to neither parent, but to a former husband of the wife who had died. Both parents, well into middle age, had just embarked, one on his fourth, the other on her third marriage. The children, who came in all sizes, and ranged from blonde nordic to jet-haired Greek, bounded around the garden, young and old as happy as any children that I have seen. To them, as Californians, their situation was not particularly odd; most of their friends had multiple parents. Indeed to them perhaps the odd family was the one which Western culture has held up as a model for two thousand years or more—the lifelong union of man and wife. But it took me a very long time to believe that they could be either happy or adjusted. And yet, were they a sign of the future, a way the world was going?

Unlike anthropologists or sociologists, historians have not studied family life very closely. Until recently we knew very little of the age at which people married in Western Europe in the centuries earlier than the nineteenth or how many children they had, or what the rates of illegitimacy might be or whether, newly wed, they lived with their parents or set up a house of their own. Few of these questions can be answered with exactitude even now, but we can make better guesses. We know even less, however, of the detailed sexual practices that marriage covered: indeed this is a subject to which historians are only just turning their attention. But we do know much more of the function of family life—its social role—particularly if we turn from the centuries to the millennia and pay attention to the broad similarities rather than the fascinating differences between one region and another: and, if we do, we realize that the family has changed far more profoundly than ever the bus load of Californians might lead us to expect.

Basically the family has fulfilled three social functions—to provide a basic labor force, to transmit property and to educate and train children not only into an accepted social pattern, but also in the work skills upon which their future subsistence would depend. Until very recent times, the vast majority of children never went to any school: their school was the family, where they learned to dig and sow and reap and herd their animals, or they learned their father's craft of smith or carpenter or potter. The unitary family was particularly good at coping with the small peasant holdings which covered most of the world's fertile regions from China to Peru. In the primitive peasant world a child of four or five could begin to earn its keep in the fields, as they still can in India and Africa: and whether Moslem, Hindu, Inca or Christian, one wife at a time was all that the bulk of the world's population could support, even though their religion permitted them more. Indeed, it was the primitive nature of peasant economy which gave the family, as we know it, its wide diffusion and its remarkable continuity.

Whether or not it existed before the neolithic revolution we shall never know, but certainly it must have gained in strength as families became rooted to the soil. Many very primitive people who live in a pre-agrarian society of hunting and food-gathering often tend to have a looser structure of marriage and the women a far greater freedom of choice and easier divorce, as with the Esquimaux, than is permitted in peasant societies. There can be little doubt that the neolithic revolution created new opportunities for the family as we know it, partly because this revolution created new property relations. More importantly it created great masses of property, beyond anything earlier societies had known. True, there were a few hunting peoples, such as the Kwakiutl Indians, who had considerable possessions—complex lodges, great pieces of copper and piles of fibre blankets, which periodically they destroyed in great battles of raging pride—but the property, personal or communal, of most primitive hunting people is usually trivial.

After the revolution in agriculture, property and its transmission lay at   5
the very heart of social relations and possessed an actuality which we find hard to grasp. Although we are much richer, possessions are more anonymous, often little more than marks in a ledger, and what we own constantly changes. Whereas for the majority of mankind over this last seven thousand years property has been deeply personal and familial: a plot of land, if not absolute ownership over it, then valuable rights in it; sometimes a house, even though it be a hovel by our standards; perhaps no more than the tools and materials of a craft, yet these possessions were the route both to survival and to betterment. Hence they were endowed with manna, bound up with the deepest roots of personality. In all societies the question of property became embedded in every aspect of family life, particularly marriage and the succession and rights of children. Because of property's vital importance, subservience of women and children to the will of the father, limited only by social custom, became the pattern of most great peasant societies. Marriage was sanctified not only by the rites of religion, but by the transmission of property. Few societies could tolerate freedom of choice in marriage—too much vital to the success or failure of a family depended on it: an ugly girl with five cows was a far fairer prospect than a pretty girl with one. And because of the sexual drives of frail human nature, the customs of marriage and of family relationships needed to be rigorously enforced. Tradition sanctified them; religion blessed them. Some societies reversed the sexually restrictive nature of permanent marriage and permitted additional wives, but such permission was meaningless to the mass of the peasantry who fought a desperate battle to support a single family. And, as we shall see, the patterns of family life were always looser for the rich and the favored.

But a family was always more than property expressed clearly and visibly in real goods; it was for thousands of years both a school and a tribunal, the basic unit of social organization whose function in modern society has been very largely taken over by the state. In most peasant societies, life is regulated by the village community, by the patriarchs of the village, and the only officer of the central government these villagers see with any regularity is the tax-gatherer; but in societies that have grown more complex, and this is particularly true of the West during the last four hundred years, life has become regulated by the nation state or by the growth in power and importance of more generalized local communities—the town or county.

This has naturally weakened the authority of heads of families, a fact that can be symbolically illustrated by change in social custom. No child in Western Europe would sit unbidden in the presence of its parents until the eighteenth century: if it did it could be sure of rebuke and punishment. No head of a household would have thought twice about beating a recalcitrant young servant or apprentice before the end of the nineteenth century. For a younger brother to marry without the consent of his eldest brother would have been regarded as a social enormity; and sisters were disposable property. All of this power has vanished. Indeed the family ties of all of us have been so loosened that we find it hard to grasp the intensity of family relationships or their complexity, they have disintegrated so rapidly this last hundred years. Now nearly every child in the Western world, male or female, is educated outside the family from five years of age. The skills they learn are rarely, if ever, transmitted by parents: and what is more they learn about the nature of their own world, its social structure and its relationships in time outside the family. For millennia the family was the great transmitter and formulator of social custom; but it now only retains a shadow of this function, usually for very young children only.

Although the economic and education functions of the family have declined, most of us feel that it provides the most satisfactory emotional basis for human beings; that a secure family life breeds stability, a capacity not only for happiness, but also to adjust to society's demands. This, too, may be based on misjudgment, for family life in the past was not remarkable for its happiness. We get few glimpses into the private lives of men and women long dead, but when we do we often find strain, frustration, petty tyranny. For so many human beings family life was a prison from which they could not escape. And although it might create deep satisfactions here and there, the majority of the rich and affluent classes of the last four hundred years in Western Europe created for themselves a double standard, particularly as far as sex was concerned. In a few cities such as Calvin's Geneva, the purity of family life might be maintained, but the aristocracies of France, Italy and Britain tolerated, without undue concern, adultery, homosexuality and that sexual freedom which, for better or worse, we consider the hallmark of modern life. Indeed the family as the basic social group began firstly to fail, except in its property relations, amongst the aristocracy.

But what we think of as a social crisis of this generation—the rapid growth of divorce, the emancipation of women and adolescents, the sexual and educational revolutions, even the revolution in eating which is undermining the family as the basis of nourishment, for over a hundred years ago the majority of Europeans never ate in public in their lives—all of these things, which are steadily making the family weaker and weaker, are the inexorable result of the changes in society itself. The family as a unit of social organization was remarkably appropriate for a less complex world of agriculture and craftsmanship, a world which stretches back some seven thousand years, but ever since industry and highly urbanized societies began to take its place, the social functions of the family have steadily weakened—and this is a process that is unlikely to be halted. And there is no historical reason to believe that human beings could be less or more happy, less or more stable. Like any other human institution the family has always been molded by the changing needs of society, sometimes slowly, sometimes fast. And that bus load of children does no more than symbolize the failure, not of marriage, but of the role of the old-fashioned family unit in a modern, urbanized, scientific and affluent society.

Even a quick skimming reveals that Plumb offers, as you anticipated he would, a historical view. He begins with a glance at one contemporary family, but you probably noticed that by the second paragraph he speaks as a historian, tracing the origins and development of the institution of the family.

Highlighting, Underlining, Annotating

Now that you have the gist of Plumb's essay, go back and reread it; this time, highlight or underline key passages as though you were marking the text so that you might later easily review it for an examination. Your purpose now is simply to make sure that you know what Plumb is getting at. You may strongly disagree with him on details or even on large matters, and you would certainly make clear your differences with him if you were to write about his essay; but for the moment your purpose is to make sure that you know what his position is. See if in each paragraph you can find a sentence that contains the topic idea of the paragraph. If you find such sentences, mark them.

Caution: Do not allow yourself to highlight or underline whole paragraphs. Before you start to mark a paragraph, read it to the end, and then go back and mark what you now see as the key word, phrase, or passage. If you simply start marking a paragraph from the beginning, you may end up marking the whole; and thus you will defeat your purpose which is to make highly visible the basic points of the essay.

You may also want to jot down, in the margins, questions or objections and you may want to circle any words that puzzle you.

Time's up. Let's talk about the underlinings and highlightings.

No two readers of the essay will make exactly the same annotations. To take a small example, a reader in Alaska would probably be more likely to mark the passage about "the Esquimaux" in paragraph 4 than would a reader in St Louis, but here is what one reader produced.

note
first
person

(I)was rather astonished when a minibus drove up to my house and out poured <u>ten children</u>. They had with them two parents, but <u>not one child had them both in</u>   *new (California)*
<u>common as mother and father</u>, and two of them belonged *style*
to neither parent, but to a former husband of the wife who had died. Both parents, well into middle age, had just embarked, one on his fourth, the other on her third marriage. The children, who came in all sizes, and ranged from blonde nordic to jet-haired Greek, bounded around the garden, young and old as happy as any children that (I) have seen. To them, as <u>Californians</u>, their situation was

not particularly odd; most of their friends had multiple
parents. Indeed to them perhaps the odd family was the
one which Western culture has held up as a model for   *old*
two thousand years or more--the lifelong union of man   *style*
and wife. But it took me a very long time to believe that
they could be either happy or adjusted. And yet, were   *who says*
they a sign of the future, a way the world was going?   *they are*
first person   Unlike anthropologists or sociologists, historians   *happy?*
again, but have not studied family life very closely. Until recently we
less knew very little of the age at which people married in
"personal" Western Europe in the centuries earlier than the
nineteenth or how many children they had, or what the
rates of illegitimacy might be or whether, newly wed,
they lived with their parents or set up a house of their
own. Few of these questions can be answered with
exactitude even now, but we can make better guesses.
We know even less, however, of the detailed sexual
practices that marriage covered: indeed this is a subject
to which historians are only just turning their attention. But
we do know much more of the function of family life--its
social role--particularly if we turn from the centuries to
the millennia and pay attention to the broad similarities
rather than the fascinating differences between one
region and another: and, if we do, we realize that the
family has changed far more profoundly than even the   *change*
bus load of Californians might lead us to expect.
              Basically the family has fulfilled three social functions--   *1. provides*
3 functions to provide a basic labor force, to transmit property and to   *labor*
educate and train children not only into an accepted social   *2. transmits*
pattern, but also in the work skills upon which their future   *property*
subsistence would depend. Until very recent times, the   *3. educates*
vast majority of children never went to any school: their   *children*
school was the family where they learned to dig and sow
and reap and herd their animals, or they learned their
father's craft of smith or carpenter or potter. The unitary   *?*
family was particularly good at coping with the small
peasant holdings which covered most of the world's fertile
regions from China to Peru. In the primitive peasant world
a child of four or five could begin to earn its keep in the
fields, as they still can in India and Africa; and whether
Moslem, Hindu, Inca or Christian, one wife at a time was all   *? couldn't*
that the bulk of the world's population could support, even   *wives earn*
though their religion permitted them more. Indeed, it was   *their keep?*
not also the primitive nature of peasant economy which gave the
religious family, as we know it, its wide diffusion and its remarkable
teachings? continuity.

Whether or not it existed before the neolithic revolution we shall never know, but certainly it must have gained in strength as families became rooted to the soil. Many very primitive people who live in a pre-agrarian society of hunting and food-gathering often tend to have a looser structure of marriage and the women a far greater freedom of choice and easier divorce, as with the Esquimaux, than is permitted in peasant societies. There can be little doubt that the neolithic revolution created new opportunities for the family as we know it, partly because this revolution created new property relations. More importantly it created great masses of property, beyond anything earlier societies had known. True, there were a few hunting peoples, such as the Kwakiutl Indians, who had considerable possessions--complex lodges, great pieces of copper and piles of fibre blankets, which periodically they destroyed in great battles of raging pride--but the property, personal or communal, of most primitive hunting people is usually trivial.

Of course different readers will find different passages of special interest and importance. Our personal histories, our beliefs, our preconceptions, our current preoccupations, to some extent determine how we read. For instance, when they come to the fifth paragraph some readers may mark Plumb's sexist language ("mankind"), and some may highlight the assertion that "Marriage was sanctified not only by the rites of religion, but by the transmission of property." Readers who are especially interested in class relations might also highlight and underline this sentence:

The patterns of family life were always looser for the rich and the favored.

Notice, by the way, that although Plumb makes this assertion he does not offer a value judgment. A reader might mark the sentence and add in the margin: *Still true, and outrageous!* Or, conversely, a reader may feel that the statement is false, and might write, *Really???*, or even *Not the rich, but the poor (free from bourgeois hangups) are sexually freer.*

As these last examples indicate, even when you simply set out to make a few notes that will help you to follow and to remember the essayist's argument, you may well find yourself making notes that record your **responses** (where you agree, what you question), notes that may start you thinking about the validity of the argument.

As we have already said, *what* you annotate will partly depend on what interests you, what your values are, and what your purpose is. True, you have read the essay because it was assigned, but Plumb's original readers read it for other reasons. It appeared first in a magazine and then in a collection of Plumb's essays. The original readers, then, were people who freely picked it up because they wanted to learn about the family or perhaps because they had read something else by Plumb, liked it, and wanted to hear more from this author.

Imagine yourself, for a moment, as a reader encountering this essay in a magazine that you have picked up. If you are reading because you want to know something about the family in an agrarian society, you'll annotate one sort of thing; if you are reading because as a child of divorced parents you were struck and possibly outraged by his first paragraph, you'll annotate another sort of thing; if you are reading because you admire Plumb as a historian, you'll annotate another sort of thing; and if you are reading because you dislike Plumb, you'll annotate something else. We remind you of a comment by Paul Valéry, quoted at the beginning of this chapter: "One reads well only when one reads with some quite personal goal in mind. It may be to acquire some power. It can be out of hatred for the author." An exaggeration, of course, but there is something to it. (In the Book of Job, Job wishes that his "adversary had written a book.")

Summarizing

In your effort to formulate a brief version of what an essayist is saying, you may want to write a summary, especially if you found the essay difficult. A good way to begin is to summarize each paragraph in a sentence or two, or in some phrases. By summarizing each paragraph, you compile—without doing any additional work—an outline of the essay. Here is a student's outline of Plumb's essay.

1.   Minibus in California: 10 children and 2 parents, but not one child was child of both adults. Different from traditional family. Sign of the way the world is going.

2.   Many things not known about the past (age of marriage, sexual practices), but something known of the function of family life.

3.   Three functions: providing a labor force, transmitting property, educating and training children. Peasant families today.

4, 5.   After neolithic (agricultural?) revolution, family strengthened because people rooted to the soil (produced masses of property: land, house, or tools of a craft). Transmission of property sanctified marriage.

6, 7.   Family was also school and basic social unit. Head of the household ruled (chose the mate for a child, etc.). In modern societies government has taken over many functions of patriarchs.

8.   Despite loss of functions, most of us still feel that a family breeds stability, happiness. May be a misjudgment; family often was a prison. And for last 400 years the rich created a double standard, at least for sex.

9.   Decline of family (divorce, emancipation of women and adoles-
       cents, etc.) is result of historic change in society itself. Family
       appropriate for agricultural society but less in industrial and
       urban societies. Busload of kids symbolizes not the failure of mar-
       riage but the loss of role for old-fashioned family in a modern
       society.

Especially if an essay is complex, writing a summary of this sort can
help you to follow the argument. Glancing over your notes, you probably
can see, fairly easily, what the writer's *main* points are, as distinct from the
subordinate points and the examples that clarify the points. Furthermore,
since your summary is now a paragraph outline, you can look it over to
see not only what it adds up to, but also how the writer shaped the material. Producing a summary, then, may be an activity that is useful to you
when you are *reading* an essay. It will almost surely help you to grasp the
essay and to remember its argument. And if you are *writing* about the
essay—perhaps to take issue with it or to amplify a point that it makes—
you may have to include in your essay a brief summary so that your readers will know what you are writing about.

How long should the summary be? Just long enough to give readers
what they need in order to follow your essay. If in a fairly long essay you
are going to take issue with several of Plumb's points, you may want to
give a fairly detailed summary—perhaps a page long.

For a short essay, however, something like the following passage
might be appropriate:

> In "The Dying Family," J. H. Plumb argues that when society
> was primarily agricultural, the family provided education and
> training, a labor force, and a way of transmitting property. In
> today's industrialized society, however, these functions are
> largely provided by the government, and the traditional family is
> no longer functional.

(For further discussion of summaries, see the entry on pages 76–77 of this
book, in "A Writer's Glossary.")

✓ Critical Thinking: Analyzing the Text

Writing a summary requires that you pay attention to the text, but it does
not require you to question the text, to think about such issues as whether
the author's assumptions are plausible, and whether evidence supports
the generations. In reading an essay, in addition to being able to summarize it accurately you must engage in **critical thinking.** "Critical" here
does not mean finding fault ("Don't be so critical") but, rather, it means

paying close attention to the ways in which the parts form the whole. In this sense, to read critically is to read analytically.

We have already said that you will probably find yourself putting question marks in the margins next to words that you don't know and that don't become clear in the context, and next to statements that you find puzzling or dubious. These marks will remind you to take action—perhaps to check a dictionary, to reread a paragraph, or to jot down your objection in the margin or at greater length in a journal.

But analytic readers also engage in another sort of questioning, though they may do so almost unconsciously. They are almost always asking themselves—or rather asking the text— several questions. You'll notice that these questions concern not only the writer's point but also the writer's craft. By asking such questions, you will learn about subject matter (for instance, about the history of the family in Plumb's essay) and also about some of the tricks of the writer's trade (for instance, effective ways of beginning). If you read actively, asking the following questions, you will find that reading is *not* a solitary activity; you are conversing with a writer.

- What is the writer's thesis?
- How does the writer support the thesis?
- What is the writer's purpose (to persuade, to rebut, to entertain, to share an experience, or whatever)?
- How do the writer's audience and purpose help shape the writing? (The place of publication is often a clue to the audience.) For instance, does the writer use humor or, on the other hand, speak earnestly? Are terms carefully defined, or does the writer assume that the audience is knowledgeable and does not need such information?
- What is the writer's tone?

These questions will help you to understand what you are reading and how writers go about their business. But you are also entitled to evaluate what you are reading, hence some other questions, of a rather different sort:

- How successful is the piece? What are its strengths and weaknesses? What do I especially like or dislike about it? Why?

We recommend that when you read an essay you ask each of these questions—not, of course, during an initial skimming, but during a second and third reading, after you have some sense of the essay.

These questions almost can be boiled down to one question:

What is the writer up to?

That is, a reader who is not content merely to take what the writer is handing out asks such questions as, Why *this* way of opening? Why *this* way of defining the term? Of course, the assumption that the writer has a purpose may be false. (We are reminded of a comment that Metternich, the keenly analytic Austrian statesman and diplomat, uttered when he learned that the Czar had died: "I wonder why he did that.") Yes, the writer may just be blundering along, but it's reasonable to begin with the assumption that the writer is competent. If under questioning the writer fails, you have at least learned that not everything in print is worthy.

Tone and Persona

Perhaps you know the line from Owen Wister's novel, *The Virginian:* "When you call me that, smile." Words spoken with a smile mean something different from the same words spoken through clenched teeth. But while speakers can communicate by facial gestures, body language, and changes in tone of voice, writers have only words in ink on paper. Somehow the writer has to help us to know whether, for instance, he or she is solemn or joking or joking in earnest.

Consider the beginning of the first paragraph of J. H. Plumb's "The Dying Family."

> I was rather astonished when a minibus drove up to my house and out poured ten children. They had with them two parents, but not one child had them both in common as mother and father, and two of them belonged to neither parent, but to a former husband of the wife who had died. Both parents, well into middle age, had just embarked, on his fourth, the other on her third marriage. The children, who came in all sizes, and ranged from blonde nordic to jet-haired Greek, bounded around the garden, young and old as happy as any children that I have seen.

Plumb's first sentence *could* have run this:

> I noted with considerable surprise the fact that when a minibus drove up to my house, ten children got out of the vehicle.

This version contains nothing that is certifiably wrong—the grammar and spelling are satisfactory—but it lacks the energy of Plumb's version. In the original, Plumb is astonished rather than surprised, and the children don't just get out of the minibus, they "pour" out. Further, the original minibus is just a minibus; it doesn't become (as it unnecessarily does, in the revised version) a "vehicle." After all, who speaks of vehicles other than perhaps police officers when they say in an official report that they "apprehended the perpetrator in a speeding vehicle"?

Notice too, in the succeeding sentences, that the children "came in all sizes." If Plumb had said that the smallest child was about three feet tall, and the largest child must have been at least five feet tall, he might have been more exact but he certainly would have been less engaging. As readers we probably enjoy the fairly colloquial tone that this distinguished professor is using.

What sort of person is Plumb? He seems to be a neighbor, chatting easily with us, not a remote professor delivering a lecture. And yet even in this paragraph, when he speaks of "two thousand years or more" of "Western culture" we realized that he is a historian who can speak with some authority. He may or may not be divorced, he may or may not be a loving parent, he may or may not be a good cook—there are countless things we don't know about him—so we can't really say what sort of person he is. We can, however, say what sort of *persona* (or personality) he conveys in his essay.

How do readers form an impression of a persona? By listening, so to speak, with a third ear, listening for the writer's attitude toward

- himself or herself,
- the subject, and
- the audience.

Still, different readers will, of course, respond differently. To take a simple example, readers who do not wish to hear arguments concerning new views of the family may dismiss Plumb as radical, or as lacking in basic moral values. But we think most readers will agree with us in saying that Plumb conveys the persona of someone who is (1) educated, (2) at least moderately engaging, (3) a good teacher, and (4) concerned with a significant issue. It's our guess, too, that Plumb hoped to be seen as this sort of person. If readers of his first paragraph conclude that he is conceited, stuffy, full of hot air, a threat to society, and so on, he has failed terribly, because he has turned his readers away.

There is a lesson for writers, too. When you reread your own drafts and essays, try to get out of yourself and into the mind of an imagined reader, say a classmate. Try to hear how your words will sound in this other person's ear; that is, try to imagine what impression this reader will form of your attitude toward yourself, your subject, and your reader.

2
A READER WRITES

All *there is to writing is having ideas. To learn to write is to learn to have ideas.*

Robert Frost

So far, the only writing that we have suggested you do is in the form of annotating, summarizing, and responding to some basic and some specific questions about the essayist's thesis and methods. All of these activities help you to think about what you are reading. "It is thinking," the philosopher John Locke wrote, "that makes what we read ours." But, of course, ultimately your thoughts will manifest themselves in your own essays, which probably will take off from one or more of the essays that you have read. Before we discuss writing about more than one essay, let's look at another essay, this one by C. S. Lewis (1898–1963).

Lewis taught English literature at Oxford and at Cambridge, but he is most widely known not for his books on literature but for his books on Christianity (*The Screwtape Letters* is one of the most famous), his children's novels (collected in a seven-volume set called *The Chronicles of Narnia*), and his science fiction (for instance, *Perelandra*). Lewis also wrote autobiographical volumes and many essays on literature and on morality. The essay printed here—the last thing that he wrote—was published in *The Saturday Evening Post* in December 1963, shortly after his death.

C. S. Lewis

We Have No "Right to Happiness"

After all," said Clare, "they had a right to happiness."

We were discussing something that once happened in our own neighborhood. Mr. A. had deserted Mrs. A. and got his divorce in order to marry Mrs. B., who had likewise got her divorce in order to marry Mr. A. And there was certainly no doubt that Mr. A. and Mrs. B. were very much in love with one another. If they continued to be in love, and if nothing went wrong with their health or their income, they might reasonably expect to be very happy.

It was equally clear that they were not happy with their old partners. Mrs. B. had adored her husband at the outset. But then he got smashed up in the war. It was thought he had lost his virility, and it was known that he had lost his job. Life with him was no longer what Mrs. B. had bargained for. Poor Mrs. A., too. She had lost her looks—and all her liveliness. It might be true, as some said, that she consumed herself by bearing his children and nursing him through the long illness that overshadowed their earlier married life.

You mustn't, by the way, imagine that A. was the sort of man who nonchalantly threw a wife away like the peel of an orange he'd sucked dry. Her suicide was a terrible shock to him. We all knew this, for he told us so himself. "But what could I do?" he said. "A man has a right to happiness. I had to take my one chance when it came."

I went away thinking about the concept of a "right to happiness."   5

At first this sounds to me as odd as a right to good luck. For I believe—whatever one school of moralists may say—that we depend for a very great deal of our happiness or misery on circumstances outside all human control. A right to happiness doesn't, for me, make much more sense than a right to be six feet tall, or to have a millionaire for your father, or to get good weather whenever you want to have a picnic.

I can understand a right as a freedom guaranteed me by the laws of the society I live in. Thus, I have a right to travel along the public roads because society gives me that freedom; that's what we mean by calling the roads "public." I can also understand a right as a claim guaranteed me by the laws, and correlative to an obligation on someone else's part. If I have a right to receive £100 from you, this is another way of saying that you have a duty to pay me £100. If the laws allow Mr. A. to desert his wife and seduce his neighbor's wife, then, by definition, Mr. A. has a legal right to do so, and we need bring in no talk about "happiness."

But of course that was not what Clare meant. She meant that he had not only a legal but a moral right to act as he did. In other words, Clare is—or would be if she thought it out—a classical moralist after the style of Thomas Aquinas, Grotius, Hooker and Locke. She believes that behind the laws of the state there is a Natural Law.[1]

I agree with her. I hold this conception to be basic to all civilization. Without it, the actual laws of the state become an absolute, as in Hegel. They cannot be criticized because there is no norm against which they should be judged.

The ancestry of Clare's maxim, "They have a right to happiness," is   10
august. In words that are cherished by all civilized men, but especially by Americans, it has been laid down that one of the rights of man is a right to "the pursuit of happiness." And now we get to the real point.

What did the writers of that august declaration mean?

It is quite certain what they did not mean. They did not mean that man was entitled to pursue happiness by any and every means—including, say, murder, rape, robbery, treason and fraud. No society could be built on such a basis.

---

[1]**Thomas Aquinas . . . Natural Law** Lewis names some philosophers and theologians from the thirteenth through the eighteenth century who believed that certain basic moral principles are evident to rational people in all periods and in all cultures. (Editors' note)

They meant "to pursue happiness by all lawful means"; that is, by all means which the Law of Nature eternally sanctions and which the laws of the nation shall sanction.

Admittedly this seems at first to reduce their maxim to the tautology that men (in pursuit of happiness) have a right to do whatever they have a right to do. But tautologies, seen against their proper historical context, are not always barren tautologies. The declaration is primarily a denial of the political principles which long governed Europe: a challenge flung down to the Austrian and Russian empires, to England before the Reform Bills, to Bourbon France.[2] It demands that whatever means of pursuing happiness are lawful for any should be lawful for all; that "man," not men of some particular caste, class, status or religion, should be free to use them. In a century when this is being unsaid by nation after nation and party after party, let us not call it a barren tautology.

But the question as to what means are "lawful"—what methods of pursuing happiness are either morally permissible by the Law of Nature or should be declared legally permissible by the legislature of a particular nation—remains exactly where it did. And on that question I disagree with Clare. I don't think it is obvious that people have the unlimited "right to happiness" which she suggests. 15

For one thing, I believe that Clare, when she says "happiness," means simply and solely "sexual happiness." Partly because women like Clare never use the word "happiness" in any other sense. But also because I never heard Clare talk about the "right" to any other kind. She was rather leftist in her politics, and would have been scandalized if anyone had defended the actions of a ruthless man-eating tycoon on the ground that his happiness consisted in making money and he was pursuing his happiness. She was also a rabid teetotaler; I never heard her excuse an alcoholic because he was happy when he was drunk.

A good many of Clare's friends, and especially her female friends, often felt—I've heard them say so—that their own happiness would be perceptibly increased by boxing her ears. I very much doubt if this would have brought her theory of a right to happiness into play.

Clare, in fact, is doing what the whole western world seems to me to have been doing for the last forty-odd years. When I was a youngster, all the progressive people were saying, "Why all this prudery? Let us treat sex just as we treat all our other impulses." I was simple-minded enough to believe they meant what they said. I have since discovered that they meant exactly the opposite. They meant that sex was to be treated as no other impulse in our nature has ever been treated by civilized people. All the others, we admit, have to be bridled. Absolute obedience to your instinct for self-preservation is what we call cowardice; to your acquisitive impulse, avarice. Even sleep must be resisted if you're a sentry. But every

[2]**England . . . France** England before the bills that liberalized representation in Parliament in the nineteenth century, and France before the French Revolution of 1789–99 (Editors' note)

unkindness and breach of faith seems to be condoned provided that the object aimed at is "four bare legs in a bed."

It is like having a morality in which stealing fruit is considered wrong—unless you steal nectarines.

And if you protest against this view you are usually met with chatter about the legitimacy and beauty and sanctity of "sex" and accused of harboring some Puritan prejudice against it as something disreputable or shameful. I deny the charge. Foam-born Venus . . . golden Aphrodite . . . Our Lady of Cyprus[3] . . . I never breathed a word against you. If I object to boys who steal my nectarines, must I be supposed to disapprove of nectarines in general? Or even of boys in general? It might, you know, be stealing that I disapproved of.

The real situation is skillfully concealed by saying that the question of Mr. A.'s "right" to desert his wife is one of "sexual morality." Robbing an orchard is not an offense against some special morality called "fruit morality." It is an offense against honesty. Mr. A.'s action is an offense against good faith (to solemn promises), against gratitude (toward one to whom he was deeply indebted) and against common humanity.

Our sexual impulses are thus being put in a position of preposterous privilege. The sexual motive is taken to condone all sorts of behavior which, if it had any other end in view, would be condemned as merciless, treacherous and unjust.

Now though I see no good reason for giving sex this privilege, I think I see a strong cause. It is this.

It is part of the nature of a strong erotic passion—as distinct from a transient fit of appetite—that it makes more towering promises than any other emotion. No doubt all our desires make promises, but not so impressively. To be in love involves the almost irresistible conviction that one will go on being in love until one dies, and that possession of the beloved will confer, not merely frequent ecstasies, but settled, fruitful, deep-rooted, lifelong happiness. Hence *all* seems to be at stake. If we miss this chance we shall have lived in vain. At the very thought of such a doom we sink into fathomless depths of self-pity.

Unfortunately these promises are found often to be quite untrue. Every experienced adult knows this to be so as regards all erotic passions (except the one he himself is feeling at the moment). We discount the world-without-end pretensions of our friends' amours easily enough. We know that such things sometimes last—and sometimes don't. And when they do last, this is not because they promised at the outset to do so. When two people achieve lasting happiness, this is not solely because they are great lovers but because they are also—I must put it crudely—good people; controlled, loyal, fairminded, mutually adaptable people.

20

25

---

[3]**Foam-born Venus . . . Aphrodite . . . Cyprus** The Roman goddess Venus was identified with the Greek goddess of love, Aphrodite. Aphrodite sprang from the foam (*aphros*), and was especially worshipped in Cyprus. (Editors' note)

If we establish a "right to (sexual) happiness" which supersedes all the ordinary rules of behavior, we do so not because of what our passion shows itself to be in experience but because of what it professes to be while we are in the grip of it. Hence, while the bad behavior is real and works miseries and degradations, the happiness which was the object of the behavior turns out again and again to be illusory. Everyone (except Mr. A. and Mrs. B.) knows that Mr. A. in a year or so may have the same reason for deserting his new wife as for deserting his old. He will feel again that all is at stake. He will see himself again as the great lover, and his pity for himself will exclude all pity for the woman.

Two further points remain.

One is this. A society in which conjugal infidelity is tolerated must always be in the long run a society adverse to women. Women, whatever a few male songs and satires may say to the contrary, are more naturally monogamous than men; it is a biological necessity. Where promiscuity prevails, they will therefore always be more often the victims than the culprits. Also, domestic happiness is more necessary to them than to us. And the quality by which they most easily hold a man, their beauty, decreases every year after they have come to maturity, but this does not happen to those qualities of personality—women don't really care twopence about our *looks*—by which we hold women. Thus in the ruthless war of promiscuity women are at a double disadvantage. They play for higher stakes and are also more likely to lose. I have no sympathy with moralists who frown at the increasing crudity of female provocativeness. These signs of desperate competition fill me with pity.

Secondly, though the "right to happiness" is chiefly claimed for the sexual impulse, it seems to me impossible that the matter should stay there. The fatal principle, once allowed in that department, must sooner or later seep through our whole lives. We thus advance toward a state of society in which not only each man but every impulse in each man claims *carte blanche*.[4] And then, though our technological skill may help us survive a little longer, our civilization will have died at heart, and will—one dare not even add "unfortunately"—be swept away.

Responding to an Essay

After you have read Lewis's essay at least twice, you may want to jot down your responses to the basic questions that we introduced on page 15 after J. H. Plumb's essay. Here they are yet again, slightly abbreviated:

- What is the writer's thesis?
- How does the writer support the thesis?
- What is the writer's purpose?

[4]*Carte blanche* full permission to act (French for "blank card") (Editors' note)

- How does the writer shape the purpose to the audience?
- What is the writer's tone?
- How successful is the piece? What are its strengths and weaknesses?

And here, to help you to think further about Lewis's essay, are some specific questions:

- Having read the entire essay, look back at Lewis's first five paragraphs and point out the ways in which he is not merely recounting an episode but is already conveying his attitude and seeking to persuade.
- Lewis argues that we do not have a "right to (sexual) happiness." What *duty* or *duties* do we have, according to Lewis?
- In paragraph 25 Lewis writes:

    > When two people achieve lasting happiness, this is not solely because they are great lovers but because they are also—I must put it crudely—good people; controlled, loyal, fairminded, mutually adaptable people.

    If you know of a couple who in your opinion have achieved "lasting happiness," do you agree with Lewis's view that their achievement is largely due to the fact that they are "good people"?
- Evaluate Lewis's comment in paragraph 28 on the differences between men and women.

If you find yourself roughing out responses to any of these questions, you may be on the way toward writing a first draft of an essay.

The Writing Process

An essay is a response to experience. J. H. Plumb saw (or says that he saw) a busload of people and was prompted to think about them and ultimately to write an essay on the family (page 6); C. S. Lewis heard (or says that he heard) someone utter a comment about a right to happiness, and he was set to thinking and then to writing about it (page 20). Their essays came out of their experience. By *experience* we do not mean only what they actually saw (since we can suspect that Plumb and Lewis may have invented the episodes they use at the start of their essays); their experience included things they had read about and had reflected on. After all, Plumb's bus and Lewis's report of Clare's remark were at most only triggers, so to speak. A good deal of previous experience and a good deal of later experience—chiefly in the form of reading and of *thinking* about what they had read—went into the production of their essays.

In short, writers think about their responses to experience. You have been actively reading their responses—engaging in a dialogue with these authors—and so you have been undergoing your own experiences. You have things to say, though on any given topic you probably are not yet certain of *all* that you have to say or of how you can best say it. You need to get further ideas, to do further thinking. How do you get ideas? The short answer is that you will get ideas if you engage in an imagined dialogue with the authors whom you are reading. When you read an essay, you will find yourself asking such questions as: What evidence supports this assertion? Is the writer starting from assumptions with which I don't agree? Why do I especially like (or dislike) this essay?

Many writers—professionals as well as students—have found it useful to get their responses down on paper, either as annotations in the margins or as entries in a journal, or both. Here, as a sample, are the annotations that one student jotted next to Lewis's third and fourth paragraphs.

It was equally clear that they were not happy with their old partners. Mrs. B. had adored her husband at the outset. But then he got smashed up in the war. It was thought he had lost his virility, and it was known that he had lost his job. Life with him was no longer what Mrs. B had bar-gained for. Poor Mrs. A., too. She had lost her looks--and all her liveliness. It might be true, as some said, that she consumed herself by bearing his children and nursing him through the long illness that overshadowed their earlier married life.

These examples are caricatures. They really defeat L's purpose

Loaded word. Makes her too calculating

You musn't, by the way, imagine that A. was the sort of man who nonchalantly threw a wife away like the peel of an orange he'd sucked dry. Her suicide was a terrible shock to him. We all knew this, for he told us so himself. "But what could I do?" he said. "A man has a right to happiness. I had to take my one chance when it came."

Is CSL making him too awful?

Annotations of this sort often are the starting point for entries in a journal.

Keeping a Journal

A journal is not a diary, a record of what the writer did during the day ("Today I read Lewis's 'We Have No 'Right to Happiness'"). Rather, a journal is a place to store some of the thoughts that you may have scribbled on a bit of paper or in the margin of the text—for instance, your initial response to the title of an essay or to something you particularly liked or disliked. It is also a place to jot down further reflections. You can record your impressions as they come to you in any order—almost as though you are talking to yourself. Since no one else is going to read your notes, you can be entirely free and at ease. The student whose annotations we reproduced a moment ago wrote the following entry in his journal:

I find Lewis's writing is very clear and in its way persuasive, but I also think that his people--A. and B. and Clare--are not real people. They are almost caricatures. Anyway, he certainly has chosen people (or invented them?) who help him make his case. What if Mrs. B.'s husband had been a wife-beater, or maybe someone who molested their daughter? Would Lewis still think Mrs. B. was wrong to leave Mr. B.?

A second student wrote a rather different entry in her journal:

Lewis at first seems to be arguing against a "right to happiness," but really he is arguing against adultery and divorce, against what we can call the Playboy morality--the idea that if a middle-aged man divorces his middle-aged wife because he now finds his young secretary attractive, he is acting maturely.

Here is a third entry:

Terrific. That story about A and B really got to me. But is it true? Does it matter if it isn't true? Probably not; there are people like the A's and the B's. Lewis really is awfully good at holding my interest. And I was really grabbed by that business about a right to happiness being as strange as a right to be six feet tall. But my question is this: I agree that we don't have a right to be six feet tall, but why, then, do we have any rights? Lewis talks about Natural Law, but what is that?

Is the idea of one husband and one wife "Natural Law"? If so, how come so many societies don't obey it? When Bertrand Russell talks about natural instincts and emotions "which we inherit from our animal ancestors," is this like Natural Law?

Still, I think Lewis is terrific. And I think he is probably right about the difference between men and women. It seems obvious to me that men care more about a woman's looks than women care about a man's looks. How can this be checked?

You might even make a journal entry in the form of a letter to the author or in the form of a dialogue. Or you might have Mr. A. and Mrs. B. give *their* versions of the story that Clare reports.

Questioning the Text Again

We have already suggested that one way to increase your understanding of an essay and to get ideas that you may use in an essay of your own is to ask questions of the selection that you have read. Let's begin by thinking about the questions we asked following C. S. Lewis's "We Have No 'Right to Happiness'" (page 20). All of these could provide topics for your own essays. Some were questions that might be asked of any essay, you'll recall—about the author's thesis, the way in which the author supports the thesis, the author's purpose, the author's persona or tone, and your evaluation of the essay. And there were questions specifically about Lewis's essay, concerning Lewis's comments on rights and his comments about the differences between men and women.

Probably the most obvious topic for an essay such as Lewis's is

What is the author's thesis, and how sound is it?

One student formulated the thesis as follows:

> We not only do not have a "right" to sexual happiness, but we probably cannot achieve lasting happiness if we allow sex to govern behavior that otherwise "would be condemned as merciless, treacherous and unjust."

An essay concerning Lewis's thesis might be narrowed, for example, to

Does Lewis give a one-sided view of divorce?

or

Does Lewis underestimate (or overestimate) the importance of sexual satisfaction?

But other topics easily come to mind, for instance:

- Lewis's methods as a writer.
- The logic of Lewis's argument.

Take the first of these three, Lewis's methods, a topic of special interest if you are trying to become a better writer. One student who planned to write about this topic made the following notes.

Summaries, Jottings, Outlines and Lists

(Parenthetic numbers refer to Lewis's paragraphs.)

1. Purpose is obviously to persuade. How does he do it?
2. Very informal manner:
   a. Begins by telling of a conversation he had (1).
   b. Often uses "I"; for instance, "I went away thinking" (5); "this sounds to me" (6); "I can understand" (7); "I was simple-minded enough to believe" (18). So the tone is personal, as if he and the reader were having a conversation.
3. Though informal, seems very educated:

    a. Cites authorities, apparently philosophers, in par. 8 (check these names); refers to Austrian, Russian, English, and French history (14).

    b. Educated vocabulary ("tautologies" in par. 14).

4.   But also uses easy examples: Mr. and Mrs. A. and Mr. and Mrs. B. in first paragraph; stealing fruit (19-21).

5.   Makes the abstract clear by being concrete. In par. 18, when he says that our impulses have to be controlled, he says, "Absolute obedience to your instinct for self-preservation is what we call cowardice. . . ."

6.   Sentences are all clear. Some are very short ("I agree with her" 9), but even the long sentences--several lines of type--are clear. Give one (or maybe two) examples?

7.   In next-to-last par., frankly speaks as a male: "domestic happiness is more necessary to them [that is, women] than to us." And "the quality by which they [that is, women] most easily hold a man," and "women don't really care twopence about our <u>looks</u>" (all in 28). Sense of a man talking heart-to-heart to men. But how might it strike a woman? Sexist? Ask Jane and Tina.

You may prefer to record your thoughts in the form of lists:

Methods:
    Examples
    Anecdote about A. and B. (par. 1)
    Stealing fruit (19-21)
Informal style:
    Uses "I" (many places)
    Also uses "we"
Clear sentences (give examples)
Vocabulary:
    Usually simple words
    A few hard words ("tautologies" in par. 14)
Beginning: an individual listening
End: rather authoritative: generalizes about men vs women

Further thinking and further readings of Lewis's essay produced more evidence, and of course the material then had to be reorganized into a clear and effective sequence, but these notes and lists were highly promising. The student who wrote them was well on the way to writing a strong first draft.

    After converting his notes into a draft and then revising the draft, an interesting—yet rather common—thing happened. The student found himself dissatisfied with his point. He now felt that he wanted to say something rather different. The annotations and the drafts, it turned out, were a way of helping him to get to a deeper response to Lewis's essay, and so he rewrote his essay, changing his focus. But we are getting ahead of our story.

Getting Ready to Write a Draft

After jotting down notes (and further notes stimulated by rereading and further thinking), you probably will be able to formulate a tentative thesis, a point such as "Lewis argues with great skill," or "Lewis does not make clear the concept of Natural Law," or "Lewis generalizes too freely," or "Lewis has a narrow idea of why people divorce." At this point most writers find it useful to clear the air by glancing over their preliminary notes and by jotting down the thesis and a few especially promising notes—brief statements of what they think their key points may be. These notes may include some key quotations that the writer thinks will help support the thesis.

Draft of an Essay

On "We Have No 'Right to Happiness'"

When I first read the title of C. S. Lewis's essay, I was interested and also somewhat resistant. Without having given much thought to it, I believe that I do have a right to happiness. I don't want to give up this right or this belief. Still I was intrigued to know what Lewis had to say. After reading the essay, it seemed entirely reasonable to say that if there is a right to happiness there are also limits to it. So I decided to look at how Lewis managed to make me change my mind--at least part way.

C. S. Lewis is persuasive, especially because of three things. First, although Lewis (a professor) is obviously very learned, he uses an informal manner that sounds very natural and honest. Second, he gives clear examples. Three, his sentences are always clear. This is true even when they are not especially short. All of these things combine together to make his essay clear and interesting. Lewis is an Englishman, not an American.

Lewis's informal manner, especially seen in his use of the first-person pronoun, appears right away. In the second sentence, when he says "We were discussing something. . . ." He uses "I" in the fifth paragraph and in many later paragraphs.

Another sign of Lewis's informality is his use of such expressions as "It might be true, as some said," and "You mustn't, by the way, imagine," and "for one thing." It sounds like an ordinary person talking, even though

Lewis also mentions the names of philosophers in paragraph 8, and in paragraph 14 mentions several historical matters.

Next I will deal with Lewis's examples. The examples help him to be clear to the reader. The essay begins with a story about four people. Two said they had a "right to happiness." In this story Lewis lets us see two people (Mr. A. and Mrs. B.) who behave very badly. They justify their behavior simply by saying they have a right to happiness. They behave so badly--Mr. A. deserts the wife who nursed him through a long illness, and Mrs. B. deserts her husband, who is a wounded veteran--that just to hear them talk about a "right to happiness" is almost enough to make you say they should not be happy and they certainly do not have a right to happiness. The example of Mr. and Mrs. A. and Mr. and Mrs. B. is the longest example that Lewis gives, but Lewis several times gives short examples. These short examples make his point clear. For instance, when he wants to show how silly it is to treat sex differently from all other impulses, he says that it is "like having a morality in which stealing fruit is considered wrong--unless you steal nectarines."

Another thing Lewis does to persuade the reader is to write very clear sentences. Some of his sentences are long—about three lines of print--but the reader has no trouble with them. Here is an example of this sort of sentence.

> A right to happiness doesn't, for me, make much more sense than a right to be six feet tall, or to have a millionaire for your father, or to get good weather whenever you want to have a picnic.

The only thing that causes any trouble is a few unfamiliar words such as "tautologies" (paragraph 14) and "tycoon" (paragraph 16), but you can understand the essay even without looking up such words.

Revising and Editing a Draft

To write a good essay you must be a good reader not only of the essay you are writing about but also of the essay you yourself are writing. We're not talking about proofreading or correcting spelling errors, though of course you must engage in those activities as well.

Revising. In revising their work, writers ask themselves such questions as:

> Do I mean what I say?
>
> Do I say what I mean? (Answering this question will cause you to ask yourself such questions as: Do I need to define my terms, add examples to clarify, reorganize the material so that a reader can grasp it?)

During this part of the process of writing, you do your best to read the draft in a skeptical frame of mind. In taking account of your doubts, you will probably unify, organize, clarify, and polish the draft.

- **Unity** is achieved partly by eliminating irrelevancies. In the second paragraph of the draft, for example, the writer says that "Lewis is an Englishman, not an American," but the fact that Lewis is English is not clearly relevant to the student's argument that Lewis writes persuasively. The statement should be deleted—or its relevance should be demonstrated.
- **Organization** is largely a matter of arranging material into a sequence that will assist the reader to grasp the point. If you reread your draft and jot down a paragraph outline of the sort shown on pages 13–14 and 28, you can then see if the draft has a reasonable organization—a structure that will let the reader move easily from the beginning to the end.
- **Clarity** is achieved largely by providing concrete details, examples, and quotations to support generalizations and by providing helpful transitions ("for instance," "furthermore," "on the other hand," "however").
- **Polish** is small-scale revision. For instance, one deletes unnecessary repetitions. In the first sentence of the second paragraph, "C. S. Lewis" can effectively be changed to "Lewis"—there really is no need to repeat his initials—and in the second sentence of the second paragraph "Lewis" can be changed to "he." Similarly, in polishing, a writer combines choppy sentences into longer sentences and breaks overly long sentences into shorter sentences.

Editing. After producing a draft that seems good enough to show to someone, writers engage in yet another activity. They edit; that is, they check the accuracy of quotations by comparing them with the original, check a dictionary for the spelling of doubtful words, check a handbook for doubtful punctuation—for instance, whether a comma or a semicolon is needed in a particular sentence.

A Revised Draft

Persuasive Strategies in C. S. Lewis's
On "~~We~~ Have No 'Right to Happiness'"

~~When I first read the title of C. S. Lewis's essay I was interested and~~
~~also somewhat resistant. Without having given much thought to it, I~~
~~believe that I do have a right to happiness. I don't want to give up this~~
~~right or this belief. Still I was intrigued to know what Lewis has to say. After~~
~~reading the essay it seemed entirely reasonable to say that if there is a~~
~~right to happiness there are also limits to it. So I decided to look at how~~
~~Lewis managed to make me change my mind, at least part way.~~

C. S. Lewis's "We Have No 'Right to Happiness" is surprisingly persuasive--
"surprisingly" because I believe in the right to happiness which is mentioned
in the Declaration of Independence. Lewis, an Englishman writing in an
American magazine, probably knew he was facing an audience who did not hold
his view, and he apparently decided to begin by stating his position as
directly as possible in his title. "We Have No 'Right to Happiness". How does
he win his reader over?

C. S. Lewis is persuasive because in addition to thinking carefully, he writes
effectively. Three features of his writing especially contribute to his
effectiveness.

~~C. S. Lewis is persuasive especially because of three things.~~ First,
although Lewis (a professor) is obviously very learned, he uses an
informal manner that ~~sounds very natural and honest~~ *helps to establish a bond between him and his reader*. Second, he gives
clear examples. ~~Third~~ *Third*, his sentences are always clear. This is true even
when they are not especially short. All of these things combine together to
make his essay clear and interesting. ~~Lewis is an Englishman, not an~~
~~American.~~

Lewis's informal manner, especially seen in his use of the first
person pronoun, appears right away-~~In~~ *in* the second sentence, when he
says "We were discussing something. . . ." He uses "I" in the fifth paragraph
and in many later paragraphs.

Another sign of Lewis's informality is his use of such expressions as
"It might be true, as some said," and "You mustn't, by the way, imagine,"

and "for one thing." It sounds like an ordinary person talking, even though

Lewis also mentions that names of philosophers in paragraph 8, and in

paragraph 14 mentions several historical matters.

As for
~~Next I will deal with Lewis's~~ examples. ~~The examples~~ *, which* help him to be

clear *, the story of Mr. & Mrs. A and Mr. & Mrs. B is a good illustration.* ~~to the reader. The essay begins with a story about four people. Two~~

~~said they~~ *Mr. A & Mrs. B both of whom believed they* had a "right to happiness." ~~In this story Lewis lets us see two~~

~~people (Mr. A and Mrs. B) who behave very badly. They justify their~~

~~behavior simply by saying they have a right to happiness~~. They behave

so badly--Mr. A deserts the wife who nursed him through a long illness,

and Mrs. B deserts her husband, who is a wounded veteran--that just hear

them talk about "right to happiness" is almost enough to make you ~~say~~
doubt that there can be such a right
~~they should not be happy and they certainly do not have a right to~~

~~happiness~~. The example of Mr. and Mrs. A and Mr. and Mrs. B is the
he
longest example that Lewis gives, but ~~Lewis~~ several times gives short
, that
examples. ~~These short examples~~ make his point clear. For instance, when

he wants to show how silly it is to treat sex differently from all other

impulses, he says that it is "like having a morality in which stealing fruit is

considered wrong--unless you steal nectarines."
Lewis's third persuasive technique
~~Another thing Lewis does to persuade the reader~~ is to write very clear

sentences. Some of his sentences are long--about three lines of print--but the

reader has no trouble with them. Here is an example of this sort of sentence.

> A right to happiness doesn't, for me, make much more
> sense than a right to be six feet tall, or to have a million-
> aire for your father, or to get good weather whenever
> you want to have a picnic.

The sentence is fairly long, partly because the second half gives three examples, but because these examples are given in a parallel construction ("to be," "or to have," "or to get") the reader easily follows the thought.

True,
~~The only thing that causes any trouble is~~ a few unfamiliar words such as
may cause a bit of trouble
tautologies (paragraph 14) and tycoon (paragraph 16)^, but ~~you~~ can
a reader
understand the essay even without looking up such words.

Of course Lewis has not absolutely proved that there is no "right to happiness," but he has made a good, clear case. The clarity, in fact, is part of the case. Everything that Lewis says here seems so obvious that a reader is almost persuaded by Lewis's voice alone.

Rethinking the Thesis: Preliminary Notes

You'll probably agree that the student improved his draft, for instance by deleting the original first paragraph and replacing it with a more focused paragraph. But, as we mentioned earlier, when the student thought further about his revision, he was still dissatisfied with it because he no longer fully believed his thesis.

He found that although he continued to admire Lewis's persuasive techniques, he remained unpersuaded by Lewis's argument. He therefore felt obliged to change the thesis of his essay from (approximately) "Lewis's chief persuasive techniques are . . ." to "Although Lewis is highly skilled as a persuasive writer, even his rhetorical skill cannot overcome certain weaknesses in his thesis."

Here are some of the annotations that the student produced after he recognized his dissatisfaction with his revised draft.

Mr. and Mrs. A. and B. may or may not be real people, but they certainly
  seem UNREAL: too neatly suited (all good or bad) to L's purpose.

  The villains: Mr. A. (he tosses out his wife after she loses her
  looks, despite the fact that she wore herself out with his
  children and nursed him through long illness; even after,
  wife commits suicide he doesn't see that he continues to talk
  selfishly); Mrs. B. (she leaves her husband when he gets
  wounded and he loses his "virility" and loses his job). Aren't
  these people a bit too awful? Are they really typical of
  people who divorce?

  The heroes--or saints? Mrs. A. (nursed husband through
  long illness, wore self out with the children); Mr. B. (injured
  in war; loses job).

  Clare: She also seems too suited to CSL's thesis; she's pretty
  terrible, and stupid too.

Lewis on Divorce: He seems to think it is always motivated by a desire for
  sex, and that it is always wrong. But what if a husband abuses his
  wife--maybe physically, or maybe verbally and emotionally? Maybe
  chronic alcoholic, refuses treatment, etc.? Or what if wife abuses hus-
  band--probably not physically, but verbally, and maybe she assaults
  kids? Or take another angle: what if woman married at too young an
  age, inexperienced, married to escape from an awful family, and
  now finds she made a mistake? Should she stay married to the man
  for life? In short, does Lewis see divorce from enough angles?

First five paragraphs are extremely interesting, but are unfair for three reasons:

1. Lewis loads the dice, showing us goodies and baddies, and then says (par. 5) that they set him to thinking about the "right to happiness";
2. He overemphasizes the importance of sex, neglects other possible reasons why people divorce;
3. His discussion of "Natural Law," is not convincing to me. I simply am not convinced that there is a "Law of Nature" that "eternally sanctions" certain things.

Sexist??? Although CSL seems to be defending women (esp. par. 28, in which he says that promiscuity puts women at a double disadvantage), there is something sort of sexist in the essay, and I imagine that this will turn off women, and maybe even men. I know that I'm a little bothered by it.

The Final Version

We won't take you through the drafts that the student wrote, but in reading the final version, below, you will notice that although some of the points from the draft are retained, the thesis, as we said, has shifted. Notice, for instance, that the first paragraph of the revised draft is used in the final version but with two significant changes: in the first sentence the student now adds that he finds Lewis's essay "finally unconvincing," and in the last sentence of the paragraph he implies that he will discuss why the essay is "not finally convincing."

Jim Weinstein

Professor Valdez

English Composition 12

Style and Argument:

An Examination of C. S. Lewis's

"We Have No 'Right to Happiness'"

C. S. Lewis's "We Have No 'Right to Happiness'" is, though finally unconvincing, surprisingly persuasive--"surprisingly" because I believe in the right to happiness, which is mentioned in the Declaration of Independence. Lewis, an Englishman writing in an American magazine, probably knew he was facing an audience who did not hold his view, and he apparently decided to begin by stating his position as directly as possible in his title: "We Have No 'Right to Happiness.'" How does he nearly win his reader over? And why is he not finally convincing?

Lewis is highly (though not entirely) persuasive because he writes effectively. Three features of his writing especially contribute to his effectiveness. First, although Lewis (a professor) is obviously very learned, he uses an informal manner that helps to establish a bond between him and his reader. Second, he gives clear examples. Third, his sentences are always clear, even when they are not especially short. All of these things combine to make his essay clear and interesting--and almost convincing.

His informal manner, especially his use of the first-person pronouns, appears right away in the second sentence, when he says "We were discussing something. . . ." He uses "I" in the fifth paragraph and in many later paragraphs. Another sign of his informality is his use of such expressions as "It might be true, as some said," and "You mustn't, by the way, imagine." It sounds like an ordinary person talking.

Most of his examples, too, seem ordinary. They make his points seem almost obvious. For instance, when he wants to show how silly it is to treat sex differently from all other impulses, he says that it is "like having a morality in which stealing fruit is considered wrong--unless you steal nectarines" (p. 23). The touch of humor drives the point home.

Still, although Lewis seems thoughtful and he makes his argument very clear, the essay somehow does not finally persuade. The trouble may largely be Mr. and Mrs. A. and B., but there are other difficulties, too.

Mr. and Mrs. A. and B. are just too simple a case, too neat an illustration. Lewis of course wanted to make a clear-cut case, but a reader does not really believe in these people. They are caricatures: Mr. A. tosses out his wife after she loses her looks (and she lost them not only through the natural process of aging but through taking care of the family), and Mrs. B. leaves her husband, a wounded veteran. Of course it is conceivable that there really were a Mr. A. and a Mrs. B., but surely the pros and cons of divorce ought not to be based on cases like this, where it is so clear that Mr. A. and Mrs. B. are irresponsible. They are, one might say, as morally stupid as Clare is. But the fact that these people are selfish and stupid and that they each get a divorce does not prove that only selfish and stupid people seek divorce.

Nor do the experiences of the A's and the B's show that people who seek a divorce always are seeking sexual pleasure. We can imagine, for instance, a woman married to a wife-beater. Does she not have a right to be free of her abusive husband, a "right to happiness"? Nor need we limit our case to physical abuse. A husband (or a wife) can abuse a spouse verbally and emotionally and can be impossibly neglectful of the children. Or we can imagine a couple who married when very young--perhaps partly for the sake of defying their parents, or maybe in order to escape from a bad family situation. In any case, we can imagine that one member of the couple now sees that a bad mistake was made. Need they stay tied to each other?

Lewis's essay is powerful, partly because it clearly advances a thesis that must seem strange to many Americans; and it is interesting, partly because Lewis makes his points clearly and he seems to be such a thoughtful and decent person. But in the end, the essay is not convincing. It is just a little too simple in its examples and in its suggestion that people who claim a right to happiness are really just saying that they want to get divorced so they can live legally with another sexual partner.

[New page]

Work Cited

Lewis, C.S. "We Have No 'Right to Happiness'." The Little Brown Reader. Eighth ed. Ed. Marcia Stubbs and Sylvan Barnet. New York: Longman, 2000. 20–24.

A Brief Overview of the Final Version

- First, a mechanical matter: The student has added a footnote, telling the reader where the essay can be found and explaining that all quotations are from this source.
- The title, though not especially engaging, is informative—more so than, say, "On an Essay by C. S. Lewis." Readers know that the writer will discuss Lewis's style and argument in a particular essay.
- The student's final essay is *not* simply a balanced debate, a statement of the pros and cons that remains inconclusive. Rather, the student argues a thesis: although Lewis's essay is in some ways admirable, it remains unconvincing.
- The student's thesis is stated early, in fact in the first paragraph. It's almost always a good idea to let your reader know early where you will be going.
- Quotations are used as evidence, not as padding. See, for example, paragraphs 3 and 4.
- The writer has kept his reader in mind. He has not summarized Lewis's essay in needless detail, but, on the other hand, he has not assumed that the reader knows the essay inside out. For instance, he does not simply assert that Mr. A. behaves very badly; rather, he reminds us that Mr. A. rejects his wife after she loses her looks. When he uses a quotation, he guides the reader to where in Lewis's essay the quotation can be found.
- He also keeps the reader in mind by using helpful transitions. In paragraph 2 notice "First," "Second," and "Third"; in paragraph 5, "Still" indicates a reversal of direction. Notice, too, that key words and phrases are repeated. Repetition of this sort, like transitions, makes it easy for the reader to follow the writer's train of thought. In the second paragraph, for example, he cites Lewis's "informal manner" as the first of three points of style. His next paragraph begins, "His informal manner . . . ." Similarly, the last sentence of paragraph 3 contains the words "ordinary person." The next paragraph begins, "Most of his examples, too, seem ordinary."
- So far we have talked about what is in the essay. But what is *not* in it is also worth comment. In the final essay, the student does *not* include all of the points he jotted down in his preliminary notes. He does not take up either Natural Law or the issue of sexism, probably because he felt unsure about both. Notes are points of departure; if when you get going you find you are going down a blind alley, don't hesitate to go back and drop the point.

✓A Checklist for Analyzing and Evaluating an Essay That You Are Writing About

When you read, try to read sympathetically, opening yourself to the writer's vision of things. But when you have finished a sympathetic reading—and an attentive reading—and you have made various sorts of notes, probably including an outline and a summary of the essay you are reading, you are ready to *analyze* the writer's methods and to *evaluate* the piece.

In **analyzing,** you will examine the relationships between the parts; that is, you will ask such questions as:

✓ What is the *topic* of the essay? Try to state it, preferably in writing, as specifically as possible. For example, broadly speaking, one might say that the subject of Lewis's essay is the right to happiness; but within this subject his topic, more specifically, is sexual freedom. Plumb's subject is the family, and his topic is the historical changes that the family has undergone.

✓ What is the essay's *thesis* (either stated or implied)? If you have located a *thesis sentence* in the essay, underline it and write *thesis* in the margin. If the thesis is implied, try to formulate it in a sentence of your own.

✓ What does the title do? What *purpose* does it suggest the writer holds?

✓ What is the function of the opening paragraph (or paragraphs)? What claim on our attention or beliefs does it make?

✓ What speaker or *persona* (see page 16–17) does the writer create, and how does the writer create it?

✓ What is the tone? Does the tone (page 16–17) shift as the essay progresses? If so, why?

✓ What *audience* is the writer addressing? The general, literate public, or a more specialized group?

✓ How is the argument set forth? By logic? By drawing on personal experience? What evidence is there that the writer is an authority on the topic? Are there other appeals to authority? What other kinds of evidence support the essay's claim? What are the author's underlying assumptions? Are they stated or implied, and are they acceptable to you, or can you challenge them?

✓ If there is a formal, explicit conclusion, underline or restate it. If the conclusion is not stated but is implied, what does the writer want us to conclude?

In **evaluating,** you will ask such questions as:

✓ Is the essay as clear as it can be, given the complexity of the material? For instance, do specific examples help to make the generalizations clear? Are crucial terms adequately defined? If the thesis is not explicitly stated, is the essay unclear or is it perhaps better because of the indirectness?

✓ If the conclusion is not stated but implied, why does the writer not state it?

✓ Is the argument (if the essay is chiefly an argument) convincing, or is it marred by faulty thinking? If statistics are used, are they sound and relevant? If authorities are quoted, are they indeed authorities (rather than just big names) on this topic?

✓ Is the essay interesting? If so, in what ways, and if not, why not— which gets us back to analysis. If there are passages of undisguised argument, for instance, are they clear without being repetitious and boring? Do specific examples clarify and enliven general assertions?

✓ If the essay includes narrative or descriptive passages, are they pertinent? Should they have been amplified, or should they have been reduced or even deleted?

✓ How is the essay organized? Is the organization effective? Does the essay build to a climax?

Another way of thinking about the criteria for evaluating an essay is to ask:

✓ Is the essay persuasive (whether because of its logic or because of the power of the speaker's personality)? and,

✓ Does the essay give pleasure?

Don't hesitate to demand that an essay give you pleasure. The author probably thought that he or she was writing well, and certainly hoped to hold your interest throughout the essay and to make you feel that you were learning something of interest. In short, the author hoped that you would like the essay. You have every right to evaluate the essay partly by considering the degree of pleasure that it affords. Of course, in your essay you cannot simply say that you enjoyed an essay or that you were bored by it. You will have to support your assertions with reasons based on evidence. To support your assertions you must have read the writer's words carefully, so we are back to an earlier point: the first thing to do if you are going to write about a piece of writing is to read it attentively, pen or pencil in hand.

As you read and reread the material that you are writing about, subjecting it to the kinds of questions we have mentioned, your understanding of it will almost surely deepen. You will probably come to feel that it is better—or worse—than you had thought at first, or in any case that it is somewhat different.

As you prepare to write your own essay and as you draft it, you are learning, feeling your way toward a considered analysis. But once having said something—whether in a mental question to yourself or in a note or a draft—you have to evaluate your thought and improve it if it doesn't stand up under further scrutiny.

3
ACADEMIC WRITING

Kinds of Prose

Traditionally, prose is said to be of four kinds: **Exposition** (its chief purpose is to explain), **Description** (it sets forth a detailed account of appearances or sensations), **Narration** (it recounts a sequence of events, telling a story), and **Persuasion** or **Argument** (it attempts to get readers to accept or act on your views). Thus, an essay or a book on how to improve our game of tennis chiefly will be an

- *exposition*—a putting forth of information.
- In fact, however, the essay or book on how to improve our game probably will also include a good deal of *description* (it will describe as accurately as possible the motion of the arm).
- and it may include some *narration* ("Tennis seems to have originated in the courts of fourteenth-century France, originally was played with balls stuffed with horse hair, and from France the game traveled to Germany and England . . . ," or "You may already be familiar with the story of how Venus Williams became the great player that she now is, but the story is worth repeating here").
- The discussion of how to improve our tennis probably will not, however, contain much *persuasive* writing, because the author assumes that the readers are already sold on the game. On the other hand, one can reasonably say that simply by writing about how to improve your game, the author is in effect persuading you to stay with the game, implicitly telling you that, gee, even *you* can become a pretty good player.

When you think about it, almost *all* writing is persuasive, since it says, in effect, "I find this interesting and I want you to find it interesting too." Even a note on a refrigerator door, "Egg salad sandwich and apple on lower shelf," is partly an attempt to persuade the reader to leave the cold roast beef and the ice cream alone. Consider for a moment Thomas Jefferson's *Declaration of Independence* (page 684). On the surface, it is chiefly *expository.* Jefferson explains why the time has come for certain people to declare their independence from England; that's the expository part, the setting forth of information, though it also includes a good deal of narration, since Jefferson tells us that the King of England did this ("He has dissolved Representative Houses repeatedly") and the king did that ("He has kept among us, in times of peace, Standing Armies"). Jefferson offers this information because he wishes to *persuade* the international community—especially the French—to support the revolution. Or consider a very different piece of writing, also by a political figure, Lincoln's *Gettysburg Address* (page 556). Surely Lincoln was not chiefly concerned with exposition or narration or description. True, he tells his hearers that "four score and seven years ago our fathers brought forth on this continent, a new nation" (narration), but they already knew *that* story; and he explains to them that they cannot dedicate the cemetery because the dead men have already hallowed it (exposition). But obviously the speech essentially is meant to celebrate the heroism of the dead, and, by reminding the audience of the heroism of the fallen soldiers, the speech seeks to inspire—to persuade—the living to continue the battle. Of these two essays, *The Declaration of Independence* is closer to academic writing than is *The Gettysburg Address.*

More about Critical Thinking: Analysis and Evaluation

In Chapter 1 we talked briefly about critical thinking and about analysis, and we now want to amplify our discussion, but first we should devote a few more words to the term "academic writing."

Exactly what is "academic writing"? *Academic* come from the Greek *Academos,* a garden near Athens where the philosopher Plato taught. Because of its connection with a great teacher, the name of the garden came to refer to any place where the arts or sciences or both are taught or fostered. Academic writing is the sort of writing done in the academy—in colleges and universities. Since each academic discipline requires its own sort of writing, however, several kinds of writing are done in an academic setting. In literature courses, students chiefly analyze and evaluate works of literature—but they may also be required to write a story, poem, or play. In sociology courses, students may be asked to analyze and evaluate the views of a particular sociologist—but they may also be asked to interview authorities or perhaps ordinary folk, and to present their findings in writing.

Still, at the heart of most academic writing—most of the writing that you will do in college—is an activity that can be called *critical thinking,* which consists chiefly of *analyzing* and *evaluating.* Exactly what is analysis? Literally, it is "separating into parts," and a good way to get going on an analysis is to ask what the parts are. Let's talk briefly about "hate speech," a topic addressed in Derek Bok's "Protecting Freedom of Expression on the Campus" (page 702), an essay that was prompted by the display of a Confederate flag hung from the window of a dormitory. Is the display of a Confederate flag "hate speech"? It's not literally speech, of course, but probably most people would agree that the act of displaying the flag might be closely comparable to verbally expressing some ideas. But exactly what is hate speech? Suppose *X* uses an ethnic term that *Y* finds offensive, but *X* says he used it playfully? Or suppose *X* admits that the word was used aggressively, and suppose we all agree that such aggressive language is bad, we still have to think about *how bad* it is. Bad enough so that it ought to be regulated by the college? Punishable by a reprimand? Suspension? Expulsion?

If in an effort to think analytically we ask ourselves such questions (and perhaps even take notes to help us advance our thoughts), we might find we are thinking along these lines:

- What is hate speech? How is it distinguished from mere unthinking expression, or high spirits? Must the speech concern race, religion, ethnicity, or sexual preference? If *X* calls *Y* a fat pig, does this show an offensive hatred of obesity? (In asking the question, "What is . . . ?" we are getting into matters of *definition*.)
- The First Amendment to the Constitution guarantees freedom of speech, but it does *not* protect *all* speech (for instance, libel, false advertising, incitements to violence). Does hate speech belong to protected speech, or does it belong to *un*protected speech? (Here we are concerned with *classification*, with trying to see to what larger class of things something belongs.)
- How bad, after all, is hate speech? Bad, yes, but probably no one would suggest that it is as bad as murder or rape, or that it should be punished by long-term jail sentences. By one day in jail? By a reprimand? (Here we are concerned with quality, with evaluation.)

As you ask yourself questions such as these, and as you seek to answer them, you will probably find that your views are changing, perhaps slightly (maybe you are refining them), perhaps radically. The writer E. M. Forster tells of a little girl who, when instructed to think before she spoke, shrewdly replied, "How do I know what I think until I hear what I say?" Only by the process of hearing what we say, and then testing and pressing further in a mental conversation with ourselves, can we hope to have ideas that our fellow students and our instructors will value. When you write an academic paper, your instructor will expect you to have done this sort of work, and if you have done it, you will recognize that you have indeed been thinking, been educating yourself. If your paper is connected to Derek Bok's essay, you may of course begin with a brief summary of his essay (we'll talk more about summaries later), in which your thinking doesn't go much beyond (1) understanding what Bok says, and (2) setting forth his thesis accurately and concisely; but soon you will get around to offering an *analysis* and probably an *evaluation*, to putting on paper the results of your serious, critical thinking.

The essays in *The Little, Brown Reader* contain a good deal of information, but chiefly you will read them not for the information they contain—as Robert Reich points out in his essay on the future of work, the world is changing and today's facts will not be tomorrow's facts; rather, you read these essays chiefly for the ideas they advance, and for the habits of thought that they display. And you will respond to them largely by setting forth arguments of your own. Writing based on serious *thinking* is what is expected of you. One of the reasons you are attending college is to acquire practice in thinking. As William Cory says (page 359), one goes to school not only for knowledge—facts, we might say—but for

the art of assuming at a moment's notice a new intellectual posture, for the art of entering quickly into another person's thought, for the habit of submit-

Sitting Bull and Buffalo Bill, 1885

ting to censure and refutation, for the art of indicating assent or dissent in graduated terms . . . .

For a moment let's put aside the writings in this book, and look at a photograph of Sitting Bull and Buffalo Bill, taken in 1886 by William McFarlane Notman. William Cody got his nickname from his work as a supplier of meat for workers on the Kansas Pacific Railway, but he got his fame from his exploits as an army scout and a fighter against the Sioux Indians. Sitting Bull, a chief of the Sioux Indians, had defeated Custer at the battle of Little Big Horn some ten years before this picture was taken, but he soon fled to Canada. In 1879 he was granted amnesty and he returned to the United States, where for a while he appeared in Buffalo Bill's Wild West Show. In 1890 whites, fearful of an Indian uprising, attempted to arrest Sitting Bull, and he was killed during the encounter.

What you have just read cannot pass for an example of critical thinking. We hope the writing is clear, but about the only thinking that we were forced to do was to decide how much information to give. Should we have added that Sitting Bull encouraged the Sioux not to sell their lands, and thus he enraged the whites? Should we have added that Buffalo Bill rode for the Pony Express? Or that he invented some of his greatest exploits? Probably none of these points needs to be made here, in a brief introduction to the photograph. In short, we made some choices—we decided go to give minimal information—and that was that. But now let's think— think critically—about the picture. We can begin (and this may sound like a contradiction) with our emotional response, our gut feelings. We are interested in this picture—but why?

We begin to ask ourselves questions, a method that, we have seen, almost always helps to develop one's thoughts. What is going on here? There are two figures, but they are so different. Buffalo Bill, head brightly illuminated, is looking off into the distance, rather like a modern-day political candidate, whose upward and outward glance implies that he or she is looking into the future. His right hand is on his heart, in a patriotic or noble gesture; his left leg is thrust forward. He wears a mammoth buckle, a fancy jacket, and shiny hip boots. His hand is above Sitting Bull's on the gun, and he is both behind Sitting Bull and (by virtue of his left leg) in front of Sitting Bull. Buffalo Bill, in short, is all show biz. If we look closely at the setting, we see that the meeting is not taking place in the great outdoors; rather, the setting is a sort of stage set, presumably in a photographer's studio.

What of Sitting Bull? Whereas Buffalo Bill clearly was striking a pose for the camera, Sitting Bull seems indifferent to the camera. Later in this chapter we will discuss comparing at length, but here we want only to mention that comparing is an excellent way to perceive what is unique about each of the things being compared. By comparing these two figures, we can more clearly see Buffalo Bill's flamboyance—and Sitting Bull's reserve. Sitting Bull seems reserved, withdrawn; his face, tilted downward, is mostly in shadow; his body seems inert; his right arm hangs lifelessly; his headdress is splendid but his trousers are baggy and his belt dangles beneath his shirt. His hand on the rifle is subordinated to Buffalo Bill's.

May we say that now we are really *thinking* about the picture? An *un*thinking description would say, "The picture shows the two figures, dividing the space approximately equally, each in costume." This statement is true, and it might indeed find a place in the early stage of an analytic essay on the photograph, but your teachers—you are writing in an academy—expect more than an accurate, neatly typed description.

Here is the final paragraph from one of the best student essays we have received on this photograph. (The earlier paragraphs specified the differences in pose, costume, and so on, along the lines that we have just set forth.)

> Buffalo Bill is obviously the dominant figure in this photograph, but he is not the outstanding one. His efforts to appear great only serve to make him appear small. His attempt to outshine Sitting Bull strikes us as faintly ridiculous. We do not

> need or want to know any more about Buffalo Bill's personality; it is spread before us in this picture. Sitting Bull's humility and dignity make him more interesting than Buffalo Bill, and make us wish to prove our intuition and to ascertain that this proud Sioux was a great chief.

Of course the photograph might lead a student to another, related topic. For instance, a student might want to know more about the photographer, William McFarlane Notman. What did Notman think the photograph said to viewers? Was Notman setting forth a compassionate statement about the American Indian? Or was he just doing a job for Buffalo Bill? One might do some research on Notman, first, perhaps, by turning to a handsome book of his photographs, *Portrait of a Period,* edited by J. Russell Harper and Stanley Triggs. Research on Notman might lead you to conclude that his pictures often subtly undermine the pretensions of his heroic sitters, or you might find, on the contrary, that Notman celebrates heroism of all kinds, white and Indian. Or you might find that, for some strange reason, his pictures of Indians are far more interesting than his pictures of whites.

If a student writing about Notman's photographs does no more than tell us that the book has 75 pictures, that they are black and white, that all are portraits, that . . . , the student is not presenting the sort of writing expected in an academic community. Such information if presented briefly is acceptable as a start, acceptable as establishing a framework, but it is only a start, it is *not* critical thinking, it is *not* academic writing.

One last example of a related essay that would exemplify critical thinking. You might want to read the entries on Sitting Bull and Buffalo Bill in two versions of the *Encyclopaedia Britannica,* the 9th edition (1911) and the most recent edition. If you do, take note of the differences between the two versions, and then think about what these differences tell us about the early twentieth century and the last decade of the twentieth century.

Joining the Conversation: Writing about Differing Views

Your instructor will probably ask you to read more than one essay in some section of this book. The chief reason for such an assignment is to stimulate you to think about some complex issue. After all, no one essay on any topic of significance can claim to say all that needs to be said about the topic. Essays that advocate similar positions on, say, capital punishment may, because of slightly different emphases, usefully supplement one another; and even two radically opposed essays may both contain material that you find is essential to a thoughtful discussion of the topic.

Let's say that you read an essay supporting the death penalty. Perhaps, as an aid to grasping the author's argument, you prepared a summary of the essay, and you notice that the writer's chief points are these:

1. The death penalty serves as a deterrent.
2. Justice requires that murderers pay an appropriate price for their crimes.

These basic points probably are supported by some evidence, but you have been reading critically, and you have wondered whether this or that piece of evidence is compelling. You have also wondered if more can't be said on the other side—not only by specific refutation of certain arguments, but perhaps also by arguments that the first essayist has not raised. You turn to a second essayist, someone who opposes the death penalty, and who (you find when you summarize the essay) in effect offers these arguments:

1. The death penalty does not serve as a deterrent.
2. If the death penalty is inflicted mistakenly, the error cannot be corrected.
3. The death penalty is imposed unequally; statistics indicate that when blacks and whites are guilty of comparable offences, blacks are more likely to be sentenced to death.

It is now evident that the two writers are and are not talking about the same thing. They are talking about the death penalty, but for the most part they are not confronting the same issues. On only one issue—deterrence—do they face each other. On this issue you will want to think hard about the evidence that each offers. Possibly you will decide that one author makes a compelling case at least on this issue, but it is also possible that you will decide that the issue cannot be resolved. Or you may find that you can make a better case than did either writer.

Think about the other arguments offered—on the one hand that justice requires the death penalty, and on the other hand that it can be mistakenly inflicted and is awarded unequally. You will not only want to think hard about each of these points, but you will also wonder why only one of the two essayists took them up. Is one or the other argument so clearly mistaken that it is not worth discussing? Or is a particular argument one that can't be proved either true of false? Or are the writers working from different **assumptions** (unexamined beliefs). For instance, the writer who argues that the death penalty is capriciously enforced may assume that race prejudice cannot be overcome, whereas a writer who rejects the argument may assume that the courts can and will see to it that the death penalty is imposed impartially. As a critical reader, you will want to be alert to the assumptions that writers make. You'll have to ask yourself often, *What assumption lies beneath this assertion?* That is, what belief is so firmly held, and is assumed to be so self-evident, that the writer does not bother to assert it? Do I share this assumption? Why?

If you are asked to compare two essays that offer sharply differing views, you probably will want to point out where the two face each other and where they don't. You probably will want also to offer an evaluation of the two. Or, depending on the assignment, you may use the two merely as a point of departure for your own essay on the topic. That is, you may want to draw on one or both—giving credit of course—and then offer your own serious thoughts.

Writing about Essays Less Directly Related: A Student's Notes and Journal Entries

Let's assume that your instructor has asked you to read Plumb's "The Dying Family" (p. 6) and Lewis's "We Have No 'Right to Happiness'" (p. 20), and has asked you to compare them. Both of these essays concern family relationships, but they do not take distinctly different positions on a single controversial topic. They are, we might say, thoughtful voices in a conversation that is consistently interesting but is wide-ranging rather than sharply focused.

Let's say that you settle on Plumb's and Lewis's attitudes toward their material. Perhaps your first thought is that Lewis very obviously offers value judgments, whereas Plumb, as a historian, simply reports what has happened in history.

On rereading the two essays, you may find yourself making notes somewhat like these notes that a student made:

1. Some of Plumb's assumptions:
    Family evolves: history a process (not static, not cyclical).
    Idea of parents wedded until death no longer needed in our urban, industrial society.
    Happiness not increasing or decreasing.

2. I'm surprised to find so many assumptions in the writings of a historian. I thought history was supposed to be an account, the "story" of what happened: in Social Studies we learned history is "value-free."

3. Some of Lewis's assumptions:
    Lewis very clearly makes assumptions, for instance, belief in the existence of "Natural Law" (par. 8) and belief that "domestic happiness is more necessary to them than to us" (to women, than to men), par. 28. Also assumes that women don't care much about men's looks (28)--but is this true? How might someone be able to prove it?

4. Big difference between Plumb and Lewis on assumptions. I think that Plumb makes assumptions but is hardly aware of them, whereas Lewis makes them and puts them right up front. With Lewis we know exactly where he stands. For instance, he obviously believes that we can use our free will to behave in ways that he considers proper. He even talks about "good people; controlled, loyal, fairminded" (25). (It's hard to imagine Plumb talking about "good people"; he only talks about whether people are "happy" or "stable.") Lewis pretty clearly believes not only that it's our job to act decently but that we can act decently. Seems not to accept the idea that we can be overwhelmed by passion or by the unconscious. Probably very anti-Freud. Anyway, his position is clear (and I agree with it). With Plumb we can hardly argue--at least I can't--since I'm not a historian. I don't know if what he says about the past really is true. but his opening paragraph strikes me as completely made up.

5. Attitudes toward change in family:
    For Lewis, a moralist, breakdown of family is a disaster; for Plumb, a fact of social evolution.

One student, whose thoughts were something like those that we have just presented, wrote two entries in his journal.

> Plumb: As I see it, he makes assumptions that pretty much go against what Lewis is arguing. Plumb looks at this family in California, and he says they are happy and he thinks everything is just fine. Well, maybe not fine, but at least he says that these children seem "as happy as any children that I have seen." I'm not so sure they are as happy as most. I know (from my own experience and from what I hear from friends) what divorced kids go through. Divorce may be normal (common, ordinary), but is it right? It seems to lead to so much unhappiness (for parents and children). Putting aside my own feelings, I can certainly see that my parents aren't especially happy with their new families. But there is Plumb, with his happy busload. Is he kidding? Or trying to fool us?

> Lewis: Lewis says we have no right to happiness--no right to divorce, remarry several times, and have families like that busload of people Plumb talks about. Lewis seems to be saying that divorce is morally wrong. Why? What are his reasons? I think he gives two: 1) it makes people unhappy (for instance, Mr. B., the wounded veteran, must have been miserable when Mrs. B. left him), and 2) it is against "Natural Law." But come to think of it, what is Natural Law? What makes divorce contrary to Natural Law? Is it really "unnatural"? Why? Lots of religions--maybe most

of them--accept divorce. And certainly governments accept it. So
what makes it unnatural? What is it that Bertrand Russell said
about our animal instinct? Check this.

The next day, after rereading Lewis's essay and the two entries, he
wrote two additional entries in his journal:

> I think that I agree with Lewis that we don't have a right to happi-
> ness, just as we don't have a right to be rich and handsome. But I
> wish Lewis had given some clear reasons instead of just saying
> that we have to remain for life with one spouse--even if we see
> that we have made a bad choice--because "Natural Law" tells us
> that we can't change. Come to think of it, Lewis <u>does</u> give some
> reasons against giving sex a special privilege: we hurt others, and
> we kid ourselves if we think each passion will last.

> Both Lewis and Plumb use short stories to make their points:
> Plumb's busload of Californians, Lewis's Mr. and Mrs. A. and Mr.
> and Mrs. B. Suppose these stories aren't true and Lewis and
> Plumb made these stories up. Does that matter?

The Student's Final Version: "Two Ways of Thinking about Today's Families"

Drawing on this material, the student drafted and revised an essay and
then submitted it to peer review. Then, in the light of the comments and
further thinking, he wrote the final version, which we give here. Our marginal comments summarize some of the strengths that we find in the finished essay. (*Note:* The original essay was, of course, double-spaced.).

Title gives a clue to topic.	Two Ways of Thinking about Today's Families
Opening paragraph names authors and essays, and indicates thesis—that the essays strongly differ.	J. H. Plumb in "The Dying Family" and C. S. Lewis in "We Have No 'Right to Happiness'" both note that today's families often consist of adults who have been divorced. But that is about as much as they would agree on. Judging from an example Plumb gives of a minibus with ten happy children, none of whom had both parents in common, Plumb thinks there is no rea- son to regret, much less to condemn, the behavior that presumably has produced this sort of family. And judg- ing from the examples Lewis gives of Mrs. B who left her wounded husband and of Mr. A who left his worn- out wife, Lewis thinks that the pursuit of happiness--sex- ual happiness at the expense of marriage--is immoral.

Despite these great differences, there are interesting similarities in the essays. The essays are both by Englishmen, are about the same length, were both written around the middle of the twentieth century, and both begin with an example. Plumb begins with his minibus of ten children and two adults, Lewis with his Mr. and Mrs. A. and Mr. and Mrs. B. Certainly both examples are striking. I'm not sure that, on rereading the essays, I believe either example is real, but they caught my attention. I must say, however, that I have more trouble believing in Plumb's happy busload than in Lewis's two couples. Putting aside my own experience as the child of divorced parents (each of whom has remarried), ten children--not two of whom have the same two parents--just seems like too many.

In addition to these relatively superficial resemblances, there is also a deeper resemblance. Plumb and Lewis are both talking about the great change in sexual behavior that came about in the twentieth century, especially in the middle of the century when divorce became respectable and common. But there is a big difference in their response. Plumb, writing as a historian, tries to understand why the change came about. Having concluded that the family no longer serves the purposes that it served in earlier periods, Plumb is not disturbed by the change. He ends his essay by saying, "And that bus load of children does no more than symbolize the failure, not of marriage, but of the role of the old-fashioned family unit in a modern, urbanized, scientific and affluent society" (11). Lewis, on the other hand, writes as a moralist. He tries to understand why the A's and B's of this world do what they do, and he sees that they behave as they do because of "the sexual impulse" (32). But Lewis does more than see what they do; he judges what they do, in particular he judges behavior against what he calls "Natural Law" (29) and "the Law of Nature" (30). And he makes it clear that he is not speaking only of sexual behavior. After saying that women are at a disadvantage in a society that tolerates conjugal infidelity, he makes a final point that goes far beyond matters of sex:

> Secondly, though the "right to happiness" is chiefly claimed for the sexual impulse, it seems to me impossible that the matter should stay

Margin notes:

Clear transition ("Despite these great differences").

Details support generalization.

Again a clear transition ("In addition to").

Quotation is used as evidence to support student's assertion that Plumb "is not disturbed."

Cites evidence.

Quotation of more than four lines is indented five spaces at left.

there. The fatal principle, once allowed in that department, must sooner or later seep through the
whole of our lives. (33)

Transition ("For
Plumb, then") by
means of brief
summary.

Parallel construc-
tion ("For Plumb .
. . For Lewis")
highlights similar-
ities and differ-
ences.

For Plumb, then, the family is something
produced by history, and it changes as history goes on.
For Lewis, the family--two adults wedded for life--is
something in accordance with Natural Law, and since
this law does not change, the nature of the family does
not change, or, rather, should not change. This
difference between the essays, of course, is far more
important than all of the similarities. Each essay is
interesting to read, and maybe each is even convincing
during the moments that someone is reading it. But
finally the essays are strongly opposed to each other,
and it is impossible to agree with both of them.

Student briefly
offers objections
to each essay.

Discloses reasons.

How is a reader to decide between the two
essays? Doubtless the earlier experience of a reader
predisposes that reader to believe certain things and not
to believe other things. Reading Plumb's essay, I find,
drawing on my experience, that I cannot believe in his
busload of happy children. Plumb does not seem to be
aware that children are greatly pained by the divorce
and remarriage of their parents. In short, Plumb seems
to me to be too satisfied that everything is just fine and
that we need not regret the loss of the old-style family.
On the other hand, Lewis does not think that everything
is just fine with the family. He sees the selfishness behind
the "right to [sexual] happiness" that for the most part has
destroyed the old-fashioned family. But Lewis rests his
case entirely on Natural Law, something that perhaps
not many people today believe in.

Student imagina-
tively extends the
discussion.

I can imagine Lewis and Plumb meeting and
having a debate. Lewis points out to Plumb that
divorce causes more unhappiness than Plumb has
admitted, and Plumb points out to Lewis that if modern
divorce causes much suffering, there must also have
been much suffering when parents did not get
divorced. Plumb and Lewis each grant the truth of
these objections, and then, in my imagined debate,
Plumb says to Lewis, "Furthermore, you build your
case on 'Natural Law,' but I don't think there really is
any such thing. I will grant that Mr. A. and Mrs. B. seem
irresponsible, but I won't grant that married adults
must for their entire lives remain with each other."
Lewis replies: "If you don't think that some things are

right--<u>always</u> right--and that some things are wrong--<u>always</u> wrong--what guides actions? You seem to care whether or not people are happy. But isn't it clear to you that some people seek their own happiness at the expense of others? What gives them such a right? If you don't believe in Natural Law, what do you believe in? Where do 'rights' come from?"

<table>
<tr><td>Transition and conclusion about the two essays.</td><td></td></tr>
</table>

And so the debate ends, not so much because they differ about whether people today are happier than people in the past, but because they differ in their assumptions. Plumb's assumption that history determines the rightness or wrongness of the family is unacceptable to Lewis, and Lewis's assumption that the family is based on Natural Law is unacceptable to Plumb.

Student intro- duces a personal note, but relates it closely to the two readings.

What is my own position? For the moment, I find <u>both</u> assumptions unacceptable. Intellectually I feel the force of Plumb's argument, but my experience tells me that he accepts the change in the family too easily. Intellectually I feel the force of Lewis's argument, but somehow I cannot convince myself that there is such a thing as Natural Law. Still, of the two writers, I feel that

Concludes with succinct refer- ences to both essays.

Lewis has a clearer picture of what people are like. I do know lots of people like Mr. and Mrs. A and Mr. and Mrs. B, but I don't know that busload of California kids.

Works Cited

Documentation

Lewis, C. S. "We Have No 'Right to Happiness.'" <u>The Little, Brown Reader</u>. Ed. Marcia Stubbs and Sylvan Barnet. 8th ed. New York: Longman, 2000. 20–24.

Plumb, J. H. "The Dying Family." <u>The Little, Brown Reader</u>. Ed. Marcia Stubbs and Sylvan Barnet. 8th ed. New York: Longman, 2000. 6–9.

Interviewing

In preparing to write about some of the essays in *The Little, Brown Reader,* you may want to interview faculty members or students, or persons not on the campus. For instance, if you are writing about the essays by Plumb and Lewis, you may want to talk to instructors who teach sociology or ethics—or you may simply want to collect the views of people who have no special knowledge but who may offer thoughtful responses. Obvious- ly topics such as divorce (pages 226–57), the value of computers in the classroom (449–64), hate speech (702–04), and almost all of the other topics addressed in this book are matters that you might profitably discuss with someone whose experience is notably different from your own.

A college campus is an ideal place to practice interviewing. Faculties are composed of experts in a variety of fields and distinguished visitors are a regular part of extracurricular life. In the next few pages, we'll offer some advice on conducting interviews and writing essays based on them. If you take our advice, you'll acquire a skill you may well put to further, more specialized use in social science courses; at the same time you'll be developing skill in asking questions and shaping materials relevant to all research and writing.

Guidelines for Conducting the Interview and Writing the Essay

You can conduct interviews over the telephone or online using electronic mail, but in the following pages we assume that you are conducting the interview face to face.

1. Finding a subject for an interview. If you are looking for an expert, in the college catalog scan the relevant department and begin to ask questions of students who have some familiarity with the department. Then, with a name or two in mind, you may want to see if these faculty members have written anything on the topic. Department secretaries are good sources of information not only about the special interests of the faculty but also about guest speakers scheduled by the department in the near future. Investigate the athletic department if you're interested in sports; or the departments of music, art, and drama, for the names of resident or visiting performing artists. Other sources of newsworthy personalities or events: the publicity office, the president's office, the college newspaper. All are potential sources for information about recent awards, or achievements, or upcoming events that may lead you to a subject for an interview, and a good story.

2. Preliminary homework. Find out as much as you can about your potential interviewee's work, from the sources we mentioned above. If the subject of your interview is a faculty member, ask the department secretary if you may see a copy of that person's vita (Latin for "life," and pronounced vee-ta). Many departments have these brief biographical sketches on file for publicity purposes. The vita will list, among other things, publications and current research interests.

3. Requesting the interview. In making your request, don't hesitate to mention that you are fulfilling an assignment, but also make evident your own interest in the person's work or area of expertise. (Showing that you already know something about the work, that you've done some preliminary homework, is persuasive evidence of your interest.) Request the interview, preferably in writing, at least a week in advance, and ask for ample time (probably an hour to an hour and a half) for a thorough interview.

4. Preparing thoroughly. If your subject is a writer, read and take notes on the publications that most interest you. Read book reviews, if available;

read reviews of performances if your subject is a performing artist. As you read, write out the questions that occur to you. As you work on them, try to phrase your questions so that they require more than a yes or no answer. A "why" or "how" question is likely to be productive, but don't be afraid of a general question such as "Tell me something about . . . ."

Revise your questions and put them in a reasonable order. Work on an opening question that you think your subject will find both easy and interesting to answer. "How did you get interested in . . ." is often a good start. Type your questions or write them boldly so that you will find them easy to refer to.

Think about how you will record the interview. Although a tape recorder may seem like a good idea, there are good reasons not to rely on one. First of all, your subject may be made uneasy by its presence and freeze up. Second, the recorder (or the operator) may malfunction, leaving you with a partial record, or nothing at all. Third, even if all goes well, when you prepare to write you will face a mass of material, some of it inaudible, and all of it daunting to transcribe.

If, despite these warnings, you decide (with your subject's permission) to tape, expect to take notes anyway. It's the only way you can be sure you will have a record of what was important to you out of all that was said. Think beforehand, then, of how you will take notes, and if you can manage to, practice by interviewing a friend. You'll probably find that you'll want to devise some system of shorthand, perhaps no more than using initials for names that frequently recur, dropping the vowels in words that you transcribe—whatever assists you to write quickly but legibly. But don't think you must transcribe every word. Be prepared to do a lot more listening than writing.

5. *Presenting yourself for the interview.* Dress appropriately, bring your prepared questions and a notebook or pad for your notes, and appear on time.

6. *Conducting the interview.* At the start of the interview, try to engage briefly in conversation, without taking notes, to put your subject at ease. Even important people can be shy. Remembering that will help keep you at ease, too. If you want to use a tape recorder, ask your subject's permission, and if it is granted, ask where the microphone may be conveniently placed.

As the interview proceeds, *keep your purpose in mind.* Are you trying to gain information about an issue or topic, or are you trying to get a portrait of a personality? Listen attentively to your subject's answers and be prepared to follow up with your own responses and spontaneous questions. Here is where your thorough preparation will pay off.

A good interview develops like a conversation. Keep in mind that your prepared questions, however essential, are not sacred. At the same time don't hesitate to steer your subject, courteously, from apparent irrelevancies (what one reporter calls "sawdust") to something that interests you more. "I'd like to hear a little more about . . ." you can say. Or, "Would you mind telling me about how you . . ." It's also perfectly acceptable to ask your subject to repeat a remark so that you can record it accurately, and if you don't understand something, don't be afraid to admit it. Experts are accustomed to knowing more than others do and are particularly happy to explain even the most elementary parts of their lore to an interested listener.

7. Concluding the interview. Near the end of the time you have agreed upon, ask your subject if he or she wishes to add any material, or to clarify something said earlier. Express your thanks and, at the appointed time, leave promptly.

8. Preparing to write. As soon as possible after the interview, review your notes, amplify them with details you wish to remember but might have failed to record, and type them up. You might have discovered during the interview, or you might see now, that there is something more that you want to read by or about your subject. Track it down and take further notes.

9. Writing the essay. In writing your first draft, think about your audience. Unless a better idea occurs to you, consider your college newspaper or magazine, or a local newspaper, as the place you hope to publish your story. Write with the readers of that publication in mind. Thinking of your readers will help you to be clear—for instance to identify names that have come up in the interview but which may be unfamiliar to your readers.

As with other writing, begin your draft with any idea that strikes you, and write at a fast clip until you have exhausted your material (or yourself).

When you revise, remember to keep your audience in mind; your material should, as it unfolds, tell a coherent and interesting story. Interviews, like conversations, tend to be delightfully circular or disorderly. But an essay, like a story, should reveal its contents in a sequence that captures and holds attention.

If you've done a thorough job of interviewing you may find that you have more notes than you can reasonably incorporate without disrupting the flow of your story. Don't be tempted to plug them in anyway. If they're really interesting, save them, perhaps by copying them into your journal; if not, chuck them out.

In introducing direct quotations from your source, choose those that are particularly characteristic, or vivid, or memorable. Paraphrase or summarize the rest of what is usable. Although the focus of your essay is almost surely the person you interviewed, it is your story, and most of it should be in your own words. Even though you must keep yourself in the background, your writing will gain in interest if your reader hears your voice as well as your subject's.

You might want to use a particularly good quotation for your conclusion. Notice that both essays we've chosen as examples conclude this way.) Now make sure that you have an attractive opening paragraph. Identifying the subject of your interview and describing the setting is one way to begin. Give your essay an attractive title. Before you prepare your final draft, read your essay aloud. You're almost certain to catch phrases you can improve, and places where a transition will help your reader to follow you without effort. Check your quotations for accuracy; check with your subject any quotations or other details you're in doubt about. Type your final draft, then edit and proofread carefully.

10. Going public. Make two copies of your finished essay, one for the person you interviewed, one for yourself. The original is for your instructor; hand it in on time.

Topic for Writing

Write an essay based on an interview. You needn't be limited in your choice of subject by the examples we've given. A very old person, a recent immigrant, the owner or manager of an interesting store or business, a veteran of the Gulf War, a gardener, are only a few of the possibilities. If you can manage to do so, include a few photographs of your subject, with appropriate captions.

Using Quotations

Our marginal comments briefly call your attention to the student's use of quotations, but here we remind you of procedures for using quotations. These procedures are not noteworthy when handled properly, but they become noticeable and even ruinous to your essay when bungled. Read over the following reminders, check them against the student's essay that you have just read, and consult them again the first few times you write about an essay.

- *Quote.* Quotations from the work under discussion provide indispensable support for your analysis.
- *Don't overquote.* Most of your essay should consist of your own words.
- *Quote briefly.* Use quotations as evidence, not as padding.
- *Comment on what you quote*—immediately before or immediately after the quotation. Make sure your reader understands why you find the quotation relevant. Don't count on the quotation to make your point for you.
- *Take care with embedded quotations* (quotations within a sentence of your own). A quotation must make good sense and must fit grammatically into the sentence of which it is a part.

Incorrect:

> Plumb says he was "astonished when a minibus drove up to my house."

(In this example, the shift from Plumb to "my" is bothersome, especially since the student uses the first person in his essay.)

Improved:

> Plumb says that he was "astonished" when he saw a minibus arrive at his house.

Or:

> Plumb says, "I was astonished when a minibus drove up to my house."

Incorrect:

> Plumb implies he is well read because "Unlike anthropologists or sociologists, historians have not studied family life very closely."

Improved:

> Plumb implies he is well read in his assertion that "Unlike anthropologists or sociologists, historians have not studied family life very closely."

- Don't try to fit a long quotation into the middle of one of your own sentences. It is almost impossible for the reader to come out of the quotation and pick up the thread of your sentence. It is better to lead into a long quotation with "Plumb says," followed by a colon, and then, after quoting, to begin a new sentence of your own.
- *Quote exactly.* Any material that you add (to make the quotation coherent with your sentence) must be in square brackets. Thus:

> Plumb says that he "was rather astonished when a minibus drove up to [his] house and out poured ten children."

An ellipsis (any material that you omit from a quotation) must be indicated by three spaced periods:

> Plumb says he "was rather astonished when a minibus drove up . . . and out poured ten children."

If you end the quotation before the end of the author's sentence, add a period and then three spaced periods to indicate the omission:

> Plumb says he "was rather astonished when a minibus drove up. . . ."

- *Quote fairly.* It would not be fair, for instance, to say that Lewis says, "After all, . . . they had a right to happiness." The words do in fact appear in Lewis's essay, but he is quoting them in order, ultimately, to refute them.
- *Identify the quotation* clearly for your reader. Use such expressions as "Lewis says," "Plumb argues."
- *Identify the source of quotations* in a list called "Works Cited."
- *Check your punctuation.* Remember: Periods and commas go *inside* the closing quotation marks, semicolons and colons go outside. Question marks and exclamation points go inside if they are part of the quotation, outside if they are your own.

✓A Checklist for Editing: Thirteen Questions to Ask Yourself

✓ Is the title of my essay at least moderately informative?

✓ Do I identify the subject of my essay (author and title) early?

✓ What is my thesis? Do I state it soon enough (perhaps even in the title) and keep it in view?

✓ Is the organization reasonable? Does each point lead into the next, without irrelevancies and without anticlimaxes?

✓ Is each paragraph unified by a topic sentence or a topic idea? Are there adequate transitions from one paragraph to the next?

✓ Are generalizations supported by appropriate concrete details, especially by brief quotations from the text?

✓ Is the opening paragraph interesting and, by its end, focused on the topic? Is the final paragraph conclusive without being repetitive?

✓ Is the tone appropriate? No sarcasm, no apologies, no condescension?

✓ If there is a summary, is it as brief as possible, given its purpose?

✓ Are the quotations accurate? Do they serve a purpose other than to add words to the essay?

✓ Is documentation provided where necessary?

✓ Are the spelling and punctuation correct? Are other mechanical matters (such as margins, spacing, and citations) in correct form? Have I proofread carefully?

✓ Is the paper properly identified—author's name, instructor's name, course number, and date?

4
WRITING AN ARGUMENT

Although in common usage an **argument** can be a noisy wrangle—baseball players argue about the umpire's decision, spouses argue about who should put out the garbage—in this chapter we mean a discourse that uses *reasons*—rather than, say, appeals to pity, or, for that matter, threats—in order to persuade readers to hold the writer's opinion, or at least to persuade readers that the writer's opinion is thoughtful and reasonable. In this sense, argument is a thoroughly respectable activity.

What distinguishes argument from **exposition** (for instance, the explanation of a process) is this: argument and exposition both consist of statements, but in argument some statements are offered as *reasons* for other statements. Essentially one builds an argument on the word *because*. Another characteristic of argument is that argument assumes there may be a substantial disagreement among informed readers. Exposition assumes that the reader is unfamiliar with the subject matter—let's say, the origins of jazz or the law concerning affirmative action—but it does *not* assume that the reader holds a different opinion. The writer of an argument, however, seeks to overcome disagreement (for instance about the value or the fairness of something) by offering reasons that are convincing or at least worth considering carefully. Here, for instance, is Supreme Court Justice Louis Brandeis concluding a justly famous argument that government may not use evidence illegally obtained by wiretapping:

> Decency, security, and liberty alike demand that government officials shall be subjected to the same rules of conduct that are commands to the citizen. In a government of laws, existence of the government will be imperilled if it fails to observe the law scrupulously. Our Government is the potent, the omnipresent teacher. For good or for ill, it teaches the whole people by its example. Crime is contagious. If the Government becomes a lawbreaker, it breeds contempt for law; it invites every man to become a law unto himself; it invites anarchy. To declare that in the administration of the criminal law the end justifies the means—to declare that the Government may commit crimes in order to secure the conviction of a private criminal—would bring terrible retribution. Against that pernicious doctrine the Court should resolutely set its face.

Notice here that Brandeis's reasoning is highlighted by his forceful style. Note the resonant use of parallel constructions ("Decency, security, and liberty," "For good or for ill," "it breeds . . . it invites," "To declare . . . to declare"), which convey a sense of dignity and authority. Notice, too, the effective variation between short and long sentences. The sentences range from three words ("Crime is contagious"—forceful because of its brevity and its alliteration) to thirty-seven words (the next-to-last sentence—impressive because of its length and especially because the meaning is suspended until the end, when we get the crucial verb and its object, "would bring terrible retribution"). Later in our discussion of argument we will talk about the importance of the writer's style.

The Aims of an Argumentative Essay

The aim might seem obvious—to persuade the reader to accept the writer's opinion. In fact, often there are other aims. First, writers draft argumentative essays partly in order to find out what they believe. In drafting a paper they come to see that certain of their unformed beliefs can't really be supported or that their beliefs need to be considerably modified. This point should not come as a surprise; in earlier chapters we have said that writers get ideas and refine their beliefs by the act of writing. Second, if you read argumentative essays in, say, *National Review* (a conservative magazine), in *The New Republic* (a liberal magazine), in *Ms.* (a feminist magazine), or in just about any magazine, you will see that much of the writing is really a matter of preaching to the converted. Good arguments may be offered, but they are offered not to persuade readers but to reassure them that the views they already hold are sound. After all, few liberals read *National Review*, few conservatives read *The New Republic*, few male chauvinists read *Ms.*, and so on.

When you write an argumentative essay, although of course you may hope to convince all readers to adopt your view, you probably also realize that the subject is complex, and that other opinions are possible. What you want to do is to set forth your viewpoint as effectively as possible, not because you believe all readers will say "Yes, of course, you have converted me," but because *you want your view to be given a hearing. You want to show that it is one that can be held by a reasonable person.* Because you are a person of good will, with an open mind, you realize that most issues are very complicated. You have formed some ideas, and now you are taking a stand and arguing on its behalf. However, you probably are not saying that no other view can possibly have the tiniest scrap of merit. As Virginia Woolf put it (with perhaps a bit of self-irony),

> When a subject is highly controversial . . . one cannot hope to tell the truth. One can only show how one came to hold whatever opinion one does hold. One can only give one's audience the chance of drawing their own conclusions as they observe the limitations, the prejudices, the idiosyncrasies of the speaker.

Again, we want to say that in drafting the paper your chief aim is to educate yourself; in offering it to readers your chief aim is to let others know that your views are worth considering because they are supported by reason. If you persuade your readers to accept your views, great; but you should at least persuade them that a reasonable person can hold these views.

Negotiating Agreements: The Approach of Carl R. Rogers

Carl H. Rogers (1902–87), best known for his book entitled *On Becoming a Person*, was a psychotherapist, not a writer, but he has exerted a great influence on teachers of writing. Rogers originally intended to become a

Protestant minister, but, as he tells in *On Becoming a Person,* during the course of a six-month visit to East Asia he came to recognize "that sincere and honest people could believe in very divergent religious doctrines." He turned to the study of psychology, and in the course of time developed the idea that a therapist must engage in "reflection," by which he meant that the therapist must reflect—must give back an image—of what the client said. (Rogers's use of the word "client" rather than patient is itself a clue to his approach; the therapist is not dealing with someone who is supposed passively to accept treatment from the all-powerful doctor.)

What has this to do with seeking to persuade a reader? Consider two lawyers arguing a case in court. Lawyer A may seem to be arguing with lawyer B, but neither lawyer really is trying to convince the other, and neither lawyer has the faintest interest in learning from the other. The lawyers are trying to persuade not each other, but the judge or jury. Similarly, the writer of a letter to a newspaper, taking issue with an editorial, probably has no thought of changing the newspaper's policy. Rather, the letter is really directed to another audience, readers of the newspaper. And we hear this sort of thing on radio and television shows with titles like *Crossfire, Firing Line,* and *Point Counterpoint.* For the most part the participants are not trying to learn from each other and are not trying to solve a complex problem, but rather are trying to convince the audience that one side is wholly right and the other side is wholly wrong. If they are talking about an issue that we don't know much about, the arguments on both sides may seem to be equally strong, and we are likely to side with the speaker whose *style* of talk (and maybe of dress) we prefer. This point is important, and we will return to it when we talk about the *persona* or character of the writer of an argument

Suppose that unlike a participant on a radio or television show, and unlike a lawyer arguing a case, speaker X really does want to persuade speaker Y; that is, X really wants to bring Y around to X's point of view, or if X is mistaken in his or her views, X really is willing to learn from Y in the course of the give and take. Rogers points out that when we engage in an argument, if we feel that our integrity or our identity is threatened, we stiffen our resistance. Normally we may *want* to grow, to develop our thoughts, to act in accordance with sound reasons, but when we are threatened we erect defenses that in fact shut us off from communication. That is, we find ourselves within a circle that not only shuts others out but that also has the unintended effect of shutting us in. We—or our opponent—may have given very good reasons, but because each party has behaved in a threatening manner, and has felt threatened by the other side, we have scarcely listened to each other, and therefore little or nothing has been communicated. (If you think about your own experience, you probably can confirm Rogers's view.)

To avoid this deplorable lack of opportunity for growth, Rogers suggests that participants in arguments need to become partners, not adversaries. Here, with Rogers's insight in mind, we can digress for a moment, and call attention to the combative terms normally associated with argument. *Debate,* for instance, is from Latin *de-* (down) and *battere* (to beat), the same word that gives us *battery,* as in "assault and battery." We *marshal* our arguments (arrange them into a military formation), and we *attack our opponents,* seeking to *rebut* (from a Latin word meaning "to butt back") or *refute* (again from a Latin word, this time meaning "to drive back") their assertions. When we are engaged in these activities, (1) we are scarcely in a position to learn from those we are talking with—really, talking *at*—and (2) we are not likely to teach them anything, because, like us, they are busy *defending* (still another military word) their own position.

Rogers suggests, therefore, that a writer who wishes to communicate (as opposed to a lawyer or a debater who merely wishes to win) needs to reduce the threat. To repeat: The participants in an argument need to become partners rather than adversaries. "Mutual communication," he says, "tends to be pointed toward solving a problem rather than attacking a person or a group."

Take abortion, for instance. We hear about "pro-life" (or "anti-abortion") people, and about "pro-choice" (or "pro-abortion") people. It may seem that there is no common ground, nothing they can agree on. But polls reveal considerable ambiguity within some people. Consider, for instance, a finding of a New York Times/CBS News poll of representative Americans, in January 1998. Participants were asked which statement came nearer to their opinion: Is abortion the same thing as murdering a child, or Is abortion not murder because the fetus really isn't a child? Half the sample chose "the same thing as murdering a child," and 38 percent chose "the fetus really isn't a child." At the same time, however, 58 percent, including a third of those who chose "murdering a child," agreed that abortion was "sometimes the best course in a bad situation." These apparently inconsistent responses have been fairly consistent for the last fifteen years; some people who consider abortion equivalent to murdering a child will grant that there are situations in which abortion is "the best course", and, we should add, many pro-choice people, people who insist that a woman has a right to choose and that her choice is not the government's business, also agree that abortion should not be lightly entered on. Take a particular case: A pregnant woman who regards abortion as "the same thing as murdering a child" learns that her baby will probably have Down Syndrome (such persons have an average IQ of about 50, are prone to hearing problems and vision problems, and have an increased risk of heart disease and leukemia). Despite her opposition to abortion, she may become one of the people who feel abortion is "sometimes the best course in a bad situation." Given the choice of bearing or aborting, she may very reluctantly decide to abort. Yet on the day we were drafting these pages we happened to come across a letter in a newspaper making a point that, however obvious, we had not thought of. The writer, Maureen K. Hogan, Executive Director of Adopt a Special Kid, reported in her letter that "There are thousands of families around the United States that would be happy to adopt such a child. . . . In 25 years, there hasn't been a single child for whom we have not been able to find a home." We can imagine that a woman who dreaded the idea of aborting a fetus but felt that she had no choice but abortion, might, on hearing this information, modify her intention, and engage in a course of behavior that she and all others concerned will find more satisfactory.

We should mention, too, that open-minded discussion between persons who hold differing views may reveal that some of their differences are verbal rather than substantial. One can wonder, for instance, if the poll would have produced the same results if the question had asked about "killing" rather than "murdering" a child. Patient, well-intentioned discussion may reveal that the parties are not as far apart as they at first seem to be; they share some ground, and once this common ground is acknowledged, differences can be discussed.

Consider, as another example, a proposal in 1997 by President Clinton to introduce voluntary national tests in reading and mathematics. Some people think this is a Bad Idea. Why?

- What is tested is what will get taught; teachers will soon start preparing students for the test, rather than teaching the things they think are important. Why would teachers do this? Because they want to look good, they want their school to stand high in the national ratings.
- A second objection is that testing introduces an unhealthy spirit of competition.
- A third objection concerns the issue of who will make the tests. Administrators? Professors of Education? The teachers who are on the firing line?
- A fourth objection is that, no matter who makes the test, the testing board would have too much power, since it would in effect determine not only what things get taught but which students get to go on to college.
- A fifth objection is that a national test would have little meaning; some states have a relatively homogenous population, whereas others have a relatively heterogenous population. A sixth objection is that test scores don't have much value. After all, we know (or do we?) that the SAT is not really a good predictor of success in school, and that tests are especially likely to fail to recognize the offbeat creative students—just look at X, who had poor grades and dropped out of school and is now recognized as a genius.

Probably all of these objections have some weight, but replies (also of varying weight) can be made to them. To take only the first two: It may be a good thing if teachers are jolted out of their parochialism and are made to become aware of the values of others, and, second, what is wrong with some competition? Competition sometimes is healthy. But after all of the pros and the cons are laid out, a Rogerian thinker will want to see what the two sides can *agree* on. They can agree, probably, that American school children ought to do better in reading and in mathematics. They can also agree, probably, that testing has some validity. And they can also agree, probably, that national testing by itself will not solve the problem. For instance, other possibilities include a longer school year, better pay for teachers (to attract better teachers), national tests for teachers, and so on. If the disputants can first establish the positions they *share,* and realize that both sides are people of good will endowed with some good ideas, they may better be able to work out their differences.

Rogers was drawing on his experience as a psychotherapist, which means he was mostly writing about the relationship between two people who were literally talking to each other, whereas a writer can at best imagine a reader. But good writers do in fact bring their readers into their writings, by such devices as "It may be said that . . ."—here one summarizes or quotes a view other than one's own. Writers genuinely interested in contributing to the solution of a problem will busy themselves not merely in asserting their position but will also inform themselves of a variety of views, by listening and by reading. And when they listen and read, they must do so with an open mind, giving the speaker or author (at least at first) the benefit of the doubt. (Rogers' term for this sort of activity is "empathic listening," i.e., comprehension so complete that it grasps not only the thoughts but also the feelings and motives of another.) That is, they will listen and read sympathetically, and they will not be too quick to evaluate. They may even, in an effort to do justice to the material, listen and read with the mind of a believer. Or, if this is asking too much, they will act in the spirit advocated by Francis Bacon: "Read not to contradict and confute; nor to believe and take for granted; nor to find talk and discourse; but to weigh and consider."

Writers genuinely interested in persuading others will educate themselves, by listening and reading. In their own writing, where they wish to contribute their views on a disputed matter, they simultaneously can reduce the psychological threat to those who hold views different from their own by doing several things: They can show sympathetic understanding of the opposing argument; they can recognize what is valid in it; and they can recognize and demonstrate that those who take a different view are nonetheless persons of goodwill.

A writer who takes Rogers seriously will, usually, in the first part of an argumentative essay

- state the problem, suggesting that it is an issue of concern, and that the reader has a stake in it;
- show respect for persons who hold differing views;
- set forth opposing positions, *stated in such a way that their proponents will agree that the statements of their positions are fair,* and

- find some shared values—that is, grant whatever validity the writer finds in those positions, for instance, by recognizing the circumstances in which they would indeed be acceptable.

Having accurately summarized other views and having granted some concessions, the writer presumably has won the reader's attention and goodwill; the writer can now

- show how those who hold other positions will benefit if they accept the writer's position.

This last point is essentially an appeal to self-interest. In the example we gave a moment ago, concerning a pregnant woman who has contemplated aborting a fetus that, if born, probably will be a baby with Down Syndrome, the appeal to self-interest might run along the lines that if she bears the child she will be free from the remorse she might feel if she had aborted it.

Sometimes, of course, the differing positions will be so far apart that no reconciliation can be proposed, in which case the writer will probably seek to show how the issue can best be solved by adopting the writer's own position. But even in such an essay it is desirable to state the opposing view in such a way that proponents of that view will agree that that is indeed their position and not a caricature of it.

Rogers, again, was a psychologist, not a teacher of writing and not a logician. In fact, his writing shares with some recent feminist theory a distrust of logic, which can be seen as masculine and aggressive, concerned with winning, even with "annihilating the opposition." Rogers offers advice not so much on winning (in the sense of conquering) but in the sense of winning over, that is, gaining converts, or at least allies.

✓A Checklist for Rogerian Argument

✓ Have I treated other views with **respect**?

✓ Have I stated at least one other view **in a way that would satisfy its proponents, and thus demonstrated my familiarity with the issue**?

✓ Have I granted **validity to any aspects of other positions, and thus demonstrated my openmindedness**?

✓ Have I pointed out the **common ground,** the ground that we share, and thus prepared the reader to listen attentively to my proposals?

✓ Have I shown how the other position will be strengthened, at least in some contexts, by accepting some aspects of my position? (In short, have I **appealed to the reader's self-interest,** by showing that proponents of the other view(s) will benefit from accepting at least part of my view?

Three Kinds of Evidence: Examples, Testimony, Statistics

Writers of arguments seek to persuade by showing that they themselves are persons of goodwill, and—our topic here—by offering evidence to support their thesis. The chief forms of evidence used in argument are:

Examples

Testimony (the citation of authorities)

Statistics

We'll briefly consider each of these.

Examples

Example is from the Latin *exemplum,* which means "something taken out." An **example** is the sort of thing, taken from among many similar things, that one selects and holds up for view, perhaps after saying "for example" or "for instance."

Three sorts of examples are especially common in written arguments:

Real examples

Invented instances

Analogies

Real examples are just what they sound like—instances that have occurred. If, for example, we are arguing that gun control won't work, we point to those states that have adopted gun control laws and that nevertheless have had no reduction in crimes using guns. Or, if one wants to support the assertion that a woman can be a capable head of state, one may find oneself pointing to women who have actually served as heads of state, such as Cleopatra, Queen Elizabeth I of England, Golda Meir (prime minister of Israel), Indira Ghandi (prime minister of India), and Margaret Thatcher (prime minister of England).

The advantage of using real examples is, clearly, that they are real. Of course, an opponent might stubbornly respond that the persons whom you name could not, for some reason or other, function as the head of state in *our* country. One might argue, for instance, that the case of Golda Meir proves nothing, since the role of women in Israeli society is different from the role of women in the United States (a country in which a majority of the citizens are Christians). And one might argue that much of Mrs. Gandhi's power came from her being the daughter of Nehru, an immensely popular Indian statesman. Even the most compelling real example inevitably will be in some ways special or particular, and in the eyes of some readers may not seem to be a fair example.

Consider, for instance, a student who is arguing that peer review should be part of the writing course, pointing out that he or she found it of great help in high school. An opponent argues that things in college are different: college students should be able to help themselves, even highly gifted college students are not competent to offer college-level instruction, and so on. Still, as the feebleness of these objections (and the objections against Meir and Gandhi indicate), real examples can be very compelling.

Invented instances are exempt from the charge that, because of some detail or other, they are not relevant as evidence. Suppose, for example, you are arguing against capital punishment, on the grounds that if an innocent person is executed, there is no way of even attempting to rectify the injustice. If you point to the case of X, you may be met with the reply that X was not in fact innocent. Rather than get tangled up in the guilt or innocence of a particular person, it may be better to argue that we can suppose—we can imagine—an innocent person convicted and executed, and we can imagine that evidence later proves the person's innocence.

Invented instances have the advantage of presenting an issue clearly, free from all of the distracting particularities (and irrelevancies) that are bound up with any real instance. But invented instances have the disadvantage of being invented, and they may seem remote from the real issues being argued.

Analogies are comparisons pointing out several resemblances between two rather different things. For instance, one might assert that a government is like a ship, and in times of stress—if the ship is to weather the storm—the authority of the captain must not be questioned.

But don't confuse an analogy with proof. An analogy is an extended comparison between two things: it can be useful in exposition, for it explains the unfamiliar by means of the familiar: "A government is like a ship, and just as a ship has a captain and a crew, so a government has . . ."; "Writing an essay is like building a house; just as an architect must begin with a plan, so the writer must. . . ." Such comparisons can be useful, helping to clarify what otherwise might be obscure, but their usefulness goes only so far. Everything is what it is, and not something else. A government is not a ship, and what is true of a captain's power need not be true of a president's power; and a writer is not an architect. Some of what is true about ships may be roughly true of governments, and some of what is true about architects may be (again, roughly) true of writers, but there are differences too. Consider the following analogy between a lighthouse and the death penalty:

> The death penalty is a warning, just like a lighthouse throwing its beams out to sea. We hear about shipwrecks, but we do not hear about the ships the lighthouse guides safely on their way. We do not have proof of the number of ships it saves, but we do not tear the lighthouse down.
>
> J. Edgar Hoover

How convincing is Hoover's analogy as an argument, that is, as a reason for retaining the death penalty?

Testimony

Testimony, or the citation of authorities, is rooted in our awareness that some people are recognized as experts. In our daily life we constantly turn to experts for guidance: we look up the spelling of a word in the dictionary, we listen to the weather forecast on the radio, we take an ailing cat to the vet for a checkup. Similarly, when we wish to become informed about controversial matters, we often turn to experts, first to help educate ourselves and then to help convince our readers.

Don't forget that *you* are an authority on many things. For example, today's newspaper includes an article about the cutback in funding for teaching the arts in elementary and secondary schools. Educators are responding that arts education is not a frill, and that in fact the arts provide the analytical thinking, teamwork, motivation, and self-discipline that most people agree are needed to reinvigorate American schools. If you have studied the arts in school—for instance, if you painted pictures or learned to play a musical instrument—you are in a position to evaluate these claims. Similarly, if you have studied in a bilingual educational program, your own testimony will be invaluable.

There are at least two reasons for offering testimony in an argument. The obvious reason is that expert opinion does (and should) carry some weight with the audience; the less obvious one is that a change of voice (if the testimony is not your own) in an essay may afford the reader a bit of pleasure. No matter how engaging our own voice may be, a fresh voice— whether that of Thomas Jefferson, Albert Einstein, or Barbara Jordan— may provide a refreshing change of tone.

But, of course, there are dangers. The chief dangers are that the words of authorities may be taken out of context or otherwise distorted, or that the authorities may not be authorities on the topic at hand. We are concerned quite rightly with what the framers of the U.S. Constitution said, but it is not entirely clear that their words can be fairly applied, on one side or the other, to such an issue as abortion. We are concerned quite rightly with what Einstein said, but it is not entirely clear that his eminence as a physicist qualifies him as an authority on, say, world peace. In a moment, when we discuss errors in reasoning, we'll have more to say about the proper and improper use of authorities.

Statistics

Statistics, another important form of evidence, are especially useful in arguments concerning social issues. If we want to argue for (or against) raising the driving age, we will probably do some research in the library, and will offer statistics about the number of accidents caused by people in certain age groups.

But a word of caution: the significance of statistics may be difficult to assess. For instance, opponents of gun control legislation have pointed out, in support of the argument that such laws are ineffectual, that homicides in Florida *increased* after Florida adopted gun control laws. Supporters of gun control laws cried "foul," arguing that in the years after adopting these laws Miami became (for reasons having nothing to do with the laws) the cocaine capital of the United States, and the rise in homicide was chiefly a reflection of murders involved in the drug trade. That is, a significant change in the population has made a comparison of the figures meaningless. This objection seems plausible, and probably the statistics therefore should carry little weight.

How Much Evidence Is Enough?

If you allow yourself ample time to write your essay, you probably will turn up plenty of evidence to illustrate your arguments, such as examples drawn from your own experience and imagination, from your reading, and from your talks with others. Examples will not only help to clarify and to support your assertions but will also provide a concreteness that will be welcome in a paper that might be, on the whole, fairly abstract. Your sense of your audience will have to guide you in making your selection of examples. Generally speaking, a single example may not fully illuminate a difficult point, and so a second example—a clincher—may be desirable. If you offer a third or fourth example you probably are succumbing to a temptation to include something that tickles your fancy. If it is as good as you think it is, the reader probably will accept the unnecessary example and may even be grateful. But before you pile on examples, try to imagine yourself in your reader's place, and ask if an example is needed. If not, ask yourself if the reader will be glad to receive the overload.

One other point: on most questions—say on the value of bilingual education or on the need for rehabilitation programs in prisons—it's not possible to make a strictly logical case, in the sense of an absolutely airtight proof. Don't assume that it is your job to make an absolute proof. What you are expected to do is to offer a reasonable argument. Remember Virginia Woolf's words: "When a subject is highly controversial . . . one cannot hope to tell the truth. One can only show how one came to hold whatever opinion one does hold."

Avoiding Fallacies

Let's further examine writing reasonable arguments by considering some obvious errors in reasoning. In logic these errors are called **fallacies** (from a Latin verb meaning "to deceive"). As Tweedledee says in *Through the Looking-Glass*, "If it were so, it would be; but as it isn't, it ain't. That's logic."

To persuade readers to accept your opinions you must persuade them that you are reliable; if your argument includes fallacies, thoughtful readers will not take you seriously. More important, if your argument includes fallacies, you are misleading yourself. When you search your draft for fallacies, you are searching for ways to improve the quality of your thinking.

1. False Authority. Don't try to borrow the prestige of authorities who are not authorities on the topic in question—for example, a heart surgeon speaking on politics. Similarly, some former authorities are no longer authorities because the problems have changed or because later knowledge has superseded their views. Adam Smith, Thomas Jefferson, Eleanor Roosevelt, and Albert Einstein remain persons of genius, but an attempt to use their opinions when you are examining modern issues—even in their fields—may be questioned. Remember the last words of John B. Sedgwick, a Union Army general at the Battle of Spotsylvania in 1864: "They couldn't hit an elephant at this dist—."

In short, before you rely on an authority, ask yourself if the person in question *is* an authority on the topic. And don't let stereotypes influence your idea of who is an authority. There is an apt Yiddish proverb: "A goat has a beard, but that doesn't make him a rabbi."

2. False Quotation. If you do quote from an authority, don't misquote. For example, you may find someone who grants that "there are strong arguments in favor of abolishing the death penalty"; but if she goes on to argue that, on balance, the arguments in favor of retaining it seem stronger to her, it is dishonest to quote her words so as to imply that she favors abolishing it.

3. Suppression of Evidence. Don't neglect evidence that is contrary to your own argument. You owe it to yourself and your reader to present all the relevant evidence. Be especially careful not to assume that every question is simply a matter of *either/or.* There may be some truth on both sides. Take the following thesis: "Grades encourage unwholesome competition and should therefore be abolished." Even if the statement about the evil effect of grading is true, it may not be the whole truth, and therefore it may not follow that grades should be abolished. One might point out that grades do other things, too: they may stimulate learning, and they may assist students by telling them how far they have progressed. One might nevertheless conclude, on balance, that the fault outweighs the benefits. But the argument will be more persuasive now that the benefits of grades have been considered.

Concede to the opposition what it deserves and then outscore the opposition. Failure to confront the opposing evidence will be noticed; your readers will keep wondering why you do not consider some particular point, and may consequently dismiss your argument. However, if you confront the opposition, you will almost surely strengthen your own argument. As Edmund Burke said two hundred years ago, "He that wrestles with us strengthens our nerves, and sharpens our skill. Our antagonist is our helper."

4. Generalization from Insufficient Evidence. In rereading a draft of an argument that you have written, try to spot your own generalizations. Ask yourself if a reasonable reader is likely to agree that the generalization is based on an adequate sample.

A visitor to a college may sit in on three classes, each taught by a different instructor, and may find all three stimulating. That's a good sign, but can we generalize and say that the teaching at this college is excellent? Are three classes a sufficient sample? If all three are offered by the Biology Department, which includes only five instructors, perhaps we can tentatively say that the teaching of biology at this institution is good. If the Biology Department contains twenty instructors, perhaps we can still say—though more tentatively—that this sample indicates that the teaching of biology is good. But what does the sample say about the teaching of other subjects at the college? It probably does say something—the institution may be much concerned with teaching across the board—but then again it may not say a great deal, since the Biology Department may be exceptionally concerned with good teaching.

5. The Genetic Fallacy. Don't assume that something can necessarily be explained in terms of its birth or origin. "He wrote the novel to make money, so it can't be any good" is not a valid inference. The value of a novel does not depend on the author's motivations in writing it. Indeed, the value or worth of a novel needs to be established by reference to other criteria. Neither the highest nor the lowest motivations guarantee the quality of the product. Another example: "Capital punishment arose in days when men sought revenge, so now it ought to be abolished." Again, an unconvincing argument: capital punishment may have some current value; for example, it may serve as a deterrent to crime. But that's another argument, and it needs evidence if it is to be believed. Be on guard, too, against the thoughtless tendency to judge people by their origins: Mr. *X* has a foreign accent, so he is probably untrustworthy or stupid or industrious.

6. Begging the Question and Circular Reasoning. Don't assume the truth of the point that you should prove. The term "begging the question" is a trifle odd. It means, in effect, "You, like a beggar, are asking me to grant you something at the outset."

Examples: "The barbaric death penalty should be abolished"; "This senseless language requirement should be dropped." Both of these statements assume what they should prove—that the death penalty is barbaric, and that the language requirement is senseless. You can, of course, make such assertions, but you must go on to prove them.

Circular reasoning is usually an extended form of begging the question. What ought to be proved is covertly assumed. Example: "*X* is the best-qualified candidate for the office, because the most informed people say so." Who are the most informed people? Those who recognize *X*'s superiority. Circular reasoning, then, normally includes intermediate steps absent from begging the question, but the two fallacies are so closely related that they can be considered one. Another example: "I feel sympathy for her because I identify with her." Despite the "because," no reason is really offered. What follows "because" is merely a restatement, in slightly different words, of what precedes; the shift of words, from *feel sympathy* to *identify with* has misled the writer into thinking she is giving a reason. Other examples: "Students are interested in courses when the subject matter and the method of presentation are interesting"; "There cannot be peace in the Middle East because the Jews and the Arabs will always fight." In each case, an assertion that ought to be proved is reasserted as a reason in support of the assertion.

7. *Post hoc ergo propter hoc.* Latin: "after this, therefore because of this." Don't assume that because *X* precedes *Y, X* must cause *Y*. For example: "He went to college and came back a boozer; college corrupted him." He might have taken up liquor even if he had not gone to college. Another example: "When a fifty-five-mile-per-hour speed limit was imposed in 1974, after the Arab embargo on oil, the number of auto fatalities decreased sharply, from 55,000 deaths in 1973 to 46,000 in 1974. Therefore, it is evident that a fifty-five-mile-per-hour speed limit—still adhered to in some states—saves lives." Not quite. Because gasoline was expensive after the embargo, the number of miles traveled decreased. The number of fatalities *per mile* remained constant. The price of gas, not the speed limit, seems responsible for the decreased number of fatalities. Moreover, the national death rate has continued to fall. Why? Several factors are at work: seat-belt and child-restraint laws, campaigns against drunk driving, improved auto design, and improved roads. Medicine, too, may have improved, so that today doctors can save accident victims who in 1974 would have died. In short, it probably is impossible to isolate the correlation between speed and safety.

8. *Argumentum ad hominem.* Here the argument is directed toward the person (*hominem* is Latin for *man*) rather than toward the issue. Don't shift from your topic to your opponent. A speaker argues against legalizing abortions, and her opponent, instead of facing the merits of the argument, attacks the character or the associations of the opponent: "You're a Catholic, aren't you?"

9. *False Assumption.* Consider the Scot who argued that Shakespeare must have been a Scot. Asked for his evidence, he replied, "The ability of the man warrants the assumption." Or take such a statement as "She goes to Yale, so she must be rich." Possibly the statement is based on faulty induction (the writer knows four Yale students, and all four are rich), but more likely he is just passing on a cliché. The Yale student in question may be on a scholarship, may be struggling to earn the money, or may be backed by parents of modest means who for eighteen years have saved money for her college education. Other examples: "I haven't heard him complain about French 10, so he must be satisfied"; "She's a writer, so she must be well read." A little thought will show how weak such assertions are; they *may* be true, but they may not.

The errors we have discussed are common. In revising your writing, try to spot them and eliminate or correct them. You have a point to make, and you should make it fairly. If you can only make it unfairly, you are doing an injustice to your reader and yourself; you should try to change your view of the topic. You don't want to be like the politician whose speech had a marginal note: "Argument weak; shout here."

Drafting An Argument

Imagining an Audience

A writer's job is made easier if the audience is known. Thus, if you are writing for the college newspaper, you can assume that your readers know certain things, and you can adopt a moderately familiar tone. Similarly, if you are writing a letter to the college trustees, you can assume that they know certain things—you will not have to tell them that the institution is a small, coeducational, undergraduate college located in northern Georgia—but you will probably adopt a somewhat more formal tone than you would use in writing for your fellow students.

Your instructor may tell you to imagine a particular audience—readers of the local newspaper, alumni, high school students, your representative in Congress, or any other group. But if your instructor does not specify an audience, you will probably do best if you imagine one of two possibilities: either write for the general reader (the person who reads *Time* or *Newsweek*) or for your classmates. Although these two audiences are similar in many respects, there is a significant difference. All of your classmates may be of the same gender or the same religion, they may be of approximately the same age, and they may come from the same area. In an essay written for your classmates, then, you may not have to explain certain things that you will indeed have to explain if you are writing for the general reader. To cite an obvious example: if the school is specialized (for instance, if it is a religious school or a military school), you can assume that your readers know certain things and share certain attitudes that you cannot assume in the general public.

Getting Started

If your essay is related to one or more of the readings in this book, of course you will read the essay(s) carefully—perhaps highlighting, underlining, annotating, summarizing, and outlining, as we suggest in our first chapter. You will question the text, and you probably will make entries in a journal, as we suggest in the second and third chapters. These entries may be ideas that come to you out of the blue, or they may emerge from conscious, critical thinking, perhaps in conversations with some of your classmates. (Critical thinking means, among other things, that you will question your own assumptions and evaluate your evidence as objectively as possible.)

Discussions—with yourself and with others—will help you to improve your ideas. At this stage, you will probably have some ideas that you did not have when you began thinking about the topic, and you will probably want to abandon some of your earlier ideas which now seem less strong than you had originally thought.

Writing a Draft

By now you probably have a fair idea of the strengths and (as you see it) the weaknesses of other positions. You also have a fair idea of what your thesis—your claim—is and what reasons you will offer to support it. And you also probably have at hand some of the supporting evidence—for instance, examples, statements by authorities, or personal experiences—that you intend to offer as support.

Some people, at this point—especially if they are writing on a word processor—like to sit down and write freely, pouring out their ideas. They then print out the material and, on rereading, highlight what seems useful, perhaps indicating in the margins how the material should be reorganized. They then (again, we are speaking of writing on a word processor) move blocks of material into some reasonable organization.

Our own preference (even though we also use a word processor when we write a first draft) is to prepare a rough outline on paper—really a list of topics. Then, after further thought, we add to it, circling items on the list and indicating (by means of arrows) better positions for these items.

Next, when we have a rough outline (perhaps a list of five or six chief items, under each of which we have written a word or phrase indicating how the point might be developed), we start writing on the word processor. It happens that our rough outline (later, much changed) for this section ran thus:

audience

   assigned? or general? or classmates

   starting

      annotating, journal? Refer to earlier chapters?

   writing

      brainstorming? outline first, then word processor

Revising

Revising a Draft

After you have written a first draft, you will read it and, almost surely, make extensive revisions. Some points will now strike you as not really worth making; others that do survive the cut you will now see as needing to be developed. You may see that you have not adequately set forth a commonly-held view that you will in effect be largely rejecting. (You now realize that you must summarize this view fairly, because many people hold it, and you now see the need to indicate that you are familiar with the view, that you see its merits, and that you think your own view is better and may at least in part be attractive even to those who hold this other view.

You may also see that the organization needs improvement. For instance, if you notice that a point you have made in the second paragraph is pretty much the same as one in the sixth paragraph, the two should be combined, rewritten, and perhaps put into an entirely new position.

Reorganizing, and providing the transitional words and phrases that make the organization clear to the reader ("moreover," "a second example," "on the other hand"), is usually not difficult, especially if you outline your draft. When you look at the outline of what you have written, you will probably see that portions of the draft have to be moved around or (in some cases) amplified or deleted, and new transitions written. Organizing an argument is so important that we will treat it separately, at some length, in a moment.

In revising, think carefully about how you use **quotations.** Keep in mind the following principles:

- Most quotations should be brief; present a long quotation only if it is extremely interesting and cannot be summarized effectively.
- Let the reader know who wrote the quotation. Identify an author who is not widely known, for example: "Judith Craft, a lawyer who specializes in constitutional matters, argues . . ."; "The warden of a maximum security prison, John Alphonso, testified that . . ."; "Anne Smith, a lesbian who has given birth to one child and adopted a second, suggests that families headed by lesbians . . . ." This sort of lead-in gives authority to the quotation.
- Let the reader know how the quotation was originally used. Examples: "Hillary Clinton argues . . ."; "The Pope rejects this view, saying . . ."; "Dr. Joycelyn Elders interprets the statistics as indicating that . . ."
- Use the present tense: "X says," *not* "X said," though of course if you are treating the passage as something from the past, use the past tense: "X wrote, twenty years ago, that . . . , but today he argues that . . . ."

After revising your draft, you may want to show it to some classmates or friends; they will doubtless give you helpful advice if you make it clear that you really do want their assistance.

Organizing An Argument

The writer of a persuasive essay almost always has to handle, in some sequence or other, the following matters:

- The background (for instance, the need to consider the issue).
- The readers' preconceptions.
- The thesis (claim).
- The evidence that supports the claim.
- The counterevidence.
- Responses to counterclaims and counterevidence (perhaps a refutation, but probably a concession that there *is* merit in the counterclaims although not as much as in the writer's thesis).
- Some sort of reaffirmation—for instance that the topic needs attention, that the thesis advanced is the most plausible or the most workable or the most moral, and that even holders of other views may find their own values strengthened by adopting the writer's view.

And here we repeat the organization that we suggested (page 65–70) for Rogerian arugment:

- state the problem, suggesting that it is an issue of concern, and that the reader has a stake in it;
- show respect for persons who hold differing views;
- set forth opposing positions, *stated in such a way that their proponents will agree that the statements of their positions, are fair,* and
- find some shared values—that is, grant whatever validity the writer finds in those positions, for instance, by recognizing the circumstances in which they would indeed be acceptable.

Having accurately summarized other views and having granted some concessions, the writer presumably has won the reader's attention and goodwill; the writer can now

- show how those who hold other positions will benefit if they accept the writer's position.

A Word about Beginnings and Endings

In the **introduction** (the first paragraph or first few paragraphs) you will usually indicate what the issue is, why it is of significance, and what your thesis is. You will also, through your tone, introduce yourself—which is to say that you will convey some sort of personality to the reader. Obviously, it is in your interest to come across as courteous, reasonable, and well informed. We will talk about this matter in a moment, when we discuss the writer's persona.

In the **ending** you probably will offer a paragraph of summary, but try to make it interesting by including something new. You might, for instance, include an interesting quotation, or reexamine a phrase from your opening paragraph in a new light. And you might appeal to your readers' self-interest, indicating how they will benefit by adopting your view.

Persona and Style

In Chapter 1 we talked about the writer's **persona**—the personality that the writer conveys through his or her words. More exactly, the persona is the image of the writer that *the readers* imagine. The writer tries to convey a certain image (courteous, fair-minded, authoritative, or all of the above, and more); but if readers find the writer discourteous, well, the writer *is* discourteous (or mean-spirited, or uninformed). It won't do for the writer, hearing of the readers' response, to insist that he or she did not mean to be discourteous (is not mean-spirited or is well-informed).

The persona is created, of course, by the impression that the words make—both the individual words and the kinds of sentences (long or short, complex or simple) in which they appear. For instance, a writer who says something like "It behooves us to exert all of our mental capacities on what I deem the primary issue of our era" will strike readers as a pompous ass. The writer may have a heart of gold and be well-informed, but he or she will still strike readers as a pompous ass—and the writer's argument will not get a very attentive hearing. A writer who uses many short sentences, much direct address to the reader, and lots of colloquial diction ("Let's get down to nuts and bolts. You've got to stop kidding yourselves. We all know what the problem is") probably will strike readers as aggressive—someone they are not keen on associating with. In short, the wrong persona can alienate readers. Even though arguments are thoughtful, the readers will be put off. We would live in a better world if we could listen objectively and separate the argument (very good) from the speaker (very unpleasant), but we can't usually do so. A hundred years ago Samuel Butler put it this way (he is overstating the case, but there is much to what he says): "We are not won by arguments that we can analyze but by tone and temper, by the manner."

Now, in fact one often *does* find aggressive writing in magazines, but this writing is, as we said earlier, a sermon addressed to the converted. The liberal readers of *The New Republic* derive pleasure from seeing conservatives roughed up a bit, just as the conservative readers of *National Review* derive pleasure from seeing liberals similarly handled. But again, these writers—utterly ignoring the principles of Carl Rogers, which we set forth on pages 65–70—are not trying to gain a hearing for their ideas; rather, they are reassuring their readers that the readers' ideas are just fine.

What kind of persona should you, as the writer of an argument, try to project? Of course you will want to be (you will *have to be*) yourself. But, just as you have different kinds of clothes, suitable for different purposes, you have several or even many selves—for instance, the self you are with a close friend, the self you are with your teachers, the self you are with customers (if you have a job), and so forth. The self that you will present in your essays—the self that you hope the readers will see from the words you put down on the page—will probably include certain specific qualities. You probably want your readers to see that you are informed and fair and are presenting a thoughtful case. You want them to be interested in hearing what you have to say. If you browse through the essays in this book, you will of course hear different voices. Although some may have an academic tone and some may sound folksy, almost all of them have one thing in common: they are the voices of people whom we would like to get to know.

An Overview: An Examination Of An Argument

Now that we have covered the ground from a more or less theoretical point of view, let's look at a specific argument. That is, let's see how one writer went about arguing her case. The writer is Barbara Mujica, a professor of Spanish at Georgetown University, in Washington, D.C. The essay originally appeared as an op-ed piece (i.e., opposite the editorial page) in *The New York Times* in 1995.

Barbara Mujica

No Comprendo

Last spring, my niece phoned me in tears. She was graduating from high school and had to make a decision. An outstanding soccer player, she was offered athletic scholarships by several colleges. So why was she crying?

My niece came to the United States from South America as a child. Although she had received good grades in her schools in Miami, she spoke English with a heavy accent and her comprehension and writing skills were deficient. She was afraid that once she left the Miami environment she would feel uncomfortable and, worse still, have difficulty keeping up with class work.

Programs that keep foreign-born children in Spanish-language classrooms for years are only part of the problem. During a visit to my niece's former school, I observed that all business, not just teaching, was conducted in Spanish. In the office, secretaries spoke to the administrators and the children in Spanish. Announcements over the public-address system were made in an English so fractured that it was almost incomprehensible.

I asked my niece's mother why, after years in public schools, her daughter had poor English skills. "It's the whole environment," she replied. "All kinds of services are available in Spanish or Spanglish. Sports and after-school activities are conducted in Spanglish. That's what the kids hear on the radio and in the street."

Until recently, immigrants made learning English a priority. But even when they didn't learn English themselves, their children grew up speaking it. Thousands of first-generation Americans still strive to learn English, but others face reduced educational and career opportunities because they have not mastered this basic skill they need to get ahead.

According to the 1990 census, 40 percent of the Hispanics born in the U.S. do not graduate from high school, and the Department of Education says that a lack of proficiency in English is an important factor in the dropout rate.

People and agencies that favor providing services only in foreign languages want to help people who do not speak English, but they may be doing them a disservice by condemning them to a linguistic ghetto from which they can not easily escape.

And my niece? She turned down all of her scholarship opportunities, deciding instead to attend a small college in Miami, where she will never have to put her English to the test.

Let's go through Mujica's argument, step by step, beginning with her title.

We think the title—Spanish for "I don't understand"—is effective. For the general reader, the term is associated with Spanish-speaking people who are weak in English. For instance, an English-speaking tourist visiting San Antonio stops someone on the street to ask where the bus station is, and the local resident replies "No comprendo." For the readers of *The New York Times* the effect of Mujica's title is perhaps slightly comic. We want to know what this professor (who is writing in an English-language newspaper) does not understand and why she is using Spanish

The first paragraph sets forth, very briefly, a personal experience that gets our attention—especially because it is puzzling: if the niece was offered several scholarships, why was she crying? In short, the paragraph gains our interest by giving us the start of a story, and it implies that this essay will be about something urgent, something that can make a young woman cry.

The second paragraph enlightens us: now we know exactly why the niece was crying, and we doubtless feel some sympathy for her. We may also become indignant with the school system, since Mujica tells us that the girl received "good grades" even though "her comprehension and writing skills were deficient." By the time we finish the essay, we can easily see that Mujica indeed is telling us that there is something wrong with the system, not with the girl.

The third paragraph openly blames programs "that keep foreign-born children in Spanish-language classrooms for years," but it goes even further, calling our attention to the fact that "all business, not just teaching, was conducted in Spanish." Mujica supports her point with concrete details: the secretaries spoke to administrators and children in Spanish, and public announcements were "made in an English so fractured that it was almost incomprehensible." (Actually this last point, about the public announcements in fractured English, somewhat undermines her statement that "all business . . . was conducted in Spanish," but perhaps the idea is that this "fractured" English really was "Spanish," English with a heavy admixture of Spanish.)

Thus far we can say that the evidence Mujica offers is largely personal. She does not tell us that 92 percent of the students in the school have such-and-such a degree of proficiency in English, or that a committee of independent investigators reported such-and-such. The evidence is the first-hand observation of the writer—her interaction with her niece and her experience as a visitor to the school. This evidence is compelling: Mujica's story, thus far, seems both truthful and moving (the niece's tears touch our hearts). On the other hand, we must realize that Mujica's essay is not addressing the arguments offered by those who support bilingual programs. (The chief argument, briefly, is that students who are not competent in English can hardly expect to do well in courses in, say, biology, if they are taught in English. Therefore, biology courses should be taught in the students' native language while they are also acquiring competence in English. A writer who accepts the principles of Carl Rogers will, of course, summarize this argument and will find some merit in it.)

The fourth paragraph adds the authority of the girl's mother. That is, Mujica in effect says, "I'm not the only one who blames the girl's poor English on the omnipresence of "Spanish or Spanglish. Look, her mother says 'That's what the kids hear on the radio and in the street.'"

The fifth paragraph, glancing at the past, asserts that immigrants used to make learning English "a priority." The assumption here is that today's immigrants can and ought to do what immigrants of the past could and did do. However, notice that Mujica cautiously modifies this view a bit by adding that even if the earlier immigrants themselves didn't learn English, their children did. Her modification is necessary, because in fact many of the earlier immigrants did not learn English. Mujica wisely avoids overstating her case.

There are at least two other things to notice in this paragraph. First, Mujica is careful not to chastise *all* of today's first-generation immigrants. She doubtless knows that if one generalizes too broadly one loses one's audience; readers will simply dismiss a writer who claims to speak unpleasant truths about whole classes of people. Second, she quietly introduces the suggestion that the school system is damaging the students *materially*; the students "face reduced . . . career opportunities . . . ." So, among other things, we are talking about serious economic matters, and she thus appeals to the readers' self-interest.

The sixth paragraph—more or less continuing this point about career opportunities—tells us that the drop-out rate is high, and that, according to the Department of Education, "a lack of proficiency in English is an important factor in the drop-out rate." What is one to make of this? Mujica cites an authority—the Board of Education—but a skeptic might say that the Board of Education says many things and its countless reports are not always convincing. Our own feeling is that there must be something to her point, but we also feel, uneasily, that her argument is weakened by the almost meaningless words, "an important factor." How important? We aren't told. We would be more impressed if we were told something like this: "The Department of Education, in a report endorsed by the governors of forty states, said that 'the chief cause of dropping out is lack of proficiency in English.'" *That* would have some weight. Still, though scarcely compelling, Mujica's statement cannot be simply brushed aside. Anyone responding to her would have to face the argument that the Department of Education sees lack of competence in English as "an important factor."

The seventh paragraph assumes that the people who are damaging the students are in fact people of good will, people who "want to help them," but (and here the economic argument returns) these people are "condemning [the students] to a linguistic ghetto." It is almost always appropriate to assume that people who hold views opposed to yours are acting from honorable intentions. First of all, they probably *do* have honorable intentions; second, by making such an assumption, you come across to your reader as a decent, fair-minded person.

The eighth (final) paragraph returns nicely to the anecdote with which the essay began, thus effectively rounding off or completing the essay. The anecdote is a sad one (or at least this is Mujica's point). But the very fact that it is sad makes it especially appropriate as a part of the argument. After all, if the niece had chosen to go, let's say, to the University of Wisconsin, Mujica's argument would collapse. The moral of such a story would be, "Even if a school keeps the student from mastering English, no great harm is done, since the student will go to a mainstream college or university anyway."

In short, although Mujica makes use of statistics and authority when (in her sixth paragraph) she mentions the Department of Education, chiefly she builds her case on personal experience. The implication is that she knows what she is talking about because she has seen it. But is personal experience enough to bring us around to her side? Perhaps so—if the person is someone of goodwill. Mujica shows that she is such a person at the outset, when she reveals herself to be a concerned aunt, and especially in paragraph 7, when she concedes that the opponents mean well.

You may of course have a very different response to Mujica's essay and to our discussion of it. Perhaps you will even be stimulated to write an argument showing that we have misread the essay. Or you may be stimulated to write an argument opposing Mujica's position.

✓A Checklist for Revising Drafts of Arguments

✓ Does the introduction let the audience know what the topic is, why the topic is of some importance, and what your thesis is?

✓ Are the terms clearly defined?

✓ Are the assumptions likely to be shared by your readers? If not, are they reasonably argued rather than merely asserted?

✓ Does the essay summarize other views fairly, and grant that they have some merit, at least in some contexts?

✓ Are the facts verifiable? Is the evidence reliable?

✓ Is the reasoning sound?

✓ Are the authorities really authorities on this matter?

✓ Are quotations no longer than they need to be, are they introduced with useful lead-ins, and do they make good reading?

✓ Are all of the substantial counterarguments recognized and effectively responded to?

✓ Is the organization effective? Does the essay begin interestingly, keep the thesis in view, and end interestingly?

✓ Is the tone appropriate? (Avoid sarcasm, present yourself as fair-minded, and assume that people who hold views opposed to yours are also fair-minded.)

Trying to Find Common Ground

Wal-Mart has a policy of not stocking compact disks whose content or whose covers they find offensive. We reprint here a short essay by William J. Bennett and C. DeLores Tucker, originally published in *The New York Times,* applauding Wal-Mart's position, and we accompany it with letters that the essay elicited from readers.

Taking into account the essay and the positions of the respondents, write a 500-word essay of your own, addressed to all of the participants in the discussion. Keeping in mind the principles set forth by Carl Rogers (pages 65–70), in your contribution to this on-going discussion try to find some common ground between writers who on the whole take opposing views. And try to show why, where you strongly differ from some respondents, you think your view is sounder than theirs, and that their own positions will in fact be strengthened if they adopt at least part of your view. (If after carefully reading the original essay and the letters you believe that there is no common ground, and that nothing can be conceded, you will of course have to take this position in your essay.)

William J. Bennett and C. DeLores Tucker

Smut-Free Stores

There is news worth celebrating on the popular-culture front. Wal-Mart, the nation's largest retailer, has refused to stock compact disks with lyrics and cover art that it finds objectionable. If the artists and the record companies want Wal-Mart to carry their albums, they can alter the product to eliminate the offensive material.

Wal-Mart has a lot of clout—it accounts for 52 million of the 615 million compact disks sold in the United States each year—and it is using that power to help clean up the music industry. For this the chain deserves great praise.

But Wal-Mart's stand has sent many in the artistic community into a tizzy. Some say that Wal-Mart is imposing a new form of censorship. But it is not forcing anyone to remove songs, change lyrics or alter artwork. It is simply saying that there are minimal standards a record company must meet if its compact disks are going to be sold at Wal-Mart.

In short, Wal-Mart is exercising quality control—which it does every day for every product. It is absurd to call this censorship. Such claims are akin to accusing a homeowner of censorship for keeping someone out of his house who intends to step all over the sofa and curse the in-laws. The issue cuts both ways: Gospel singers are not invited to perform at raunchy nightclubs, but the fact that they are not welcome does not mean they are being censored.

Many artists consider any change to their original work an assault on their artistic integrity. But they have a choice: Clean up your lyrics, or your product won't be sold at Wal-Mart. Some artists refuse, but they are the exception. Of course, there are those who have changed their work for financial reasons but who have the chutzpah to whine that "Wal-Mart made us do it!" This is not censorship; this is greed combined with self-righteousness.

Some have charged that Wal-Mart's policy will have a chilling effect on artists' creativity. Nina Crowley, executive director of the Massachusetts Music Industry Coalition, says that some young performers "are wondering if they are going to have to change what they do if they want to make any money." Translation: Wal-Mart is creating market pressure to elevate the quality and standards of what is being sold to children. The response from many of us is: It's about time.

Another argument from the recording companies is that they already met their responsibilities when they agreed (reluctantly) to put "parental advisory" labels on recordings that use profanity or glorify violence. Warning labels are probably better than nothing, but not much better. An analogy: If a toxic- waste dump is polluting the environment, would nearby residents be mollified if the corporate polluters agreed merely to put up a sign saying, "Danger: Toxic Waste"? Of course not.

For years, concerned parents and politicians of both parties have asked the recording industry to stop selling music with lyrics that are so vile that newspapers refuse to print them. We have appealed to simple decency and their sense of corporate responsibility. But for the most part our appeals have fallen on deaf ears. Corporations like BMG, Sony, Time Warner and MCA continue to peddle filth for profit—so we will continue to exercise our First Amendment rights to criticize them for doing so.

The controversy over Wal-Mart is a perfect illustration of the intellectual confusion and moral obtuseness of the record companies. They still don't get it.

Two days after the essay appeared, the following responses were printed.

Wal-Mart Is Opening a New Gate to Censorship

To the Editor:

In "Wal-Mart's Free Choice" (Op-Ed, Dec. 9), William J. Bennett and C. DeLores Tucker make several telling points about censorship and the commercial culture. What is troublesome about their views is their blanket deference to censorship by retailers to dictate the content of music, videos and books. Mr. Bennett and Ms. Tucker endorse virtuous business censorship. But what about less ennobling censorship, say of an overtly political character? Is that equally acceptable?

When major distribution outlets like Wal-Mart refuse to carry a particular compact disk, video or book because of its message, that decision traces back to the artist. For example, a record company may well disfavor lyrics that offend the major outlets. Or a book publisher may shy away from topics disfavored by marketing giants. Such decisions are especially objectionable when, as in the case of Wal-Mart, a C.D. is banned because it criticizes the marketing practices of these outlets.

Today, the threat of private censorship by retailers and advertisers is far too great to countenance by way of carte blanche deference—even when such deference seems morally and culturally warranted.

RONALD K. L. COLLINS
Tacoma, Wash., Dec. 9, 1996

Too Much Protecting?

To the Editor:

By comparing recordings that use profanity to a toxic-waste dump, William J. Bennett and C. DeLores Tucker (Op-Ed, Dec. 9) seem to believe that once someone is exposed to such material, the damage is real and irreversible. Such overprotectiveness might be forgiven if one is dealing exclusively with impressionable young children. The rub is that not a few adults purchase their music at Wal-Mart as well.

While seeming to serve children's best interest, Wal-Mart is dumbing down its music selection to the lowest common denominator, so that anyone responsible for his or her own mind has no choice but to buy only what's intended to "protect" adolescents. And if enough retailers believe that purveying such pablum is lucrative enough, there's not much to stop them from extending a "sanitized for your protection" policy to books, too, which I find a truly frightening prospect.

It is curious that Mr. Bennett advocates greater parental guidance of their children's lives in some situations but here he is happy to let some anonymous corporate bureaucrat decide what's best for America's children.

ROGER C. GEISSLER
Philadelphia, Dec. 9, 1996

Music vs. Money

To the Editor:

Contrary to William J. Bennett and C. DeLores Tucker (Op-Ed, Dec. 9), Wal-Mart's policy has not sent the artistic community into a "tizzy." The policy has sent the record industry into a tizzy.

Recording "artists" are not in the business of producing art. They work for a big corporation known as a record label. If the records don't sell, they get fired, no mater how artistic their product.

It is amazing that these entertainers, especially the young ones, don't understand the "contract with the devil" record labels offer them. Sure, they get paid heaps for doing what they love, but they also have to satisfy somebody in a business suit who cares exactly zero about music (like Wal-Mart). Ultimately, the bottom line takes precedent over free expression, Dr. Faustus. Surprise, surprise, surprise.

SCOTT CARGLE
Artistic Director
The Shakespeare Project
New York, Dec. 9, 1996

Wal-Mart's Rights

To the Editor:

The Constitution guarantees the right to free expression. It does not guarantee everybody equal access to the marketplace to peddle their ideas

Wal-Mart is exercising its right of free expression by creating an environment where families will not be offended by lyrics or cover art. Artists who do not want to comply with Wal-Mart's standards can try to sell their material elsewhere. It is not everybody's right to sell products at Wal-Mart, but it is Wal-Mart's right to control the environment in its stores.

MARY P. WALKER
College Station, Tex., Dec. 9, 1996

5
READING AND WRITING ABOUT PICTURES

I *am after the one unique picture whose composition possesses such vigor and richness, and whose content so radiates outwards from it, that this single picture is a whole story in itself.*

Henri Cartier-Bresson

The Language Of Pictures

It may sound odd to talk about "reading" pictures and about the "language" of pictures, but pictures, like words, convey messages. Advertisers know this, and that's why their advertisements for soft drinks include images of attractive young couples frolicking at the beach. The not-so-hidden message is that consumers of these products are healthy, prosperous, relaxed, and strongly attractive to people of the opposite sex.

Like compositions made of words—stories, poems, even vigorous sentences—many paintings are carefully constructed things, built up in a certain way in order to make a statement. To cite an obvious example, in medieval religious pictures Jesus or Mary may be shown larger than the surrounding figures to indicate their greater spiritual status. But even in realistic paintings the more important figures are likely to be given a greater share of the light or a more central position than the lesser figures. Such devices of composition are fairly evident in paintings, but we occasionally forget that photographs too are almost always constructed things. The photographer—even the amateur just taking a candid snapshot—adjusts a pillow under the baby's head, or suggests that the subject may want to step out of the shadow , and then the photographer backs up a little and bends his or her knees before clicking the shutter. Even when photographing something inanimate, the photographer searches for the best view, waits for a cloud to pass, and perhaps pushes out of the range of the camera some trash that would spoil the effect of a lovely fern growing beside a rock. Minor White was speaking for almost all photographers when he said, "I don't take pictures, I make them."

And we often make our photographs for a particular purpose—perhaps to have a souvenir of a trip, or to show what we look like in uniform, or to show grandparents what the new baby looks like. Even professional photographers have a variety of purposes—for instance to provide wedding portraits, to report the news, to sell automobiles, or to record some visual phenomena that they think must be recorded. Sometimes these purposes can be mingled. During the depression of the early 1930s, for instance, the Resettlement Administration employed photographers such as Dorothea Lange to help convince the nation that migrant workers and dispossessed farmers needed help. These photographers were, so to speak, selling something, but they were also reporting the news and serving a noble social purpose. Later in this chapter we will reproduce Lange's most famous picture, *Migrant Mother,* along with some comments on it that students wrote in journals. We will follow these entries from journals with a finished essay, submitted by a student at the end of the term.

But before we get to Lange's photograph, we will give some questions that may help you to think about pictures.

What are some of the basic things to look for in understanding the language of pictures? One can begin almost anywhere, but let's begin with the relationship among the parts:

> Do the figures share the space evenly, or does one figure overpower another, taking most of the space or the light?

> Are the figures harmoniously related, perhaps by a similar stance or shared action? Or are they opposed, perhaps by diagonals thrusting at each other? Generally speaking, diagonals may suggest instability, except when they form a triangle resting on its base. Horizontal lines suggest stability, as do vertical lines when connected by a horizontal line. Circular lines are often associated with motion, and sometimes—especially by men—with the female body and fertility. These simple formulas, however, must be applied cautiously, for they are not always appropriate.

> In a landscape, what is the relation between humans and nature? Are the figures at ease in nature, or are they dwarfed by it? Are they earthbound, beneath the horizon, or (because the viewpoint is low) do they stand out against the horizon and perhaps seem in touch with the heavens, or at least with open air? Do the natural objects in the landscape somehow reflect the emotions of the figures in it?

> If the picture is a portrait, how do the furnishings and the background and the angle of the head or the posture of the head and body (as well, of course, as the facial expression) contribute to our sense of the character of the person portrayed?

> What is the effect of light in the picture? Does it produce sharp contrasts, brightly illuminating some parts and throwing others into darkness? Or does it, by means of gentle gradations, unify most or all of the parts? Does the light seem theatrical or natural, disturbing or comforting? If the picture is in color, is the color realistic or is it expressive, or both?

You can stimulate responses to pictures by asking yourself two kinds of questions:

1. *What is this doing?* Why is this figure here and not there, why is this tree so brightly illuminated, why are shadows omitted, why is this seated figure leaning forward like that?

2. *Why do I have this response?* Why do I find this figure pathetic, this landscape oppressive, this child revoltingly sentimental but that child fascinating?

The first of these questions, "What is this doing?" requires you to identify yourself with the artist, wondering perhaps whether the fence or the side of the house is the better background for this figure, or whether both figures should sit or stand. The second question, "Why do I have this response?" requires you to trust your feelings. If you are amused, repelled, unnerved, or soothed, assume that these responses are appropriate and follow them up—at least until further study of the work provides other responses.

Thinking About Dorothea Lange's
Migrant Mother, Nipomo, California

Let's look now at a photograph by Dorothea Lange, an American photographer who made her reputation with photographs of migrant laborers in California during the depression that began in 1929. Lange's *Migrant Mother, Nipomo, California* (1936) is probably the best-known image of the period. One of our students made the following entry in his journal. (The student was given no information about the photograph other than the name of the photographer and the title of the picture.)

> This woman seems to be thinking. In a way, the picture reminds me of a statue called The Thinker, of a seated man who is bent over, with his chin resting on his fist. But I wouldn't say that this photograph is really so much about thinking as it is about other things. I'd say that it is about several other things. First (but not really in any particular order), fear. The children must be afraid, since they have turned to their mother. Second, the picture is about love. The children press against their mother, sure of her love. The mother does not actually show her love--for instance, by kissing them, or even hugging them--but you feel she loves them. Third, the picture is about hopelessness. The mother doesn't seem to be able to offer any comfort. Probably they have very little food; maybe they are homeless. I'd say the picture is also about courage. Although the picture seems to me to show hopelessness, I also think the mother, even though she does not know how she will be able to help her children shows great strength in her face. She also has a lot of dignity. She hasn't broken down in front of the children: she is going to do her best to get through the day and the next day and the next.

Another student wrote:

> I remember from American Lit that good literature is not sentimental. (When we discussed the word, we concluded that

Eyes of the Nation
Vincent Virga, 1997

"sentimental" meant "sickeningly sweet.") Some people might think that Lange's picture, showing a mother and two little children, is sentimental, but I don't think so. Although the children must be upset, and maybe they even are crying, the mother seems to be very strong. I feel that with a mother like this, the children are in very good hands. She is not "sickeningly sweet." She may be almost overcome with despair, but she doesn't seem to ask us to pity her.

A third student wrote:

It's like those pictures of the homeless in the newspapers and on TV. A photographer sees some man sleeping in a cardboard box, or a woman with shopping bags sitting in a doorway, and he takes their picture. I suppose the photographer could say that he is calling the public's attention to "the plight of the homeless," but I'm not convinced that he's doing anything more than making money by selling photographs. Homeless people have almost no privacy, and then some photographer comes along and invades even their doorways and cardboard houses. Sometimes the people are sleeping, or even if they are awake they may be in so much despair that they don't bother to tell the photographer to get lost. Or they may be mentally ill and don't know what's happening. In the case of this picture, the woman is not asleep, but she seems so preoccupied that she isn't aware of the photographer. Maybe she has just been told there is no work for her, or maybe she has been told she can't stay if she keeps the children. Should the photographer have intruded on this woman's sorrow? This picture may be art, but it bothers me.

All of these entries seem to us to be thoughtful, interesting, and helpful, though of course even taken together they do not provide the last word.

Here are a few additional points. First, it happens that Lange has written about the picture. She said that she had spent the winter of 1935–36 taking photographs of migrants, and now, in March, she was preparing to drive five hundred miles to her home when she noticed a sign that said, "Pea-Pickers Camp." Having already taken hundreds of pictures, she drove on for twenty miles, but something preyed on her mind, and she made a U-turn and visited the camp. Here is part of what she wrote.

> I saw and approached the hungry and desperate mother, as if drawn by a magnet. I do not remember how I explained my presence or my camera to her, but I do remember she asked me no questions. I made five exposures, working closer and closer from the same direction. I did not ask her name or her history. She told me her age, that she was thirty-two. She said that they had been living on frozen vegetables from the surrounding fields, and birds that the children killed. She had just sold the tires from her car to buy food. There she sat in that lean-to tent with her children huddled around her, and seemed to know that my pictures might help her, and so she helped me. There was a sort of equality about it. . . . What I am trying to tell other photographers is that had I not been deeply involved in my undertaking on that field trip, I would not have had to turn back. What I am trying to say is that I believe this inner compulsion to be the vital ingredient in our work.

Lange does not say anything about posing the woman and her child, and we can assume that she had too much decency to ask a woman and children in these circumstances to arrange themselves into an interesting pictorial composition. Furthermore, it seems obvious that unlike, say, a figure in a wedding portrait, the woman is not striking a pose. She has not deliberately prepared herself for a picture that will represent her to the public. Nevertheless, the composition—the way things are put together— certainly contributes to the significance of the picture. Of course the subject matter, a mother with children, may suggest the traditional Madonna and Child of the Middle Ages and the Renaissance, but the resemblance is not just in the subject matter. Lange's photograph may remind us of paintings in which the Madonna and the infant Jesus form a unified composition, their heads and limbs harmonizing and echoing each other.

The photograph, with its near-balance—a child on each side, the mother's bare left arm balanced by the child's bare arm, the mother's hand at one side of her neck echoed by the child's hand at the other side—achieves a stability, or harmony, that helps make the painfulness of the subject acceptable. That is, although the subject may be painful, it is possible to take some pleasure in the way in which it is presented. That the faces of the children are turned away probably helps make the subject acceptable. If we saw not only the woman's face but also the faces of two hungry children, we might feel that Lange was tugging too vigorously at our heartstrings. Finally, speaking of faces, it is worth mentioning that the woman does not look at us. Of course we don't know why, but we can guess that she takes no notice of us because she is preoccupied with issues far beyond us.

A Sample Essay by a Student

We have already given extracts from the journals of three students. A week after the journals were due, students were asked to write essays on the picture. Notice in the following essay that the student draws not only on his own experience as an amateur photographer but also on material that he found in the college library.

Did Dorothea Lange Pose Her Subject for Migrant Mother?

In doing research for this essay, I was surprised to find that Dorothea Lange's Migrant Mother (figure A) is one of six pictures of this woman and her children. Migrant Mother is so much an image of the period, an icon of the Depression, that it is hard to believe it exists in any other form than the one we all know.[1]

In addition to the famous picture, four other pictures of this subject (figures B-E) are illustrated in a recent book, Vincent Virga's Eyes of the

[1] Curiously, Lange in her short essay on the picture, "The Assignment I'll Never Forget: Migrant Mother," in Popular Photography 46 (February 1960): 43, says that she made five exposures. A slightly abridged version of the essay is reprinted in Milton Meltzer, Dorothea Lange: A Photographer's Life (New York: Farrar Straus Giroux 1978): 132-33. Because Meltzer's book is more available than the magazine, when I quote from the article I quote from his book.

Nation, and still another picture (figure F) is illustrated in Karen
Tsujimoto's Dorothea Lange. When you think about it, it is not surprising
that Lange would take several pictures of this woman and her children,
anyone who takes snapshots knows that if photographers have the
opportunity they will take several pictures of a subject. What is surprising
is that the picture we all know, the one that has become an icon for the
period, is so much more moving than the others.

    Two of the pictures include an older child, apparently a teenager,
sitting in a chair, so in a sense they are "truer" to the fact, because they
give us more information about the family. The trunk, for instance, tells us
that he people are on the move, and the setting--a messy field, with a
shabby tent or lean-to--tells us that they are homeless. But sometimes less
is more; the pictures showing the tent, trunk, and all of the children seem
to sprawl. Perhaps we find ourselves wondering why people who seem to
have only a trunk and some canvas would carry with them so bulky an

object as a rocker. In saying that the two more inclusive pictures are less effective--less impressive, less moving--than the others, then, I don't think that I am simply expressing a personal preference. I think that most or maybe even all viewers would agree.

Putting aside the two pictures that show the setting, and also putting aside for the moment the most famous picture, we probably can agree that the three remaining pictures of the woman are approximately equally effective, one viewer might prefer one picture, another viewer another, but compared with the two that show the larger setting, all three of these pictures have the advantage of emphasizing the mother-and-child motif. But the remaining picture, the famous one, surely is far more memorable than even the other three close-up pictures. Why? Partly, perhaps, because it is a *closer* view, eliminating the tent pole and most of the hanging cloth. Partly it is more effective because the children have turned their faces from the camera, thereby conveying their isolation from everything in the world except their mother. And partly it is more effective because the woman, touching the side of her face, has a faraway look of anxiety.

Thinking about this picture in the context of the other five, if one has a cynical mind one might wonder if Lange staged it. And this is exactly what Charles J. Shindo says she did, in his recent book:

> In the course of this encounter Lange took six exposures, starting with a long shot of the lean-to with the mother and four children inside. . . . For the final shot Lange called back another of the children and had the children lean upon their mother with their backs to the camera. The woman raised her hand to her chin and struck the now famous pose of the Migrant Mother. . . . (50)

What evidence does Shindo give for his claim that "Lange called back another of the children" and that she "had the children lean upon their mother"? Absolutely none. He does not cite Lange, or an eyewitness, or anyone who suggests that Lange customarily posed her subjects. He ignores the basic evidence, Lange's own words about how she took the picture:

> I saw and approached the hungry and desperate mother, as if drawn by a magnet. I do not remember how I explained my presence of my camera to her, but I do remember she asked me no questions. I made five exposures, working closer and closer from the same direction. I did not ask her name or her history. She told me her age, that she was 32. She said that they had been living on frozen vegetables from the surrounding fields, and birds that the children killed. She had just sold the tires from her car to buy food. There she sat in that lean-to tent with her children huddled around her, and seemed to know that my pictures might help her, and so she helped me. There was a sort of equality about it.
>
> The pea crop at Nipomo had frozen and there was no work for anybody. But I did not approach the tents and shelters of other stranded pea-pickers. It was not necessary; I knew I had recorded the essence of my assignment. . . . (qtd. in Meltzer 133)

This is the <u>only</u> eye-witness account of how Lange photographed the woman and her children. Of course she may not have been telling the truth, but none of her contemporaries ever challenged the truth of her statement. Furthermore, everything that we know about Lange suggests that she did not pose her subjects. For instance, Rondal Partridge, a longtime friend and sometimes a co-worker, gave this description of Lange's method: "She did not ask people to hold a pose or repeat an action, instead she might ask a question: 'How much does that bag of cotton weigh?' And the man, wanting to give her a precise answer, would lift it onto the scales and Lange would make her photograph" (qtd. in Ohrn 61).

Rondal Partridge's comment harmonizes with comments that Lange herself made about her method. Asked about her approach to photography, she said, "First--hands off! Whatever I photograph, I do not molest or tamper with or arrange" (qtd. in Dixon 68). Elsewhere she explained that since she worked with a large camera, "You have to wait until certain decisions are made by the subject--what he's going to give to the camera, which is a very important decision; and the photographer-- what he's going to choose to take" (qtd. in Ohrn 233). If I may add a personal comment, I want to say that as an amateur portrait photographer I know from my experience and from talking to other photographers, that posed photographs just don't come out successfully. You can't say to children, "Turn your faces toward your mother," and then say to the mother, "Please put your hand on your cheek," and get a good picture. Every photographer quickly learns that when the photographer specifies the poses, the pictures will be lifeless. The way to get a picture that is convincing is, as Lange's friend said, for the photographer to engage in some talk with the subject, which allows the subject to respond in some significant way. I imagine that while Lange talked, the children may have become uneasy at the sight of the woman with the big camera, and they may have turned and sought the security of their mother. (This is only a guess, but it is very different from Shindo's assertion, made without evidence, that "Lange called back another of the children and had the children lean upon their mother with their backs to the camera"). And perhaps Lange asked the woman something like, "What do you think you will do now?" or "Do you think you can get a friend to give your family a hitch to another work-site?" or some such thing, and the woman responded naturally. Again my view is different from Shindo's, who says that the woman "struck the pose of the Migrant Mother," where "struck the pose," in the context of his preceding sentences about Lange coldly setting up the image, suggests that the whole thing is a performance, with Lange as stage-manager and the woman as the chief actor.

Anyone who has read a book about Dorothea Lange, and has studied Lange's numerous comments about her ways of working in Dorothea Lange, ed. Howard M. Levin and Katherine Northrup, knows that posing figures was utterly foreign to her. In 1923 she posted on her darkroom door these words from Francis Bacon, and they guided her for the remaining thirty-odd years of her career:

> The contemplation of things as they are
>
> without substitution or imposture
>
> without error or confusion
>
> is in itself a nobler thing
>
> than a whole harvest of invention. (qtd. in Stein 59)

In her photography Lange sought to show the viewer "things as they are." She believed it was nobler to show life as it is than it is to invent compositions.

There are, of course, questions about this picture, such as "Exactly what is the mother thinking about?" Is she thinking that the situation is hopeless? Or that somehow she and the children will get through? Does her face show despair, or does it show determination? These are questions that we cannot answer definitively. But if we ask the question, "Did Lange tell the children and the woman how to position themselves?" we must answer that all of the evidence suggests that she did not set the scene. She spoke to the woman, and she moved about, looking for the best shot, but a picture as great as this one can only have come from (to repeat Lange's own belief) what the subject is "going to give to the camera" and what the photographer is "going to choose to take."

Works Cited

Dixon, Daniel. "Dorothea Lange." Modern Photography 16 (Dec 1952). 68-77, 138-41.

Levin, Howard M., and Katherine Northrup. Dorothea Lange. 2 vols. Glencoe: Text-Fiche Press, 1980.

Meltzer, Milton. Dorothea Lange: A Photographer's Life. New York: Farrar,
1978.

Ohrn, Karin Becker. Dorothea Lange and the Documentary Tradition.
Baton Rouge: Louisiana State UP, 1980.

Shindo, Charles J. Dust Bowl Migrants in the American Imagination.
Lawrence: UP of Kansas, 1997.

Stein, Sally. "Peculiar Grace: Dorothea Lange and the Testimony of the
Body." Dorothea Lange: A Visual Life. Ed. Elizabeth Partridge. Washington, D. C.: Smithsonian Institution, 1994. 57-89.

A Short Published Essay on a Photograph

Recently the Mariners' Museum at Newport News, Virginia, held an exhibition of photographs concerned with seafaring. If you have visited a
maritime museum, you probably were strongly attracted and perhaps
even moved by paintings and models of old vessels, by whaling gear, by
quaint uniforms, and by strongly carved ships' figureheads. One doesn't
usually think of photographs in such a museum, but the Mariners' Museum, endowed with a large collection of photographs, decided to exhibit
some of them and then to publish a book with one hundred pictures, each
with a brief commentary. Who would read such a book? More precisely,
who would look at such a book, since the immediate appeal is the pictures, not the text? Most obviously, anyone interested in life at sea, or in
photography, or in both. You may not have a passion for either topic, but
look at Clifton Guthrie's photograph of the ship called *Juan Sebastian de
Elcano*, think about it for a moment, and then read Richard Benson's short
essay.

Richard Benson

Juan Sebastian de Elcano

 T he white ship whose figurehead we see is a trainer, built by Spain
for the betterment of her young seafaring officer candidates. These ships

Juan Sebastian de Elcano
Clifton Guthrie

sail about, not really going anywhere, and when the men are not up in the rigging learning fear and respect for the sea they can be found employed in the three activities shown here. First is the pastime of leaning back in some nook of the ship, with a companion, and passing the long days peering about and commenting on wharfside life. Second is carrying on the constant battle to prevent the ship from rusting away; this is what the man suspended in the rope bosun's chair is doing. Whether scraping or painting, the crew of any steel or iron ship must continually fight rust caused by the corrosive salt water in which the ship lives. Third is the ceremony of dressing up in fine clothes, complete with gold buttons and stripes of rank, that all military men must do to display their human version of the ruffled feathers or raised antlers that adorn so many creatures that fight.

The flattening structure of the photograph, which puts the four men and the ornate figurehead all on the same picture plane, binds the people up in a linear web. Most of this visual network is drawn by strands of wire rope, or cable, but common rope—or line as it is called at sea—is visible as well, holding our sailor suspended in his chair. The most surprising line of all in the picture is the white, featureless bobstay that runs diagonally from lower right to upper left. This is a solid shaft that reaches to the end of the bowsprit from its anchor point low down on the stem of the ship, and it counteracts the immense upward pull that the bowsprit must sustain from the forestays that support the ship's masts and headsails. By matching the tension of the cables that reach up to the masthead, this rod ensures that the bowsprit is in compression only, so the wood supports a load that can be easily handled, in the same way that a structural column holds up the weight of a heavy floor or lintel. The white rod is acting like another piece of line—it could just as well be a length of massive cable—but because of its forward location half in the water, this structural element is subject to corrosion of the worst sort. The twisted fine wires of a cable would suffer from destructive rust that would be hard to see or prevent; the use of a smooth, round shaft instead, which can be painted and easily examined, avoids the potential catastrophe of a failure in the most highly tensioned point in the ship's rig.

The first thing we want to mention about Benson's essay is that, perhaps surprisingly, he does *not* talk about the figurehead or the shield beneath it (perhaps the emblem of a Spanish naval academy?) or the decorative carving on the prow that leads into the figurehead. Benson's interests apparently are elsewhere. The first lesson we can learn, then, is that there is (of course) not *one* thing to say about a picture, but many possible things; writers say what interests them, and different writers have different interests. When you look at and then write about pictures in *The Little, Brown Reader,* write about what interests you; you are not expected to have the same response as the person whose name follows yours in the alphabetic class list.

Benson talks chiefly about two topics, the figures in the picture, and a "linear web"—ropes and cables—that binds the figures together and that in fact binds a ship. Not surprisingly, in this two-paragraph essay he devotes one paragraph to each topic. The first paragraph is thoroughly delightful analysis of the seafaring life as it is revealed in this picture. It is analytic because it studies the parts (three in number) and relates them to the whole (life at sea); it is delightful because (a) it is clear ("first," "second," "third"), because (b) it is informative (for instance, it tells us that sailors fight a "constant battle to prevent the ship from rusting away"), because (c) it makes us see things freshly (training ships, such as this one, "sail about, not really going anywhere"), and because (d) the clear, informative writing that makes us see things freshly also says something that is deeply true: We must learn "fear and respect for the sea."

What we have just said is heavy-handed, especially when compared with Benson's light touch. Consider the last sentence of his first paragraph:

Third is the ceremony of dressing up in fine clothes, complete with gold buttons and stripes of rank, that all military men must do to display their human version of the ruffled feathers or raised antlers that adorn so many creatures that fight.

Benson here goes far beyond the photograph; indeed, most of us writing about this picture probably would have had nothing to say about the uniformed figure at the bottom—but all readers will agree, we think, that Benson has said something of considerable interest.

Having given his readers (in a highly engaging way) a good deal to think about, concerning not only life at sea but also concerning aggression in human nature, in his second paragraph Benson turns to more mechanical matters, the functions of a ship's lines. For many readers this paragraph is less interesting than the first, but even these readers may agree that Benson's knowledge and his concern to tell the truth—to make clear the life-and-death importance of that "smooth, round shaft"—are compelling. A line might be drawn connecting his last sentence in his last paragraph, with its reference to "potential catastrophe," to something he said in his first paragraph—that sailors must learn "fear and respect for the sea."

Last Words

If your instructor asks you to write about a picture—perhaps one in this book—and if even after thinking about the questions on pages 93–94 you don't quite know where to begin, you may want to think about it partly in terms of one of the following remarks by distinguished photographers. (But remember: a remark need not be true just because it was made by someone who is highly regarded as a photographer.)

A great photograph is a full expression of what one feels about what is being photographed in the deepest sense, and is, thereby, a true expression of what one feels about life in its entirety.

Ansel Adams

It's the subject-matter that counts. I'm interested in revealing the subject in a new way to intensify it.

Harry Callahan

Documentary photography records the social scene of our time. It mirrors the present and documents for the future. Its focus is man in his relations to mankind.

Dorothea Lange

Photography is the simultaneous recognition, in a fraction of a second, of the significance of an event as well as of the precise organization of forms which give that event its proper expression.

Henri Cartier-Bresson

I am a passionate lover of the snapshot because of all photographic images it comes closest to truth. The snapshot is a specific spiritual moment. . . . What the eye sees is different from what the camera records. Whereas the eye sees in three dimensions, images are projected on a surface of two dimensions, which for every image-maker is a great problem. The snap-shooter disregards this problem, and the result is that his pictures have an apparent disorder and imperfection, which is exactly their appeal and their style. . . . Out of this imbalance, and out of this not knowing, and out of this real innocence toward the medium comes an enormous vitality and expression of life.

Lisette Model

Or you might begin by thinking about a statement by Janet Malcolm, who in *Diana and Nikon* (a book about photography) said:

If "the camera can't lie," neither is it inclined to tell the truth, since it can reflect only the usually ambiguous, and sometimes outright deceitful surface of reality.

Exercise: Find a picture that interest you, and write two or three paragraphs about it. Say whatever you want to say, but, like Benson, you may want to take a picture that allows you to draw on your technical knowledge, so that you can educate your reader. If you read any specialized magazines, for instance about sports or computers or automobiles or fashion or beekeeping, you probably know more about this area than the average person. From a magazine on this topic, take a picture that interests you—a picture that (a) stimulates you to reflect, as Benson does in his first paragraph, and that (b) allows you to educate your reader by elucidating technical details, as Benson does in his second paragraph.

6
MEMOIRS: DISCOVERING THE PAST

Short Views

Know myself? If I knew my self, I'd run away.
      Johann Wolfgang von Goethe

The true art of memory is the art of attention.
      Samuel Johnson

The charm, one might say the genius of memory, is that it is choosy, chancy, and temperamental: It rejects the edifying cathedral and indelibly photographs the small boy outside, chewing a hunk of melon in the dust.
      Elizabeth Bowen

Our memory is like a shop in the window of which is exposed now one, now another photograph of the same person. And as a rule the most recent exhibit remains for some time the only one to be seen.
      Marcel Proust

It's a pleasure to share one's memories. Everything remembered is dear, endearing, touching, precious. At least the past is safe—though we didn't know it at the time. We know it now. Because it's in the past; because we have survived.
      Susan Sontag

Not the power to remember, but its very opposite, the power to forget, is a necessary condition for our existence.
      Sholem Asch

Memory is the thing you forget with.
      Alexander Chase

A retentive memory may be a good thing, but the ability to forget is the true token of greatness.
> **Elbert Hubbard**

Better by far you should forget and smile
Than that you should remember and be sad.
> **Christina Rossetti**

We are now at the 24th of March 1856, and from this point of time, my journal, let us renew our daily intercourse without looking back. Looking back was not intended by nature, evidently, from the fact that our eyes are in our faces and not in our hind heads. Look straight before you, then, Jane Carlyle, and, if possible, not over the heads of things either, away into the distant vague. Look, above all, at the duty nearest hand, and what's more, do it. Ah, the spirit is willing, but the flesh is weak, and four weeks of illness have made mine weak as water.
> **Jane Welsh Carlyle**

I did, I think, nothing.
> **Evelyn Waugh**

Went to bed, and slept dreamlessly, but not refreshingly. Awoke, and up an hour before being called; but dawdled three hours in dressing. When one subtracts from life infancy (which is vegetation)—sleep, eating, and swilling—buttoning and unbuttoning—how much remains of downright existence? The summer of a dormouse.
> **Lord Byron**

To be able to enjoy one's past life is to live twice.
> **Martial**

Memory . . . is the diary that we all carry about with us.
> **Oscar Wilde**

St. Augustine

Augustine (354–430) was born in a Roman territory in what is now Algeria, of Roman-African stock. His mother was a Christian, but his father was a pagan, and Augustine did not become converted to Christianity until 386, when, studying philosophy in Milan, he heard a divine voice tell him to read the Scriptures. He picked them up, and the line that most struck him was: "But put ye on the Lord Jesus Christ, and make not provision for the flesh to fulfill the lusts thereof." Augustine was baptized the next year, and, after further study, he returned to Africa, where he in time became Bishop of Hippo. Our selection comes from Book II of his Confessions.

The Love of Evil

He Commits Theft with His Companions, Not Urged on by Poverty, but from a Certain Distaste of Well-doing

Theft is punished by Thy law, O Lord, and by the law written in men's hearts, which iniquity itself cannot blot out. For what thief will suffer a thief? Even a rich thief will not suffer him who is driven to it by want. Yet had I a desire to commit robbery, and did so, compelled neither by hunger, nor poverty, but through a distaste for well-doing, and a lustiness of iniquity. For I pilfered that of which I had already sufficient, and much better. Nor did I desire to enjoy what I pilfered, but the theft and sin itself. There was a pear-tree close to our vineyard, heavily laden with fruit, which was tempting neither for its color nor its flavor. To shake and rob this some of us wanton young fellows went, late one night (having, according to our disgraceful habit, prolonged our games in the streets until then), and carried away great loads, not to eat ourselves, but to fling to the very swine, having only eaten some of them; and to do this pleased us all the more because it was not permitted. Behold my heart, O my God; behold my heart, which Thou hadst pity upon when in the bottomless pit. Behold, now, let my heart tell Thee what it was seeking there, that I should be gratuitously wanton, having no inducement to evil but the evil itself. It was foul, and I loved it. I loved to perish. I loved my own error—not that for which I erred; but the error itself. Base soul, falling from Thy firmament to utter destruction—not seeking aught through the shame but the shame itself!

 Topics for Critical Thinking and Writing:

1. How does Augustine account for his sin?

2. What reasons does he offer?

3. How plausible do you find his confession?

Mary Karr

*Mary Karr is a poet and essayist who has won numerous prizes, awards, and grants for her work.
In* The Liars' Club, *published by Penguin in 1995, she describes a troubled and at times traumatic childhood with her parents and sister in East Texas. Critics have called her memoir "dazzling"
and "wickedly funny."*

*Ms. Karr teaches literature and creative writing at Syracuse University, and lives with her
son in upstate New York.*

Texas, 1961

Maybe it's wrong to blame the arrival of Grandma Moore for much
of the worst hurt in my family, but she was such a ring-tailed bitch that I
do. She sat like some dissipated empress in Mother's huge art deco chair
(mint-green vinyl with square black arms), which she turned to face right
out of our front picture window like she was about to start issuing proclamations any minute.

All day, she doled out criticisms that set my mother to scurrying
around with her face set so tight her mouth was a hyphen. The drapes
were awful; let's make some new. When was the last time we'd cleaned
our windows? (Never.) Had Mother put on weight? She seemed pudged
up. I looked plumb like a wetback I was so dark. (Lecia had managed to
come out blond like her people, but Grandma never got over my looking
vaguely Indian like Daddy.) And I was *pore-looking,* a term she reserved for
underfed farm animals and the hookworm-ridden Cajun kids we saw trying to catch crawfish on summer afternoons on the edge of Taylor's
Bayou. (Marvalene Seesacque once described her incentive for crawdadding all day: "You don't catch, you don't eat.")

In a house where I often opened a can of tamales for breakfast and ate
them cold (I remember sucking the cuminy tomato sauce off the paper
each one was wrapped in) Grandma cut out a *Reader's Digest* story on the
four major food groups and taped it to the refrigerator. Suddenly our family dinners involved dishes you saw on TV, like meatloaf—stuff you had
to light the oven to make, which Mother normally didn't even bother
doing for Thanksgiving.

Our family's habit of eating meals in the middle of my parents' bed
also broke overnight. Mother had made the bed extra big by stitching two
mattresses together and using coat hangers to hook up their frames. She'd
said that she needed some spread-out space because of the humidity, a
word Lecia and I misheard for a long time as *stupidity.* (Hence, our tendency to say, *It ain't the heat, it's the stupidity.*) It was the biggest bed I ever saw,
and filled their whole bedroom wall-to-wall. She had to stitch up special
sheets for it, and even the chest of drawers had to be put out in the hall. The
only pieces of furniture that still fit next to the bed were a standing brass

ashtray shaped like a Viking ship on Daddy's side and a tall black reading lamp next to a wobbly tower of hardback books on Mother's.

Anyway, the four of us tended to eat our family meals sitting cross-legged on the edges of that bed. We faced opposite walls, our backs together, looking like some four-headed totem, our plates balanced on the spot of quilt between our legs. Mother called it picnic-style, but since I've been grown, I recall it as just plain odd. I've often longed to take out an ad in a major metropolitan paper and ask whether anybody else's family ate back-to-back in the parents' bed, and what such a habit might signify.

With Grandma there, we used not just the table but table linens. Mother hired a black woman named Mae Brown to wash and iron the tablecloth and napkins when they got greased up. And we couldn't just come in out of the heat at midday and pull off our clothes anymore with Grandma there. We'd had this habit of stripping down to underwear or putting on pajamas in the house, no matter what the time. In the serious heat, we'd lie for hours half-naked on the wooden floor in front of the black blade-fan sucking chipped ice out of wadded-up dish towels. Now Grandma even tried to get us to keep shoes and socks on. Plus we had to take baths every night. One of these first baths ended with the old woman holding me in a rough towel on her lap while she scrubbed at my neck with fingernail-polish remover. (It had supposedly accumulated quite a crust.)

She undertook to supervise our religious training, which had until then consisted of sporadic visits to Christian Science Sunday school alternating with the exercises from a book Mother had on yoga postures. (I could sustain a full-lotus position at five.) Grandma bought Lecia and me each white leather Bibles that zipped shut. "If you read three chapters a day and five on Sunday, you can read the Holy Bible in one year," she said. I don't remember ever unzipping mine once after unwrapping it, for Grandma was prone to abandoning any project that came to seem too daunting, as making us into Christians must have seemed.

Much later, when Mother could be brought to talk about her own childhood, she told stories about how peculiar her mother's habits had been. Grandma Moore didn't sound like such a religious fanatic back then. She just seemed like a fanatic in general. For instance, she had once sent away for a detective-training kit from a magazine. The plan was for her and Mother to spy on their neighbors—this, back when the Lubbock population still fit into three digits. According to Mother, this surveillance went on for weeks. Grandma would stirrup Mother up to the parson's curtained windows—and not because of any suspected adultery or flagrant sinning, but to find out whether his wife did her cakes from scratch or not. She kept the answers to these kinds of questions in an alphabetized log of prominent families. She would also zero in on some particular person who troubled her and keep track of all his comings and goings for weeks on end. She knew the procedure for taking fingerprints and kept Mother's on a recipe card, in case she was ever kidnapped. Grandma even began to collect little forensic envelopes of hair and dust that she found on people's furniture when she visited them. Mother said that for the better part of a year, they'd be taking tea at some lady's house, when her mother would suddenly sneak an envelope with something like a dustball in it into the pocket of her pinafore. Whatever became of this *evidence* Mother couldn't say. The whole detective-training deal got dropped as abruptly as it had been undertaken.

When Grandma came to our house, she brought with her that same kind of slightly deranged scrutiny. Before, our lives had been closed to outsiders. The noise of my parents' fights might leak out through the screens at night, and I might guess at the neighbors' scorn, but nobody really asked after our family, about Mother's being Nervous. We didn't go to church. No one came to visit. We probably seemed as blurry to the rest of the neighborhood as bad TV. Suddenly Grandma was staring at us with laser-blue eyes from behind her horn rims, saying *Can I make a suggestion?* or beginning every sentence with *Why don't you . . . ?*

Also, she was herself secretive. She bustled around as if she had some   10 earnest agenda, but God knows what it was. She carried, for instance, an enormous black alligator doctor's bag, which held, along with the regular lady stuff in there—cosmetics and little peony-embroidered hankies—an honest-to-God hacksaw. It was the kind you see only in B movies, when criminals need it to saw through jail bars. Lest you think I fabricate, Lecia saw it, too. We even had a standing joke that we were keeping Grandma prisoner, and she was planning to bust out.

I had always thought that what I lacked in my family was some attentive, brownie-baking female to keep my hair curled and generally Donna-Reed over me. But my behavior got worse with Grandma's new order. I became a nail-biter. My tantrums escalated to the point where even Daddy didn't think they were funny anymore. I tore down the new drapes they'd hung across the dining room windows and clawed scratch marks down both of Lecia's cheeks. Beating me didn't seem to discourage me one whit. Though I was a world-famous crybaby, I refused to cry during spankings. I still can recall Daddy holding a small horse quirt, my calves striped with its imprint and stinging and my saying, "Go on and hit me then, if it makes you feel like a man to beat on a little girl like me." End of spanking.

Lecia was both better-tempered and better at kissing ass than I was, so she fared better. But the pressure must have gotten to her too. It was during Grandma's residency that my sister stuffed me struggling into the clothes hamper that pulled out from the bathroom wall, and left me screaming among the mildewed towels till Mae Brown came back from getting groceries. Also, she took to plastering down her bangs with so much hair spray that neither wind nor rain could move them. (I called her Helmet-head.) And she lengthened all her skirts so her knees didn't show anymore. In pictures from then, she looks like a child trying to impersonate an adult and coming out some strange gargoyle neither adult nor child. Once she even had me climb up on her shoulders, then draped a brown corduroy painter's smock to hang from my shoulders to her knees. We staggered from house to house pretending we were some lady collecting for the American Cancer Society. I remember holding a coffee can out to various strangers as I listed side to side on her shoulders. We didn't clear a dime.

In fairness to Grandma, she was dying of cancer at fifty, which can't do much for your disposition. Still, I remember not one tender feeling for or from her. Her cheek was withered like a bad apple and smelled of hyacinth. I had to be physically forced to kiss this cheek, even though I was prone to throwing my arms around the neck of any vaguely friendly grown-up—vacuum-cleaner salesman, mechanic, checkout lady.

The worst part wasn't all the change she brought, but the silence that came with it. Nobody said anything about how we'd lived before. It felt as if the changes themselves had just swept over us like some great wave, flattening whatever we'd once been. I somehow knew that suggesting a dinner in the middle of the bed, or stripping down when I came in from playing, would have thrown such a pall of shame over the household that I couldn't even consider it. Clearly, we had, all this time, been doing everything all wrong.

✎ Topics for Critical Thinking and Writing:

1. In the opening sentence of this section of her memoir, Karr calls Grandma Moore "a ring-tailed bitch." Do you remember how you felt, reading that description? Were you surprised? How do you explain your reaction, whatever it was?

2. How did Mary feel about her parents? About her sister? What passages best reveal how she felt about them?

3. Karr doesn't reveal until her next-to-last paragraph that her grandmother was dying of cancer. Should she have revealed this earlier? What does the narrative gain (or lose) by her postponing this revelation?

4. Imagine that you were a social worker in East Texas and the Karrs were on your case list. In three or four sentences, describe the family.

5. How does Karr feel about her childhood? Is she angry? Regretful? Stoic? Note some instances of humor in her account. How do they help you to understand her feelings?

6. A writing assignment: Think of a relative or close family friend whom you disliked or who made you uncomfortable. Write an account of that person within your family, including two or three incidents that reveal the person as you then perceived him or her.

Frank McCourt

Frank McCourt was born in Brooklyn to Irish immigrant parents. The family returned to Ireland, settling in a Limerick slum, enduring bitter poverty. The father, when he worked, drank away his wages; the mother, Angela, repeatedly pregnant, nursed her sick infants and was forced to beg for money to feed them. McCourt returned to America at 19, where he was later joined by his mother and 3 surviving brothers. Frank managed to get a college education and then taught writing in high schools in New York City. He published Angela's Ashes, *his first book, at the age of 66. It has sold several million copies and has won numerous awards, including a Pulitzer Prize.*

Brooklyn and Limerick

Brooklyn

When Dad gets a job Mam is cheerful and she sings,

> Anyone can see why I wanted your kiss,
> It had to be and the reason is this
> Could it be true, someone like you
> Could love me, love me?

When Dad brings home the first week's wages Mam is delighted she can pay the lovely Italian man in the grocery shop and she can hold her head up again because there's nothing worse in the world than to owe and be beholden to anyone. She cleans the kitchen, washes the mugs and plates, brushes crumbs and bits of food from the table, cleans out the icebox and orders a fresh block of ice from another Italian. She buys toilet paper that we can take down the hall to the lavatory and that, she says, is better than having the headlines from the *Daily News* blackening your arse. She boils water on the stove and spends a day at a great tin tub washing our shirts and socks, diapers for the twins, our two sheets, our three towels. She hangs everything out on the clotheslines behind the apartment house and we can watch the clothes dance in wind and sun. She says you wouldn't want the neighbors to know what you have in the way of a wash but there's nothing like the sweetness of clothes dried by the sun.

When Dad brings home the first week's wages on a Friday night we know the weekend will be wonderful. On Saturday night Mam will boil water on the stove and wash us in the great tin tub and Dad will dry us. Malachy will turn around and show his behind. Dad will pretend to be shocked and we'll all laugh. Mam will make hot cocoa and we'll be able to stay up while Dad tells us a story out of his head. All we have to do is say a name, Mr. MacAdorey or Mr. Leibowitz down the hall, and Dad will have the two of them rowing up a river in Brazil chased by Indians with green noses and puce shoulders. On nights like that we can drift off to sleep knowing there will be a breakfast of eggs, fried tomatoes and fried bread, tea with lashings of sugar and milk and, later in the day, a big dinner of mashed potatoes, peas and ham, and a trifle Mam makes, layers of fruit and warm delicious custard on a cake soaked in sherry.

When Dad brings home the first week's wages and the weather is fine Mam takes us to the playground. She sits on a bench and talks to Minnie MacAdorey. She tells Minnie stories about characters in Limerick and Minnie tells her about characters in Belfast and they laugh because there are funny people in Ireland, North and South. Then they teach each other sad songs and Malachy and I leave the swings and seesaws to sit with them on the bench and sing,

> A group of young soldiers one night in a camp
> Were talking of sweethearts they had.
> All seemed so merry except one young lad,
> And he was downhearted and sad.
> Come and join us, said one of the boys,
> Surely there's someone for you.
> But Ned shook his head and proudly he said
> I am in love with two, Each like a mother to me,
> From neither of them shall I part.
> For one is my mother, God bless her and love her,
> The other is my sweetheart.

Malachy and I sing that song and Mam and Minnie laugh till they cry   5
at the way Malachy takes a deep bow and holds his arms out to Mam at the end. Dan MacAdorey comes along on his way home from work and says Rudy Vallee better start worrying about the competition.

When we go home Mam makes tea and bread and jam or mashed potatoes with butter and salt. Dad drinks the tea and eats nothing. Mam says, God above, How can you work all day and not eat? He says, The tea is enough. She says, You'll ruin your health, and he tells her again that food is a shock to the system. He drinks his tea and tells us stories and shows us letters and words in the *Daily News* or he smokes a cigarette, stares at the wall, runs his tongue over his lips.

When Dad's job goes into the third week he does not bring home the wages. On Friday night we wait for him and Mam gives us bread and tea. The darkness comes down and the lights come on along Classon Avenue. Other men with jobs are home already and having eggs for dinner because you can't have meat on a Friday. You can hear the families talking upstairs and downstairs and down the hall and Bing Crosby is singing on the radio, Brother, can you spare a dime?

Malachy and I play with the twins. We know Mam won't sing Anyone can see why I wanted your kiss. She sits at the kitchen table talking to herself, What am I going to do? till it's late and Dad rolls up the stairs singing Roddy McCorley. He pushes in the door and calls for us, Where are my troops? Where are my four warriors?

Mam says, Leave those boys alone. They're gone to bed half hungry because you have to fill your belly with whiskey.

He comes to the bedroom door. Up, boys, up. A nickel for everyone   10
who promises to die for Ireland.

Deep in Canadian woods we met
From one bright island flown.
Great is the land we tread, but yet
Our hearts are with our own.

Up, boys, up. Francis, Malachy, Oliver, Eugene. The Red Branch
Knights, the Fenian Men, the IRA. Up, up.

Mam is at the kitchen table, shaking, her hair hanging damp, her face
wet. Can't you leave them alone? she says. Jesus, Mary and Joseph, isn't it
enough that you come home without a penny in your pocket without
making fools of the children on top of it?

She comes to us. Go back to bed, she says.

I want them up, he says. I want them ready for the day Ireland will be
free from the center to the sea.

Don't cross me, she says, for if you do it'll be a sorry day in your moth-   15
er's house.

He pulls his cap down over his face and cries, My poor mother. Poor
Ireland. Och, what are we going to do?

Mam says, You're pure stone mad, and she tells us again to go to bed.

On the morning of the fourth Friday of Dad's job Mam asks him if
he'll be home tonight with his wages or will he drink everything again?
He looks at us and shakes his head at Mam as if to say, Och, you should-
n't talk like that in front of the children.

Mam keeps at him. I'm asking you, Are you coming home so that we
can have a bit of supper or will it be midnight with no money in your
pocket and you singing Kevin Barry and the rest of the sad songs?

He puts on his cap, shoves his hands into his trouser pockets, sighs   20
and looks up at the ceiling. I told you before I'll be home, he says.

Later in the day Mam dresses us. She puts the twins into the pram and
off we go through the long streets of Brooklyn. Sometimes she lets
Malachy sit in the pram when he's tired of trotting along beside her. She
tells me I'm too big for the pram. I could tell her I have pains in my legs
from trying to keep up with her but she's not singing and I know this is
not the day to be talking about my pains.

We come to a big gate where there's a man standing in a box with windows all around. Mam talks to the man. She wants to know if she can go
inside to where the men are paid and maybe they'd give her some of
Dad's wages so he wouldn't spend it in the bars. The man shakes his head.
I'm sorry, lady, but if we did that we'd have half the wives in Brooklyn
storming the place. Lotta men have the drinking problem but there's nothing we can do long as they show up sober and do their work.

We wait across the street. Mam lets me sit on the sidewalk with my
back against the wall. She gives the twins their bottles of water and sugar

but Malachy and I have to wait till she gets money from Dad and we can go to the Italian for tea and bread and eggs.

When the whistle blows at half five men in caps and overalls swarm through the gate, their faces and hands black from the work. Mam tells us watch carefully for Dad because she can hardly see across the street herself, her eyes are that bad. There are dozens of men, then a few, then none. Mam is crying, Why couldn't ye see him? Are ye blind or what?

She goes back to the man in the box. Are you sure there wouldn't be   25
one man left inside?

No, lady, he says. They're out. I don't know how he got past you.

We go back through the long streets of Brooklyn. The twins hold up their bottles and cry for more water and sugar. Malachy says he's hungry and Mam tells him wait a little, we'll get money from Dad and we'll all have a nice supper. We'll go to the Italian and get eggs and make toast with the flames on the stove and we'll have jam on it. Oh, we will, and we'll all be nice and warm.

It's dark on Atlantic Avenue and all the bars around the Long Island Railroad Station are bright and noisy. We go from bar to bar looking for Dad. Mam leaves us outside with the pram while she goes in or she sends me. There are crowds of noisy men and stale smells that remind me of Dad when he comes home with the smell of the whiskey on him.

The man behind the bar says, Yeah, sonny, whaddya want? You're not supposeta be in here, y'know.

I'm looking for my father. Is my father here?   30

Naw, sonny, how'd I know dat? Who's your fawdah?

His name is Malachy and he sings Kevin Barry.

Malarkey?

No, Malachy.

Malachy? And he sings Kevin Barry?   35

He calls out to the men in the bar, Youse guys, youse know guy Malachy what sings Kevin Barry?

Men shake their heads. One says he knew a guy Michael sang Kevin Barry but he died of the drink which he had because of his war wounds.

The barman says, Jeez, Pete, I didn't ax ya to tell me history o' da woild, did I? Naw, kid. We don't let people sing in here. Causes trouble. Specially the Irish. Let 'em sing, next the fists are flying. Besides, I never hoid a name like dat Malachy. Naw, kid, no Malachy here.

The man called Pete holds his glass toward me. Here, kid, have a sip, but the barman says, Whaddya doin', Pete? Tryina get the kid drunk? Do that again, Pete, an' I'll come out an' break y'ass.

Mam tries all the bars around the station before she gives up. She   40
leans against a wall and cries. Jesus, we still have to walk all the way to Classon Avenue and I have four starving children. She sends me back into the bar where Pete offered me the sip to see if the barman would fill the twins' bottles with water and maybe a little sugar in each. The men in the bar think it's very funny that the barman should be filling baby bottles but

he's big and he tells them shut their lip. He tells me babies should be drinking milk not water and when I tell him Mam doesn't have the money he empties the baby bottles and fills them with milk. He says, Tell ya mom they need that for the teeth an' bones. Ya drink water an' sugar an' all ya get is rickets. Tell ya Mom.

Mam is happy with the milk. She says she knows all about teeth and bones and rickets but beggars can't be choosers.

When we reach Classon Avenue she goes straight to the Italian grocery shop. She tells the man her husband is late tonight, that he's probably working overtime, and would it be at all possible to get a few things and she'll be sure to see him tomorrow?

The Italian says, Missus, you always pay your bill sooner or later and you can have anything you like in this store.

Oh, she says, I don't want much.

Anything you like, missus, because I know you're an honest woman and you got a bunch o'nice kids there.   45

We have eggs and toast and jam though we're so weary walking the long streets of Brooklyn we can barely move our jaws to chew. The twins fall asleep after eating and Mam lays them on the bed to change their diapers. She sends me down the hall to rinse the dirty diapers in the lavatory so that they can be hung up to dry and used the next day. Malachy helps her wash the twins' bottoms though he's ready to fall asleep himself.

I crawl into bed with Malachy and the twins. I look out at Mam at the kitchen table, smoking a cigarette, drinking tea, and crying. I want to get up and tell her I'll be a man soon and I'll get a job in the place with the big gate and I'll come home every Friday night with money for eggs and toast and jam and she can sing again Anyone can see why I wanted your kiss.

The next week Dad loses the job. He comes home that Friday night, throws his wages on the table and says to Mam, Are you happy now? You hang around the gate complaining and accusing and they sack me. They were looking for an excuse and you gave it to them.

He takes a few dollars from his wages and goes out. He comes home late roaring and singing. The twins cry and Mam shushes them and cries a long time herself.

Limerick

On a Saturday morning Mam finishes her tea and says, You're going to dance.   50

Dance? Why?

You're seven years old, you made your First Communion, and now 'tis time for the dancing. I'm taking you down to Catherine Street to Mrs. O'Connor's Irish dancing classes. You'll go there every Saturday morning and that'll keep you off the streets. That'll keep you from wandering around Limerick with hooligans.

She tells me wash my face not forgetting ears and neck, comb my hair, blow my nose, take the look off my face, what look? never mind, just take it off, put on my stockings and my First Communion shoes which, she says, are destroyed because I can't pass a canister or a rock without kicking it. She's worn out standing in the queue at the St. Vincent de Paul Society begging for boots for me and Malachy so that we can wear out the toes with the kicking. Your father says it's never too early to learn the songs and dances of your ancestors.

What's ancestors?

Never mind, she says, you're going to dance.   55

I wonder how I can die for Ireland if I have to sing and dance for Ireland, too. I wonder why they never say, You can eat sweets and stay home from school and go swimming for Ireland.

Mam says, Don't get smart or I'll warm your ear.

Cyril Benson dances. He has medals hanging from his shoulders to his kneecaps. He wins contests all over Ireland and he looks lovely in his saffron kilt. He's a credit to his mother and he gets his name in the paper all the time and you can be sure he brings home the odd few pounds. You don't see him roaming the streets kicking everything in sight till the toes hang out of his boots, oh, no, he's a good boy, dancing for his poor mother.

Mam wets an old towel and scrubs my face till it stings, she wraps the towel around her finger and sticks it in my ears and claims there's enough wax there to grow potatoes, she wets my hair to make it lie down, she tells me shut up and stop the whinging, that these dancing lessons will cost her sixpence every Saturday, which I could have earned bringing Bill Galvin his dinner and God knows she can barely afford it. I try to tell her, Ah, Mam, sure you don't have to send me to dancing school when you could be smoking a nice Woodbine and having a cup of tea, but she says, Oh, aren't you clever. You're going to dance if I have to give up the fags forever.

If my pals see my mother dragging me through the streets to an Irish   60
dancing class I'll be disgraced entirely. They think it's all right to dance and pretend you're Fred Astaire because you can jump all over the screen with Ginger Rogers. There is no Ginger Rogers in Irish dancing and you can't jump all over. You stand straight up and down and keep your arms against yourself and kick your legs up and around and never smile. My uncle Pa Keating said Irish dancers look like they have steel rods up their arses, but I can't say that to Mam, she'd kill me.

There's a gramophone in Mrs. O'Connor's playing an Irish jig or a reel and boys and girls are dancing around kicking their legs out and keeping their hands to their sides. Mrs. O'Connor is a great fat woman and when she stops the record to show the steps all the fat from her chin to her ankles jiggles and I wonder how she can teach the dancing. She comes over to my mother and says, So, this is little Frankie? I think we have the makings of a dancer here. Boys and girls, do we have the makings of a dancer here?

We do, Mrs. O'Connor.

Mam says, I have the sixpence, Mrs. O'Connor.

Ah, yes, Mrs. McCourt, hold on a minute.

She waddles to a table and brings back the head of a black boy with 65
kinky hair, big eyes, huge red lips and an open mouth. She tells me put the
sixpence in the mouth and take my hand out before the black boy bites me.
All the boys and girls watch and they have little smiles. I drop in the sixpence and pull my hand back before the mouth snaps shut. Everyone
laughs and I know they wanted to see my hand caught in the mouth. Mrs.
O'Connor gasps and laughs and says to my mother, Isn't that a howl,
now? Mam says it's a howl. She tells me behave myself and come home
dancing.

I don't want to stay in this place where Mrs. O'Connor can't take the
sixpence herself instead of letting me nearly lose my hand in the black
boy's mouth. I don't want to stay in this place where you have to stand in
line with boys and girls, straighten your back, hands by your sides, look
ahead, don't look down, move your feet, move your feet, look at Cyril,
look at Cyril, and there goes Cyril, all dressed up in his saffron kilt and the
medals jingling, medals for this and medals for that and the girls love
Cyril and Mrs. O'Connor loves Cyril for didn't he bring her fame and did-
n't she teach him every step he knows, oh, dance, Cyril, dance, oh, Jesus,
he floats around the room, he's an angel out of heaven and stop the frowning, Frankie McCourt, or you'll have a puss on you like a pound of tripe,
dance, Frankie, dance, pick up your feet for the love o'Jesus, onetwothreefourfivesixseven onetwothree and a onetwothree, Maura, will you help
that Frankie McCourt before he ties his two feet around his poll entirely,
help him, Maura.

Maura is a big girl about ten. She dances up to me with her white teeth
and her dancer's dress with all the gold and yellow and green figures that
are supposed to come from olden times and she says, Give me your hand,
little boy, and she wheels me around the room till I'm dizzy and making a
pure eejit of myself and blushing and foolish till I want to cry but I'm
saved when the record stops and the gramophone goes hoosh hoosh.

Mrs. O'Connor says, Oh, thank you, Maura, and next week, Cyril, you
can show Frankie a few of the steps that made you famous. Next week,
boys and girls, and don't forget the sixpence for the little black boy.

Boys and girls leave together. I make my own way down the stairs
and out the door hoping my pals won't see me with boys who wear kilts
and girls with white teeth and fancy dresses from olden times.

Mam is having tea with Bridey Hannon, her friend from next door. 70
Mam says, What did you learn? and makes me dance around the kitchen,
onetwothreefourfivesixseven onetwothree and a onetwothree. She has a
good laugh with Bridey. That's not too bad for your first time. In a month
you'll be like a regular Cyril Benson.

I don't want to be Cyril Benson. I want to be Fred Astaire.

They turn hysterical, laughing and squirting tea out of their mouths,
Jesus love him, says Bridey. Doesn't he have a great notion of himself. Fred
Astaire how are you.

Mam says Fred Astaire went to his lessons every Saturday and didn't go around kicking the toes out of his boots and if I wanted to be like him I'd have to go to Mrs. O'Connor's every week.

The fourth Saturday morning Billy Campbell knocks at our door. Mrs. McCourt, can Frankie come out and play? Mam tells him, No, Billy. Frankie is going to his dancing lesson.

He waits for me at the bottom of Barrack Hill. He wants to know why I'm dancing, that everyone knows dancing is a sissy thing and I'll wind up like Cyril Benson wearing a kilt and medals and dancing all over with girls. He says next thing I'll be sitting in the kitchen knitting socks. He says dancing will destroy me and I won't be fit to play any kind of football, soccer, rugby or Gaelic football itself because the dancing teaches you to run like a sissy and everyone will laugh.   75

I tell him I'm finished with the dancing, that I have sixpence in my pocket for Mrs. O'Connor that's supposed to go into the black boy's mouth, that I'm going to the Lyric Cinema instead. Sixpence will get the two of us in with tuppence left over for two squares of Cleeves' toffee, and we have a great time looking at *Riders of the Purple Sage*.

Dad is sitting by the fire with Mam and they want to know what steps I learned today and what they're called. I already did "The Siege of Ennis" and "The Walls of Limerick," which are real dances. Now I have to make up names and dances. Mam says she never heard of a dance called "The Siege of Dingle" but if that's what I learned go ahead, dance it, and I dance around the kitchen with my hands down by my sides making my own music, diddley eye di eye di eye diddley eye do you do you, Dad and Mam clapping in time with my feet. Dad says, Och, that's a fine dance and you'll be a powerful Irish dancer and a credit to the men who died for their country. Mam says, That wasn't much for a sixpence.

Next week it's a George Raft film and the week after that a cowboy film with George O'Brien. Then it's James Cagney and I can't take Billy because I want to get a bar of chocolate to go with my Cleeves' toffee and I'm having a great time till there's a terrible pain in my jaw and it's a tooth out of my gum stuck in my toffee and the pain is killing me. Still, I can't waste the toffee so I pull out the tooth and put it in my pocket and chew the toffee on the other side of my mouth blood and all. There's pain on one side and delicious toffee on the other and I remember what my uncle Pa Keating would say, There are times when you wouldn't know whether to shit or go blind.

I have to go home now and worry because you can't go through the world short a tooth without your mother knowing. Mothers know everything and she's always looking into our mouths to see if there's any class of disease. She's there by the fire and Dad is there and they're asking me the same old questions, the dance and the name of the dance. I tell them I learned "The Walls of Cork" and I dance around the kitchen trying to hum a made-up tune and dying with the pain of my tooth. Mam says, "Walls o' Cork," my eye, there's no such dance, and Dad says, Come over here. Stand there before me. Tell us the truth, Did you go to your dancing classes today?

I can't tell a lie anymore because my gum is killing me and there's   80
blood in my mouth. Besides, I know they know everything and that's
what they're telling me now. Some snake of a boy from the dancing school
saw me going to the Lyric Cinema and told and Mrs. O'Connor sent a note
to say she hadn't seen me in ages and was I all right because I had great
promise and could follow in the footsteps of the great Cyril Benson.

Dad doesn't care about my tooth or anything. He says I'm going to
confession and drags me over to the Redemptorist church because it's Saturday and confessions go on all day. He tells me I'm a bad boy, he's
ashamed of me that I went to the pictures instead of learning Ireland's
national dances, the jig, the reel, the dances that men and women fought
and died for down those sad centuries. He says there's many a young man
that was hanged and now moldering in a lime pit that would be glad to
rise up and dance the Irish dance.

The priest is old and I have to yell my sins at him and he tells me I'm
a hooligan for going to the pictures instead of my dancing lessons
although he thinks himself that dancing is a dangerous thing almost as
bad as the films, that it stirs up thoughts sinful in themselves, but even if
dancing is an abomination I sinned by taking my mother's sixpence and
lying and there's a hot place in hell for the likes of me, say a decade of the
rosary and ask God's forgiveness for you're dancing at the gates of hell
itself, child.

✎ Topics for Critical Thinking and Writing:

1. *Angela's Ashes,* the book from which these selections come, is flooded with
memories of poverty, hunger, alcoholism, depression, and infant death.
Nevertheless, the book has been an international bestseller ever since it
was published in 1996. What qualities do you detect in these early episodes
that account for the enormous popularity of this dark memoir?

2. Notice that McCourt persistently uses the present tense. Reread a passage
or two and then try to describe the effect of the present tense. One way to
think about it is to recast some sentences using the past tense. Then try to
describe the difference.

3. When you were a child did you ever use money given to you for one purpose on another? An easier question, did you ever lie about where you had
spent an afternoon or an evening? Write a brief essay, 3 to 4 pages,
describing your experience. Try to capture your voice at your age at the
time of the incident.

Vladimir Nabokov

Vladimir Nabokov (pronounced VlaDEEmir NaBOHKoff) was born in Russia in 1899, the son of rich aristocrats. In the 1920s and 1930s he lived in Berlin and Paris. In 1940 he came to the United States, where Lolita *(1955), a novel, brought him fame. Among Nabokov's other works are novels, stories, critical studies, translations, and* Speak, Memory *(from which we give a selection), a memoir of childhood in Czarist Russia and of college years in England. Nabokov died in 1977.*

Speak, Memory

Few things indeed have I known in the way of emotion or appetite, ambition or achievement, that could surpass in richness and strength the excitement of entomological exploration. From the very first it had a great many intertwinkling facets. One of them was the acute desire to be alone, since any companion, no matter how quiet, interfered with the concentrated enjoyment of my mania. Its gratification admitted of no compromise or exception. Already when I was ten, tutors and governesses knew that the morning was mine and cautiously kept away.

In this connection, I remember the visit of a schoolmate, a boy of whom I was very fond and with whom I had excellent fun. He arrived one summer night from a town some fifty miles away. His father had recently perished in an accident, the family was ruined and the stout-hearted lad, not being able to afford the price of a railway ticket, had bicycled all those miles to spend a few days with me.

On the morning following his arrival, I did everything I could to get out of the house for my morning hike without his knowing where I had gone. Breakfastless, with hysterical haste, I gathered my net, pillboxes, sailor cap, and escaped through the window. Once in the forest, I was safe; but still I walked on, my calves quaking, my eyes full of scalding tears, the whole of me twitching with shame and self-disgust, as I visualized my poor friend, with his long pale face and black tie, moping in the hot garden—patting the panting dogs for want of something better to do, and trying hard to justify my absence to himself.

Let me look at my demon objectively. With the exception of my parents, no one really understood my obsession, and it was many years before I met a fellow-sufferer. One of the first things I learned was not to depend on others for the growth of my collection. Aunts, however, kept making me ridiculous presents—such as Denton mounts of resplendent but really quite ordinary insects. Our country doctor, with whom I had left the pupae of a rare moth when I went on a journey abroad, wrote me that everything had hatched finely; but in reality a mouse had got at the precious pupae, and upon my return the deceitful old man produced some common Tortoise-shell butterflies, which, I presume, he had hurriedly caught in his garden and popped into the breeding cage as plausible substitutes (so *he* thought). Better than he, was an enthusiastic kitchen boy who would sometimes borrow my equipment and come back two hours later in triumph with a bagful of seething invertebrate life and several additional items. Loosening the mouth of the net which he had tied up with a string, he would pour out his cornucopian spoil—a mass of grasshoppers, some sand, the two parts of a mushroom he had thriftily plucked on the way home, more grasshoppers, more sand, and one battered Cabbage butterfly.

I also found out very soon that an entomologist indulging in his quiet quest was apt to provoke strange reactions in other creatures. How often, when a picnic had been arranged, and I would be self-consciously trying to get my humble implements unnoticed into the tar-smelling charabanc (a tar preparation was used to keep flies away from the horses) or the tea-smelling Opel convertible (benzine forty years ago smelled that way), some cousin or aunt of mine would remark: "Must you *really* take that net with you? Can't you enjoy yourself like a normal boy? Don't you think you are spoiling everybody's pleasure?" Near a sign *Nach Bodenlaube,* at Bad Kissingen, Bavaria, just as I was about to join for a long walk my father and majestic old Muromtsev (who, four years before, in 1906, had been President of the first Russian Parliament), the latter turned his marble head toward me, a vulnerable boy of eleven, and said with his famous solemnity: "Come with us by all means, but do not chase butterflies, child. It mars the rhythm of the walk." On a path above the Black Sea, in the Crimea, among shrubs in waxy bloom, in March, 1919, a bow-legged Bolshevik sentry attempted to arrest me for signaling (with my net, he said) to a British warship. In the summer of 1929, every time I walked through a village in the Eastern Pyrenees, which I was exploring lepidopterologically, and happened to look back, I would see in my wake the villagers frozen in the various attitudes my passage had caught them in, as if I were Sodom and they Lot's wife. A decade later, in the Maritime Alps, I once noticed the grass undulate in a serpentine way behind me because a fat rural policeman was wriggling after me on his belly to find out if I were not trapping song birds. America has shown even more of this morbid interest in my doings than other countries have—perhaps because I was in my forties when I came here to live, and the older the man, the queerer he looks with a butterfly net in his hand. Stern farmers have drawn my attention to *No Fishing* signs; from cars passing me on the highway have come wild howls of derision; sleepy dogs, though unmindful of the worst bum, have perked up and come at me, snarling; tiny tots have pointed me out to their puzzled mammas; broadminded vacationists have asked me whether I was catching bugs for bait; and one morning on a wasteland, lit by tall yuccas in bloom, near Santa Fé, a big, black mare followed me for more than a mile.

✎ Topics for Critical Thinking and Writing

1. In the first paragraph, what devices does Nabokov use to suggest that his hobby is special, something precious?
2. Nabokov begins his fourth paragraph thus: "Let me look at my demon objectively." Check a dictionary to see how many meanings of "demon" might fit. How objective is the rest of the paragraph?
3. Nabokov's passion does not prevent him from being amusing—not only about others but also about himself. Point out some examples of self-irony. How do we know that he is nevertheless serious?

Black Elk

Black Elk, a wichasha wakon (holy man) of the Oglala Sioux, as a small boy witnessed the battle of the Little Bighorn (1876). He lived to see his people all but annihilated and his hopes for them extinguished. In 1931, toward the end of his life, he told his life story to the poet and scholar John G. Neihardt to preserve a sacred vision given him. Another excerpt from Black Elk Speaks *appears on page 219.*

"War Games" (editors' title) is from Black Elk Speaks.

War Games

When it was summer again we were camping on the Rosebud, and I did not feel so much afraid, because the Wasichus seemed farther away and there was peace there in the valley and there was plenty of meat. But all the boys from five or six years up were playing war. The little boys would gather together from the different bands of the tribe and fight each other with mud balls that they threw with willow sticks. And the big boys played the game called Throwing-Them-Off-Their-Horses, which is a battle all but the killing; and sometimes they got hurt. The horsebacks from the different bands would line up and charge upon each other, yelling; and when the ponies came together on the run, they would rear and flounder and scream in a big dust, and the riders would seize each other, wrestling until one side had lost all its men, for those who fell upon the ground were counted dead.

When I was older, I, too, often played this game. We were always naked when we played it, just as warriors are when they go into battle if it is not too cold, because they are swifter without clothes. Once I fell off on my back right in the middle of a bed of prickly pears, and it took my mother a long while to pick all the stickers out of me. I was still too little to play war that summer, but I can remember watching the other boys, and I thought that when we all grew up and were big together, maybe we could kill all the Wasichus or drive them far away from our country. . . .

There was a war game that we little boys played after a big hunt. We went out a little way from the village and built some grass tepees, playing we were enemies and this was our village. We had an adviser, and when it got dark he would order us to go and steal some dried meat from the big people. He would hold a stick up to us and we had to bite off a piece of it. If we bit a big piece we had to get a big piece of meat, and if we bit a little piece, we did not have to get so much. Then we started for the big people's village, crawling on our bellies, and when we got back without getting caught, we would have a big feast and a dance and make kill talks, telling of our brave deeds like warriors. Once, I remember, I had no brave deed to tell. I crawled up to a leaning tree beside a tepee and there was meat hanging on the limbs. I wanted a tongue I saw up there in the moonlight, so I climbed up. But just as I was about to reach it, the man in the tepee yelled "Ye-a-a!" He was saying this to his dog, who was stealing some meat too, but I thought the man had seen me, and I was so scared I fell out of the tree and ran away crying.

Then we used to have what we called a chapped breast dance. Our adviser would look us over to see whose breast was burned most from not having it covered with the robe we wore; and the boy chosen would lead the dance while we all sang like this:

I have a chapped breast.
My breast is red.
My breast is yellow.

And we practiced endurance too. Our adviser would put dry sunflower seeds on our wrists. These were lit at the top, and we had to let them burn clear down to the skin. They hurt and made sores, but if we knocked them off or cried Owh!, we would be called women.

✎ Topics for Critical Thinking and Writing

1. Notice the subjective passages in Black Elk's descriptions of the games he played as a child. What do they reveal about Black Elk as a child and as an adult? How appropriate are these revelations to his topic?
2. The Duke of Wellington is reported to have said that the battle of Waterloo was won on the playing fields of Eton. Try to describe a game that is a small version of an adult activity and that teaches adult habits—good or bad. As an experiment, write the description as objectively as you can. Then rewrite it, allowing your description to reveal your attitudes—as a child and now—to the game, to other children, and to the adult world.

Richard Wright

Richard Wright (1908–60), the grandson of a slave and the son of an impoverished sharecropper family, was born on a cotton plantation near Natchez, Mississippi. He dropped out of school after completing the ninth grade, took a variety of odd jobs, and in 1927 moved to Chicago, where he worked as a porter, dishwasher, and postal clerk. In 1937 he moved to New York, where he became the Harlem editor of The Daily Worker, *a Communist newspaper. In 1947 he and his family moved to Paris, where they lived until he suffered a fatal heart attack in 1960.*

With Native Son *(1940), a militant novel attacking racism, Wright became the first African-American writer to reach a large white audience. His next best-selling work was an autobiography,* Black Boy *(1945), part of which we reprint below. (The title is the editors'.)*

Writing and Reading

The eighth grade days flowed in their hungry path and I grew more conscious of myself; I sat in classes, bored, wondering, dreaming. One long dry afternoon I took out my composition book and told myself that I would write a story; it was sheer idleness that led me to it. What would the story be about? It resolved itself into a plot about a villain who wanted a widow's home and I called it *The Voodoo of Hell's Half-Acre*. It was crudely atmospheric, emotional, intuitively psychological, and stemmed from pure feeling. I finished it in three days and then wondered what to do with it.

The local Negro newspaper! That's it . . . I sailed into the office and shoved my ragged composition book under the nose of the man who called himself the editor.

"What is that?" he asked.

"A story," I said.

"A news story?"   5

"No, fiction."

"All right. I'll read it," he said.

He pushed my composition book back on his desk and looked at me curiously, sucking at his pipe.

"But I want you to read it *now*," I said.

He blinked. I had no idea how newspapers were run. I thought that   10
one took a story to an editor and he sat down then and there and read it and said yes or no.

"I'll read this and let you know about it tomorrow," he said.

I was disappointed; I had taken time to write it and he seemed distant and uninterested.

"Give me the story," I said, reaching for it.

He turned from me, took up the book and read ten pages or more.

"Won't you come in tomorrow?" he asked. "I'll have it finished then."   15

I honestly relented.

"All right," I said. "I'll stop in tomorrow."

I left with the conviction that he would not read it. Now, where else could I take it after he had turned it down? The next afternoon, en route to my job, I stepped into the newspaper office.

"Where's my story?" I asked.

"It's in galleys," he said.   20

"What's that?" I asked; I did not know what galleys were.

"It's set up in type," he said. "We're publishing it."

"How much money will I get?" I asked, excited.

"We can't pay for manuscript," he said.

"But you sell your papers for money," I said with logic.   25

"Yes, but we're young in business," he explained.

"But you're asking me to *give* you my story, but you don't *give* your papers away," I said.

He laughed.

"Look, you're just starting. This story will put your name before our readers. Now, that's something," he said.

"But if the story is good enough to sell to your readers, then you ought   30
to give me some of the money you get from it," I insisted.

He laughed again and I sensed that I was amusing him.

"I'm going to offer you something more valuable than money," he said. "I'll give you a chance to learn to write."

I was pleased, but I still thought he was taking advantage of me.

"When will you publish my story?"

"I'm dividing it into three installments," he said.   35

"The first installment appears this week. But the main thing is this: Will you get news for me on a space rate basis?"

"I work mornings and evenings for three dollars a week," I said.

"Oh," he said. "Then you better keep that. But what are you doing this summer?"

"Nothing."

"Then come to see me before you take another job," he said. "And   40
write some more stories."

A few days later my classmates came to me with baffled eyes, holding copies of the *Southern Register* in their hands.

"Did you really write that story?" they asked me.

"Yes."

"Why?"

"Because I wanted to."   45

"Where did you get it from?"

"I made it up."

"You didn't. You copied it out of a book."

"If I had, no one would publish it."

"But what are they publishing it for?"   50

"So people can read it."

"Who told you to do that?"

"Nobody."

"Then why did you do it?"

"Because I wanted to," I said again.   55

They were convinced that I had not told them the truth. We had never had any instruction in literary matters at school; the literature of the nation or the Negro had never been mentioned. My schoolmates could not understand why anyone would want to write a story; and, above all, they could not understand why I had called it *The Voodoo of Hell's Half-Acre.* The mood out of which a story was written was the most alien thing conceivable to them. They looked at me with new eyes, and a distance, a suspiciousness came between us. If I had thought anything in writing the story, I had thought that perhaps it would make me more acceptable to them, and now it was cutting me off from them more completely than ever.

At home the effects were no less disturbing. Granny came into my room early one morning and sat on the edge of my bed.

"Richard, what is this you're putting in the papers?" she asked.

"A story," I said.

"About what?"   60

"It's just a story, granny."

"But they tell me it's been in three times."

"It's the same story. It's in three parts."

"But what is it about?" she insisted.

I hedged, fearful of getting into a religious argument.   65

"It's just a story I made up," I said.

"Then it's a lie," she said.

"Oh, Christ," I said.

"You must get out of this house if you take the name of the Lord in vain," she said.

"Granny, please . . . I'm sorry," I pleaded. "But it's hard to tell you about   70 the story. You see, granny, everybody knows that the story isn't true, but . . ."

"Then why write it?" she asked.

"Because people might want to read it."

"That's the Devil's work," she said and left.

My mother also was worried.

"Son, you ought to be more serious," she said. "You're growing up   75 now and you won't be able to get jobs if you let people think that you're weak-minded. Suppose the superintendent of schools would ask you to teach here in Jackson, and he found out that you had been writing stories?"

I could not answer her.

"I'll be all right, mama," I said.

Uncle Tom, though surprised, was highly critical and contemptuous. The story had no point, he said. And whoever heard of a story by the title of *The Voodoo of Hell's Half-Acre*? Aunt Addie said that it was a sin for anyone to use the word "hell" and that what was wrong with me was that I had nobody to guide me. She blamed the whole thing upon my upbringing.

In the end I was so angry that I refused to talk about the story. From no quarter, with the exception of the Negro newspaper editor, had there come a single encouraging word. It was rumored that the principal wanted to know why I had used the word "hell." I felt that I had committed a crime. Had I been conscious of the full extent to which I was pushing against the current of my environment, I would have been frightened altogether out of my attempts at writing. But my reactions were limited to the attitude of the people about me, and I did not speculate or generalize.

I dreamed of going north and writing books, novels. The North 80
symbolized to me all that I had not felt and seen; it had no relation
whatever to what actually existed. Yet, by imagining a place where
everything was possible, I kept hope alive in me. But where had I got
this notion of doing something in the future, of going away from home
and accomplishing something that would be recognized by others? I
had, of course, read my Horatio Alger stories, my pulp stories, and I
knew my Get-Rich-Quick Wallingford series from cover to cover,
though I had sense enough not to hope to get rich; even to my naïve
imagination that possibility was too remote. I knew that I lived in a
country in which the aspirations of black people were limited, marked-
off. Yet I felt that I had to go somewhere and do something to redeem
my being alive.

I was building up in me a dream which the entire educational system
of the South had been rigged to stifle. I was feeling the very thing that the
state of Mississippi had spent millions of dollars to make sure that I would
never feel; I was becoming aware of the thing that the Jim Crow laws had
been drafted and passed to keep out of my consciousness; I was acting on
impulses that southern senators in the nation's capital had striven to keep
out of Negro life; I was beginning to dream the dreams that the state had
said were wrong, that the schools had said were taboo.

Had I been articulate about my ultimate aspirations, no doubt someone would have told me what I was bargaining for; but nobody seemed to
know, and least of all did I. My classmates felt that I was doing something
that was vaguely wrong, but they did not know how to express it. As the
outside world grew more meaningful, I became more concerned, tense;
and my classmates and my teachers would say: "Why do you ask so many
questions?" Or: "Keep quiet."

I was in my fifteenth year; in terms of schooling I was far behind the
average youth of the nation, but I did not know that. In me was shaping a
yearning for a kind of consciousness, a mode of being that the way of life
about me had said could not be, must not be, and upon which the penalty
of death had been placed. Somewhere in the dead of the southern night
my life had switched onto the wrong track and, without my knowing it,
the locomotive of my heart was rushing down a dangerously steep slope,
heading for a collision, heedless of the warning red lights that blinked all
about me, the sirens and the bells and the screams that filled the air . . . .

One morning I arrived early at work and went into the bank lobby
where the Negro porter was mopping. I stood at a counter and picked up
the Memphis *Commercial Appeal* and began my free reading of the press. I
came finally to the editorial page and saw an article dealing with one H. L.
Mencken. I knew by hearsay that he was the editor of the *American Mer-
cury*, but aside from that I knew nothing about him. The article was a furious denunciation of Mencken, concluding with one, hot, short sentence:
Mencken is a fool.

I wondered what on earth this Mencken had done to call down upon   85
him the scorn of the South. The only people I had ever heard denounced
in the South were Negroes, and this man was not a Negro. Then what
ideas did Mencken hold that made a newspaper like the *Commercial Appeal*
castigate him publicly? Undoubtedly he must be advocating ideas that the
South did not like. Were there, then, people other than Negroes who criticized the South? I knew that during the Civil War the South had hated
northern whites, but I had not encountered such hate during my life.
Knowing no more of Mencken than I did at that moment, I felt a vague
sympathy for him. Had not the South, which had assigned me the role of
a non-man, cast at him its hardest words?

Now, how could I find out about this Mencken? There was a huge
library near the riverfront, but I knew that Negroes were not allowed to
patronize its shelves any more than they were the parks and playgrounds
of the city. I had gone into the library several times to get books for the
white men on the job. Which of them would now help me to get books?
And how could I read them without causing concern to the white men
with whom I worked? I had so far been successful in hiding my thoughts
and feelings from them, but I knew that I would create hostility if I went
about this business of reading in a clumsy way.

I weighed the personalities of the men on the job. There was Don, a
Jew; but I distrusted him. His position was not much better than mine and
I knew that he was uneasy and insecure; he had always treated me in an
offhand, bantering way that barely concealed his contempt. I was afraid to
ask him to help me to get books; his frantic desire to demonstrate a racial
solidarity with the whites against Negroes might make him betray me.

Then how about the boss? No, he was a Baptist and I had the suspicion that he would not be quite able to comprehend why a black boy
would want to read Mencken. There were other white men on the job
whose attitudes showed clearly that they were Kluxers or sympathizers,
and they were out of the question.

There remained only one man whose attitude did not fit into an anti-
Negro category, for I had heard the white men refer to him as a "Pope
lover." He was an Irish Catholic and was hated by the white Southerners.
I knew that he read books, because I had got him volumes from the library
several times. Since he, too, was an object of hatred, I felt that he might
refuse me but would hardly betray me. I hesitated, weighing and balancing the imponderable realities.

One morning I paused before the Catholic fellow's desk.   90

"I want to ask you a favor," I whispered to him.

"What is it?"

"I want to read. I can't get books from the library. I wonder if you'd let
me use your card?"

He looked at me suspiciously.

"My card is full most of the time," he said.   95

"I see," I said and waited, posing my question silently.

"You're not trying to get me into trouble, are you, boy?" he asked, staring at me.

"Oh, no, sir."

"What book do you want?"

"A book by H. L. Mencken."   100

"Which one?"

"I don't know. Has he written more than one?"

"He has written several."

"I didn't know that."

"What makes you want to read Mencken?"   105

"Oh, I just saw his name in the newspaper," I said.

"It's good of you to want to read," he said. "But you ought to read the right things."

I said nothing. Would he want to supervise my reading?

"Let me think," he said. "I'll figure out something."

I turned from him and he called me back. He stared at me quizzically.   110

"Richard, don't mention this to the other white men," he said.

"I understand," I said. "I won't say a word."

A few days later he called me to him.

"I've got a card in my wife's name," he said. "Here's mine."

"Thank you, sir."   115

"Do you think you can manage it?"

"I'll manage fine," I said.

"If they suspect you, you'll get in trouble," he said.

"I'll write the same kind of notes to the library that you wrote when you sent me for books," I told him. "I'll sign your name."

He laughed.   120

"Go ahead. Let me see what you get," he said.

That afternoon I addressed myself to forging a note. Now, what were the names of books written by H. L. Mencken? I did not know any of them. I finally wrote what I thought would be a foolproof note: *Dear Madam: Will you please let this nigger boy*—I used the word "nigger" to make the librarian feel that I could not possibly be the author of the note—*have some books by H. L. Mencken?* I forged the white man's name.

I entered the library as I had always done when on errands for whites, but I felt that I would somehow slip up and betray myself. I doffed my hat, stood a respectful distance from the desk, looked as unbookish as possible, and waited for the white patrons to be taken care of. When the desk was clear of people, I still waited. The white librarian looked at me.

"What do you want, boy?"

As though I did not possess the power of speech, I stepped forward   125
and simply handed her the forged note, not parting my lips.

"What books by Mencken does he want?" she asked.

"I don't know, ma'am," I said, avoiding her eyes.

"Who gave you this card?"

"Mr. Falk," I said.

"Where is he?"   130

"He's at work, at the M——— Optical Company," I said. "I've been in here for him before."

"I remember," the woman said. "But he never wrote notes like this."

Oh, God, she's suspicious. Perhaps she would not let me have the books? If she had turned her back at that moment, I would have ducked out the door and never gone back. Then I thought of a bold idea.

'You can call him up, ma'am," I said, my heart pounding.

"You're not using these books, are you?" she asked pointedly.   135

"Oh, no, ma'am. I can't read."

"I don't know what he wants by Mencken," she said under her breath.

I knew now that I had won; she was thinking of other things and the race question had gone out of her mind. She went to the shelves. Once or twice she looked over her shoulder at me, as though she was still doubtful. Finally she came forward with two books in her hand.

"I'm sending him two books," she said. "But tell Mr. Falk to come in next time, or send me the names of the books he wants. I don't know what he wants to read."

I said nothing. She stamped the card and handed me the books. Not   140
daring to glance at them, I went out of the library, fearing that the woman would call me back for further questioning. A block away from the library I opened one of the books and read a title: *A Book of Prefaces*. I was nearing my nineteenth birthday and I did not know how to pronounce the word "preface." I thumbed the pages and saw strange words and strange names. I shook my head, disappointed. I looked at the other book; it was called *Prejudices*. I knew what that word meant; I had heard it all my life. And right off I was on guard against Mencken's books. Why would a man want to call a book *Prejudices*? The word was so stained with all my memories of racial hate that I could not conceive of anybody using it for a title. Perhaps I had made a mistake about Mencken? A man who had prejudices must be wrong.

When I showed the books to Mr. Falk, he looked at me and frowned.

"That librarian might telephone you," I warned him.

"That's all right," he said. "But when you're through reading those books, I want you to tell me what you get out of them."

That night in my rented room, while letting the hot water run over my can of pork and beans in the sink, I opened *A Book of Prefaces* and began to read. I was jarred and shocked by the style, the clear, clean, sweeping sentences. Why did he write like that? And how did one write like that? I pictured the man as a raging demon, slashing with his pen, consumed with hate, denouncing everything American, extolling everything European or German, laughing at the weaknesses of people, mocking God, authority. What was this? I stood up, trying to realize what reality lay behind the meaning of the words . . . Yes, this man was fighting, fighting with words. He was using words as a weapon, using them as one would use a club. Could words be weapons? Well, yes, for here they were. Then, maybe, perhaps, I could use them as a weapon? No. It frightened me. I read on and what amazed me was not what he said, but how on earth anybody had the courage to say it.

Occasionally I glanced up to reassure myself that I was alone in the room. Who were these men about whom Mencken was talking so passionately? Who was Anatole France? Joseph Conrad? Sinclair Lewis, Sherwood Anderson, Dostoevski, George Moore, Gustave Flaubert, Maupassant, Tolstoy, Frank Harris, Mark Twain, Thomas Hardy, Arnold Bennett, Stephen Crane, Zola, Norris, Gorky, Bergson, Ibsen, Balzac, Bernard Shaw, Dumas, Poe, Thomas Mann, O. Henry, Dreiser, H. G. Wells, Gogol, T. S. Eliot, Gide, Baudelaire, Edgar Lee Masters, Stendhal, Turgenev, Huneker, Nietzsche, and scores of others? Were these men real? Did they exist or had they existed? And how did one pronounce their names?

I ran across many words whose meanings I did not know, and I either looked them up in a dictionary or, before I had a chance to do that, encountered the word in a context that made its meaning clear. But what strange world was this? I concluded the book with the conviction that I had somehow overlooked something terribly important in life. I had once tried to write, had once reveled in feeling, had let my crude imagination roam, but the impulse to dream had been slowly beaten out of me by experience. Now it surged up again and I hungered for books, new ways of looking and seeing. It was not a matter of believing or disbelieving what I read, but of feeling something new, of being affected by something that made the look of the world different.

As dawn broke I ate my pork and beans, feeling dopey, sleepy. I went to work, but the mood of the book would not die; it lingered, coloring everything I saw, heard, did. I now felt that I knew what the white men were feeling. Merely because I had read a book that had spoken of how they lived and thought, I identified myself with that book. I felt vaguely guilty. Would I, filled with bookish notions, act in a manner that would make the whites dislike me?

I forged more notes and my trips to the library became frequent. Reading grew into a passion. My first serious novel was Sinclair Lewis's *Main Street*. It made me see my boss, Mr. Gerald, and identify him as an American type. I would smile when I saw him lugging his golf bags into the office. I had always felt a vast distance separating me from the boss, and now I felt closer to him, though still distant. I felt now that I knew him, that I could feel the very limits of his narrow life. And this had happened because I had read a novel about a mythical man called George F. Babbitt.

The plots and stories in the novels did not interest me so much as the point of view revealed. I gave myself over to each novel without reserve, without trying to criticize it; it was enough for me to see and feel something different. And for me, everything was something different. Reading was like a drug, a dope. The novels created moods in which I lived for days. But I could not conquer my sense of guilt, my feeling that the white men around me knew that I was changing, that I had begun to regard them differently.

Whenever I brought a book to the job, I wrapped it in newspaper—a [150] habit that was to persist for years in other cities and under other circumstances. But some of the white men pried into my packages when I was absent and they questioned me.

"Boy, what are you reading those books for?"

"Oh, I don't know, sir."

"That's deep stuff you're reading, boy."

"I'm just killing time, sir."

"You'll addle your brains if you don't watch out." [155]

I read Dreiser's *Jennie Gerhardt* and *Sister Carrie* and they revived in me a vivid sense of my mother's suffering; I was overwhelmed. I grew silent, wondering about the life around me. It would have been impossible for me to have told anyone what I derived from these novels, for it was nothing less than a sense of life itself. All my life had shaped me for the realism, the naturalism of the modern novel, and I could not read enough of them.

Steeped in new moods and ideas, I bought a ream of paper and tried to write; but nothing would come, or what did come was flat beyond telling. I discovered that more than desire and feeling were necessary to write and I dropped the idea. Yet I still wondered how it was possible to know people sufficiently to write about them? Could I ever learn about life and people? To me, with my vast ignorance, my Jim Crow station in life, it seemed a task impossible of achievement. I now knew what being a Negro meant. I could endure the hunger. I had learned to live with hate. But to feel that there were feelings denied me, that the very breath of life itself was beyond my reach, that more than anything else hurt, wounded me. I had a new hunger.

In buoying me up, reading also cast me down, made me see what was possible, what I had missed. My tension returned, new, terrible, bitter, surging, almost too great to be contained. I no longer *felt* that the world about me was hostile, killing; I *knew* it. A million times I asked myself what I could do to save myself, and there were no answers. I seemed forever condemned, ringed by walls.

I did not discuss my reading with Mr. Falk, who had lent me his library card; it would have meant talking about myself and that would have been too painful. I smiled each day, fighting desperately to maintain my old behavior, to keep my disposition seemingly sunny. But some of the white men discerned that I had begun to brood.

"Wake up there, boy!" Mr. Olin said one day. [160]

"Sir!" I answered for the lack of a better word.

"You act like you've stolen something," he said.

I laughed in the way I knew he expected me to laugh, but I resolved to be more conscious of myself, to watch my every act, to guard and hide the new knowledge that was dawning within me.

If I went north, would it be possible for me to build a new life then? But how could a man build a life upon vague, unformed yearnings? I wanted to write and I did not even know the English language. I bought English grammars and found them dull. I felt that I was getting a better sense of the language from novels than from grammars. I read hard, discarding a writer as soon as I felt that I had grasped his point of view. At night the printed page stood before my eyes in sleep.

Mrs. Moss, my landlady, asked me one Sunday morning: 165

"Son, what is this you keep on reading?"

"Oh, nothing. Just novels."

"What you get out of 'em?"

"I'm just killing time," I said.

"I hope you know your own mind," she said in a tone which implied 170 that she doubted if I had a mind.

I knew of no Negroes who read the books I liked and I wondered if any Negroes ever thought of them. I knew that there were Negro doctors, lawyers, newspapermen, but I never saw any of them. When I read a Negro newspaper I never caught the faintest echo of my preoccupation in its pages. I felt trapped and occasionally, for a few days, I would stop reading. But a vague hunger would come over me for books, books that opened up new avenues of feeling and seeing, and again I would forge another note to the white librarian. Again I would read and wonder as only the naïve and unlettered can read and wonder, feeling that I carried a secret, criminal burden about with me each day.

That winter my mother and brother came and we set up house-keeping, buying furniture on the installment plan, being cheated and yet knowing no way to avoid it. I began to eat warm food and to my surprise found that regular meals enabled me to read faster. I may have lived through many illnesses and survived them, never suspecting that I was ill. My brother obtained a job and we began to save toward the trip north, plotting our time, setting tentative dates for departure. I told none of the white men on the job that I was planning to go north; I knew that the moment they felt I was thinking of the North they would change toward me. It would have made them feel that I did not like the life I was living, and because my life was completely conditioned by what they said or did, it would have been tantamount to challenging them.

I could calculate my chances for life in the South as a Negro fairly clearly now.

I could fight the southern whites by organizing with other Negroes, as my grandfather had done. But I knew that I could never win that way; there were many whites and there were but few blacks. They were strong and we were weak. Outright black rebellion could never win. If I fought openly I would die and I did not want to die. News of lynchings were frequent.

I could submit and live the life of a genial slave, but that was impossi- 175 ble. All of my life had shaped me to live by my own feelings and thoughts. I could make up to Bess and marry her and inherit the house. But that, too, would be the life of a slave; if I did that, I would crush to death something within me, and I would hate myself as much as I knew the whites already hated those who had submitted. Neither could I ever willingly present myself to be kicked, as Shorty had done. I would rather have died than do that.

I could drain off my restlessness by fighting with Shorty and Harrison. I had seen many Negroes solve the problem of being black by transferring their hatred of themselves to others with a black skin and fighting them. I would have to be cold to do that, and I was not cold and I could never be.

I could, of course, forget what I had read, thrust the whites out of my mind, forget them; and find release from anxiety and longing in sex and alcohol. But the memory of how my father had conducted himself made that course repugnant. If I did not want others to violate my life, how could I voluntarily violate it myself?

I had no hope whatever of being a professional man. Not only had I been so conditioned that I did not desire it, but the fulfillment of such an ambition was beyond my capabilities. Well-to-do Negroes lived in a world that was almost as alien to me as the world inhabited by whites.

What, then, was there? I held my life in my mind, in my consciousness each day, feeling at times that I would stumble and drop it, spill it forever. My reading had created a vast sense of distance between me and the world in which I lived and tried to make a living, and that sense of distance was increasing each day. My days and nights were one long, quiet, continuously contained dream of terror, tension, and anxiety. I wondered how long I could bear it.

✎ Topics for Critical Thinking and Writing:

1. In this section of his autobiography, Wright recounts his illegal use of the public library. Why was his use of the library illegal? And why was the library so important to him? Compare Wright's experience with your own introduction to a public library.

2. At the end of the first part of the narrative (paragraph 83), Wright tells of his "yearning for a kind of consciousness, a mode of being . . . upon which the penalty of death had been placed." To what extent can we change the consciousness that we have? Is Wright exaggerating when he says that "the penalty of death had been placed" on the changes he desires?

3. Wright frequently uses dialogue to tell his story. Select a passage of dialogue, of about a page, and then summarize it without using dialogue. Then, in a brief paragraph, explain what has been gained or lost. We suggest Wright's conversations with the editor of the newspaper or with "the Catholic fellow."

Doris Kearns Goodwin

Doris Kearns Goodwin was born in Rockville Centre, New York, in 1943, and educated at Colby College (BA) and Harvard University (Ph.D). As an undergraduate she served in Washington as a State Department intern, and between college and graduate school she served as a House of Representatives intern. In 1968, the year she received her Ph.D., she served as special assistant to President Lyndon Johnson—a rather remarkable appointment, since Johnson offered it to her knowing that in 1967 she had published an article urging the Democrats not to renominate him for the 1968 election.

One product of her work with Johnson was a highly acclaimed biography (which she published under the name of Doris Helen Kearns), Lyndon Johnson and the American Dream *(1976). She has also written two more books which are widely regarded as major works:* The Fitzgeralds and the Kennedys: An American Saga *(1987) and* No Ordinary Time: Franklin and Eleanor Roosevelt *(1994), which won the Pulitzer Prize in 1995.* Wait Till Next Year, *her book about the Dodgers and her memories of baseball, the source of the following passage, was published in 1997. Goodwin is a regular panelist on television programs and was the first woman journalist to enter the locker room of the Boston Red Sox.*

Fan

My continuing love of baseball is inseparably linked to memories of my father. On summer nights, when he came home from work, the two of us would sit together on our porch, reliving that day's Brooklyn Dodger game, which I had permanently preserved in the large red scorebook he'd given me for my seventh birthday.

I can still remember how proud I was when I first mastered all the miniature symbols that allowed me to record every movement, play by play, of our favorite players, Jackie Robinson and Duke Snider. Pee Wee Reese and Gil Hodges. With the scorebook spread between us, my dad would ask me questions about different plays, whether a strikeout was called or swinging, and if I'd been careful in my scoring, I would know the answers. At such moments, when he smiled at me, I could not help but smile, too, for he had one of those contagious smiles that started in his eyes and traveled across his face, leaving laugh lines on either side of his mouth.

Sometimes a particular play would trigger in my dad a memory of a similar situation framed forever in his mind, and suddenly we were back in time recalling the Dodgers of his childhood—Casey Stengel, Zack Wheat, and Jimmy Johnston. Mingling together the present and the past, our conversations nurtured within me an irresistible fascination with history, which has remained to this day.

It fell to me to be the family scorekeeper not only because I was the third daughter and youngest child, but because my idea of a perfect afternoon was lying in front of our ten-inch-screen television, watching baseball. What is more, there was real power in being the one to keep score. For all through my early childhood, my father kept from me the knowledge that the daily papers printed daily box scores, permitting me to imagine that without my symbolic renderings of all the games he had missed while he was at work, he would never have been able to follow the Dodgers in the only proper way a team should be followed, day by day, inning by inning. In other words, without me, his love for baseball would be forever unrequited.

In our neighborhood in Rockville Centre, New York, allegiance was   5 equally divided among Dodger, Yankee, and Giant fans. As families emigrated from different parts of the city to the suburbs of Long Island, the old loyalties remained intact, creating rival enclaves on every street. Born and bred in Brooklyn, my father would always love the Dodgers, fear the Giants, and hate the abominable Yankees.

The butcher shop in our neighborhood was owned by a father and son, Old Joe and Young Joe Schmidt. They were both rabid Giant fans, as was Max, the man in charge of the vegetables. Knowing how much I loved baseball, they all took great delight in teasing me. They called me Ragmop, in honor of my unruly hair, and they constantly made fun of my Dodgers. I'd pretend to be angry, but the truth was that I loved going into their shop; I loved the sawdust on the floor, the sides of beef hanging from the ceiling, the enormous walk-in freezer behind the counter. And most of all, I loved the attention I received.

During the glorious summer of 1951, when I was eight years old and the Dodgers seemed invincible, I visited my friends in the butcher shop every day. Jackie Robinson was awesome that year, hitting .338; Roy Campanella was the MVP; Gil Hodges hit 40 homers. It seemed that no one could beat us. But then, in the third week of August, the Giants began an astonishing stretch that whittled the Dodger lead away until the season ended in a tie.

When the deciding play-off began, I was so nervous I couldn't sit by the television. Each time the Giants came to bat in the early innings, I left the room, returning only when I knew they were out and the Dodgers were up. I began to relax slightly as the Dodgers pulled ahead 4–1, but when the Giants came to bat in the last of the ninth, I could hear the beating of my heart. Then, as Bobby Thomson stepped to the plate, with one run in and two men on base, my sister Charlotte predicted that he would hit a home run and win the game for the Giants. When Thomson did precisely that, crushing Ralph Branca's pitch into the left field stand, I thought for a moment my sister had made it happen and I hated her with all my heart.

In the days that followed, I refused to go into the butcher shop, unable to face the mocking laughter that I imagined would accompany my first steps into the store. I was wrong. After a week's absence, a bouquet of flowers arrived at my door. "Ragmop, come back," the card read. "We miss you. Your friends at Bryn Mawr Meat Market."

"Wait till next year," my father consoled, repeating a refrain that   10 would become all too familiar in the years ahead. But at eight years of age, it was easy to gamble in expectation, to believe that as soon as winter gave way to spring, a splendid new season would begin.

This indomitable belief in the future was vitally important to me when I was a child, for my mother's life was slowly ebbing away. The rheumatic fever she had when she was young had left her heart permanently damaged; every year, it seemed, she suffered another heart attack, which sent her to the hospital for days or weeks at a time. I was never made privy to the full extent of her illness; on the contrary, I took great comfort from the ritual of knowing that each time she went away, she came back. It's only a matter of time. I kept telling myself, as the ambulance carried her away, until she'll walk through the door again and everything will be all right.

In my prayers, the Dodgers figured prominently. Every night I said two sets of Hail Marys and Our Fathers. Believing that each prayer was worth a certain number of days off my inevitable sentence to purgatory, I dedicated the first set of prayers to my account in heaven. At the end of the week I would add up my nightly prayers and fold the total into a note. "Dear God. I have said 935 days worth of prayers this week. Please put this to my account. I live at 125 Southard Avenue." My second set of prayers was directed toward more earthly desires, chief among them the wish for the Dodgers to win the World Series at least once before I died.

It took tens of thousands of Hail Marys and Our Fathers, but finally on October 4, 1955, the Dodgers won their first-ever world championship. It was one of the happiest moments of my life, made all the more special because this time, I predicted the outcome. In the sixth inning, Sandy Amoros made a spectacular catch in left field of a wicked fly ball that would have tied the score with two Yankee runs. I knew then that the Dodgers would win, just as, on other occasions, a failed sacrifice or a double play signaled an inevitable loss.

Everything happened quickly after that until, stunningly, it was the bottom of the ninth with the Dodgers up 2–0. And this time there was no Bobby Thomson to destroy the cherished dreams of delirious Brooklyn fans. When my father came home that night, we celebrated by recreating the entire game, play by play, and there was more. When the newspaper arrived on our lawn the next morning with the fabulous headline THIS *IS* NEXT YEAR, we relished every word as if we were hearing about the game for the first time.

Things fell apart all too quickly after that magical summer. When I first heard the rumor that Brooklyn owner Walter O'Malley was contemplating taking the Dodgers to Los Angeles, I refused to believe it, assuming he was simply jockeying for a new stadium. I hated all the talk about the need for a new stadium. When they said Ebbets Field was too small, too dilapidated, I took it as a personal insult. I couldn't imagine a more beautiful place.

I dreamed one night I was being ushered into O'Malley's office to make the case for Brooklyn. He was standing behind his desk, a diabolic look on his face that chilled my heart. But as I started to talk, his face softened and when I finished, he threw his arms around me and promised to stay at Ebbets Field. I had saved the Dodgers for Brooklyn!

In reality, of course, neither I nor anyone else could prevent the unforgivable O'Malley from completing his invidious act of betrayal. When the move was officially announced in the fall of 1957, I felt as if I, too, were

15

being uprooted. Never again to sit in the stands at Ebbets Field, never again to watch the papers for the first news out of spring training, it was impossible to imagine.

My sense of being uprooted was real. As the 1958 season got under way, a weird, empty season with neither the Dodgers nor the Giants in New York, my mother suffered another heart attack. As before, she was taken away, but this time she didn't return. Six months later, we sold our house and moved to an apartment. My father couldn't bear sleeping in his bedroom without my mother.

Suddenly, my feelings for baseball seemed an aspect of my departing youth, to be discarded along with my childhood freckles and my collection of *Archie* comics. I didn't entirely forget about baseball during those last years in high school, but without a team to root for, my emotions became detached; my heart wasn't in it anymore.

Then, one September day, having settled in Massachusetts while get-   20
ting my Ph.D. at Harvard, I agreed, half reluctantly, to go to Fenway Park. There it was again: the cozy ball field scaled to human dimensions so that every word of encouragement and every scornful yell could be heard on the field; the fervent crowd that could, with equal passion, curse a player for today's failures after cheering his heroics the day before; the team that always seemed to break your heart in the last weeks of the season. It was love at first sight as I found myself directing all my old intensities toward my new team—the Boston Red Sox.

By this time, my dad had become a Mets fan so there was no need to feel guilty about my new love. Indeed, my return to baseball reinforced the old link between my father and me: providing endlessly absorbing topics for conversation. Once again our talks produced a sequence of mental images, vivid recollections of similar plays from the past; once again, we were united by an easy affection.

In the summer of 1972, while I was still single and teaching at Harvard, my father died. He had just settled down in his favorite chair to watch the Mets when he suffered a fatal heart attack. I remember the inconsolable feeling that the children I hoped to have someday would never know this extraordinary man, who had given me such steadfast love for so many years.

When I got married and had children my passion for the Sox assumed a strange urgency: at times I felt almost as if I were circling back to my childhood, as I found myself following the same rituals with my sons that I had practiced with my father. At Fenway Park, there are a number of ramps one can take to get from the crowded concession stands selling hot dogs, Cokes, tacos, and beer to the interior of the park itself. Ramp 33 is "my" ramp—with a curious attachment to a ritual my father followed by entering Ebbets Field at the same angle each time, I find myself walking up exactly the same ramp every game so that my first sight of the field comes at the same angle.

Indeed, sometimes when I close my eyes against the sun as I sit with my boys at Fenway, I am suddenly back at Ebbets Field, a young girl once more in the presence of my father, watching the players of my youth on the grassy field below. There is magic in these moments, for when I open my eyes and see my sons in the place where my father once sat, I feel an invisible bond among our three generations, an anchor of loyalty linking my sons to the grandfather whose face they have never seen, but whose person they have come to know through this most timeless of all sports.

When the Sox won the pennant in 1986, my boys were absolutely certain they would win the World Series. I, of course, was less sure, having been at the edge of victory so many times before only to see my hopes dashed at the final moment. Yet by the sixth game, with the Sox leading 3 games to 2 over the Mets and ahead 5–3 in the bottom of the tenth, I told my husband to break out the champagne. Then, of course, in an agonizing replay of the Bobby Thomson fiasco, Boston first baseman Bill Buckner let a routine grounder slip through his legs and the Mets came back to win both the game and the World Series.

I tried to control my emotions but I couldn't. "Mom, it's all right," my boys consoled me. "They'll win next year. Don't worry."

Oh, my God, I thought. These kids don't know yet that the Sox haven't won since 1918, that this may be as close as they will ever come in any of our lifetimes. Suddenly I felt possessed of a terrible wisdom that I did not ever want to impart to my children.

"Right," I said. "Wait till next year."

✎ Topics for Critical Thinking and Writing

1. In paragraph 17 Goodwin says "neither I nor anyone else could prevent the unforgivable O'Malley from completing his invidious act of betrayal." What was O'Malley's "act of betrayal"? And how would you characterize Goodwin's style here?
2. In paragraph 20 how does Goodwin characterize baseball? What does she *leave out* of her characterization? In a paragraph try to create an impression of a game, focusing on a particular angle to highlight.
3. In her next-to-last paragraph Goodwin writes of a "terrible wisdom" but does not define it. What was the wisdom?
4. If you ever have been a fan of baseball or some other sport, write a narrative essay explaining how you came to be a fan and whether or not your enthusiasm continues.

Frank Conroy

Frank Conroy, currently the director of the University of Iowa Writers' Workshop, has received fellowships from the Guggenheim and Rockefeller foundations and from the National Council for the Arts. His autobiography Stop-Time *was nominated in 1967 for a National Book Award and was the first manuscript project on the Internet homepage of The Writer's Workshop. He has written three other books and numerous essays and short stories. His avocation is playing jazz piano.*

A Yo-Yo Going Down

The common yo-yo is crudely made, with a thick shank between two widely spaced wooden disks. The string is knotted or stapled to the shank. With such an instrument nothing can be done except the simple up-down movement. My yo-yo, on the other hand, was a perfectly balanced construction of hard wood, slightly weighted, flat, with only a sixteenth of an inch between the halves. The string was not attached to the shank, but looped over it in such a way as to allow the wooden part to spin freely on its own axis. The gyroscopic effect thus created kept the yo-yo stable in all attitudes.

I started at the beginning of the book and quickly mastered the novice, intermediate, and advanced stages, practicing all day every day in the woods across the street from my house. Hour after hour of practice, never moving to the next trick until the one at hand was mastered.

The string was tied to my middle finger, just behind the nail. As I threw—with your palm up, make a fist; throw down your hand, fingers unfolding, as if you were casting grain—a short bit of string would tighten across the sensitive pad of flesh at the tip of my finger. That was the critical area. After a number of weeks I could interpret the condition of the string, the presence of any imperfections on the shank, but most importantly the exact amount of spin or inertial energy left in the yo-yo at any given moment—all from that bit of string on my fingertip. As the throwing motion became more and more natural I found I could make the yo-yo "sleep" for an astonishing length of time—fourteen or fifteen seconds—and still have enough spin left to bring it back to my hand. Gradually the basic moves became reflexes. Sleeping, twirling, swinging, and precise aim. Without thinking, without even looking, I could run through trick after trick involving various combinations of the elemental skills, switching from one to the other in a smooth continuous flow. On particularly good days I would hum a tune under my breath and do it all in time to the music.

Flicking the yo-yo expressed something. The sudden, potentially comic extension of one's arm to twice its length. The precise neatness of it, intrinsically soothing, as if relieving an inner tension too slight to be noticeable, the way a man might hitch up his pants simply to enact a reassuring gesture. It felt good. The comfortable weight in one's hand, the smooth, rapid-descent down the string, ending with a barely audible snap as the yo-yo hung balanced, spinning, pregnant with force and the slave of one's fingertip. That it was vaguely masturbatory seems inescapable. I doubt that half the pubescent boys in America could have been captured by any other means, as, in the heat of the fad, half of them were. A single Loop-the-Loop might represent, in some mysterious way, the act of masturbation, but to break down the entire repertoire into the three stages of throw, trick, and return representing erection, climax, and detumescence seems immoderate.

The greatest pleasure in yo-yoing was an abstract pleasure—watching   5
the dramatization of simply physical laws, and realizing they would
never fail if a trick was done correctly. The geometric purity of it! The
string wasn't just a string, it was a tool in the enactment of theorems. It
was a line, an idea. And the top was an entirely different sort of idea, a
gyroscope, capable of storing energy and of interacting with the line. I
remember the first time I did a particularly lovely trick, one in which the
sleeping yo-yo is swung from right to left while the string is interrupted
by an extended index finger. Momentum carries the yo-yo in a circular
path around the finger, but instead of completing the arc the yo-yo falls on
the taut string between the performer's hands, where it continues to spin
in an upright position. My pleasure at that moment was as much from the
beauty of the experiment as from pride. Snapping apart my hands I sent
the yo-yo into the air above my head, bouncing it off nothing, back into
my palm.

I practiced the yo-yo because it pleased me to do so, without the
slightest application of will power. It wasn't ambition that drove me, but
the nature of yo-yoing. The yo-yo represented my first organized attempt
to control the outside world. It fascinated me because I could see my
progress in clearly defined stages, and because the intimacy of it, the
almost spooky closeness I began to feel with the instrument in my hand,
seemed to ensure that nothing irrelevant would interfere. I was, in the language of jazz, "up tight" with my yo-yo, and finally free, in one small area
at least, of the paralyzing sloppiness of life in general.

The first significant problem arose in the attempt to do fifty consecutive Loop-the-Loops. After ten or fifteen the yo-yo invariably started to
lean and the throws became less clean, resulting in loss of control. I almost
skipped the whole thing because fifty seemed excessive. Ten made the
point. But there it was, written out in the book. To qualify as an expert you
had to do fifty, so fifty I would do.

It took me two days, and I wouldn't have spent a moment more. All
those Loop-the-Loops were hard on the strings. Time after time the shank
cut them and the yo-yo went sailing off into the air. It was irritating, not
only because of the expense (strings were a nickel each, and fabricating
your own was unsatisfactory), but because a random element had been
introduced. About the only unforeseeable disaster in yo-yoing was to
have your string break, and here was a trick designed to do exactly that.
Twenty-five would have been enough. If you could do twenty-five clean
Loop-the-Loops you could do fifty or a hundred. I supposed they were
simply trying to sell strings and went back to the more interesting tricks.

The witty nonsense of Eating Spaghetti, the surprise of The Twirl, the
complex neatness of Cannonball, Backwards Round the World, or
Halfway Round the World—I could do them all, without false starts or
sloppy endings. I could do every trick in the book. Perfectly.

The day was marked on the kitchen calendar (God Gave Us Bluebell   10
Natural Bottled Gas). I got on my bike and rode into town. Pedaling along

the highway I worked out with the yo-yo to break in a new string. The twins were appearing at the dime store.

I could hear the crowd before I turned the corner. Kids were coming on bikes and on foot from every corner of town, rushing down the streets like madmen. Three or four policemen were busy keeping the street clear directly in front of the store, and in a small open space around the doors some of the more adept kids were running through their tricks, showing off to the general audience or stopping to compare notes with their peers. Standing at the edge with my yo-yo safe in my pocket, it didn't take me long to see I had them all covered. A boy in a sailor hat could do some of the harder tricks, but he missed too often to be a serious threat. I went inside.

As Ramos and Ricardo performed I watched their hands carefully, noticing little differences in style, and technique. Ricardo was a shade classier, I thought, although Ramos held an edge in the showy two-handed stuff. When they were through we went outside for the contest.

"Everybody in the alley!" Ramos shouted, his head bobbing an inch or two above the others. "Contest starting now in the alley!" A hundred excited children followed the twins into an alley beside the dime store and lined up against the wall.

"Attention all kids!" Ramos yelled, facing us from the middle of the street like a drill sergeant. "To qualify for contest you got to Rock the Cradle. You got to rock yo-yo in cradle four time. Four time! Okay? Three time no good. Okay. Everybody happy?" There were murmurs of disappointment and some of the kids stepped out of line. The rest of us closed ranks. Yo-yos flicked nervously as we waited. "Winner receive grand prize. Special Black Beauty Prize Yo-Yo with Diamonds," said Ramos, gesturing to his brother who smiled and held up the prize, turning it in the air so we could see the four stones set on each side. ("The crowd gasped . . ." I want to write. Of course they didn't. They didn't make a sound, but the impact of the diamond yo-yo was obvious.) We'd never seen anything like it. One imagined how the stones would gleam as it revolved, and how much prettier the tricks would be. The ultimate yo-yo! The only one in town! Who knew what feats were possible with such an instrument? All around me a fierce, nervous resolve was settling into the contestants, suddenly skittish as race-horses.

"Ricardo will show trick with Grand Prize Yo-Yo. Rock the Cradle four time!"   15

"One!" cried Ramos.

"Two!" the kids joined in.

"Three!" It was really beautiful. He did it so slowly you would have thought he had all the time in the world. I counted seconds under my breath to see how long he made it sleep.

"Four!" said the crowd.

"Thirteen" I said to myself as the yo-yo snapped back into his hand.   20
Thirteen seconds. Excellent time for that particular trick.

"Attention all kids!" Ramos announced. "Contest start now at head of line."

The first boy did a sloppy job of gathering his string but managed to rock the cradle quickly four times.

"Okay." Ramos tapped him on the shoulder and moved to the next boy, who fumbled. "Out." Ricardo followed, doing an occasional Loop-the-Loop with the diamond yo-yo. "Out . . . out . . . okay," said Ramos as he worked down the line.

There was something about the man's inexorable advance that unnerved me. His decisions were fast, and there was no appeal. To my surprise I felt my palms begin to sweat. Closer and closer he came, his voice growing louder, and then suddenly he was standing in front of me. Amazed, I stared at him. It was as if he'd appeared out of thin air.

"What happen boy, you swarrow bubble gum?"   25

The laughter jolted me out of it. Blushing, I threw down my yo-yo and executed a slow Rock the Cradle, counting the four passes and hesitating a moment at the end so as not to appear rushed.

"Okay." He tapped my shoulder. "Good."

I wiped my hands on my blue jeans and watched him move down the line. "Out . . . out . . . out." He had a large mole on the back of his neck.

Seven boys qualified. Coming back, Ramos called out, "Next trick Backward Round the World! Okay? Go!"

The first two boys missed, but the third was the kid in the sailor hat.   30
Glancing quickly to see that no one was behind him, he hunched up his shoulder, threw, and just barely made the catch. There was some loose string in his hand, but not enough to disqualify him.

Number four missed, as did number five, and it was my turn. I stepped forward, threw the yo-yo almost straight up over my head, and as it began to fall pulled very gently to add some speed. It zipped neatly behind my legs and there was nothing more to do. My head turned to one side, I stood absolutely still and watched the yo-yo come in over my shoulder and slap into my hand. I added a Loop-the-Loop just to show the tightness of the string.

"Did you see that?" I heard someone say.

Number seven missed, so it was between myself and the boy in the sailor hat. His hair was bleached by the sun and combed up over his forehead in a pompadour, held from behind by the white hat. He was a year or two older than me. Blinking his blue eyes nervously, he adjusted the tension of his string.

"Next trick Cannonball! Cannonball! You go first this time," Ramos said to me.

Kids had gathered in a circle around us, those in front quiet and atten-   35
tive, those in back jumping up and down to get a view. "Move back for room," Ricardo said, pushing them back. "More room, please."

I stepped into the center and paused, looking down at the ground. It was a difficult trick. The yo-yo had to land exactly on the string and there was a chance I'd miss the first time. I knew I wouldn't miss twice. "Can I have one practice?"

Ramos and Ricardo consulted in their mother tongue, and then Ramos held up his hands. "Attention all kids! Each boy have one practice before trick."

The crowd was then silent, watching me. I took a deep breath and threw, following the fall of the yo-yo with my eyes, turning slightly, matador-fashion, as it passed me. My finger caught the string, the yo-yo came up and over, and missed. Without pausing I threw again. "Second time," I yelled, so there would be no misunderstanding. The circle had been too big. This time I made it small, sacrificing beauty for security. The yo-yo fell where it belonged and spun for a moment. (A moment I don't rush, my arms widespread, my eyes locked on the spinning toy. The Trick! There it is, brief and magic right before your eyes! My hands are frozen in the middle of a deaf-and-dumb sentence, holding the whole airy, tenuous statement aloft for everyone to see.) With a quick snap I broke up the trick and made my catch.

Ramos nodded. "Okay. Very good. Now next boy."

Sailor-hat stepped forward, wiping his nose with the back of his hand. 40 He threw once to clear the string.

"One practice," said Ramos.

He nodded.

"C'mon Bobby," someone said. "You can do it."

Bobby threw the yo-yo out to the side, made his move, and missed. "Damn," he whispered. (He said "dahyum.") The second time he got halfway through the trick before his yo-yo ran out of gas and fell impotently off the string. He picked it up and walked away, winding slowly.

Ramos came over and held my hand in the air. "The winner!" he 45 yelled. "Grand prize Black Beauty Diamond Yo-Yo will now be awarded."

Ricardo stood in front of me. "Take off old yo-yo." I loosened the knot and slipped it off. "Put out hand." I held out my hand and he looped the new string on my finger, just behind the nail, where the mark was. "You like Black Beauty," he said, smiling as he stepped back. "Diamond make pretty colors in the sun."

"Thank you," I said.

"Very good with yo-yo. Later we have contest for whole town. Winner go to Miami for State Championship. Maybe you win. Okay?"

"Okay." I nodded. "Thank you."

A few kids came up to look at Black Beauty. I threw it once or twice to 50 get the feel. It seemed a bit heavier than my old one. Ramos and Ricardo were surrounded as the kids called out their favorite tricks.

"Do Pickpocket! Pickpocket!"

"Do the Double Cannonball!"

"Ramos! Ramos! Do the Turkish Army!"

Smiling, waving their hands to ward off the barrage of requests, the twins worked their way through the crowd toward the mouth of the alley. I watched them moving away and was immediately struck by a wave of fierce and irrational panic. "Wait," I yelled, pushing through after them. "Wait!"

I caught them on the street. 55

"No more today," Ricardo said, and then paused when he saw it was me. "Okay. The champ. What's wrong? Yo-yo no good?"

"No. It's fine."

"Good. You take care of it."

"I wanted to ask when the contest is. The one where you get to go to Miami."

"Later. After school begins." They began to move away. "We have to go home now." 60

"Just one more thing," I said, walking after them. "What is the hardest trick you know?"

Ricardo laughed. "Hardest trick is killing flies in air."

"No, no. I mean a real trick."

They stopped and looked at me. "There is a very hard trick," Ricardo said. "I don't do it, but Ramos does. Because you won the contest he will show you. But only once, so watch carefully."

We stepped into the lobby of the Sunset Theater. Ramos cleared his 65
string. "Watch," he said, and threw. The trick started out like a Cannonball, and then unexpectedly folded up, opened again, and as I watched breathlessly the entire complex web spun around in the air, propelled by Ramos' two hands making slow circles like a swimmer. The end was like the end of a Cannonball.

"That's beautiful," I said, genuinely awed. "What's it called?"

"The Universe."

"The Universe," I repeated.

"Because it goes around and around," said Ramos, "like the planets."

✎ Topics for Critical Thinking and Writing

1. In paragraph 6 Conroy says "The yo-yo represented my first organized attempt to control the outside world." Try to explain what he means by this. Then reflect on your own attempts "to control the outside world." Write a journal entry recording what comes to mind. (One of the editors of *The Little, Brown Reader* obsssessively practiced doing cartwheels when she was six or seven; the other became a magician.)

2. From paragraph 15 to the end of the passage Conroy uses dialogue. Why do you suppose he does this; what effect does the dialogue have? Why did he not use dialogue earlier?

3. In paragraph 14 Conroy writes "('The crowd gasped . . . I want to write . . . .)." Read the rest of this passage and then try to evaluate his technique as a writer here.

4. Conroy has written "Life happens to all of us. Art answers back." He was doubtless talking about writing as his "art." How well, though, does this motto apply to his mastery of the yo-yo?

5. In a brief essay (750 to 1000 words) compare Conroy's narrative with Richard Wright's (136–46).

Natalie Zemon Davis

Natalie Zemon Davis is currently associated with the University of Toronto. She is Professor of History Emeritus at Princeton University and has taught at several universities, including Brown, the University of California at Berkeley, and Yale. A specialist in the history of early modern France and in interdisciplinary courses in history and anthropology, and history and film, she has also pioneered in the history of women. She has written four important books, including The Return of Martin Guerre, *but she is regarded by many preeminently as an essayist. She has received numerous awards, honors, and honorary degrees. She lives with her husband, a mathematician, in Toronto. They have three children and three grandchildren.*

We reprint the opening pages of the 1997 Charles Homer Haskins Lecture for the American Council of Learned Societies.

A Life of Learning

"**A** life of learning?" "But I've only begun," I protested to myself when I received Stanley Katz's kind invitation to deliver this year's Charles Homer Haskins lecture. Why such a reaction? I wondered after I had accepted. I have no shyness about my 68 years; I use them whenever it is to my advantage. I am not falsely modest about the knowledge I have acquired over the decades: I can tell the difference between the girl who sat crosslegged, reading *The Renaissance of the Twelfth Century* in her Smith College carrel, and the mature scholar who, absorbed in an archival register, gets stiff after only an hour of immobility. I am confident about the tools of my trade, and yet there are vast landscapes where I have to work like a neophyte to find my way. Recounting my tale this evening may help me discover where such a scholarly style comes from.

The historical past was not discussed around my dinner table when I was a girl in Detroit in the 1930s. The bookshelves were filled with the stories, novels and especially the plays beloved of my father and the popular ethical works that my mother found uplifting. That learned Talmudists had been ancestors to my mother in Russia I heard only years later from an elderly cousin in Tel Aviv. Born in the United States—my mother in Burlington, Vermont, my father in Detroit—my parents had the characteristic time frame of the children of immigrants of that period: loyalty to the present and the future. What was important was being an eminently successful American, while holding staunchly to one's Jewish identity: for instance, getting on the University of Michigan tennis team (as did my father), and then having to fight for your "M" because the tennis coach had never given a letter to a Jew before.

The past was a secret too unpleasant for children to know. My brother and I might get hints of it from the whispered word "pogrom" at grandfather's house, from post cards that sometimes came in with unrecognizable lettering and faraway stamps, and from the Yiddish my mother spoke to her older sister when she didn't want us to understand. Later when I visited Russia and Poland, I found out that the childhood foods that I had thought were distinctly Jewish—rye bread, sour cream and cottage cheese—were just standard Eastern European fare. Later I even discovered that my family had a nineteenth-century American past. They were settlers in out-of-the-way places: Lake Champlain peddlers on my mother's side, founding the first synagogue in Burlington in the 1880s; and with my paternal great-grandfather running a general store in Elk Rapids, Michigan in the 1870s–1880s, buying land from the Ojibwa Indians, and, when he wanted to be part of a Jewish *minyan* on the Sabbath, riding the twenty miles to Traverse City before sundown.

My father, Julian Zemon, was a businessman, selling textiles wholesale to the automobile manufacturers around Detroit. My mother, Helen Lamport, stopped working at the family office, and devoted herself to her children, her family's interests, her garden, her golf, Hadassah. My parents bought a house distant from the Jewish quarter and we lived a few *landsleit* scattered among the gentiles. Sometimes it was easy to put my two worlds together, as when I rooted for the Detroit Tigers: Mickey Cochrane, captain of the team, lived around the corner while the Tigers' homerun hero was Hank Greenberg. Sometimes the worlds strained in opposition, as at Christmas time, when the Zemon house was one of the few without lights along the street. I shook my head at the stubborn wrong-headedness of our neighbors, and hoped that the true Messiah would come in my day to enlighten them.

It was a middle-class life that we lived, the Depression hardly leaving a trace on these comfortable houses into which people of color entered only to clean, iron, or serve at the table. But politics erupted there nonetheless. On the radio, when in between listening to Jack Benny and Fred Allen, we heard news of the bombing in Spain and the sounds of Hitler's German tirades. In the grade-school yard, where the first German refugees appeared, two Jewish boys in the exotic garb of lederhosen, who spat when children were mean to them. On the sidewalks, where a classmate came up when I was walking with my girlfriends and pointed his finger at me: "*You* are a Jew," he said. "So what?" I answered. My first memories of the Europe that would one day be my historian's home were full of terror.

My parents decided to send me to a private girls' high-school in the suburbs of Detroit—Kingswood School Cranbrook—my brother Stanley following to the boys' school a few years afterward. Kingswood was an exclusive school in those days, with girls from wealthy Detroit families and a quota of about two Jews per class (it was somewhat higher at the boys' school). Now my two worlds had little overlap. On the one hand, I plunged into life at the school, making good friends, trying to do my best at hockey and on the tennis court, and becoming, to my delight, president of the student council. On the other hand, we high-school girls were beginning to date and it was unthinkable on either side that a Jewish girl could go out with a non-Jewish boy. My social life was with Jewish young people from the public schools in Detroit. At the weekly Christian chapel at Kingswood, I crossed my fingers during prayers and hymns lest my Old Testament God be angry at me.

I loved my studies at Kingswood: the Latin and French, the Shakespeare plays, the algebra, and especially the surprises of history, from the ancient civilizations to modern Europe to the history of America. I liked to underline, to outline, to memorize facts and time charts—all the things that are supposed to turn high-school students off and make them hate history. Even better was to learn about Athenian democracy, the Enlightenment, the French Revolution and the American Revolution! I had never realized the extent of human aspiration in the past, the hope to make things better, an important counter-weight to the war raging across the Atlantic. As for Jewish history, a Detroit boyfriend urged me to read a biography of the Zionist founder Theodore Herzl, which helped me understand why my maternal grandmother had left America for Palestine. But the ancestral home I felt closest to was Europe.

My high school years were also a time of ethical and political growth, strands of development that wind in and out of my life of learning. I had come to Kingswood with a strong sense of community service—mostly acquired in years of summer camp—of volunteering with alacrity, of being a good sport. How to put this together with my intense desire to excel, to get the best grades, which made me ever the competitor of, rather than the cooperator with my cohort? I read Ralph Waldo Emerson's "Compensation" at the suggestion of my Religion teacher, and found an approach that undermined strict rankings. "The farmer imagines power and place are fine things, but the President has paid dear for his White House." There are many ways to contribute to society, each to be respected; the important thing is to excel wherever you are placed.

The rankings for which I had no tolerance were those constantly made by the Detroit bourgeoisie, which for me was the Jewish bourgeoisie I met at parties and at the country club. From my isolated perch, I inveighed against their materialism, constant ranking of clothes, automobiles (I refused to learn to drive), and money. I condemned heavy pancake make-up and nose operations with as much vigor as a Renaissance treatise against the hypocrisy and masking at a princely court.

There were options, however. I began to get to know some of the really 10
smart students at Central High, virtually an all-Jewish school, and some of the young people clustered around a Jewish leftist teacher at Wayne University. And in my own house, my father usually voted Democratic and subscribed to *PM*, where I devoured the liberal views of Max Lerner and I. F. Stone. In the fall of my senior year, there was a mock election in my class at Kingswood, and my best friend and I were the two Democrats against 41 Republicans. At the last moment I deserted her and voted for the Socialist Norman Thomas. That spring and summer, all of us were out in the streets of Detroit to mark the end of the war in Europe and then in the Pacific and to wonder at the mushroom cloud that had suddenly entered our lives.

Smith College was an exhilarating place in the years right after World War II. Young women came there from all over the United States and beyond, and a significant number of them were on scholarships. Jews were a minority—maybe ten percent of the freshmen—but still more numerous than at Kingswood, and for the first time there were a few young women of color in my circle. We were activists, the class of 1949, concerned about the rebuilding of Europe, supporting the new United Nations, and creating a lasting peace in the face of the atomic bomb. Even after events began to split us along political lines—the beginnings of the Cold War, the establishment of the Communist regime in Czechoslovakia, HUAC and the Hollywood Ten—hope for the future was not extinguished and friendships remained strong. The mood was in contrast with the silences that fell only a year after we graduated, with the start of the Korean War and the intensification of the Red Hunt.

My psychological and intellectual economy was carried over from my high-school days, but now with some structural differences. I still wanted to be part of the center of the community and also to be its critic, but now the source of the critical spirit came from seeing myself as part of an intellectual elite and from a more fully developed political-ethical vision. Sometimes when I wrote songs for the annual Rally Day shows (a Smith College carnival), I could do both things at the same time. I still felt as if I belonged to two worlds, but now it was not so much being Jewish that created the tension between them, but being part of the political left.

Marxist socialism was a revelation when I heard about it in my freshman year from Judy Mogil, herself fresh from Music and Art High School and all the sophistication of New York City. Here was a solution to the ferocious competition that set one individual against the other, one nation against the other; here was a way to obliterate crass materialism and allow people to enjoy the work they did. I imagined a future where changed structures truly transformed human behavior; "from each according to his ability to each according to his need" (today we'd say his or her) seemed a better slogan than Emerson's Compensation. So along with serving on the college Judicial Board, I joined organizations like the American Youth for Democracy, the Marxist discussion group, and the Young Progressives, not exactly mass movements at Smith. "You're just the kind of person they'd put away," one of my professors said to me, holding up the Stalinist camps as a rebuke to my activities. He was right, of course, I would have been a prisoner if I'd lived in the Soviet Union, but Russia was then a distant and for me unimportant example. America was near, and within the frame of my Utopian idealism, I worked with my comrades on the concrete issues of racism, union rights, and free speech.

The free realm for me, however—the privileged realm—was my studies. English, Russian and French literature: I lived in the *maison française* and we talked excitedly of André Gide and Albert Camus and Jean-Paul Sartre. And especially there was history with my teacher Leona Gabel, a Bryn Mawr PhD of years before, who was editing the *Commentaries* of Pope Pius II and teaching what were then vanguard courses, informed by the scholarship of European emigrés. With the utmost decorum, sometimes even lecturing in a hat, Leona Gabel told us of the wondrous aspirations of Renaissance philosophy, of Pico della Mirandola's observation (which I believed and still believe) that "man" could fall to the level of the beasts, but also rise to the level of the angels; of Machiavelli's hard-boiled politics; and of Luther's courageous call to another path. In seminar, she led us quietly through a comparison of the turbulent English, French, and Russian Revolutions and their dénouement in dictatorship. Now I began to read primary sources, following the French Revolution day by day through *Le Moniteur,* which seemed to me even more fascinating than Marcel Proust's *À la recherche du temps perdu.* Satisfying both political loyalties and scholarly appetite, I chose the most radical possible philosopher for my senior honors thesis: the rational Aristotelian Pietro Pomponazzi, who denied the immortality of the soul and who (interestingly enough for a double-minded person like myself) deflected persecution by a two-truth theory. Marx's thought also offered some big ways to organize the past, a vision quite missing from our courses, and even led me to Giambattista Vico's *New Science,* with its proto-anthropological view of culture. Before I graduated, I also read Marc Bloch's *Strange Defeat* and learned that an historian can be a hero.

Given my interest for the last twenty-five years in the history of women, I ask myself whether I felt any deprivation in my undergraduate days because my Smith College courses virtually never talked about women. I don't recall that I did, and thinking about our attitudes and situation in those years, I understand why. In my circle in the post-war 1940s, we felt we had the same political and intellectual interests as men, and any group of smart men and women with the same political values would see the world in the same way. If I had read Mary Beard's *Women as Force in History* when it came out in 1946, I would have appreciated how she drew on Jacob Burckhardt and others to show women as historical and civilizing actors, but I would have been troubled by her separating them from men, by what I would have seen as historical fragmentation.

And yet, Leona Gabel and the Smith setting were providing us women with some of the sense of difference and support that we needed if we were to survive later as intellectuals and professional women. Whatever the discourse was about Renaissance "man," it came from the lips of a woman, was heard by women's ears, and discussed in a classroom of women. Women could evidently decide what was true. And I suspect we took, and at some level were intended by Miss Gabel to take, the symbols of "man's" potentiality and applied them to ourselves. Somehow we saw our female bodies inscribed inside Leonardo da Vinci's famous circle (immodest though that pose was for a woman) and sensed ourselves as free agents.

In the summer of 1948, at the end of my junior year, my agency was put to the test when I met Chandler Davis. I had gone to Harvard Summer School to study the philosophy of science, and I came across Chan at a meeting of Students for Wallace (the Progressive Party candidate for President). He had been in the Navy V–12 during the war and was now in his second year of graduate work in mathematics at Harvard. He was handsome, smart, on the left, and liked intelligent women. Besides math and science, he was interested in music, poetry, and science fiction, so we had much to talk about. He was also the first radical male student I had met who enjoyed what I considered "normal" activities like tennis and ping-pong. But he was not Jewish: his ancestors were old Massachusetts Unitarians and Pennsylvania Quakers. And he was not rich: his parents were professors and teachers. After three weeks Chandler proposed to me; after six weeks we got married at the Boston City Hall. I was 19; Chan had just turned 22.

Needless to say, this was a scandal. Chandler's family welcomed a Jewish daughter-in-law into their fold; their household was always crowded anyway with Jewish refugees and Jewish leftists. My parents, and especially my mother, were horrified that I should marry a non-Jew. We remained in good touch with my brother, now a student himself at Harvard, and finally with my father, but it was many years before my mother accepted my marriage or even my role as a scholar.

Now such events must be told for a *woman's* life of learning. On the one hand, I embarked on my graduate work without a female cheering section. Even Miss Gabel feared my marriage tolled the knell of my history career, though she never said it right out. Her generation had taken a different path; how could I ever be a scholar if I were traipsing after my husband amid the clutter of children? On the other hand, I had a husband early along, who truly believed in women's careers; and who was genuinely committed to sharing household tasks and parenting. We began a lifelong conversation about politics, history, science, and literature. And now it seemed to me my vocational path was set. I had planned to get a doctorate in history, but was thinking of putting it to work in documentary films. Since Chan was going on to university teaching, I thought, "OK, I'll become a professor instead."

✎ Topics for Critical Thinking and Writing:

1. In "A Life of Learning," Davis attempts to discover the roots of her life as a scholar. What seem to you to be the most important facts or events in her life that predisposed her to that role? What were the earliest?
2. "I belonged to two worlds," Davis writes, and defines what she means first in one way and then in another. What does she mean, each time?
3. "I belonged to two worlds." Write your own memoir, of any time (or times) in your life so far, so that your readers understand what those two worlds were, and what they meant and continue to mean to you.

Eudora Welty

Eudora Welty was born in 1909 in Jackson, Mississippi. Although she earned a bachelor's degree at the University of Wisconsin, and she spent a year studying advertising in New York City at the Columbia University Graduate School of Business, she has lived almost all of her life in Jackson.
In the preface to her Collected Stories *she says:*

> I have been told, both in approval and in accusation, that I seem to love all my characters. What I do in writing of any character is to try to enter into the mind, heart and skin of a human being who is not myself. Whether this happens to be a man or a woman, old or young, with skin black or white, the primary challenge lies in making the jump itself. It is the act of a writer's imagination that I set most high.

In addition to writing stories and novels, Welty has written a book about fiction, The Eye of the Story *(1977), and a memoir,* One Writer's Beginnings *(1984), from which we reprint the following excerpt.*

The Secret

It was when my mother came out onto the sleeping porch to tell me goodnight that her trial came. The sudden silence in the double bed meant my younger brothers had both keeled over in sleep, and I in the single bed at my end of the porch would be lying electrified, waiting for this to be the night when she'd tell me what she'd promised for so long. Just as she bent to kiss me I grabbed her and asked: "Where do babies come from?"

My poor mother! But something saved her every time. Almost any night I put the baby question to her, suddenly, as if the whole outdoors exploded, Professor Holt would start to sing. The Holts lived next door; he taught penmanship (the Palmer Method), typing, bookkeeping and shorthand at the high school. His excitable voice traveled out of their dining-room windows across the two driveways between our houses, and up to our upstairs sleeping porch. His wife, usually so quiet and gentle, was his uncannily spirited accompanist at the piano. "High-ho! Come to the Fair!" he'd sing, unless he sang "Oho ye oho ye, who's bound for the ferry, the briar's in bud and the sun's going down!"

"Dear, this isn't a very good time for you to hear Mother, is it?"

She couldn't get started. As soon as she'd whisper something, Professor Holt galloped into the chorus, "And 'tis but a penny to Twickenham town!" "Isn't that enough?" she'd ask me. She'd told me that the mother and the father had to both *want* the baby. This couldn't be enough. I knew she was not trying to fib to me, for she never did fib, but also I could not help but know she was not really *telling* me. And more than that, I was afraid of what I was going to hear next. This was partly because she wanted to tell me in the dark. I thought *she* might be afraid. In something like childish hopelessness I thought she probably *couldn't* tell, just as she *couldn't* lie.

On the night we came the closest to having it over with, she started to   5
tell me without being asked, and I ruined it by yelling, "Mother, look at
the lightning bugs!"

In those days, the dark was dark. And all the dark out there was filled
with the soft, near lights of lightning bugs. They were everywhere, flashing on the slow, horizontal move, on the upswings, rising and subsiding
in the soundless dark. Lightning bugs signaled and answered back without a stop, from down below all the way to the top of our sycamore tree.
My mother just gave me a businesslike kiss and went on back to Daddy in
their room at the front of the house. Distracted by lightning bugs, I had
missed my chance. The fact is she never did tell me.

I doubt that any child I knew ever was told by her mother any more
than I was about babies. In fact, I doubt that her own mother ever told her
any more than she told me, though there were five brothers who were
born after Mother, one after the other, and she was taking care of babies all
her childhood.

Not being able to bring herself to open that door to reveal its secret,
one of those days, she opened another door.

In my mother's bottom bureau drawer in her bedroom she kept
treasures of hers in boxes, and had given me permission to play with
one of them—a switch of her own chestnut-colored hair, kept in a heavy
bright braid that coiled around like a snake inside a cardboard box. I
hung it from her doorknob and unplaited it; it fell in ripples nearly to
the floor, and it satisfied the Rapunzel in me to comb it out. But one day
I noticed in the same drawer a small white cardboard box such as her
engraved calling cards came in from the printing house. It was tightly
closed, but I opened it, to find to my puzzlement and covetousness two
polished buffalo nickels, embedded in white cotton. I rushed with this
opened box to my mother and asked if I could run out and spend the
nickels.

"No!" she exclaimed in a most passionate way. She seized the box into   10
her own hands. I begged her; somehow I had started to cry. Then she sat
down, drew me to her, and told me that I had had a little brother who had
come before I did, and who had died as a baby before I was born. And
these two nickels that I'd wanted to claim as my find were his. They had
lain on his eyelids, for a purpose untold and unimaginable. "He was a fine
little baby, my first baby, and he shouldn't have died. But he did. It was
because your mother almost died at the same time," she told me. "In looking after me, they too nearly forgot about the little baby."

She'd told me the wrong secret—not how babies could come but how
they could die, how they could be forgotten about.

I wondered in after years: how could my mother have kept those two
coins? Yet how could someone like herself have disposed of them in any
way at all? She suffered from a morbid streak which in all the life of the
family reached out on occasions—the worst occasions—and touched us,

clung around us, making it worse for her; her unbearable moments could find nowhere to go.

The future story writer in the child I was must have taken unconscious note and stored it away then: one secret is liable to be revealed in the place of another that is harder to tell, and the substitute secret when nakedly exposed is often the more appalling.

Perhaps telling me what she did was made easier for my mother by the two secrets, told and still not told, being connected in her deepest feeling, more intimately than anyone ever knew, perhaps even herself. So far as I remember now, this is the only time this baby was ever mentioned in my presence. So far as I can remember, and I've tried, he was never mentioned in the presence of my father, for whom he had been named. I am only certain that my father, who could never bear pain very well, would not have been able to bear it.

It was my father (my mother told me at some later date) who saved   15 her own life, after that baby was born. She had in fact been given up by the doctor, as she had long been unable to take any nourishment. (That was the illness when they'd cut her hair, which formed the switch in the same bureau drawer.) What had struck her was septicemia, in those days nearly always fatal. What my father did was to try champagne.

I once wondered where he, who'd come not very long before from an Ohio farm, had ever heard of such a remedy, such a measure. Or perhaps as far as he was concerned he invented it, out of the strength of desperation. It would have been desperation augmented because champagne couldn't be bought in Jackson. But somehow he knew what to do about that too. He telephoned to Canton, forty miles north, to an Italian orchard grower, Mr. Trolio, told him the necessity, and asked, begged, that he put a bottle of his wine on Number 3, which was due in a few minutes to stop in Canton to "take on water" (my father knew everything about train schedules). My father would be waiting to meet the train in Jackson. Mr. Trolio did—he sent the bottle in a bucket of ice and my father snatched it off the baggage car. He offered my mother a glass of chilled champagne and she drank it and kept it down. She was to live, after all.

Now, her hair was long again, it would reach in a braid down her back, and now I was her child. She hadn't died. And when I came, I hadn't died either. Would she ever? Would I ever? I couldn't face *ever*. I must have rushed into her lap, demanding her like a baby. And she had to put her first-born aside again, for me.

✎ Topics for Critical Thinking and Writing

1. Welty writes "I doubt that any child I knew ever was told by her mother any more than I was about babies." This was probably true for her generation. How true is it of yours?

2. In the biographical note we quote Welty as saying: "What I do in writing of any character is to try to enter into the mind, heart and skin of a human being who is not myself." Here she is doubtless writing about her fiction, but how well does her note apply to her portrait of her mother? In your own words, describe Welty's mother and then explain where in the manuscript you located the evidence.

3. What secret or secrets were there in your family or among your friends? Write an essay, 750 to 1000 words, describing your attempt to have the secret disclosed and your success or failure.

Tobias Wolff

Tobias Wolff was born in Alabama in 1945, but be grew up in the state of Washington. He left high school before graduating, served as an apprentice seaman and as a weight-guesser in a carnival, and then joined the army, where he served four years as a paratrooper. After his discharge from the army, he hired private tutors to enable him to pass the entrance degree to Oxford University. At Oxford be did spectacularly well, graduating with First Class Honors in English. Wolff has written stories, novels, and an autobiography (This Boy's Life); he now teaches writing at Syracuse University.

Powder

Just before Christmas my father took me skiing at Mount Baker. He'd had to fight for the privilege of my company, because my mother was still angry with him for sneaking me into a nightclub during his last visit, to see Thelonius Monk.

He wouldn't give up. He promised, hand on heart, to take good care of me and have me home for dinner on Christmas Eve, and she relented. But as we were checking out of the lodge that morning it began to snow, and in this snow he observed some quality that made it necessary for us to get in one last run. We got in several last runs. He was indifferent to my fretting. Snow whirled around us in bitter, blinding squalls, hissing like sand, and still we skied. As the lift bore us to the peak yet again, my father looked at his watch and said: "Criminey. This'll have to be a fast one."

By now I couldn't see the trail. There was no point in trying. I stuck to him like white on rice and did what he did and somehow made it to the bottom without sailing off a cliff. We returned our skis and my father put chains on the Austin-Healy white I swayed from foot to foot, clapping my mittens and wishing I were home. I could see everything. The green tablecloth, the plates with the holly pattern, the red candles waiting to be lit.

We passed a diner on our way out. "You want some soup?" my father asked. I shook my head. "Buck up," he said. "I'll get you there. Right, doctor?"

I was supposed to say, "Right, doctor," but I didn't say anything.

5

A state trooper waved us down outside the resort. A pair of sawhorses were blocking the road. The trooper came up to our car and bent down to my father's window. His face was bleached by the cold. Snowflakes clung to his eyebrows and to the fur trim of his jacket and cap.

"Don't tell me," my father said.

The trooper told him. The road was closed. It might get cleared, it might not. Storm took everyone by surprise. So much, so fast. Hard to get people moving. Christmas Eve. What can you do?

My father said: "Look. We're talking about four, five inches. I've taken this car through worse than that."

The trooper straightened up, boots creaking. His face was out of sight   10 but I could hear him. "The road is closed."

My father sat with both hands on the wheel, rubbing the wood with his thumbs. He looked at the barricade for a long time. He seemed to be trying to master the idea of it. Then he thanked the trooper, and with a weird, old-maidy show of caution turned the car around. "Your mother will never forgive me for this," he said.

"We should have left before," I said. "Doctor."

He didn't speak to me again until we were in a booth at the diner, waiting for our burgers. "She won't forgive me," he said. "Do you understand? Never."

"I guess," I said, but no guesswork was required; she wouldn't forgive him.

"I can't let that happen." He bent toward me. "I'll tell you what I   15 want. I want us to be all together again. Is that what you want?"

"Yes, sir."

He bumped my chin with his knuckles. "That's all I needed to hear."

When we finished eating he went to the pay phone in the back of the diner, then joined me in the booth again. I figured he'd called my mother, but he didn't give a report. He sipped at his coffee and stared out the window at the empty road. "Come on, come on," he said. A little while later he said, "Come on!" When the trooper's car went past, lights flashing, he got up and dropped some money on the check. "O.K. Vámonos."

The wind had died. The snow was falling straight down, less of it now; lighter. We drove away from the resort, right up to the barricade. "Move it," my father told me. When I looked at him he said, "What are you waiting for?" I got out and dragged one of the sawhorses aside, then put it back after he drove through. He pushed the door open for me. "Now you're an accomplice," he said. "We go down together." He put the car into gear and gave me a look. "Joke, doctor."

"Funny, doctor."   20

Down the first long stretch I watched the road behind us, to see if the trooper was on our tail. The barricade vanished. Then there was nothing but snow: snow on the road, snow kicking up from the chains, snow on the trees, snow in the sky; and our trail in the snow. I faced around and had a shock. The lie of the road behind us had been marked by our own

tracks, but there were no tracks ahead of us. My father was breaking virgin snow between a line of tall trees. He was humming "Stars Fell on
Alabama." I felt snow brush along the floorboards under my feet. To keep
my hands from shaking, I clamped them between my knees.

My father grunted in a thoughtful way and said, "Don't ever try this
yourself."

"I won't."

"That's what you say now, but someday you'll get your license and
then you'll think you can do anything. Only you won't be able to do this.
You need, I don't know—a certain instinct."

"Maybe I have it."   25

"You don't. You have your strong points, but not . . . this. I only mention it, because I don't want you to get the idea this is something just anybody can do. I'm a great driver. That's not a virtue, O.K.? It's just a fact,
and one you should be aware of. Of course you have to give the old heap
some credit, too—there aren't many cars I'd try this with. Listen!"

I listened. I heard the slap of the chains, the stiff, jerky rasps of the
wipers, the purr of the engine. It really did purr. The car was almost new.
My father couldn't afford it, and kept promising to sell it, but here it was.

I said, "Where do you think that policeman went to?"

"Are you warm enough?" He reached over and cranked up the blow-
er. Then he turned off the wipers. We didn't need them. The clouds had
brightened. A few sparse, feathery flakes drifted into our slipstream and
were swept away. We left the trees and entered a broad field of snow that
ran level for a while and then tilted sharply downward. Orange stakes
had been planted at intervals in two parallel lines and my father steered a
course between them, though they were far enough apart to leave considerable doubt in my mind as to where exactly the road lay. He was humming again, doing little scat riffs around the melody.

"O.K. then. What are my strong points?"   30

"Don't get me started," he said. "It'd take all day."

"Oh, right. Name one."

"Easy. You always think ahead."

True. I always thought ahead. I was a boy who kept his clothes on
numbered hangers to insure proper rotation. I bothered my teachers for
homework assignments far ahead of their due dates so I could make up
schedules. I thought ahead, and that was why I knew that there would be
other troopers waiting for us at the end of our ride, if we got there. What I
did not know was that my father would wheedle and plead his way past
them—he didn't sing "O Tannenbaum" but just about—and get me home
for dinner, buying a little more time before my mother decided to make
the split final. I knew we'd get caught; I was resigned to it. And maybe for
this reason I stopped moping and began to enjoy myself.

Why not? This was one for the books. Like being in a speedboat, but   35
better. You can't go downhill in a boat. And it was all ours. And it kept
coming, the laden trees, the unbroken surface of snow, the sudden white

vistas. Here and there I saw hints of the road, ditches, fences, stakes, but not so many that I could have found my way. But then I didn't have to. My father was driving. My father in his 48th year, rumpled, kind, bankrupt of honor, flushed with certainty. He was a great driver. All persuasion, no coercion. Such subtlety at the wheel, such tactful pedalwork. I actually trusted him. And the best was yet to come—the switchbacks and hairpins. Impossible to describe. Except maybe to say this: If you haven't driven fresh powder, you haven't driven.

✎ Topics for Critical Thinking and Writing

1. How would you characterize the father?
2. How does the boy feel about his father?

Countee Cullen

Countee Cullen (1903–46) was born Countee Porter in New York City, raised by his grandmother, and then adopted by the Reverend Frederick A. Cullen, a Methodist minister in Harlem. Cullen received a bachelor's degree from New York University (Phi Beta Kappa) and a master's degree from Harvard. He earned his living as a high school teacher of French, but his literary gifts were recognized in his own day.

Incident
(For Eric Walrond)

Once riding in old Baltimore,
   Heart-filled, head-filled with glee.
I saw a Baltimorean
   Keep looking straight at me.   4

Now I was eight and very small.
   And he was no whit bigger.
And so I smiled, but he poked out
   His tongue, and called me, "Nigger."   8

I saw the whole of Baltimore
   From May until December;
Of all the things that happened there
   That's all that I remember.   12

Topics for Critical Thinking and Writing

1. How would you define an "incident"? A serious occurrence? A minor occurrence, or what? Think about the word, and then think about Cullen's use of it as a title for the event recorded in this poem. Test out one or two other possible titles as a way of helping yourself to see the strengths or weaknesses of Cullen's title.

2. The dedicatee, Eric Walrond (1898–1966), was an African-American essayist and writer of fiction, who in an essay, "On Being Black," had described his experiences of racial prejudice. How does the presence of the dedication bear on our response to Cullen's account of the "incident"?

3. What is the tone of the poem? Indifferent? Angry? Or what? What do you think is the speaker's attitude toward the "incident"? What is your attitude?

4. Ezra Pound, poet and critic, once defined literature as "news that *stays* news." What do you think he meant by this? Do you think that the definition fits Cullen's poem?

7
ALL IN THE FAMILY

Sonia
Joanne Leonard, 1966

Why One's Parents Got Married
R. Chast

Short Views

After a certain age, the more one becomes oneself, the more obvious one's family traits become.
    Marcel Proust

All happy families resemble one another; every unhappy family is unhappy in its own fashion.
    Leo Tolstoy, *Anna Karenina*

On Tuesday, March 31, he and I dined at General Paoli's. A question was started, whether the state of marriage was natural to man. Johnson. "Sir, it is so far from being natural for a man and woman to live in a state of marriage, that we find all the motives which they have for remaining in that connection, and the restraints which civilized society imposes to prevent separation, are hardly sufficient to keep them together." The General said, that in a state of nature a man and woman uniting together would form a strong and constant affection, by the mutual pleasure each would receive; and that the same causes of dissension would not arise between them, as occur between husband and wife in a civilized state. Johnson. "Sir, they would have dissensions enough, though of another kind. One would choose to go a hunting in this wood, the other in that; one would choose to go a fishing in this lake, the other in that; or, perhaps, one would choose to go a hunting, when the other would choose to go a fishing; and so they would part. Besides, Sir, a savage man and a savage woman meet by chance; and when the man sees another woman that pleases him better, he will leave the first."
    James Boswell

Marriage is the best of human statuses and the worst, and it will continue to be. And that is why, though its future in some form or other is as assured as anything can be, this future is as equivocal as its past. The demands that men and women make on marriage will never be fully met; they cannot be.
    Jessie Bernard

A slavish bondage to parents cramps every faculty of the mind; and Mr. Locke very judiciously observes, that "if the mind be curbed and humbled too much in children, if their spirits be abased and broken much by too strict an hand over them, they lose all their vigour and industry." This strict hand may in some degree account for the weakness of women; for girls, from various causes, are more kept down by their parents, in every sense of the word, than boys. The duty expected from them is, like all the duties arbitrarily imposed on women, more from a sense of propriety, more out of respect for decorum, than reason; and thus taught slavishly to submit to their parents, they are prepared for the slavery of marriage. I may be told that a number of women are not slaves in the marriage state. True, but they then become tyrants; for it is not rational freedom, but a lawless kind of power resembling the authority exercised by the favourites of absolute monarchs, which they obtain by debasing means.

Mary Wollstonecraft

Nobody who has not been in the interior of a family can say what the difficulties of any individual of that family may be.

Jane Austen, *Emma*

When I was young enough to still spend a long time buttoning my shoes in the morning, I'd listen toward the hall: Daddy upstairs was shaving in the bathroom and Mother downstairs was frying the bacon. They would begin whistling back and forth to each other up and down the stairwell. My father would whistle his phrase, my mother would try to whistle, then hum hers back. It was their duet. I drew my buttonhook in and out and listened to it—I knew it was "The Merry Widow." The difference was, their song almost floated with laughter: how different from the record, which growled from the beginning, as if the Victrola were only slowly being wound up. They kept it running between them, up and down the stairs where I was now just about ready to run clattering down and show them my shoes.

Eudora Welty

Lewis Coser

Lewis Coser, born in Berlin in 1913, was educated at the Sorbonne in Paris and at Columbia University, where he received a Ph.D. in sociology in .1954. For many years he taught at the State University of New York, Stony Brook, where he held the title Distinguished Professor. The passage given below is from a textbook designed for college students.

The Family

Following the French anthropologist Claude Lévi-Strauss, we can define the family as a group manifesting these characteristics: it finds its origin in marriage; it consists of husband, wife and children born in their wedlock—though other relatives may find their place close to that nuclear group; and the members of the group are united by moral, legal, economic, religious, and social rights and obligations. These include a network of sexual rights and prohibitions and a variety of socially patterned feelings such as love, attraction, piety, awe, and so on.

The family is among the few universal institutions of mankind. No known society lacks small kinship groups of parents and children related through the process of reproduction. But recognition of the universality of this institution must immediately be followed by the acknowledgment that its forms are exceedingly varied. The fact that many family organizations are not monogamic, as in the West, led many nineteenth-century observers to the erroneous conclusion that in "early" stages of evolution there existed no families, and that "group marriage," institutionalized promiscuity, prevailed. This is emphatically not the case; even though patterned wife-lending shocked the sensibilities of Victorian anthropologists, such an institution is evidently predicated on the fact that men have wives in the first place. No matter what their specific forms, families in all known societies have performed major social functions—reproduction, maintenance, socialization, and social placement of the young.

Families may be monogamous or polygamous—there are systems where no man is entitled to several wives and others where several husbands share one wife. A society may recognize primarily the small nuclear, conjugal unit of husband and wife with their immediate descendants or it may institutionalize the large extended family linking several generations and emphasizing consanguinity more than the conjugal bond. Residence after marriage may be matrilocal, patrilocal or neolocal; exchanges of goods and services between families at the time of marriage may be based on bride price, groom price or an equal exchange; endogamous or exogamous regulations may indicate who is and who is not eligible for marriage; the choice of a mate may be controlled by parents or it may be left in large measure to the young persons concerned. These are but a few of the many differences which characterize family structures in variant societies.

 Topics for Critical Thinking and Writing

1. At the end of paragraph 2, Coser writes: "No matter what their specific forms, families in all known societies have performed major social func-tions—reproduction, maintenance, socialization, and social placement of the young." What does "socialization" mean? How does it differ from "social placement of the young"? What specific forms does each take in our soci-ety?

2. What examples can you give of "moral, legal, economic, religious, and social rights and obligations" (paragraph 1) that unite members of a family?

3. Compare Coser and Plumb (pages 6–9) on the social functions of the fami-ly. According to Plumb, what responsibility does the family in our society have in performing the social functions Coser lists? How do other institu-tions compete with the family in performing some of these functions?

4. As you read other selections in this chapter, what variations in form of the family do you encounter? Are there any variations in form that Coser did not mention or anticipate?

William J. Doherty

William J. Doherty is a family therapist and director of the Marriage and Family Programs at the University of Minnesota. We reprint a passage from his book, The Intentional Family *(1997).*

Doherty explains intentional *thus: "An intentional family is one whose members create a working plan for maintaining and building family ties, and then implements the plan as best they can."*

Rituals of Passage: Weddings

Most family rituals occur at home, away from the gaze and judg-ment of the community. No one is around to evaluate the quality of your family dinner or bedtime rituals. But weddings and funerals are planned by the family to share with their community, which is why they are so packed with meaning and stress.

Weddings and funerals have always been public events because they are too important to be left to individuals. We all have a stake in the start of a new family and in the death of a member of the community. But being intentional about these two central family rituals, in the face of communi-ty traditions and pressures, is a major challenge for families.

Weddings

Wedding rituals occur in every human society because marriage in its various forms has enormous social significance. In the Western world, the weddings of royalty and the upper class were always highly ritualized because of their political importance. By the eighteenth century, families of the middle class were also celebrating weddings in a big way. But it wasn't until the nineteenth century in Europe and America that almost all families, rich and poor, began putting substantial time and resources into weddings. It was during this period that what we think of as the "traditional wedding" came into being.

The traditional wedding is American society's classic example of a rite of passage. Anthropologists studying premodern cultures realized that rituals served as transitions from one state of being to another, for example, from childhood to adolescence. (Confirmations and bar mitzvahs serve the same purpose today for Christians and Jews, respectively.) Traditional rites of passage involved a separation from the community, a transitional event, and then reemergence with a new social identity. In other words, you go away, you are transformed, and you return with a new role in the community.[1] Traditional wedding ceremonies in volved all three stages.

Although there are regional, ethnic, and religious variations, the general outline of a traditional American wedding ceremony is as follows: At the outset, the groom stands at the front of the church with his best man, awaiting his bride. Before that, he has been mingling about, whereas the bride is in seclusion getting prepared. Immediate family members are escorted to their assigned places on either side of the aisle. There is a pause. The rite of transition begins in earnest when the music shifts and the bride's party starts walking down the aisle. The first high point of the ritual occurs when the bride appears, resplendent in a white gown, accompanied by her father or other significant man. The couple are reunited at the front when the parents hand her over to her groom. The rite of transition culminates with the couple's exchange of vows in solemn tones in front of a member of the clergy. Sometimes at the end of the service, particularly if the woman has taken the man's family name, the clergyperson introduces the couple to the congregation as Mr. and Mrs. They are now legally and religiously married, with all the accompanying rights and responsibilities, before God and the state. The transformation of identity now complete, the couple walk back down the aisle in more informal fashion to joyous music. The receiving line then initiates the postceremony rituals of congratulations and celebration.

---

[1] Arnold van Gennep was the anthropologist who pioneered the study of rites of passage. See *The Rites of Passage* (Chicago: University of Chicago Press), 1960, originally published in 1909.

However, this traditional wedding ritual is packed with a number of fascinating contradictions:[2]

- *Traditional weddings are public ceremonies that are nevertheless organized by individual families.* Virtually every other public ceremony in our society is organized by clergy, officials, or other professionals. No wonder families feel so much pressure, and why they rely on wedding guides and other "expert" opinions.
- *Weddings follow strict guidelines of propriety, with a personal touch.* Dear Abby and Ann Landers have made a living responding to irate family members and guests who all have complaints about violations of wedding protocol, everything from the invitations to what the bride wore and the lack of thank-you notes. Although there are clear rights and wrongs in traditional weddings, the couple is also expected to put its own stamp on the ritual in details such as the invitations, flowers, cake, music, wedding attire, vows, and order of service. These personal choices must also be "correct," that is, not out of line with community expectations. The double-bind is thus manifest: To be unoriginal is to not measure up, but to be too original is to invite social disapproval.
- *Even couples with little religious affiliation often want religious weddings.* Couples who do not make time for the "sacred" in their daily lives nevertheless frequently want this religious aspect to their weddings. In American society, only religious surroundings make possible the traditional wedding pomp and circumstance of the majestic bridal procession up a long aisle, high-vaulted ceilings, the engulfing organ music, and the sense that something profound and holy is occurring. An office wedding by a justice of the peace carries far less ritual power. The traditional wedding ritual is even more potent if held at the place of one's baptism, bar mitzvah or bat mitzvah, and the weddings and funerals of loved ones. The walls reverberate with family memories.
- *Traditional religious weddings combine the sense of the sacred and the sexual, elements that are rarely connected in society.* In all cultures and all religions, the sexual bond is what makes marriage unique. Sexual themes, therefore, pervade the wedding ritual, from the presumed virginity of the bride in her white gown and the readings from the erotic Song of Songs in the Bible to the expectation that the bride and groom will exchange a lover's kiss. The couple is expected to consummate their union on the wedding night. Traditional religious rituals also refer to the outcome of their sexual activity—children, the continuity of the family, and the community. Failure to

10

---

[2]See Diana Leonard Barker, "A Proper Wedding," in Marie Corbin (ed.), *The Couple* (New York: Penguin Books), 1978, pp. 56–77; and Diane Leonard Barker, *Sex and Generation: A Study of Courtship and Wedding* (New York: Tavistock Publications), 1980.

consummate the marriage is in fact grounds for annulment in most religions. This combination of the sacred and the sexual gives weddings special power in our consciousness.

- *The couple are elevated and celebrated by the community, but also teased and embarrassed.* After honoring the bride and groom with gifts and special attention, guests at the traditional wedding reception expect the couple to submit to embarrassing, silly rituals such as feeding each other cake, dancing on command, having people pay to dance with them, removing and tossing a garter belt, having to kiss whenever the guests tinkle their glasses, and enduring practical jokes as they prepare to leave for their honeymoon. The same kinds of rituals occur in many other cultures; in Hindu weddings, for example, the couple is required to play various games for the benefit of the guests. It is as if the community wants to remind the couple not to feel above those who know and love them the best.
- *Weddings in contemporary society are expected to bring a man and woman together as equal partners in marriage, but the traditional ceremony suggests an imbalance.* The bride's white dress is the key symbol. The white color symbolizes youth and virginity, two elements not regarded as important for the groom. She purchases her dress, often at considerable expense, and is expected to keep it. The groom generally rents his tuxedo unless he happens to own one. The bride is the object of much more attention than the groom before, during, and after the ceremony. In the traditional ceremony, she is given away by her family; no one gives him away. In the past, she received a ring; he did not. In many cases, she still changes her family name to his. All of these elements make it clear that the change in identity is more significant for the woman than for the man, implying that her status in the world will be dependent on his. Although most contemporary couples aspire to equality in marriage, they enthusiastically go through a ritual that emphasizes the woman's inequality.[3]
- *Traditionally only first marriages are allowed the full ritual.* Actually, the key is the bride's prior marriages, not the groom's. A woman supposedly only has the right to wear white once. After that, she is expected to be more discreet about what she wears—she is clearly no longer a virgin—and what she expects in the way of attention and gifts. If the man has been married three times before but the woman has never been married, they are still eligible to have a traditional wedding—another clear illustration of how a wedding is thought to change a woman's identity more than a man's. But Intentional Couples today sometimes ignore these strictures for second marriages and have all the bells and whistles at their wedding. I

[3]*Ibid.*, p. 71.

know one woman who had eloped for her first wedding and decided to do make the second one a grand production. It was her
groom's first marriage and he was all for it.

✎ Topics for Critical Thinking and Writing

1. In these pages, Doherty lists what he calls the "fascinating contradictions" of
   the traditional wedding ritual. What are the contradictions? Were you
   aware that these contradictions existed? Which of them strikes you as most
   interesting?
2. If you have been married, how many of the contradictions that Doherty lists
   did your wedding ritual include? If you expect (sometime) to be married,
   how traditional do you want your wedding to be?
3. In an essay of about 750 words, report a wedding that you have attended.
   Comment on the contradictions—or lack of contradictions—that you
   observed and remember.

Gabrielle Glaser

Gabrielle Glaser is the author of a recent book, Strangers to the Tribe: Portraits of Interfaith Marriage *(1997). We reprint an essay that was originally published in* The New York Times Magazine
in 1997.

Scenes from an Intermarriage

As Alfred and Eileen Ono sit down late one evening to discuss their
family's religious life, even the seating arrangement seems to reveal their
spiritual divide. On one side of their sumptuous living room in Portland,
Ore., Eileen settles into a comfortable wing chair. Al is across from her, on
the couch, next to their 22-year-old daughter, Sarah. From time to time
during the conversation, father and daughter link hands.

Sarah and her 18-year-old brother, Alistair, a college freshman, have
been raised in the Buddhist faith of their Japanese-American father.
Eileen, a Middle Westerner with Dutch, Lithuanian and German roots, has
remained a Catholic. The Onos decided how to raise the children long ago,
even before they were married, and Eileen insists that her solitary spiritu-
ality is of little import. But the religious differences in this family, in which
both children shave their heads in the style of Buddhist monks and nuns,
exert a gravitational pull on each relationship—between the parents and
the children, between the siblings and between husband and wife.

Perhaps surprisingly, it is Eileen who is most relaxed about the family's
complicated spiritual life. Over the years, her husband has become more
doctrinaire. When Sarah was in her early teens and interested in Catholi-

cism, for example, Al insisted that she continue to attend temple every Sunday. Then, in college, when she dated a devout Irish Catholic and began going to Mass with him, Al expressed his disappointment outright.

The Onos say that they try to live up to the ideal of tolerance in all matters. But it isn't any easier for them than it is for the other 33 million Americans who live in interfaith households. The United States, founded by religious dissidents and shaped by a Christian revival in the 19th century, has evolved into a rich religious pluralism. As racial and ethnic barriers have become hazier, intermarriage has become more common: according to recent surveys, 52 percent of Jews, 32 percent of Catholics and 57 percent of Buddhists marry outside the faith.

Many couples split their religious differences in the interest of family harmony, but the Onos' choice not to is evident the moment you enter their splendid turn-of-the-century home. A gold Japanese panel rests on the living room mantel, and in the library sits a black lacquer *obutsudan,* or Buddhist shrine, where Alistair, Sarah and Al recite chants over prayer beads. The three practice Jodoshinshu, a form of Japanese Buddhism, although in recent years Sarah has also included elements of Tibetan Buddhism. (Alistair refers teasingly to Sarah's interest in Tibetan Buddhism as an "upper-middle-class white thing.")

Al, a gentle man with thick gray hair and a kind but intense face, speaks in the drawn-out vowels of his native Minnesota. His parents, George and Masaye, were born in California; their marriage was arranged by a matchmaker. They later settled in St. Louis Park, and helped to found the state's first Buddhist temple. Growing up, Al flourished there and relished the simple truths of his faith: There is suffering. There is a cause for suffering. Suffering can be overcome by thinking and living in the right way. His Buddhism, which he describes as "logical and linear," built on wisdom, knowledge, truth and compassion, filters into all aspects of his life: as a doctor—he has a thriving OB-GYN practice in Portland—a father and a husband. "When patients come to me and say, 'Oh, my God, it's cancer, I should have come to you sooner,'" Al says, "I say: 'This is not because you've done anything wrong or because you missed your last appointment. Don't blame yourself. Bodies are always changing. Now it's time to put it back on track.'"

Eileen, on the other hand, has always had questions about her faith. A plain-spoken woman with pale, luminous skin and large, hazel eyes, she was raised in a Minnesota farming town where about half the population was Catholic. As a child, she liked the music and pageantry the church offered, but some things didn't make sense to her. "I'd go to confession and have to make up sins," she says. "I just hadn't done anything horrible." By the time she married, Eileen had also begun to find much of church doctrine—on birth control and the role of women, for example—outdated. Still, she considers herself Catholic. "It's how I was brought up, and it's in my soul," she says.

From time to time, she has second thoughts about the choice she made 27 years ago to raise children in a religion not her own. "I sometimes wish we could be all the same thing," she says softly. "Sure, I do." Sometimes an "Our Father" or "Hail, Mary" will cross her lips before she falls asleep, or when she learns that someone has died. But she rarely goes to church, and like the crossword puzzles she does on Sunday mornings when the rest of her family is at temple, or the meticulous squares of fabric she sews together in her award-winning quilts, Eileen's faith lies apart, boxed and separate, from the rest of her family. "I'm happy with how my spiritual life is," she says. She pauses, then adds, "It's others who have a problem with it."

Those others included her relatives, at least at first. When Al and Eileen began dating in the late 1960's as students at the University of Minnesota, their parents couldn't believe the relationship was serious. When Al told his parents of the couple's plans to marry, his parents accepted the announcement with grim resignation. Eileen's parents reacted with similar reticence.

The wedding was to take place in Minneapolis, and the closest English-speaking Buddhist clergyman lived hundreds of miles away, in Chicago, so the couple settled on a Catholic priest. They were married in a campus chapel, amid burlap banners reading "Peace" and "Love." Led by the priest, they recited Buddhist wedding vows, emphasizing not love or miracles but truth, honor and respect.   10

Yet the occasion did not flow as smoothly as they had hoped. Eileen's father, an Army veteran, had been stationed in the Philippines during World War II, and after the surrender had hunted the country for Japanese deserters. After several glasses of Champagne at the reception, he approached George Ono's best friend with a powerful slap on the back. "Whoever would have guessed that my daughter would be marrying a Jap 25 years after I was over there shooting at them?" he declared. Eileen and Al stared at each other in disbelief. "We'd been so worried about the religious aspects of the wedding that we had overlooked the racial ones," Eileen says. "Our families had always been very cordial to each other." There were other not-so-subtle messages. As a gift, an aunt gave them a plaster statue of Christ, engraved with their names and wedding date.

The couple moved to Portland, and a few years after Sarah's birth the family started going to the Oregon Buddhist Temple there. But at first it was Eileen who took the children to and from services—while Al, caught up in building his medical practice, rarely went. Over time, she began to feel a resistance to being so involved and told Al that he would have to take the lead. "I don't care if you're in the middle of a delivery, you're going to have to be the point man on this," she finally said to him. When Al started going, she stopped.

Sometimes during the ride to temple an image would flash through his head. Of all things, he envisioned a Norman Rockwell painting he once saw, of a family driving off to church, all together. He would dismiss the picture by reminding himself: "But she's not Japanese! She doesn't even relate to this stuff. This was the agreement."

These days, Eileen attends temple occasionally and has incorporated Buddhist thought into her life as a *hakujin,* or white person, as she jokingly calls herself. Indeed, the flies she once swatted are now gently shooed outdoors, in keeping with the Buddhist belief that all forms of life deserve dignity and respect. "They get several chances," she says with a smile. But she has retained a few of her rituals, and Christmas is one of them. The family chooses a tree together, and on Dec. 24 Al and Sarah attend midnight Mass—because they like the music. Eileen doesn't go. "I'm not practicing Catholicism, so I don't feel good just going to church for the highlights," she says, "but I do encourage them to go." The next morning, the whole family opens presents together.

Al says that Christ embodied the wisdom and compassion to which   15
Buddhists aspire, so honoring his birthday has never been an issue. Even so, the holiday Eileen loved as a child, and dreamed of sharing someday with her children, is a bit of a compromise. But religious differences can't take all of the blame: Dec. 25 is also Alistair's birthday, and at noon the day turns from celebrating Christ's arrival to celebrating Alistair's.

Other holidays follow Japanese tradition. For New Year's, Al spends days preparing a feast of special rice cakes and sashimi, and the family toasts one another with sake. "It's never been, 'Well, if you get sushi, tomorrow we have to have schnitzel,'" Eileen says. "I never denied my heritage. It just wasn't a big deal."

Her children's upbringing was a world away from memorizing catechism lessons. Sarah and Alistair spent Sundays at dharma school, learning to chant and meditate. At home, they drank green tea and, as toddlers, learned to use chopsticks. (So accustomed was the family to eating rice at every meal that Alistair thought mashed potatoes were a delicacy. "I thought there was a religious meaning to having them at Thanksgiving," he says with a grin. "That's the only time we ever had them.")

Yet growing up Buddhist in Portland wasn't easy. Children taunted Sarah and Alistair on the playground. In his advanced-placement English class, Alistair once suggested that perhaps not everyone was able to recognize Biblical allusions in literature. The teacher replied, "If you don't know the story of Moses, you don't belong here."

Sarah, a recent graduate of Connecticut College, is back at home doing part-time work while she looks for a job. As a child, she could see only what her religion didn't offer her. "Buddhism didn't have any perks," she says. "Until high school, it was weird. There's no Buddhist rite of passage. My Jewish friends got bas mitzvahs, my Catholic friends got big parties at their first Communion. When you're " or 10, you don't want to be anything but what your friends are." So she "tried out" Catholicism and at night would drop to her knees, hands clasped together, and pray at her bedside. She thought it might be easier to "talk to God" than to sit in silent meditation and clear her head of all thoughts. She even attended Catholic summer camp. Her friends taught her prayers, walked her through the steps of Mass, including Communion. She wanted, she says, "to pass," and told people that her mother was Catholic. When a counselor found out that Sarah had taken Communion without being Catholic, she scolded her. Sarah was mortified.

In time, Sarah, a small woman with delicate Asian features, made [20] peace with Buddhism. She studied in Asia for several months and welcomed living in a Buddhist society. Her faith, she says, has taught her one true thing: "to focus on the present."

In some ways, Eileen and Al's decision to raise their children as Buddhists was reinforced by society at large. Because of their Japanese surname and their tea-with-cream-colored skin, both Alistair and Sarah say that they found themselves identifying more readily with their Asian roots than their European ones. Alistair in particular has immersed himself in Japanese culture and credits the dynamic young minister at the Portland temple with inspiring his deeper involvement in Buddhism. At a special ceremony last spring, he received his Buddhist name, a great honor. Days later, he had the name, Gu-Sen—"widespread proclamation"—tattooed in Japanese on his lower back.

Yet guilt also lurks behind Alistair's enthusiasm for his father's faith and heritage. He half-facetiously calls himself a "mama's boy," and frequently E-mails Eileen from college; he worries that he has neglected her in some way. When a high-school history teacher gave out an assignment to research family trees, Alistair filled out the Ono branches practically by heart. When he asked his mother for help with her side, she pulled out photo albums and scrapbooks and recounted details of little-known relatives. "I had never asked about them before," he says. "I felt kind of bad."

Al, too, wonders quietly if he has inadvertently dampened his wife's religious life or her ties to her culture. They don't talk about it much; Al shies from confrontation. But he does remember that on a trip to Ireland some years ago they stumbled one afternoon into a stone church in the middle of Mass. Al turned to Eileen and asked, "Do you want to take Communion?" She brushed him off, he says, by saying she couldn't, since she hadn't been to confession in years. "Was it that she didn't want to be bothered?" he wonders. "Or was it just too complicated with me there, and she didn't want to mess with it?"

What may become of the religious divide between Al and Eileen now, with both children grown, is hard to say. Their marriage is a solid one. They take trips together, go to movies, make elaborate meals, enjoy their children. As middle age gives way to senior discounts, however, the Onos are likely to have disquieting moments. For them, death poses yet another separation. "I don't necessarily believe that God will forgive all at the last minute," Eileen says. "But I do think our spirits go somewhere." Al shakes his head gently. "I'm not so sure there's any connection between this life and another one. The Buddhist perspective doesn't believe we'll all be together again somewhere. I kid Eileen sometimes, telling her: 'Gee, Eileen, if you get last rites, you'll go to heaven. We'll all go to hell, so we'll still be in different places.'"

✎ Topics for Critical Thinking and Writing

1. Glaser writes of the Ono family's "complicated spiritual life" (paragraph 3). What are the complications, and what produces them?
2. Glaser casts her first paragraph in the present tense. What advantage does this focus give her?
3. Think of an intermarriage with which you are acquainted, in your family or among your friends. Then jot down a list of "scenes" that represent it; for example, religious services, holidays, weddings, funerals. Would you label the intermarriage "complicated"?
4. In an essay of 750 to 1000 words, write your own "Scenes from an Intermarriage" through which you reveal its ease, or strains, or both.

Florence Trefethen

Florence Trefethen holds degrees from Bryn Mawr and the University of Cambridge. She has taught English at Tufts University and was for many years executive editor for books published by the Council on East Asian Studies at Harvard University. Her poems and short stories appear frequently.

This essay was originally published in the Washington Post.

Points of a Lifelong Triangle
Reflections of an Adoptive Mother

I have a friend who's a social worker. Her clients include a group of women who've given up a child for adoption. Their ages range widely, and the moment of surrender may have been long ago or last year. They form a birth mothers' support group.

My friend says their meetings are suffused with sorrow, sometimes bitterness. They describe their lost children and the new parents as ambling through life happily, selfishly, and with never a thought for the origins left behind. As an adoptive mother, I find that picture distorted.

I think of the biological father rarely, envisioning him as the dashing young fellow he must have been at the time he sired our daughter. But scarcely a day goes by when the birth mother is not in my thoughts, growing older as I do.

She's been with me from the start. When Gwyned was placed with us on probation, there was always the threat that the birth mother might change her mind and snatch our baby back. She loomed as a fearsome adversary. I pictured her wild-eyed, manic, appearing in the courtroom a moment before the final decree, shouting, "She's mine, and her name is Monica!" Our papers were approved, however, without incident.

Those papers contain my signature and my husband's. The birth parents' signatures were folded under so that we never learned their names. The papers are dated Dec. 30, 1953, and are locked away in a Maryland court house, apparently inviolate. We received a "birth certificate" proclaiming that Gwyned was born to me and my husband on May 8, 1953, in Garfield Memorial Hospital, Washington, D.C. 5

What is a birthday like for an adopted daughter who's 1 or 4 or 10 or 16 or all the years between and after? Just like birthdays for other children—parties, presents, friends and family gathered to celebrate. But for me there was always a special poignancy when lighting the candles on the cake. I, the mother in residence, would think of that first mother, wondering where she was, knowing she was remembering the day. I wanted to call out to her and say, "Look how delightful Gwyned is! Thank you." My hands always shook as I carried the cake to the table, trying not to quaver as I started singing "Happy Birthday."

Gwyned didn't seem to care. She grew up in a neighborhood and attended a school where there were several adopted children. No big deal, she said. In fact, she implied that there was a special cachet to being "selected." Though she knew better, I think she fantasized about our walking down an aisle lined with bassinets until we came to her and said, "That's the one!"

When Gwyned acquired a figure, it turned out to be more svelte than the figures in my family; I imagined the birth mother trim in bikinis, mini skirts and other fashions I avoided. Gwyned took to singing in choruses, acting in plays; the birth mother became the repository of performing talents I'd never possessed. Gwyned liked skiing and running and in college elected "self defense" in gym; the birth mother assumed the dimensions of a sportswoman, perhaps Olympics material.

With the approach of Gwyned's wedding, I grew restless, then frantic. Ought we try to contact that birth mother, to assure her everything had turned out well, possibly to invite her to the marriage? I struggled with these questions through sleepless nights and finally consulted a psychiatrist. He offered a common-sense suggestion I wish I'd thought of in my anxiety: "Why don't you ask Gwyned?" I did. She said she'd just as soon leave things as they were. She spoke as though that issue was closed. But later in life she changed her mind. After giving birth to her own children, she began to wonder about physical traits and medical histories.

At the same time, large-scale changes were in motion. Mothers were locating long-lost children; adult adoptees were searching for parents, combing registers, placing ads; associations were established to facilitate these investigations and, it was hoped, ultimate reunions. Some agencies and some states offered help to the searchers. Others clung to the conditions in force at the time of adoption—usually an unbreachable barrier between birth parents and adoptive parents. 10

"Can't I get the name of at least one of my parents?" Gwyned asked. "With a name, I could search." She presented herself at the adoption agency; they declined to reveal that information. She petitioned the court and had a hearing before the judge; he said he did not want "to disturb the birth mother." In the hope that our support might be useful, my husband and I wrote to both agency and judge, to no avail.

It's difficult to sort out the rights and wrongs in a case like this. Gwyned feels compelled to close a loop that's been open all her life. She gets encouragement from support groups but also pain, since they usually include happy birth mothers and adult adoptees who have found each other. My heart aches as I observe her thus far futile efforts to pinpoint anyone who can help her, any clue that might lead to success. Sometimes I feel guilty for having failed, in the initial wonder of acquiring a marvelous child, to anticipate that the secrecy then imposed might one day frustrate us all.

Yet we can understand the adamance of the adoption agency and the court. They are simply adhering to the rules in force nearly four decades ago when the decree became final. They were parties to a contract and are loath to break it. Perhaps they may even feel they are sparing us grief. Indeed, the birth mother, if located, might not wish to be disturbed, might reject Gwyned. Or she could prove to be a disappointment.

I doubt it, though. She's been in my mind and my mind's eye for 37 years, and I'm convinced she's a sad but lovely lady. Whatever her name, and whether or not we ever find her, she, Gwyned and I are the points of a triangle that will endure all our lives.

✎ Topics for Critical Thinking and Writing

1. Do you agree with the decisions made by the adoption agency and the judge? Why or why not? Do you know of any instances of reunions between the birth parent and a child? If so, how do they influence your opinion about the advisability of agencies and courts facilitating such reunions?

2. The father is mentioned only briefly, in the first sentence of the third paragraph, and to our knowledge is rarely the parent sought by adopted children. Nor do we hear or read of adopted sons seeking their birth parents. What do you make of this phenomenon? Or do you know of exceptions to our generalizations?

3. The essay is about a controversial point—should agencies and courts reveal the names of birth parents to the children whom they surrendered? But it is also about Gwyned, about the birth mother, and about the author. How would you characterize the author? What do you think the author's purposes in writing the essay were?

4. Consider the title (including the subtitle) and the opening and the concluding paragraphs. What does the title lead you to expect? What does the first paragraph suggest about birth mothers and the author's attitude toward them? How does the concluding paragraph change or enrich your reading (or rereading) of the title and the first paragraph?

5. Imagine that you are one of Gwyned's birth parents—since you are imagining, you can choose either gender—and you have happened on this article.

What do you imagine you would feel or would do? Write a letter (but don't, of course, mail it) to Florence or Gwyned Trefethen, or to the editor of *The Washington Post* (you can ask to have your name withheld), explaining what you feel and what you plan or do not plan to do.

Anonymous

The anonymous author of this essay has revealed only that he was forty when he wrote it, is married, and is the father of three children. The essay originally appeared in The New Republic, *a magazine regarded by some as liberal.*

Confessions of an Erstwhile Child

Some years ago I attempted to introduce a class of Upward Bound students to political theory via More's *Utopia*. It was a mistake: I taught precious little theory and earned More a class full of undying enemies on account of two of his ideas. The first, that all members of a Utopian family were subject to the lifelong authority of its eldest male. The second, the Utopian provision that should a child wish to follow a profession different from that of his family, he could be transferred by adoption to a family that practiced the desired trade. My students were not impressed with my claim that the one provision softened the other and made for a fair compromise—for what causes most of our quarrels with our parents but our choice of life-patterns, of occupation? In objecting to the first provision my students were picturing themselves as children, subject to an unyielding authority. But on the second provision they surprised me by taking the parents' role and arguing that this form of ad lib adoption denied them a fundamental right of ownership over their children. It occurred to me that these reactions were two parts of the same pathology: having suffered the discipline of unreasonable parents, one has earned the right to be unreasonable in turn to one's children. The phenomenon has well-known parallels, such as frantic martinets who have risen from the ranks. Having served time as property, my Upward Bound students wanted theirs back as proprietors. I shuddered. It hardly takes an advanced course in Freudian psychology to realize that the perpetuation, generation after generation, of psychic lesions must go right to this source, the philosophically dubious notion that children are the property of their biological parents, compounded with the unphilosophic certitude so many parents harbor, that their children must serve an apprenticeship as like their own as they can manage.

The idea of the child as property has always bothered me, for personal reasons I shall outline. I lack the feeling that I own my children and I have always scoffed at the idea that what they are and do is a continuation or a rejection of my being. I like them, I sympathize with them, I acknowledge the obligation to support them for a term of years—but I am not so fond or foolish as to regard a biological tie as a lien on their loyalty or respect, nor to imagine that I am equipped with preternatural powers of guidance as to their success and happiness. Beyond inculcating some of the obvious social protocols required in civilized life, who am I to pronounce on what makes for a happy or successful life? How many of us can say that we have successfully managed our own lives? Can we do better with our children? I am unimpressed, to say no more, with parents who have no great track record, presuming to oracular powers in regard to their children's lives.

The current debate over the Equal Rights Amendment frequently turns to custody questions. Opponents of ERA have made the horrifying discovery that ERA will spell the end of the mother's presumed rights of custody in divorce or separation cases, and that fathers may begin custody rights. Indeed a few odd cases have been so settled recently in anticipation of the ratification of ERA. If ratified, ERA would be an extremely blunt instrument for calling the whole idea of custody into question, but I for one will applaud anything that serves to begin debate. As important as equal rights between adults may be, I think that the rights of children are a far more serious and unattended need. To me, custody by natural parents, far from being a presumed right only re-examined in case of collapsing marriages, should be viewed as a privilege.

At this point I have to explain why I can so calmly contemplate the denial of so-called parental rights.

I am the only child of two harsh and combative personalities who   5
married, seemingly, in order to have a sparring partner always at hand. My parents have had no other consistent or lasting aim in life but to win out over each other in a contest of wills. They still live, vigorous and angry septuagenarians, their ferocity little blunted by age or human respect. My earliest memories—almost my sole memories—are of unending combat, in which I was sometimes an appalled spectator, more often a hopeless negotiator in a war of no quarter, and most often a bystander accused of covert belligerency on behalf of one side or the other, and frequently of both! I grew up with two supposed adults who were absorbed in their hatreds and recriminations to the exclusion of almost all other reality. Not only did I pass by almost unnoticed in their struggle, the Depression and World War II passed them by equally unnoticed. I figured mainly as a practice target for sarcasm and invective, and occasionally as the ultimate culprit responsible for their unhappiness. ("If it weren't for you," my mother would sometimes say, "I could leave that SOB," a remark belied by her refusal to leave the SOB during these 20 long years since I left their "shelter.")

The reader may ask, "How did you survive if your parents' house was all that bad?" I have three answers. First, I survived by the moral equivalent of running away to sea or the circus, i.e., by burying myself in books and study, especially in the history of faraway and (I thought) more idealistic times than our own, and by consciously shaping my life and tastes to be as different as possible from those of my parents (this was a reproach to them, they knew, and it formed the basis of a whole secondary area of conflict and misunderstanding). Second, I survived because statistically most people "survive" horrible families, but survival can be a qualified term, as it is in my case by a permanently impaired digestive system and an unnatural sensitivity to raised voices. And third, though I found solace in schooling and the rationality, cooperation and basic fairness in teachers that I missed in my parents, I must now question whether it is healthy for a child to count so heavily on schooling for the love and approval that he deserves from his home and family. Even if schooling can do this well, in later life it means that one is loyal and affectionate toward schooling, not toward parents, who may in some sense need affection even if they don't "deserve" it. I am not unaware that however fair and rational I may be in reaction to my parents' counter-examples, I am a very cold-hearted man. I might have done better transferred to a new family, not just by receiving love, but through learning to give it—a lack I mourn as much or more than my failure to receive.

It is little wonder then that I have an acquired immunity to the notion that parental custody is by and large a preferable thing. In my case, almost anything else would have been preferable, including even a rather callously run orphanage—anything for a little peace and quiet. Some people are simply unfit, under any conditions, to be parents, even if, indeed especially if, they maintain the charade of a viable marriage. My parents had no moral right to custody of children, and I cannot believe that my experience is unique or particularly isolated. There are all too many such marriages, in which some form of horror, congenial enough to adults too sick or crazed to recognize it, works its daily ruination on children. Surely thousands of children conclude at age 10 or 11, as I did, that marriage is simply an institution in which people are free to be as beastly as they have a mind to, which may lead either to a rejection of marriage or to a decision to reduplicate a sick marriage a second time, with another generation of victims. It is time to consider the rights of the victims.

How to implement a nascent theory of justice for children is difficult to say. One cannot imagine taking the word of a five-year-old against his parents, but what about a ten- or twelve-year-old? At *some* point, children should have the right to escape the dominance of impossible parents. The matter used to be easier than it has been since World War I. The time-honored solution—for boys—of running away from home has been made infeasible by economic conditions, fingerprints, social security and minimum wage laws. No apprenticeship system exists any more, much less its upper-class medieval version—with required exchange of boys at puberty among noble families to serve as pages and so forth. The adoption system contemplated in More's *Utopia* is a half-remembered echo of a medieval life, in which society, wiser than its theory, decreed a general exchange of children at or just before puberty, whether through apprenticeship or page-service, or more informal arrangements, like going to a university at 14 or running away with troubadors or gypsies.

Exchanging children is a wisely conceived safety valve against a too traumatic involvement between the biological parent and the child. Children need an alternative to living all their formative life in the same biological unit. They should have the right to petition for release from some sorts of families, to join other families, or to engage in other sorts of relationships that may provide equivalent service but may not be organized as a family. The nuclear family, after all, is not such an old or proven vehicle. Phillippe Aries' book, *Centuries of Childhood,* made the important point that the idea of helpless childhood is itself a notion of recent origin, that grew up simultaneously in the 16th and 17th centuries with the small and tight-knit nuclear family, sealed off from the world by another recent invention, "privacy." The older *extended* family (which is the kind More knew about) was probably more authoritarian on paper but much less productive of dependency in actual operation. There ought to be more than one way a youngster can enter adult society with more than half of his sanity left. At least no one should be forced to remain in a no-win game against a couple of crazy parents for 15–18 years. At 10 or 12, children in really messy situations should have the legal right to petition for removal from impossible families, and those rights should be reasonably easy to exercise. (This goes on de facto among the poor, of course, but it is not legal, and usually carries both stigma and danger.) The minimum wage laws should be modified to exempt such persons, especially if they wish to continue their education, working perhaps for public agencies, if they have no other means of support. If their parents can support them, then the equivalent of child support should be charged them to maintain their children, not in luxury, but adequately. Adoption of older children should be facilitated by easing of legal procedures (designed mainly to govern the adoption of *infants*) plus tax advantages for those willing to adopt older children on grounds of goodwill. Indeed children wishing to escape impossible family situations should be allowed a fair degree of initiative in finding and negotiating with possible future families.

Obviously the risk of rackets would be very high unless the exact terms of such provisions were framed very carefully, but the possibility of rackets is less frightening to anyone who thinks about it for long than the dangers of the present situation, which are evident and unrelieved by any signs of improvement. In barely a century this country has changed from a relatively loose society in which Huckleberry Finns were not uncommon, to a society of tense, airless nuclear families in which unhealthy and neurotic tendencies, once spawned in a family, tend to repeat themselves at a magnifying and accelerating rate. We may soon gain the distinction of being the only nation on earth to need not just medicare but "psychi-care." We have invested far too heavily in the unproved "equity" called the nuclear family; that stock is about to crash and we ought to begin finding escape options. In colonial days many New England colonies passed laws imposing fines or extra taxes on parents who kept their children under their own roofs after age 15 or 16, on the sensible notion that a person of that age ought to be out and doing on his own, whether going to Yale or apprenticing in a foundry. Even without the benefit of Freud, the colonial fathers had a good sense of what was wrong with a closely bound and centripetal family structure—it concentrates craziness like compound interest, and so they hit it with monetary penalties, a proper Protestant response, intolerant at once of both mystery and excuses. But this was the last gasp of a medieval and fundamentally Catholic idea that children, God help them, while they may be the children of *these* particular parents biologically, spiritually are the children of God, and more appositely are the children of the entire community, for which the entire community takes responsibility. The unguessed secret of the middle ages was not that monasteries relieved parents of unwanted children; more frequently, they relieved children of unwanted parents!

✎ Topics for Critical Thinking and Writing

1. What is the author's thesis? (Quote the thesis sentence.) Apart from his own experience, what evidence or other means does he offer to persuade you to accept his thesis?
2. What part does the *tone* of his article play in persuading you to agree with him or in alienating you? Does his tone strike you, perhaps, as vigorous or belligerent, as ironic or bitter, as reasonable or hysterical?
3. The author admits (paragraph 6) that he is "a very cold-hearted man." Do you remember your initial reaction to that sentence? What was it? Overall, does the author strengthen or jeopardize his argument by this admission? Explain.
4. If you did not find the article persuasive, did you find it interesting? Can you explain why?

Julie Matthaei

Julie Matthaei teaches economics at Wellesley College and is active with the Economic Literacy Project of Women for Economic Justice of Boston. She is the author of An Economic History of Women in America *and is working on a book entitled* Beyond Sex and Blood: Economy, Family, and the Breakdown of the "Natural" Family.

Political Economy and Family Policy

Our current, "natural" family system, based on biological similarities and differences, is in crisis. Not only are its institutions breaking down, they are also under attack as unjust, unequal, and unfree. The "natural" family system needs to be replaced by a consciously social family system; this means socializing parenting costs and pursuing policies which attack the sexual division of Labor and better integrate economic and family life.

The family plays a central role in the distribution of income and wealth in our society, reproducing class, race, and gender inequalities. This paper will 1) present a radical and feminist analysis of the "traditional" family system, 2) discuss the recent breakdown of this system, 3) present a radical and feminist critique of the traditional family system, and 4) indicate social policies which would build a family system more consistent with the principles of equality, freedom, and social justice.

The "Natural" Family

The development of capitalism and wage labor in the nineteenth-century U.S. brought with it new familial institutions. The family continued to be patriarchal—ruled by the husband/father—but was less defined by and involved in commodity production, either as a family firm, or as a family enslaved to producing for others. The family emerged as an increasingly personal and feminine sphere, physically separate and distinct from the competitive and masculine economy (Matthaei 1982). Since, in the nineteenth century, "scientific" explanations of social life were replacing the former religious ones, the new familial institutions were viewed as "natural," and stress was placed on their determination by biological similarities and differences. This "natural,"[1] family system has three, interconnected parts:

1. *"Natural" Marriage.* Marriage is seen as a union of naturally different and complementary beings: men/males and women/females (biological sex and social gender are equated). Men and women are believed to be instinctually heterosexual; those who form homosexual liaisons are viewed as unnatural and perverted.[2] Men are seen as natural bread-winners, competing in the economy, and women as natural homemakers, caring for their husbands and children in the home, and segregated into

[1]*Natural* is in quotes because the "natural" family system is actually a social product.
[2]In contrast, previous times viewed homosexual attractions as natural (and shared by all) but immoral and not to be acted on (Weeks 1979).

dead-end, low paid "women's jobs." Forced into this sexual division of labor, men and women need one another to be socially complete, and in order to undertake the essential function of marriage, which is seen as . . .

2. *"Natural" Parenting.* Parenting is seen as the biological production   5
of offspring, a process in which adults pass on their identities and wealth to their children, to "their own flesh and blood." Children are seen as the responsibility and property of their parents. Women/females are seen as naturally endowed with special maternal instincts which make them more qualified than men/males for parenting.

3. *"Natural" Community.* Connected to the view of family life as natural is a white racist view of society which divides people into races and views whites as the biologically superior race. Whites rationalize their political and economic domination of people of color not only as natural but also as part of "white man's burden to civilize the savages."[3] Races and white supremacy are perpetuated as social entities by the prohibition of racial intermarriage; by the passing down of wealth or poverty, language and culture to one's children; and by racially segregated institutions such as housing and job markets.

The Breakdown of the "Natural" Family System

In the last fifteen years, the "natural" family system has been breaking down and coming under increasing attack by feminists and others.

1. *Married women have entered the labor force and "men's jobs" in growing numbers, challenging the "natural" sexual division of labor.* Now over half of married women are in paid jobs at any one time. Women are demanding entry into the better-paid "men's jobs," and pressing their husbands to do "women's work" in the home. The "natural" marriage union between a bread-winning husband and a homemaking wife has become the exception rather than the rule, characterizing only 29% of husband/wife couples in 1985 (Current Population Reports March 1985).

2. *Married women's labor force participation has created a crisis in day care: there is a severe shortage of day care facilities, especially affordable ones.* In New York, for example, between 830,000 and 1.2 million preschool and school-age children vie for the fewer than 135,000 available licensed child care placements (Select Committee on Children 1987). The shortage of day care, combined with the absence of flexible jobs, forces parents to use make-shift arrangements: 2.1 million or 7% of 5–13-year-olds whose mothers work outside the home are admittedly left unsupervised; actual numbers are much higher (Children's Defense Fund 1987).

3. *Growing numbers are not living in husband/wife families;* only 57% of all   10
households include married couples. Adults are marrying later, spending

---

[3]Similarly, whites in the Eugenics movement argued that poor whites had inferior genes, and worked to limit their reproduction (Gould 1981).

more time living alone (23.4% of all households) or with friends or lovers. Homosexuality appears to be on the rise, and gays are coming out of the closet and demanding their rights. Marriages have become very unstable; divorce rates more than tripled between 1960 and 1982, more than doubling the number of female-headed households (1986 and 1987 Statistical Abstracts).

4. *"Natural" parenting is on the wane.* Divorces create "unnatural" female-headed households, most with dependent children. Unwed mothering has increased to comprise 1 in 5 births and over half of all births among blacks (1987 Statistical Abstract). Remarriages create "unatural" families, with step-parents and -siblings. More "unnatural" is the trend for sterile couples, gays, and singles to obtain children through artificial insemination, surrogate mothers, and inter-country inter-racial adoptions.

What do these trends mean? Members of the so-called Moral Majority interpret them as the breakdown of *the* family; their solution, embodied in the Family Protection Act of the late 1970s and early 1980s, is to put the "natural" family back together: encourage marriage; discourage divorce, unwed mothering, homosexuality; and get married women out of men's jobs and back into the home. The radical perspective is the opposite; the "natural" family is only one of many possible family systems, a very oppressive and ineffective one at that, as the next section will show. Growing numbers are rejecting the "natural" family system, and trying to create alternative family structures. What society needs is a radical family policy to focus and facilitate this process of dismantling of the old family system and constructing a new and more liberated one.

The Radical Critique of the "Natural" Family

The radical critique of the "natural" family has many prongs. All of these are underlain by a common claim—the "natural" family is not natural, necessary, or optimal, and a more adequate family system needs to be developed.

1. *The "natural" family system is not natural.* Biological differences in skin color or sex organs, and biological similarities between parent and child, do not necessitate a particular family form, or hierarchy and difference between the sexes and races. Past family systems have been very different from the "natural" family.[4] It is not nature but our society which is

---

[4]Among the Rangiroa, adopted children were given equal status and rights as biological offspring, and considered "one belly" (from the same mother) with one another and with their other siblings (Sahlins 1976). In the New England and Southern colonies, mothering among the wealthy was essentially biological, producing one's husband's children, who were then nursed and cared for by poor white or slave women. Mead (1935) found societies where men and women shared the early care of children. Many societies see polygamy as the norm for marriage; others have allowed females to live as men and take wives after having cross-sex dreams (Blackwood 1984). Among the ancient Greeks, the highest form of love for an adult man was homosexual love for a younger man.

producing and reproducing the "natural" family, and its associated institutions of gender and race difference and inequality, through parenting practices, laws, labor market structures, and culture.

2. *The "natural" family system is classist and racist.* The conception of the "natural" family is generated by the dominant culture of upper-class, native-born whites, who then claim it applies to all. Since being a man means bread-winning and supporting a homebound homemaker and children, men without "family wage" jobs due to unemployment, class, or race discrimination are seen (and often see themselves) as less than manly. Black women, forced into the labor force to compensate for their husbands' lack of economic opportunity, are viewed as unfeminine, castrating "matriarchs," and the extended and chosen family system which blacks have developed to combat poverty and economic insecurity is condemned as deviant (Stack 1974). The inability of the poor to properly parent their children because of their meager resources is seen as a fault in their characters, and they are criticized for having children at all, as if the poor do not have a right to parent.

3. *The "natural" family system impoverishes female-headed households.* Women and children face high risks of poverty. Married women are to specialize in unpaid homemaking and mothering, complementing their husbands' bread-winning. Divorce or widowhood leaves women with little access to income, but with major if not full emotional and financial responsibility for the children.[5] "Women's jobs" do not pay enough to cover child care and keep female households with young children out of poverty. The present welfare system (Aid to Families with Dependent Children), structured to support the "natural" family system, does not even provide female-headed families with poverty-level income. The result: the majority of black and Hispanic female-headed families (50 and 53%, respectively), and 27% of white female-headed families, are poor. Children are penalized the most: 54% of children in such families are poor (Current Population Reports 1985).

4. *"Natural" marriage creates inequality between the sexes.* Since wives are relegated to unpaid housework and low paid jobs, they are economically dependent upon their husbands. Fear of losing this financial support can force women into subservience to their husbands, and into staying in unsatisfying marriages. Indeed, some feminists see "natural" marriage as a struggle in which men have gained the upper hand by monopolizing the higher-paid jobs (Hartmann 1981). Whatever its origins, "natural" marriage is clearly unequal, making mutual love and respect difficult.

5. *"Natural" parenting is oppressive and unjust.* Along with financial responsibility, parents are given almost total power over children. Children have no rights, and no system through which they can complain about mistreatment or find alternative parents (Rodham 1976). In a society

[5]In 1983, only 35% of mothers caring for their children with absent fathers received any child support, and the average yearly payment was only $2,341; only 6% of separated or divorced women received any alimony (1987 Statistical Abstract).

where most men are under the power of bosses, and women under that of their husbands, parenting provides an arena where adults have total power and authority. It is easy to forget one's children's needs and use or abuse them to fill one's own needs. What results is not only an epidemic of child physical and sexual abuse,[6] but also the training of each child to accept and participate in hierarchical and authoritarian systems, from schools to workplaces to politics (Miller 1981).

6. *The "natural" family perpetuates inequality between families* through the generations, because parents pass down their economic position to their children. Inheritance keeps ownership of the means of production in the hands of a few, mostly white, families.[7] Children born into higher-income families receive better nutrition, housing, health care, and schooling than their poor counterparts, have the "insurance" of wealthy relatives to back them up and encourage risk-taking, and can expect to inherit wealth. On the other hand, 11 million children (one in five) must live without even the most basic goods and services (Current Population Reports 1985). This is not only unjust but also irrational: it is in society's interest to guarantee quality health care and education to its future workers and citizens.

7. *The "natural" family system discourages the formation of alternative families, while forcing many into unwanted "natural" families.* Its broad and virulent anti-gay discrimination from education, employment, housing, and marriage laws to media images—makes it very difficult for people to love and share their lives with people of the same sex. It discriminates against couples who are unable to have children biologically by treating adoption and artificial insemination as "unnatural" and undesirable options. On the other hand, the "natural" family's equation of sex, reproduction, and marriage creates unwanted children by creating opposition to sex education, birth control for unmarried teens, and abortion. Forty percent of all births are mistimed or unwanted—for those under 24, a disastrous 53%—forcing millions of women into premature or unwanted motherhood and/or marriages (1987 Statistical Abstract).

Conceptualizing a Social Family System

The "natural" family system is inadequate, oppressive, and is coming apart at the seams. At the same time, all need the love and warmth and sharing and parenting which family relationships provide.[8] Hence criticism is not enough; an *alternative* and better vision of family life needs to

---

[6]The media have focussed on child abuse by strangers—on day care scandals and missing children—whereas the vast majority of children are abused by their parents or relatives (Eliasoph 1986).

[7]The wealthiest 2.4% of households owns 65% of the income-producing wealth (Edwards, Reich, Weisskopf 1986).

[8]Some feminists and gays have taken an "anti-family" position, as if the "natural" family is the only family form (Barrett and McIntosh 1982); however they usually advocate some alternative, family-like institutions.

be delineated, along with a set of concrete policies to bring such a new family system into being.

The oppressiveness of the "natural" family system was accepted because its institutions were seen as natural and inevitable. Our new family system would be a *consciously* social one, its institutions developed through study, discussion, struggle and compromise, and continually criticized and improved so as to maximize freedom, equality, self-fulfillment, democracy, and justice. Here are some of the central principles of such a system; while it may appear utopian, many are living out parts of this vision now.

Social Marriage. Marriage would become a symmetrical relationship between whole, equal, and socially independent human beings, each participating in a similar range of familial, economic and political activities.[9] Its basis would be mutual love of the other, i.e., liking of, respect for, and sexual attraction to the person the other is, as providing the reason for intimate sharing of lives and living spaces and, if desired, parenting. Couples would not be expected to stay together "for better or for worse . . . as long as ye both shall live"; nor would they need to, since each would have earnings.

Social Parenting. Parenting would be recognized as a quintessentially social activity which, by shaping our unconsciousnesses, bodies, and minds, shapes the future of our society. Society would ensure that each child is well cared for and educated, since the upbringing of children as physically and psychologically healthy, creative, educated, and socially-conscious citizens is essential both to society's well-being, and to our belief in equal opportunity. This would include providing children and their parents with economic and institutional support, as well as seeking out optimal parenting practices and educating prospective parents in them.

Social Community. Cultural and economic differences between groups of people would be acknowledged to be social rather than natural products. All human beings would be recognized as equally human citizens of the world, and a concept of basic human rights, both political and economic, developed. Intercultural marriages would be encouraged to further social understanding.

Bringing the Social Family into Being: A Policy Checklist

Although the "natural" family system is in decline, the social family system cannot replace it unless there are many changes in our economic and social institutions. Here are some of the policies which will help bring about these changes; many are now in place in other countries.

---

[9]If this seems far-fetched, an October 1977 CBS–*New York Times* National Survey found that 50% of 30–44 year olds, and 67% of 18–29-year-olds, preferred a symmetrical marriage (of a man and woman who both had jobs, did housework, and cared for the children) over the traditional, complementary one.

1. *Policies which socialize parenting*
   a. *Policies which establish the right of all adults to choose when and if they wish to parent.* Universal sex education and parenting training for adolescents, as well as access of all to free, safe, 100% effective birth control, abortions, and adoption placement, are needed to make every child a wanted child. At the same time, society must recognize the right of those who are infertile, gay, or single to parent, and support the development of alternative modes of obtaining children from adoption to artificial insemination and in-vitro fertilization.[10] The right to parent must also be protected by programs to help low-income parents with the costs of child-rearing (see 1b). Finally, the right to parent must be seen as socially established, rather than inhering in the genetic connection between a parent and a child; parenting rights must be revocable if a parent neglects or abuses a child, and society should seek to prevent child abuse through an effective system of child advocates and parenting support and training.
   b. *Policies which ensure a basic, social inheritance for every child.* The best way to ensure healthy and provided-for children is to ensure this health and income to all families through a system of national health insurance and a combination of anti-poverty measures, from full employment, to comparable worth, to a guaranteed annual income. In addition, since having children does increase a family's poverty risk, family allowances should be provided to parents according to need.[11] Furthermore, all children need to have access to high quality, free or sliding-scale education, from preschool day care when their parents are at work, to elementary and secondary school and college. This "social inheritance" program would be paid for by high inheritance taxes and very progressive income and/or luxury taxes. Such taxes would, in themselves, help reduce the present gross inequalities of opportunity among children.[12]
   c. *Policies which socialize child-care costs: government- and business-subsidized day care.* Making quality child care available and

[10]Most doctors refuse to artificially inseminate single or lesbian women. The developing practice of surrogate mothering is very controversial among feminists and radicals. Since eggs can be fertilized outside of a womb, and embryos can be raised in incubators from the age of a few months, there are many other possibilities, including impregnating men, or even producing infants entirely outside of human bodies, as Marge Piercy (1976) and Shulamith Firestone (1970) have envisioned.

[11]Sweden and France give housing allowances to parents (Kamerman and Kahn 1979); many European countries have national health insurance and family allowances. Swedish policy is to guarantee all citizens a minimum standard of living (Ibid.); in the U. S., the needy only receive support through "entitlement" programs, which require certain qualifications (such as being a female household head with children) other than being poor, and which do not, in any event, raise incomes up to the poverty level.

[12]See Chester (1982) for a review of Western thought on inheritance.

affordable to all should be the joint financial responsibility of business and government, since it benefits both employers and society at large. A few trend-setting employers now provide child-care benefits to their workers, having found that these more than pay for themselves by decreasing worker absenteeism, increasing productivity, and attracting top workers (Blau and Ferber 1986). Current federal funding through Title 20 is woefully inadequate; many states are serving less than 30% of their eligible populations (Select Committee on Children 1987). One survey found that ¼ of all full-time homemakers, and ½ of all single parents, were kept from employment and training programs by the unavailability of child care (Cal. Governor's Task Force on Child Care 1986). Again, Sweden provides the example to follow: the government pays "0% of the child-care costs of public day care centers, which are used by over half of children with employed mothers (Blau and Ferber 1986).

On the other hand, to permit parents with job commitments to spend more time with their children, especially their infants, a system of paid leaves from work without loss of one's job or seniority must be established. The U.S. does not even have laws guaranteeing prospective parents an *unpaid* leave when they have or adopt a child.[13] In a few states, women can use their temporary disability insurance to pay for 4 to 10 weeks of pregnancy/infant care leave (Kamerman et al. 1983). Again, Sweden is the model in this area, with: 1) paid, year-long parental leaves, 2) up to 60 days a year paid leave to care for sick children, and 3) the right for all full-time employed parents with children under 8 to reduce their work weeks (with reduced pay) to 30 hours a week (Ginsberg 1983). Radicals have advocated a shorter work week without reduction in pay as a solution to unemployment and low productivity, for it would create more jobs, reduce unemployment, and increase output (Bowles, Gordon, and Weisskopf 1983); a consideration of the needs of parents makes such policies even more desirable. Other innovations which allow adults to combine work with parenting are flex-time and flex-place (working at home); the extension of health, pension, and other benefits to part-time workers; and the cafeteria benefit plan, which allows dual-career couples to eliminate doubly-covered benefits in favor of more of other benefits, such as leaves or child-care support (Farley 1983; Kamerman and Hayes 1982).

2. *Policies to support egalitarian, symmetrical marriages* in which partners participate equally in parenting, housework, the labor force, and political life.[14]

---

[13]Kamerman and Kingston (in Kamerman and Hayes 1982) found that paid maternity leave was available to fewer than one-third of all employed women in 1978, and averaged only about six weeks of benefits.
[14]Cuba encourages such marriages through its "Family Code," adopted in 1975 (Randall 1981); however, it still discriminates against gay couples.

a. *Comparable worth, affirmative action, increased unionization.* Comparable worth would increase the pay of women's jobs to that of men's jobs requiring comparable skill, effort, and responsibility. Affirmative action encourages women to enter into traditionally masculine jobs. Women need to organize in unions to fight for the above, and for general wage increases; one platform is "solidarity wages," again practiced in Sweden, in which workers agree to take part of their wage increase to reduce inequalities among them. Together these policies would stop the segregation of women into low-paid, dead-end, less-satisfying jobs, reduce women's economic dependence upon men, and encourage more similar work and family participation by the sexes.

b. *Socialization of parenting* (see #1 above) would support symmetrical marriage, for it would allow adults to combine parenting with labor force commitments, reducing the pressure to specialize as in "natural" marriage.

c. *Repeal of the laws that discourage formation of "unnatural" marriages and non-traditional households.* This includes repealing sodomy laws and advocating legislation prohibiting discrimination against gays in employment, housing, insurance, foster parenting, adoption, and other areas.[15] Gay relationships must be legitimized in marriage laws, to give spouses health insurance, pension, inheritance, and other benefits and rights enjoyed by heterosexual spouses.[16] The repeal of co-residence laws, which in many states prohibit the cohabitation of more than two unrelated adults, is needed to allow the formation of non-biologically-based extended families.

d. *Individual rather than joint taxation of married couples.* Our present income tax system is progressive and married couples are discouraged from entering the labor force since, when a woman's earnings raise the household's tax bracket, much of her earnings are paid to the government in taxes.[17] Taxing adults individually (as is currently done in Sweden), rather than jointly, would instead encourage both members of a couple to participate in the labor force.

---

[15]Sodomy laws, which outlaw forms of "unnatural sex" (e.g., anal intercourse and oral/genital sex, either heterosexual or homosexual), still exist in many states, and were recently upheld by the Supreme Court, although they are seldom enforced. Many cities and a few states have passed gay rights legislation, and more and more employers have extended their non-discrimination policy to include sexual preference or orientation.

[16]In June 1987, the Swedish Parliament approved a bill which gave gay couples the same rights as heterosexuals married by common law; it will allow couples to sign housing leases as couples, regulate the division of property after a break-up, and grant lovers the right to inherit property in the absence of a will (*Gay Community News*, June 14–20, 1987).

[17]Even though the recent tax reform reduced the progressivity of the tax system, and a 1983 reform exempted 10% of the income of the lower-earning partner from taxation, the "marriage penalty" persists (Blau and Ferber 1986).

e. *Policies to aid the casualties of the "natural" marriage system.* Until the above changes are achieved, women and children will continue to face high poverty risks when they live in female-headed households. Many feminists advocate the strengthening of alimony and child-support laws; however, this both reinforces the "natural" marriage notion that husbands should be the main providers, and reproduces class and race inequality, because wives' and children's incomes depend on that of their husbands/fathers. Extensive welfare reform, combined with the policies above, is a better solution.

3. *Policies to create social community.* Labor market reforms (2a) must always aim at eliminating both race and sex segregation and discrimination. These, along with social inheritance policies, will go far in stopping the economic reproduction of racial inequality in the U.S. The decline of "natural" parenting views of children as "one's own flesh and blood" will foster, and in turn be fostered by, the decline of conceptions of race, as both are replaced by a view of a human community reproduced through social parenting.

Bibliography

Barrett, Michele, and Mary McIntosh. 1982. *The Anti-Social Family.* London: New Left Books.

Blackwood, Evelyn. 1984. Sexuality and Gender in Certain Native Tribes: The Case of Cross-Gender Females. *Signs* 10(1):27–42.

Blau, Francine, and Marianne Ferber. 1986. *The Economics of Women, Men, and Work.* Englewood Cliffs, N.J.: Prentice-Hall.

Bowles, Samuel, David M. Gordon, and Thomas E. Weisskopf. 1983. *Beyond the Wasteland: A Democratic Alternative to Economic Decline.* New York: Anchor Doubleday.

Chester, Ronald. 1982. *Inheritance, Wealth, and Society.* Bloomington: Indiana University Press.

Children's Defense Fund. 1987. Unpublished paper.

Edwards, Richard, Michael Reich, and Thomas Weisskopf. 1986. *The Capitalist System.* Englewood Cliffs, N.J.: Prentice-Hall. Third Edition.

Eliasoph, Nina. 1986. Drive-In Mortality, Child Abuse, and the Media. *Socialist Review* #90, 16(6):7–31.

Farley, Jennie, ed. 1983. *The Woman in Management.* New York: ILR Press.

Firestone, Shulamith. 1970. *The Dialectic of Sex.* New York: Morrow.

Ginsberg, Helen. 1983. *Full Employment and Public Policy: The United States and Sweden.* Lexington, Mass.: D.C. Heath and Co.

Gould, Stephen J. 1981. *The Mismeasure of Man.* New York: Norton.

Hartmann, Heidi. 1981. The Unhappy Marriage of Marxism and Feminism. In *Women and Revolution: A Discussion of the Unhappy Marriage of Marxism and Feminism,* Lydia Sargent (ed.), pp. 1–41. Boston: South End Press.

Kamerman, Sheila, and Alfred Kahn. 1979. *Family Policy: Government and Families in Fourteen Countries.* New York: Columbia University Press.

Kamerman, Sheila, and Cheryl Hayes, eds. 1982. *Families That Work: Children in a Changing World.* Washington: National Academy Press.

Kamerman, Sheila, et al., eds. 1983. *Maternity Policies and Working Women.* New York: Columbia University Press.

Matthaei, Julie. 1982. *An Economic History of Women in America: Women's Work, the Sexual Division of Labor, and the Development of Capitalism.* New York: Schocken Books.

Mead, Margaret. 1935. *Sex and Temperament in Three Primitive Societies.* New York: William Morrow and Co.

Miller, Alice. 1981. *The Drama of the Gifted Child,* trans. by Ruth Ward. New York: Basic Books.

Piercy, Marge. 1976. *Woman on the Edge of Time.* New York: Fawcett.

Randall, Margaret. 1981. *Women in Cuba: Twenty Years Later.* New York: Smyrna Press.

Rodham, Hillary. 1976. Children under the Law. In *Rethinking Childhood,* Arlene Skolnick (ed.). Boston: Little, Brown and Co.

Sahlins, Marshall. 1976. *The Use and Abuse of Biology: An Anthropological Critique of Sociobiology.* Ann Arbor: University of Michigan Press.

Select Committee on Children, Youth and Families, U.S. House of Representatives. 1987. Fact Sheet: Hearing on Child Care, Key to Employment in a Changing Economy. March 10.

Stack, Carol. 1974. *All Our Kin.* New York: Harper & Row.

U.S. Bureau of the Census, Current Population Reports. 1985. Household and Family Characteristics: March 1985.

—. 1985. Money Income and Poverty Status of Families and Persons in the United States.

—. 1986, 1987. Statistical Abstract of the United States.

Weeks, Jeffrey. 1979. *Coming Out: Homosexual Politics in Britain, from the Nineteenth Century to the Present.* London: Quartet Books.

✎ Topics for Critical Thinking and Writing

1. What, if anything, strikes you as "radical" in Matthaei's "radical analysis" of the "'natural' family" (paragraph 3)? Do any parts of this analysis strike you as unfair, misleading, or wrong? If so, which parts, and what do you find wrong with them?

2. In paragraph 7 Matthaei says that "adults are marrying later." Assuming this statement to be true, what do you think are the causes? What do you think may be the consequences, good and bad?

3. In paragraph 10 Matthaei denies that the "natural" family is natural. Do you think she proves her case? If not, in what way(s) does she fail?

4. Matthaei argues (paragraph 18) that the idea of the "natural" family can lead easily to child abuse. Can one argue in response that the "natural" family is better suited to assist children in growing into healthy, responsible,

happy adults than is any conceivable alternative arrangement? If you think so, what arguments might you offer? (For an interesting argument that children should be granted legal rights to escape impossible families, see "Confessions of an Erstwhile Child," page 192.)

5. In paragraph 20 Matthaei argues that the idea of the "natural" family "discriminates against couples who are unable to have children biologically." Is she saying that all adults—including the sterile, the infertile, and those who do not wish to engage in heterosexual sex—have a right to have children? If she is saying this, on what might she base this right? In her next paragraph she says that "all need the love and warmth and sharing and parenting which family relationships provide." Is this need perhaps the basis for a right—possessed by all adults—to have children? (See also the discussion in paragraph 24.)

6. Much of the essay is devoted to arguing on behalf of various kinds of equality. For example, in paragraph 23, in discussing "social marriage," Matthaei says that "marriage would become a symmetrical relationship between whole, equal, and socially independent human beings." The two persons involved would participate "in a similar range of familial, economic, and political activities." But what if both persons do not share an interest in, for example, political activities? Should they therefore not marry? Or suppose that one person enjoyed the world of paid work and the other preferred to engage, at least for a while, chiefly in the role of parenting and housekeeping. Do you think such a marriage would be inherently unstable?

7. In paragraph 29, Matthaei argues for programs and policies that would redistribute wealth—for example, a guaranteed annual income. Suppose someone argued (or at least asserted) that he or she saw no reason to support the families of the poor. What reply might you make?

8. Matthaei apparently sees marriage as involving only two adults. Do you assume that she rejects polygamy (a practice not unknown in the United States and elsewhere)? And what about polyandry (one woman with two or more husbands)? If you accept Matthaei's arguments, or most of them, how do *you* feel about polygamy and polyandry? What argument(s) can you imagine for these?

Andrew Sullivan

Andrew Sullivan grew up in England, but he earned a doctorate in government at Harvard University. Sullivan for several years served as the editor of The New Republic, *where the following essay was originally published in 1989.*

Here Comes the Groom
A (Conservative) Case for Gay Marriage

Last month in New York, a court ruled that a gay lover had the right to stay in his deceased partner's rent-control apartment because the lover qualified as a member of the deceased's family. The ruling deftly annoyed almost everybody. Conservatives saw judicial activism in favor of gay rent control: three reasons to be appalled. Chastened liberals (such as the *New York Times* editorial page), while endorsing the recognition of gay relationships, also worried about the abuse of already stretched entitlements that the ruling threatened. What neither side quite contemplated is that they both might be right, and that the way to tackle the issue of unconventional relationships in conventional society is to try something both more radical and more conservative than putting courts in the business of deciding what is and is not a family. That alternative is the legalization of civil gay marriage.

The New York rent-control case did not go anywhere near that far, which is the problem. The rent-control regulations merely stipulated that a "family" member had the right to remain in the apartment. The judge ruled that to all intents and purposes a gay lover is part of his lover's family, inasmuch as a "family" merely means an interwoven social life, emotional commitment, and some level of financial interdependence.

It's a principle now well established around the country. Several cities have "domestic partnership" laws, which allow relationships that do not fit into the category of heterosexual marriage to be registered with the city and qualify for benefits that up till now have been reserved for straight married couples. San Francisco, Berkeley, Madison, and Los Angeles all have legislation, as does the politically correct Washington, D.C. suburb, Takoma Park. In these cities, a variety of interpersonal arrangements qualify for health insurance, bereavement leave, insurance, annuity and pension rights, housing rights (such as rent-control apartments), adoption and inheritance rights. Eventually, according to gay lobby groups, the aim is to include federal income tax and veterans' benefits as well. A recent case even involved the right to use a family member's accumulated frequent-flier points. Gays are not the only beneficiaries; heterosexual "live-togethers" also qualify.

There's an argument, of course, that the current legal advantages extended to married people unfairly discriminate against people who've shaped their lives in less conventional arrangements. But it doesn't take a genius to see that enshrining in the law a vague principle like "domestic partnership" is an invitation to qualify at little personal cost for a vast array of entitlements otherwise kept crudely under control.

To be sure, potential DPs have to prove financial interdependence, shared living arrangements, and a commitment to mutual caring. But they don't need to have a sexual relationship or even closely mirror old-style marriage. In principle, an elderly woman and her live-in nurse could qualify. A couple of uneuphemistically confirmed bachelors could be DPs. So could two close college students, a pair of seminarians, or a couple of frat buddies. Left as it is, the concept of domestic partnership could open a Pandora's box of litigation and subjective judicial decision-making about who qualifies. You either are or are not married; it's not a complex question. Whether you are in a "domestic partnership" is not so clear.

More important, the concept of domestic partnership chips away at the prestige of traditional relationships and undermines the priority we give them. This priority is not necessarily a product of heterosexism. Consider heterosexual couples. Society has good reason to extend legal advantages to heterosexuals who choose the formal sanction of marriage over simply living together. They make a deeper commitment to one another and to society; in exchange, society extends certain benefits to them. Marriage provides an anchor, if an arbitrary and weak one, in the chaos of sex and relationships to which we are all prone. It provides a mechanism for emotional stability, economic security, and the healthy rearing of the next generation. We rig the law in its favor not because we disparage all forms of relationships other than the nuclear family, but because we recognize that not to promote marriage would be to ask too much of human virtue. In the context of the weakened family's effect upon the poor, it might also invite social disintegration. One of the worst products of the New Right's "family values" campaign is that its extremism and hatred of diversity has disguised this more measured and more convincing case for the importance of the marital bond.

The concept of domestic partnership ignores these concerns, indeed directly attacks them. This is a pity, since one of its most important objectives—providing some civil recognition for gay relationships—is a noble cause and one completely compatible with the defense of the family. But the way to go about it is not to undermine straight marriage; it is to legalize old-style marriage for gays.

The gay movement has ducked this issue primarily out of fear of division. Much of the gay leadership clings to notions of gay life as essentially outsider, antibourgeois, radical.[1] Marriage, for them, is co-optation into straight society. For the Stonewall generation, it is hard to see how this vision of conflict will ever fundamentally change. But for many other gays—my guess, a majority—while they don't deny the importance of rebellion twenty years ago and are grateful for what was done, there's now the sense of a new opportunity. A need to rebel has quietly ceded to a desire to belong. To be gay and to be bourgeois no longer seems such an absurd proposition. Certainly since AIDS, to be gay and to be responsible has become a necessity.

[1]The Stonewall Inn was a gay bar in New York City. When the police closed it in June 1966, the gays did not submit (as they had done in the past) but attacked the police. The event is regarded as a turning point in gay history.

Gay marriage squares several circles at the heart of the domestic partnership debate. Unlike domestic partnership, it allows for recognition of gay relationships, while casting no aspersions on traditional marriage. It merely asks that gays be allowed to join in. Unlike domestic partnership, it doesn't open up avenues for heterosexuals to get benefits without the responsibilities of marriage, or a nightmare of definitional litigation. And unlike domestic partnership, it harnesses to an already established social convention the yearnings for stability and acceptance among a fast-maturing gay community.

Gay marriage also places more responsibilities upon gays: It says for the first time that gay relationships are not better or worse than straight relationships, and that the same is expected of them. And it's clear and dignified. There's a legal benefit to a clear, common symbol of commitment. There's also a personal benefit. One of the ironies of domestic partnership is that it's not only more complicated than marriage, it's more demanding, requiring an elaborate statement of intent to qualify. It amounts to a substantial invasion of privacy. Why, after all, should gays be required to prove commitment before they get married in a way we would never dream of asking of straights?

Legalizing gay marriage would offer homosexuals the same deal society now offers heterosexuals: general social approval and specific legal advantages in exchange for a deeper and harder-to-extract-yourself-from commitment to another human being. Like straight marriage, it would foster social cohesion, emotional security, and economic prudence. Since there's no reason gays should not be allowed to adopt or be foster parents, it could also help nurture children. And its introduction would not be some sort of radical break with social custom. As it has become more acceptable for gay people to acknowledge their loves publicly, more and more have committed themselves to one another for life in full view of their families and their friends. A law institutionalizing gay marriage would merely reinforce a healthy social trend. It would also, in the wake of AIDS, qualify as a genuine public health measure. Those conservatives who deplore promiscuity among some homosexuals should be among the first to support it. Burke[2] could have written a powerful case for it.

The argument that gay marriage would subtly undermine the unique legitimacy of straight marriage is based upon a fallacy. For heterosexuals, straight marriage would remain the most significant—and only legal—social bond. Gay marriage could only delegitimize straight marriage if it were a real alternative to it, and this is clearly not true. To put it bluntly, there's precious little evidence that straights could be persuaded by any law to have sex with—let alone marry—someone of their own sex. The only possible effect of this sort would be to persuade gay men and women who force themselves into heterosexual marriage (often at appalling cost to themselves and their families) to find a focus for their family instincts in

10

---

[2]Edmund Burke (1729–97), conservative British politician.

a more personally positive environment. But this is clearly a plus, not a minus: Gay marriage could both avoid a lot of tortured families and create the possibility for many happier ones. It is not, in short, a denial of family values. It's an extension of them.

Of course, some would claim that any legal recognition of homosexuality is a de facto attack upon heterosexuality. But even the most hardened conservatives recognize that gays are a permanent minority and aren't likely to go away. Since persecution is not an option in a civilized society, why not coax gays into traditional values rather than rail incoherently against them?

There's a less elaborate argument for gay marriage: It's good for gays. It provides role models for young gay people who, after the exhilaration of coming out, can easily lapse into short-term relationships and insecurity with no tangible goal in sight. My own guess is that most gays would embrace such a goal with as much (if not more) commitment as straights. Even in our society as it is, many lesbian relationships are virtual textbook cases of monogamous commitment. Legal gay marriage could also help bridge the gulf often found between gays and their parents. It could bring the essence of gay life—a gay couple—into the heart of the traditional straight family in a way the family can most understand and the gay offspring can most easily acknowledge. It could do as much to heal the gay-straight rift as any amount of gay rights legislation.

If these arguments sound socially conservative, that's no accident. It's   15
one of the richest ironies of our society's blind spot toward gays that essentially conservative social goals should have the appearance of being so radical. But gay marriage is not a radical step. It avoids the mess of domestic partnership: it is humane; it is conservative in the best sense of the word. It's also practical. Given the fact that we already allow legal gay relationships, what possible social goal is advanced by framing the law to encourage those relationships to be unfaithful, undeveloped, and insecure?

✎ Topics for Critical Thinking and Writing

1. In his second paragraph Sullivan summarizes a judge's definition of a family. How satisfactory do you find the definition? Explain.
2. What is "conservative"—Sullivan's word, in his title—about this case for gay and lesbian marriages?
3. A common argument in support of the financial privileges that the state awards to the traditional family is that it is in the state's interest for children to be brought up by adults committed to each other. However, divorce is now common, and, of course, many married couples do not have children, for one reason or another. Can any justification, then, be offered for allowing a spouse—but not an unmarried heterosexual or homosexual lover—to inherit without payment of taxes the partner's share of property jointly held?

4. In Sullivan's view why is marriage better than mere cohabitation? What is your view of this matter?
5. In paragraph 11 Sullivan says that "there's no reason gays should not be allowed to adopt or be foster parents." This issue is highly controversial. Construct the strongest argument you can, on one side or the other. (Remember, a strong argument faces the opposing arguments.)
6. In his next-to-last paragraph Sullivan says that "legal gay marriage could also help bridge the gulf often found between gays and their parents." If you are aware of gays who are separated from their parents by a "gulf," do you think that legal marriage might reduce that gulf? Explain.

Arlie Hochschild

Arlie Hochschild, born in Boston in 1940, holds a bachelor's degree from Swarthmore and a Ph.D. from the University of California, Berkeley, where he is now a professor in the Department of Sociology. He is the author of several important books, including The Second Shift: Working Parents and the Revolution at Home *(1989, written with Anne Machung). The material that we give below comes from this book.*

The Second Shift: Employed Women Are Putting in Another Day of Work at Home

Every American household bears the footprints of economic and cultural trends that originate far outside its walls. A rise in intlation eroding the earning power of the male wage, an expanding service sector opening up jobs for women, and the inroads made by women into many professions—all these changes do not simply go on around the American family. They occur *within* a marriage or living-together arrangement and transform it. Problems between couples, problems that seem "unique" or "marital," are often the individual ripples of powerful economic and cultural shock waves. Quarrels between husbands and wives in households across the nation result mainly from a friction between faster-changing women and slower-changing men.

The exodus of women from the home to the workplace has not been accompanied by a new view of marriage and work that would make this transition smooth. Most workplaces have remained inflexible in the face of the changing needs of workers with families, and most men have yet to really adapt to the changes in women. I call the strain caused by the disparity between the change in women and the absence of change elsewhere the "stalled revolution."

If women begin to do less at home because they have less time, if men do little more, and if the work of raising children and tending a home requires roughly the same effort, then the questions of who does what at home and of what "needs doing" become a source of deep tension in a marriage.

Over the past 30 years in the United States, more and more women have begun to work outside the home, and more have divorced. While some commentators conclude that women's work *causes* divorce, my research into changes in the American family suggests something else. Since all the wives in the families I studied (over an eight-year period) worked outside the home, the fact that they worked did not account for why some marriages were happy and others were not. What *did* contribute to happiness was the husband's willingness to do the work at home. Whether they were traditional or more egalitarian in their relationship, couples were happier when the men did a sizable share of housework and child care.

In one study of 600 couples filing for divorce, researcher George Levinger found that the second most common reason women cited for wanting to divorce—after "mental cruelty"—was their husbands' "neglect of home or children." Women mentioned this reason more often than financial problems, physical abuse, drinking, or infidelity.   5

A happy marriage is supported by a couple's being economically secure, by their enjoying a supportive community, and by their having compatible needs and values. But these days it may also depend on a shared appreciation of the work it takes to nurture others. As the role of the homemaker is being abandoned by many women, the homemaker's work has been continually devalued and passed on to low-paid housekeepers, baby-sitters, or day-care workers. Long devalued by men, the contribution of cooking, cleaning, and care-giving is now being devalued as mere drudgery by many women, too.

In the era of the stalled revolution, one way to make housework and child care more valued is for men to share in that work. Many working mothers are already doing all they can at home. Now it's time for men to make the move.

If more mothers of young children are working at full-time jobs outside the home, and if most couples can't afford household help, who's doing the work at home? Adding together the time it takes to do a paid job and to do housework and child care and using estimates from major studies on time use done in the 1960s and 1970s. I found that women worked roughly 15 more hours each week than men. Over a year, they worked an extra month of 24-hour days. Over a dozen years, it was an extra year of 24-hour days. Most women without children spend much more time than men on housework. Women with children devote more time to both housework and child care. Just as there is a wage gap between men and women in the workplace, there is a "leisure gap" between them at home. Most women work one shift at the office or factory and a "second shift" at home.

In my research, I interviewed and observed 52 couples over an eight-year period as they cooked dinner, shopped, bathed their children, and in general struggled to find enough time to make their complex lives work. The women I interviewed seemed to be far more deeply torn between the demands of work and family than were their husbands. They talked more about the abiding conflict between work and family. They felt the second shift was *their* issue, and most of their husbands agreed. When I telephoned one husband to arrange an interview with him, explaining that I wanted to ask him how he managed work and family life, he replied genially, "Oh, this will *really* interest my *wife*."

Men who shared the load at home seemed just as pressed for time as their wives, and as torn between the demands of career and small children. But of the men I surveyed, the majority did not share the load at home. Some refused outright. Others refused more passively. often offering a loving shoulder to lean on, or an understanding ear, as their working wife faced the conflict they both saw as hers. At first it seemed to me that the problem of the second shift *was* hers. But I came to realize that those husbands who helped very little at home were often just as deeply affected as their wives—through the resentment their wives felt toward them and through their own need to steel themselves against that resentment.

A clear example of this phenomenon is Evan Holt, a warehouse furniture salesman who did very little housework and played with his four-year-old son, Joey, only at his convenience. His wife, Nancy, did the second shift, but she resented it keenly and half-consciously expressed her frustration and rage by losing interest in sex and becoming overly absorbed in Joey.

Even when husbands happily shared the work, their wives *felt* more responsible for home and children. More women than men kept track of doctor's appointments and arranged for kids' playmates to come over. More mothers than fathers worried about a child's Halloween costume or a birthday present for a school friend. They were more likely to think about their children while at work and to check in by phone with the baby-sitter.

Partly hecause of this, more women felt torn between two kinds of urgency, between the need to soothe a child's fear of being left at day-care and the need to show the boss she's "serious" at work. Twenty percent of the men in my study shared housework equally. Seventy percent did a substantial amount (less than half of it, but more than a third), and 10 percent did less than a third. But even when couples more equitably share the work at home, women do two thirds of the daily jobs at home, such as cooking and cleaning up—jobs that fix them into a rigid routine. Most women cook dinner, for instance, while men change the oil in the family car. But, as one mother pointed out, dinner needs to be prepared every evening around six o'clock, whereas the car oil needs to be changed every six months, with no particular deadline. Women do more child care than men, and men repair more household appliances. A child needs to be tended to daily, whereas the repair of household appliances can often wait, said the men, "until I have time." Men thus have more control over

10

when they make their contributions than women do. They may be very busy with family chores, but, like the executive who tells his secretary to "hold my calls," the man has more control over his time.

Another reason why women may feel under more strain than men is that women more often do two things at once—for example, write checks and return phone calls, vacuum and keep an eye on a three-year-old, fold laundry and think out the shopping list. Men more often will either cook dinner *or* watch the kids. Women more often do both at the same time.

Beyond doing more at home, women also devote proportionately more of their time at home to housework than men and proportionately less of it to child care. Of all the time men spend working at home, a growing amount of it goes to child care. Since most parents prefer to tend to their children than to clean house, men do more of what they'd rather do. More men than women take their children on "fun" outings to the park, the zoo, the movies. Women spend more time on maintenance, such as feeding and bathing children—enjoyable activities, to be sure, but often less leisurely or "special" than going to the zoo. Men also do fewer of the most undesirable household chores, such as scrubbing the toilet.

As a result, women tend to talk more intensely about being overtired, sick, and emotionally drained. Many women interviewed were fixated on the topic of sleep. They talked about how much they could "get by on": six and a half, seven, seven and a half, less, more. They talked about who they knew who needed more or less. Some apologized for how much sleep they needed—"I'm afraid I need eight hours of sleep"—as if eight was "too much." They talked about how to avoid fully waking up when a child called them at night, and how to get back to sleep. These women talked about sleep the way a hungry person talks about food.

If, all in all, the two-job family is suffering from a speedup of work and family life, working mothers are its primary victims. It is ironic, then, that often it falls to women to be the time-and-motion experts of family life. As I observed families inside their homes, I noticed it was often the mother who rushed children, saying, "Hurry up! It's time to go." "Finish your cereal now," "You can do that later," or "Let's go!" When a bath needed to be crammed into a slot between 7:45 and 8:00, it was often the mother who called out. "Let's see who can take their bath the quickest!" Often a younger child would rush out, scurrying to be first in bed, while the older and wiser one stalled, resistant, sometimes resentful: "Mother is always rushing us." Sadly, women are more often the lightning rods for family tensions aroused by this speedup of work and family life. They are the villains in a process in which they are also the primary victims. More than the longer hours and the lack of sleep, this is the saddest cost to women of their extra month of work each year.

Raising children in a nuclear family is still the overwhelming preference of most people. Yet in the face of new problems for this family model we have not created an adequate support system so that the nuclear family can do its job well in the era of the two-career couple. Corporations have done little to accommodate the needs of working parents, and the government has done little to prod them.

We really need, as sociologist Frank Furstenberg has suggested, a Marshall Plan for the family. After World War II we saw that it was in our best interests to aid the war-torn nations of Europe. Now—it seems obvious in an era of growing concern over drugs, crime, and family instability—it is in our best interests to aid the overworked two-job families right here at home. We should look to other nations for a model of what could be done. In Sweden, for example, upon the birth of a child every working couple is entitled to 12 months of paid parental leave—nine months at 90 percent of the worker's salary, plus an additional three months at about three hundred dollars a month. The mother and father are free to divide this year off between them as they wish. Working parents of a child under eight have the opportunity to work no more than six hours a day, at six hours' pay. Parental insurance offers parents money for work time lost while visiting a child's school or caring for a sick child. That's a true pro-family policy.

A pro-family policy in the United States could give tax breaks to companies that encourage job sharing, part-time work, flex time, and family leave for new parents. By implementing comparable worth policies we could increase pay scales for "women's" jobs. Another key element of a pro-family policy would be instituting fewer-hour, more flexible options—called "family phases"—for all regular jobs filled by parents of young children.

Day-care centers could be made more warm and creative through generous public and private funding. If the best form of day-care comes from the attention of elderly neighbors, students, or grandparents, these people could be paid to care for children through social programs.

In these ways, the American government would create a safer environment for the two-job family. If the government encouraged corporations to consider the long-range interests of workers and their families, they would save on long-range costs caused by absenteeism, turnover, juvenile delinquency, mental illness, and welfare support for single mothers.

These are real pro-family reforms. If they seem utopian today, we should remember that in the past the eight-hour day, the abolition of child labor, and the vote for women seemed utopian, too. Among top-rated employers listed in *The 100 Best Companies to Work for in America* are many offering country-club memberships, first-class air travel, and million-dollar fitness centers. But only a handful offer job sharing, flex time, or part-time work. Not one provides on-site day-care, and only three offer child-care deductions: Control Data, Polaroid, and Honeywell. In his book *Megatrends*, John Naisbitt reports that 83 percent of corporate executives believed that more men feel the need to share the responsibilities of parenting; yet only 9 percent of corporations offer paternity leave.

20

Public strategies are linked to private ones. Economic and cultural trends bear on family relations in ways it would be useful for all of us to understand. The happiest two-job marriages I saw during my research were ones in which men and women shared the housework and parenting. What couples called good communication often meant that they were good at saying thanks to one another for small aspects of taking care of the family. Making it to the school play, helping a child read, cooking dinner in good spirit, remembering the grocery list, taking responsibility for cleaning up the bedrooms—these were the silver and gold of the marital exchange. Until now, couples committed to an equal sharing of housework and child care have been rare. But, if we as a culture come to see the urgent need of meeting the new problems posed by the second shift, and if society and government begin to shape new policies that allow working parents more flexibility, then we will be making some progress toward happier times at home and work. And as the young learn by example, many more women and men will be able to enjoy the pleasure that arises when family life is family life, and not a second shift.

✎ Topics for Critical Thinking and Writing

1. Here is Hochschild's opening sentence: "Every American household bears the footprints of economic and cultural trends that originate outside its walls." Explain what Hochschild means and then, using the household you know best, test the truth of Hochschild's sentence.
2. What does Hochschild mean by the phrase "stalled revolution"?
3. Hochschild writes that "Most workplaces have remained inflexible in the face of the changing needs of workers with families" (second paragraph). Assuming that he is correct, why do you think this is so?
4. The rest of the sentence we just quoted is "and most men have yet to really adapt to the changes in women." To what changes does he refer? And do you think he is right? If so, how do you account for the failure of men to adapt?
5. According to Hochschild, women "are the villains in a process in which they are also the primary victims." What does he mean? In your own experience, have you been aware that women have been cast as the villains?
6. Hochschild lists conditions in Sweden for working families and refers to them as a "pro-family policy." What are some of the conditions? Why, in your opinion, does a similar pro-family policy not exist in the United States?
7. In your own family, what was the division of labor for raising children and doing household chores? Who did what (and how often)? Write a brief essay (500–750 words) in which you reveal both the division of labor and your attitude toward it.

Black Elk

Black Elk, a wichasha wakon *(holy man) of the Oglala Sioux, as a small boy witnessed the battle of the Little Bighorn (1876). He lived to see his people all but annihilated and his hopes for
them extinguished. In 1931, toward the end of his life, he told his life story to the poet and scholar
John G. Neihardt to preserve a sacred vision given him.*
"High Horse's Courting" is a comic interlude in Black Elk Speaks, *a predominantly tragic
memoir.*

High Horse's Courting

You know, in the old days, it was not very easy to get a girl when
you wanted to be married. Sometimes it was hard work for a young man
and he had to stand a great deal. Say I am a young man and I have seen a
young girl who looks so beautiful to me that I feel all sick when I think
about her. I cannot just go and tell her about it and then get married if she
is willing. I have to be a very sneaky fellow to talk to her at all, and after I
have managed to talk to her, that is only the beginning.

Probably for a long time I have been feeling sick about a certain girl
because I love her so much, but she will not even look at me, and her parents keep a good watch over her. But I keep feeling worse and worse all
the time; so maybe I sneak up to her tepee in the dark and wait until she
comes out. Maybe I just wait there all night and don't get any sleep at all
and she does not come out. Then I feel sicker than ever about her.

Maybe I hide in the brush by a spring where she sometimes goes to
get water, and when she comes by, if nobody is looking, then I jump out
and hold her and just make her listen to me. If she likes me too, I can tell
that from the way she acts, for she is very bashful and maybe will not say
a word or even look at me the first time. So I let her go, and then maybe I
sneak around until I can see her father alone, and I tell him how many
horses I can give him for his beautiful girl, and by now I am feeling so sick
that maybe I would give him all the horses in the world if I had them.

Well, this young man I am telling about was called High Horse, and
there was a girl in the village who looked so beautiful to him that he was just
sick all over from thinking about her so much and he was getting sicker all
the time. The girl was very shy, and her parents thought a great deal of her
because they were not young any more and this was the only child they had.
So they watched her all day long, and they fixed it so that she would be safe
at night too when they were asleep. They thought so much of her that they
had made a rawhide bed for her to sleep in, and after they knew that High
Horse was sneaking around after her, they took rawhide thongs and tied the
girl in bed at night so that nobody could steal her when they were asleep, for
they were not sure but that their girl might really want to be stolen.

Well, after High Horse had been sneaking around a good while and
hiding and waiting for the girl and getting sicker all the time, he finally

5

caught her alone and made her talk to him. Then he found out that she liked him maybe a little. Of course this did not make him feel well. It made him sicker than ever, but now he felt as brave as a bison bull, and so he went right to her father and said he loved the girl so much that he would give two good horses for her—one of them young and the other one not so very old.

But the old man just waved his hand, meaning for High Horse to go away and quit talking foolishness like that.

High Horse was feeling sicker than ever about it; but there was another young fellow who said he would loan High Horse two ponies and when he got some more horses, why, he could just give them back for the ones he had borrowed.

Then High Horse went back to the old man and said he would give four horses for the girl—two of them young and the other two not hardly old at all. But the old man just waved his hand and would not say anything.

So High Horse sneaked around until he could talk to the girl again, and he asked her to run away with him. He told her he thought he would just fall over and die if she did not. But she said she would not do that; she wanted to be bought like a fine woman. You see she thought a great deal of herself too.

That made High Horse feel so very sick that he could not eat a bite, and he went around with his head hanging down as though he might just fall down and die any time.

Red Deer was another young fellow, and he and High Horse were great comrades, always doing things together. Red Deer saw how High Horse was acting, and he said: "Cousin, what is the matter? Are you sick in the belly? You look as though you were going to die.

Then High Horse told Red Deer how it was, and said he thought he could not stay alive much longer if he could not marry the girl pretty quick.

Red Deer thought awhile about it, and then he said: "Cousin, I have a plan, and if you are man enough to do as I tell you, then everything will be all right. She will not run away with you; her old man will not take four horses; and four horses are all you can get. You must steal her and run away with her. Then afterwhile you can come back and the old man cannot do anything because she will be your woman. Probably she wants you to steal her anyway."

So they planned what High Horse had to do, and he said he loved the girl so much that he was man enough to do anything Red Deer or anybody else could think up. So this is what they did.

That night late they sneaked up to the girl's tepee and waited until it sounded inside as though the old man and the old woman and the girl were sound asleep. Then High Horse crawled under the tepee with a knife. He had to cut the rawhide thongs first, and then Red Deer, who was pulling up the stakes around that side of the tepee, was going to help drag the girl outside and gag her. After that, High Horse could put her across his pony in front of him and hurry out of there and be happy all the rest of his life.

10

15

When High Horse had crawled inside, he felt so nervous that he could hear his heart drumming, and it seemed so loud he felt sure it would 'waken the old folks. But it did not, and afterwhile he began cutting the thongs. Every time he cut one it made a pop and nearly scared him to death. But he was getting along all right and all the thongs were cut down as far as the girl's thighs, when he became so nervous that his knife slipped and stuck the girl. She gave a big, loud yell. Then the old folks jumped up and yelled too. By this time High Horse was outside, and he and Red Deer were running away like antelope. The old man and some other people chased the young men but they got away in the dark and nobody knew who it was.

Well, if you ever wanted a beautiful girl you will know how sick High Horse was now. It was very bad the way he felt, and it looked as though he would starve even if he did not drop over dead sometime.

Red Deer kept thinking about this, and after a few days he went to High Horse and said: "Cousin, take courage! I have another plan, and I am sure, if you are man enough, we can steal her this time." And High Horse said: "I am man enough to do anything anybody can think up, if I can only get that girl."

So this is what they did.

They went away from the village alone, and Red Deer made High   20
Horse strip naked. Then he painted High Horse solid white all over, and after that he painted black stripes all over the white and put black rings around High Horse's eyes. High Horse looked terrible. He looked so terrible that when Red Deer was through painting and took a good look at what he had done, he said it scared even him a little.

"Now," Red Deer said, "if you get caught again, everybody will be so scared they will think you are a bad spirit and will be afraid to chase you."

So when the night was getting old and everybody was sound asleep, they sneaked back to the girl's tepee. High Horse crawled in with his knife, as before, and Red Deer waited outside, ready to drag the girl out and gag her when High Horse had all the thongs cut.

High Horse crept up by the girl's bed and began cutting at the thongs. But he kept thinking, "If they see me they will shoot me because I look so terrible." The girl was restless and kept squirming around in bed, and when a thong was cut, it popped. So High Horse worked very slowly and carefully.

But he must have made some noise, for suddenly the old woman awoke and said to her old man: "Old Man, wake up! There is somebody in this tepee!" But the old man was sleepy and didn't want to be bothered. He said: "Of course there is somebody in this tepee. Go to sleep and don't bother me." Then he snored some more.

But High Horse was so scared by now that he lay very still and as flat   25
to the ground as he could. Now, you see, he had not been sleeping very well for a long time because he was so sick about the girl. And while he was lying there waiting for the old woman to snore, he just forgot everything, even how beautiful the girl was. Red Deer who was lying outside

ready to do his part, wondered and wondered what had happened in there, but he did not dare call out to High Horse.

Afterwhile the day began to break and Red Deer had to leave with the two ponies he had staked there for his comrade and girl, or somebody would see him.

So he left.

Now when it was getting light in the tepee, the girl awoke and the first thing she saw was a terrible animal, all white with black stripes on it, lying asleep beside her bed. So she screamed, and then the old woman screamed and the old man yelled. High Horse jumped up, scared almost to death, and he nearly knocked the tepee down getting out of there.

People were coming running from all over the village with guns and bows and axes, and everybody was yelling.

By now High Horse was running so fast that he hardly touched the ground at all, and he looked so terrible that the people fled from him and let him run. Some braves wanted to shoot at him, but the others said he might be some sacred being and it would bring bad trouble to kill him.   30

High Horse made for the river that was near, and in among the brush he found a hollow tree and dived into it. Afterwhile some braves came there and he could hear them saying that it was some bad spirit that had come out of the water and gone back in again.

That morning the people were ordered to break camp and move away from there. So they did, while High Horse was hiding in his hollow tree.

Now Red Deer had been watching all this from his own tepee and trying to look as though he were as much surprised and scared as all the others. So when the camp moved, he sneaked back to where he had seen his comrade disappear. When he was down there in the brush, he called, and High Horse answered, because he knew his friend's voice. They washed off the paint from High Horse and sat down on the river bank to talk about their troubles.

High Horse said he never would go back to the village as long as he lived and he did not care what happened to him now. He said he was going to go on the war-path all by himself. Red Deer said: "No, cousin, you are not going on the war-path alone, because I am going with you."

So Red Deer got everything ready, and at night they started out on the   35
war-path all alone. After several days they came to a Crow camp just about sundown, and when it was dark they sneaked up to where the Crow horses were grazing, killed the horse guard, who was not thinking about enemies because he thought all the Lakotas were far away, and drove off about a hundred horses.

They got a big start because all the Crow horses stampeded and it was probably morning before the Crow warriors could catch any horses to ride. Red Deer and High Horse fled with their herd three days and nights before they reached the village of their people. Then they drove the whole herd right into the village and up in front of the girl's tepee. The old man was there, and High Horse called out to him and asked if he thought maybe that would be enough horses for his girl. The old man did not wave him away that time. It was not the horses that he wanted. What he wanted was a son who was a real man and good for something.

So High Horse got his girl after all, and I think he deserved her.

 Topics for Critical Thinking and Writing

Although High Horse's behavior is amusing and at times ridiculous, how does Black Elk make it clear that he is not ridiculing the young man, but is instead in sympathy with him? Consider the following questions:

1. What is the effect of the first three paragraphs? Think about the first two sentences, and then the passage beginning "Say I am a young man . . ." and ending ". . . I would give him all the horses in the world if I had them."
2. Describe the behavior of the young girl and of her father and mother. How do they contribute to the comedy? How does their behavior affect your understanding of Black Elk's attitude toward High Horse?
3. What is the function of Red Deer?
4. The narrative consists of several episodes. List them in the order in which they occur and then describe the narrative's structure. How does this structure affect the tone?

Jamaica Kincaid

Jamaica Kincaid was born in 1949 in St. Johns, Antigua, in the West Indies. She was educated at the Princess Margaret School in Antigua and, briefly, at Westchester Community College and Franconia College. Since 1974 she has been a contributor to The New Yorker, *where "Girl" first was published. "Girl" was later included in the first of Kincaid's six books,* At the Bottom of the River.*

Ms. Kincaid informs us that "benna," mentioned early in "Girl," refers to "songs of the sort your parents didn't want you to sing, at first calypso and later rock and roll."

Girl

Wash the white clothes on Monday and put them on the stone heap; wash the color clothes on Tuesday and put them on the clothesline to dry; don't walk barehead in the hot sun; cook pumpkin fritters in very hot sweet oil; soak your little clothes right after you take them off; when buying cotton to make yourself a nice blouse, be sure that it doesn't have gum on it, because that way it won't hold up well after a wash; soak salt fish overnight before you cook it; is it true that you sing benna in Sunday school?; always eat your food in such a way that it won't turn someone else's stomach; on Sundays try to walk like a lady and not like the slut you are so bent on becoming; don't sing benna in Sunday school; you mustn't speak to wharf-rat boys, not even to give directions; don't eat fruits on the street—flies will follow you; *but I don't sing benna on Sundays at all and never in Sunday school;* this is how to sew on a button; this is how to make a buttonhole for the button you have just sewed on; this is how to hem a dress when you see the hem coming down and so to prevent yourself from looking like the slut I know you are so bent on becoming; this is how you iron your father's khaki shirt so that it doesn't have a crease; this is how you iron your father's khaki pants so that they don't have a crease; this is how you grow okra—far from the house, because okra tree harbors red ants; when you are growing dasheen, make sure it gets plenty of water or else it makes your throat itch when you are eating it; this is how you sweep a corner; this is how you sweep a whole house; this is how you sweep a yard; this is how you smile to someone you don't like too much; this is how you smile to someone you don't like at all; this is how you smile to someone you like completely; this is how you set a table for tea; this is how you set a table for dinner; this is how you set a table for dinner with an important guest; this is how you set a table for lunch; this is how you set a table for breakfast; this is how to behave in the presence of men who don't know you very well, and this way they won't recognize immediately the slut I have warned you against becoming; be sure to wash every day, even if it is with your own spit; don't squat down to play marbles—you are not a boy, you know; don't pick people's flowers—you might catch something; don't throw stones at blackbirds, because it might not be a blackbird at all; this is how to make a bread pudding; this is how to make doukona; this is how to make pepper pot; this is how to make a good medicine for a cold; this is how to make a good medicine to throw away a child before it even becomes a child; this is how to catch a fish; this is how to throw back a fish you don't like, and that way something bad won't fall on you; this is how to bully a man; this is how a man bullies you; this is how to love a man, and if this doesn't work there are other ways, and if they don't work don't feel too bad about giving up; this is how to spit up in the air if you feel like it, and this is how to move quick so that it doesn't fall on you; this is how to make ends meet; always squeeze bread to make sure it's fresh; *but what if the baker won't let me feel the bread?;* you mean to say that after all you are really going to be the kind of woman who the baker won't let near the bread?

✎ Topic for Critical Thinking and Writing

In a paragraph, identify the two characters whose voices we hear in this story. Explain what we know about them (their circumstances and their relationship). Cite specific evidence from the text. For example, what is the effect of the frequent repetition of "this is how"? Are there other words or phrases frequently repeated?

Try reading a section of "Girl" out loud in a rhythmical pattern, giving the principal and the second voices. Then reread the story, trying to incorporate this rhythm mentally into your reading. How does this rhythm contribute to the overall effect of the story? How does it compare to or contrast with speech rhythms that are familiar to you?

Sharon Olds

Sharon Olds was born in San Francisco in 1942 and was educated at Stanford University and Columbia University. She has published several volumes of poetry and has received major awards.

I Go Back to May 1937

I see them standing at the formal gates of their colleges,
I see my father strolling out
under the ochre sandstone arch, the
red tiles glinting like bent
plates of blood behind his head, I   5
see my mother with a few light books at her hip
standing at the pillar made of tiny bricks with the
wrought-iron gate still open behind her, its
sword-tips black in the May air,
they are about to graduate, they are about to get married,   10
they are kids, they are dumb, all they know is they are
innocent, they would never hurt anybody.
I want to go up to them and say Stop,
don't do it—she's the wrong woman,
he's the wrong man, you are going to do things   15
you cannot imagine you would ever do,
you are going to do bad things to children,
you are going to suffer in ways you never heard of,
you are going to want to die. I want to go
up to them there in the late May sunlight and say it,   20
her hungry pretty blank face turning to me,
his pitiful beautiful untouched body,
his arrogant handsome blind face turning to me,
his pitiful beautiful untouched body,
but I don't do it. I want to live. I   25
take them up like the male and female
paper dolls and bang them together
at the hips like chips of flint as if to
strike sparks from them, I say
Do what you are going to do, and I will tell about it.

[1987]

✎ Topics for Critical Thinking and Writing

1. Having read the poem, how do you understand its title? How does Olds seem to define "I"? What does she mean by "Go Back to"? And why "May 1937"?
2. In the first line Olds says, "I see them." *How* does she see them? Actually? In imagination? In photographs? Or can't we know?
3. Consider the comparisons, such as the simile in lines 4–5 ("red tiles glinting like bent/plates of blood") and the metaphor in lines 8–9 (the uprights of the wrought-iron fence are "sword-tips"). What do they tell us about the speaker's view of things?
4. Observe where the sentences of the poem begin and end. Can you explain these sentence boundaries? What shifts of meaning or mood accompany the end of one sentence and the beginning of the next?
5. How are the mother and father characterized when young? Are these characterizations consistent or inconsistent with the violent emotions of lines 13–19?
6. How do you read the last line? Do you feel that the speaker is, for example, angry, or vengeful, or sympathetic, or resigned? How do you interpret "and I will tell about it"? To whom will she "tell about it," and how?

A Casebook on Divorce

Peter D. Kramer

Peter D. Kramer, a clinical professor of psychiatry at Brown University, is the author of "Listening to Prozac" and the forthcoming "Should You Leave?"

Divorce and Our National Values

How shall we resolve a marital crisis? Consider an example from the advice column of Ann Landers. An "Iowa Wife" wrote to ask what she should do about her husband's habit, after 30 years of marriage, of reading magazines at table when the couple dined out. Ann Landers advised the wife to engage her husband by studying subjects of interest to him.

Readers from around the country protested. A "14-Year-Old Girl in Pennsylvania" crystallized the objections: "You told the wife to read up on sports or business, whatever he was interested in, even though it might be boring to her. Doesn't that defeat the basic idea of being your own self?" Chastened, Ann Landers changed course, updated her stance: Reading at table is a hostile act, perhaps even grounds for divorce.

When it comes to marriage, Ann Landers seems a reasonable barometer of our values. In practical terms, reading the sports pages might work for some Iowa wife—but we do not believe that is how spouses ought to behave. Only the second response, consider divorce, expresses our overriding respect for autonomy, for the unique and separate self.

Look south now from Iowa and Pennsylvania to Louisiana, where a new law allows couples to opt for a "covenant marriage"—terminable only after a lengthy separation or because of adultery, abandonment, abuse or imprisonment. The law has been praised by many as an expedient against the epidemic of divorce and an incarnation of our "traditional values."

Whether the law will lower the divorce rate is an empirical question to be decided in the future, but it is not too soon to ask: Does covenant marriage express the values we live by? 5

History seems to say no. American literature's one great self-help book is "walden," a paean to self-reliance and an homage to Henry David Thoreau's favorite preacher, Ralph Waldo Emerson, who declaimed: "Say to them, O father, O mother, O wife, O brother, O friend, I have lived with you after appearances hitherto. Henceforward, I am the truth's. . . . I must be myself. I cannot break my self any longer for you, or you."

The economic philosophy we proudly export, fundamentalist capitalism, says that society functions best when members act in a self-interested manner. The nation's founding document is a bill of divorcement. Autonomy is the characteristic American virtue.

As a psychiatrist, I see this value embedded in our psychotherapy, the craft that both shapes and expresses the prevailing common sense. In the early 1970's, Carl Rogers, known as the "Psychologist of America," encapsulated the post–World War II version of our ideals: A successful marriage is one that increases the "self-actualization" of each member. Of a failed union, he wrote: "If Jennifer had from the first insisted on being her true self, the marriage would have had much more strife and much more hope."

Rogers was expressing the predominant viewpoint; for most of the past 50 years, enhanced autonomy has been a goal of psychotherapy. Erik Erikson began the trend by boldly proclaiming that the search for identity had become as important in his time as the study of sexuality was in Freud's. Later, Murray Bowen, a founder of family therapy, invoked a scale of maturity whose measure is a person's ability to maintain his or her beliefs in the face of family pressures. The useful response to crises within couples, Bowen suggested, is to hold fast to your values and challenge your partner to rise to meet your level of maturity.

But autonomy was a value for men only, and largely it was pseudo-   10
autonomy, the successful man propped up by the indentured wife and over-
burdened mother. (No doubt Thoreau sent his clothes home for laundering.)

The self-help movement, beginning in the 1970's, extended this American ideal to women. Once both partners are allowed to be autonomous,
the continuation of marriage becomes more truly voluntary. In this sense,
an increase in divorce signals social progress.

It signals social progress, except that divorce is itself destructive. So it
seems to me the question is whether any other compelling value counter-
balances the siren song of self-improvement.

Turning again to psychotherapy, we do hear arguments for a different
type of American value. Answering Erikson's call for individual identity,
Helen Merrell Lynd, a sociologist at Sarah Lawrence College, wrote, "Nor
must complete finding of one-self . . . precede finding oneself in and
through other persons."

Her belief entered psychiatry through the writings of her pupil, Jean
Baker Miller. A professor of psychiatry at Boston University, Dr. Miller
faults most psychotherapy for elevating autonomy at the expense of qualities important to women, such as mutuality. To feel connected (when
there is genuine give-and-take) is to feel worth. Miller wants a transformed culture in which mutuality "is valued as highly as, or more highly
than, self-enhancement."

Mutuality is an ideal the culture believes it should honor but does not   15
quite. Ours is a society that does a half-hearted job of inculcating compromise, which is to say that we still teach these skills mainly to women.
Much of psychotherapy addresses the troubles of those who make great
efforts at compromise only to be taken advantage of by selfish partners.

Often the more vulnerable spouse requires rescue through the sort of
move Ann Landers recommends, vigorous self-assertion, and even divorce.

Mutuality is a worthy ideal, one that might serve as a fit complement
and counterbalance to our celebration of the self. But if we do not reward
it elsewhere—if in the school and office and marketplace, we celebrate
self-assertion—it seems worrisome to ask the institution of marriage to
play by different rules.

What is insidious about Louisiana's covenant marriage is that, contrary to claims on its behalf, it is out of touch with our traditional values:
self-expression, self-fulfillment, self-reliance.

The Louisiana law invites couples to lash themselves to a morality the
broader culture does not support, an arrangement that creates a potential
for terrible tensions.

Though we profess abhorrence of divorce, I suspect that the divorce   20
rate reflects our national values with great exactness, and that conventional modern marriage—an eternal commitment with loopholes
galore—expresses precisely the degree of loss of autonomy that we are
able to tolerate.

Barbara S. Cain

Older Children and Divorce

 T hey were more sanguine about Laura. She was, after all, in college and on the far side of growing up. They said she had loosened her tether to the family and was no longer hostage to the twists of their fate. They allowed that she would be shaken for a time by their divorce, but insisted that before long she would find her balance and regain her stride. Her younger brothers, on the other hand, were a constant source of nagging concern. At home and in the eye of the storm, they were in closer range and at higher risk. But Laura, they said, was less vulnerable. Not to worry, Laura would be fine.

So go the prevailing attitudes toward college-age children of a midlife divorce. Moreover, these assumptions appear to be shared by social scientists and cultural tribunes who have rigorously investigated the impact of divorce on younger children but have, nevertheless, overlooked the plight of a college-age population, even though statistics show increased incidence of divorce during midlife, thereby involving greater numbers of young adult offspring.

In an effort to narrow this gap in the literature, a study was launched in 1984 at the University of California at San Diego and the University of Michigan at Ann Arbor—in which 50 college students between the ages of 18 and 26 were interviewed by this writer, who reported the findings in the journal *Psychiatry* in May 1989. There were obvious differences among the students, their families and each individual divorce process, but recurrent themes and threads of discourse wove themselves within and across the interviews with striking regularity.

Perhaps most consistent among them were the students' initial reactions to news of their parents' divorce. All but three in the study recalled an immediate state of shock followed by a lingering sense of disbelief. Even those who grew up amid a turbulent marriage were incredulous when a separation was announced.

"I shouldn't have been surprised," a 20-year-old woman reflected. "I used to hear them argue night after night. I used to hear Mom cry and Dad take off in the car. I used to lie awake until he came back, but he always did come back, so I just assumed they would carry on like that for the rest of their lives."   5

Others who had observed their parents slowly disengage solaced themselves with the belief that though a marriage of more than two decades might inevitably lose its luster it would not necessarily lose its life. "Sure, I noticed them drift apart," a 21-year-old woman remarked. "But then I surveyed the marriages in our neighborhood, and nobody was exactly hearing violins, so I relaxed and told myself that Mom and

Dad were like every other couple who had spent half their lives in one relationship."

An unexpected finding was that more than half the youngsters surveyed had glorified the marriage preceding its breach, claiming theirs was "the all-American family," their parents were "the ideal couple"—and "the envy of everyone they knew."

"I mean I wasn't exactly naïve about divorce," a 19-year-old woman explained. "Half my friends grew up with a single parent, but my Mom and Dad were considered Mr. and Mrs. Perfect Couple. So when they split up, all our friends were just as freaked out as I was."

When the veil of denial began to lift and reality took hold, these young adults experienced a profound sense of loss. They felt bereft of the family of childhood, the one in the photo album, the one whose members shared the same history, the same humor, the same address. Many described in graphic detail the wrenching pain when the family house was sold, when the furniture was divided and delivered to two separate addresses, neither of which "would ever be home."

"Nothing really sank in," explained a 20-year-old man, "until I watched the movers denude the house I lived in for most of my life. And then I sat on the bare floor and stared at the marks on the wall which outlined the places where our furniture used to be. And I cried until I couldn't see those borders anymore." Clearly the dismantling of the family house symbolized in stark relief the final dismantling of the family itself.

As each parent began living with new partners, the young adults surveyed said that they felt estranged from the resented interloper and displaced by the new mate's younger (often live-in) children. Others felt virtually evicted from the parents' new homes, which simply could not accommodate two sets of children during over-lapping visits.

"When neither Mom nor Dad had room for me during spring break," a 19-year-old man recalled, "it finally hit me that I no longer had a home to go back to and, like it or not, I'd better get my act together because it was, 'Welcome to the adult world, kid, you're now completely on your own.'"

Because the divorce represented the first sobering crisis in their young adult lives, many in the study believed it marked the end of an era of trust and ushered in a new apprehension about life's unforeseen calamities. They reported an unprecedented preoccupation with death, disease and crippling disabilities. They became self-described cynics, and began scanning relationships for subterfuge. "I used to believe what people said," a 22-year-old woman recalled. "I used to trust my roommates. I used to trust my boyfriends, and now I know I also used to be certifiably 'judgment impaired.'"

Striking among this age group was the way in which harsh moral opprobrium became the conduit through which anger toward parents was expressed. Pejoratives like irresponsible, self-indulgent and hypocritical punctuated the interviews.

"You accept as an article of faith that your parents will stay together   15
until they die," explained a thoughtful 20-year-old woman, "and then
they pull the rug out from under you and you want to scream out" and
ask, "How can you break the very rules you yourselves wrote?"

Many described being gripped by an unforgiving fury toward parents
who they felt had deprived them of a home, a family and that inseparable
parental pair they assumed would always be there, together, at birthdays,
holidays and vacations at home. Furthermore, they viewed these losses to
have been preventable, hence they deeply resented learning of the decision when it was a fait accompli. And they upbraided their parents for
excluding them from a process they might have otherwise reversed.

"Why didn't they tell me they were having trouble?" one young
woman asked in barely muted exasperation. "If I had known, I would
have helped them find a marriage counselor. If they were unhappy then
why didn't they do something about it? My dad spent more time fixing his
car than he ever did his marriage."

Most in the study blamed the parent who initiated the break and
relentlessly hectored that parent for explanations. "Every day I'd ask my
mother 'Why,'" one young woman recalled, "and no answer ever made
sense. They all sounded so feeble, and so absolutely wrong."

The young adults surveyed were most staggered by the apparent
moral reversals in their parents' behavior. In stunned disbelief, a 20-year-
old woman discovered her "buttoned up, Bible-carrying" mother in bed
with a man two years older than her son. Another student witnessed his
ambitious, seemingly conscience-ridden father walk away from his family and his lucrative law firm for destinations unknown. As though looking
through lenses badly out of focus, many gazed upon parents they no
longer recognized and struggled over which image was false, which
authentic.

"Was the old Mom just hiding under the real one that was coming out   20
now?" a 21-year-old man wondered. "Was that tender, loving person all a
lie? Was I just not seeing what I didn't want to see? And if that's true, then
how am I supposed to trust what I think I see now?"

Upon observing their mothers' unbridled sexuality, several young
women withdrew from romantic relationships, retreated to solitary study,
became abstemious and, in Anna Freud's words, declared war on the pursuit of pleasure.

In sharp contrast, others plunged into hedonism, flaunting their indul-
gences, daring their parents to forbid activity that mirrored their own. A
20-year-old woman launched a series of sexual liaisons with older married
men. A 19-year-old moved in with a graduate student after knowing him
for 10 days. And a 22-year-old male dropped out of school to deal in drugs.

In response to their parents' apparent moral inversion, a small subgroup temporarily took refuge in a protective nihilism, reasoning that illusions that never form are illusions that never shatter. "Since their breakup
I don't pin my hopes on anything anymore," a disenchanted young man

declared. "And I no longer have a secret dream. What will be will be. Since I can't change any of that, why even try and why even care?"

At variance with the familiar loyalty conflict observed in younger children of divorce, most young adults considered one parent worthy of blame, the other worthy of compassion. Several openly stated they were sorely tempted to sever ties permanently with the parent who initiated the break. And when asked, "What would you advise someone your age whose parents were divorcing?" many answered, "Do not write one parent off totally, even though you might be tempted to at the time of the split."

Several said they feigned an affectionate tie to the rejected parent simply because of financial need. "Between you and me," a spunky 19-year-old man confessed, "I can't wait till I'm self-supporting, so then I won't have to humor my father with a phony song and dance every time my tuition is due." And a number reported that their overt condemnation of their father cost them a long-enjoyed relationship with paternal grandparents as battle lines between "his" and "her" side of the family were drawn.

25

Despite their censoriousness and ascriptions of blame, these young adults staunchly insisted that each parent honor their attempted neutrality. "I refused to let my Mom put down my Dad," one 23-year-old man declared emphatically, "and I artfully dodged every invitation to spy on one and report to the other."

Remarks such as these suggest that, whatever else, these college-age youngsters are better able than younger children to remove themselves from the internecine warfare and resist colluding with the parent "spurned" in excoriating the parent blamed.

In sharp contrast to younger children of divorce who frequently hold themselves responsible for the separation, the young adults surveyed did not reveal even the slightest traces of guilt or blame. Though most were certain they had not caused their parents' divorce, several lamented having failed to prevent it. A 19-year-old woman believed that had she managed her mother's domestic chores more effectively, her mother would not have ended her marriage in favor of her career. And a 21-year-old woman chided herself for not noticing her parents' estrangement: "Sometimes I still wonder if I had paid more attention to *them*, maybe we would all still be *us*."

And because each youngster in the study was living away from home at the time of the separation, many believed that their parents had literally "stayed together for the sake of the children." Indeed, several parents did not disabuse their children of this notion. When a 20-year-old man accused his father of being foolishly head-strong in abruptly ending his 25-year marriage, his father informed him that he had wanted to end his marriage for more than 20 years but had waited until his son was grown and gone.

Three in the study proudly announced that they were responsible for their parents' separations and celebrated the fact that they urged upon their mothers a much overdue separation from chronically abusive alcoholic fathers. "Do I feel responsible for my parents splitting? You bet I do," one 24-year-old man trumpeted. "And my only regret is not pushing for it sooner."

30

With few exceptions, the young adults surveyed described an unremitting concern for their single parents, particularly the one who opposed the break. They dropped courses, cut classes, extended weekends away from school in an effort to bolster the spirit of the parent at home. "I flew home so often," one young man mused, "I was awarded three free tickets in less than one year."

In striking role reversals, these youngsters disavowed their own wish for support and ministered to their parents instead. They nurtured mothers who cried in their arms, they discouraged fathers from reckless decisions, they variously counseled, succored, reassured and advised. And many reported they were unable to resume the natural rhythms of their lives until their parents were clearly back on track.

"I was nervous most of the time I wasn't with my Mom," a 20-year-old man explained. ". . . I called her constantly and went home as often as I could. . . . Deep down, I was worried she'd take her own life or accidentally smash the car as she was thinking about Dad or money or being too old and too fat to start over again."

These young adults also assumed the role of proxies. "After the split, I felt I was wearing a thousand hats," a 19-year-old woman recalled. "In one day I could be a college student, my mother's therapist, my dad's escort and my brother's mother. Small wonder I was a little ditzy that year."

After their parents had parted, some of those surveyed recalled allowing themselves to return to a recently relinquished parent-child relationship in which they "tolerated" parental overprotection from the "spurned" partner. They no longer balked at queries about eating habits and dating behavior. "If Mom's happier treating me like a kid, I'm willing to be that for her," a 20-year-old man admitted. "She just lost her husband, the least I can do is let her have her kid." Others described a quasi-symbiotic relationship with one or the other parent in which both parent and child were by turns both host and parasite.

Though many felt compelled to rescue their parents, several baldly stated that they deeply resented the "hysterical calls in the middle of the night," the incessant ruminations about "the same old stuff." It is noteworthy, however, that those who were enraged by parental pleas and demands felt, nonetheless, obliged to leave school at times and comfort the beleaguered parent at home. As a young woman stated succinctly, "If I stayed at school, I was worried about my Mom; if I went home I was worried about me."

Perhaps the most uniform finding in this study was the radically altered attitudes toward love and marriage held by many following their parents' divorce.

When a young woman's parents separated soon after their 20th anniversary, she created her own theory of marriage: "People marry in order to have children, and parenthood is what holds a marriage together. When children are grown and gone, marriage no longer has a reason for being and couples will then drift apart and the marriage will slowly die. If couples stay together even after their last child leaves home, then they are truly in love and they are the lucky few."

Several categorically forswore marriage, vowing to spare themselves and their unborn children the pain and dislocation they had recently endured. Others allowed for a long-term live-in relationship but pledged to forestall indefinitely a legally binding commitment. A disenchanted young man spoke for many: "Since their divorce, I'm gun-shy about love and spastic about marriage. To me, getting married is like walking over a minefield, you know it's going to explode . . . you just don't know when!"

Those who were already involved in longstanding romances felt their parents' divorce cast a long shadow on their own relationship. As a 20-year-old woman explained: "You become super alert to everything your boyfriend does. You suddenly notice his wandering eye as you walk together across campus. You start resenting it when he yawns or fidgets or looks at his watch while you're talking. And you spend a whole lot of time holding your breath braced for the moment when he hits you with, 'I mean I really like you, but I really need more space.'"

Some young women withdrew from boyfriends they suddenly suspected as being unfaithful, indifferent or increasingly remote. Others demanded premature commitments or promises thereof. And many abruptly aborted solid relationships in an effort to actively master what they believed they might otherwise helplessly endure.

With rare exception, most in the study feared they were destined to repeat their parents' mistakes, a concern frequently reinforced by the parents themselves. "You're attracted to the same kind of charming Don Juan who did me in," one mother admonished. "Beware of the womanizer just like your father or you'll be dumped in your 40's, just like me." Many of the youngsters deeply resented these apocalyptic, cautionary tales. Others felt burdened by having to wrestle with the ghosts of their parents' past. "Most people meet, fall in love and marry," a 21-year-old lamented, "but I have to find someone who convinces my mother he's not my father and then he has to fit the job description of a saint."

Whereas most felt fated to repeat their parents' past, many were determined to avoid the perils their parents did not. Many pledged never to let feelings fester until "they explode in everybody's face." They planned a "playmate relationship" in order to avoid the pallor of their parents' middle years. In an effort to revise their parents' history, some feared they would submit a potential partner to such dissecting scrutiny no mortal would qualify, and marriage would be forever postponed.

Nevertheless, when asked at the close of their interviews, "Where do you see yourself 10 years from now?" many of those who earlier had denounced marriage stated unhesitatingly that they would in all probability "be married with kids and a house of my own."

Not every divorce was emotionally wrenching. It was least disruptive when the parents' decision was mutual and their initial rancor was relatively shortlived. Youngsters fared best when their attachment to each parent was honored by the other, when their quest for neutrality was respected and when their relationship with each parent remained virtually unmarred. Few were so fortunate, however.

Friendship and religion were great comforts for many, but the majority said that soul-baring marathons with siblings clearly offered the greatest amount of comfort with the least amount of shame.

"I couldn't have made it without my sister," one college junior recalled. "Talking to friends was like going public, but with my sister it was safe, it was private, and a lifeline for us both."

Whether or not the profound sense of loss, the disillusionment, the revised attitudes toward love and marriage remain an enduring legacy of parental divorce for college-age youngsters, only future studies can determine. It should be noted, however, that most of these youngsters unsuccessfully disguised a deep and abiding wish to marry, to have children and to recapture the family of childhood—the one in the picture frame, animated, intertwined and inseparable.

Diane Medved

Diane Medved was born in 1951 in Los Angeles and educated (B.A., M.A., and Ph.D.) at the University of California, Los Angeles. She is a licensed clinical therapist and the author of three books: Children, To Have or Have Not? *(1982, under the name of Diane C. Elvenstar),* First Comes Love: Deciding Whether or Not to Get Married *(1983, also under the name of Elvenstar), and (under the name of Medved)* The Case against Divorce *(1989), in which the material that we reprint here appears.*

The Case Against Divorce

I have to start with a confession: This isn't the book I set out to write.

I planned to write something consistent with my previous professional experience—helping people with decision making. In ten years as a psychologist, I've run scores of workshops that specialized in weighing the pros and cons of major life choices. I've even published books on two of life's major turning points: whether or not to have a child and whether or not to get married. When I conceptualized this book on divorce, it was in that mold—a guide to help people decide if separation is appropriate.

I based this concept on some firmly held assumptions and beliefs. For example, I started this project believing that people who suffer over an extended period in unhappy marriages ought to get out. In my private practice, I'd seen plenty of struggling couples, and in every case, I anguished along with them when they described manipulation, lack of attention, or emotional dissatisfaction. I knew from their stories, as well as from my own experience, the heart-wrenching desperation that precedes separating and the liberation that leaving represents. I originally thought that staying together in turmoil was ultimately more traumatic than simply making the break.

I was convinced that recent no-fault divorce laws were a praiseworthy step toward simplifying a legally, psychologically, and emotionally punishing process. I thought that striking down taboos about divorce was another part of the ongoing enlightenment of the women's, civil rights, and human potential movements of the last twenty-five years. I had learned early in my graduate school training that crisis fosters growth, and therefore I assumed that the jolt of divorce almost always brings beneficial psychological change.

To my utter befuddlement, the extensive research I conducted for this   5
book brought me to one inescapable and irrefutable conclusion: I had been wrong. The statistics and anecdotes I gathered forced me to scuttle my well-prepared plans. I had to face the fact that writing a "morally neutral" book showing divorce to be just another option—a life choice no better or worse than staying married—would be irreparably damaging to the audience I wanted to help.

The change came as I shifted my focus from still-married couples in conflict, who made up the bulk of my practice, to now-single individuals who had already received their decrees.

I asked questions—and got some predictable answers: Are you glad you divorced? Yes. Do you regret getting your divorce? No. I was pleased that the responses to these two questions confirmed my original thinking.

But then I plumbed beneath the surface: What kind of contact do you have with your ex-spouse? How has the divorce affected your children? What kinds of experiences have you had in the dating world since your divorce? How has your style of living changed?

"Oh, everything's fine, fine," the respondents at first insisted. Everyone was without a doubt stronger and more hearty than ever.

But my questions kept coming. And the truth was difficult to avoid.   10
Often in a rush of tears, they described the suffering and anguish they had endured—nights of fantasies about the husband or wife who left them; days of guilt after abandoning a once-devoted mate. They talked about the nuts-and-bolts of daily life, of uprooting, of shifting to an apartment and splitting possessions, of balancing parental duties with now-pressing work demands. They spoke of changing relationships with their children, who moved from innocent babes to confidants to arbitrators and sometimes to scapegoats.

And they mourned a part of themselves never to be recaptured. The part they had once invested in a marital or family unit was now destroyed. Wearily, they told of the transformation of the optimism and enthusiasm they had devoted to the now-crushed marriage to bitterness, skepticism, and self-preservation. "Never again," echoed my respondents. "Never again will I combine my income with another's." "Never again will I trust my spouse away overnight." "Never again will I believe someone when he says 'I'll take care of you.'"

I didn't want to hear it. I wanted to hear that they got past their divorces and emerged better for it. And while the women and men I spoke to were more sure of themselves and capable of living independently, I also heard that they had gained this self-reliance out of painful necessity, not out of free choice.

For given a choice, they preferred to be married. Everyone said he or she wanted to find somebody new. Many women were panic-stricken, afraid they would not find the "right" man before their childbearing years were lost. Others had become so jaded that they lamented the sobering truth that they were unlikely to find another mate at all. With their new-found strength, they all said they would survive; all said they were perfectly content with themselves and the lives they'd recently reconstructed. Still, there was regret. "Looking back now, do you think that you could have made it work with your first husband?" I asked.

"Well, he was crazy," they'd begin. "He was a slob. He was unromantic. He only thought of himself and his career. But knowing what I know now . . . yes, I probably could have made it work."

I was aghast. But the more I heard these or similar words, and the more I read from the library, the more I was forced to concede that the ruinous stories of my divorced clients and interviewees were true. Divorce was catastrophic—but not in the commonly acceptable terms of a simple year or two thrown away. I found that the mere contemplation of divorce—the acceptance of it as an imminent option (rather than dedication to working on a wounded marriage) is debilitating. The process of evaluating the injuries—of cajoling and pleading and threatening—is emotionally exhausting. The physical act of packing a bag and moving out is traumatic. And from there the trauma escalates.

15

Quite simply, I discovered in my research that the process and aftermath of divorce is so pervasively disastrous—to body, mind, and spirit—that in an overwhelming number of cases, the "cure" that it brings is surely worse than marriage's "disease."

Of course, there are exceptions. There are times when divorce is clearly the only recourse. When physical or mental abuse exists. When emotional cruelty or neglect becomes intolerable. When one partner adamantly refuses to stay in the marriage or withdraws to the point where in reality you're alone.

I used to think that the range of situations when divorce is appropriate encompassed quite a bit more than that. But when I look at the balance of the bad and the good that divorced individuals endure, my only possible conclusion is that people could be spared enormous suffering if they scotched their permissive acceptance of divorce and viewed marriage as a serious, lifelong commitment, a bond not to be entered into—or wriggled out of—lightly.

The old wedding vows read "for better or for worse . . . until death do us part." They now commonly intone, "through good times and bad . . . as long as our love shall last." Until recently, I nodded at the "improvement"; now I soberly acknowledge the wisdom in the message of the past.

Too Late for Marleen

The grim stories of crippled couples whom I interviewed for this book got   20
me thinking about the permanent distrust, anguish, and bitterness divorce
brings. But the catalyst coalescing these thoughts was a simple workaday
lunch with a friend I've known for about eight years. Marleen Gaines, a
school district administrator, is a handsome woman of forty who wears
sophisticated silks, renews season tickets to the symphony, and stays
sharp on the decisions of the courts, cabinet, and city council. When a
mutual friend originally introduced us, I instantly clicked into Marleen's
quick wit, upbeat attitude, and direct, self-confident zest. But as we sat
down to salads at a cafe near my office, her usual sunny veneer gave way
to a depressing monotone of desolation.

Three years ago, Marleen startled her friends by suddenly walking
out of her nine-year marriage. At the time she left him, her husband Bob,
now forty-two, seemed unbearably boring, uneducated, and unmotivated
to achieve. Marleen wanted more of a dynamo, a brilliant intellectual she
could admire, successful in his career. She met lots of these stimulating
men at the office, and casual flirtations suggested to her that once she was
free to pursue them, she would have plenty of opportunities for a more
satisfying marriage.

But after three years single, she has found only frustration—and the
humiliating realization that at her age, she is considered witty and glib but
not especially desirable. There were a couple of flings with married men
and an unrequited crush on her self-absorbed boss, who encouraged her
attention merely to further inflate his swollen ego. She fell in love with a
coworker, who treasured her company so much he told her every excruciating detail of his romantic exploits and eventual engagement. Meanwhile, her three closest friends remarried one by one and had stylishly
late-in-life babies.

Now alone in a rambling house in San Bernardino with only her three
dogs for companionship, she yearns for the simple warmth of Bob's presence. Though he was a college dropout and works now as a supermarket
manager, Bob had his virtues. Always gentle and good-natured, he doted
on Marleen and provided consistent encouragement. He may not have
been the go-getter she desired, but he had an intuitive intelligence and a
good, steady income to maintain their comfortable lifestyle.

It took all this time for Marleen to realize her mistake. At first, Bob had
begged her to return; rebuked, he rebounded into one, then another serious relationship. He now lives with a woman who's pushing for marriage,
and he's grown quite fond of her two teenage sons. When they speak
every few weeks, Bob confesses to Marleen that his current companion
"can be a pain" and swears that Marleen is the only woman he's ever
"really" loved. Now Marleen has asked for a reconciliation, but weak-
willed Bob is too dominated in his new world to leave, and Marleen, realizing that "possession is nine-tenths of the law," has resigned herself to the
fact that he's not coming back.

Divorces Are Forever

Sitting in the restaurant trying to console my friend, I was struck by the   25
frequency with which I've heard stories similar to hers—not only in my
workshops and clinical psychology practice, but increasingly in everyday
social chatter. It's a well-known U.S. Census Bureau statistic that half of all
marriages fail; equally well-publicized is how both men and women suffer financially as a result. Sociologist Leonore Weitzman found that
women's standard of living declines by a whopping 73 percent in the first
year after divorce, and those who are mothers are further saddled with
additional child care and logistics chores.

While everyone laments the immediate trauma of "going through a
divorce," more discomfiting is the alarming news of its lingering emotional
and psychological effects. Research by the California Children of Divorce
Project headed by Judith Wallerstein, for example, shows an especially dismal future for women forty and over—even ten years after the divorce. Half
of the women studied at that distant point could be diagnosed as "clinically
depressed," and all were moderately or severely lonely, despite the fact that
50 percent of them had initiated the divorce themselves. Exacerbating their
malaise might be alarming new statistics on their chances of finding another husband—chances *Newsweek* magazine (June 1986) claims are so low that
these women face a greater likelihood of being struck by a terrorist!

Uncovering these facts during the preparation of this book only made
me determined to probe reactions to divorce further. I jotted down some
ideas and then developed an informal questionnaire that I distributed to
an unscientific but diverse sample of two hundred people who had been
separated or divorced. The results brought home undeniably that the
effects of divorce last a lifetime. And they are in actuality far worse than
we care to confront.

Everyone has some understanding of the pain of divorce. And yet, in
these days of disposable marriage, at one time or another every married
person contemplates separation. It may be in the heat of an argument, or
during a fantasy about a more perfect mate. It may appear amid recurrent
minor irritations, or it may come as the cumulative result of larger problems stored away for years. Everyone in the throes of a flirtation or affair
considers the possibility of chucking the safe and boring for the exciting
and glamorous. And people on the cusp of new success are tempted to
leave reminders of the less glorious past and begin anew.

Clashing with this casual attitude toward divorce is America's
reclaiming of traditional values. Religion has gained renewed respectability. Women who cried "career first" are now honoring their maternal
instincts and realizing they may not be able to "have it all." Conservative
politics have recently attracted many of yesterday's liberals. All college
students, once esoterically majoring in philosophy and sociology, are taking the most direct routes to their MBAs.

Personal lives are more conservative as well, due to the sheer terror   30
provoked by the specter of AIDS. People are practicing "safe sex" not only

with frank conversation prior to intimacy and with the use of condoms, but through definite changes in outlook toward recreational sex. A 1987 bestseller, taken seriously enough to be the subject of a day's discussion on the Oprah Winfrey television talk show and a return appearance by the author, advocated sexual abstinence before marriage. In addition, a representative national survey of twelve hundred college students undertaken by *Glamour* magazine revealed that "the AIDS epidemic is a serious damper on sexual activity: about half of all college students say the threat of AIDS has caused them to change their sexual habits."

The AIDS scare and the broader shift toward conservative attitudes, however, seem distant to couples in the throes of conjugal combat. In the midst of a shouting match, a gloriously portrayed single life and freedom from the oppression of a particular spouse call much more loudly. Unfortunately, veterans of divorce like my friend Marleen, who yearn for families and secure, permanent relationships, now see that they have been sadly duped by those compelling myths, which suggest that divorce "can open up new horizons," that the dating scene is exciting, and that bright, attractive people will always find new partners with whom to share their lives.

It's finally time to renounce—openly and clearly—these self-serving platitudes about independence and fulfillment and look at the reality of divorce. We act too frequently as if every infirm marriage deserves to die, based simply upon the emotional report of one distressed partner. Rather than viewing a separation first with alarm, we're full of sympathy for a divorcing friend, and we offer understanding of the temporary insanity involved in severing old ties.

Still influenced by the "do your own thing" era, we don't act constructively. We don't take the husband (or wife) by the shoulders and shake him. We don't shout in his ear that he might be making a disastrous mistake. Even if we care immensely about him, we feel it's too intrusively "judgmental" to do more than step back and say, "Okay, if that's what you want," and close our eyes to the consequences. My research suggests that this is more cruelty than friendship.

Even Winners Pay the Price

Some people who know me well ask how I could take this position, having been divorced and then happily remarried myself. It is partially because I have faced divorce that I can speak with some authority. It is true that I am one of the very lucky few who entered the chancy world of potential happiness or permanent pain and was ultimately given a break. But there are so many others—just as bright, just as desirable or more so— who bitterly ask why their "best years" must be spent alone. Even though I found a satisfying relationship, I am still paying the price of my divorce.

It is difficult for me to discuss something as personal as my own   35
divorce, partially because I now invest so much in the new life I have cre-

ated. I also don't like writing about my divorce because I am embarrassed and ashamed, and those feelings are painful to express.

Though my ex-husband and I were constitutionally quite different, we were nevertheless also the same in many ways, or at least had grown that way over the years. And because we shared our adolescence and formative adult period, we had a bond I found excruciating to discard. Unfortunately, like almost all of the divorced couples I have seen and researched, we cannot manage that ridiculous myth of being "just friends." So in becoming divorced, I severed an important extension of myself, negating a crucial and memorable chunk of my history and development. It is an enormous loss.

I am humiliated and mortified at failing in a relationship others at one time held exemplary. My divorce clashes with the self-image I work earnestly to cultivate: that I am triumphant in my endeavors, that the things I attempt are not only worthwhile but likely to succeed. By divorcing, I have proven myself inept—at least once—in perhaps the most crucial arena, one which by profession is my stock-in-trade—the ability to analyze choices and proceed wisely.

My divorce would have been bad enough were I able to keep my downfall a secret, like the dieter who sneaks a bag of cookies while driving on the anonymous freeway. But I am embarrassed further because of the public discredit and the possibility that former admirers now view me as diminished. Whether or not my associates really do see my character as smirched, or whether they are truly forgiving, is not as relevant as the fact that I *feel* I am now less worthy of their regard.

For those who do go on to build a second life, the future, built more on hope than confidence, may falter. Only about half of those I interviewed who remarried stayed with the second spouse or reported conjugal satisfaction; many found themselves reeling from their first marriages years later and admitted repeating the same mistakes.

The book *Crazy Time* by Abigail Trafford describes the weeks and   40 months after separation, when typically people replay those crushing moments over and over in their minds. The one who is rejected remembers the years together in measured fragments, dissecting every retort, every misplaced movement, for signs of failure or symbols of flawed passion.

The one who leaves in search of something better is so wracked by guilt and remorse that he can do nothing more than look ahead, shielding himself from the overwhelming self-loathing and embarrassment of looking at his past. Like Pharaoh, who refused the Jews' pleas for freedom even when confronted by the convincing pressure of the ten plagues, a spouse who negates his marriage must harden his heart against it. He must bury all the love that still exists for his partner, even if he realizes that it is love shaped by gratitude rather than attraction. The safe and cozy, welcoming home that the estranged partner once provided must be temporarily barred from consciousness. Years of striving together for the success of the other, for the enhancement of the unit, must be eliminated from the mind.

No one ever emerges from a divorce unscathed—he or she is inevitably permanently harmed.

That the divorced end up even more unhappy is not their fault. They're told by innumerable subtle and direct messages that they ought to be "mad as hell and unwilling to take it anymore," to paraphrase the inciteful slogan of the movie *Network*. They're encouraged by magazines sold at checkout stands to dissect their relationships. They're led by business-seeking shrinks to believe they can't possibly be fulfilled unless they're undergoing turmoil and instigating change.

I've read more than fifty books off my local public library shelves that comfort and cheer on those involved in divorce. These volumes take you step-by-step through the court procedure and tell you what stages of distress your "normal" child will endure. These books ease you like silk into the singles game and tout your "new freedom" as if it, rather than marriage, is the ultimate means toward fulfillment.

I write this book as a counterbalance, to shake a few shoulders, with   45
hopes that I might spare some children helplessness and some partners pain. I want to expose the forces that strive to hide the damage of divorce. Too many people think "If only I could be out of this marriage . . ." and conclude that sentence with their own private miracles. To repeat: It's not their fault; they're victims of propaganda. But the lure lets them down, for after they buy it they inevitably remain the same people, with the same problem-solving skills, values, and styles of relating to another. And so they can't help but choose and shape new relationships into duplications of their spoiled romance. How can they be expected to see that divorce is, with very few exceptions, the wrong way to improve their lives?

And so this book is for everyone who is now focusing on some infuriating characteristic of their mate and thinking, "I can't take this much longer." It is for those who have already packed and moved out, either physically or emotionally, who look ahead and therefore can't see that their brightest path lies behind them. It is for those who have been hurt, whose wounds are so painful that they simply want to run away, and for others who see signs and want to prevent a breakup before the repairs become too overwhelming.

Perhaps you or someone you know has uttered something similar to one or more of these lines:

> "Our fights are getting so fierce, the good times don't seem worth the arguments anymore."
> "Sure I love him. But I know I could do better."
> "I've found the love of my life—I have to get out of my marriage because I just can't end this affair and give up such a good thing."
> "I've been smothered in this marriage too long—I need to go off on my own and prove myself."
> "I don't respect or admire her anymore."
> "He's been bugging me for a long time. I've just stuck it out for the sake of the children."

When any of these statements are used long after the fact—years beyond a final decree—there's nothing to be done. But in many other cases, it may not be too late. I've found that none of these sentiments automatically signals an irreparable tear in the basic fiber of a marriage. If you hear someone for whom you have any feeling at all hinting at separation, instead of tacitly endorsing the move, instantly protest. Nearly every marriage has something worth preserving, something that can be restored. Revitalizing a relationship brings triumph and ongoing reward; and as you'll see, avoiding divorce spares those concerned from the greatest trauma of their lives.

The Case Against Divorce

Of course, nobody *wants* to get divorced. Or does he? Joseph Epstein, in *Divorced in America*, recognizes the respectability of divorce: "In some circles, not to have gone through a divorce seems more exceptional than having gone through one; here living out one's days within the confines of a single marriage might even be thought to show an insufficiency of imagination, evidence that one is possibly a bit callow emotionally."

God forbid we appear emotionally callow! How dare we assume that those in the same dreary marriage they claim to have treasured for years could have gotten a lot out of it! The unspoken popular wisdom declares that only by undergoing this rite of psychological passage can anyone mature. I've heard the tales of postdivorce development: people who finally find themselves; who finally learn to be self-sufficient; who finally achieve independence. It is true that after divorce women especially, and men to some extent, report emotional growth. But they won't admit that they might have blossomed even more had they gathered the gumption to stick with and heal the marriage.

Of course, it's useless to speculate about what might have been accomplished in any particular relationship. But some things we *do* know—and these comprise the major arguments in the case against divorce: 50

1. *Divorce hurts you.* Divorce brings out selfishness, hostility, and vindictiveness. It ruins your idealism about marriage. It leaves emotional scars from which you can never be free. It costs a bunch of money—and significantly reduces your standard of living.
2. *Divorce hurts those around you.* It devastates your children for at least two years and probably for life. It hurts your family by splitting it in two; both family and friends are compelled to take sides. It forces you to be hardened against people you once loved. It rips the fabric of our society, each divorce providing another example of marriage devalued.
3. *The single life isn't what it's cracked up to be.* Ask anyone—the "swinging singles" life is full of frustration, rejection, and disappointment. The

Mr. and Ms. Right you assume waits for you may be only a futile fantasy. Even a successful affair that bridges you from one marriage to another often becomes merely a second failure.

4. *Staying married is better for you.* You don't have to disrupt your life for two to seven years; instead, solving marital problems provides a sense of teamwork and stands as a concrete accomplishment that enhances problem-solving skills in the larger world. Marriage is statistically proven to be the best status for your health, divorce the worst. Marriage gives you something to show for your time on earth—children (usually) and a bond built on continuity and history.

I don't expect that everyone will agree with what I've found. It's largely a matter of values and also one of semantics. For example, I write that a family is worth preserving, and therefore it is worth compromising your goals or habits to save your marriage. Others holding different values might say that no marriage is worth burying your "true self" by dashing the goals you truly desire or stifling your personal inclinations. Obviously, it's not so easy to make a marriage work. But few achievements are as major or lasting.

Tony Perkins, Joe Cook, Anita Blair, Lynne Gold-Bikin

We reprint a discussion that was televised on The Newshour with Jim Lehrer, *on August 20, 1997. Perkins is a Louisiana state representative; Cook is with the American Civil Liberties Union; Blair is with the Independent Women's Forum; Gold-Bikin is a family law attorney. The moderator was Elizabeth Farnsworth.*

Symposium: Death Do Us Part?

Elizabeth Farnsworth: Finally tonight, a new marriage law in Louisiana. We begin with some background.

Elizabeth Farnsworth: Millions of Americans tie the knot every year, pledging to stay together till death do us part, but nearly half of all marriages fail. Divorce rates in the United States are the highest of any western nation, having climbed 34 percent in the decade between 1970 and 1990. Some in Louisiana argued couples weren't taking their vows seriously because it was so easy to marry.

Bishop Paul Morton, St. Stephen Baptist Church, New Orleans: I'm surprised people have not literally opened up some places where you can rent wedding rings because it's just—we take it so lightly.

Elizabeth Farnsworth: In June, the Louisiana legislature dealt with the problem head on. It passed a law which went into effect last week allowing couples to choose a new kind of union called "Covenant Marriage."

Bishop Paul Morton: You have that document as it relates to the "Covenant Marriage"—

Elizabeth Farnsworth: A Covenant Marriage is harder to enter and escape than a standard marriage. Couples must prove they've had premarital counseling and pledge to seek help if the marriage turns rocky. A standard marriage in Louisiana, which couples can still choose, allows divorce after a six-month separation or immediately if one spouse is guilty of adultery or has been sentenced to prison or death. But a Covenant Marriage can't be dissolved unless the couple is separated for two years or can show proof of adultery, abandonment, physical abuse, or if one spouse is sentenced for a felony conviction. Catholic and Episcopal bishops and some Baptist ministers in Louisiana are considering making the Covenant Marriage license a requirement for weddings in their churches. Louisiana is the first state to offer two marriage options, but at least nine other states are also exploring ways to make it tougher to divorce.

Elizabeth Farnsworth: Now, four different perspectives on Covenant Marriages. Louisiana Rep. Tony Perkins, a Republican from Baton Rouge, was the primary sponsor of the legislation creating the covenant option. Joe Cook is the executive director of the American Civil Liberties Union in Louisiana. Lynne Gold-Bikin is the former chair of the American Bar Association's Family Law Section, and Anita Blair is executive vice president of the Independent Women's Forum, a women's policy organization here in Washington. Thank you all for being with us.

Rep. Perkins, this is your legislation. Why did you think it was necessary?

State Rep. Tony Perkins, (R) Louisiana (Baton Rouge): Well, legislatures around the country are continually dealing with issues trying to create new laws to address teenage pregnancy, juvenile delinquency, child poverty, a number of these issues. And now what the social sciences are telling us that these issues trace right back to broken homes. And so government has a vested interest in trying to keep families together. And this bill is not about making divorce more difficult. Its focus is on prevention and on treatment, on making marriages more successful by providing premarital counseling, and encouraging counsel when a couple runs into difficulty. And it's by their own choice. So we think it's a good step in the right direction on shifting our culture back to one of marriage versus one of divorce.

Elizabeth Farnsworth: Joe Cook, the ACLU in Louisiana vigorously opposed this. Why?

Joe Cook, ACLU, Louisiana (New Orleans): Well, because what we have in this case is the state enforcing religious doctrine. Originally, the bill started out by Rep. Perkins where the only grounds for divorce were abandonment and adultery. Those are biblical grounds. The other grounds were added as it went through the process over Mr. Perkins' objections. The state should not be in the business of enforcing religious doctrine. And, as the bill came out of law, it is more difficult to get a divorce on other grounds than it is on abandonment and adultery. Secondly, this particular law now is not in the best interest of women and children.

Elizabeth Farnsworth: Okay. Let's come back to that. Let me go back to Rep. Perkins once more—before we go on. What about that? Does it enforce religious doctrine?

State Rep. Tony Perkins: No, it certainly does not. This deals with the civil contract aspect of marriage. And Joe knows. He's seen the legislative process. You never start out with a piece of legislation as you want to end up, or else you wouldn't have anything worth having. And so we started out with a very tightly worded document. And I'll add this. It is not for the first time actually in Louisiana law we have an expanded grounds for divorce. We actually are elevating to the same level as adultery and abandonment, as Joe pointed out, physical and sexual abuse. Domestic violence for the first time is being recognized in Louisiana law as serious of a breach as adultery.

Elizabeth Farnsworth: Joe Cook, go ahead with your second point.

Joe Cook: Well, the second point is it's not in the best interest, especially of women and children, who usually find themselves trapped in a bad marriage situation. If the children are being emotionally abused, it's going to be very difficult to prove in a court of law to, first of all, even get a separation agreement, the same thing for physical abuse of a woman. You'll have to have photographs, perhaps, if the woman is battered, witnesses to come forward and air the dirty linen of the marriage in public. And that's not in the best interest of children, to have them go through this kind of situation. And there's no study, scientific studies, that have been done to compare children who had to stay in these kinds of abusive and neglectful situations, as opposed to children who have gotten—where there have been divorces.

Elizabeth Farnsworth: Rep. Perkins, how do you answer that?

State Rep. Tony Perkins: That's a red herring. The issue is: Are we going to make marriages more successful? Women and children have suffered under no-fault divorce. What this does, this provides every avenue of escape, and it puts the person who's been offended in the driver's seat. They're the ones that will be able to make the decision, not the one who is the abuser but the one who is the abused. And certainly if a woman has enough of evidence to get a restraining order currently to protect herself, she certainly has enough evidence to get a legal separation or divorce under this law.

Elizabeth Farnsworth: All right. We're going to expand this discussion now. Anita Blair, do you agree that divorce is this serious a problem and that this is one way to solve it?

Anita Blair, Independent Women's Forum: I certainly agree that divorce is this serious a problem. In my role as a policy organization in Washington I hear from people across the country. And what I see is an America under no-fault divorce that has a leading broken heart.

Elizabeth Farnsworth: Explain no-fault divorce for us.

Anita Blair: No-fault divorce is essentially a contract under which either person may unilaterally pull out without taking into account the feelings of the other person. And this is the predominant kind of complaint that I hear, whether it's a husband or a wife, you know, my spouse woke up one day, didn't want to be married anymore; I had no choice; I was forced into a divorce. And that is the post no-fault America that we live in.

Elizabeth Farnsworth: How would this change that, though? That still could happen. You just have to wait longer.

Anita Blair: It still can happen. I don't think that the Louisiana law is perfect. It is not going to outlaw divorce in America. But it's a step in the right direction. It's a statement by the state that says we recognize the importance of marriage and the role that we have played in making divorce so easy to get and, therefore, devaluing marriage. And so we're going to, you know, give people the option to have the kind of marriage that they want. If they feel committed, then we will support their commitment. And I think it's a wonderful statement in the state of Louisiana that says we recognize how important marriage is, and we're going to support it.

Elizabeth Farnsworth: Ms. Gold-Bikin, how do you see it? How important a problem is divorce, and is this the way to get at it?

Lynne Gold-Bikin, Family Law Attorney (Philadelphia): Well, let me start off by telling you that, of course, divorce is a problem, but let's go back to what Rep. Perkins said in the first place, which is we're concerned about the impact on children. And Mr. Cook points out very well that we have never had a study that shows the impact of a bad marriage on children. We only look at the children of divorce. Divorce does not hurt children. Parents hurt children. There are a lot of children who have come out of good divorces, if we can use those words, parents who mutually agree to separate and do not pull the children back and forth like pieces of Turkish taffy.

Elizabeth Farnsworth: So, let me just interrupt for one minute. So, you're objecting to the premise that divorce is to blame for the broken hearts and all the things that people—

Lynne Gold-Bikin: Oh, absolutely. And the idea that this wonderful law that Mr. Perkins has proposed is going to give the abused the right to control or the idea that this will give the person who doesn't want the marriage some say, let's keep in mind that when we had only fault divorce in this country the person who didn't want the marriage had the say. So, all we've done now is recognize the realities of a situation; that when someone is unhappy in a marriage, they're going to leave, whether it be a legal separation, a legal divorce, or moving across town, which is what people did in the 70's and the 60's when they didn't like their marriage. We ought to work on marriage. I don't disagree with that, but it's a little bit late—excuse me—it's a little bit late to start working on the marriage when the wedding dress is bought and the invitations are out. We should start working on relationships in third and fourth grade, in fifth and sixth grade, like the American Bar Association is trying to do with the partners program. We have developed a program to teach people about relationships.

Elizabeth Farnsworth: I'll come back to you with some suggestions for solutions in a second.
    Rep. Perkins, how do you respond to her criticism?

State Rep. Tony Perkins: Well—

Elizabeth Farnsworth: That divorce may not be the problem and that this is not the way to treat it, even if it is a problem.

State Rep. Tony Perkins: I guess, in her view, we would just leave it the way it is. I suggest that we have to take steps to make our families stronger and make marriage more successful. It is a problem. And our children are suffering. The study done recently by Judith Wallerstein that tracked families over a 25-year period of divorce showed that the impact on children of divorce actually grew over time, spanning a period of three decades, having a tremendous impact on their lives. And these were families that were well educated, that had finances, that were well adapted. You can imagine, when you go down a scale on education and finances, that the impact grows even stronger.

Elizabeth Farnsworth: Ms. Gold-Bikin.

Lynne Gold-Bikin: The problem is that people are going to get divorced whether the state tells them they can or not. That's not the issue. We ought to make marriages stronger, but it's not up to the state to do that.

State Rep. Tony Perkins: The state is giving them an option.

Lynne Gold-Bikin: Excuse me. The state is not giving them an option. People are going to be manipulated into this so-called Covenant Marriage, and it is—

Elizabeth Farnsworth: Why? Explain why—

Lynne Gold-Bikin: Why? Because—

Elizabeth Farnsworth: —you think there's no option.

Lynne Gold-Bikin: I'm going to tell you why. Because first of all, a regular marriage is for life. To say that—to give it a different label, this is a slippery slope on the way to doing away with a no-fault divorce. This is to try to give control to a vindictive person in a relationship. You know, the idea that one person ends a marriage is naive. It takes two to end a marriage. It takes two people to make each other unhappy, and you don't start training people to get divorced, or to have a good marriage just before they get married. This is not the—

Elizabeth Farnsworth: Okay.

Lynne Gold-Bikin: —place for the state.

Elizabeth Farnsworth: Let me go to—

Lynne Gold-Bikin: Keep the state out of the relationship.

Elizabeth Farnsworth: —Anita Hall for a minute. Anita Hall, do you think that this is one step towards ending no-fault divorce; that this is a—there has been the view expressed that this is sort of a backdoor way of ending no-fault divorce.

Anita Blair: There are a lot of people who wouldn't object to that. In fact, there are numerous groups across the country, Americans for Divorce Reform—

Elizabeth Farnsworth: I'm sorry, Anita Blair. I'm sorry.

Anita Blair: That's okay. Americans for Divorce Reform has been formed, and they are across the United States. They would like to see no-fault divorce done away with, and the institution of marriage thereby strengthened and given more value. There are lots of—you know, for people that want to live together or want to share economic benefits or something like that, you know, there is a legal thing for them, and it's called partnership. And I think that Ms. Bikin is trying to say that there is—there is marriage and then there is something that the state recognizes. But, you know, in our society they walk hand in hand. And if the state is going to support this wonderful social institution of marriage, it's got to get on the ball and say, we're not going—we are going to enforce the parties' expectation that it's going to be mutual and exclusive and forever.

Lynne Gold-Bikin: But what if one of the parties doesn't work at it?

Elizabeth Farnsworth: Excuse me. Joe Cook has been trying to get in here. Joe Cook.

Joe Cook: Yes. This particular law is a solution in search—in search of a problem to solve. Louisiana already has one of the lowest divorce rates in the nation, according to research done by the Children's Rights Council out of Washington, D.C., however, we do rank 49th in the quality of life for children in this state. We should be doing something to improve family life. And we could do that by lifting children out of poverty, one of the highest poverty rates in the nation, by improving our graduation rates, by improving our infant mortality rate and our teenage pregnancy rate. This particular bill does nothing to address those issues.

Elizabeth Farnsworth: Rep. Perkins, why didn't you address those issues? Why choose this issue to center on?

State Rep. Tony Perkins: This is addressing those issues. That's exactly what is the—what comes out of broken homes. And while Louisiana is about 11th in terms of having to lower divorce rates, we still have a problem with divorce. And it's a national problem. And it's an issue that needs to be addressed at some point and some time. And this is the beginning of addressing it. All of those issues that Joe brought out are issues that relate to single-parent homes where children are more likely to be in poverty, less educated, have poor health, and at a greater risk for violence and for involvement in criminal activity. That's what this addressed.

Lynne Gold-Bikin: Excuse me. That's not what the statistics show.

Elizabeth Farnsworth: Joe Cook first and then we'll go to Ms. Gold-Bikin.

Joe Cook: Well, that's untrue. The majority of people in this state are already married, and the majority of children who have the problems that I just addressed come out of homes where there's a marriage. And that just doesn't hold up. So what we should be doing is certainly trying to improve the family and home life in this state and in this nation, but you cannot legislate good marriages. And that's what we are trying to do here in this case by the religious right wing.

Elizabeth Farnsworth: Anita Blair first and then I'll go back to you, Ms. Gold-Bikin.

Anita Blair: I would be very surprised if it were true that many of the children that are disadvantaged are in a two-parent, intact home. We have a terrible problem with illegitimacy today. And one of the reasons is that there's no reason to get married if you're not going to accomplish the security that you want. And no-fault takes away the security, so why get married?

Elizabeth Farnsworth: Do you see this—Ms. Blair—

Lynne Gold-Bikin: Excuse me. That's absolutely untrue. And I really would like to jump in here—

Elizabeth Farnsworth: Go ahead.

Lynne Gold-Bikin: —and say to you that you can't blame no-fault divorce for the problems. You have to look at the fact that the media holds up the perfect marriage that nobody can meet; that we have people moving away all over the country from families and communities so you no longer have a support system. You've got people living a lot longer. You've got fifty, sixty, seventy-year marriages. So you cannot blame no-fault divorce for the rise in the problems. You've got to look at the society as a whole. But if you want to work on marriage, start working on relationships early on, not when people are getting married. And keep the state out of it.

Elizabeth Farnsworth: Ms. Blair.

Anita Blair: Well, we could work on it by shortening life spans. Is that the suggestion?

Lynne Gold-Bikin: Not at all.

Anita Blair: I mean, this is something that we can do and Louisiana ought to be congratulated for taking a step in the right direction. It may or may not be the perfect thing to do, but it acknowledges problems, and it works toward the solution.

Elizabeth Farnsworth: Ms. Blair, do you expect now for other states to do this, and for this to be something that is a national phenomenon?

Anita Blair: Yes. I think Louisiana kind of broke through the political log-jam here. Many other states had tried to do away with no-fault divorce, but Louisiana has this very interesting combination of two kinds of marriage and a menu for people who may want to get married that allows people who might not be totally against no-fault divorce to, nonetheless, get on the bandwagon for counseling and making a bigger commitment.

Elizabeth Farnsworth: And Joe Cook, do you expect the ACLU and other organizations to oppose this around the country as it becomes—if it does become a phenomenon?

Joe Cook: Well, absolutely. We've already received a complaint from a Christian minister who wants to challenge this particular law in Louisiana. And we're going to be researching it to see if it can be challenged. This is not in the best interest of women and children especially. And it's a throwback to the days before we had no-fault divorce, where people were trapped in abusive and neglectful situations and that is certainly worse than getting a divorce and getting away from it.

Elizabeth Farnsworth: All right. Well, thank you all very much for being with us.

Celia E. Rothenberg

Celia E. Rothenberg graduated from Wellesley College in 1991. A history major with a special interest in the lives of Middle Eastern women, she was awarded a Marshall fellowship and is now studying modern Middle Eastern history at Oxford. She has served as an intern in an Israeli-Palestinian women's peace group in Jerusalem, and she plans to continue working for understanding between these two groups.

Rothenberg wrote the following essay while she was an undergraduate.

Child of Divorce

Over this past winter vacation my parents, brother, and I spent a few days together—a rare event now that the four of us live in four different states. As I watched my parents and brother engage in our usual laughter and reminiscing, accompanied by an occasional tear at a past both bitter and sweet, I listened more closely than ever before to what is a frequent topic of discussion, our relationship as a family.

Perhaps because my parents divorced when I was a small child, it seems to surprise my friends that my family's recollections of those years are filled with many pleasant memories. After all, those who don't know my family have reason to assume that the memories of growing up with divorced parents in some tough economic times might be rather dreary. In fact, however, my memories center on the results of the thoughtfulness and conscious effort exerted by both my parents to create a sense of love and protection for my brother and me. I have always felt that my family was a team, a team that sometimes fumbled, and sometimes seemed to have two, three, or even four captains, and a team that underwent a change in plan mid-game, but a team nevertheless. It is only recently, however, that I have realized how much patience and understanding went into achieving that sense of belonging and love, and how achieving it was part of the long and often painful process for us of divorce and healing.

My parents divorced, after fifteen years of marriage, when I was six. I have nearly no memories of living in a two-parent household. From the time of my earliest memories, my mother has always studied or worked full time. Immediately after the divorce, she, like many women who find themselves single after many years as a "housewife," went back to school. My brother at the time was twelve. Although I remember my Cinderella-shaped cake for my seventh birthday, a few of my favorite pets, and a well-loved school teacher, I remember very little of my mom's return to school, or my own or brother's adjustment to our new surroundings. Perhaps the gaps in my memory serve as some kind of mental defense mechanism to protect me from the reality of the harder times; no matter the reason for my memory voids, however, my brother's recollections are so vivid, and my mom and dad so open about those years, that my scattered memories have been augmented by their story-telling—to the point that I often confuse my memories with theirs.

It is only recently, in fact, that I have realized how difficult the initial years following the divorce were for my mother, brother and father. Over this past winter vacation, my mom told me for the first time how taxing even the simplest tasks seemed to be. For example, locking the doors to our new, small house conjured up all the difficulties and sadnesses of this new beginning. Because my dad had customarily locked up, she had rarely been the one to lock each lock and turn off each light. Doing these tasks in a new house in a new city was a constant reminder of her changed circumstances. Late in the evening she would carefully plot the order in which to turn off the lights, so as not to be alone in the dark. She would lock a door, and then a window, pausing in between the locks to distract her mind from the task at hand—and the frightening and lonely feelings these new responsibilities brought with them.

My family now openly recalls that those years were a difficult time of   5
adjustment to new schools, a new city, and a new life. We had moved from
a small suburb of St. Louis to Champaign-Urbana, a community largely
centered on the life of the University of Illinois. Our first house in Cham-
paign and my mom's tuition for the Master's degree in Library and Information Science were largely financed by the sale of the lovely Steinway
baby grand piano that had graced my parents' living room since before I
was born. Before the divorce, my father was an attorney until he found
himself in legal difficulties, which ultimately led him to give up the practice of law. His reduced income and my mom's tuition bills placed us
under a great financial strain.

My brother, who was twelve at the time of the divorce, particularly
recalls how difficult communication was between the three of us and
my father, and at times even among the three of us. To help ease the tension of my dad's monthly visits and maintain a relationship which
included some fun, my brother and dad played checkers through the
mail. They carefully conceived of a plan of multiple paper copies of the
checker board and colored pencils for their game. One of my few early
memories of those years focusses on the checker board we set up on the
dining room table to represent the game my brother and dad played on
paper. One evening, the cat we brought with us from (as my mother
often said) our "other life," jumped on the board, knocking the pieces all
over the table. Steve was inconsolable, and only a prolonged long-distance phone call to figure out where each piece belonged resolved the
situation.

That first year my brother escaped into a world of books, often reading fiction and plays when he should have been doing homework, a coping behavior he practiced until he was nearly through high school.

But even the deepest hurts can heal over time. With encouragement
and support from both my parents, Steve channeled his considerable energy and anger into planning for an early graduation from high school and
a year in Israel between high school and college. The only conditions set
were that he had to earn enough money to buy his own plane ticket and
he had to have a college acceptance letter in hand before he left. These
goals gave him something to work for at a time when he felt that he had
lost friends and status in coming to a new, very different, and less comfortable environment than had been part of his early days.

As for me, perhaps because I was six years younger, I appeared to go
blithely along, oblivious to most of the tensions and strains that Steve
seemed to feel. With my mother studying for her classes and Steve spending almost all his time reading, I became an avid reader myself, almost in
self defense. I found new friends and reveled in my new elementary school,
a magnet school where we studied French every day. I wrote long, detailed
stories of a young girl who lived on a farm with both parents and a dozen
brothers and sisters and a beautiful horse. Perhaps I, too, was seeking some
consolation in an imaginary life far removed from our little house.

It can take years for wounds to heal, and I am happy to say that my family healed more quickly than most. Perhaps we got past that initial phase early on because my parents did not make too many mistakes. They avoided some common pitfalls of divorcing families. The divorce was quick—the process was completed a few months after my parents sold their house and moved to their new homes—there were no court battles, no screaming fights, no wrenching decisions that we children were required to make. Steve and I were never asked—or allowed—to choose sides or express a preference for one parent over the other. Although my own memories are blurry, the few recollections I have of those first five years focus on my dad's regular monthly visits (he lived a few hours away by car). By the time I was ten, he was spending nearly every weekend with us at the house, a pattern which continued for the next decade, until I was out of high school and off to Wellesley.

Nothing worthwhile, my mother has always told me, is ever easy. It could not have always been easy for either of my parents to spend so much of their free time together when they had chosen to create separate lives, but at the time Steve and I rarely saw anything but civility and fondness. As parents they were determined not to let their children suffer for mistakes they may have made in their marriage. It is one of their greatest gifts to Steve and me, for it was the ultimate lesson in learning about the commitment and cost of love and the lifelong responsibilities of family.

The stories we have accumulated over the years have become more hilarious as I have grown older. My dad, determined not to be a "Disneyland daddy," showing up on the weekends for shopping and dinners out, was not uncomfortable in our new home. In fact, he helped us figure out how to do various home improvement projects. Under his direction, we rewired our house (and nearly electrocuted Steve in the process), insulated our attic (the family story lingers that we nearly blew off the roof), and painted the house (and, of course, ourselves). Our projects probably didn't save us very much money, since we seemed to spend as much money on fixing the mistakes we made as on the project itself, yet we were not merely building the house, or growing gardens, or mowing the lawn. We were rebuilding our lives, making memories, and creating a sense of togetherness.

My own clear and more complete memories begin at the age of eleven, when my mother, brother, and I began a new life-style, which reflected a newly achieved flexibility and confidence in our ability to manage our lives. When my brother entered the University of Illinois, we moved into a big old house and I began high school. The house was what a real estate broker fondly calls a "fixer-upper," and was perfect for my mom's income (she worked for the University after she finished her Master's degree) and our need for space for friends of mine and Steve's. Steve, in particular, brought home countless Jewish college students whom he knew from his involvement in the campus Jewish student organization. They often needed a good meal, a shoulder to lean on, an opinion on a paper, or a good night's sleep.

I remember our dining room on Shabbos, furnished with a dining room set probably beautiful in my grandmother's day but battered after three generations of use, packed with college students eating dinner. I remember vividly the talk and the laughter, the jesting and the endless debates. My mom was not only an intellectual support for those students but also an inspiration, someone who had experienced a marriage gone bad, the trials and tribulations of parenting alone (at least during the week), and the tough economics of a single-parent household. Conversations stretched from the abstract to the concrete, from the politics of the Eastern bloc to the intricacies of love and sex.

Over the years it has become clear that the divorce, although traumatic, opened our minds, enriched our relationships with each other, and loosened restraints we did not know we were subject to. I vividly remember my high school years as a busy time full of my friends and my brothers' who simply enjoyed being around the house. The slightly chaotic, easy-going atmosphere of the house was fostered in large part by our mom; she had disliked the isolated feeling of life in suburbia when she was married. She wanted to create a different atmos-phere for Steve and me, a place where young people were comfortable to come and go.

My friends in high school were fascinated by my home, and I enjoyed it as much as they did. My dad was able to watch us grow and change from weekend to weekend, his place secure and comfortable at the head of the Shabbos table surrounded by students. He helped us with science projects, participated in countless car-pools, and, most of all, was there when we needed him. Although from the point of view of the Census Bureau we were a "single parent household," in actuality we were a *family* that happened to have divorced parents. Perhaps our experience was not typical of some families in which there has been a divorce, but the labels obscure our understanding of the needs and hopes of all families, which I think are probably the same, divorced or not. My parent's expectations for Steve and me were not altered by their marital status, nor do I think that Steve and I let them get away with very much on the excuse that they were divorced!

I have always loved my family, but I find that I admire each of them increasingly as time goes on. Now, when we gather from different corners of the country and world during vacations a few times a year, we admit that the best and the worst, but always the most precious times, were when we were together on the weekends in that big old house, sometimes with the students and sometimes with only each other. On special occasions, we have a (very patient) long-distance operator connect the four of us on the same phone line, and we talk as if there is no tomorrow. We are fiercely proud of one another; I often have to restrain myself from blurting out the merits of my exceptional family to my unsuspecting friends.

At times I wonder how different we would be if we had not gone through the divorce, but for that question I can conjure up no really meaningful speculation. I know that we immensely value our time together, freely share our money (or, I should say, our student loans, as my brother is

15

now in law school, my mom is a full-time doctoral student and my father shoulders the Wellesley burden), and exorbitantly rejoice in each other's company. What more could any of us want from family? So often, it seems to me, I see families that do not realize they possess a great wealth—time. They are together all the time. They don't miss the moments of their mother/father/brother/sister's lives that are irreplacable.

There is no question that it is often difficult to be a family. My own family's life took a path with an unexpected curve. We weathered times of tough adjustments, economic difficulties, and typical adolescent rebellion. Through it all, though, there was a guiding (if unspoken until many years later) principle of life: family is family forever, and there is no escaping either the trials or the rewards. My parents expect my brother and me to extend ourselves and do work that in some way will bring more light into the world. I have parents who, on modest incomes and budgets, have endowed me with dreams and a sense that the impossible is possible. I have parents for whom I am extremely grateful.

When I told my family that Wellesley asked me to write an article on growing up in a single parent household, they responded in their typical chaotic fashion. My brother forced each of us to sit and write a page about the "Single-Parent Thing" before he let us eat dinner. My mother began plotting a book made up of chapters written from the different perspectives of mother, father, son, and daughter in the single-parent household. My dad insisted we discuss it over dinner (and promised to write his page immediately after dessert). In the end, I took their contributions with me back to Wellesley and wrote down my own feelings, late at night in Munger Hall.

8
IDENTITIES

*Grandfather and Grandchildren Awaiting Evacuation Bus, Hayward,
California, May 9, 1942*
Dorothea Lange

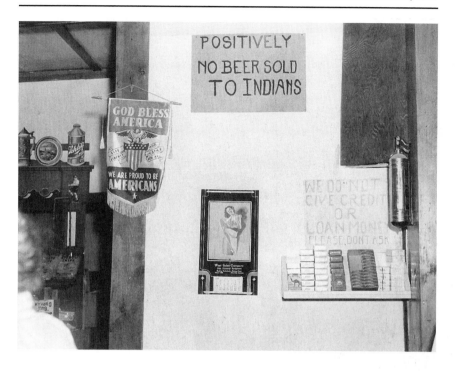

Short Views

In every known society, the male's need for achievement can be recognized. Men may cook, or weave, or dress dolls or hunt hummingbirds, but if such activities are appropriate occupations of men, then the whole society, men and women alike, votes them as important. When the same occupations are performed by women, they are regarded as less important.

Margaret Mead

There is no female mind. The brain is not an organ of sex. As well speak of a female liver.

Charlotte Perkins Gilman

This has always been a man's world, and none of the reasons hitherto brought forward in explanation of this fact has seemed adequate.

Simone de Beauvoir

We all have been put into categories which fix us in a position which lasts the whole of our lives. Girls are called "feminine" beings and are taught the appropriate feminine behavior; boys are labelled "masculine" and have their behavior defined for them too. No one escapes. Failure to conform to our assigned behavior means that we feel wrong and bad about ourselves. We are not encouraged to break the laws of sex and gender; and certainly no one questions whether the demands of society are contrary to the demands of being human. There ought to be questions asked, though. For what society does is not in our best interest as persons. Society's interest is concerned with how effective we will be as economic and political and cultural supports, not how human we will be.

Heather Formaini

America is God's crucible, the great melting pot where all the races of Europe are melting and re-forming.

Israel Zangwill

No metaphor can capture completely the complexity of ethnic dynamics in the U. S. "Melting pot" ignores the persistence and reconfiguration of ethnicity over the generations. "Mosaic," much more apt for pluralistic societies such as Kenya or India, is too static a metaphor; it fails to take into account the easy penetration of many ethnic boundaries. Nor is "salad bowl" appropriate; the ingredients of a salad bowl are mixed but do not change. "Rainbow" is a tantalizing metaphor, but rainbows disappear. "Symphony," like "rainbow," implies near perfect harmony; both fail to take into account the variety and range of ethnic conflict in the United States.

The most accurately descriptive metaphor, the one that best explains the dynamics of ethnicity, is "kaleidoscope." American ethnicity is kaleidoscopic, i.e. "complex and varied, changing form, pattern, color . . . continually shifting from one set of relations to another; rapidly changing." When a kaleidoscope is in motion, the parts give the appearance of rapid change and extensive variety in color and shape and in their interrelationships. The viewer sees an endless variety of variegated patterns, just as takes place on the American ethnic landscape.
   Lawrence Fuchs

We have room for but one language here and that is the English language, for we intend to see that the crucible turns out our people as Americans, of American nationality and not as dwellers in a polyglot boarding house, and we have room for but one loyalty and that is a loyalty to the American people.
   Theodore Roosevelt

I cannot say too often—any man who carries a hyphen about him carries a dagger which he is ready to plunge into the vitals of the Republic.
   Woodrow Wilson

Capitalism is a machine for the suppression of one class by another.
   Vladimir I. Lenin

Through our own efforts and concerted good faith in learning to know, thus to respect, the wonderfully rich and diverse subcommunities of America, we can establish a new vision of America: a place where "community" may mean many things, yet retains its deeper spiritual significance. We may even learn to coincide with the 500th anniversary of the "discovery" of America by Columbus, that America, in its magnificent variety, has yet to be discovered.
   Joyce Carol Oates

I have a dream that my four little children will one day live in a nation where they will not be judged by the color of their skin but by the content of their character.

Martin Luther King, Jr.

Light came to me when I realized that I did not have to consider any racial group as a whole. God made them duck by duck and that was the only way I could see them.

Zora Neale Hurston

Racism is so universal in this country, so wide-spread and deep-seated, that it is invisible because it is so normal.

Shirley Chisholm

Stephen Jay Gould

Stephen Jay Gould, born in 1941, is a professor of geology at Harvard University, where he teaches paleontology, biology, and the history of science. The essays he has written for the magazine Natural History *have been collected in five highly readable books.*

Women's Brains

In the Prelude to *Middlemarch,* George Eliot lamented the unfulfilled lives of talented women:

> Some have felt that these blundering lives are due to the inconvenient indefiniteness with which the Supreme Power has fashioned the natures of women: if there were one level of feminine incompetence as strict as the ability to count three and no more, the social lot of women might be treated with scientific certitude.

Eliot goes on to discount the idea of innate limitation, but while she wrote in 1872, the leaders of European anthropometry were trying to measure "with scientific certitude" the inferiority of women. Anthropometry, or measurement of the human body, is not so fashionable a field these days, but it dominated the human sciences for much of the nineteenth century and remained popular until intelligence testing replaced skull measurement as a favored device for making invidious comparisons among races, classes, and sexes. Craniometry, or measurement of the skull, commanded the most attention and respect. Its unquestioned leader, Paul Broca (1824–80), professor of clinical surgery at the Faculty of Medicine in Paris, gathered a school of disciples and imitators around himself. Their work, so meticulous and apparently irrefutable, exerted great influence and won high esteem as a jewel of nineteenth-century science.

Broca's work seemed particularly invulnerable to refutation. Had he not measured with the most scrupulous care and accuracy? (Indeed, he had. I have the greatest respect for Broca's meticulous procedure. His numbers are sound. But science is an inferential exercise, not a catalog of facts. Numbers, by themselves, specify nothing. All depends upon what you do with them.) Broca depicted himself as an apostle of objectivity, a man who bowed before facts and cast aside superstition and sentimentality. He declared that "there is no faith, however respectable, no interest, however legitimate, which must not accommodate itself to the progress of human knowledge and bend before truth." Women, like it or not, had smaller brains than men and, therefore, could not equal them in intelligence. This fact, Broca argued, may reinforce a common prejudice in male society, but it is also a scientific truth. L. Manouvrier, a black sheep in Broca's fold, rejected the inferiority of women and wrote with feeling about the burden imposed upon them by Broca's numbers:

> Women displayed their talents and their diplomas. They also invoked philosophical authorities. But they were opposed by *numbers* unknown to Condorcet or to John Stuart Mill. These numbers fell upon poor women like a sledge hammer, and they were accompanied by commentaries and sarcasms more ferocious than the most misogynist imprecations of certain church fathers. The theologians had asked if women had a soul. Several centuries later, some scientists were ready to refuse them a human intelligence.

Broca's argument rested upon two sets of data: the larger brains of men in modern societies, and a supposed increase in male superiority through time. His most extensive data came from autopsies performed personally in four Parisian hospitals. For 292 male brains, he calculated an average weight of 1,325 grams; 140 female brains averaged 1,144 grams for a difference of 181 grams, or 14 percent of the male weight. Broca understood, of course, that part of this difference could be attributed to the greater height of males. Yet he made no attempt to measure the effect of size alone and actually stated that it cannot account for the entire difference because we know, a priori, that women are not as intelligent as men (a premise that the data were supposed to test, not rest upon):

We might ask if the small size of the female brain depends exclusively upon the small size of her body. Tiedemann has proposed this explanation. But we must not forget that women are, on the average, a little less intelligent than men, a difference which we should not exaggerate but which is, nonetheless, real. We are therefore permitted to suppose that the relatively small size of the female brain depends in part upon her physical inferiority and in part upon her intellectual inferiority.

In 1873, the year after Eliot published *Middlemarch,* Broca measured the   5
cranial capacities of prehistoric skulls from L'Homme Mort cave. Here he found a difference of only 99.5 cubic centimeters between males and females, while modern populations range from 129.5 to 220.7. Topinard, Broca's chief disciple, explained the increasing discrepancy through time as a result of differing evolutionary pressures upon dominant men and passive women:

> The man who fights for two or more in the struggle for existence, who has all the responsibility and the cares of tomorrow, who is constantly active in combating the environment and human rivals, needs more brain than the woman whom he must protect and nourish, the sedentary woman, lacking any interior occupations, whose role is to raise children, love, and be passive.

In 1879, Gustave Le Bon, chief misogynist of Broca's school, used these data to publish what must be the most vicious attack upon women in modern scientific literature (no one can top Aristotle). I do not claim his views were representative of Broca's school, but they were published in France's most respected anthropological journal. Le Bon concluded

> In the most intelligent races, as among the Parisians, there are a large number of women whose brains are closer in size to those of gorillas than to the most developed male brains. This inferiority is so obvious that no one can contest it for a moment; only its degree is worth discussion. All psychologists who have studied the intelligence of women, as well as poets and novelists, recognize today that they represent the most inferior forms of human evolution and that they are closer to children and savages than to an adult, civilized man. They excel in fickleness, inconstancy, absence of thought and logic, and incapacity to reason. Without doubt there exist some distinguished women, very superior to the average man, but they are as exceptional as the birth of any monstrosity, as, for example, of a gorilla with two heads; consequently, we may neglect them entirely.

Nor did Le Bon shrink from the social implications of his views. He was horrified by the proposal of some American reformers to grant women higher education on the same basis as men:

> A desire to give them the same education, and, as a consequence, to propose the same goals for them, is a dangerous chimera. . . . The day when, misun-

derstanding the inferior occupations which nature has given her, women leave the home and take part in our battles; on this day a social revolution will begin, and everything that maintains the sacred ties of the family will disappear.

Sound familiar?[1]

I have reexamined Broca's data, the basis for all this derivative pronouncement, and I find his numbers sound but his interpretation ill-founded, to say the least. The data supporting his claim for increased difference through time can be easily dismissed. Broca based his contention on the samples from L'Homme Mort alone—only seven male and six female skulls in all. Never have so little data yielded such far ranging conclusions.

In 1888, Topinard published Broca's more extensive data on the Parisian hospitals. Since Broca recorded height and age as well as brain size, we may use modern statistics to remove their effect. Brain weight decreases with age, and Broca's women were, on average, considerably older than his men. Brain weight increases with height, and his average man was almost half a foot taller than his average woman. I used multiple regression, a technique that allowed me to assess simultaneously the influence of height and age upon brain size. In an analysis of the data for women, I found that, at average male height and age, a woman's brain would weigh 1,212 grams. Correction for height and age reduces Broca's measured difference of 181 grams by more than a third, to 113 grams.

I don't know what to make of this remaining difference because I cannot assess other factors known to influence brain size in a major way. Cause of death has an important effect: degenerative disease often entails a substantial diminution of brain size. (This effect is separate from the decrease attributed to age alone.) Eugene Schreider, also working with Broca's data, found that men killed in accidents had brains weighing, on average, 60 grams more than men dying of infectious diseases. The best modern data I can find (from American hospitals) records a full 100-gram difference between death by degenerative arteriosclerosis and by violence or accident. Since so many of Broca's subjects were very elderly women, we may assume that lengthy degenerative disease was more common among them than among the men.

More importantly, modern students of brain size still have not agreed on a proper measure for eliminating the powerful effect of body size. Height is partly adequate, but men and women of the same height do not share the same body build. Weight is even worse than height, because most of its variation reflects nutrition rather than intrinsic size—fat versus skinny exerts little influence upon the brain. Manouvrier took up this subject in the 1880s and argued that muscular mass and force should be used.

[1]When I wrote this essay, I assumed that Le Bon was a marginal, if colorful, figure. I have since learned that he was a leading scientist, one of the founders of social psychology, and best known for a seminal study on crowd behavior, still cited today (*La psychologie des foules*, 1895), and for his work on unconscious motivation.

He tried to measure this elusive property in various ways and found a marked difference in favor of men, even in men and women of the same height. When he corrected for what he called "sexual mass," women actually came out slightly ahead in brain size.

Thus, the corrected 113-gram difference is surely too large; the true figure is probably close to zero and may as well favor women as men. And 113 grams, by the way, is exactly the average difference between a 5 foot 4 inch and a 6 foot 4 inch male in Broca's data. We would not (especially us short folks) want to ascribe greater intelligence to tall men. In short, who knows what to do with Broca's data? They certainly don't permit any confident claim that men have bigger brains than women.

To appreciate the social role of Broca and his school, we must recognize that his statements about the brains of women do not reflect an isolated prejudice toward a single disadvantaged group. They must be weighed in the context of a general theory that supported contemporary social distinctions as biologically ordained. Women, blacks, and poor people suffered the same disparagement, but women bore the brunt of Broca's argument because he had easier access to data on women's brains. Women were singularly denigrated but they also stood as surrogates for other disenfranchised groups. As one of Broca's disciples wrote in 1881: "Men of the black races have a brain scarcely heavier than that of white women." This juxtaposition extended into many other realms of anthropological argument, particularly to claims that, anatomically and emotionally, both women and blacks were like white children—and that white children, by the theory of recapitulation, represented an ancestral (primitive) adult stage of human evolution. I do not regard as empty rhetoric the claim that women's battles are for all of us.

Maria Montessori did not confine her activities to educational reform for young children. She lectured on anthropology for several years at the University of Rome, and wrote an influential book entitled *Pedagogical Anthropology* (English edition, 1913). Montessori was no egalitarian. She supported most of Broca's work and the theory of innate criminality proposed by her compatriot Cesare Lombroso. She measured the circumference of children's heads in her schools and inferred that the best prospects had bigger brains. But she had no use for Broca's conclusions about women. She discussed Manouvrier's work at length and made much of his tentative claim that women, after proper correction of the data, had slightly larger brains than men. Women, she concluded, were intellectually superior, but men had prevailed heretofore by dint of physical force. Since technology has abolished force as an instrument of power, the era of women may soon be upon us: "In such an epoch there will really be superior human beings, there will really be men strong in morality and in sentiment. Perhaps in this way the reign of women is approaching, when the enigma of her anthropological superiority will be deciphered. Woman was always the custodian of human sentiment, morality and honor."

This represents one possible antidote to "scientific" claims for the con-   15
stitutional inferiority of certain groups. One may affirm the validity of biological distinctions but argue that the data have been misinterpreted by
prejudiced men with a stake in the outcome, and that disadvantaged
groups are truly superior. In recent years, Elaine Morgan has followed this
strategy in her *Descent of Woman,* a speculative reconstruction of human
prehistory from the woman's point of view—and as farcical as more
famous tall tales by and for men.

I prefer another strategy. Montessori and Morgan followed Broca's
philosophy to reach a more congenial conclusion. I would rather label the
whole enterprise of setting a biological value upon groups for what it is:
irrelevant and highly injurious. George Eliot well appreciated the special
tragedy that biological labeling imposed upon members of disadvantaged
groups. She expressed it for people like herself—women of extraordinary
talent. I would apply it more widely—not only to those whose dreams are
flouted but also to those who never realize that they may dream—but I
cannot match her prose. In conclusion, then, the rest of Eliot's prelude to
Middlemarch:

> The limits of variation are really much wider than anyone would imagine
> from the sameness of women's coiffure and the favorite love stories in prose
> and verse. Here and there a cygnet is reared uneasily among the ducklings
> in the brown pond, and never finds the living stream in fellowship with its
> own oary-footed kind. Here and there is born a Saint Theresa, foundress of
> nothing, whose loving heartbeats and sobs after an unattained goodness
> tremble off and are dispersed among hindrances instead of centering in
> some long-recognizable deed.

✑ Topics for Critical Thinking and Writing

1. What is your understanding of anthropometry from paragraph 2? According to Gould, what does intelligence testing have in common with anthropometry? Characterize his attitude toward both. How does he reveal his
   attitude in this paragraph?
2. In paragraph 3, what does Gould mean when he says, "But science is an
   inferential exercise, not a catalog of facts"?
3. In paragraph 13 Gould says, "I do not regard as empty rhetoric the claim that
   women's battles are for all of us." What does he mean? What foundation for
   this opinion have this paragraph and paragraph 2 provided?
4. Who was Maria Montessori, and what does her work have to do with
   Gould's argument? If her relevance is not entirely clear to you, or was not
   on first reading, what might Gould have done to make it clearer?
5. What, according to Gould, are the social consequences of what he calls in
   paragraph 16 *biological labeling*? If on the whole you agree with him, what
   is the basis of your agreement?

6. In paragraph 13 Gould refers to the "social role of Broca and his school." What does he mean by that? On the basis of this essay (and others of Gould's that you may have read) formulate in a sentence or two the social role of Gould.

Yona Zeldis McDonough

Yona Zeldis McDonough is the author of Anne Frank, *a biography for children. The essay that we reprint originally appeared in* The New York Times Magazine, *on January 25, 1998.*

What Barbie Really Taught Me

Now that my son is 6 and inextricably linked to the grade-school social circuit, he gets invited to birthday parties. Whenever I telephone to say he is coming, I ask about gifts. And whenever the child is a girl, I secretly hope the answer will be the dirty little word I am longing to hear. The word is Barbie.

No such luck. In our Park Slope, Brooklyn, neighborhood, there is a bias against the doll. "My daughter loves her, but I can't stand her," laments one mother. "I won't let her in the house," asserts another. "Oh, please!" sniffs a third.

But I love Barbie. I loved her in 1963, when she made her entrance into my life. She had a Jackie Kennedy bouffant hairdo. Her pouty mouth gave her a look both knowing and sullen. She belonged to a grown-up world of cocktail dresses, cigarette smoke and perfume. I loved her in the years that followed, too, when she developed bendable joints, a twist-'n'-turn waist, long, ash-blond hair and lifelike lashes.

I've heard all the arguments against Barbie: she's an airhead, she's an insatiable consumer—of tarty clothes, a dream house filled with pink furniture, a Barbie-mobile—who teaches girls there is nothing in life quite so exciting as shopping. Her body, with its no-way-in-the-world breasts, wasp waist and endless legs, defies all human proportion. But at 6, I inchoately understood Barbie's appeal: pure sex. My other dolls were either babies or little girls, with flat chests and chubby legs. Even the other so-called fashion dolls—Tammy, in her aqua and white playsuit, and Tressy, with that useless hank of hair—couldn't compete. Barbie was clearly a woman, and a woman was what I longed to be.

When I was 8 and had just learned about menstruation, I fashioned a   5
small sanitary napkin for Barbie out of neatly folded tissues. Rubber bands held it in place. "Look," said my bemused mother, "Barbie's got her

little period. Now she can have a baby." I was disappointed, but my girl-friends snickered in a way that satisfied me. You see, we all wanted Barbie to be, well, dirty.

Our Barbies had sex, at least our childish version of it. They hugged and kissed the few available boy dolls we had—clean-cut and oh-so-square Ken, the more relaxed and sexy Allan. Our Barbies also danced, pranced and strutted, but mostly they stripped. An adult friend tells me how she used to put her Barbie's low-backed bathing suit on backward, so the doll's breasts were exposed. I dressed mine in her candy-striped baby-sitter's apron—and nothing else. Girls respond intuitively to the doll's sexuality, and it lets them play out those roles in an endlessly compelling and yet ultimately safe manner.

I've also heard that Barbie is a poor role model. Is there such wide-spread contempt for the intelligence of children that we really imagine they are stupid enough to be shaped by a doll? Girls learn how to be women from the women around them. Most often this means Mom. Mine eschewed beauty parlors. She was a painter who wore her long, black hair loose, her earrings big and dangling and her lipstick dark. She made me a Paris bistro birthday party, with candles stuck in old wine bottles. Instead of games, she read T.S. Eliot to the group of enchanted 10-year-olds. My mother, not an 11½-inch doll, was the most powerful female role model in my life. What she thought of Barbie I really don't know, but she had the good sense to back off and let me use the doll my own way.

Barbie now exists in a variety of "serious" incarnations: teacher, Olympic athlete, dentist. And later this year we'll even get to see the Real-ly Rad Barbie, a doll whose breasts and hips will be smaller and whose waist will be thicker, thus reflecting a more real (as if children want their toys to be real) female body. I personally don't think any of this matters one iota. Girls will still know the reason they love her, a reason that has nothing to do with new professions or a subtly amended figure.

Fortunately, my Barbie love will no longer have to content itself with buying gifts for my son's female friends. I have a daughter now, and although she is just 2, she already has a half-dozen Barbies. They are, along with various articles of clothing, furniture and other accouterments, packed away like so many sleeping princesses in translucent pink plastic boxes that line my basement shelves. The magic for which they wait is not the prince's gentle kiss. It is the heart and mind of my little girl as she picks them up and begins to play.

✎ Topics for Critical Thinking and Writing

1. Evaluate the first two paragraphs of the essay as opening paragraphs. Did they hold your interest? Why, or why not? Are they appropriate to the rest of the essay?

2. In paragraph 4 McDonough says that she has heard various arguments against Barbie, and she summarizes them. Had you heard these views? Or others? In any case, in an essay of 500 words set forth the arguments and indicate how much validity you find in them. Or take some other toy—perhaps G. I. Joe, or water pistols—and evaluate arguments that you have heard offered against them.

3. At the end of paragraph 6 McDonough suggests that Barbie serves a useful function: "Girls respond intuitively to the doll's sexuality, and it lets them play out those roles in an endlessly compelling and yet ultimately safe manner." In a paragraph indicate the degree to which you agree, and why. Or take some toy that is popular with boys, and explain its popularity and its value.

Katha Pollitt

Katha Pollitt (b. 1949) writes chiefly on literary, political, and social topics. In addition to writing essays, she writes poetry; her first collection of poems, Antarctic Traveller *(1982), won the National Book Critics Circle Award. She publishes widely, especially in* The Nation, The New Yorker, *and* The New York Times. *We reprint an article that originally appeared in* The New York Times Magazine.

Why Boys Don't Play with Dolls

It's twenty-eight years since the founding of NOW,[1] and boys still like trucks and girls still like dolls. Increasingly, we are told that the source of these robust preferences must lie outside society—in prenatal hormonal influences, brain chemistry, genes—and that feminism has reached its natural limits. What else could possibly explain the love of preschool girls for party dresses or the desire of toddler boys to own more guns than Mark from Michigan?

True, recent studies claim to show small cognitive differences between the sexes: He gets around by orienting himself in space; she does it by remembering landmarks. Time will tell if any deserve the hoopla with which each is invariably greeted, over the protests of the researchers themselves. But even if the results hold up (and the history of such research is not encouraging), we don't need studies of sex-differentiated brain activity in reading, say, to understand why boys and girls still seem so unalike.

The feminist movement has done much for some women, and something for every woman, but it has hardly turned America into a playground free of sex roles. It hasn't even got women to stop dieting or men to stop interrupting them.

[1]**Now** National Organization for Women (editors' note)

Instead of looking at kids to "prove" that differences in behavior by sex are innate, we can look at the ways we raise kids as an index to how unfinished the feminist revolution really is, and how tentatively it is embraced even by adults who fully expect their daughters to enter previously male-dominated professions and their sons to change diapers.

I'm at a children's birthday party. "I'm sorry," one mom silently mouths to the mother of the birthday girl, who has just torn open her present—Tropical Splash Barbie. Now, you can love Barbie or you can hate Barbie, and there are feminists in both camps. But *apologize* for Barbie? Inflict Barbie, against your own convictions, on the child of a friend you know will be none too pleased?

Every mother in that room had spent years becoming a person who had to be taken seriously, not least by herself. Even the most attractive, I'm willing to bet, had suffered over her body's failure to fit the impossible American ideal. Given all that, it seems crazy to transmit Barbie to the next generation. Yet to reject her is to say that what Barbie represents— being sexy, thin, stylish—is unimportant, which is obviously not true, and children know it's not true.

Women's looks matter terribly in this society, and so Barbie, however ambivalently, must be passed along. After all, there are worse toys. The Cut and Style Barbie styling head, for example, a grotesque object intended to encourage "hair play." The grown-ups who give that probably apologize, too.

How happy would most parents be to have a child who flouted sex conventions? I know a lot of women, feminists, who complain in a comical, eyeball-rolling way about their sons' passion for sports: the ruined weekends, obnoxious coaches, macho values. But they would not think of discouraging their sons from participating in this activity they find so foolish. Or do they? Their husbands are sports fans, too, and they like their husbands a lot.

Could it be that even sports-resistant moms see athletics as part of manliness? That if their sons wanted to spend the weekend writing up their diaries, or reading, or baking, they'd find it disturbing? Too antisocial? Too lonely? Too gay?

Theories of innate differences in behavior are appealing. They let parents off the hook—no small recommendation in a culture that holds moms, and sometimes even dads, responsible for their children's every misstep on the road to bliss and success.

They allow grown-ups to take the path of least resistance to the dominant culture, which always requires less psychic effort, even if it means more actual work: Just ask the working mother who comes home exhausted and nonetheless finds it easier to pick up her son's socks than make him do it himself. They let families buy for their children, without *too* much guilt, the unbelievably sexist junk that the kids, who have been watching commercials since birth, understandably crave.

But the thing the theories do most of all is tell adults that the *adult* world—in which moms and dads still play by many of the old rules even as they question and fidget and chafe against them—is the way it's supposed to be. A girl with a doll and a boy with a truck "explain" why men are from Mars and women are from Venus, why wives do housework and husbands just don't understand.

The paradox is that the world of rigid and hierarchical sex roles evoked by determinist theories is already passing away. Three-year-olds may indeed insist that doctors are male and nurses female, even if their own mother is a physician. Six-year-olds know better. These days, something like half of all medical students are female, and male applications to nursing school are inching upward. When tomorrow's three-year-olds play doctor, who's to say how they'll assign the roles?

With sex roles, as in every area of life, people aspire to what is possible, and conform to what is necessary. But these are not fixed, especially today. Biological determinism may reassure some adults about their present, but it is feminism, the ideology of flexible and converging sex roles, that fits our children's future. And the kids, somehow, know this.

That's why, if you look carefully, you'll find that for every kid who   15 fits a stereotype, there's another who's breaking one down. Sometimes it's the same kid—the boy who skateboards *and* takes cooking in his afterschool program; the girl who collects stuffed animals *and* A-pluses in science.

Feminists are often accused of imposing their "agenda" on children. Isn't that what adults always do, consciously and unconsciously? Kids aren't born religious, or polite, or kind, or able to remember where they put their sneakers. Inculcating these behaviors, and the values behind them, is a tremendous amount of work, involving many adults. We don't have a choice, really, about *whether* we should give our children messages about what it means to be male and female—they're bombarded with them from morning till night.

✎ Topics for Critical Thinking and Writing

1. In a paragraph set forth Pollitt's answer to the question she poses in her title.
2. In paragraph 7 Pollitt says, "Women's looks matter terribly in this society." Do you agree with this generalization? If they do matter "terribly," do they matter more than men's? What evidence can you give, one way or the other? Set forth your answer in an essay of 250 words.
3. Look at the last sentence in paragraph 12: "A girl with a doll and a boy with a truck 'explain' why men are from Mars and women are from Venus, why wives do housework and husbands just don't understand." Why does Pollitt put "explain" within quotation marks? What is she getting at by speaking of Mars and Venus? "Do housework" and "don't understand" are not the parallel construction that a reader probably

expects. Do you think Pollitt's writing is deficient here, or is the variation purposeful? Explain.

4. In paragraph 14 Pollitt says that "the ideology of flexible and converging sex roles" is the one that "fits our children's future." What would be examples of "flexible and converging sex roles"? And do you agree that this ideology is the one that suits the immediate future? Why?

5. Do you believe that you have been influenced by Barbie or by any other toy? Explain.

6. In her final paragraph Pollitt says that adults always impose an "agenda" on their children, consciously or unconsciously. What agenda did your parents (or other adults charged with your upbringing) impose or try to impose. What was your response? As you think back on it, were the agenda and the responses appropriate? Set forth your answers in an essay of 500 to 750 words.

7. If you have heard that "brain chemistry" or "genes" (paragraph 1) account for "innate differences in behavior" (paragraph 10) in boys and girls, in a paragraph set forth the view, and in another paragraph evaluate it, drawing perhaps on your reading of Pollitt's essay.

Malcolm Gladwell

Malcolm Gladwell is a staff writer for the New Yorker *magazine. We reprint another of his essays on page 587.*

The Sports Taboo

The education of any athlete begins, in part, with an education in the racial taxonomy of his chosen sport—in the subtle, unwritten rules about what whites are supposed to be good at and what blacks are supposed to be good at. In football, whites play quarterback and blacks play running back; in baseball whites pitch and blacks play the outfield. I grew up in Canada, where my brother Geoffrey and I ran high-school track, and in Canada the rule of running was that anything under the quarter-mile belonged to the West Indies. This didn't mean that white people didn't run the sprints. But the expectation was that they would never win, and, sure enough, they rarely did. There was just a handful of West Indian immigrants in Ontario at that point—clustered in and around Toronto—but they *owned* Canadian sprinting, setting up under the stands at every major championship, cranking up the reggae on their boom boxes, and then humiliating everyone else on the track. My brother and I weren't from Toronto, so we weren't part of that scene. But our West Indian heritage meant that we got to share in the swagger. Geoffrey was a magnificent runner, with powerful legs and a barrel chest, and when he was warming up he used to do that exaggerated, slow-motion jog that the white guys would try to do and never quite pull off. I was a miler, which was a little outside the West Indian range. But, the way I figured it, the rules meant that no one should ever out-kick me over the final two hundred metres of any race. And in the golden summer of my fourteenth year, when my running career prematurely peaked, no one ever did.

When I started running, there was a quarter-miler just a few years older than I was by the name of Arnold Stotz. He was a bulldog of a runner, hugely talented, and each year that he moved through the sprinting ranks he invariably broke the existing four-hundred-metre record in his age class. Stotz was white, though, and every time I saw the results of a big track meet I'd keep an eye out for his name, because I was convinced that he could not keep winning. It was as if I saw his whiteness as a degenerative disease, which would eventually claim and cripple him. I never asked him whether he felt the same anxiety, but I can't imagine that he didn't. There was only so long that anyone could defy the rules. One day, at the provincial championships, I looked up at the results board and Stotz was gone.

Talking openly about the racial dimension of sports in this way, of course, is considered unseemly. It's all right to say that blacks dominate sports because they lack opportunities elsewhere. That's the "Hoop Dreams" line, which says whites are allowed to acknowledge black athletic success as long as they feel guilty about it. What you're not supposed to say is what we were saying in my track days—that we were better *because* we were black, because of something intrinsic to being black. Nobody said anything like that publicly last month when Tiger Woods won the Masters or when, a week later, African men claimed thirteen out of the top twenty places in the Boston Marathon. Nor is it likely to come up this month, when African-Americans will make up eighty per cent of the players on the floor for the N.B.A. playoffs. When the popular television sports commentator Jimmy (the Greek) Snyder did break this taboo, in 1988—infamously ruminating on the size and significance of black thighs—one prominent N.A.A.C.P. official said that his remarks "could set race relations back a hundred years." The assumption is that the whole project of trying to get us to treat each other the same will be undermined if we don't all agree that under the skin we actually are the same.

The point of this, presumably, is to put our discussion of sports on a par with legal notions of racial equality, which would be a fine idea except that civil-rights law governs matters like housing and employment and the sports taboo covers matters like what can be said about someone's jump shot. In his much heralded new book "Darwin's Athletes," the University of Texas scholar John Hoberman tries to argue that these two things are the same, that it's impossible to speak of black physical superiority without implying intellectual inferiority. But it isn't long before the argument starts to get ridiculous. "The spectacle of black athleticism," he writes, inevitably turns into "a highly public image of black retardation." Oh, really? What, exactly, about Tiger Woods's victory in the Masters resembled "a highly public image of black retardation"? Today's black athletes are multimillion-dollar corporate pitchmen, with talk shows and sneaker deals and publicity machines and almost daily media opportunities to share their thoughts with the world, and it's very hard to see how all this contrives to make them look stupid. Hoberman spends a lot of time trying to inflate the significance of sports, arguing that how we talk about events on the baseball diamond or the track has grave consequences for how we talk about race in general. Here he is, for example, on Jackie Robinson:

> The sheer volume of sentimental and intellectual energy that has been invested in the mythic saga of Jackie Robinson has discouraged further thinking about what his career did and did not accomplish. . . . Black America has paid a high and largely unacknowledged price for the extraordinary prominence given the black athlete rather than other black men of action (such as military pilots and astronauts), who represent modern aptitudes in ways that athletes cannot.

Please. Black America has paid a high and largely unacknowledged   5
price for a long list of things, and having great athletes is far from the top of the list. Sometimes a baseball player is just a baseball player, and sometimes an observation about racial difference is just an observation about racial difference. Few object when medical scientists talk about the significant epidemiological differences between blacks and whites—the fact that blacks have a higher incidence of hypertension than whites and twice as many black males die of diabetes and prostate cancer as white males, that breast tumors appear to grow faster in black women than in white women, that black girls show signs of puberty sooner than white girls. So why aren't we allowed to say that there might be athletically significant differences between blacks and whites?

According to the medical evidence, African-Americans seem to have, on the average, greater bone mass than do white Americans—a difference that suggests greater muscle mass. Black men have slightly higher circulating levels of testosterone and human-growth hormone than their white counterparts, and blacks over all tend to have proportionally slimmer hips, wider shoulders, and longer legs. In one study, the Swedish physiologist Bengt Saltin compared a group of Kenyan distance runners with a group of Swedish distance runners and found interesting differences in muscle composition: Saltin reported that the Africans appeared to have more blood-carrying capillaries and more mitochondria (the body's cellular power plant) in the fibres of their quadriceps. Another study found that, while black South African distance runners ran at the same speed as white South African runners, they were able to use more oxygen—eighty-nine per cent versus eighty-one per cent—over extended periods: somehow, they were able to exert themselves more. Such evidence suggested that there were physical differences in black athletes which have a bearing on activities like running and jumping, which should hardly come as a surprise to anyone who follows competitive sports.

To use track as an example—since track is probably the purest measure of athletic ability—Africans recorded fifteen out of the twenty fastest times last year in the men's ten-thousand-metre event. In the five thousand metres, eighteen out of the twenty fastest times were recorded by Africans. In the fifteen hundred metres, thirteen out of the twenty fastest times were African, and in the sprints, in the men's hundred metres, you have to go all the way down to the twenty-third place in the world rankings—to Geir Moen, of Norway—before you find a white face. There is a point at which it becomes foolish to deny the fact of black athletic prowess, and even more foolish to banish speculation on the topic. Clearly, something is going on. The question is what.

If we are to decide what to make of the differences between blacks and whites, we first have to decide what to make of the word "difference," which can mean any number of things. A useful case study is to compare the ability of men and women in math. If you give a large, representative sample of male and female students a standardized math test, their mean scores will come out pretty much the same. But if you look at the margins, at the very best and the very worst students, sharp differences emerge. In the math portion of an achievement test conducted by Project Talent—a nationwide survey of fifteen-year-olds—there were 1.3 boys for every girl in the top ten per cent, 1.5 boys for every girl in the top five per cent, and seven boys for every girl in the top one per cent. In the fifty-six-year history of the Putnam Mathematical Competition, which has been described as the Olympics of college math, all but one of the winners have been male. Conversely, if you look at people with the very lowest math ability, you'll find more boys than girls there, too. In other words, although the average math ability of boys and girls is the same, the distribution isn't: there are more males than females at the bottom of the pile, more males than females at the top of the pile, and fewer males than females in the middle. Statisticians refer to this as a difference in variability.

This pattern, as it turns out, is repeated in almost every conceivable area of gender difference. Boys are more variable than girls on the College Board entrance exam and in routine elementary-school spelling tests. Male mortality patterns are more variable than female patterns; that is, many more men die in early and middle age than women, who tend to die in more of a concentrated clump toward the end of life. The problem is that variability differences are regularly confused with average differences. If men had higher average math scores than women, you could say they were better at the subject. But because they are only more variable the word "better" seems inappropriate.

The same holds true for differences between the races. A racist stereotype is the assertion of average difference—it's the claim that the typical white is superior to the typical black. It allows a white man to assume that the black man he passes on the street is stupider than he is. By contrast, if what racists believed was that black intelligence was simply more variable than white intelligence, then it would be impossible for them to construct a stereotype about black intelligence at all. They wouldn't be able to generalize. If they wanted to believe that there were a lot of blacks dumber than whites, they would also have to believe that there were a lot of blacks smarter than they were. This distinction is critical to understanding the relation between race and athletic performance. What are we seeing when we remark black domination of élite sporting events—an average difference between the races or merely a difference in variability?

This question has been explored by geneticists and physical anthropologists, and some of the most notable work has been conducted over the past few years by Kenneth Kidd, at Yale. Kidd and his colleagues have been taking DNA samples from two African Pygmy tribes in Zaire and the Central African Republic and comparing them with DNA samples taken from populations all over the world. What they have been looking for is variants—subtle differences between the DNA of one person and another—and what they have found is fascinating. "I would say, without a doubt, that in almost any single African population—a tribe or however you want to define it—there is more genetic variation than in all the rest of the world put together," Kidd told me. In a sample of fifty Pygmies, for example, you might find nine variants in one stretch of DNA. In a sample of hundreds of people from around the rest of the world, you might find only a total of six variants in that same stretch of DNA—and probably every one of those six variants would also be found in the Pygmies. If everyone in the world was wiped out except Africans, in other words, almost all the human genetic diversity would be preserved.

The likelihood is that these results reflect Africa's status as the homeland of *Homo sapiens:* since every human population outside Africa is essentially a subset of the original African population, it makes sense that everyone in such a population would be a genetic subset of Africans, too. So you can expect groups of Africans to be more variable in respect to almost anything that has a genetic component. If, for example, your genes control how you react to aspirin, you'd expect to see more Africans than whites for whom one aspirin stops a bad headache, more for whom no amount of aspirin works, more who are allergic to aspirin, and more who need to take, say, four aspirin at a time to get any benefit—but far fewer Africans for whom the standard two-aspirin dose would work well. And to the extent that running is influenced by genetic factors you would expect to see more really fast blacks—and more really slow blacks—than

10

whites but far fewer Africans of merely average speed. Blacks are like boys. Whites are like girls.

There is nothing particularly scary about this fact, and certainly nothing to warrant the kind of gag order on talk of racial differences which is now in place. What it means is that comparing élite athletes of different races tells you very little about the races themselves. A few years ago, for example, a prominent scientist argued for black athletic supremacy by pointing out that there had never been a white Michael Jordan. True. But, as the Yale anthropologist Jonathan Marks has noted, until recently there was no black Michael Jordan, either. Michael Jordan, like Tiger Woods or Wayne Gretzky or Cal Ripken, is one of the best players in his sport not because he's like the other members of his own ethnic group but precisely because he's not like them—or like anyone else, for that matter. Élite athletes are élite athletes because, in some sense, they are on the fringes of genetic variability. As it happens, African populations seem to create more of these genetic outliers than white populations do, and this is what underpins the claim that blacks are better athletes than whites. But that's all the claim amounts to. It doesn't say anything at all about the rest of us, of all races, muddling around in the genetic middle.

There is a second consideration to keep in mind when we compare blacks and whites. Take the men's hundred-metre final at the Atlanta Olympics. Every runner in that race was of either Western African or Southern African descent, as you would expect if Africans had some genetic affinity for sprinting. But suppose we forget about skin color and look just at country of origin. The eight-man final was made up of two African-Americans, two Africans (one from Namibia and one from Nigeria), a Trinidadian, a Canadian of Jamaican descent, an Englishman of Jamaican descent, and a Jamaican. The race was won by the Jamaican-Canadian, in world-record time, with the Namibian coming in second and the Trinidadian third. The sprint relay—the 4×100—was won by a team from Canada, consisting of the Jamaican-Canadian from the final, a Haitian-Canadian, a Trinidadian-Canadian, and another Jamaican-Canadian. Now it appears that African heritage is important as an initial determinant of sprinting ability, but also that the most important advantage of all is some kind of cultural or environmental factor associated with the Caribbean.

Or consider, in a completely different realm, the problem of hypertension. Black Americans have a higher incidence of hypertension than white Americans, even after you control for every conceivable variable, including income, diet, and weight, so it's tempting to conclude that there is something about being of African descent that makes blacks prone to hypertension. But it turns out that although some Caribbean countries have a problem with hypertension, others—Jamaica, St. Kitts, and the Bahamas—don't. It also turns out that people in Liberia and Nigeria—two countries where many New World slaves came from—have similar and perhaps even lower blood-pressure rates than white North Americans, 15 while studies of Zulus, Indians, and whites in Durban, South Africa, showed that urban white males had the highest hypertension rates and urban white females had the lowest. So it's likely that the disease has nothing at all to do with Africanness.

The same is true for the distinctive muscle characteristic observed when Kenyans were compared with Swedes. Saltin, the Swedish physiologist, subsequently found many of the same characteristics in Nordic skiers who train at high altitudes and Nordic runners who train in very hilly regions—conditions, in other words, that resemble the mountainous regions of Kenya's Rift Valley, where so many of the country's distance runners come from. The key factor seems to be Kenya, not genes.

Lots of things that seem to be genetic in origin, then, actually aren't. Similarly, lots of things that we wouldn't normally think might affect athletic ability actually do. Once again, the social-science literature on male and female math achievement is instructive. Psychologists argue that when it comes to subjects like math, boys tend to engage in what's known as ability attribution. A boy who is doing well will attribute his success to the fact that he's good at math, and if he's doing badly he'll blame his teacher or his own lack of motivation—anything but his ability. That makes it easy for him to bounce back from failure or disappointment, and gives him a lot of confidence in the face of a tough new challenge. After all, if you think you do well in math because you're good at math, what's stopping you from being good at, say, algebra, or advanced calculus? On the other hand, if you ask a girl why she is doing well in math she will say, more often than not, that she succeeds because she works hard. If she's doing poorly, she'll say she isn't smart enough. This, as should be obvious, is a self-defeating attitude. Psychologists call it "learned helplessness"— the state in which failure is perceived as insurmountable. Girls who engage in effort attribution learn helplessness because in the face of a more difficult task like algebra or advanced calculus they can conceive of no solution. They're convinced that they can't work harder, because they think they're working as hard as they can, and that they can't rely on their intelligence, because they never thought they were that smart to begin with. In fact, one of the fascinating findings of attribution research is that the smarter girls are, the more likely they are to fall into this trap. High achievers are sometimes the most helpless. Here, surely, is part of the explanation for greater math variability among males. The female math whizzes, the ones who should be competing in the top one and two per cent with their male counterparts, are the ones most often paralyzed by a lack of confidence in their own aptitude. They think they belong only in the intellectual middle.

The striking thing about these descriptions of male and female stereotyping in math, though, is how similar they are to black and white stereotyping in athletics—to the unwritten rules holding that blacks achieve through natural ability and whites through effort. Here's how *Sports Illustrated* described, in a recent article, the white basketball player Steve Kerr, who plays alongside Michael Jordan for the Chicago Bulls. According to the magazine, Kerr is a "hard-working overachiever," distinguished by his "work ethic and heady play" and by a shooting style "born of a million practice shots." Bear in mind that Kerr is one of the best shooters in basketball today, and a key player on what is arguably one of the finest basketball teams in history. Bear in mind, too, that there is no evidence that Kerr works any harder than his teammates, least of all Jordan himself, whose work habits are legendary. But you'd never guess that from the article. It concludes, "All over America, whenever quicker, stronger gym rats see Kerr in action, they must wonder, How can that guy be out there instead of me?"

There are real consequences to this stereotyping. As the psychologists Carol Dweck and Barbara Licht write of high-achieving schoolgirls, "[They] may view themselves as so motivated and well disciplined that they cannot entertain the possibility that they did poorly on an academic task because of insufficient effort. Since blaming the teacher would also be out of character, blaming their abilities when they confront difficulty may seem like the most reasonable option." If you substitute the words "white athletes" for "girls" and "coach" for "teacher," I think you have part of the reason that so many white athletes are underrepresented at the highest levels of professional sports. Whites have been saddled with the athletic equivalent of learned helplessness—the idea that it is all but fruitless to try and compete at the highest levels, because they have only effort on their side. The causes of athletic and gender discrimination may be diverse, but its effects are not. Once again, blacks are like boys, and whites are like girls.

When I was in college, I once met an old acquaintance from my high-school running days. Both of us had long since quit track, and we talked about a recurrent fantasy we found we'd both had for getting back into shape. It was that we would go away somewhere remote for a year and do nothing but train, so that when the year was up we might finally know how good we were. Neither of us had any intention of doing this, though, which is why it was a fantasy. In adolescence, athletic excess has a certain appeal—during high school, I happily spent Sunday afternoons running up and down snow-covered sandhills—but with most of us that obsessiveness soon begins to fade. Athletic success depends on having the right genes and on a self-reinforcing belief in one's own ability. But it also depends on a rare form of tunnel vision. To be a great athlete, you have to *care*, and what was obvious to us both was that neither of us cared anymore. This is the last piece of the puzzle about what we mean when we say one group is better at something than another: sometimes different groups care about different things. Of the seven hundred men who play major-league baseball, for example, eighty-six come from either the Dominican Republic or Puerto Rico, even though those two islands have a combined population of only eleven million. But then baseball is something that Dominicans and Puerto Ricans care about—and you can say the

20

same thing about African-Americans and basketball, West Indians and sprinting, Canadians and hockey, and Russians and chess. Desire is the great intangible in performance, and unlike genes or psychological affect we can't measure it and trace its implications. This is the problem, in the end, with the question of whether blacks are better at sports than whites. It's not that it's offensive, or that it leads to discrimination. It's that, in some sense, it's not a terribly interesting question; "better" promises a tidier explanation than can ever be provided.

I quit competitive running when I was sixteen—just after the summer I had qualified for the Ontario track team in my age class. Late that August, we had travelled to St. John's, Newfoundland, for the Canadian championships. In those days, I was whippet-thin, as milers often are, five feet six and not much more than a hundred pounds, and I could skim along the ground so lightly that I barely needed to catch my breath. I had two white friends on that team, both distance runners, too, and both, improbably, even smaller and lighter than I was. Every morning, the three of us would run through the streets of St. John's, charging up the hills and flying down the other side. One of these friends went on to have a distinguished college running career, the other became a world-class miler; that summer, I myself was the Canadian record holder in the fifteen hundred metres for my age class. We were almost terrifyingly competitive, without a shred of doubt in our ability, and as we raced along we never stopped talking and joking, just to prove how absurdly easy we found running to be. I thought of us all as equals. Then, on the last day of our stay in St. John's, we ran to the bottom of Signal Hill, which is the town's principal geographical landmark—an abrupt outcrop as steep as anything in San Francisco. We stopped at the base, and the two of them turned to me and announced that we were all going to run straight up Signal Hill *backward*. I don't know whether I had more running ability than those two or whether my Africanness gave me any genetic advantage over their whiteness. What I do know is that such questions were irrelevant, because, as I realized, they were willing to go to far greater lengths to develop their talent. They ran up the hill backward. I ran home.

✎ Topics for Critical Thinking and Writing

1. In paragraph 6 Gladwell, referring to scientific studies, says that one difference between blacks and whites "suggests" something, and another study found that blacks "appeared" to have a certain quality. We notice the cautious words. Should Gladwell have refrained from citing these studies, which apparently are not conclusive? Why, or why not?
2. Why in an article about athletes does Gladwell discuss (paragraph 17) the attitudes of boys and girls with respect to achievement in mathematics?
3. In a paragraph explain why, in your view, "the claim that blacks are better athletes than whites" (paragraph 13) is taboo.

4. In paragraphs 3 and 4 Gladwell implies that Tiger Woods is black—and indeed he is widely perceived as black. In fact his father is half African-American, one quarter Native American, and one quarter Chinese; his mother is half Thai, one quarter Chinese, and one quarter white. In an essay of 250 words explain why, in your view, Tiger Woods is often regarded as black.
5. Gladwell devotes his long final paragraph to an anecdote about running backward. What is the point of the anecdote? In an essay of 250 words set forth the point, and indicate why this paragraph does or does not make an effective ending to the essay.

Carol Tavris

Carol Tavris, born in Los Angeles in 1944, holds a bachelor's degree from Brandeis University and a Ph.D. from the University of Michigan. Among her many publications are The Female Experience *(1973),* Anger: the Misunderstood Emotion *(1983), and* The Mismeasure of Woman: Why Women Are Not the Better Sex, the Inferior Sex, or the Opposite Sex, and How Using Men as the Yardstick for Normalcy Has Given Women the Short End of the Stick *(1992). We reprint an essay that first appeared in* The New York Times *in 1997.*

How Friendship Was "Feminized"

Once upon a time and not so very long ago, everyone thought that men had the great and true-blue friendships. The cultural references stretched through time and art: Damon and Pythias, Hamlet and Horatio, Butch Cassidy and the Sundance Kid. The Lone Ranger never rode off with anyone but Tonto, and Laurel never once abandoned Hardy in whatever fine mess he got them into.

Male friendships were said to grow from the deep roots of shared experience and faithful camaraderie, whereas women's friendships were portrayed as shallow, trivial and competitive, like Scarlett O'Hara's with her sisters. Women, it was commonly claimed, would sell each other out for the right guy, and even for a good time with the wrong one.

Some social scientists told us that this difference was hard-wired, a result of our evolutionary history. In the early 1970's, for example, the anthropologist Lionel Tiger argued in "Men in Groups" that "male bonding" originated in prehistoric male hunting groups and was carried on today in equivalent pack-like activities: sports, politics, business and war.

Apparently, women's evolutionary task of rummaging around in the garden to gather the odd yam or kumquat was a solo effort, so females do not bond in the same way. Women prattle on about their feelings, went the stereotype, but men act.

My, how times have changed. Today, we are deluged in the wave of   5
best-selling books that celebrate female friendships—"Girlfriends," "Sisters," "Mothers and Daughters" and its clever clone, "Daughters and
Mothers." The success of this genre is partly because the book market is so
oriented to female readers these days.

But it is also a likely result of two trends that began in the 1970's and
1980's: Female scholars began to dispel the men-are-better stereotype in
all domains and women became the majority of psychotherapists. The
result was a positive reassessment of the qualities associated with women,
including a "feminizing" of definitions of intimacy and friendship.

Accordingly, female friendships are now celebrated as the deep and
abiding ones, based as they are on shared feelings and confidences. Male
friendships are scorned as superficial, based as they are on shared interests in, say, the Mets and Michelle Pfeiffer.

In our psychologized culture, "intimacy" is defined as what many
women like to do with their friends: talk, express feelings and disclose
worries. Psychologists, most of whom are good talkers, validate this definition as the true measure of intimacy. For example, in a study of "intimacy maturity" in marriage, published in the *Journal of Personality and Social
Psychology,* researchers equated "most mature" with "most verbally
expressive." As a woman, I naturally think this is a perfectly sensible
equation, but I also know it is an incomplete one. To label people mature
or immature, you also have to know how they actually behave toward
others.

What about all the men and women who support their families, put
the wishes of other family members ahead of their own or act in moral and
considerate ways when conflicts arise? They are surely mature, even if
they are inarticulate or do not express their feelings easily. Indeed, what
about all the men and women who define intimacy in terms of deeds
rather than words: sharing activities, helping one another or enjoying
companionable silence? Too bad for them. That's a "male" definition, and
out of favor in these talky times.

Years ago, my husband had to have some worrisome medical tests,   10
and the night before he was to go to the hospital we went to dinner with
one of his best friends who was visiting from England. I watched, fascinated, as male stoicism combined with English reserve produced a decidedly unfemale-like encounter. They laughed, they told stories, they
argued about movies, they reminisced. Neither mentioned the hospital,
their worries or their affection for each other. They didn't need to.

It is true that women's style of intimacy has many benefits. A large
body of research in health psychology and social psychology finds that
women's greater willingness to talk about feelings improves their mental
and physical health and makes it easier to ask for help.

But as psychologists like Susan Nolen-Hoeksema of Stanford University have shown, women's fondness for ruminating about feelings can
also prolong depression, anxiety and anger. And it can keep women stuck

in bad jobs or relationships, instead of getting out of them or doing what is necessary to make them better.

Books and movies that validate women's friendships are overdue, and welcome as long as they don't simply invert the stereotype. Playing the women-are-better game is fun, but it blinds us to the universal need for intimacy and the many forms that friendship takes. Maybe men could learn a thing or two about friendship from women. But who is to say that women couldn't learn a thing or two from them in exchange?

✎ Topics for Critical Thinking and Writing

1. Evaluate Tavris's first paragraph as an opening paragraph. (In your evaluation you may want to consider such topics as: Did it attract your interest? Is it clear? Is it appropriate to what follows?)
2. In a sentence or two, formulate Tavris's thesis.
3. How would you characterize Tavris's style? Formal? Chatty? Vulgar? Or what? In a paragraph set forth your view, supporting it with specific examples drawn from her essay.
4. In her first paragraph Tavris cites some famous examples of male friendships. What additional examples can you cite? What comparable examples of female friendship can you cite? If female examples come less easily to mind, why do you suppose this is so?
5. Drawing on your own experience, write an essay (250–500 words) on male versus female friendships. Since your experience now includes familiarity with Tavris's essay, you can, if you wish, make use of it in your own writing. You may even want to put your essay into the form of a reply to hers.
6. Take one of the following passages and write an essay of 500 words, using the quotation as an epigraph.

Friendships, in general, are suddenly contracted, and therefore it is no wonder they are easily dissolved.

Joseph Addison (1974)

No man can be friends with a woman he finds attractive. He always wants to have sex with her. Sex is always out there. Friendship is ultimately doomed and that is the end of the story.

Nora Ephron (1989)

If a man does not make new acquaintance as he advances through life, he will soon find himself left alone. A man, Sir, should keep his friendship in constant repair.

Samuel Johnson (1755. *Note:* Johnson probably is using "man" generically, to stand for any human being. Take the remark as *not* referring only to men.)

Scott Russell Sanders

Scott Russell Sanders first published this essay in Milkweek Chronicle, *Spring/Summer 1984, and then reprinted it in his book,* Paradise of Bombs.

The Men We Carry in Our Minds ... and How They Differ from the Real Lives of Most Men

"This must be a hard time for women," I say to my friend Anneke. "They have so many paths to choose from, and so many voices calling them."

"I think it's a lot harder for men," she replies.

"How do you figure that?"

"The women I know feel excited, innocent, like crusaders in a just cause. The men I know are eaten up with guilt."

"Women feel such pressure to be everything, do everything," I say. "Career, kids, art, politics. Have their babies and get back to the office a week later. It's as if they're trying to overcome a million years' worth of evolution in one lifetime." 5

"But we help one another. And we have this deep-down sense that we're in the *right*—we've been held back, passed over, used—while men feel they're in the wrong. Men are the ones who've been discredited, who have to search their souls."

I search my soul. I discover guilty feelings aplenty—toward the poor, the Vietnamese, Native Americans, the whales, an endless list of debts. But toward women I feel something more confused, a snarl of shame, envy, wary tenderness, and amazement. This muddle troubles me. To hide my unease I say, "You're right, it's tough being a man these days."

"Don't laugh," Anneke frowns at me. "I wouldn't be a man for anything. It's much easier being the victim. All the victim has to do is break free. The persecutor has to live with his past."

How deep is that past? I find myself wondering. How much of an inheritance do I have to throw off?

When I was a boy growing up on the back roads of Tennessee and Ohio, the men I knew labored with their bodies. They were marginal farmers, just scraping by, or welders, steelworkers, carpenters; they swept floors, dug ditches, mined coal, or drove trucks, their forearms ropy with muscle; they trained horses, stoked furnaces, made tires, stood on assembly lines wrestling parts onto cars and refrigerators. They got up before light, worked all day long whatever the weather, and when they came home at night they looked as though somebody had been whipping them. 10

In the evenings and on weekends they worked on their own places, tilling gardens that were lumpy with clay, fixing broken-down cars, hammering on houses that were always too drafty, too leaky, too small.

The bodies of the men I knew were twisted and maimed in ways visible and invisible. The nails of their hands were black and split, the hands tattooed with scars. Some had lost fingers. Heavy lifting had given many of them finicky backs and guts weak from hernias. Racing against conveyor belts had given them ulcers. Their ankles and knees ached from years of standing on concrete. Anyone who had worked for long around machines was hard of hearing. They squinted, and the skin of their faces was creased like the leather of old work gloves. There were times, studying them, when I dreaded growing up. Most of them coughed, from dust or cigarettes, and most of them drank cheap wine or whiskey, so their eyes looked bloodshot and bruised. The fathers of my friends always seemed older than the mothers. Men wore out sooner. Only women lived into old age.

As a boy I also knew another sort of men, who did not sweat and break down like mules. They were soldiers, and so far as I could tell they scarcely worked at all. But when the shooting started, many of them would die. This was what soldiers were *for*, just as a hammer was for driving nails.

Warriors and toilers: these seemed, in my boyhood vision, to be the chief destinies for men. They weren't the only destinies, as I learned from having a few male teachers, from reading books, and from watching television. But the men on television—the politicians, the astronauts, the generals, the savvy lawyers, the philosophical doctors, the bosses who gave orders to both soldiers and laborers—seemed as remote and unreal to me as the figures in Renaissance tapestries. I could no more imagine growing up to become one of these cool, potent creatures than I could imagine becoming a prince.

A nearer and more hopeful example was that of my father, who had escaped from a red-dirt farm to a tire factory, and from the assembly line to the front office. Eventually he dressed in a white shirt and tie. He carried himself as if he had been born to work with his mind. But his body, remembering the earlier years of slogging work, began to give out on him in his fifties, and it quit on him entirely before he turned 65.

A scholarship enabled me not only to attend college, a rare enough feat in my circle, but even to study in a university meant for the children of the rich. Here I met for the first time young men who had assumed from birth that they would lead lives of comfort and power. And for the first time I met women who told me that men were guilty of having kept all the joys and privileges of the earth for themselves. I was baffled. What privileges? What joys? I thought about the maimed, dismal lives of most of the men back home. What had they stolen from their wives and daughters? The right to go five days a week, 12 months a year, for 30 or 40 years to a steel mill or a coal mine? The right to drop bombs and die in war? The right to feel every leak in the roof, every gap in the fence,

15

every cough in the engine as a wound they must mend? The right to feel, when the layoff comes or the plant shuts down, not only afraid but ashamed?

I was slow to understand the deep grievances of women. This was because, as a boy, I had envied them. Before college, the only people I had ever known who were interested in art or music or literature, the only ones who read books, the only ones who ever seemed to enjoy a sense of ease and grace were the mothers and daughters. Like the men-folk, they fretted about money, they scrimped and made do. But, when the pay stopped coming in, they were not the ones who had failed. Nor did they have to go to war, and that seemed to me a blessed fact. By comparison with the narrow, ironclad days of fathers, there was an expansiveness, I thought, in the days of mothers. They went to see neighbors, to shop in town, to run errands at school, at the library, at church. No doubt, had I looked harder at their lives, I would have envied them less. It was not my fate to become a woman, so it was easier for me to see the graces. I didn't see, then, what a prison a house could be, since houses seemed to me brighter, handsomer places than any factory. I did not realize—because such things were never spoken of—how often women suffered from men's bullying. Even then I could see how exhausting it was for a mother to cater all day to the needs of young children. But if I had been asked, as a boy, to choose between tending a baby and tending a machine, I think I would have chosen the baby. (Having now tended both, I know I would choose the baby.)

So I was baffled when the women at college accused me and my sex of having cornered the world's pleasures. I think something like my bafflement has been felt by other boys (and by girls as well) who grew up in dirt-poor farm country, in mining country, in black ghettos, in Hispanic barrios, in the shadows of factories, in Third World nations—any place where the fate of men is just as grim and bleak as the fate of women.

When the women I met at college thought about the joys and privileges of men, they did not carry in their minds the sort of men I had known in my childhood. They thought of their fathers, who were bankers, physicians, architects, stockbrokers, the big wheels of the big cities. They were never laid off, never short of cash at month's end, never lined up for welfare. These fathers made decisions that mattered. They ran the world.

The daughters of such men wanted to share in this power, this glory. So did I. They yearned for a say over their future, for jobs worthy of their abilities, for the right to live at peace, unmolested, whole. Yes, I thought, yes yes. The difference between me and these daughters was that they saw me, because of my sex, as destined from birth to become like their fathers, and therefore as an enemy to their desires. But I knew better. I wasn't an enemy, in fact or in feeling. I was an ally. If I had known, then, how to tell them so, would they have believed me? Would they now?

✎ Topics for Critical Thinking and Writing

1. Look at Sanders' introductory paragraphs (1–9). What do you think he hoped to accomplish by these paragraphs? To put it another way, suppose the essay began with paragraph 10, "When I was a boy growing up . . . ." What would be changed or lost?
2. Look at the second sentence of paragraph 10. It's a rather long sentence, with three independent clauses and lists of parallel phrases. How would you describe the verbs he uses? What effect does the structure of the sentence produce?
3. What is the topic sentence of paragraph 11? How does Sanders develop the paragraph, and what does the paragraph contribute to his argument?
4. What advantages did women enjoy that Sanders says he envied when he was a boy? What disadvantages does he mention (in paragraph 15)? What disadvantages does he *not* mention?
5. In paragraphs 16, 17, and 18, Sanders shifts from focusing on issues of gender to issues of class. How has he prepared us for this shift?
6. Evaluate Sanders' argument. How would you answer the questions he poses in his final paragraph?
7. When you were growing up, which lives seemed to have the most advantages or disadvantages, those of men or of women? Why did you think so? Did your opinion change as you grew older? Explain.

Paul Theroux

Paul Theroux was born in 1941 in Medford, Massachusetts, and was educated at the University of Maine, the University of Massachusetts, and Syracuse University. He served as a Peace Corps volunteer in Africa and has spent much of his adult life abroad, in Africa, Asia, Europe, and Central America. Though best known as a novelist and writer of travel books, he is also a poet and essayist. This essay originally appeared in The New York Times Magazine.

The Male Myth

There is a pathetic sentence in the chapter "Fetishism" in Dr. Norman Cameron's book *Personality Development and Psychopathology*. It goes: "Fetishists are nearly always men; and their commonest fetish is a woman's shoe." I cannot read that sentence without thinking that it is just one more awful thing about being a man—and perhaps it is the most important thing to know about us.

I have always disliked being a man. The whole idea of manhood in America is pitiful, a little like having to wear an ill-fitting coat for one's entire life. (By contrast, I imagine femininity to be an oppressive sense of nakedness.) Even the expression "Be a man!" strikes me as insulting and abusive. It means: Be stupid, be unfeeling, obedient and soldierly, and stop thinking. Man means "manly"—how can one think "about men" without considering the terrible ambition of manliness? And yet it is part of every man's life. It is a hideous and crippling lie; it not only insists on difference and connives at superiority, it is also by its very nature destructive—emotionally damaging and socially harmful.

The youth who is subverted, as most are, into believing in the masculine ideal is effectively separated from women—it is the most savage tribal logic—and he spends the rest of his life finding women a riddle and a nuisance. Of course, there is a female version of this male affliction. It begins with mothers encouraging little girls to say (to other adults), "Do you like my new dress?" In a sense, girls are traditionally urged to please adults with a kind of coquettishness, while boys are enjoined to behave like monkeys toward each other. The 9-year-old coquette proceeds to become womanish in a subtle power game in which she learns to be sexually indispensable, socially decorative and always alert to a man's sense of inadequacy.

Femininity—being ladylike—implies needing a man as witness and seducer; but masculinity celebrates the exclusive company of men. That is why it is so grotesque; and that is also why there is no manliness without inadequacy—because it denies men the natural friendship of women.

It is very hard to imagine any concept of manliness that does not belittle women, and it begins very early. At an age when I wanted to meet girls—let's say the treacherous years of 13 to 16—I was told to take up a sport, get more fresh air, join the Boy Scouts, and I was urged not to read so much. It was the 1950's and, if you asked too many questions about sex, you were sent to camp—boy's camp, of course; the nightmare. Nothing is more unnatural or prisonlike than a boys' camp, but if it were not for them, we would have no Elks' Lodges, no pool-rooms, no boxing matches, no marines.   5

And perhaps no sports as we know them. Everyone is aware of how few in number are the athletes who behave like gentlemen. Just as high-school basketball teaches you how to be a poor loser, the manly attitude toward sports seems to be little more than a recipe for creating bad marriages, social misfits, moral degenerates, sadists, latent rapists and just plain louts. I regard high-school sports as a drug far worse than marijuana, and it is the reason that the average tennis champion, say, is a pathetic oaf.

Any objective study would find the quest for manliness essentially right wing, puritanical, cowardly, neurotic and fueled largely by a fear of women. It is also certainly philistine. There is no book hater like a Little League coach. But, indeed, all the creative arts are obnoxious to the manly ideal, because at their best the arts are pursued by uncompetitive and essentially solitary people. It makes it very hard for a creative youngster, for any boy who expresses the desire to be alone seems to be saying that there is something wrong with him.

It ought to be clear by now that I have an objection to the way we turn boys into men. It does not surprise me that when the President of the United States has his customary weekend off, he dresses like a cowboy—it is both a measure of his insecurity and his willingness to please. In many ways, American culture does little more for a man than prepare him for modeling clothes in the L. L. Bean catalogue. I take this as a personal insult because for many years I found it impossible to admit to myself that I wanted to be a writer. It was my guilty secret, because being a writer was incompatible with being a man.

There are people who might deny this, but that is because the American writer, typically, has been so at pains to prove his manliness. But first there was a fear that writing was not a manly profession—indeed, not a profession at all. (The paradox in American letters is that it has always been easier for a woman to write and for a man to be published.) Growing up, I had thought of sports as wasteful and humiliating, and the idea of manliness as a bore. My wanting to become a writer was not a flight from that oppressive role playing, but I quickly saw that it was at odds with it. Everything in stereotyped manliness goes against the life of the mind. The Hemingway personality is too tedious to go into here, but certainly it was not until this aberrant behavior was examined by feminists in the 1960's that any male writer dared question the pugnacity in Hemingway's fiction. All that bullfighting and arm-wrestling and elephant shooting diminished Hemingway as a writer: One cannot be a male writer without first proving that one is a man.

It is normal in America for a man to be dismissive or even somewhat apologetic about being a writer. Various factors make it easier. There is a heartiness about journalism that makes it acceptable—journalism is the manliest form of American writing and, therefore, the profession the most independent-minded women seek (yes, it is an illusion, but that is my point). Fiction writing is equated with a kind of dispirited failure and is only manly when it produces wealth. Money is masculinity. So is drinking. Being a drunkard is another assertion, if misplaced, of manliness. The American male writer is traditionally proud of his heavy drinking. But we are also very literal-minded people. A man proves his manhood in America in old-fashioned ways. He kills lions, like Hemingway; or he hunts ducks, like Nathanael West; or he makes pronouncements, like "A man should carry enough knife to defend himself with," as James Jones is said to have once told an interviewer. And we are familiar with the lengths to which Norman Mailer is prepared, in his endearing way, to prove that he is just as much a monster as the next man.

When the novelist John Irving was revealed as a wrestler, people took him to be a very serious writer. But what interests me is that it is inconceivable that any woman writer would be shown in such a posture. How surprised we would be if Joyce Carol Oates were revealed as a sumo wrestler or Joan Didion enjoyed pumping iron. "Lives in New York City with her three children" is the typical woman-writer's biographical note, for just as the male writer must prove he has achieved a sort of muscular manhood, the woman writer—or rather her publicists—must prove her motherhood.

10

There would be no point in saying any of this if it were not generally accepted that to be a man is somehow—even now in feminist-influenced America—a privilege. It is on the contrary an unmerciful and punishing burden. Being a man is bad enough; being manly is appalling. It is the sinister silliness of men's fashions that inspires the so-called dress code of the Ritz-Carlton Hotel in Boston. It is the institutionalized cheating in college sports. It is a pathetic and primitive insecurity.

And this is also why men often object to feminism, but are afraid to explain why: Of course women have a justified grievance, but most men believe—and with reason—that their lives are much worse.

✎ Topics for Critical Thinking and Writing

1. In paragraph 6 Theroux says that "high-school basketball teaches you how to be a poor loser." Think about this, and then write a paragraph that in effect offers a definition of a "poor loser" but that also shows how a high school sport teaches one to be a poor loser.
2. Theroux speaks of "the Hemingway personality" and of "the pugnacity in Hemingway's fiction." If you have read a work by Hemingway, write a paragraph in which you explain (to someone unfamiliar with Hemingway) what Theroux is talking about.
3. Let's assume that a reader says he or she doesn't quite understand Theroux's final paragraph. Write a paragraph explaining it.
4. Theroux makes some deliberately provocative statements, for example:

   Nothing is more unnatural or prisonlike than a boys' camp.

   Everyone is aware of how few in number are the athletes who behave like gentlemen.

   The quest for manliness . . . [is] fueled largely by a fear of women.

   Choose one such statement from the essay and consider what you would need to do to argue effectively against it. You needn't produce the argument, but simply consider how such an argument might be constructed.

Andrew Lam

Andrew Lam is an associate editor of the Pacific News Service. *This essay originally appeared as an op-ed piece in* The New York Times *in 1993.*

Goodbye, Saigon, Finally

Flipping through my United States passport as if it were a comic book, the customs man at the Noi Bai Airport, near Hanoi, appeared curious. "Brother, when did you leave Vietnam?"

"One day before National Defeat Day," I said without thinking. It was an exile's expression, not his.

"God! When did that happen?"

"The 30th of April, 1975."

"But, brother, don't you mean National Liberation Day?"   5

If this conversation had occurred a decade earlier, the difference would have created a dangerous gap between the Vietnamese and the returning Vietnamese-American. But this happened in 1992, when the walls were down, and as I studied the smiling young official, it occurred to me that there was something about this moment, an epiphany. "Yes, brother, I suppose I do mean liberation day."

Not everyone remembers the date with humor. It marked the Vietnamese diaspora, boat people, refugees.

On April 29, 1975, my family and I escaped from Saigon in a crowded C–130. We arrived in Guam the next day, to hear the BBC's tragic account of Saigon's demise: U.S. helicopters flying over the chaotic city, Vietcong tanks rolling in, Vietnamese climbing over the gate into the U.S. Embassy, boats fleeing down the Saigon River toward the South China Sea.

In time, April 30 became the birth date of an exile's culture built on defeatism and a sense of tragic ending. For a while, many Vietnamese in America talked of revenge, of blood debts, of the exile's anguish. Their songs had nostalgic titles: "The Day When I Return" and "Oh, Mother Vietnam, We Are Still Here."

April 30, 1976: A child of 12 with nationalistic fervor, I stood in front of   10
San Francisco City Hall with other refugees. I waved the gold flag with three horizontal red stripes. I shouted (to no one in particular): "Give us back South Vietnam!"

April 30, 1979: An uncle told me there was an American plan to retake our homeland by force: "The way Douglas MacArthur did for the South Koreans in the 50's." My 17-year-old brother declared that he would join the anti-Communist guerrilla movement in Vietnam. My father sighed.

April 30, 1983: I stayed awake all night with Vietnamese classmates from Berkeley to listen to monotonous speeches by angry old men. "National defeat must be avenged by sweat and blood!" one vowed.

But through the years, April 30 has come to symbolize something entirely different to me. Although I sometimes mourn the loss of home and land, it's the American landscape and what it offers that solidify my hyphenated identity. This date of tragic ending, from an optimist's point of view, is also an American rebirth, something close to the Fourth of July.

I remember whispering to a young countryman during one of those monotonous April 30 rallies in the mid-1980's: "Even as the old man speaks of patriotic repatriation, we've already become Americans."

Assimilation, education, the English language, the American "I"—   15
these have carried me and many others further from that beloved tropical country than the C–130 ever could. Each optimistic step the young Vietnamese takes toward America is tempered with a little betrayal of Little

Saigon's parochialism, its sentimentalities and the old man's outdated passion.

When did this happen? Who knows? One night, America quietly seeps in and takes hold of one's mind and body, and the Vietnamese soul of sorrows slowly fades away. In the morning, the Vietnamese American speaks a new language of materialism: his vocabulary includes terms like career choices, down payment, escrow, overtime.

My brother never made it to the Indochinese jungle. The would-be guerrilla fighter became instead a civil engineer. My talk of endless possibilities is punctuated with favorite verbs—transcend, redefine, become. "I want to become a writer," I declared to my parents one morning. My mother gasped.

April 30, 1975: defeat or liberation?

"It was a day of joyous victory," said a retired Communist official in Hanoi. "We fought and realized Uncle Ho's dream of national independence." Then he asked for Marlboro cigarettes and a few precious dollars.

Nhon Nguyen, a real state salesman in San Jose, a former South Vietnamese naval officer, said: "I could never forget the date. So many people died. So much blood. I could never tolerate Communism, you know." 20

Mai Huong, a young Vietnamese woman in Saigon, said that, of course, it was National Liberation Day. "But it's the South," she said with a wink, "that liberated the North." Indeed, conservative Uncle Ho has slowly admitted defeat to entrepreneurial and cosmopolitan Miss Saigon. She has taken her meaning from a different uncle, you know, Uncle Sam.

"April 30, 1975?" said Bobby To, my 22 year-old cousin in San Francisco. "I don't know that date. I don't remember Vietnam at all." April 29, 1992, is more meaningful to him, Bobby said. "It's when the race riots broke out all over our country. To me it's more realistic to worry about what's going on over here than there."

Sighing, the customs man, who offered me a ride into Hanoi, said: "In truth, there are no liberators. We are all defeated here." There is no job, no future, no direction, only a sense of collective malaise, something akin to the death of the national soul. He added: "You're lucky, brother. You left Vietnam and became an American."

April 30, 1993: My friends and I plan to watch *Gone with the Wind* for the umpteenth time and look for a scene of our unrequited romantic longings: Scarlett, teary-eyed with wind-blown hair, returning to forlorn Tara. We no longer can. Children of defeat, self-liberating adults, we promise to hug instead and recount to each other our own stories of flight.

✎ Topics for Critical Thinking and Writing

1. Lam sets up at once the distinction between National Defeat Day and National Liberation Day and calls the moment for him an *epiphany*. How does he do it? And what is an epiphany?

2. In paragraph 8 Lam remembers the escape from Vietnam in 1975, and then April 30 in 1976, 1979, 1983. Assuming that you were not around to notice those dates—or even if you were—what techniques does Lam use to make them vivid?

3. In paragraph 15 Lam says "Each optimistic step the young Vietnamese takes toward America is tempered with a little betrayal of Little Saigon's parochialism, its sentimentalities and the old man's outdated passion." What does he mean?

4. At the essay's conclusion, Lam says that he and his friends will watch *Gone with the Wind* and "recount to each other our own stories of flight." Why do they watch *Gone with the Wind* (instead of a Vietnamese film)? What does Lam's choice of the film tell us?

5. If you have a story similar to Lam's, or one that in many ways is opposed to Lam's, try to tell it in an essay that begins with a narrative and may end with one too.

Bharati Mukherjee

Bharati Mukherjee, born in Calcutta, India, in 1940, spent much of her childhood in London with her parents and sisters, but returned to India in 1951. She earned a bachelor's and a master's degree in India, then moved to London, and to the United States, where she studied for a doctorate at the University of Iowa Writers Workshop. At Iowa she met and married a novelist, and the couple later moved to Canada. While living in Canada she published two novels, and in 1980 she came to the United States to teach at the University of Iowa. She has also taught at Skidmore College, Queens College, and at Columbia University. We reprint an essay that originally appeared in The New York Times.

Two Ways to Belong in America

This is a tale of two sisters from Calcutta, Mira and Bharati, who have lived in the United States for some 35 years, but who find themselves on different sides in the current debate over the status of immigrants. I am an American citizen and she is not. I am moved that thousands of long-term residents are finally taking the oath of citizenship. She is not.

Mira arrived in Detroit in 1960 to study child psychology and pre-school education. I followed her a year later to study creative writing at the University of Iowa. When we left India, we were almost identical in appearance and attitude. We dressed alike, in saris; we expressed identical views on politics, social issues, love and marriage in the same Calcutta convent-school accent. We would endure our two years in America, secure our degrees, then return to India to marry the grooms of our father's choosing.

Instead, Mira married an Indian student in 1962 who was getting his business administration degree at Wayne State University. They soon acquired the labor certifications necessary for the green card of hassle-free residence and employment.

Mira still lives in Detroit, works in the Southfield, Mich., school system, and has become nationally recognized for her contributions in the fields of pre-school education and parent-teacher relationships. After 36 years as a legal immigrant in this country, she clings passionately to her Indian citizenship and hopes to go home to India when she retires.

In Iowa City in 1963, I married a fellow student, an American of Canadian parentage. Because of the accident of his North Dakota birth, I bypassed labor-certification requirements and the race-related "quota" system that favored the applicant's country of origin over his or her merit. I was prepared for (and even welcomed) the emotional strain that came with marrying outside my ethnic community. In 33 years of marriage, we have lived in every part of North America. By choosing a husband who was not my father's selection, I was opting for fluidity, self-invention, blue jeans and T-shirts, and renouncing 3,000 years (at least) of caste-observant, "pure culture" marriage in the Mukherjee family. My books have often been read as unapologetic (and in some quarters over-enthusiastic) texts for cultural and psychological "mongrelization." It's a word I celebrate.

Mira and I have stayed sisterly close by phone. In our regular Sunday morning conversations, we are unguardedly affectionate. I am her only blood relative on this continent. We expect to see each other through the looming crises of aging and ill health without being asked. Long before Vice President Gore's "Citizenship U.S.A." drive, we'd had our polite arguments over the ethics of retaining an overseas citizenship while expecting the permanent protection and economic benefits that come with living and working in America.

Like well-raised sisters, we never said what was really on our minds, but we probably pitied one another. She, for the lack of structure in my life, the erasure of Indianness, the absence of an unvarying daily core. I, for the narrowness of her perspective, her uninvolvement with the mythic depths or the superficial pop culture of this society. But, now, with the scapegoating of "aliens" (documented or illegal) on the increase, and the targeting of long-term legal immigrants like Mira for new scrutiny and new self-consciousness, she and I find ourselves unable to maintain the same polite discretion. We were always unacknowledged adversaries, and we are now, more than ever, sisters.

"I feel used," Mira raged on the phone the other night. "I feel manipulated and discarded. This is such an unfair way to treat a person who was invited to stay and work here because of her talent. My employer went to the I.N.S. and petitioned for the labor certification. For over 30 years, I've invested my creativity and professional skills into the improvement of *this* country's pre-school system. I've obeyed all the rules, I've paid my taxes, I love my work, I love my students, I love the friends I've made. How dare America now change its rules in midstream? If America wants to make new rules curtailing benefits of legal immigrants, they should apply only to immigrants who arrive after those rules are already in place."

To my ears, it sounded like the description of a long-enduring, comfortable yet loveless marriage, without risk or recklessness. Have we the right to demand, and to expect, that we be loved? (That, to me, is the subtext of the arguments by immigration advocates.) My sister is an expatriate, professionally generous and creative, socially courteous and gracious, and that's as far as her Americanization can go. She is here to maintain an identity, not to transform it.

I asked her if she would follow the example of others who have decided to become citizens because of the anti-immigration bills in Congress. And here, she surprised me. "If America wants to play the manipulative game, I'll play it too," she snapped. "I'll become a U.S. citizen for now, then change back to Indian when I'm ready to go home. I feel some kind of irrational attachment to India that I don't to America. Until all this hysteria against legal immigrants, I was totally happy. Having my green card meant I could visit any place in the world I wanted to and then come back to a job that's satisfying and that I do very well." 10

In one family, from two sisters alike as peas in a pod, there could not be a wider divergence of immigrant experience. America spoke to me—I married it—I embraced the demotion from expatriate aristocrat to immigrant nobody, surrendering those thousands of years of "pure culture," the saris, the delightfully accented English. She retained them all. Which of us is the freak?

Mira's voice, I realize, is the voice not just of the immigrant South Asian community but of an immigrant community of the millions who have stayed rooted in one job, one city, one house, one ancestral culture, one cuisine, for the entirety of their productive years. She speaks for greater numbers than I possibly can. Only the fluency of her English and the anger, rather than fear, born of confidence from her education, differentiate her from the seamstresses, the domestics, the technicians, the shop owners, the millions of hard-working but effectively silenced documented immigrants as well as their less fortunate "illegal" brothers and sisters.

Nearly 20 years ago, when I was living in my husband's ancestral homeland of Canada, I was always well-employed but never allowed to feel part of the local Quebec or larger Canadian society. Then, through a Green Paper that invited a national referendum on the unwanted side effects of "nontraditional" immigration, the Government officially turned against its immigrant communities, particularly those from South Asia.

I felt then the same sense of betrayal that Mira feels now. I will never forget the pain of that sudden turning, and the casual racist outbursts the Green Paper elicited. That sense of betrayal had its desired effect and drove me, and thousands like me, from the country.

Mira and I differ, however, in the ways in which we hope to interact with the country that we have chosen to live in. She is happier to live in 15

America as expatriate Indian than as an immigrant American. I need to feel like a part of the community I have adopted (as I tried to feel in Canada as well). I need to put roots down, to vote and make the difference that I can. The price that the immigrant willingly pays, and that the exile avoids, is the trauma of self-transformation.

✎ Topics for Critical Thinking and Writing

1. Analyze the first paragraph as an opening paragraph? Why do you think it is or is not effective? (Some suggestions: Does the phrase "a tale of two sisters" ring a bell? Do the variations in the lengths of the sentences contribute to the meaning?)

2. Given what you now know about Mira, do you think she has a case? List her arguments and evaluate each. If you believe they don't add up to much, do you think she should be required to leave? Set forth your evaluation of her arguments, and your view about granting permanent status to aliens who do not wish to become citizens, in an essay of 500 words.

3. If you are an American citizen, can you imagine living most of your adult life in another country—perhaps because you believe you are contributing a needed skill, or perhaps because your spouse is a citizen of that country—and *not* becoming a citizen, even though you enjoy your life there? Or put the reverse question: Can you imagine *becoming* a citizen of that country? Perhaps much would depend on the country. Choose a country that you are likely to find highly attractive, and in an essay of 500 words set forth your position.

4. Mukherjee in her final paragraph speaks of the "price" that the immigrant willingly pays when he or she becomes a citizen. Interview two immigrants who have become citizens, and report their views on what (if anything) it cost them spiritually to become a citizen. (On interviewing, see page 56–60.)

Emily Tsao

Emily Tsao wrote this essay when she was a sophomore at Yale University. It was originally published in a daily newspaper, The Washington Post.

Thoughts of an Oriental Girl

I am an Oriental girl. Excuse me, I forgot to use my politically correct dictionary. Let me rephrase that, I am an Asian-American woman. Yes, that sounds about right. Excuse me again; I mean politically correct.

When I first stepped onto the campus scene last year, I, like many other anxious freshmen, wanted to fit in. I wanted to wear the right clothes, carry the right bookbag and, most important, say the right things. Speaking to upperclassmen, however, I realized that I had no command of the proper "PC" language.

Girls, it became clear, were to be called women. Freshmen who were girls were to be called freshwomen. Mixed groups of both sexes were to be labeled freshpeople, and upperclassmen were to be referred to as upperclasspeople. Orientals were to be called Asian Americans, blacks were to be called African Americans and Hispanics Latinos.

To me, most of this seemed pointless. Being called a girl doesn't bother me. I'm 18 years old. My mom is a woman. I'm her kid. I don't expect her to refer to me as a woman.

I have always referred to my female friends as girls, and still do. I want my boyfriend to call me his girlfriend, not his woman friend.   5

My friends and I refer to the male students at college as boys or guys. Never men. Kevin Costner and Robert Redford are men. Men don't drink themselves sick at keg parties every weekend, ask Dad for money, or take laundry home to Mom.

For 12 years of high school and grade school, the female students were always girls and the males were boys. Why does going to college with these same peers suddenly make me a woman and the boys men? I certainly don't feel much older or wiser than I did last year. When people refer to me as a woman, I turn around to see who might be standing behind me.

Another fad now is for people to spell women with a "y" in place of the "e"—"womyn." These people want to take the "men" out of "women." Next perhaps they'll invent "femyle."

I've always been gender conscious with my language when it seemed logical. In third grade I referred to the mailman as a mailperson because our mail was sometimes delivered by a woman. I don't think I ever said mailwoman, though, because it just didn't sound right.

From elementary through high school, I told people I was Chinese,   10
and if I wanted to refer to all Asians, I used the word "Orientals." I guess I was young and foolish and didn't know any better.

At college I was told that the proper label for me was Asian American, that "Oriental" was a word to describe furniture, not people. But what is the difference? All Asians are still being clumped together, even though each group—Chinese, Korean, Japanese, Indians, Vietnamese and Filipinos, to name just a few—comes from a different country with a different language and culture.

The new "PC" term to describe Asian Americans and all other minorities is "people of color." The reason, I am told, is that the "minority" population has grown to be the majority. But even if that's true, the phrase seems contradictory. Since many African Americans no longer want to be referred to as blacks, why should the term for minorities once again refer to skin color? The same is true for Asians, most of whom find the label "yellow" more offensive than Oriental. And isn't white also a color?

As long as we're throwing out all the old labels, why not replace "white" with "European American." Wasps could be EAASPS (European-American Anglo Saxon Protestants). Well, maybe not. Minority groups want new labels to give themselves a more positive image, but unless the stereotypes disappear as well, is it really going to help very much?

Look at the word "sophomore," which comes from Greek roots meaning "wise fool." PC-conscious sophomores ought to revolt against this offensive phrase. I, however, will not be among them. Changing the word won't make me any smarter, humbler or wiser.

✎ Topics for Critical Thinking and Writing

1. Tsao doesn't comment on stereotypical views of persons of Asian background, but one commonly hears that the chief stereotypes are these: The men are asexual, effeminate, and sly; the women are malevolent (Dragon Lady) or passive (Madam Butterfly). If you are familiar with any of the images that perhaps have helped to perpetuate these or other stereotypes, set forth your response, for instance to a Charlie Chan film (the clever Asian).

2. In paragraph 11 Tsao rightly insists that "each group—Chinese, Korean, Japanese, Indians, Vietnamese and Filipinos, to name just a few—comes from a different country with a different language and culture." If we can speak of "culture"—whether Chinese or Anglo or Italian or Italian American—how does culture differ from stereotypical behavior?

3. In her first three paragraphs Tsao says that the word "Oriental" is now in disfavor, but she doesn't say why. The reasons apparently are two: (1) The word (from Latin *oriri*, "to arise") means, in effect, the east, where the sun arises. The word is now regarded as Eurocentric; China, Korea, and Japan are eastern relative to Europe, but they are not eastern in an absolute sense. (2) "Oriental," used of Chinese, Koreans, Japanese, Indonesians and others, suggests racial identity, and overlooks important cultural differences. The preferred terms today are East Asia and East Asian. Given this background, do you think it is foolish to abandon the terms "Orient" and "Oriental"? In an essay of 250 words set forth your response.

4. In paragraph 3 Tsao talks about the word "freshman." If you were a college dean or president, in other words someone in a position to set the tone for the institution, would you abandon "freshman" and "freshwoman" for "freshperson," or perhaps for "first-year student"? In a paragraph explain why you would or would not drop "freshman" for all first-year students.

5. In paragraph 12 Tsao comments on the use of the term "people of color." Does the term seem to you to have some value, or is it something we should avoid using? Set forth your views in one or two paragraphs.

David Mura

David Mura (b. 1952) is a sansei, *a third-generation Japanese-American. In addition to publishing a book of poems, he has published* A Male Grief *(a study of pornography),* Turning Japanese *(a memoir of his visit to Japan), and* Where the Body Meets Memory: An Odyssey of Race, Sexuality and Identity. *Mura has received several awards, including a US/Japan Creative Artist Fellowship, and an NEA Literature Fellowship. The essay that we reprint appeared originally in* The New York Times.

How America Unsexes the Asian Male

The Japanese-American actor Marc Hayashi once said to me: "Every culture needs its eunuchs. And we're it. Asian-American men are the eunuchs of America." I felt an instant shock of recognition.

To my chagrin, I came close to being one such eunuch on screen in the Coen brothers' movie "Fargo."

The call for the role seemed perfect: a Japanese-American man, in his late 30's, a bit portly, who speaks with a Minnesota accent.

I am a sansei, a third-generation Japanese-American. I've lived in Minnesota for 20 years. Though not portly, I'm not thin. A writer and a performance artist, I had done one small film for PBS.

After I passed the first two readings, my wife and I talked about what other parts might follow and even joked about moving to Hollywood. But in the end, the Coens found another Asian-American actor.   5

But when I saw the much-acclaimed "Fargo," I said to myself, "Thank God I didn't get the part." The character I would have played is Mike Yanagita, a Japanese-American who speaks with a thick Minnesota accent and awkwardly attempts a pass at an old high school friend, Marge Gunderson, a rural police chief who is visibly pregnant.

He then tells of marrying a mutual acquaintance from high school and of her recent death from cancer. A few scenes later, Marge learns that this marriage was fiction: the acquaintance is not only alive, but has also complained to the police that Mike has been harassing her.

The Japanese-American character has no relevance to Marge's investigation. He is there mainly for humor. The humor is based on his derangement and his obvious illusions that Marge or their acquaintance would ever find him attractive.

I recognized this character as only the latest in a long line of Asian and Asian-American male nerds. Often, as in "Fargo," such a character will pant after white women, ridiculous in his desires. In the movies, as in the culture as a whole, Asian-American men seem to have no sexual clout. Or sexual presence.

Americans rarely talk about race and sex together. It's still taboo. Yet,   10
I often wonder what people make of me and my wife, who is three-quar-

ters WASP and one-quarter Hungarian Jew. Recently we went shopping with my sister Linda and our children. Several people, all white, mistook Linda for the wife, the mother. Was that because many whites find it difficult to picture an Asian-American man with a white woman?

In fiction, when East meets West, it is almost always a Western man meeting an Asian woman. There is constant reinforcement for the image of the East as feminine and the stereotype of Asian women as exotic, submissive and sensual. From "Madama Butterfly" to "The Karate Kid, Part II" and "Miss Saigon," the white man who falls in love with an Asian woman has been used to proffer the view that racial barriers cannot block the heart's affections.

But such pairings simply place white men at the screen's center and reinforce a hierarchy of power and sexual attractiveness. They play on the stereotype of the East as feminine. And where does that leave Asian men?

A salient feature of the play "M. Butterfly" is that it affirms this feminine view of Asian men. In it, a French diplomat conducts a lengthy love affair with someone he believes is a woman but is actually a Chinese transvestite. The affair proves that Asian manhood is indeed difficult to find, at least for white Westerners. And when the "mistress" strips to a highly buffed and masculine body, it is not just the diplomat who gasps, but the audience as well.

And the stereotypes continue. In the sitcom "All-American Girl," Margaret Cho played a hip Korean-American who dated white boys in defiance of her mother's wishes. The brother was a studious, obsequious geek who dated no one.

Asian and Asian-American men are simply not seen as attractive or sexual beings by the mainstream culture. What could be attractive about the horny, thick-glassed, nerdy Asian guy, ridiculous in his desires for white women?

15

How little things change. As a boy I watched Mickey Rooney as the Japanese buffoon neighbor in "Breakfast at Tiffany's" and knew I never wanted to be associated with this snarling, bucktoothed creature who shouted at Audrey Hepburn, "Miss Gorrightry, Miss Gorrightry," and panted when she offered to let him photograph her; I identified with John Wayne against the Japs; in "Have Gun Will Travel," I was a cowboy like Paladin, not the Chinese messenger who ran into the hotel lobby shouting, "Terragram for Mr. Paradin."

To me as a child, Asian features, Asian accents—these were all undesirable. They weren't part of my image of a real all-American boy.

For a while this seemed to work. My parents, interned during World War II, wanted to distance themselves from their ethnic roots. We lived in an all-white suburb, where I generally felt like one of the crowd. Then came adolescence, and my first boy-girl party. As usual, I was the only Asian-American and person of color in the room. But when we began to play spin the bottle, I felt a new sense of difference from the others. And then the bottle I'd spun pointed to a girl I had a crush on, and she refused to kiss me.

Did that have to do with race? I had no language to express how race factored into the way the others perceived me, nor did they. But if the culture had told me Asian men were nerds or goofy houseboys, the white kids at the party must have received the same message.

In college, in the early 1970's, my reaction to the sexual place assigned   20
to me took the form of compulsive sexuality: rampant promiscuity with white women and an obsession with pornography. There was definitely a racial component to it: my desires focused specifically on white women. I thought if I was with a white woman, then I would be as "good" as a white guy.

It took me years to figure out what was going on. It helped to read Frantz Fanon, the great Caribbean author and psychiatrist. In "Black Skin, White Masks," he writes of how the black man who constantly sleeps with white women has the illusion that his feelings of inferiority will somehow be erased by this act.

Gradually, I began to ask questions about how I learned what was sexually attractive and what images the culture gave me of myself.

How, for instance, does race factor in attraction? A popular way around such questions is to say that love sees no color.

I don't believe that. We are taught to see and process race early on. Race may not be the sole determinant in interracial relationships, but it is a factor. When I look at my wife, for example, I'm aware my desires for her cannot be separated from the ways the culture has inculcated me with standards of white beauty.

And when I told Alexs Pate, an African-American novelist, about   25
Marc Hayashi's comment about the eunuchization of Asian-American men, he replied, "And black men are the sexual demons."

One is undersexed, the other, oversexed. Everyone knows who possesses a normal, healthy sense of sexuality.

Recently, after a panel discussion on "identity art," an elderly white man came up and complimented me on a performance I'd appeared in with my friend Alexs. Then he asked, "Weren't you in 'Fargo,' too?"

"No," I replied. "That wasn't me."

✎ Topics for Critical Thinking and Writing

1. In paragraph 9 Mura says that the Japanese-American in *Fargo* is one of "a long line of Asian and Asian-American male nerds." He goes on: "In the movies, as in the culture as a whole, Asian-American men seem to have no sexual clout. Or sexual presence." What examples can you give to support his generalizations? What counter examples (perhaps Bruce Lee, the *kung fu* man)? In short, do you think Mura's point here is sound? Why?

2. In paragraph 11 Mura says, "In fiction, when East meets West, it is almost always a Western man meeting an Asian woman." He is probably right—but why do you think this is so?

3. Mura in paragraph 14 speaks of "stereotypes." In a sentence or two define "stereotype." If indeed there are cultural patterns—let's say ethnic patterns in which certain groups are justly known for their displays of affection, or their reserved manner, or their sense of humor, or whatever—is one speaking of stereotypes if one comments on these patterns?

4. "Race may not be the sole determinant in interracial relationships, but it is a factor." Does this generalization strike you as true? How would one go about supporting or refuting it? Is it different from saying, "Class may not be the sole determinant . . . ," or "Education may not be the sole determinant, . . . ," or "Age may not be the sole determinant . . ."?

5. In paragraphs 18–19 Mura reports a childhood experience that he suggests was based on race. If you have ever had a somewhat comparable experience—it may have been based on religion, or even on a geographical difference within the United States—set forth the experience. Consider writing three paragraphs: a lead-in, the narrative of the experience, and finally a reflection on it.

6. If among your friends or family you know of a marriage between a white and an Asian or a white and an Asian-American, ask the couple to read Mura's essay and then interview them, finding out their responses. Report the results of your interview in an essay of 750 words. (On interviews, see page 56–60.)

Dennis Altman

We print an excerpt from an article that originally appeared in the New Internationalist *in November, 1989.*

Why Are Gay Men So Feared?

Gay men are the victims of insults, prejudice, abuse, violence, sometimes murder. Why are gay men hated by so many other men? Some maintain that homosexuality is unnatural or a threat to the family. But celibacy is also unnatural, yet nuns and priests are not regularly attacked. And there is also a good case to be made that homosexuality, actually *strengthens* the family by liberating some adults from childbearing duties and so increasing the pool of adults available to look after children.

But the real objection to homosexuality (and lesbianism) is undoubtedly more deep-seated: It is threatening because it seems to challenge the conventional roles governing a person's sex, and the female and male roles in society. The assertion of homosexual identity clearly challenges the apparent naturalness of gender roles.

Men are particularly prone to use anger and violence against those they think are undermining their masculinity. And it is here that we can find at least some of the roots of homophobia and gay-bashing.

As Freud understood, most societies are built upon a set of relationships between men: Most powerful institutions like parliaments and business corporations are male-dominated. And this "male bonding" demands a certain degree of sexual sublimation.

In many societies, the links between men are much stronger than the relations that link them to women. But these bonds are social rather than individual, and for this reason need to be strictly governed. Armies, for example, depend upon a very strong sense of male solidarity, though this does not allow for too close an emotional tie between any *specific* pair of men.

Thus the most extreme homophobia is often found among tightly knit groups of men, who need to deny any sexual component to their bonding as well as boost their group solidarity by turning violently on "fags" or "queers," who are defined as completely alien. This is a phenomenon found among teenage gangs, policemen, and soldiers. A particularly prominent example of this was Germany's Nazi Party, which shortly after coming to power purged those of its members who were tempted to turn the hypermasculinity of Nazism into an excuse for overt homosexual behavior.

Many observers of sexual violence have argued that the most virulent queer-basher is attacking the homosexual potential in himself—a potential that he has learned to suppress. Because homosexuality is "un-masculine," those who struggle with feelings of homosexuality (often unacknowledged) will be particularly tempted to resolve them through "masculine" expressions of violence. In court cases involving violence against gay men, the idea of preserving one's male honor is often pleaded as a defense.

Homophobia has effects that go far beyond those individuals against whom it is directed. Like racism and sexism, it is an expression of hatred that harms the perpetrator as well as the victim; the insecurities, fears, and sexual hang-ups that lead young men to go out looking for "fags" to beat up are dangerous to the entire society.

Those societies that are best able to accept homosexuals are also societies that are able to accept assertive women and gentle men, and they tend to be less prone to the violence produced by hypermasculinity.

✎ Topics for Critical Thinking and Writing

1. Before you read this essay, had it occurred to you that gay men are "feared"? What other attitudes toward gay men does Altman suggest?
2. Does Altman believe that homosexuality is unnatural? Does he offer any evidence that it either is or is not unnatural? How, in this context, might *natural* and *unnatural* be defined?
3. In a sentence or two state the answer that Altman gives to the question that he poses in his title. How convincing do you find it?

4. Does the logic of Altman's argument lead you to infer that lesbians are feared? Do you think they *are* feared? What do you think that Altman might say in reply to this question?

Gloria Naylor

Gloria Naylor—university teacher, essayist, and novelist—holds an M.A. in Afro-American Studies from Yale University. Her first novel, The Women of Brewster Place *(1983), won an American Book Award. "A Question of Language" originally appeared in* The New York Times.

A Question of Language

Language is the subject. It is the written form with which I've managed to keep the wolf away from the door and, in diaries, to keep my sanity. In spite of this, I consider the written word inferior to the spoken, and much of the frustration experienced by novelists is the awareness that whatever we manage to capture in even the most transcendent passages falls far short of the richness of life. Dialogue achieves its power in the dynamics of a fleeting moment of sight, sound, smell, and touch.

I'm not going to enter the debate here about whether it is language that shapes reality or vice versa. That battle is doomed to be waged whenever we seek intermittent reprieve from the chicken and egg dispute. I will simply take the position that the spoken word, like the written word, amounts to a nonsensical arrangement of sounds or letters without a consensus that assigns "meaning." And building from the meanings of what we hear, we order reality. Words themselves are innocuous; it is the consensus that gives them true power.

I remember the first time I heard the word *nigger.* In my third-grade class, our math tests were being passed down the rows, and as I handed the papers to a little boy in back of me, I remarked that once again he had received a much lower mark than I did. He snatched his test from me and spit out that word. Had he called me a nymphomaniac or a necrophiliac, I couldn't have been more puzzled. I didn't know what a nigger was, but I knew that whatever it meant, it was something he shouldn't have called me. This was verified when I raised my hand, and in a loud voice repeated what he had said and watched the teacher scold him for using a "bad" word. I was later to go home and ask the inevitable question that every black parent must face—"Mommy, what does 'nigger' mean?"

And what exactly did it mean? Thinking back, I realize that this could not have been the first time the word was used in my presence. I was part of a large extended family that had migrated from the rural South after World War II and formed a close-knit network that gravitated around my

maternal grandparents. Their ground-floor apartment in one of the buildings they owned in Harlem was a weekend mecca for my immediate family, along with countless aunts, uncles, and cousins who brought along
assorted friends. It was a bustling and open house with assorted neighbors and tenants popping in and out to exchange bits of gossip, pick up an
old quarrel or referee the ongoing checkers game in which my grandmother cheated shamelessly. They were all there to let down their hair and
put up their feet after a week of labor in the factories, laundries, and ship-
yards of New York.

Amid the clamor, which could reach deafening proportions—two or   5
three conversations going on simultaneously, punctuated by the sound of
a baby's crying somewhere in the back rooms or out on the street—there
was still a rigid set of rules about what was said and how. Older children
were sent out of the living room when it was time to get into the juicy
details about "you-know-who" up on the third floor who had gone and
gotten herself "p·r·e·g·n·a·n·t!" But my parents, knowing that I could spell
well beyond my years, always demanded that I follow the others out to
play. Beyond sexual misconduct and death, everything else was considered harmless for our young ears. And so among the anecdotes of the tri-
umphs and disappointments in the various workings of their lives, the
word *nigger* was used in my presence, but it was set within contexts and
inflections that caused it to register in my mind as something else.

In the singular, the word was always applied to a man who had distinguished himself in some situation that brought their approval for his
strength, intelligence, or drive:

"Did Johnny really do that?"

"I'm telling you, that nigger pulled in $6,000 of overtime last year.
Said he got enough for a down payment on a house."

When used with a possessive adjective by a woman—"my nigger"—
it became a term of endearment for husband or boyfriend. But it could be
more than just a term applied to a man. In their mouths it became the pure
essence of manhood—a disembodied force that channeled their past history of struggle and present survival against the odds into a victorious
statement of being: "Yeah, that old foreman found out quick enough—you
don't mess with a nigger."

In the plural, it became a description of some group within the com-   10
munity that had overstepped the bounds of decency as my family defined
it: Parents who neglected their children, a drunken couple who fought in
public, people who simply refused to look for work, those with excessively dirty mouths or unkempt households were all "trifling niggers." This
particular circle could forgive hard times, unemployment, the occasional
bout of depression—they had gone through all of that themselves—but
the unforgivable sin was lack of self-respect.

A woman could never be a *nigger* in the singular, with its connotation
of confirming worth. The noun *girl* was its closest equivalent in that sense,
but only when used in direct address and regardless of the gender doing

the addressing. *Girl* was a token of respect for a woman. The one-syllable word was drawn out to sound like three in recognition of the extra ounce of wit, nerve or daring that the woman had shown in the situation under discussion.

"G·i·r·l, stop. You mean you said that to his face?"

But if the word was used in a third-person reference or shortened so that it almost snapped out of the mouth, it always involved some element of communal disapproval. And age became an important factor in these exchanges. It was only between individuals of the same generation, or from an older person to a younger (but never the other way around), that "girl" would be considered a compliment.

I don't agree with the argument that use of the word *nigger* at this social stratum of the black community was an internalization of racism. The dynamics were the exact opposite: the people in my grandmother's living room took a word that whites used to signify worthlessness or degradation and rendered it impotent. Gathering there together, they transformed *nigger* to signify the varied and complex human beings they knew themselves to be. If the word was to disappear totally from the mouths of even the most liberal of white society, no one in that room was naive enough to believe it would disappear from white minds. Meeting the word head-on, they proved it had absolutely nothing to do with the way they were determined to live their lives.

So there must have been dozens of times that the word *nigger* was spo- 15
ken in front of me before I reached the third grade. But I didn't "hear" it until it was said by a small pair of lips that had already learned it could be a way to humiliate me. That was the word I went home and asked my mother about. And since she knew that I had to grow up in America, she took me in her lap and explained.

✎ Topics for Critical Thinking and Writing

1. Why, according to Naylor (in paragraph 1) is written language inferior to spoken language? Can you think of any way or any circumstance in which written language is superior? How does Naylor's essay support her position here? Or does it?

2. In paragraph 2 Naylor says "Words themselves are innocuous; it is the consensus that gives them true power." What does this mean? In the rest of the essay Naylor discusses meanings of the word *nigger*. To what extent does her discussion demonstrate that consensus "assigns meaning" and gives words power.

3. If as a child you were the victim of an ethnic slur, explain how you reacted to it and how others (perhaps a parent or teacher) reacted to it. Or, if you ever delivered an ethnic slur, explain how you felt then and how you feel now about the incident or incidents.

Jeanne Wakatsuki Houston

Jeanne Wakatsuki, the daughter of immigrants from Japan, was born in Inglewood, California. When she was seven, the Japanese attack on Pearl Harbor aroused such fear and resentment that Japanese and Japanese Americans on the Pacific coast of the United States were relocated, and her family was forced to spend three-and-a-half years at Manzanar, a camp in Owens Valley, California. Later she graduated from San Jose State University, married James D. Houston, and took up writing as a career.

Her first book, written with her husband, was Farewell to Manzanar *(1973), a memoir of her experience of the years during World War II. We reprint an essay from a later collection,* Beyond Manzanar *(1985).*

Double Identity

The memories surrounding my awareness of being female fall into two categories: those of the period before World War II, when the family made up my life, and those after the war when I entered puberty, and my world expanded to include the ways and values of my Caucasian peers. I did not think about my Asian-ness and how it influenced my self-image as a female until I married.

In remembering myself as a small child, I find it hard to separate myself from the entity of the family. I was too young to be given "duties" according to my sex, and I was unaware that this was the organizational basis for operating the family. I took it for granted that every-one just did what had to be done to keep things running smoothly. My five older sisters helped my mother with domestic duties. My four older brothers helped my father in the fishing business. What I vaguely recall about the sensibility surrounding our sex differences was that my sisters and I all liked to please our brothers. Moreover, we tried to attract positive attention from Papa. A smile or affectionate pat from him was like a gift from heaven. Somehow, we never felt this way about Mama. We took her love for granted. But there was something special about Papa.

I never identified this as one of the blessings of maleness. After all, I played with my brother Kiyo, two years older than myself, and I never felt there was anything special about him. I could even make him cry. My older brothers were fun-loving, boisterous and very kind to me, especially when I made them laugh with my imitations of Carmen Miranda dancing, or Bonnie Baker singing "Oh, Johnny." But Papa was different. His specialness came not from being male, but from being the authority.

After the war, and the closing of the camps, my world drastically changed. The family had disintegrated, my father was no longer "God-like" despite my mother's attempt to sustain that pre-war image of him. I was spending most of my time with my new Caucasian friends and learning new values that clashed with the values of my parents. It was also time that I assumed the duties girls were supposed to do—cooking, cleaning the house, washing and ironing clothes. I remember washing and ironing my brothers' shirts, careful to press the collars correctly, trying not to displease them. I cannot ever remember my brothers performing domestic chores while I lived at home. Yet, even though they may not have been working "out there," as the men were supposed to do, I did not resent it. It would have embarrassed me to see my brothers doing the dishes. Their reciprocation came in a different way. They were very protective of me and made me feel good and important for being a female. If my brother Ray had extra money, he would sometimes buy me a sexy sweater like my Caucasian friends wore, which Mama wouldn't buy for me. My brothers taught me to ride a bicycle, to drive a car, took me to my first dance, and proudly introduced me to their friends.

Although the family had changed, my identity as a female within it   5
did not differ much from my older sisters' who grew up before the war. The males and females supported each other but for different reasons. No longer was the survival of the family as a group our primary objective; we cooperated to help each other survive "out there" in the complicated world that had weakened Papa.

We were living in Long Beach then. My brothers encouraged me to run for school office, to try out for majorette and song leader, and to run for Queen of various festivities. They were proud that I was breaking social barriers still closed to them. It was acceptable for an Oriental male to excel academically and in sports. But to gain recognition socially in a society that had been fed the stereotyped model of the Asian male as cook, houseboy or crazed *Kamikaze* pilot, was almost impossible. The more alluring myth of mystery and exotica that surrounds the Oriental female made it easier, though no less inwardly painful.

Whenever I succeeded in the *hakujin*[1] world, my brothers were supportive, whereas Papa would be disdainful, undermined by my obvious capitulation to the ways of the West. I wanted to be like my Caucasian friends. Not only did I want to look like them, I wanted to act like them. I tried hard to be outgoing and socially aggressive, and to act confidently, like my girl friends. At home I was careful not to show these traits to my father. For him it was bad enough that I did not even look very Japanese; I was too big, and I walked too assertively. My breasts were large, and besides that I showed them off with those sweaters the *hakujin* girls wore! My behavior at home was never calm and serene, but around my father I still tried to be as Japanese as I could.

As I passed puberty and grew more interested in boys, I soon became aware that an Oriental female evoked a certain kind of interest from males. I was still too young to understand how or why an Oriental female fascinated Caucasian men, and of course, far too young to see then that it was a form of "not being seen." My brothers would warn me, "Don't trust the *hakujin* boys. They only want one thing. They'll treat you like a servant and expect you to wait on them hand and foot. They don't know how to be nice to you." My brothers never dated Caucasian girls. In fact, I never

[1]*hakujin*, Caucasian.

really dated Caucasian boys until I went to college. In high school, I used to sneak out to dances and parties where I would meet them. I wouldn't even dare to think what Papa would do if he knew.

What my brothers were saying was that I should not act towards Caucasian males as I did towards them. I must not "wait on them" or allow them to think I would, because they wouldn't understand. In other words, be a Japanese female around Japanese men and act *hakujin* around Caucasian men. This double identity within a "double standard" resulted not only in confusion of my role or roles as female, but also in who or what I was racially. With the admonitions of my brothers lurking deep in my consciousness, I would try to be aggressive, assertive and "come on strong" towards Caucasian men. I mustn't let them think I was submissive, passive and all-giving, like Madame Butterfly.[2] With Asian males I would tone down my natural enthusiasm and settle into patterns instilled in me through the models of my mother and my sisters. I was not comfortable in either role.

I found I was more physically attracted to Caucasian men. Although   10
T.V. and film were not nearly as pervasive as they are now, we still had an abundance of movie magazines and films from which to garner our idols for crushes and fantasy. For years I was madly in love with Lon McAllister and Alan Ladd. Bruce Lee and O.J. Simpson were absent from the idol-making media. Asian men became like "family" to me: they were my brothers. Of course, no one was like my father. He was so powerful. The only men who might possess some of that power were those whose control and dominance over his life diminished his. Those would be the men who interested me.

Although I was attracted to males who looked like someone in a Coca-Cola ad, I yearned for the expressions of their potency to be like that of Japanese men, like that of my father: unpredictable, dominant, and brilliant—yet sensitive and poetic. I wanted a blond Samurai.[3]

When I met him during those college years in San Jose, I was surprised to see how readily my mother accepted the idea of our getting married. My father had passed away, but I was still concerned about her reaction. All of my married brothers and sisters had Japanese American mates. I would be the first to marry a Caucasian. "He's a strong man and will protect you. I'm all for it," she said. Her main concern for me was survival. Knowing that my world was the world of the *hakujin,* she wanted me to be protected, even if it meant marriage to one. It was 1957, and inter-racial couples were a rare sight to see. She felt that my husband-to-be was strong because he was acting against the norms of his culture, perhaps even against his parent's wishes. From her vantage point, where family and group opinion outweighed the individual's, this willingness to oppose them was truly a show of strength.

When we first married I wondered if I should lay out his socks and underwear every morning like my mother used to do. But my brothers'

---

[2]*Madame Butterfly:* In Puccini's opera with this title, a young Japanese woman falls in love with an American naval officer in Japan, becomes pregnant, and is abandoned by him.
[3]*Samurai:* A member of the Japanese warrior class.

warning would float up from the past: don't be subservient to Caucasian men or they will take advantage. So I compromised and laid them out whenever I thought to do it . . . which grew less and less often as the years passed. His first reaction to this wifely gesture was to be uncomfortably pleased. Then he was puzzled by its sporadic occurrence, which did not seem to be an act of apology, or a sign that I wanted something. On the days when I felt I should be a good Japanese wife, I did it. On other days, when I felt American and assertive, I did not.

When my mother visited us, as she often did, I had to be on good behavior, much to my husband's pleasure and surprise. I would jump up from the table to fill his empty water glass (if she hadn't beat me to it) or butter his roll. If I didn't notice that his plate needed refilling, she would kick me under the table and reprimand me with a disapproving look. Needless to say, we never had mother-in-law problems. He would often ask with hope in his voice "when is your mother coming to visit?"

Despite the fact that early in our marriage we had become aware of the "images" we had married and were trying to relate to each other as the real people we were, he still hoped deep in his heart that I was his exotic, mysterious but ever available *Cho-Cho san*.[4] And I still saw him as my Anglo Samurai, wielding his sword of integrity, slaying the dragons that prevented my acceptance as an equal human being in his world, now mine.   15

* * *

My mother dutifully served my father throughout their marriage. I never felt she resented it. I served my brothers and father and did not resent it. I was made to feel not only important for performing duties of my role, but absolutely integral for the functioning of the family. I realized a very basic difference in attitude between Japanese and American culture towards serving another. In my family, to serve another could be uplifting, a gracious gesture that elevated oneself. For many white Americans it seems that serving another is degrading, an indication of dependency or weakness in character, or a low place in the social ladder. To be ardently considerate is to be "self-effacing" or apologetic.

My father used to say, "Serving humanity is the greatest virtue. Giving service of yourself is more worthy than selling the service or goods of another." He would prefer that we be maids in someone's home, serving someone well, than be salesgirls where our function would be to exchange someone else's goods, handling money. Perhaps it was his way to rationalize and give pride to the occupations open to us as Orientals. Nevertheless, his words have stayed with me, giving me spiritual sustenance at times when I perceived that my willingness to give was misconstrued as a need to be liked or an act of manipulation to get something.

I was talking about this subject with an Asian American woman friend, recently widowed, whose husband had also been Asian American. He had been a prominent surgeon, highly thought of in the community where we

---

[4]*Cho-Cho san,* Madam Butterfly.

live. She is forty-two, third generation Chinese, born in San Francisco, articulate, intelligent and a professional therapist for educationally handicapped children. She "confessed" her reticence to let her Caucasian friends know she served her husband. "There is such a stereotyped view that is laid on us. They just don't understand *why* we do what we do!"

She told me of an incident when she remarked to a Caucasian friend that she polished her husband's shoes. Her friend turned on her in mock fury and said, "Don't you dare let my husband know you do that!" My friend said she felt ashamed, humiliated, that she had somehow betrayed this woman by seeming subordinate to her husband.

"I served him in many ways," she said. "Even though he was a graduate of Stanford and professionally successful, he drove himself to work harder and longer to compete because he felt he was handicapped by being Chinese. You know our Asian men, the ones raised with values from the old country are not equipped to compete like white American men. They are not conditioned to be outwardly aggressive and competitive. It was agony for my husband, and I knew he was out there doing it for us, so I tried to make it easier for him at home." As I looked at her I could see her compassion, and for a flickering moment I saw my mother. A generation had passed, but some things had not changed that much.

My husband and I often joke that the reason we have stayed married for so long is that we continually mystify each other with responses and attitudes that are plainly due to our different backgrounds. For years I frustrated him with unpredictable silences and accusative looks. I felt a great reluctance to tell him what I wanted or what needed to be done in the home. I was inwardly furious that I was being put into the position of having to *tell* him what to do. I felt my femaleness, in the Japanese sense, was being degraded. I did not want to be the authority. That would be humiliating for him and for me. He, on the other hand, considering the home to be under my dominion, in the American sense, did not dare to impose on me what he thought I wanted. He wanted me to tell him or make a list, like his parents.

Entertaining socially was also confusing. Up to recent times, I still hesitated to sit at one head of our rectangular dining table when my husband sat at the other end. It seemed right to be seated next to him, helping him serve the food. Sometimes I did it anyway, but only with our close friends who didn't misread my physical placement as psychological subservience.

At dinner parties I always served the men first, until I noticed the women glaring at me. I became self-conscious about it and would try to remember to serve the women first. Sometimes I would forget and automatically turn to a man. I would catch myself abruptly, dropping a bowl of soup all over him. Then I would have to serve him first anyway, as a gesture of apology. My unconscious Japanese instinct still managed to get what it wanted.

Now I just entertain according to how I feel that day. If my Japanese sensibility is stronger I act accordingly and feel comfortable. If I want to go all-American I can do that too. I have come to accept the cultural hybridness of my personality, to recognize it as a strength and not weakness. Because I am culturally neither pure Japanese nor pure American does not mean I am less of a person. It means I have been enriched with the heritage of both.

As I look back on my marriage and try to compare it to the marriage of my parents, it seems ludicrous to do so—like comparing a sailboat to a jet airliner. Both get you there, but one depends on the natural element of wind and the other on modern technology. What does emerge as a basic difference is directly related to the Japanese concept of cooperation for group survival and the American value of competition for the survival of the individual. My Japanese family cooperated to survive economically and spiritually. Although sibling rivalry was subtly present, it was never allowed the ferocity of expression we allow our children. I see our children compete with each other. I have felt my husband and I compete with each other—not always in obvious ways, such as professional recognition or in the comparison of role responsibilities, but in attitudes toward self-fulfillment. "I love you more than you love me," or "My doing nothing is more boring than your doing nothing."

Competition does provide some challenge and excitement in life. Yet carried to extremes in personal relationships it can become destructive. How can you fully trust someone you are in competition with? And when trust breaks down, isolation and alienation set in.

I find another basic difference between my mother and myself in how we relate to sons. I try very consciously not to indulge my son, as my mother indulged my brothers. My natural inclination is to do as she did. So I try to restrain it. In fact, I find myself being harder on him, afraid that my constrained Japanese training to please the male might surface, crippling instead of equipping him for future relationships with females who may not be of my background, hampering his emotional survival in the competitive and independent world he will face when he leaves the nest.

How my present attitudes will affect my children in later years remains to be seen. My world is radically different from mother's world, and all indications point to an even wider difference in our world from our children's. Whereas my family's struggle and part of my own was racially based, I do not foresee a similar struggle for our children. Their bi-racialness is, indeed, a factor in their identity and self-image, but I feel their struggle will be more to sustain human dignity in a world rapidly dehumanizing itself with mechanization and technology. My hope is they have inherited that essential trait ethnic minorities in this country have so sharply honed: a strong will to survive.

✎ Topics for Critical Thinking and Writing

1. In her fifth paragraph Jeanne Wakatsuki Houston recalls how her brothers and sisters cooperated to "help each other survive 'out there' in the compli-

cated world that had weakened Papa." What do we suppose had happened to reduce Papa's "Godlike" image? And in the next paragraph, Houston speaks of how her brothers encouraged her "to run for school office, to try out for majorette and song leader, and to run for Queen of various festivities." How had her brothers encouraged her here?

2. Houston tells us in paragraph 7 that, although now past puberty, she was "still too young to understand how or why an Oriental female fascinated Caucasian men." Nowadays, Houston would probably not use the word *Oriental*. Can you explain why? (Hint: See the entry on *Orient* in "A Writer's Glossary.")

3. We are told that there are differences in the Houston household that stem from the writer and her husband coming from different cultures. Which of these differences most resemble those that are *not* a result of being a Japanese/American couple? Can you explain why?

4. In her last paragraph Houston projects some differences for her children from those of her world with her husband. What are these differences? Do you find them similar to the challenges you face or not? Explain.

5. Houston contrasts her Japanese environment, which emphasized service in her family, with the Caucasian environment, which emphasizes competition. She calls it her *cultural hybridness* and is proud of it. Compare this essay with Fan Shen's, page 417. Is he also proud of his "hybridness"? Explain.

Brent Staples

Brent Staples, born in 1951, holds a Ph.D. in psychology from the University of Chicago. He taught briefly and then turned to journalism. He is now assistant metropolitan editor at The New York Times. *We reprint an essay that appeared in this paper in 1994.*

The "Scientific" War on the Poor

Everyone knows the stereotype of the fair-haired executive who owes the office with the view and the six-figure salary to an accident of birth—like relatives in the halls of power. What about merit, for heaven's sake? Why not give I.Q. tests, grant the best jobs to those who score well and send the laggards to the mailroom?

That would never happen, nor should it. I.Q. scores in themselves tell you almost nothing. This was clearly explained by the Frenchman Alfred Binet, who invented the first usable I.Q. test in 1905. The test had one purpose: to help identify learning-disabled children who needed special schools. Binet warned that a "brutal pessimism" would follow if his test was ever mistaken as a measure of a fixed, unchangeable intelligence.

You wouldn't know it from the I.Q. worship in progress today, but using the tests to draw finer distinctions than Binet intended amounts to overreaching, if not scientific fraud. Most scientists concede that they don't really know what "intelligence" is. Whatever it might be, paper and pencil tests aren't the tenth of it.

The fair-haired executive gets a pass for other reasons entirely. First, because the world works more on insiderism and inherited privilege than on "pure merit," whatever that might be. Second, because the charge of innate stupidity has historically been reserved for the poor.

That charge surfaced during the immigrant influx of the teens and 20's, and again during the affirmative-action 60's and 70's—both times when America found "scientific" justifications of poverty very appealing. Misgivings about the "underclass" have made them appealing again. By way of example, consider Senator Daniel Patrick Moynihan's ludicrous claim that out-of-wedlock births in modern America amounted to the creation of a new species.

Alfred Binet's American imitators embraced "brutal pessimism" right away. In 1912, after Eastern and Southern Europeans began to out-number Northern Europeans at Ellis Island, immigration authorities asked the psychologist Henry Goddard to do "quality control," through intelligence testing. Goddard and his colleagues believed that Nordic peoples were civilization's best and that the rest were genetically second-rate or worse. The test was merely a means of proving it.

Not surprisingly, Goddard's testing of what he called a representative sample of immigrants showed that 80 percent of all Jews, Italians and Hungarians and nearly 90 percent of Russians were "feeble-minded." As a result, hundreds each year were deported.

At the start of World War I, two million draftees were also tested. The results showed a gap between blacks and whites, but at the time, few were interested. The passion then was proving a connection between "mental deficiency" and national origin among white immigrants. The testers didn't bother with translation; non-English-speakers were instructed in pantomime.

Once again, British immigrants were classified as first-rate, with Poles, Italians and Russians labeled stupid and undesirable. The data were published by the National Academy of Sciences in 1921, and contributed to the introduction of temporary limits on immigration. I.Q. hysteria also resulted in sterilization laws that were enforced only against the poor.

The I.Q. believers worked with messianic zeal. Like many before him, the British psychologist Sir Cyril Burt went way beyond science in defense of his beliefs. Burt alleged that intelligence was so wired into the genes, so indifferent to environment, that identical twins reared apart had virtually identical I.Q. scores. Statisticians now agree that Burt made much of it up.

The I.Q. worshipers of today remain essentially unchanged from Goddard's time. Despite the impression that there is something new in

The Bell Curve, its authors, Charles Murray and Richard Herrnstein, have merely reasserted the long-unproven claim that I.Q. is mainly inherited. The language is calmer, the statistical gimmicks slicker, but the truth remains the same: There exist no plausible data to make the case. Belief to the contrary rests mainly on brutal preconceptions about poverty, but also on a basic confusion between pseudoscience and the real thing.

✎ Topics for Critical Thinking and Writing

1. In his first paragraph Staples outlines the "stereotype of the fair-haired executive who owes the office with the view and the six-figure salary to an accident of birth." Why, he asks, don't we give I. Q. tests for such jobs? In the next paragraph, however, he says "That would never happen, nor should it." Why does he believe that it should *not* happen? Do *you* believe it should or should not happen? Why?

2. In paragraph 5 Staples mentions two earlier times when "'scientific' justifications of poverty" were appealing. Why were these "justifications" appealing? Why are they appealing now? And why does Staples use quotation marks around "scientific"?

3. What happened in 1912 on Ellis Island that prompted authorities to ask Henry Goddard for "quality control." What did he do? Staples offers no examples for the "affirmative-action 60's and 70's." Should he have?

4. In his last paragraph Staples states that "brutal preconceptions about poverty" underlie arguments for I.Q. scores. If Staples had removed the word *brutal,* would the sentence remain the same?

Amy Tan

Amy Tan was born in 1952 in Oakland, California, two-and-a-half years after her parents had emigrated from China. She attended Linfield College in Oregon and then California State University at San Jose, where she shifted her major from premedical studies to English. After earning a master's degree in linguistics from San Jose, Tan worked as a language consultant and then as a freelance business writer. In 1985, having decided to try her hand at fiction, she joined the Squaw Valley Community of Writers, a fiction workshop. In 1989 she published her first novel, The Joy Luck Club, *a collection of sixteen interwoven stories. In 1991 she published a second novel,* The Kitchen God's Wife.*

The essay that we reprint appeared in* Life *magazine in April 1991.*

Courtesy Amy Tan

Snapshot: Lost Lives of Women

When I first saw this photo as a child, I thought it was exotic and re-mote, of a faraway time and place, with people who had no connection to my American life. Look at their bound feet! Look at that funny lady with the plucked forehead!

The solemn little girl is, in fact, my mother. And leaning against the rock is my grandmother, Jingmei. "She called me Baobei," my mother told me. "It means Treasure."

The picture was taken in Hangzhou, and my mother believes the year was 1922, possibly spring or fall, judging by the clothes. At first glance, it appears the women are on a pleasure outing.

But see the white bands on their skirts? The white shoes? They are in mourning. My mother's grandmother, known to the others as Divong, "The Replacement Wife," has recently died. The women have come to this place, a Buddhist retreat, to perform yet another ceremony for Divong. Monks hired for the occasion have chanted the proper words. And the women and little girl have walked in circles clutching smoky sticks of incense. They knelt and prayed, then burned a huge pile of spirit money so that Divong might ascend to a higher position in her new world.

This is also a picture of secrets and tragedies, the reasons that warn-   5 ings have been passed along in our family like heirlooms. Each of these women suffered a terrible fate, my mother said. And they were not peasant women but big city people, very modern. They went to dance halls and wore stylish clothes. They were supposed to be the lucky ones.

Look at the pretty woman with her finger on her cheek. She is my mother's second cousin, Nunu Aiji, "Precious Auntie." You cannot see this, but Nunu Aiyi's entire face was scarred from smallpox. Lucky for her, a year or so after this picture was taken, she received marriage proposals from two families. She turned down a lawyer and married another man. Later she divorced her husband, a daring thing for a woman to do. But then, finding no means to support herself or her young daughter, Nunu eventually accepted the lawyer's second proposal—to become his number two concubine. "Where else could she go?" my mother asked. "Some people said she was lucky the lawyer still wanted her."

Now look at the small woman with a sour face (*third from left*). There's a reason that Jyou Ma, "Uncle's Wife," looks this way. Her husband, my great-uncle often complained that his family had chosen an ugly woman for his wife. To show his displeasure, he often insulted Jyou Ma's cooking. One time Great-Uncle tipped over a pot of boiling soup, which fell all over his niece's four-year-old neck and nearly killed her. My mother was the little niece, and she still has that soup scar on her neck. Great-Uncle's family eventually chose a pretty woman for his second wife. But the complaints about Jyou Ma's cooking did not stop.

Doomma, "Big Mother," is the regal-looking woman seated on a rock. (The woman with the plucked forehead, far left, is a servant, remembered only as someone who cleaned but did not cook.) Doomma was the daughter of my great-grandfather and Nu-pei, "The Original Wife." She was shunned by Divong, "The Replacement Wife," for being "too strong," and loved by Divong's daughter, my grandmother. Doomma's first daughter was born with a hunchback—a sign, some said, of Doomma's own crooked nature. Why else did she remarry, disobeying her family's orders to remain a widow forever? And why did Doomma later kill herself, using some mysterious means that caused her to die slowly over three days? "Doomma died the same way she lived," my mother said, "strong, suffering lots."

Jingmei, my own grandmother, lived only a few more years after this picture was taken. She was the widow of a poor scholar, a man who had the misfortune of dying from influenza when he was about to be appointed a vice-magistrate. In 1924 or so, a rich man, who liked to collect pretty women, raped my grandmother and thereby forced her into becoming one of his concubines. My grandmother, now an outcast, took her young daughter to live with her on an island outside of Shanghai. She left her son behind, to save his face. After she gave birth to another son she killed herself by swallowing raw opium buried in the New Year's rice cakes. The young daughter who wept at her deathbed was my mother.

At my grandmother's funeral, monks tied chains to my mother's ankles so she would not fly away with her mother's ghost. "I tried to take them off," my mother said. "I was her treasure. I was her life."

10

My mother could never talk about any of this, even with her closest friends. "Don't tell anyone," she once said to me. "People don't understand. A concubine was like some kind prostitute. My mother was a good woman, high-class. She had no choice."

I told her I understood.

"How can you understand?" she said, suddenly angry. "You did not live in China then. You do not know what it's like to have no position in life. I was her daughter. We had no face! We belonged to nobody! This is a shame I can never push off my back." By the end of the outburst, she was crying.

On a recent trip with my mother to Beijing, I learned that my uncle found a way to push the shame off his back. He was the son my grandmother left behind. In 1936 he joined the Communist party—in large part, he told me, to overthrow the society that forced his mother into concubinage. He published a story about his mother. I told him I had written about my grandmother in a book of fiction. We agreed that my grandmother is the source of strength running through our family. My mother cried to hear this.

My mother believes my grandmother is also my muse, that she helps me write. "Does she still visit you often?" she asked while I was writing my second book. And then she added shyly, "Does she say anything about me?"

"Yes," I told her. "She has lots to say. I am writing it down."

This is the picture I see when I write. These are the secrets I was supposed to keep. These are the women who never let me forget why stories need to be told.

✎ Topics for Critical Thinking and Writing

1. Consider the title of this essay. Why are the women's lives described as "lost lives"? Can you imagine a companion piece, "Lost Lives of Men"? If not, why not?

2. In paragraph 5, what does Tan communicate by "And they were not peasant women but big city people, very modern"? What does she imply about the lives of those who *were* peasants?

3. In the fifth paragraph and in the last, Tan refers to "secrets" that she "was supposed to keep." What were the secrets? Why does she reveal them?

4. In the first paragraph Tan reports, "When I first saw this photo as a child, I thought it was exotic and remote, of a faraway time and place, with people who had no connection to my American life." What does she imply in this paragraph about their "connection to [her] American life" now? Where in the essay is that connection revealed or explained?

5. If you are lucky enough to have photographs of your ancestors, explore the images of the people in them and what you have been told about their lives. Do you feel "connected" or not? Explain.

Liliana Heker

Liliana Heker, born in Argentina in 1943, achieved fame in 1966 with the publication of her first book. She has continued to write fiction, and she has also been influential in her role as the editor of a literary magazine. "The Stolen Party," first published in Spanish in 1982, was translated and printed in Other Fires: Short Fiction by Latin American Women *(1985), edited and translated by Alberto Manguel.*

The Stolen Party

As soon as she arrived she went straight to the kitchen to see if the monkey was there. It was: what a relief! She wouldn't have liked to admit that her mother had been right. *Monkeys at a birthday?* her mother had sneered. *Get away with you, believing any nonsense you're told!* She was cross, but not because of the monkey, the girl thought; it's just because of the party.

"I don't like you going," she told her. "It's a rich people's party."

"Rich people go to Heaven too," said the girl, who studied religion at school.

"Get away with Heaven," said the mother. "The problem with you, young lady, is that you like to fart higher than your ass."

The girl didn't approve of the way her mother spoke. She was barely   5
nine, and one of the best in her class.

"I'm going because I've been invited," she said. "And I've been invited because Luciana is my friend. So there."

"Ah yes, your friend," her mother grumbled. She paused. "Listen, Rosaura," she said at last. "That one's not your friend. You know what you are to them? The maid's daughter, that's what."

Rosaura blinked hard: she wasn't going to cry. Then she yelled: "Shut up! You know nothing about being friends!"

Every afternoon she used to go to Luciana's house and they would both finish their homework while Rosaura's mother did the cleaning. They had their tea in the kitchen and they told each other secrets. Rosaura loved everything in the big house, and she also loved the people who lived there.

"I'm going because it will be the most lovely party in the whole world,   10
Luciana told me it would. There will be a magician, and he will bring a monkey and everything."

The mother swung around to take a good look at her child, and pompously put her hands on her hips.

"Monkeys at a birthday?" she said. "Get away with you, believing any nonsense you're told!"

Rosaura was deeply offended. She thought it unfair of her mother to accuse other people of being liars simply because they were rich. Rosaura too wanted to be rich, of course. If one day she managed to live in a beautiful palace, would her mother stop loving her? She felt very sad. She wanted to go to that party more than anything else in the world.

"I'll die if I don't go," she whispered, almost without moving her lips.

And she wasn't sure whether she had been heard, but on the morning   15
of the party she discovered that her mother had starched her Christmas
dress. And in the afternoon, after washing her hair, her mother rinsed it in
apple vinegar so that it would be all nice and shiny. Before going out,
Rosaura admired herself in the mirror, with her white dress and glossy
hair, and thought she looked terribly pretty.

Señora Ines also seemed to notice. As soon as she saw her, she said:

"How lovely you look today, Rosaura."

Rosaura gave her starched skirt a slight toss with her hands and walked
into the party with a firm step. She said hello to Luciana and asked about
the monkey. Luciana put on a secretive look and whispered into Rosaura's
ear: "He's in the kitchen. But don't tell anyone, because it's a surprise."

Rosaura wanted to make sure. Carefully she entered the kitchen and
there she saw it: deep in thought, inside its cage. It looked so funny that the
girl stood there for a while, watching it, and later, every so often, she would
slip out of the party unseen and go and admire it. Rosaura was the only one
allowed into the kitchen. Señora Ines had said: "You yes, but not the others,
they're much too boisterous, they might break something." Rosaura had
never broken anything. She even managed the jug of orange juice, carrying
it from the kitchen into the dining room. She held it carefully and didn't
spill a single drop. And Señora Ines had said: "Are you sure you can manage a jug as big as that?" Of course she could manage. She wasn't a but-
terfingers, like the others. Like that blonde girl with the bow in her hair. As
soon as she saw Rosaura, the girl with the bow, had said:

"And you? Who are you?"   20

"I'm a friend of Luciana," said Rosaura.

"No," said the girl with the bow, "you are not a friend of Luciana
because I'm her cousin and I know all her friends. And I don't know you."

"So what," said Rosaura. "I come here every afternoon with my mother and we do our homework together."

"You and your mother do your homework together?" asked the girl,
laughing.

"I and Luciana do our homework together," said Rosaura, very seri-   25
ously.

The girl with the bow shrugged her shoulders.

"That's not being friends," she said. "Do you go to school together?"

"No."

"So where do you know her from?" said the girl, getting impatient.

Rosaura remembered her mother's words perfectly. She took a deep   30
breath.

"I'm the daughter of the employee," she said.

Her mother had said very clearly: "If someone asks, you say you're
the daughter of the employee; that's all." She also told her to add: "And
proud of it." But Rosaura thought that never in her life would she dare say
something of the sort.

"What employee?" said the girl with the bow. "Employee in a shop?"

"No," said Rosaura angrily. "My mother doesn't sell anything in any shop, so there."

"So how come she's an employee?" said the girl with the bow.

Just then Señora Ines arrived saying *shh shh*, and asked Rosaura if she   35
wouldn't mind helping serve out the hotdogs, as she knew the house so much better than the others.

"See?" said Rosaura to the girl with the bow, and when no one was looking she kicked her in the shin.

Apart from the girl with the bow, all the others were delightful. The one she liked best was Luciana, with her golden birthday crown; and then the boys. Rosaura won the sack race, and nobody managed to catch her when they played tag. When they split into two teams to play charades, all the boys wanted her for their side. Rosaura felt she had never been so happy in all her life.

But the best was still to come. The best came after Luciana blew out the candles. First the cake. Señora Ines had asked her to help pass the cake around, and Rosaura had enjoyed the task immensely, because everyone called out to her, shouting "Me, me!" Rosaura remembered a story in which there was a queen who had the power of life or death over her subjects. She had always loved that, having the power of life or death. To Luciana and the boys she gave the largest pieces, and to the girl with the bow she gave a slice so thin one could see through it.

After the cake came the magician, tall and bony, with a fine red cape.   40
A true magician: he could untie handkerchiefs by blowing on them and make a chain with links that had no openings. He could guess what cards were pulled out from a pack, and the monkey was his assistant. He called the monkey "partner." "Let's see here, partner," he would say, "turn over a card." And, "Don't run away, partner: time to work now."

The final trick was wonderful. One of the children had to hold the monkey in his arms and the magician said he would make him disappear.

"What, the boy?" they all shouted.

"No, the monkey!" shouted back the magician.

Rosaura thought that this was truly the most amusing party in the whole world.

The magician asked a small fat boy to come and help, but the small fat   45
boy got frightened almost at once and dropped the monkey on the floor. The magician picked him up carefully, whispered something in his ear, and the monkey nodded almost as if he understood.

"You mustn't be so unmanly, my friend," the magician said to the fat boy.

"What's unmanly?" said the fat boy.

The magician turned around as if to look for spies.

"A sissy," said the magician. "Go sit down."

Then he stared at all the faces, one by one. Rosaura felt her heart tremble.   50

"You, with the Spanish eyes," said the magician. And everyone saw that he was pointing at her.

She wasn't afraid. Neither holding the monkey, nor when the magician made him vanish; not even when, at the end, the magician flung his red cape over Rosaura's head and uttered a few magic words . . . and the monkey reappeared, chattering happily, in her arms. The children clapped furiously. And before Rosaura returned to her seat, the magician said:

"Thank you very much, my little countess."

She was so pleased with the compliment that a while later, when her mother came to fetch her, that was the first thing she told her.

"I helped the magician and he said to me, 'Thank you very much, my little countess.'"

It was strange because up to then Rosaura had thought that she was angry with her mother. All along Rosaura had imagined that she would say to her: "See that the monkey wasn't a lie?" But instead she was so thrilled that she told her mother all about the wonderful magician.

Her mother tapped her on the head and said: "So now we're a countess!"

But one could see that she was beaming.

And now they both stood in the entrance, because a moment ago Señora Ines, smiling, had said: "Please wait here a second."

Her mother suddenly seemed worried.

"What is it?" she asked Rosaura.

"What is what?" said Rosaura. "It's nothing; she just wants to get the presents for those who are leaving, see?"

She pointed at the fat boy and at a girl with pigtails who were also waiting there, next to their mothers. And she explained about the presents. She knew, because she had been watching those who left before her. When one of the girls was about to leave, Señora Ines would give her a bracelet. When a boy left, Señora Ines gave him a yo-yo. Rosaura preferred the yo-yo because it sparkled, but she didn't mention that to her mother. Her mother might have said: "So why don't you ask for one, you blockhead?" That's what her mother was like. Rosaura didn't feel like explaining that she'd be horribly ashamed to be the odd one out. Instead she said:

"I was the best-behaved at the party."

And she said no more because Señora Ines came out into the hall with two bags, one pink and one blue.

First she went up to the fat boy, gave him a yo-yo out of the blue bag, and the fat boy left with his mother. Then she went up to the girl and gave her a bracelet out of the pink bag, and the girl with the pigtails left as well.

Finally she came up to Rosaura and her mother. She had a big smile on her face and Rosaura liked that. Señora Ines looked down at her, then looked up at her mother, and then said something that made Rosaura proud:

"What a marvelous daughter you have, Herminia."

For an instant, Rosaura thought that she'd give her two presents: the bracelet and the yo-yo. Señora Ines bent down as if about to look for something. Rosaura also leaned forward, stretching out her arm. But she never completed the movement.

Señora Ines didn't look in the pink bag. Nor did she look in the blue bag. Instead she rummaged in her purse. In her hand appeared two bills.

"You really and truly earned this," she said handing them over. "Thank you for all your help, my pet."

Rosaura felt her arms stiffen, stick close to her body, and then she noticed her mother's hand on her shoulder. Instinctively she pressed herself against her mother's body. That was all. Except her eyes. Rosaura's eyes had a cold, clear look that fixed itself on Señora Ines's face.

Señora Ines, motionless, stood there with her hand outstretched. As if she didn't dare draw it back. As if the slightest change might shatter an infinitely delicate balance.

✏️ Topics for Critical Thinking and Writing

1. The first paragraph tells us, correctly, that Rosaura's mother is wrong about the monkey. By the time the story is over, is the mother right about anything? If so, what?
2. Characterize Señora Ines. Why does she offer Rosaura money instead of a yo-yo or a bracelet? By the way, do you assume she is speaking deceptively when she tells Rosaura that she bars other children from the kitchen on the grounds that "they might break something"? On what do you base your view?
3. What do you make of the last paragraph? Why does Señora Ines stand with her hand outstretched, "as if she didn't dare draw it back"? What "infinitely delicate balance" might be shattered?

Pat Mora

Pat Mora did her undergraduate work at Texas Western College and then earned a master's degree at the University of Texas at El Paso, where she later served as Assistant to the Vice President for Academic Affairs, Director of the University Museum, and then (1981–89) as Assistant to the President. She has published essays on Hispanic culture as well as a children's book, Tomás and the Library Lady, *but she is best known for her books of poems. Mora has received several awards, including one from the Southwest Council of Latin American Studies.*

Immigrants

wrap their babies in the American flag,
feed them mashed hot dogs and apple pie,
name them Bill and Daisy,
buy them blonde dolls that blink blue
eyes or a football and tiny cleats   5
before the baby can even walk,
speak to them in thick English,
   hallo, babee, hallo.
whisper in Spanish or Polish
when the babies sleep, whisper

in a dark parent bed, that dark
parent fear, "Will they like   10
our boy, our girl, our fine american
boy, our fine american girl?"

Topics for Critical Thinking and Writing

1. To say that someone—for example, a politician—"wraps himself in the American flag" is to suggest disapproval or even anger or contempt. What behavior does the phrase usually describe? What does Mora mean when she says
   that immigrants "wrap their babies in the American flag"?
2. What do you suppose is Mora's attitude toward the immigrants? Do you
   think the poet fully approves of their hopes? On what do you base your
   answer?
3. Does Mora's description of the behavior of immigrants ring true of the
   immigrant group you are part of or know best? What is your attitude
   toward their efforts to assimilate? Explain in an essay of 750 to 1000 words.

A Casebook on Race

Because *The Columbia Encyclopedia* is amazingly comprehensive and,
for its size, relatively inexpensive, many people rightly believe that (like a
good dictionary) it should be part of one's home reference library. We
reprint the unsigned essay on "Race."

Race

Race, one of the group of populations constituting humanity. The
differences among races are essentially biological and are marked by the
hereditary transmission of physical characteristics. Genetically a race may
be defined as a group with gene frequencies differing from those of the
other groups in the human species (see HEREDITY; GENETICS; GENE). However, the genes responsible for the hereditary differences between humans are few when compared with the vast number of genes common to
all human beings regardless of the race to which they belong. All human
groups belong to the same species (*Homo sapiens*) and are mutually fertile.
The term *race* is inappropriate when applied to national, religious, geographic, linguistic, or cultural groups, nor can the biological criteria of
race be equated with any mental characteristics such as intelligence, per-

sonality, or character. Races arose as a result of MUTATION, selection, and adaptational changes in human populations. Most scholars hold that there has been a common evolution for all races and that differentiation occurred relatively late in history. Even to classify humans on the basis of physiological traits is difficult, for the coexistence of races since earliest times through conquests, invasions, migrations, and mass deportations has produced a heterogeneous world population. Nevertheless, by limiting the criteria to such traits as skin pigmentation, color and form of hair, shape of head, stature, and form of nose, most anthropologists agree on the existence of three relatively distinct groups: the Caucasoid, the Mongoloid, and the Negroid. The Caucasoid, found in Europe, N Africa, and the Middle East to N India, is characterized as pale reddish white to olive brown in color, of medium to tall stature, with a long or broad head form. The hair is light blond to dark brown in color, of a fine texture, and straight or wavy. The color of the eyes is light blue to dark brown and the nose bridge is usually high. The Mongoloid race, including most peoples of E Asia and the Indians of the Americas, has been described as saffron to yellow or reddish brown in color, of medium stature, with a broad head form. The hair is dark, straight, and coarse; body hair is sparse. The eyes are black to dark brown. The epicanthic fold, imparting an almond shape to the eye, is common, and the nose bridge is usually low or medium. The Negroid race is characterized by brown to brown-black skin, usually a long head form, varying stature, and thick, everted lips. The hair is dark and coarse, usually kinky. The eyes are dark, the nose bridge low, and the nostrils broad. To the Negroid race belong the peoples of Africa south of the Sahara, the Pygmy groups of Indonesia, and the inhabitants of New Guinea and Melanesia. Each of these broad groups can be divided into subgroups. General agreement is lacking as to the classification of such people as the aborigines of Australia, the Dravidian people of S India, the Polynesians, and the Ainu of N Japan. Attempts have been made to classify humans since the 17th cent., when scholars first began to separate types of flora and fauna. Johann Friedrich BLUMENBACH was the first to divide mankind according to skin color. In the 19th and early 20th cent., men such as Joseph Arthur GOBINEAU and Houston Stewart CHAMBERLAIN, mainly interested in pressing forward the supposed superiority of their own kind of culture or nationality, began to attribute cultural and psychological values to race. This approach, called racism, culminated in the vicious racial doctrines of Nazi Germany, and especially in ANTI-SEMITISM. This same approach complicated the INTEGRATION movement in the United States and underlies segregation policies in the Republic of South Africa (see APARTHEID). See Ruth Benedict, *Race: Science and Politics* (rev. ed. 1943, repr. 1968); C. S. Coon, *The Origin of Races* (1962) and *Living Races of Man* (1965); Margaret Mead et al., ed., *Science and the Concept of Race* (1968); S. M. Garn, ed., *Readings on Race* (2d ed. 1968) and *Human Races* (3d ed. 1971); J. C. King, *The Biology of Race* (1971); L. L. Cavalli-Sforza, *The Origin and Differentiation of Human Races* (1972).

W. E. B. Du Bois

W. E. B. Du Bois (1868–1963) was born in Great Barrington, Massachusetts, a small town where he seems to have had a relatively happy early childhood—though in grade school he was shocked to learn that his classmates considered him different because of his color. In 1885 he went to Fisk University, in Nashville, Tennessee; and then, for doctoral work, he studied history at Harvard University and sociology at the University of Berlin. His doctoral dissertation, The Suppression of the Slave Trade in the United States of America, *was published in* Harvard Historical Studies *in 1896. In the following year he delivered to the American Negro Academy the lecture that we reprint below.*

Although Du Bois had embarked on a scholarly career, he became increasingly concerned with the injustices of contemporary society, and his subsequent writings were directed at a general public. From 1910 to the mid-1930s he edited The Crisis, *the journal of the National Association for the Advancement of Colored People. Although he energetically solicited the writings of other people, he wrote so many essays for the journal that he can almost be said to be its author as well as its editor. Eventually Du Bois joined the Communist party, and in 1963 he left the United States for Ghana, where he died.*

The Conservation of Races

The American Negro has always felt an intense personal interest in discussions as to the origins and destinies of races: primarily because back of most discussions of race with which he is familiar, have lurked certain assumptions as to his natural abilities, as to his political, intellectual and moral status, which he felt were wrong. He has, consequently, been led to deprecate and minimize race distinctions, to believe intensely that out of one blood God created all nations, and to speak of human brotherhood as though it were the possibility of an already dawning tomorrow.

Nevertheless, in our calmer moments we must acknowledge that human beings are divided into races; that in this country the two most extreme types of the world's races have met, and the resulting problem as to the future relations of these types is not only of intense and living interest to us, but forms an epoch in the history of mankind.

It is necessary, therefore, in planning our movements, in guiding our future development, that at times we rise above the pressing, but smaller questions of separate schools and cars, wage-discrimination and lynch law, to survey the whole question of race in human philosophy and to lay, on a basis of broad knowledge and careful insight, those large lines of policy and higher ideals which may form our guiding lines and boundaries in the practical difficulties of everyday. For it is certain that all human striving must recognize the hard limits of natural law, and that any striving, no matter how intense and earnest, which is against the constitution of the world, is vain. The question, then, which we must seriously consider is this: what is the real meaning of race; what has, in the past, been the law of race development, and what lessons has the past history of race development to teach the rising Negro people?

When we thus come to inquire into the essential difference of races we find it hard to come at once to any definite conclusion. Many criteria of race differences have in the past been proposed, as color, hair, cranial measurements and language. And manifestly, in each of these respects, human beings differ widely. They vary in color, for instance, from the marble-like pallor of the Scandinavian to the rich, dark brown of the Zulu, passing by the creamy Slav, the yellow Chinese, the light brown Sicilian and the brown Egyptian. Men vary, too, in the texture of hair from the obstinately straight hair of the Chinese to the obstinately tufted and frizzled hair of the Bushman. In measurement of heads, again, men vary; from the broad-headed Tartar to the medium-headed European and the narrow-headed Hottentot; or, again in language, from the highly-inflected Roman tongue to the monosyllabic Chinese. All these physical characteristics are patent enough, and if they agreed with each other it would be very easy to classify mankind. Unfortunately for scientists, however, these criteria of race are most exasperatingly intermingled. Color does not agree with texture of hair, for many of the dark races have straight hair; nor does color agree with the breadth of the head, for the yellow Tartar has a broader head than the German; nor, again, has the science of language as yet succeeded in clearing up the relative authority of these various and contradictory criteria.

The final word of science, so far, is that we have at least two, perhaps   5
three, great families of human beings—the whites and Negroes, possibly the yellow race. That other races have arisen from the intermingling of the blood of these two. This broad division of the world's races which men like [Thomas Henry] Huxley and [Friedrich] Raetzel have introduced as more nearly true than the old five-race scheme of [Johann-Friedrich] Blumenbach, is nothing more than an acknowledgement that, so far as purely physical characteristics are concerned, the differences between men do not explain all the differences of their history. It declares, as Darwin himself said, that great as is the physical unlikeness of the various races of men, their likenesses are greater, and upon this rests the whole scientific doctrine of human brotherhood.

Although the wonderful developments of human history teach that the grosser physical differences of color, hair and bone go but a short way toward explaining the different roles which groups of men have played in human progress, yet there are differences—subtle, delicate and elusive, though they may be—which have silently but definitely separated men into groups. While these subtle forces have generally followed the natural cleavage of common blood, descent and physical peculiarities, they have at other times swept across and ignored these. At all times, however, they have divided human beings into races, which, while they perhaps transcend scientific definition, nevertheless, are clearly defined to the eye of the historian and sociologist.

If this be true, then the history of the world is the history, not of individuals, but of groups, not of nations, but of races, and he who ignores or seeks to override the race idea in human history ignores and overrides the central thought of all history. What, then, is a race? It is a vast family of human beings, generally of common blood and language, always of common history, traditions and impulses, who are both voluntarily and involuntarily striving together for the accomplishment of certain more or less vividly conceived ideals of life.

Turning to real history, there can be no doubt, first, as to the widespread, nay, universal, prevalence of the race idea, the race spirit, the race ideal, and as to its efficiency as the vastest and most ingenious invention for human progress. We, who have been reared and trained under the individualistic philosophy of the Declaration of Independence and the laissez-faire philosophy of Adam Smith, are loath to see and loath to acknowledge this patent fact of human history. We see the Pharaohs, Caesars, Toussaints and Napoleons of history and forget the vast races of which they were but epitomized expressions. We are apt to think in our American impatience, that while it may have been true in the past that closed race groups made history, that here in conglomerate America *nous avons changé tout cela*—we have changed all that, and have no need of this ancient instrument of progress. This assumption of which the Negro people are especially fond cannot be established by a careful consideration of history.

We find upon the world's stage today eight distinctly differentiated races, in the sense in which history tells us the word must be used. They are the Slavs of Eastern Europe, the Teutons of middle Europe, the English of Great Britain and America, the Romance nations of Southern and Western Europe, the Negroes of Africa and America, the Somitic people of Western Asia and Northern Africa, the Hindoos of Central Asia and the Mongolians of Eastern Asia. There are, of course, other minor race groups, [such] as the American Indians, the Esquimaux and the South Sea Islanders; these larger races, too, are far from homogeneous; the Slav includes the Czech, the Magyar, the Pole and the Russian; the Teuton includes the German, the Scandinavian and the Dutch; the English include the Scotch, the Irish and the conglomerate American. Under Romance nations the widely-differing Frenchman, Italian, Sicilian and Spaniard are comprehended. The term Negro is, perhaps, the most indefinite of all, combining the Mulattoes and Zamboes of America and the Egyptians, Bantus and Bushmen of Africa. Among the Hindoos are traces of widely differing nations, while the great Chinese, Tartar, Korean and Japanese families fall under the one designation—Mongolian.

The question now is: What is the real distinction between these nations? Is it the physical differences of blood, color and cranial measurements? Certainly we must all acknowledge that physical differences play a great part, and that, with wide exceptions and qualifications, these eight great races of today follow the cleavage of physical race distinctions; the English and Teuton represent the white variety of mankind; the Mongolian, the yellow; the Negroes, the black. Between these are many crosses and mixtures, where Mongolian and Teuton have blended into the Slav, and other mixtures have produced the Romance nations and the Semites. But while race differences have followed mainly physical race lines, yet no mere physical distinctions would really define or explain the deeper differences—the cohesiveness and continuity of these groups. The deeper differences are spiritual, psychical, differences—undoubtedly based on the physical, but infinitely transcending them. The forces that bind together the Teuton nations are, then, first, their race identity and common blood; secondly, and more important, a common history, common laws and religion, similar habits of thought and a conscious striving together for certain ideals of life. The whole process which has brought about these race differentiations has been a growth, and the great characteristic of this growth has been the differentiation of spiritual and mental differences between great races of mankind and the integration of physical differences.

The age of nomadic tribes of closely related individuals represents the maximum of physical differences. They were practically vast families, and there were as many groups as families. As the families came together to form cities the physical differences lessened, purity of blood was replaced by the requirement of domicile, and all who lived within the city bounds became gradually to be regarded as members of the group; i.e., there was a slight and slow breaking down of physical barriers. This, however, was accompanied by an increase of the spiritual and social differences between cities. This city became husbandmen; this, merchants; another, warriors; and so on. The *ideals of life* for which the different cities struggled were different.

When at last cities began to coalesce into nations there was another breaking down of barriers which separated groups of men. The larger and broader differences of color, hair and physical proportions were not by any means ignored, but myriads of minor differences disappeared, and the sociological and historical races of men began to approximate the present division of races as indicated by physical researches. At the same time the spiritual and psychical differences of race groups which constituted the nations became deep and decisive. The English nation stood for constitutional liberty and commercial freedom; the German nation for science and philosophy; the Romance nations stood for literature and art, and the other race groups are striving, each in its own way, to develop for civilization its particular message, its particular ideal, which shall help to guide the world nearer and nearer that perfection of human life for which we all long, that "one far-off Divine event."

This has been the function of the race differences up to the present time. What shall be its function in the future? Manifestly some of the great races of today—particularly the Negro race—have not as yet given to civilization the full spiritual message which they are capable of giving. I will not say that the Negro race has as yet given no message to the world, for it is still a mooted question among scientists as to just how far Egyptian civilization was Negro in its origin; if it was not wholly Negro, it was certainly very closely allied. Be that as it may, however, the fact still remains that the full, complete Negro message of the whole Negro race has not as yet been given to the world: that the messages and ideal of the yellow race have not been completed, and that the striving of the mighty Slavs has but begun.

The question is, then: how shall this message be delivered; how shall these various ideals be realized? The answer is plain: by the development of these race groups, not as individuals, but as races. For the development of Japanese genius, Japanese literature and art, Japanese spirit, only Japanese, bound and welded together, Japanese inspired by one vast ideal, can work out in its fullness the wonderful message which Japan has for the nations of the earth. For the development of Negro genius, of Negro literature and art, of Negro spirit, only Negroes bound and welded together, Negroes inspired by one vast ideal, can work out in its fullness the great message we have for humanity. We cannot reverse history; we are subject to the same natural laws as other races, and if the Negro is ever to be a factor in the world's history—if among the gaily-colored banners that deck the broad ramparts of civilization is to hang one uncompromising black, then it must be placed there by black hands, fashioned by black heads and hallowed by the travail of two hundred million black hearts beating in one glad song of jubilee.

For this reason, the advance guard of the Negro people—the eight million people of Negro blood in the United States of America—must soon come to realize that if they are to take their just place in the van of Pan-Negroism, then their destiny is *not* absorption by the white Americans. That if in America it is to be proven for the first time in the modern world that not only are Negroes capable of evolving individual men like Toussaint the Saviour, but are a nation stored with wonderful possibilities of culture, then their destiny is not a servile imitation of Anglo-Saxon culture, but a stalwart originality which shall unswervingly follow Negro ideals.

It may, however, be objected here that the situation of our race in America renders this attitude impossible; that our sole hope of salvation lies in our being able to lose our race identity in the commingled blood of the nation; and that any other course would merely increase the friction of races which we call race prejudice, and against which we have so long and so earnestly fought.

Here, then, is the dilemma, and it is a puzzling one, I admit. No Negro who has given earnest thought to the situation of his people in America has failed, at some time in life, to find himself at these cross-roads; has failed to ask himself at some time: what, after all, am I? Am I an American or am I a Negro? Can I be both? Or is it my duty to cease to be a Negro as soon as possible and be an American? If I strive as a Negro, am I not perpetuating the very cleft that threatens and separates black and white America? Is not my only possible practical aim the subduction of all that is Negro in me to the American? Does my black blood place upon me any more obligation to assert my nationality than German, or Irish or Italian blood would?

It is such incessant self-questioning, and the hesitation that arises from it, that is making the present period a time of vacillation and contradiction for the American Negro; combined race action is stifled, race responsibility is shirked, race enterprises languish, and the best blood, the best talent, the best energy of the Negro people cannot be marshaled to do the bidding of the race. They stand back to make room for every rascal and demagogue who chooses to cloak his selfish devilry under the veil of race pride.

Is this right? Is it rational? Is it good policy? Have we in America a distinct mission as a race—a distinct sphere of action and an opportunity for race development, or is self-obliteration the highest end to which Negro blood dare aspire?

If we carefully consider what race prejudice really is, we find it, historically, to be nothing but the friction between different groups of people; it is the difference in aim, in feeling, in ideals of two different races; if, now, this difference exists touching territory, laws, language, or even religion, it is manifest that these people cannot live in the same territory without fatal collision; but if, on the other hand, there is substantial agreement in laws, language and religion; if there is a satisfactory adjustment of economic life, then there is no reason why, in the same country and on the same street, two or three great national ideals might not thrive and develop, that men of different races might not strive together for their race ideals as well, perhaps even better, than in isolation. [20]

Here, it seems to me, is the reading of the riddle that puzzles so many of us. We are Americans, not only by birth and by citizenship, but by our political ideals, our language, our religion. Farther than that, our Americanism does not go. At that point, we are Negroes, members of a vast historic race that from the very dawn of creation has slept, but half awakening in the dark forests of its African fatherland. We are the first fruits of this new nation, the harbinger of that black tomorrow which is yet destined to soften the whiteness of the Teutonic today. We are that people whose subtle sense of song has given America its only American music, its only American fairy tales, its only touch of pathos and humor amid its mad money-getting plutocracy. As such, it is our duty to conserve our physical powers, our intellectual endowments, our spiritual ideals; as a race we must strive by race organization, by race solidarity, by race unity to the realization of that broader humanity which freely recognizes differences in men, but sternly deprecates inequality in their opportunities of development.

For the accomplishment of these ends we need race organizations: Negro colleges, Negro newspapers, Negro business organizations, a Negro school of literature and art, and an intellectual clearing house, for all these products of the Negro mind, which we may call a Negro Academy. Not only is all this necessary for positive advance, it is absolutely imperative for negative defense. Let us not deceive ourselves at our situation in this country. Weighted with a heritage of moral iniquity from our past history, hard pressed in the economic world by foreign immigrants and native prejudice, hated here, despised there and pitied everywhere; our one haven of refuge is ourselves, and but one means of advance, our own belief in our great destiny, our own implicit trust in our ability and worth.

There is no power under God's high heaven that can stop the advance of eight thousand thousand honest, earnest, inspired and united people. But—and here is the rub—they *must* be honest, fearlessly criticizing their own faults, zealously correcting them; they must be *earnest*. No people that laughs at itself, and ridicules itself, and wishes to God it was anything but itself ever wrote its name in history; it *must* be inspired with the Divine faith of our black mothers, that out of the blood and dust of battle will march a victorious host, a mighty nation, a peculiar people, to speak to the nations of earth a Divine truth that shall make them free. And such a people must be united; not merely united for the organized theft of political spoils, not united to disgrace religion with whoremongers and ward-heelers; not united merely to protest and pass resolutions, but united to stop the ravages of consumption among the Negro people, united to keep black boys from loafing, gambling and crime; united to guard the purity of black women and to reduce that vast army of black prostitutes that is today marching to hell; and united in serious organizations, to determine by careful conference and thoughtful interchange of opinion the broad lines of policy and action for the American Negro.

This is the reason for being which the American Negro Academy has. It aims at once to be the epitome and expression of the intellect of the black-blooded people of America, the exponent of the race ideals of one of the world's great races. As such, the Academy must, if successful, be:

   a.   Representative in character.
   b.   Impartial in conduct.
   c.   Firm in leadership.

It must be representative in character; not in that it represents all interests or all factions, but in that it seeks to comprise something of the *best* thought, the most unselfish striving and the highest ideals. There are scattered in forgotten nooks and corners throughout the land, Negroes of some considerable training, of high minds, and high motives, who are unknown to their fellows, who exert far too little influence. These the Negro Academy should strive to bring into touch with each other and to give them a common mouthpiece.

The Academy should be impartial in conduct; while it aims to exalt the people it should aim to do so by truth—not by lies, by honesty—not by flattery. It should continually impress the fact upon the Negro people that they must not expect to have things done for them—they *must do for themselves;* that they have on their hands a vast work of self-reformation to do, and that a little less complaint and whining, and a little more dogged work and manly striving would do us more credit and benefit than a thousand Force or Civil Rights bills.

Finally, the American Negro Academy must point out a practical path of advance to the Negro people; there lie before every Negro today hundreds of questions of policy and right which must be settled and which each one settles now, not in accordance with any rule, but by impulse or individual preference; for instance: what should be the attitude of Negroes toward the educational qualification for voters? What should be our attitude toward separate schools? How should we meet discriminations on railways and in hotels? Such questions need not so much specific answers for each part as a general expression of policy, and nobody should be better fitted to announce such a policy than a representative honest Negro Academy.

All this, however, must come in time after careful organization and long conference. The immediate work before us should be practical and have direct bearing upon the situation of the Negro. The historical work of collecting the laws of the United States and of the various states of the Union with regard to the Negro is a work of such magnitude and importance that no body but one like this could think of undertaking it. If we could accomplish that one task we would justify our existence.

In the field of sociology an appalling work lies before us. First, we must unflinchingly and bravely face the truth, not with apologies, but with solemn earnestness. The Negro Academy ought to sound a note of warning that would echo in every black cabin in the land: *unless we conquer our present vices they will conquer us;* we are diseased, we are developing criminal tendencies, and an alarmingly large percentage of our men and women are sexually impure. The Negro Academy should stand and proclaim this over the housetops, crying with Garrison: *I will not equivocate, I will not retreat a single inch, and I will be heard.* The Academy should seek to gather about it the talented, unselfish men, the pure and noble-minded women, to fight an army of devils that disgraces our manhood and our womanhood. There does not stand today upon God's earth a race more capable in muscle, in intellect, in morals, than the American Negro, if he will bend his energies in the right direction; if he will

> Burst his birth's invidious bar
> And grasp the skirts of happy chance,
> And breast the blows of circumstance,
>   And grapple with his evil star.

In science and morals, I have indicated two fields of work for the Academy. Finally, in practical policy, I wish to suggest the following *Academy Creed:* 30

1. We believe that the Negro people, as a race, have a contribution to make to civilization and humanity, which no other race can make.
2. We believe it the duty of the Americans of Negro descent, as a body, to maintain their race identity until this mission of the Negro people is accomplished, and the ideal of human brotherhood has become a practical possibility.
3. We believe that, unless modern civilization is a failure, it is entirely feasible and practicable for two races in such essential political, economic and religious harmony as the white and colored people of America, to develop side by side in peace and mutual happiness, the peculiar contribution which each has to make to the culture of their common country.
4. As a means to this end we advocate, not such social equality between these races as would disregard human likes and dislikes, but such a social equilibrium as would, throughout all the complicated relations of life, give due and just consideration to culture, ability, and moral worth, whether they be found under white or black skins.
5. We believe that the first and greatest step toward the settlement of the present friction between the races—commonly called the Negro prob-

lem—lies in the correction of the immorality, crime and laziness among the Negroes themselves, which still remains as a heritage from slavery. We believe that only earnest and long continued efforts on our own part can cure these social ills.

6. We believe that the second great step toward a better adjustment of the relations between the races should be a more impartial selection of ability in the economic and intellectual world, and a greater respect for personal liberty and worth, regardless of race. We believe that only earnest efforts on the part of the white people of this country will bring much needed reform in these matters.

7. On the basis of the foregoing declaration, and firmly believing in our high destiny, we, as American Negroes, are resolved to strive in every honorable way for the realization of the best and highest aims, for the development of strong manhood and pure womanhood, and for the rearing of a race ideal in America and Africa, to the glory of God and the uplifting of the Negro people.

Sharon Begley

Sharon Begley, a senior writer for Newsweek, *published this essay in an issue (February 13, 1995) whose cover story was "What Color Is Black?"*

Three Is Not Enough

To most Americans race is as plain as the color of the nose on your face. Sure, some light-skinned blacks, in some neighborhoods, are taken for Italians, and some Turks are confused with Argentines. But even in the children of biracial couples, racial ancestry is writ large—in the hue of the skin and the shape of the lips, the size of the brow and the bridge of the nose. It is no harder to trace than it is to judge which basic colors in a box of Crayolas were combined to make tangerine or burnt umber. Even with racial mixing, the existence of primary races is as obvious as the existence of primary colors.

Or is it? C. Loring Brace has his own ideas about where race resides, and it isn't in skin color. If our eyes could perceive more than the superficial, we might find race in chromosome 11: there lies the gene for hemoglobin. If you divide humankind by which of two forms of the gene each person has, then equatorial Africans, Italians and Greeks fall into the "sickle-cell race"; Swedes and South Africa's Xhosas (Nelson Mandela's ethnic group) are in the healthy-hemoglobin race. Or do you prefer to group people by whether they have epicanthic eye folds, which produce the "Asian" eye? Then the !Kung San (Bushmen) belong with the Japanese and Chinese. Depending on which trait you choose to demarcate races, "you won't get anything that remotely tracks conventional [race] categories," says anthropologist Alan Goodman, dean of natural science at Hampshire College.

The notion of race is under withering attack for political and cultural reasons—not to mention practical ones like what to label the child of a Ghanaian and a Norwegian. But scientists got there first. Their doubts about the conventional racial categories—black, white, Asian—have nothing to do with a sappy "we are all the same" ideology. Just the reverse. "Human variation is very, very real," says Goodman. "But race, as a way of organizing [what we know about that variation], is incredibly simplified and bastardized." Worse, it does not come close to explaining the astounding diversity of humankind—not its origins, not its extent, not its meaning. "There is no organizing principle by which you could put 5 billion people into so few categories in a way that would tell you anything important about humankind's diversity," says Michigan's Brace, who will lay out the case against race at the annual meeting of the American Association for the Advancement of Science.

About 70 percent of cultural anthropologists, and half of physical anthropologists, reject race as a biological category, according to a 1989 survey by Central Michigan University anthropologist Leonard Liebermnan and colleagues. The truths of science are not decided by majority vote, of course. Empirical evidence, woven into a theoretical whole, is what matters. The threads of the argument against the standard racial categories:

• **Genes:** In 1972, population biologist Richard Lewontin of Harvard University laid out the genetic case against race. Analyzing 17 genetic markers in 168 populations such as Austrians, Thais and Apaches, he found that there is more genetic difference within one race than there is between that race and another. Only 6.3 percent of the genetic differences could be explained by the individuals' belonging to different races. That is, if you pick at random any two "blacks" walking along the street, and analyze their 23 pairs of chromosomes, you will probably find that their genes have less in common than do the genes of one of them with that of a random "white" person. Last year the Human Genome Diversity Project used 1990s genetics to extend Lewontin's analysis. Its conclusion: genetic variation from one individual to another of the same "race" swamps the average differences between racial groupings. The more we learn about humankind's genetic differences, says geneticist Luca Cavalli-Sforza of Stanford University, who chairs the committee that directs the biodiversity project, the more we see that they have almost nothing to do with what we call race.

• **Traits:** As sickle-cell "races" and epicanthic-fold "races" show, there are as many ways to group people as there are traits. That is because "racial" traits are what statisticians call non-concordant. Lack of concordance means that sorting people according to *these* traits produces different groupings than you get in sorting them by *those* (equally valid) traits. When biologist Jared Diamond of UCLA surveyed half a dozen traits for a recent issue of *Discover* magazine, he found that, depending on which traits you pick, you can form very surprising "races." Take the scooped-out shape of the back of the front teeth, a standard "Asian" trait. Native

Americans and Swedes have these shovel-shaped incisors, too, and so would fall in the same race. Is biochemistry better? Norwegians, Arabians, north Indians and the Fulani of northern Nigeria, notes Diamond, fall into the "lactase race" (the lactase enzyme digests milk sugar). Everyone else—other Africans, Japanese, Native Americans—forms the "lactase-deprived race" (their ancestors did not drink milk from cows or goats and hence never evolved the lactase gene). How about blood types, the familiar A, B and O groups? Then Germans and New Guineans, populations that have the same percentages of each type, are in one race; Estonians and Japanese comprise a separate one for the same reason, notes anthropologist Jonathan Marks of Yale University. Depending on which traits are chosen, "we could place Swedes in the same race as either Xhosas, Fulani, the Ainu of Japan or Italians," writes Diamond.

• **Subjectivity:** If race is a valid biological concept, anyone in any culture should be able to look at any individual and say, Aha, you are a . . . It should not be the case, as French tennis star Yannick Noah said a few years ago, that "in Africa I am white, and in France I am black" (his mother is French and his father is from Cameroon). "While biological traits give the impression that race is a biological unit of nature," says anthropologist George Armelagos of Emory University, "it remains a cultural construct. The boundaries between races depends on the classifier's own cultural norms."

• **Evolution:** Scholars who believe in the biological validity of race argue that the groupings reflect human pre-history. That is, populations that evolved together, and separately from others, constitute a race. This school of thought holds that blacks should all be in one race because they are descended from people who stayed on the continent where humanity began. Asians, epitomized by the Chinese, should be another race because they are the children of groups who walked north and east until they reached the Pacific. Whites of the pale, blond variety should be another because their ancestors filled Europe. Because of their appearance, these populations represent the extremes, the archetypes, of human diversity— the reds, blues and yellows from which you can make every other hue. "But if you use these archetypes as your groups you have classified only a very tiny proportion of the world's people, which is not very useful," says Marks, whose incisive new book "Human Biodiversity" deconstructs race. "Also, as people walked out of Africa, they were differentiating along the way. Equating 'extreme' with 'primordial' is not supported by history."

Often, shared traits are a sign of shared heritage—racial heritage. "Shared traits are not random," says Alice Brues, an anthropologist at the University of Colorado. "Within a continent, you of course have a number of variants [on basic traits], but some are characteristic of the larger area, too. So it's natural to look for these major divisions. It simplifies your thinking." A wide distribution of traits, however, makes them suspect as evidence of a shared heritage. The dark skin of Somalis and Ghanaians, for instance, indicates that they evolved under the same selective force (a sunny climate). But that's all it shows. It does *not* show that they are any more closely related, in the sense of sharing more genes, than either is to Greeks. Calling Somalis and Ghanaians "black" therefore sheds no further light on their evolution-ary history and implies—wrongly—that they are more closely related to each other than either is to someone of a different "race." Similarly, the long noses of North Africans and northern Europeans reveal that they evolved in dry or cold climates (the nose moistens air before the air reaches the lungs, and longer noses moisten more air). The tall, thin bodies of Kenya's Masai evolved to dissipate heat; Eskimos evolved short, squat bodies to retain it. Calling these peoples "different races" adds nothing to that understanding.

Where did the three standard racial divisions come from? They entered 10 the social, and scientific, consciousness during the Age of Exploration. Loring Brace doesn't think it's a coincidence that the standard races represent peo-ples who, as he puts it, "lived at the end of the Europeans' trade routes"—in Africa and China—in the days after Prince Henry the Navigator set sail. Before Europeans took to the seas, there was little perception of races. If vil-lagers began to look different to an Englishman riding a horse from France to Italy and on to Greece, the change was too subtle to inspire notions of races. But if the English sailor left Lisbon Harbor and dropped anchor off the King-dom of Niger, people looked so different he felt compelled to invent a scheme to explain the world—and, perhaps, distance himself from the Africans.

This habit of sorting the world's peoples into a small number of groups got its first scientific gloss from Swedish taxonomist Carolus Lin-naeus. (Linnaeus is best known for his system of classifying living things by genus and species—*Escherichia coli*, *Homo sapiens* and the rest.) In 1758 he declared that humanity falls into four races: white (Europeans), red (Native Americans), dark (Asians) and black (Africans). Linnaeus said that Native Americans (who in the 1940s got grouped with Asians) were ruled by custom. Africans were indolent and negligent, and Europeans were inventive and gentle, said Linnaeus. Leave aside the racist under-tones (not to mention the oddity of ascribing gentleness to the group that perpetrated the Crusades and Inquisition): that alone should not under-mine its validity. More worrisome is that the notion and the specifics of race predate genetics, evolutionary biology and the science of human ori-gins. With the revolutions in those fields, how is it that the 18th-century scheme of race retains its powerful hold? Consider these arguments:

- **If I parachute into Nairobi, I know I'm not in Oslo:** Colorado's Alice Brues uses this image to argue that denying the reality of race flies in the face of common sense. But the parachutists, if they were familiar with the great range of human diversity, could also tell that they were in Nairo-bi rather than Abidjan—east Africans don't look much like west Africans. They could also tell they were in Istanbul rather than Oslo, even though Turks and Norwegians are both called Caucasian.

- **DOA, male, 58119 . . . black:** When U.S. police call in a forensic anthropologist to identify the race of a skeleton, the scientist comes through 80 to 85 percent of the time. If race has no biological validity, how can the sleuths get it right so often? The forensic anthropologist could, with enough information about bone structure and genetic markers, iden-tify the region from which the corpse came—south and west Africa,

Southeast Asia and China, Northern and Western Europe. It just so happens that the police would call corpses from the first two countries black, from the middle two Asian, and the last pair white. But lumping these six distinct populations into three groups of two serves no biological purpose, only a social convention. The larger grouping may reflect how society views humankind's diversity, but does not explain it.

*   **African-Americans have more hypertension:** If race is not real, how can researchers say that blacks have higher rates of infant mortality, lower rates of osteoporosis and a higher incidence of hypertension? Because a social construct can have biological effects, says epidemiologist Robert Hahn of the U.S. Centers for Disease Control and Prevention. Consider hypertension among African-Americans. Roughly 34 percent have high blood pressure, compared with about 16 percent of whites. But William Dressler finds the greatest incidence of hypertension among blacks who are upwardly mobile achievers. "That's probably because in mundane interactions, from the bank to the grocery store, they are treated in ways that do not coincide with their self-image as respectable achievers," says Dressler, an anthropologist at the University of Alabama. "And the upwardly mobile are more likely to encounter discriminatory white culture." Lab studies show that stressful situations—like being followed in grocery stores as if you were a shoplifter—elevate blood pressure and lead to vascular changes that cause hypertension. "In this case, race captures social factors such as the experience of discrimination," says sociologist David Williams of the University of Michigan. Further evidence that hypertension has more to do with society than with biology: black Africans have among the lowest rates of hypertension in the world.

If race is not a biological explanation of hypertension, can it offer a   15 biological explanation of something as complex as intelligence? Psychologists are among the strongest proponents of retaining the three conventional racial categories. It organizes and explains their data in the most parsimonious way, as Charles Murray and Richard Herrnstein argue in "The Bell Curve." But anthropologists say that such conclusions are built on a foundation of sand. If nothing else, argues Brace, every ethnic group evolved under conditions where intelligence was a requirement for survival. If there are intelligence "genes," they must be in all ethnic groups equally: differences in intelligence must be a cultural and social artifact.

Scientists who doubt the biological meaningfulness of race are not nihilists. They just prefer another way of capturing, and explaining, the great diversity of humankind. Even today most of the world's peoples marry within their own group. Intramarriage preserves features—fleshy lips, small ears, wide-set eyes—that arose by a chance genetic mutation long ago. Grouping people by geographic origins—better known as ethnicity—"is more correct both in a statistical sense and in understanding the history of human variation," says Hampshire's Goodman. Ethnicity also serves as a proxy for differences—from diet to a history of discrimination—that can have real biological and behavioral effects.

In a 1942 book, anthropologist Ashley Montagu called race "Man's Most Dangerous Myth." If it is, then our most ingenuous myth must be that we sort humankind into groups in order to understand the meaning and origin of humankind's diversity. That isn't the reason at all; a greater number of smaller groupings, like ethnicities, does a better job. The obsession with broad categories is so powerful as to seem a neurological imperative. Changing our thinking about race will require a revolution in thought as profound, and profoundly unsettling, as anything science has ever demanded. What these researchers are talking about is changing the way in which we see the world—and each other. But before that can happen, we must do more than understand the biologist's suspicions about race. We must ask science, also, why it is that we are so intent on sorting humanity into so few groups—us and Other—in the first place.

Stanley Crouch

Stanley Crouch, born in Los Angeles in 1945, is a playwright, actor, drummer and band leader, and author of several books of social criticism in which he explores such topics as feminism, black power, and the films of Spike Lee. In his early years he was a black nationalist, but he is now regarded as conservative—though his essays almost always contain surprises even for readers who think they are familiar with his work.

Race Is Over

Even though error, chance and ambition are at the nub of the human future, I am fairly sure that race, as we currently obsess over it, will cease to mean as much 100 years from today. The reasons are basic—some technological, others cultural. We all know that electronic media have broken down many barriers, that they were even central to the fall of the Soviet Union because satellite dishes made it impossible for the Government to control images and ideas about life outside the country. People there began to realize how far behind they were from the rest of the modern world. The international flow of images and information will continue to make for a greater and greater swirl of influences. It will increasingly change life on the globe and also change our American sense of race.

In our present love of the mutually exclusive, and our pretense that we are something less than a culturally miscegenated people, we forget our tendency to seek out the exotic until it becomes a basic cultural taste, the way pizza or sushi or tacos have become ordinary fare. This approach guarantees that those who live on this soil a century from now will see and accept many, many manifestations of cultural mixings and additions.

In that future, definition by racial, ethnic and sexual groups will most probably have ceased to be the foundation of special-interest power. Ten decades up the road, few people will take seriously, accept or submit to any forms of segregation that are marching under the intellectually ragged flag of "diversity." The idea that your background will determine your occupation, taste, romantic preference or any other thing will dissolve in favor of your perceived identity as defined by your class, livelihood and cultural preferences. Americans of the future will find themselves surrounded in every direction by people who are part Asian, part Latin, part African, part European, part American Indian. What such people will look like is beyond my imagination, but the sweep of body types, combinations of facial features, hair textures, eye colors and what are now unexpected skin tones will be far more common, primarily because the current paranoia over mixed marriages should by then be largely a superstition of the past.

In his essay "The Little Man at Chehaw Station," Ralph Ellison described a young "light-skinned, blue-eyed, Afro-American-featured individual who could have been taken for anything from a sun-tinged white Anglo-Saxon, an Egyptian, or a mixed-breed American Indian . . . ." He used the young man as an example of our central problem—"the challenge of arriving at an adequate definition of American cultural identity . . . ." While the youth's feet and legs were covered by riding boots and breeches, he wore a multicolored dashiki and "a black homburg hat tilted at a jaunty angle." For Ellison, "his clashing of styles nevertheless sounded an integrative, vernacular tone, an American compulsion to improvise upon the given."

The vernacular tone Ellison wrote of is what makes us improvise   5
upon whatever we actually like about one another, no matter how we might pretend we feel about people who are superficially different. Furthermore, the social movements of minorities and women have greatly aided our getting beyond the always culturally inaccurate idea that the United States is "a white man's country."

We sometimes forget how much the Pilgrims learned from the American Indians, or look at those lessons in only the dullest terms of exploitation, not as a fundamental aspect of our American identity. We forget that by the time James Fenimore Cooper was inventing his back-woodsmen, there were white men who had lived so closely to the land and to the American Indian that the white man was, often quite proudly, a cultural mulatto. We forget that we could not have had the cowboy without the Mexican vaquero. We don't know that our most original art-music, jazz, is a combination of African, European and Latin elements. Few people are aware that when the Swiss psychoanalyst Carl Jung came to this country he observed that white people walked, talked and laughed like Negroes. He also reported that the two dominant figures in the dreams of his white American patients were the Negro and the American Indian.

Are we destined to become one bland nation of interchangeables? I do not think so. What will fall away over the coming decades, I believe, is our present tendency to mistake something borrowed for   something ethnically "authentic." Regions will remain regions and within them we will find what we always find: variations on the overall style and pulsation. As the density of cross-influences progresses, we will get far beyond the troubles the Census Bureau now has with racial categories, which are growing because we are so hung up on the barbed wire of tribalism and because we fear absorption, or "assimilation." We look at so-called "assimilation" as some form of oppression, some loss of identity, even a way of "selling out." In certain cases and at certain times, that may have been more than somewhat true. If you didn't speak with a particular command of the language—or at a subdued volume—you might have been dismissed as crude. If you hadn't been educated in what were considered the "right places," you were seen as some sort of a peasant.

But anyone who has observed the dressing, speaking and dancing styles of Americans since 1960 can easily recognize the sometimes startling influences that run from the top to the bottom, the bottom to the top. Educated people of whatever ethnic group use slang and terms scooped out from the disciplines of psychology, economics and art criticism. In fact, one of the few interesting things about the rap idiom is that some rappers pull together a much richer vocabulary than has ever existed in black pop music, while peppering it to extremes with repulsive vulgarity.

One hundred years from today, Americans are likely to look back on the ethnic difficulties of our time as quizzically as we look at earlier periods of human history, when misapprehension defined the reality. There will still be squabbling, and those who supposedly speak in the interest of one group or another will hector the gullible into some kind of self-obsession that will influence the local and national dialogues. But those squabbles are basic to upward mobility and competition. It is the very nature of upward mobility and competition to ease away superficial distinctions in the interest of getting the job done. We already see this in the integration of the workplace, in the rise of women and in the increase of corporations that grant spousal-equivalent benefits to homosexuals because they want to keep their best workers, no matter what they do privately as consenting adults. In the march of the world economy, the imbalances that result from hysterical xenophobia will largely melt away because Americans will be far too busy standing up to the challenges of getting as many international customers for their wares as they can. That is, if they're lucky.

Edward Rothstein

Edward Rothstein writes regularly for The New York Times, *where this article appeared, on December 14, 1997.*

Ethnicity and Disney: It's a Whole New Myth

In Julie Taymor's triumphant Broadway reinterpretation of the Walt Disney Company's "Lion King," the movie's shamanesque baboon,

Rafiki, is transmuted into a Zulu-chanting priestess, an African griot-storyteller, hooting and hollering, grunting knowingly and guiding the young lion Simba to his destiny. In the show, Rafiki is thrust to the story's center, just as the generic African background of the animated feature film is thrust into the foreground by Ms. Taymor, with muscular dance and music, ritualistic images and carnivalesque ensemble pieces.

With this new ethnic emphasis, Rafiki's closest Disney ancestor may be James Baskett, who starred as the black plantation-style storyteller Uncle Remus in "Song of the South" 51 years ago. That film has never been released on video and probably never will be (it is available only on laser disk from Japan). In it, Mr. Baskett, whose voice was known from the "Amos 'n' Andy" radio show, charmed the movie's post-Reconstruction Southern children with Joel Chandler Harris's vernacular tales of Brer Rabbit and Brer Fox. His performance won him a special Oscar, but the charm had its limits. *The New Yorker* said that the film consisted of "the purest sheep-dip about happy days on the old plantation." Adam Clayton Powell Jr. said it was an "insult to American minorities" and to "everything that America as a whole stands for."

The ethnic romance of the Broadway "Lion King," with its mixture of Zulu chant and songs by Elton John and Tim Rice, might also have turned into caricature. But it was saved by Ms. Taymor's genius, along with something else: the show's attitude toward ethnicity is not patronizing because ethnicity is no longer being treated as the mark of an outsider. Instead, ethnicity defines a society itself.

This represents a major change in the Disney vision of ethnicity, which is no small matter. Disney films may be the only cultural experience shared by American children, while ethnicity and race are probably the most charged words in American politics.

Ethnically defined characters have been a crucial part of Disney films for many years, both before Walt Disney died in 1966 and after. These characters include the broadly sketched black-American crows of "Dumbo" (1941) singing "I be done seen 'bout everything"; the alley cats of "Aristocats" (1970), who break out into an infectious jazz rendition of "Ev'rybody Wants to Be a Cat," led by the voice of Scatman Crothers; and Sebastian the crab in "The Little Mermaid" (1989), sung by Samuel E. Wright, who gives advice to a calypso beat ("Go on and kiss the girl"). Isn't there also a hint of caricature of black Americans when the Ape King in "The Jungle Book" (1967) yearns to learn the secret of civilization and sings (in the voice of Louis Prima), "I wan'na be like you"?

And not just black culture has preoccupied the Disney empire. Throughout the films—pre-Walt and post, animated and live action—ethnic types abound, sometimes associated with national caricatures and even social class. "The Three Caballeros" (1945) is a veritable tour of Latin American stereotypes. "Peter Pan" (1953) has an "Injun" powwow, "Pocahontas" (1995) an American Indian potlatch. In "Mary Poppins" (1964), the middle-class Banks family comes up against the Cockney chimney sweep Bert. "Aladdin" (1992) offended some viewers with its references to Arab culture. "The Hunchback of Notre-Dame" (1996) has the magically beguiling Gypsy Esmeralda.

Why is ethnicity so central to the Disney oeuvre? The word ethnic, which comes from the Greek word ethnos, meaning heathen or pagan, is a title given to an outsider and implies condescension: the ethnic heathen has rejected the civilized mainstream and has also been rejected by it. And the Disney ethnic character has tended to be interpreted as evidence of racism and insularity shared by Walt Disney and generations of Disney animators, writers and directors.

But while American racial attitudes have changed dramatically over the course of Disney history, the nature of the Disney view of ethnicity has been remarkably consistent until recently. And despite whiffs of condescension (and rare mean-spiritedness, as in the portrait of the Siamese cats in "Lady and the Tramp" in 1955), the ethnic character is treated with unusual affection. The Disney ethnic characters are loaded down by cliché—in accent, character and mannerism—but are also admired, even envied (they also get the best songs).

The crows in "Dumbo," for example, are more knowledgeable and witty than any of the flying elephant's circus colleagues. The alley cats in "Aristocats" turn out to be the heroes, possessing far more important skills than the upper-crust "white" kittens. Esmeralda, the Gypsy of "Hunchback," comprehends the trials of Quasimodo because of her own beleaguered ethnic status.

This is no accident. Ethnicity involves complicated relationships between an outsider and a supposed center, between an immigrant and the mainstream, an aspiring lower class and a complacent middle. And these relationships are often the very subjects of the films themselves. Disney movies do not just incorporate ethnicity; they are, in a broad sense, about it. 10

This is true even if the key characters are not explicitly ethnic. Dumbo is a misfit, Pinocchio a boy without a purpose. Ariel the mermaid is out of place in her underwater world, yearning to be human. In "Beauty and the Beast," Belle is "so different from the rest of us." The outsider—the hunchback, the child, the disenfranchised princess, the beast—struggles to join the center or change it.

Meanwhile, the identifiably ethnic characters aid in those struggles: Geppetto tries to help Pinocchio become a boy; Sebastian helps the little mermaid become human; the dwarfs help Snow White; the inner-city cats help the Aristocats. The typical Disney film presents a joint triumph: the ethnic character ends up becoming mainstream, and the mainstream ends up learning from and accepting the ethnic character.

In this light, the Disney oeuvre seems an embodiment of old-fashioned liberalism, something that seems bizarre given Walt Disney's reputation as a man of the right (any chance of his obtaining true liberal credentials ended with his anti-Communist testimony before the House Un-American Activities Committee in 1947). Still, until the recent past, when their view of ethnicity began to shift, Disney films—reaching back to "Dumbo," and even encompassing the paternalistic "Song of the South"—proclaimed a melting-pot liberalism. The dominant idea was not conformity but mutual accommodation.

Walt Disney's latest biographer, Steven Watts, points out in his forthcoming book, "The Magic Kingdom," that in the 1950's the Disney studios also engaged in an almost radical celebration of American self-reliance. But this tendency, too, became a celebration of the melting pot, in which ethnic characters, like the Mexican-born Zorro, were heroic iconoclasts. In Disneyland, Disney envisioned an idealized America that incorporated exotic lands and foreign climes. Even the star of "The Mickey Mouse Club" on television was the young Italian-American Annette Funicello.

In fact, in contrast with many other popular forms of entertainment, few ethnic characters, even in the early Disney films, are villains. In "Bambi" (1942), which in its eco pieties anticipates "The Lion King," the enemy is man himself, the hunter and fire maker. In "Dumbo" the most unlikable characters are the other elephants, who dislike anyone different from themselves. In "Hunchback," the villain hates Gypsies, the poor and the crippled. Evil is far more often associated with pretense and social climbing than with being ethnically different.

This then was the central myth of the Disney entertainment empire, a variation on the American dream that tapped into children's fantasies and adult political hopes. In a way, it was almost opposite of the grandly popular myths of opera that dominated 19th-century European culture.

Opera, like Disney genre films, came into its own with the efforts to create unified nations out of disparate peoples. But in opera, the outsider often threatens the social order and the conflict between the ethnic character (think Carmen) and the mainstream (think Don José) often ended in tragedy. No triumph came without pain and complication. Disney's optimism allowed none of this; the view of society was ethnically rich, but it was a civilization without discontents.

Such optimism couldn't be sustained. In the 90's, the Disney myth started to dissolve leading to a string of meandering, strained films. Ethnicity remained prominent in "Aladdin," as if out of habit, but was unrelated to anything else in the film. "Pocahontas" signaled the first real signs of change, overturning Disney liberalism and exchanging it for assertions of ethnic independence. The film "The Lion King" rejected the Disney myth more completely by focusing on a new notion of ethnicity: its hero was not an outsider yearning to join the center or thriving outside it but a disinherited heir who had to recapture his ethnic kingdom. "The Lion King" is not about accommodation and influence but about ethnic identity.

This means that the outsider is not someone to be admired or learned from, like the Tramp or Uncle Remus or Sebastian. He is a villain who threatens the ethnic future. Scar is literally a heathen, a pagan who rejects the Circle of Life and African animal society; he is portrayed as an ethnic caricature who is really an anti-ethnic. Simba tells Scar he is strange; the villain replies in a precious drawl, "You have no idea."

Partly because the film never makes much of Simba's native culture, 20
the ethnic stakes never seem very high. But Ms. Taymor has fully uncov-
ered the new Disney myth with her production's African-style celebra-
tions and chants. The film's subtext comes to the surface. The ethnic world
is being threatened by Scar; it is that world that Simba must preserve by
accepting his identity and celebrating its centrality.

This transformation of the Disney myth reflects changes in the larger
society as well. The melting pot is out; ethnic identity is in. Accommodation is no longer the issue; self-assertion is. But nuance is hardly more
plentiful. It will be revealing to see what happens if Disney comes through
with its proposed version of Verdi's opera "Aida." That opera focuses on
the demands made by ethnic and national identity and their conflicts with
personal desire. Private and public clash; tragedy emerges from the fray.

Will Disney allow itself to reveal the dangers behind its new myth? Is
there room in the Disney universe for a sense of complication, or even for
old-style reconciliation? The issues are not Disney's alone.

Eric Liu

Eric Liu, born in the United States of Chinese immigrant parents, published The Accidental Asian:
Notes of Native Speaker *(a collection of essays on racial identity) in 1998, when he was twenty-
nine, a student at Harvard Law School. Liu had already contributed essays to several national
magazines, and he had edited an anthology,* Next: Young American Writers on the New Generation. *We give an excerpt from* The Accidental Asian. *The title of the extract is our own.*

Our Problem Isn't Just "Race" in the Abstract

The "Negro problem," wrote Norman Podhoretz in 1963, would
not be solved unless color itself disappeared: "and that means not
integration, it means assimilation, it means—let the brutal word come
out—miscegenation." Coming after a lengthy confession of his tortured
feelings toward blacks—and coming at a time when nineteen states still
had antimiscegenation statutes on the books—Podhoretz's call for a
"wholesale merging of the two races" seemed not just bold but desperate.
Politics had failed us, he was conceding; now we could find hope only in
the unlikely prospect of intermarriage.

Podhoretz's famous essay was regarded as peculiar at the time, but
today it seems like prophecy. We are intermarrying in unprecedented
numbers. Between 1970 and 1992 the number of mixed-race marriages
quadrupled. We are mixing our genes with such abandon that the Census
Bureau considered adding a new "multiracial" category to the forms in

the year 2000. It settled instead on a potentially more radical solution: allowing people to check as many boxes as they wish.

These changes have provoked strong reactions from civil rights activists who fear that many minorities will defect from their old categories, thus diluting colored political clout. But the debate, properly framed, isn't about "light flight." It's about our very conception of race. For the new rules are an admission that the five points of what David Hollinger calls the "ethnoracial pentagon" (black, white, Asian, Hispanic, Native American) aren't fixed or divinely ordained, but fickle and all too man-made.

Race, you see, is a fiction. As a matter of biology it has no meaningful basis. Genetic variations within any race far exceed the variations between the races, and genetic similarities among the races swamp both. The power of race, however, derives not from its pseudoscientific markings but from its social trappings. It is as an *ideology* that race matters, indeed matters so much that the biologists' protestations fall away like Copernican claims in the age of Ptolemy.

The hope is that the emergence of a mixed-race community will help   5
obliterate our antiquated notions of racial difference. I'm all for that. I certainly won't want to infect my Chinese-Scottish-Irish-Jewish children with bloodline fever. I won't force them to choose among ill-fitting racial uniforms. That said, though, there is reason to wonder whether miscegenation alone can ever, as one commentator put it, "blow the lid off of race."

Foremost is this reality: racialism is awfully adaptive. No matter how quickly demographics change, we seem to find a way to sustain our jerry-built pigmentocracy. Take the term "Hispanic." Ever since it was added to the census in 1977, we've been told that "Hispanic" is merely a linguistic category, that Hispanics "can be of any race." Today, amid a boom in the Hispanic population, we hear that caveat the same way smokers read the surgeon general's warning. Heterogeneous Hispanics—who ought to have exposed the flimsiness of racial categories—became in the popular mind just another homogeneous race.

Could this happen to people of mixed descent? Their very existence as a group is premised on the idea of *transcending* race. Moreover, they have less reason to cohere than Hispanics ever had: they include every conceivable combination of genes and are not bound together by another language. Still, in a nation accustomed to thinking of "official races," people of mixed descent could come to be regarded as a bloc of their own.

One possibility is that multiracials, over time, will find themselves deemed a middleman race. Their presence, like that of the "coloreds" in old South Africa, wouldn't undermine racialism; it would reinforce it, by fleshing out a rough white-black caste system. Again, however, the sheer diversity of the multiracial population would probably prevent this from happening.

Yet this same diversity makes it possible that multiracials will replicate within their ranks the "white-makes-right" mentality that prevails all around them. Thus we might see a hierarchy take hold in which a mixed child with "white" blood would be the social better of a mixed child without such blood. In this scenario, multiracials wouldn't be a distinct group; they'd be distributed across a continuum of color.

Perhaps such a continuum is preferable to a simple black-white 10 dichotomy. Brazilians, for instance, with their many gradations of *tipo*, or "type," behold with disdain our crude bifurcation of race. But no amount of baloney-slicing changes the fact that, in Brazil, whitening remains the ideal. It is still better for a woman to be a *branca* (light skin, hair without tight curls, thin lips, narrow nose) than a *morena* (tan skin, wavy hair, thicker lips, broader nose); and better to be a *morena* than a *mulata* (darker skin, tightly curled hair). Subverting racial labels is not the same as subverting racism.

Still another possibility is that whites will do to the multiracials what the Democrats or Republicans have traditionally done to third-party movements: absorb their most "desirable" elements and leave the rest on the fringe. It's quite possible, as the sociologist Mary Waters suggests, that the ranks of the white will simply expand to include the "lighter" or more "culturally white" of the multiracials.

All these scenarios, far-fetched as they may sound, should remind us that our problem isn't just "race" in the abstract; it's the idea of the "white race" in particular. So long as we speak of whiteness as the social norm and "passing" as the option of choice, no amount of census reshuffling will truly matter.

We return, then, to the question of politics. Perhaps we should abolish racial classification altogether. Perhaps we need more class-based variants of affirmative action. Perhaps we need a form of national service to counter the effects of resegregation. Whatever it takes, though, we need to do more than marry one another if we are ever to rid our society of color-consciousness. "The way of politics," Podhoretz lamented, "is slow and bitter." Indeed. But it is the only lasting way. Our ideology of "blood," like blood itself, is too fluid, too changeable, and too easily diverted to be remade by lovers alone.

9
TEACHING AND LEARNING

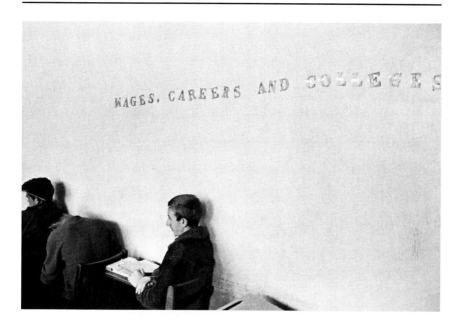

Short Views

Knowledge is power.
   Francis Bacon

Hard students are commonly troubled with gouts, catarrahs, rheums, cachexia, bradypepsia, bad eyes, stone, and collick, crudities, oppilations, vertigo, winds, consumptions, and all such diseases as come by over-much sitting: they are most part lean, dry, ill-colored . . . and all through immoderate pains and extraordinary studies.
   Robert Burton

In my opinion, the only justification for high schools is as therapeutic halfway houses for the deranged. Normal adolescents can find themselves and grow further only by coping with the jobs, sex, and chances of the real world—it is useless to feed them curricular imitations. I would simply abolish the high schools, substituting apprenticeships and other alternatives and protecting the young from gross exploitation by putting the school money directly in their pockets. The very few who have authentic scholarly interests will gravitate to their own libraries, teachers, and academies, as they always did in the past, when they could afford it. In organic communities, adolescents cluster together in their own youth houses, for their fun and games and loud music, without bothering sober folk. I see no reason whatsoever for adults to set up or direct such nests or to be there at all unless invited.
   Paul Goodman

I can judge one of the main effects of personal grading by the attitudes of students who land in my remedial course in college. They hate and fear writing more than anything else they have had to do in school. If they see a blank sheet of paper on which they are expected to write something, they look as though they want to scream. Apparently they have never written anything that anyone thought was good. At least, no one ever told them that anything in their writing was good. All their teachers looked for were mistakes, and there are so many kinds of mistakes in writing that their students despair of ever learning to avoid them.

   The attitude toward writing that these students have developed is well illustrated by a story told by the Russian writer Chekhov about a kitten that was given to his uncle. The uncle wanted to make the kitten a champion killer of mice, so while it was still very young, he showed it a live mouse in a cage. Since the kitten's hunting instinct had not yet developed, it examined the mouse curiously but without any hostility. The uncle wanted to teach it that such fraternizing with the enemy was wrong, so he slapped the kitten, scolded it, and sent it away in disgrace. The next day the same mouse was shown to the kitten again. This time the kitten regarded it rather fearfully but without any aggressive intent. Again the uncle slapped it, scolded it, and sent it away. This treatment went on day after day. After some time, as soon as the kitten saw or smelled that mouse, it screamed and tried to climb up the walls. At that point the uncle lost patience and gave the kitten away, saying that it was stupid and would never learn. Of course the kitten had learned perfectly, and had learned exactly what it had been taught, but unfortunately not what the uncle intended to teach. "I can sympathize with that kitten," says Chekhov, "because that same uncle tried to teach me Latin."

Paul B. Diederich

A woman came to Rabbi Israel, the great maggid or teacher in Koznitz, and told him, with many tears, that she had been married a dozen years and still had not borne a son. "What are you willing to do about it?" he asked her. She did not know what to say. "My mother," so the maggid told her, "was aging and still had no child. Then she heard that the holy Baal Shem was stopping over in Apt in the course of a journey. She hurried to his inn and begged him to pray she might bear a son. 'What are you willing to do about it?' he asked. 'My husband is a poor book-binder,' she replied, 'but I do have one fine thing that I shall give to the rabbi.' She went home as fast as she could and fetched her good cape, her 'Katinka,' which was carefully stowed away in a chest. But when she returned to the inn with it, she heard that the Baal Shem had already left for Mezbizh. She immediately set out after him and since she had no money to ride, she walked from town to town with her 'Katinka' until she came to Mezbizh. The Baal Shem took the cape and hung it on the wall. 'It is well,' he said. My mother walked all the way back, from town to town, until she reached Apt. A year later, I was born."

"I, too," cried the woman, "will bring you a cape of mine so that I may get a son."

"That won't work," said the maggid. "You heard the story. My mother had no story to go by."

Hasidic Tale

You go to a great school not for knowledge so much as for arts and habits; for the habit of attention, for the art of expression, for the art of assuming at a moment's notice a new intellectual posture, for the art of entering quickly into another person's thought, for the habit of submitting to censure and refutation, for the art of indicating assent or dissent in graduated terms, for the habit of regarding minute points of accuracy, for the habit of working out what is possible in a given time, for taste, for discrimination, for mental courage and mental soberness. Above all, you go to a great school for self-knowledge.

William Cory

How people keep correcting us when we are young! There's always some bad habit or other they tell us we ought to get over. Yet most bad habits are tools to help us through life.

Johann Wolfgang von Goethe

Supposing anyone were to suggest that the best results for the individual and society could be derived through compulsory feeding, would not the most ignorant rebel against such a stupid procedure? And yet the stomach has far greater adaptability to almost any situation than the brain. With all that, we find it quite natural to have compulsory mental feeding.

Indeed, we actually consider ourselves superior to other nations, because we have evolved a compulsory brain tube through which, for a certain number of hours every day, and for so many years, we can force into the child's mind a large quantity of mental nutrition.

. . . The great harm done by our system of education is not so much that it teaches nothing worth knowing, that it helps to perpetuate privileged classes, that it assists them in the criminal procedure of robbing and exploiting the masses; the harm of the system lies in its boastful proclamation that it stands for true education, thereby enslaving the masses a great deal more than could an absolute ruler.

Emma Goldman

The education of women should always be relative to that of men. To please, to be useful to us, to make us love and esteem them, to educate us when young, to take care of us when grown up; to advise, to console us, to render our lives easy and agreeable. These are the duties of women at all times, and what they should be taught in their infancy.

Jean Jacques Rousseau, *Emile*

If Johnny can't learn because he is hungry, that's the fault of poverty. But if Johnny can't pay attention because he is sleepy, that's the fault of parents.

What does it matter if we have a new book or an old book, if we open neither?

Jesse Jackson

Universities are, of course, hostile to geniuses.
>   **Ralph Waldo Emerson**

The man who can make hard things easy is the educator.
>   **Ralph Waldo Emerson**

It is perhaps idle to wonder what, from my present point of view, would have been an ideal education. If I could provide such a curriculum for my own children they, in their turn, might find it all a bore. But the fantasy of what I would have liked to learn as a child may be revealing, since I feel unequipped by education for problems that lie outside the cloistered, literary domain in which I am competent and at home. Looking back, then, I would have arranged for myself to be taught survival techniques for both natural and urban wildernesses. I would want to have been instructed in self-hypnosis, in *aikido* (the esoteric and purely self-defensive style of judo), in elementary medicine, in sexual hygiene, in vegetable gardening, in astronomy, navigation, and sailing; in cookery and clothesmaking, in metalwork and carpentry, in drawing and painting, in printing and typography, in botany and biology, in optics and acoustics, in semantics and psychology, in mysticism and yoga, in electronics and mathematical fantasy, in drama and dancing, in singing and in playing an instrument by ear; in wandering, in advanced daydreaming, in prestidigitation, in techniques of escape from bondage, in disguise, in conversation with birds and beasts, in ventriloquism, in French and German conversation, in planetary history, in morphology, and in classical Chinese. Actually, the main thing left out of my education was a proper love for my own body, because one feared to cherish anything so obviously mortal and prone to sickness.
>   **Alan Watts**

Education! Which of the various me's do you propose to educate, and which do you propose to suppress?
>   **D. H. Lawrence**

Think about the kind of world you want to live and work in. What do you need to know to build the world? Demand that your teachers teach you that.
>   **Prince Kropotkin**

The entire object of true education is to make people not merely *do* the right things, but *enjoy* the right things.
>   **John Ruskin**

Learning without thought is labor lost; thought without learning is dangerous.
Confucius

Nan-in, a Japanese master during the Meiji era (1868–1912), received a university professor who came to inquire about Zen.

Nan-in served tea. He poured his visitor's cup full, and then kept on pouring.

The professor watched the overflow until he no longer could restrain himself. "It is overfull. No more will go in!"

"Like this cup," Nan-in said, "you are full of your own opinions and speculations. How can I show you Zen unless you first empty your cup?"
Anonymous Zen Anecdote

I think [Raymond Weaver] first attracted my attention as someone worth watching when, while we were both new instructors, I heard from a bewildered freshman about the quiz he had just given. The first question written on the blackboard was, "Which of the required readings in this course did you find least interesting?" Then, after members of the class had had ten minutes in which to expatiate on what was certainly to many a congenial topic, he wrote the second question: "To what defect in yourself do you attribute this lack of interest?"
Joseph Wood Krutch

It is not sufficiently understood that a child's education should include at least a rudimentary grasp of religion, sex, and money. Without a basic knowledge of these three primary facts in a normal human being's life—subjects which stir the emotions, create events and opportunities, and if they do not wholly decide must greatly influence an individual's personality—no human being's education can have a safe foundation.
Phyllis Bottome

Plato

Plato (427–347 B.C.), born in Athens, the son of an aristocratic family, wrote thirty dialogues in which Socrates is the chief speaker. Socrates, about twenty-five years older than Plato, was a philosopher who called himself a gadfly to Athenians. For his efforts at stinging them into thought, the Athenians executed him in 399 B.C. "The Myth of the Cave" is the beginning of Book VII of Plato's dialogue entitled The Republic. *Socrates is talking with Glaucon.*

For Plato, true knowledge is philosophic insight or awareness of the Good, not mere opinion or the knack of getting along in this world by remembering how things have usually worked in the past. To illustrate his idea that awareness of the Good is different from the ability to recognize the things of this shabby world, Plato (through his spokesman Socrates) resorts to an allegory: men imprisoned in a cave see on a wall in front of them the shadows or images of objects that are really behind them, and they hear echoes, not real voices. (The shadows are caused by the light from a fire behind the objects, and the echoes by the cave's acoustical properties.) The prisoners, unable to perceive the real objects and the real voices, mistakenly think that the shadows and the echoes are real, and some of them grow highly adept at dealing with this illusory world. Were Plato writing today, he might have made the cave a movie theater: we see on the screen in front of us images caused by an object (film, passing in front of light) that is behind us. Moreover, the film itself is an illusory image, for it bears only the traces of a yet more real world—the world that was photographed—outside of the movie theater. And when we leave the theater to go into the real world, our eyes have become so accustomed to the illusory world that we at first blink with discomfort—just as Plato's freed prisoners do when they move out of the cave—at the real world of bright day, and we long for the familiar darkness. So too, Plato suggests, dwellers in ignorance may prefer the familiar shadows of their unenlightened world ("the world of becoming") to the bright world of the eternal Good ("the world of being") that education reveals.

We have just used the word education. *You will notice that the first sentence in the translation (by Benjamin Jowett) says that the myth will show "how far our nature is enlightened or unenlightened." In the original Greek the words here translated* enlightened *and* unenlightened *are* paideia *and* apaideusia. *No translation can fully catch the exact meanings of these elusive words. Depending on the context,* paideia *may be translated as* enlightenment, education, civilization, culture, knowledge of the good.

The Myth of the Cave

And now, I said, let me show in a figure how far our nature is enlightened or unenlightened—Behold! human beings living in an underground den, which has a mouth open toward the light and reaching all along the den; here they have been from their childhood, and have their legs and necks chained so that they cannot move, and can only see before them, being prevented by the chains from turning round their heads. Above and behind them a fire is blazing at a distance, and between the fire and the prisoners there is a raised way; and you will see, if you look, a low wall built along the way, like the screen which marionette players have in front of them, over which they show the puppets.

I see.

And do you see, I said, men passing along the wall carrying all sorts of vessels, and statues and figures of animals made of wood and stone and various materials, which appear over the wall? Some of them are talking, others silent.

You have shown me a strange image, and they are strange prisoners.

Like ourselves, I replied; and they see only their own shadows, or the shadows of one another, which the fire throws on the opposite wall of the cave?

True, he said; how could they see anything but the shadows if they were never allowed to move their heads?

And of the objects which are being carried in like manner they would only see the shadows?

Yes, he said.

And if they were able to converse with one another, would they not suppose that they were naming what was actually before them?

Very true.

And suppose further that the prison had an echo which came from the other side, would they not be sure when one of the passersby spoke that the voice which they heard came from the passing shadow?

No question, he replied.

To them, I said, the truth would be literally nothing but the shadows of the images.

That is certain.

And now look again, and see what will naturally follow if the prisoners are released and disabused of their error. At first, when any of them is liberated and compelled suddenly to stand up and turn his neck round and walk and look toward the light, he will suffer sharp pains; the glare will distress him, and he will be unable to see the realities of which in his former state he had seen the shadows; and then conceive some one saying to him, that what he saw before was an illusion, but that now, when he is approaching nearer to being and his eye is turned toward more real existence, he has a clearer vision—what will be his reply? And you may further imagine that his instructor is pointing to the objects as they pass and requiring him to name them—will he not be perplexed? Will he not fancy that the shadows which he formerly saw are truer than the objects which are now shown to him?

Far truer.

And if he is compelled to look straight at the light, will he not have a pain in his eyes which will make him turn away to take refuge in the objects of vision which he can see, and which he will conceive to be in reality clearer than the things which are now being shown to him?

True, he said.

And suppose once more, that he is reluctantly dragged up a steep and rugged ascent, and held fast until he is forced into the presence of the sun himself, is he not likely to be pained and irritated? When he approaches the light his eyes will be dazzled, and he will not be able to see anything at all of what are now called realities.

Not all in a moment, he said.   20

He will require to grow accustomed to the sight of the upper world. And first he will see the shadows best, next the reflections of men and other objects in the water, and then the objects themselves; then he will gaze upon the light of the moon and the stars and the spangled heaven; and he will see the sky and the stars by night better than the sun or the light of the sun by day?

Certainly.

Last of all he will be able to see the sun, and not mere reflections of him in the water, but he will see him in his own proper place, and not in another; and he will contemplate him as he is.

Certainly.

He will then proceed to argue that this is he who gives the season and   25 the years, and is the guardian of all that is in the visible world, and in a certain way the cause of all things which he and his fellows have been accustomed to behold?

Clearly, he said, he would first see the sun and then reason about him.

And when he remembered his old habitation, and the wisdom of the den and his fellow-prisoners, do you not suppose that he would felicitate himself on the change, and pity them?

Certainly, he would.

And if they were in the habit of conferring honors among themselves on those who were quickest to observe the passing shadows and to remark which of them went before, and which followed after, and which were together; and who were therefore best able to draw conclusions as to the future, do you think that he would care for such honors and glories, or envy the possessors of them? Would he not say with Homer,

> Better to be the poor servant of a poor master,

and to endure anything, rather than think as they do and live after their manner?

Yes, he said, I think that he would rather suffer anything than enter-   30 tain these false notions and live in this miserable manner.

Imagine once more, I said, such an one coming suddenly out of the sun to be replaced in his old situation; would he not be certain to have his eyes full of darkness?

To be sure, he said.

And if there were a contest, and he had to compete in measuring the shadows with the prisoners who had never moved out of the den, while his sight was still weak, and before his eyes had become steady (and the time which would be needed to acquire this new habit of sight might be very considerable), would he not be ridiculous? Men would say of him that up he went and down he came without his eyes; and that it was better not even to think of ascending; and if any one tried to loose another and lead him up to the light, let them only catch the offender, and they would put him to death.

No question, he said.

This entire allegory, I said, you may now append, dear Glaucon, to the previous argument; the prison-house is the world of sight, the light of the fire is the sun, and you will not misapprehend me if you interpret the journey upwards to be the ascent of the soul into the intellectual world according to my poor belief, which, at your desire, I have expressed— whether rightly or wrongly God knows. But, whether true or false, my opinion is that in the world of knowledge the idea of good appears last of all, and is seen only with an effort; and, when seen, is also inferred to be the universal author of all things beautiful and right, parent of light and of the lord of light in this visible world, and the immediate source of reason and truth in the intellectual; and that this is the power upon which he who would act rationally either in public or private life must have his eye fixed. 35

I agree, he said, as far as I am able to understand you.

Moreover, I said, you must not wonder that those who attain to this beatific vision are unwilling to descend to human affairs; for their souls are ever hastening into the upper world where they desire to dwell; which desire of theirs is very natural, if our allegory may be trusted.

Yes, very natural.

And is there anything surprising in one who passes from divine contemplations to the evil state of man, misbehaving himself in a ridiculous manner; if, while his eyes are blinking and before he has become accustomed to the surrounding darkness, he is compelled to fight in courts of law, or in other places, about the images or the shadows of images of justice, and is endeavoring to meet the conceptions of those who have never yet seen absolute justice?

Anything but surprising, he replied. 40

Any one who has common sense will remember that the bewilderments of the eyes are of two kinds, and arise from two causes, either from coming out of the light or from going into the light, which is true of the mind's eye, quite as much as of the bodily eye; and he who remembers this when he sees any one whose vision is perplexed and weak, will not be too ready to laugh; he will first ask whether that soul of man has come out of the brighter life, and is unable to see because unaccustomed to the dark, or having turned from darkness to the day is dazzled by excess of light. And he will count the one happy in his condition and state of being, and he will pity the other; or, if he have a mind to laugh at the soul which comes from below into the light, there will be more reason in this than in the laugh which greets him who returns from above out of the light into the den.

That, he said, is a very just distinction.

But then, if I am right, certain professors of education must be wrong when they say that they can put a knowledge into the soul which was not there before, like sight into blind eyes.

They undoubtedly say this, he replied.

Whereas, our argument shows that the power and capacity of learn-   45
ing exists in the soul already; and that just as the eye was unable to turn from darkness to light without the whole body, so too the instrument of knowledge can only by the movement of the whole soul be turned from the world of becoming into that of being, and learn by degrees to endure the sight of being, and of the brightest and best of being, or in other words, of the good.

Very true.

And must there not be some art which will effect conversion in the easiest and quickest manner; not implanting the faculty of sight, for that exists already, but has been turned in the wrong direction, and is looking away from the truth?

Yes, he said, such an art may be presumed.

And whereas the other so-called virtues of the soul seem to be akin to bodily qualities, for even when they are not originally innate they can be implanted later by habit and exercise, the virtue of wisdom more than anything else contains a divine element which always remains, and by this conversion is rendered useful and profitable; or, on the other hand, hurtful and useless. Did you never observe the narrow intelligence flashing from the keen eye of a clever rogue—how eager he is, how clearly his paltry soul sees the way to his end; he is the reverse of blind, but his keen eyesight is forced into the service of evil, and he is mischievous in proportion to his cleverness?

Very true, he said.   50

But what if there had been a circumcision of such natures in the days of their youth; and they had been severed from those sensual pleasures, such as eating and drinking, which, like leaden weights, were attached to them at their birth, and which drag them down and turn the vision of their souls upon the things that are below—if, I say, they had been released from these impediments and turned in the opposite direction, the very same faculty in them would have seen the truth as keenly as they see what their eyes are turned to now.

Very likely.

Yes, I said; and there is another thing which is likely, or rather a necessary inference from what has preceded, that neither the uneducated and uninformed of the truth, nor yet those who never make an end of their education, will be able ministers of State; not the former, because they have no single aim of duty which is the rule of all their actions, private as well as public; nor the latter, because they will not act at all except upon compulsion, fancying that they are already dwelling apart in the islands of the blest.

Very true, he replied.

Then, I said, the business of us who are the founders of the State will 55
be to compel the best minds to attain that knowledge which we have
already shown to be the greatest of all—they must continue to ascend
until they arrive at the good; but when they have ascended and seen
enough we must not allow them to do as they do now.

What do you mean?

I mean that they remain in the upper world: but this must not be
allowed; they must be made to descend again among the prisoners in the
den, and partake of their labors and honors, whether they are worth having or not.

But is not this unjust? he said; ought we to give them a worse life,
when they might have a better?

You have again forgotten, my friend, I said, the intention of the legislator, who did not aim at making any one class in the State happy above the
rest; the happiness was to be in the whole State, and he held the citizens
together by persuasion and necessity, making them benefactors of the
State, and therefore benefactors of one another; to this end he created them,
not to please themselves, but to be his instruments in binding up the State.

True, he said, I had forgotten. 60

Observe, Glaucon, that there will be no justice in compelling our
philosophers to have a care and providence of others; we shall explain to
them that in other States, men of their class are not obliged to share in the
toils of politics: and this is reasonable, for they grow up at their own sweet
will, and the government would rather not have them. Being self-taught,
they cannot be expected to show any gratitude for a culture which they
have never received. But we have brought you into the world to be rulers
of the hive, kings of yourselves and of the other citizens, and have educated you far better and more perfectly than they have been educated, and
you are better able to share in the double duty. Wherefore each of you,
when his turn comes, must go down to the general underground abode,
and get the habit of seeing in the dark. When you have acquired the habit,
you will see ten thousand times better than the inhabitants of the den, and
you will know what the several images are, and what they represent,
because you have seen the beautiful and just and good in their truth. And
thus our State which is also yours will be a reality, and not a dream only,
and will be administered in a spirit unlike that of other States, in which
men fight with one another about shadows only and are distracted in the
struggle for power, which in their eyes is a great good. Whereas the truth
is that the State in which the rulers are most reluctant to govern is always
the best and most quietly governed, and the State in which they are most
eager, the worst.

Quite true, he replied.

And will our pupils, when they hear this, refuse to take their turn at
the toils of State, when they are allowed to spend the greater part of their
time with one another in the heavenly light?

Impossible, he answered; for they are just men, and the commands which we impose upon them are just; there can be no doubt that every one of them will take office as a stern necessity, and not after the fashion of our present rulers of State.

Yes, my friend, I said; and there lies the point. You must contrive for your future rulers another and a better life than that of a ruler, and then you may have a well-ordered State; for only in the State which offers this, will they rule who are truly rich, not in silver and gold, but in virtue and wisdom, which are the true blessings of life. Whereas if they go to the administration of public affairs, poor and hungering after their own private advantage, thinking that hence they are to snatch the chief good, order there can never be; for they will be fighting about office, and the civil and domestic broils which thus arise will be the ruin of the rulers themselves and of the whole State.

Most true, he replied.

And the only life which looks down upon the life of political ambition is that of true philosophy. Do you know of any other?

Indeed, I do not, he said.

And those who govern ought not to be lovers of the task? For, if they are, there will be rival lovers, and they will fight.

No question.

Who then are those whom we shall compel to be guardians? Surely they will be the men who are wisest about affairs of State, and by whom the State is best administered, and who at the same time have other honors and another and a better life than that of politics?

They are the men, and I will choose them, he replied.

And now shall we consider in what way such guardians will be produced, and how they are to be brought from darkness to light—as some are said to have ascended from the world below to the gods?

By all means, he replied.

The process, I said, is not the turning over of an oyster-shell,[1] but the turning round of a soul passing from a day which is little better than night to the true day of being, that is, the ascent from below which we affirm to be true philosophy?

Quite so.

✎ Topics for Critical Thinking and Writing

1. Plato is not merely reporting one of Socrates' conversations; he is teaching. What advantages does a dialogue have over a narrative or an essay as a way of teaching philosophy? How is the form of a dialogue especially suited to solving a problem?

---

[1]An allusion to a game in which two parties fled or pursued according as an oyster shell that was thrown into the air fell with the dark or light side uppermost. (Translator's note)

2. If you don't know the etymology of the word *conversion,* look it up in a dictionary. How is the etymology appropriate to Plato's idea about education?

3. In paragraph 19, describing the prisoner as "reluctantly dragged" upward and "forced" to look at the sun, Socrates asks: "Is he not likely to be pained and irritated?" Can you recall experiencing pain and irritation while learning something you later were glad to have learned? Can you recall learning something new *without* experiencing pain and irritation?

4. "The State in which rulers are most reluctant to govern is always the best and most quietly governed, and the State in which they are most eager, the worst" (paragraph 61). What does Socrates mean? Using examples from contemporary politics, defend this proposition or argue against it.

5. Can you account for the power of this myth or fable? In our introductory comment (page 363), we tried to clarify the message by saying that a movie theater might serve as well as a cave. But, in fact, if the story were recast using a movie theater, would the emotional power be the same? Why or why not?

6. The metaphors of education as conversion and ascent are linked by the metaphor of light. Consider such expressions as "I see" (meaning "I understand") and "Let me give an illustration" (from the Latin *in* = in, and *lustrare* = to make bright). What other expressions about light are used metaphorically to describe intellectual comprehension?

Richard Rodriguez

Richard Rodriguez, the son of immigrants from Mexico, was born in San Francisco in 1944. He was educated at Stanford University, Columbia University, and the University of California, Berkeley, where he specialized in English literature of the Renaissance. In his book, The Hunger of Memory *(1982), he reports how his progress in the Anglo world was accompanied by estrangement from the Spanish-speaking world. We print an excerpt from the book; the title of the excerpt is our own.*

Public and Private Language

Supporters of bilingual education today imply that students like me miss a great deal by not being taught in their family's language. What they seem not to recognize is that, as a socially disadvantaged child, I considered Spanish to be a private language. What I needed to learn in school was that I had the right—and the obligation—to speak the public language of *los gringos.* The odd truth is that my first-grade classmates could have become bilingual, in the conventional sense of that word, more easily than I. Had they been taught (as upper-middle-class children are often taught early) a second language like Spanish or French, they could have regarded it simply as that: another public language. In my case such bilingualism could not have been so quickly achieved. What I did not believe was that I could speak a single public language.

Without question, it would have pleased me to hear my teachers address me in Spanish when I entered the classroom. I would have felt much less afraid. I would have trusted them and responded with ease. But I would have delayed—for how long postponed?—having to learn the language of public society. I would have evaded—and for how long could I have afforded to delay?—learning the great lesson of school, that I had a public identity.

Fortunately, my teachers were unsentimental about their responsibility. What they understood was that I needed to speak a public language. So their voices would search me out, asking me questions. Each time I'd hear them, I'd look up in surprise to see a nun's face frowning at me. I'd mumble, not really meaning to answer. The nun would persist, "Richard, stand up. Don't look at the floor. Speak up. Speak to the entire class, not just to me!" But I couldn't believe that the English language was mine to use. (In part, I did not want to believe it.) I continued to mumble. I resisted the teacher's demands. (Did I somehow suspect that once I learned public language my pleasing family life would be changed?) Silent, waiting for the bell to sound, I remained dazed, diffident, afraid.

Because I wrongly imagined that English was intrinsically a public language and Spanish an intrinsically private one, I easily noted the difference between classroom language and the language of home. At school, words were directed to a general audience of listeners. ("Boys and girls.") Words were meaningfully ordered. And the point was not self-expression alone but to make oneself understood by many others. The teacher quizzed: "Boys and girls, why do we use that word in this sentence? Could we think of a better word to use there? Would the sentence change its meaning if the words were differently arranged? And wasn't there a better way of saying much the same thing?" (I couldn't say. I wouldn't try to say.)

Three months. Five. Half a year passed. Unsmiling, ever watchful, my   5
teachers noted my silence. They began to connect my behavior with the difficult progress my older sister and brother were making. Until one Saturday morning three nuns arrived at the house to talk to our parents. Stiffly, they sat on the blue living room sofa. From the doorway of another room, spying the visitors, I noted the incongruity—the clash of two worlds, the faces and voices of school intruding upon the familiar setting of home. I overheard one voice gently wondering, "Do your children speak only Spanish at home, Mrs. Rodriguez?" While another voice added, "That Richard especially seems so timid and shy."

That Rich-heard!

With great tact the visitors continued, "Is it possible for you and your husband to encourage your children to practice their English when they are home?" Of course, my parents complied. What would they not do for their children's well-being? And how could they have questioned the Church's authority which those women represented? In an instant, they agreed to give up the language (the sounds) that had revealed and accentuated our family's closeness. The moment after the visitors left, the change was observed. *"Ahora,* speak to us *en inglés,"* my father and mother united to tell us.

At first, it seemed a kind of game. After dinner each night, the family gathered to practice "our" English. (It was still then *inglés,* a language foreign to us, so we felt drawn as strangers to it.) Laughing, we would try to define words we could not pronounce. We played with strange English sounds, often over-anglicizing our pronunciations. And we filled the smiling gaps of our sentences with familiar Spanish sounds. But that was cheating, somebody shouted. Everyone laughed. In school, meanwhile, like my brother and sister, I was required to attend a daily tutoring session. I needed a full year of special attention. I also needed my teachers to keep my attention from straying in class by calling out, *Rich-heard*—their English voices slowly prying loose my ties to my other name, its three notes. *Ri-car-do.* Most of all I needed to hear my mother and father speak to me in a moment of seriousness in broken—suddenly heartbreaking—English. The scene was inevitable: One Saturday morning I entered the kitchen where my parents were talking in Spanish. I did not realize that they were talking in Spanish however until, at the moment they saw me, I heard their voices change to speak English. Those *gringo* sounds they uttered startled me. Pushed me away. In that moment of trivial misunderstanding and profound insight, I felt my throat twisted by unsounded grief. I turned quickly and left the room. But I had no place to escape to with Spanish. (The spell was broken.) My brother and sisters were speaking English in another part of the house.

Again and again in the days following, increasingly angry, I was obliged to hear my mother and father: "Speak to us *en inglés." (Speak).* Only then did I determine to learn classroom English. Weeks after, it happened: One day in school I raised my hand to volunteer an answer. I spoke out in a loud voice. And I did not think it remarkable when the entire class understood. That day, I moved very far from the disadvantaged child I had been only days earlier. The belief, the calming assurance that I belonged in public, had at last taken hold.

Shortly after, I stopped hearing the high and loud sounds of *los grin-* 10
gos. A more and more confident speaker of English, I didn't trouble to listen to *how* strangers sounded, speaking to me. And there simply were too many English-speaking people in my day for me to hear American accents anymore. Conversations quickened. Listening to persons who sounded eccentrically pitched voices, I usually noted their sounds for an initial few seconds before I concentrated on *what* they were saying. Conversations became content-full. Transparent. Hearing someone's *tone* of voice—angry or questioning or sarcastic or happy or sad—I didn't distinguish it from the words it expressed. Sound and word were thus tightly wedded.

At the end of a day, I was often bemused, always relieved, to realize how "silent," though crowded with words, my day in public had been. (This public silence measured and quickened the change in my life.)

At last, seven years old, I came to believe what had been technically true since my birth: I was an American citizen.

But the special feeling of closeness at home was diminished by then. Gone was the desperate, urgent, intense feeling of being at home: rare was the experience of feeling myself individualized by family intimates. We remained a loving family, but one greatly changed. No longer so close; no longer bound tight by the pleasing and troubling knowledge of our public separateness. Neither my older brother nor sister rushed home after school anymore. Nor did I. When I arrived home there would often be neighborhood kids in the house. Or the house would be empty of sounds.

Following the dramatic Americanization of their children, even my parents grew more publicly confident. Especially my mother. She learned the names of all the people on our block. And she decided we needed to have a telephone installed in the house. My father continued to use the word *gringo*. But it was no longer charged with the old bitterness or distrust. (Stripped of any emotional content, the word simply became a name for those Americans not of Hispanic descent.) Hearing him, sometimes, I wasn't sure if he was pronouncing the Spanish word *gringo* or saying gringo in English.

Matching the silence I started hearing in public was a new quiet at home. The family's quiet was partly due to the fact that, as we children learned more and more English, we shared fewer and fewer words with our parents. Sentences needed to be spoken slowly when a child addressed his mother or father. (Often the parent wouldn't understand.) The child would need to repeat himself. (Still the parent misunderstood.) The young voice, frustrated, would end up saying, "Never mind"—the subject was closed. Dinners would be noisy with the clinking of knives and forks against dishes. My mother would smile softly between her remarks; my father at the other end of the table would chew and chew at his food, while he stared over the heads of his children.

My *mother!* My *father!* After English became my primary language, I   15
no longer knew what words to use in addressing my parents. The old Spanish words (those tender accents of sound) I had used earlier—*mamá* and *papá*—I couldn't use anymore. They would have been too painful reminders of how much had changed in my life. On the other hand, the words I heard neighborhood kids call *their* parents seemed equally unsatisfactory. *Mother* and *Father*; *Ma, Papa, Pa, Dad, Pop* (how I hated the all-American sound of that last word especially)—all these terms I felt were unsuitable, not really terms of address for *my* parents. As a result, I never used them at home. Whenever I'd speak to my parents, I would try to get their attention with eye contact alone. In public conversations, I'd refer to "my parents" or "my mother and father."

My mother and father, for their part, responded differently, as their children spoke to them less. She grew restless, seemed troubled and anxious at the scarcity of words exchanged in the house. It was she who would question me about my day when I came home from school. She smiled at small talk. She pried at the edges of my sentences to get me to say something more. (What?) She'd stopped her children's talking. By contrast, my father seemed reconciled to the new quiet. Though his English improved somewhat, he retired into silence. At dinner he spoke very little. One night his children and even his wife helplessly giggled at his garbled English pronunciation of the Catholic Grace before Meals. Thereafter he made his wife recite the prayer at the start of each meal, even on formal occasions, when there were guests in the house. Hers became the public voice of the family. On official business, it was she, not my father, one would usually hear on the phone or in stores, talking to strangers. His children grew so accustomed to his silence that, years later, they would speak routinely of his shyness. (My mother would often try to explain: Both his parents died when he was eight. He was raised by an uncle who treated him like little more than a menial servant. He was never encouraged to speak. He grew up alone. A man of few words.) But my father was not shy, I realized, when I'd watch him speaking Spanish with relatives. Using Spanish, he was quickly effusive. Especially when talking with other men, his voice would spark, flicker, flare alive with sounds. In Spanish, he expressed ideas and feelings he rarely revealed in English. With firm Spanish sounds, he conveyed confidence and authority English would never allow him.

The silence at home, however, was finally more than a literal silence. Fewer words passed between parent and child, but more profound was the silence that resulted from my inattention to sounds. At about the time I no longer bothered to listen with care to the sounds of English in public, I grew careless about listening to the sounds family members made when they spoke. Most of the time I heard someone speaking at home and didn't distinguish his sounds from the words people uttered in public. I didn't even pay much attention to my parents' accented and ungrammatical speech. At least not at home. Only when I was with them in public would I grow alert to their accents. Though, even then, their sounds caused me less and less concern. For I was increasingly confident of my own public identity.

I would have been happier about my public success had I not sometimes recalled what it had been like earlier, when my family had conveyed its intimacy through a set of conveniently private sounds. Sometimes in public, hearing a stranger, I'd hark back to my past. A Mexican farmworker approached me downtown to ask directions to somewhere. "Hijito . . . ?" he said. And his voice summoned deep longing. Another time, standing beside my mother in the visiting room of a Carmelite convent, before the dense screen which rendered the nuns shadowy figures, I heard several Spanish-speaking nuns—their busy, singsong overlapping voices—assure us that yes, yes, we were remembered, all our family was remembered in their prayers. (Their voices echoed faraway family sounds.) Another day, a dark-faced old woman—her hand light on my shoulder—steadied herself against me as she boarded a bus. She murmured something I couldn't quite comprehend. Her Spanish voice came near, like the face of a never-before-seen relative in the instant before I was kissed. Her voice, like so many of the Spanish voices I'd hear in public, recalled the golden age of my youth. Hearing Spanish then, I continued to be a careful, if sad, listener to sounds. Hearing a Spanish-speaking family walking behind me, I turned to look. I smiled for an instant, before my glance found the Hispanic-looking faces of strangers in the crowd going by.

✎ Topics for Critical Thinking and Writing

1. We have called this selection from Richard Rodriguez's *The Hunger of Memory* "Public and Private Language," and, indeed, the words occur often in the text. But, from reading these pages, how would you identify what is "public language" and what is "private"? What words and images would you associate with each?

2. In his first paragraph Rodriguez identifies himself as a "socially disadvantaged child." What does he mean?

3. At the end of his second paragraph Rodriguez identifies "the great lesson of school," that he "had a public identity." What does Rodriguez mean by his "public identity," and would you say that your elementary school also aided you in achieving one? Explain.

4. In his eleventh and twelfth paragraphs Rodriguez comes "to believe what had been technically true since [his] birth—he was now an "American citizen." He seems to associate this truth with a change in his family relationships. Was there a period in your life when you felt such a change in your family—with or without a change in language? If so, how would you characterize it?

Ernest van den Haag

Ernest van den Haag, born in 1914 in The Hague, Netherlands, came to the United States in 1940 and became a U.S. citizen in 1947. During a long and highly productive career, he practiced psychoanalysis and taught psychology, sociology, and law at several universities. Though he is now retired as a psychoanalyst and as a teacher, he continues to write.

In the following essay, reprinted from the National Review, *van den Haag offers several steps to help youngsters learn more—the first of which is for adults to decide that children ought to learn.*

Why Do American Kids Learn So Little?

American children learn far less in school than European and Japanese children do, although America spends far more per pupil. Why is so little education achieved for so much money? The answer may lie in a major oddity in the American creed.

Europeans have always regarded children as barbarians to be painfully civilized by schooling. Childhood is thought to be merely, or mainly, a means to adult achievement. Children are apprentice adults. Schools are to teach them what they will need, even if they cannot see the use of it: language (including grammar), arithmetic, science, history, classics. In Europe there are hardly any of those undemanding classes so frequent in the U.S., such as current events, or home economics.

Of course, the young have never liked the stern demands the schools made. They have preferred to enjoy being young—*gaudeamus igitur juvenes dum sumus*,[1] the students sang—instead of using their young years to prepare for adult careers. But the young could sing all they wanted (in the Latin they learned in school), they had little choice. Without parental support—inheritance and connections—they could never hope to make their way in the world, for which the schools served as gatekeepers. Thus, in Europe—and in Japan, which has swallowed the European idea hook, line, and sinker—the power of the older generation is used to make children spend most of their time doing schoolwork. Occasionally they have rebelled, but, on the whole, they have submitted, become literate, and gone on their way.

In America, however, youth is seen as an end in itself, never merely a means to adult achievement. Children rarely are expected to work at anything they don't enjoy. Teachers are expected to "motivate" their students and to make learning a pleasure, even if this means going easy on unavoidably tedious stretches. The young themselves tend to see adulthood as a hard-to-avoid postscript, almost a decline. Many adults nostalgically agree.

Parents seldom can make unwilling children do homework, and   5
teachers wisely don't ask for what they can't get. To demand vexatious schoolwork of children seems almost immoral in the American context.

Unlike Europeans, Americans do not expect their children to continue in their own social position: they regard their children as the hope of the future. Far from imposing the civilization of the past, education is to help the young to "find themselves," to unfold their innate creativity. The young

---

[1]*gaudeamus igitur juvenes dum sumus,* let us be joyful while we are young (Latin, from a medieval university song).

will do better if less encumbered by the past. Margaret Mead even told parents that they must learn from the young, who "have the knowledge."

To most Americans the future always has been more real than the past. This notion makes teaching hard, for teaching requires, at least temporarily, submission to the authority of ancient ideas, and of teachers who transmit them. All learning initially must rest on the authority of the past; after all, the past is all that can be learned.

Pupils must first accept the teachers' authority. Teachers cannot explain to an eight-year-old why words are spelled as they are, or why two and two make four, not five. It is only after much material has been absorbed by rote—children fortunately like learning by rote, although progressive teachers don't like to let them—that students can begin to examine critically and usefully what they are learning. If the authority of the older generation is weak, little knowledge will be absorbed.

We largely let students elect the classes they prefer, assuming that they know enough to fashion their own curriculum, although they cannot yet have learned how to evaluate the importance of various kinds of knowledge. Of course, they elect the easy classes, sometimes of dubious value. They get the same credit toward a diploma for easy classes as they get for harder ones, the same for Contemporary Drama as for Advanced Algebra.

Via Media[2]

There must be a reasonable middle way between a joyous childhood and an exclusively instrumental use of it, a way of combining the civilizing influence of science, history, and literature with the enjoyment of youth. The young must learn to learn as well as to play. Some even may enjoy learning once they try it. Is there anything that can be done to bring about the necessary changes? Consider some beginning steps.   10

Public schools currently have a monopoly on tax money, which they jealously guard, and because public schools do not compete with one another—pupils are assigned—each public school is in a near monopoly position. The usual effects of monopoly occur: shoddy products at high cost to the involuntary purchasers (taxpayers). A voucher system, entitling parents to choose any public school in the state for their children—and, later on, any approved private school as well—would introduce some competition and might eliminate the worst effects of the monopoly. Schools never should be subsidized; *schooling* should be, by granting vouchers to parents.

Other monopoly features should be dismantled as well. Currently nobody, however capable, is allowed to teach without first attending courses in education. This functions as a barrier to entry, strengthening the entrenched monopoly defended by unions. Private schools hire teachers

[2]*Via Media*, the middle way (Latin).

able to teach their subjects well, in spite (or because) of not having attended a school of education. Usually these teachers are much less well paid than public-school teachers; yet their students, on the average, learn more according to all available tests.

In other countries children spend more time in school. It has been suggested therefore that the school day should be lengthened and summer vacations shortened. I doubt that this will help much. It is not that children spend too little time in school; rather, they learn too little in the time they spend. More homework might indeed help, if only marginally.

What ails American schools is not lack of money. We spend much more per pupil (adjusted for inflation) than we did in the past, and far more than other countries do. But the returns in learning are remarkably low. Where does the money go? Far too much goes into non-teaching activities. There is far too much administration, as can be shown irrefutably by comparing the ratio of teaching to non-teaching personnel in private and public schools. I do not claim that these administrators, counselors, et al. do not work hard. Rather, the work doesn't contribute much to the education of children. They keep each other busy.

Then there is the quality of the teachers themselves. Children cannot   15
learn much from teachers who do not command basic skills. Scandalously few do.

Teachers have some reasonable complaints. They get many children from homes to which learning is as alien as discipline. Still, most children can learn to spell and to read, can learn elementary grammar and arithmetic—if teachers are allowed to impose the necessary discipline, as they are not now. There are some things that can be learned by doing—in fact, only by doing: carefulness, punctuality, manners, discipline are among them. Anybody can acquire these; but schools make little effort to help. They do not feel they are charged with helping to forge the character of students, many of whom graduate functionally illiterate, with slovenly work habits and manners.

Minimum requirements for a high-school diploma (to which each school should be able to add its own) should be imposed by every state, fulfilled only by passing examinations, including essay tests, graded by teachers from schools other than the one attended by the student.

Public schools also should be allowed to expel students unwilling to learn (or to submit to discipline), as private schools are now. Contrary to much opinion, not only would the schools be better off, the expelled students themselves are likely to do better by not being kept when schooling is unproductive for them.

We should stop assuming complacently that our children are being educated just because we have many schools with lots of teachers and myriad administrators. Currently they learn very little, not because they are stupid, but because they are taught very little. It is easier that way for everybody, the kids, the teachers, the parents. But we can't afford it any longer. If we want to avoid a rapid decline of America we must make sure that our children are educated rather than just entertained and kept in school. This will require more changes than I proposed. But we have to begin somewhere.

✎ Topics for Critical Thinking and Writing

1. Do you agree with van den Haag (paragraph 2) that courses in current events and home economics are necessarily "undemanding"? Explain.
2. In paragraph 4 van den Haag speaks of "unavoidably tedious stretches," and in paragraph 5 of "vexatious schoolwork." Do you agree that there must be such things? If so, how would you as a teacher proceed? Or do you assume that material is "tedious" and "vexatious" only because it is not properly taught? If so, give an example of how a skilled teacher presented material that might otherwise have been tedious or vexatious and made it exciting or enjoyable.
3. In paragraph 6 van den Haag quotes what he implies is a wrong-headed statement by Margaret Mead, to the effect that parents must learn from their young, who "have the knowledge." He does not cite his source, but do you think that he has said enough to indicate that the idea is preposterous? Or on the other hand do you think that the young do indeed have certain kinds of "knowledge" and that their parents can learn some things from them? Explain.
4. Do you agree with the remarks in paragraph 8 about authority and rote learning? If not, explain your position.
5. In paragraph 9 van den Haag dismisses the idea of youngsters electing courses. Drawing on your own experience in secondary school, evaluate his reason.
6. As you look back on your elementary or high school education, what do you think were the greatest strengths? The greatest weaknesses? (You may want to compare one kind of schooling with the other.)
7. Van den Haag implies that many teachers "do not command basic skills." Drawing on your experience, do you agree? (If you write about particular teachers, do not use their real names.)
8. In paragraph 16 van den Haag suggests that schools should teach "carefulness, punctuality, manners, discipline"—in short, aspects of character. Do you agree? Did some or all of your teachers teach any or all of these things? Explain.
9. Consider the strategies that van den Haag uses in his final paragraph. Do you think it provides a good ending for this argumentative essay? Explain.

Maya Angelou

Maya Angelou, born in St. Louis, Missouri, in 1938, grew up in Arkansas and California. She studied music, dance, and drama (she had a role in the televised version of Alex Haley's Roots), and she is now a professor of American studies at Wake Forest University. She has also worked as a cook, streetcar conductor, and waitress. In addition to writing books of poetry, she has written five autobiographical volumes.

*   "Graduation" (editors' title) comes from her first autobiography,* I Know Why the Caged Bird Sings *(1969).*

Graduation

The children in Stamps trembled visibly with anticipation. Some adults were excited too, but to be certain the whole young population had come down with graduation epidemic. Large classes were graduating from both the grammar school and the high school. Even those who were years removed from their own day of glorious release were anxious to help with preparations as a kind of dry run. The junior students who were moving into the vacating classes' chairs were tradition-bound to show their talents for leadership and management. They strutted through the school and around the campus exerting pressure on the lower grades. Their authority was so new that occasionally if they pressed a little too hard it had to be overlooked. After all, next term was coming, and it never hurt a sixth grader to have a play sister in the eighth grade, or a tenth-year student to be able to call a twelfth grader Bubba. So all was endured in a spirit of shared understanding. But the graduating classes themselves were the nobility. Like travelers with exotic destinations on their minds, the graduates were remarkably forgetful. They came to school without their books, or tablets or even pencils. Volunteers fell over themselves to secure replacements for the missing equipment. When accepted, the willing workers might or might not be thanked, and it was of no importance to the pregraduation rites. Even teachers were respectful of the now quiet and aging seniors, and tended to speak to them, if not as equals, as beings only slightly lower than themselves. After tests were returned and grades given, the student body, which acted like an extended family, knew who did well, who excelled, and what piteous ones had failed.

Unlike the white high school, Lafayette County Training School distinguished itself by having neither lawn, nor hedges, nor tennis court, nor climbing ivy. Its two buildings (main classrooms, the grade school and home economics) were set on a dirt hill with no fence to limit either its boundaries or those of bordering farms. There was a large expanse to the left of the school which was used alternately as a baseball diamond or a basketball court. Rusty hoops on the swaying poles represented the permanent recreational equipment, although bats and balls could be borrowed from the P.E. teacher if the borrower was qualified and if the diamond wasn't occupied.

Over this rocky area relieved by a few shady tall persimmon trees the graduating class walked. The girls often held hands and no longer bothered to speak to the lower students. There was a sadness about them, as if this old world was not their home and they were bound for higher ground. The boys, on the other hand, had become more friendly, more outgoing. A decided change from the closed attitude they projected while studying for finals. Now they seemed not ready to give up the old school, the familiar paths and classrooms. Only a small percentage would be continuing on to college—one of the South's A & M (agricultural and mechanical) schools, which trained Negro youths to be carpenters, farmers, handymen, masons, maids, cooks and baby nurses. Their future rode heavily on their shoulders, and blinded them to the collective joy that had pervaded the lives of the boys and girls in the grammar school graduating class.

Parents who could afford it had ordered new shoes and ready-made clothes for themselves from Sears and Roebuck or Montgomery Ward. They also engaged the best seamstresses to make the floating graduating dresses and to cut down secondhand pants which would be pressed to a military slickness for the important event.

Oh, it was important, all right. Whitefolks would attend the ceremony, and two or three would speak of God and home, and the Southern way of life, and Mrs. Parsons, the principal's wife, would play the graduation march while the lower-grade graduates paraded down the aisles and took their seats below the platform. The high school seniors would wait in empty classrooms to make their dramatic entrance.

5

In the Store I was the person of the moment. The birthday girl. The center. Bailey had graduated the year before, although to do so he had had to forfeit all pleasures to make up for his time lost in Baton Rouge.

My class was wearing butter-yellow piqué dresses, and Momma launched out on mine. She smocked the yoke into tiny crisscrossing puckers, then shirred the rest of the bodice. Her dark fingers ducked in and out of the lemony cloth as she embroidered raised daisies around the hem. Before she considered herself finished she had added a crocheted cuff on the puff sleeves, and a pointy crocheted collar.

I was going to be lovely. A walking model of all the various styles of fine hand sewing and it didn't worry me that I was only twelve years old and merely graduating from the eighth grade. Besides, many teachers in Arkansas Negro schools had only that diploma and were licensed to impart wisdom.

The days had become longer and more noticeable. The faded beige of former times had been replaced with strong and sure colors. I began to see my classmates' clothes, their skin tones, and the dust that waved off pussy willows. Clouds that lazed across the sky were objects of great concern to

me. Their shiftier shapes might have held a message that in my new happiness and with a little bit of time I'd soon decipher. During that period I
looked at the arch of heaven so religiously my neck kept a steady ache. I
had taken to smiling more often, and my jaws hurt from the unaccustomed activity. Between the two physical sore spots, I suppose I could
have been uncomfortable, but that was not the case. As a member of the
winning team (the graduating class of 1940) I had outdistanced unpleasant sensations by miles. I was headed for the freedom of open fields.

Youth and social approval allied themselves with me and we tram-   10
meled memories of slights and insults. The wind of our swift passage
remodeled my features. Lost tears were pounded to mud and then to dust.
Years of withdrawal were brushed aside and left behind, as hanging ropes
of parasitic moss.

My work alone had awarded me a top place and I was going to be one
of the first called in the graduating ceremonies. On the classroom blackboard, as well as on the bulletin board in the auditorium, there were blue
stars and white stars and red stars. No absences, no tardinesses, and my
academic work was among the best of the year. I could say the preamble
to the Constitution even faster than Bailey. We timed ourselves often:
"WethepeopleoftheUnitedStatesinordertoformamoreperfectunion . . ."   I
had memorized the Presidents of the United States from Washington to
Roosevelt in chronological as well as alphabetical order.

My hair pleased me too. Gradually the black mass had lengthened
and thickened, so that it kept at last to its braided pattern, and I didn't
have to yank my scalp off when I tried to comb it.

Louise and I had rehearsed the exercises until we tired out ourselves.
Henry Reed was class valedictorian. He was a small, very black boy with
hooded eyes, a long, broad nose and an oddly shaped head. I had admired
him for years because each term he and I vied for the best grades in our
class. Most often he bested me, but instead of being disappointed I was
pleased that we shared top places between us. Like many Southern Black
children, he lived with his grandmother, who was as strict as Momma and
as kind as she knew how to be. He was courteous, respectful and soft-spo-
ken to elders, but on the playground he chose to play the roughest games.
I admired him. Anyone I reckoned, sufficiently afraid or sufficiently dull
could be polite. But to be able to operate at a top level with both adults and
children was admirable.

His valedictory speech was entitled "To Be or Not To Be." The rigid
tenth-grade teacher helped him to write it. He'd been working on the dramatic stresses for months.

The weeks until graduation were filled with heady activities. A group   15
of small children were to be presented in a play about buttercups and
daisies and bunny rabbits. They could be heard throughout the building
practicing their hops and their little songs that sounded like silver bells.
The older girls (non-graduates, of course) were assigned the task of making refreshments for the night's festivities. A tangy scent of ginger, cinna-

mon, nutmeg and chocolate wafted around the home economics building as the budding cooks made samples for themselves and their teachers.

In every corner of the workshop, axes and saws split fresh timber as the woodshop boys made sets and stage scenery. Only the graduates were left out of the general bustle. We were free to sit in the library at the back of the building or look in quite detachedly, naturally, on the measures being taken for our event.

Even the minister preached on graduation the Sunday before. His subject was, "Let your light so shine that men will see your good works and praise your Father, Who is in Heaven." Although the sermon was purported to be addresses to us, he used the occasion to speak to back-sliders, gamblers, and general ne'er-do-wells. But since he had called our names at the beginning of the service we were mollified.

Among Negroes the tradition was to give presents to children going only from one grade to another. How much more important this was when the person was graduating at the top of the class. Uncle Willie and Momma had sent away for a Mickey Mouse watch like Bailey's. Louise gave me four embroidered handkerchiefs. (I gave her three crocheted doilies.) Mrs. Sneed, the minister's wife, made me an underskirt to wear for graduation, and near-ly every customer gave me a nickel or maybe even a dime with the instruc-tion "Keep on moving to higher ground," or some such encouragement.

Amazingly the great day finally dawned and I was out of bed before I knew it. I threw open the back door to see it more clearly, but Momma said, "Sister, come away from that door and put your robe on."

I hoped the memory of that morning would never leave me. Sunlight was itself still young, and the day had none of the insistence maturity would bring it in a few hours. In my robe and barefoot in the backyard, under cover of going to see about my new beans, I gave myself up to the gentle warmth and thanked God that no matter what evil I had done in my life He had allowed me to live to see this day. Somewhere in my fatal-ism I had expected to die, accidentally, and never have the chance to walk up the stairs in the auditorium and gracefully receive my hard-earned diploma. Out of God's merciful bosom I had won reprieve. 20

Bailey came out in his robe and gave me a box wrapped in Christmas paper. He said he had saved his money for months to pay for it. It felt like a box of chocolates, but I knew Bailey wouldn't save money to buy candy when we had all we could want under our noses.

He was as proud of the gift as I. It was a soft-leather-bound copy of a collection of poems by Edgar Allan Poe, or, as Bailey and I called him, "Eap." I turned to "Annabel Lee" and we walked up and down the garden rows, the cool dirt between our toes, reciting the beautifully sad lines.

Momma made a Sunday breakfast although it was only Friday. After we finished the blessing, I opened my eyes to find the watch on my plate. It was a dream of a day. Everything went smoothly and to my credit. I did-n't have to be reminded or scolded for anything. Near evening I was too jittery to attend to chores, so Bailey volunteered to do all before his bath.

Days before, we had made a sign for the Store and as we turned out the lights Momma hung the cardboard over the doorknob. It read clearly: CLOSED. GRADUATION.

My dress fitted perfectly and everyone said that I looked like a sun-   25 beam in it. On the hill, going toward the school, Bailey walked behind with Uncle Willie, who muttered, "Go on, Ju." He wanted him to walk ahead with us because it embarrassed him to have to walk so slowly. Bailey said he'd let the ladies walk together, and the men would bring up the rear. We all laughed, nicely.

Little children dashed by out of the dark like fireflies. Their crepe-paper dresses and butterfly wings were not made for running and we heard more than one rip, dryly, and the regretful "uh uh" that followed.

The school blazed without gaiety. The windows seemed cold and unfriendly from the lower hill. A sense of ill-fated timing crept over me, and if Momma hadn't reached for my hand I would have drifted back to Bailey and Uncle Willie, and possibly beyond. She made a few slow jokes about my feet getting cold, and tugged me along to the now-strange building.

Around the front steps, assurance came back. There were my fellow "greats," the graduating class. Hair brushed back, legs oiled, new dresses and pressed pleats, fresh pocket handkerchiefs and little hand-bags, all homesewn. Oh, we were up to snuff, all right. I joined my comrades and didn't even see my family go in to find seats in the crowded auditorium.

The school band struck up a march and all classes filed in as had been rehearsed. We stood in front of our seats, as assigned, and on a signal from the choir director, we sat. No sooner had this been accomplished than the band started to play the national anthem. We rose again and sang the song, after which we recited the pledge of allegiance. We remained standing for a brief minute before the choir director and the principal signaled to us, rather desperately I thought, to take our seats. The command was so unusual that our carefully rehearsed and smooth-running machine was thrown off. For a full minute we fumbled for our chairs and bumped into each other awkwardly. Habits change or solidify under pressure, so in our state of nervous tension we had been ready to follow our usual assembly pattern: the American National Anthem, then the pledge of allegiance, then the song every Black person I knew called the Negro National Anthem. All done in the same key, with the same passion and most often standing on the same foot.

Finding my seat at last, I was overcome with a presentiment of worse   30 things to come. Something unrehearsed, unplanned, was going to happen, and we were going to be made to look bad. I distinctly remember being explicit in the choice of pronoun. It was "we," the graduating class, the unit, that concerned me then.

The principal welcomed "parents and friends" and asked the Baptist minister to lead us in prayer. His invocation was brief and punchy, and for a second I thought we were getting back on the high road to right action. When the principal came back to the dais, however, his voice had changed. Sounds always affected me profoundly and the principal's voice was one of my favorites. During assembly it melted and lowed weakly into the audience. It had not been in my plan to listen to him, but my curiosity was piqued and I straightened up to give him my attention.

He was talking about Booker T. Washington, our "late great leader," who said we can be as close as the fingers on the hand, etc. . . . Then he said a few vague things about friendship and the friendship of kindly people to those less fortunate than themselves. With that his voice near-ly faded, thin, away. Like a river diminishing to a stream and then to a trickle. But he cleared his throat and said, "Our speaker tonight, who is also our friend, came from Texarkana to deliver the commencement address, but due to the irregularity of the train schedule, he's going to, as they say, 'speak and run.'" He said that we understood and wanted the man to know that we were most grateful for the time he was able to give us and then something about how we were willing always to adjust to another's program, and without more ado—"I give you Mr. Edward Donleavy."

Not one but two white men came through the door offstage. The short-er one walked to the speaker's platform, and the tall one moved over to the center seat and sat down. But that was our principal's seat, and already occupied. The dislodged gentleman bounced around for a long breath or two before the Baptist minister gave him his chair, then with more dignity than the situation deserved, the minister walked off the stage.

Donleavy looked at the audience once (on reflection, I'm sure that he wanted only to reassure himself that we were really there), adjusted his glasses and began to read from a sheaf of papers.

He was glad "to be here and to see the work going on just as it was in   35
the other schools."

At the first "Amen" from the audience I willed the offender to imme-diate death by choking on the word. But Amen's and Yes, sir's began to fall around the room like rain through a ragged umbrella.

He told us of the wonderful changes we children in Stamps had in store. The Central School (naturally, the white school was Central) had already been granted improvements that would be in use in the fall. A well-known artist was coming from Little Rock to teach art to them. They were going to have the newest microscopes and chemistry equipment for their laboratory. Mr. Donleavy didn't leave us long in the dark over who made these improvements available to Central High. Nor were we to be ignored in the general betterment scheme he had in mind.

He said that he had pointed out to people at a very high level that one of the first-line football tacklers at Arkansas Agricultural and Mechanical College had graduated from good old Lafayette County Training School. Here fewer Amen's were heard. Those few that did break through lay dully in the air with the heaviness of habit.

He went on to praise us. He went on to say how he had bragged that "one of the best basketball players at Fisk sank his first ball right here at Lafayette County Training School."

The white kids were going to have a chance to become Galileos and   40
Madame Curies and Edisons and Gauguins, and our boys (the girls weren't even in on it) would try to be Jesse Owenses and Joe Louises.

Owens and the Brown Bomber were great heroes in our world, but what school official in the white-goddom of Little Rock had the right to decide that those two men must be our only heroes? Who decided that for Henry Reed to become a scientist he had to work like George Washington Carver, as a bootblack, to buy a lousy microscope? Bailey was obviously always going to be too small to be an athlete, so which concrete angel glued to what county seat had decided that if my brother wanted to become a lawyer he had to first pay penance for his skin by picking cotton and hoeing corn and studying correspondence books at night for twenty years?

The man's dead words fell like bricks around the auditorium and too many settled in my belly. Constrained by hard-learned manners I couldn't look behind me, but to my left and right the proud graduating class of 1940 had dropped their heads. Every girl in my row had found something new to do with her handkerchief. Some folded the tiny squares into love knots, some into triangles, but most were wadding them, then pressing them flat on their yellow laps.

On the dais, the ancient tragedy was being replayed. Professor Parsons sat, a sculptor's reject, rigid. His large, heavy body seemed devoid of will or willingness, and his eyes said he was no longer with us. The other teachers examined the flag (which was draped stage right) or their notes, or the windows which opened on our now-famous playing diamond.

Graduation, the hush-hush magic time of frills and gifts and congratulations and diplomas, was finished for me before my name was called. The accomplishment was nothing. The meticulous maps, drawn in three colors of ink, learning and spelling decasyllabic words, memorizing the whole of *The Rape of Lucrece*—it was nothing. Donleavy had exposed us.

We were maids and farmers, handymen and washerwomen, and any-   45
thing higher that we aspired to was farcical and presumptuous. Then I wished that Gabriel Prosser and Nat Turner had killed all white-folks in their beds and that Abraham Lincoln had been assassinated before the signing of the Emancipation Proclamation, and that Harriet Tubman had been killed by that blow on her head and Christopher Columbus had drowned in the *Santa Maria*.

It was awful to be Negro and have no control over my life. It was brutal to be young and already trained to sit quietly and listen to charges brought against my color and no chance of defense. We should all be dead. I thought I should like to see us all dead, one on top of the other. A pyramid of flesh with the whitefolks on the bottom, as the broad base, then the Indians with their silly tomahawks and teepees and wigwams and treaties, the Negroes with their mops and recipes and cotton sacks and spirituals sticking out of their mouths. The Dutch children should all stumble in their wooden shoes and break their necks. The French should choke to death on the Louisiana Purchase (1803) while silkworms ate all the Chinese with their stupid pigtails. As a species, we were an abomination. All of us.

Donleavy was running for election, and assured our parents that if he won we could count on having the only colored paved playing field in that part of Arkansas. Also—he never looked up to acknowledge the grunts of acceptance—also, we were bound to get some new equipment for the home economics building and the workshop.

He finished, and since there was no need to give any more than the most perfunctory thank-you's, he nodded to the men on the stage, and the tall white man who was never introduced joined him at the door. They left with the attitude that now they were off to something really important. (The graduation ceremonies at Lafayette County Training School had been a mere preliminary.)

The ugliness they left was palpable. An uninvited guest who wouldn't leave. The choir was summoned and sang a modern arrangement of "Onward, Christian Soldiers," with new words pertaining to graduates seeking their place in the world. But it didn't work. Elouise, the daughter of the Baptist minister, recited "Invictus," and I could have cried at the impertinence of "I am the master of my fate, I am the captain of my soul."

My name had lost its ring of familiarity and I had to be nudged to go and receive my diploma. All my preparations had fled. I neither marched up to the stage like a conquering Amazon, nor did I look in the audience for Bailey's nod of approval. Marguerite Johnson, I heard the name again, my honors were read, there were noises in the audience of appreciation, and I took my place on the stage as rehearsed. 50

I thought about colors I hated: ecru, puce, lavender, beige and black.

There was shuffling and rustling around me, then Henry Reed was giving his valedictory address, "To Be or Not to Be." Hadn't he heard the whitefolks? We couldn't *be,* so the question was a waste of time. Henry's voice came out clear and strong. I feared to look at him. Hadn't he got the message? There was no "nobler in the mind" for Negroes because the world didn't think we had minds, and they let us know it. "Outrageous fortune"? Now, that was a joke. When the ceremony was over I had to tell Henry Reed some things. That is, if I still cared. Not "rub," Henry, "erase." "Ah, there's the erase." Us.

Henry had been a good student in elocution. His voice rose on tides of promise and fell on waves of warnings. The English teacher had helped him to create a sermon winging through Hamlet's soliloquy. To be a man, a doer, a builder, a leader, or to be a tool, an unfunny joke, a crusher of funky toadstools. I marveled that Henry could go through with the speech as if we had a choice.

I had been listening and silently rebutting each sentence with my eyes closed; then there was a hush, which in an audience warns that something unplanned is happening. I looked up and saw Henry Reed, the conservative, the proper, the A student, turn his back to the audience and turn to us (the proud graduating class of 1940) and sing, nearly speaking,

> *Lift ev'ry voice and sing*
> *Till earth and heaven ring*
> *Ring with the harmonies of Liberty . . .*

It was the poem written by James Weldon Johnson. It was the music   55
composed by J. Rosamond Johnson. It was the Negro National Anthem. Out of habit we were singing it.

Our mothers and fathers stood in the dark hall and joined the hymn of encouragement. A kindergarten teacher led the small children onto the stage and the buttercups and daisies and bunny rabbits marked time and tried to follow:

> *Stony the road we trod*
> *Bitter the chastening rod*
> *Felt in the days when hope, unborn, had died.*
> *Yet with a steady beat*
> *Have not our weary feet*
> *Come to the place for which our fathers sighed?*

Every child I knew had learned that song with his ABC's and along with "Jesus Loves Me This I Know." But I personally had never heard it before. Never heard the words, despite the thousands of times I had sung them. Never thought they had anything to do with me.

On the other hand, the words of Patrick Henry had made such an impression on me that I had been able to stretch myself tall and trembling and say, "I know not what course others may take, but as for me, give me liberty or give me death."

And now I heard, really for the first time:

> *We have come over a way that with tears has been watered,*
> *We have come, treading our path through the blood of the*
> *slaughtered.*

While echoes of the song shivered in the air, Henry Reed bowed his   60
head, said "Thank you," and returned to his place in the line. The tears that slipped down many faces were not wiped away in shame.

We were on top again. As always, again. We survived. The depths had been icy and dark, but now a bright sun spoke to our souls. I was no longer simply a member of the proud graduating class of 1940; I was a proud member of the wonderful, beautiful Negro race.

Oh, Black known and unknown poets, how often have your auctioned pains sustained us? Who will compute the lonely nights made less lonely by your songs, or the empty pots made less tragic by your tales?

If we were a people much given to revealing secrets, we might raise monuments and sacrifice to the memories of our poets, but slavery cured us of that weakness. It may be enough, however, to have it said that we survive in exact relationship to the dedication of our poets (include preachers, musicians and blues singers).

✎ Topics for Critical Thinking and Writing

1. In paragraph 1 notice such overstatements as "glorious release," "the graduating classes themselves were the nobility," and "exotic destinations." Find further examples in the next few pages. What do you think is the function of this diction?
2. Characterize the writer as you perceive her through paragraph 28. Support your characterization with references to specific passages. Next, characterize her in paragraph 46, which begins "It was awful to be Negro." Next, characterize her on the basis of the entire essay. Finally, in a sentence, try to describe the change, telling the main attitudes or moods that she goes through.
3. How would you define *poets* as Angelou uses the word in the last sentence?

Neil Postman

Neil Postman, born in New York City in 1931, has taught in elementary and secondary schools and is now a professor of communication arts and sciences at New York University.

Order in the Classroom

William O'Connor, who is unknown to me in a personal way, was once a member of the Boston School Committee, in which capacity he made the following remark: "We have no inferior education in our schools. What we have been getting is an inferior type of student."

The remark is easy to ridicule, and I have had some fun with it in the past. But there are a couple of senses in which it is perfectly sound.

In the first place, a classroom is a technique for the achievement of certain kinds of learning. It is a workable technique provided that both the teacher and the student have the skill and, particularly, the attitudes that are fundamental to it. Among these, from the student's point of view, are tolerance for delayed gratification, a certain measure of respect for and fear of authority, and a willingness to accommodate one's individual desires to the interests of group cohesion and purpose. These attitudes cannot be taught easily in school because they are a necessary component of the teaching situation itself. The problem is not unlike trying to find out how to spell a word by looking it up in the dictionary. If you do not know how a word is spelled, it is hard to look it up. In the same way, little can be taught in school unless these attitudes are present. And if they are not, to teach them is difficult.

Obviously, such attitudes must be learned during the years before a child starts school; that is, in the home. This is the real meaning of the phrase "preschool education." If a child is not made ready at home for the classroom experience, he or she usually cannot benefit from any normal school program. Just as important, the school is defenseless against such a child, who, typically, is a source of disorder in a situation that requires order. I raise this issue because education reform is impossible without order in the classroom. Without the attitudes that lead to order, the classroom is an entirely impotent technique. Therefore, one possible translation of Mr. O'Connor's remark is, "We have a useful technique for educating youth but too many of them have not been provided at home with the attitudes necessary for the technique to work."

In still another way Mr. O'Connor's remark makes plain sense. The   5
electronic media, with their emphasis on visual imagery, immediacy, non-linearity, and fragmentation, do not give support to the attitudes that are fundamental to the classroom; that is, Mr. O'Connor's remark can be translated as, "We would not have an inferior education if it were the nineteenth century. Our problem is that we have been getting students who are products of the twentieth century." But there is nothing nonsensical about this, either. The nineteenth century had much to recommend it, and we certainly may be permitted to allow it to exert an influence on the twentieth. The classroom is a nineteenth-century invention, and we ought to prize what it has to offer. It is one of the few social organizations left to us in which sequence, social order, hierarchy, continuity, and deferred pleasure are important.

The problem of disorder in the classroom is created largely by two factors: a dissolving family structure, out of which come youngsters who are "unfit" for the presuppositions of a classroom; and a radically altered information environment, which undermines the foundation of school. The question, then, is, What should be done about the increasing tendency toward disorder in the classroom?

Liberal reformers, such as Kenneth Keniston, have answers, of a sort. Keniston argues that economic reforms should be made so that the integrity and authority of the family can be restored. He believes that poverty is the main cause of family dissolution, and that by improving the economic situation of families, we may kindle a sense of order and aspiration in the lives of children. Some of the reforms he suggests in his book *All Our Children* seem practical, although they are long-range and offer no immediate response to the problem of present disorder. Some

Utopians, such as Ivan Illich, have offered other solutions; for example, dissolving the schools altogether, or so completely restructuring the school environment that its traditional assumptions are rendered irrelevant. To paraphrase Karl Kraus's epigram about psychoanalysis, these proposals are the Utopian disease of which they consider themselves the cure.

One of the best answers comes from Dr. Howard Hurwitz, who is neither a liberal reformer nor a Utopian. It is a good solution, I believe, because it tries to respond to the needs not only of children who are unprepared for school because of parental failure but of children of all backgrounds who are being made strangers to the assumptions of school by the biases of the electronic media.

During the eleven years Dr. Hurwitz was principal at Long Island City High School, the average number of suspensions each year was three, while in many New York City high schools the average runs close to one hundred. Also, during his tenure, not one instance of an assault on a teacher was reported, and daily student attendance averaged better than 90 percent, which in the context of the New York City school scene represents a riot of devotion.

Although I consider some of Dr. Hurwitz's curriculum ideas uninspired and even wrong-headed, he understands a few things of overriding importance that many educators of more expansive imagination do not. The first is that educators must devote at least as much attention to the immediate consequences of disorder as to its abstract causes. Whatever the causes of disorder and alienation, the consequences are severe and, if not curbed, result in making the school impotent. At the risk of becoming a symbol of reaction, Hurwitz ran "a tight ship." He holds to the belief, for example, that a child's right to an education is terminated at the point where the child interferes with the right of other children to have one.

Dr. Hurwitz also understands that disorder expands proportionately to the tolerance for it, and that children of all kinds of home backgrounds can learn, in varying degrees, to function in situations where disorder is not tolerated at all. He does not believe that it is inevitably or only the children of the poor who are disorderly. In spite of what the "revisionist" education historians may say, poor people still regard school as an avenue of social and economic advancement for their children, and do not object in the least to its being an orderly and structured experience.

All this adds up to the common sense view that the school ought not to accommodate itself to disorder, or to the biases of other communication systems. The children of the poor are likely to continue to be with us. Some parents will fail to assume competent responsibility for the preschool education of their children. The media will increase the intensity of their fragmenting influence. Educators must live with these facts. But Dr. Hurwitz believes that as a technique for learning, the classroom can work if students are oriented toward its assumptions, not the other way around. William O'Connor, wherever he is, would probably agree. And so do I. The school is not an extension of the street, the movie theater, a rock concert, or a playground. And it is certainly not an extension of the psychiatric clinic. It is a special environment that requires the enforcement of certain traditional rules of controlled group interaction. The school may be the only remaining public situation in which such rules have any meaning, and it would be a grave mistake to change those rules because some children find them hard or cannot function within them. Children who cannot ought to be removed from the environment in the interests of those who can.

Wholesale suspensions, however, are a symptom of disorder, not a cure for it. And what makes Hurwitz's school noteworthy is the small number of suspensions that have been necessary. This is not the result of his having "good" students or "bad" students. It is the result of his having created an unambiguous, rigorous, and serious attitude—a nineteenth-century attitude, if you will—toward what constitutes acceptable school behavior. In other words, Dr. Hurwitz's school turns out to be a place where children of all backgrounds—fit and unfit—can function, or can learn to function, and where the biases of our information environment are emphatically opposed.

At this point I should like to leave the particulars of Dr. Hurwitz's solution and, retaining their spirit, indicate some particulars of my own.

Let us start, for instance, with the idea of a dress code. A dress code   15
signifies that school is a special place in which special kinds of behavior are required. The way one dresses is an indication of an attitude toward a situation. And the way one is *expected* to dress indicates what that attitude ought to be. You would not wear dungarees and a T-shirt that says "Feel Me" when attending a church wedding. That would be considered an outrage against the tone and meaning of the situation. The school has every right and reason, I believe, to expect the same sort of consideration.

Those who are inclined to think this is a superficial point are probably forgetting that symbols not only reflect our feelings but to some extent create them. One's kneeling in church, for example, reflects a sense of reverence but also engenders reverence. If we want school to *feel* like a special place, we can find no better way to begin than by requiring students to dress in a manner befitting the seriousness of the enterprise and the institution. I should include teachers in this requirement. I know of one high school in which the principal has put forward a dress code of sorts for teachers. (He has not, apparently, had the courage to propose one for the students.) For males the requirement is merely a jacket and tie. One of his teachers bitterly complained to me that such a regulation infringed upon his civil rights. And yet, this teacher will accept without complaint the same regulation when it is enforced by an elegant restaurant. His complaint and his acquiescence tell a great deal about how he values schools and how he values restaurants.

I do not have in mind, for students, uniforms of the type sometimes worn in parochial schools. I am referring here to some reasonable standard of dress which would mark school as a place of dignity and seriousness. And I might add that I do not believe for one moment the argument that poor people would be unable to clothe their children properly if such a code were in force. Furthermore, I do not believe that poor people have advanced that argument. It is an argument that middle-class education critics have made on behalf of the poor.

Another argument advanced in behalf of the poor and oppressed is the students' right to their own language. I have never heard this argument come from parents whose children are not competent to use Standard English. It is an argument, once again, put forward by "liberal" education critics whose children *are* competent in Standard English but who in some curious way wish to express their solidarity with and charity for those who are less capable. It is a case of pure condescension, and I do not think teachers should be taken in by it. Like the mode of dress, the mode of language in school ought to be relatively formal and exemplary, and therefore markedly different from the custom in less rigorous places. It is particularly important that teachers should avoid trying to win their students' affection by adopting the language of youth. Such teachers frequently win only the contempt of their students, who sense that the language of teachers and the language of students ought to be different; that is to say, the world of adults is different from the world of children.

In this connection, it is worth saying that the modern conception of childhood is a product of the sixteenth century, as Philippe Aries has documented in his *The Centuries of Childhood*. Prior to that century, children as young as six and seven were treated in all important respects as if they were adults. Their language, their dress, their legal status, their responsibilities, their labor, were much the same as those of adults. The concept of childhood as an identifiable stage in human growth began to develop in the sixteenth century and has continued into our own times. However, with the emergence of electronic media of communication, a reversal of this trend seems to be taking place. In a culture in which the distribution of information is almost wholly undifferentiated, age categories begin to disappear. Television, in itself, may bring an end to childhood. In truth, there is no such thing as "children's programming," at least not for children over the age of eight or nine. Everyone sees and hears the same things. We have already reached a point where crimes of youth are indistinguishable from those of adults, and we may soon reach a point where the punishments will be the same.

I raise this point because the school is one of our few remaining institutions based on firm distinctions between childhood and adulthood, and on the assumption that adults have something of value to teach the young. That is why teachers must avoid emulating in dress and speech the style of the young. It is also why the school ought to be a place for what we

20

might call "manners education": the adults in school ought to be concerned with teaching youth a standard of civilized interaction.

Again those who are inclined to regard this as superficial may be underestimating the power of media such as television and radio to teach how one is to conduct oneself in public. In a general sense, the media "unprepare" the young for behavior in groups. A young man who goes through the day with a radio affixed to his ear is learning to be indifferent to any shared sound. A young woman who can turn off a television program that does not suit her needs at the moment is learning impatience with any stimulus that is not responsive to her interests.

But school is not a radio station or a television program. It is a social situation requiring the subordination of one's own impulses and interests to those of the group. In a word, manners. As a rule, elementary school teachers will exert considerable effort in teaching manners. I believe they refer to this effort as "socializing the child." But it is astonishing how precipitously this effort is diminished at higher levels. It is certainly neglected in the high schools, and where it is not, there is usually an excessive concern for "bad habits," such as smoking, drinking, and in some nineteenth-century schools, swearing. But, as William James noted, our virtues are as habitual as our vices. Where is the attention given to the "Good morning" habit, to the "I beg your pardon" habit, to the "Please forgive the interruption" habit?

The most civilized high school class I have ever seen was one in which students and teacher said "Good morning" to each other and in which the students stood up when they had something to say. The teacher, moreover, thanked each student for any contribution made to the class, did not sit with his feet on the desk, and did not interrupt a student unless he had asked permission to do so. The students, in turn, did not interrupt each other, or chew gum, or read comic books when they were bored. To avoid being a burden to others when one is bored is the essence of civilized behavior.

Of this teacher, I might also say that he made no attempt to entertain his students or model his classroom along the lines of a TV program. He was concerned not only to teach his students manners but to teach them how to attend in a classroom, which is partly a matter of manners but also necessary to their intellectual development. One of the more serious difficulties teachers now face in the classroom results from the fact that their students suffer media-shortened attention spans and have become accustomed, also through intense media exposure, to novelty, variety, and entertainment. Some teachers have made desperate attempts to keep their students "tuned in" by fashioning their classes along the lines of *Sesame Street* or the *Tonight* show. They tell jokes. They change the pace. They show films, play records, and avoid *anything* that would take more than eight minutes. Although their motivation is understandable, this is what their students least need. However difficult it may be, the teacher must try to achieve student attention and even enthusiasm through the attraction of ideas, not razzmatazz. Those who think I am speaking here in favor of "dull" classes may themselves, through media exposure, have lost an understanding of the potential for excitement contained in an idea. The media (one prays) are not so powerful that they can obliterate in the young, particularly in the adolescent, what William James referred to as a "theoretic instinct," a need to know reasons, causes, abstract conceptions. Such an "instinct" can be seen in its earliest stages in what he calls the "sporadic metaphysical inquiries of children as to who made God, and why they have five fingers . . . ."

I trust that the reader is not misled by what I have been saying. As I   25
see it, nothing in any of the above leads to the conclusion that I favor a classroom that is authoritarian or coldhearted, or dominated by a teacher insensitive to students and how they learn. I merely want to affirm the importance of the classroom as a special place, aloof from the biases of the media; a place in which the uses of the intellect are given prominence in a setting of elevated language, civilized manners, and respect for social symbols.

✎ Topics for Critical Thinking and Writing

1. In paragraph 3 what does Postman mean by "tolerance for delayed gratification"? By the way, two paragraphs later Postman uses an expression that is approximately synonymous with "delayed gratification." What is this expression?
2. Postman in part blames "the electronic media," because (he says in paragraph 5) they emphasize "fragmentation." Does he give any examples in his essay? Do you think you know what he means? And do you think he is right?
3. Who is Postman's audience? High school students? Parents and teachers? Professors of education? And who is Postman—that is, putting aside the biographical note on page 389, what sort of person does the author of the essay reveal himself to be? A frustrated high school teacher? A professor of education? An intelligent layperson? Does he seem to know what he is talking about?
4. In paragraph 10 we are told, with approval, that a principal named Dr. Howard Hurwitz "ran 'a tight ship.'" First, make sure that you know what the phrase means, and then write an essay of five hundred words evaluating the degree of success of some instructor or administrator who ran a tight ship in your school. Your essay will, of course, have to give us a sense of what the instructor or administrator did, as well as your evaluation of the results of his or her teaching or administrating.
5. If you disagree with Postman on the value of a dress code, set forth your disagreement in a persuasive essay of five hundred words.
6. Write an editorial—as an alumnus or alumna—for your high school newspaper, summarizing Postman's essay in a paragraph, and then compar-

ing your school with Postman's idea of a good school, and, finally, evaluating your school and Postman's essay. You may, for example, conclude that, thank heavens, your school was nothing like Postman's ideal school.

Merry White

Merry White is the author of The Japanese Educational Challenge *(1987) and* Japan: The Material Child *(1993). She is also the author of a book on noodles. White, who has served as an administrator of Harvard's East Asian Studies Program, now teaches anthropology at Boston University. This essay was originally published in 1984, hence the salaries specified in paragraph 19 and comments on world trends must be adjusted in view of later developments.*

Japanese Education
How Do They Do It?

Japan has become the new reference point for the developing nations and the West, and comparisons with Japan cause increasing wonder and sometimes envy. Travel agents continue to profit from the curiosity of Americans, particularly businessmen, who take regular tours of Japan seeking the secrets of Japanese industry. They come back with photographs and full notebooks, convinced they have learned secrets that can be transplanted to their own companies.

Even the Japanese have entered the pop-sociological search for the secrets of their own success; their journalists suggest that they emphasize problem *prevention* while Americans make up for their lack of prescience and care through *remediation* (in the case of cars, recalls for flawed models). The explanation given by a European Economic Community report—that the Japanese are workaholics willing, masochistically, to live in "rabbit hutches" without complaint—was met with amused derision in Japan. But it seems that those who do not look for transportable "secrets" are nonetheless willing to believe that the source of Japanese success is genetic, and thus completely untransferable. There are alternatives to these positions, and an examination of Japanese education provides us with a backdrop for considering them.

The Social Consensus

The attention given to the decline of both American industry and American education has not yet led to an awareness here of the close relationship between the development of people and the development of society, an awareness we see everywhere in Japanese thought and institutions, and whose effects we can see in the individual achievements of Japanese children. If Americans realized how powerful the relationship is between Japanese school achievement and social and economic successes we might see the same kind of protectionist language aimed at the Japanese educational system that we see directed at their automobile industry. ("The Japanese must stop producing such able and committed students because *it isn't fair.*")

The Japanese understand how important it is to have not just a high level of literacy (which they have had since well before modernization), but also a high level of education in the whole population. It has been said that the Japanese high school graduate is as well educated as an American college graduate, and indeed it is impressive that any worker on the factory floor can be expected to understand statistical material, work from complex graphs and charts, and perform sophisticated mathematical operations. This consensus that education is important, however simple it may sound, is the single most important contributor to the success of Japanese schools. Across the population, among parents, at all institutional and bureaucratic levels, and highest on the list of national priorities, is the stress on excellence in education. This is not just rhetoric. If the consensus, societal mobilization, and personal commitment—all focused on education—are not available to Americans, the reason is not genetic, nor are we locked in an immutable cultural pattern. We simply have not mobilized around our children.

There are dear advantages to being a Japanese child: a homogeneous   5
population focused on perpetuating its cultural identity; an occupational system where selection and promotion are based on educational credentials; a relatively equal distribution of educational opportunities; a universal core curriculum; highly trained and rewarded teachers; and families, especially mothers, devoted to enhancing the life chances of children and working cooperatively with the educational system. Finally, there are high standards for performance in every sector, and a carefully graded series of performance expectations in the school curriculum.

It is clear from these assertions that the measurable cognitive achievements of Japanese education represent only part of the picture. The American press stresses these achievements and accounts for them in terms of government expenditures, longer school years, and early use of homework. While the International Association for the Evaluation of Educational Achievement (IEA) test scores certainly indicate that Japanese children are testing higher than any children in the world (especially in math and science), and while some researchers have even claimed that Japanese children on average score 11 points more than American children on IQ tests, the social and psychological dimensions of Japanese education are similarly impressive and are primary contributors to cognitive achievement. The support given by family and teachers to the emotional and behavioral development of the child provides a base for the child's acquisition of knowledge and problem-solving skills. But beyond this, the Japanese think a major function of education is the development of a happy, engaged, and secure child, able to work hard and cooperate with others.

Inside the Japanese School

In order to understand the context of the Japanese educational system, some basic information is necessary:

1. Education is compulsory for ages six to 15, or through lower secondary school. (Age is almost always correlated with grade level, by the way, because only rarely is a child "kept back" and almost never "put ahead.") Non-compulsory high school attendance (both public and private) is nearly universal, at 98 percent.

2. There is extensive "non-official" private education. Increasing numbers of children attend pre-schools. Currently, about 95 percent of the five-year olds are in kindergarten or nursery school, 70 percent of the four-year olds and 10 percent of three-year olds. Many older children attend *juku* (after school classes) as well. These are private classes in a great variety of subjects, but most enhance and reinforce the material to be learned for high school or college entrance examinations. There are also *yobiko* (cram schools) for those taking an extra year between high school and college to prepare for the exams.

3. While competition for entrance to the most prestigious universities is very stiff, nearly 40 percent of the college-age group attend college or university. (The rates are slightly higher for women, since many attend two-year junior colleges.)

4. Japanese children attend school 240 days a year, compared to 180 in the U.S. Many children spend Sundays in study or tutoring, and vacation classes are also available. Children do not necessarily see this as oppressive, and younger children often ask their parents to send them to *juku* as a way of being with their friends after school. Homework starts in first grade, and children in Japan spend more time in home study than children in any other country except Taiwan. In Japan, 8 percent of the high school seniors spend less than five hours per week on homework, compared to 65 percent of American seniors.[1]

5. Primary and lower secondary schools provide what we would call a core curriculum: a required and comprehensive course of study progressing along a logical path, with attention given to children's developmental levels. In elementary and lower secondary school, language learning dominates the school curriculum, and takes up the greatest number of classroom hours, particularly from second to fourth grade. The large number of characters to be learned requires an emphasis on memorization and drill that is not exhibited in the rest of the curriculum. Arithmetic and

10

---

[1]Thomas Rohlen, *Japan's High Schools* (Berkeley: University of California Press, 1983), p. 277.

math are next in number of class hours, followed by social studies. The curriculum includes regular physical education and morning exercise as part of a "whole-child" program. In high school all students take Japanese, English, math, science, and social studies each year, and all students have had courses in chemistry, biology, physics, and earth sciences. All high school students take calculus.

6. Computers and other technology do not play a large role in schools. The calculator is used, but has not replaced mental calculations or, for that matter, the abacus. There is no national program to develop high technology skills in children. Americans spend much more money on science and technology in the schools; the Japanese spend more on teacher training and salaries.

These features should be seen in the context of a history of emphasis on education in Japan. To begin with, an interest in mass (or at least widespread) education greatly antedated the introduction of Western schools to Japan. Literacy, numeracy, and a moral education were considered important for people of all classes. When Western style universal compulsory schooling was introduced in 1872, it was after a deliberate and wide-ranging search throughout the world that resulted in a selection of features from German, French, and American educational systems that would advance Japan's modernization and complement her culture. While uniform, centralized schooling was an import, it eventually brought out Japan's already refined powers of adaptation—not the ability to adapt to a new mode as much as *the ability to adapt the foreign mode to Japanese needs and conditions.*

Also striking was the rapidity with which Japan developed a modern   15
educational system and made it truly universal. In 1873, one year after the Education Act, there was 28 percent enrollment in primary schools, but by 1904 enrollment had already reached 98 percent—one percent less than the current rate. The rush to educate children was buttressed both by the wish to catch up with the West and by a cultural interest in schooling.

A Truly National System

Tradition, ideology, and international competition are not, however, the only motive forces in Japanese education: other factors are as significant. First, Japan has a relatively homogeneous population. Racially and economically there is little variety. Minority groups, such as Koreans and the former out-castes, exist and do suffer some discrimination, but all children have equal access to good schooling. Income is more evenly distributed in Japan than in America and most people (96 percent in a recent Prime Minister's Office poll) consider themselves middle class. There are few remaining regional differences that affect the educational system, except perhaps local accents.

Second, educational financing and planning are centralized. While American educational policy sees the responsibility for schooling as a local matter, Japanese planners can rely on a centralized source of funding, curriculum guidance, and textbook selection. In terms of educational spending as a percentage of total GNP, the U.S. and Japan are not so far apart: The U.S. devotes 6.8 percent of its GNP to education, and Japan devotes 8.6 percent. But in Japan about 50 percent of this is national funding, while in the U.S. the federal government provides only 8 percent of the total expenditure on education, most of which is applied to special education, not to core schooling. Moreover, in the U.S. there exist no national institutions to build a consensus on what and how our children are taught. The most significant outcome of centralization in Japan is the even distribution of resources and quality instruction across the country. National planners and policymakers can mobilize a highly qualified teaching force and offer incentives that make even the most remote areas attractive to good teachers.

Third (but perhaps most important in the comparison with the United States), teachers enjoy respect and high status, job security, and good pay. More than in any other country, teachers in Japan are highly qualified: Their mastery of their fields is the major job qualification, and all have at least a bachelor's degree in their specialty. Moreover, they have a high degree of professional involvement as teachers: 74 percent are said to belong to some professional teachers' association in which teaching methods and curriculum are actively discussed.[2]

Teachers are hired for life, at starting salaries equivalent to starting salaries for college graduates in the corporate world. Elementary and junior high school teachers earn $18,200 per year on the average, high school teachers $19,000. Compared to other Japanese public sector workers, who earn an average of $16,800, this is a high salary, but it is less than that of managers in large companies or bureaucrats in prestigious ministries. In comparison with American teachers, whose salaries average $17,600, it is an absolutely higher wage. The difference is especially striking when one considers that over all professions, salaries are lower in Japan than in the U.S. In fact, American teachers' salaries are near the bottom of the scale of jobs requiring a college degree. Relative status and prestige correlate with salary in both countries. Japanese teachers' pay increases, as elsewhere in Japan, are tied to a seniority ladder, and older "master teachers" are given extra pay as teacher supervisors in each subject.[3]

Japanese teachers see their work as permanent: Teaching is not a   20
waystation on a path to other careers. Teachers work hard at improving their skills and knowledge of their subject, and attend refresher courses and upgrading programs provided by the Ministry of Education. While

---

[2]William Cummings, *Education and Equality in Japan* (Princeton: Princeton University Press, 1980), p. 159.
[3]There is a debate in Japan today concerning rewarding good teachers with higher pay: Professor Sumiko Iwao, of Keio University, reports that when quality is measured in yen, the commitment of teachers to good teaching declines.

there are tendencies, encouraged by the Teachers' Union, to downplay the traditional image of the "devoted, selfless teacher" (since this is seen as exploitative), and to redefine the teacher as a wage laborer with regular hours, rather than as a member of a "sacred" profession, teachers still regularly work overtime and see their job's sphere extending beyond classroom instruction. Classes are large: The average is about 40 students to one teacher. Teachers feel responsible for their students' discipline, behavior, morality, and for their general social adjustment as well as for their cognitive development. They are "on duty" after school hours and during vacations, and supervise vacation play and study. They visit their students' families at home, and are available to parents with questions and anxieties about their children. The Teachers' Union protests strongly against this extensive role, but both teachers and parents reinforce this role, tied as it is to the high status of the teacher.

Fourth, there is strong ideological and institutional support for education because the occupational system relies on schools to select the right person for the right organization. Note that this is not the same as the "right job" or "slot": A new company recruit, almost always a recent graduate, is not expected to have a skill or special identity, but to be appropriate in general educational background and character for a company. The company then trains recruits in the skills they will need, as well as in the company style. Of course, the basic skill level of the population of high school and college graduates is extremely high. But the important fact is that the social consensus supports an educational system that creates a committed, productive labor force. And although the emphasis seems to be on educational credentials, the quality of graduates possessing these credentials is indisputably high.

Mom

The background I have presented—of national consensus, institutional centralization, and fiscal support—alone does not explain the successes of Japanese education. There are other, less tangible factors that derive from cultural conceptions of development and learning, the valued role of maternal support, and psychological factors in Japanese pedagogy, and which distinguish it from American schooling.

The role of mothers is especially important. The average Japanese mother feels her child has the potential for success: Children are believed to be born with no distinguishing abilities (or disabilities) and can be mobilized to achieve and perform at high levels. Effort and commitment are required, and, at least at the beginning, it is the mother's job to engage the child. One way of looking at Japanese child development is to look at the words and concepts related to parental goals for their children. A "good child" has the following, frequently invoked characteristics: He is *otonashii* (mild or gentle), *sunao* (compliant, obedient, and cooperative), *akarui* (bright, alert), and *genki* (energetic and spirited). *Sunao* has frequently been translated as "obedient," but it would be more appropriate to use "open minded," "nonresistant," or "authentic in intent and cooperative in spirit." The English word "obedience" implies subordination and lack of self-determination, but *sunao* assumes that what we call compliance (with a negative connotation) is really cooperation, an act of affirmation of the self. A child who is *sunao* has not yielded his personal autonomy for the sake of cooperation; cooperation does not imply giving up the self, but in fact implies that working with others is the appropriate setting for expressing and enhancing the self.

One encourages a *sunao* child through the technique, especially used by mothers and elementary school teachers, of *wakaraseru*, or "getting the child to understand." The basic principle of child rearing seems to be: Never go against the child. *Wakaraseru* is often a long-term process that ultimately engages the child in the mother's goals, and makes her goals the child's own, thus producing an authentic cooperation, as in *sunao*. The distinction between external, social expectations and the child's own personal goals becomes blurred from this point on. An American might see this manipulation of the child through what we would call "indulgence" as preventing him from having a strong will of his own, but the Japanese mother sees long term benefits of self-motivated cooperation and real commitment.

Japanese mothers are active teachers as well, and have a real curriculum for their pre-school children: Games, teaching aids, ordinary activities are all focused on the child's development. There are counting games for very small babies, songs to help children learn new words, devices to focus the child's concentration. Parents buy an average of two or three new books every month for their preschoolers, and there are about 40 monthly activity magazines for preschoolers, very highly subscribed. The result is that most, at least most urban children, can read and write the phonetic syllabary before they enter school, and can do simple computations.

Maternal involvement becomes much more extensive and "serious" once she and the child enter the elementary school community. In addition to formal involvement in frequent ceremonies and school events, PTA meetings and visiting days, the mother spends much time each day helping the child with homework (sometimes to the point at which the teachers joke that they are really grading the mothers by proxy). There are classes for mothers, called *mamajuku*, that prepare mothers in subjects their children are studying. Homework is considered above all a means for developing a sense of responsibility in the child, and like much in early childhood education, it is seen as a device to train character.

The Japanese phenomenon of maternal involvement recently surfaced in Riverdale, New York, where many Japanese families have settled. School teachers and principals there noted that each Japanese family was purchasing two sets of textbooks. On inquiring, they found that the second set was for the mother, who could better coach her child if she worked during the day to keep up with his lessons. These teachers said that children entering in September with no English ability finished in June at the top of their classes in every subject.

The effort mothers put into their children's examinations has been given a high profile by the press. This is called the *kyoiku mama* syndrome—the mother invested in her children's progress. In contrast to Western theories of achievement, which emphasize individual effort and ability, the Japanese consider academic achievement to be an outgrowth of an interdependent network of cooperative effort and planning. The caricature of the mother's over-investment, however, portrays a woman who has totally identified with her child's success or failure, and who has no separate identity of her own. The press emphasizes the negative aspects of this involvement with accounts of maternal nervous breakdowns, reporting a murder by a mother of the child next-door, who made too much noise while her child was studying. But the press also feeds the mother's investment by exhorting her to prepare a good work environment for the studying child, to subscribe to special exam-preparation magazines, to hire tutors, and to prepare a nutritious and exam-appropriate diet.

High-schoolers from outlying areas taking entrance exams in Tokyo come with their mothers to stay in special rooms put aside by hotels. They are provided with special food, study rooms, counselors, and tension-release rooms, all meant to supply home-care away from home. The home study-desk bought by most parents for their smaller children symbolizes the hovering care and intensity of the mother's involvement: All models have a high front and half-sides, cutting out distractions and enclosing the workspace in womb-like protection. There is a built-in study light, shelves, a clock, electric pencil sharpener, and builtin calculator. The most popular model includes a push-button connecting to a buzzer in the kitchen to summon mother for help or for a snack.

How Do You Feel about Cubing?

Not much work has been done yet to analyze the relationship between the strongly supportive learning atmosphere and high achievement in Japan. In the home, mothers train small children in a disciplined, committed use of energy through what Takeo Doi has called the encouragement of "positive dependency"; in the schools as well there is a recognition that attention to the child's emotional relationship to his work, peers, and teachers is necessary for learning.

A look at a Japanese classroom yields some concrete examples of this. Many Westerners believe that Japanese educational successes are due to an emphasis on rote learning and memorization, that the classroom is rigidly disciplined. This is far from reality. An American teacher walking into a fourth grade science class in Japan would be horrified: children all talking at once, leaping and calling for the teacher's attention. The typical

American's response is to wonder, "who's in control of this room?" But if one understands the content of the lively chatter, it is clear that all the noise and movement is focused on the work itself—children are shouting out answers, suggesting other methods, exclaiming in excitement over results, and not gossiping, teasing, or planning games for recess. As long as it is the result of this engagement, the teacher is not concerned over the noise, which may measure a teacher's success. (It has been estimated that American teachers spend about 60 percent of class time on organizing, controlling, and disciplining the class, while Japanese teachers spend only 10 percent.)

A fifth grade math class I observed reveals some elements of this pedagogy. The day I visited, the class was presented with a general statement about cubing. Before any concrete facts, formulae, or even drawings were displayed, the teacher asked the class to take out their math diaries and spend a few minutes writing down their feelings and anticipations over this new concept. It is hard for me to imagine an American math teacher beginning a lesson with an exhortation to examine one's emotional predispositions about cubing (but that may be only because my own math training was antediluvian).

After that, the teacher asked for conjectures from the children about the surface and volume of a cube and asked for some ideas about formulae for calculation. The teacher asked the class to cluster into its component *han* (working groups) of four or five children each, and gave out materials for measurement and construction. One group left the room with large pieces of cardboard, to construct a model of a cubic meter. The groups worked internally on solutions to problems set by the teacher and competed with each other to finish first. After a while, the cubic meter group returned, groaning under the bulk of its model, and everyone gasped over its size. (There were many comments and guesses as to how many children could fit inside.) The teacher then set the whole class a very challenging problem, well over their heads, and gave them the rest of the class time to work on it. The class ended without a solution, but the teacher made no particular effort to get or give an answer, although she exhorted them to be energetic. (It was several days before the class got the answer—there was no deadline but the excitement did not flag.)

Several characteristics of this class deserve highlighting. First, there was attention to feelings and predispositions, provision of facts, and opportunities for discovery. The teacher preferred to focus on process, engagement, commitment, and performance rather than on discipline (in our sense) and production. Second, the *han:* Assignments are made to groups, not to individuals (this is also true at the workplace) although individual progress and achievement are closely monitored. Children are supported, praised, and allowed to make mistakes through trial and error within the group. The group is also pitted against other groups, and the group's success is each person's triumph, and vice versa. Groups are made up by the teacher and are designed to include a mixture of skill levels—there is a *hancho* (leader) whose job it is to choreograph the group's work, to encourage the slower members, and to act as a reporter to the class at large.

Japanese teachers seem to recognize the emotional as well as the intellectual aspects of engagement. Japanese pedagogy (and maternal socialization) are based on the belief that effort is the most important factor in achievement, and that the teacher's job is to get the child to commit himself positively and energetically to hard work. This emphasis is most explicit in elementary school, but persists later as a prerequisite for the self-discipline and effort children exhibit in high school.

American educational rhetoric does invoke "the whole child," does seek "self-expression," and does promote emotional engagement in "discovery learning." But Japanese teaching style, at least in primary schools, effectively employs an engaging, challenging teaching style that surpasses most American attempts. In the cubing class, I was struck by the spontaneity, excitement, and (to American eyes) "unruly" dedication of the children to the new idea, and impressed with the teacher's ability to create this positive mood. It could be a cultural difference: We usually separate cognition and emotional affect, and then devise artificial means of reintroducing "feeling" into learning. It is rather like the way canned fruit juices are produced—first denatured by the preserving process and then topped up with chemical vitamins to replace what was lost.

The Role of Competition

The frequent accusation that Japanese education involves children in hellish competition must also be examined. In the elementary school classroom, competition is negotiated by means of the *han*. The educational system tries to accommodate both the ideology of harmony and the interest in hierarchy and ranking. The introduction of graded, competitive Western modes of education into societies where minimizing differences between people is valued has often produced severe social and psychological dislocation (as in Africa and other parts of the Third World). In Japan, the importance of the modern educational system as a talent selector and the need to preserve harmony and homogeneity have produced complementary rather than conflicting forces. The regular classroom is a place where the individual does not stick out, but where individual needs are met and goals are set. Children are not held back nor advanced by ability: the cohesion of the age group is said to be more important. Teachers focus on pulling up the slower learners, rather than tracking the class to suit different abilities. For the most part, teachers and the school system refuse to engage in examination preparation hysteria. Part of the reason for this is pressure from the Teachers' Union, a very large and powerful labor union which consistently resists any moves away from the egalitarian and undifferentiating mode of learning. Turning teachers into drill instructors is said to be dehumanizing, and the process of cramming a poor substitute for education.

So where is the competitive selection principle served? In the *juku. Juku* are tough competitive classes, often with up to 500 in one lecture hall. The most prestigious are themselves very selective and there are examinations (and preparation courses for these) to enter the *juku.* Some *juku* specialize in particular universities' entrance exams, and they will boast of their rate of admission into their universities. It is estimated that one third of all primary school students and one half of all secondary school students attend *juku,* but in Tokyo the rate rises to 86 percent of junior high school students. The "king of *juku,*" Furukawa Noboru, the creator of a vast chain of such classes, says that *juku* are necessary to bridge the gap of present realities in Japan. He says that public schools do not face the fact of competition, and that ignoring the reality does not help children. The Ministry of Education usually ignores this non-accredited alternative and complementary system, and permits this functional division to take the pressure off the public schools. While there is considerable grumbling by parents, and while it is clear that the *juku* introduce an inegalitarian element into the process of schooling (since they do cost money), they do, by their separation from the regular school, permit the persistence of more traditional modes of learning, while allowing for a fast track in the examinations.

It is important to note that in Japan there really is only one moment of critical importance to one's career chances—the entrance examination to college. There are few opportunities to change paths or retool. Americans' belief that one can be recreated at any time in life, that the self-made person can get ahead, simply is not possible in Japan—thus the intense focus on examinations.

The Problems—In Context

This rapid tour through the Japanese educational system cannot neglect   40
the problems. However, two things must be kept in mind when considering these well-publicized difficulties: One is that although problems do exist, the statistical reality is that, compared to the West, Japan still looks very good indeed. The other is that the Japanese themselves tend to be quite critical, and educational problems are given attention. But this attention should be seen in context: Not that people are not truly concerned about real problems, but that the anxiety seems related to a sense of national insecurity. The Japanese focus on educational issues may emanate from a sense of the importance of intellectual development in a society where there are few other resources. Any educational problem seems to put the nation truly at risk.

Japanese parents are critical and watchful of the schools and are not complacent about their children's successes. There was a telling example of this in a recent comparative study of American and Japanese education.

Mothers in Minneapolis and in Sendai, roughly comparable cities, were asked to evaluate their children's school experiences. The Minneapolis mothers consistently answered that the schools were fine and that their children were doing well, while the Sendai mothers were very critical of their schools and worried that their children were not performing up to potential. Whose children were, in objective tests, doing better? The Sendai group—in fact so much better that the poorest performer in the Japanese group was well ahead of the best in the American group. Mothers in Japan and the U.S. have very different perspectives on performance: Japanese mothers attribute failure to lack of effort while American mothers explain it as lack of ability. Japanese children have an external standard of excellence to which they can aspire, while an American child normally can only say he will "do his best."

Problems have surfaced, of course. Psychotherapists report a syndrome among children related to school and examination pressure. School phobia, psychosomatic symptoms, and juvenile suicide are most frequently reported. Japan does lead the world in school-related suicides for the 15- to 19-year old age group, at about 300 per year. Recently, the "battered teacher" and "battered parent" syndromes have received much attention. There are cases where teenagers have attacked or killed parents and teachers, and these have been related to examination pressure. The numbers involved in these cases are very small—at least in comparison with American delinquency patterns and other juvenile pathologies. Dropouts, drug use, and violent juvenile crimes are almost non-existent in Japan. The crimes reported in one year among school-age children in Osaka, for example, are equal to those reported in one day in New York.

Criticism leveled at Japanese education by Western observers focuses on what they regard as a suppression of genius and individuality, and a lack of attention to the development of creativity in children. The first may indeed be a problem—for the geniuses—because there is little provision for tracking them to their best advantage. There has been discussion of introducing tracking so that individual ability can be better served, but this has not been implemented. The superbright may indeed be disadvantaged.

On the other hand, creativity and innovation *are* encouraged, but their manifestations may be different from those an American observer would expect. We must look at our own assumptions, to see if they are too limited. Americans see creativity in children as a fragile blossom that is stifled by rigid educational systems or adult standards. Creativity involves a necessary break with traditional content and methods, and implies the creation of a new idea or artifact. Whether creativity is in the child or in the teaching, and how it is to be measured, are questions no one has answered satisfactorily. Why we emphasize it is another question, probably related to our theories of progress and the importance we attach to unique accomplishments that push society forward. The fact is that, if anything, our schools do less to encourage creativity than do the Japanese, especially in the arts. All children in Japan learn two instruments and how to read music in elementary school, have regular drawing and painting classes, and work in small groups to create projects they themselves devise. It is true, though, that if everyone must be a soloist or composer to be considered creative, then most Japanese are not encouraged to be creative.

It is not enough to claim that the Japanese have been successful in   45
training children to take exams at the expense of a broader education. And it is not at all appropriate to say that they are unable to develop children's individuality and create the geniuses who make scientific breakthroughs. The first is untrue and the second remains to be shown as false by the Japanese themselves, who are now mobilizing to produce more scientists and technologists. In fact, the scales are tipped in favor of Japan, and to represent it otherwise would be a distortion.

The success of the Japanese model has led to its use in other rapidly developing countries, including South Korea, Taiwan, and Singapore. There, education is seen as the linchpin for development, and attention to children has meant the allocation of considerable resources to schools. The results are similar to those seen in Japanese schools: highly motivated, hard-working students who like school and who have achieved very high scores on international achievement tests.

Seeing Ourselves through Japanese Eyes

What *America* can learn from Japan is rather an open question. We can, to begin with, learn more *about* Japan, and in doing so, learn more about ourselves. Japanese advancements of the past 20 years were based on American principles of productivity (such as "quality control"), not on samurai management skills and zen austerities. Looking for Japanese secrets, or worse, protesting that they are inhuman or unfair, will not get us very far. They have shown they can adjust programs and policies to the needs and resources of the times; we must do the same. We need to regain the scientific literacy we lost and reacquire the concrete skills and participatory techniques we need. We should see Japan as establishing a new standard, not as a model to be emulated. To match that standard we have to aim at general excellence, develop a long-term view, and act consistently over time with regard to our children's education.

✎ Topics for Critical Thinking and Writing

1. In paragraph 4 White contrasts Japanese commitment to education with our own. Where in our society might one look for evidence of commitment or lack of commitment to education?
2. In paragraph 5 White lists many "clear advantages to being a Japanese child." Considering your education, or any other grounds you choose, which of these "advantages" would you like to have? Are there any you would

gladly do without? Can you explain why? How many of the Japanese advantages appear to be dependent on the first that White lists, "a homogeneous population"? Are you aware of advantages to growing up in a heterogeneous population? (For an explanation of Japanese homogeneity, see paragraph 16.)

3. At the end of paragraph 6 White says that "the Japanese think a major function of education is the development of a happy, engaged, and secure child, able to work hard and cooperate with others." Complete the following sentence: "Americans think a major function of education is . . ."

4. In paragraph 11 White discusses the amount of time Japanese students spend on homework. What were your own experiences with homework? Did homework contribute significantly to your education? Were there assignments you now regard as counterproductive?

5. In paragraph 13 White says that computers do not play a large role in Japanese schools. If computers played a fairly large role in your education, what do you think you learned from them, aside from how to operate them?

6. In paragraph 18 White reports that Japanese teachers are highly qualified. Do you think that, on the whole, your high school teachers were highly qualified? If you were able to do so, what measures would you take to insure well-qualified teachers in *all* American high schools? (White's paragraph 19 may provide some ideas.)

7. In paragraph 32 White briefly describes a math class about to study cubing. Does the procedure followed in the class strike you as being of any value? Why or why not? And what about the procedure described in the next paragraph? (In thinking about this, consider also White's comments in paragraphs 34–35). Looking back at a class in which you learned a good deal, what "elements of this pedagogy" (White's words, paragraph 32) made the class successful?

8. In paragraph 37 White says that children in Japanese schools are almost never held back or advanced because of ability, and there is no tracking system. What do you think of this system? (Consider also paragraphs 43 and 44.)

9. In paragraph 39 White writes of the belief of Americans that "one can be recreated at any time in life, that the self-made person can get ahead." To what extent do you share these beliefs? To what extent did the schools you attended promote them?

10. Japan has produced relatively few winners of the Nobel Prize. Did White's essay help you to understand why this might be so? Do you take the lack of Nobel Prize winners to be a significant criticism of the Japanese educational system?

11. Given the great differences between our societies, what, if anything, do you think our educational system can learn from the Japanese system? (For example, we are far less homogeneous. And the mothers in our society often hold paying jobs, whereas few Japanese mothers do. Further, two thirds of our teenagers hold part-time jobs, whereas almost no Japanese teenagers hold jobs.)

Robert Coles

Robert Coles is a psychiatrist and a professor at Harvard. He is the author of many books, includ-ing Children of Crisis *(5 volumes, 1967–77), which won the Pulitzer Prize, and* The Spiritual Lives of Children *(1990). "On Raising Moral Children" is an excerpt from* The Moral Intelli-gence of Children, *published by Random House in 1997.*

On Raising Moral Children

The Child as Witness

I first heard the term "moral intelligence" many years ago, from Rustin McIntosh, a distinguished pediatrician who was teaching a group of us how to work with young patients who were quite ill. When we asked him to explain what he had in mind by that phrase, "moral intelligence," he did not respond with an elegantly precise definition. Rather, he told us about boys and girls he'd known and treated who had it—who were "good," who were kind, who thought about others, who extended them-selves toward those others, who were "smart" that way. He told us stories of clinical moments he found unforgettable: a girl dying of leukemia who worried about the "burden" she'd put upon her terribly saddened moth-er; a boy who lost the effective use of his right arm due to an automobile injury, and who felt sorry less for himself than he did for his dad, who loved baseball, loved coaching his son and others in a neighborhood Little League team.

Moral intelligence isn't only acquired by memorization of rules and regulations, by dint of abstract classroom discussion or kitchen compli-ance. We grow morally as a consequence of learning how to be with oth-ers, how to behave in this world, a learning prompted by taking to heart what we have seen and heard. The child is an ever attentive witness of grownup morality.

Of course, some children don't explicitly tell us what they have wit-nessed, the sense they've made of us, our moral ways of being. It can be hard for our sons and daughters to stand up to us, their parents, and teachers, point things out that trouble them. I once realized this all too memorably when I was driving my nine-year-old son to the hospital. He had injured himself in an accident—he had disobeyed his mother and me by "playing" with some carpentry tools we had set aside in our garage. I was upset because he'd sustained a deep cut that obviously would require surgical attention and that he'd ignored our "rule." I raced with him to the hospital on a rainy morning, careless that my car was splash-ing pedestrians, and at one point, I ignored a yellow light, then a red light. Amidst this headlong rush to an emergency ward, my son said, "Dad, if we're not careful, we'll make more trouble on our way to getting out of trouble."

A boy was pointing out, tactfully, respectfully, and yes, a bit fearfully, a major irony—that this effort to get us out of "trouble" could lead to more trouble; and he was also giving me a reproving as well as an anxious look: be careful, lest you hurt people on your all too hurried journey. I realized the ethical implications of my son's admonitory if not admonishing remark: there's something important at stake here, the lives of others. A boy had reached outside himself, thought of those others, no matter his own ordeal, with its justification of a heightened self-regard. That is what our children can offer us and what we can offer them—a chance to learn from them, even as we try to teach them.

Day One

"I think we start sending signals to our kids from Day One," said a mother in one of my discussion groups. "My sister, Maisie, has a son who had a great appetite right from the beginning. They're going along fine—six months, seven months, and you know what? He'd be sitting in the bassinet or the high chair, and he'd gulp down that milk, and as he got bigger, and had a little more control, he started throwing the bottle away, throwing it on the floor. He knew what he was doing, he heard the 'bang', the 'thump', and he was obviously pleased with himself. A neighbor told my sister, 'He's just flexing his muscles, so let him do it—be glad he's like that.' But Maisie said no, no; she said she wasn't going to let her kid get the idea that he could behave like that: toss something away, when he was through with it, and see other people come running to clean up the mess he'd made! You know what she did? She didn't shout or get real tough with him; she just made sure she was there, right there, her hand ready, as the baby took his last bit of milk, and she took the bottle from him, while talking to him, or cleaning his face. In a while, the baby lost interest—she tested him a few times by not being so quick to ease the bottle away. Now, to my mind, my sister had started teaching her son right versus wrong— how he should behave, and what he shouldn't do, as early as it was, as young as the boy was."

Maisie had been smart enough to move in her mind from a boy who teased his mother, so she saw it, to an older child who had a similarly cavalier attitude toward his parents and others in authority. The parent has an opportunity to teach even a baby under one, and certainly a baby who is two or three, how to come to terms with wishes and yearnings, with times of disappointment and frustration that are part of love, of life. Some lucky babies have parents who show them love, and who love, in return—but do not become slaves to their child's demands, nor to their own nervous wish, natural for all of us, to give as much as we have, and as often as we can, to our sons and daughters. Other parents are less sure of themselves,

5

or are lacking in self-restraint, and so let concern and affection deteriorate into an indulgence that can turn a child's head.

The Age of Conscience

In elementary school, maybe as never before or ever afterwards, the child becomes an intensely moral creature, quite interested in figuring out the reasons of this world—how and why things work, but also, how and why he or she should behave in various situations. "This is the age of conscience," Anna Freud once observed to me, and she went further: "This is the age that a child's conscience is built—or isn't; it is the time when a child's character is built and consolidated, or isn't." These are the years when a new world of knowledge and possibility arrives in the form of books, music, art, athletics, and, of course, the teachers and coaches who offer all that, the fellow students who share in the experiences. These are years of magic, of eager, lively searching on the part of children, whose parents and teachers are often hard put to keep up with them, as they try to understand things.

I once asked a six-year-old boy about his keen interest in telescopes. "When I look in it," he said, "it's like going on a long trip, and I'm far away, but I'm still here too." That child then took me on another kind of voyage, further into his mind and the thinking of other children than I had thought possible. "Those stars," he told me, "are moving fast, even if it looks like they're not moving one inch. A friend of mine said that God is keeping them from bumping into each other, but I told him, no, God isn't like that. He lets things happen—he doesn't keep interfering! He made everything, and then everything is on its own, and people too. In Sunday school, they say it's up to you, whether you'll be good or bad, and it's like that with the stars: they keep moving, and if they go off track, that's because something has gone wrong—it's an accident, it's not God falling asleep, or getting mad, something like that." He decided to complete his presentation: "Here it's different—there are people here. We're the star with people! That's why we could mess things up. The stars could hit each other—one star gets in the way of the other. That would be bad luck for both of them. But we could do something bad to this place, this star—and it would be as bad as if another star hit it, worse even!" A boy seemingly detoured by intellectual inclination from this planet's problems in favor of abiding interests in other planets was quite interested in addressing the biggest questions confronting all of us human beings—how our behavior might influence the very nature of existence.

Adolescence

Young people coming of age quite naturally command a good deal of our notice. They are understandably self-conscious, hence apt to call attention to themselves (while often claiming to want no such thing), and they bring us back to our own momentous time of adolescence—a second birth of sorts, only now accompanied by a blaze of self-awareness. Perhaps no other aspect of our life has prompted more writing on the part of our novelists, social scientists, journalists—it is as if these youths, in their habits, their interests, their language and dress, their music and politics, and not least, their developing sexuality, have a hold on us that is tied to our own memories.

Even if they have a good number of friends, many young people have   10 a loneliness that has to do with a self-imposed judgment of sorts: I am pushed and pulled by an array of urges, yearnings, worries, fears, that I can't share with anyone, really. This sense of utter difference makes for a certain moodiness well known among adolescents, who are, after all, constantly trying to figure out exactly how they ought to and might live.

I remember a young man of 15 who engaged in light banter, only to shut down, keep shaking his head, refuse to talk at all when his own life became the subject at hand. (He had stopped going to school, begun using large amounts of pot; he sat in his room for hours, listening to rock music.) After calling him, to myself, a host of psychiatric names—withdrawn, depressed, possibly psychotic—I asked him about his head-shaking behavior. I wondered whom he was thereby addressing. He did reply: "No one." I hesitated, gulped a bit as I took a chance: "Not yourself?" He looked right at me now in a sustained stare, for the first time. "Why do you say that?"

I decided not to answer the question in the manner that I was trained to reply—an account of what I had surmised about him, what I thought was happening inside him. Instead, with some unease, I heard myself saying this: "I've been there; I remember being there, when I felt I couldn't say a word to anyone." I can still remember those words, still remember feeling that I ought not have spoken them—a breach in "technique." The young man kept staring at me, didn't speak, at least through his mouth. When he took out his handkerchief and wiped his eyes, I realized they had begun to fill.

From there, we began a very gradual climb upward, step by step. As Anna Freud told me, "We are not miracle workers, who can say something, and—presto!—the trouble in a life has vanished. But I have noticed that in most of the adolescents that I see, in most of them a real effort at understanding . . . can go a long way."

To Parents and Teachers

Ralph Waldo Emerson once said, "Character is higher than intellect." Marian, a student of mine several years ago, much admired Emerson. She had arrived at Harvard from the Midwest and was trying hard to work her way through college by cleaning the rooms of her fellow students. Again and again she met classmates who had forgotten the meaning of please, of thank you, no matter their high SAT scores. They did not hesitate to be rude, even crude toward her. One day she was not so subtly propositioned by a young man she knew to be very bright. She quit her job, and was preparing to quit going to school. She came to see me full of anxiety and anger. "I've been taking all these philosophy courses," she said to me at one point, "and we talk about what's true, what's important, what's good. Well, how do you teach people to be good?"

Rather obviously, community service offers us all a chance to put our money where our mouths are. Books and classroom discussion, the skepticism of Marian notwithstanding, can be of help in this matter. But ultimately we must heed the advice of Henry James. When asked by his nephew what he ought to do in life, James replied, "Three things in human life are important. The first is to be kind. The second is to be kind. And the third is to be kind." The key to those words is the hortatory verb—the insistence that one find an existence that enables one to be kind. How to do so? By wading in, over and over, with that purpose in mind, with a willingness to sail on, tacking and tacking again, helped by those we aim to help, guided by our moral yearnings on behalf of others, on behalf of ourselves with others: a commitment to others that won't avoid squalls and periods of drift, a commitment that will become the heart of the journey itself.

✎ Topics for Critical Thinking and Writing

1. Rustin McIntosh, from whom Coles first heard the term "moral intelligence," does not define it. Based on Cole's article, how would you define it? And how do children acquire it?
2. In his third and fourth paragraphs, Coles relates a personal anecdote. What is it, and what point is he making through it? What other anecdotes does he use, and why does he use them?
3. In his final paragraph, Coles uses a metaphor. What is it? Evaluate its effectiveness.
4. In a paragraph or two reveal through an anecdote a moral lesson.

Mary Field Belenky, Blythe McVicker Clinchy, Nancy Rule Goldberger, and Jill Mattuck Tarule

Mary Belenky is an assistant research professor at the University of Vermont, Blythe Clinchy is a professor of psychology at Wellesley College, Nancy Goldberger is a visiting scholar in psychology at New York University, and Jill Tarule is Dean of Education at the University of Vermont. The essay printed here is part of Chapter 9 of their book, Women's Ways of Knowing, *a study of how women's intellectual abilities develop. (The title of the extract is the editors'.)*

How Women Learn

We begin with the reminiscences of two ordinary women, each recalling an hour during her first year at college. One of them, now middle-aged, remembered the first meeting of an introductory science course. The professor marched into the lecture hall, placed upon his desk a large jar filled with dried beans, and invited the students to guess how many beans the jar contained. After listening to an enthusiastic chorus of wildly inaccurate estimates the professor smiled a thin, dry smile, revealed the correct answer, and announced, "You have just learned an important lesson about science. Never trust the evidence of your own senses."

Thirty years later, the woman could guess what the professor had in mind. He saw himself, perhaps, as inviting his students to embark upon an exciting voyage into a mysterious underworld invisible to the naked eye, accessible only through scientific method and scientific instruments. But the seventeen-year-old girl could not accept or even hear the invitation. Her sense of herself as a knower was shaky, and it was based on the belief that she could use her own firsthand experience as a source of truth. This man was saying that this belief was fallacious. He was taking away her only tool for knowing and providing her with no substitute. "I remember feeling small and scared," the woman says, "and I did the only thing I could do. I dropped the course that afternoon, and I haven't gone near science since."

The second woman, in her first year at college, told a superficially similar but profoundly different story about a philosophy class she had attended just a month or two before the interview. The teacher came into class carrying a large cardboard cube. She placed it on the desk in front of her and asked the class what it was. They said it was a cube. She asked what a cube was, and they said a cube contained six equal square sides. She asked how they knew that this object contained six equal square sides. By looking at it, they said. "But how do you know?" the teacher asked again. She pointed to the side facing her and, therefore, invisible to the students; then she lifted the cube and pointed to the side that had been face down on the desk, and, therefore, also invisible. "We can't look at all six sides of a cube at once, can we? So we can't exactly *see* a cube. And yet, you're right. You know it's a cube. But you know it not just because you have eyes but because you have intelligence. You invent the sides you cannot see. You use your intelligence to create the 'truth' about cubes."

The student said to the interviewer,

It blew my mind. You'll think I'm nuts, but I ran back to the dorm and I called my boyfriend and I said, "Listen, this is just incredible," and I told him all about it. I'm not sure he could see why I was so excited. I'm not sure

I understand it myself. But I really felt, for the first time, like I was really in college, like I was—I don't know—sort of *grown up.*

Both stories are about the limitations of firsthand experience as a source of knowledge—we cannot simply see the truth about either the jar of beans or the cube—but there is a difference. We can know the truth about cubes. Indeed, the students did know it. As the science professor pointed out, the students were wrong about the beans; their senses had deceived them. But, as the philosophy teacher pointed out, the students were right about the cube; their minds had served them well. 5

The science professor was the only person in the room who knew how many beans were in that jar. Theoretically, the knowledge was available to the students; they could have counted the beans. But faced with that tedious prospect, most would doubtless take the professor's word for it. He is authority. They had to rely upon his knowledge rather than their own. On the other hand, every member of the philosophy class knew that the cube had six sides. They were all colleagues.

The science professor exercised his authority in a benign fashion, promising the students that he would provide them with the tools they needed to excavate invisible truths. Similarly, the philosophy teacher planned to teach her students the skills of philosophical analysis, but she was at pains to assure them that they already possessed the tools to construct some powerful truths. They had built cubes on their own, using only their own powers of inference, without the aid of elaborate procedures or fancy apparatus or even a teacher. Although a teacher might have told them once that a cube contained six equal square sides, they did not have to take the teacher's word for it; they could have easily verified it for themselves.

The lesson the science professor wanted to teach is that experience is a source of error. Taught in isolation, this lesson diminished the student, rendering her dumb and dependent. The philosophy teacher's lesson was that although raw experience is insufficient, by reflecting upon it the student could arrive at truth. It was a lesson that made the student feel more powerful ("sort of grown up").

No doubt it is true that, as the professor in May Sarton's novel *The Small Room* says, the "art" of being a student requires humility. But the woman we interviewed did not find the science lesson humbling; she found it humiliating. Arrogance was not then and is not now her natural habitat. Like most of the women in our sample she lacked confidence in herself as a thinker; and the kind of learning the science teacher demanded was not only painful but crippling.

In thinking about the education of women, Adrienne Rich writes, "Suppose we were to ask ourselves, simply: What does a woman need to know?" A woman, like any other human being, does need to know that the mind makes mistakes; but our interviews have convinced us that every woman, regardless of age, social class, ethnicity, and academic 10 achievement, needs to know that she is capable of intelligent thought, and she needs to know it right away. Perhaps men learn this lesson before going to college, or perhaps they can wait until they have proved themselves to hear it; we do not know. We do know that many of the women we interviewed had not yet learned it.

✎ Topics for Critical Thinking and Writing

1. How is the professor in the first anecdote characterized? Look particularly at the words used in paragraphs 1 and 2 to describe him. How is the student characterized? Look back at the first sentence: Why do the writers use the word *ordinary* to describe both students? Why did they not simply say, "We begin with the reminiscences of two women"?

2. In paragraph 5 the writers say, "Both stories are about the limitations of firsthand experience as a source of knowledge." What else do the stories have in common? What are the important differences? What particular difference is most relevant to the main point of the essay?

3. Look again at paragraph 6. The science teacher is described as being "authority." The students "had to rely upon his knowledge rather than their own." Is this relationship between teacher and students more likely in science courses than in philosophy or literature courses? Is it inevitable in sciences courses? If so, why?

4. What is the main point of the concluding paragraph? Do the two anecdotes support this point? To what extent does your own experience confirm it or not confirm it?

Fan Shen

Fan Shen came to the United States from the People's Republic of China. A translator and writer, he also teaches at Rockland Community College in Suffern, New York.

The Classroom and the Wider Culture
Identity as a Key to Learning English Composition

One day in June 1975, when I walked into the aircraft factory where I was working as an electrician, I saw many large-letter posters on the walls and many people parading around the workshops shouting slogans like "Down with the word 'I'!" and "Trust in masses and the Party!" I then remembered that a new political campaign called "Against Individualism" was scheduled to begin that day. Ten years later, I got back my first English composition paper at the University of Nebraska—Lincoln. The professor's first comments were: "Why did you always use 'we' instead of 'I'?" and "Your paper would be stronger if you eliminated some sentences in the passive voice." The clashes between my Chinese background and the requirements of English composition had begun. At the center of this mental struggle, which has lasted several years and is still not completely over, is the prolonged, uphill battle to recapture "myself."

In this paper I will try to describe and explore this experience of reconciling my Chinese identity with an English identity dictated by the rules of English composition. I want to show how my cultural background shaped—and shapes—my approaches to my writing in English and how writing in English redefined—and redefines—my *ideological* and *logical* identities. By "ideological identity" I mean the system of values that I acquired (consciously and unconsciously) from my social and cultural background. And by "logical identity" I mean the natural (or Oriental) way I organize and express my thoughts in writing. Both had to be modified or redefined in learning English composition. Becoming aware of the process of redefinition of these different identities is a mode of learning that has helped me in my efforts to write in English, and, I hope, will be of help to teachers of English composition in this country. In presenting my case for this view, I will use examples from both my composition courses and literature courses, for I believe that writing papers for both kinds of courses contributed to the development of my "English identity." Although what I will describe is based on personal experience, many Chinese students whom I talked to said that they had had the same or similar experiences in their initial stages of learning to write in English.

Identity of the Self: Ideological and Cultural

Starting with the first English paper I wrote, I found that learning to compose in English is not an isolated classroom activity, but a social and cultural experience. The rules of English composition encapsulate values that are absent in, or sometimes contradictory to, the values of other societies (in my case, China). Therefore, learning the rules of English composition is, to a certain extent, learning the values of Anglo-American society. In writing classes in the United States I found that I had to reprogram my mind, to redefine some of the basic concepts and values that I had about myself, about society, and about the universe, values that had been imprinted and reinforced in my mind by my cultural background, and that had been part of me all my life.

Rule number one in English composition is: Be yourself. (More than one composition instructor has told me, "Just write what *you* think.") The values behind this rule, it seems to me, are based on the principle of protecting and promoting individuality (and private property) in this country.

The instruction was probably crystal clear to students raised on these values, but, as a guideline of composition, it was not very clear or useful to me when I first heard it. First of all, the image or meaning that I attached to the word "I" or "myself" was, as I found out, different from that of my English teacher. In China, "I" is always subordinated to "We"—be it the working class, the Party, the country, or some other collective body. Both political pressure and literary tradition require that "I" be somewhat hidden or buried in writings and speeches; presenting the "self" too obviously would give people the impression of being disrespectful of the Communist Party in political writings and boastful in scholarly writings. The word "I" has often been identified with another "bad" word, "individualism," which has become a synonym for selfishness in China. For a long time the words "self" and "individualism" have had negative connotations in my mind, and the negative force of the words naturally extended to the field of literary studies. As a result, even if I had brilliant ideas, the "I" in my papers always had to show some modesty by not competing with or trying to stand above the names of ancient and modern authoritative figures. Appealing to Mao or other Marxist authorities became the required way (as well as the most "forceful" or "persuasive" way) to prove one's point in written discourse. I remember that in China I had even committed what I can call "reversed plagiarism"—here, I suppose it would be called "forgery"—when I was in middle school: willfully attributing some of my thoughts to "experts" when I needed some arguments but could not find a suitable quotation from a literary or political "giant."

Now, in America, I had to learn to accept the words "I" and "self" as   5
something glorious (as Whitman did), or at least something not to be ashamed of or embarrassed about. It was the first and probably biggest step I took into English composition and critical writing. Acting upon my professor's suggestion, I intentionally tried to show my "individuality" and to "glorify" "I" in my papers by using as many "I's" as possible—"I think," "I believe," "I see"—and deliberately cut out quotations from authorities. It was rather painful to hand in such "pompous" (I mean immodest) papers to my instructors. But to an extent it worked. After a while I became more comfortable with only "the shadow of myself." I felt more at ease to put down *my* thoughts without looking over my shoulder to worry about the attitudes of my teachers or the reactions of the Party secretaries, and to speak out as "bluntly" and "immodestly" as my American instructors demanded.

But writing many "I's" was only the beginning of the process of redefining myself. Speaking of redefining myself is, in an important sense, speaking of redefining the word "I." By such a redefinition I mean not only the change in how I envisioned myself, but also the change in how *I* perceived the world. The old "I" used to embody only one set of values, but now it had to embody multiple sets of values. To be truly "myself," which I knew was a key to my success in learning English composition, meant *not to be my Chinese self* at all. That is to say, when I write in English

I have to wrestle with and abandon (at least temporarily) the whole system of ideology which previously defined me in myself. I had to forget Marxist doctrines (even though I do not see myself as a Marxist by choice) and the Party lines imprinted in my mind and familiarize myself with a system of capitalist/bourgeois values. I had to put aside an ideology of collectivism and adopt the values of individualism. In composition as well as in literature classes, I had to make a fundamental adjustment: If I used to examine society and literary materials through the microscopes of Marxist dialectical materialism and historical materialism, I now had to learn to look through the microscopes the other way around, i.e., to learn to look at and understand the world from the point of view of "idealism." (I must add here that there are American professors who use a Marxist approach in their teaching.)

The word "idealism," which affects my view of both myself and the universe, is loaded with social connotations, and can serve as a good example of how redefining a key word can be a pivotal part of redefining my ideological identity as a whole.

To me, idealism is the philosophical foundation of the dictum of English composition: "Be yourself." In order to write good English, I knew that I had to be myself, which actually meant not to be my Chinese self. It meant that I had to create an English self and be *that* self. And to be that English self, I felt, I had to understand and accept idealism the way a Westerner does. That is to say, I had to accept the way a Westerner sees himself in relation to the universe and society. On the one hand, I knew a lot about idealism. But on the other hand, I knew nothing about it. I mean I knew a lot about idealism through the propaganda and objections of its opponent, Marxism, but I knew little about it from its own point of view. When I thought of the word "materialism"—which is a major part of Marxism and in China has repeatedly been "shown" to be the absolute truth—there were always positive connotations, and words like "right," "true," etc., flashed in my mind. On the other hand, the word "idealism" always came to me with the dark connotations that surround words like "absurd," "illogical," "wrong," etc. In China "idealism" is depicted as a ferocious and ridiculous enemy of Marxist philosophy. Idealism, as the simplified definition imprinted in my mind had it, is the view that the material world does not exist; that all that exists is the mind and its ideas. It is just the opposite of Marxist dialectical materialism which sees the mind as a product of the material world. It is not too difficult to see that idealism, with its idea that mind is of primary importance, provides a philosophical foundation for the Western emphasis on the value of individual human minds, and hence individual human beings. Therefore, my final acceptance of myself as of primary importance—an importance that overshadowed that of authority figures in English composition—was, I decided, dependent on an acceptance of idealism.

My struggle with idealism came mainly from my efforts to understand and to write about works such as Coleridge's *Biographia Literaria* and Emerson's "Over-Soul." For a long time I was frustrated and puzzled by the idealism expressed by Coleridge and Emerson—given their ideas, such as "I think, therefore I am" (Coleridge obviously borrowed from Descartes) and "the transparent eyeball" (Emerson's view of himself)—because in my mind, drenched as it was in dialectical materialism, there was always a little voice whispering in my ear "You are, therefore you think." I could not see how human consciousness, which is not material, could create apples and trees. My intellectual conscience refused to let me believe that the human mind is the primary world and the material world secondary. Finally, I had to imagine that I was looking at a world with my head upside down. When I imagined that I was in a new body (born with the head upside down) it was easier to forget biases imprinted in my sub-consciousness about idealism, the mind, and my former self. Starting from scratch, the new inverted self—which I called my "English Self" and into which I have transformed myself—could understand and *accept,* with ease, idealism as "the truth" and "himself" (i.e., my English Self) as the "creator" of the world.

Here is how I created my new "English Self." I played a "game" similar   10
to ones played by mental therapists. First I made a list of (simplified) features about writing associated with my old identity (the Chinese Self), both ideological and logical, and then beside the first list I added a column of features about writing associated with my new identity (the English Self). After that I pictured myself getting out of my old identity, the timid, humble, modest Chinese "I," and creeping into my new identity (often in the form of a new skin or a mask), the confident, assertive, and aggressive English "I." The new "Self" helped me to remember and accept the different rules of Chinese and English composition and the values that underpin these rules. In a sense, creating an English Self is a way of reconciling my old cultural values with the new values required by English writing, without losing the former.

An interesting structural but not material parallel to my experiences in this regard has been well described by Min-zhan Lu in her important article, "From Silence to Words: Writing as Struggle" (*College English* 49 [April 1987]: 437–48). Min-zhan Lu talks about struggles between two selves, an open self and a secret self, and between two discourses, a mainstream Marxist discourse and a bourgeois discourse her parents wanted her to learn. But her struggle was different from mine. Her Chinese self was severely constrained and suppressed by mainstream cultural discourse, but never interfused with it. Her experiences, then, were not representative of those of the majority of the younger generation who, like me, were brought up on only one discourse. I came to English composition as a Chinese person, in the fullest sense of the term, with a Chinese identity already fully formed.

Identity of the Mind: Illogical and Alogical

In learning to write in English, besides wrestling with a different ideological system, I found that I had to wrestle with a logical system very different from the blueprint of logic at the back of my mind. By "logical system" I mean two things: the Chinese way of thinking I used to approach my theme or topic in written discourse, and the Chinese critical/logical way to develop a theme or topic. By English rules, the first is illogical, for it is the opposite of the English way of approaching a topic; the second is alogical (nonlogical), for it mainly uses mental pictures instead of words as a critical vehicle.

The Illogical Pattern In English composition, an essential rule for the logical organization of a piece of writing is the use of a "topic sentence." In Chinese composition, "from surface to core" is an essential rule, a rule which means that one ought to reach a topic gradually and "systematically" instead of "abruptly."

The concept of a topic sentence, it seems to me, is symbolic of the values of a busy people in an industrialized society, rushing to get things done, hoping to attract and satisfy the busy reader very quickly. Thinking back, I realized that I did not fully understand the virtue of the concept until my life began to rush at the speed of everyone else's in this country. Chinese composition, on the other hand, seems to embody the values of a leisurely paced rural society whose inhabitants have the time to chew and taste a topic slowly. In Chinese composition, an introduction explaining how and why one chooses this topic is not only acceptable, but often regarded as necessary. It arouses the reader's interest in the topic little by little (and this is seen as a virtue of composition) and gives him/her a sense of refinement. The famous Robert B. Kaplan "noodles" contrasting a spiral Oriental thought process with a straight-line Western approach ("Cultural Thought Patterns in Inter-Cultural Education," *Readings on English as a Second Language,* ed. Kenneth Croft, 2nd ed., Winthrop, 1980, 403–10) may be too simplistic to capture the preferred pattern of writing in English, but I think they still express some truth about Oriental writing. A Chinese writer often clears the surrounding bushes before attacking the real target. This bush-clearing pattern in Chinese writing goes back two thousand years to Kong Fuzi (Confucius). Before doing anything, Kong says in his *Luen Yu (Analects),* one first needs to call things by their proper names (expressed by his phrase "Zheng Ming"). In other words, before touching one's main thesis, one should first state the "conditions" of composition: how, why, and when the piece is being composed. All of this will serve as a proper foundation on which to build the "house" of the piece. In the two thousand years after Kong, this principle of composition was gradually formalized (especially through the formal essays required by imperial examinations) and became known as "Ba Gu," or the eight-legged essay. The logic of Chinese composition, exemplified by the eight-legged essay, is like the peeling of an onion: Layer after layer is removed until the reader finally arrives at the central point, the core.

Ba Gu still influences modern Chinese writing. Carolyn Matalene has   15
an excellent discussion of this logical (or illogical) structure and its influence on her Chinese students' efforts to write in English ("Contrastive Rhetoric: An American Writing Teacher in China," *College English* 47 [November 1985]: 789–808). A recent Chinese textbook for composition

lists six essential steps (factors) for writing a narrative essay, steps to be taken in this order: time, place, character, event, cause, and consequence (*Yuwen Jichu Zhishi Liushi Jiang [Sixty Lessons on the Basics of the Chinese Language]*, ed. Beijing Research Institute of Education, Beijing Publishing House, 1981, 525–609). Most Chinese students (including me) are taught to follow this sequence in composition.

The straightforward approach to composition in English seemed to me, at first, illogical. One could not jump to the topic. One had to walk step by step to reach the topic. In several of my early papers I found that the Chinese approach—the bush-clearing approach—persisted, and I had considerable difficulty writing (and in fact understanding) topic sentences. In what I deemed to be topic sentences, I grudgingly gave out themes. Today, those papers look to me like Chinese papers with forced or false English openings. For example, in a narrative paper on a trip to New York, I wrote the forced/false topic sentence, "A trip to New York in winter is boring." In the next few paragraphs, I talked about the weather, the people who went with me, and so on, before I talked about what I learned from the trip. My real thesis was that one could always learn something even on a boring trip.

The Alogical Pattern In learning English composition, I found that there was yet another cultural blueprint affecting my logical thinking. I found from my early papers that very often I was unconsciously under the influence of a Chinese critical approach called the creation of "yijing," which is totally non-Western. The direct translation of the word "yijing" is: yi, "mind or consciousness," and jing, "environment." An ancient approach which has existed in China for many centuries and is still the subject of much discussion, yijing is a complicated concept that defies a universal definition. But most critics in China nowadays seem to agree on one point, that yijing is the critical approach that separates Chinese literature and criticism from Western literature and criticism. Roughly speaking, yijing is the process of creating a pictorial environment while reading a piece of literature. Many critics in China believe that yijing is a creative process of inducing oneself, while reading a piece of literature or looking at a piece of art, to create mental pictures, in order to reach a unity of nature, the author, and the reader. Therefore, it is by its very nature both creative and critical. According to the theory, this nonverbal, pictorial process leads directly to a higher ground of beauty and morality. Almost all critics in China agree that yijing is not a process of logical thinking—it is not a process of moving from the premises of an argument to its conclusion, which is the foundation of Western criticism. According to yijing, the process of criticizing a piece of art or literary work has to involve the process of creation on the reader's part. In yijing, verbal thoughts and pictorial thoughts are one. Thinking is conducted largely in pictures and then "transcribed" into words. (Ezra Pound once tried to capture the creative aspect of yijing in poems such as "In a Station of the Metro." He also tried to capture the critical aspect of it in his theory of imagism and vorticism, even though he did not know the term "yijing.") One characteristic of the yijing approach to criticism, therefore, is that it often includes a description of the created mental pictures on the part of the reader/critic and his/her mental attempt to bridge (unite) the literary work, the pictures, with ultimate beauty and peace.

In looking back at my critical papers for various classes, I discovered that I unconsciously used the approach of yijing, especially in some of my earlier papers when I seemed not yet to have been in the grip of Western logical critical approaches. I wrote, for instance, an essay entitled "Wordsworth's Sound and Imagination: The Snowdon Episode." In the major part of the essay I described the pictures that flashed in my mind while I was reading passages in Wordsworth's long poem, *The Prelude.*

> I saw three climbers (myself among them) winding up the mountain in silence "at the dead of night," absorbed in their "private thoughts." The sky was full of blocks of clouds of different colors, freely changing their shapes, like oily pigments disturbed in a bucket of water. All of a sudden, the moonlight broke the darkness "like a flash," lighting up the mountain tops. Under the "naked moon," the band saw a vast sea of mist and vapor, a silent ocean. Then the silence was abruptly broken, and we heard the "roaring of waters, torrents, streams/Innumerable, roaring with one voice" from a "blue chasm," a fracture in the vapor of the sea. It was a joyful revelation of divine truth to the human mind: the bright, "naked" moon sheds the light of "higher reasons" and "spiritual love" upon us; the vast ocean of mist looked like a thin curtain through which we vaguely saw the infinity of nature beyond; and the sounds of roaring waters coming out of the chasm of vapor cast us into the boundless spring of imagination from the depth of the human heart. Evoked by the divine light from above, the human spring of imagination is joined by the natural spring and becomes a sustaining source of energy, feeding "upon infinity" while transcending infinity at the same time.

Here I was describing my own experience more than Wordsworth's. The picture described by the poet is taken over and developed by the reader. The imagination of the author and the imagination of the reader are thus joined together. There was no "because" or "therefore" in the paper. There was little *logic.* And I thought it was (and it is) criticism. This seems to me a typical (but simplified) example of the yijing approach. (Incidentally, the instructor, a kind professor, found the paper interesting, though a bit "strange.")

In another paper of mine, "The Note of Life: Williams's 'The Orchestra'," I found myself describing my experiences of pictures of nature while reading William Carlos Williams's poem "The Orchestra." I "painted" these fleeting pictures and described the feelings that seemed to lead me to an understanding of a harmony, a "common tone," between man and nature. A paragraph from that paper reads: 20

The poem first struck me as a musical fairy tale. With rich musical sounds in my ear, I seemed to be walking in a solitary, dense forest on a spring morning. No sound from human society could be heard. I was now sitting under a giant pine tree, ready to hear the grand concert of Nature. With the sun slowly rising from the east, the cello (the creeping creek) and the clarinet (the rustling pine trees) started with a slow overture. Enthusiastically the violinists (the twittering birds) and the French horn (the mumbling cow) "interpose[d] their voices," and the bass (bears) got in at the wrong time. The orchestra did not stop, they continued to play. The musicians of Nature do not always play in harmony. "Together, unattuned," they have to seek "a common tone" as they play along. The symphony of Nature is like the symphony of human life: both consist of random notes seeking a "common tone." For the symphony of life

Love is that common tone
shall raise his fiery head
and sound his note.

Again, the logical pattern of this paper, the "pictorial criticism," is illogical to Western minds but "logical" to those acquainted with yijing. (Perhaps I should not even use the words "logical" and "think" because they are so conceptually tied up with "words" and with culturally-based conceptions, and therefore very misleading if not useless in a discussion of yijing. Maybe I should simply say that yijing is neither illogical nor logical, but alogical.)

I am not saying that such a pattern of "alogical" thinking is wrong—in fact some English instructors find it interesting and acceptable—but it is very non-Western. Since I was in this country to learn the English language and English literature, I had to abandon Chinese "pictorial logic," and to learn Western "verbal logic."

If I Had to Start Again

The change is profound: Through my understanding of new meanings of words like "individualism," "idealism," and "I," I began to accept the underlying concepts and values of American writing, and by learning to use "topic sentences" I began to accept a new logic. Thus, when I write papers in English, I am able to obey all the general rules of English composition. In doing this I feel that I am writing through, with, and because of a new identity. I welcome the change, for it has added a new dimension to me and to my view of the world. I am not saying that I have entirely lost my Chinese identity. In fact I feel that I will never lose it. Any time I write in Chinese, I resume my old identity, and obey the rules of Chinese composition such as "Make the 'I' modest," and "Beat around the bush before attacking the central topic." It is necessary for me to have such a Chinese identity in order to write authentic Chinese. (I have seen people who, after learning to write in English, use English logic and sentence patterning to write Chinese. They produce very awkward Chinese texts.) But when I write in English, I imagine myself slipping into a new "skin," and I let the "I" behave much more aggressively and knock the topic right on the head. Being conscious of these different identities has helped me to reconcile different systems of values and logic, and has played a pivotal role in my learning to compose in English.

Looking back, I realize that the process of learning to write in English is in fact a process of creating and defining a new identity and balancing it with the old identity. The process of learning English composition would have been easier if I had realized this earlier and consciously sought to compare the two different identities required by the two writing systems from two different cultures. It is fine and perhaps even necessary for American composition teachers to teach about topic sentences, paragraphs, the use of punctuation, documentation, and so on, but can anyone design exercises sensitive to the ideological and logical differences that students like me experience—and design them so they can be introduced at an early stage of an English composition class? As I pointed out earlier, the traditional advice "Just be yourself" is not clear and helpful to students from Korea, China, Vietnam, or India. From "Be yourself" we are likely to hear either "Forget your cultural habit of writing" or "Write as you would write in your own language." But neither of the two is what the instructor meant or what we want to do. It would be helpful if he or she pointed out the different cultural/ideological connotations of the word "I," the connotations that exist in a group-centered culture and an individual-centered culture. To sharpen the contrast, it might be useful to design papers on topics like "The Individual vs. The Group: China vs. America" or "Different 'I's' in Different Cultures."

Carolyn Matalene mentioned in her article (789) an incident concerning American businessmen who presented their Chinese hosts with gifts of cheddar cheese, not knowing that the Chinese generally do not like cheese. Liking cheddar cheese may not be essential to writing English prose, but being truly accustomed to the social norms that stand behind ideas such as the English "I" and the logical pattern of English composition—call it "compositional cheddar cheese"—is essential to writing in English. Matalene does not provide an "elixir" to help her Chinese students like English "compositional cheese," but rather recommends, as do I, that composition teachers not be afraid to give foreign students English "cheese," but to make sure to hand it out slowly, sympathetically, and fully realizing that it tastes very peculiar in the mouths of those used to a very different cuisine.

25

✑ Topics for Critical Thinking and Writing

1. In his second paragraph Fan Shen says, "I will try to describe and explore this experience of reconciling my Chinese identity with an English identity." What does the article tell us is part of a "Chinese identity," and what is

part of an "English identity"? How does your experience in answering this question account for the value of beginning his article with two narratives?

2. His article is based, primarily, on "personal experience." Is this part of his "English identity" or "Chinese identity"? Explain.

3. In paragraph 4 Fan Shen says that "Rule number one in English composition is: Be yourself." Whether you are from the United States or from another culture, try to explain why "being yourself" is (or is not) difficult when you enter college writing. Why did Fan Shen find it difficult?

4. Does Fan Shen's explanation (paragraphs 13–15) of the value of the topic sentence in English help to explain it to you, or do you have some other account of it? Explain.

5. In his next-to-last paragraph Fan Shen suggests topics for instructors to assign to international students. One of the two, "Different 'I's' in Different Cultures," strikes us as a good project to assign to native students as well as those from other cultures. We suggest here that you write a journal entry taking notes on the "different 'I's" you have experienced before attending college and now. If it suits you to do this, divide your journal entry in two down the middle, taking notes on the "I" before and the "I" after.

Paul Goodman

Paul Goodman (1911–72) received his bachelor's degree from City College in New York and his Ph.D. from the University of Chicago. He taught in several colleges and universities, and he was a prolific writer on literature, politics, and education. Goodman's view that students were victims of a corrupt society made him especially popular on campuses—even in the 1960s when students tended to distrust anyone over thirty. "A Proposal to Abolish Grading" (editors' title) is an extract from Compulsory Miseducation and the Community of Scholars *(1966).*

A Proposal to Abolish Grading

Let half a dozen of the prestigious Universities—Chicago, Stanford, the Ivy League—abolish grading, and use testing only and entirely for pedagogic purposes as teachers see fit.

Anyone who knows the frantic temper of the present schools will understand the transvaluation of values that would be effected by this modest innovation. For most of the students, the competitive grade has come to be the essence. The naïve teacher points to the beauty of the subject and the ingenuity of the research; the shrewd student asks if he is responsible for that on the final exam.

Let me at once dispose of an objection whose unanimity is quite fascinating. I think that the great majority of professors agree that grading hinders teaching and creates a bad spirit, going as far as cheating and plagiarizing. I have before me the collection of essays, *Examining in Harvard College,* and this is the consensus. It is uniformly asserted, however, that the grading is inevitable; for how else will the graduate schools, the foundations the corporations *know* whom to accept, reward, hire? How will the talent scouts know whom to tap?

By testing the applicants, of course, according to the specific task-requirements of the inducting institution, just as applicants for the Civil Service or for licenses in medicine, law, and architecture are tested. Why should Harvard professors do the testing *for* corporations and graduate-schools?

The objection is ludicrous. Dean Whitla, of the Harvard Office of Tests,   5
points out that the scholastic-aptitude and achievement tests used for *admission* to Harvard are a super-excellent index for all-around Harvard performance, better than high-school grades or particular Harvard course-grades. Presumably, these college-entrance tests are tailored for what Harvard and similar institutions want. By the same logic, would not an employer do far better to apply his own job-aptitude test rather than to rely on the vagaries of Harvard sectionmen. Indeed, I doubt that many employers bother to look at such grades; they are more likely to be interested merely in the fact of a Harvard diploma, whatever that connotes to them. The grades have most of their weight with the graduate schools— here, as elsewhere, the system runs mainly for its own sake.

It is really necessary to remind our academics of the ancient history of Examination. In the medieval university, the whole point of the gruelling trial of the candidate was whether or not to accept him as a peer. His disputation and lecture for the Master's was just that, a masterpiece to enter the guild. It was not to make comparative evaluations. It was not to weed out and select for an extra-mural licensor or employer. It was certainly not to pit one young fellow against another in an ugly competition. My philosophic impression is that the medievals thought they knew what a good job of work was and that we are competitive because we do not know. But the more status is achieved by largely irrelevant competitive evaluation, the less will we ever know.

(Of course, our American examinations never did have this purely guild orientation, just as our faculties have rarely had absolute autonomy; the examining was to satisfy Overseers, Elders, distant Regents—and they as paternal superiors have always doted on giving grades, rather than accepting peers. But I submit that this set-up itself makes it impossible for the student to *become* a master, to *have* grown up, and to commence on his own. He will always be making A or B for some overseer. And in the present atmosphere, he will always be climbing on his friend's neck.)

Perhaps the chief objectors to abolishing grading would be the students and their parents. The parents should be simply disregarded; their anxiety has done enough damage already. For the students, it seems to me that a primary duty of the university is to deprive them of their props, their dependence on extrinsic valuation and motivation, and to force them to confront the difficult enterprise itself and finally lose themselves in it.

A miserable effect of grading is to nullify the various uses of testing. Testing, for both student and teacher, is a means of structuring, and also of finding out what is blank or wrong and what has been assimilated and can be taken for granted. Review—including high-pressure review—is a means of bringing together the fragments, so that there are flashes of synoptic insight.

There are several good reasons for testing, and kinds of test. But if the   10 aim is to discover weakness, what is the point of down-grading and punishing it, and thereby inviting the student to conceal his weakness, by faking and bulling, if not cheating? The natural conclusion of synthesis is the insight itself, not a grade for having had it. For the important purpose of placement, if one can establish in the student the belief that one is testing *not* to grade and make invidious comparisons but for his own advantage, the student should normally seek his own level, where he is challenged and yet capable, rather than trying to get by. If the student dares to accept himself as he is, a teacher's grade is a crude instrument compared with a student's self-awareness. But it is rare in our universities that students are encouraged to notice objectively their vast confusion. Unlike Socrates, our teachers rely on power-drives rather than shame and ingenuous idealism.

Many students are lazy, so teachers try to goad or threaten them by grading. In the long run this must do more harm than good. Laziness is a character-defense. It may be a way of avoiding learning, in order to protect the conceit that one is already perfect (deeper, the despair that one *never* can). It may be a way of avoiding just the risk of failing and being down-graded. Sometimes it is a way of politely saying, "I won't." But since it is the authoritarian grown-up demands that have created such attitudes in the first place, why repeat the trauma? There comes a time when we must treat people as adult, laziness and all. It is one thing courageously to fire a do-nothing out of your class; it is quite another thing to evaluate him with a lordly F.

Most important of all, it is often obvious that balking in doing the work, especially among bright young people who get to great universities, means exactly what it says: The work does not suit me, not this subject, or not at this time, or not in this school, or not in school altogether. The student might not be bookish; he might be school-tired; perhaps his development ought now to take another direction. Yet unfortunately, if such a student is intelligent and is not sure of himself, he *can* be bullied into passing, and this obscures everything. My hunch is that I am describing a common situation. What a grim waste of young life and teacherly effort! Such a student will retain nothing of what he has "passed" in. Sometimes he must get mononucleosis to tell his story and be believed.

And ironically, the converse is also probably commonly true. A student flunks and is mechanically weeded out, who is really ready and eager to learn in a scholastic setting, but he has not quite caught on. A good teacher can recognize the situation, but the computer wreaks its will.

Topics for Critical Thinking and Writing

1. In his opening paragraph Goodman limits his suggestion about grading and testing to "half a dozen of the prestigious Universities." Does he offer any reason for this limitation? Can you?
2. In paragraph 3 Goodman says that "the great majority of professors agree that grading hinders teaching." What evidence does he offer to support this claim? What arguments might be made that grading assists teaching? Should Goodman have made them?
3. As a student, have grades helped you to learn, or have grades hindered you? Explain.
4. If you have been a student in an ungraded course, describe the course and evaluate the experience.

Patricia Nelson Limerick

Patricia Nelson Limerick was born in Banning, California, in 1951 and was educated at the University of California at Santa Cruz and Yale. She has taught history at Yale, Harvard, and the University of Colorado (her special interests are Western history, American Indian history, and environmental history), but she is also interested in the teaching of writing and in (as this essay reveals) students. "The Phenomenon of Phantom Students" was originally published in the Harvard Gazette, *a weekly publication for the university community.*

The Phenomenon of Phantom Students
Diagnosis and Treatment

On any number of occasions, students have told me that I am the first and only professor they have spoken to. This was, at first, flattering. Then curiosity began to replace vanity. How had conversation between teacher and student become, for many students, a novelty? These students conducted themselves as if the University were a museum: the professors on display, the students at a distance, directing any questions to the museum's guides and guards—the graduate students.

The museum model is not University policy. No "guide for instructors" tells professors to cultivate aloofness and keep students in their place. No "guide for undergraduates" tells them to speak to graduate students and only approach professors on extremely solemn and serious business.

This is not University policy, and it is by no means the experience of all Harvard students. Many confidently talk to their professors; in occasional cases, introducing a measure of shyness and humility would not be altogether unfortunate. I have no notion what the actual statistics are, but it is my impression that the disengaged are no insignificant minority. Harvard has an abundance of factors creating phantoms—my term for the radically disengaged, those staying resolutely on the academic periphery, taking large lecture classes, writing survivalist papers and exams. Phantomhood—even in its milder versions—is a significant problem and deserves the University's attention.

What creates phantoms? They tell remarkably similar stories. In the basic narrative, the freshman arrives with the familiar doubt: did Admissions make a mistake? Paradoxically, the doubt coexists with vanity; high school was easy, and Harvard won't be much worse for an individual of such certified achievement. Then, in the basic phantom story, a paper comes back with a devastating grade. Since a direct nerve connects the student's prose to his self-respect and dignity, and since the Expository Writing Program stands as the Ellis Island of Harvard, many of these initial injuries involve Expos.

Crucial Fork

The crucial fork in the road comes here: the paper, more than likely produced in good faith, is a disaster; the student has been judged by standards he doesn't understand. The split outcome really cannot be overdramatized: one route goes direct to defeat, resignation, and cynicism; the other offers a struggle, rewriting, and very probably, the learning of new skills.

Some of those new skills involve writing, but for this subject, the significant skill involves conversation—direct, productive—in which the grader of the paper says precisely and clearly how the paper went wrong, and how the author can make it better. (On the instructor's side, if there is any more intellectually demanding exercise in the academic world than this, I don't know what it is.) One successful round of this kind of dialogue has, I think, an immunizing effect; on the occasion of the next disastrous paper, the precedent set makes another collapse unlikely.

For the representative phantom, though, any number of things go wrong. Even if the instructor clearly explains the paper's problems, panic keeps the phantom from hearing. Conversation with instructors becomes an unhappy experience, avoided by anyone with any sense, in which papers are picked on to no particular result.

The essential groundwork completed, the phantom can become a part of a community in which groups of the radically disengaged make their unfortunate academic status a matter of pride or, alternatively, the phantom can think of himself as uniquely and distinctively cut off from the University. In either case, the crucial transition is complete: from thinking, "I *may* be the fluke in Admissions," the student has moved on to certainty:

"I *am* the fluke." From here on, the prospect for positive student/faculty contact meets the unpassable obstacle: the student's own fatalism.

I draw here a portrait of extreme cases—with academic underperformance part of the package. There are a substantial number of individuals doing perfectly competent academic work who still would choose a visit to the dentist over a visit to a professor. Usually, no particular unhappy event explains their shyness, and one could certainly argue that their situation is not particularly unfortunate. They are doing the reading, and writing their papers, and getting solid educations. But they are missing something. Recently, my course assistant arranged for me to have lunch with a recently graduated student who had been in my class; four years of a good academic performance, and she had never spoken to a professor. She was a remarkable person, involved over a long time in volunteer work for the homeless. I think both she and Harvard would have profited had she been comfortable talking with professors.

Student/Faculty Contact

I address myself here to the problem of student/faculty contact in the case   10
of students both with and without academic problems. Reading and writing with both ease and intensity are fundamental goals; speaking with ease and intensity should be in the package.

How are students to be persuaded to talk to professors? This encouragement should not offer false advertising. One simply cannot say that all professors are at heart accessible and friendly. Some of them are certifiably grumpy, and many of them are shy. They are still worth talking to.

With a major interest in Indian/White relations, I cannot resist thinking anthropologically. White people and Indian people still confront each other through a fog of stereotypes (all Indians are noble and in touch with nature, or, alternatively, all Indians are demoralized and in touch with alcohol), and the impulse to provide a comparable analysis for student/professor relations is irresistible. Images have equal powers in both situations.

Commonly Held Student Myths about Professors

1a. *Professors Must Be Asked Specific, Better Yet, Bibliographic Questions.* Professors do not converse like ordinary people. To speak their language, you must address them in this fashion: "Professor X, I was very interested in your remarks about the unification of the Northwest Company and the Hudson's Bay Company in 1821, and I wondered if you might direct me to further reading." If you do not have a specific question like this, then you have no business troubling a professor.

1b. *Professors Only Like to Talk about Senior Theses.* This proposition was brought home to me at a Quincy House gathering. A number of students and I were speaking on a general, humane topic (sports?) when they discovered my hidden identity. The truth out, they began to tell me about their senior theses. The evening, I felt, became something of a busman's holiday.

2. *Professors Only Want to Talk with Other Elegant, Learned and Brilliant Conversationalists.* (Numbers 1 and 2 may appear to be contradictory, but they often coexist.) Living in the intellectual equivalent of Mt. McKinley or Mt. Whitney, professors do not like to descend the mountain to talk to the lowlanders. They are used to sophisticated, erudite conversation, in contrast to which normal speech sounds embarrassingly flat and pedestrian. Even if they seem to tolerate the speech of mortals, professors are inwardly thinking how stupid it sounds. They have, in their distinguished careers, heard nearly every insight there is. If a new idea seems to occur to a student in 1983, it can be assumed that the professor first heard that idea sometime in the 1950s. Having a memory built on the order of a steel trap, the professor does not need to hear it again.

3. *If I Speak to a Professor, He Will Probably (and Maybe Rightly) Assume That I Am a Grade-grubbing Toady.* (The students, of course, use a more vivid term.) This belief actually concerns attitudes to other students: dependent, hypocritical drudges hang around professors, asking insincere questions, and seeking recommendation letters; students with integrity keep their distance and avoid the dishonor of visibly trying to make an impression.

Countering these three assumptions does not require a debasing of professional status; respect for achievement and authority, and excessive deference and fear are two different matters. Number 1 and #2 are both extremely widespread, and #3 has, I think, the greatest power over phantoms. In the further reaches of phantomhood, these assumptions rest on considerable hostility toward the institution, a basic act of self-defense in which the individual reasons (if that's the word): "Harvard has ignored and injured me; well, Harvard is stupid anyway." We are dealing here, in other words, with wounded dignity, a condition not known for bringing out the finest in human behavior.

In the last eight years, I have seen many phantoms emerge from hiding; I have enormous faith in their potential for recovery. Nothing encouraged me more than the Committee on College Life meeting last spring. I had promised to bring expert witnesses—verifiable phantoms. Having made the promise, I began to regret it. If these individuals barely had the courage to talk to me, how would they face a panel of five professors, two deans and five students? Would any consent to appear? The first five I called said yes—without reluctance. At the committee, they spoke with frankness and energy. To be equally frank, that amazed me—I evidently expected that I would have to act as their interpreter. They were, instead, perfectly capable of speaking for themselves.

There is a fairly reliable personal solution to the problem of phantom-hood for faculty to follow:

1. *Discover the phantoms* (midterm grade sheets locate the ones with academic problems; reports from course assistants and from professorial visits to sections identify the others). 20

2. *Contact them.*

3. *Get an acknowledgment of the condition of phantomhood, directly and briefly.* (Don't milk it for its misery, which is often at a pretty high level.)

4. *Engage them in a specific project—ideally, rewriting a paper.* Here, the instructor is most productive when she uses her own enthusiasm for the subject to launch a discussion of the ideas in the paper, so that the student slides, without perceiving it, into what was hitherto unimaginable—"an intellectual conversation with a professor."

5. *Keep a careful eye out for achievement on the part of the student, during the conversation, and comment on it.* This is only in part "encouragement"—the primary goal is to help the individual penetrate the mysterious standards of what constitutes "insight" or a "a solid point."

6. *Hold out for concrete evidence of recovery—a successfully rewritten paper, for instance.* These second drafts are almost without exception much better papers—primarily because the student now has what was wholly lacking before—faith in a living, actual audience. 25

7. *Encourage a wide application of the new principles.* The student's logical next step is to say to the instructor, "I can work with you because you are different from the others." Resist this. The sports analogy is the best: you may need a coach at the start of learning a sport, but you do not need a coach at your elbow for the rest of your career in that sport. Professors, like most other individuals, like snowflakes, are all different. That, surely, is part of their charm.

Phantoms are not beyond understanding, and certainly not beyond recovery. But there is another, equally complex party to the basic transactions of student/faculty contact. We might now take up the question of the genesis of shyness, harriedness and grumpiness in professors.

How nice to lead a leisured life in a book-lined office, I used to think, chatting, reading and (if *real* work meant actually teaching classes) working only a few hours a week. Cross the line into professorhood, and the plot thickens considerably. Those few minutes a week in class rest on hours of preparation. Reading exams and papers closely eats up time. Then, of course, there is "one's own work"—research and writing for promised articles and books. Add to this, participation in professional organizations and department and University committees, and one's leisured time in the book-lined office often comes down to checking the datebook to see where one is due next.

That is in part why professors can seem grumpy and aloof, even when they are genuinely committed to teaching. Phantoms, and prospective phantoms, should be advised not to take personal injury when cut short by an individual who will have to stay up most of the night revising the next day's lecture and writing recommendation letters. Schedule a meeting for a time when the universe at least gives the illusion of being a bit more in the professor's control, and try not to resent any accidental rudeness.

More important, phantoms should be encouraged to use empathy in understanding the professors. Phantoms are, after all, experts in shyness; shyness, while not universal in the professorial population, is no stranger. Consider the pattern: the individual is initially drawn to the world of books and private contemplation, communicating more often through writing than through speech. How nice, the susceptible individual thinks, that there is a profession that encourages and supports this retreat to private intellectual exertion. And that promise seems to hold for the initial years of graduate school, and then, abruptly, the treachery stands exposed. One has to walk into a classroom, cause everyone else to fall silent, and become the center of attention. It is a shy person's nightmare, and individuals evolve the best mechanisms for dealing with it that they can. Once the mechanisms are in place, the individual holds on to them. It is undeniably more dignified to seem aloof and uncaring than to seem scared and shy.

I write as a reformed phantom myself—one, happily, in the category in which academic problems did not play a part. My papers carried me through college and graduate school; I was a veritable sphinx in classes. Occupying—initially to my horror—the teacher's chair, phantomhood became a luxury I could not afford.

A few years ago, when I had just started teaching, an old professor of mine from Santa Cruz came to Yale for the year. "We're so fragmented at Santa Cruz," he said, "I am really looking forward to having hard-hitting intellectual conversations again."

"Hard-hitting intellectual conversations?" I didn't seem to have ever had one. It was a concept beyond the reach of an only partially recovered phantom.

Seven or eight years later, I am thoroughly addicted to the kind of conversations I thought I would never have. They provide the core of vitality for the university, the only real cement that makes such a collection of disparate individuals into a community. I want the phantoms included in the community.

✎ Topics for Critical Thinking and Writing

1. Limerick mentions that after receiving an essay with a "devastating grade," a student finds that "conversation with instructors becomes an unhappy experience, avoided by anyone with any sense." If on some occasion your good sense deserted you and you therefore engaged in conversation with an instructor, was the conversation profitable? Why, or why not?

2. Let's assume that you find this essay interesting, and not simply because of the subject matter. *Why* is it interesting? What are some of the rhetorical devices that the author uses to engage your attention?
3. In paragraph 4 Limerick refers to the Expository Writing Program as "the Ellis Island of Harvard." Explain the metaphor. In the same paragraph she says: "A direct nerve connects the student's prose to his self-respect." Again, explain the metaphor and then try to explain why, for most of us, it rings true.
4. In paragraph 3 Limerick mentions, but does not define or explain, something she labels "survivalist papers and exams." In a paragraph invent a definition for this term, using both Limerick's essay and your own experience as sources.
5. Without naming or in any other way clearly identifying the instructor, write an essay of five hundred words in which you explain why—at least for that instructor—you are a phantom student. Or, on the other hand, write an essay explaining why you have enjoyed conversing with an instructor. *Hint:* a few bits of dialogue will probably be effective.
6. Write a dialogue of an imaginary conference between a composition teacher and a phantom. (Even though this is an exercise in writing pure fiction, you may use one of your own essays as a prop.)

E. B. White

E[lwyn] B[rooks] White (1899–1985) wrote poetry and fiction, but he is most widely known as an essayist and as the coauthor (with William Strunk, Jr.) of Elements of Style. *After a long career at* The New Yorker *he retired to Maine, but he continued to write until the year before his death at the age of 86.*

Education

I have an increasing admiration for the teacher in the country school where we have a third-grade scholar in attendance. She not only undertakes to instruct her charges in all the subjects of the first three grades, but she manages to function quietly and effectively as a guardian of their health, their clothes, their habits, their mothers, and their snowball engagements. She has been doing this sort of Augean task for twenty years, and is both kind and wise. She cooks for the children on the stove that heats the room, and she can cool their passions or warm their soup with equal competence. She conceives their costumes, cleans up their messes, and shares their confidences. My boy already regards his teacher as his great friend, and I think tells her a great deal more than he tells us.

The shift from city school to country school was something we worried about quietly all last summer. I have always rather favored public school over private school, if only because in public school you meet a greater variety of children. This bias of mine, I suspect, is partly an attempt to justify my own past (I never knew anything but public schools) and partly an involuntary defense against getting kicked in the shins by a young ceramist on his way to the kiln. My wife was unacquainted with public schools, never having been exposed (in her early life) to anything more public than the washroom of Miss Winsor's. Regardless of our backgrounds, we both knew that the change in schools was something that concerned not us but the scholar himself. We hoped it would work out all right. In New York our son went to a medium-priced private institution with semi-progressive ideas of education, and modern plumbing. He learned fast, kept well, and we were satisfied. It was an electric, colorful, regimented existence with moments of pleasurable pause and giddy incident. The day the Christmas angel fainted and had to be carried out by one of the Wise Men was educational in the highest sense of the term. Our scholar gave imitations of it around the house for weeks afterward, and I doubt if it ever goes completely out of his mind.

His days were rich in formal experience. Wearing overalls and an old sweater (the accepted uniform of the private seminary), he sallied forth at morn accompanied by a nurse or a parent and walked (or was pulled) two blocks to a corner where the school bus made a flag stop. This flashy vehicle was as punctual as death: seeing us waiting at the cold curb, it would sweep to a halt, open its mouth, suck the boy in, and spring away with an angry growl. It was a good deal like a train picking up a bag of mail. At school the scholar was worked on for six or seven hours by half a dozen teachers and a nurse, and was revived on orange juice in mid-morning. In a cinder court he played games supervised by an athletic instructor, and in a cafeteria he ate lunch worked out by a dietitian. He soon learned to read with gratifying facility and discernment and to make Indian weapons of a semi-deadly nature. Whenever one of his classmates fell low of a fever the news was put on the wires and there were breathless phone calls to physicians, discussing periods of incubation and allied magic.

In the country all one can say is that the situation is different, and somehow more casual. Dressed in corduroys, sweatshirt, and short rubber boots, and carrying a tin dinner-pail, our scholar departs at the crack of dawn for the village school, two and a half miles down the road, next to the cemetery. When the road is open and the car will start, he makes the journey by motor, courtesy of his old man. When the snow is deep or the motor is dead or both, he makes it on the hoof. In the afternoons he walks or hitches all or part of the way home in fair weather, gets transported in foul. The schoolhouse is a two-room frame building, bungalow type, shingles stained a burnt brown with weather-resistant stain. It has a chemical toilet in the basement and two teachers above the stairs. One takes the first three grades, the other the fourth, fifth, and sixth. They have little or no time for individual instruction, and no time at all for the esoteric. They teach what they know themselves, just as fast and as hard as they can manage. The pupils sit still at their desks in class, and do their milling around outdoors during recess.

There is no supervised play. They play cops and robbers (only they   5 call it "Jail") and throw things at one another—snowballs in winter, rose hips in fall. It seems to satisfy them. They also construct darts, pinwheels, and "pick-up sticks" (jackstraws), and the school itself does a brisk trade in penny candy, which is for sale right in the classroom and which contains "surprises." The most highly prized surprise is a fake cigarette, made of cardboard, fiendishly lifelike.

The memory of how apprehensive we were at the beginning is still strong. The boy was nervous about the change too. The tension, on that first fair morning in September when we drove him to school, almost blew the windows out of the sedan. And when later we picked him up on the road, wandering along with his little blue lunch-pail, and got his laconic report "All right" in answer to our inquiry about how the day had gone, our relief was vast. Now, after almost a year of it, the only difference we can discover in the two school experiences is that in the country he sleeps better at night—and *that* probably is more the air than the education. When grilled on the subject of school-in-country vs. school-in-city, he replied that the chief difference is that the day seems to go so much quicker in the country. "Just like lightning," he reported.

✎ Topics for Critical Thinking and Writing

1. Which school, public or private, does White prefer? Since White doesn't state his preference outright, from what evidence were you able to infer it?
2. In the first half of paragraph 2 White admits to a bias in favor of public schools, and he speculates, half-seriously, about the origins of his bias. If his intention here is not simply to amuse us, what is it?
3. What is White's strongest argument in favor of the school he prefers? Where in the essay do you find it?

LeAlan Jones and Lloyd Newman

The following material comes from Our America: Life and Death on the South Side of Chicago *(1997). This book started as two radio documentaries,* Ghetto Life 101 *and* Remorse: The 14 Stories of Eric Morse *(the second episode refers to the death of Morse, who was dropped from the fourteenth floor of an apartment building).*

The book had an unusual origin. In 1993 a professional writer, David Isay, decided to hire some youngsters to tape record "sound portraits" in Chicago public housing. He settled on LeAlan

Jones (13 years old) and Lloyd Newman (14 years old), who for seven days in March recorded material. Isay then edited it, and the boys recorded their own narration. The two radio programs were aired in 1996, and then turned into a book, Our America, *in the following year.*

Interview at Donoghue Elementary School

We're both in eighth grade at Donoghue Elementary School, fixing to graduate in a couple of months. There are twenty-eight kids in our homeroom class, and it's pretty rowdy most of the time.

But in our classes we're a bunch of smart kids. If you could just hear some of the things we talk about—ooh, we have some heavy discussions! We talk about the government. We talk about the president, what Bush is doing when the cameras aren't around, how JFK got assassinated, what they did to Mike Tyson, and how William Kennedy Smith got off. We've always been doing that—since third grade. Man, it might not look like it, but we read the newspapers. We're smart kids!

Ms. Margaret A. Tolson has been the principal at Donoghue since 1991. We interviewed her in the front office about her job and our school.

Is it hard being a principal in this neighborhood?
Ms. Tolson: Yes, it's difficult. Not so much because the children are really any different. It's difficult because of the publicity that surrounds our housing development and community. People set their minds, before they come here, to expect problems, and generally you get what you expect. There *is* danger in and around the school. You all live in it every day. That means if we work here, we work in it. So that makes it difficult. And we have difficulty convincing you that we believe in you, that we don't believe that you will grow up to be members of gangs, that you can achieve anything that you want to achieve. We have to convince you of that every day. And you don't believe that we believe you're smart.

So it's very difficult. It's difficult for some teachers to see the skills that you have. But one of the reasons I'm here is to help to train teachers to look at the gifts that you bring with you. Many of you get up in the morning, deal with whether or not an elevator is working, you may dress a brother or sister, may stop at the store to get some breakfast. Those are all skills that can be used in education. But it's a matter of showing you that it is a skill. Many of you cook, and you cook quite well considering what you use to create meals. We can use the measurements in math, we can use labels in reading. But it's a matter of training a teacher so that she can pull all of that out of you and use it for education. So yes, it's difficult. But can it be done? Sure.

5

LeAlan: *Do you see any gang activities here that you would see in the movies like* **West Side Story?**
At times, yes. I know that I have some gang members. But they come to school and many of them try to be halfway respectful while they're here.

You all have a decision to make about gangs, whether or not it's going to be a part of your life. I hope it won't. But I also hoped that you wouldn't see the guns and the shootings. But have you experience it? Yes. We have children who have been killed. We have children who have been shot on the street in front of school. As a matter of fact, the first summer that I arrived, within the first week we had a drive-by shooting at the front door. Then we had another drive-by shooting within two days that started over near your house, Lloyd. I sent you all out the back door that day. So yes, we've seen some of the things like you see in the movies. Do they happen every day? No.

LeAlan: *Do you hear kids talk about some of the things they see that you didn't see at a young age?*
Oh yes. I have some of my students who know more about gangs, guns, and sex than I do, because they have observed things. I have kindergartners who can tell you about sexual intercourse, who can tell you about guns and gangs, but cannot read and have not found a great many things in their life enjoyable. I would hope that none of you would have to see a family member get shot in front of you, but I know I have plenty of students who have seen that. I would hope that none of you would have to experience having hepatitis or AIDS. But I know that I have students who have to deal with that. They know about a lot of things I would wish they would never see.

Lloyd: *Ms. Margaret A. Tolson, what does the "A" stand for in your name?*
Armstrong. It's my middle name.

Lloyd: *Could you describe us?*
Let me see. . . . . Lloyd. Lloyd is a quiet young man in school who could do a lot more things if he would believe in himself. He should speak up a little more often about his ideas, because Lloyd has a lot of ideas and a lot of things that he is capable of doing.

LeAlan is a very expressive young man. He has opinions about things. He thinks in depth. He takes a look at situations around him. He observes carefully. You challenge things, which is good. You will listen to someone else's side but you won't necessarily accept it.

Lloyd: *What do you think we'll be when we grow up?*
LeAlan will be a politician. Lloyd, I think you will be behind the scenes—probably a businessman and a millionaire and I'll have to come borrow money from you in my old age.

Lloyd: *Are there any classes that you call the baddest class in Donoghue?*

No. Now, are my eighth graders my most rambunctious group? Yes. You all keep me challenged every day, to say the least.

Lloyd: *What do you think of the people in eighth grade? What will they become in life?*
Well, if they're true to form for Donoghue, they will become politicians, lawyers, judges, doctors, secretaries, teachers in the classrooms at Donoghue. They will become expert workmen, technicians—most anything that they want to become.

15

Lloyd: *Mrs. Tolson, what percentage of the students do you think are going to fall down?*
How many are not going to make it? I'd say maybe about five to six percent.

•   •   •

One day my buddy Stevie grabbed my mike and started goofing. He did a whole fake radio broadcast pretending he was David Duke:

Stevie: (pretending he's David Duke): I'm your host, David Duke, the host of this show, *The Lifestyles of the Nice and White.* We're just going to talk about how much I hate niggers. See, all niggers deserve to die. Want a good way to kill a nigger? You tie him to a tree and pour hot tar all over him, or you get a knife and cut all the way up to his throat, or you can just lynch the guy real tight around the neck until his head pops open. That's forty good ways to kill a nigger. I'm your host David Duke.
One day me and my friend J. Edgar Hoover were walking through the woods, and a black man came up and said, "Hey, white man, what are you doing in our territory? This is black man's territory!" And we said, "This is our land, nigger, we brought you here . . . ." Then the niggers started throwing rocks at us. So I did my Klansman call and Klansmen started coming out of the sewers and out of the trees. The niggers started running. And we said, "Now we got you!" And started shooting. Winchester rifles. And we just blew their brains out. Two of them got away, but we caught them later on. We dragged one of them out of his house, put him on a cross, and burned his black ass crisp! The other one? Had to use the bloodhounds. Very good dogs! We caught that nigger in Harlem, tied him to a tree, poured hot tar all over him, stuck a match in his ass, and cut out his esophagus. Then we lynched that black motherfucker. That's one way to kill a nigger. Remember: you can never trust a nigger, because niggers aren't trustworthy, O.K.? I'm your host, David Duke, signing off.

✎ Topics for Critical Thinking and Writing

1. We reprint here 9 questions that LeAlan and Lloyd asked their elementary school principal. In 3 or 4 words, characterize their questions.
2. How do Ms. Tolson's answers help to characterize LeAlan and Lloyd?

3. In 2 or 3 sentences, describe the neighborhood of Donoghue Elementary School.
4. How do you imagine LeAlan and Lloyd learned to conduct an interview?
5. Imagine that you were planning to interview your elementary school principal. Write 6 to 8 questions that you would ask. Then, in 3 or 4 sentences, explain how you arrived at the questions.

Toni Cade Bambara

Toni Cade Bambara (1939–95), an African-American writer, was born in New York City in 1939, received her B.A. from Queens College in 1959 and her M.A. from City College in 1964. Both schools are part of the City University of New York. She taught at Livingston College of Rutgers University, and served as writer in residence at Spelman College in Atlanta.

The Lesson

Back in the days when everyone was old and stupid or young and foolish and me and Sugar were the only ones just right, this lady moved on our block with nappy hair and proper speech and no makeup. And quite naturally we laughed at her, laughed the way we did at the junk man who went about his business like he was some bigtime president and his sorry-ass horse his secretary. And we kinda hated her too, hated the way we did the winos who cluttered up our parks and pissed on our handball walls and stank up our hallways and stairs so you couldn't halfway play hide-and-seek without a goddamn gas mask. Miss Moore was her name. The only woman on the block with no first name. And she was black as hell, cept for her feet, which were fish-white and spooky. And she was always planning these boring-ass things for us to do, us being my cousin, mostly, who lived on the block cause we all moved North the same time and to the same apartment then spread out gradual to breathe. And our parents would yank our heads into some kinda shape and crisp up our clothes so we'd be presentable for travel with Miss Moore, who always looked like she was going to church, though she never did. Which is just one of the things the grownups talked about when they talked behind her back like a dog. But when she came calling with some sachet she'd sewed up or some gingerbread she'd made or some book, why then they'd all be too embarrassed to turn her down and we'd get handed over all spruced up. She'd been to college and said it was only right that she should take responsibility for the young ones' education, and she not even related by marriage or blood. So they'd go for it. Specially Aunt Gretchen. She was the main gofer in the family. You got some ole dumb shit foolishness you want somebody to go for, you send for Aunt Gretchen. She been screwed into the go-along for so long, it's a blood-deep natural thing with her. Which is how she got saddled with me and Sugar and Junior in the first place while our mothers were in a la-de-da apartment up the block having a good ole time.

So this one day Miss Moore rounds us all up at the mailbox and it's puredee hot and she's knockin herself out about arithmetic. And school suppose to let up in summer I heard, but she don't never let up. And the starch in my pinafore scratching the shit outta me and I'm really hating this nappy-head bitch and her goddamn college degree. I'd much rather go to the pool or to the show where it's cool. So me and Sugar leaning on the mailbox being surly, which is a Miss Moore word. And Flyboy checking out what everybody brought for lunch. And Fat Butt already wasting his peanut-butter-and-jelly sandwich like the pig he is. And Junebug punchin on Q.T.'s arm for potato chips. And Rosie Giraffe shifting from one hip to the other waiting for somebody to step on her foot or ask her if she from Georgia so she can kick ass, preferably Mercedes'. And Miss Moore asking us do we know what money is, like we a bunch of retards. I mean real money, she say, like it's only poker chips or monopoly papers we lay on the grocer. So right away I'm tired of this and say so. And would much rather snatch Sugar and go to the Sunset and terrorize the West Indian kids and take their hair ribbons and their money too. And Miss Moore files that remark away for next week's lesson on brotherhood, I can tell. And finally I say we oughta get to the subway cause it's cooler and besides we might meet some cute boys. Sugar done swiped her mama's lipstick, so we ready.

So we heading down the street and she's boring us silly about what things cost and what our parents make and how much goes for rent and how money ain't divided up right in this country. And then she gets to the part about we all poor and live in the slums, which I don't feature. And I'm ready to speak on that, but she steps out in the street and hails two cabs just like that. Then she hustles half the crew in with her and hands me a five-dollar bill and tells me to calculate 10 percent tip for the driver. And we're off. Me and Sugar and Junebug and Flyboy hangin out the window and hollering to everybody, putting lipstick on each other cause Flyboy a faggot anyway, and making farts with our sweaty armpits. But I'm mostly trying to figure how to spend this money. But they all fascinated with the meter ticking and Junebug starts laying bets to how much it'll read when Flyboy can't hold his breath no more. Then Sugar lays bets as to how much it'll be when we get there. So I'm stuck. Don't nobody want to go for my plan, which is to jump out at the next light and run off to the first bar-b-que we can find. Then the driver tells us to get the hell out cause we there already. And the meter reads eighty-five cents. And I'm stalling to figure out the tip and Sugar say give him a dime. And I decide he don't need it as bad as I do, so later for him. But then he tries to take off with Junebug's foot still in the door so we talk about his mama something ferocious. Then we check out that we on Fifth Avenue and everybody dressed up in stockings. One lady in a fur coat, hot as it is. White folks crazy.

"This is the place," Miss Moore say, presenting it to us in the voice she uses at the museum. "Let's look in the windows before we go in."

"Can we steal?" Sugar asks very serious like she's getting the ground rules squared away before she plays. "I beg your pardon," say Miss Moore, and we fall out. So she leads us around the windows of the toy store and me and Sugar screamin, "This is mine, that's mine, I gotta have that, that was made for me, I was born for that," till Big Butt drowns us out.

"Hey, I'm goin to buy that there."

"That there? You don't even know what it is, stupid."

"I do so," he say punchin on Rosie Giraffe. "It's a microscope."

"Whatcha gonna do with a microscope, fool?"

"Look at things."

"Like what, Ronald?" ask Miss Moore. And Big Butt ain't got the first notion. So here go Miss Moore gabbing about the thousands of bacteria in a drop of water and the somethinorother in a speck of blood and the million and one living things in the air around us is invisible to the naked eye. And what she say that for? Junebug go to town on that "naked" and we rolling. Then Miss Moore ask what it cost. So we all jam into the window smudgin it up and the price tag say $300. So then she ask how long'd take for Big Butt and Junebug to save up their allowances. "Too long," I say. "Yeh," adds Sugar, "outgrown it by that time." And Miss Moore say no, you never outgrow learning instruments. "Why, even medical students and interns and," blah, blah, blah. And we ready to choke Big Butt for bringing it up in the first damn place.

"This here costs four hundred eighty dollars," say Rosie Giraffe. So we pile up all over her to see what she pointin out. My eyes tell me it's a chunk of glass cracked with something heavy, and different-color inks dripped into the splits, then the whole thing put into a oven or something. But for $480 it don't make sense.

"That's a paperweight made of semi-precious stones fused together under tremendous pressure," she explains slowly, and her hands doing the mining and all the factory work.

"So what's a paperweight?" asks Rosie Giraffe.

"To weigh paper with, dumbbell," say Flyboy, the wise man from the East.

"Not exactly," say Miss Moore, which is what she say when you warm or way off too. "It's to weigh paper down so it won't scatter and make your desk untidy." So right away me and Sugar curtsy to each other and then to Mercedes who is more the tidy type.

"We don't keep paper on top of the desk in my class," say Junebug, figuring Miss Moore crazy or lyin one.

"At home, then," she say. "Don't you have a calendar and a pencil case and a blotter and a letter-opener on your desk at home where you do your homework?" And she know damn well what our homes look like cause she nosys around in them every chance she gets.

"I don't even have a desk," say Junebug. "Do we?"

"No. And I don't get no homework neither," says Big Butt.

"And I don't even have a home," say Flyboy like he do at school to keep the white folks off his back and sorry for him. Send this poor kid to camp posters, is his specialty.

"I do," says Mercedes. "I have a box of stationery on my desk and a picture of my cat. My godmother bought the stationery and the desk. There's a big rose on each sheet and the envelopes smell like roses."

"Who wants to know about your smelly-ass stationery," say Rosie Giraffe fore I can get my two cents in.

"It's important to have a work area all your own so that . . ."

"Will you look at this sailboat, please," say Flyboy, cuttin her off and pointin to the thing like it was his. So once again we tumble all over each other to gaze at this magnificent thing in the toy store which is just big enough to maybe sail two kittens across the pond if you strap them to the posts tight. We all start reciting the price tag like we in assembly. "Hand-crafted sailboat of fiberglass at one thousand one hundred ninety-five dollars."

"Unbelievable," I hear myself say and am really stunned. I read it again for myself just in case the group recitation put me in a trance. Same thing. For some reason this pisses me off. We look at Miss Moore and she lookin at us, waiting for I dunno what.

"Who'd pay all that when you can buy a sailboat set for a quarter at Pop's, a tube of glue for a dime, and a ball of string for eight cents? It must have a motor and a whole lot else besides," I say. "My sailboat cost me about fifty cents."

"But will it take water?" say Mercedes with her smart ass.

"Took mine to Alley Pond Park once," say Flyboy. "String broke. Lost it. Pity."

"Sailed mine in Central Park and it keeled over and sank. Had to ask my father for another dollar."

"And you got the strap," laugh Big Butt. "The jerk didn't even have a string on it. My old man wailed on his behind."

Little Q.T. was staring hard at the sailboat and you could see he wanted it bad. But he too little and somebody'd just take it from him. So what the hell. "This boat for kids, Miss Moore?"

"Parents silly to buy something like that just to get all broke up," say Rosie Giraffe.

"That much money it should last forever," I figure.

"My father'd buy it for me if I wanted it."

"Your father, my ass," say Rosie Giraffe getting a chance to finally push Mercedes.

"Must be rich people shop here," say Q.T.

"You are a very bright boy," say Flyboy. "What was your first clue?" And he rap him on the head with the back of his knuckles, since Q.T. the only one he could get away with. Though Q.T. liable to come up behind you years later and get his licks in when you half expect it.

"What I want to know is," I says to Miss Moore though I never talk to her, I wouldn't give the bitch that satisfaction, "is how much a real boat costs? I figure a thousand'd get you a yacht any day."

"Why don't you check that out," she says, "and report back to the group?" Which really pains my ass. If you gonna mess up a perfectly good swim day least you could do is have some answers. "Let's go in," she say like she got something up her sleeve. Only she don't lead the way. So me and Sugar turn the corner to where the entrance is, but when we get there I kinda hang back. Not that I'm scared, what's there to be afraid of, just a toy store. But I feel funny, shame. But what I got to be shamed about? Got as much right to go in as anybody. But somehow I can't seem to get hold of the door, so I step away for Sugar to lead. But she hangs back too. And I look at her and she looks at me and this is ridiculous. I mean, damn, I have never ever been shy about doing nothing or going nowhere. But then Mercedes steps up and then Rosie Giraffe and Big Butt crowd in behind and shove, and next thing we all stuffed into the doorway with only Mercedes squeezing past us, smoothing out her jumper and walking right down the aisle. Then the rest of us tumble in like a glued-together jigsaw done all wrong. And people lookin at us. And it's like the time me and Sugar crashed into the Catholic church on a dare. But once we got in there and everything so hushed and holy and the candles and the bowin and the handkerchiefs on all the drooping heads, I just couldn't go through with the plan. Which was for me to run up to the altar and do a tap dance while Sugar played the nose flute and messed around in the holy water. And Sugar kept givin me the elbow. Then later teased me so bad I tied her up in the shower and turned it on and locked her in. And she'd be there till this day if Aunt Gretchen hadn't finally figured I was lyin about the boarder takin a shower.

Same thing in the store. We all walkin on tiptoe and hardly touchin the games and puzzles and things. And I watched Miss Moore who is steady watchin us like she waitin for a sign. Like Mama Drewery watches the sky and sniffs the air and takes note of just how much slant is in the bird formation. Then me and Sugar bump smack into each other, so busy gazing at the toys, 'specially the sailboat. But we don't laugh and go into our fat-lady bump-stomach routine. We just stare at that price tag. Then Sugar run a finger over the whole boat. And I'm jealous and want to hit her. Maybe not her, but I sure want to punch somebody in the mouth.

"Whatcha bring us here for, Miss Moore?"

"You sound angry, Sylvia. Are you mad about something?" Givin me one of them grins like she tellin a grown-up joke that never turns out to be funny. And she's lookin very closely at me like maybe she plannin to do my portrait from memory. I'm mad, but I won't give her that satisfaction. So I slouch around the store bein very bored and say, "Let's go."

Me and Sugar at the back of the train watchin the tracks whizzin by large then small then gettin gobbled up in the dark. I'm thinkin about this tricky toy I saw in the store. A clown that somersaults on a bar then does chin-ups just cause you yank lightly at his leg. Cost $35. I could see me askin my mother for a $35 birthday clown. "You wanna who that costs what?" she'd say, cocking her head to the side to get a better view of the hole in my head. Thirty-five dollars and the whole household could go visit Granddaddy Nelson in the country. Thirty-five dollars would pay for the rent and the piano bill too. Who are these people that spend that much for performing clowns and $1000 for toy sailboats? What kinda work they do and how they live and how come we ain't in on it? Where we are is who we are, Miss Moore always pointin out. But it don't necessarily have to be that way, she always adds then waits for somebody to say that poor people have to wake up and demand their share of the pie and don't none of us know what kind of pie she talkin about in the first damn place. But she ain't so smart cause I still got her four dollars from the taxi and she sure ain't gettin it. Messin up my day with this shit. Sugar nudges me in my pocket and winks.

Miss Moore lines us up in front of the mailbox where we started from,   45 seem like years ago, and I got a headache for thinkin so hard. And we lean all over each other so we can hold up under the draggy-ass lecture she always finishes us off with at the end before we thank her for borin us to tears. But she just looks at us like she readin tea leaves. Finally she say, "Well, what do you think of F. A. O. Schwartz?"

Rosie Giraffe mumbles, "White folks crazy."

"I'd like to go there again when I get my birthday money," says Mercedes, and we shove her out the pack so she has to lean on the mailbox by herself.

"I'd like a shower. Tiring day," say Flyboy.

Then Sugar surprises me by sayin, "You know, Miss Moore, I don't think all of us here put together eat in a year what that sailboat costs." And Miss Moore lights up like somebody goosed her. "And?" she say, urging Sugar on. Only I'm standin on her foot so she don't continue.

"Imagine for a minute what kind of society, it is in which some people   50 can spend on a toy what it would cost to feed a family of six or seven. What do you think?"

"I think," say Sugar pushing me off her feet like she never done before, cause I whip her ass in a minute, "that this is not much of a democracy if you ask me. Equal chance to pursue happiness means an equal crack at the dough, don't it?" Miss Moore is besides herself and I am disgusted with Sugar's treachery. So I stand on her foot one more time to see if she'll shove me. She shuts up, and Miss Moore looks at me, sorrowfully I'm thinkin. And somethin weird is goin on, I can feel it in my chest.

"Anybody else learn anything today?" lookin dead at me. I walk away and Sugar has to run to catch up and don't even seem to notice when I shrug her arm off my shoulder.

"Well, we got four dollars anyway," she says.

"Uh hunh."

"We could go to Hascombs and get half a chocolate layer and then go   55
to the Sunset and still have plenty money for potato chips and ice cream
sodas."

"Uh hunh."

"Race you to Hascombs," she say.

We start down the block and she gets ahead which is O.K. by me cause
I'm going to the West End and then over to the Drive to think this day
through. She can run if she want to and even run faster. But ain't nobody
gonna beat me at nuthin.

✎ Topics for Critical Thinking and Writing

1. What is the point of Miss Moore's lesson? Why does Sylvia resist it?
2. Describe the relationship between Sugar and Sylvia. What is Sugar's function in the story?
3. What does the last line of the story suggest?

Wu-tsu Fa-yen

Wu-tsu Fa-yen (1025–1104) was a Chinese Zen Buddhist priest. More exactly, he was a Ch'an priest: Zen is Japanese for the Chinese Ch'an.

The practitioner of Zen (to use the more common name) seeks satori, "enlightenment" or "awakening." The awakening is from a world of blind strivings (including those of reason and of morality). The awakened being, free from a sense of the self in opposition to all other things, perceives the unity of all things. Wu-tsu belonged to the branch of Zen that uses "shock therapy, the purpose of which is to jolt the student out of his analytical and conceptual way of thinking and lead him back to his natural and spontaneous faculty" (Kenneth Ch'en, Buddhism in China *[1964, rptd. 1972], p. 359).*

The title of this story, from The Sayings of Goso Hōyen, *is the editors'.*

Zen and the Art of Burglary

If people ask me what Zen is like, I will say that it is like learning the
art of burglary. The son of a burglar saw his father growing older and
thought, "If he is unable to carry on his profession, who will be the breadwinner of the family, except myself? I must learn the trade." He intimated
the idea to his father, who approved of it.

One night the father took the son to a big house, broke through the
fence, entered the house, and, opening one of the large chests, told the
son to go in and pick out the clothing. As soon as the son got into it, the
father dropped the lid and securely applied the lock. The father now
came out to the courtyard and loudly knocked at the door, waking up the
whole family; then he quietly slipped away by the hole in the fence. The

residents got excited and lighted candles, but they found that the burglar had already gone.

The son, who remained all the time securely confined in the chest, thought of his cruel father. He was greatly mortified, then a fine idea flashed upon him. He made a noise like the gnawing of a rat. The family told the maid to take a candle and examine the chest. When the lid was unlocked, out came the prisoner, who blew out the light, pushed away the maid, and fled. The people ran after him. Noticing a well by the road, he picked up a large stone and threw it into the water. The pursuers all gathered around the well trying to find the burglar drowning himself in the dark hole.

In the meantime he went safely back to his father's house. He blamed his father deeply for his narrow escape. Said the father, "Be not offended, my son. Just tell me how you got out of it." When the son told him all about his adventures, the father remarked, "There you are, you have learned the art."

 Topics for Critical Thinking and Writing

1. What assumptions about knowledge did the father make? Can you think of any of your own experiences that substantiate these assumptions?
2. Is there anything you have studied or are studying to which Zen pedagogical methods would be applicable? If so, explain by setting forth a sample lesson.

A Casebook on Computers in the Schools

David Gelernter

David Gelernter, a professor of computer science at Yale University, originally published this essay in The New Republic *in 1994.*

Unplugged

Over the last decade an estimated $2 billion has been spent on more than 2 million computers for America's classrooms. That's not surprising.

We constantly hear from Washington that the schools are in trouble and that computers are a godsend. Within the education establishment, in poor as well as rich schools, the machines are awaited with nearly religious awe. An inner-city principal bragged to a teacher friend of mine recently that his school "has a computer in every classroom . . . despite being in a bad neighborhood!"

Computers should be in the schools. They have the potential to accomplish great things. With the right software, they could help make science tangible or teach neglected topics like art and music. They could help students form a concrete idea of society by displaying on screen a version of the city in which they live—a picture that tracks real life moment by moment.

In practice, however, computers make our worst educational nightmares come true. While we bemoan the decline of literacy, computers discount words in favor of pictures and pictures in favor of video. While we fret about the decreasing cogency of public debate, computers dismiss linear argument and promote fast, shallow romps across the information landscape. While we worry about basic skills, we allow into the classroom software that will do a student's arithmetic or correct his spelling.

Take multimedia. The idea of multimedia is to combine text, sound and pictures in a single package that you browse on screen. You don't just *read* Shakespeare; you watch actors performing, listen to songs, view Elizabethan buildings. What's wrong with that? By offering children candy-coated books, multimedia is guaranteed to sour them on unsweetened reading. It makes the printed page look even more boring than it used to look. Sure, books will be available in the classroom, too—but they'll have all the appeal of a dusty piano to a teen who has a Walkman handy.

So what if the little nippers don't read? If they're watching Olivier   5 instead, what do they lose? The text, the written word along with all of its attendant pleasures. Besides, a book is more portable than a computer, has a higher-resolution display, can be written on and dog-eared and is comparatively dirt cheap.

Hypermedia, multimedia's comrade in the struggle for a brave new classroom, is just as troubling. It's a way of presenting documents on screen without imposing a linear start-to-finish order. Disembodied paragraphs are linked by theme; after reading one about the First World War, for example, you might be able to choose another about the technology of battleships, or the life of Woodrow Wilson, or hemlines in the '20s. This is another cute idea that is good in minor ways and terrible in major ones. Teaching children to understand the orderly unfolding of a plot or a logical argument is a crucial part of education. Authors don't merely agglomerate paragraphs; they work hard to make the narrative read a certain way, prove a particular point. To turn a book or a document into hypertext is to invite readers to ignore exactly what counts—the story.

The real problem, again, is the accentuation of already bad habits. Dynamiting documents into disjointed paragraphs is one more expression of the sorry fact that sustained argument is not our style. If you're a newspaper or magazine editor and your readership is dwindling, what's the solution? Shorter pieces. If you're a politician and you want to get elected, what do you need? Tasty sound bites. Logical presentation be damned.

Another software species, "allow me" programs, is not much better. These programs correct spelling and, by applying canned grammatical and stylistic rules, fix prose. In terms of promoting basic skills, though, they have all the virtues of a pocket calculator.

In Kentucky, as *The Wall Street Journal* recently reported, students in grades K–3 are mixed together regardless of age in a relaxed environment. It works great, the *Journal* says. Yes, scores on computation tests have dropped 10 percent at one school, but not to worry: "Drilling addition and subtraction in an age of calculators is a waste of time," the principal reassures us. Meanwhile, a Japanese educator informs University of Wisconsin mathematician Richard Akey that in his country, "calculators are not used in elementary or junior high school because the primary emphasis is on helping students develop their mental abilities." No wonder Japanese kids blow the pants off American kids in math. Do we really think "drilling addition and subtraction in an age of calculators is a waste of time"? If we do, then "drilling reading in an age of multimedia is a waste of time" can't be far behind.

Prose-correcting programs are also a little ghoulish, like asking a computer for tips on improving your personality. On the other hand, I ran this article through a spell-checker, so how can I ban the use of such programs in schools? Because to misspell is human; to have no idea of correct spelling is to be semiliterate.

There's no denying that computers have the potential to perform inspiring feats in the classroom. If we are ever to see that potential realized, however, we ought to agree on three conditions. First, there should be a completely new crop of children's software. Most of today's offerings show no imagination. There are hundreds of similar reading and geography and arithmetic programs, but almost nothing on electricity or physics or architecture. Also, they abuse the technical capacities of new media to glitz up old forms instead of creating new ones. Why not build a time-travel program that gives kids a feel for how history is structured by zooming you backward? A spectrum program that lets users twirl a frequency knob to see what happens?

Second, computers should be used only during recess or relaxation periods. Treat them as fillips, not as surrogate teachers. When I was in school in the '60s, we all loved educational films. When we saw a movie in class, everybody won: teachers didn't have to teach, and pupils didn't have to learn. I suspect that classroom computers are popular today for the same reasons.

Most important, educators should learn what parents and most teachers already know: you cannot teach a child anything unless you look him in the face. We should not forget what computers are. Like books—better

10

in some ways, worse in others—they are devices that help children mobilize their own resources and learn for themselves. The computer's potential to do good is modestly greater than a book's in some areas. Its potential to do harm is vastly greater, across the board.

Clifford Stoll

Clifford Stoll (b. 1950), an astrophysicist, is the author of Silicon Snake Oil: Thoughts on the Information Highway. *The following essay originally appeared in* The New York Times, *May 19, 1996. We follow the essay with four letters that were written in response.*

Invest in Humanware

Remember filmstrips? I used to look forward to Wednesday afternoons when our fifth-grade teacher would dim the lights, pull down the screen and advance the projector to an electronic beep. All the pupils loved filmstrips. For the next hour, we didn't have to think.

Teachers liked them, too. With arms folded in the back of the class, they didn't have to teach. The principal approved. Filmstrips were proof that Public School 61 in Buffalo was at the cutting edge of educational technology. Parents demanded filmstrips, the modern, multimedia way to bring the latest information into the classroom. It was a win-win approach that bypassed textbooks and old-style classrooms. But no learning took place.

You've likely seen as many filmstrips as I have. O.K., name three that had a lasting effect on your life. Now name three teachers who did.

Yesterday's filmstrip has morphed into today's school computer. Promoted as a solution to the crisis in the classroom, computers have been welcomed uncritically across the educational spectrum. So uncritically that, astonishingly, school libraries, art studies and music rooms are being replaced by computer labs.

President Clinton promotes the wiring of the nation's high schools. Elementary schools seek grants for hardware and software. Colleges invest in video teaching systems. Yet the value of these expensive gizmos to the classroom is unproved and rests on dubious assumptions.

What's most important in a classroom? A good teacher interacting with motivated students. Anything that separates them—filmstrips, instructional videos, multimedia displays, E-mail TV sets, interactive computers—is of questionable education value.

Yes, kids love these high-tech devices and play happily with them for hours. But just because children do something willingly doesn't mean that it engages their minds. Indeed, most software for children turns lessons into games. The popular arithmetic program Math Blaster simulates an arcade shoot-'em-down, complete with enemy flying saucers. Such

5

instant gratification keeps the kids clicking icons while discouraging any sense of studiousness or sustained mental effort.

Plop a kid down before such a program, and the message is, "You have to learn the math tables, so play with this computer." Teach the same lesson with flash cards, and a different message comes through: "You're important to me, and this subject is so useful that I'll spend an hour teaching you arithmetic."

Computers promise short cuts to higher grades and painless learning. Today's edutainment software comes shrink-wrapped in the magic mantra: "makes learning fun."

Equating learning with fun says that if you don't enjoy yourself,   10 you're not learning. I disagree. Most learning isn't fun. Learning takes work. Discipline. Responsibility—you have to do your homework. Commitment, from both teacher and student. There's no short cut to a quality education. And the payoff isn't an adrenaline rush but a deep satisfaction arriving weeks, months or years later.

Anyway, what good are these glitzy gadgets to a child who can't pay attention in class, won't read more than a paragraph and is unable to write analytically?

Still, isn't it great that the Internet brings the latest events into classrooms? Maybe. Perhaps some teachers lack information, but most have plenty, thank you. Rather, there is too little class time to cover what's available. A shortage of information simply isn't a problem.

There's a wide gulf between data and information. The former lacks organization, content, context, timeliness and accuracy. The Internet delivers plenty of data and precious little information. Lacking critical thinking, kids are on-screen innocents who confuse form with content, sense with sensibility, ponderous words with weighty thoughts.

Sure, students can search the Web, gathering information for assignments. The result? Instead of synthesizing a report from library sources, they often take the short cut, copying what's on line.

It's no surprise when a ninth grader turns in a history paper duplicat-   15 ed from a CD-ROM encyclopedia or a college sophomore turns in an English composition taken straight from the Internet. The copy-and-paste mentality of computing works against creativity.

Computing encourages the tyranny of the right answer. But the price of rigid thinking is whimsy lost, inventiveness snubbed, curiosity thwarted. Learning doesn't quantify well and it shouldn't be a competitive sport. Students who can explain their reasons for picking wrong answers contribute more to classroom dialogue than those who seldom make errors. To my way of thinking, mistakes are more interesting than correct answers. And problems more important than solutions.

Promoters of the Internet tell us that the World Wide Web brings students closer together through instant communications. But the drab reality of spending hours at a keyboard is one of isolation. While reaching out to faraway strangers, we're distanced from classmates, teachers and family. Somehow, I feel it's more important to pen a thank-you note to a friend than to upload E-mail to someone across the ocean.

One of the most common—and illogical—arguments for computers in the classroom is that they'll soon be everywhere, so shouldn't they be in schools? One might as well say that since cars play such a crucial role in our society, shouldn't we make driver's ed central to the curriculum?

Anyway, computer skills aren't tough to learn. Millions have taught themselves at home. In school, it's better to learn how Shakespeare processed words than how Microsoft does.

The Gosh-Wow attitude of multimedia turns science and math into a spectator sport, substituting pictures of test tubes for the real thing. Which teaches more: watching a video about the heat of crystallization or dissolving potassium nitrate in water and touching the side of the beaker?   20

What exactly is being taught using computers? On the surface, pupils learn to read, type and use programs. I'll bet that they're really learning something else. How to stare at a monitor for hours on end. To accept what a machine says without arguing. That the world is a passive, pre-programmed place, where you need only click the mouse to get the right answer. That relationships—developed over E-mail—are transitory and shallow. That discipline isn't necessary when you can zap frustrations with a keystroke. That legible handwriting, grammar, analytic thought and human dealings don't matter.

Looking for simple ways to help in the classroom? Eliminate interruptions from school intercoms. Make classes smaller. Respect teachers as essential professionals with tough jobs. Protest multiple-choice exams, which discourage writing and analytic thinking. If we must push technology into the classroom, let's give teachers their own photocopiers so they can avoid the long wait in the school office.

For decades, we've welcomed each new technology—stereopticons, lantern slides, motion pictures, filmstrips and videotapes—as a way to improve teaching. Each has promised better students and easier learning. None has succeeded. Except that it is even more expensive, I suspect that classroom computing isn't much different.

Judith Bruk, Robert P. DeSieno, Robert M. Berkman, Melvin Dubnik

Letters Responding to Clifford Stoll

To the Editor:

Make no mistake. I am a fan of Clifford Stoll. His book "Cuckoo's Egg" was required reading for my City University of New York students in new communications technologies. However, Mr. Stoll's article "Invest in Humanware" (Op-Ed, May 19) struck a raw nerve. For Mr. Stoll to criticize the use of computers in the classroom and join the ranks of those who say that "everything was better in the good old days when I was a kid" disappoints me.

The suggestion that flash cards delivered a message of warmth and caring is mind-boggling. On the human torture scale, I rate teaching math with flash cards just above placing bamboo shoots under the fingernails.

Although I graduated from high school as an "outstanding senior," my study skills were nonexistent and my concentration poor. All this without exposure to a computer.

I will venture to say that many students faced with today's "drill and kill" computer programs will survive as well. A good many will go on to develop solid analytical skills and excel academically. This will be because of their chance assignment to good teachers along the way, as was my good fortune.

Are computer programs currently used in the classroom dreadful? Here I would agree with Mr. Stoll, and so would most teachers using them. What Mr. Stoll suggests is that these teachers don't know how dreadful some of these programs are. They do. But they are constantly striving to improve education with any tool at hand, be it a Bunsen burner or a modem.

After introducing my own students to on-line services and the ocean of data that is at their disposal, I insisted that they learn only one thing: access to information means nothing if you don't ask the right questions.

Judith Bruk
Bellevue, Wash., May 20, 1996

The writer, creator of the Classroom Prodigy on-line service, is a producer for the Microsoft Network.

To the Editor:

What Clifford Stoll (Op-Ed, May 19) omits is the capacity for interaction that computers deliver, the potential for engaging students more deeply in their own learning.

So, for example, in the sciences, it is possible to launch students into discussions of first principles and then, with electronic spreadsheets or computer algebra systems, guide them to stimulating variations on a theme that help them understand the subtleties of what they study.

I have used electronic mail lists to encourage shared note taking for class and to foster exchanges of views among students and faculty. These "listserves" tell me what students have learned in my classes and what they have misunderstood.

I've used graphics software to create images for my classes that reveal far more than I've been able to do without this technology.

Does this technology enhance the education of all students? Of course   5 not. To a significant degree, education is a solo enterprise. For those students who do wish to learn, computers can be a way to help them soar a little higher and see a little further.

> Robert P. DeSieno
> Saratoga Springs, N.Y., May 20, 1996
> *The writer is a professor of computer science at Skidmore College.*

To the Editor:
I find some irony in that Clifford Stoll, an astrophysicist, is so critical of computers in education (Op-Ed, May 19). If Mr. Stoll were to apply the same argument to his chosen profession, black holes would have to be dismissed as some theory, advanced by raving lunatics, because nobody has ever seen one.

Just because Mr. Stoll has never seen computers used in meaningful ways in the classroom does not mean it isn't being done.

Over the past 12 years, I have seen computers make a real difference in how children use and understand information. I have seen children create detailed, polished research projects far beyond what I could have produced when I was their age, because the labor of editing and rewriting stood in my way.

I have seen children learn more about algebraic equations in two weeks than I did in a year, because the computer freed them from plotting hundreds of points by hand. I have seen children design computer programs portraying natural phenomena that not even my best shoe-box diorama could show.

It is true that a computer cannot replace a good teacher in the classroom,   5 but what a good teacher can do with a computer in a classroom is boundless.

> Robert M. Berkman
> Brooklyn, May 19, 1996
> *The writer is an adjunct professor of mathematics and science education at Brooklyn College.*

To the Editor:
Clifford Stoll (Op-Ed, May 19) is on target. The computer seems no more effective than any of the other high-tech gadgets adapted to the classroom in the electronic age.

The problem is not that these instruments are used to replace teaching but rather to reproduce it. To the child, it matters not whether the talking head is a physical being standing in front of the room or a filmstrip narrator. Underlying the use of the expensive gizmos is a model of education based on an "I send, you receive" model no different from the pedagogy of Charles Dickens's Mr. Gradgrind.

Nor has the "game" approach worked. Despite the efforts of educational software developers, creating a truly entertaining game for most children involves hiding the substantive content of the lesson.

But Mr. Stoll is off base in his failure to address the potential that computer technology has to enhance education not by reproducing or supplementing it, but by transforming the learning process. With widespread access to the Internet, the new technology can challenge the ineffective send-receive model by making creative use of improving interactive multimedia features.

The good teacher is one who creates students out of pupils and nurtures a desire to learn. Present-day educational techniques accomplish this so rarely that the success of a student is more likely to be associated with genetic or socioeconomic factors than with good teaching.

If appropriately applied, computer technology can help create an educational process focused on developing lifelong students who can apply an internalized commitment to learning.

Melvin Dubnick
Princeton Jct., N.J., May 19, 1996

The writer is a professor of political science and public administration at Rutgers University.

David Rothenberg

David Rothenberg, a professor of philosophy at the New Jersey Institute of Technology, is the author of Hand's End: Technology and the Limits of Nature *(1993).*

The following essay was originally published in The Chronicle of Higher Education, *a journal read chiefly by college and university teachers and administrators.*

How the Web Destroys the Quality of Students' Research Papers

Sometimes I look forward to the end-of-semester rush, when students' final papers come streaming into my office and mailbox. I could have hundreds of pages of original thought to read and evaluate. Once in a while, it *is* truly exciting, and brilliant words are typed across a page in response to a question I've asked the class to discuss.

But this past semester was different. I noticed a disturbing decline in both the quality of the writing and the originality of the thoughts expressed. What had happened since last fall? Did I ask worse questions? Were my students unusually lazy? No. My class had fallen victim to the latest easy way of writing a paper: doing their research on the World-Wide Web.

It's easy to spot a research paper that is based primarily on information collected from the Web. First, the bibliography cites no books, just articles or pointers to places in that virtual land somewhere off any map: http://www.etc. Then a strange preponderance of material in the bibliography is curiously out of date. A lot of stuff on the Web that is advertised as timely is actually at least a few years old. (One student submitted a research paper last semester in which all of his sources were articles published between September and December 1995; that was probably the time span of the Web page on which he found them.)

Another clue is the beautiful pictures and graphs that are inserted neatly into the body of the student's text. They look impressive, as though they were the result of careful work and analysis, but actually they often bear little relation to the precise subject of the paper. Cut and pasted from the vast realm of what's out there for the taking, they masquerade as original work.

5

Accompanying them are unattributed quotes (in which one can't tell who made the statement or in what context) and curiously detailed references to the kinds of things that are easy to find on the Web (pages and pages of federal documents, corporate propaganda, or snippets of commentary by people whose credibility is difficult to assess). Sadly, one finds few references to careful, in-depth commentaries on the subject of the paper, the kind of analysis that requires a book, rather than an article, for its full development.

Don't get me wrong, I'm no neo-Luddite. I am as enchanted as anyone else by the potential of this new technology to provide instant information. But too much of what passes for information these days is simply *advertising* for information. Screen after screen shows you where you can find out more, how you can connect to this place or that. The acts of linking and networking and randomly jumping from here to there become as exciting or rewarding as actually finding anything of intellectual value.

Search engines, with their half-baked algorithms, are closer to slot machines than to library catalogues. You throw your query to the wind, and who knows what will come back to you? You may get 234,468 supposed references to whatever you want to know. Perhaps one in a thousand might actually help you. But it's easy to be sidetracked or frustrated as you try to go through those Web pages one by one. Unfortunately, they're not arranged in order of importance.

What I'm describing is the hunt-and-peck method of writing a paper. We all know that word processing makes many first drafts look far more polished than they are. If the paper doesn't reach the assigned five pages, readjust the margin, change the font size, and . . . *voila!* Of course, those machinations take up time that the student could have spent revising the paper. With programs to check one's spelling and grammar now standard features on most computers, one wonders why students make any mistakes at all. But errors are as prevalent as ever, no matter how crisp the typeface. Instead of becoming perfectionists, too many students have become slackers, preferring to let the machine do their work for them.

What the Web adds to the shortcuts made possible by word processing is to make research look too easy. You toss a query to the machine, wait a few minutes, and suddenly a lot of possible sources of information appear on your screen. Instead of books that you have to check out of the library, read carefully, understand, synthesize, and then tactfully excerpt, these sources are quips, blips, pictures, and short summaries that may be downloaded magically to the dorm-room computer screen. Fabulous! How simple! The only problem is that a paper consisting of summaries of summaries is bound to be fragmented and superficial, and to demonstrate more of a random montage than an ability to sustain an argument through 10 to 15 double-spaced pages.

10

Of course, you can't blame the students for ignoring books. When college libraries are diverting funds from books to computer technology that will be obsolete in two years at most, they send a clear message to students: Don't read, just connect. Surf. Download. Cut and paste. Originality becomes hard to separate from plagiarism if no author is cited on a Web page. Clearly, the words are up for grabs, and students much prefer the fabulous jumble to the hard work of stopping to think and make sense of what they've read.

Libraries used to be repositories of words and ideas. Now they are seen as centers for the retrieval of information. Some of this information comes from other, bigger libraries, in the form of books that can take time to obtain through interlibrary loan. What happens to the many students (some things never change) who scramble to write a paper the night before it's due? The computer screen, the gateway to the world sitting right on their desks, promises instant access—but actually offers only a pale, two-dimensional version of a real library.

But it's also my fault. I take much of the blame for the decline in the quality of student research in my classes. I need to teach students how to read, to take time with language and ideas, to work through arguments, to synthesize disparate sources to come up with original thought. I need to help my students understand how to assess sources to determine their credibility, as well as to trust their own ideas more than snippets of thought that materialize on a screen. The placelessness of the Web leads to an ethereal randomness of thought. Gone are the pathways of logic and passion, the sense of the progress of an argument. Chance holds sway, and it more often misses than hits. Judgment must be taught, as well as the methods of exploration.

I'm seeing my students' attention spans wane and their ability to reason for themselves decline. I wish that the university's computer system would crash for a day, so that I could encourage them to go outside, sit under a tree, and read a really good book—from start to finish. I'd like them to sit for a while and ponder what it means to live in a world where some things get easier and easier so rapidly that we can hardly keep track of how easy they're getting, while other tasks remain as hard as ever—such as doing research and writing a good paper that teaches the writer something in the process. Knowledge does not emerge in a vacuum, but we do need silence and space for sustained thought. Next semester, I'm going to urge my students to turn off their glowing boxes and think, if only once in a while.

Richard Cummins, Sharon Stoerger, Kenneth J. Zanca, Jere L. Bacharach

Letters Responding to David Rothenberg

To the Editor:

David Rothenberg's thoughtful essay includes the common fallacy of giving the World-Wide Web far too much power over our lives and consciousness ("*How the Web Destroys the Quality of Students' Research Papers*," Point of View, August 15). Too often, the assumption is that this technology somehow induces states of mind for which there is no remedy. But the Web is simply a tool that needs to be used strategically by teachers who have carefully thought through the outcomes they expect from their students. Even the metaphor of a web implies this, and it is up to the student to become either the spider or the fly.

Actually, it is often poor course design that impedes student performance to a far greater extent. Realistically, the Web no more "destroys the quality of students' research papers" than does television, the blackboard, the overhead projector, the way that poorly designed research assignments are routinely handed out to students, or the rote way that some teachers present their materials. In terms of quality, where does the buck stop? I would hope at the professor's desk, where the questions about what is acceptable research need to be discussed and answered for the student's edification, while the professor makes it clear that grades will directly reflect those standards.

Professor Rothenberg's general points, however, are well stated, and I admire his willingness to accept the challenge of what I consider the hard job of *real* teaching. This includes teaching students "how to read, to take time with language and ideas, to work through arguments, to synthesize disparate sources to come up with original thought ... [and] how to assess sources to determine their credibility." This is difficult and important work, and it teaches students how to sort the wheat from the chaff in *any* kind of resource.

In truth, there are as many rotten books and worthless journal articles in libraries as there are rotten sources on the Internet. The particular medium will matter less and less with the preponderance of cheap printers. To suggest that the Web is solely a source of ephemeral advertisements about information is a specious generalization. It sounds great, but closer examination reveals it to be too sweeping an assessment—one that, additionally, fails to account for the Web's future development as a scholarly resource.

5

We should not allow the spider of popular culture to spin us up in a web of helplessness and despair by allowing the Internet to become so personified that it takes on extraordinary powers. It's just a bunch of interconnected computers. In addition to delineating how it may prevent students (and teachers) from thinking clearly and well, we need to place the onus of education back on the students and insist that they perform to certain standards by intelligently using available tools and technologies: books, journals, computers, and so forth . . . .

These issues will become increasingly important as the waves of the so-called age of information approach flood stage in the years ahead. Among the dikes, sandbags, and navigation equipment that a college can offer are truly rigorous courses in both rhetoric and critical thinking, which all college students should be required to complete. Indeed, the Web may very

well turn out to be precisely the burr under the saddle that compels everyone in education to return to our mission, which is teaching people how to
think in disciplined ways.

Richard Cummins
Director of Information Technology Applications
Columbia Basin College
Pasco, Wash.

To the Editor:

I think David Rothenberg was looking for a scapegoat to explain the poor
quality of his students' papers. I cannot believe that this is the first semester he has received poor papers. Nor do I believe that "students have
become slackers" because of the invention of computers.

The problem is not computers. Many students have never been taught
how to even begin the research process, let alone produce an acceptable
paper. You cannot assume that your students have been in the library or
know the first thing about finding books or journal articles. Students need
to be guided and taught how to do research. A library-instruction session,
combined with very specific requirements for the assignment, will probably result in a higher-quality product.

Mr. Rothenberg seems to believe that all books contain better information
than any other resource, especially any resource on the Web. I work in a
library that has been weeding out books that are so out-of-date that they
provide incorrect data. Certain subjects have changed over the years, such
as the role of women and the portrayal of African Americans. Some students will take any book off the shelf just as easily as they take information
off the Web. Some believe that if it's in print, it has to be true. Critical-eval-
uation skills need to be taught in the classroom and in the library. This is
applicable to print as well as Web resources.

Today's library is rapidly changing because of new technological
advances. This is not necessarily a bad thing. Libraries have always been
places to retrieve information. Full-text data bases and the Web supplement existing collections. This allows patrons to access more resources,
not fewer . . . .

I believe librarians and instructors need to work together to help students   5
through the research process and to critically evaluate retrieved resources.
Boundaries and guidelines need to be set in order to have a successful
assignment. If you do not want Web resources used, state that in the

assignment. We need to accept the Web as yet another resource rather than deeming it an evil destroyer.

Sharon Stoerger
Public Services Librarian
Learning Resources Center
Danville Area Community College
Danville, Ill.

To the Editor:

David Rothenberg might benefit from the following three suggestions before giving any further Internet-related research projects:

* Refer students to resources specifically addressing the "how to" of Internet research. I can recommend two print aids—*Official Netscape Guide to Internet Research* and *Internet Homework Helper*—and several on-line aids in this area. The latter are less advanced than the former.

One on-line tutorial—www.digitalthink.com—gives two free lessons on structuring a research query. The Indianapolis-Marion County Public Library also provides a list of free tutorials (see www.imcpl.lib.in.us/). Teachers interested in learning how to use the Internet for research can take a look at www.studyweb.com and www.teachers.net.

* Not all search engines are created equal. Excite rates "hits," ranking them in order of agreement with search terms. Better to teach students how to use Boolean operators (which are very simple to learn) in making their search requests more focused, thus avoiding the "234,468 supposed references to whatever you want to know."

* I have avoided the demon that snagged Professor Rothenberg by insisting that all research papers have a balance of components: one-third books, one-third periodical literature, one-third Web resources. I grade down for any overloading with Internet sources. If students want to use more Web material, they must also increase their use of other materials.

I agree with Rothenberg that many students are lazy and look to the Internet as a short cut and "easy way" of getting these kinds of assignments done. This search for short cuts has been going on since "trots" for Caesar's *The Gallic Wars* and Cliffs Notes. Any tool can be abused. It is imperative that instructors learn how to use the Internet before sending students "out there" to conduct research. If students know that you know how to use the Internet responsibly, there is at least the possibility that they will conform to your standards for its use.

Kenneth J. Zanca
Professor of Philosophy
Marymount College
Rancho Palos Verdes, Cal.

To the Editor:

David Rothenberg's article ends on the wrong note. Rather than urging his students to "turn off their glowing boxes and think," I would urge him to have his students turn *on* their glowing boxes and think. The exercise would start with his own article, or any other article or book in any scholarly field.

The goal would be to establish a set of criteria for evaluating the printed material: Who wrote it, what can we learn about the author, is it dated, where was it published, is the publication subject to review, etc.? Evaluating criteria would then be established for the printed piece itself: What is the subject matter discussed, what are the perspectives or biases of the author(s), can the information be checked for accuracy by comparing it with other examples or data, etc.?

Once the students have established criteria for evaluating the printed material, I would assign them the same task for a Web site. For example, can they identify the author(s), the date the material was gathered, the biases or perspective of the author(s), the accuracy of the material, etc.? Finally, how would they compare the effectiveness of the evaluating criteria for printed material with their effectiveness for electronic sources? This exercise allows the students to discover the problems and limitations in using electronic sources.

Jan Alexander (Janet.E.Alexander@widener.edu) and Marsha Tate (Marsha.A.Tate@widener.edu), reference librarians at Wolgram Memorial Library at Widener University, have developed a series of exercises and criteria for comparing resources in print with those on the Web (http://www.science.widener.edu/~withers/webeval.htm). I have found their work very helpful. Also helpful is a class developed at the University of Washington for teaching these skills (http://weber.u.washington.edu/~libr560/NETEVAL/).

Jere L. Bacharach
Director
Henry M. Jackson School of International Studies
Professor of History
University of Washington
Seattle

10
WORK AND PLAY

467

Children
Helen Levitt, 1940

Short Views

Work and play are words used to describe the same thing under differing conditions.
  Mark Twain

The Battle of Waterloo was won on the playing fields of Eton.
  Attributed to the Duke of Wellington

The competitive spirit goes by many names. Most simply and directly, it is called "the work ethic." As the name implies, the work ethic holds that labor is good in itself; that a man or woman at work not only makes a contribution to his fellow man, but becomes a better person by virtue of the act of working. That work ethic is ingrained in the American character. That is why most of us consider it immoral to be lazy or slothful—even if a person is well off enough not to have to work or deliberately avoids work by going on welfare.
  Richard Milhous Nixon

In the laws of political economy, the alienation of the worker from his product is expressed as follows: the more the worker produces, the less he has to consume; the more value he creates, the more valueless, the more unworthy he becomes; the better formed is his product, the more deformed becomes the worker; the more civilized his product, the more brutalized becomes the worker; the mightier the work, the more powerless the worker; the more ingenious the work, the duller becomes the worker and the more he becomes nature's bondsman.

Political economy conceals the alienation inherent in labor by avoiding any mention of the evil effects of work on those who work. Thus, whereas labor produces miracles for the rich, for the worker it produces destitution. Labor produces palaces, but for the worker, hovels. It produces beauty, but it cripples the worker. It replaces labor by machines, but how does it treat the worker? By throwing some workers back into a barbarous kind of work, and by turning the rest into machines. It produces intelligence, but for the worker, stupidity and cretinism.
  Karl Marx

My young men shall never work. Men who work cannot dream, and wisdom comes in dreams.
Smohalla, of the Nez Perce

Everyone who is prosperous or successful must have dreamed of something. It is not because he is a good worker that he is prosperous, but because he dreamed.
Lost Star, of the Maricopa

The possible quantity of play depends on the possible quantity of pay.
John Ruskin

It can't be just a job. It's not worth playing just for money. It's a way of life. When we were kids there was the release in playing, the sweetness in being able to move and control your body. This is what play is. Beating somebody is secondary. When I was a kid, to really *move* was my delight. I felt released because I could move around anybody. I was free.
Eric Nesterenko, Professional Hockey Player

Winning is not the most important thing; it's everything.
Vince Lombardi

The games don't matter to me. I have no interest in the games. The only things that interested me in sports were the issues. I was interested in Muhammad Ali, in Jackie Roosevelt Robinson, in Curtis Flood. That's the kind of thing that mattered to me. Curtis Flood's assault on baseball, the reserve clause. I remember going to see Flood, who was tending bar in a place called The Rustic Inn. . . . He told me, "There's something in my heart and in my mind that says, 'No, you can't trade me. You can't sell me. This is the United States of America, and I will not be traded as a slave.'" I was fulfilled by his attitude and his behavior. That mattered to me. I was never interested in these silly games. I can't think of anything less important in life than who wins or loses a game. There are certain causes in sports that transcend sport, that have to do with constitutional law, that have to do with the nature of society.
Howard Cosell

Serious sport has nothing to do with fair play. It is bound up with hatred, jealousy, boastfulness, disregard of all rules and sadistic pleasure in witnessing violence: in other words, it is war minus the shooting.
    George Orwell

The maturity of man—that means to have reacquired the seriousness that one has as a child at play.
    Friedrich Nietzsche

I see great things in baseball. It's our game—the American game. It will take our people out-of-doors, fill them with oxygen, give them a larger physical stoicism. Tend to relieve us from being a nervous, dyspeptic set. Repair these losses, and be a blessing to us.
    Walt Whitman

It's great because it has no clock. You can play forever. You can't kill that clock or run a few plays up the middle as you can do in the other sports.
    It's great because it is a sport of rigid, complex rules, but every field is unique. No park is the same, and no other sport can make that claim.
    It's great because you can do things in foul territory; you can win a game, you can lose a game, outside the field.
    It's great because it not only follows the rhythms of the seasons but it is as much about loss as it is about winning. The greatest baseball players fail seven times out of ten.
    It's great because you can't go to your best player every time as you can in other sports. Even Babe Ruth came up only once every nine times.
    Ken Burns

The boys throw stones at the frogs in sport, but the frogs die not in sport but in earnest.
    Bion

Bertrand Russell

Bertrand Russell (1872–1970) was educated at Trinity College, Cambridge. He published his first book. The Study of German Social Democracy, *in 1896; subsequent books on mathematics and on philosophy quickly established his international reputation. His pacifist opposition to World War I cost him his appointment at Trinity College and won him a prison sentence of six months. While serving this sentence he wrote his* Introduction to Mathematical Philosophy. *In 1940 an appointment to teach at the College of the City of New York was withdrawn because of Russell's unorthodox moral views. But he was not always treated shabbily; he won numerous awards, including (in 1950) a Nobel Prize. After World War II he devoted most of his energy to warning the world about the dangers of nuclear war.*

In reading the first sentence of the essay that we reprint, you should know that the essay comes from a book called The Conquest of Happiness, *published in 1930.*

Work

Whether work should be placed among the causes of happiness or among the causes of unhappiness may perhaps be regarded as a doubtful question. There is certainly much work which is exceedingly irksome, and an excess of work is always very painful. I think, however, that, provided work is not excessive in amount, even the dullest work is to most people less painful than idleness. There are in work all grades, from mere relief of tedium up to the profoundest delights, according to the nature of the work and the abilities of the worker. Most of the work that most people have to do is not in itself interesting, but even such work has certain great advantages. To begin with, it fills a good many hours of the day without the need of deciding what one shall do. Most people, when they are left free to fill their own time according to their own choice, are at a loss to think of anything sufficiently pleasant to be worth doing. And whatever they decide on, they are troubled by the feeling that something else would have been pleasanter. To be able to fill leisure intelligently is the last product of civilization, and at present very few people have reached this level. Moreover the exercise of choice is in itself tiresome. Except to people with unusual initiative it is positively agreeable to be told what to do at each hour of the day, provided the orders are not too unpleasant. Most of the idle rich suffer unspeakable boredom as the price of their freedom from drudgery. At times, they may find relief by hunting big game in Africa, or by flying round the world, but the number of such sensations is limited, especially after youth is past. Accordingly the more intelligent rich men work nearly as hard as if they were poor, while rich women for the most part keep themselves busy with innumerable trifles of whose earth-shaking importance they are firmly persuaded.

Work therefore is desirable, first and foremost, as a preventive of boredom, for the boredom that a man feels when he is doing necessary though uninteresting work is as nothing in comparison with the boredom that he feels when he has nothing to do with his days. With this advantage of work another is associated, namely that it makes holidays much more delicious when they come. Provided a man does not have to work so hard as to impair his vigor, he is likely to find far more zest in his free time than an idle man could possibly find.

The second advantage of most paid work and of some unpaid work is that it gives chances of success and opportunities for ambition. In most work success is measured by income, and while our capitalistic society continues, this is inevitable. It is only where the best work is concerned that this measure ceases to be the natural one to apply. The desire that men feel to increase their income is quite as much a desire for success as for the extra comforts that a higher income can procure. However dull work may be, it becomes bearable if it is a means of building up a reputation, whether in the world at large or only in one's own circle. Continuity of purpose is one of the most essential ingredients of happiness in the long run, and for most men this comes chiefly through their work. In this respect those women whose lives are occupied with housework are much less fortunate than men, or than women who work outside the home. The domesticated wife does not receive wages, has no means of bettering herself, is taken for granted by her husband (who sees practically nothing of what she does), and is valued by him not for her housework but for quite other qualities. Of course this does not apply to those women who are sufficiently well-to-do to make beautiful houses and beautiful gardens and become the envy of their neighbors; but such women are comparatively few, and for the great majority housework cannot bring as much satisfaction as work of other kinds brings to men and to professional women.

The satisfaction of killing time and of affording some outlet, however modest, for ambition, belongs to most work, and is sufficient to make even a man whose work is dull happier on the average than a man who has no work at all. But when work is interesting, it is capable of giving satisfaction of a far higher order than mere relief from tedium. The kinds of work in which there is some interest may be arranged in a hierarchy. I shall begin with those which are only mildly interesting and end with those that are worthy to absorb the whole energies of a great man.

Two chief elements make work interesting; first, the exercise of skill,   5
and second, construction.

Every man who has acquired some unusual skill enjoys exercising it until it has become a matter of course, or until he can no longer improve himself. This motive to activity begins in early childhood: a boy who can stand on his head becomes reluctant to stand on his feet. A great deal of work gives the same pleasure that is to be derived from games of skill. The work of a lawyer or a politician must contain in a more delectable form a great deal of the same pleasure that is to be derived from playing bridge. Here of course there is not only the exercise of skill but the outwitting of a skilled opponent. Even where this competitive element is absent, however, the performance of difficult feats is agreeable. A man who can do stunts in an aeroplane finds the pleasure so great that for the sake of it he is willing to risk his life. I imagine that an able surgeon, in spite of the painful circumstances in which his work is done, derives satisfaction from the exquisite precision of his operations. The same kind of pleasure, though in a less intense form, is to be derived from a great deal of work of a humbler kind. All skilled work can be pleasurable, provided the skill required is either variable or capable of indefinite improvement. If these conditions are absent, it will cease to be interesting when a man has acquired his maximum skill. A man who runs three-mile races will cease to find pleasure in this occupation when he passes the age at which he can beat his own previous record. Fortunately there is a very considerable amount of work in which new circumstances call for new skill and a man can go on improving, at any rate until he has reached middle age. In some kinds of skilled work, such as politics, for example, it seems that men are at their best between sixty and seventy, the reason being that in such occupations a wide experience of other men is essential. For this reason successful politicians are apt to be happier at the age of seventy than any other men of equal age. Their only competitors in this respect are the men who are the heads of big businesses.

There is, however, another element possessed by the best work, which is even more important as a source of happiness than is the exercise of skill. This is the element of constructiveness. In some work, though by no means in most, something is built up which remains as a monument when the work is completed. We may distinguish construction from destruction by the following criterion. In construction the initial state of affairs is comparatively haphazard, while the final state of affairs embodies a purpose: in destruction the reverse is the case; the initial state of affairs embodies a purpose, while the final state of affairs is haphazard, that is to say, all that is intended by the destroyer is to produce a state of affairs which does not embody a certain purpose. This criterion applies in the most literal and obvious case, namely the construction and destruction of buildings. In constructing a building a previously made plan is carried out, whereas in destroying it no one decides exactly how the materials are to lie when the demolition is complete. Destruction is of course necessary very often as a preliminary to subsequent construction; in that case it is part of a whole which is constructive. But not infrequently a man will engage in activities of which the purpose is destructive without regard to any construction that may come after. Frequently he will conceal this from himself by the belief that he is only sweeping away in order to build afresh, but it is generally possible to unmask this pretense, when it is a pretense, by asking him what the subsequent construction is to be. On this subject it will be found that he will speak vaguely and without enthusiasm, whereas on the preliminary destruction he has spoken precisely and with zest. This applies to not a few revolutionaries and militarists and other apostles of violence. They are actuated, usually without their own knowledge, by hatred: the destruction of what they hate is their real purpose, and they are comparatively indifferent to the question what is to come after it. Now I cannot deny that in the work of destruction as in the work of construction there may be joy. It is a fiercer joy, perhaps at moments more intense, but it is less profoundly satisfying, since the result is one in which little satisfaction is to be found. You kill your enemy, and when he is dead your occupation is gone, and the satisfaction that you derive from victory quickly fades. The work of construction, on the other hand, when completed is delightful to contemplate, and moreover is never so fully completed that there is nothing further to do about it. The most satisfactory purposes are those that lead on indefinitely from one success to another without ever coming to a dead end; and in this respect it will be found that construction is a greater source of happiness than destruction. Perhaps it would be more correct to say that those who find satisfaction in construction find in it greater satisfaction than the lovers of destruction can find in destruction, for if once you have become filled with hate you will not easily derive from construction the pleasure which another man would derive from it.

At the same time few things are so likely to cure the habit of hatred as the opportunity to do constructive work of an important kind.

The satisfaction to be derived from success in a great constructive enterprise is one of the most massive that life has to offer, although unfortunately in its highest forms it is open only to men of exceptional ability. Nothing can rob a man of the happiness of successful achievement in an important piece of work, unless it be the proof that after all his work was bad. There are many forms of such satisfaction. The man who by a scheme of irrigation has caused the wilderness to blossom like the rose enjoys it in one of its most tangible forms. The creation of an organization may be a work of supreme importance. So is the work of those few statesmen who have devoted their lives to producing order out of chaos, of whom Lenin is the supreme type in our day. The most obvious examples are artists and men of science. Shakespeare says of his verse: "So long as men can breathe, or eyes can see, so long lives this." And it cannot be doubted that the thought consoled him for misfortune. In his sonnets he maintains that the thought of his friend reconciled him to life, but I cannot help suspecting that the sonnets he wrote to his friend were even more effective for this purpose than the friend himself. Great artists and great men of science do work which is in itself delightful; while they are doing it, it secures them the respect of those whose respect is worth having, which gives them the most fundamental kind of power, namely power over men's thoughts and feelings. They have also the most solid reasons for thinking well of themselves. This combination of fortunate circumstances ought, one would think, to be enough to make any man happy. Nevertheless it is not so. Michael Angelo, for example, was a profoundly unhappy man, and maintained (not, I am sure, with truth) that he would not have troubled to produce works of art if he had not had to pay the debts of his impecunious relations. The power to produce great art is very often, though by no means always, associated with a temperamental unhappiness, so great that but for the joy which the artist derives from his work, he would be driven to suicide. We cannot, therefore, maintain that even the greatest work must make a man happy; we can only maintain that it must make him less unhappy. Men of science, however, are far less often temperamentally unhappy than artists are, and in the main the men who do great work in science are happy men, whose happiness is derived primarily from their work.

One of the causes of unhappiness among intellectuals in the present day is that so many of them, especially those whose skill is literary, find no opportunity for the independent exercise of their talents, but have to hire themselves out to rich corporations directed by Philistines, who insist upon their producing what they themselves regard as pernicious nonsense. If you were to inquire among journalists in either England or America whether they believed in the policy of the newspaper for which they worked, you would find, I believe, that only a small minority do so; the rest, for the sake of a livelihood, prostitute their skill to purposes which they believe to be harmful. Such work cannot bring any real satisfaction, and in the course of reconciling himself to the doing of it, a man has to make himself so cynical that he can no longer derive whole-hearted satisfaction from anything whatever. I cannot condemn men who undertake work of this sort, since starvation is too serious an alternative, but I think that where it is possible to do work that is satisfactory to a man's constructive impulses without entirely starving, he will be well advised from the point of view of his own happiness if he chooses it in preference to work much more highly paid but not seeming to him worth doing on its own account. Without self-respect genuine happiness is scarcely possible. And the man who is ashamed of his work can hardly achieve self-respect.

The satisfaction of constructive work, though it may, as things are, be the privilege of a minority, can nevertheless be the privilege of a quite large minority. Any man who is his own master in his work can feel it; so can any man whose work appears to him useful and requires considerable skill. The production of satisfactory children is a difficult constructive work capable of affording profound satisfaction. Any woman who has achieved this can feel that as a result of her labor the world contains something of value which it would not otherwise contain.

Human beings differ profoundly in regard to the tendency to regard their lives as a whole. To some men it is natural to do so, and essential to happiness to be able to do so with some satisfaction. To others life is a series of detached incidents without directed movement and without unity. I think the former sort are more likely to achieve happiness than the latter, since they will gradually build up those circumstances from which they can derive contentment and self-respect, whereas the others will be blown about by the winds of circumstances now this way, now that, without ever arriving at any haven. The habit of viewing life as a whole is an essential part both of wisdom and of true morality, and is one of the things which ought to be encouraged in education. Consistent purpose is not enough to make life happy, but it is an almost indispensable condition of a happy life. And consistent purpose embodies itself mainly in work.

✎ Topics for Critical Thinking and Writing

1. Russell says (paragraph 3): "The desire that men feel to increase their income is quite as much a desire for success as for the extra comforts that a higher income can procure." In its context, what does *success* mean? In your experience, do Russell's words ring true? Why or why not?

2. In paragraphs 7–11 Russell develops a contrast between what he calls "destructive" and "constructive" work. Is the contrast clarified by the examples he offers? What examples from your own experience or knowledge can you add?

3. In paragraph 10 Russell speaks of workers who "prostitute their skills to purposes which they believe to be harmful." What work does he use as an example here? What other examples can you offer? Imagine yourself doing work that you do not respect or that you even find "harmful." Then imagine being offered work that you do respect but at a much lower salary. How helpful would you find Russell's advice? What would you do? (Specific examples of work that you respect and work that you don't respect will help you to form a clear idea of the choice and a clear argument to support it.)

4. What new point does Russell introduce in his last paragraph? How well does this last paragraph work as a conclusion?

5. Russell is generally admired for his exceptionally clear prose. List some of the devices that make for clarity in this essay.

6. Through most of his essay, Russell writes as if only men were engaged in work. What references to women working do you find? From these references and from the predominant references to men, would you describe Russell as sexist? Why or why not?

7. Compare Russell with Steinem (page 484) on the value of work.

W. H. Auden

W[ystan] H[ugh] Auden (1907–73) was born and educated in England. In 1939 he came to the United States and became an American citizen, but in 1972 he returned to England to live. Although Auden established his reputation chiefly with his poetry, he also wrote excellent plays, libretti, and essays.

One of Auden's most unusual works, A Certain World: A Commonplace Book, *is an anthology of some of his favorite passages from other people's books, along with brief reflections on his reading. The passage we print here begins with a reference to Hannah Arendt's* The Human Condition.

Work, Labor, and Play

So far as I know, Miss Hannah Arendt was the first person to define the essential difference between work and labor. To be happy, a man must feel, firstly, free and, secondly, important. He cannot be really happy if he is compelled by society to do what he does not enjoy doing, or if what he enjoys doing is ignored by society as of no value or importance. In a society where slavery in the strict sense has been abolished, the sign that what a man does is of social value is that he is paid money to do it, but a laborer today can rightly be called a wage slave. A man is a laborer if the job society offers him is of no interest to himself but he is compelled to take it by the necessity of earning a living and supporting his family.

The antithesis to labor is play. When we play a game, we enjoy what we are doing, otherwise we should not play it, but it is a purely private activity; society could not care less whether we play it or not.

Between labor and play stands work. A man is a worker if he is personally interested in the job which society pays him to do; what from the point of view of society is necessary labor is from his own point of view voluntary play. Whether a job is to be classified as labor or work depends, not on the job itself, but on the tastes of the individual who undertakes it. The difference does not, for example, coincide with the difference between a manual and a mental job; a gardener or a cobbler may be a worker, a bank clerk a laborer. Which a man is can be seen from his attitude toward leisure. To a worker, leisure means simply the hours he needs to relax and rest in order to work efficiently. He is therefore more likely to take too little leisure than too much; workers die of coronaries and forget their wives' birthdays. To the laborer, on the other hand, leisure means freedom from compulsion, so that it is natural for him to imagine that the fewer hours he has to spend laboring, and the more hours he is free to play, the better.

What percentage of the population in a modern technological society are, like myself, in the fortunate position of being workers? At a guess I would say sixteen per cent, and I do not think that figure is likely to get bigger in the future.

Technology and the division of labor have done two things: by eliminating in many fields the need for special strength or skill; they have made a very large number of paid occupations which formerly were enjoyable work into boring labor, and by increasing productivity they have reduced the number of necessary laboring hours. It is already possible to imagine a society in which the majority of the population, that is to

5

say, its laborers, will have almost as much leisure as in earlier times was enjoyed by the aristocracy. When one recalls how aristocracies in the past actually behaved, the prospect is not cheerful. Indeed, the problem of dealing with boredom may be even more difficult for such a future mass society than it was for aristocracies. The latter, for example, ritualized their time; there was a season to shoot grouse, a season to spend in town, etc. The masses are more likely to replace an unchanging ritual by fashion which it will be in the economic interest of certain people to change as often as possible. Again, the masses cannot go in for hunting, for very soon there would be no animals left to hunt. For other aristocratic amuse-ments like gambling, dueling, and warfare, it may be only too easy to find equivalents in dangerous driving, drug-taking, and senseless acts of vio-lence. Workers seldom commit acts of violence, because they can put their aggression into their work, be it physical like the work of a smith, or mental like the work of a scientist or an artist. The role of aggression in mental work is aptly expressed by the phrase "getting one's teeth into a problem."

Topics for Critical Thinking and Writing

1. Some readers have had trouble following Auden in his first three para-graphs, although by the end of the third paragraph the difficulties have dis-appeared. Can you summarize the first paragraph in a sentence? If you think that the development of the idea in these first three paragraphs could be clearer, insert the necessary phrases or sentences, or indicate with arrows the places to which sentences should be moved.
2. Compare Auden with Russell (page 472) on the relationship between work and happiness.

Malcolm X

Malcolm X, born Malcolm Little in Nebraska in 1925, was the son of a Baptist minister. He com-pleted the eighth grade, but then he got into trouble and was sent to a reformatory. After his release he became a thief, dope peddler, and pimp. In 1944 he was sent to jail, where he spent six and a half years. During his years in jail he became a convert to the Black Muslim faith. Paroled in 1950, he served as a minister and founded Muslim temples throughout the United States. In 1964, however, he broke with Elijah Muhammad, leader of the Black Muslims and a powerful advocate of separation of whites and blacks. Malcolm X formed a new group, the Organization of Afro-American Unity, but a year later he was assassinated in New York. His Auto-biography, written with Alex Haley, was published in 1964. Haley (1921–92) is also the author of Roots, a study tracing a black family back through seven generations.

The Shoeshine Boy (editors' title) is from The Autobiography of Malcolm X, chapter 3.

The Shoeshine Boy

When I got home, Ella said there had been a telephone call from somebody named Shorty. He had left a message that over at the Roseland State Ballroom, the shoeshine boy was quitting that night, and Shorty had told him to hold the job for me.

"Malcolm, you haven't had any experience shining shoes," Ella said. Her expression and tone of voice told me she wasn't happy about my taking that job. I didn't particularly care, because I was already speechless thinking about being somewhere close to the greatest bands in the world. I didn't even wait to eat any dinner.

The ballroom was all lighted when I got there. A man at the front door was letting in members of Benny Goodman's band. I told him I wanted to see the shoeshine boy, Freddie.

"You're going to be the new one?" he asked. I said I thought I was, and he laughed, "Well, maybe you'll hit the numbers and get a Cadillac, too." He told me that I'd find Freddie upstairs in the men's room on the second floor.

But downstairs before I went up, I stepped over and snatched a glimpse inside the ballroom. I just couldn't believe the size of that waxed floor! At the far end, under the soft, rose-colored lights, was the bandstand with the Benny Goodman musicians moving around, laughing and talking, arranging their horns and stands.

A wiry, brown-skinned, conked fellow upstairs in the men's room greeted me. "You Shorty's homeboy?" I said I was, and he said he was Freddie. "Good old boy," he said. "He called me, he just heard I hit the big number, and he figured right I'd be quitting." I told Freddie what the man at the front door had said about a Cadillac. He laughed and said, "Burns them white cats up when you get yourself something. Yeah, I told them I was going to get me one—just to bug them."

Freddie then said for me to pay close attention, that he was going to be busy and for me to watch but not get in the way, and he'd try to get me ready to take over at the next dance, a couple of nights later.

As Freddie busied himself setting up the shoeshine stand, he told me, "Get here early . . . your shoeshine rags and brushes by this footstand . . . your polish bottles, paste wax, suede brushes over here . . . everything in place, you get rushed, you never need to waste motion . . ."

While you shined shoes, I learned, you also kept watch on customers inside, leaving the urinals. You darted over and offered a small white hand towel. "A lot of cats who ain't planning to wash their hands, sometimes you can run up with a towel and shame them. Your towels are real-

5

ly your best hustle in here. Cost you a penny apiece to launder—you always get at least a nickel tip."

The shoeshine customers, and any from the inside rest room who took   10
a towel, you whiskbroomed a couple of licks. "A nickel or a dime tip, just give 'em that," Freddie said. "But for two bits, Uncle Tom a little—white cats especially like that. I've had them to come back two, three times a dance."

From down below, the sound of the music had begun floating up. I guess I stood transfixed. "You never seen a big dance?" asked Freddie. "Run on awhile, and watch."

There were a few couples already dancing under the rose-covered lights. But even more exciting to me was the crowd thronging in. The most glamorous-looking white women I'd ever seen—young ones, old ones, white cats buying tickets at the window, sticking big wads of green bills back into their pockets, checking the women's coats, and taking their arms and squiring them inside.

Freddie had some early customers when I got back upstairs. Between the shoeshine stand and thrusting towels to me just as they approached the wash basin, Freddie seemed to be doing four things at once. "Here, you can take over the whiskbroom," he said, "just two or three licks—but let 'em feel it."

When things slowed a little, he said, "You ain't seen nothing tonight. You wait until you see a spooks' dance! Man, our own people carry *on!*" Whenever he had a moment, he kept schooling me. "Shoelaces, this drawer here. You just starting out, I'm going to make these to you as a present. Buy them for a nickel a pair, tell cats they need laces if they do, and charge two bits."

Every Benny Goodman record I'd ever heard in my life, it seemed,   15
was filtering faintly into where we were. During another customer lull, Freddie let me slip back outside again to listen. Peggy Lee was at the mike singing. Beautiful! She had just joined the band and she was from North Dakota and had been singing with a group in Chicago when Mrs. Benny Goodman discovered her, we had heard some customers say. She finished the song and the crowd burst into applause. She was a big hit.

"It knocked me out, too, when I first broke in here," Freddie said, grinning, when I went back in there. "But, look, you ever shined any shoes?" He laughed when I said I hadn't, excepting my own. "Well, let's get to work. I never had neither." Freddie got on the stand and went to work on his own shoes. Brush, liquid polish, brush, paste wax, shine rag, lacquer sole dressing . . . step by step, Freddie showed me what to do.

"But you got to get a whole lot faster. You can't waste time!" Freddie showed me how fast on my own shoes. Then, because business was tapering off, he had time to give me a demonstration of how to make the shine rag pop like a firecracker. "Dig the action?" he asked. He did it in slow motion. I got down and tried it on his shoes. I had the principle of it. "Just got to do it faster," Freddie said. "It's a jive noise, that's all. Cats tip better, they figure you're knocking yourself out!"

✎ Topics for Critical Thinking and Writing

1. In this selection Malcolm X is more concerned with Benny Goodman than with learning about shining shoes. Freddie is concerned with teaching Malcolm the trade. What are we concerned with in this selection?
2. How would you characterize Freddie's attitude toward his job?
3. In paragraph 17 Freddie demonstrates a "jive noise." Using evidence from this selection, the library, mother wit, or what you will, define *jive*.
4. On what date did Malcolm begin his apprenticeship as a shoeshine boy? How did you arrive at that date?

Richard Benson

In Chapter 5, "The Language of Pictures," we reproduced Richard Benson's analysis of a photograph in the collection of the Mariners' Museum, Newport News, Virginia. Here is another of his analyses, of another photo in the same collection.

First Wing Panel Made by Girls. Naval Aircraft Factory, Phila. Pa., 1918

The title of this photograph is very carefully typed on the back of the original print in the Museum's collection. It could easily have been changed to the more appropriate "women," but this would alter the significance of the picture, which presages such sweeping change in our society. "Girls" was a common word in 1918, a holdover from earlier times when men ruled by muscle power and women kept to the home and hearth, doing the real work. The twentieth century has finally started to alter this state of affairs, and here we can see a beginning of the change in a wartime Philadelphia factory. The wing panel is a beautifully made thing, with metal struts, tensioned cable diagonals, and smooth wooden outer surfaces. It has been carefully engineered, and perhaps there was some idea that women could produce such a delicate and precise object better than men. Whether they ended up in industry because of a notion like this, or simply due to a lack of male labor, women began to find

First Wing Panel Made by Girls
Naval Aircraft Factory, Phila. Pa., 1918

openings in American factories around this time, and much of our country has been constructed by them ever since.

The rectangular bricks of the wall and the similarly shaped lights of the factory's glass windows are reminders of how much the right angle has served us in manufacturing. It is as though the ruler and drawing board tended to design only geometric forms. One striking aspect of this picture is how differently the human beings are shaped than the things that surround them. The photograph is almost a perfect gridwork of lines, and the living creatures that have created this Euclidean world stand out as oddly shaped, non-idealized strangers. The wing panel is really quite primitive, because in plan view it too would be completely rectilinear. Within ten years engineers would understand that successful flying machinery needed less of the right angle and more of the sort of complex curved forms that characterize the organic world. The photograph foreshadows this watershed as well: industry was coming to realize that the form of its creations could no longer be determined by the nature of convenient materials at hand, nor hide within old and comfortable patterns of design.

✎ Topics for Critical Thinking and Writing

1. In his first paragraph Benson says, "The wing panel is a beautifully made thing . . . ." He probably means not only that it is beautifully *made,* that is, carefully constructed, but also—look at the rest of his sentence—that this constructed object itself is beautiful. Would you agree that this wing panel is beautiful? If so, why? If not, why not? Describe any object that is the product of work—an automobile, a chair, a lamp, whatever—and in an essay of 500 words explain why it is or is not beautiful. (If possible, attach a photograph with your essay.)

2. Benson offers sociological comment, aesthetic analysis, and a bit of the history of technology. Do you find his comments stimulating and worth considering, or do they seem uninformed or farfetched or otherwise of little interest? Explain, in an essay of 250 to 500 words.

Gloria Steinem

Gloria Steinem was born in Toledo in 1934 and educated at Smith College. An active figure in politics, civil rights affairs, and feminist issues, she was a co-founder of the Women's Action Alliance and a co-founder and editor of Ms. *magazine. We reprint an essay from one of her books,* Outrageous Acts and Everyday Rebellions *(1983).*

The Importance of Work

Toward the end of the 1970s, *The Wall Street Journal* devoted an eight-part, front-page series to "the working woman"—that is, the influx of women into the paid-labor force—as the greatest change in American life since the Industrial Revolution.

Many women readers greeted both the news and the definition with cynicism. After all, women have always worked. If all the productive work of human maintenance that women do in the home were valued at its replacement cost, the gross national product of the United States would go up by 26 percent. It's just that we are now more likely than ever before to leave our poorly rewarded, low-security, high-risk job of homemaking (though we're still trying to explain that it's a perfectly good one and that the problem is male society's refusal both to do it and to give it an economic value) for more secure, independent, and better-paid jobs outside the home.

Obviously, the real work revolution won't come until all productive work is rewarded—including child rearing and other jobs done in the home—and men are integrated into so-called women's work as well as vice versa. But the radical change being touted by the *Journal* and other media is one part of that long integration process: the unprecedented flood of women into salaried jobs, that is, into the labor force as it has been male-defined and previously occupied by men. We are already more than 41 percent of it—the highest proportion in history. Given the fact that women also make up a whopping 69 percent of the "discouraged labor force" (that is, people who need jobs but don't get counted in the unemployment statistics because they've given up looking), plus an official female unemployment rate that is substantially higher than men's, it's clear that we could expand to become fully half of the national work force by 1990.

Faced with this determination of women to find a little independence and to be paid and honored for our work, experts have rushed to ask: "Why?" It's a question rarely directed at male workers. Their basic motivations of survival and personal satisfaction are taken for granted. Indeed, men are regarded as "odd" and therefore subjects for sociological study and journalistic reports only when they *don't* have work, even if they are rich and don't need jobs or are poor and can't find them. Nonetheless, pollsters and sociologists have gone to great expense to prove that women work outside the home because of dire financial need, or if we persist despite the presence of a wage-earning male, out of some desire to buy "little extras" for our families, or even out of good old-fashioned penis envy.

Job interviewers and even our own families may still ask salaried women the big "Why?" If we have small children at home or are in some job regarded as "men's work," the incidence of such questions increases. Condescending or accusatory versions of "What's a nice girl like you doing in a place like this?" have not disappeared from the workplace.   5

How do we answer these assumptions that we are "working" out of some pressing or peculiar need? Do we feel okay about arguing that it's as natural for us to have salaried jobs as for our husbands—whether or not we have young children at home? Can we enjoy strong career ambitions without worrying about being thought "unfeminine"? When we confront men's growing resentment of women competing in the work force (often in the form of such guilt-producing accusations as "You're taking men's jobs away" or "You're damaging your children"), do we simply state that a decent job is a basic human right for everybody?

I'm afraid the answer is often no. As individuals and as a movement, we tend to retreat into some version of a tactically questionable defense: "Womenworkbecausewehaveto." The phrase has become one word, one key on the typewriter—an economic form of the socially "feminine" stance of passivity and self-sacrifice. Under attack, we still tend to present ourselves as creatures of economic necessity and familial devotion. "Womenworkbecausewehaveto" has become the easiest thing to say.

Like most truisms, this one is easy to prove with statistics. Economic need *is* the most consistent work motive—for women as well as men. In 1976, for instance, 43 percent of all women in the paid-labor force were single, widowed, separated, or divorced, and working to support themselves and their dependents. An additional 21 percent were married to men who had earned less than ten thousand dollars in the previous year, the minimum then required to support a family of four. In fact, if you take men's pensions, stocks, real estate, and various forms of accumulated wealth into account, a good statistical case can be made that there are more women who "have" to work (that is, who have neither the accumulated wealth, nor husbands whose work or wealth can support them for the rest of their lives) than there are men with the same need. If we were going to ask one group "Do you really need this job?" we should ask men.

But the first weakness of the whole "have to work" defense is its deceptiveness. Anyone who has ever experienced dehumanized life on welfare or any other confidence-shaking dependency knows that a paid job may be preferable to the dole, even when the hand-out is coming from a family member. Yet the will and self-confidence to work on one's own can diminish as dependency and fear increase. That may explain why—contrary to the "have to" rationale—wives of men who earn less than three thousand dollars a year are actually *less* likely to be employed than wives whose husbands make ten thousand dollars a year or more.

Furthermore, the greatest proportion of employed wives is found   10
among families with a total household income of twenty-five to fifty thousand dollars a year. This is the statistical underpinning used by some sociologists to prove that women's work is mainly important for boosting families into the middle or upper middle class. Thus, women's incomes are largely used for buying "luxuries" and "little extras": a neat double-whammy that renders us secondary within our families, and makes our jobs expendable in hard times. We may even go along with this interpretation (at least, up to the point of getting fired so a male can have our job). It preserves a husbandly ego-need to be seen as the primary breadwinner, and still allows us a safe "feminine" excuse for working.

But there are often rewards that we're not confessing. As noted in *The Two-Career Couple,* by Francine and Douglas Hall: "Women who hold jobs by choice, even blue-collar routine jobs, are more satisfied with their lives than are the full-time housewives."

In addition to personal satisfaction, there is also society's need for all its members' talents. Suppose that jobs were given out on only a "have to work" basis to both women and men—one job per household. It would be unthinkable to lose the unique abilities of, for instance, Eleanor Holmes Norton, the distinguished chair of the Equal Employment Opportunity Commission. But would we then be forced to question the important work of her husband, Edward Norton, who is also a distinguished lawyer? Since men earn more than twice as much as women on the average, the wife in most households would be more likely to give up her job.

Does that mean the nation could do as well without millions of its nurses, teachers, and secretaries? Or that the rare man who earns less than his wife should give up his job?

It was this kind of waste of human talents on a society-wide scale that traumatized millions of unemployed or underemployed Americans during the Depression. Then, a one-job-per-household rule seemed somewhat justified, yet the concept was used to displace women workers only, create intolerable dependencies, and waste female talent that the country needed. That Depression experience, plus the energy and example of women who were finally allowed to work during the manpower shortage created by World War II, led Congress to reinterpret the meaning of the country's full-employment goal in its Economic Act of 1946. Full employment was officially defined as "the employment of those who want to work, without regard to whether their employment is, by some definition, necessary. This goal applies equally to men and to women." Since bad economic times are again creating a resentment of employed women—as well as creating more need for women to be employed—we need such a goal more than ever. Women are again being caught in a tragic double bind: We are required to be strong and then punished for our strength.

Clearly, anything less than government and popular commitment to this 1946 definition of full employment will leave the less powerful groups, whoever they may be, in danger. Almost as important as the financial penalty paid by the powerless is the suffering that comes from being shut out of paid and recognized work. Without it, we lose much of our self-respect and our ability to prove that we are alive by making some difference in the world. That's just as true for the suburban woman as it is for the unemployed steel worker.

But it won't be easy to give up the passive defense of "weworkbe- causewehaveto." 15

When a woman who is struggling to support her children and grand-children on welfare sees her neighbor working as a waitress, even though that neighbor's husband has a job, she may feel resentful; and the waitress (of course, not the waitress's husband) may feel guilty. Yet unless we establish the obligation to provide a job for everyone who is willing and able to work, that welfare woman may herself be penalized by policies that give out only one public-service job per household. She and her daughter will have to make a painful and divisive decision about which of them gets that precious job, and the whole household will have to survive on only one salary.

A job as a human right is a principle that applies to men as well as women. But women have more cause to fight for it. The phenomenon of the "working woman" has been held responsible for everything from an increase in male impotence (which turned out, incidentally, to be attributable to medication for high blood pressure) to the rising cost of steak (which was due to high energy costs and beef import restrictions, not women's refusal to prepare the cheaper, slower-cooking cuts). Unless we

see a job as part of every citizen's right to autonomy and personal fulfillment, we will continue to be vulnerable to someone else's idea of what
"need" is, and whose "need" counts the most.

In many ways, women who do not have to work for simple survival,
but who choose to do so nonetheless, are on the frontier of asserting this
right for all women. Those with well-to-do husbands are dangerously
easy for us to resent and put down. It's easier still to resent women from
families of inherited wealth, even though men generally control and benefit from that wealth. (There is no Rockefeller Sisters Fund, no J. P. Morgan & Daughters, and sons-in-law may be the ones who really sleep their
way to power.) But to prevent a woman whose husband or father is
wealthy from earning her own living, and from gaining the self-confidence that comes with that ability, is to keep her needful of that unearned
power and less willing to disperse it. Moreover, it is to lose forever her
unique talents.

Perhaps modern feminists have been guilty of a kind of reverse snob-
bism that keeps us from reaching out to the wives and daughters of
wealthy men; yet it was exactly such women who refused the restrictions
of class and financed the first wave of feminist revolution.

For most of us, however, "womenworkbecausewehaveto" is just true   20
enough to be seductive as a personal defense.

If we use it without also staking out the larger human right to a job,
however, we will never achieve that right. And we will always be subject
to the false argument that independence for women is a luxury affordable only in good economic times. Alternatives to layoffs will not be
explored, acceptable unemployment will always be used to frighten
those with jobs into accepting low wages, and we will never remedy the
real cost, both to families and to the country, of dependent women and a
massive loss of talent.

Worst of all, we may never learn to find productive, honored work as
a natural part of ourselves and as one of life's basic pleasures.

✎ Topics for Critical Thinking and Writing

1. In paragraph 2 Steinem characterizes homemaking as a "poorly rewarded,
   low-security, high-risk job." How might she justify each of these descriptions
   of homemaking? Do you agree that homemaking is rightly classified as a
   job? If so, do you agree with her description of it?

2. Restate in your own words Steinem's explanation (paragraph 9) of why
   "wives of men who earn *less* than three thousand dollars a year are actually *less* likely to be employed than wives whose husbands make ten thousand dollars a year or more." The salary figures are, of course, out of date.
   Is the point nevertheless still valid? Explain.

3. To whom does Steinem appear to address her remarks? Cite evidence for
   your answer. In your opinion, is this audience likely to find her argument

persuasive? Would a different audience find it more or less persuasive? Explain.

4. In addition to arguments, what persuasive devices does Steinem use? How, for example, does she persuade you that she speaks with authority? What other authorities does she cite? How would you characterize her diction and tone, for instance in paragraph 18? (On diction, and tone, see pages 16–17.)

5. Steinem suggests two reasons for working: "personal satisfaction" and "society's need for all its members' talents." Suppose that you had no financial need to work. Do you imagine that you would choose to work in order to gain "personal satisfaction"? Or, again if you had no need to work, would you assume that you are morally obligated to contribute to society by engaging in paid work?

6. Summarize, in a paragraph of about 100 to 150 words, Steinem's argument that it is entirely proper for wealthy women to work for pay. In the course of your paragraph, you may quote briefly from the essay.

7. Compare Steinem with Russell (page 472) on the value of work.

Felice N. Schwartz

Felice N. Schwartz is founder and president of Catalyst, a not-for-profit organization that works with corporations to foster the career development of women.

In 1989 Schwartz published in the Harvard Business Review *an article that was widely interpreted as advising women to limit their expectations of advancement if they entered the business world. The controversy was reported in the newspapers, and Schwartz took the opportunity to reach a mass audience by writing an essay—printed below—for* The New York Times.

The "Mommy Track" Isn't Anti-Woman

"The cost of employing women in business is greater than the cost of employing men."

This sentence, the first of my recent article in the *Harvard Business Review,* has provoked an extraordinary debate, now labeled by others "the Mommy track." The purpose of the article was to urge employers to create policies that help mothers balance career and family responsibilities, and to eliminate barriers to female productivity and advancement.

But two fears have emerged in the debate. One is that, by raising the issue that it costs more to employ women, we will not be hired and promoted. The other is the fear that if working mothers are offered a variety of career paths, including a part-time option, all women will be left with the primary responsibility for child care.

Acknowledging that there are costs associated with employing women will not lead companies to put women in dead-end jobs. Time taken from work for childbearing, recovery and child care, as well the counterproductive attitudes and practices women face in a male-dominated workplace, do take their toll on women's productivity. But in our competitive marketplace, the costs of employing women pale beside the payoffs.

Current "baby-bust" demographics compel companies to employ women at every level, no matter what the cost. Why? Women comprise half the talent and competence in the country. The idea that companies are looking for excuses to send women home again is untrue. Companies are looking for solutions, not excuses.

Over and over, corporate leaders tell me that their most pressing concern is not why but *how* to respond cost-effectively to the needs of women. Some take bold steps to provide women with the flexibility and family supports they need; others implement ground-breaking programs to remove barriers to women's leadership. The farsighted do both.

Their programs address the needs of women as individuals. There can be no one career "track" to which women, or men, can be expected to adhere throughout their lives. Few can know from the start to what degree they will be committed to career or to family. Raising the issue of the costs of employing women motivates companies to find solutions that work for individuals with diverse and sometimes changing goals and needs.

The second fear voiced in this debate is that making alternative career paths available to women may freeze them in the role of primary caretakers of children.

Today, men are more involved in their children's upbringing, from fixing breakfast to picking up kids at school—enriching our children's lives. But despite increased sharing of parental responsibilities, women remain at the center of family life. According to a recent study, 54 percent of married women who work full-time said child care was their responsibility—contrasted with two percent of surveyed men.

The danger of charting our direction on the basis of wishful thinking is clear. Whether or not men play a greater role in child rearing, companies must reduce the family-related stresses on working women. The flexibility companies provide for women now will be a model in the very near future for men—thus women will not be forced to continue to take primary responsibility for child care. Giving men flexibility will benefit companies in many ways, including greater women's productivity.

What I advocate is that companies create options that allow employees to set their own pace, strive for the top, find satisfaction at the midlevel or cut back for a period of time—not to be penalized for wanting to make a substantial commitment to family. Achievement should not be a function of whether an employee has children. Success is the reward of talent, hard work and commitment.

What benefits women benefits companies. In reducing the cost of employing women—by clearing obstacles to their advancement and providing family benefits—companies create an environment in which all can succeed. But employers will not be motivated to reduce the costs if it remains taboo to discuss them. Only by putting the facts on the table will employers and women—and men—be able to form a partnership in addressing the issues.

 ## Topics for Critical Thinking and Writing

Read the following letters, and then consult the topics on page 495.

Pat Schroeder, Lois Brenner, Hope Dellon, Anita M. Harris, Peg McAuley Byrd

The following letters were published in The New York Times *shortly after Schwartz's article appeared.*

Letters Responding to Felice N. Schwartz

To the Editor:

Felice N. Schwartz might have had the best of intentions when she wrote "Management Women and the New Facts of Life" for the *Harvard Business Review* and reiterated her thesis in "The 'Mommy Track' Isn't Anti-Woman" (Op-Ed, March 22). Her arguments, however, are hardly supported by her scholarship, which relies on unidentified studies at unnamed corporations about undefined "turnover" rates, assertions that begin with phrases like "we know" and "what we know to be true," and an undocumented assumption that women in business cost more.

The linchpin of Ms. Schwartz's thesis is an unidentified study at a single multinational corporation where the turnover rate for female managers was allegedly two and a half times that for male managers. Ms. Schwartz does not say whether the actual rates were an insignificant 1 percent for men and 2.5 percent for women, a significant 40 percent for men and 100 percent for women or something between. Moreover, she fails to explore the reasons for the difference. These might include poor personnel policies, like rigid relocation demands or a lack of parental leave, better job opportunities at other corporations or downturns in the company's fortunes that prompted more recently hired female managers to seek greener pastures.

Ms. Schwartz cites a second unidentified study (apparently of all female employees, not just managers) at another unnamed company, where "half of the women who take maternity leave return to their jobs late or not at all." That is, half returned as scheduled, and an unspecified number did not return, but for unexplained reasons.

Singling out turnover rates among female employees, whether clerks or managers, is a dubious approach. The days of an employee's spending 50 years with a single employer and retiring with a gold watch and a handshake are over. (Indeed, thanks to the buyout, merger and acquisition mania of the 1980s, the days of a company's lasting even a few years under the same ownership, management or even the same name, are diminishing.)

A January 1983 Bureau of Labor Statistics job-tenure survey that represented 54 million male and 42 million female workers reported that fewer that 10 percent of workers of either sex had been with their current employers 25 years or more. Of the 14 million male and 9.5 million female managers and executives covered by the survey, the median tenure was 6.6 years for males and 4.7 years for females.

The survey also showed that 60 percent of the male managers and executives and 74 percent of their female counterparts had the same employer for 9 years or less. Only 11 percent of the males and 3 percent of the females had the same employer for 25 years or more.

In short, few men or women remain with one employer for their entire careers, and women's somewhat lower managerial tenures might be explained partly by women's having only recently entered the executive ranks in significant numbers.

If Ms. Schwartz's scholarship is suspect, her two-track career model (future mommies in this corner, future nonmommies in that corner) is quaint—indeed Victorian—in view of what businesses are doing for men and women.

Impelled by the changing American work force and striving to remain competitive, corporations like U S West, I.B.M., A.T.&T., Time Inc., Corning Glass, Quaker Oats and Merck have concluded that productivity and family obligations are not mutually exclusive, that the almighty dollar and the family are not enemies. To accommodate these new realities companies have instituted such employment practices as parental leave, flexible and part-time schedules, sabbaticals, child care, telecommuting and job sharing.

But workers are not the only beneficiaries of these new practices. Employers are finding that meeting the needs of employees makes companies more productive and more competitive.

Pat Schroeder
Member of Congress, 1st Dist., Colo.
Washington, March 27, 1989

To the Editor:

Corporations may welcome Felice Schwartz's discovery of the "career and family" woman and "her willingness to accept lower pay and little advancement in return for a flexible schedule" (news story, March 8), but such women should consider the recent history of divorce laws before agreeing to this definition.

Although the law says marriage is an economic partnership that values child rearing and other domestic contributions as well as earning power, the reality is that when a marriage ends, women are not adequately compensated for having devoted themselves to their families at the expense of pursuing their career development.

If young women are going to be doubly penalized this way for choosing "the mommy track," they would do well to look closely at the experience of a generation of middle-aged women who have been left divorced and financially derailed by that choice.

Lois Brenner
New York, March 19, 1989

The writer of the following letter heads the family law department of a law firm and is co-author of not-yet-published book on divorce for women.

To the Editor:

Felice N. Schwartz, in her attempt to persuade us that "The 'Mommy Track' Isn't Anti-Woman" (Op-Ed, March 22), cites an intriguing statistic. According to a recent study, she says, 54 percent of married women working full-time regard child care as their responsibility, whereas only 2 percent of men say the same.

Does this mean that 46 percent of women in these circumstances see child care as a shared responsibility—presumably because men are sharing in the work? While not a majority, such a figure would be a significant enough minority to lend force to the argument for the importance of making businesses more responsive to the needs of both mothers and fathers—and, perhaps more compellingly, to the needs of the nation's children.

While Ms. Schwartz's assurance that "current 'baby-bust' demographics compel companies to employ women at every level" may be true, it is also true that few mothers have reached the top.

The idea of tracks has always had its limitations—whether in junior high school or in the corporate world. But if we must have such tracks in business, the chances of discrimination are surely much less for a "parent track" than for a "mommy track." Corporations may or may not believe that they can get along without mothers in high places, but they must realize that they cannot function without parents.

Hope Dellon
New York, March 24, 1989

To the Editor:

Another problem with Felice Schwartz's proposal to track working women according to the likelihood they will want to raise children is that it is impossible to tell ahead of time which women are which.

In interviewing highly successful career women in predominantly male fields, I found that some women who as late as age 34 said adamantly that they did not want children had, by 40, had them. One executive who had had her tubes tied at 29, with the idea that she wanted a career and no children was, at 35, about to be married; she wanted desperately to have the ligation reversed and was seriously contemplating a completely different line of work.

Women who in their 20's had expected to quit work to have families found themselves in their 30's still single or divorced and enjoying their careers. Most women, married or single, with or without children, expressed ambivalence both about children and about their careers.

The problem is not that women don't know what they want, but that women, like men, grow and change along the life cycle. Stereotyping women early on into mothers and nonmothers would hamper their ability to develop fully both as individuals and as productive employees.

Even worse, it would perpetuate a cycle in which generations of   5
women have been depreciated, divided and weakened through a paradoxical message that says women are inferior if they—and unless they—compete in terms that are set by and for men.

Anita M. Harris
Cambridge, Mass., March 13, 1989

The writer of the following letter, an assistant professor of communications at Simmons College in Boston, is completing a book on professional women.

To the Editor:

While I mostly agree with your response to "Management Women and the New Facts of Life" (editorial, March 13), your perspective does not include or explore the profoundly different attitudes men and women have toward money, which is, after all, why people work. There has been a spate of surveys highlighting these different attitudes.

Men see money as a means to power, heightening their visibility for selection for leadership within society. Looked at this way, the insatiable appetite for money, frequently bordering on greed, makes sense, albeit an insane sense. Capital accumulation is seen as primarily a male activity.

Women, on the other hand, see money as a means of power to purchase. Money purchases food, clothing, shelter or the means of nurturing. This idea too has its insane side, giving rise to gross materialism. Excessive spending is seen as a female trait.

Both these traits cross gender, but a greater number fall within a male-female perspective.

Women cannot satisfy their primary need, nurturing family and soci-   5
ety, with the same single-minded directness that men can bring to their primary need of territory (capital accumulation). The marketplace, a male invention, reflects this bias, presenting women with unnatural choices, creating for them a practical as well as psychological disadvantage.

We must force the news media to include differing economic attitudes in covering the brave woman who daily deals with the multifaceted pressures of family life and living up to her potential as described by others.

Peg McAuley Byrd
Madison, N.J., March 20, 1989

✎ Topics for Critical Thinking and Writing

1. In paragraph 5 Schwartz says that "baby-bust' demographics compel companies to employ women at every level, no matter what the cost." Exactly what does she mean?
2. In paragraph 9 Schwartz says that "Today, men are more involved in their children's upbringing . . . ." One often hears comparable statements, but are they true? How would one verify such a statement? In any case, if *you* have any reason to agree or disagree with the statement, express the grounds. To what extent do you think men *ought* to be involved in child-rearing?
3. Schwartz begins her final paragraph by asserting. "What benefits women benefits companies." What evidence or arguments does she offer to support this claim? Or do you think the point is self-evident and needs no support?
4. List the three most cogent arguments the letter-writers make against Schwartz's position.
5. Imagine that you are Schwartz. Write a letter to *The New York Times* in which you reply to one of the letters.

Milton Friedman

Milton Friedman, born in Brooklyn in 1912, is a graduate of Rutgers University, the University of Chicago, and Columbia University. A leading conservative economist, Friedman has had considerable influence on economic thought in America through his popular writings (he wrote a regular column in Newsweek) *his numerous scholarly writings and his presence on national committees.*

The Social Responsibility of Business Is to Increase Its Profits

When I hear businessmen speak eloquently about the "social responsibilities of business in a free-enterprise system," I am reminded of the wonderful line about the Frenchman who discovered at the age of 70 that he had been speaking prose all his life. The businessmen believe that they are defending free enterprise when they declaim that business is not concerned "merely" with profit but also with promoting desirable "social" ends; that business has a "social conscience" and takes seriously its responsibilities for providing employment, eliminating discrimination, avoiding pollution and whatever else may be the catchwords of the contemporary crop of reformers. In fact they are—or would be if they or anyone else took them seriously—preaching pure and unadulterated socialism. Businessmen who talk this way are unwitting puppets of the intellectual forces that have been undermining the basis of a free society these past decades.

The discussions of the "social responsibilities of business" are notable for their analytical looseness and lack of rigor. What does it mean to say that "business" has responsibilities? Only people can have responsibilities. A corporation is an artificial person and in this sense may have artificial responsibilities, but "business" as a whole cannot be said to have responsibilities, even in this vague sense. The first step toward clarity in examining the doctrine of the social responsibility of business is to ask precisely what it implies for whom.

Presumably, the individuals who are to be responsible are businessmen, which means individual proprietors or corporate executives. Most of the discussion of social responsibility is directed at corporations, so in what follows I shall mostly neglect the individual proprietors and speak of corporate executives.

In a free-enterprise, private-property system, a corporate executive is an employee of the owners of the business. He has direct responsibility to his employers. That responsibility is to conduct the business in accordance with their desires, which generally will be to make as much money as possible while conforming to the basic rules of the society, both those embodied in law and those embodied in ethical custom. Of course, in some cases his employers may have a different objective. A group of persons might establish a corporation for an eleemosynary purpose—for example, a hospital or a school. The manager of such a corporation will not have money profit as his objectives but the rendering of certain services.

In either case, the key point is that, in his capacity as a corporate executive, the manager is the agent of the individuals who own the corporation or establish the eleemosynary institution, and his primary responsibility is to them.

Needless to say, this does not mean that it is easy to judge how well he is performing his task. But at least the criterion of performance is straightforward, and the persons among whom a voluntary contractual arrangement exists are clearly defined.

Of course, the corporate executive is also a person in his own right. As a person, he may have many other responsibilities that he recognizes or assumes voluntarily—to his family, his conscience, his feelings of charity, his church, his clubs, his city, his country. He may feel impelled by these responsibilities to devote part of his income to causes he regards as worthy, to refuse to work for particular corporations, even to leave his job, for example, to join his country's armed forces. If we wish, we may refer to some of these responsibilities as "social responsibilities." But in these respects he is acting as a principal, not an agent; he is spending his own money or time or energy, not the money of his employers or the time or energy he has contracted to devote to their purposes. If these are "social responsibilities," they are the social responsibilities of individuals, not of business.

What does it mean to say that the corporate executive has a "social responsibility" in his capacity as businessman? If this statement is not pure rhetoric, it must mean that he is to act in some way that is not in the interest of his employers. For example, that he is to refrain from increasing the price of the product in order to contribute to the social objective of preventing inflation, even though a price increase would be in the best interests of the corporation. Or that he is to make expenditures on reducing pollution beyond the amount that is in the best interests of the corporation or that is required by law in order to contribute to the social objective of improving the environment. Or that, at the expense of corporate profits, he is to hire "hardcore" unemployed instead of better qualified available workmen to contribute to the social objective of reducing poverty.

In each of these cases, the corporate executive would be spending someone else's money for a general social interest. Insofar as his actions in accord with his "social responsibility" reduce returns to stockholders, he is spending their money. Insofar as his actions raise the price to customers, he is spending the customers' money. Insofar as his actions lower the wages of some employees, he is spending their money.

The stockholders or the customers or the employees could separately   10
spend their own money on the particular action if they wished to do so. The executive is exercising a distinct "social responsibility," rather than serving as an agent of the stockholders or the customers or the employees, only if he spends the money in a different way than they would have spent it.

But if he does this, he is in effect imposing taxes, on the one hand, and deciding how the tax proceeds shall be spent, on the other.

This process raises political questions on two levels: principle and consequences. On the level of political principle, the imposition of taxes and the expenditure of tax proceeds are governmental functions. We have established elaborate constitutional, parliamentary and judicial provisions to control these functions, to assure that taxes are imposed so far as possible in accordance with the preferences and desires of the public—after all, "taxation without representation" was one of the battle cries of the American Revolution. We have a system of checks and balances to separate the legislative function of imposing taxes and enacting expenditures from the executive function of collecting taxes and administering expenditure programs and from the judicial function of mediating disputes and interpreting the law.

Here the businessman—self-selected or appointed directly or indirectly by stockholders—is to be simultaneously legislator, executive and jurist. He is to decide whom to tax by how much and for what purpose, and he is to spend the proceeds—all this guided only by general exhortations from on high to restrain inflation, improve the environment, fight poverty and so on and on.

The whole justification for permitting the corporate executive to be selected by the stockholders is that the executive is an agent serving the interests of his principal. This justification disappears when the corporate executive imposes taxes and spends the proceeds for "social" purposes. He becomes in effect a public employee, a civil servant, even though he remains in name an employee of a private enterprise. On grounds of political principle, it is intolerable that such civil servants—insofar as their actions in the name of social responsibility are real and not just window-dressing,—should be selected as they are now. If they are to be civil servants, then they must be elected through a political process. If they are to impose taxes and make expenditures to foster "social" objectives, then political machinery must be set up to make the assessment of taxes and to determine through a political process the objectives to be served.

This is the basic reason why the doctrine of "social responsibility" involves the acceptance of the socialist view that political mechanisms, not market mechanisms, are the appropriate way to determine the allocation of scarce resources to alternative uses.   15

On the grounds of consequences, can the corporate executive in fact discharge his alleged "social responsibilities"? On the other hand, suppose he could get away with spending the stockholders' or customers' or employees' money. How is he to know how to spend it? He is told that he must contribute to fighting inflation. How is he to know what action of his will contribute to that end? He is presumably an expert in running his company—in producing a product or selling it or financing it. But nothing about his selection makes him an expert on inflation. Will his holding down the price of his product reduce inflationary pressure? Or, by leaving more spending power in the hands of his customers, simply divert it elsewhere? Or, by forcing him to produce less because of the lower price, will it simply contribute to shortages? Even if he could answer these questions, how much cost is he justified in imposing on his stockholders, customers and employees for this social purpose? What is his appropriate share and what is the appropriate share of others?

And, whether he wants to or not, can he get away with spending his stockholders', customers' or employees' money? Will not the stockholders fire him? (Either the present ones or those who take over when his actions in the name of social responsibility have reduced the corporation's profits and the price of its stock.) His customers and his employees can desert him for other producers and employers less scrupulous in exercising their social responsibilities.

This facet of "social responsibility" doctrine is brought into sharp relief when the doctrine is used to justify wage restraint by trade unions. The conflict of interest is naked and clear when union officials are asked to subordinate the interest of their members to some more general purpose. If the union officials try to enforce wage restraint, the consequence is likely to be wildcat strikes, rank-and-file revolts and the emergence of strong competitors for their jobs. We thus have the ironic phenomenon that union leaders—at least in the U.S.—have objected to Government interference with the market far more consistently and courageously than have business leaders.

The difficulty of exercising "social responsibility" illustrates, of course, the great virtue of private competitive enterprise—it forces people to be responsible for their own actions and makes it difficult for them to "exploit" other people for either selfish or unselfish purposes. They can do good—but only at their own expense.

Many a reader who has followed the argument this far may be tempted to remonstrate that it is all well and good to speak of Government's having the responsibility to impose taxes and determine expenditures for such "social" purposes as controlling pollution or training the hard-core unemployed, but that the problems are too urgent to wait on the slow course of political processes, that the exercise of social responsibility by businessmen is a quicker and surer way to solve pressing current problems.

Aside from the question of fact—I share Adam Smith's skepticism about the benefits that can be expected from "those who affected to trade for the public good"—this argument must be rejected on grounds of principle. What it amounts to is an assertion that those who favor the taxes and expenditures in question have failed to persuade a majority of their fellow citizens to be of like mind and that they are seeking to attain by undemocratic procedures what they cannot attain by democratic procedures. In a free society, it is hard for "evil" people to do "evil," especially since one man's good is another's evil.

I have, for simplicity, concentrated on the special case of the corporate executive, except only for the brief digression on trade unions. But precisely the same argument applies to the newer phenomenon of calling upon stockholders to require corporations to exercise social responsibility (the recent G.M. crusade for example). In most of these cases, what is in effect involved is some stockholders trying to get other stockholders (or customers or employees) to contribute against their will to "social" causes favored by the activists. Insofar as they succeed, they are again imposing taxes and spending the proceeds.

The situation of the individual proprietor is somewhat different. If he acts to reduce the returns of his enterprise in order to exercise his "social responsibility," he is spending his own money, not someone else's. If he wishes to spend his money on such purposes, that is his right, and I cannot see that there is any objection to his doing so. In the process, he, too, may impose costs on employees and customers. However, because he is far less likely than a large corporation or union to have monopolistic power, any such side effects will tend to be minor.

Of course, in practice the doctrine of social responsibility is frequently a cloak for actions that are justified on other grounds rather than a reason for those actions.

To illustrate, it may well be in the long-run interest of a corporation that is a major employer in a small community to devote resources to providing amenities to that community or to improving its government. That may make it easier to attract desirable employees, it may reduce the wage bill or lessen losses from pilferage and sabotage or have other worthwhile effects. Or it may be that, given the laws about the deductibility of corporate charitable contributions, the stockholders can contribute more to charities they favor by having the corporation make the gift than by doing it themselves, since they can in that way contribute an amount that would otherwise have been paid as corporate taxes.

In each of these—and many similar—cases, there is a strong temptation to rationalize these actions as an exercise of "social responsibility." In the present climate of opinion, with its widepread aversion to "capitalism," "profits," the "soulless corporation" and so on, this is one way for a corporation to generate goodwill as a byproduct of expenditures that are entirely justified in its own self-interest.

It would be inconsistent of me to call on corporate executives to refrain from this hypocritical window-dressing because it harms the foundations of a free society. That would be to call on them to exercise a "social responsibility"! If our institutions and the attitudes of the public make it in their self-interest to cloak their actions in this way, I cannot summon much indignation to denounce them. At the same time, I can express admiration for those individual proprietors or owners of closely held corporations or stockholders of more broadly held corporations who disdain such tactics as approaching fraud.

Whether blameworthy or not, the use of the cloak of social responsibility, and the nonsense spoken in its name by influential and prestigious businessmen, does clearly harm the foundations of a free society. I have been impressed time and again by the schizophrenic character of many businessmen. They are capable of being extremely far-sighted and clear-headed in matters that are internal to their businesses. They are incredibly short-sighted and muddle-headed in matters that are outside their businesses but affect the possible survival of business in general. This short-sightedness is strikingly exemplified in the calls from many businessmen for wage and price guidelines or controls or income policies. There is nothing that could do more in a brief period to destroy a market system and replace it by a centrally controlled system than effective governmental control of prices and wages.

The short-sightedness is also exemplified in speeches by businessmen on social responsibility. This may gain them kudos in the short run. But it helps to strengthen the already too prevalent view that the pursuit of profits is wicked and immoral and must be curbed and controlled by external forces. Once this view is adopted, the external forces that curb the market will not be the social consciences, however highly developed, of the pontificating executives; it will be the iron fist of Government bureaucrats. Here, as with price and wage controls, businessmen seem to me to reveal a suicidal impulse.

The political principle that underlies the market mechanism is unanimity. In an ideal free market resting on private property, no individual can coerce any other, all cooperation is voluntary, all parties to such cooperation benefit or they need not participate. There are no values, no

30

"social" responsibilities in any sense other than the shared values and responsibilities of individuals. Society is a collection of individuals and of the various groups they voluntarily form.

The political principle that underlies the political mechanism is conformity. The individual must serve a more general social interest—whether that be determined by a church or a dictator or a majority. The individual may have a vote and say in what is to be done, but if he is overruled, he must conform. It is appropriate for some to require others to contribute to a general social purpose whether they wish to or not.

Unfortunately, unanimity is not always feasible. There are some respects in which conformity appears unavoidable, so I do not see how one can avoid the use of the political mechanism altogether.

But the doctrine of "social responsibility" taken seriously would extend the scope of the political mechanism to every human activity. It does not differ in philosophy from the most explicitly collectivist doctrine. It differs only by professing to believe that collectivist ends can be attained without collectivist means. That is why, in my book "Capitalism and Freedom," I have called it a "fundamentally subversive doctrine" in a free society, and have said that in such a society, "there is one and only one social responsibility of business—to use its resources and engage in activities designed to increase its profits so long as it stays within the rules of the game, which is to say, engages in open and free competition without deception or fraud."

✎ Topics for Critical Thinking and Writing

1. Friedman says that corporate executives who spend the corporation's money "for a general social interest" are "in effect imposing taxes . . . and deciding how the tax proceeds shall be spent . . ." (paragraphs 9 and 11). Is the use of the word *tax* effective? Is it fair? (Notice that paragraphs 12, 13, and 14, as well as some later paragraphs, also speak of taxes.)

2. "The socialist view," Friedman says in paragraph 15, is "that political mechanisms, not market mechanisms, are the appropriate way to determine the allocation of scarce resources to alternative uses." Suppose a fellow student told you that he or she found this passage puzzling. How would you clarify it?

3. Some persons in business have replied to Friedman by arguing that because the owners of today's corporations are rarely involved in running them, the corporations can properly be viewed not as private property but as social institutions able to formulate goals of their own. These people argue that the managers of a corporation are public trustees of a multipurpose organization, and their job is to use their power to promote the interests not only of stockholders but of employees and of the general public. What do you think are the strengths and the weaknesses of this reply?

4. Does Friedman argue that corporations have no responsibilities?
5. In *Religion and the Rise of Capitalism,* R. H. Tawney said that "economic organization must allow for the fact that, unless industry is to be paralyzed by
   recurrent revolts on the part of outraged human nature, it must satisfy criteria which are not purely economic." Do you think Friedman would agree?
   Why, or why not?

Barbara Ehrenreich and Annette Fuentes

Barbara Ehrenreich writes regularly for the New York Times *and for* Ms. *magazine. Annette
Fuentes, the editor of* Sisterhood Is Global, *has also written for* Ms., *where this article originally
appeared.*

Life on the Global Assembly Line

In Ciudad Juárez, Mexico, Anna M. rises at 5 A.M. to feed her son before
starting on the two-hour bus trip to the maquiladora (factory). He will spend
the day along with four other children in a neighbor's one-room home.
Anna's husband, frustrated by being unable to find work for himself, left for
the United States six months ago. She wonders, as she carefully applies her
new lip gloss, whether she ought to consider herself still married. It might be
good to take a night course, become a secretary. But she seldom gets home
before eight at night, and the factory, where she stitches brassieres that will
be sold in the United States through J. C. Penney, pays only $48 a week.
In Penang, Malaysia, Julie K. is up before the three other young women with
whom she shares a room, and starts heating the leftover rice from last night's
supper. She looks good in the company's green-trimmed uniform, and she's
proud to work in a modern, American-owned factory. Only not quite so
proud as when she started working three years ago—she thinks as she
squints out the door at a passing group of women. Her job involves peering
all day through a microscope, bonding hair-thin gold wires to a silicon chip
destined to end up inside a pocket calculator, and at 21, she is afraid she can
no longer see very clearly.

Every morning, between four and seven, thousands of women like
Anna and Julie head out for the day shift. In Ciudad Juárez, they crowd
into *ruteras* (rundown vans) for the trip from the slum neighborhoods to
the industrial parks on the outskirts of the city. In Penang they squeeze, 60
or more at a time, into buses for the trip from the village to the low, modern factory buildings of the Bayan Lepas free trade zone. In Taiwan, they
walk from the dormitories—where the night shift is already asleep in the
still-warm beds—through the checkpoints in the high fence surrounding
the factory zone.

This is the world's new industrial proletariat: young, female, Third
World. Viewed from the "first world," they are still faceless, genderless

"cheap labor," signaling their existence only through a label or tiny imprint,—"made in Hong Kong," or Taiwan, Korea, the Dominican Republic, Mexico, the Philippines. But they may be one of the most strategic blocs of womanpower in the world of the 1980s. Conservatively, there are 2 million Third World female industrial workers employed now, millions more looking for work, and their numbers are rising every year. Anyone whose image of Third World women features picturesque peasants with babies slung on their backs should be prepared to update it. Just in the last decade, Third World women have become a critical element in the global economy and a key "resource" for expanding multinational corporations.

It doesn't take more than second-grade arithmetic to understand   5 what's happening. In the United States, an assembly-line worker is likely to earn, depending on her length of employment, between $3.10 and $5 an hour. In many Third World countries, a woman doing the same work will earn $3 to $5 a *day*. According to the magazine *Business Asia*, in 1976 the average hourly wage for unskilled work (male or female) was 55 cents in Hong Kong, 52 cents in South Korea, 32 cents in the Philippines, and 17 cents in Indonesia. The logic of the situation is compelling: why pay someone in Massachusetts $5 an hour to do what someone in Manila will do for $2.50 a day? Or, as a corollary, why pay a male worker anywhere to do what a female worker will do for 40 to 60 percent less?

And so, almost everything that can be packed up is being moved out to the Third World; not heavy industry, but just about anything light enough to travel—garment manufacture, textiles, toys, footwear, pharmaceuticals, wigs, appliance parts, tape decks, computer components, plastic goods. In some industries, like garment and textile, American jobs are lost in the process, and the biggest losers are women, often black and Hispanic. But what's going on is much more than a matter of runaway shops. Economists are talking about a "new international division of labor," in which the process of production is broken down and the fragments are dispersed to different parts of the world. In general, the low-skilled jobs are farmed out to the Third World, where labor costs are minuscule, while control over the overall process and technology remains safely at company headquarters in "first world" countries like the United States and Japan.

The American electronics industry provides a classic example: circuits are printed on silicon wafers and tested in California; then the wafers are shipped to Asia for the labor-intensive process by which they are cut into tiny chips and bonded to circuit boards; final assembly into products such as calculators or military equipment usually takes place in the United States. Garment manufacture too is often broken into geographically separated steps, with the most repetitive, labor-intensive jobs going to the poor countries of the southern hemisphere. Most Third World countries welcome whatever jobs come their way in the new division of labor, and the major international development agencies—like the World Bank and the United States Agency for International Development (AID)—encourage them to take what they can get.

So much any economist could tell you. What is less often noted is the *gender* breakdown of the emerging international division of labor. Eighty to 90 percent of the low-skilled assembly jobs that go to the Third World are performed by women—in a remarkable switch from earlier patterns of foreign-dominated industrialization. Until now, "development" under the aegis of foreign corporations has usually meant more jobs for men and—compared to traditional agricultural society—a diminished economic status for women. But multinational corporations and Third World governments alike consider assembly-line work—whether the product is Barbie dolls or missile parts—to be "women's work."

One reason is that women can, in many countries, still be legally paid less than men. But the sheer tedium of the jobs adds to the multinationals' preference for women workers—a preference made clear, for example, by this ad from a Mexican newspaper: *We need female workers; older than 17, younger than 30; single and without children; minimum education primary school, maximum education one year of preparatory school [high school]: available for all shifts.*

It's an article of faith with management that only women can do, or will do, the monotonous, painstaking work that American business is exporting to the Third World. Bill Mitchell, whose job is to attract United States businesses to the Bermudez Industrial Park in Ciudad Juárez told us with a certain macho pride: "A man just won't stay in this tedious kind of work. He'd walk out in a couple of hours." The personnel manager of a light assembly plant in Taiwan told anthropologist Linda Gail Arrigo: "Young male workers are too restless and impatient to do monotonous work with no career value. If displeased, they sabotage the machines and even threaten the foreman. But girls? At most, they cry a little."   10

In fact, the American businessmen we talked to claimed that Third World women genuinely enjoy doing the very things that would drive a man to assault and sabotage. "You should watch these kids going into work" Bill Mitchell told us. "You don't have any sullenness here. They smile." A top-level management consultant who specializes in advising American companies on where to relocate their factories gave us this global generalization: "The [factory] girls genuinely enjoy themselves. They're away from their families. They have spending money. They can buy motorbikes, whatever. Of course it's a regulated experience too—with dormitories to live in—so it's a healthful experience."

What is the real experience of the women in the emerging Third World industrial work force? The conventional Western stereotypes leap to mind: You can't really compare, the standards are so different. . . . Everything's easier in warm countries. . . . They really don't have any alternatives. . . . Commenting on the low wages his company pays its women workers in Singapore, a Hewlett-Packard vice-president said, "They live much differently here than we do . . . ." But the differences are ultimately very simple. To start with, they have less money.

The great majority of the women in the new Third World work force live at or near the subsistence level for one person, whether they work for a multinational corporation or a locally owned factory. In the Philippines, for example, starting wages in U.S.-owned electronics plants are between $34 to $46 a month, compared to a cost of living of $37 a month; in Indonesia the starting wages are actually about $7 a month less than the cost of living. "Living," in these cases, should be interpreted minimally: a diet of rice, dried fish, and water—a Coke might cost a half-day's wages—lodging in a room occupied by four or more other people. Rachael Grossman, a researcher with the Southeast Asia Resource Center, found women employees of U.S. multinational firms in Malaysia and the Philippines living four to eight in a room in boardinghouses, or squeezing into tiny extensions built onto squatter huts near the factory. Where companies do provide dormitories for their employees, they are not of the "healthful," collegiate variety implied by our corporate informant. Staff from the American Friends Service Committee report that dormitory space is "likely to be crowded, with bed rotation paralleling shift rotation—while one shift works, another sleeps, as many as twenty to a room." In one case in Thailand, they found the dormitory "filthy," with workers forced to find their own place to sleep among "splintered floorboards, rusting sheets of metal, and scraps of dirty cloth."

Wages do increase with seniority, but the money does not go to pay for studio apartments or, very likely, motorbikes. A 1970 study of young women factory workers in Hong Kong found that 88 percent of them were turning more than half their earnings over to their parents. In areas that are still largely agricultural (such as parts of the Philippines and Malaysia), or places where male unemployment runs high (such as northern Mexico), a woman factory worker may be the sole source of cash income for an entire extended family.

But wages on a par with what an 11-year-old American could earn on a paper route, and living conditions resembling what Engels found in nineteenth-century Manchester are only part of the story. The rest begins at the factory gate. The work that multinational corporations export to the Third World is not only the most tedious, but often the most hazardous part of the production process. The countries they go to are, for the most part, those that will guarantee no interference from health and safety inspectors, trade unions, or even free-lance reformers. As a result, most Third World factory women work under conditions that already have broken or will break their health—or their nerves—within a few years, and often before they've worked long enough to earn any more than a subsistence wage.

Consider first the electronics industry, which is generally thought to be the safest and cleanest of the exported industries. The factory buildings are low and modern, like those one might find in a suburban American industrial park. Inside, rows of young women, neatly dressed in the company uniform or T-shirt, work quietly at their stations. There is air conditioning (not for the women's comfort, but to protect the delicate semiconductor parts they work with), and high-volume piped-in Bee Gees hits (not so much for entertainment, as to prevent talking).

For many Third World women, electronics is a prestige occupation, at least compared to other kinds of factory work. They are unlikely to know that in the United States the National Institute on Occupational Safety and Health (NIOSH) has placed electronics on its select list of "high health-risk industries using the greatest number of toxic substances." If electronics assembly work is risky here, it is doubly so in countries where there is no equivalent of NIOSH to even issue warnings. In many plants toxic chemicals and solvents sit in open containers, filling the work area with fumes that can literally knock you out. "We have been told of cases where ten to twelve women passed out at once," an AFSC field worker in northern Mexico told us, "and the newspapers report this as 'mass hysteria.'"

In one stage of the electronics assembly process, the workers have to dip the circuits into open vats of acid. According to Irene Johnson and Carol Bragg, who toured the National Semiconductor plant in Penang, Malaysia, the women who do the dipping "wear rubber gloves and boots, but these sometimes leak, and burns are common." Occasionally, whole fingers are lost. More commonly, what electronics workers lose is the 20/20 vision they are required to have when they are hired. Most electronics workers spend seven to nine hours a day peering through microscopes, straining to meet their quotas. One study in South Korea found that most electronics assembly workers developed severe eye problems after only one year of employment: 88 percent had chronic conjunctivitis; 44 percent became nearsighted; and 19 percent developed astigmatism. A manager for Hewlett-Packard's Malaysia plant, in an interview with Rachael Grossman, denied that there were any eye problems: "These girls are used to working with 'scopes.' We've found no eye problems. But it sure makes me dizzy to look through those things."

Electronics, recall, is the "cleanest" of the exported industries. Conditions in the garment and textile industry rival those of any nineteenth-century sweatshop. The firms, generally local subcontractors to large American chains such as J. C. Penney and Sears, as well as smaller manufacturers, are usually even more indifferent to the health of their employees than the multinationals. Some of the worst conditions have been documented in South Korea, where the garment and textile industries have helped spark that country's "economic miracle." Workers are packed into poorly lit rooms, where summer temperatures rise above 100 degrees. Textile dust, which can cause permanent lung damage, fills the air. When there are rush orders, management may require forced overtime of as much as 48 hours at a stretch, and if that seems to go beyond the limits of human endurance, pep pills and amphetamine injections are thoughtfully provided. In her diary (originally published in a magazine now banned by the South Korean government) Min Chong Suk, 30, a sewing-machine operator, wrote of working from 7 A.M. to 11:30 P.M. in a garment factory: "When [the apprentices] shake the waste threads from the clothes, the whole room fills with dust, and it is hard to breathe. Since we've been working in such dusty air, there have been increasing numbers of people getting tuberculosis, bronchitis, and eye diseases. Since we are women, it makes us so sad when we have pale, unhealthy, wrinkled faces like dried-up spinach. . . . It seems to me that no one knows our blood dissolves into the threads and seams, with sighs and sorrow."

In all the exported industries, the most invidious, inescapable health hazard is stress. On their home ground United States corporations are not likely to sacrifice productivity for human comfort. On someone else's home ground, however, anything goes. Lunch breaks may be barely long enough for a woman to stand in line at the canteen or hawkers' stalls. Visits to the bathroom are treated as privilege; in some cases, workers must raise their hands for permission to use the toilet, and waits up to a half hour are common. Rotating shifts—the day shift one week, the night shift the next— wreak havoc with sleep patterns. Because inaccuracies or failure to meet production quotas can mean substantial pay losses, the pressures are quickly internalized; stomach ailments and nervous problems are not unusual in the multinationals' Third World female work force. In some situations, good work is as likely to be punished as slow or shoddy work. Correspondent Michael Flannery, writing for the AFL-CIO's *American Federationist,* tells the story of 23-year-old Basilia Altagracia, a seamstress who stitched collars onto ladies' blouses in the La Romana (Dominican Republic) free trade zone (a heavily guarded industrial zone owned by Gulf & Western Industries, Inc.):

"A nimble veteran seamstress, Miss Altagracia eventually began to earn as much as $5.75 a day. . . . 'I was exceeding my piecework quota by a lot.' . . . But then, Altagracia said, her plant supervisor, a Cuban emigré, called her into his office. 'He said I was doing a fine job, but that I and some other of the women were making too much money, and he was being forced to lower what we earned for each piece we sewed.' On the best days, she now can clear barely $3, she said. 'I was earning less, so I started working six and seven days a week. But I was tired and I could not work as fast as before.' " Within a few months, she was too ill to work at all.

As if poor health and the stress of factory life weren't enough to drive women into early retirement, management actually encourages a high turnover in many industries. "As you know, when seniority rises, wages rise," the management consultant to U.S. multinationals told us. He explained that it's cheaper to train a fresh supply of teenagers than to pay experienced women higher wages. "Older" women, aged 23 or 24, are likely to be laid off and not rehired.

We estimate, based on fragmentary data from several sources, that the multinational corporations may already have used up (cast off) as many as 6 million Third World workers—women who are too ill, too old (30 is over the hill in most industries), or too exhausted to be useful any more. Few "retire" with any transferable skills or savings. The lucky ones find husbands.

The unlucky ones find themselves at the margins of society—as bar girls, "hostesses," or prostitutes.

At 21, Julie's greatest fear is that she will never be able to find a husband. She 25 *knows that just being a "factory girl" is enough to give anyone a bad reputation. When she first started working at the electronics company, her father refused to speak to her for three months. Now every time she leaves Penang to go back to visit her home village she has to put up with a lecture on morality from her older brother—not to mention a barrage of lewd remarks from men outside her family. If they knew that she had actually gone out on a few dates, that she had been to a discotheque, that she had once kissed a young man who said he was a student. . . . Julie's stomach tightens as she imagines her family's reaction. She tries to concentrate on the kind of man she would like to marry: an engineer or technician of some sort, someone who had been to California, where the company headquarters are located and where even the grandmothers wear tight pants and lipstick— someone who had a good attitude about women. But if she ends up having to wear glasses, like her cousin who worked three years at the "scopes," she might as well forget about finding anyone to marry her.*

One of the most serious occupational hazards that Julie and millions of women like her may face is the lifelong stigma of having been a "factory girl." Most of the cultures favored by multinational corporations in their search for cheap labor are patriarchal in the grand old style: any young woman who is not under the wing of a father, husband, or older brother must be "loose." High levels of unemployment among men, as in Mexico, contribute to male resentment of working women. (Ironically, in some places the multinationals have increased male unemployment—for example, by paving over fishing and farming villages to make way for industrial parks.) Add to all this the fact that certain companies—American electronics firms are in the lead—actively promote Western-style sexual objectification as a means of insuring employee loyalty: there are company-sponsored cosmetics classes, "guess whose legs these are" contests, and swim-suit-style beauty contests where the prize might be a free night *for two* in a fancy hotel. Corporate-promoted Westernization only heightens the hostility many men feel toward any independent working women—having a job is bad enough, wearing jeans and mascara to work is going too far.

Anthropologist Patricia Fernandez, who has worked in a *maquiladora* herself, believes that the stigmatization of working women serves, indirectly, to keep them in line. "You have to think of the kind of socialization that girls experience in a very Catholic—or, for that matter, Muslim—society. The fear of having a 'reputation' is enough to make a lot of women bend over backward to be 'respectable' and ladylike, which is just what management wants." She points out that in northern Mexico, the tabloids delight in playing up stories of alleged vice in the *maquiladoras*—indiscriminate sex on the job, epidemics of venereal disease, fetuses found in factory rest rooms. "I worry about this because there are those who treat you differently as soon as they know you have a job at a *maquiladora*," one woman told Fernandez. "Maybe they think that if you have to work, there is a chance you're a whore."

And there is always a chance you'll wind up as one. Probably only a small minority of Third World factory workers turn to prostitution when their working days come to an end. But it is, as for women everywhere, the employment of last resort, the only thing to do when the factories don't need you and traditional society won't—or, for economic reasons, can't—take you back. In the Philippines, the brothel business is expanding as fast as the factory system. If they can't use you one way, they can use you another.

✎ Topics for Critical Thinking and Writing

1. Consider the title of the essay. When you first saw it, what connotations did "global assembly line" immediately suggest? Now that you have finished reading the essay, evaluate the title.

2. Before you read this essay, what was your image of the multinational corporation? Was it mostly positive, or negative, or neutral? To what extent has the article affected the way you think about multinational corporations? If, for example, you were offered a managerial job in a multinational, would you be inclined to ask questions about their employment practices abroad that you might not have asked before reading this article?

3. Paragraph 1, which gives us a quick portrait of Anna, tells us that "Anna's husband, frustrated by being unable to find work for himself, left for the United States six months ago." Why do the authors bother to include this detail? Is it in any way relevant to their thesis, or is it simply for human interest?

4. According to paragraph 10, management believes "that only women can do, or will do, the monotonous, painstaking work that American business is exporting to the Third World." Do the authors of the essay believe this? Do you believe that women by nature—or by training—are more suited than men "to do monotonous work with no career value"?

5. Paragraph 11 reports some statements businessmen offer as reasons why Third World women supposedly enjoy their jobs. Do you think these reasons (or some of them) have any merit? Do paragraphs 12–14 and 17–21 adequately refute these reasons?

6. In paragraph 14 we learn that 88 percent of the young female workers in Hong Kong turned more than half of their wages over to their parents. What conclusions can one reasonably draw from this assertion?

7. Why do you suppose that Julie (paragraphs 2 and 25) works in a factory?
8. In paragraph 26 the author tells us that "high levels of unemployment among men, as in Mexico, contribute to male resentment of working women." Does this analysis strike you as probably true? If so, what do you think American business can do about the Mexican economy?
9. What is the effect of using the second person pronoun (*you*) in the final paragraph?
10. Given what you have read about the working conditions of women in Third World countries, when you buy your next sweater (or tennis racquet or calculator or whatever) will you reject products made in Third World countries?

John S. Fielden

John S. Fielden, formerly an associate editor of the Harvard Business Review—*the journal in which this essay first appeared—is now University Professor of Management at the University of Alabama.*

"What Do You Mean You Don't Like My Style"

In large corporations all over the country, people are playing a game of paddleball—with drafts of letters instead of balls. Volley after volley goes back and forth between those who sign the letters and those who actually write them. It's a game nobody likes, but it continues, and we pay for it. The workday has no extra time for such unproductiveness. What causes this round robin of revision?

Typos? Factual misstatements? Poor format? No. *Style* does. Ask yourself how often you hear statements like these:

"It takes new assistants about a year to learn my style. Until they do, I have no choice but to bounce letters back for revision. I won't sign a letter if it doesn't sound like me."

"I find it difficult, almost impossible, to write letters for my boss's signature. The boss's style is different from mine."

In companies where managers primarily write their own letters, confusion about style also reigns. Someone sends out a letter and hears later that the reaction was not at all the one desired. It is reported that the reader doesn't like the writer's "tone." A colleague looks over a copy of the letter and says, "No wonder the reader doesn't like this letter. You shouldn't have said things the way you did. You used the wrong style for a letter like this." "Style?" the writer says. "What's wrong with my style?" "I don't know" is the response. "I just don't like the way you said things."

Everybody talks about style, but almost nobody understands the meaning of the word in the business environment. And this lack of understanding hurts both those who write letters for another's signature and those who write for themselves. Neither knows where to turn for help. Strunk and White's marvelous book *The Elements of Style* devotes only a few pages to a discussion of style, and that concerns only literary style.[1] Books like the Chicago *Manual of Style*[2] seem to define style as all the technical points they cover, from abbreviations and capitalizations to footnotes and bibliographies. And dictionary definitions are usually too vague to be helpful.

Even such a general definition as this offers scant help, although perhaps it comes closest to how business people use the word:

5

> Style is "the way something is said or done, as distinguished from its substance."[3]

Managers signing drafts written by subordinates, and the subordinates themselves, already know that they have trouble agreeing on "the way things should be said." What, for instance, is meant by "way"? In trying to find that way, both managers and subordinates are chasing a will-o'-the-wisp. There is no magical way, no perfect, universal way of writing things that will fend off criticism of style. There *is* no one style of writing in business that is appropriate in all situations and for all readers, even though managers and subordinates usually talk and behave as if there were.

But why all the confusion? Isn't style really the way we say things? Certainly it is. Then writing style must be made up of the particular words we select to express our ideas and the types of sentences and paragraphs we put together to convey those ideas. What else could it be? Writing has no tone of voice or body gesture to impart additional meanings. In written communication, tone comes from what a reader reads into the words and sentences used.

Words express more than *denotations,* the definitions found in dictionaries. They also carry *connotations.* In the feelings and images associated with each word lies the capacity a writing style has for producing an emotional reaction in a reader. And in that capacity lies the tone of a piece of writing. Style is largely a matter of tone. The writer uses a style; the reader infers a communication's tone. Tone comes from what a reader reads into the words and sentences a writer uses.

---

[1]William Strunk, Jr., and E. B. White, *The Elements of Style* (New York: Macmillan, 1979).
[2]*A Manual of Style* (Chicago: University of Chicago Press, 1969).
[3]*The American Heritage Dictionary of the English Language* (Boston: American Heritage and Houghton Mifflin, 1969).

In the business environment, tone is especially important. Business writing is not literary writing. Literary artists use unique styles to "express" themselves to a general audience. Business people write to particular persons in particular situations, not so much to express themselves as to accomplish particular purposes, "to get a job done." If a reader doesn't like a novelist's tone, nothing much can happen to the writer short of failing to sell some books. In the business situation, however, an offensive style may not only prevent a sale but may also turn away a customer, work against a promotion, or even cost you a job.

While style can be distinguished from substance, it cannot be   10
divorced from substance. In business writing, style cannot be divorced from the circumstances under which something is written or from the likes, dislikes, position, and power of the reader.

A workable definition of style in business writing would be something like this:

> Style is that choice of words, sentences, and paragraph format which by virtue of being appropriate to the situation and to the power positions of both writer and reader produces the desired reaction and result.

Let's take a case and see what we can learn from it. Assume that you are an executive in a very large information-processing company. You receive the following letter:

Mr. (Ms.) Leslie J. Cash
XYZ Corporation
Main Street
Anytown, U.S.A.

Dear Leslie:

As you know, I respect your professional opinion highly. The advice your people have given us at ABC Corporation as we have moved into a comprehensive information system over the past three years has been very helpful. I'm writing to you now, however, in my role as chairman of the executive committee of the trustees of our hospital. We at Community General Hospital have decided to establish a skilled volunteer data processing evaluation team to assess proposals to automate our hospital's information flow.

I have suggested your name to my committee. I know you could get real satisfaction from helping your community as a member of this evaluation team. Please say yes. I look forward to being able to count on your advice. Let me hear from you soon.

Frank J. Scalpel
Chairman
Executive Committee
Community General Hospital
Anytown, U.S.A.

If you accepted the appointment mentioned in this letter, you would have a conflict of interest. You are an executive at XYZ, Inc. You know that XYZ will submit a proposal to install a comprehensive information system for the hospital. Mr. Scalpel is the vice president of finance at ABC Corp., a very good customer of yours. You know him well since you have worked with him on community programs as well as in the business world.

I can think of four typical responses to Scalpel's letter. Each says essentially the same thing, but each is written in a different business style:

Response 1

Mr. Frank J. Scalpel
Chairman, Executive Committee
Community General Hospital
Anytown, U.S.A.
Dear Frank,
As you realize, this litigious age often makes it necessary for large companies to take stringent measures not only to avoid conflicts of interest on the part of their employees but also to preclude even the very suggestion of conflict. And, since my company intends to submit a proposal with reference to automating the hospital's information flow, it would not appear seemly for me to be part of an evaluation team assessing competitors' proposals. Even if I were to excuse myself from consideration of the XYZ proposal, I would still be vulnerable to charges that I gave short shrift to competitors' offerings.

If there is any other way that I can serve the committee that will not raise this conflict-of-interest specter, you know that I would find it pleasurable to be of service, as always.
Sincerely,

Response 2

Dear Frank,
Your comments relative to your respect for my professional opinion are most appreciated. Moreover, your invitation to serve on the hospital's data processing evaluation team is received with gratitude, albeit with some concern.

The evaluation team must be composed of persons free of alliance with any of the vendors submitting proposals. For that reason, it is felt that my services on the team could be construed as a conflict of interest.

Perhaps help can be given in some other way. Again, please be assured that your invitation has been appreciated.
Sincerely,

Response 3

Dear Frank,
Thank you for suggesting my name as a possible member of your data processing evaluation team. I wish I could serve, but I cannot.

XYZ intends, naturally, to submit a proposal to automate the hospital's information flow. You can see the position of conflict I would be in if I were on the evaluation team.

Just let me know of any other way I can be of help. You know I would be more than willing. Thanks again for the invitation.
Cordially,

Response 4
Dear Frank,
Thanks for the kind words and the invitation. Sure wish I could say yes. Can't, though.

XYZ intends to submit a sure-fire proposal on automating the hospital's information. Shouldn't be judge and advocate at the same time!

Any other way I can help, Frank—just ask. Thanks again.
Cordially,

What Do You Think of These Letters?

Which letter has the style you like best? Check off the response you pre-   15
fer.

Response	1	2	3	4
	☐	☐	☐	☐

Which letter has the style resembling the one you customarily use? Again, check off your choice.

Response	1	2	3	4
	☐	☐	☐	☐

Which terms best describe the style of each letter? Check the appropriate boxes.

Response 1   ☐ Colorful   ☐ Passive   ☐ Personal
             ☐ Dull   ☐ Forceful   ☐ Impersonal
Response 2   ☐ Colorful   ☐ Passive   ☐ Personal
             ☐ Dull   ☐ Forceful   ☐ Impersonal
Response 3   ☐ Colorful   ☐ Passive   ☐ Personal
             ☐ Dull   ☐ Forceful   ☐ Impersonal
Response 4   ☐ Colorful   ☐ Passive   ☐ Personal
             ☐ Dull   ☐ Forceful   ☐ Impersonal

Let's Compare Reactions

Now that you've given your reactions, let's compare them with some of mine.

Response 1 seems cold, impersonal, complex. Most business people would, I think, react somewhat negatively to this style because it seems to push the reader away from the writer. Its word choice has a cerebral quality that, while flattering to the reader's intelligence, also parades the writer's.

Response 2 is fairly cool, quite impersonal, and somewhat complex.   20
Readers' reactions will probably be neither strongly positive nor strongly negative. This style of writing is "blah" because it is heavily passive. Instead of saying "I appreciate your comments," it says "Your comments are most appreciated"; instead of "I think that my service could be construed as a conflict of interest," it says "It is felt that my service could be

construed . . . ." The use of the passive voice subordinates writers modestly to the back of sentences or causes them to disappear.

This is the impersonal, passive style of writing that many with engineering, mathematics, or scientific backgrounds feel most comfortable using. It is harmless, but it is certainly not colorful; nor is it forceful or interesting.

Response 3 illustrates the style of writing that most high-level executives use. It is simple; it is personal; it is warm without being syrupy; it is forceful, like a firm handshake. Almost everybody in business likes this style, although lower-level managers often find themselves afraid to write so forthrightly (and, as a result, often find themselves retreating into the styles of responses 1 and 2—the style of 1 to make themselves look "smart" to superiors and the style of 2 to appear unbossy and fairly impersonal). Persons who find response 2 congenial may feel a bit dubious about the appropriateness of response 3. (Although I have no way of proving this judgment, I would guess that more readers in high positions— perhaps more owner-managers—would like response 3 than would readers who are still in lower positions.)

Response 4 goes beyond being forceful; it is annoyingly self-confident and breezy. It is colorful and conversational to an extreme, and it is so intensely personal and warm that many business people would be offended, even if they were very close acquaintances of Frank Scalpel's. "It sounds like an advertising person's chitchat," some would probably say.

As you compared your responses with mine, did you say, "What difference does it make which style *I* like or which most resembles *my* customary style? What matters is which style will go over best with Mr. Scalpel in this situation"? If you did, we're getting somewhere.

Earlier, when we defined business writing style, some may have wanted to add, "And that style should sound like me." This was left out for a good reason. Circumstances not only alter cases; they alter the "you" that it is wise for your style to project. Sometimes it's wise to be forceful; at other times it's suicidal. Sometimes being sprightly and colorful is appropriate; at other times it's ludicrous. There are times to be personal and times to be impersonal.

Not understanding this matter of style and tone is why the big corporation game of paddleball between managers and subordinates goes on and on. The subordinate tries to imitate the boss's style, but in actuality— unless the boss is extremely insensitive—he or she has no single style for all circumstances and for all readers. What usually happens is that after several tries, the subordinate writes a letter that the boss signs. "Aha!" the subordinate says. "So that's what the boss wants!" And then the subordinate tries to use that style for all situations and readers. Later, the superior begins rejecting drafts written in the very style he or she professed liking before. Both parties throw up their hands.

This volleying is foolish and wasteful. Both superior and subordinate have to recognize that in business writing, style cannot be considered apart from the given situation or from the person to whom the writing is directed. Expert writers select the style that fits a particular reader and the type of writing situation with which they are faced. In business, people often face the following writing situations:

Positive situations.

Saying yes or conveying good news.

Situations where some action is asked of the reader.

Giving orders or persuading someone to do as requested.

Information-conveying situations.

Giving the price of ten widgets, for example.

Negative situations.

Saying no or relaying bad news.

In each of these situations, the choice of style is of strategic importance.

In positive situations, a writer can relax on all fronts. Readers are usually so pleased to hear the good news that they pay little attention to anything else. Yet it is possible for someone to communicate good news in such a cold, impersonal, roundabout, and almost begrudging way that the reader becomes upset.

Action-request situations involve a form of bargaining. In a situation   30
where the writer holds all the power, he or she can use a forceful commanding style. When the writer holds no power over the reader, though, actions have to be asked for and the reader persuaded, not ordered. In such cases, a forceful style will not be suitable at all.

In information-conveying situations, getting the message across forcefully and straightforwardly is best. Such situations are not usually charged emotionally.

In negative situations, diplomacy becomes very important. The right style depends on the relative positions of the person saying no and the person being told no.

For instance, if you were Leslie Cash, the person in the example at the beginning of the article whom Frank Scalpel was inviting to serve on a hospital's evaluation team, you would be in a situation of having to say no to a very important customer of your company. You would also be in a doubly sensitive situation because it is unlikely that Mr. Scalpel would fail to recognize that he is asking you to enter a conflict-of-interest situation. He is probably asking you *anyway*. Therefore, you would not only have to tell him no, but you would have to avoid telling him that he has asked you to do something that is highly unethical. In this instance, you would be faced with communicating two negative messages at once or else not giving Scalpel any sensible reason for refusing to serve.

Now that we've thought about the strategic implications of style, let's go back to look at each of the responses to Scalpel's request and ask ourselves which is best.

Do we *want* to be personal and warm? Usually yes. But in this situation? Do we want to communicate clearly and directly and forcefully? Usually yes. But here? Do we want to appear as if we're brushing aside the conflict, as the third response does? Or do we want to approach that issue long-windedly, as in the first response, or passively, as in the second? What is the strategically appropriate style?

In the abstract, we have no way of knowing which of these responses will go over best with Mr. Scalpel. The choice is a matter of judgment in a concrete situation. Judging the situation accurately is what separates successful from unsuccessful executive communicators.

Looking at the situation with strategy in mind, we note that in the first response, the writer draws back from being close, knowing that it is necessary to reject not only one but two of the reader's requests. By using legalistic phraseology and Latinate vocabulary, the writer lowers the personal nature of the communication and transforms it into a formal statement. It gives an abstract, textbook-like response that removes the tone of personal rejection.

The very fact that response 1 is difficult to read and dull in impact may be a strategic asset in this type of negative situation. But if in this situation a subordinate presented response 1 to you for your signature, would it be appropriate for you to reject it because it is not written in the style *you* happen to *like* best in the abstract—say, the style of response 3?

Now let's look at response 2. Again, we see that a lack of personal warmth may be quite appropriate to the situation at hand. Almost immediately, the letter draws back into impersonality. And by using the passive constantly, the writer avoids the need to say "I must say no." Furthermore, the term *construed* reinforces the passive in the second paragraph. This term is a very weak but possibly a strategically wise way of implying that *some* persons (*other* people, not the writer) could interpret Scalpel's request as an invitation to participate in an improper action. Now we can see that, instead of seeming dull and lacking in personal warmth as it did in the abstract, response 2 may be the type of letter we would be wise to send out, that is, when we have taken the whole situation into careful consideration and not just our personal likes and dislikes.

The third response, and to even greater extent the fourth, have styles that are strategically inappropriate for this situation. In fact, Scalpel might well regard the colorful style of the fourth response as highly offensive. Both responses directly and forcefully point out the obvious conflict, but by being so direct each runs the risk of subtly offending him. (The third response is "you can see the position of conflict I'd be in if I were on the evaluation team," and the fourth is "Shouldn't be judge and advocate at the same time!") We could make a pretty strong argument that the direct, forceful, candid style of the third response and the breezy, warm, colorful, intensely personal "advertising" style of the fourth response may both prove ineffectual in a delicate, negative situation such as this.

At this point, readers may say, "All right. I'm convinced. I need to adjust my style to what is appropriate in each situation. And I also need to give directions to others to let them know how to adjust their styles. But I haven't the foggiest notion of how to do either!" Some suggestions for varying your writing style follow. I am not implying that a communication must be written in one style only. A letter to be read aloud at a colleague's retirement party, for instance, may call not only for a warm, personal style but for colorfulness as well. A long analytic report may require a passive, impersonal style, but the persuasive cover letter may call for recommendations being presented in a very forceful style.

For a Forceful Style

This style is usually appropriate only in situations where the writer has the power, such as in action requests in the form of orders or when you are saying no firmly but politely to a subordinate.

> Use the active voice. Have your sentences do something to people and to objects, not just lie there having things done to them; have them give orders: "Correct this error immediately" (you-understood is the subject) instead of "A correction should be made" (which leaves the reader wondering, made by whom).

> Step up front and be counted: "I have decided not to recommend you for promotion" instead of "Unfortunately, a positive recommendation for your promotion is not forthcoming."

> Do not beat around the bush or act like a politician. If something needs to be said, say it directly.

> Write most of your sentences in subject-verb-object order. Do not weaken them by putting namby-pamby phrases before the subject: "I have decided to fund your project" instead of "After much deliberation and weighing of the pros and cons, I have decided to fund your project."

> Do not weaken sentences by relegating the point or the action to a subordinate clause: If your point is that your company has won a contract, say "Acme won the contract, although the bidding was intense and highly competitive," not "Although Acme won the contract, the bidding was intense and highly competitive."

> Adopt a tone of confidence and surety about what you say by avoiding weasel words like: "Possibly," "maybe," "perhaps," "It could be concluded that . . ." "Some might conclude that . . ."

For a Passive Style

This style is often appropriate in negative situations and in situations where the writer is in a lower position than the reader.

Avoid the imperative—never give an order: Say "A more effective and time-conserving presentation of ideas should be devised before our next meeting" as opposed to "Do a better job of presenting your ideas at our next meeting. Respect my time and get right to the point."

Use the passive voice heavily because it subordinates the subject to the end of the sentence or buries the subject entirely. The passive is especially handy when you are in a low-power position and need to convey negative information to a reader who is in a higher position (an important customer, for instance): Say "Valuable resources are being wasted" instead of "Valuable resources are being wasted by your company" or, even worse, "You are wasting valuable resources."

Avoid taking responsibility for negative statements by attributing them to faceless, impersonal "others": Say "It is more than possible that several objections to your proposed plans might be raised by some observers" or "Several objections might be raised by those hostile to your plans" instead of "I have several objections to your plans."

Use weasel words, especially if the reader is in a high-power position and will not like what you are saying.

Use long sentences and heavy paragraphs to slow down the reader's comprehension of sensitive or negative information.

For a Personal Style

This style is usually appropriate in good-news and persuasive action-request situations.

Use the active voice, which puts you, as the writer, at the front of sentences: "Thank you very much for your comments" or "I appreciated your comments" instead of "Your comments were very much appreciated by me" or the even more impersonal "Your comments were very much appreciated."

Use persons' names (first names, when appropriate) instead of referring to them by title: "Bill James attended the meeting" instead of "Acme's director attended the meeting."

Use personal pronouns—especially "you" and "I"—when you are saying positive things: "I so much appreciate the work you've done" as opposed to "The work you've done is appreciated."

Use short sentences that capture the rhythm of ordinary conversation: "I discussed your proposal with Frank. He's all for it!" as opposed to "This is to inform you that your proposal was taken up at Friday's meeting and that it was regarded with favor."

Use contractions ("can't," "won't," "shouldn't") to sound informal and conversational.

Direct questions to the reader: "Just ask yourself, how would your company like to save $10,000?"

Interject positive personal thoughts and references that will make the reader know that this letter is really to him or her and not some type of form letter sent to just anyone.

For an Impersonal Style

This style is usually appropriate in negative and information-conveying situations. It's always appropriate in technical and scientific writing and usually when you are writing to technical readers.

Avoid using persons' names, especially first names. Refer to people, if at all, by title or job description: "I would like to know what you think of this plan" instead of "What do you think of this, Herb?" "Our vice president of finance" or "the finance department," not "Ms. Jones."

Avoid using personal pronouns, especially "you" and "I" ("we" may be all right because the corporate we is faceless and impersonal): "The logistics are difficult, and the idea may not work" instead of "I think you have planned things so that the logistics are difficult and your idea may not work." "We wonder if the idea will work" rather than "I don't think the idea will work."

Use the passive voice to make yourself conveniently disappear when desirable: "An error in the calculations has been made" instead of "I think your calculations are wrong."

Make some of your sentences complex and some paragraphs long; avoid the brisk, direct, simple-sentence style of conversation.

For a Colorful Style

Sometimes a lively style is appropriate in good-news situations. It is most commonly found in the highly persuasive writing of advertisements and sales letters.

Insert some adjectives and adverbs: Instead of "This proposal will save corporate resources," write "This (hard-hitting) (productivity-building) (money-saving) proposal will (easily) (surely) (quickly) (immediately) save our (hard-earned) (increasingly scarce) (carefully guarded) corporate resources."

If appropriate, use a metaphor (A is B) or a simile (A is like B) to make a point: "Truly this program is a miracle of logical design." "Our solution strikes at the very root of Acme's problems." "This program is like magic in its ability to . . . ."

For a Less Colorful Style

By avoiding adjectives, adverbs, metaphors, and figures of speech, you can make your style less colorful. Such a style is appropriate for ordinary business writing and also results from:

Blending the impersonal style with the passive style.

Employing words that remove any semblance of wit, liveliness, and vigor from the writing.

Please bear in mind that these six styles are not mutually exclusive. There is some overlap. A passive style is usually far more impersonal than personal and also not very colorful. A forceful style is likely to be more personal than impersonal, and a colorful style is likely to be fairly forceful. Nevertheless, these styles are distinct enough to justify talking about them. If we fail to make such distinctions, style becomes a catchall term that means nothing specific. Even if not precise, these distinctions enable us to talk about style and its elements and to learn to write appropriately for each situation.

What conclusions can we draw from this discussion? Simply that, whether you write your own letters or have to manage the writing of subordinates, to be an effective communicator, you must realize that:

1. Each style has an impact on the reader.
2. Style communicates to readers almost as much as the content of a message.
3. Style cannot be isolated from a situation.
4. Generalizing about which style is the best in all situations is impossible.
5. Style must be altered to suit the circumstances.
6. Style must be discussed sensibly in the work situation.

These conclusions will be of obvious help to managers who write their own letters. But what help will these conclusions be to managers who direct assistants in the writing of letters? In many instances, writing assignments go directly to subordinates for handling. Often, manager and

50

assistant have no chance to discuss style strategy together. In such cases, rather than merely submitting a response for a signature, the subordinate would be wise to append a note: e.g., "This is a very sensitive situation, I think. Therefore, I deliberately drew back into a largely impersonal and passive style." At least, the boss will not jump to the conclusion that the assistant has written a letter of low impact by accident.

When they do route writing assignments to assistants, superiors could save much valuable time and prevent mutual distress if they told the subordinates what style seemed strategically wise in each situation. Playing guessing games also wastes money.

And if, as is often the case, neither superior nor subordinate has a clear sense of what style is best, the two can agree to draft a response in one style first, and if that doesn't sound right, to adjust the style appropriately.

Those who write their own letters can try drafting several responses to tough but important situations, each in a different style. It's wise to sleep on them and then decide which sounds best.

Whether you write for yourself or for someone else, it is extremely unlikely that in difficult situations a first draft will be signed by you or anyone else. Only the amateur expects writing perfection on the first try. By learning to control your style and to engineer the tone of your communications, you can make your writing effective.

✎ Topics for Critical Thinking and Writing

1. Characterize the style of Fielden's first two paragraphs. (His essay, of course, says much about style, but for a brief additional discussion of style you may wish to consult page 875 in the glossary.)
2. In paragraph 11 Fielden offers what he calls a "workable definition of style in business writing." Do you find this definition workable for other forms of writing as well—for example, term papers, editorials in the school newspaper, love letters? Why, or why not?
3. If you disagree with Fielden's analysis of any of the four letters Leslie Cash drafts to send to Frank Scalpel, explain the basis of your disagreement.
4. Many textbooks urge students to avoid using the passive voice, but in paragraph 43 Fielden says that the passive "is often appropriate in negative situations and in situations where the writer is in a lower position than the reader." Look at his examples and then evaluate his advice.
5. This essay appeared in the *Harvard Business Review* and has been one of its most popular reprints. Explain why, in your opinion, it has been popular, or why you find its popularity surprising.
6. Let's assume that Cash sent Scalpel the third letter. You are Scalpel; write a letter to Cash acknowledging receipt of Cash's letter. In fact, write two letters, one a poor letter and one a good letter.

7. In discussing "strategy," Fielden writes in paragraph 25: "Sometimes it's wise to be forceful; at other times it's suicidal. Sometimes being sprightly and colorful is appropriate; at other times it's ludicrous. There are times to be personal and times to be impersonal." Try to recall examples from your own experience (whether writing or speaking) that illustrate one or more of these circumstances. Then write a paragraph combining Fielden's sentence (which you should feel free to modify) with your illustration of it.

Henry Louis Gates, Jr.

Henry Louis Gates, Jr., born in West Virginia in 1950, holds degrees from Yale University and Clare College in Cambridge, England. Returning to the United States, Gates quickly established a reputation as a leading scholar of African-American literature. He is now chair of Harvard's program in African-American Studies, and he is also the director of the W. E. B. Du Bois Institute.
*   We reprint an essay that originally appeared in* Sports Illustrated.

Delusions of Grandeur

Standing at the bar of an all-black VFW post in my home-town of Piedmont, W.Va., I offered five dollars to anyone who could tell me how many African-American professional athletes were at work today. There are 35 million African-Americans, I said.

"Ten million!" yelled one intrepid soul, too far into his cups.

"No way . . . more like 500,000," said another.

"You mean *all* professional sports," someone interjected, "including golf and tennis, but not counting the brothers from Puerto Rico?" Everyone laughed.

"Fifty thousand, minimum," was another guess.   5

Here are the facts:

There are 1,200 black professional athletes in the U.S.

There are 12 times more black lawyers than black athletes.

There are 2 1/2 times more black dentists than black athletes.

There are 15 times more black doctors than black athletes.   10

Nobody in my local VFW believed these statistics; in fact, few people would believe them if they weren't reading them in the pages of *Sports Illustrated.* In spite of these statistics, too many African-American youngsters still believe that they have a much better chance of becoming another Magic Johnson or Michael Jordan than they do of matching the achievements of Baltimore Mayor Kurt Schmoke or neurosurgeon Dr. Benjamin Carson, both of whom, like Johnson and Jordan, are black.

In reality, an African-American youngster has about as much chance of becoming a professional athlete as he or she does of winning the lottery. The tragedy for our people, however, is that few of us accept that truth.

Let me confess that I love sports. Like most black people of my generation—I'm 40—I was raised to revere the great black athletic heroes, and I never tired of listening to the stories of triumph and defeat that, for blacks, amount to a collective epic much like those of the ancient Greeks: Joe Louis's demolition of Max Schmeling; Satchel Paige's dazzling repertoire of pitches; Jesse Owens's in-your-face performance in Hitler's 1936 Olympics; Willie Mays's over-the-shoulder basket catch; Jackie Robinson's quiet strength when assaulted by racist taunts; and a thousand other grand tales.

Nevertheless, the blind pursuit of attainment in sports is having a devastating effect on our people. Imbued with a belief that our principal avenue to fame and profit is through sport, and seduced by a win-at-any-cost system that corrupts even elementary school students, far too many black kids treat basketball courts and football fields as if they were classrooms in an alternative school system. "O.K., I flunked English," a young athlete will say. "But I got an A plus in slam-dunking."

The failure of our public schools to educate athletes is part and parcel   15
of the schools' failure to educate almost everyone. A recent survey of the Philadelphia school system, for example, stated that "more than half of all students in the third, fifth and eighth grades cannot perform minimum math and language tasks." One in four middle school students in that city fails to pass to the next grade each year. It is a sad truth that such statistics are repeated in cities throughout the nation. Young athletes—particularly young black athletes—are especially ill-served. Many of them are functionally illiterate, yet they are passed along from year to year for the greater glory of good old Hometown High. We should not be surprised to learn, then, that only 26.6% of black athletes at the collegiate level earn their degrees. For every successful educated black professional athlete, there are thousands of dead and wounded. Yet young blacks continue to aspire to careers as athletes, and it's no wonder why; when the University of North Carolina recently commissioned a sculptor to create archetypes of its student body, guess which ethnic group was selected to represent athletes?

Those relatively few black athletes who do make it in the professional ranks must be prevailed upon to play a significant role in the education of all of our young people, athlete and nonathlete alike. While some have done so, many others have shirked their social obligations: to earmark small percentages of their incomes for the United Negro College Fund; to appear on television for educational purposes rather than merely to sell sneakers; to let children know the message that becoming a lawyer, a teacher or a doctor does more good for our people than winning the Super Bowl; and to form productive liaisons with educators to help forge solutions to the many ills that beset the black community. These are merely a few modest proposals.

A similar burden falls upon successful blacks in all walks of life. Each of us must strive to make our young people understand the realities. Tell them to cheer Bo Jackson but to emulate novelist Toni Morrison or businessman Reginald Lewis or historian John Hope Franklin or Spelman College president Johnetta Cole—the list is long.

Of course, society as a whole bears responsibility as well. Until colleges stop using young blacks as cannon fodder in the big-business wars of so-called nonprofessional sports, until training a young black's mind becomes as important as training his or her body, we will continue to perpetuate a system akin to that of the Roman gladiators, sacrificing a class of people for the entertainment of the mob.

✎ Topics for Critical Thinking and Writing

1. Strictly speaking, the first five paragraphs are not necessary to Gates's argument. Why do you suppose he included them? Evaluate his strategy for opening the essay.

2. In his next-to-last paragraph Gates says that "successful blacks in all walks of life" have a special obligation. In his last paragraph he widens his vision, saying that "society as a whole bears responsibility as well." Two questions: (a) In what ways is society responsible? (b) How effective do you think the final paragraph is, and why? (Consider especially the comparison to gladiatorial games.)

3. In paragraph 13 Gates mentions Joe Louis, Satchel Paige, Jesse Owens, Willie Mays, and Jackie Robinson. Do a little research on one of these men and write a short paragraph explaining Gates's reference to him. For instance, *when* did Joe Louis defeat Max Schmeling (and who *was* Schmeling)—in what year, in what round, and with what sort of punches?

4. In paragraph 13 Gates says the he "never tired of listening to the stories of triumph and defeat that, for blacks, amount to a collective epic much like those of the ancient Greeks . . . ." The appeal of stories of triumph is evident, but what is the appeal of stories of defeat? If you are familiar with stories of defeat that concern your heritage, analyze the sources of their appeal.

John Updike

John Updike (b. 1932) grew up in Shillington, Pennsylvania, where his father was a teacher and his mother was a writer. After receiving a B.A. degree from Harvard he studied drawing at Oxford for a year, but an offer from The New Yorker *magazine brought him back to the United States. He at first served as a reporter for the magazine, but soon began contributing poetry, essays, and fiction. Today he is one of America's most prolific and well-known writers.*

The Bliss of Golf

I never touched a club until I was twenty-five. Then, on a shady lawn in Wellesley, a kind of aunt-in-law showed me how to hold her driver and told me, after one swoop at a phantom ball, that I had a wonderful natural swing. Since that fatal encouragement, in many weathers inner and outer, amid many a green and winding landscape, I have asked myself what the peculiar bliss of this demanding game is, a bliss that at times threatens to relegate all the rest of life, including those sexual concerns that Freud claims are paramount and those even more basic needs that Marx insists must be met, to the shadows.

The immensities of space, beside which even polo and baseball are constricted pastimes, must be part of it. To see one's ball gallop two hundred and more yards down the fairway, or see it fly from the face of an 8-iron clear across an entire copse of maples in full autumnal flare, is to join one's soul with the vastness that, contemplated from another angle, intimidates the spirit, and makes one feel small. As it moves through the adventures of a golf match, the human body, like Alice's in Wonderland, experiences an intoxicating relativity—huge in relation to the ball, tiny in relation to the course, exactly matched to that of the other players. From this relativity is struck a silent music that rings to the treetops and runs through a Wagnerian array of changes as each hole evokes its set of shots, dwindling down to the final putt. The clubs in their nice gradations suggest organ pipes.

There is a bliss to the equipment—the festive polyester slacks, the menacing and elevating cleated shoes, the dainty little gauntlet the left hand gets to wear, the leathery adhesion of the grips and the riflelike purity of the shafts, the impeccable lustre of the (pre–Day-Glo orange) ball. The uniform sits light, unlike the monstrous armor of the skier or the football player, and cloaks us in a colorful individuality—not for the golfer the humiliating uniforms, cooked up by press agents and tyrannic owners, inflicted upon baseball players. We feel, dressed for golf, knightly, charging toward distant pennants past dragon-shaped hazards. The green when it receives us is soft, fine, gently undulating, maidenly.

A beautiful simplicity distinguishes the game's objective and the scoring. One stroke, count one. William Faulkner's *The Sound and the Fury* opens with an idiot watching a game of golf, and he grasps the essence well enough: "They took the flag out, and they were hitting. Then they put the flag back and they went to the table, and he hit and the other hit." That's how it goes; golf appeals to the idiot in us, and the child. What child does not grasp the pleasure-principle of miniature golf? Just how childlike golf players become is proven by their frequent inability to count past five. There is a lovable injustice, a comic democracy, in the equality, for purposes of scoring, of a three-hundred-yard smash from an elevated tee and a three-inch tap-in. Or, let's not forget, a total whiff—the most comical stroke of all. A ground-out in baseball or a tennis ball whapped into the net is not especially amusing; but bad shots in golf are endless fun—at least the other fellow's are. The duck hook, the banana slice, the topped dribble, the no-explode explosion shot, the arboreal ricochet, the sky ball, the majestic OB, the pondside scuff-and-splash, the deep-grass squirt, the cart-path shank, the skull, the fat hit, the thin hit, the stubbed putt—what a wealth of mirth is to be had in an afternoon's witnessing of such varied miseries, all produced in a twinkling of an eye by the infallible laws of physics!

And the bliss of the swing. The one that feels effortless and produces   5
a shot of miraculous straightness and soar. "I'll take it," we say modestly, searching about with a demure blush for the spun-away tee. Just a few shots a round keep us coming back; what other sport offers such sudden splendor in exchange for so few calories of expended energy? In those instants of whizz, ascent, hover, and fall, an ideal self seems mirrored. If we have that one shot in us, we must have thousands more—the problem is to get them out, to *let* them out. To concentrate, to take one's time, to move the weight across, to keep the elbow in, to save the wrist-cock for the hitting area, to keep one's head still, down, and as full of serenity as a Zen monk's: an ambitious program, but a basically spiritual one, which does not require the muscularity and shapeliness of youth. What other sport holds out hope of improvement to a man or a woman over fifty? True, the pros begin to falter at around forty, but it is their putting nerves that go, not their swings. For a duffer like the abovesigned, the room for improvement is so vast that three lifetimes could be spent roaming the fairways carving away at it, convinced that perfection lies just over the next rise. And that hope, perhaps, is the kindest bliss of all that golf bestows upon its devotees.

✎ Topics for Critical Thinking and Writing

1. Updike uses the word "bliss," usually associated with a religious experience, in his title. Where else in the essay do you find religious terms? How seriously does Updike want us to take these religious references?
2. Notice the structure of Updike's first paragraph, especially the length of the sentences. What prevents the length of the last sentence from being overwhelming?
3. Describe the organization of Updike's essay. Write a sentence or a phrase for each paragraph, indicating its content.
4. In the third paragraph, Updike lists the golfer's equipment. What other lists does he offer? To what extent did the lists add to your pleasure in reading "The Bliss of Golf"?
5. Write a brief essay (500–750 words) analyzing the pleasure of a sport or game you enjoy either participating in or observing. Use Updike's organization as a guide for your essay.

Terry McDonell

Terry McDonell, the editor and publisher of Sports Afield *magazine, published this essay in* The New York Times.

Hunters Are Not Gun Nuts

Not so long ago, we were a nation of hunters. Our wild lands and animals appeared endless. Our Presidents were known as sportsmen and wrote books bragging about their exploits.

Today, our wildlife is under great pressure and our politicians spend brief moments in the field holding shotgun or rod aloft to television cameras, cynically hunting for votes.

There are still real hunters in America, of course. The number of hunters has stabilized at about 7 percent of the population since 1937 (6.9 million then, 15.5 million now). But these hunters are not seen clearly. The media increasingly resorts to cartoon stereotypes of hunters, and this hurts them. They are not mean-spirited rednecks or drunken Bubbas, and they are tired of offhanded references to Bambi.

They live in a food chain that they understand clearly, and they husband their game. In 1900, less than half a million white-tailed deer remained in this country; today, the whitetail population exceeds 18 million. In 1907, only about 40,000 elk could be counted; the elk population in 10 Western states now totals more than 800,000. In the early 1900's, the wild turkey population was under 100,000 and falling fast; at last count, there were more than 4.5 million. Less than 50 years ago, there were only 12,000 pronghorn antelope left. Since then the population has increased to more than a million.

This is good news for everyone, and sportsmen should be given credit for a lot of it. They have certainly paid for it. Each day, through license revenues, excise taxes and other income sources like Duck Stamps, sportsmen contribute $3 million to wildlife conservation efforts—more than $1 billion a year.

Through some 10,000 private groups they give an additional $300 million each year. Disappearing wildlife habitat is their issue, and effective game management is their goal.

No wonder they bristle when some fashion model or lobbyist accuses them of murder for thinning herds that would otherwise be virtually wiped out by winter kill. Nothing about hunting is simple, least of all the mind of the predator. Not to recognize this is to miss the point of a new hunting ethos that is as strong in the deer and elk camps of Pennsylvania and Wyoming as it is dimly perceived in the plastic-shoe section of Bloomingdale's and the health-food bistros of South Beach.

The men and women in the hunting camps are after much more than their quarry, and they are fed up with not being recognized as the strong and dedicated conservationists they are. And lately they have become even more frustrated with talk show patter about how dangerous they are.

Hunters do not join citizen's militias. They look at gun control as an urban-rural issue. And most of them agree that waiting periods and background checks are good safeguards to attach to firearm purchases.

The wilderness thrills them even as they see the social and political environment for hunting changing more rapidly than the natural world itself.   10

They nurture their traditions as vigorously as their grandfathers and grandmothers do, but they are saddened by what they anticipate for their grandchildren.

Sometimes, sitting silently in the forest or climbing in the mountains, it occurs to them that they do not want to go home. They have begun to think of themselves as an endangered species. I know this because I am a hunter.

✎ Topics for Critical Thinking and Writing

1. How does McDonell characterize "real hunters"? How does he characterize opponents of hunting?
2. In his third paragraph McDonell cites the increase in white-tailed deer, elk, wild turkey, and pronghorn antelope. How does he account for these increases in wildlife? How reasonable do you find his account?
3. In his seventh paragraph McDonell says "Nothing about hunting is simple, least of all the mind of the predator." What do you think he means?
4. Characterize McDonell's style. Putting aside your own views on hunting, how persuasive do you find his argument?

Margaret A. Whitney

Margaret A. Whitney wrote this essay while she was a doctoral candidate at Rensselaer Polytechnic Institute, in Troy, New York. It was originally published in The New York Times Magazine.

Playing to Win

My daughter is an athlete. Nowadays, this statement won't strike many parents as unusual, but it does me. Until her freshman year in high school, Ann was only marginally interested in sport of any kind. When she played, she didn't swing hard, often dropped the ball, and had an annoying habit of tittering on field or court.

Indifference combined with another factor that did not bode well for a sports career. Ann was growing up to be beautiful. By the eighth grade, nature and orthodontics had produced a 5-foot-8-inch, 125-pound, brown-eyed beauty with a wonderful smile. People told her, too. And, as many young women know, it is considered a satisfactory accomplishment to be pretty and stay pretty. Then you can simply sit still and enjoy the unconditional positive regard. Ann loved the attention too, and didn't consider it demeaning when she was awarded "Best Hair," female category, in the eighth-grade yearbook.

So it came as a surprise when she became a jock. The first indication that athletic indifference had ended came when she joined the high-school cross-country team. She signed up in early September and ran third for the team within three days. Not only that. After one of those 3.1-mile races up hill and down dale on a rainy November afternoon, Ann came home muddy and bedraggled. Her hair was plastered to her head, and the mascara she had applied so carefully that morning ran in dark circles under her eyes. This is it, I thought. Wait until Lady Astor sees herself. But the kid with the best eighth-grade hair went on to finish the season and subsequently letter in cross-country, soccer, basketball and softball.

I love sports, she tells anyone who will listen. So do I, though my midlife quest for a doctorate leaves me little time for either playing or watching. My love of sports is bound up with the goals in my life and my hopes for my three daughters. I have begun to hear the message of sports. It is very different from many messages that women receive about living, and I think it is good.

My husband, for example, talked to Ann differently when he realized   5
that she was a serious competitor and not just someone who wanted to get in shape so she'd look good in a prom dress. Be aggressive, he'd advise. Go for the ball. Be intense.

Be intense. She came in for some of the most scathing criticism from her dad, when, during basketball season, her intensity waned. You're pretending to play hard, he said. You like it on the bench? Do you like to watch while your teammates play?

I would think, how is this kid reacting to such advice? For years, she'd been told at home, at school, by countless advertisements, "Be quiet, Be good, Be still." When teachers reported that Ann was too talkative, not obedient enough, too flighty. When I dressed her up in frilly dresses and admonished her not to get dirty. When ideals of femininity are still, quiet, cool females in ads whose vacantness passes for sophistication. How can any adolescent girl know what she's up against? Have you ever really noticed intensity? It is neither quiet nor good. And it's definitely not pretty.

In the end, her intensity revived. At half time, she'd look for her father, and he would come out of the bleachers to discuss tough defense, finding the open player, squaring up on her jump shot. I'd watch them at the edge of the court, a tall man and a tall girl, talking about how to play.

Of course I'm particularly sensitive at this point in my life to messages about trying hard, being active, getting better through individual and team effort. Ann, you could barely handle a basketball two years ago. Now you're bringing the ball up against the press. Two defenders are after you. You must dribble, stop, pass. We're depending on you. We need you to help us. I wonder if my own paroxysms of uncertainty would be eased had more people urged me—be active, go for it!

Not that dangers don't lurk for the females of her generation. I occa-   10
sionally run this horror show in my own mental movie theater: an unctu-
ous but handsome lawyer-like drone of a young man spies my Ann. Hmmm, he says unconsciously to himself, good gene pool, and wouldn't she go well with my BMW and the condo? Then I see Ann with a great new hairdo kissing the drone goodbyehoney and setting off to the nearest mall with splendid-looking children to spend money.

But the other night she came home from softball tryouts at 6 in the evening. The dark circles under her eyes were from exhaustion, not make-up. I tried too hard today, she says. I feel like I'm going to puke.

After she has revived, she explains. She wants to play a particular posi-tion. There is competition for it. I can't let anybody else get my spot, she says, I've got to prove that I can do it. Later we find out that she has not got-ten the much-wanted third-base position, but she will start with the varsity team. My husband talks about the machinations of coaches and tells her to keep trying. You're doing fine, he says. She gets that I-am-going-to-keep-try-ing look on her face. The horror-show vision of Ann-as-Stepford-Wife fades.

Of course, Ann doesn't realize the changes she has wrought, the power of her self-definition. I'm an athlete, Ma, she tells me when I sug-gest participation in the school play or the yearbook. But she has really caused us all to rethink our views of existence: her younger sisters who consider sports a natural activity for females, her father whose advocacy of women has increased, and me. Because when I doubt my own abilities, I say to myself, Get intense, Margaret. Do you like to sit on the bench?

And my intensity revives.

I am not suggesting that participation in sports is the answer for all   15
young women. It is not easy—the losing, jealousy, raw competition and intense personal criticism of performance.

And I don't wish to imply that the sports scene is a morality play either. Girls' sports can be funny. You can't forget that out on that field are a bunch of people who know the meaning of the word cute. During one game, I noticed that Ann had a blue ribbon tied on her ponytail, and it dawned on me that every girl on the team had an identical bow. Somehow I can't picture the Celtics gathered in the locker room of the Boston Garden agreeing to wear the same color sweatbands.

No, what has struck me, amazed me and made me hold my breath in wonder and in hope is both the ideal of sport and the reality of a young girl not afraid to do her best.

I watch her bringing the ball up the court. We yell encouragement from the stands, though I know she doesn't hear us. Her face is red with exertion, and her body is concentrated on the task. She dribbles, draws the defense to her, passes, runs. A teammate passes the ball back to her. They've beaten the press. She heads toward the hoop. Her father watches her, her sisters watch her, I watch her. And I think, drive, Ann, drive.

✎ Topics for Critical Thinking and Writing

1. In her second paragraph Whitney claims that "nature and orthodontics had produced a . . . brown-eyed beauty with a wonderful smile." We find (and hope that you find) this passage amusing. What other instances of humor do you find in "Playing to Win"? Humor is always agreeable. Does it have any other function in this essay?
2. In her fourth paragraph Whitney says "I have begun to hear the message of sports." Does she say what that message is? If not, can you put it in your own words?
3. In her tenth paragraph Whitney implies that "dangers" "lurk" for females of her daughter's generation. What are the dangers?
4. In paragraph 16 Whitney mentions the blue ribbon Ann wore on her pony-tail. Why does she mention it? What is her point?
5. In her final paragraph, Whitney uses the present tense. Why? What is the effect?
6. In paragraph 7 Whitney refers to "countless advertisements" in which women are portrayed as "still, quiet, cool" and vacant. Whitney's essay was published in 1988. Are women still so portrayed? Look at a half dozen ads and then choose one to write about. In the first paragraph, describe the ad clearly enough so that someone who hasn't seen it can make a reasonably good sketch of it. In the second paragraph, analyze the ad, revealing what the composition and text say and imply about women. Indicate in your first paragraph the source of the ad, and include a copy of the ad with your essay.

Sir Thomas More

Sir Thomas More (1478–1535) was an extremely able English administrator and diplomat who rose to high rank in the government of King Henry VIII, but when he opposed the King's break with Roman Catholicism (Henry demanded that his subjects recognize him as Supreme Head of the Church), More was beheaded. Four hundred years later, in 1935, he was canonized.

More wrote Utopia *in Latin (the international language of the Renaissance) in 1516. The word is Greek for* no place, *with a pun on the Greek prefix,* eu, *meaning "good," so More's Utopia is both "no where" and a "good place." The Greek-sounding names for officials in this imaginary land—a syphogrant is elected by a group of thirty households, and a tranibor governs a group of ten syphogrants—have no meaning. Though the book is fictional, setting forth a playful vision of an ideal society, there is no story; it is not a novel but a sort of essay.*

"Work and Play" (editors' title) represents about one-tenth of the book.

Work and Play in Utopia

Their Occupations

Agriculture is the one occupation at which everyone works, men and women alike, with no exceptions. They are trained in it from childhood, partly in the schools where they learn theory, and partly through field trips to nearby farms, which make something like a game of practical instruction. On these trips they not only watch the work being done, but frequently pitch in and get a workout by doing the jobs themselves.

Besides farm work (which, as I said, everybody performs), each person is taught a particular trade of his own, such as wool-working, linen-making, masonry, metal-work, or carpentry. There is no other craft that is practiced by any considerable number of them. Throughout the island people wear, and down through the centuries they have always worn, the same style of clothing, except for the distinction between the sexes, and between married and unmarried persons. Their clothing is attractive, does not hamper bodily movement, and serves for warm as well as cold weather; what is more, each household can make its own.

Every person (and this includes women as well as men) learns a second trade, besides agriculture. As the weaker sex, women practice the lighter crafts, such as working in wool or linen; the heavier crafts are assigned to the men. As a rule, the son is trained to his father's craft; for which most feel a natural inclination. But if anyone is attracted to another occupation, he is transferred by adoption into a family practicing the trade he prefers. When anyone makes such a change, both his father and the authorities make sure that he is assigned to a grave and responsible householder. After a man has learned one trade, if he wants to learn another, he gets the same permission. When he has learned both, he pursues whichever he likes better, unless the city needs one more than the other.

The chief and almost the only business of the syphogrants is to manage matters so that no one sits around in idleness, and assure that everyone works hard at his trade. But no one has to exhaust himself with endless toil from early morning to late at night, as if he were a beast of burden. Such wretchedness, really worse than slavery, is the common lot of workmen in all countries, except Utopia. Of the day's twenty-four hours, the Utopians devote only six to work. They work three hours before noon, when they go to dinner. After dinner they rest for a couple of hours, then go to work for another three hours. Then they have supper, and at eight o'clock (counting the first hour after noon as one), they go to bed and sleep eight hours.

The other hours of the day, when they are not working, eating, or sleeping, are left to each man's individual discretion, provided he does not waste them in roistering or sloth, but uses them busily in some occupation that pleases him. Generally these periods are devoted to intellectual activ-

5

ity. For they have an established custom of giving public lectures before daybreak; attendance at these lectures is required only of those who have been specially chosen to devote themselves to learning, but a great many other people, both men a.id women, choose voluntarily to attend. Depending on their interests, some go to one lecture, some to another. But if anyone would rather devote his spare time to his trade, as many do who don't care for the intellectual life, this is not discouraged; in fact, such persons are commended as especially useful to the commonwealth.

After supper, they devote an hour to recreation, in their gardens when the weather is fine, or during winter weather in the common halls where they have their meals. There they either play music or amuse themselves with conversation. They know nothing about gambling with dice, or other such foolish and ruinous games. They do play two games not unlike our own chess. One is a battle of numbers, in which one number captures another. The other is a game in which the vices fight a battle against the virtues. The game is set up to show how the vices oppose one another, yet readily combine against the virtues; then, what vices oppose what virtues, how they try to assault them openly or undermine them in secret; how the virtues can break the strength of the vices or turn their purposes to good; and finally, by what means one side or the other gains the victory.

But in all this, you may get a wrong impression, if we don't go back and consider one point more carefully. Because they allot only six hours to work, you might think the necessities of life would be in scant supply. This is far from the case. Their working hours are ample to provide not only enough but more than enough of the necessities and even the conveniences of life. You will easily appreciate this if you consider how large a part of the population in other countries exists without doing any work at all. In the first place, hardly any of the women, who are a full half of the population, work; or, if they do, then as a rule their husbands lie snoring in the bed. Then there is a great lazy gang of priests and so-called religious men. Add to them all the rich, especially the landlords, who are commonly called gentlemen and nobility. Include with them their retainers, that mob of swaggering bullies. Finally, reckon in with these the sturdy and lusty beggars, who go about feigning some disease as an excuse for their idleness. You will certainly find that the things which satisfy our needs are produced by far fewer hands than you had supposed.

And now consider how few of those who do work are doing really essential things. For where money is the standard of everything, many superfluous trades are bound to be carried on simply to satisfy luxury and licentiousness. Suppose the multitude of those who now work were limited to a few trades, and set to producing more and more of those conveniences and commodities that nature really requires. They would be bound to produce so much that the prices would drop, and the workmen would be unable to gain a living. But suppose again that all the workers in useless trades were put to useful ones, and that all the idlers (who now guzzle twice as much as the workingmen who make what they consume) were assigned to productive tasks—well, you can easily see how little time each man would have to spend working, in order to produce all the goods that human needs and conveniences require—yes, and human pleasure too, as long as it's true and natural pleasure.

The experience of Utopia makes this perfectly apparent. In each city and its surrounding countryside barely five hundred of those men and women whose age and strength make them fit for work are exempted from it. Among these are the syphogrants, who by law are free not to work; yet they don't take advantage of the privilege, preferring to set a good example to their fellow-citizens. Some others are permanently exempted from work so that they may devote themselves to study, but only on the recommendation of the priests and through a secret vote of the syphogrants. If any of these scholars disappoints their hopes, he becomes a workman again. On the other hand, it happens from time to time that a craftsman devotes his leisure so earnestly to study, and makes such progress as a result, that he is relieved of manual labor, and promoted to the class of learned men. From this class of scholars are chosen ambassadors, priests, tranibors, and the prince himself, who used to be called Barzanes, but in their modern tongue is known as Ademus. Since all the rest of the population is neither idle nor occupied in useless trades, it is easy to see why they produce so much in so short a working day.

Apart from all this, in several of the necessary crafts their way of life   10 requires less total labor than does that of people elsewhere. In other countries, building and repairing houses requires the constant work of many men, because what a father has built, his thriftless heirs lets fall into ruin; and then his successor has to repair, at great expense, what could easily have been maintained at a very small charge. Further, even when a man has built a splendid house at large cost, someone else may think he has finer taste, let the first house fall to ruin, and then build another one somewhere else for just as much money. But among the Utopians, where everything has been established, and the commonwealth is carefully regulated, building a brand-new home on a new site is a rare event. They are not only quick to repair damage, but foresighted in preventing it. The result is that their buildings last for a very long time with minimum repairs; and the carpenters and masons sometimes have so little to do, that they are set to hewing timber and cutting stone in case some future need for it should arise.

Consider, too, how little labor their clothing requires. Their work clothes are loose garments made of leather which last as long as seven years. When they go out in public, they cover these rough working-clothes with a cloak. Throughout the entire island, everyone wears the same colored cloak, which is the color of natural wool. As a result, they not only need less wool than people in other countries, but what they do need is less expensive. They use linen cloth most, because it requires least labor. They like linen cloth to be white and wool cloth to be clean; but they put no price on fineness of texture. Elsewhere a man is not satisfied with four or five woolen cloaks of different colors and as many silk shirts, or if he's a show-off, even ten of each are not enough. But a Utopian is content with a single cloak, and generally wears it for two seasons. There is no reason at all why he should want any others, for if he had them, he would not be better protected against the cold, nor would he appear in any way better dressed.

When there is an abundance of everything, as a result of everyone working at useful trades, and nobody consuming to excess, then great numbers of the people often go out to work on the roads, if any of them need repairing. And when there is no need even for this sort of public work, then the officials very often proclaim a short work day, since they never force their citizens to perform useless labor. The chief aim of their constitution and government is that, whenever public needs permit, all citizens should be free, so far as possible, to withdraw their time and energy from the service of the body, and devote themselves to the freedom and culture of the mind. For that, they think, is the real happiness of life. . . .

Their Moral Philosophy

They conclude, after carefully considering and weighing the matter, that all our actions and the virtues exercised within them look toward pleasure and happiness at their ultimate end.

By pleasure they understand every state or movement of body or mind in which man naturally finds delight. They are right in considering man's appetites natural. By simply following his senses and his right reason a man may discover what is pleasant by nature—it is a delight which does not injure others, which does not preclude a greater pleasure, and which is not followed by pain. But a pleasure which is against nature, and which men call "delightful" only by the emptiest of fictions (as if one could change the real nature of things just by changing their names), does not really make for happiness; in fact they say, it destroys happiness. And the reason is that men whose minds are filled with false ideas of pleasure have no room left for true and genuine delight. As a matter of fact, there are a great many things which have no sweetness in them, but are mainly or entirely bitter—yet which through the perverse enticements of evil lusts are considered very great pleasures, and even the supreme goals of life.

Among those who pursue this false pleasure the Utopians include 15 those whom I mentioned before, the men who think themselves finer fellows because they wear finer clothes. These people are twice mistaken: first in thinking their clothes better than anyone else's, and then in thinking themselves better because of their clothes. As far as a coat's usefulness goes, what does it matter if it was woven of thin thread or thick? Yet they act as if they were set apart by nature herself, rather than their own fantasies; they strut about, and put on airs. Because they have a fancy suit, they think themselves entitled to honors they would never have expected if they were poorly dressed, and they get very angry if someone passes them by without showing special respect.

It is the same kind of absurdity to be pleased by empty, ceremonial honors. What true and natural pleasure can you get from someone's bent knee or bared head? Will the creaks in your own knees be eased thereby, or the madness in your head? The phantom of false pleasure is illustrated by other men who run mad with delight over their own blue blood, plume themselves on their nobility, and applaud themselves for all their rich ancestors (the only ancestors worth having nowadays), and all their ancient family estates. Even if they don't have the shred of an estate themselves, or if they've squandered every penny of their inheritance, they don't consider themselves a bit less noble.

In the same class the Utopians put those people I described before, who are mad for jewelry and gems, and think themselves divinely happy if they find a good specimen, especially of the sort which happens to be fashionable in their country at the time—for stones vary in value from one market to another. The collector will not make an offer for the stone till it's taken out of its setting, and even then he will not buy unless the dealer guarantees and gives security that it is a true and genuine stone. What he fears is that his eyes will be deceived by a counterfeit. But if you consider the matter, why should a counterfeit give any less pleasure when your eyes cannot distinguish it from a real gem? Both should be of equal value to you, as they would be, in fact, to a blind man.

Speaking of false pleasure, what about those who pile up money, not because they want to do anything with the heap, but so they can sit and look at it? Is that true pleasure they experience, or aren't they simply cheated by a show of pleasure? Or what of those with the opposite vice, the men who hide away money they will never use and perhaps never even see again? In their anxiety to hold onto their money, they actually lose it. For what else happens when you deprive yourself, and perhaps other people too, of a chance to use money, by burying it in the ground? And yet when the miser has hidden his treasure, he exults over it as if his mind were now free to rejoice. Suppose someone stole it, and the miser died ten years later, knowing nothing of the theft. During all those ten years, what did it matter whether the money was stolen or not? In either case, it was equally useless to the owner.

To these false and foolish pleasures they add gambling, which they have heard about, though they've never tried it, as well as hunting and hawking. What pleasure can there be, they wonder, in throwing dice on a table? If there were any pleasure in the action, wouldn't doing it over and over again quickly make one tired of it? What pleasure can there be in listening to the barking and yelping of dogs—isn't that rather a disgusting noise? Is there any more real pleasure when a dog chases a rabbit than there is when a dog chases a dog? If what you like is fast running, there's plenty of that in both cases; they're just about the same. But if what you really want is slaughter, if you want to see a living creature torn apart under your eyes, then the whole thing is wrong. You ought to feel nothing but pity when you see the hare fleeing from the hound, the weak creature tormented by the stronger, the fearful and timid beast brutalized by the savage one, the harmless hare killed by the cruel dog. The Utopians, who regard this whole activity of hunting as unworthy of free men, have assigned it, accordingly, to their butchers, who as I said before, are all slaves. In their eyes, hunting is the lowest thing even butchers can do. In the slaughterhouse, their work is more useful and honest—besides which, they kill animals only from necessity; but in hunting they seek merely their own pleasure from the killing and mutilating of some poor little creature. Taking such relish in the sight of death, even if it's only beasts, reveals, in the opinion of the Utopians, a cruel disposition. Or if he isn't cruel to start with, the hunter quickly becomes so through the constant practice of such brutal pleasures.

Most men consider these activities, and countless others like them, to   20 be pleasures; but the Utopians say flatly they have nothing at all to do with real pleasure since there's nothing naturally pleasant about them. They often please the senses, and in this they are like pleasure, but that does not alter their basic nature. The enjoyment doesn't arise from the experience itself, but only from the perverse mind of the individual, as a result of which he mistakes the bitter for the sweet, just as pregnant women, whose taste has been turned awry, sometimes think pitch and tallow taste sweeter than honey. A man's taste may be similarly depraved, by disease or by custom, but that does not change the nature of pleasure, or of anything else.

✎ Topics for Critical Thinking and Writing

1. What does More assume are the only functions of clothing? Do you agree with More, or do you find other important reasons why people wear the clothes that they wear?
2. The "work ethic" assumes that labor is good in itself—that there is some sort of virtue in work. (See Nixon's remark on page 469.) Further, many people assume that work, at least certain kinds of work done under certain conditions, affords happiness to the worker. What does More's attitude seem to be on these two related points?
3. What is More's opinion of hunting? What arguments in support of hunting are commonly offered? In your opinion, does More successfully counter those arguments?
4. In approximately five hundred words set forth More's assumptions about the sources of happiness.
5. More says that each Utopian is free to do what he wishes with leisure hours, "provided he does not waste them in roistering or sloth." (By the way, since the Utopians work six hours a day, if they sleep eight hours they have ten

hours of free time.) In five hundred words develop an argument for or against this proviso concerning the pursuit of happiness. (You may want to recall that our own government to some degree regulates our pleasure, for instance by outlawing bullfights.)

6. Note the passage (paragraph 6) in which More describes two games enjoyed by Utopians. Imitating More's style in describing the second game, write a paragraph describing a video game as a Utopian or anti-Utopian recreation.

Marie Winn

Marie Winn, born in Czechoslovakia in 1936, came to New York when she was still a child. She later graduated from Radcliffe College and then did further academic work at Columbia University. Our selection comes from Childhood without Children *(1983), a book based in part on interviews with hundreds of children and parents.*

The End of Play

Of all the changes that have altered the topography of childhood, the most dramatic has been the disappearance of childhood play. Whereas a decade or two ago children were easily distinguished from the adult world by the very nature of their play, today children's occupations do not differ greatly from adult diversions.

Infants and toddlers, to be sure, continue to follow certain timeless patterns of manipulation and exploration; adolescents, too, have not changed their free-time habits so very much, turning as they ever have towards adult pastimes and amusements in their drive for autonomy, self-mastery, and sexual discovery. It is among the ranks of school-age children, those six-to-twelve-year-olds who once avidly filled their free moments with childhood play, that the greatest change is evident. In the place of traditional, sometimes ancient childhood games that were still popular a generation ago, in the place of fantasy and make-believe play— "You be the mommy and I'll be the daddy"—doll play or toy-soldier play, jump-rope play, ball-bouncing play, today's children have substituted television viewing and, most recently, video games.

Many parents have misgivings about the influence of television. They sense that a steady and time-consuming exposure to passive entertainment might damage the ability to play imaginatively and resourcefully, or prevent this ability from developing in the first place. A mother of two school-age children recalls: "When I was growing up, we used to go out into the vacant lots and make up week-long dramas and sagas. This was during third, fourth, fifth grades. But my own kids have never done that sort of thing, and somehow it bothers me. I wish we had cut down on the TV years ago, and maybe the kids would have learned how to play."

The testimony of parents who eliminate television for periods of time strengthens the connection between children's television watching and changed play patterns. Many parents discover that when their children don't have television to fill their free time, they resort to the old kinds of imaginative, traditional "children's play." Moreover, these parents often observe that under such circumstances "they begin to seem more like children" or "they act more childlike." Clearly, a part of the definition of childhood, in adults' minds, resides in the nature of children's play.

Children themselves sometimes recognize the link between play and their own special definition as children. In an interview about children's books with four ten-year-old girls, one of them said: "I read this story about a girl my age growing up twenty years ago—you know, in 1960 or so,—and she seemed so much younger than me in her behavior. Like she might be playing with dolls, or playing all sorts of children's games, or jump-roping or something." The other girls all agreed that they had noticed a similar discrepancy between themselves and fictional children in books of the past: those children seemed more like children. "So what do *you* do in your spare time, if you don't play with dolls or play make-believe games or jump rope or do things kids did twenty years ago?" they were asked. They laughed and answered, "We watch TV."

But perhaps other societal factors have caused children to give up play. Children's greater exposure to adult realities, their knowledge of adult sexuality, for instance, might make them more sophisticated, less likely to play like children. Evidence from the counterculture communes of the sixties and seventies adds weight to the argument that it is television above all that has eliminated children's play. Studies of children raised in a variety of such communes, all television-free, showed the little communards continuing to fill their time with those forms of play that have all but vanished from the lives of conventionally reared American children. And yet these counterculture kids were casually exposed to all sorts of adult matters—drug taking, sexual intercourse. Indeed, they sometimes incorporated these matters into their play: "We're mating," a pair of six-year-olds told a reporter to explain their curious bumps and grinds. Nevertheless, to all observers the commune children preserved a distinctly childlike and even innocent demeanor, an impression that was produced mainly by the fact that they spent most of their time playing. Their play defined them as belonging to a special world of childhood.

Not all children have lost the desire to engage in the old-style childhood play. But so long as the most popular, most dominant members of the peer group, who are often the most socially precocious, are "beyond" playing, then a common desire to conform makes it harder for those children who still have the drive to play to go ahead and do so. Parents often report that their children seem ashamed of previously common forms of play and hide their involvement with such play from their peers. "My fifth-grader still plays with dolls," a mother tells, "but she keeps them hidden in the basement where nobody will see them." This social check on the play instinct serves to hasten the end of childhood for even the least advanced children.

What seems to have replaced play in the lives of great numbers of preadolescents these days, starting as early as fourth grade, is a burgeoning interest in boy-girl interactions—"going out" or "going together." These activities do not necessarily involve going anywhere or doing anything sexual, but nevertheless are the first stage of a sexual process that used to commence at puberty or even later. Those more sophisticated children who are already involved in such manifestly unchildlike interest make plain their low opinion of their peers who still *play*. "Some of the kids in the class are real weird," a fifth-grade boy states. "They're not interested in going out, just in trucks and stuff, or games pretending they're monsters. Some of them don't even *try* to be cool."

Video Games versus Marbles

Is there really any great difference, one might ask, between that gang of kids playing video games by the hour at their local candy store these days and those small fry who used to hang around together spending equal amounts of time playing marbles? It is easy to see a similarity between the two activities: each requires a certain amount of manual dexterity, each is almost as much fun to watch as to play, each is simple and yet challenging enough for that middle-childhood age group for whom time can be so oppressive if unfilled.

One significant difference between the modern pre-teen fad of video   10
games and the once popular but now almost extinct pastime of marbles is economic: playing video games costs twenty-five cents for approximately three minutes of play; playing marbles, after a small initial investment, is free. The children who frequent video-game machines require a considerable outlay of quarters to subsidize their fun; two, three, or four dollars is not an unusual expenditure for an eight-or nine-year-old spending an hour or two with his friends playing Asteroids or Pac-Man or Space Invaders. For most of the children the money comes from their weekly allowance. Some augment this amount by enterprising commercial ventures—trading and selling comic books, or doing chores around the house for extra money.

But what difference does it make *where* the money comes from? Why should that make video games any less satisfactory as an amusement for children? In fact, having to pay for the entertainment, whatever the source of the money, and having its duration limited by one's financial resources changes the nature of the game, in a subtle way diminishing the satisfactions it offers. Money and time become intertwined, as they so often are in the adult world and as, in the past, they almost never were in the child's world. For the child playing marbles, meanwhile, time has a far more care-free quality, bounded only by the requirements to be home by suppertime or by dark.

But the video-game-playing child has an additional burden—a burden of choice, of knowing that the money used for playing Pac-Man could have been saved for Christmas, could have been used to buy something tangible, perhaps something "worthwhile," as his parents might say, rather than being "wasted" on video games. There is a certain sense of adultness that spending money imparts, a feeling of being a consumer, which distinguishes a game with a price from its counterparts among the traditional childhood games children once played at no cost.

There are other differences as well. Unlike child-initiated and child-organized games such as marbles, video games are adult-created mechanisms not entirely within the child's control, and thus less likely to impart a sense of mastery and fulfillment: the coin may get jammed, the machine may go haywire, the little blobs may stop eating the funny little dots. Then the child must go to the storekeeper to complain, to get his money back. He may be "ripped off" and simply lose his quarter, much as his parents are when they buy a faulty appliance. This possibility of disaster gives the child's play a certain weight that marbles never imposed on its light-hearted players.

Even if a child has a video game at home requiring no coin outlay, the play it provides is less than optimal. The noise level of the machine is high—too high, usually, for the child to conduct a conversation easily with another child. And yet, according to its enthusiasts, this very noisiness is a part of the game's attraction. The loud whizzes, crashes, and whirrs of the video-game machine "blow the mind" and create an excitement that is quite apart from the excitement generated simply by trying to win a game. A traditional childhood game such as marbles, on the other hand, has little built-in stimulation; the excitement of playing is generated entirely by the players' own actions. And while the pace of a game of marbles is close to the child's natural physiological rhythms, the frenzied activities of video games serve to "rev up" the child in an artificial way, almost in the way a stimulant or an amphetamine might. Meanwhile the perceptual impact of a video game is similar to that of watching television—the action, after all, takes place on a television screen—causing the eye to defocus slightly and creating a certain alteration in the child's natural state of consciousness.

Parents' instinctive reaction to their children's involvement with video games provides another clue to the difference between this contemporary form of play and the more traditional pastimes such as marbles. While parents, indeed most adults, derive open pleasure from watching children at play, most parents today are not delighted to watch their kids flicking away at the Pac-Man machine. This does not seem to them to be real play. As a mother of two school-age children anxiously explains, "We used to do real childhood sorts of things when I was a kid. We'd build forts and put on crazy plays and make up new languages, and just generally we *played*. But today my kids don't play that way at all. They like video games and of course they still go in for sports outdoors. They go roller skating and ice skating and skiing and all. But they don't seem to really *play*."

Some of this feeling may represent a certain nostalgia for the past and the old generation's resistance to the different ways of the new. But it is more likely that most adults have an instinctive understanding of the importance of play in their own childhood. This feeling stokes their fears that their children are being deprived of something irreplaceable when they flip the levers on the video machines to manipulate the electronic images rather than flick their fingers to send a marble shooting towards another marble.

Play Deprivation

In addition to television's influence, some parents and teachers ascribe children's diminished drive to play to recent changes in the school curriculum, especially in the early grades.

"Kindergarten, traditionally a playful port of entry into formal school, is becoming more academic, with children being taught specific skills, taking tests, and occasionally even having homework," begins a report on new directions in early childhood education. Since 1970, according to the United States census, the proportion of three- and four-year-olds enrolled in school has risen dramatically, from 20.5 percent to 36.7 percent in 1980, and these nursery schools have largely joined the push towards academic acceleration in the early grades. Moreover, middle-class nursery schools in recent years have introduced substantial doses of academic material into their daily programs, often using those particular devices originally intended to help culturally deprived preschoolers in compensatory programs such as Headstart to catch up with their middleclass peers. Indeed, some of the increased focus on academic skills in nursery schools and kindergartens is related to the widespread popularity among young children and their parents of *Sesame Street*, a program originally intended to help deprived children attain academic skills, but universally watched by middle-class toddlers as well.

Parents of the *Sesame Street* generation often demand a "serious," skill-centered program for their preschoolers in school, afraid that the old-fashioned, play-centered curriculum will bore their alphabet-spouting, number-chanting four- and five-year-olds. A few parents, especially those whose children have not attended television classes or nursery school, complain of the high-powered pace of kindergarten these days. A father whose five-year-old daughter attends a public kindergarten declares: "There's a lot more pressure put on little kids these days than when we were kids, that's for sure. My daughter never went to nursery school and never watched *Sesame*, and she had a lot of trouble when she entered kindergarten this fall. By October, just a month and a half into the program, she was already flunking. The teacher told us our daughter couldn't keep up with the other kids. And believe me, she's a bright kid! All the other kids were getting gold stars and smiley faces for their work, and every day Emily would come home in tears because she didn't get a gold star. Remember when we were in kindergarten? We were *children* then. We were allowed just to play!"

A kindergarten teacher confirms the trend towards early academic   20
pressure. "We're expected by the dictates of the school system to push a lot of curriculum," she explains. "Kids in our kindergarten can't sit around playing with blocks any more. We've just managed to squeeze in one hour of free play a week, on Fridays."

The diminished emphasis on fantasy and play and imaginative activities in early childhood education and the increased focus on early academic-skill acquisition have helped to change childhood from a play-centered time of life to one more closely resembling the style of adulthood: purposeful, success-centered, competitive. The likelihood is that these preschool "workers" will not metamorphose back into players when they move on to grade school. This decline in play is surely one of the reasons why so many teachers today comment that their third- or fourth-graders act like tired businessmen instead of like children.

What might be the consequences of this change in children's play? Children's propensity to engage in that extraordinary series of behaviors characterized as "play" is perhaps the single great dividing line between childhood and adulthood, and has probably been so throughout history. The make-believe games anthropologists have recorded of children in primitive societies around the world attest to the universality of play and to the uniqueness of this activity to the immature members of each society. But in those societies, and probably in Western society before the middle or late eighteenth century, there was always a certain similarity between children's play and adult work. The child's imaginative play took the form of imitation of various aspects of adult life, culminating in the gradual transformation of the child's play from make-believe work to *real* work. At this point, in primitive societies or in our own society of the past, the child took her or his place in the adult work world and the distinctions between adulthood and childhood virtually vanished. But in today's technologically advanced society there is no place for the child in the adult work world. There are not enough jobs, even of the most menial kind, to go around for adults, much less for children. The child must continue to be dependent on adults for many years while gaining the knowledge and skills necessary to become a working member of society.

This is not a new situation for children. For centuries children have endured a prolonged period of dependence long after the helplessness of early childhood is over. But until recent years children remained childlike and playful far longer than they do today. Kept isolated from the adult world as a result of deliberate secrecy and protectiveness, they continued to find pleasure in socially sanctioned childish activities until the imperatives of adolescence led them to strike out for independence and self-sufficiency.

Today, however, with children's inclusion in the adult world both through the instrument of television and as a result of a deliberately preparatory, integrative style of child rearing, the old forms of play no longer seem to provide children with enough excitement and stimulation. What then are these so-called children to do for fulfillment if their desire to play has been vitiated and yet their entry into the working world of adulthood must be delayed for many years? The answer is precisely to get involved in those areas that cause contemporary parents so much distress: addictive television viewing during the school years followed, in adolescence or even before, by a search for similar oblivion via alcohol and drugs; exploration of the world of sensuality and sexuality before achieving the emotional maturity necessary for altruistic relationships.

Psychiatrists have observed among children in recent years a marked   25
increase in the occurrence of depression, a state long considered antithetical to the nature of childhood. Perhaps this phenomenon is at least somewhat connected with the current sense of uselessness and alienation that children feel, a sense that play may once upon a time have kept in abeyance.

✎ Topics for Critical Thinking and Writing

1. In a sentence or two sum up Winn's thesis.
2. When you were a child, what did you do in your "spare time"? Judging from your own experience, is Winn's first paragraph true, or at least roughly true?
3. Assuming that children today do indeed spend many hours watching television and playing video games, is it true that these activities "do not differ greatly from adult diversions"? To test Winn's assertion, list the diversions of adults and of children that you know of from your own experience. Are the two lists indeed strikingly similar? Or do the lists reveal important differences? Explain.
4. Winn's argument is largely composed of a series of comparisons between the play of children before access to TV and after; between traditional and contemporary kindergarten; between childhood in "primitive" (and our own preindustrial) society and in technologically advanced societies. List the points she makes to develop each of these comparisons. How well does each comparison support her thesis?
5. Winn obviously prefers that children play by making up stories rather than watching television. What reasons can be given to prefer making up stories, or reading stories in a book, to watching stories on television? Winn does not mention being read to by an adult as an activity of childhood. Draw your own comparison between traditional bedtime story-reading and nighttime TV-watching. Would such a comparison have strengthened or weakened Winn's argument?

6. Speaking of video games (paragraph 11), Winn argues that "having to pay for the entertainment . . . changes the nature of the game, in a subtle way diminishing the satisfactions it offers." Can one reply that having to pay helps a child to appreciate the value of money? In short, can it be argued that paying for one's pleasure is a way of becoming mature?

W. H. Auden

W[ystan] H[ugh] Auden (1907–73) was born and educated in England. In 1939 he came to the United States and later became an American citizen; but in 1972 he returned to England to live. Auden established his reputation chiefly with his poetry, but he also wrote plays, libretti, and essays (we include two of his essays in this book), all bearing the stamp of his highly original mind.

The Unknown Citizen

(To JS/07/M/378 This Marble Monument Is Erected by the State)

He was found by the Bureau of Statistics to be
One against whom there was no official complaint,
And all the reports on his conduct agree
That, in the modern sense of an old-fashioned word, he was a saint,
For in everything he did he served the Greater Community.   5
Except for the War till the day he retired
He worked in a factory and never got fired,
But satisfied his employers, Fudge Motors Inc.
Yet he wasn't a scab or odd in his views,
For his Union reports that he paid his dues,   10
(Our report on his Union shows it was sound)
And our Social Psychology workers found
That he was popular with his mates and liked a drink.
The press are convinced that he bought a paper every day
And that his reactions to advertisements were normal in
     every way.   15
Policies taken out in his name prove that he was fully insured,
And his Health-card shows he was once in hospital but left it cured.
Both Producers Research and High-Grade Living declare
He was fully sensible to the advantages of the Installment Plan
And had everything necessary to the Modern Man,   20
A phonograph, radio, a car and a frigidaire.
Our researchers into Public Opinion are content
That he held the proper opinions for the time of year;

When there was peace, he was for peace; when there was war, he
    went.
He was married and added five children to the population,   25
Which our Eugenist says was the right number for a parent of his
    generation,
And our teachers report that he never interfered with their
    education.
Was he free? Was he happy? The question is absurd:
Had anything been wrong, we should certainly have heard.

✎ Topics for Critical Thinking and Writing

1. Who is the speaker, and on what occasion is he supposed to be speaking?
2. What do the words "The Unknown Citizen" suggest to you?
3. How does Auden suggest that he doesn't share the attitudes of the speaker and is, in fact, satirizing them? What else does he satirize?
4. If Auden were writing the poem today, what might he substitute for "Install-ment Plan" in line 19 and the items listed in line 21?
5. Explicate the last two lines.
6. Write a tribute to The Unknown Student or The Unknown Professor or Politician or Professional Athlete or some other object of your well-deserved scorn.

11
MESSAGES

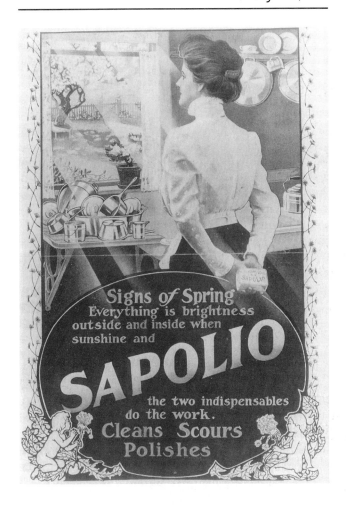

Just what is it that makes today's homes so different, so appealing?
Richard Hamilton, 1956

Short Views

Men . . . employ speech only to conceal their thoughts.
Voltaire

We must be as clear as our natural reticence allows us to be.
Marianne Moore

To change your language you must change your life.
Derek Walcott

If you saw a bullet hit a bird, and he told you he wasn't shot, you might weep at his courtesy, but you would certainly doubt his word.
Emily Dickinson

Language is political. That's why you and me, my Brother and Sister, that's why we sposed to choke our natural self into the weird, lying, barbarous, unreal, white speech and writing habits that the schools lay down like holy law. Because, in other words, the powerful don't play; they mean to keep that power, and those who are the powerless (you and me) better shape up—mimic/ape/suck—in the very image of the powerful, or the powerful will destroy you—you and our children.
June Jordan

While I am thinking about metaphor, a flock of purple finches arrives on the lawn. Since I haven't seen these birds for some years, I am only fairly sure of their being in fact purple finches, so I get down Peterson's *Field Guide* and read his description: "Male: About size of House Sparrow, rosy-red, brightest on head and rump." That checks quite well, but his next remark—"a sparrow dipped in raspberry juice," is decisive: it fits. I look out the window again, and now I know that I am seeing purple finches.
Howard Nemerov

We will understand the world, and preserve ourselves and our values in it, only insofar as we have a language that is alert and responsive to it, and careful of it. I mean that literally. When we give our plows such brand names as "Sod Blaster," we are imposing on their use conceptual limits which raise the likelihood that they will be used destructively. When we speak of man's "war against nature," or of a "peace offensive," we are accepting the limitations of a metaphor that suggests, and even proposes, violent solutions. When students ask for the right of "participatory input" at the meetings of a faculty organization, they are thinking of democratic process, but they are *speaking* of a convocation of robots, and are thus devaluing the very traditions that they invoke.

Wendell Berry

Sticks and stones will break my bones, but words will never hurt me.

Anonymous

Language both reflects and shapes society. The textbook on American government that consistently uses male pronouns for the president, even when not referring to a specific individual (e.g., "a president may cast his veto"), reflects the fact that all our presidents have so far been men. But it also shapes a society in which the idea of a female president somehow "doesn't sound right."

Rosalie Maggio

I keep six honest serving men
(They taught me all I knew);
Their names are What and Why and When
And How and Where and Who.

Rudyard Kipling

The search is for the just word, the happy phrase, that will give expression to the thought, but somehow the thought itself is transfigured by the phrase when found.

Benjamin Cardozo

"Wild and Free." An American dream-phrase loosing images: a long-maned stallion racing across the grasslands, a V of Canada Geese high and honking, a squirrel chattering and leaping limb to limb overhead in an oak. It also sounds like an ad for a Harley-Davidson. Both words, profoundly political and sensitive as they are, have become consumer baubles.

Gary Snyder

The current flows fast and furious. It issues in a spate of words from the loudspeakers and the politicians. Every day they tell us that we are a free people fighting to defend freedom. That is the current that has whirled the young airman up into the sky and keeps him circulating there among the clouds. Down here, with a roof to cover us and a gasmask handy, it is our business to punctuate gasbags and discover the seeds of truth.

Virginia Woolf (writing in 1940)

There can be too much communication between people.

Ann Beattie

Abraham Lincoln

Abraham Lincoln (1809–65), sixteenth president of the United States, is not usually thought of as a writer, but his published speeches and writings comprise about 1,078,000 words, the equivalent of about four thousand pages of double-spaced typing. They were all composed without the assistance of a speech writer.

The Gettysburg campaign—a series of battles fought near Gettysburg in southeastern Pennsylvania—took place in June and July of 1863. Each side lost something like twenty-three thousand men. The battle is regarded as a turning point in the war, but the Confederate army escaped and the war continued until April, 1865.

On November 19, 1863, Lincoln delivered a short speech (printed below) at the dedication of a national cemetery on the battlefield at Gettysburg.

Address at the Dedication of the Gettysburg National Cemetery

Four score and seven years ago our fathers brought forth on this continent, a new nation, conceived in Liberty, and dedicated to the proposition that all men are created equal.

Now we are engaged in a great civil war; testing whether that nation, or any nation so conceived and so dedicated, can long endure. We are met on a great battlefield of that war. We have come to dedicate a portion of that field as a final resting-place for those who here gave their lives that that nation might live. It is altogether fitting and proper that we should do this.

But, in a larger sense, we cannot dedicate—we cannot consecrate—we cannot hallow—this ground. The brave men, living and dead, who struggled here have consecrated it, far above our poor power to add or detract. The world will little note, nor long remember, what we say here, but it can never forget what they did here. It is for us the living, rather, to be dedicated here to the unfinished work which they who fought here have thus far so nobly advanced. It is rather for us to be here dedicated to the great task remaining before us—that from these honored dead we take increased devotion to that cause for which they gave the last full measure of devotion; that we here highly resolve that these dead shall not have died in vain; that this nation, under God, shall have a new birth of freedom; and that government of the people, by the people, for the people, shall not perish from the earth.

Gilbert Highet

Gilbert Highet (1906–78) was born in Glasgow, Scotland, and was educated at Glasgow University and at Oxford University. In 1937 he came to the United States, and in 1951 he was naturalized. Until his retirement in 1972 he taught Latin, Greek, and comparative literature at Columbia University. In addition to writing scholarly studies of classical authors, he wrote several general and more popular books.

The Gettysburg Address

Fourscore and seven years ago. . . .

These five words stand at the entrance to the best-known monument of American prose, one of the finest utterances in the entire language, and surely one of the greatest speeches in all history. Greatness is like granite: it is molded in fire, and it lasts for many centuries.

Fourscore and seven years ago. . . . It is strange to think that President Lincoln was looking back to the 4th of July 1776, and that he and his speech are now further removed from us than he himself was from George Washington and the Declaration of Independence. Fourscore and seven years before the Gettysburg Address, a small group of patriots signed the Declaration. Fourscore and seven years after the Gettysburg Address, it was the year 1950, and that date is already receding rapidly into our troubled, adventurous, and valiant past.

Inadequately prepared and at first scarcely realized in its full importance, the dedication of the graveyard at Gettysburg was one of the supreme moments of American history. The battle itself had been a turning point of the war. On the 4th of July 1863, General Meade repelled Lee's invasion of Pennsylvania. Although he did not follow up his victory, he had broken one of the most formidable aggressive enterprises of the Confederate armies. Losses were heavy on both sides. Thousands of dead were left on the field, and thousands of wounded died in the hot days following the battle. At first, their burial was more or less haphazard; but thoughtful men gradually came to feel that an adequate burying place and memorial were required. These were established by an interstate commission that autumn, and the finest speaker in the North was invited to dedicate them. This was the scholar and statesman Edward Everett of Harvard. He made a good speech—which is still extant: not at all academic, it is full of close strategic analysis and deep historical understanding.

Lincoln was not invited to speak, at first. Although people knew him as an effective debater, they were not sure whether he was capable of making a serious speech on such a solemn occasion. But one of the impressive things about Lincoln's career is that he constantly strove to *grow*. He was anxious to appear on that occasion and to say something worthy of it. (Also, it has been suggested, he was anxious to remove the impression that he did not know how to behave properly—an impression which had been strengthened by a shocking story about his clowning on the battlefield of Antietam the previous year.) Therefore when he was invited he took considerable care with his speech. He drafted rather more than half of it in the White House before leaving, finished it in the hotel at Gettysburg the night before the ceremony (not in the train, as sometimes reported), and wrote a fair copy next morning.

There are many accounts of the day itself, 19 November 1863. There are many descriptions of Lincoln, all showing the same curious blend of grandeur and awkwardness, or lack of dignity, or—it would be best to call it humility. In the procession he rode horseback: a tall lean man in a high plug hat, straddling a short horse, with his feet too near the ground. He arrived before the chief speaker, and had to wait patiently for half an hour or more. His own speech came right at the end of a long and exhausting ceremony, lasted less than three minutes, and made little impression on the audience. In part this was because they were tired, in part because (as eyewitnesses said) he ended almost before they knew he had begun, and in part because he did not speak the Address, but read it, very slowly, in a thin high voice, with a marked Kentucky accent, pronouncing "to" as "toe" and dropping his final R's.

Some people of course were alert enough to be impressed. Everett congratulated him at once. But most of the newspapers paid little attention to the speech, and some sneered at it. The *Patriot and Union* of Harrisburg wrote, "We pass over the silly remarks of the President; for the credit of the nation we are willing . . . that they shall no more be repeated or thought of"; and the London *Times* said, "The ceremony was rendered ludicrous by some of the sallies of that poor President Lincoln," calling his

5

remarks "dull and commonplace." The first commendation of the Address came in a single sentence of the Chicago *Tribune,* and the first discriminating and detailed praise of it appeared in the Springfield *Republican,* the Providence *Journal,* and the Philadelphia *Bulletin.* However, three weeks after the ceremony and then again the following spring, the editor of *Harper's Weekly* published a sincere and thorough eulogy of the Address, and soon it was attaining recognition as a masterpiece.

At the time, Lincoln could not care much about the reception of his words. He was exhausted and ill. In the train back to Washington, he lay down with a wet towel on his head. He had caught smallpox. At that moment he was incubating it, and he was stricken down soon after he reentered the White House. Fortunately it was a mild attack, and it evoked one of his best jokes: he told his visitors, "At last I have something I can give to everybody."

He had more than that to give to everybody. He was a unique person, far greater than most people realize until they read his life with care. The wisdom of his policy, the sources of his statesmanship—these were things too complex to be discussed in a brief essay. But we can say something about the Gettysburg Address as a work of art.[1]

A work of art. Yes: for Lincoln was a literary artist, trained both by others and by himself. The textbooks he used as a boy were full of difficult exercises and skillful devices in formal rhetoric, stressing the qualities he practiced in his own speaking: antithesis, parallelism, and verbal harmony. Then he read and reread many admirable models of thought and expression: the King James Bible, the essays of Bacon, the best plays of Shakespeare. His favorites were *Hamlet, Lear, Macbeth, Richard III,* and *Henry VIII,* which he had read dozens of times. He loved reading aloud, too, and spent hours reading poetry to his friends. (He told his partner Herndon that he preferred getting the sense of any document by reading it aloud.) Therefore his serious speeches are important parts of the long and noble classical tradition of oratory which begins in Greece, runs through Rome to the modern world, and is still capable (if we do not neglect it) of producing masterpieces.

The first proof of this is that the Gettysburg Address is full of quotations—or rather of adaptations—which give it strength. It is partly religious, partly (in the highest sense) political: therefore it is interwoven with memories of the Bible and memories of American history. The first and the last words are Biblical cadences. Normally Lincoln did not say "fourscore" when he meant eighty; but on this solemn occasion he recalled the important dates in the Bible—such as the age of Abraham when his first son was born to him, and he was "fourscore and six years old." Similarly, he did not say there was a chance that democracy might die out: he recalled the

10

[1]For further reference, see W. E. Barton, *Lincoln at Gettysburg* (Indianapolis: Bobbs-Merrill, 1930); R. P. Basler, "Abraham Lincoln's Rhetoric." *American Literature* 11 (1939–40), 167–82; and L. E. Robinson, *Abraham Lincoln as a Man of Letters* (Chicago, 1918).

somber phrasing in the Book of Job—where Bildad speaks of the destruction of one who shall vanish without a trace, and says that "his branch shall be cut off; his remembrance shall perish from the earth." Then again, the famous description of our State as "government of the people, by the people, for the people" was adumbrated by Daniel Webster in 1830 (he spoke of "the people's government, made for the people, made by the people, and answerable to the people") and then elaborated in 1854 by the abolitionist Theodore Parker (as "government of all the people, by all the people, for all the people"). There is good reason to think that Lincoln took the important phrase "under God" (which he interpolated at the last moment) from Weems, the biographer of Washington; and we know that it had been used at least once by Washington himself.

Analyzing the Address further, we find that it is based on a highly imaginative theme, or group of themes. The subject is—how can we put it so as not to disfigure it?—the subject is the kinship of life and death, that mysterious linkage which we see sometimes as the physical succession of birth and death in our world, sometimes as the contrast, which is perhaps a unity, between death and immortality. The first sentence is concerned with birth:

Our *fathers brought forth a new* nation, *conceived* in liberty.

The final phrase but one expresses the hope that

this nation, under God, shall have a *new birth* of freedom.

And that last phrase of all speaks of continuing life as the triumph over death. Again and again throughout the speech, this mystical contrast and kinship reappear: "those who *gave their lives* that that nation might *live,*" "the brave men *living and dead,*" and so in the central assertion that the dead have already consecrated their own burial place, while "it is for us, the *living,* rather to be dedicated . . . to the great task remaining." The Gettysburg Address is a prose poem; it belongs to the same world as the great elegies, and the adagios of Beethoven.

Its structure, however, is that of a skillfully contrived speech. The oratorical pattern is perfectly clear. Lincoln describes the occasion, dedicates the ground, and then draws a larger conclusion by calling on his hearers to dedicate themselves to the preservation of the Union. But within that, we can trace his constant use of at least two important rhetorical devices.

The first of these is *antithesis:* opposition, contrast. The speech is full of it. Listen:

The world will little	*note*		
nor long	*remember*	what	*we say* here
but it can never	*forget*	what	*they did* here

And so in nearly every sentence: "brave men, *living* and *dead*"; "to *add* or *detract*." There is the antithesis of the Founding Fathers and men of Lincoln's own time:

Our *fathers brought forth* a new nation ...

now *we* are testing whether that nation ... can *long endure.*

And there is the more terrible antithesis of those who have already died and those who still live to do their duty. Now, antithesis is the figure of contrast and conflict. Lincoln was speaking in the midst of a great civil war.

The other important pattern is different. It is technically called *tricolon*—the division of an idea into three harmonious parts, usually of increasing power. The most famous phrase of the Address is a tricolon:

government of the people
        by the people
        for the people.
The most solemn sentence is a tricolon:

we cannot dedicate
we cannot consecrate
we cannot hallow   this ground.
And above all, the last sentence (which has sometimes been criticized as too complex) is essentially two parallel phrases, with a tricolon growing out of the second and then producing another tricolon: a trunk, three branches, and a cluster of flowers. Lincoln says that it is for his hearers to be dedicated to the great task remaining before them. Then he goes on.

that from these honored dead

—apparently he means "in such a way that from these honored dead"—

we take increased devotion to that cause.

Next, he restates this more briefly:

that we here highly resolve . . . .

And now the actual resolution follows, in three parts of growing intensity:

that these dead shall not have died in vain

that this nation, under God, shall have a new birth of freedom and that (one more tricolon)

> government of the people
> > by the people
> > for the people
> shall not perish from the earth.

Now, the tricolon is the figure which, through division, emphasizes basic harmony and unity. Lincoln used antithesis because he was speaking to a people at war. He used the tricolon because he was hoping, planning, praying for peace.

No one thinks that when he was drafting the Gettysburg Address, Lincoln deliberately looked up these quotations and consciously chose these particular patterns of thought. No, he chose the theme. From its development and from the emotional tone of the entire occasion, all the rest followed, or grew—by that marvelous process of choice and rejection which is essential to artistic creation. It does not spoil such a work of art to analyze it as closely as we have done; it is altogether fitting and proper that we should do this: for it helps us to penetrate more deeply into the rich meaning of the Gettysburg Address, and it allows us the very rare privilege of watching the workings of a great man's mind.

✎ Topics for Critical Thinking and Writing

1. At the start of his essay, after quoting the opening words of Lincoln's speech, Highet uses a metaphor and a simile: he says that the words "stand at the entrance to the best-known monument," and that "greatness is like granite: it is molded in fire, and it lasts for many centuries." Are these figures of speech effective? Why or why not? How are the two figures related to each other?
2. Analyze the structure of Highet's essay.
3. This essay was a talk given on the radio, presumably to a large general public. Find passages in the essay that suggest oral delivery to an unspecialized audience. How would you describe Highet's tone?
4. It has been suggested that "government of the people, by the people" is redundant; a government *of* the people, it is argued, must be the same as a government *by* the people. Did Lincoln repeat himself merely to get a triad: "of the people, by the people, for the people"? If so, is this a fault? Or can it be argued that "government of the people" really means "government over the people"? If so, what does the entire expression mean?
5. Highet claims that Lincoln was not only a great statesman but also a literary artist. According to Highet, what was Lincoln's training as a literary artist? Highet implies that such training is still available. To what extent has it been available to you? Traditionally, studying "admirable models of thought and expression," including poetry, was an important part of writing

instruction, but it is less common now. Should such study be included in writing courses? Why, or why not?

6. In paragraph 11 Highet points out that "the Gettysburg Address is full of quotations—or rather of adaptations," and he analyzes several examples of Lincoln's adaptations of sources. How is such adaptation different from plagiarism? Or is it?

Francis Pharcellus Church

In 1897 Francis Pharcellus Church, a journalist who wrote for the New York Sun, *wrote a response to a letter by Virginia O'Hanlon, an eight-year-old. Virginia had written:*

> Dear Editor: I am 8 years old. Some of my little friends say there is no Santa Claus. Papa says "If you see it in *The Sun* it's so." Please tell me the truth, is there a Santa Claus?
> Virginia O'Hanlon, 115 West 95th Street

Rising to the challenge, Church produced an essay that is known, or at least known of, even today.

Yes, Virginia, There Is a Santa Claus

Virginia, your little friends are wrong. They have been affected by the skepticism of a skeptical age. They do not believe except [what] they see. They think that nothing can be which is not comprehensible by their little minds. All minds, Virginia, whether they be men's or children's, are little. In this great universe of ours man is a mere insect, an ant, in his intellect, as compared with the boundless world about him, as measured by the intelligence capable of grasping the whole of truth and knowledge.

Yes, Virginia, there is a Santa Claus. He exists as certainly as love and generosity and devotion exist, and you know that they abound and give to your life its highest beauty and joy. Alas! how dreary would be the world if there were no Santa Claus! It would be as dreary as if there were no Virginias. There would be no childlike faith then, no poetry, no romance to make tolerable this existence. We should have no enjoyment, except in sense and sight. The eternal light with which childhood fills the world would be extinguished.

Not believe in Santa Claus! You might as well not believe in fairies! You might get your papa to hire men to watch in all the chimneys on Christmas Eve to catch Santa Claus, but even if they did not see Santa Claus coming down, what would that prove? Nobody sees Santa Claus, but that is no sign that there is no Santa Claus. The most real things in the world are those that neither children nor men can see. Did you ever see fairies dancing on the lawn? Of course not, but that's no proof that they are not there. Nobody can conceive or imagine all the wonders there are unseen and unseeable in the world.

You tear apart the baby's rattle and see what makes the noise inside, but there is a veil covering the unseen world which not the strongest man, nor even the united strength of all the strongest men that ever lived, could tear apart. Only faith, fancy, poetry, love, romance, can push aside that curtain and view and picture the supernal beauty and glory beyond. Is it all real? Ah, Virginia, in all this world there is nothing else real and abiding. No Santa Claus! Thank God! he lives, and he lives forever. A thousand years from now, Virginia, nay, ten times ten thousand years from now, he will continue to make glad the heart of childhood.

Thomas Vinciguerra

On the one hundredth anniversary of the appearance in the New York Sun *of an editorial replying to Virginia O'Hanlon's question about the existence of Santa Claus,* The New York Times *ran the following essay.*

Yes, Virginia, a Thousand Times Yes

It was exactly 100 years ago today when The New York Sun responded to the plaintive inquiry of Virginia O'Hanlon, an 8-year-old whose "little friends" had told her the unthinkable when she returned to school that fall. "Please tell me the truth," Virginia wrote at the urging of her father, a New York City police surgeon and deputy coroner. "Is there a Santa Claus?"

For all who are pure of heart, "Yes, Virginia, there is a Santa Claus" has been the only possible answer since Sept. 21, 1897, when the world learned something about the power of journalism and of the human capacity to believe.

Just try to quote from any other newspaper editorial. The endurance of "Is There a Santa Claus?" seems to suggest that what most readers of editorial pages care about most are ruminations on singular subjects like blizzards or the death of a princess. For such observations can constitute a national gathering of sorts, validating emotions that people want to share but can't quite express.

"'Yes, Virginia' is the ultimate feel-good editorial," said John Tebbel, a former chairman of the New York University journalism department. But "Yes, Virginia"—both the phrase and the editorial—resonates beyond

Dec. 25. Translated into some 20 languages and even set to music, the editorial somehow evokes a universal recognition of mystical affirmation, be it of the painfully obvious or the painfully remote.

The author was Francis Pharcellus Church, a sardonic Columbia College graduate and a veteran writer at *The Sun,* a popular daily notable in those days for its lively writing and human interest features. Mr. Church, whose personal motto was "Endeavor to clear your mind of cant," reportedly "bristled and pooh-poohed" when his editor, Edward P. Mitchell, handed him Virginia's letter and asked him to reply. Yet Mr. Church produced a masterpiece—under deadline, and in fewer than 500 words.

Viewed critically, Mr. Church's magnum opus is a sentimental mix of tautology, syllogism and fantasy. "If I saw it cold," said the author's cousin, Richard Church Thompson of Gaithersburg, Md., "my temptation would be to shorten it up. Every time I read it, I get hung up on the word 'supernal.'" (It means heavenly, by the way.)

But it is precisely because "Yes, Virginia" does not bear close scrutiny that it is a true sleight of rhetorical hand—and, therefore, magical. "What this child is doing is knocking on the door of the adult world and asking to be let in." said Howell Raines, editor of the editorial page of *The New York Times.* "And what this editor is doing is protecting her—and his adult readers."

William David Sloan, a journalism professor at the University of Arkansas, once put it this way in *The Masthead,* the journal of the National Conference of Editorial Writers: "Had he denied Santa Claus, he might have torn down the fanciful world of many youngsters and tampered with the values and traditions many people consider important. Had he affirmed Santa Claus matter-of-factly, he would have contributed no ideas of lasting significance. What Church did was sustain a child's hope while giving her a statement of ideals that are worthwhile for the adult. He did not simply continue a myth. He gave a reason for believing."

The historian Stephen Nissenbaum thinks "Yes, Virginia" is concerned not so much with faith in Santa Claus as with faith in faith. "The late 19th century was a period of vexing religious doubt for many middle-class Americans," Mr. Nissenbaum wrote in "The Battle for Christmas" (Knopf, 1996), "and one characteristic solution was to think that God must exist simply because people so badly needed Him to." When Mr. Church referred to "the skepticism of a skeptical age," Mr. Nissenbaum said in an interview, he was speaking to grown-ups.

"Yes, Virginia" has, of course, outlived its two principals (Mr. Church died in 1906, Virginia in 1971). Come Christmastime, however, the Century Club in Manhattan, of which Mr. Church was a member, and the Gannett Newseum in Rosslyn, Va., will offer retrospective displays.

Could "Yes, Virginia" be written today? Yes, said Stephen Simurda, a journalism professor at the University of Massachusetts in Amherst, but "whether anyone would notice it, sadly, I doubt it. Unless someone bought the rights and made a TV movie."

Bob Haiman, president emeritus of the Poynter Institute for Media Studies in St. Petersburg, Fla., and the chairman of the 1997 Pulitzer Prize jury for editorial writing, said: "Do you suppose there are any 8-year-olds left in America who still believe in Santa Claus? One can only hope. And after all, hope is what good editorial pages are all about.

✎ Topics for Critical Thinking and Writing

1. In a paragraph, try to summarize Church's argument. Then evaluate both his argument and his style.
2. In paragraph 12, Vinciguerra quotes the chairman of the 1997 Pulitzer Prize jury for editorial writing, who asked "Do you suppose there are any 8-year-olds left in America who still believe in Santa Claus?" What is your answer to that question? If you believed in Santa Claus, how old were you when you stopped believing, and how did you feel about that change in you?
3. In paragraph 3 of Church's answer to Virginia, Church says "Not believe in Santa Claus! You might as well not believe in fairies!" It's been a while since we've met anyone of any age who believed in fairies—except, of course, for the Tooth Fairy. Write a paragraph or two on your own experience with the Tooth Fairy. (We would particularly like to know how much money she left per tooth.)
4. If you are not enthralled by Church's letter, write a letter of your own to Virginia. (Ours begins: "Virginia, Grow Up, Please!" You may borrow our beginning, and our attitude, if you like.)
5. Compose an e-mail addressed to your hometown newspaper with a query similar to Virginia's (e.g., Do aliens exist? Do they visit planet earth?) and then, imagining that you are an editor of that newspaper, compose an e-mail with your answer (500 words).

George Orwell

George Orwell (1903–50) was the pen name adopted by Eric Blair, an Englishman born in India. Orwell was educated at Eton, in England, but in 1921 he went back to the East and served for five years as a police officer in Burma. He then returned to Europe, doing odd jobs while writing novels and stories. In 1936 he fought in the Spanish Civil War on the side of the Republicans, an experience reported in Homage to Catalonia *(1938). His last years were spent writing in England.*

Politics and the English Language

Most people who bother with the matter at all would admit that the English language is in a bad way, but it is generally assumed that we cannot by conscious action do anything about it. Our civilization is decadent and our language—so the argument runs—must inevitably share in the general collapse. It follows that any struggle against the abuse of language is a sentimental archaism, like preferring candles to electric light or hansom cabs to aeroplanes. Underneath this lies the half-conscious belief that language is a natural growth and not an instrument which we shape for our own purposes.

Now, it is clear that the decline of a language must ultimately have political and economic causes: it is not due simply to the bad influence of this or that individual writer. But an effect can become a cause, reinforcing the original cause and producing the same effect in an intensified form, and so on indefinitely. A man may take to drink because he feels himself to be a failure, and then fail all the more completely because he drinks. It is rather the same thing that is happening to the English language. It becomes ugly and inaccurate because our thoughts are foolish, but the slovenliness of our language makes it easier for us to have foolish thoughts. The point is that the process is reversible. Modern English, especially written English, is full of bad habits which spread by imitation and which can be avoided if one is willing to take the necessary trouble. If one gets rid of these habits one can think more clearly, and to think clearly is a necessary first step towards political regeneration: so that the fight against bad English is not frivolous and is not the exclusive concern of professional writers. I will come back to this presently, and I hope that by that time the meaning of what I have said here will have become clearer. Meanwhile, here are five specimens of the English language as it is now habitually written.

These five passages have not been picked out because they are especially bad—I could have quoted far worse if I had chosen—but because they illustrate various of the mental vices from which we now suffer. They are a little below the average, but are fairly representative samples. I number them so that I can refer back to them when necessary:

1. I am not, indeed, sure whether it is not true to say that the Milton who once seemed not unlike a seventeenth-century Shelley had not become, out of an experience ever more bitter in each year, more alien [*sic*] to the founder of that Jesuit sect which nothing could induce him to tolerate.

   Professor Harold Laski (Essay in *Freedom of Expression*)

2. Above all, we cannot play ducks and drakes with a native battery of idioms which prescribes such egregious collocations of vocables as the Basic *put up with* for *tolerate* or *put at a loss* for *bewilder*.

   Professor Lancelot Hogben (*Interglossa*)

3. On the one side we have the free personality: by definition it is not neurotic, for it has neither conflict nor dream. Its desires, such as they are, are transparent, for they are just what institutional approval keeps in the forefront of consciousness; another institutional pattern would alter their number and intensity; there is little in them that is natural, irreducible, or culturally dangerous. But *on the other side,* the social bond itself is noticing but the mutual reflection of these self-secure integrities. Recall the

definition of love. Is not this the very picture of a small academic? Where is there a place in this hall of mirrors for either personality or fraternity?

Essay on Psychology in *Politics* (New York)

4. All the "best people" from the gentlemen's clubs, and all the frantic fascist captains, united in common hatred of Socialism and bestial horror of the rising tide of the mass revolutionary movement, have turned to acts of provocation, to foul incendiarism, to medieval legends of poisoned wells, to legalize their own destruction of proletarian organizations, and rouse the agitated petty, bourgeoisie to chauvinistic fervor on behalf of the fight against the revolutionary way out of the crisis.

Communist Pamphlet

5. If a new spirit *is* to be infused into this old country, there is one thorny and contentious reform which must be tackled, and that is the humanization and galvanization of the B.B.C. Timidity here will bespeak canker and atrophy of the soul. The heart of Britain may be sound and of strong beat, for instance, but the British lion's roar at present is like that of Bottom in Shakespeare's *Midsummer Night's Dream*—as gentle as any sucking dove. A virile new Britain cannot continue indefinitely to be traduced in the eyes, or rather ears, of the world by the effete languors of Langham Place, brazenly masquerading as "standard English." When the voice of Britain is heard at nine o'clock, better far and infinitely less ludicrous to hear aitches honestly dropped than the present priggish, inflated, inhibited, school-ma'amish arch braying of blameless bashful mewing maidens!

Letter in *Tribune*

Each of these passages has faults of its own, but, quite apart from avoidable ugliness, two qualities are common to all of them. The first is staleness of imagery; the other is lack of precision. The writer either has a meaning and cannot express it, or he inadvertently says something else, or he is almost indifferent as to whether his words mean anything or not. This mixture of vagueness and sheer incompetence is the most marked characteristic of modern English prose, and especially of any kind of political writing. As soon as certain topics are raised, the concrete melts into the abstract and no one seems able to think of turns of speech that are not hackneyed: prose consists less and less of *words* chosen for the sake of their meaning, and more and more of *phrases* tacked together like the sections of a prefabricated henhouse. I list below, with notes and examples, various of the tricks by means of which the work of prose-construction is habitually dodged:

Dying Metaphors

A newly invented metaphor assists thought by evoking a visual image, while on the other hand a metaphor which is technically "dead" (e.g., *iron resolution*) has in effect reverted to being an ordinary word and can gener-

5

ally be used without loss of vividness. But in between these two classes there is a huge dump of worn-out metaphors which have lost all evocative power and are merely used because they save people the trouble of inventing phrases for themselves. Examples are: *Ring the changes on, take up the cudgels for, toe the line, ride roughshod over, stand shoulder to shoulder with, play into the hands of, no axe to grind, grist to the mill, fishing in troubled waters, on the order of the day, Achilles' heel, swan song, hotbed.* Many of these are used without knowledge of their meaning (what is a "rift," for instance?), and incompatible metaphors are frequently mixed, a sure sign that the writer is not interested in what he is saying. Some metaphors now current have been twisted out of their original meaning without those who use them even being aware of the fact. For example, *toe the line* is sometimes written *tow the line.* Another example is the *hammer and the anvil,* now always used with the implication that the anvil gets the worst of it. In real life it is always the anvil that breaks the hammer, never the other way about: a writer who stopped to think what he was saying would be aware of this, and would avoid perverting the original phrase.

Operators or Verbal False Limbs

These save the trouble of picking out appropriate verbs and nouns, and at the same time pad each sentence with extra syllables which give it an appearance of symmetry. Characteristic phrases are *render inoperative, militate against, make contact with, be subjected to, give rise to, give grounds for, have the effect of, play a leading part (role) in, make itself felt, take effect, exhibit a tendency to, serve the purpose of, etc., etc.* The keynote is the elimination of simple verbs. Instead of being a single word, such as *break, stop, spoil, mend, kill,* a verb becomes *a phrase,* made up of a noun or adjective tacked on to some general-purpose verb such as *prove, serve, form, play, render.* In addition, the passive voice is wherever possible used in preference to the active, and noun constructions are used instead of gerunds (*by examination of* instead of *by examining*). The range of verbs is further cut down by means of the *-ize* and *de-* formations, and the banal statements are given an appearance of profundity by means of the *not un-* formation. Simple conjunctions and prepositions are replaced by such phrases as *with respect to, having regard to, the fact that, by dint of, in view of, in the interests of, on the hypothesis that;* and the ends of sentences are saved from anticlimax by such resounding common-places as *greatly to be desired, cannot be left out of account, a development to be expected in the near future, deserving of serious consideration, brought to a satisfactory conclusion,* and so on and so forth.

Pretentious Diction

Words like *phenomenon, element, individual* (as noun), *objective, categorical, effective, virtual, basic, primary, promote, constitute, exhibit, exploit, utilize, eliminate, liquidate,* are used to dress up simple statements and give an air of scientific impartiality to biased judgments. Adjectives like *epoch-making, epic, historic, unforgettable, triumphant, age-old, inevitable, inexorable, veritable,* are used to dignify the sordid processes of international politics, while writing that aims at glorifying war usually takes on an archaic color, its characteristic words being: *realm, throne, chariot, mailed fist, trident, sword, shield, buckler, banner, jackboot, clarion.* Foreign words and expressions such as *cul de sac, ancien regime, deus ex machina, mutatis mutandis, status quo, gleichschaltung, weltanschauung,* are used to give an air of culture and elegance. Except for the useful abbreviations *i.e., e.g.,* and *etc.,* there is no real need for any of the hundreds of foreign phrases now current in English. Bad writers, and especially scientific, political and sociological writers, are nearly always haunted by the notion that Latin or Greek words are grander than Saxon ones, and unnecessary words like *expedite, ameliorate, predict, extraneous, deracinated, clandestine, subaqueous* and hundreds of others constantly gain ground from their Anglo-Saxon opposite numbers.[1] The jargon peculiar to Marxist writing (*hyena, hangman, cannibal, petty bourgeois, these gentry, lacquey, flunkey, mad dog, White Guard,* etc.) consists largely of words and phrases translated from Russian, German or French; but the normal way of coining a new word is to use a Latin or Greek root with the appropriate affix and, where necessary, the *-ize* formation. It is often easier to make up words of this kind (*deregionalize, impermissible, extramarital, nonfragmentary* and so forth) than to think up the English words that will cover one's meaning. The result, in general, is an increase in slovenliness and vagueness.

Meaningless Words

In certain kinds of writing, particularly in art criticism and literary criticism, it is normal to come across long passages which are almost completely lacking in meaning.[2] Words like *romantic, plastic, values, human, dead, sentimental, natural, vitality,* as used in art criticism, are strictly meaningless, in the sense that they not only do not point to any discoverable object, but are hardly ever expected to do so by the reader. When one critic writes, "The outstanding feature of Mr. X's work is its living quality," while another writes, "the immediately striking thing about Mr. X's work is its peculiar deadness," the reader accepts this as a simple difference of

---

[1]An interesting illustration of this is the way in which the English flower names which were in use till very recently are being ousted by Greek ones, *snapdragon* becoming *antirrhinum, forget-me-not* becoming *myosotis,* etc. It is hard to see any practical reason for this change of fashion: it is probably due to an instinctive turning-away from the more homely word and a vague feeling that the Greek word is scientific.

[2]*Example:* "Comfort's catholicity of perception and image, strangely Whitmanesque in range, almost the exact opposite in aesthetic compulsion, continues to evoke that trembling atmospheric accumulative hinting at a cruel, an inexorably serene timelessness. . . . Wrey Gardiner scores by aiming at simple bull's-eyes with precision. Only they are not simple, and through this contented sadness runs more than the surface bitter-sweet of resignation." (*Poetry Quarterly*)

opinion. If words like *black* and *white* were involved, instead of the jargon words *dead* and *living,* he would see at once that language was being used in an improper way. Many political words are similarly abused. The word *Fascism* has now no meaning except in so far as it signifies "something not desirable." The words *democracy, socialism, freedom, patriotic, realistic, justice,* have each of them several different meanings which cannot be reconciled with one another. In the case of a word like *democracy,* not only is there no agreed definition, but the attempt to make one is resisted from all sides. It is almost universally felt that when we call a country democratic we are praising it: consequently the defenders of every kind of régime claim that it is a democracy, and fear that they might have to stop using the word if it were tied down to any one meaning. Words of this kind are often used in a consciously dishonest way. That is, the person who uses them has his own private definition, but allows his hearer to think he means something quite different. Statements like *Marshal Pétain was a true patriot, The Soviet Press is the freest in the world, The Catholic Church is opposed to persecution,* are almost always made with intent to deceive. Other words used in variable meanings, in most cases more or less dishonestly, are: *class, totalitarian, science, progressive, reactionary, bourgeois, equality.*

Now that I have made this catalogue of swindles and perversions, let me give another example of the kind of writing that they lead to. This time it must of its nature be an imaginary one. I am going to translate a passage of good English into modern English of the worst sort. Here is a well-known verse from *Ecclesiastes:*

> I returned and saw under the sun, that the race is not to the swift, nor the battle to the strong, neither yet bread to the wise, nor yet riches to men of understanding, nor yet favour to men of skill; but time and chance happeneth to them all.

Here it is in modern English:

> Objective consideration of contemporary phenomena compels the conclusion that success or failure in competitive activities exhibits no tendency to be commensurate with innate capacity, but that a considerable element of the unpredictable must invariably be taken into account.

This is a parody, but not a very gross one. Exhibit (3), above, for instance, contains several patches of the same kind of English. It will be seen that I have not made a full translation. The beginning and ending of the sentence follow the original meaning fairly closely, but in the middle the concrete illustrations—race, battle, bread—dissolve into the vague phrase "success or failure in competitive activities." This had to be so, because no modern writer of the kind I am discussing—no one capable of using phrases like "objective consideration of contemporary phenomena"—would ever tabulate his thoughts in that precise and detailed way. The whole tendency of modern prose is away from concreteness. Now

10

analyze these two sentences a little more closely. The first contains forty-nine words but only sixty syllables, and all its words are those of everyday life. The second contains thirty-eight words of ninety syllables: eighteen of its words are from Latin roots, and one from Greek. The first sentence contains six vivid images, and only one phrase ("time and chance") that could be called vague. The second contains not a single fresh, arresting phrase, and in spite of its ninety syllables it gives only a shortened version of the meaning contained in the first. Yet without a doubt it is the second kind of sentence that is gaining ground in modern English. I do not want to exaggerate. This kind of writing is not yet universal, and outcrops of simplicity will occur here and there in the worst-written page. Still, if you or I were told to write a few lines on the uncertainty of human fortunes, we should probably come much nearer to my imaginary sentence than to the one from *Ecclesiastes.*

As I have tried to show, modern writing at its worst does not consist in picking out words for the sake of their meaning and inventing images in order to make the meaning clearer. It consists in gumming together long strips of words which have already been set in order by someone else, and making the results presentable by sheer humbug. The attraction of this way of writing is that it is easy. It is easier—even quicker, once you have the habit—to say *In my opinion it is not an unjustifiable assumption that* than to say *I think.* If you use ready-made phrases, you not only don't have to hunt about for words; you also don't have to bother with the rhythms of your sentences, since these phrases are generally so arranged as to be more or less euphonious. When you are composing in a hurry—when you are dictating to a stenographer, for instance, or making a public speech—it is natural to fall into a pretentious, Latinized style. Tags like *a consideration which we should do well to bear in mind* or *a conclusion to which all of us would readily assent* will save many a sentence from coming down with a bump. By using stale metaphors, similes and idioms, you save much mental effort, at the cost of leaving your meaning vague, not only for your reader but for yourself. This is the significance of mixed metaphors. The sole aim of a metaphor is to call up a visual image. When these images clash—as in *The Fascist octopus has sung its swan song, the jackboot is thrown into the melting pot*—it can be taken as certain that the writer is not seeing a mental image of the objects he is naming; in other words he is not really thinking. Look again at the examples I gave at the beginning of this essay. Professor Laski (1) uses five negatives in fifty-three words. One of these is superfluous, making nonsense of the whole passage, and in addition there is the slip *alien* for *akin,* making further nonsense, and several avoidable pieces of clumsiness which increase the general vagueness. Professor Hogben (2) plays ducks and drakes with a battery which is able to write prescriptions, and while, disapproving of the everyday phrase *put up with,* is unwilling to look *egregious* up in the dictionary and see what it means; (3), if one takes an uncharitable attitude towards it, is simply meaningless: probably one could work out its intended meaning by reading the whole of the article in which it occurs. In (4), the writer knows more or less what he wants to say, but an accumulation of stale phrases chokes him like tea leaves blocking a sink. In (5), words and meaning have almost parted company. People who write in this manner usually have a general emotional meaning—they dislike one thing and want to express solidarity with another—but they are not interested in the detail of what they are saying. A scrupulous writer, in every sentence that he writes, will ask himself at least four questions, thus: What am I trying to say? What words will express it? What image or idiom will make it clearer? Is this image fresh enough to have an effect? And he will probably ask himself two more: Could I put it more shortly? Have I said anything that is avoidably ugly? But you are not obliged to go to all this trouble. You can shirk it by simply throwing your mind open and letting the ready-made phrases come crowding in. They will construct your sentences for you—even think your thoughts for you, to a certain extent—and at need they will perform the important service of partially concealing your meaning even from yourself. It is at this point that the special connection between politics and the debasement of language becomes clear.

In our time it is broadly true that political writing is bad writing. Where it is not true, it will generally be found that the writer is some kind of rebel, expressing his private opinions and not a "party line." Orthodoxy, of whatever color, seems to demand a lifeless, imitative style. The political dialects to be found in pamphlets, leading articles, manifestos, White Papers and the speeches of undersecretaries do, of course, vary from party to party, but they are all alike in that one almost never finds in them a fresh, vivid, homemade turn of speech. When one watches some tired hack on the platform mechanically repeating the familiar phrases—*bestial atrocities, iron heel, bloodstained tyranny, free peoples of the world, stand shoulder to shoulder*—one often has a curious feeling that one is not watching a live human being but some kind of dummy: a feeling which suddenly becomes stronger at moments when the light catches the speaker's spectacles and turns them into blank discs which seem to have no eyes behind them. And this is not altogether fanciful. A speaker who uses that kind of phraseology has gone some distance towards turning himself into a machine. The appropriate noises are coming out of his larynx, but his brain is not involved as it would be if he were choosing his words for himself. If the speech he is making is one that he is accustomed to make over and over again, he may be almost unconscious of what he is saying, as one is when one utters the responses in church. And this reduced state of consciousness, if not indispensable, is at any rate favorable to political conformity.

In our time, political speech and writing are largely the defense of the indefensible. Things like the continuance of British rule in India, the Russian purges and deportations, the dropping of the atom bombs on Japan, can indeed be defended, but only by arguments which are too brutal for most people to face, and which do not square with the professed aims of political parties. Thus political language has to consist largely of euphemism, question-begging and sheer cloudy vagueness. Defenseless villages are bombarded from the air, the inhabitants driven out into the countryside, the cattle machine-gunned, the huts set on fire with incendiary bullets: this is called *pacification*. Millions of peasants are robbed of their farms and sent trudging along the roads with no more than they can carry: this is called *transfer of population* or *rectification of frontiers*. People are imprisoned for years without trial, or shot in the back of the neck or sent to die of scurvy in Arctic lumber camps: this is called *elimination of unreliable elements*. Such phraseology is needed if one wants to name things without calling up mental pictures of them. Consider for instance some comfortable English professor defending Russian totalitarianism. He cannot say outright, "I believe in killing off your opponents when you can get good results by doing so." Probably, therefore, he will say something like this:

> While freely conceding that the Soviet regime exhibits certain features which the humanitarian may be inclined to deplore, we must, I think, agree that a certain curtailment of the right to political opposition is an unavoidable concomitant of transitional periods, and that the rigors which the Russian people have been called upon to undergo have been amply justified in the sphere of concrete achievement.

The inflated style is itself a kind of euphemism. A mass of Latin words falls upon the facts like soft snow, blurring the outlines and covering up all the details. The great enemy of clear language is insincerity. When there is a gap between one's real and one's declared aims, one turns as it were instinctively to long words and exhausted idioms, like a cuttlefish squirting out ink. In our age there is no such thing as "keeping out of politics." All issues are political issues, and politics itself is a mass of lies, evasions, folly, hatred and schizophrenia. When the general atmosphere is bad, language must suffer. I should expect to find—this is a guess which I have not sufficient knowledge to verify—that the German, Russian and Italian languages have all deteriorated in the last ten to fifteen years, as a result of dictatorship.

But if thought corrupts language, language can also corrupt thought. 15 A bad usage can spread by tradition and imitation, even among people who should and do know better. The debased language that I have been discussing is in some ways very convenient. Phrases like *a not unjustifiable assumption, leaves much to be desired, would serve no good purpose, a consideration which we should do well to bear in mind,* are a continuous temptation, a packet of aspirins always at one's elbow. Look back through this essay, and for certain you will find that I have again and again committed the very faults I am protesting against. By this morning's post I have received a pamphlet dealing with conditions in Germany. The author tells me that he "felt impelled" to write it. I open it at random, and here is almost the first sentence that I see: "[The Allies] have an opportunity not only of achieving a radical transformation of Germany's social and political structure in such a way as to avoid a nationalistic reaction in Germany itself, but at the same time of laying the foundations of cooperative and unified Europe." You see, he "feels impelled" to write—feels, presumably, that he has something new to say—and yet his words, like cavalry horses answering the bugle, group themselves automatically into the familiar dreary pattern. This invasion of one's mind by ready-made phrases (*lay the foundations, achieve a radical transformation*) can only be prevented if one is constantly on guard against them, and every such phrase anaesthetizes a portion of one's brain.

I said earlier that the decadence of our language is probably curable. Those who deny this would argue, if they produced an argument at all, that language merely reflects existing social conditions, and that we cannot influence its development by any direct tinkering with words and constructions. So far as the general tone or spirit of a language goes, this may be true, but it is not true in detail. Silly words and expressions have often disappeared, not through any evolutionary process but owing to the conscious action of a minority. Two recent examples were *explore every avenue* and *leave no stone unturned*, which were killed by the jeers of a few journalists. There is a long list of fly-blown metaphors which could similarly be got rid of if enough people would interest themselves in the job; and it should also be possible to laugh the *not un-* formation out of existence,[3] to reduce the amount of Latin and Greek in the average sentence, to drive out foreign phrases and strayed scientific words, and, in general, to make pretentiousness unfashionable. But all these are minor points. The defense of the English language implies more than this, and perhaps it is best to start by saying what it does *not* imply.

To begin with it has nothing to do with archaism, with the salvaging of obsolete words and turns of speech, or with the setting up of a "standard English" which must never be departed from. On the contrary, it is especially concerned with the scrapping of every word or idiom which has outworn its usefulness. It has nothing to do with correct grammar and syntax, which are of no importance so long as one makes one's meaning clear, or with the avoidance of Americanisms, or with having what is called a "good prose style." On the other hand it is not concerned with fake simplicity and the attempt to make written English colloquial. Nor does it even imply in every case preferring the Saxon word to the Latin one, though it does imply using the fewest and shortest words that will cover one's meaning. What is above all needed is to let the meaning choose the word, and not the other way about. In prose, the worst thing one can do with words is to surrender to them. When you think of a concrete object, you think wordlessly, and then, if you want to describe the thing you have been visualizing you probably hunt about till you find the exact words that seem to fit in. When you think of something abstract you

[3] One can cure oneself of the *not un-* formation by memorizing this sentence: *A not unblack dog was chasing a not unsmall rabbit across a not ungreen field.*

are more inclined to use words from the start, and unless you make a conscious effort to prevent it, the existing dialect will come rushing in and do the job for you, at the expense of blurring or even changing your meaning. Probably it is better to put off using words as long as possible and get one's meaning as clear as one can through pictures or sensations. Afterwards one can choose—not simply accept—the phrases that will best cover the meaning, and then switch round and decide what impression one's words are likely to make on another person. This last effort of the mind cuts out all stale or mixed images, all prefabricated phrases, needless repetitions, and humbug and vagueness generally. But one can often be in doubt about the effect of a word or a phrase, and one needs rules that one can rely on when instinct fails. I think the following rules will cover most cases:

1. Never use a metaphor, simile or other figure of speech which you are used to seeing in print.
2. Never use a long word where a short one will do.
3. If it is possible to cut a word out, always cut it out.
4. Never use the passive where you can use the active.
5. Never use a foreign phrase, a scientific word or a jargon word if you can think of an everyday English equivalent.
6. Break any of these rules sooner than say anything outright barbarous.

These rules sound elementary, and so they are, but they demand a deep change of attitude in anyone who has grown used to writing in the style now fashionable. One could keep all of them and still write bad English, but one could not write the kind of stuff that I quoted in those five specimens at the beginning of this article.

I have not here been considering the literary use of language, but merely language as an instrument for expressing and not for concealing or preventing thought. Stuart Chase and others have come near to claiming that all abstract words are meaningless, and have used this as a pretext for advocating a kind of political quietism. Since you don't know what Fascism is, how can you struggle against Fascism? One need not swallow such absurdities as this, but one ought to recognize that the present political chaos is connected with the decay of language, and that one can probably bring about some improvement by starting at the verbal end. If you simplify your English, you are freed from the worst follies of orthodoxy. You cannot speak any of the necessary dialects, and when you make a stupid remark its stupidity will be obvious, even to yourself. Political language—and with variations this is true of all political parties, from Conservatives to Anarchists—is designed to make lies sound truthful and murder respectable, and to give an appearance of solidity to pure wind. One cannot change this all in a moment, but one can at least change one's own habits, and from time to time, one can even, if one jeers loudly enough, send some worn-out and useless phrase—some *jackboot, Achilles' heel, hotbed, melting pot, acid test, veritable inferno* or other lump of verbal refuse—into the dustbin where it belongs.

Topics for Critical Thinking and Writing

1. Revise one or two of Orwell's examples of bad writing.
2. Examine Orwell's metaphors. Do they fulfill his requirements for good writing?
3. Look again Orwell's grotesque revision (paragraph 9) of a passage from the Bible. Write a similar version of another passage from the Bible.
4. Can you recall any occasion when you have used words, in writing or speaking, in a consciously dishonest way? If so, can you explain why, or go further and justify your behavior?
5. In paragraph 2 Orwell says, "Written English is full of bad habits which spread by imitation." Are you aware of having acquired any bad writing habits by imitation? If so, imitation of what or whom?

Nicholas Negroponte

Nicholas Negroponte, born in 1943, holds degrees in architecture from the Massachusetts Institute of Technology, where he now teaches. Among his influential books are The Architecture Machine *and (the source of the following brief essay)* Being Digital *(1995)*

Being Asynchronous

A face-to-face or telephone conversation is real time and synchronous. Telephone tag is a game played to find the opportunity to be synchronous. Ironically, this is often done for exchanges, which themselves require no synchrony whatsoever, and could just as well be handled by non-real-time message passing. Historically, asynchronous communication, like letter writing, has tended to be more formal and less off-the-cuff exchanges. This is changing with voice mail and answering machines.

I have met people who claim they cannot understand how they (and we all) lived without answering machines at home and voice mail at the office. The advantage is less about voice and more about off-line processing and time shifting. It is about leaving messages versus engaging somebody needlessly in online discussion. In fact, answering machines are designed slightly backward. They should not only activate when you are not there or don't want to be there, but they should *always* answer the telephone and give the caller the opportunity to simply leave a message.

One of the enormous attractions of e-mail is that it is not interruptive like a telephone. You can process it at your leisure, and for this reason you may reply to messages that would not stand a chance in hell of getting through the secretarial defenses of corporate, telephonic life.

E-mail is exploding in popularity because it is *both* an asynchronous and a computer-readable medium. The latter is particularly important, because interface agents will use those bits to prioritize and deliver messages differently. Who sent the message and what it is about could determine the order in which you see it—no different from the current secretarial screening that allows a call from your six-year-old daughter to go right through, while the CEO of the XYZ Corporation is put on hold. Even on a busy workday, personal e-mail messages might drift to the top of the heap.

Not nearly as much of our communications need to be contemporaneous or in real time. We are constantly interrupted or forced into being punctual for things that truly do not merit such immediacy or promptness. We are forced into regular rhythms, not because we finished eating at 8:59 p.m., but because the TV program is about to start in one minute. Our great-grandchildren will understand our going to the theater at a given hour to benefit from the collective presence of human actors, but they will not understand the synchronous experiencing of television signals in the privacy of our home—until they look at the bizarre economic model behind it.

5

✎ Topics for Critical Thinking and Writing

1. Rephrase in your own words Negroponte's first sentence. How might his obscure diction be explained or justified?
2. Do you agree with Negroponte that "answering machines should *always* answer the telephone"? Explain.
3. Whom is Negroponte addressing in paragraph 3? Does the attraction of e-mail he cites apply to anyone else? Explain.
4. When did you start to use e-mail? How do you currently use it? What advantages (or disadvantages) do you find in "being asynchronous"?

Robin Lakoff

Robin Lakoff was born in 1943 and educated at Radcliffe College and Harvard University. A professor of linguistics at the University of California at Berkeley, she has been especially interested in the language that women use. The essay that we give here was first published in Ms. *magazine in 1974.*

You Are What You Say

Women's language is that pleasant (dainty?), euphemistic never-aggressive way of talking we learned as little girls. Cultural bias was built into the language we were allowed to speak, the subjects we were allowed to speak about, and the ways we were spoken of. Having learned our linguistic lesson well, we go out in the world, only to discover that we are communicative cripples—damned if we do, and damned if we don't.

If we refuse to talk "like a lady," we are ridiculed and criticized for being unfeminine. ("She thinks like a man" is, at best, a left-handed compliment.) If we do learn all the fuzzy-headed, unassertive language of our sex, we are ridiculed for being unable to think clearly, unable to take part in a serious discussion, and therefore unfit to hold a position of power.

It doesn't take much of this for a woman to begin feeling she deserves such treatment because of inadequacies in her own intelligence and education.

"Women's language" shows up in all levels of English. For example, women are encouraged and allowed to make far more precise discriminations in naming colors than men do. Words like *mauve, beige, ecru, aquamarine, lavender,* and so on, are unremarkable in a woman's active vocabulary, but largely absent from that of most men. I know of no evidence suggesting that women actually *see* a wider range of colors than men do. It is simply that fine discriminations of this sort are relevant to women's vocabularies, but not to men's; to men, who control most of the interesting affairs of the world, such distinctions are trivial—irrelevant.

In the area of syntax, we find similar gender-related peculiarities of speech. There is one construction, in particular, that women use conversationally far more than men: the tag question. A tag is midway between an outright statement and a yes-no question; it is less assertive than the former, but more confident than the latter.

A *flat statement* indicates confidence in the speaker's knowledge and is fairly certain to be believed; a *question* indicates a lack of knowledge on some point and implies that the gap in the speaker's knowledge can and will be remedied by an answer. For example, if, at a Little League game, I have had my glasses off, I can legitimately ask someone else: "Was the player out at third?" A *tag question,* being intermediate between statement and question, is used when the speaker is stating a claim, but lacks full confidence in the truth of that claim. So if I say, "Is Joan here?" I will probably not be surprised if my respondent answers "no"; but if I say, "Joan is here, isn't she?" instead, chances are I am already biased in favor of a positive answer, wanting only confirmation. I still want a response, but I have enough knowledge (or think I have) to predict that response. A tag question, then, might be thought of as a statement that doesn't demand to be

5

believed by anyone but the speaker, a way of giving leeway, of not forcing the addressee to go along with the views of the speaker.

Another common use of the tag question is in small talk when the speaker is trying to elicit conversation: "Sure is hot here, isn't it?"

But in discussing personal feelings or opinions, only the speaker normally has any way of knowing the correct answer. Sentences such as "I have a headache, don't I?" are clearly ridiculous. But there are other examples where it is the speaker's opinions, rather than perceptions, for which corroboration is sought, as in "The situation in Southeast Asia is terrible, isn't it?"

While there are, of course, other possible interpretations of a sentence like this, one possibility is that the speaker has a particular answer in mind "yes" or "no"—but is reluctant to state it baldly. This sort of tag question is much more apt to be used by women than by men in conversation. Why is this the case?

The tag question allows a speaker to avoid commitment, and thereby   10
avoid conflict with the addressee. The problem is that, by so doing, speakers may also give the impression of not really being sure of themselves, or looking to the addressee for confirmation of their views. This uncertainty is reinforced in more subliminal ways, too. There is a peculiar sentence-intonation pattern, used almost exclusively by women, as far as I know, which changes a declarative answer into a question. The effect of using the rising inflection typical of a yes-no question is to imply that the speaker is seeking confirmation, even though the speaker is clearly the only one who has the requisite information, which is why the question was put to her in the first place:

(Q) When will dinner be ready?
(A) Oh . . . around six o'clock . . . ?

It is as though the second speaker was saying, "Six o'clock—if that's okay with you, if you agree." The person being addressed is put in the position of having to provide confirmation. One likely consequence of this sort of speech pattern in a woman is that, often unbeknownst to herself, the speaker builds a reputation of tentativeness, and others will refrain from taking her seriously or trusting her with any real responsibilities, since she "can't make up her mind," and "isn't sure of herself."

Such idiosyncrasies may explain why women's language sounds much more "polite" than men's. It is polite to leave a decision open, not impose your mind, or views, or claims, or anyone else. So a tag question is a kind of polite statement, in that it does not force agreement or belief on the addressee. In the same way a request is a polite command, in that it does not force obedience on the addressee, but rather suggests something be done as a favor to the speaker. A clearly stated order implies a threat of certain consequences if it is not followed, and—even more impolite—implies that the speaker is in a superior position and able to enforce the order. By couching wishes in the form of a request, on the other hand, a speaker implies that if the request is not carried out, only the speaker will suffer; noncompliance cannot harm the addressee. So the decision is really left up to the addressee. The distinction becomes clear in these examples:

Close the door.

Please close the door.

Will you close the door?

Will you please close the door?

Won't you close the door?

In the same ways as words and speech patterns used *by* women undermine her image, those used to *describe* women make matters even worse. Often a word may be used of both men and women (and perhaps of things as well); but when it is applied to women, it assumes a special meaning that, by implication rather than outright assertion, is derogatory to women as a group.

The use of euphemisms has this effect. A euphemism is a substitute for a word that has acquired a bad connotation by association with something unpleasant or embarrassing. But almost as soon as the new word comes into common usage, it takes on the same old bad connotations, since feelings about the things or people referred to are not altered by a change of name; thus new euphemisms must be constantly found.

There is one euphemism for *woman* still very much alive. The word, of course, is *lady. Lady* has a masculine counterpart, namely *gentleman*, occasionally shortened to *gent*. But for some reason *lady* is very much commoner than *gent(leman)*.

The decision to use *lady* rather than *woman*, or vice versa, may considerably alter the sense of a sentence, as the following examples show: 15

   a. A woman (lady) I know is a dean at Berkeley.
   b. A woman (lady) I know makes amazing things out of shoelaces and old boxes.

The use of *lady* in (a) imparts a frivolous, or nonserious, tone to the sentence: the matter under discussion is not one of great moment. Similarly, in (b), using *lady* here would suggest that the speaker considered the "amazing things" not to be serious art, but merely a hobby or an aberration. If *woman* is used, she might be a serious sculptor. To say *lady doctor* is very condescending, since no one ever says *gentleman doctor* or even *man doctor*. For example, mention in the San Francisco *Chronicle* of January 31, 1972, of Madalyn Murray O'Hair as the *lady atheist* reduces her position to that of scatterbrained eccentric. Even *woman atheist* is scarcely defensible: sex is irrelevant to her philosophical position.

Many women argue that, on the other hand, *lady* carries with it overtones recalling the age of chivalry: conferring exalted stature on the person so referred to. This makes the term seem polite at first, but we must also remember that these implications are perilous: they suggest that a "lady" is helpless, and cannot do things by herself.

Lady can also be used to infer frivolousness, as in titles of organizations. Those that have a serious purpose (not merely that of enabling "the ladies" to spend time with one another) cannot use the word *lady* in their titles, but less serious ones may. Compare the *Ladies' Auxiliary* of a men's group, or the *Thursday Evening Ladies' Browning and Garden Society* with *Ladies' Liberation* or *Ladies' Strike for Peace*.

What is curious about this split is that *lady* is in origin a euphemism—a substitute that puts a better face on something people find uncomfortable—for *woman*. What kind of euphemism is it that subtly denigrates the people to whom it refers? Perhaps *lady* functions as a euphemism for *woman* because it does not contain the sexual implications present in *woman:* it is not "embarrassing" in that way. If this is so, we may expect that, in the future, *lady* will replace woman as the primary word for the human female, since *woman* will have become too blatantly sexual. That this distinction is already made in some contexts at least is shown in the following examples, where you can try replacing *woman* with *lady:*

a. She's only twelve, but she's already a woman.
b. After ten years in jail, Harry wanted to find a woman.
c. She's my woman, see, so don't mess around with her.

Another common substitute for *woman* is *girl*. One seldom hears a man past the age of adolescence referred to as a boy, save in expressions like "going out with the boys," which are meant to suggest an air of adolescent frivolity and irresponsibility. But women of all ages are "girls": one can have a man—not a boy—Friday, but only a girl—never a woman or even a lady—Friday; women have girlfriends, but men do not—in a nonsexual sense—have boyfriends. It may be that this use of *girl* is euphemistic in the same way the use of *lady* is: in stressing the idea of immaturity, it removes the sexual connotations lurking in *woman. Girl* brings to mind irresponsibility: you don't send a girl to do a woman's errand (or even, for that matter, a boy's errand). She is a person who is both too immature and too far from real life to be entrusted with responsibilities or with decisions of any serious or important nature.

Now let's take a pair of words which, in terms of the possible relationships in an earlier society, were simple male-female equivalents, analogous to *bull: cow.* Suppose we find that, for independent reasons, society has changed in such a way that the original meanings now are irrelevant. Yet the words have not been discarded, but have acquired new meanings, metaphorically related to their original senses. But suppose these new metaphorical uses are no longer parallel to each other. By seeing where the parallelism breaks down, we discover something about the different roles played by men and women in this culture. One good example of such a divergence through time is found in the pair, *master: mistress.* Once used with reference to one's power over servants, these

20

words have become unusable today in their original master-servant sense as the relationship has become less prevalent in our society. But the words are still common.

Unless used with reference to animals, *master* now generally refers to a man who has acquired consummate ability in some field, normally nonsexual. But its feminine counterpart cannot be used this way. It is practically restricted to its sexual sense of "paramour." We start out with two terms, both roughly paraphrasable as "one who has power over another." But the masculine form, once one person is no longer able to have absolute power over another, becomes usable metaphorically in the sense of "having power over *something*." *Master* requires as its object only the name of some activity, something inanimate and abstract. But *mistress* requires a masculine noun in the possessive to precede it. One cannot say: "Rhonda is a mistress." One must be *someone's* mistress. A man is defined by what he does, a woman by her sexuality, that is, in terms of one particular aspect of her relationship to men. It is one thing to be an *old master* like Hans Holbein,[1] and another to be an *old mistress.*

The same is true of the words *spinster* and *bachelor*—gender words for "one who is not married." The resemblance ends with the definition. While *bachelor* is a neuter term, often used as a compliment, *spinster* normally is used pejoratively, with connotations of prissiness, fussiness, and so on. To be a bachelor implies that one has a choice of marrying or not, and this is what makes the idea of a bachelor existence attractive, in the popular literature. He has been pursued and has successfully eluded his pursuers. But a spinster is one who has not been pursued, or at least not seriously. She is old, unwanted goods. The metaphorical connotations of *bachelor* generally suggest sexual freedom; of *spinster,* puritanism or celibacy.

These examples could be multiplied. It is generally considered a *faux pas,* in society, to congratulate a woman on her engagement, while it is correct to congratulate her fiancé. Why is this? The reason seems to be that it is impolite to remind people of things that may be uncomfortable to them. To congratulate a woman on her engagement is really to say, "Thank goodness! You had a close call!" For the man, on the other hand, there was no such danger. His choosing to marry is viewed as a good thing, but not something essential.

The linguistic double standards holds throughout the life of the relationship. After marriage, bachelor and spinster become man and wife, not man and woman. The woman whose husband dies remains "John's widow"; John, however, is never "Mary's widower."   25

Finally, why is it that salesclerks and others are so quick to call women customers "dear," "honey," and other terms of endearment they really have no business using? A male customer would never put up with it. But

---

[1]German painter of the sixteenth century.

women, like children, are supposed to enjoy these endearments, rather than being offended by them.

In more ways than one, it's time to speak up.

✎ Topics for Critical Thinking and Writing

1. Lakoff's first example of "women's language" (paragraph 4) has to do with colors. She says that women are more likely than men to use such words as *mauve, beige,* and *lavender* not because women see a wider range of colors but because men, "who control most of the interesting affairs of the world," regard distinctions of color as trivial and presumably leave them to the women. How adequate does this explanation seem to you?

2. For a day or so, try to notice if Lakoff's suggestion is correct that women are more inclined than men to use "tag questions" and to use a "rising inflection" with a declarative sentence. Jot down examples you hear, and write an essay of about five hundred words, either supporting or refuting Lakoff.

3. While you are eavesdropping, you might notice, too, whether or not in mixed company women talk more than men. Many men assume that "women talk a lot," but is it true? If, for instance, you spend an evening with an adult couple, try to form an impression about which of the two does more of the talking. Of course this is too small a sample to allow for a generalization; still, it is worth thinking about. If you are at a meeting—perhaps a meeting of a committee with men and women—again try to see whether the males or the females do most of the talking. Try also to see whether one sex interrupts the other more often than the other way around. And try to make some sense out of your findings.

4. In paragraph 11 Lakoff says, "Women's language sounds much more 'polite' than men's," and she implies that this politeness is a way of seeming weak. Do you associate politeness with weakness?

5. The essay originally appeared in *Ms.,* a feminist magazine, rather than in an academic journal devoted to language or to sociology. Why do you suppose she chose *Ms.?* What would you say Lakoff's purpose was in writing and publishing the essay?

6. This essay was first published in 1974. Do you think it is dated? You might begin by asking yourself if women today use "women's language."

Barbara Lawrence

Barbara Lawrence was born in Hanover, New Hampshire, and educated at Connecticut College and New York University. She teaches at the State University of New York, at Old Westbury. This essay first appeared in The New York Times.

Four-letter Words Can Hurt You

Why should any words be called obscene? Don't they all describe natural human functions? Am I trying to tell them, my students demand, that the "strong, earthy, gut-honest"—or, if they are fans of Norman Mailer, the "rich, liberating, existential"—language they use to describe sexual activity isn't preferable to "phony-sounding, middle-class words like 'intercourse' and 'copulate'?" "Cop You Late!" they say with fancy inflections and gagging grimaces. "Now, what is *that* supposed to mean?"

Well, what is it supposed to mean? And why indeed should one group of words describing human functions and human organs be acceptable in ordinary conversation and another, describing presumably the same organs and functions, be tabooed—so much so, in fact, that some of these words still cannot appear in print in many parts of the English-speaking world?

The argument that these taboos exist only because of "sexual hangups" (middle-class, middle-age, feminist), or even that they are a result of class oppression (the contempt of the Norman conquerors for the language of their Anglo-Saxon serfs), ignores a much more likely explanation, it seems to me, and that is the sources and functions of the words themselves.

The best known of the tabooed sexual verbs, for example, comes from the German *ficken,* meaning "to strike"; combined, according to Partridge's etymological dictionary *Origins,* with the Latin sexual verb *futuere;* associated in turn with the Latin *fustis,* "a staff or cudgel"; the Celtic *buc,* "a point, hence to pierce"; the Irish *bot,* "the male member"; the Latin *battuere,* "to beat"; the Gaelic *batair,* "a cudgeller"; the Early Irish *bualaim,* "I strike"; and so forth. It is one of what etymologists sometimes call "the sadistic group of words for the man's part in copulation."

The brutality of this word, then, and its equivalents ("screw," "bang," etc.), is not an illusion of the middle class or a crotchet of Women's Liberation. In their origins and imagery these words carry undeniably painful, if not sadistic, implications, the object of which is almost always female. Consider, for example, what a "screw" actually does to the wood it penetrates; what a painful, even mutilating, activity this kind of analogy suggests. "Screw" is particularly interesting in this context, since the noun, according to Partridge, comes from words meaning "groove," "nut," "ditch," "breeding sow," "scrofula" and "swelling," while the verb, besides its explicit imagery, has antecedent associations to "write on," "scratch," "scarify," and so forth—a revealing fusion of a mechanical or painful action with an obviously denigrated object.

Not all obscene words, of course, are as implicitly sadistic or denigrating to women as these, but all that I know seem to serve a similar purpose: to reduce the human organism (especially the female organism) and human functions (especially sexual and procreative) to their least organic, most mechanical dimension; to substitute a trivializing or deforming resemblance for the complex human reality of what is being described.

Tabooed male descriptives, when they are not openly denigrating to women, often serve to divorce a male organ or function from any significant interaction with the female. Take the word "testes," for example, suggesting "witnesses" (from the Latin *testis*) to the sexual and procreative strengths of the male organ; and the obscene counterpart of this word, which suggests little more than a mechanical shape. Or compare almost any of the "rich," "liberating" sexual verbs, so fashionable today among male writers, with that much-derided Latin word "copulate" ("to bind or join together") or even that Anglo-Saxon phrase (which seems to have had no trouble surviving the Norman Conquest) "make love."

How arrogantly self-involved the tabooed words seem in comparison to either of the other terms, and how contemptuous of the female partner. Understandably so, of course, if she is only a "skirt," a "broad," a "chick," a "pussycat" or a "piece." If she is, in other words, no more than her skirt, or what her skirt conceals; no more than a breeder, or the broadest part of her; no more than a piece of a human being or a "piece of tail."

The most severely tabooed of all the female descriptives, incidentally, are those like a "piece of tail," which suggest (either explicitly or through antecedents) that there is no significant difference between the female channel through which we are all conceived and born and the anal outlet common to both sexes—a distinction that pornographers have always enjoyed obscuring.

This effort to deny women their biological identity, their individuality, their humanness, is such an important aspect of obscene language that one can only marvel at how seldom, in an era preoccupied with definitions of obscenity, this fact is brought to our attention. One problem, of course, is that many of the people in the best position to do this (critics, teachers, writers) are so reluctant today to admit that they are angered or shocked by obscenity. Bored, maybe, unimpressed, aesthetically, displeased, but—no matter how brutal or denigrating the material—never angered, never shocked.

And yet how eloquently angered, how piously shocked many of these same people become if denigrating language is used about any minority group other than women; if the obscenities are racial or ethnic, that is, rather than sexual. Words like "coon," "kike," "spic," "wop," after all, deform identity, deny individuality and humanness in almost exactly the same way that sexual vulgarisms and obscenities do.

No one that I know, least of all my students, would fail to question the values of a society whose literature and entertainment rested heavily on racial or ethnic pejoratives. Are the values of a society whose literature and entertainment rest as heavily as ours on sexual pejoratives any less questionable?

Topics for Critical Thinking and Writing

1. In addition to giving evidence to support her view, what persuasive devices (such as irony, analogy) does Lawrence use? (On irony, see page 872–73; on analogy, see page 868.)

2. Examine your own use or nonuse of four-letter words. How and when did you learn to use them or to avoid using them? If you have reasons to avoid them other than the ones Lawrence provides, what are they? If you do use such words, under what circumstances are you likely to use them? Will Lawrence's analysis persuade you to avoid them altogether? Why or why not?

Malcolm Gladwell

Malcolm Gladwell is a staff writer for The New Yorker. *We reprint another of his essays on page 277.*

Chip Thrills

Anyone who stands on a New York City subway platform on a hot summer day experiences what the historian Edward Tenner has called a rearranging effect. Subway platforms seem as if they ought to be cool places, since they are underground and are shielded from the sun. Actually, they're anything but. Come summer, they can be as much as ten degrees hotter than the street above, in part because the air-conditioners inside subway cars pump out so much hot air that they turn the rest of the subway system into an oven. In other words, we need air-conditioners on subway cars because air-conditioners on subway cars have made stations so hot that subway cars need to be air-conditioned. It's a bit like the definition the Viennese writer karl Kraus famously gave of psychoanalysis: "the disease of which it purports to be the cure."

Not all technological advances result in this kind of problem, of course. But it happens often enough so that when someone comes along making spectacular claims in behalf of a new technology—the way, for example, parents' groups, television executives, and politicians are now jumping up and down in excitement over the so-called V-chip—it's worth asking whether that technology really solves the problem or simply rearranges the hot air from the car to the platform.

The V-chip, as is well known, is the little piece of computer hardware that, by law, will be put inside every new television receiver, beginning perhaps as early as next year. Parents will push the V-chip button on their remote, punch in a password, pull up what looks like an ATM menu of ratings categories, and then program that particular TV set to receive from then on only the shows they deem acceptable. The Motion Picture Association of America has proposed a variation on its age-based movie ratings for the V-chip, while others argue for categories that break down shows by content. The end result, though, is the same: the V-chip will give interested parents a chance to exercise some degree of control over the electronic stranger in their living room. Now, what could be wrong with that?

Well, nothing—at least, for those inside the subway car. But there are at least two potential rearranging effects worth thinking about. One of them results from the fact that the V-chip is likely to increase the amount of sex and violence on television, not decrease it. In the 1992 Cable Act, there is a provision that requires cable operators to take all "patently offensive" sexual programming on their leased-access channels, lump it together on a single channel, and then block that channel from general distribution unless customers specifically ask to receive it. But last June the Supreme Court, in *Denver Area Educational Telecommunications Consortium, Inc., et al. v. Federal Communications Commission, et al.*, struck down that provision. Why? Because the V-chip is on its way, and, as Justice Breyer argued, allowing people to block offensive programming for themselves infringes on free-speech rights far less than having cable operators block it for them. And the networks? No doubt they'll clean up shows aimed at young families in order to avoid getting V-zapped, but for other shows— those targeted at adult audiences—the V-chip removes the need to show any restraint at all.

This is where the rearranging effect comes in. TV is nice and cool for those with a V-chip. But hot, humid TV isn't going away. It's simply being pushed onto people without a V-chip. And who are those people? In the short run, they're people who aren't rich enough to buy a new television set as long as the old one is still working. In the long run, they're parents who don't care what their children watch. This is not an insubstantial group. According to one recent study, somewhere between twenty and twenty-seven per cent of the parents of four- to six-year-olds never restrict their children's viewing hours, never decide what programs they can watch, never change the channel when something objectionable comes on, and never forbid the watching of certain programs. It has apparently never occurred to these parents that television can be a bad influence, and it strains credulity to think that the advent of the V-chip is going to wake them up. Yet their families—mainly lower-income, ill-educated—are the very ones most in need of protection from television violence. Here is a rearranging effect with a vengeance: not only does the V-chip make television worse, it makes television worse precisely for those already most vulnerable to its excesses.

And then there is the second rearranging effect. The V-chip is a response to the increasingly violent content of television programming, but content is only half the story. The second—and largely ignored—

5

problem with television is that children watch too much of it and, as a result, spend less time in creative play, less time interacting with other children, less time reading, and less time doing their homework. Watching television for four or five hours a day is a very bad thing for children, even if every minute of what they watch is brilliant educational programming.

The V-chip addresses the problem of content but not the problem of time. In fact, it's conceivable that for concerned parents the effect of solving the former will be to exacerbate the latter. Over the past thirty years, television has become steadily more violent, and middle-class parents have become steadily more vigilant about monitoring their children's viewing, yet the amount of time children spend watching television has *still* increased, to the point where children under eleven now watch something like thirty hours of TV a week. Soon, thanks to technology, parents will be able to permanently screen out undesirable shows, and will never again have to worry about their children's watching sex and violence and hearing bad language. Parents will be able to relax about content. How much more will viewing time increase now?

This is not to say we shouldn't have a V-chip, any more than we shouldn't air-condition subway cars. The lesson of the subway paradox is simply that if we are going to cool the trains we might give a bit of thought to improving the ventilation of the stations as well; and the lesson of the V-chip is much the same. V-chips will work only if parents can be induced to use them, especially parents not currently convinced of television's dangers. And, now that we are thinking about a V-chip, we should also think about a T-chip—a time chip—to make sure that we aren't simply rearranging the content problem into a viewing-time problem. Past a certain point, after all, the only solution is to turn the damn thing off.

✎ Topics for Critical Thinking and Writing

1. Comment on the title of this essay. Do you find it enticing? clever? suitable? Explain.
2. What is "a rearranging effect."? Evaluate Gladwell's use of the term as a strategy for his argument.
3. In paragraph 2 what attitude toward the V-chip do you discern?
4. What arguments does Gladwell offer against the V-chip? How persuasive do you find them?
5. If you were a parent would you want a V-chip in your television set and, if so, how would you use it? Explain your answers in 500 to 750 words, using TV shows you know and your own experience for evidence.

Edward T. Hall

Edward T. Hall, born in Missouri in 1914, was for many years a professor of anthropology at Northwestern University.

Hall is especially concerned with "proxemics," a word derived from the Latin proximus, *"nearest." Proxemics is the study of people's responses to spatial relationships—for example, their ways of marking out their territory in public places and their responses to what they consider to be crowding. In these pages from his book,* The Hidden Dimension *(1966), Hall suggests that Arabs and Westerners must understand the proxemic customs of each other's culture; without such understanding, other communications between them are likely to be misunderstood.*

Proxemics in the Arab World

In spite of over two thousand years of contact, Westerners and Arabs still do not understand each other. Proxemic research reveals some insights into this difficulty. Americans in the Middle East are immediately struck by two conflicting sensations. In public they are compressed and overwhelmed by smells, crowding, and high noise levels; in Arab homes Americans are apt to rattle around, feeling exposed and often somewhat inadequate because of too much space! (The Arab houses and apartments of the middle and upper classes which Americans stationed abroad commonly occupy are much larger than the dwellings such Americans usually inhabit.) Both the high sensory stimulation which is experienced in public places and the basic insecurity which comes from being in a dwelling that is too large provide Americans with an introduction to the sensory world of the Arab.

Behavior in Public

Pushing and shoving in public places is characteristic of Middle Eastern culture. Yet it is not entirely what Americans think it is (being pushy and rude) but stems from a different set of assumptions concerning not only the relations between people but how one experiences the body as well. Paradoxically, Arabs consider northern Europeans and Americans pushy, too. This was very puzzling to me when I started investigating these two views. How could Americans who stand aside and avoid touching be considered pushy? I used to ask Arabs to explain this paradox. None of my subjects was able to tell me specifically what particulars of American behavior were responsible, yet they all agreed that the impression was widespread among Arabs. After repeated unsuccessful attempts to gain insight into the cognitive world of the Arab on this particular point, I filed it away as a question that only time would answer. When the answer came, it was because of a seemingly inconsequential annoyance.

While waiting for a friend in a Washington, D.C. hotel lobby and wanting to be both visible and alone, I had seated myself in a solitary chair

outside the normal stream of traffic. In such a setting most Americans follow a rule, which is all the more binding because we seldom think about
it, that can be stated as follows: as soon as a person stops or is seated in a
public place, there balloons around him a small sphere of privacy which is
considered inviolate. The size of the sphere varies with the degree of
crowding, the age, sex, and the importance of the person, as well as the
general surroundings. Anyone who enters this zone and stays there is
intruding. In fact, a stranger who intrudes, even for a specific purpose,
acknowledges the fact that he has intruded by beginning his request with
"Pardon me, but can you tell me . . . ?"

To continue, as I waited in the deserted lobby, a stranger walked up to
where I was sitting and stood close enough so that not only could I easily
touch him but I could even hear him breathing. In addition, the dark mass
of his body filled the peripheral field of vision on my left side. If the lobby
had been crowded with people, I would have understood his behavior,
but in an empty lobby his presence made me exceedingly uncomfortable.
Feeling annoyed by this intrusion, I moved my body in such a way as to
communicate annoyance. Strangely enough, instead of moving away, my
actions seemed only to encourage him, because he moved even closer. In
spite of the temptation to escape the annoyance, I put aside thoughts of
abandoning my post, thinking, "To hell with it. Why should I move? I was
here first and I'm not going to let this fellow drive me out even if he is a
boor." Fortunately, a group of people soon arrived whom my tormentor
immediately joined. Their mannerisms explained his behavior, for I knew
from both speech and gestures that they were Arabs. I had not been able
to make this crucial identification by looking at my subject when he was
alone because he wasn't talking and he was wearing American clothes.

In describing the scene later to an Arab colleague, two contrasting pat- 5
terns emerged. My concept and my feelings about my own circle of privacy in a "public" place immediately struck my Arab friend as strange and
puzzling. He said, "After all, it's a public place, isn't it?" Pursuing this line
of inquiry, I found that an Arab thought I had no rights whatsoever by
virtue of occupying a given spot; neither my place nor my body was inviolate! For the Arab, there is no such thing as an intrusion in public. Public
means public. With this insight, a great range of Arab behavior that had
been puzzling, annoying, and sometimes even frightening began to make
sense. I learned, for example, that if A is standing on a street corner and B
wants his spot, B is within his rights if he does what he can to make A
uncomfortable enough to move. In Beirut only the hardy sit in the last row
in a movie theater, because there are usually standees who want seats and
who push and shove and make such a nuisance that most people give up
and leave. Seen in this light, the Arab who "intruded" on my space in the
hotel lobby had apparently selected it for the very reason I had: it was a
good place to watch two doors and the elevator. My show of annoyance,
instead of driving him away, had only encouraged him. He thought he
was about to get me to move.

Another silent source of friction between Americans and Arabs is in an area that Americans treat very informally—the manners and rights of the road. In general, in the United States we tend to defer to the vehicle that is bigger, more powerful, faster, and heavily laden. While a pedestrian walking along a road may feel annoyed he will not think it unusual to step aside for a fast-moving automobile. He knows that because he is moving he does not have the right to the space around him that he has when he is standing still (as I was in the hotel lobby). It appears that the reverse is true with the Arabs who apparently *take on rights to space as they move*. For someone else to move into a space an Arab is also moving into is a violation of his rights. It is infuriating to an Arab to have someone else cut in front of him on the highway. It is the American's cavalier treatment of moving space that makes the Arab call him aggressive and pushy.

Concepts of Privacy

The experience described above and many others suggested to me that Arabs might actually have a wholly contrasting set of assumptions concerning the body and the rights associated with it. Certainly the Arab tendency to shove and push each other in public and to feel and pinch women in public conveyances would not be tolerated by Westerners. It appeared to me that they must not have any concept of a private zone outside the body. This proved to be precisely the case.

In the Western world, the person is synonymous with an individual inside a skin. And in northern Europe generally, the skin and even the clothes may be inviolate. You need permission to touch either if you are a stranger. This rule applies in some parts of France, where the mere touching of another person during an argument used to be legally defined as assault. For the Arab the location of the person in relation to the body is quite different. The person exists somewhere down inside the body. The ego is not completely hidden, however, because it can be reached very easily with an insult. It is protected from touch but not from words. The dissociation of the body and the ego may explain why the public amputation of a thief's hand is tolerated as standard punishment in Saudi Arabia. It also sheds light on why an Arab employer living in a modern apartment can provide his servant with a room that is a box-like cubicle approximately 5 by 10 by 4 feet in size that is not only hung from the ceiling to conserve floor space but has an opening so that the servant can be spied on.

As one might suspect, deep orientations toward the self such as the one just described are also reflected in the language. This was brought to my attention one afternoon when an Arab colleague who is the author of an Arab-English dictionary arrived in my office and threw himself into a chair in a state of obvious exhaustion. When I asked him what had been going on, he said: "I have spent the entire afternoon trying to find the Arab equivalent of the English word 'rape.' There is no such word in Arabic. All my sources, both written and spoken, can come up with no more than an approximation, such as 'He took her against her will.' There is nothing in Arabic approaching your meaning as it is expressed in that one word."

Differing concepts of the placement of the ego in relation to the body   10
are not easily grasped. Once an idea like this is accepted, however, it is possible to understand many other facets of Arab life that would otherwise be difficult to explain. One of these is the high population density of Arab cities like Cairo, Beirut, and Damascus. According to the animal studies described [elsewhere], the Arabs should be living in a perpetual behavioral sink. While it is probable that Arabs are suffering from population pressures, it is also just as possible that continued pressure from the desert has resulted in a cultural adaptation to high density which takes the form described above. Tucking the ego down inside the body shell not only would permit higher population densities but would explain why it is that Arab communications are stepped up as much as they are when compared to northern European communication patterns. Not only is the sheer noise level much higher, but the piercing look of the eyes, the touch of the hands, and the mutual bathing in the warm moist breath during conversation represent stepped-up sensory inputs to a level which many Europeans find unbearably intense.

The Arab dream is for lots of space in the home, which unfortunately many Arabs cannot afford. Yet when he has space, it is very different from what one finds in most American homes. Arab spaces inside their upper middle-class homes are tremendous by our standards. They avoid partitions because Arabs *do not like to be alone.* The form of the home is such as to hold the family together inside a single protective shell, because Arabs are deeply involved with each other. Their personalities are intermingled and take nourishment from each other like the roots and soil. If one is not with people and actively involved in some way, one is deprived of life. An old Arab saying reflects this value: "Paradise without people should not be entered because it is Hell." Therefore, Arabs in the United States often feel socially and sensorially deprived and long to be back where there is human warmth and contact.

Since there is no physical privacy as we know it in the Arab family, not even a word for privacy, one could expect that the Arabs might use some other means to be alone. Their way to be alone is to stop talking. Like the English, an Arab who shuts himself off in this way is not indicating that anything is wrong or that he is withdrawing, only that he wants to be alone with his own thoughts or does not want to be intruded upon. One subject said that her father would come and go for days at a time without saying a word, and no one in the family thought anything of it. Yet for this very reason, an Arab exchange student visiting a Kansas farm failed to pick up the cue that his American hosts were mad at him when they gave him the "silent treatment." He only discovered something was wrong when they took him to town and tried forcibly to put him on a bus to Washington, D.C., the headquarters of the exchange program responsible for his presence in the U.S.

Arab Personal Distances

Like everyone else in the world, Arabs are unable to formulate specific rules for their informal behavior patterns. In fact, they often deny that there are any rules, and they are made anxious by suggestions that such is the case. Therefore, in order to determine how the Arab sets distances, I investigated the use of each sense separately. Gradually, definite and distinctive behavioral patterns began to emerge.

Olfaction occupies a prominent place in the Arab life. Not only is it one of the distance-setting mechanisms, but it is a vital part of a complex system of behavior. Arabs consistently breathe on people when they talk. However, this habit is more than a matter of different manners. To the Arab good smells are pleasing and a way of being involved with each other. To smell one's friend is not only nice but desirable, for to deny him your breath is to act ashamed. Americans, on the other hand, trained as they are not to breathe in people's faces, automatically communicate shame in trying to be polite. Who would expect that when our highest diplomats are putting on their best manners they are also communicating shame? Yet this is what occurs constantly, because diplomacy is not only "eyeball to eyeball" but breath to breath.

By stressing olfaction, Arabs do not try to eliminate all the body's   15
odors, only to enhance them and use them in building human relationships. Nor are they self-conscious about telling others when they don't like the way they smell. A man leaving his house in the morning may be told by his uncle, "Habib, your stomach is sour and your breath doesn't smell too good. Better not talk too close to people today." Smell is even considered in the choice of a mate. When couples are being matched for marriage, the man's go-between will sometimes ask to smell the girl, who may be turned down if she doesn't "smell nice." Arabs recognize that smell and disposition may be linked.

In a word, the olfactory boundary performs two roles in Arab life. It enfolds those who want to relate and separates those who don't. The Arab finds it essential to stay inside the olfactory zone as a means of keeping tab on changes in emotion. What is more, he may feel crowded as soon as he smells something unpleasant. While not much is known about "olfactory crowding," this may prove to be as significant as any other variable in the crowding complex because it is tied directly to the body chemistry and hence to the state of health and emotions. It is not surprising, therefore, that the olfactory boundary constitutes for the Arabs an informal distance-setting mechanism in contrast to the visual mechanisms of the Westerner.

Facing and Not Facing

One of my earliest discoveries in the field of intercultural communication was that the position of the bodies of people in conversation varies with the culture. Even so, it used to puzzle me that a special Arab friend seemed unable to walk and talk at the same time. After years in the United States, he could not bring himself to stroll along, facing forward while talking. Our progress would be arrested while he edged ahead, cutting slightly in front of me and turning sideways so we could see each other. Once in this position, he would stop. His behavior was explained when I learned that for the Arabs to view the other person peripherally is regarded as impolite, and to sit or stand back-to-back is considered very rude. You must be involved when interacting with Arabs who are friends.

One mistaken American notion is that Arabs conduct all conversations at close distances. This is not the case at all. On social occasions, they may sit on opposite sides of the room and talk across the room to each other. They are, however, apt to take offense when Americans use what are to them ambiguous distances, such as the four- to seven-foot social-consultative distance. They frequently complain that Americans are cold or aloof or "don't care." This was what an elderly Arab diplomat in an American hospital thought when the American nurses used "professional" distance. He had the feeling that he was being ignored, that they might not take good care of him. Another Arab subject remarked, referring to American behavior, "What's the matter? Do I smell bad? Or are they afraid of me?"

Arabs who interact with Americans report experiencing a certain flatness traceable in part to a very different use of the eyes in private and in public as well as between friends and strangers. Even though it is rude for a guest to walk around the Arab home eying things, Arabs look at each other in ways which seem hostile or challenging to the American. One Arab informant said that he was in constant hot water with Americans because of the way he looked at them without the slightest intention of offending. In fact, he had on several occasions barely avoided fights with American men who apparently thought their masculinity was being challenged because of the way he was looking at them. As noted earlier, Arabs look each other in the eye when talking with an intensity that makes most Americans highly uncomfortable.

Involvement

As the reader must gather by now, Arabs are involved with each other on   20
many different levels simultaneously. Privacy in a public place is foreign to them. Business transactions in the bazaar, for example, are not just between buyer and seller, but are participated in by everyone. Anyone who is standing around may join in. If a grownup sees a boy breaking a window, he must stop him even if he doesn't know him. Involvement and participation are expressed in other ways as well. If two men are fighting, the crowd must intervene. On the political level, *to fail to intervene* when trouble is brewing is to take sides, which is what our State Department always seems to be doing. Given the fact that few people in the world

today are even remotely aware of the cultural mold that forms their thoughts, it is normal for Arabs to view *our* behavior as though it stemmed from *their* own hidden set of assumptions.

Feelings about Enclosed Spaces

In the course of my interviews with Arabs the term "tomb" kept cropping up in conjunction with enclosed space. In a word, Arabs don't mind being crowded by people but hate to be hemmed in by walls. They show a much greater overt sensitivity to architectural crowding than we do. Enclosed space must meet at least three requirements that I know of if it is to satisfy the Arabs: there must be plenty of unobstructed space in which to move around (possibly as much as a thousand square feet); very high ceilings—so high in fact that they do not normally impinge on the visual field; and, in addition, there must be an unobstructed view. It was spaces such as these in which the Americans referred to earlier felt so uncomfortable. One sees the Arab's need for a view expressed in many ways, even negatively, for to cut off a neighbor's view is one of the most effective ways of spiting him. In Beirut one can see what is known locally as the "spite house." It is nothing more than a thick, fourstory wall, built at the end of a long fight between neighbors, on a narrow strip of land, for the express purpose of denying a view of the Mediterranean to any house built on the land behind. According to one of my informants, there is also a house on a small plot of land between Beirut and Damascus which is completely surrounded by a neighbor's wall built high enough to cut off the view from all windows!

Boundaries

Proxemic patterns tell us other things about Arab culture. For example, the whole concept of the boundary as an abstraction is almost impossible to pin down. In one sense, there are no boundaries. "Edges" of towns, yes, but permanent boundaries out in the country (hidden lines), no. In the course of my work with Arab subjects I had a difficult time translating our concept of a boundary into terms which could be equated with theirs. In order to clarify the distinctions between the two very different definitions, I thought it might be helpful to pinpoint acts which constituted trespass. To date, I have been unable to discover anything even remotely resembling our own legal concept of trespass.

Arab behavior in regard to their own real estate is apparently an extension of, and therefore consistent with, their approach to the body. My subjects simply failed to respond whenever trespass was mentioned. They didn't seem to understand what I meant by this term. This may be explained by the fact that they organize relationships with each other according to closed social systems rather than spatially. For thousands of years Moslems, Marinites, Druses, and Jews have lived in their own villages, each with strong kin affiliations. Their hierarchy of loyalties is: first to one's self, then to kinsman, townsman, or tribesman, coreligionist and/or countryman. Anyone not in these categories is a stranger. Strangers and enemies are very closely linked, if not synonymous, in Arab thought. Trespass in this context is a matter of who you are, rather than a piece of land or a space with a boundary that can be denied to anyone and everyone, friend and foe alike.

In summary, proxemic patterns differ. By examining them it is possible to reveal hidden cultural frames that determine the structure of a given people's perceptual world. Perceiving the world differently leads to differential definitions of what constitutes crowded living, different interpersonal relations, and a different approach to both local and international politics.

✎ Topics for Critical Thinking and Writing

1. According to Hall, why do Arabs think Americans are pushy? And, again according to Hall, why do Arabs not consider themselves pushy?
2. Explain what Hall means by "cognitive world" (paragraph 2); by "ego" (paragraph 10); by "behavioral sink" (in the same paragraph). Then explain, for the benefit of someone who does not understand the terms, how you know what Hall means by each.
3. In paragraph 9 Hall points out that there is no Arabic equivalent of the English word *rape*. Can you provide an example of a similar gap in English or in another language? Does a cultural difference account for the linguistic difference?
4. In paragraph 3 Hall says of a rule that it "is all the more binding because we seldom think about it." Is this generally true of rules? What examples or counterexamples support your view?

Deborah Tannen

Deborah Tannen holds a Ph.D. in linguistics from the University of California, Berkeley, and is an associate professor of linguistics at Georgetown University. She is the author of scholarly articles and books as well as of popular articles in such magazines as New York *and* Vogue. *We reprint a chapter from one of her books,* That's Not What I Meant!

The Workings of Conversational Style

The Meaning Is the Metamessage

You're sitting at a bar—or in a coffee shop or at a party—and suddenly you feel lonely. You wonder, "What do all these people find to talk about that's so important?" Usually the answer is, Nothing. Nothing that's so important. But people don't wait until they have something important to say in order to talk.

Very little of what is said is important for the information expressed in the words. But that doesn't mean that the talk isn't important. It's crucially important, as a way of showing that we are involved with each other, and how we feel about being involved. Our talk is saying something about our relationship.

Information conveyed by the meanings of words is the message. What is communicated about relationships—attitudes toward each other, the occasion, and what we are saying—is the metamessage. And it's metamessages that we react to most strongly. If someone says, "I'm not angry," and his jaw is set hard and his words seem to be squeezed out in a hiss, you won't believe the message that he's not angry; you'll believe the metamessage conveyed by the way he said it—that he is. Comments like "It's not what you said but the way you said it" or "Why did you say it like that?" or "Obviously it's not nothing; something's wrong" are responses to metamessages of talk.

Many of us dismiss talk that does not convey important information as worthless—meaningless small talk if it's a social setting or "empty rhetoric" if it's public. Such admonitions as "Skip the small talk," "Get to the point," or "Why don't you say what you mean?" may seem to be reasonable. But they are reasonable only if information is all that counts. This attitude toward talk ignores the fact that people are emotionally involved with each other and that talking is the major way we establish, maintain, monitor, and adjust our relationships.

Whereas words convey information, how we speak those words— 5 how loud, how fast, with what intonation and emphasis—communicates what we think we're doing when we speak: teasing, flirting, explaining, or chastising; whether we're feeling friendly, angry, or quizzical; whether we want to get closer or back off. In other words, how we say what we say communicates social meanings.

Although we continually respond to social meaning in conversation, we have a hard time talking about it because it does not reside in the dictionary definitions of words, and most of us have unwavering faith in the gospel according to the dictionary. It is always difficult to talk about—even to see or think about—forces and processes for which we have no names, even if we feel their impact. Linguistics provides terms that describe the processes of communication and therefore make it possible to see, talk, and think about them.

This chapter introduces some of the linguistic terms that give names to concepts that are crucial for understanding communication—and therefore relationships. In addition to the concept of metamessages—underlying it, in a sense—there are universal human needs that motivate communication: the needs to be connected to others and to be left alone. Trying to honor these conflicting needs puts us in a double bind. The linguistic concept of politeness accounts for the way we serve these needs and react to the double bind—through metamessages in our talk.

Involvement and Independence

The philosopher Schopenhauer gave an often-quoted example of porcupines trying to get through a cold winter. They huddle together for warmth, but their sharp quills prick each other, so they pull away. But then they get cold. They have to keep adjusting their closeness and distance to keep from freezing and from getting pricked by their fellow porcupines—the source of both comfort and pain.

We need to get close to each other to have a sense of community, to feel we're not alone in the world. But we need to keep our distance from each other to preserve our independence, so others don't impose on or engulf us. This duality reflects the human condition. We are individual and social creatures. We need other people to survive, but we want to survive as individuals.

Another way to look at this duality is that we are all the same—and all different. There is comfort in being understood and pain in the impossibility of being understood completely. But there is also comfort in being different—special and unique—and pain in being the same as everyone else, just another cog on the wheel.

Valuing Involvement and Independence

We all keep balancing the needs for involvement and independence, but individuals as well as cultures place different relative values on these needs and have different ways of expressing those values. America as a nation has glorified individuality, especially for men. This is in stark contrast to people in many parts of the world outside Western Europe, who more often glorify involvement in family and clan, for women and men.

The independent pioneers—and later our image of them—have served us well. The glorification of independence served the general progress of the nation as (traditionally male) individuals have been willing to leave their hometowns—the comfort of the familiar and familial—to find opportunity, get the best education, travel, work wherever they could find the best jobs or wherever their jobs sent them. The yearning for involvement enticed (traditionally female) individuals to join them.

The values of the group are reflected in personal values. Many Americans, especially (but not only) American men, place more emphasis on their need for independence and less on their need for social involvement. This often entails paying less attention to the metamessage level of talk—the level that comments on relationships—focusing instead on the information level. The attitude may go as far as the conviction that only the information level really counts—or is really there. It is then a logical conclusion that talk not rich in information should be dispensed with. Thus, many daughters and sons of all ages, calling their parents, find that their fathers want to exchange whatever information is needed and then hang up, but their mothers want to chat, to "keep in touch."

American men's information-focused approach to talk has shaped the American way of doing business. Most Americans think it's best to "get down to brass tacks" as soon as possible, and not "waste time" in small talk (social talk) or "beating around the bush." But this doesn't work very well in business dealings with Greek, Japanese, or Arab counterparts for whom "small talk" is necessary to establish the social relationship that must provide the foundation for conducting business.

Another expression of this difference—one that costs American   15
tourists huge amounts of money—is our inability to understand the logic behind bargaining. If the African, Indian, Arab, South American, or Mediterranean seller wants to sell a product, and the tourist wants to buy it, why not set a fair price and let the sale proceed? Because the sale is only one part of the interaction. Just as important, if not more so, is the interaction that goes on during the bargaining: an artful way for buyer and seller to reaffirm their recognition that they're dealing with—and that they are—humans, not machines.

Believing that only the information level of communication is important and real also lets men down when it comes to maintaining personal relationships. From day to day, there often isn't any significant news to talk about. Women are negatively stereotyped as frivolously talking at length without conveying significant information. Yet their ability to keep talking to each other makes it possible for them to maintain close friendships. *Washington Post* columnist Richard Cohen observed that he and the other men he knows don't really have friends in the sense that women have them. This may be at least partly because they don't talk to each other if they can't think of some substantive topic to talk about. As a result, many men find themselves without personal contacts when they retire.

The Double Bind

No matter what relative value we place on involvement and independence, and how we express these values, people, like porcupines, are always balancing the conflicting needs for both. But the porcupine metaphor is a little misleading because it suggests a sequence: alternately drawing close and pulling back. Our needs for involvement and independence—to be connected and to be separate—are not sequential but simultaneous. We must serve both needs at once in all we say.

And that is why we find ourselves in a double bind. Anything we say to show we're involved with others is in itself a threat to our (and their) individuality. And anything we say to show we're keeping our distance from others is in itself a threat to our (and their) need for involvement. It's not just a conflict—feeling torn between two alternatives—or ambivalence—feeling two ways about one thing. It's a double bind because whatever we do to serve one need necessarily violates the other. And we can't step out of the circle. If we try to withdraw by not communicating, we hit the force field of our need for involvement and are hurled back in.

Because of this double bind, communication will never be perfect; we cannot reach stasis. We have no choice but to keep trying to balance independence and involvement, freedom and safety, the familiar and the strange—continually making adjustments as we list to one side or the other. The way we make these adjustments in our talk can be understood as politeness phenomena.

Information and Politeness in Talk

A language philosopher, H. P. Grice, codified the rules by which conversation would be constructed if information were its only point: 20

Say as much as necessary and no more.

Tell the truth.

Be relevant.

Be clear.

These make perfect sense—until we start to listen to and think about real conversations. For one thing, all the seeming absolutes underlying these injunctions are really relative. How much is necessary? Which truth? What is relevant? What is clear?

But even if we could agree on these values, we wouldn't want simply to blurt out what we mean, because we're juggling the needs for involvement and independence. If what we mean shows involvement, we want to temper it to show we're not imposing. If what we mean shows distance, we want to temper it with involvement to show we're not rejecting. If we state what we want to believe, others may not agree or may not want the same thing, so our statement could introduce disharmony; therefore we prefer to get an idea of what others want or think, or how they feel about what we want or think, before we commit ourselves to—maybe even before we make up our minds about—what we mean.

This broad concept of the social goals we serve when we talk is called "politeness" by linguists and anthropologists—not the pinky-in-the-air idea of politeness, but a deeper sense of trying to take into account the effect of what we say on other people.

Linguist Robin Lakoff devised another set of rules that describe the motivations behind politeness—that is, how we adjust what we say to take into account its effects on others. Here they are as Lakoff presents them:

1. Don't impose; keep your distance.
2. Give options; let the other person have a say.
3. Be friendly; maintain camaraderie.

Following Rule 3, Be friendly, makes others comfortable by serving their need for involvement. Following Rule 1, Don't impose, makes others comfortable by serving their need for independence. Rule 2, Give options, falls between Rules 1 and 3. People differ with respect to which rules they tend to apply, and when, and how.

To see how these rules work, let's consider a fairly trivial but common conversation. If you offer me something to drink, I may say, "No, thanks," even though I am thirsty. In some societies this is expected; you insist, and I give in after about the third offer. This is polite in the sense of Rule 1, Don't impose. If you expect this form of politeness and I accept on the first offer, you will think I'm too forward—or dying of thirst. If you don't expect this form of politeness, and I use it, you will take my refusal at face value—and I might indeed die of thirst while waiting for you to ask again.

I may also say, in response to your offer, "I'll have whatever you're   25 having." This is polite in the sense of Rule 2, Give options: I'm letting you decide what to give me. If I do this, but you expect me to refuse the first offer, you may still think I'm pushy. But if you expect Rule 3, Be friendly, you may think me wishy-washy. Don't I know what I want?

Exercising Rule 3-style politeness, Be friendly, I might respond to your offer of something to drink by saying, "Yes, thanks, some apple juice, please." In fact, if this is my style of politeness, I might not wait for you to offer at all, but ask right off, "Have you got anything to drink?," or even head straight for your kitchen, throw open the refrigerator door, and call out, "Got any juice?"

If you and I both feel this is appropriate, my doing it will reinforce our rapport because we both subscribe to the rule of breaking rules; not having to follow the more formal rule sends a metamessage: "We are such good friends, we don't have to stand on ceremony." But if you don't subscribe to this brand of politeness, or don't want to get that chummy with me, you will be offended by my way of being friendly. If we have only recently met, that could be the beginning of the end of our friendship.

Of course, these aren't actually rules, but senses we have of the "natural" way to speak. We don't think of ourselves as following rules, or even (except in formal situations) of being polite. We simply talk in ways that seem obviously appropriate at the time they pop out of our mouths—seemingly self-evident ways of being a good person.

Yet our use of these "rules" is not unconscious. If asked about why we said one thing or another in this way or that, we are likely to explain that we spoke the way we did "to be nice" or "friendly" or "considerate." These are commonsense terms for what linguists refer to, collectively, as politeness—ways of taking into account the effect on others of what we say.

The rules, or senses, of politeness are not mutually exclusive. We don't   30 choose one and ignore the others. Rather we balance them all to be appropriately friendly without imposing, to keep appropriate distance without appearing aloof.

Negotiating the offer of a drink is a fairly trivial matter, though the importance of such fleeting conversations should not be underestimated.

The way we talk in countless such daily encounters is part of what constitutes our image of ourselves, and it is on the basis of such encounters that we form our impressions of each other. They have a powerful cumulative effect on our personal and interactive lives.

Furthermore, the process of balancing these conflicting senses of politeness—serving involvement and independence—is the basis for the most consequential of interactions as well as the most trivial. Let's consider the linguistic means we have of serving these needs—and their inherent indeterminacy, which means they can easily let us down.

The Two-Edged Sword of Politeness

Sue was planning to visit Amy in a distant city, but shortly before she was supposed to arrive, Sue called and canceled. Although Amy felt disappointed, she tried to be understanding. Being polite by not imposing, and respecting Sue's need for independence, Amy said it was really okay if Sue didn't come. Sue was very depressed at that time, and she got more depressed. She took Amy's considerateness—a sign of caring, respecting Sue's independence—as indifference—not caring at all, a lack of involvement. Amy later felt partly responsible for Sue's depression because she hadn't insisted that Sue visit. This confusion was easy to fall into and hard to climb out of because ways of showing caring and indifference are inherently ambiguous.

You can be nice to some one either by showing your involvement or by not imposing. And you can be mean by refusing to show involvement—cutting her off—or by imposing—being "inconsiderate." You can show someone you're angry by shouting at her—imposing—or refusing to talk to her at all: the silent activity called snubbing.

You can be kind by saying something or by saying nothing. For example, if someone has suffered a misfortune—failed an exam, lost a job, or contracted a disease—you may show sympathy by expressing your concern in words or by deliberately not mentioning it to avoid causing pain by bringing it up. If everyone takes the latter approach, silence becomes a chamber in which the ill, the bereaved, and the unemployed are isolated.

If you choose to avoid mentioning a misfortune, you run the risk of seeming to have forgotten, or of not caring. You may try to circumvent that interpretation by casting a knowing glance, making an indirect reference, or softening the impact with euphemisms ("your situation"), hedges and hesitations ("your . . . um . . . well . . . er . . . you know"), or apologies ("I hope you don't mind my mentioning this"). But meaningful glances and verbal hedging can themselves offend by sending the metamessage "This is too terrible to mention" or "Your condition is shameful." A person thus shielded may feel like shouting, "Why don't you just say it!?"

An American couple visited the husband's brother in Germany, where he was living with a German girlfriend. One evening during dinner, the girlfriend asked the brother where he had taken his American guests that day. Upon hearing that we had taken them to the concentration camp at

Dachau, she exclaimed in revulsion that that was an awful place to take them; why would he do such a stupid thing? The brother cut off her exclamations by whispering to her while glancing at the American woman. His girlfriend immediately stopped complaining and nodded in understanding, also casting glances at the American, who was not appreciative of their discretion. Instead, she was offended by the assumption that being Jewish is cause for whispering and furtive glances.

Any attempt to soften the impact of what is said can have the opposite effect. For example, a writer recalled the impression that a colleague had written something extremely critical about the manuscript of her book. Preparing to revise the manuscript, she returned to his comments and was surprised to see that the criticism was very mild indeed. The guilty word was the one that preceded the comment, not the comment itself. By beginning the sentence with "Frankly," her colleague sent a metamessage: "Steel yourself. This is going to hurt a lot."

Such layers of meaning are always at work in conversation; anything you say or don't say sends metamessages that become part of the meaning of the conversation.

Mixed Metamessages at Home

Parental love puts relative emphasis on involvement, but as children grow   40
up, most parents give more and more signs of love by respecting their independence. Usually this comes too late for the children's tastes. The teenager who resents being told to put on a sweater or eat breakfast interprets the parent's sign of involvement as an imposition. Although this isn't in the message, the teenager hears a metamessage to the effect "You're still a child who needs to be told how to take care of yourself."

Partners in intimate relationships often differ about how they balance involvement and independence. There are those who show love by making sure the other eats right, dresses warmly, or doesn't drive alone at night. There are others who feel this is imposing and treating them like children. And there are those who feel that their partners don't care about them because they aren't concerned with what they eat, wear, or do. What may be meant as a show of respect for their independence is taken as lack of involvement—which it also might be.

Maxwell wants to be left alone, and Samantha wants attention. So she gives him attention, and he leaves her alone. The adage "Do unto others as you would have others do unto you" may be the source of a lot of anguish and misunderstanding if the doer and the done unto have different styles.

Samantha and Maxwell might feel differently if the other acted differently. He may want to be left alone precisely because she gives him so much attention, and she may want attention precisely because he leaves her alone. With a doting spouse she might find herself craving to be left alone, and with an independent spouse, he might find himself craving attention. It's important to remember that others' ways of talking to you are partly a reaction to your style, just as your style with them is partly a reaction to their style—with you.

The ways we show our involvement and considerateness in talk seem self-evidently appropriate. And in interpreting what others say, we assume they mean what we would mean if we said the same thing in the same way. If we don't think about differences in conversational style, we see no reason to question this. Nor do we question whether what we perceive as considerate or inconsiderate, loving or not, was *intended* to be so.

In trying to come to an understanding with someone who has misinterpreted our intentions, we often end up in a deadlock, reduced to childlike insistence:

"You said so."

"I said no such thing!"

"You did! I heard you!"

"Don't tell me what I said."

In fact, both parties may be sincere—and both may be right. He recalls what he meant, and she recalls what she heard. But what he intended was not what she understood—which was what she would have meant if she had said what he said in the way he said it.

These paradoxical metamessages are recursive and potentially confusing in all conversations. In a series of conversations between the same people, each encounter bears the burdens as well as the fruits of earlier ones. The fruits of ongoing relationships are an ever-increasing sense of understanding based on less and less talk. This is one of the great joys of intimate conversations. But the burdens include the incremental confusion and disappointment of past misunderstandings, and hardening conviction of the other's irrationality or ill will.

The benefits of repeated communication need no explanation; all our conventional wisdom about "getting to know each other," "working it out," and "speaking the same language" gives us ways to talk about and understand that happy situation. But we need some help—and some terms and concepts—to understand why communicating over time doesn't always result in understanding each other better, and why some times it begins to seem that one or the other is speaking in tongues.

Mixed Metamessages across Cultures

The danger of misinterpretation is greatest, of course, among speakers who actually speak different native tongues, or come from different cultural backgrounds, because cultural difference necessarily implies different assumptions about natural and obvious ways to be polite.

Anthropologist Thomas Kochman gives the example of a white office worker who appeared with a bandaged arm and felt rejected because her black fellow worker didn't mention it. The (doubly) wounded worker assumed that her silent colleague didn't notice or didn't care. But the co-worker was purposely not calling attention to something her colleague might not want to talk about. She let her decide whether or not to mention it: being considerate by not imposing. Kochman says, based on his research, that these differences reflect recognizable black and white styles.

An American woman visiting England was repeatedly offended—   50
even, on bad days, enraged—when Britishers ignored her in settings in which she thought they should pay attention. For example, she was sitting at a booth in a railroad-station cafeteria. A couple began to settle into the opposite seat in the same booth. They unloaded their luggage; they laid their coats on the seat; he asked what she would like to eat and went off to get it; she slid into the booth facing the American. And throughout all this, they showed no sign of having noticed that someone was already sitting in the booth.

When the British woman lit up a cigarette, the American had a concrete object for her anger. She began ostentatiously looking around for another table to move to. Of course there was none; that's why the British couple had sat in her booth in the first place. The smoker immediately crushed out her cigarette and apologized. This showed that she had noticed that someone else was sitting in the booth, and that she was not inclined to disturb her. But then she went back to pretending the American wasn't there, a ruse in which her husband collaborated when he returned with their food and they ate it.

To the American, politeness requires talk between strangers forced to share a booth in a cafeteria, if only a fleeting "Do you mind if I sit down?" or a conventional "Is anyone sitting here?" even if it's obvious no one is. The omission of such talk seemed to her like dreadful rudeness. The American couldn't see that another system of politeness was at work. (She could see nothing but red.) By not acknowledging her presence, the British couple freed her from the obligation to acknowledge theirs. The American expected a show of involvement; they were being polite by not imposing.

An American man who had lived for years in Japan explained a similar politeness ethic. He lived, as many Japanese do, in frightfully close quarters—a tiny room separated from neighboring rooms by paper-thin walls. In this case the walls were literally made of paper. In order to preserve privacy in this most unprivate situation, his Japanese neighbors simply acted as if no one else lived there. They never showed signs of having overheard conversations, and if, while walking down the hall, they caught a neighbor with the door open, they steadfastly glued their gaze ahead as if they were alone in a desert. The American confessed to feeling what I believe most Americans would feel if a next-door neighbor passed within a few feet without acknowledging their presence—snubbed. But he realized that the intention was not rudeness by omitting to show involvement, but politeness by not imposing.

The fate of the earth depends on cross-cultural communication. Nations must reach agreements, and agreements are made by individual representatives of nations sitting down and talking to each other—public analogues of private conversations. The processes are the same, and so are the pitfalls. Only the possible consequences are more extreme.

We Need the Eggs

Despite the fact that talking to each other frequently fails to yield the understanding we seek, we keep at it, just as nations keep trying to negotiate and reach agreement. Woody Allen knows why, and tells, in his film *Annie Hall,* which ends with a joke that is heard voice over:

> This guy goes to a psychiatrist and says, "Doc my brother's crazy. He thinks he's a chicken." And the doctor says, "Well, why don't you turn him in?" And the guy says, "I would, but I need the eggs." Well, I guess that's pretty much how I feel about relationships.

Even though intimate as well as fleeting conversations don't yield the perfect communication we crave—and we can see from past experience and from the analysis presented here that they can't—we still keep hoping and trying because we need the eggs of involvement and independence. The communication chicken can't give us these golden eggs because of the double bind: Closeness threatens our lives as individuals, and our real differences as individuals threaten our needs to be connected to other people.

But because we can't step out of the situation—the human situation—we keep trying to balance these needs. We do it by not saying exactly what we mean in our messages, while at the same time negotiating what we mean in metamessages. Metamessages depend for their meaning on subtle linguistic signals and devices.

Notes

[The page references have been changed to accord with pages in *The Little, Brown Reader,* 8th ed., and the bibliographic citations have been amplified where necessary.]

> pp. 597, 600. The terms *metamessage* and *double bind* are found in Gregory Bateson, *Steps to an Ecology of Mind* (1972). For Bateson, a double bind entailed contradictory orders at different levels: the message and metamessage conflict. I use the term, as do other linguists (for example, Scollon, "The Rythmic Integration of Ordinary Talk," in *Analyzing Discourse: Text and Talk,* Deborah Tannen, ed. [1981]), simply to describe the state of receiving contradictory orders without being able to step out of the situation.

p. 599. I am grateful to Pamela Gerloff for bringing to my attention Bettelheim's reference (in *Surviving* [1979]) to Schopenhauer's porcupine metaphor.

p. 599. Mary Catherine Bateson, *With a Daughters Eye: A Memoir of Margaret Mead and Gregory Bateson* (1984), discusses G. Bateson's idea that living systems (biological processes as well as human interaction) never achieve a static state of balance, but achieve balance only as a series of adjustments within a range.

p. 601. For his conversational maxims see H. P. Grice, "Logic and Conservation," rptd. in *Syntax and Semantics*, vol. 3, *Speech Acts*, eds. Peter Cole and Jerry Morgan (1975).

p. 601. Lakoff's original statement of the rules of politeness is in Lakoff, "The Logic of Politeness, or Minding Your P's and Q's," *Papers from the Ninth Regional Meeting of the Chicago Linguistics Society* (1973). She also presents this system in the context of discussing male/female differences (Lakoff, *Language and Woman's Place* [1975]). Penelope Brown and Stephen Levinson, "Universals in Language Usage: Politeness Phenomena," in *Questions and Politeness*, ed. Esther Goody (1978), provide an extended and formalized discussion of politeness phenomena.

p. 606. Thomas Kochman presents an extended analysis of *Black and White Styles in Conflict* (1981).

p. 607. The quotation from *Annie Hall* is taken from the screenplay by Woody Allen and Marshall Brickman in *Four Films of Woody Allen* (NY: Random House, 1982).

✎ Topics for Critical Thinking and Writing

1. Tannen begins this chapter using the second person ("You're sitting at a bar—or in a coffee shop or at a party—and suddenly you feel lonely. You wonder . . ."), a usage often prohibited in high school English classes and textbooks. How well do you think it works here? Try to make the same point without using the second person. *Have* you made the same point? What has been left out?

2. How does Tannen define *metamessages*? The word will not appear in most dictionaries, but we can probably guess what it means, even without Tannen's explanation. What does *meta* usually mean as a prefix to a word? (Most dictionaries do define *meta* as a prefix.)

3. Why, according to Tannen, has the word *metamessages* been invented? What other linguistic terms does she introduce, and what do they mean?

4. What is the example of porcupines introduced to explain? Why do you suppose it is easier to remember the example than to remember what it explains?

5. In paragraph 11, Tannen says "individuals as well as cultures place different relative values" on the "needs for involvement and independence." In the same paragraph and in the next several paragraphs, she says that Americans glorify independence and she offers an historical explanation of the glorification of independence and other values that flow from it. What does she assume here about "Americans," American culture, and American history?
6. In paragraph 16, Tannen contrasts women talking to women and men talking to men. What does she *assume* here, in addition to what she says, about the differences? On the whole, do you agree with her about women's talk and men's talk?
7. In paragraphs 47–53 Tannen talks about misinterpretations between persons of different cultural backgrounds. If possible, provide an example from your own experience.
8. Write an essay or a journal entry analyzing an encounter which illustrates the "double bind," a "politeness phenomenon," or "mixed metamessages," as Tannen defines these terms and situations. Or summarize this chapter in 750 words.

Steven Pinker

Steven Pinker, professor of brain and cognitive sciences at the Massachusetts Institute of Technology, is the author of The Language Instinct *(1994). We reprint an essay that originally appeared in* The New York Times, *5 April 1994.*

The Game of the Name

The *Los Angeles Times*'s new "Guidelines on Racial and Ethnic Identification," for its writers and editors, bans or restricts some 150 words and phrases such as "birth defect," "Chinese fire drill," "crazy," "dark continent," "stepchild," "WASP" and "to welsh."

Defying such politically correct sensibilities, *The Economist* allows the use of variants of "he" for both sexes (as in "everyone should watch his language"), and "crippled" for disabled people.

One side says that language insidiously shapes attitudes and that vigilance against subtle offense is necessary to eliminate prejudice. The other bristles at legislating language, seeing a corrosion of clarity and expressiveness at best, and thought control at worst, changing the way reporters render events and opinions.

Both arguments make assumptions about language and how it relates to thoughts and attitudes—a connection first made in 1946 by George Orwell in his essay "Politics and the English Language," which suggested that euphemisms, clichés and vague writing could be used to reinforce orthodoxy and defend the indefensible. We understand language and thought better than we did in Orwell's time, and our discoveries offer insights about the P.C. controversy.

First, words are not thoughts. Despite the appeal of the theory that   5
language determines thought, no cognitive scientist believes it. People coin new words, grapple for *le mot juste*[1], translate from other languages and ridicule or defend P.C. terms. None of this would be possible if the ideas expressed by words were identical to the words themselves. This should alleviate anxiety on both sides, reminding us that we are talking about style manuals, not brain programming.

Second, words are arbitrary. The word "duck" does not look, walk or quack like a duck, but we all know it means duck because we have memorized an arbitrary association between a sound and a meaning.

Some words can be built out of smaller pieces and their meanings can be discerned by examining how the pieces are arranged (a dishwasher washes dishes), but even complex words turn opaque, and people become oblivious to the logic of their derivation, memorizing them as arbitrary symbols. (Who last thought of "breakfast" as "breaking a fast"?)

The Los Angeles Times style manual seems to assume that readers are reflexive etymologists; for it bans "invalid" (literally "not valid" and thus an offensive reference to a disabled person), "New World" (ignores the indigenous cultures that preceded Columbus's voyage) and "Dutch treat" (offensive, presumably, to Netherlanders). But I doubt if Americans associate the dozen-odd idioms in which Dutch means "ersatz" ("Dutch uncle," "Dutch oven") with the Dutch; presumably, the sting has worn off in the three centuries since the English coined such terms to tweak their naval rivals.

The bewildering feature of political correctness is the mandated replacement of formerly unexceptionable terms by new ones: "Negro" by "black" by "African-American"; "Spanish-American" by "Hispanic" by "Latino"; "slum" by "ghetto" by "inner city" by, according to *The Los Angeles Times*, "slum" again.

How should a thoughtful person react to this carousel? Respect means   10
treating people as they wish to be treated, beginning with names. That is why there is a clear need for guidelines. One wonders, though, why *The Los Angeles Times*'s style panel apparently did not consult those it defends. Many deaf people insist on being called "deaf," not "individuals who cannot hear," and as one who was taught to revere the Wailing Wall, I was surprised to learn that the term is "highly offensive" rather than merely obsolete.

But if users of new ethnic terms have responsibilities, so do those who promulgate the terms. What are their motives? What are the effects?

Occasionally, neologisms are defended with some semantic rationale: "black" emphasized parity with the corresponding "white." "Native

---

[1]*Le mot juste,* the most suitable word.

American" reminds us of who was here first and eschews the inaccurate European label "Indian." But when new terms replace ones that had been justified in their own day with equal moral force and when offensive and sanctioned terms are near-synonyms—"colored people," "people of color"; "Afro-American," "African-American"; Negro (Spanish for "black"), "black"—something else must be driving the process.

To a linguist, the phenomenon is familiar: the euphemism treadmill. People invent new "polite" words to refer to emotionally laden or distasteful things, but the euphemism becomes tainted by association and the new one that must be found acquires its own negative connotations.

"Water closet" becomes "toilet" (originally a term for any body care, as in "toilet kit"), which becomes "bathroom," which becomes "rest room," which becomes "lavatory." "Garbage collection" turns into "sanitation," which turns into "environmental services."

The euphemism treadmill shows that concepts, not words, are in charge: give a concept a new name, and the name becomes colored by the concept; the concept does not become freshened by the name. (We will know we have achieved equality and mutual respect when names for minorities stay put.) 15

People learn a word by witnessing other people using it, so when they use a word, they provide a history of their reading and listening. Using the latest term for a minority often shows not sensitivity but subscribing to the right magazines or going to the right cocktail parties.

Shifts in terms have an unfortunate side effect. Many people who don't have a drop of malice or prejudice but happen to be older or distant from university, media and government spheres find themselves tainted as bigots for innocently using passé terms like "Oriental" or "crippled." Arbiters of the changing linguistic fashions must ask themselves whether this stigmatization is really what they set out to accomplish.

Topic for Critical Thinking and Discussion

In paragraph 8 Pinker expresses the opinion that because three centuries have passed since the English used the term *Dutch* to refer to something that is not quite the real thing, the term is no longer offensive. Do you suppose that an American of Dutch ancestry is bothered by such a term as *Dutch oven* (a heavy pot with a cover)? In any case, does the length of time since a phrase was originated have anything to do with whether the phrase is offensive today? Explain.

Richard A. Hawley

Richard Hawley was born in Chicago in 1945 and was educated at Middlebury College, Cambridge University, and Case Western Reserve University. Since 1968 he has taught at University School, Hunting Valley, Ohio, where he is now the headmaster. In addition to writing books on adolescence and issues in teaching, Hawley has written a half-dozen works of fiction and nonfiction, two volumes of poetry, and an opera libretto.

Television and Adolescents
A Teacher's View

Ever since its novelty wore off in the fifties, we have all known, really, that television in its commercial form wasn't up to much good. This isn't to say that millions of people don't still depend on it, but dependency is hardly a sign of virtue. Except for Marshall McLuhan's grab-bag theoretics, few claims have been advanced for the improving effects of television. In fact, recently there has been a flurry of publishing activity, most notably Marie Winn's *The Plug-in Drug,* about television as a cause of downright mental erosion. But what I think Marie Winn and others need is a concrete, closely observed, and intensely felt illustration of the larger thesis. That's what I offer here.

Television has a way of intruding into our lives, and last year it intruded into my life and into the life of the school where I work in a way that many of us there will never forget. We had all taken our seats for morning assembly. The usual announcements were read, after which the morning's senior speaker was introduced. Like many independent schools, ours requires each senior to address the student body in some manner before he graduates. Since public speaking is not a widely distributed gift these days, the senior speeches are infrequently a source of much interest or intentional amusement.

As the curtains parted, we could see that the speaker had opted for a skit. On the stage were a covered table and a number of cooking implements. Out stepped the speaker wearing an apron and chef's hat, which very quickly established that he was going to satirize one of my colleagues who has a national reputation as a gourmet chef. Since this colleague is also a man who can take a joke, the prospects for the skit seemed bright. But not for long.

At first, I think almost all of us pretended that we didn't hear, that we were making too much of certain, possibly accidental, double entendres. But then came the direct statements and a few blatant physical gestures. Then it was clear! This boy was standing before five hundred of us making fun of what he suggested at some length was the deviant sexual nature of one of his teachers. The response to this was at first stupefaction, then some outbursts of laughter (the groaning kind of laughter that says, "I don't believe you said that"), then a quieting, as the speech progressed, to periodic oohs (the kind that say, "You *did* say that, and you're in for it").

When he had finished, there was a nearly nauseating level of tension afloat. As the students filed off to class, I made my way backstage to find the speaker. It had by now dawned on him that he had done something wrong, even seriously wrong. We met in my office.

5

He expressed remorse at having offended a teacher whom he said he particularly liked. (Before the conference I had checked briefly with the teacher and found him badly flustered and deeply hurt.) The remorse was, I felt, genuine. But something was decidedly missing in the boy's explanation of how he came to think that such a presentation might, under any circumstances, have been appropriate. He hadn't, he admitted, really thought about it, and some of his friends thought the idea was funny, and, well, he didn't know. When it occurred to him that serious school action was in the offing, he protested that in no way had he intended the sexual references to be taken seriously—they were, you know, a joke.

I pointed out to him that the objects of such jokes have no way to respond: To ignore the insinuation might affirm its validity; on the other hand, to object vigorously would draw additional attention to the offense and sustain the embarrassment connected with it. I pointed out further that sometimes innocent parties *never* regain their stature after being offended in this manner, and that the injured party was, at the very least, in for a terrible day of school.

The boy became reflective and said, "Was it *that* bad? You can see worse on 'Saturday Night Live'." I told him I doubted this, but if it were true, and were I in a position to judge, I would be in favor of expelling "Saturday Night Live" from the air. He left the office, and subsequently endured the appropriate consequences.

For my part, I resolved to turn on "Saturday Night Live," and when I did, I realized the student had spoken truly. The show's quick-succession, absurdist comedy spots depended for their appeal on establishing an almost dangerous sense of inappropriateness: exactly that sense created by our senior speaker. To me, for some years a lapsed viewer, it seemed that both the variety and specificity of sexual innuendo had developed considerably since, say, the once daring Smothers Brothers show of the sixties. What struck me more, however, was how many punch lines and visual gags depended on suddenly introducing the idea of injury or violent death.

I happened to tune in the night a funny caption was put over the documentary shot of Middle Eastern political partisans being dragged to death behind an automobile. Was this funny? I asked my students. They said it was "sick" and laughed. Does this kind of fun trivialize crisis? Trivialize cruelty? Inure us to both? Or is it, you know, a joke? 10

The right things were said, I think, to our students about the boy's speech. But I can't say the situation improved. Not more than a couple of weeks later, a speaker garbed in a woman's tennis dress took the podium and began to talk humorously about the transsexual tennis player Renee Richards. I can't think of a subject harder for an adolescent to discuss before an adolescent audience. Rarely noted for their confidence and breadth of vision in matters of human sexuality, adolescents are unlikely to be objective, sympathetic, or (let me tell you) funny about so disturbing a phenomenon as sex change. This particular boy, whose inflection is very flat and whose normal countenance is especially stony, managed to convey almost a sense of bitterness in making his string of insulting and, in his reference to genitals and to menstruation, awfully tasteless cracks.

So there it was again: the inappropriateness, the tension. This time the injured party was remote from our particular world, so the hastily arranged conference with the boy turned on general considerations of taste and judgment. This time, however, the speaker was recalcitrant: We could disapprove of his speech and discipline him if we chose, but we ought to know that we could hear the same thing on television.

At that moment something clicked for me. Not only did my brief exposure to "Saturday Night Live" convince me that, yes, I would hear the same thing on television, but I was suddenly struck with the realization that he was using television as an arbiter of taste—that is, *as an arbiter of good taste.* I began to see in this premise a common ground upon which he and I could at least argue. Both of us were in agreement that what is broadcast over television ought to be acceptable; our point of disagreement was his feeling that broadcasting something over television *made* it acceptable. Alarming as such a feeling is to me, it is not hard to see how it has developed over the past few decades.

Until the middle sixties, with the exception of the very earthiest plays and novels, the values of home and school and the values of the popular culture were fairly continuous; if anything, radio, television, and motion pictures were more staid than real life. Of course, all this would change very quickly—not because change was requested or even consented to, but because it wasn't, perhaps couldn't be, resisted. And suddenly there it all was at once: the most embarrassing expletives as common speech; every imaginable kind of sexual coupling depicted in ever-increasing candor; obsessively specific wounds, mutilations.

These formerly unacceptable kinds of stimulation made their way   15
more easily into the relatively insulated world of print and film than they did into the more communal world of the television set. Television is typically viewed in homes, and what is communally seen and heard must be communally integrated, or there will be friction. Since American households—set-holds?—share this communal experience for an estimated two to seven hours per day, the potential for friction is considerable. This is why, on grounds of taste, criticism of television programming tends to be more bitter and more relentless than criticism of books and films.

Television foes and partisans alike continue to advise, with some reason, that those who object to certain programs ought not to watch them. But given the impossibility of monitoring the set at all hours, control over the amount and quality of viewing is difficult to maintain even in principled, surveillant households. Too, some viewers will insist on being their brother's keeper. Not everyone who is convinced that what is beaming over the national airwaves is inhumane, unscrupulous, or scurrilous is going to fight to the death for the networks' right to be so.

For many people, television is no longer on the polite side of real life. This is an obvious observation about a novel development, one whose consequences are only just dawning on us. A realist or an existentialist may argue that the unflappably suburban world of "Father Knows Best" revealed none of the complex, ambivalent, and often irrational forces at work in real families: But it is hard to argue that "Father Knows Best" in any way *contributed* to those dark forces. On the contrary, it is possible to argue—although one hesitates to carry it too far—that the theme of Father Knowing Best serves as a psychologically soothing backdrop to the prickly dynamics of real family life. And while today's most highly rated shows suggest that the prevailing seventies' theme is Nobody Knows Anything, there are still apparently enough viewers who like Father Knowing Best to support series like "The Waltons" and "Little House on the Prairie."

Sometimes the theme is compromised in a typical seventies' manner, of which "James at 16" provides a good example: The parents are cast very much in the Robert Young–Jane Wyatt mold, but their son James is, to borrow a phrase, kind of now. By far the most interesting thing he did was to lose his virginity on prime time. The fifteen-going-on-sixteen-year-old boys I work with, many of them at least as sophisticated as James, typically hold on to their virginity a bit longer, until the disposition of their sexual feelings is under surer control. The best clinical evidence maintains that the process of bringing newly emergent sexuality under control is *inherently* delicate and troublesome. James' television plunge planted the anxiety-provoking notion in the mind of the adolescent viewer that he was sexually lagging behind not only the precocious kid down the block, but the Average American Boy character of James. (One was allowed to be less anxious when Father Knew Best.)

Why shouldn't television make people anxious? say the producers of programs that make people anxious. After all, the *world* is anxious. (An awfully self-serving position: Programs that arouse anxiety are relevant; those that don't are enjoyable.) Before long, this line of argument begins to lay claim that programs which bring up irritating subjects in an irritating manner are performing a valuable social mission. Norman Lear, the producer of comedies such as "All in the Family" and "Maude," makes such a claim. According to the Lear formula, a controversial topic will be raised, tossed around for laughs, then either discarded or resolved. Resolution occurs when one of the characters tolerates or forgives the controversial person or practice, while some other character, usually a combination of lovable old coot and ass, does not.

As many critics have pointed out, this is only apparent resolution. 20
Nothing much really happens to a racial or sexual conflict when it is laughed at (a device that is supposed to soften outright slurring and stereotyping), discarded, tolerated, or forgiven. The idea that "if we can

joke about it this way, we have taken a humanitarian stride" is mistaken. There is plenty of evidence, particularly among the student population, that, for one thing, race relations are more strained today than they were a decade ago. No one would want to claim that racism among youth disappeared during the politically active sixties; however, a claim can be made that when a student was confronted then with having made a racial slur, he seemed to be aware of having violated a standard.

Who is to say that Archie Bunker hath no sting? More and more television comedians, in the manner of Don Rickles, seek *only* to sting. It is really an empirical question, not a matter of taste, whether or not it is harmless, much less healing, to denigrate everybody, including oneself. A hit song by Randy Newman insults small people: this is no parody of unkindness or bigotry, but the real thing. My students understand it perfectly and parrot it enthusiastically. Rebuked, they grimace in exasperation. Nothing in their youthful experience tells them that bigotry is a sign of cultural regression ("It isn't bigotry; it's, you know, a joke"). They prefer to see whatever wicked delights crop up in the media as a progressive casting off of prudish inhibitions. According to such a view, progress is whatever happens next.

Toleration of the intolerable is always worrying, but it is especially so when it takes place among the young, in whom we want to invest so much hope. Tolerating the intolerable is part of a dynamic, not a static, process; the intolerable, when it is nurtured, grows.

Which brings me back to the senior speeches. Two so thoroughly inappropriate presentations in a single year represented a high count for us, so we were not ready, at least I wasn't, for the third.

This time the talk was about a summer spent working on a ranch, and the format was that of a commentary with slides. No apparent harm in this, but there were a number of factors working against the speech's success. The first was that the speaker was renowned for being a card, a reputation the welcoming ovation insisted he live up to. Second, he had not adequately rehearsed the projection of the slides, so that they tended to appear out of order and askew, the effect of which was to provide a subtextual comedy of visual non sequiturs. Third, he chose to capitalize on the audience's nearly unrestrained hilarity by playing up certain questionable references.

The speaker made a fairly good, not too inappropriate crack about a   25 slide which depicted a bull mounting a cow—"Sometimes the corrals get so crowded we have to stack the cattle on top of one another." But he chose to exploit his references to the gelding of bulls. There were, in all, four jokey and brutal evocations of this process which served to keep the image of bull genitalia before our minds for quite a few minutes. Since laughter had already been spent, the castration jokes were met with a kind of nervous applause. Bolstered by this, the speaker closed with a coda to the effect that he would be available after assembly to anybody who wanted tips on "cutting meat."

Since I happened to be in charge that day, I sent him home. It seemed to me, in light of the various reprisals and forewarnings connected with the previous speeches, that this particular performance, though perhaps less offensive in its specific references than the other two, ought to be the last straw. The speaker had clearly exceeded anything required by either schoolboy or cowboy saltiness. He had created an anything-goes atmosphere, and then he had let it go—for which he was applauded. "That was great!" said the boy next to me on the way out of the auditorium.

That morning and afterward scores of students, most, but not all, of them civil, hastened to let me know that they felt it was unfair to have sent the speaker home. Not one of them failed to remind me that I could see worse on television. Had I never seen "Saturday Night Live"? That afternoon an opinion poll went up requesting signatures from those who disapproved of the action I had taken and, in an opposing column, those who approved. Within the hour, hundreds expressed disapproval, only one approved.

For a day or two at school there was an animated atmosphere of martyrdom (the speaker's, not mine), but it dissipated rapidly, possibly because the right to make castration jokes from the stage was not, as a cause, very catalytic. The banished speaker, a very likable boy, returned, was received warmly, and apologized not at all cringingly.

In the calm that has followed, my colleagues and I have taken pains to stress to our students, especially at the commencement of the new school year, that whenever somebody addresses an assembly, it is a special occasion. Speakers are expected to observe definite standards when they speak or perform; audiences are expected to be courteous and restrained. Humor at someone else's expense is out, unless it is prearranged with the party lampooned, and even then it ought not to be inhumane. Excretory and copulatory humor is out; it's too easy. Preparation is important. Being persuasive is important. Being controversial is important. Being funny is a delight to all, though it is harder than it looks.

Perhaps these expectations are high. However, schools, especially parochial and independent schools, are gloriously unencumbered in setting such standards: Schools are often *chosen* for the standards they set, the difference they represent. One of the things schools have an opportunity to be different from is television, for although we are all wired into it and it feels public, like the law, it is actually private, like a door-to-door salesman. We don't have to buy the goods.

Since children who watch a fair amount of television will quite naturally assume they are being told and shown the truth, it seems to me crucial that they are exposed to models who view it selectively and critically, who judge it by criteria other than its potential to engage. My own experience has been that students are surprised, but not hostile, when television programming is harshly judged. I think they may even come to like the idea that they themselves, at their discriminating best, are in the process of becoming people television ought to measure up to.

✎ Topics for Critical Thinking and Writing

1. In paragraph 10 Hawley refers to a "comedy spot" on *Saturday Night Live,* which his students labeled "sick" humor. He then asks "Does this kind of fun trivialize crisis? Trivialize cruelty? Inure us to both?" Reread the paragraph and explain how you might respond to Hawley's questions. If you can think of a recent example of similar humor, explain your response to it as well.

2. In paragraph 14 Hawley refers to a sudden change in what became acceptable on television and film. All at once, he says, there were "the most embarrassing expletives as common speech; every imaginable kind of sexual coupling depicted in ever-increasing candor; obsessively specific wounds, mutilations." Are these forms of "unacceptable kinds of stimulation" (paragraph 15) available in the films and television shows of the nineties? If so, how do you feel about them? Are there actions (including speech) that you also find unacceptable?

3. Why, according to Hawley, is criticism of television programming "more bitter and more relentless than criticism of books and films"? Try to recall the last public controversy over taste. Was it over a television show, or some other form of popular entertainment?

4. In paragraph 16, what does Hawley seem to suggest that viewers can do about objectionable television programs? What does he mean by "some viewers will insist on being their brother's keeper"?

5. In paragraph 17 Hawley comments on the family values represented in shows popular in the sixties and seventies, such as "Father Knows Best," "The Waltons," and "Little House on the Prairie." What generalizations can you make about families in shows of the nineties? If you have seen reruns of the earlier shows, have you bean struck by any differences in representations of family life then and now?

6. In paragraphs 20–22, Hawley implies that popular culture (his examples include a popular singer, a television show, and a comedian seen primarily on television) promotes the "toleration of the intolerable," particularly of racial and sexual bigotry. Using some current examples in which racial and sexual conflicts are represented, would you argue that they tend to reinforce bigotry, reduce it, or leave the audience's biases unaffected?

7. Hawley argues for restrictions in students' behavior and speech. How does he defend such restrictions on freedom? How would you feel about attending a school with such restrictions? How does the school you currently attend deal with speech or behavior containing racial, ethnic, or sexual slurs? What is your attitude toward current policy?

8. Hawley reveals that his school is "independent." What else can we infer about the school, its student body, teachers, parents, administration? How do these inferences affect your willingness to accept Hawley's argument?

Stevie Smith

Stevie Smith (1902–71) was born Florence Margaret Smith in England. Her first book was a novel, published in 1936, but she is best known for her several volumes of poetry.

Not Waving but Drowning

Nobody heard him, the dead man,
But still he lay moaning:
I was much further out than you thought
And not waving but drowning.

Poor chap, he always loved larking   5
And now he's dead
It must have been too cold for him his heart gave way,
They said

Oh, no no no, it was too cold always
(Still the dead one lay moaning)   10
I was much too far out all my life
And not waving but drowning.

 Topics for Critical Thinking and Writing

1. The first line, "Nobody heard him, the dead man," is, of course, literally true. Dead men do not speak. In what other ways is it true?
2. Who are "they" whose voices we hear in the second stanza? What does the punctuation—or lack of it—in line 7 tell us of their feelings for the dead man? What effect is produced by the brevity of line 6? of line 8?
3. In the last stanza, does the man reproach himself, or others, or simply bemoan his fate? What was the cause of his death?

12
ART AND LIFE

the Checkered House is old,
this as it looked in 1853,
     It was the Headquarters of
General Baum in the revolution
war, and afterwards He used
it as a Hospital,
     then it was a stoping place
for the stage,
     where they changed Horses every
two miles,
     oh we traveled fast in those
     days,

Place de l'Europe, Paris, 1932
Henri Cartier-Bresson

Short Views

Art for art's sake.
> **Théophile Gautier**

What is art, that it should have a sake?
> **Samuel Butler**

Art for art's sake is an empty phrase. Art for the sake of the true, art for the sake of the good and the beautiful, that is the faith I am searching for.
> **George Sand (Amandine Aurore Lucie Dupin)**

The end of reading is not more books but more life.
> **Holbrook Jackson**

The storyteller's own experience of people and things, whether for good or ill—not only what he has passed through himself, but even events which he has only witnessed or been told of—has moved the writer to an emotion so passionate that he can no longer keep it shut up in his heart. Again and again something in his own life or in that around him will seem to the writer so important that he cannot bear to let it pass into oblivion. There must never come a time, he feels, when people do not know about it.
> **Lady Murasaki,** *The Tale of Genji*

If I had to give young writers advice, I'd say don't listen to writers talking about writing.
> **Lillian Hellman**

Artistic growth is, more than anything else, a refining of the sense of truthfulness. The stupid believe that to be truthful is easy; only the artist, the great artist, knows how difficult it is.
> **Willa Cather**

Art, it seems to me, should simplify. That, indeed, is very nearly the whole of the higher artistic process; finding what conventions of form and what detail one can do without and yet preserve the spirit of the whole—so that all that one has suppressed and cut away is there to the reader's consciousness as much as if it were in type on the page.
>   **Willa Cather**

I think art, literature, fiction, poetry, what it is, makes justice in the world. That's why it almost always has to be on the side of the underdog.
>   **Grace Paley**

Literature is news that stays news.
>   **Ezra Pound**

The two worst sins of bad taste in fiction are pornography and sentimentality. One is too much sex and the other is too much sentiment.
>   **Flannery O'Connor**

It is easier to understand a nation by listening to its music than by learning its language.
>   **Anonymous**

What's swinging in words? If a guy makes you pat your foot and if you feel it down your back, you don't have to ask anybody if that's good music or not. You can always feel it.
>   **Miles Davis**

It started with the moans and groans of the people in the cotton fields. Before it got the name of soul, men were sellin' watermelons and vegetables on a wagon drawn by a mule, hollerin' "watermelon!" with a cry in their voices. And the man on the railroad track layin' crossties—every time they hit the hammer it was with a sad feelin', but with a beat. And the Baptist preacher— he the one who had the soul—he give out the meter, a long and short meter, and the old mothers of the church would reply. This musical thing has been here since America been here. This is trial and tribulation music.
>   **Mahalia Jackson**

If art does not enlarge men's sympathies, it does nothing morally.
George Eliot

You don't take a photograph, you make it.
Ansel Adams

A good painter is to paint two main things, namely, man and the working of man's mind. The first is easy, the second difficult, for it is to be represented through the gestures and movements of the limbs.
Leonardo da Vinci

I like pretty things the best, what's the use of painting a picture if it isn't something nice? So I think real hard till I think of something real pretty, and then I paint it. I like to paint old timey things, historical landmarks of long ago, bridges, mills and hostelries, those old time homes, there are a few left, and they are going fast. I do them all from memory, most of them are day dreams, as it were.
Grandma Moses

The truest expression of a people is in its dances and its music. Bodies never lie.
Agnes De Mille

Dancing is like bank robbery, it takes split-second timing.
Twyla Tharp

Oscar Wilde

Oscar Wilde (1854–1900), born in Dublin, studied classics at Trinity College, Dublin, and then at Oxford. After graduating in 1878 he settled in London, where he achieved fame as a wit and as an advocate of the Aesthetic Movement, whose creed can (with some injustice, of course) be summarized as "Art for Art's Sake." (One contemporary drily asked, "What is art, that it should have a sake?" Two other contemporaries, Gilbert and Sullivan, spoofed the Aesthetic Movement in their comic opera Patience.) *But Wilde was not merely a talker, he was a writer; among his notable works are a witty discussion of the nature of imaginative literature,* The Decay of Lying *(1879); a novel,* The Picture of Dorian Gray *(1891); and several comedies that hold the stage even today,* Lady Windermere's Fan *(1892),* An Ideal Husband *(1895), and his masterpiece* The Importance of Being Earnest *(1895).*

Soon after Earnest *opened, Wilde became involved in a sensational and disastrous court battle. The Marquess of Queensbury (the father of the young man who was Wilde's lover) in effect accused Wilde of homosexuality, and Wilde sued him for libel. During the trial evidence was presented establishing Wilde's homosexuality, and Wilde lost the case. He was then arrested and convicted—homosexual practices were illegal—and he was sentenced to two years in jail at hard labor. Such was his disgrace that his plays were withdrawn from the stage. When Wilde was released he emigrated to France, where he lived his last three years under an assumed name.*

Preface to *The Picture of Dorian Gray*

The artist is the creator of beautiful things.

To reveal art and conceal the artist is art's aim.

The critic is he who can translate into another manner or a new material his impression of beautiful things.

The highest, as the lowest, form of criticism is a mode of autobiography.

Those who find ugly meaning in beautiful things are corrupt without being charming. This is a fault.   5

Those who find beautiful meanings in beautiful things are the cultivated. For these there is hope.

They are the elect to whom beautiful things mean only Beauty.

There is no such thing as a moral or an immoral book.

Books are well written, or badly written. That is all.

The nineteenth-century dislike of Realism is the rage of Caliban[1] seeing his own face in a glass.   10

The nineteenth-century dislike of Romanticism is the rage of Caliban not seeking his own face in a glass.

The moral life of man forms part of the subject matter of the artist, but the morality of art consists in the perfect use of an imperfect medium. No artist desires to prove anything. Even things that are true can be proved.

No artist has ethical sympathies. An ethical sympathy in an artist is an unpardonable mannerism of style.

No artist is ever morbid. The artist can express everything.

Thought and language are to the artist instruments of an art.   15

Vice and Virtue are to the artist materials for an art.

From the point of view of form, the type of all the arts is the art of the musician. From the point of view of feeling, the actor's craft is the type.

[1]**Caliban** a brutish figure in Shakespeare's play *The Tempest*

All art is at once surface and symbol.

Those who go beneath the surface do so at their peril.

Those who read the symbol do so at their peril.   20

It is the spectator, and not life, that art really mirrors.

Diversity of opinion about a work of art shows that the work is new, complex, and vital.

When critics disagree the artist is in accord with himself.

We can forgive a man for making a useful thing as long as he does not admire it. The only excuse for making a useless thing is that one admires it intensely.

All art is quite useless.   25

✎ Topics for Critical Thinking and Writing

1. Wilde ends by saying, "all art is quite useless." Can you accept this view? Why or why not? (If you are inclined to think that a novel or a play may be useful because it may teach us something about life, what do you say about other works of art, such as a wordless musical composition, or a still life painting, or a song such as one sung by the Beatles or Bruce Springsteen? What "use" might such a work have?

2. Wilde says (paragraph 4) that "criticism is a mode of autobiography." Do you suppose that when you offer criticism—whether in a conversation with a friend about a movie you saw last night, or in a course paper on a story, poem, or play—you are in some measure offering autobiography? In a paragraph explain what Wilde probably means, and in a second paragraph evaluate the idea.

3. "There is no such thing as a moral or an immoral book./Books are well written, or badly written. That is all" (8–9). In an essay of 500 words evaluate the view. Whichever side you take, try to see the opposing point of view, state it as fairly as possible, and then respond to it.

4. Perhaps the two books that have most often offended persons concerned with the school curriculum are Shakespeare's *The Merchant of Venice* and Mark Twain's *The Adventures of Huckleberry Finn*. Their defenders usually argue that the former is not anti-Semitic, and the latter is not racist, but they do recognize that the content of the books disturbs many people. If you have read a book whose content is disturbing, in an essay of 250 words indicate whether you think it can be judged purely on the basis of whether it is "well written, or badly written." Or you may want to argue that a "well written" book must reveal a sound view of life, and that a "badly written" book must reveal a false view.

5. "No artist has ethical sympathies" (13). It is sometimes said that part of the greatness of Shakespeare is that his villains (for instance, Claudius in *Hamlet*, and Macbeth and Richard III in the plays named for them) are as exciting and as interesting to us as are his heroes and heroines, and this is at least partly so because Shakespeare was able to get into their minds, was able to see things from their point of view, and was able, so to speak, to

walk in their shoes. If you are familiar with a play by Shakespeare, in an essay of 500 words comment on the degree to which he does or does not reveal "ethical sympathies."

Lou Jacobs Jr.

Lou Jacobs, Jr., Photographer and the author of several books on photography, is a frequent contributor of essays on the topic to The New York Times, *where this piece originally appeared.*

What Qualities Does a Good Photograph Have?

When amateur and professional photographers get together they often discuss equipment and techniques at some length, but it is not often that photographers take time to consider what makes a good picture.

Many photographic organizations list criteria similar to those described below when judging pictures submitted in a competition. Judges may offer opinions like "The composition is off balance," or "The expressions on peoples' faces tell the story well." But photographic criticism is not an exact art. In the media, critics tend to use esoteric terms that even an "in" group doesn't always grasp.

Therefore it's important to the average photographer that he or she develop a basis for understanding and verbalizing how pictures succeed or fail in their visual way, or how they happen to be a near-miss. The latter term describes an image that has some, but not enough, of the visual virtues discussed below.

Of course "a good picture" is a relative description because it's subjective, as is the judgement of all the qualities mentioned in the list that follows. However, there is enough agreement in the tastes of a variety of people to make certain standards general and valid, though the characteristics of a good picture are subject to flexible interpretation. A little honest controversy about the visual success of a print or slide can be a healthy thing.

Impact: This descriptive word comprises a collection of the qualities   5 that help make a photograph appealing, interesting, impressive, or memorable. For instance, Ansel Adams' "Moonrise, Hernandez, NM" is a famous image that has been selling for astronomical prices at auctions because it has enormous pictorial or visual impact—among other reasons. The picture's impact evolves from many qualities such as the drama of the light, the mood invoked, and the magic sense of realism.

Moonrise, Hernandez, New Mexico, 1941
Ansel Adams

It is possible to translate such qualities into your own photographs when you consider how the subjects were treated, whether landscapes or people. Too seldom do we meet dramatic opportunities in nature as grand as those in "Moonrise," but with a well developed artistic sensitivity, ideal conditions can be captured on film.

Human Interest: Here is another rather general term to encompass emotional qualities, action, and things that people do which appeal to a lot of viewers. A shot of your children laughing or a picture of vendors in a marketplace might both show outstanding human interest. The success of such a photograph depends on how you compose it, on lighting, on timing to catch vivid expressions, and perhaps on camera angle or choice of lens. All of these ingredients of a good picture are coming up on the list.

There is another aspect of human interest in your own or others' photographs. Sometimes the unusualness of a subject and the way it's presented overshadows adequate technique. For instance, a good sports picture showing peak action in a scrimmage or a definitive play in baseball has intrinsic appeal.

A photograph of a pretty girl, a baby, and a sunset are in the same category, because in each case the subject matter grabs the viewer's attention.

As a result, a mediocre composition, inferior lighting, a messy back-ground, or other technical or esthetic weaknesses are ignored or excused because the subject is striking.

It's a good feeling when you can distinguish between the subject in a   10
photograph and the way it was treated.

Galleries and museums often hang photographs that are "different," but they're not necessarily worthy of distinction. Many offbeat pho-tographs we see are likely not to have lasting visual value, while fine pho-tographs like those of Ansel Adams or Cartier-Bresson will still be admired in future decades.

Effective Composition: Like other qualities that underlie a good picture, composition can be controversial. There are somewhat conventional prin-ciples of design that we follow because they seem "natural," like placing the horizon line or a figure off-center to avoid a static effect.

But really effective composition is usually derived from the subject, and generally the urge to keep composition as simple as possible pays off. That's why plain backgrounds are often best for portraits, and if you relate someone to his/her environment, simplicity is also a virtue. Composition may be dynamic, placid, or somewhere between.

Study the compositional tendencies of fine photographers and painters for guidance. Be daring and experimental at times too, because a "safe" composition may also be dull.

Spontaneity: This characteristic of a good picture is related to human   15
interest, realism and involvement. When you are involved with the sub-ject, as you might be in photographing an aged father or mother, you prize most the images that include spontaneous expressions and emotional reactions. Get people involved with each other, too, so they forget the cam-era and your pictures are likely to be more believable—and credibility is often a pictorial asset.

If your camera lens is not fast enough to shoot at let's say 1/60th of a second at f/2.8, then you need flash. But you get more spontaneity when people aren't posed, waiting for the flash to go off. Natural light also adds to the realistic impression you capture of people and places, since flash-on-camera has an unavoidably artificial look in most cases.

Lighting: Certainly we have to shoot sometimes when the light is not pictorial, so we do the best we can. A tripod is often the answer to long exposures and exciting photographs. In some situations the light improves if we have the time and patience to wait. Outdoors plan to shoot when the sun is low in the early morning, and at sunset time. Mountains, buildings and people are more dramatic in low-angle light. Details lost in shadows don't seem to matter when the light quality itself is beautiful.

Lighting also helps to create mood, another element of a good picture. Mood is understandably an ethearial quality which includes mystery, gai-ety, somberness, and other emotional aspects. Effective photographs may capitalize on the mood of a place especially when it's dramatic.

Color: In a painting a pronounced feeling of light and shadow is called chiaroscuro, and in photographs such effects are augmented by color which may be in strong contrasts, or part of important forms. Outstanding pictures may also be softly colored in pastels that can be as appealing as bright hues.

We tend to take color in photographs for granted, but we don't have to settle for literal color when a colored filter or a switch in film may improve a situation. Next time it rains, shoot some pictures through a car window or windshield, or keep your camera dry and shoot on foot—using indoor color film. The cold blue effects, particularly in slides, are terrific. You may later use an 85B filter to correct the color for normal outdoor or flash use.   20

Keep in mind that "pretty" or striking color may influence us to take pictures where there really is no worthwhile image. And when you view prints and slides, realize that theatrical color can influence your judgment about the total quality of a picture. A beautiful girl in brightly colored clothes, or an exotic South Seas beach scene may be photographed with creative skill, or insensitively, no matter how appealing the color is.

Contrast: Outstanding pictures may be based on the fact that they contain various contrasting elements, such as large and small, near and far, old and new, bright and subtle color, etc. In taking pictures and evaluating them, keep the contrast range in mind, although these values are often integral with other aspects of the picture.

Camera Angle and Choice of Lens: If someone standing next to you shoots a mid-town Manhattan street with a 50mm lens on a 35mm camera, and you do the same scene with a 35mm or 105mm lens from a crouch rather than standing, you might get a better picture. You can dramatize a subject through your choice of camera angle and lens focal length to alter perspective as well as the relationship of things in the scene. Distortion created this way can be pictorially exciting—or awkward and distracting. You may get good pictures by taking risks in visual ways, and later deciding if what you tried seems to work.

Imagination and Creativity: These two attributes of people who take pictures might have been first on the list if they were not abused words. Look each one up in the dictionary. Ponder how you would apply the definitions to your own pictures and to photographs you see in books or exhibitions.

It takes imagination to see the commonplace in an artistic way, but a certain amount of imagination and creativity should be involved every time we press the shutter button. These human capabilities are basic to understanding the other qualities that make good pictures.   25

✎ Topics for Critical Thinking and Writing

1. Evaluate the title and the first paragraph.
2. In paragraph 4 Jacobs says, "Of course 'a good picture' is a relative description because it's subjective . . . ." Do you agree? Look, for instance, at

Dorothea Lange's photographs of a migrant laborer and her children, on page 94–100. Would you be willing to argue that the famous picture (the one showing the children turned away from the camera) is clearly—objectively—a better picture than one of the other pictures? Explain.

3. In paragraph 5 Jacobs praises Ansel Adams's *Moonrise, Hernandez, NM,* but this picture, showing a cemetery with crosses illumined by a silvery moon, has been disparaged by some critics on the grounds that it is sentimental. How would you define sentimentality? And is it a bad thing in a photograph? Explain.

4. In paragraph 7 Jacobs speaks of "human interest," and he cites a picture of "children laughing or a picture of vendors in a marketplace." Given these examples, what does "human interest" seem to mean? What might be some examples of photographs of people that do *not* have "human interest"?

5. In paragraph 23 Jacobs says that "you can dramatize a subject through your choice of camera angle . . . ." Find an example of such a photo in a newspaper or newsmagazine, or perhaps in this book, and explain how the camera angle "dramatizes" the subject.

6. Take a photo, perhaps one in this book, and in 500 words analyze and evaluate it in Jacobs's terms. Then consider whether Jacobs's essay has helped you to see and enjoy the photograph.

7. Write your own short essay (250–500 words) on "What Qualities Does a Good Photograph Have?" Illustrate it with photocopies of two or three photographs, from this book or from any other source that you wish to draw on. (You may want to choose two examples of good photographs, or one of a good photograph and one of a poor photograph.)

Mary Beard

Mary Beard, of Newnham College, Cambridge, wrote this essay for a volume called Issues in World Literature. *The book included illustrations, and the essay was intended to help viewers look at unfamiliar works of art.*

Culturally Variable Ways of Seeing: Art and Literature

We tend to take the process of *looking* very much for granted; and we rarely stop to reflect on how we make sense of what we see. It is a striking contrast with our engagement in the process of *reading*. Not only do most of us still remember the struggles of first learning to read, the difficulties of decoding those baffling symbols on the page, but even as well-practiced, adult readers we constantly remind ourselves of the problems of understanding and interpreting texts: when was this text written? Does its age affect our understanding? Who was it written for? Why? What language was it first written in? What difference does the translation make? So, for example, we would hardly try to read the Psalms, the Acts of Buddha, or the Koran without recollecting that these are religious texts, part of a system of beliefs that we perhaps do not share. Nor would we seriously try to read early Chinese love poetry, or attempt to understand the passions of Racine's *Phaedra* or Shakespeare's Prospero without any thought for their historical context: however immediate, even modern, the emotions expressed might at first seem, our reading is almost inevitably affected by the knowledge that "being in love" in ancient China or Elizabethan England may have been quite a different experience (governed by quite different rules and constraints) from "being in love" in the contemporary West.

Compare the very casual approach we take to looking. We are often happy to look without thinking, and to allow ourselves to enjoy images as "pure," with little regard for their context, history, or cultural difference. We may admire, for example, the glittering icons of Byzantium without reflecting on their original purpose as devotional, religious images, just as we often enjoy the luxuriant miniatures of ladies at the Indian court without considering the social and economic circumstances that produced such images. Of course, we are not always so casual. Some images do remain for us firmly rooted in their historical context, or in the ideology that created them. If someone, for example, chose reproductions of Nazi art as home decoration, even now that would be a strident political statement; we would hardly believe any claim that it was just an aesthetic admiration for the paintings. Similarly with Picasso's *Guernica:* few viewers consider the painting without at the same time reflecting on the atrocities of the Spanish Civil War that were its inspiration. But all the same, a glance at most dormitory walls (with their wild juxtapositions of images—postcards of Botticelli next to Salvador Dali, native American textiles next to Hokusai waves) suggests that in the visual field "anything goes."

This atmosphere of free play can be liberating. It allows us to use the images *for ourselves,* without becoming lost in the intricacies of historical context or original purpose; it allows us to fix the images freely into our own personal stories ("this postcard is a souvenir of the time when I . . ." or "This poster reminds me of . . ."). But at the same time the casualness tends to conceal from us the processes which lie behind the ways we make sense of, judge, and rank the images we see. It encourages us not to examine our *rules for looking.* These are the rules that govern things as basic as our classification of artistic production ("major art," "minor arts," "art," "artefact," "craft," "Western art," "tribal art," and so on), the language we use to discuss this production, and the value we choose to give it.

The aim of this essay is to bring out into the open some of these rules for looking. It tries to show not only that such rules do exist, however concealed they may be in everyday life, but also that—as the title suggests—

they are *culturally variable;* that is, they are not universal but differ from one culture or cultural subgroup to another. It follows from this variability that the rules themselves may be a source of disagreement or conflict within any society—but particularly within the diffuse amalgam of cultures that makes up modern North America and many other modern-nation states. This essay examines some of the cases where such conflict has become open, even fierce; and it tries to show that these instances of explicit disagreement about our "ways of seeing" are not just peculiar exceptions, but can help us more generally to uncover the rules that underlie our practice of viewing—rules that normally remain concealed, implicit, and unexamined.

The focus of what follows is the museum and art gallery. It is not, of   5
course, the case that art exists only within those institutions. There are all kinds of visual images in private houses, in churches, in dormitories, in hospitals. But nevertheless, over the last two hundred years the museum has become the privileged location for art; the museum is the place we now look to as the guardian of art, the place whose rules play a large part in defining our ways of seeing. As is obvious, the vast majority of the pictures in this book illustrate objects or paintings that (whatever their original location) are now housed in museums.

In the mid 1980s a large exhibition of Hispanic art was shown in various galleries across the United States. It gathered together probably the most comprehensive collection of contemporary paintings and sculptures produced by American artists of Hispanic descent ever to be shown in major national museums. The exhibition's organizers had set out to bring before a wider American public the work of artists normally neglected by mainstream art institutions, and to assert the importance of Hispanic art as part of contemporary American culture. They almost certainly did not foresee the intense controversies that the exhibition would arouse.

The terms of the conflict were very clear. On the one hand there were the well-intentioned, liberal aims of the organizers who saw themselves as expanding the range of the traditional art museum, widening the horizons of the American museum-going public, and at the same time doing justice to Hispanic artists by granting them their rightful place in great national institutions. On the other hand there were those who objected to the cultural imperialism of the mainstream galleries, which (as they saw it) were attempting to take over, domesticate, and so depoliticize Chicano artistic productions. To turn Hispanic art into "Art," to pull murals off street walls and place them as "museum objects" in the institutions of the dominant culture was, so the argument went, to undermine the whole significance of the Hispanic art movement. The rightful place of Hispanic art, in other words, was on the streets, not in the museum.

This debate is part of an irresolvable series of questions about the place of Hispanic art and about how we should look at it. Should Hispanic art always exist on the margins of the dominant artistic culture? How can that dominant culture recognize the work of Hispanic artists without merely appropriating them? Why would Chicano artists *want* to show their work in the Metropolitan Museum? Or why, on the other hand, should they be content never to be shown there? Why should "we" not be free to display and view Hispanic art wherever and however we want? Who has the right to decide where this art belongs? But underlying these questions, even wider issues come into play: namely, the fact that the context in which we view art *matters;* that a painting hung on a museum wall necessarily means something different from the same painting displayed in the street; that we process and understand images in one way when we view them in the calm, quiet, reverent atmosphere of the art museum and in quite other ways when we see them at the back of the parking lot.

It is easy enough to recognize these various options and differences when we are thinking of contemporary art, within the society with which we are most familiar. So even if we do not wholeheartedly agree with the complaints of some of the Chicano artists, we can readily understand what is at stake in their objections. It is rather more difficult to see the force of such issues immediately when we are viewing art that was produced at much greater distance from us—centuries old, perhaps, or from an unfamiliar foreign culture. But here, too, conflict, choices, and options in viewing lie just beneath the surface. How can we recapture them for ourselves?

Imagine that you are in an art museum looking at a painting by an   10 artist of the Italian Renaissance; let's suppose it is *The Baptism of Christ* by Piero della Francesca (1416?–1492). How does the museum encourage you to see and understand this picture? What story does it try to construct around it? Maybe the label beside the painting is very brief, telling you only the name of the artist, the title, and date of the work of art; maybe there is not much explicit guidance about "how to look." Nevertheless the chances are that the whole layout and atmosphere of the museum has already given you clearer instructions about how and *what* to see than you realize.

The mere fact that this painting is in a major public gallery has already told you it is "important"—culturally, historically, aesthetically. It is a chosen object, here for you to admire. And it is surrounded, no doubt, by other paintings of the Italian Renaissance: a period defined as "great," a cultural peak in the history of the West, the age that first recaptured the genius of classical antiquity. You are here admiring the painting not just on its own, but also as a symbol of the cultural production of its age. There are, however, other issues that the museum is encouraging you to bear in mind. The paintings are arranged in chronological order: you meet fourteenth-century art before fifteenth-century; fifteenth-century art before sixteenth. You are being asked to assign Piero his place in the *development* of art, to consider how far his treatment of, say, perspective marks an "advance" on his predecessors; you are being taught to look at this painting as a representative of the history of artistic style and technique.

What, though, of the subject matter and context? You may already have reacted somewhat differently to Piero's *Baptism* according to your religious beliefs—Christian, atheist, Moslem, Jew. But what happens if you discover (or perhaps the museum label tells you) that this picture was originally part of a church altarpiece, that it was painted to be the backdrop of the most holy Christian ceremonies? What difference does this make to the way you see it? Instantly then, whatever your own beliefs, you understand that another way of looking is possible. This painting was once a focus of *religious* reverence—not just the *cultural* reverence of today's museum visitor. The scene depicted was a central moment of the Christian faith—not just (as it is for many viewers today) a matter for intellectual "decoding" ("Baptism: Christ in center, John the Baptist to the side").

It is not, of course, only *one* more way of looking that is possible. The original viewers may have been no more homogeneous in their attitudes than we are. Some would perhaps have doubted the Christian faith—and have found it hard to feel any sense of devotion here. Others, with their own private conception of Christ, might simply have been disappointed with Piero's version. The options are almost limitless—although necessarily different from most of the options open to the modern museum-goer.

These considerations are not meant to suggest that the original setting and interpretation of a painting is the only "correct" one. After all, we could never accurately recover the original interpretations of Piero's *Baptism;* we can at best only pretend to be fifteenth-century Italians. We have necessarily made our own new contexts and meanings for paintings of this type. The questions that have been raised, however, are meant to suggest that we should reflect much more carefully on how our ways of seeing are determined and how they vary. Why do we see as we do? As was so clear in the controversies over the exhibition of Hispanic art, the context of our viewing *makes a difference:* new contexts produce new ways of seeing; new ways of seeing produce new meanings.

An exhibition at the New York Center for African Art in 1987 set out to challenge some of the way we classify different types of art, and at the same time to reveal the power of museum display in forming our ways of seeing. A prize exhibit was a very cheap, ordinary hunting net from Zaire. It was laid out on its own, on a low platform, under spot-lighting—the kind of treatment usually reserved for the rarest and most precious objects. The questions being posed here were very simple: How do we now classify this net? What happens when we display it as "art" rather than as cheap "artefact"? Is it still an "ordinary" hunting net, or has it been transformed? And if it has been transformed, what has brought about the transformation?

This was, of course, in some senses a "trick"—a trick that obviously worked rather well, as several dealers in tribal art were drawn to inquire from the Center where they might acquire another such marvelous net! But, as the questions suggest, it had an important point in highlighting the arbitrariness of our normal division between "native craft" and "art"; and in showing the power of museum display in creating "Art" out of the most humble object. Different styles of display can entirely change the way we

15

see what we see. Imagine how humble the net would have remained if it had been displayed in a museum case packed full of other pieces of hunting equipment, and with background information on hunting practices among the Zande people.

These issues of status, valuation, and display are not restricted to the problems of tribal art/craft. They have a much wider resonance in many different areas of the visual arts. Consider, for example, the "masterpieces" of ancient Greek ceramics—the painted vases produced largely in Athens between the sixth and fourth centuries B.C.E., elegantly decorated with scenes drawn from Greek myth and everyday life. These vases are now treated as major works of art: their painters (who sometimes signed their pieces) are discussed by scholars in much the same terms as the painters of the Italian Renaissance; the stylistic details of the painting are minutely compared from vase to vase, influence and imitation from one to another carefully detected; individual vases are given spot-lit, star treatment in most museums. Paradoxically, though, in the ancient world itself the production of these ceramics was a low-grade "craft" activity. Unlike their renowned sculptors or painters on wood or canvas, the men who decorated these vases were, to the Greeks, craftsmen, not artists.

There are various reasons why we have come to value these vase paintings so highly—and so differently from the society that created them. Perhaps the most obvious lies in the accidents of survival: none of the major Greek paintings on wood have survived—we know of them only through the descriptions given by ancient writers; if we want to get any idea of the character of Greek painting, we are *forced* to concentrate on (and so in the process over-value) these paintings on vases. But others might argue that our modern appreciation of these objects as "art" is in fact a proper revaluation of their quality—that the Greeks themselves, in thinking of them as mundane "craft," quite simply failed to recognize their artistic genius. Whatever the underlying reasons, though, it is clear that the modern display of these objects in museums (pride of place in the museum case, shining spotlights onto a single prize specimen) serves to reinforce their high status. The way they are displayed (and so the way that we see them) makes them seem self-evidently "Art."

Could we reverse that valuation? If we consistently displayed these objects in a different way, would we start to think differently about them? Imagine how it would be if they were shown in the case piled one upon another, as if in a cheap china store—not single objects for our admiration. What if we changed their labels and called them "pots," not "vases"? What if we surrounded them with information not about their "artists" or their "painterly technique," but about their domestic use, or about the pottery "industry" in ancient Athens? These changes would, of course, be "tricks," like the "trick" of the Zaire hunting net. But they are tricks that would almost certainly work in making us think quite differently about the objects on display. We would find that we had quite different things to say about these vases or pots, a quite different sense of their value. That in itself should reveal to us how fragile and how variable our judgment of visual objects is.

Explicit conflicts about *how to look* are rare. In other words, the rules   20
we intuit for processing what we see usually do their job very well; they veil from us the sometimes arbitrary, sometimes very loaded choices that we make in classifying and judging the visual world. So, for example, the political agenda that underlies the term "women's craft" or "native craft" (rather than "women's *art*" or "black *art*") is something that most of the time, for most of us, passes unnoticed. But thinking about such conflicts, when they do become explicit, can help to make us aware of the choices that we (or someone on our behalf) are always, necessarily, making when we think about, describe, classify, and *view* works of art.

Topics for Critical Thinking and Writing

1. In paragraph 2 Beard suggests that the walls of a dormitory room suggest "the visual equivalent of 'anything goes.' " Think about the walls in your room, whether in a dormitory or not. Is there a unifying taste or them? Or does the variety itself say something? (In her third paragraph Beard offers a comment that you may find helpful in thinking about these questions.)
2. In paragraph 3 Beard speaks of "art" and of "craft." In your view, what, if anything, is the difference? (See also Beard's paragraphs 16–18.) Consider such items as a handmade quilt, a handmade chair, flowers made out of beads on wire, beaded moccasins, a braided leather belt.
3. In paragraphs 6–8 Beard tells of the controversy concerning an exhibition of Hispanic art. (By the way, what does *Hispanic* mean? Is a Spanish-speaking Indian from Guatemala a Hispanic person? A Spanish-speaking black from Cuba?) Write a paragraph answering her question, "Why would Chicano artists *want* to show their work in the Metropolitan Museum?" Write a second paragraph answering another of her questions, "Or why, on the other hand, should they be content never to be shown there?"
4. Think about a photograph you like very much, taken by you or by a friend or member of your family. In 250 words answer the question, Is it art? Why, or why not.

W. E. B. Du Bois

W. E. B. Du Bois (1868–1963) was born in Massachusetts, where he seems to have had a relatively happy early childhood—though in grade school he was shocked to learn that his classmates considered him different because of his color. In 1885 he went to Fisk University in

Nashville, Tennessee; and then, for doctoral work, he studied history at Harvard University and sociology at the University of Berlin. His doctoral dissertation, The Suppression of the Slave Trade in the United States of America, *was published in* Harvard Historical Studies *in 1896.*

Although Du Bois had embarked on a scholarly career, he became increasingly concerned with the injustices of contemporary society, and his writings were now directed at a general public. In 1903 he published The Souls of Black Folk, *a book challenging Booker T. Washington's more resigned position. From 1910 to the mid-1930s he edited* The Crisis, *the journal of the* National Association for the Advancement of Colored People. *Although he energetically solicited the writings of other people, he wrote so many essays for the journal that he can almost be said to be its author as well as its editor. Eventually Du Bois joined the Communist party, and in 1963 he left the United States for Ghana, where he died.*

We reprint part of chapter 14 from The Souls of Black Folk.

Of the Sorrow Songs

> I walk through the churchyard
>   To lay this body down;
> I know moon-rise, I know star-rise;
> I walk in the moonlight, I walk in the starlight;
> I'll lie in the grave and stretch out my arms,
> I'll go to judgment in the evening of the day,
> And my soul and thy soul shall meet that day,
>   When I lay this body down.
>
> Negro Song

They that walked in darkness sang songs in the olden days—Sorrow Songs—for they were weary at heart. And so before each thought that I have written in this book I have set a phrase, a haunting echo of these weird old songs in which the soul of the black slave spoke to men. Ever since I was a child these songs have stirred me strangely. They came out of the South unknown to me, one by one, and yet at once I knew them as of me and of mine. Then in after years when I came to Nashville I saw the great temple builded of these songs towering over the pale city. To me Jubilee Hall seemed ever made of the songs themselves, and its bricks were red with the blood and dust of toil. Out of them rose for me morning, noon, and night, bursts of wonderful melody, full of the voices of my brothers and sisters, full of the voices of the past.

Little of beauty has America given the world save the rude grandeur God himself stamped on her bosom; the human spirit in this new world has expressed itself in vigor and ingenuity rather than in beauty. And so by fateful chance the Negro folk-song—the rhythmic cry of the slave— stands to-day not simply as the sole American music, but as the most beautiful expression of human experience born this side the seas. It has been neglected, it has been, and is, half despised, and above all it has been persistently mistaken and misunderstood; but notwithstanding, it still remains as the singular spiritual heritage of the nation and the greatest gift of the Negro people.

Away back in the thirties the melody of these slave songs stirred the nation, but the songs were soon half forgotten. Some, like "Near the lake where drooped the willow," passed into current airs and their source was forgotten; others were caricatured on the "minstrel" stage and their memory died away. Then in war-time came the singular Port Royal experiment after the capture of Hilton Head, and perhaps for the first time the North met the Southern slave face to face and heart to heart with no third witness. The Sea Islands of the Carolinas, where they met, were filled with a black folk of primitive type, touched and moulded less by the world about them than any others outside the Black Belt. Their appearance was uncouth, their language funny, but their hearts were human and their singing stirred men with a mighty power. Thomas Wentworth Higginson hastened to tell of these songs, and Miss McKim and others urged upon the world their rare beauty. But the world listened only half credulously until the Fisk Jubilee Singers sang the slave songs so deeply into the world's heart that it can never wholly forget them again.

There was once a blacksmith's son born at Cadiz, New York, who in the changes of time taught school in Ohio and helped defend Cincinnati from Kirby Smith. Then he fought at Chancellorsville and Gettysburg and finally served in the Freedman's Bureau at Nashville. Here he formed a Sunday-school class of black children in 1866, and sang with them and taught them to sing. And then they taught him to sing, and when once the glory of the Jubilee songs passed into the soul of George L. White, he knew his life-work was to let those Negroes sing to the world as they had sung to him. So in 1871 the pilgrimage of the Fisk Jubilee Singers began. North to Cincinnati they rode,—four half-clothed black boys and five girl-women,—led by a man with a cause and a purpose. They stopped at Wilberforce, the oldest of Negro schools, where a black bishop blessed them. Then they went, fighting cold and starvation, shut out of hotels, and cheerfully sneered at, ever northward; and ever the magic of their song kept thrilling hearts, until a burst of applause in the Congregational Council at Oberlin revealed them to the world. They came to New York and Henry Ward Beecher dared to welcome them, even though the metropolitan dailies sneered at his "Nigger Minstrels." So their songs conquered till they sang across the land and across the sea, before Queen and Kaiser, in Scotland and Ireland, Holland and Switzerland. Seven years they sang, and brought back a hundred and fifty thousand dollars to found Fisk University.

* * *

The words that are left to us are not without interest, and, cleared of evident dross, they conceal much of real poetry and meaning beneath conventional theology and unmeaning rhapsody. Like all primitive folk, the slave stood near to Nature's heart. Life was a "rough and rolling sea" like the brown Atlantic of the Sea Islands; the "Wilderness" was the home of God, and the "lonesome valley" led to the way of life. "Winter'll soon be over," was the picture of life and death to a tropical imagination. The sudden wild thunder-storms of the South awed and impressed the Negroes,—at times the rumbling seemed to them "mournful," at times imperious:

> "My Lord calls me,
> He calls me by the thunder,
> The trumpet sounds it in my soul."

The monotonous toil and exposure is painted in many words. One sees the ploughmen in the hot, moist furrow, singing:

> "Dere's no rain to wet you,
> Dere's no sun to burn you,
> Oh, push along, believer,
> I want to go home."

The bowed and bent old man cries, with thrice-repeated wail:

> "O Lord, keep me from sinking down,"

and he rebukes the devil of doubt who can whisper:

> "Jesus is dead and God's gone away."

Yet the soul-hunger is there, the restlessness of the savage, the wail of the wanderer, and the plaint is put in one little phrase:
My soul wants something that's new, that's new.

Of death the Negro showed little fear, but talked of it familiarly and even fondly as simply a crossing of the waters, perhaps—who knows?— back to his ancient forests again. Later days transfigured his fatalism, and amid the dust and dirt the toiler sang:

> "Dust, dust and ashes, fly over my grave,
> But the Lord shall bear my spirit home."

The things evidently borrowed from the surrounding world undergo characteristic change when they enter the mouth of the slave. Especially is this true of Bible phrases. "Weep, O captive daughter of Zion," is quaintly turned into "Zion, weep-a-low," and the wheels of Ezekiel are turned every way in the mystic dreaming of the slave, till he says:

> "There's a little wheel a-turnin' in-a-my heart."

As in olden time, the words of these hymns were improvised by some   10
leading minstrel of the religious band. The circumstances of the gathering,
however, the rhythm of the songs, and the limitations of allowable
thought, confined the poetry for the most part to single or double lines,
and they seldom were expanded to quatrains or longer tales, although
there are some few examples of sustained efforts, chiefly paraphrases of
the Bible. Three short series of verses have always attracted me,—the one
that heads this chapter, of one line of which Thomas Wentworth Higginson has fittingly said, "Never, it seems to me, since man first lived and suffered was his infinite longing for peace uttered more plaintively." The second and third are descriptions of the Last Judgment,—the one a late
improvisation, with some traces of outside influence:

> "Oh, the stars in the elements are falling,
> And the moon drips away into blood,
> And the ransomed of the Lord are returning unto God,
> Blessed be the name of the Lord."

And the other earlier and homelier picture from the low coast lands:

> "Michael, haul the boat ashore,
> Then you'll hear the horn they blow,
> Then you'll hear the trumpet sound,
> Trumpet sound the world around,
> Trumpet sound for rich and poor,
> Trumpet sound for Jubilee,
> Trumpet sound for you and me."

Through all the sorrow of the Sorrow Songs there breathes a hope—
a faith in the ultimate justice of things. The minor cadences of despair
change often to triumph and calm confidence. Sometimes it is faith in
life, sometimes a faith in death, sometimes assurance of boundless justice in some fair world beyond. But whichever it is, the meaning is
always clear: that sometime, somewhere, men will judge men by their
souls and not by their skins. Is such a hope justified? Do the Sorrow
Songs sing true?

The silently growing assumption of this age is that the probation of
races is past, and that the backward races of to-day are of proven ineffi-
ciency and not worth the saving. Such an assumption is the arrogance of
peoples irreverent toward Time and ignorant of the deeds of men. A thousand years ago such an assumption, easily possible, would have made it
difficult for the Teuton to prove his right to life. Two thousand years ago
such dogmatism, readily welcome, would have scouted the idea of blond
races ever leading civilization. So wofully unorganized is sociological
knowledge that the meaning of progress, the meaning of "swift" and
"slow" in human doing, and the limits of human perfectability, are veiled,

unanswered sphinxes on the shores of science. Why should Æschylus have sung two thousand years before Shakespeare was born? Why has civilization flourished in Europe, and flickered, flamed, and died in Africa? So long as the world stands meekly dumb before such questions, shall this nation proclaim its ignorance and unhallowed prejudices by denying freedom of opportunity to those who brought the Sorrow Songs to the Seats of the Mighty?

Your country? How came it yours? Before the Pilgrims landed we were here. Here we have brought our three gifts and mingled them with yours: a gift of story and song—soft, stirring melody in an ill-harmonized and unmelodious land; the gift of sweat and brawn to beat back the wilderness, conquer the soil, and lay the foundations of this vast economic empire two hundred years earlier than your weak hands could have done it; the third, a gift of the Spirit. Around us the history of the land has centered for thrice a hundred years; out of the nation's heart we have called all that was best to throttle and subdue all that was worst; fire and blood, prayer and sacrifice, have billowed over this people, and they have found peace only in the altars of the God of Right. Nor has our gift of the Spirit been merely passive. Actively we have woven ourselves with the very warp and woof of this nation,—we fought their battles, shared their sorrow, mingled our blood with theirs, and generation after generation have pleaded with a headstrong, careless people to despise not Justice, Mercy, and Truth, lest the nation be smitten with a curse. Our song, our toil, our cheer, and warning have been given to this nation in blood-brotherhood. Are not these gifts worth the giving? Is not this work and striving? Would America have been America without her Negro people?

Even so is the hope that sang in the songs of my fathers well sung. If somewhere in this whirl and chaos of things there dwells Eternal Good, pitiful yet masterful, then anon in His good time America shall rend the Veil and the prisoned shall be free. Free, free as the sunshine trickling down the morning into these high windows of mine, free as yonder fresh young voices welling up to me from the caverns of brick and mortar below—welling with song, instinct with life, tremulous treble and darkening bass. My children, my little children, are singing to the sunshine, and thus they sing:

> Let us cheer the weary traveller,
> Cheer the weary traveller,
> Let us cheer the weary traveller
> Along the heavenly way.

And the traveller girds himself, and sets his face toward the Morning, 15 and goes his way.

[1903]

Topics for Critical Thinking and Writing

1. Du Bois uses some terms that may disconcert a reader, such as *primitive* and *backward races.* Look especially closely at the passages in which these terms occur and then summarize Du Bois's view of the African Americans of his time. Look closely, too, at passages in which he discusses white attitudes toward African Americans, and summarize his views of these whites also.
2. Read the three spirituals quoted below—or, better, hear a performance of spirituals. To what extent has Du Bois helped you (if he has) to understand and enjoy these works?
3. Alain Locke (1886–1954), African-American educator and literary critic and historian, in *The Negro and His Music,* says of the spirituals,

> Over-emphasize the melodic elements of a spiritual, and you get a sentimental ballad a la Stephen Foster. Stress the harmony and you get a cloying glee or "barber-shop" chorus. Over-emphasize, on the other hand, the rhythmic idiom and instantly you secularize the product and it becomes a syncopated shout, with the religious tone and mood completely evaporated.

If you are familiar with performances of spirituals, test the performances against Locke's words—or test Locke's words against the performances.

Anonymous

Three Spirituals

A Note on Spirituals

Spirituals, or Sorrow Songs, by slaves in the United States, seem to have been created chiefly in the first half of the nineteenth century. Their origins are still a matter of some dispute, but probably most students of the subject agree that the songs represent a distinctive fusion of African rhythms with white hymns; and, of course, many of the texts derive ultimately from Biblical sources. One of the chief themes is the desire for release, sometimes presented with imagery drawn from ancient Israel. Examples include references to crossing the River Jordan (a river that runs from north of the Sea of Galilee to the Dead Sea), the release of the Israelites from slavery in Egypt (Exodus), Jonah's release from the whale (Book of Jonah), and Daniel's deliverance from a fiery furnace and from the lions' den (Book of Daniel, chapters 3 and 6).

The texts were collected and published especially in the 1860s, for instance in *Slave Songs of the United States* (1867). These books usually sought to reproduce the singers' pronunciation, and we have followed the early texts here.

Deep River

Deep river, my home is over Jordan, Deep river,
Lord, I want to cross over into campground,
Lord, I want to cross over into campground,
Lord, I want to cross over into campground.
Oh, chillun, Oh, don't you want to go to that gospel feast,   5
That promised land, that land, where all is peace?
Walk into heaven, and take my seat,
And cast my crown at Jesus feet,
Lord, I want to cross over into campground,
Lord, I want to cross over into campground,   10
Lord, I want to cross over into campground.
Deep river, my home is over Jordan, Deep river
Lord, I want to cross over into campground,
Lord, I want to cross over into campground,
Lord, I want to cross over into campground, Lord!   15

Go Down, Moses

When Israel was in Egypt's land,
    Let my people go;
Oppressed so hard they could not stand,
    Let my people go.

Chorus:
Go down, Moses, way down in Egypt's land;   5
Tell old Pharoah, to let my people go.
Thus saith the Lord, bold Moses said,
    Let my people go;
If not I'll smite your first born dead,
    Let my people go.   10
No more shall they in bondage toil,
    Let my people go;
Let them come out with Egypt's spoil,
    Let my people go.
O'twas a dark and dismal night,   15
    Let my people go;
When Moses led the Israelites,
    Let my people go.

The Lord told Moses what to do,
    Let my people go;   20
To lead the children of Israel through,
    Let my people go.

O come along, Moses, you won't get lost,
    Let my people go;
Stretch our your rod and come across,   25
    Let my people go.

As Israel stood by the water side,
    Let my people go;
At the command of God it did divide,
    Let my people go.   30

And when they reached the other side,
    Let my people go;
They sang a song of triumph o'er,
    Let my people go.

You won't get lost in the wilderness,   35
    Let my people go;
With a lighted candle in your breast,
    Let my people go.

O let us all from bondage flee,
    Let my people go;   40
And let us all in Christ be free,
    Let my people go.

We need not always weep and moan,
    Let my people go;
And wear these slavery chains forlorn,   45
    Let my people go.

What a beautiful morning that will be,
    Let my people go;
When time breaks up in eternity,
    Let my people go.   50

Didn't My Lord Deliver Daniel

Didn't my Lord deliver Daniel, deliver Daniel, deliver Daniel,
Didn't my Lord deliver Daniel,
    An' why not every man.
He delivered Daniel from de lion's den,
Jonah from de belly of de whale,   5
An' de Hebrew chillun from de fiery furnace,
An' why not every man.

Didn't my Lord deliver Daniel, deliver Daniel, deliver Daniel,
Didn't my Lord deliver Daniel,
    An' why not every man.   10
De moon run down in a purple stream,
De sun forbear to shine,
An' every star disappear,
King Jesus shall-a be mine.
    (Refrain)
De win' blows eas' an' de win' blows wes'   15
It blows like de judgament day,
An' every po' soul dat never did pray
'll be glad to pray dat day.
    (Refrain)
I set my foot on de Gospel ship,
An de ship begin to sail,   20
It landed me over on Canaan's shore,[1]
An' I'll never come back no mo'.
    (Refrain)

 Topic for Critical Thinking and Writing

As we mention in our introductory note, we give the texts of the songs as they were printed in the second half of the nineteenth century, when an effort to indicate pronunciation was made (e.g., *chillun* for *children*). If you were printing the songs, would you retain these attempts to indicate pronunciation. What, if anything, is gained by keeping them? What, if any, unintentional side effects are produced?

John Simon

John Simon, born in Yugoslavia in 1925, received his higher education in the United States. He has written criticism of plays, books, and films for several magazines, as well as a book on Ingmar Bergman. We reprint an article from New York *magazine—a periodical aimed not only at New Yorkers but at all middle-class, general-interest readers.*

Triumph over Death

Why is dance enjoying such all-but-unprecedented popularity in our time? At least partly, I think, because of the withdrawal of the word

---

[1]**Canaan's shore,** *Canaan* is the ancient name of a territory that included part of what is now Israel.

from our culture—or, more precisely, our withdrawal from the word. Whether in or out of school, Dick and Jane write, read, and express themselves orally with increasing difficulty. One of the consequences is that, among the arts, the wholly or largely nonverbal ones become favored—especially dance, where the body has it all over the mind. In the fine arts and in serious music, the mind seems to make greater demands than in dance, whose only appreciable competition comes from the movies, where the word appears to be undemanding and the visuals are seemingly all that matters. Highly kinetic, then, is what dance and film are: forms, as it were, of body language, which may yet become our lingua franca.

In the domain of dance, ballet is unquestioned king, because it is the least earthbound, the most death-defying, form of dance: it appears to defeat the laws of gravity, defy death itself. The danseur noble[1] at the height of an entrechat or jeté, the ballerina carried aloft but looking more airborne than handheld, are no longer a little lower than the angels, but fully of their company. Even a simple pas de bourrée, perfectly executed, conveys a skimming along the surface of the earth rather than a walk or run upon it; it is perhaps a water bird skittering along the mirror of a lake. And dancers are always young and beautiful. Just as at a university only the sedentary faculty ages, watching students who are always twentyish come and go, at the ballet only the audience grows old. The faces and bodies may not belong to the same dancers—although, in another way, they do, for the perfectly stylized steps, highly dramatic makeup, and formalized costumes bestow their own uniformity and continuity—but those privileged beings up there are forever beautiful and young.

So our two greatest limitations are overcome before our eyes: we become like unto the angels who need not touch ground, and do not have to die. I think it is no accident that three of the greatest, ever-popular story ballets deal with the triumph over death. In *Swan Lake*, the wicked enchanter and the demanding parent are both bested as the lovers float off into shared immortality. In *Giselle*, the beloved remains faithful to her deceitful lover beyond death, rises from her tomb to save his life, and thus binds him to herself forever. In *The Sleeping Beauty*, Prince Charming awakens the heroine from a sleep perilously resembling death. Even the fourth hardy perennial, *The Nutcracker*, takes us back to the ageless world of childhood, whose animated toys, benign fairies, and transfigured children mortality cannot touch.

It is easier to project ourselves into dancers than into actors. Dancers, especially in ballet, are abstract: they symbolize rather than express, they are mythic rather than specific. The particular words of Shakespeare's Ophelia may leave some audiences cold, but an Ophelia balletically transmuted into a symbol of unfulfilled yearning is an image for everybody.

---

[1]**Danseur noble,** leading male dancer in a ballet company; an **entrechat** is a leap during which the dancer crosses his feet a number of times, a **jeté** is a leap from one foot to the other.

Louis MacNeice's poem, "Les Sylphides," begins, significantly, "Life in a day: he took his girl to the ballet"; stanza three runs: "Now, he thought, we are floating—ageless, oarless—/Now there is no separation, from now on/You will be wearing white/Satin and a real sash/Under the waltzing trees." It seems noteworthy how many extremely obese people there are among balletomanes; they, more than anyone, want to think themselves disembodied sylphs. But all of us, regardless of weight, size, and age, would like to soar, be lighter than air, than care.

✎ Topics for Critical Thinking and Writing

1. Simon offers no evidence that dance is "enjoying . . . all but unprecedented popularity." Should he have? Explain.
2. In his first paragraph Simon makes a distinction between verbal and non-verbal arts. What are some examples of verbal arts? What are some non-verbal arts other than those he mentions?
3. What contrasts does Simon find between ballet and other forms of dance, and between dance and other theatrical forms?
4. In the first paragraph Simon speaks of "our withdrawal from the word." What does he mean? In the last paragraph he quotes from a poem. How can this apparent inconsistency be explained?
5. How would you characterize the readers Simon addresses in this essay? On what evidence do you base your characterization?

Perri Klass

Perri Klass, a physician and a writer of fiction and nonfiction, was born in Trinidad in 1958 and educated in the United States. In the essay that we reprint, from The New York Times, *Klass considers the view that Disney's* The Lion King, *with its themes of patricide and guilt, may be too upsetting for small children.*

King of the Jungle

Last summer, people worried about whether the dinosaurs in *Jurassic Park* were too frightening for children. This summer, some may look at, *The Lion King* and wonder if the death of the father lion is too traumatic. In the first case, the worry was that brilliant special effects would leave children frightened of animals they know do not really walk the earth; in the second, that a well-told story would have children identifying with an animated lion cub and his grief and guilt over the loss of his father.

In *The Lion King*, which opened on Wednesday, Mufasa, the king of beasts, is trampled in a wildebeest stampede as he saves his little cub,

Simba. Mufasa's evil brother, Scar, who provoked the stampede to kill his brother and take over the lion kingdom, convinces Simba that he killed his father. The distraught cub leaves home, nearly dies and wanders the veldt until he grows up enough to return and challenge his usurping uncle.

Many reviewers have specifically noted the potentially frightening aspects of the movie. Janet Maslin, writing in *The New York Times*, referred to "Mufasa's disturbing on-screen death" and wondered if the film "really warranted a G rating." Terrence Rafferty, writing in *The New Yorker,* said the film dredged up "deep-seated insecurities and terrors." Richard Corliss, in *Time* magazine, said, "Get ready to explain to the kids why a good father should die violently and why a child should have to witness the death." And *Variety* pointed to "scenes of truly terrifying animal-kingdom violence that should cause parents to think twice before bringing along the 'Little Mermaid' set."

Hamlet with fur. An animated movie with the potential to move its audience, adults and children, to make them wonder and worry and cheer and, yes, cry. Isn't that what stories are supposed to do, on the page, on the stage or on the screen?

If children's entertainment is purged of the powerful, we risk homogenization, predictability and boredom, and we deprive children of any real understanding of the cathartic and emotional potentials of narrative. As Marie Antoinette once remarked, "Let them watch Barney."   5

So this is a Disney cartoon about animals in which a loving parent dies. Surely we've had this discussion before, at some point in our collective cultural pageant. In fact, the world is full of adults who think that the death of Bambi's mother is too upsetting for small children. Too sad. Too scary. There will be parents who feel that *The Lion King* may be too upsetting for children, too; a movie about lions is a little, well, redder in tooth and claw than a movie about a deer. As Timon the meerkat says—and there is no way to convey how much exasperation Nathan Lane gets into his voice—Carnivores!"

I myself tend to worry more about human villains, both in real life and at the movies. By my standards, *Snow White* is the much more upsetting movie. There is nothing in *The Lion King* that can compare to a wicked queen who wants to kill her stepdaughter for being too beautiful or to a huntsman ordered to kill the girl and cut her heart out. And for that matter, are two lions fighting for control as scary as Cruella De Vil, who, in *101 Dalmatians,* wants to kill the puppies and make them into coats?

Do we really want to protect our children from being saddened or scared or even upset by movies—or by books? Do we want to eliminate surprise, reversal, tragedy, conflict and leave children with stories in which they can be smugly confident that the good will always be rewarded and the bad always punished? Children don't have to sit through "Friday the 13th" at a tender age, but neither do they need an unending diet of wholesomely bland entertainment. A child who is worried, truly worried, about the outcome of a book is a child who is learning to understand what pulls someone into literature, and in fact it is a triumph that in an age of special effects and interactive videos, words on a page still have the power to move children.

Similarly, in an age when cartoons and live action films are full of bang'-em-on-the-head violence that has no true dramatic impact, this is a movie in which a noble character dies and is truly mourned. And when we talk about children made sad by a movie, we are talking about children being moved by things that are not really happening to real people, and that is what art and drama and literature are all about. Those children are recognizing a character and feeling for that character, and that is a giant step toward empathy.

Maria Tatar, professor of German studies at Harvard and the author of *Off With Their Heads! Fairy Tales and the Culture of Childhood*, points out that stories and folk tales have always offered children a way to consider and even control death and other difficult and forbidden topics. "Kids can handle almost anything if they're authorized to see it, talk about it," she says. "They're much smarter than we give them credit for."   10

Barry Zuckerman, chairman of the department of pediatrics at Boston City Hospital and an expert on child development, agrees that these stories offer children an opportunity to master troubling issues. "It's not bad for children to be exposed to stressful things. They can cope by having a parent available, so they can cuddle up to a parent who provides safety and security."

And if a child responds to *The Lion King* on some level that is deeper and more intense than a pow-pow Saturday morning cartoon, that is because the people who made this movie are trying for something more complex here, and children know it.

What there is in *The Lion King*, along with sometimes breathtaking animation and well-cast voices, is an interesting mix of *Hamlet, Bambi* and *The Jungle Book,* all shot through with some contemporary sensibility about men who can't grow up. Is this just a late-20th-century take on *Hamlet* imbued with self-help books and actualization therapy? Instead of a young man who could not make up his mind, we have a young man who cannot share his feelings and has trouble with commitment. Still, when the ghost of the dead king appears to the young lion and charges him to depose his treacherous uncle to reclaim the kingdom, you can't help looking around for Rosencrantz and Guildenstern (played here by a wart hog and a meerkat).

Yes, the father dies. And there is a stampede, which is some kind of heroic triumph of animation. But the stampede is not so much scary as it is inexorable, an animal-world event, even if it is provoked by the evil uncle and his hyena henchmen.

Yes, the cub is tortured by guilt, thinking that he started the wildebeests running and is therefore responsible for his father's death. But even small children will have no trouble identifying whose fault it really is; Jeremy Irons gives the evil uncle, Scar, a personality worthy of the long and distinguished line of Disney cartoon villains. And cartoon villains   15 have always had a certain license to be evil, just because they are not real people, and children can see that they are not.

In *The Lion King*, they aren't people at all. It's always a little tricky to know how children absorb animal stories. *Born Free* was the great lion movie of my childhood, another movie about a lion cub who loses a parent, and I can dimly recall discussions of whether the hunting (and eating) scenes were too strong for children. In addition to the loss of Bambi's mother, there is Babar's mother, killed by a wicked hunter on the third page of *The Story of Babar*; within two pages, Babar is consoling himself by buying new clothes. In my experience, children are interested in the death of Babar's mother, and then quickly curious about Babar's new clothes.

I cried when Bambi's mother was shot, but my son, who was then 4, did not; he was interested in what would happen next. Parents are terrified of dying and leaving their child unprotected. For children, the issues are often different.

Note it was Bambi's and Babar's *mothers* who were killed off. Most Disney cartoon features have not included mothers at all; the title character in *The Little Mermaid* has only a father, as do Princess Jasmine in *Aladdin* and Belle in *Beauty and the Beast*. Snow White and Cinderella, of course, have evil stepmothers. Bambi has a mother, but she dies; Dumbo's mother spends most of the movie locked up.

In *The Lion King*, it is the father who dies. Though this may be dictated by the plot structure of *Hamlet*, it is connected to the movie's 90's-style celebration of the involved dad. Bambi's father, after all, was the archetypal distant father of the 1940's, the kind of stag who would stay out of sight and let his son take the hard knocks, and only show up the end to point the way to manhood. But Mufasa in *The Lion King* is there romping with his cub, offering sensitive advice about what it means to be the King of Beasts: "I'm only brave when I have to be," he tells his admiring son.

Will children see the deeper themes—Disney describes the movie as "allegorical"—or will they simply be entertained by the surface story? Will they understand the central moral, that Simba has to confess the guilt he has been hiding, and has to give up his carefree bachelor-hood and accept the responsibilities of leadership? Well, some children will understand some of it. And some of this New-Age-tinged message is there for adults, as are the numerous and clever animated references, from the Busby Berkeley animal acrobatics to the Leni Riefenstahl Nuremberg rally scene in which Scar reviews his hyena troops. You don't have to understand these associations to appreciate the scenes, and, similarly, most of the worrying about Oedipal overtones, guilt and responsibility will be done by parents.

It all comes down to what is real and what is not-real, which can admittedly be a complex question for children. A few months ago my 4-year-old daughter, Josephine, was going to her first opera. Her opera-loving but perhaps overambitious father prepared her as carefully as possible, playing his favorite recording of *La Traviata*, a little each day, explaining the story, showing her a photograph of Maria Callas, and teaching Josephine to listen for her voice of voices. Toward the end of the week, I came into the living room to find Josephine sobbing hysterically on the couch, with the music blaring and her father looking flummoxed.

Why was she crying? "Because Maria Callas is dying!" she wailed. And it was hard to know exactly how to comfort her; when her father told her that no, Callas was just playing the part of a woman who was dying, Josephine promptly asked, "So Maria Callas did not die?" Then, of course, he had to explain that as a matter of fact she was dead—and Josephine was in tears again.

She was eventually comforted, and went on to enjoy the opera tremendously, probably because Maria Callas did not die in our local production.

Children do, in general, understand the difference between real people and cartoon characters. And they understand the difference between people and animals. And these differences give movie makers a certain latitude to explore themes and scenes that they couldn't really touch in a live action movie for children.

Are there some children, maybe children trader 4, who could be too upset by this movie? Probably.   25

Will I take Josephine, my own 4-year-old? Certainly, and I would have taken her a year ago. The bad guys get it most satisfactorily in the end, and none of the sweet, cute, funny little fellows get hurt—the bird Zazu is actually endowed with cartoon invulnerability and can emerge unscathed from a lion's mouth or a boiling pot. Children may be made sad by the film, as their parents certainly will be, and they may find the villains scary, but they will also be interested and amused and involved, and that, after all, is the point of art.

Some children may make it through the death of Mufasa, and then fall apart at the final apocalyptic battle between lions and hyenas, which goes on a little too long for the just-keep-your-eyes-closed crowd (the ones who were traumatized by the wolves in *Beauty and the Beast*). I myself did not go to see *Jaws* as an adult, since I was a fairly timid ocean swimmer who did not want to watch images that would make me even more wary. On the other hand, I had no problem sending my 9-year-old to *Jurassic Park* last summer; I wouldn't really mind if he ended up very scared of live dinosaurs.

But let us, for heaven's sake, not start worrying that it's a problem if children respond to art with sadness or dismay or even fear, as long as these emotions can be discussed, as long as the sad can be comforted and the frightened reassured.

And if you do have a child who identifies too completely with Bambi or Simba, you can practice some reassurances, just to see how they feel. Then decide which you would be more comfortable saying: "Darling, I promise, there are no bad men with guns," or "Darling, I promise, there won't be a wildebeest stampede."

✎ Topics for Critical Thinking and Writing

1. In her fourth paragraph Klass says that literature is "supposed" to make audiences "wonder and worry and cheer and, yes, cry." Much of Klass's essay is in effect addressed to someone whose position might be summarized as saying, "Perhaps *adult* literature is supposed to do these things, but not children's literature." List Klass's arguments. Which is the strongest? The weakest? Why?
2. Think back to your childhood and recall a book or film (or perhaps even an event at a circus or fair) that in some ways distressed you. Do you now feel that you should not have been put through this experience, or that an adult should in some way have helped you to cope with it? Explain.
3. Evaluate Klass's final paragraph as a concluding paragraph.

Margo Jefferson

Margo Jefferson regularly writes books reviews and essays about the arts for The New York Times. *The following essay appeared in the* Times *shortly after Sinatra died.*

Sinatra, Not a Myth but a Man, and One among Many

Monotheism doesn't suit the world of popular music; that world has too many great performers. The pleasure I have always taken in Frank Sinatra's best singing is being tainted by the "thou shalt have no other singer" eulogies and by the cultural studies, conferences and papers still to come.

Rock-and-roll never stopped me from loving the truly wonderful Sinatra recordings of the 1950's. And loving those recordings never stopped me from lamenting and resenting the songs, the singing and the persona that appeared in the mid-60's and prevailed until his death. The voice and the man grew coarse. The easy swagger became belligerent, and the melancholy turned brashly sentimental.

Artists don't need to be remembered for anything but their best work. But they don't need to have that work enshrined in a mythology that places them above all others and will soon pass into (and pass itself off as) history and criticism.

Jule Styne was a good songwriter, but how can anyone let his famous comment about Sinatra stand? Sinatra brought style to popular singing,

Styne proclaimed: "Before Sinatra, songs were just sung straight and without much panache. Crosby had a little sense of style, but Sinatra was the one who went the whole way."

This is stupefying. The tradition of popular and jazz singing that produced Sinatra was invented in the 1920's by Louis Armstrong, Bing Crosby and Ethel Waters, with major input from assorted blues, nightclub and musical-theater performers. That tradition was extended and developed in the 1930's when Billie Holiday and Ella Fitzgerald led the innovations, with significant contributions from Connee Boswell, Mildred Bailey, Lee Wiley and Jimmy Rushing. (Rushing was largely a blues singer; and it's true that Sinatra didn't sing blues. But we're going for a full aerial view here, and the blues, with its mingling of lyricism and bravado, is a crucial part of the mix.) This was a golden age of singing, and it was filled—crammed, bursting—with panache, invention and all kinds of style.

It has been said that before Sinatra, singers tended to sound as though they barely knew the band they were working with. And of course that was true of mediocre to bad singers. It certainly wasn't true of the singers just named. Nor was it true of fine singers a cut or two below. Ivie Anderson certainly knew Duke Ellington's band, Helen Humes knew Count Basie's and Helen Forrest knew Benny Goodman's.

Sinatra was certainly the man when it came to reviving a big-band tradition that had all but capsized during World War II. And when it came to what the critic Gary Giddins has aptly called the rhythmic midground between pop gentility and jazz swing, Sinatra had the taste, skill and clout to bring audiences there, away from a mainstream glutted with slush and treacle.

He wasn't the first to discover that fruitful ground, but he retooled and refreshed it. He didn't invent dramatic naturalism either, but he deepened and extended its range and became our best singer in that tradition.

Peggy Lee is a close second. Her phrasing and rhythm are just as good, her intonation is better, and she can trump him in subtlety, but she doesn't have his vocal or temperamental force. And let us not forget that there is another song tradition that Sinatra admired and learned from but does not belong in: the nonnaturalistic, call it abstractly expressionist, tradition fathered by Armstrong and developed in quite different ways by Holiday, Fitzgerald and in Sinatra's era by Nat (King) Cole.

Innovative jazz and mainstream popular music grew further and further apart in the 1940's and 50's. Jazz singers still had their pop hits, but you certainly couldn't say that singers like Anita O'Day, Billy Eckstine, Sarah Vaughan or Mel Tormé were at the center of the culture's consciousness; they were on its vigorous borders or in its vanguard. Of the mainstream performers who made their names in the war and postwar years, Sinatra, Ms. Lee and Cole (despite the trash he sometimes had to record) were the hit makers who kept the jazz-pop links center stage. (Doris Day was a very good singer, but she concentrated on movies, not recordings.)

Sinatra's other great gift, of course, was his sexual charisma. Whatever he sang, it was there. The jaunty manliness was sexy; so was the melancholy introspection; so was the edgy rebelliousness one saw most clearly in his best film performances. He was a star, and he had what real stars have: the ability to take their gifts, their limitations and their influences and mold them into a unified whole called My Personality. The force of that personality is what makes Sinatra unforgettable.

But why claim, as some do, that Sinatra was the first popular singer to think of himself as an artist? Surely we don't still believe, given the evidence of the work they put in (the practicing, the jam sessions, the attention paid to opera singers, actors, horn players and their own own peers), that the masters of the preceding generation didn't know they were artists. Holiday, Armstrong and Mabel Mercer—the English song-actress nonpareil whom Sinatra called a major influence along with Holiday and Tommy Dorsey—all wore an armor of modesty in public, but that shouldn't fool us anymore. They knew their worth.

It has been very unpleasant reading these eulogies to see how segregated, racially and sexually, views of popular music remain. And wearying to have to note that nearly all of the pre-Sinatra innovators who are left out of this musical hagiography are blacks and women. In my generation this is called the Elvis Presley syndrome. The setting: A fertile but largely unformed musical world. The action: He arrives.

It makes one remember that preferential treatment based on race and gender has always been the norm in American life; it is only the beneficiaries who have changed in the last few decades. For all of his talent and drive, Sinatra benefited greatly from the preferential treatment given his race and gender, as if by natural right in those days. (So, for all of his greatness as a dancer, did Fred Astaire.) Not only did Sinatra have unparalleled power in the music industry, he got to act out a lavish drama of masculinity that thrilled the entire culture.

What black man could have gotten away with such cocky brashness   15 and become a star of that magnitude? (Witness the unusually passive public demeanor of Cole.) What woman of either race could have? They simply could not have seized the imagination and approval of a mass audience with such open displays of power and nose-thumbing.

Sinatra was a great performer because he joined kinetic musical force to what looked and sounded like pure naturalism. It was also his great good fortune to come of age in a time when the world still considered whiteness and maleness the best and most natural of states.

✎ Topics for Critical Thinking and Writing:

1. Jefferson traces Sinatra's style to previous singers. What aspects of Sinatra's style does she analyze, and to whom is he indebted for them?
2. In paragraph 8 Jefferson writes of dramatic naturalism without defining it. How would you define it? With what other song tradition does Jefferson compare dramatic naturalism?

3. What does Jefferson mean by "the Elvis Presley syndrome" and how does this term apply to Sinatra?

4. Jefferson accuses popular music critics of racial and sexual segregation. What does she mean?

5. In a parenthetical remark, Jefferson suggests that Fred Astaire, like Sinatra, benefited from racial and sexual segregation. In an essay of 500 to 750 words, analyze the style of a popular artist—a musical performer or a dancer—tracing the influence of other performers. Did the performer you are analyzing benefit from or suffer from racial and sexual segregation?

Amy Tan

Amy Tan was born in Oakland, California, in 1952, of Chinese parents. She recalls that as a child she felt "shame and self-hate. There is this myth that America is a melting pot, but what happens in assimilation is that we end up deliberately choosing the American things—hot dogs and apple pie—and ignoring the Chinese offerings." After her father's death she and her mother moved to Switzerland, but she returned to the United States and went to college in Oregon, and then moved to San Francisco. While working as a writer of computer manuals she began to write a series of interlocking short stories, one of which was published in a little magazine. The complete group was published as The Joy Luck Club *(1989); among her later books are a novel,* The Kitchen God's Wife *(1992), and a book for children,* The Moon Lady *(1992).*

In the Canon, For All the Wrong Reasons

Several years ago I learned that I had passed a new literary milestone. I had made it to the Halls of Education under the rubric of "Multicultural Literature," also known in many schools as "Required Reading."

Thanks to this development, I now meet students who proudly tell me they're doing their essays, term papers, or master's theses on me. By that they mean that they are analyzing not just my books but me—my gradeschool achievements, youthful indiscretions, marital status, as well as the movies I watched as a child, the slings and arrows I suffered as a minority, and so forth—all of which, with the hindsight of classroom literary investigation, prove to contain many Chinese omens that made it inevitable that I would become a writer.

Once I read a master's thesis on feminist writings, which included examples from *The Joy Luck Club*. The student noted that I had often used the number four, something on the order of thirty-two or thirty-six times—in any case, a number divisible by four. She pointed out that there were four mothers, four daughters, four sections of the book, four stories per section. Furthermore, there were four sides to a mah jong table, four directions of the wind, four players. More important, she postulated, my use of the number four was a symbol for the four stages of psychological development, which corresponded in uncanny ways to the four stages of some type of Buddhist philosophy I had never heard of before. The student recalled that the story contained a character called Fourth Wife, symbolizing death, and a four-year-old girl with a feisty spirit, symbolizing regeneration.

In short, her literary sleuthing went on to reveal a mystical and rather Byzantine puzzle, which, once explained, proved to be completely brilliant and precisely logical. She wrote me a letter and asked if her analysis had been correct. How I longed to say "absolutely."

The truth is, if there are symbols in my work they exist largely by accident or through someone else's interpretive design. If I wrote of "an orange moon rising on a dark night," I would more likely ask myself later if the image was a cliché, not whether it was a symbol for the feminine force rising in anger, as one master's thesis postulated. To plant symbols like that, you need a plan, good organizational skills, and a prescient understanding of the story you are about to write. Sadly, I lack those traits.

All this is by way of saying that I don't claim my use of the number four to be a brilliant symbolic device. In fact, now that it's been pointed out to me in rather astonishing ways, I consider my overuse of the number to be a flaw.

Reviewers and students have enlightened me about not only how I write but why I write. Apparently, I am driven to capture the immigrant experience, to demystify Chinese culture, to point out the differences between Chinese and American culture, even to pave the way for other Asian American writers.

If only I were that noble. Contrary to what is assumed by some students, reporters, and community organizations wishing to bestow honors on me, I am not an expert on China, Chinese culture, mah jong, the psychology of mothers and daughters, generation gaps, immigration, illegal aliens, assimilation, acculturation, racial tension, Tiananmen Square, the Most Favored Nation trade agreements, human rights, Pacific Rim economics, the purported one million missing baby girls of China, the future of Hong Kong after 1997, or, I am sorry to say, Chinese cooking. Certainly I have personal opinions on many of these topics, but by no means do my sentiments and my world of make-believe make me an expert.

So I am alarmed when reviewers and educators assume that my very personal, specific, and fictional stories are meant to be representative down to the nth detail not just of Chinese Americans but, sometimes, of all Asian culture. Is Jane Smiley's *A Thousand Acres* supposed to be taken as representative of all of American culture? If so, in what ways? Are all

American fathers tyrannical? Do all American sisters betray one another? Are all American conscientious objectors flaky in love relationships?

Over the years my editor has received hundreds of permissions   10
requests from publishers of college textbooks and multicultural anthologies, all of them wishing to reprint my work for "educational purposes." One publisher wanted to include an excerpt from *The Joy Luck Club*, a scene in which a Chinese woman invites her non-Chinese boyfriend to her parents' house for dinner. The boyfriend brings a bottle of wine as a gift and commits a number of social gaffes at the dinner table. Students were supposed to read this excerpt, then answer the following question: "If you are invited to a Chinese family's house for dinner, should you bring a bottle of wine?"

In many respects, I am proud to be on the reading lists for courses such as Ethnic Studies, Asian American Studies, Asian American Literature, Asian American History, Women's Literature, Feminist Studies, Feminist Writers of Color, and so forth. What writer wouldn't want her work to be read? I also take a certain perverse glee in imagining countless students, sleepless at three in the morning, trying to read *The Joy Luck Club* for the next day's midterm. Yet I'm also not altogether comfortable about my book's status as required reading.

Let me relate a conversation I had with a professor at a school in southern California. He told me he uses my books in his literature class but he makes it a point to lambast those passages that depict China as backward or unattractive. He objects to any descriptions that have to do with spitting, filth, poverty, or superstitions. I asked him if China in the 1930s and 1940s was free of these elements. He said, No, such descriptions are true; but he still believes it is "the obligation of the writer of ethnic literature to create positive, progressive images."

I secretly shuddered and thought, Oh well, that's southern California for you. But then, a short time later, I met a student from UC Berkeley, a school that I myself attended. The student was standing in line at a book signing. When his turn came, he swaggered up to me, then took two steps back and said in a loud voice, "Don't you think you have a responsibility to write about Chinese men as positive role models?"

In the past, I've tried to ignore the potshots. A *Washington Post* reporter once asked me what I thought of another Asian American writer calling me something on the order of "a running dog whore sucking on the tit of the imperialist white pigs."

"Well," I said, "you can't please everyone, can you?" I pointed out   15
that readers are free to interpret a book as they please, and that they are free to appreciate or not appreciate the result. Besides, reacting to your critics makes a writer look defensive, petulant, and like an all-around bad sport.

But lately I've started thinking it's wrong to take such a laissez-faire attitude. Lately I've come to think that I must say something, not so much to defend myself and my work but to express my hopes for American literature, for what it has the potential to become in the twenty-first century—that is, a truly American literature, democratic in the way it includes many colorful voices.

Until recently, I didn't think it was important for writers to express their private intentions in order for their work to be appreciated; I believed that any analysis of my intentions belonged behind the closed doors of literature classes. But I've come to realize that the study of literature does have its effect on how books are being read, and thus on what might be read, published, and written in the future. For that reason, I do believe writers today must talk about their intentions—if for no other reason than to serve as an antidote to what others say our intentions should be.

For the record, I don't write to dig a hole and fill it with symbols. I don't write stories as ethnic themes. I don't write to represent life in general. And I certainly don't write because I have answers. If I knew everything there is to know about mothers and daughters, Chinese and Americans, I wouldn't have any stories left to imagine. If I had to write about only positive role models, I wouldn't have enough imagination left to finish the first story. If I knew what to do about immigration, I would be a sociologist or a politician and not a long-winded storyteller.

So why do I write?

Because my childhood disturbed me, pained me, made me ask foolish   20
questions. And the questions still echo. Why does my mother always talk about killing herself? Why did my father and brother have to die? If I die, can I be reborn into a happy family? Those early obsessions led to a belief that writing could be my salvation, providing me with the sort of freedom and danger, satisfaction and discomfort, truth and contradiction I can't find in anything else in life.

I write to discover the past for myself. I don't write to change the future for others. And if others are moved by my work—if they love their mothers more, scold their daughters less, or divorce their husbands who were not positive role models—I'm often surprised, usually grateful to hear from kind readers. But I don't take either credit or blame for changing their lives for better or for worse.

Writing, for me, is an act of faith, a hope that I will discover what I mean by "truth." I also think of reading as an act of faith, a hope that I will discover something remarkable about ordinary life, about myself. And if the writer and the reader discover the same thing, if they have that connection, the act of faith has resulted in an act of magic. To me, that's the mystery and the wonder of both life and fiction—the connection between two individuals who discover in the end that they are more the same than they are different.

And if that doesn't happen, it's nobody's fault. There are still plenty of other books on the shelf. Choose what you like.

✎ Topics for Critical Thinking and Writing

1. In paragraph 11 Tan mentions that her books are "required reading" in various courses. What qualities, in your view, should a book of fiction have if it is to be required reading?

2. In paragraph 21 Tan says she doesn't expect her books to influence her readers. Have you ever read a work that has indeed shaped your thoughts or actions in even the slightest degree? If so, explain. If not, explain why you read anything, other than to kill time.

3. The patterns that critics see, Tan says in her first six paragraphs, are not present or, if present, are accidental. Are you convinced, or do you think (1) she may be speaking tongue-in-cheek, or (2) she may not be aware of how her unconscious mind works? In an essay of 250 words indicate why you do or do not accept at face value her words on this point.

4. Tan says (paragraph 15) that "readers are free to interpret a book as they please." She goes on, however, in paragraph 16 to indicate that she no longer holds this "laissez-faire" attitude. Do you believe that your interpretation of a work should coincide with the author's? In an essay of 250 words, explain why, or why not.

5. In paragraph 18 Tan says she cannot write a story with only "positive role models." Can you think of a work of literature that includes a character from a minority group who is not a "positive" role model? (Many people believe that Shylock in Shakespeare's *The Merchant of Venice* is such an example.) If you are familiar with such a work, do you think that members of the minority group are right to find the depiction offensive? Should such a work not be taught in high school, and perhaps not even in college? Explain, in an essay of 500 words.

Eudora Welty

Eudora Welty was born in Jackson, Mississippi, in 1909. Although she earned a bachelor's degree at the University of Wisconsin and spent a year studying advertising in New York City at the Columbia University Graduate School of Business, she has lived almost all of her life in Jackson.
In the preface to her Collected Stories *she says.*

I have been told, both in approval and in accusation, that I seem to love all my characters. What I do in writing of any character is to try to enter into the mind, heart and skin of a human being who is not myself. Whether this happens to be a man or a woman, old or young, with skin black or white, the primary challenge lies in making the jump itself. It is the act of a writer's imagination that I set most high.

In addition to writing stories and novels. Welty has written a book about fiction. The Eye of the Story *(1977), and a memoir,* One Writer's Beginnings *(1984). Here is one of her stories, 'A Worn Path,' followed by her discussion of the work, in* The Eye of the Story.

A Worn Path

It was December—a bright frozen day in the early morning. Far out in the country there was an old Negro woman with her head tied in a red rag, coming along a path through the pinewoods. Her name was Phoenix Jackson. She was very old and small and she walked slowly in the dark pine shadows, moving a little from side to side in her steps, with the balanced heaviness and lightness of a pendulum in a grandfather clock. She carried a thin, small cane made from an umbrella, and with this she kept tapping the frozen earth in front of her. This made a grave and persistent noise in the still air, that seemed meditative like the chirping of a solitary little bird.

She wore a dark striped dress reaching down to her shoe tops, and an equally long apron of bleached sugar sacks, with a full pocket: all neat and tidy, but every time she took a step she might have fallen over her shoe-laces, which dragged from her unlaced shoes. She looked straight ahead. Her eyes were blue with age. Her skin had a pattern all its own of numberless branching wrinkles and as though a whole little tree stood in the middle of her forehead, but a golden color ran underneath, and the two knobs of her cheeks were illuminated by a yellow burning under the dark. Under the red rag her hair came down on her neck in the frailest of ringlets, still black, and with an odor like copper.

Now and then there was a quivering in the thicket. Old Phoenix said, "Out of my way, all you foxes, owls, beetles, jack rabbits, coons, and wild animals! . . . Keep out from under these feet, little bob-whites. . . . Keep the big wild hogs out of my path. Don't let none of those come running my direction. I got a long way." Under her small black-freckled hand her cane, limber as a buggy whip, would switch at the brush as if to rouse up any hiding things.

On she went. The woods were deep and still. The sun made the pine needles almost too bright to look at, up where the wind rocked. The cones dropped as light as feathers. Down in the hollow was the mourning dove—it was not too late for him.

The path ran up a hill. "Seem like there is chains about my feet, time I get this far," she said, in the voice of argument old people keep to use with themselves. "Something always take a hold of me on this hill—pleads I should stay."

After she got to the top she turned and gave a full, severe look behind her where she had come. "Up through pines," she said at length. "Now down through oaks."

Her eyes opened their widest, and she started down gently. But before she got to the bottom of the hill a bush caught her dress.

Her fingers were busy and intent, but her skirts were full and long, so that before she could pull them free in one place they were caught in another. It was not possible to allow the dress to tear. "I in the thorny bush," she said. "Thorns, you doing your appointed work. Never want to let folks pass—no sir. Old eyes thought you was a pretty little *green* bush."

Finally, trembling all over, she stood free, and after a moment dared to stoop for her cane.

"Sun so high!" she cried, leaning back and looking, while the thick tears went over her eyes. "The time getting all gone here."

At the foot of this hill was a place where a log was laid across the creek.

"Now comes the trial," said Phoenix.

Putting her right foot out, she mounted the log and shut her eyes. Lifting her skirt, levelling her cane fiercely before her, like a festival figure in some parade, she began to march across. Then she opened her eyes and she was safe on the other side.

"I wasn't as old as I thought," she said.

But she sat down to rest. She spread her skirts on the bank around her and folded her hands over her knees. Up above her was a tree in a pearly cloud of mistletoe. She did not dare to close her eyes, and when a little boy brought her a little plate with a slice of marble-cake on it she spoke to him. "That would be acceptable," she said. But when she went to take it there was just her own hand in the air.

So she left that tree, and had to go through a barbed-wire fence. There she had to creep and crawl, spreading her knees and stretching her fingers like a baby trying to climb the steps. But she talked loudly to herself: she could not let her dress be torn now, so late in the day, and she could not pay for having her arm or leg sawed off if she got caught fast where she was.

At last she was safe through the fence and risen up out in the clearing. Big dead trees, like black men with one arm, were standing in the purple stalks of the withered cotton field. There sat a buzzard.

"Who you watching?"

In the furrow she made her way along.

"Glad this not the season for bulls," she said, looking sideways, "and the good Lord made his snakes to curl up and sleep in the winter. A pleasure I don't see no two-headed snake coming around that tree, where it come once. It took a while to get by him, back in the summer."

She passed through the old cotton and went into a field of dead corn. It whispered and shook and was taller than her head. "Through the maze now," she said, for there was no path.

Then there was something tall, black, and skinny there, moving before her.

At first she took it for a man. It could have been a man dancing in the field. But she stood still and listened, and it did not make a sound. It was as silent as a ghost.

"Ghost," she said sharply, "who be you the ghost of? For I have heard of nary death close by."

But there was no answer—only the ragged dancing in the wind.

She shut her eyes, reached out her hand, and touched a sleeve. She found a coat and inside that an emptiness, cold as ice.

"You scarecrow," she said. Her face lighted. "I ought to be shut up for good," she said with laughter. "My senses is gone, I too old. I the oldest people I ever know. Dance, old scarecrow," she said, "while I dancing with you."

She kicked her foot over the furrow, and with mouth drawn down, shook her head once or twice in a little strutting way. Some husks blew down and whirled in streamers about her skirts.

Then she went on, parting her way from side to side with the cane, through the whispering field. At last she came to the end, to a wagon truck where the silver grass blew between the red ruts. The quail were walking around like pullets, seeming all dainty and unseen.

"Walk pretty," she said. "This the easy place. This the easy going."   30

She followed the track, swaying through the quiet bare fields, through the little strings of trees silver in their dead leaves, past cabins silver from weather, with the doors and windows boarded shut, all like old women under a spell sitting there. "I walking in their sleep," she said, nodding her head vigorously.

In a ravine she went where a spring was silently flowing through a hollow log. Old Phoenix bent and drank. "Sweet-gum makes the water sweet," she said, and drank more. "Nobody know who made this well, for it was here when I was born."

The track crossed a swampy part where the moss hung as white as lace from every limb. "Sleep on, alligators, and blow your bubbles." Then the track went into the road.

Deep, deep the road went down between the high green-colored banks. Overhead the live-oaks met, and it was as dark as a cave.

A black dog with a lolling tongue came up out of the weeds by the   35 ditch. She was meditating, and not ready, and when he came at her she only hit him a little with her cane. Over she went in the ditch, like a little puff of milk-weed.

Down there, her senses drifted away. A dream visited her, and she reached her hand up, but nothing reached down and gave her a pull. So she lay there and presently went to talking. "Old woman," she said to herself, "that black dog come up out of the weeds to stall you off, and now there he sitting on his fine tail, smiling at you."

A white man finally came along and found her—a hunter, a young man, with his dog on a chain.

"Well, Granny!" he laughed, "what are you doing there?"

"Lying on my back like a June-bug waiting to be turned over, mister," she said, reaching up her hand.

He lifted her up, gave her a swing in the air, and set her down. "Any-   40 thing broken, Granny?"

"No sir, them old dead weeds is springy enough," said Phoenix, when she had got her breath. "I thank you for your trouble."

"Where do you live, Granny?" he asked, while the two dogs were growling at each other.

"Away back yonder, sir, behind the ridge. You can't even see it from here."

"On your way home?"

"No, sir, I going to town." 45

"Why, that's too far! That's as far as I walk when I come out myself, and I get something for my trouble." He patted the stuffed bag he carried, and there hung down a little closed claw. It was one of the bob-whites, with its beak hooked bitterly to show it was dead. "Now you go on home, Granny!"

"I bound to go to town, mister," said Phoenix. "The time come around."

He gave another laugh, filling the whole landscape. "I know you old colored people! Wouldn't miss going to town to see Santa Claus!"

But something held Old Phoenix very still. The deep lines in her face went into a fierce and different radiation. Without warning, she had seen with her own eyes a flashing nickel fall out of the man's pocket onto the ground.

"How old are you, Granny?" he was saying. 50

"There is no telling, mister," she said, "no telling."

Then she gave a little cry and clapped her hands and said, "Git on away from here, dog! Look! Look at that dog!" She laughed as if in admiration. "He ain't scared of nobody. He a big black dog." She whispered, "Sic him!"

"Watch me get rid of that cur," said the man. "Sic him, Pete! Sic him!"

Phoenix heard the dogs fighting, and heard the man running and throwing sticks. She even heard a gunshot. But she was slowly bending forward by that time, further and further forward, the lids stretched down over her eyes, as if she were doing this in her sleep. Her chin was lowered almost to her knees. The yellow palm of her hand came out from the fold of her apron. Her fingers slid down and along the ground under the piece of money with the grace and care they would have in lifting an egg from under a sitting hen. Then she slowly straightened up, she stood erect, and the nickel was in her apron pocket. A bird flew by. Her lips moved. "God watching me the whole time, I come to stealing."

The man came back, and his own dog panted about them. "Well, I 55 scared him off that time," he said, and then he laughed and lifted his gun and pointed it at Phoenix.

She stood straight and faced him.

"Doesn't the gun scare you?" he said, still pointing it.

"No, sir. I seen plenty go off closer by, in my day, and for less than what I done," she said, holding utterly still.

He smiled, and shouldered the gun. "Well, Granny," he said, "You must be a hundred years old, and scared of nothing. I'd give you a dime if I had any money with me. But you take my advice and stay home, and nothing will happen to you."

"I bound to go on my way, mister," said Phoenix. She inclined her 60 head in the red rag. Then they went in different directions, but she could hear the gun shooting again and again over the hill.

She walked on. The shadows hung from the oak trees to the road like curtains. Then she smelled wood-smoke, and smelled the river, and she saw a steeple and the cabins on their steep steps. Dozens of little black children whirled around her. There ahead was Natchez shining. Bells were ringing. She walked on.

In the paved city it was Christmas time. There were red and green electric lights strung and crisscrossed everywhere, and all turned on in the daytime. Old Phoenix would have been lost if she had not distrusted her eyesight and depended on her feet to know where to take her.

She paused quietly on the sidewalk where people were passing by. A lady came along in the crowd, carrying an armful of red-, green-, and silver-wrapped presents; she gave off perfume like the red roses in hot summer, and Phoenix stopped her.

"Please, missy, will you lace up my shoe?" She held up her foot.

"What do you want, Grandma?"   65

"See my shoe," said Phoenix. "Do all right for out in the country, but wouldn't look right to go in a big building."

"Stand still then, Grandma," said the lady. She put her packages down on the sidewalk beside her and laced and tied both shoes tightly.

"Can't lace 'em with a cane," said Phoenix. "Thank you, missy. I doesn't mind asking a nice lady to tie up my shoe, when I gets out on the street."

Moving slowly and from side to side, she went into the big building and into a tower of steps, where she walked up and around and around until her feet knew to stop.

She entered a door, and there she saw nailed up on the wall the docu-   70
ment that had been stamped with the gold seal and framed in the gold frame, which matched the dream that was hung up in her head.

"Here I be," she said. There was a fixed and ceremonial stiffness over her body.

"A charity case, I suppose," said an attendant who sat at the desk before her.

But Phoenix only looked above her head. There was sweat on her face, the wrinkles in her skin shone like a bright net.

"Speak up, Grandma," the woman said. "What's your name? We must have your history, you know. Have you been here before? What seems to be the trouble with you?"

Old Phoenix only gave a twitch to her face as if a fly were bothering   75
her.

"Are you deaf?" cried the attendant.

But then the nurse came in.

"Oh, that's just old Aunt Phoenix," she said. "She doesn't come for herself—she has a little grandson. She makes these trips just as regular as clockwork. She lives away back off the old Natchez Trace." She bent down. "Well, Aunt Phoenix, why don't you just take a seat? We won't keep you standing after your long trip." She pointed.

The old woman sat down, bolt upright in the chair.

"Now, how is the boy?" asked the nurse.   80

Old Phoenix did not speak.

"I said, how is the boy?"

But Phoenix only waited and stared straight ahead, her face very solemn and withdrawn into the rigidity.

"Is his throat any better?" asked the nurse. "Aunt Phoenix, don't you hear me? Is your grandson's throat any better since the last time you came for the medicine?"

With her hands on her knees, the old woman waited, silent, erect and motionless, just as if she were in armor.   85

"You mustn't take up our time this way, Aunt Phoenix," the nurse said. "Tell us quickly about your grandson, and get it over. He isn't dead, is he?"

At last there came a flicker and then a flame of comprehension across her face, and she spoke.

"My grandson. It was my memory had left me. There I sat and forgot why I made my long trip."

"Forgot?" The nurse frowned. "After you came so far?"

Then Phoenix was like an old woman begging a dignified forgiveness   90
for waking up frightened in the night. "I never did go to school. I was too old at the Surrender," she said in a soft voice. "I'm an old woman without an education. It was my memory fail me. My little grandson, he is just the same, and I forgot it in the coming."

"Throat never heals, does it?" said the nurse, speaking in a loud, sure voice to Old Phoenix. By now she had a card with something written on it, a little list. "Yes. Swallowed lye. When was it—January—two-three years ago—"

Phoenix spoke unasked now. "No, missy, he not dead, he just the same. Every little while his throat begin to close up again, and he not able to swallow. He not get his breath. He not able to help himself. So the time come around, and I go on another trip for the soothing medicine."

"All right. The doctor said as long as you came to get it, you could have it," said the nurse. "But it's an obstinate case."

"My little grandson, he sit up there in the house all wrapped up, waiting by himself," Phoenix went on. "We is the only two left in the world. He suffer and it don't seem to put him back at all. He got a sweet look. He going to last. He wear a little patch quilt and peep out holding his mouth open like a little bird. I remembers so plain now. I not going to forget him again, no, the whole enduring time. I could tell him from all the others in creation."

"All right." The nurse was trying to hush her now. She brought her a   95
bottle of medicine. "Charity," she said, making a check mark in a book.

Old Phoenix held the bottle close to her eyes and then carefully put it into her pocket.

"I thank you," she said.

"It's Christmas time, Grandma," said the attendant. "Could I give you a few pennies out of my purse?"

"Five pennies is a nickel," said Phoenix stiffly.

"Here's a nickel," said the attendant.   100

Phoenix rose carefully and held out her hand. She received the nickel and then fished the other nickel out of her pocket and laid it beside the new one. She stared at her palm closely, with her head on one side.

Then she gave a tap with her cane on the floor.

"This is what come to me to do," she said. "I going to the store and buy my child a little windmill they sells, made out of paper. He going to find it hard to believe there such a thing in the world. I'll march myself back where he waiting, holding it straight up in this hand."

She lifted her free hand, gave a little nod, turned round, and walked out of the doctor's office. Then her slow step began on the stairs, going down.

✎ Topics for Critical Thinking and Writing

1. If you do not know the legend of the phoenix, look it up in a dictionary or, better, in an encyclopedia. Then carefully reread the story to learn whether the story in any way connects with the legend.
2. Characterize the hunter.
3. What would be lost if the episode (with all of its dialogue) of Phoenix falling into the ditch and being helped out of it by the hunter were omitted?
4. Is Christmas a particularly appropriate time in which to set the story? Why or why not?
5. What do you make of the title?

Eudora Welty

Is Phoenix Jackson's Grandson Really Dead?

A story writer is more than happy to be read by students; the fact that these serious readers think and feel something in response to his work he finds life-giving. At the same time he may not always be able to reply to their specific questions in kind. I wondered if it might clarify something, for both the questioners and myself, if I set down a general reply to the question that comes to me most often in the mail, from both students and their teachers, after some classroom discussion. The unrivaled favorite is this: "Is Phoenix Jackson's grandson really *dead*?"

It refers to a short story I wrote years ago called "A Worn Path," which tells of a day's journey an old woman makes on foot from deep in the country into town and into a doctor's office on behalf of her little grandson; he is at home, periodically ill, and periodically she comes for his medicine; they give it to her as usual, she receives it and starts the journey back.

I had not meant to mystify readers by withholding any fact; it is not a writer's business to tease. The story is told through Phoenix's mind as she undertakes her errand. As the author at one with the character as I tell it, I must assume that the boy is alive. As the reader, you are free to think as you like, of course: The story invites you to believe that no matter what happens, Phoenix for as long as she is able to walk and can hold to her purpose will make her journey. The *possibility* that she would keep on even if he were dead is there in her devotion and its single-minded, single-track errand. Certainly the *artistic* truth, which should be good enough for the fact, lies in Phoenix's own answer to that question. When the nurse asks, "He isn't dead, is he?" she speaks for herself: "He still the same. He going to last."

The grandchild is the incentive. But it is the journey, the going of the errand, that is the story, and the question is not whether the grandchild is in reality alive or dead. It doesn't affect the outcome of the story or its meaning from start to finish. But it is not the question itself that has struck me as much as the idea, almost without exception implied in the asking, that for Phoenix's grandson to be dead would somehow make the story "better."

It's *all right,* I want to say to the students who write to me, for things   5
to be what they appear to be, and for words to mean what they say. It's all right, too, for words and appearances to mean more than one thing— ambiguity is a fact of life. A fiction writer's responsibility covers not only what he presents as the facts of a given story but what he chooses to stir up as their implications; in the end, these implications, too, become facts, in the larger, fictional sense. But it is not all right, not in good faith, for things *not* to mean what they say.

The grandson's plight was real and it made the truth of the story, which is the story of an errand of love carried out. If the child no longer lived, the truth would persist in the "wornness" of the path. But his being dead can't increase the truth of the story, can't affect it one way or the other. I think I signal this, because the end of the story has been reached before Old Phoenix gets home again: she simply starts back. To the question "Is the grandson really dead?" I could reply that it doesn't make any difference. I could also say that I did not make him up in order to let him play a trick on Phoenix. But my best answer would be: "*Phoenix* is alive."

The origin of a story is sometimes a trustworthy clue to the author— or can provide him with the clue—to its key image; maybe in this case it will do the same for the reader. One day I saw a solitary old woman like Phoenix. She was walking; I saw her, at middle distance, in a winter country landscape, and watched her slowly make her way across my line of vision. That sight of her made me write the story. I invented an errand for her, but that only seemed a living part of the figure she was herself: What errand other than for someone else could be making her go? And her going was the first thing, her persisting in her landscape was the real thing, and the first and the real were what I wanted and worked to keep. I brought her up close enough, by imagination, to describe her face, make her present to the eyes, but the full-length figure moving across the winter fields was the indelible one and the image to keep, and the perspective extending into the vanishing distance the true one to hold in mind.

I invented for my character, as I wrote, some passing adventures— some dreams and harassments and a small triumph or two, some jolts to her pride, some flights of fancy to console her, one or two encounters to scare her, a moment that gave her cause to feel ashamed, a moment to dance and preen—for it had to be a *journey,* and all these things belonged to that, parts of life's uncertainty.

A narrative line is in its deeper sense, of course, the tracing out of a meaning, and the real continuity of a story lies in this probing forward. The real dramatic force of a story depends on the strength of the emotion that has set it going. The emotional value is the measure of the reach of the story. What gives any such content to "A Worn Path" is not its circumstances but its *subject:* the deep-grained habit of love.

What I hoped would come clear was that in the whole surround of   10 this story, the world it threads through, the only certain thing at all is the worn path. The habit of love cuts through confusion and stumbles or contrives its way out of difficulty, it remembers the way even when it forgets, for a dumfounded moment, its reason for being. The path is the thing that matters.

Her victory—old Phoenix's—is when she sees the diploma in the doctor's office, when she finds "nailed up on the wall the document that had been stamped with the gold seal and framed in the gold frame, which matched the dream that was hung up in her head." The return with the medicine is just a matter of retracing her own footsteps. It is the part of the journey, and of the story, that can now go without saying.

In the matter of function, old Phoenix's way might even do as a sort of parallel to your way of work if you are a writer of stories. The way to get there is the all-important, all-absorbing problem, and this problem is your reason for undertaking the story. Your only guide, too, is your sureness about your subject, about what this subject is. Like Phoenix, you work all your life to find your way, through all the obstructions and the false appearances and the upsets you may have brought on yourself, to reach a meaning—using inventions of your imagination, perhaps helped out by your dreams and bits of good luck. And finally too, like Phoenix, you have to assume that what you are working in aid of is life, not death.

But you would make the trip anyway—wouldn't you?—just on hope.

✎ Topics for Critical Thinking and Writing

1. In paragraph 4 Welty suggests that those who ask the question about the grandson imply "that for Phoenix's grandson to be dead would somehow make the story 'better.' " Why might anyone think this? And *would* the story be better if the grandson were dead? Explain your answer.
2. Did Welty's comment increase your enjoyment and your understanding of her story? If so, offer specific details.
3. Although it seems natural to want to hear what authors have to say about their work, consider the possibility that authors may consciously or unconsciously misrepresent their work. (The painter Claes Oldenburg said that anyone who pays attention to what artists write about their pictures ought to have his eyes examined.) Do you think, therefore, that we should ignore what writers say about their works? Explain.

Robert Frost

Robert Frost (1874–1963) was born in California. After his father's death in 1885 Frost's mother brought the family to New England, where she taught in high schools in Massachusetts and New Hampshire. Frost studied for part of one term at Dartmouth College in New Hampshire, then did odd jobs (including teaching), and from 1897 to 1899 was enrolled as a special student at Harvard. He later farmed in New Hampshire, published a few poems in local newspapers, left the farm and taught again, and in 1912 left for England, where he hoped to achieve more popular success as a writer. By 1915 he had won a considerable reputation, and he returned to the United States, settling on a farm in New Hampshire and cultivating the image of the country-wise farmer-poet. In fact he was well read in the classics, in the Bible, and in English and American literature.

Among Frost's many comments about literature, here are three: "Writing is unboring to the extent that it is dramatic"; "Every poem is . . . a figure of the will braving alien entanglements"; and, finally, a poem "begins in delight and ends in wisdom. . . . It runs a course of lucky events, and ends in a clarification of life—not necessarily a great clarification, such as sects and cults are founded on, but in a momentary stay against confusion."

The Aim Was Song

Before man came to blow it right
    The wind once blew itself untaught,
And did its loudest day and night
    In any rough place where it caught.

Man came to tell it what was wrong: 5
    It hadn't found the place to blow;
It blew too hard—the aim was song.
    And listen—how it ought to go!

He took a little in his mouth,
    And held it long enough for north   10
To be converted into south,
    And then by measure blew it forth.

By measure. It was word and note,
    The wind the wind had meant to be—
A little through the lips and throat.   15
    The aim was song—the wind could see.

[1923]

Topics for Critical Thinking and Writing

1. Frost is telling a playful fable about the invention of "song." According to the fable, what are the essentials of song?
2. In a journal entry, or in a note of about one typed page, extend Frost's fable to cover some other kind or kinds of art, for instance architecture or music or dance. To what degree, if any, are his comments on "song" relevant to other forms?

13
LAW AND ORDER

Cell of a Modern Prison, U.S.A., 1975
Henri Cartier-Bresson

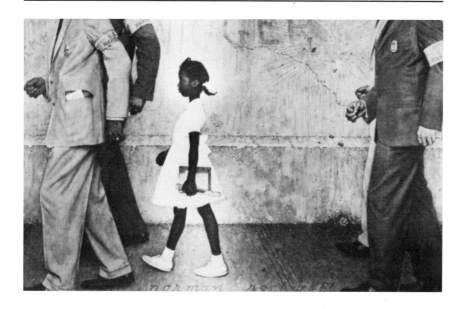

Short Views

The trouble for the thief is not how to steal the bugle, but where to blow it.
African proverb

Whether there was ever a significant increase in crime and when it might have occurred is puzzling, since the phrase, "the land is full of bloody crimes and the city full of violence," did not appear in a recent Chicago newspaper but in a report on a crime wave in the promised land about 600 B.C. as recorded in Ezekiel VII:23. The logical possibility of an ever-increasing crime wave becomes more doubtful when we consider the biblical origin of humankind: Adam, Eve and Cain committed the worst offenses possible and after Abel was killed, all survivors—or 75 percent of the first four human beings—had criminal records. In spite of all righteous claims to the opposite, this crime wave seems to have subsided, never to reach its biblical heights again. It is simpler and more correct to state that crime has always existed but statistics have not.
Kurt Weis and Michael F. Milakovich

Whoever desires to found a state and give it laws, must start with assuming that all men are bad and ever ready to display their vicious nature, whenever they may find occasion for it.
Niccolò Machiavelli

It is questionable whether, when we break a murderer on the wheel, we aren't lapsing into precisely the mistake of the child who hits the chair he bumps into.
G. C. Lichtenberg

If a man were permitted to make all the ballads, he need not care who should make the laws of a nation.
Andrew Fletcher

Nature has given women so much power that the law has very wisely given them very little.
Samuel Johnson

I asked him whether, as a moralist, he did not think that the practice of the law, in some degree, hurt the nice feeling of honesty. JOHNSON. "Why no, Sir, if you act properly. You are not to deceive your clients with false representations of your opinion: you are not to tell lies to a judge." BOSWELL. "But what do you think of supporting a cause which you know to be bad?" JOHNSON. "Sir, you do not know it to be good or bad till the Judge determines it. I have said that you are to state facts fairly; so that your thinking, or what you call knowing, a cause to be bad, must be from reasoning, must be from your supposing your arguments to be weak and inconclusive. But, Sir, that is not enough. An argument which does not convince yourself, may convince the Judge to whom you urge it; and if it does convince him, why, then, Sir, you are wrong, and he is right. It is his business to judge; and you are not to be confident in your own opinion that a cause is bad, but to say all you can for your client, and then hear the Judge's opinion." BOSWELL. "But, Sir, does not affecting a warmth when you have no warmth, and appearing to be clearly of one opinion when you are in reality of another opinion, does not such dissimulation impair one's honesty? Is there not some danger that a lawyer may put on the same mask in common life, in the intercourse with his friends?" JOHNSON. "Why no, Sir. Everybody knows you are paid for affecting warmth for your client; and it is, therefore, properly no dissimulation: the moment you come from the bar you resume your usual behaviour. Sir, a man will no more carry the artifice of the bar into the common intercourse of society, than a man who is paid for tumbling upon his hands will continue to tumble upon his hands when he should walk on his feet."

James Boswell

One law for the ox and the ass is oppression.

William Blake

The law, in its majestic equality, forbids the rich as well as the poor to sleep under bridges, to beg in the streets, and to steal bread.

Anatole France

Decency, security and liberty alike demand that government officials shall be subjected to the same rules of conduct that are commands to the citizen. In a government of laws, existence of the government will be imperilled if it fails to observe the law scrupulously. Our Government is the potent, the omnipresent teacher. For good or for ill, it teaches the whole people by its example. Crime is contagious. If the Government becomes a lawbreaker, it breeds contempt for law; it invites every man to become a law unto himself; it invites anarchy. To declare that in the administration of the criminal law the end justifies the means—to declare that the Government may commit crimes in order to secure the conviction of a private criminal—would bring terrible retribution. Against that pernicious doctrine this Court should resolutely set its face.

Louis D. Brandeis

The trouble about fighting for human freedom is that you have to spend much of your life defending sons of bitches; for oppressive laws are always aimed at them originally, and oppression must be stopped in the beginning if it is to be stopped at all.

H. L. Mencken

Censorship upholds the dignity of the profession, know what I mean?

Mae West

Thomas Jefferson

Thomas Jefferson (1743–1826), governor of Virginia and the third president of the United States, devoted most of his adult life, until his retirement, to the service of Virginia and of the nation. The spirit and the wording of the Declaration are almost entirely Jefferson's.

The Declaration of Independence

In CONGRESS, July 4, 1776.
The Unanimous Declaration of the Thirteen United States of America.

When in the Course of human events, it becomes necessary for one people to dissolve the political bands which have connected them with another, and to assume among the powers of the earth, the separate and equal station to which the Laws of Nature and of Nature's God entitle them, a decent respect to the opinions of mankind requires that they should declare the causes which impel them to the separation.

We hold these truths to be self-evident, that all men are created equal, that they are endowed by their Creator with certain unalienable Rights, that among these are Life, Liberty and the pursuit of Happiness.

That to secure these rights, Governments are instituted among Men, deriving their just powers from the consent of the governed.

That whenever any Form of Government becomes destructive of these ends, it is the Right of the People to alter or to abolish it, and to institute new Government, laying its foundation on such principles and organizing its powers in such form, as to them shall seem most likely to effect their Safety and Happiness. Prudence, indeed, will dictate that Governments long established should not be changed for light and transient causes; and accordingly all experience hath shewn, that mankind are more disposed to suffer, while evils are sufferable, than to right themselves by abolishing the forms to which they are accustomed. But when a long train of abuses and usurpations, pursuing invariably the same Object evinces a design to reduce them under absolute Despotism, it is their right, it is their duty, to throw off such Government, and to provide new Guards for their future security.

Such has been the patient sufferance of these Colonies; and such is now the necessity which constrains them to alter their former Systems of Government. The history of the present King of Great Britain is a history of repeated injuries and usurpations, all having in direct object the establishment of an absolute Tyranny over these States. To prove this, let Facts be submitted to a candid world.

He has refused his Assent to Laws, the most wholesome and necessary for the public good.

He has forbidden his Governors to pass Laws of immediate and pressing importance, unless suspended in their operation till his Assent should be obtained; and when so suspended, he has utterly neglected to attend to them.

He has refused to pass other Laws for the accommodation of large districts of people, unless those people would relinquish the right of Representation in the Legislature, a right inestimable to them and formidable to tyrants only.

He has called together legislative bodies at places unusual, uncomfortable, and distant from the depository of their public Records, for the sole purpose of fatiguing them into compliance with his measures.

He has dissolved Representative Houses repeatedly, for opposing with manly firmness his invasions on the rights of people.

He has refused for a long time, after such dissolutions, to cause others to be elected; whereby the Legislative powers, incapable of Annihilation, have returned to the People at large for their exercise; the State remaining in the mean time exposed to all the dangers of invasion from without, and convulsions within.

He has endeavoured to prevent the population of these States; for that purpose obstructing the Laws for Naturalization of Foreigners; refusing to pass others to encourage their migrations hither, and raising the conditions of new Appropriations of Lands.

He has obstructed the Administration of Justice, by refusing his Assent to Laws for establishing Judiciary powers.

He has made Judges dependent on his Will alone, for the tenure of their offices, and the amount and payment of their salaries.

He has erected a multitude of New Offices, and sent hither swarms of Officers to harass our people, and eat out their substance.   15

He has kept among us, in times of peace, Standing Armies without the Consent of our legislatures.

He has affected to render the Military independent of and superior to the Civil power.

He has combined with others to subject us to a jurisdiction foreign to our constitution, and unacknowledged by our laws; giving his Assent to their Acts of pretended Legislation:

For Quartering large bodies of armed troops among us:

For Protecting them, by a mock Trial, from punishment for any Murders which they should commit on the Inhabitants of these States: 20

For cutting off our Trade with all parts of the world:

For imposing Taxes on us without our Consent:

For depriving us in many cases, of the benefits of Trial by Jury:

For transporting us beyond Seas to be tried for pretended offences:

For abolishing the free System of English Laws in a neighbouring Province, establishing therein an Arbitrary government, and enlarging its Boundaries so as to render it at once an example and fit instrument for introducing the same absolute rule into these Colonies: 25

For taking away our Charters, abolishing our most valuable Laws, and altering fundamentally the Forms of our Governments:

For suspending our own Legislatures, and declaring themselves invested with power to legislate for us in all cases whatsoever.

He has abdicated Government here, by declaring us out of his Protection and waging War against us:

He has plundered our seas, ravaged our Coasts, burnt our towns, and destroyed the lives of our people.

He is at this time transporting large Armies of foreign Mercenaries to compleat the works of death, desolation and tyranny, already begun with circumstances of Cruelty & perfidy scarcely paralleled in the most barbarous ages, and totally unworthy the Head of a civilized nation.   30

He has constrained our fellow Citizens taken Captive on the high Seas to bear Arms against their Country, to become the executioners of their friends and Brethren, or to fall themselves by their Hands.

He has excited domestic insurrections amongst us, and has endeavoured to bring on the inhabitants of our frontiers, the merciless Indian Savages, whose known rule of warfare, is an undistinguished destruction of all ages, sexes and conditions. In every stage of these Oppressions We have Petitioned for Redress in the most humble terms: Our repeated Petitions have been answered only by repeated injury. A Prince, whose character is thus marked by every act which may define a Tyrant, is unfit to be the ruler of a free people. Nor have We been wanting in attentions to our British brethren. We have warned them from time to time of attempts by their legislature to extend an unwarrantable jurisdiction over us. We have reminded them of the circumstances of our emigration and settlement here. We have appealed to their native justice and magnanimity, and we have conjured them by the ties of our common kindred to disavow these usurpations, which, would inevitably interrupt our connections and correspondence. They too have been deaf to the voice of justice and of consanguinity. We must, therefore, acquiesce in the necessity, which denounces our Separation, and hold them, as we hold the rest of mankind, Enemies in War, in Peace Friends.

We, THEREFORE, the Representatives of the UNITED STATES OF AMERICA, in General Congress Assembled, appealing to the Supreme Judge of the world for the rectitude of our intentions, do, in the Name and by Authority of the good People of these Colonies, solemnly publish and declare, That these United Colonies are, and of Right ought to be FREE AND INDEPENDENT STATES; that they are Absolved from all Allegiance to the British Crown, and that all political connection between them and the State of Great Britain, is and ought to be totally dissolved; and that as Free and Independent States, they have full Power to levy War, conclude Peace, contract Alliances, establish Commerce, and to do all other Acts and Things which Independent States may of right do.

And for the support of this Declaration, with a firm reliance on the protection of divine Providence, we mutually pledge to each other our Lives, our Fortunes and our sacred Honor.

✎ Topics for Critical Thinking and Writing

1. What audience is being addressed in the Declaration of Independence? Cite passages in the text that support your answer.
2. The Library of Congress has the original manuscript of the rough draft of the Declaration. This manuscript itself includes revisions that are indicated below, but it was later further revised. We print the first part of the second paragraph of the draft and, after it, the corresponding part of the final version. Try to account for the changes within the draft, and from the revised draft to the final version.

> self evident,
> We hold these truths to be ~~seared & undeniable~~, that all men are creat-
> they are endowed by their creator
> ed equal ~~& independent,~~ that ~~from that equal creation they derive~~
>
> ~~equal rights some of which are in rights~~   with
> rights; that   these
> inherent & inalienable among ~~which~~ are ~~the preservation of~~ life, liber-
>
> ty, & the pursuit of happiness.

> We hold these Truths to be self-evident, that all men are created equal, that they are endowed by their Creator with certain unalienable Rights, that among these are Life, Liberty and the pursuit of Happiness.

In a paragraph evaluate the changes. Try to put yourself into Jefferson's mind and see if you can sense why Jefferson made the changes.

3. In a paragraph define *happiness,* and then in a second paragraph explain why, in your opinion, Jefferson spoke of "the pursuit of happiness" rather than of "happiness."

4. In "We Have No 'Right to Happiness'" (pages 20–24) C. S. Lewis discusses the meaning of "the pursuit of happiness" in the Declaration and a current misinterpretation of the phrase. How does he explain and define the phrase? How does his interpretation differ from what he considers an erroneous interpretation?

5. What assumptions lie behind the numerous specific reasons that are given to justify the rebellion? Set forth the gist of the argument of the Declaration using the form of reasoning known as a *syllogism,* which consists of a major premise (such as "All men are mortal"), a minor premise ("Socrates is a man"), and a conclusion ("Therefore, Socrates is mortal"). For a brief discussion of syllogisms, see page 869 (deduction).

6. In a paragraph argue that the assertion that "all Men are created equal" is nonsense, or, on the other hand, that it makes sense.

7. If every person has an unalienable right to life, how can capital punishment be reconciled with the Declaration of Independence? You need not in fact be a supporter of capital punishment; simply offer the best defense you can think of, in an effort to make it harmonious with the Declaration.

Martin Luther King, Jr.

Martin Luther King, Jr. (1929–68), clergyman and civil rights leader, achieved national fame in 1955–56 when he led the boycott against segregated bus lines in Montgomery, Alabama. His policy of passive resistance succeeded in Montgomery, and King then organized the Southern Christian Leadership Conference in order to extend his efforts. In 1964 he was awarded the Nobel Peace Prize, but he continued to encounter strong opposition. On April 4, 1968, while in Memphis to support striking sanitation workers, he was shot and killed.

Nonviolent Resistance

Oppressed people deal with their oppression in three characteristic ways. One way is acquiescence: the oppressed resign themselves to their doom. They tacitly adjust themselves to oppression, and thereby become conditioned to it. In every movement toward freedom some of the oppressed prefer to remain oppressed. Almost 2800 years ago Moses set out to lead the children of Israel from the slavery of Egypt to the freedom of the promised land. He soon discovered that slaves do not always welcome their deliverers. They become accustomed to being slaves. They would rather bear those ills they have, as Shakespeare pointed out, than flee to others that they know not of. They prefer the "fleshpots of Egypt" to the ordeals of emancipation.

There is such a thing as the freedom of exhaustion. Some people are so worn down by the yoke of oppression that they give up. A few years ago in the slum areas of Atlanta, a Negro guitarist used to sing almost daily: "Ben down so long that down don't bother me." This is the type of negative freedom and resignation that often engulfs the life of the oppressed.

But this is not the way out. To accept passively an unjust system is to cooperate with that system; thereby the oppressed become as evil as the oppressor. Noncooperation with evil is as much a moral obligation as is cooperation with good. The oppressed must never allow the conscience of the oppressor to slumber. Religion reminds every man that he is his brother's keeper. To accept injustice or segregation passively is to say to the oppressor that his actions are morally right. It is a way of allowing his conscience to fall asleep. At this moment the oppressed fails to be his brother's keeper. So acquiescence—while often the easier way—is not the moral way. It is the way of the coward. The Negro cannot win the respect of his oppressor by acquiescing; he merely increases the oppressor's arrogance and contempt. Acquiescence is interpreted as proof of the Negro's inferiority. The Negro cannot win the respect of the white people of the South or the peoples of the world if he is willing to sell the future of his children for his personal and immediate comfort and safety.

A second way that oppressed people sometimes deal with oppression is to resort to physical violence and corroding hatred. Violence often brings about momentary results. Nations have frequently won their independence in battle. But in spite of temporary victories, violence never brings permanent peace. It solves no social problem; it merely creates new and more complicated ones.

Violence as a way of achieving racial justice is both impractical and   5
immoral. It is impractical because it is a descending spiral ending in destruction for all. The old law of an eye for an eye leaves everybody blind. It is immoral because it seeks to humiliate the opponent rather than win his understanding; it seeks to annihilate rather than to convert. Violence is immoral because it thrives on hatred rather than love. It destroys community and makes brotherhood impossible. It leaves society in monologue rather than dialogue. Violence ends by defeating itself. It creates bitterness in the survivors and brutality in the destroyers. A voice echoes through time saying to every potential Peter, "Put up your sword." History is cluttered with the wreckage of nations that failed to follow his command.

If the American Negro and other victims of oppression succumb to the temptation of using violence in the struggle for freedom, future generations will be the recipients of a desolate night of bitterness, and our chief legacy to them will be an endless reign of meaningless chaos. Violence is not the way.

The third way open to oppressed people in their quest for freedom is the way of nonviolent resistance. Like the synthesis in Hegelian philosophy, the principle of nonviolent resistance seeks to reconcile the truths of two opposites—acquiescence and violence—while avoiding the extremes and immoralities of both. The nonviolent resister agrees with the person who acquiesces that one should not be physically aggressive toward his opponent; but he balances the equation by agreeing with the person of violence that evil must be resisted. He avoids the nonresistance of the former and the violent resistance of the latter. With nonviolent resistance, no individual or group need submit to any wrong, nor need anyone resort to violence in order to right a wrong.

It seems to me that this is the method that must guide the actions of the Negro in the present crisis in race relations. Through nonviolent resistance the Negro will be able to rise to the noble height of opposing the unjust system while loving the perpetrators of the system. The Negro must work passionately and unrelentingly for full stature as a citizen, but he must not use inferior methods to gain it. He must never come to terms with falsehood, malice, hate, or destruction.

Nonviolent resistance makes it possible for the Negro to remain in the South and struggle for his rights. The Negro's problem will not be solved by running away. He cannot listen to the glib suggestion of those who would urge him to migrate en masse to other sections of the country. By grasping his great opportunity in the South he can make a lasting contribution to the moral strength of the nation and set a sublime example of courage for generations yet unborn.

By nonviolent resistance, the Negro can also enlist all men of good will in his struggle for equality. The problem is not a purely racial one, with Negroes set against whites. In the end, it is not a struggle between people at all, but a tension between justice and injustice. Nonviolent resistance is not aimed against oppressors but against oppression. Under its banner consciences, not racial groups, are enlisted.

If the Negro is to achieve the goal of integration, he must organize himself into a militant and nonviolent mass movement. All three elements are indispensable. The movement for equality and justice can only be a success if it has both a mass and militant character; the barriers to be overcome require both. Nonviolence is an imperative in order to bring about ultimate community.

A mass movement of militant quality that is not at the same time committed to nonviolence tends to generate conflict, which in turn breeds anarchy. The support of the participants and the sympathy of the uncommitted are both inhibited by the threat that bloodshed will engulf the community. This reaction in turn encourages the opposition to threaten and resort to force. When, however, the mass movement repudiates violence while moving resolutely toward its goal, its opponents are revealed as the instigators and practitioners of violence if it occurs. Then public support is magnetically attracted to the advocates of nonviolence, while those who employ violence are literally disarmed by overwhelming sentiment against their stand.

Only through a nonviolent approach can the fears of the white community be mitigated. A guilt-ridden white minority lives in fear that if the Negro should ever attain power, he would act without restraint or pity to revenge the injustices and brutality of the years. It is something like a parent who continually mistreats a son. One day that parent raises his hand to strike the son, only to discover that the son is now as tall as he is. The parent is suddenly afraid—fearful that the son will use his new physical power to repay his parent for all the blows of the past.

The Negro, once a helpless child, has now grown up politically, culturally, and economically. Many white men fear retaliation. The job of the Negro is to show them that they have nothing to fear, that the Negro understands and forgives and is ready to forget the past. He must convince the white man that all he seeks is justice, *for both himself and the white man*. A mass movement exercising nonviolence is an object lesson in power under discipline, a demonstration to the white community that if such a movement attained a degree of strength, it would use its power creatively and not vengefully.

Nonviolence can touch men where the law cannot reach them. When   15
the law regulates behavior it plays an indirect part in molding public sentiment. The enforcement of the law is itself a form of peaceful persuasion. But the law needs help. The courts can order desegregation of the public schools. But what can be done to mitigate the fears, to disperse the hatred, violence, and irrationality gathered around school integration, to take the initiative out of the hands of racial demagogues, to release respect for the law? In the end, for laws to be obeyed, men must believe they are right.

Here nonviolence comes in as the ultimate form of persuasion. It is the method which seeks to implement the just law by appealing to the conscience of the great decent majority who through blindness, fear, pride, or irrationality have allowed their consciences to sleep.

The nonviolent resisters can summarize their message in the following simple terms: We will take direct action against injustice without waiting for other agencies to act. We will not obey unjust laws or submit to unjust practices. We will do this peacefully, openly, cheerfully because our aim is to persuade. We adopt the means of nonviolence because our end is a community at peace with itself. We will try to persuade with our words, but if our words fail, we will try to persuade with our acts. We will always be willing to talk and seek fair compromise, but we are ready to suffer when necessary and even risk our lives to become witnesses to the truth as we see it.

The way of nonviolence means a willingness to suffer and sacrifice. It may mean going to jail. If such is the case the resister must be willing to fill the jail houses of the South. It may even mean physical death. But if physical death is the price that a man must pay to free his children and his white brethren from a permanent death of the spirit, then nothing could be more redemptive.

Topics for Critical Thinking and Writing

1. In the first paragraph, the passage about Moses and the children of Israel is not strictly necessary; the essential idea of the paragraph is stated in the previous sentence. Why, then, does King add this material? And why the quotation from Shakespeare?
2. Pick out two or three sentences that seem to you to be especially effective and analyze the sources of their power. You can choose either isolated sentences or (because King often effectively links sentences with repetition of words or of constructions) consecutive ones.
3. In a paragraph set forth your understanding of what nonviolent resistance is. Use whatever examples from your own experience or reading you find useful. In a second paragraph, explain how Maya Angelou's "Graduation" (page 380) offers an example of nonviolent resistance.

Linda M. Hasselstrom

Linda M. Hasselstrom, a South Dakota rancher, writer, and environmentalist, has wielded a gun as a last resort, but she has never used it. Her essay first appeared in High Country News *and later appeared in a somewhat longer form in a collection of her essays,* Land Circle: Writings Collected from the Land *(Golden, Col.: Fulcrum, 1991).*

Ms. Hasselstrom has asked us to indicate that her choices for self-defense are based on a particular set of circumstances, that she does not advocate handgun ownership, and that she is not a member of any group that advocates handgun use.

A Peaceful Woman Explains Why She Carries a Gun

I am a peace-loving woman. But several events in the past 10 years have convinced me I'm safer when I carry a pistol. This was a personal decision, but because handgun possession is a controversial subject, perhaps my reasoning will interest others.

I live in western South Dakota on a ranch 25 miles from the nearest large town: for several years I spent winters alone here. As a free-lance writer, I travel alone a lot—more than 100,000 miles by car in the last four years. With women freer than ever before to travel alone, the odds of our encountering trouble seem to have risen. And help, in the West, can be hours away. Distances are great, roads are deserted, and the terrain is often too exposed to offer hiding places.

A woman who travels alone is advised, usually by men, to protect herself by avoiding bars and other "dangerous situations," by approaching her car like an Indian scout, by locking doors and windows. But these precautions aren't always enough. I spent years following them and still found myself in dangerous situations. I began to resent the idea that just because I am female, I have to be extra careful.

A few years ago, with another woman, I camped for several weeks in the West. We discussed self-defense, but neither of us had taken a course in it. She was against firearms, and local police told us Mace was illegal. So we armed ourselves with spray cans of deodorant tucked into our sleeping bags. We never used our improvised Mace because we were lucky enough to camp beside people who came to our aid when men harassed us. But on one occasion we visited a national park where our assigned space was less than 15 feet from other campers. When we returned from a walk, we found our closest neighbors were two young men. As we gathered our cooking gear, they drank beer and loudly discussed what they would do to us after dark. Nearby campers, even families, ignored them; rangers strolled past, unconcerned. When we asked the rangers point-blank if they would protect us, one of them patted my shoulder and said, "Don't worry, girls. They're just kidding." At dusk we drove out of the park and hid our camp in the woods a few miles away. The illegal spot was lovely, but our enjoyment of that park was ruined. I returned from the trip determined to reconsider the options available for protecting myself.

At that time, I lived alone on the ranch and taught night classes in   5
town. Along a city street I often traveled, a woman had a flat tire, called for help on her CB radio, and got a rapist who left her beaten. She was afraid to call for help again and stayed in her car until morning. For that reason, as well as because CBs work best along line-of-sight, which wouldn't help much in the rolling hills where I live, I ruled out a CB.

As I drove home one night, a car followed me. It passed me on a narrow bridge while a passenger flashed a blinding spotlight in my face. I braked sharply. The car stopped, angled across the bridge, and four men jumped out. I realized the locked doors were useless if they broke the windows of my pickup. I started forward, hoping to knock their car aside so I could pass. Just then another car appeared, and the men hastily got back in their car. They continued to follow me, passing and repassing. I dared not go home because no one else was there. I passed no lighted houses. Finally they pulled over to the roadside, and I decided to use their tactic: fear. Speeding, the pickup horn blaring, I swerved as close to them as I dared as I roared past. It worked: they turned off the highway. But I was frightened and angry. Even in my vehicle I was too vulnerable.

Other incidents occurred over the years. One day I glanced out a field below my house and saw a man with a shotgun walking toward a pond full of ducks. I drove down and explained that the land was posted. I politely asked him to leave. He stared at me, and the muzzle of the shotgun began to rise. In a moment of utter clarity I realized that I was alone on the ranch, and that he could shoot me and simply drive away. The moment passed; the man left.

One night, I returned home from teaching a class to find deep tire ruts in the wet ground of my yard, garbage in the driveway, and a large gas tank empty. A light shone in the house; I couldn't remember leaving it on. I was too embarrassed to drive to a neighboring ranch and wake someone up. An hour of cautious exploration convinced me the house was safe, but once inside, with the doors locked, I was still afraid. I kept thinking of how vulnerable I felt, prowling around my own house in the dark.

My first positive step was to take a kung fu class, which teaches evasive or protective action when someone enters your space without permission. I learned to move confidently, scanning for possible attackers. I learned how to assess danger and techniques for avoiding it without combat.

I also learned that one must practice several hours a day to be good at   10
kung fu. By that time I had married George; when I practiced with him, I learned how *close* you must be to your attacker to use martial arts, and decided a 120-pound woman dare not let a six-foot, 220-pound attacker get that close unless she is very, very good at self-defense. I have since read articles by several women who were extremely well trained in the martial arts, but were raped and beaten anyway.

I thought back over the times in my life when I had been attacked or threatened and tried to be realistic about my own behavior, searching for anything that had allowed me to become a victim. Overall, I was convinced that I had not been at fault. I don't believe myself to be either paranoid or a risk-taker, but I wanted more protection.

With some reluctance I decided to try carrying a pistol. George had always carried one, despite his size and his training in martial arts. I practiced shooting until I was sure I could hit an attacker who moved close enough to endanger me. Then I bought a license from the county sheriff, making it legal for me to carry the gun concealed.

But I was not yet ready to defend myself. George taught me that the most important preparation was mental: convincing myself I could actually *shoot a person.* Few of us wish to hurt or kill another human being. But there is no point in having a gun—in fact, gun possession might increase your danger—unless you know you can use it. I got in the habit of rehearsing, as I drove or walked, the precise conditions that would be required before I would shoot someone.

People who have not grown up with the idea that they are capable of protecting themselves—in other words, most women—might have to work hard to convince themselves of their ability, and of the necessity. Handgun ownership need not turn us into gun-slingers, but it can be part of believing in, and relying on, *ourselves* for protection.

To be useful, a pistol has to be available. In my car, it's within instant reach. When I enter a deserted rest stop at night, it's in my purse, with my hand on the grip. When I walk from a dark parking lot into a motel, it's in my hand, under a coat. At home, it's on the headboard. In short, I take it with me almost everywhere I go alone.

Just carrying a pistol is no protection; avoidance is still the best approach to trouble. Subconsciously watching for signs of danger, I believe I've become more alert. Handgun use, not unlike driving, becomes instinctive. Each time I've drawn my gun—I have never fired it at another human being—I've simply found it in my hand.

I was driving the half-mile to the highway mailbox one day when I saw a vehicle parked about midway down the road. Several men were standing in the ditch, relieving themselves. I have no objection to emergency urination, but I noticed they'd dumped several dozen beer cans in the road. Besides being ugly, cans can slash a cow's feet or stomach.

The men noticed me before they finished and made quite a performance out of zipping their trousers while walking toward me. All four of them gathered around my small foreign car, and one of them demanded what the hell I wanted.

"This is private land. I'd appreciate it if you'd pick up the beer cans."

"What beer cans?" said the belligerent one, putting both hands on the car door and leaning in my window. His face was inches from mine, and the beer fumes were strong. The others laughed. One tried the passenger door, locked; another put his foot on the hood and rocked the car. They circled, lightly thumping the roof, discussing my good fortune in meeting them and the benefits they were likely to bestow upon me. I felt very small and very trapped and they knew it.

"The ones you just threw out," I said politely.

"I don't see no beer cans. Why don't you get out here and show them to me, honey?" said the belligerent one, reaching for the handle inside my door.

"Right over there," I said, still being polite, "—there, and over there." I pointed with the pistol, which I'd slipped under my thigh. Within one minute the cans and the men were back in the car and headed down the road.

I believe this incident illustrates several important principles. The men were trespassing and knew it; their judgment may have been impaired by alcohol. Their response to the polite request of a woman alone was to use their size, numbers, and sex to inspire fear. The pistol was a response in the same language. Politeness didn't work; I couldn't match them in size or number. Out of the car, I'd have been more vulnerable. The

15

20

pistol just changed the balance of power. It worked again recently when I was driving in a desolate part of Wyoming. A man played cat-and-mouse with me for 30 miles, ultimately trying to run me off the road. When his car passed mine with only two inches to spare, I showed him my pistol, and he disappeared.

When I got my pistol, I told my husband, revising the old Colt slogan. "God made men *and women*, but Sam Colt made them equal." Recently I have seen a gunmaker's ad with a similar sentiment. Perhaps this is an idea whose time has come, though the pacifist inside me will be saddened if the only way women can achieve equality is by carrying weapons.   25

We must treat a firearm's power with caution. "Power tends to corrupt, and absolute power corrupts absolutely," as a man (Lord Acton) once said. A pistol is not the only way to avoid being raped or murdered in today's world, but, intelligently wielded, it can shift the balance of power and provide a measure of safety.

✎ Topics for Critical Thinking and Writing

1. In her first eight paragraphs, Hasselstrom sketches the kinds of experiences that ultimately caused her to carry a gun. Do you find her account of those experiences persuasive? Do they, in your opinion, justify her decision? If not, why not?

2. In paragraph 13 Hasselstrom introduces an idea that perhaps takes a reader by surprise. Do you think it is true, by and large, that a person who decides to carry a gun must, by means of "rehearsing," prepare himself or herself to use it? Whether or not you think it is true, what is the effect of her introducing this idea? Does it make her account more, or less, persuasive?

3. In paragraphs 17–23 Hasselstrom recounts an episode when her gun frightened off several belligerent and probably slightly intoxicated men. Do you think that this episode serves (as Hasselstrom doubtless thinks it does) as clear support for her position? What counterargument(s) can you imagine?

4. What devices does Hasselstrom use, as a writer, to convince her reader that she is not aggressive or gun-crazy?

Byron R. White

In January 1985 a majority of the United States Supreme Court, in a case called New Jersey v. T.L.O. *(a student's initials), ruled six to three that a school official's search of a student suspected of disobeying a school regulation does not violate the Fourth Amendment's protection against unreasonable searches and seizures.*

The case originated thus: an assistant principal in a New Jersey high school opened the purse of a fourteen-year-old girl who had been caught violating school rules by smoking in the lavatory. The girl denied that she ever smoked, and the assistant principal thought that the contents of her purse would show whether or not she was lying. The purse was found to contain cig-

arettes, marijuana, and some notes that seemed to indicate that she sold marijuana to other students. The school then called the police.

   The case went through three lower courts; almost five years after the event occurred, the
case reached the Supreme Court. Associate Justice Byron R. White wrote the majority opinion,
joined by Chief Justice Warren E. Burger and by Associate Justices Lewis F. Powell, Jr., William H.
Rehnquist, and Sandra Day O'Connor. Associate Justice Harry A. Blackmun concurred in a separate opinion. Associate Justices William J. Brennan, Jr., John Paul Stevens, and Thurgood Marshall dissented in part.

The Majority Opinion of the Supreme Court in *New Jersey v. T.L.O* [On the Right to Search Students]

In determining whether the search at issue in this case violated the
Fourth Amendment, we are faced initially with the question whether that
amendment's prohibition on unreasonable searches and seizures applies
to searches conducted by public school officials. We hold that it does.

It is now beyond dispute that "the Federal Constitution, by virtue of
the 14th Amendment, prohibits unreasonable searches and seizures by
state officers." Equally indisputable is the proposition that the 14th
Amendment protects the rights of students against encroachment by public school officials.

On reargument, however, the State of New Jersey has argued that the
history of the Fourth Amendment indicates that the amendment was
intended to regulate only searches and seizures carried out by law
enforcement officers; accordingly, although public school officials are con-
cededly state agents for purposes of the 14th Amendment, the Fourth
Amendment creates no rights enforceable against them.

But this Court has never limited the amendment's prohibition on
unreasonable searches and seizures to operations conducted by the police.
Rather, the Court has long spoken of the Fourth Amendment's strictures
as restraints imposed upon "governmental action"—that is, "upon the
activities of sovereign authority." Accordingly, we have held the Fourth
Amendment applicable to the activities of civil as well as criminal authorities: building inspectors, OSHA inspectors, and even firemen entering
privately owned premises to battle a fire, are all subject to the restraints
imposed by the Fourth Amendment.

Notwithstanding the general applicability of the Fourth Amendment   5
to the activities of civil authorities, a few courts have concluded that
school officials are exempt from the dictates of the Fourth Amendment by
virtue of the special nature of their authority over schoolchildren. Teachers and school administrators, it is said, act *in loco parentis* [i.e., in place of

a parent] in their dealings with students: their authority is that of the parent, not the State, and is therefore not subject to the limits of the Fourth Amendment.

Such reasoning is in tension with contemporary reality and the teachings of this Court. We have held school officials subject to the commands of the First Amendment, and the Due Process Clause of the 14th Amendment. If school authorities are state actors for purposes of the constitutional guarantees of freedom of expression and due process, it is difficult to understand why they should be deemed to be exercising parental rather than public authority when conducting searches of their students.

In carrying out searches and other disciplinary functions pursuant to such policies, school officials act as representatives of the State, not merely as surrogates for the parents, and they cannot claim the parents' immunity from the strictures of the Fourth Amendment.

To hold that the Fourth Amendment applies to searches conducted by school authorities is only to begin the inquiry into the standards governing such searches. Although the underlying command of the Fourth Amendment is always that searches and seizures be reasonable, what is reasonable depends on the context within which a search takes place.

[Standard of Reasonableness]

The determination of the standard of reasonableness governing any specific class of searches requires balancing the need to search against the invasion which the search entails. On one side of the balance are arrayed the individual's legitimate expectations of privacy and personal security; on the other, the government's need for effective methods to deal with breaches of public order.

We have recognized that even a limited search of the person is a substantial invasion of privacy. A search of a child's person or of a closed purse or other bag carried on her person, no less than a similar search carried out on an adult, is undoubtedly a severe violation of subjective expectations of privacy.   10

Of course, the Fourth Amendment does not protect subjective expectations of privacy that are unreasonable or otherwise "illegitimate." The State of New Jersey has argued that because of the pervasive supervision to which children in the schools are necessarily subject, a child has virtually no legitimate expectation of privacy in articles of personal property "unnecessarily" carried into a school. This argument has two factual premises: (1) the fundamental incompatibility of expectations of privacy with the maintenance of a sound educational environment; and (2) the minimal interest of the child in bringing any items of personal property into the school. Both premises are severely flawed.

Although this Court may take notice of the difficulty of maintaining discipline in the public schools today, the situation is not so dire that students in the schools may claim no legitimate expectations of privacy.

[Privacy and Discipline]

Against the child's interest in privacy must be set the substantial interest of teachers and administrators in maintaining discipline in the classroom and on school grounds. Maintaining order in the classroom has never been easy, but in recent years, school disorder has often taken particularly ugly forms; drug use and violent crime in the schools have become major social problems. Accordingly, we have recognized that maintaining security and order in the schools requires a certain degree of flexibility in school disciplinary procedures, and we have respected the value of preserving the informality of the student-teacher relationship.

How, then, should we strike the balance between the schoolchild's legitimate expectations of privacy and the school's equally legitimate need to maintain an environment in which learning can take place? It is evident that the school setting requires some easing of the restrictions to which searches by public authorities are ordinarily subject. The warrant requirement, in particular, is unsuited to the school environment; requiring a teacher to obtain a warrant before searching a child suspected of an infraction of school rules (or of the criminal law) would unduly interfere with the maintenance of the swift and informal disciplinary procedures needed in the schools. We hold today that school officials need not obtain a warrant before searching a student who is under their authority.

The school setting also requires some modification of the level of suspicion of illicit activity needed to justify a search. Ordinarily, a search—even one that may permissibly be carried out without a warrant—must be based upon "probable cause" to believe that a violation of the law has occurred. However, "probable cause" is not an irreducible requirement of a valid search.

15

[Balancing of Interests]

The fundamental command of the Fourth Amendment is that searches and seizures be reasonable, and although "both the concept of probable cause and the requirement of a warrant bear on the reasonableness of a search, . . . in certain limited circumstances neither is required." Thus, we have in a number of cases recognized the legality of searches and seizures based on suspicions that, although "reasonable," do not rise to the level of probable cause. Where a careful balancing of governmental and private interests suggests that the public interest is best served by a Fourth

Amendment standard of reasonableness that stops short of probable cause, we have not hesitated to adopt such a standard.

We join the majority of courts that have examined this issue in concluding that the accommodation of the privacy interests of schoolchildren with the substantial need of teachers and administrators for freedom to maintain order in the schools does not require strict adherence to the requirement that searches be based on probable cause to believe that the subject of the search has violated or is violating the law.

Rather, the legality of a search of a student should depend simply on the reasonableness, under all the circumstances, of the search. Determining the reasonableness of any search involves a twofold inquiry; first, one must consider "whether the . . . action was justified at its inception," second, one must determine whether the search as actually conducted "was reasonably related in scope to the circumstances which justified the interference in the first place."

Under ordinary circumstances, a search of a student by a teacher or other school official will be "justified at its inception" when there are reasonable grounds for suspecting that the search will turn up evidence that the student has violated or is violating either the law or the rules of the school. Such a search will be permissible in its scope when the measures adopted are reasonably related to the objectives of the search and not excessively intrusive in light of the age and sex of the student and the nature of the infraction.

This standard will, we trust, neither unduly burden the efforts of   20
school authorities to maintain order in their schools nor authorize unrestrained intrusions upon the privacy of schoolchildren. By focusing attention on the question of reasonableness, the standard will spare teachers and school administrators the necessity of schooling themselves in the niceties of probable cause and permit them to regulate their conduct according to the dictates of reason and common sense. At the same time, the reasonableness standard should insure that the interests of students will be invaded no more than is necessary to achieve the legitimate end of preserving order in the schools.

There remains the question of the legality of the search in this case. We recognize that the "reasonable grounds" standard applied by the New Jersey Supreme Court in its consideration of this question is not substantially different from the standard that we have adopted today. Nonetheless, we believe that the New Jersey court's application of that standard to strike down the search of T.L.O.'s purse reflects a somewhat crabbed notion of reasonableness. Our review of the facts surrounding the search leads us to conclude that the search was in no sense unreasonable for Fourth Amendment purposes. [End of majority opinion][1]

---

[1]Questions on this selection appear on page 701.

John Paul Stevens

Dissent in the Case of *New Jersey v. T.L.O.*

The majority holds that "a search of a student by a teacher or other school official will be 'justified at its inception' when there are reasonable grounds for suspecting that the search will turn up evidence *that the student has violated or is violating either the law or the rules of the school.*"

This standard will permit teachers and school administrators to search students when they suspect that the search will reveal evidence of [violation of] even the most trivial school regulation or precatory guideline for students' behavior. For the Court, a search for curlers and sunglasses in order to enforce the school dress code is apparently just as important as a search for evidence of heroin addiction or violent gang activity.

A standard better attuned to this concern would permit teachers and school administrators to search a student when they have reason to believe that the search will uncover *evidence that the student is violating the law or engaging in conduct that is seriously disruptive of school order or the educational process.*

A standard that varies the extent of the permissible intrusion with the gravity of the suspected offense is also more consistent with common-law experience and this Court's precedent. Criminal law has traditionally recognized a distinction between essentially regulatory offenses and serious violations of the peace, and graduated the response of the criminal justice system depending on the character of the violation.

✎ Topics for Critical Thinking and Writing

1. In the majority opinion Justice White says (paragraph 14) that it is "evident that the school setting requires some easing of the restrictions to which searches by public authorities are ordinarily subject." Does White offer evidence supporting what he says is "evident"? List the evidence, if you can find it in White, or if you can think of any.
2. In paragraph 20 Justice White writes of a "reasonableness standard." What does he mean by this phrase? (See paragraphs 18–20.)
3. Considering your own experience of school life as well as the arguments of Justice White and Justice Stevens, do you, on the whole, agree with the majority decision or with the dissent? What, in your opinion, are the chief issues? Explain.

4. Some forty years before this case, Justice Robert H. Jackson argued that the schools have a special responsibility for adhering to the Constitution: "That they are educating the young for citizenship is reason for scrupulous protection of constitutional freedoms of the individual, if we are not to strangle the free mind at its source and teach youth to discount important principles of our government as mere platitudes." Similarly, in 1967, in an analogous case involving another female pupil, Justice Brennan argued that "The lesson the school authorities taught her that day will undoubtedly make a greater impression than the one her teacher had hoped to convey.... Schools cannot expect their students to learn the lessons of good citizenship when the school authorities themselves disregard the fundamental principles underpinning our constitutional freedoms." Do you find these arguments compelling? Why or why not?

Derek Bok

Derek Bok was born in 1930 in Bryn Mawr, Pennsylvania, and was educated at Stanford and Harvard, where he received a law degree. He taught law at Harvard, then served as dean of the law school, and held the office of president of Harvard from 1971 to 1991. The essay that we give here was published in a Boston newspaper, prompted by the display of Confederate flags hung from the window of a dormitory room.

Protecting Freedom of Expression on the Campus

For several years, universities have been struggling with the problem of trying to reconcile the rights of free speech with the desire to avoid racial tension. In recent weeks, such a controversy has sprung up at Harvard. Two students hung Confederate flags in public view, upsetting students who equate the Confederacy with slavery. A third student tried to protest the flags by displaying a swastika.

These incidents have provoked much discussion and disagreement. Some students have urged that Harvard require the removal of symbols that offend many members of the community. Others reply that such symbols are a form of free speech and should be protected.

Different universities have resolved similar conflicts in different ways. Some have enacted codes to protect their communities from forms of speech that are deemed to be insensitive to the feelings of other groups. Some have refused to impose such restrictions.

It is important to distinguish between the appropriateness of such communications and their status under the First Amendment. The fact that speech is protected by the First Amendment does not necessarily mean that it is right, proper, or civil. I am sure that the vast majority of Harvard students believe that hanging a Confederate flag in public view—or displaying a swastika in response—is insensitive and unwise because any satisfaction it gives to the students who display these symbols is far outweighed by the discomfort it causes to many others.

I share this view and regret that the students involved saw fit to behave in this fashion. Whether or not they merely wished to manifest their pride in the South—or to demonstrate the insensitivity of hanging Confederate flags by mounting another offensive symbol in return—they must have known that they would upset many fellow students and ignore the decent regard for the feelings of others so essential to building and preserving a strong and harmonious community.

To disapprove of a particular form of communication, however, is not enough to justify prohibiting it. We are faced with a clear example of the conflict between our commitment to free speech and our desire to foster a community founded on mutual respect. Our society has wrestled with this problem for many years. Interpreting the First Amendment, the Supreme Court has clearly struck the balance in favor of free speech.

While communities do have the right to regulate speech in order to uphold aesthetic standards (avoiding defacement of buildings) or to protect the public from disturbing noise, rules of this kind must be applied across the board and cannot be enforced selectively to prohibit certain kinds of messages but not others.

Under the Supreme Court's rulings, as I read them, the display of swastikas or Confederate flags clearly falls within the protection of the free-speech clause of the First Amendment and cannot be forbidden simply because it offends the feelings of many members of the community. These rulings apply to all agencies of government, including public universities.

Although it is unclear to what extent the First Amendment is enforceable against private institutions, I have difficulty understanding why a university such as Harvard should have less free speech than the surrounding society—or than a public university.

One reason why the power of censorship is so dangerous is that it is extremely difficult to decide when a particular communication is offensive enough to warrant prohibition or to weigh the degree of offensiveness against the potential value of the communication. If we begin to forbid flags, it is only a short step to prohibiting offensive speakers.

I suspect that no community will become humane and caring by restricting what its members can say. The worst offenders will simply find other ways to irritate and insult.

In addition, once we start to declare certain things "offensive," with all the excitement and attention that will follow, I fear that much ingenuity will be exerted trying to test the limits, much time will be expended trying to draw tenuous distinctions, and the resulting publicity will eventually attract more attention to the offensive material than would ever have occurred otherwise.

Rather than prohibit such communications, with all the resulting risks, it would be better to ignore them, since students would then have little reason to create such displays and would soon abandon them. If this response is not possible—and one can understand why—the wisest course is to speak with those who perform insensitive acts and try to help them understand the effects of their actions on others.

Appropriate officials and faculty members should take the lead, as the Harvard House Masters have already done in this case. In talking with students, they should seek to educate and persuade, rather than resort to ridicule or intimidation, recognizing that only persuasion is likely to produce a lasting, beneficial effect. Through such effects, I believe that we act in the manner most consistent with our ideals as an educational institution and most calculated to help us create a truly understanding, supportive community.

✎ Topics for Critical Thinking and Writing

1. In paragraph 8 Bok argues that "the display of swastikas or of Confederate flags clearly falls within the free-speech clause of the First Amendment and cannot be forbidden simply because it offends the feelings of many members of the community." Suppose someone replied thus: "The display of swastikas or of Confederate flags—symbols loaded with meaning—is, to a Jew or an African-American, at least equivalent to a slap in the face. Such a display is, in short, an act of violence." What would you reply, and how would you support your response?

2. Do you find Bok persuasive? Support your answer with evidence about the points of his argument and his techniques of argument.

3. What rules, if any, does your school have concerning limitations of speech? What rules, if any, would you propose?

4. Compare Bok with Hawley (page 612) on reasons for and against limitations on students' freedom of speech.

Stephen Bates

Stephen Bates, Annenberg Senior Fellow, holds a law degree from Harvard Law School. He is the co-author of The Spot: The Rise of Political Advertising on Television *(1984) and the author of* The Media and Congress *(1987),* If No News, Send Rumors: Anecdotes of American Journalism *(1989), and* Battleground: One Mother's Crusade, the Religious Right, and the Struggle for Control of Our Classrooms *(1993).*

The Internet: The Next Front in the Book Wars

In two suburban Chicago high schools this year, students are analyzing satellite photos of current weather, tracking wildfires in California, questioning atmospheric scientists about their research and collaborating on writing projects with students thousands of miles away. "The Internet is making the school a more integral part of the world," said Barry Fishman, manager of the federally funded CoVis Network which provides the schools' Internet hookup.

But the Internet is also bringing seamier elements of the world into the schoolhouse. Sooner or later, Mr. Fishman and other educators realize, people will complain about what the Internet is making available to schoolchildren and the ceaseless battles over schoolbooks will soar into cyberspace.

The cyberspace battles may prove especially contentious, because the Internet contains a great many works not found on the shelves of most schools. "The School Stopper's Textbook," for instance, tells how to short-circuit electrical wiring, set off explosives in school plumbing and "break into your school at night and burn it down."

"The Big Book of Mischief" features detailed bomb-making instructions.

"Suicide Methods," based in part on Derek Humphry's book "Final 5 Exit," comprehensively analyzes various ways of killing oneself.

A drug archive offers recipes for marijuana brownies and a guide to constructing "bongs, pipes and other wonderful contraptions."

On several archives and Usenet discussion groups, hackers provide tips on breaking into computer networks, telephone systems and cash machines.

Some Usenet groups contain pornographic stories; others have photos of naked men, women and, occasionally, children.

"I don't think parents have ever had quite this challenge before," said Steve Bennett, an author who has developed computer activities for children. "You think your kid is mastering the Internet so he'll be ready for a technically sophisticated job—then you find he's got 'Popular Gynecology' up on the screen."

Schools can keep a pornographic book off the library shelf by not buy- 10 ing it, but they can't keep it from entering the building through cyberspace. The Internet is a headless web of computer networks, designed by Defense Department contractors in the 1960's to withstand nuclear war. Limiting a user's access to material on it is nearly impossible. "The Net interprets censorship as damage and routes around it," said John Gilmore, a leading activist for freedom of speech in cyberspace.

So when educators contemplate bringing the Internet into public schools, "the situation is essentially all or nothing," said Libby Black, director of the Boulder Valley School District's Internet Project in Colorado, which provides Internet accounts to more than 1,600 public school students. Like the fledgling CoVis and other publicly and privately funded networks that provide information services to schools, Boulder Valley excludes the "alt.sex" discussion groups from Usenet's "alternative" hierarchy, but an enterprising user can venture out on the Internet and find a network that does receive them. Even from the confines of an E-mail-only account, a student can instruct several automated systems to send Usenet posts, including those from the alt.sex groups, by return mail. It is the electronic equivalent of interlibrary loan, only beyond the librarian's control.

"You can't prevent it," said Peg Szady, who teaches a course on the Internet at Monta Vista High School in Cupertino, Calif. "There's just no way."

Consequently, schools must rely on discipline and supervision. Early on in the CoVis project, Mr. Fishman sat down with teachers at the two pilot schools. "We attempted to get a sense of how we could educate people to use these tools for good, and minimize people using them for resources not directly related to improving education," he said.

The result is a network-use policy that the student and a parent must sign. The form stipulates that "network use is primarily intended for the support of project work conducted in participating CoVis classes, and far less significantly for other purposes that students and teachers determine to be of educational value."

Other schools send permission forms home with students. The   15
Poudre School District in Fort Collins, Colo., alerts parents to the possibility of "defamatory, inaccurate, abusive, obscene, profane, sexually oriented, threatening, racially offensive, or illegal material" on-line. At Monta Vista, the policy instructs students not to access "areas of cyberspace that would be offensive to any students, teachers, or parents." Many schools limit students' electronic speech, prohibiting profanity, sexually oriented remarks, advertising, political lobbying and "flames" (vituperative verbal attacks). Violators can lose their accounts.

Some systems monitor students' use of the Internet. At Long Island's Oceanside High School, students must fill out a form summarizing each on-line session. Students at several schools in Chicago will soon log onto their Internet accounts using "smartcards," which will record their online movements for subsequent review by teachers. At the Poudre District in Fort Collins, administrators reserve the right to examine users' E-mail and other files. "You really have to do that with kids," said Larry Buchanan, a Poudre educational technologies specialist. "When they know somebody's watching them, they behave differently."

Schools impose such restrictions "to cover their butts," in the view of Russell Smith, a technology consultant for the state of Texas who has reviewed several schools' written policies. "Nobody wants to get sued."

The fear of litigation has a basis. "Some jurisdictions have laws that place a duty on everyone, not just schools, to prevent minors from being exposed to sexually related materials," said Mike Goodwin, online counsel of the Electronic Frontier Foundation. "Even if the material is not legally obscene—for instance, *Playboy* magazine—it may be that a party can be liable for giving that kind of sexually oriented material to a minor." Some states also prohibit "exposing minors to dangerous material or information," he added, but the courts have not definitively ruled on the constitutionality of such laws.

The seamy material on the Internet has not yet generated litigation, or in fact much controversy. At the relatively few schools now offering Internet accounts, students have had their accounts suspended for hacking, abusive E-mail and similar misbehavior more frequently than for accessing objectionable photos and texts.

Even so, educators know that cyberspace has the potential to ignite a   20
sizable controversy. "The nightmare [public school educators] have," Steve Cisler, a senior scientist in the Apple Computer library, wrote in a newsletter last year, "is of some legislator waving around a raunchy [digitized] image 'paid for with tax dollars and found on the State Educational Network,' or reading some choice posting from alt.sex.necrophilia." The furor becomes increasingly likely as more and more schools put students on-line frequently with accounts they can access from home, beyond the scrutiny of school officialdom—and as the public schools' traditional critics begin paying attention to the Internet.

"There's a lot of fundamentalist groups out there," said Mr. Smith, the Texas consultant. "I don't think they know what's up with the Internet yet."

Representatives of three conservative organizations—Concerned Women for America, Focus on the Family and the American Family Association—said they had not yet studied Internet access in public schools.

Conservative Christians won't be the only ones to take offense. Indeed, most protests so far in universities rather than public schools have come from other groups, according to a list prepared by Carl Kadie, co-editor of the electronic periodical *Computers and Academic Freedom News.*

Women have complained about the newsgroups devoted to pornographic photos and sex chatter, and several universities have banned them. In 1989 Stanford banned a Usenet discussion group over a joke that some users deemed anti-Semitic; accused of censorship, the university later backed down. In September of this year, the Education Department's Office for Civil Rights contended that a males-only on-line discussion group at a California junior college violated Federal anti-discrimination law.

Whether the complaints come from the right or the left, the Inter-   25
net's online community generally supports absolute freedom of inquiry. The phrase "information wants to be free" is a commonplace of Usenet discussions.

Mirroring that viewpoint, some civil libertarians have decried efforts to restrict how students use the Internet. In a statement issued in August, the Minnesota Coalition Against Censorship called for all public school students to enjoy unfettered Internet privileges, including access to "information that some have identified as controversial or of potential harm."

Most anti-censorship organizations are still studying the issue. "It's incredibly complex," said Candace Morgan, chairwoman of the American Library Association's Intellectual Freedom Committee. "The most difficult situations are those faced by school libraries."

People for the American Way, a liberal public-interest group, generally takes the position that no library materials should be kept from children, according to Leslie Harris, the organization's director of public policy. But, she added, pornographic images and some other materials on the Internet "may require a different answer."

"We are generally not for restrictions," said Roz Udow of the National Coalition Against Censorship. "But the Internet changes everything—it makes it all so accessible."

Meanwhile, computer engineers are looking for technical fixes. One   30
approach is a "reverse firewall." Whereas a firewall keeps outsiders from entering a computer system, a reverse firewall would keep users from going beyond a few uncontroversial zones on the Internet, according to Denis Newman, director of education network systems at BBN Systems and Technologies. BBN, he said, is at work on a prototype. Other companies are also pursuing technical solutions, according to Nelson Heller, publisher of a newsletter on educational technology.

Mr. Fishman of CoVis thinks that network architecture won't provide the answer. "Roadblocks end up taking away what's valuable—the ability of students to perform tasks that their teachers couldn't even conceive of," he said. In his view, the better approach is for educators to "spend time up front thinking about what objections people might raise, then try to defuse those concerns through education."

He hopes that educators succeed in pre-empting the protests. "Losing the Internet in schools just because of some information on it—and we're really talking about a small percentage of the total information—it's a pretty bad investment," he said. "If a student was smuggling dirty pictures in their science textbook, would we take away all the science textbooks?"

✎ Topics for Critical Thinking and Writing

1. It is widely agreed that the government has a compelling interest ("compelling interest" is a common legal term) in protecting children from pornography. Does this position in effect mean that schools should not make use of the Internet?

2. The final paragraph sets forth an analogy, which is offered as an argument. How convincing do you find this argument? Explain.

3. In paragraph 16 Bates says that some schools use a device that monitors the student's online movement, and that teachers review the account. In an

essay of 500 words indicate whether you believe this practice is appropriate. Support your position with arguments.

4. In paragraph 17 a technology consultant says—doubtless correctly—that schools employ restrictions because they fear they may be sued. But let's assume that a school does not have restrictions in place, and a parent sues on the grounds that the student has viewed sexually explicit material in school. You are a lawyer, take the side of the defense or of the plaintiff—the choice is yours—and present your argument to the jury, in about 500 words.

Barbara L. Keller

Barbara L. Keller, a lawyer, late at night experienced a break-in, but she nevertheless argues that guns, far from being a good means of self-defense, add to the likelihood that the innocent will be harmed.

Frontiersmen Are History

Late on a Friday night, I had a personal introduction to terror. My 11-year-old daughter and I were playing Scrabble. My husband had just phoned to let us know he was grounded in Dallas by bad weather. A moment later my front doorbell rang loudly and repeatedly. I stood up, wondering who in God's name was ringing at 1 o'clock in the morning. Then I heard the sound of shattering glass. Someone was breaking into my house.

As I grabbed my daughter and dashed out the side door to my neighbor's to call the police, she began to cry. "Mom! What about the boys?" My three sons—3, 4 and a mentally handicapped 8-year-old—were asleep upstairs. I had made a split-second decision to leave them and run for help. To go to them, or the phone, would have taken me right into harm's way. Being eight months pregnant, I couldn't carry them two at a time to safety. The minutes it took until the police arrived seemed like years. I wasn't permitted to enter the house until the officers had secured it. I stood on the sidewalk, fearing for my sons' safety and worrying about their reaction if they awoke to find armed policemen trooping through their bedroom. Blessedly, the boys slept through it, and the would-be intruders ran off without entering the house.

In the aftermath of what was for me a horribly traumatic experience, my husband and I considered and once again rejected the idea of buying a gun for protection. Police officers have told me a gun is not a particularly good defense strategy, especially where there are small children in the home. If the gun isn't loaded—or the ammunition isn't very nearby—it's not likely to be much help in a situation needing a fast reaction. Yet if it is loaded and handy, it poses a serious threat to children—and others.

Like most residents of Baton Rouge, I have strong views on gun control. Unlike most, I am for it. You have to understand that this is Louisiana. We have been characterized humorously, but I fear accurately, as a society of good ole boys who consider the shotguns displayed in the back of the pickup as a God-given right and a status symbol. We don't much care for being told what to do, especially by the government. During the trial of Rodney Peairs, acquitted of killing a Japanese exchange student who he mistakenly thought was invading his home on Halloween in 1992, a local news program conducted a telephone poll on the question of gun control. At that time, 68 percent of the respondents opposed stricter controls. Such measures routinely fail in our legislature, as they do in Congress.

One result is that we have criminals armed with semiautomatic and   5 assault weapons and a police force that is seriously outgunned. Our options, as I see them, are three: maintain the status quo, make it more difficult for criminals to obtain these weapons, or provide them to the police as well. The status quo is to me unacceptable, and the notion of a police force armed with assault rifles roaming the streets of Baton Rouge does not bring solace to my soul. It terrifies me. That leaves the option of gun control.

Why does this prospect engender such hysteria? I do not propose to outlaw guns—only to make them more difficult to obtain. No one with a criminal record or history of violent mental illness—and no child—should by law be able to purchase a gun. And *no one* has a compelling need to buy an assault weapon.

None of this may make a hill of beans of difference, directly, in the case of a homeowner protecting himself from real or perceived threats. But indirectly it can. We should rethink our cultural heritage and the historical gunslinger's mentality of "a Smith & Wesson beats four aces." We've outgrown the frontier spirit and the need of weapons for survival. In Baton Rouge, I am a definite oddity in not allowing my children, including my normal, rambunctious little boys, to play at shooting people. I don't want my children to think of guns as problem solvers. Nor do I favor the simplistic depictions of good guys versus bad guys.

What really frightens me is that if I were faced with the prospect of imminent harm to myself or my children and had a gun at the ready, I would reach for it, despite my feelings against using firearms for personal protection. Panic is a compelling emotion and basically incompatible with reason. It is tempting fate severely to keep a powerful weapon available to deal with panic-inducing circumstances. The police are trained in when and how to shoot, and innocent people can still fall victim to an officer's adrenaline surge.

I will for a very long time remember the sound of glass breaking and feel all over again the fear mingled with disbelief of that Friday night. If I'd owned a gun, I undoubtedly would have used it—probably to my own detriment. I do not know if the young men who so thoroughly violated my sense of safety were armed. I do know that if I'd had a gun, and had actually confronted them, they would have been more likely to harm me, and my children. It would have been I who escalated the potential for violence, and I would have had to live with the consequences—just like Rodney Peairs.

Although I have felt the terror of helplessness, owning a handgun is something I cannot do. And the "Shoot first, ask questions later" approach is an attitude I don't want to teach my children. Guns are like cars. We are so inured to their power we tend to treat them irresponsibly. We see them as commodities that we have a right to own and use as we please. Instead, we should limit the "right to bear arms" so that only trained, responsible citizens can buy guns for sport, recreation and protection—while those who would be most likely to use weapons detrimentally will have a much harder time getting them. Most of all, we need to reconsider our entire love affair with guns and the ways that this passion destroys innocent lives.

✎ Topics for Critical Thinking and Writing

1. Evaluate Keller's first two paragraphs as an opening for her essay.
2. Keller's title ("Frontiersmen Are History") is explained in her seventh paragraph ("We've outgrown the frontier spirit"). Exactly what does she mean? Do you accept the implicit assumption? Why, or why not?
3. If you had been in Keller's position when she heard the doorbell ring and the glass shatter, what would you have done? Loudly announce that you were armed—even if you weren't?
4. In her final paragraph Keller says that "the 'Shoot first, ask questions later' approach is an attitude that I don't want to teach my children." Suppose someone said to you that if you hear an intruder in the house, this lesson is entirely appropriate. In an essay of 500 words set forth your response.

Don B. Kates

Don B. Kates, a civil-liberties lawyer and criminologist, is the editor of Firearms and Violence. *The following essay, arguing that "widespread gun ownership is a net benefit for society," was first published in a conservative magazine,* National Review, *in 1995.*

Shot Down

Criminologists, criminals, and cops all have a professional interest in crime. It is therefore significant that criminological research has generally validated the skepticism of both police and criminals about the effectiveness of gun control. Yet the consensus among these three sets of professionals has received little attention in the popular media.

Surprisingly, in light of the fervent support for stringent gun control that many academics expressed in the 1960s, serious research in this area did not begin until the 1970s. That research demonstrates that no amount of control over mere weaponry can overcome the fundamental socio-cultural and economic determinants of crime. Indeed, the evidence indicates that banning gun possession by the general public is actually counterproductive.

The most prolific researcher in this area is Gary Kleck of Florida State University's School of Criminology. His encyclopedic 1991 book, *Point Blank: Guns and Violence in America,* has won high praise even from academics distressed by its findings. Broadly speaking, those findings are: 1) Gun possession by ordinary citizens is not a problem; the perpetrators of gun crime and accidents are aberrant individuals with histories of substance abuse, violence, felonies, and other dangerous behavior. 2) While outlawing possession of guns by such people is plainly sensible, it can bring at best marginal benefit as long as the fundamental determinants of their behavior remain unchanged. 3) Because guns empower the weak against the strong, and because victims are generally weaker than felons, widespread gun ownership is a net benefit for society.

Based on surveys of both the general populace and incarcerated felons, Kleck finds that gun-armed victims rout criminals three to four times more often than gun-armed criminals attack victims. And a victim who resists with a gun is only half as likely to be injured as a victim who submits—and far less likely to be robbed or raped.

In 1993 the American Society of Criminology declared Kleck's book   5
the single most important contribution to criminological research in the previous three years. Kleck's findings are so unimpeachable that critics often resort to ad hominem attacks. They falsely accuse Kleck of being a National Rifle Association member, minion, or even employee. In fact, Kleck, a liberal Democrat and opponent of the death penalty, is a member not of the NRA but of Amnesty International and the American Civil Liberties Union (ACLU). Moreover, Kleck started out on the other side of the gun-control debate. In a 1991 speech to the National Academy of Sciences, he said:

> When I began my research on guns in 1976, like most academics, I was a believer in the "anti-gun" thesis. . . . It seemed then like self-evident common sense which hardly needed to be empirically tested. . . . [But] the best currently available evidence, imperfect though it is (and must always be), indicates that general gun availability has no measurable net positive effect on rates of homicide, suicide, robbery, assault, rape, or burglary in the U.S. . . .
> Further, when victims have guns, it is less likely aggressors will attack or injure them and less likely they will lose property in a robbery. . . . The positive associations often found between aggregate levels of violence and gun own-

ership appear to be primarily due to violence increasing gun ownership, rather than the reverse.

Other scholars have also changed their views. University of Maryland political scientist Ted Robert Gurr and State University of New York criminologist Hans Toch were closely associated with the Eisenhower Commission, which concluded in the Sixties that "reducing the availability of the handgun will reduce firearms violence." Based on subsequent research, however, each now repudiates this judgment. "When used for protection," Toch writes, "firearms can seriously inhibit aggression and can provide a psychological buffer against the fear of crime. Furthermore, the fact that national patterns show little violent crime where guns are most dense implies that guns do not elicit aggression in any meaningful way. Quite the contrary, these findings suggest that high saturations of guns in places, or something correlated with that condition, inhibit illegal aggression."

Gurr has come to believe that handgun prohibition "would criminalize much of the citizenry but have only marginal effects on criminals," while "overemphasis on such proposals diverts attention from the kinds of conditions that are responsible for much of our crime, such as persisting poverty for the black underclass and some whites and Hispanics." Gurr adds that "guns can be an effective defense," noting that UCLA historian Roger McGrath's evidence from the 19th-century American West "shows that widespread gun ownership deterred" acquisitive crimes. "Modern studies," he writes, "also show that widespread gun ownership deters crime. . . . Convicted robbers and burglars report that they are deterred when they think their potential targets are armed."

Indeed, felons have consistently said that banning handguns would make their lives safer and easier by disarming victims without affecting their own ability to obtain weapons. "Ban guns," said a typical convict interviewed by New York University criminologist Ernest van den Haag in the mid 1970s. "I'd love it. I'm an armed robber."

In 1982 the Chicago suburb of Morton Grove received nationwide publicity for enacting the nation's first handgun ban. Surprisingly little attention was paid to two remarkable responses. One was a letter an inmate in a Florida prison wrote the editor of a local newspaper: "If guns are banned, then I as a criminal feel a lot safer. When a thief breaks into someone's house or property, the first thing to worry about is getting shot by the owner. But now, it seems we won't have to worry about that anymore." Branding it a "fantasy that just because guns are outlawed we, the crooks, can't get guns," the author asserted that "the only people who can't are the ones we victimize. . . . Drugs are against the law. Does that stop us? It's also against the law to rob and steal. But does a law stop us? One more thing: I thank you, the public, for giving me this fine opportunity to further my criminal career."

Similarly, the editor of the inmate newspaper at the Illinois Correctional Center in Menard "made it a point to get the views of those in the real   10 know—convicts here for armed robbery, some of them extremely professional individuals with years of experience in their chosen field. The[y] . . . were unanimous that you in Morton Grove are making things a bit easier for us. . . . [The] law is meaningless and useless in curbing crime. However, it is very effective in curbing the general populace. This coming from 'hardened criminals,' professionals, convicts . . . someone should listen!"

Perhaps the National Institute of Justice did listen. In 1983 it funded a survey of two thousand felons in state prisons across the U.S. In addition to overwhelmingly endorsing the views set out above, 39 per cent of the felons in the NIJ survey said they had aborted at least one crime because they believed the intended victim was armed; 8 per cent had done so "many" times; 34 per cent had been "scared off, shot at, wounded, or captured by an armed victim"; and 69 per cent knew at least one acquaintance who had had such an experience.

Thirty-four per cent of the felons said that in contemplating a crime they either "often" or "regularly" worried that they "might get shot at by the victim." Asked about criminals in general, 56 per cent of the inmates agreed that "a criminal is not going to mess around with a victim he knows is armed with a gun"; 57 per cent agreed that "most criminals are more worried about meeting an armed victim than they are about running into the police"; 58 per cent agreed that "a store owner who is known to keep a gun on the premises is not going to get robbed very often"; and 74 per cent agreed that "one reason burglars avoid houses when people are home is that they fear being shot during the crime."

Since 1976 the District of Columbia has had the country's most extreme gun law: no civilian may buy or carry a handgun, nor may *any* gun be kept loaded or assembled in a home for self-defense. Nevertheless, Washington has one of the highest homicide rates in the country. In 1992 *Washington Post* reporters interviewed the 114 inmates in D.C.'s Lorton Prison who had been convicted of at least one gun crime. The consensus was clear: "Gun control is not the answer, the inmates agreed." And they anticipated no difficulty obtaining an illegal gun. Though many claimed to want to go straight, 25 per cent flatly said they would get a gun as soon as they emerged from prison.

A week later a newspaper in Syracuse found similar opinions when it combined a survey of inmates in a nearby maximum-security prison with a survey of police officers in the local department. The two groups concurred that tougher gun laws would have no effect on crime; neither would banning assault weapons.

This congruence of opinion contradicts the impression that several prominent police chiefs have created that cops generally oppose civilian gun ownership. The truth is that these police chiefs were appointed precisely because their views sharply diverged from their peers'. Furthermore, strong political pressure tends to silence police administrators who oppose gun bans. In the mid 1980s Maurice Turner became Washington, D.C.'s first black police chief. When reporters inquired into the new chief's

15

opinion of D.C.'s severe gun law, he replied that it was not just useless but actually promoted crime, since felons knew it had rendered victims defenseless. When his remarks were reported, he was called on the carpet by Mayor Marion Barry, who told him banning guns was a city policy that he was forbidden to criticize. Thereafter Chief Turner refused to comment on gun control (until he retired, whereupon he reiterated his previous views).

Boston Police Chief Robert DiGrazia, on the other hand, did sincerely champion the banning and confiscation of handguns. In 1976 he had his research division poll police opinion nationwide, hoping the results would support a Massachusetts ballot initiative to ban handguns. Thinking patrol officers would oppose the initiative, he limited the poll to administrators. Yet the survey found "a substantial majority of the respondents looked favorably on the general possession of handguns by the citizenry (excludes those with criminal records [or] history of mental instability). Strong approval was also elicited from the police administrators concerning possession of handguns in the home or place of business." The poll confirmed Chief DiGrazia's views in only one respect: the administrators agreed that officers who dealt with crime on the streets would be even more opposed to banning handguns.

This pattern has been confirmed by subsequent polling. For instance, in *Law Enforcement Technology* magazine's 1991 poll of two thousand cops across the nation, 76 per cent of street officers believed that licenses to carry concealed handguns for protection should be issued to every trained, responsible adult applicant; only 59 per cent of managers agreed. Ninety-one per cent of street officers opposed banning semi-automatic "assault rifles," compared to 66 per cent of top management. On the other hand, 94 per cent of street officers felt that private citizens should keep handguns in their homes and offices for self-defense, and 93 per cent of top management agreed. Over all, 93 per cent of the respondents supported defensive ownership of handguns, 85 per cent felt gun control had little potential to reduce crime, 79 per cent opposed banning "assault weapons," and 63 per cent supported widespread carrying of concealed handguns by trained civilians.

Every year since 1988, the National Association of Chiefs of Police has polled the nation's more than fifteen thousand police agencies, with a response rate of 10 per cent or more. The respondents have consistently said that their departments are understaffed and unable to adequately protect individuals; that law-abiding, responsible adults should have the right to own "any type of firearm" for self-defense; and that banning guns will not reduce crime. In these and other surveys police generally support moderate controls, such as background checks, designed to exclude felons from gun ownership to the extent possible without obstructing defensive ownership by law-abiding citizens.

It's possible, of course, that the cops, the criminals, and the criminologists are mistaken about gun control. But given the remarkable consensus, it's time to reconsider the casual assumption that weapons cause crime.

✎ Topics for Critical Thinking and Writing

1. In his second paragraph Kates says that "no amount" of gun control can "overcome . . . crime." Probably even the most zealous advocates of gun control would agree, and they would explain that it's not a matter of over-coming crime but of reducing it. Do you believe Kates's essay suffers from overstatement? Explain.
2. In his third paragraph Kates calls attention to Gary Kleck's finding that "Gun possession by ordinary citizens is not a problem." But accidents *do* occur; it is not unusual to read a newspaper account of a child who is killed by a loaded gun in the house. *Is* this a "problem"? Explain.
3. Advocates of gun control usually offer, as one of their arguments, evidence that armed homeowners sometimes are injured (or injure family members) by their own weapons. Does Kate face this argument? If so, what is his response? If not, is his own argument weakened?
4. Let's assume that there is no overwhelming evidence one way or the other concerning crime and laws concerning gun ownership. In an essay of 500 words set forth your own position, explaining why you hold it.

Mitsuye Yamada

Mitsuye Yamada, the daughter of Japanese immigrants to the United States, was born in Japan in 1923, during her mother's return visit to her native land. Yamada was raised in Seattle, but in 1942 she and her family were incarcerated and then relocated in a camp in Idaho, when Executive Order 9066 gave military authorities the right to remove any and all persons from "military areas." In 1954 she became an American citizen. A visiting professor of English in the Asian American Studies Program at the University of California, Irvine, she is the author of poems and stories.

To the Lady

The one in San Francisco who asked:
Why did the Japanese Americans let
the government put them in
those camps without protest?

Come to think of it I   5
    should've run off to Canada
    should've hijacked a plane to Algeria
    should've pulled myself up from my
    bra straps
    and kicked'm in the groin   10

should've bombed a bank
should've tried self-immolation
should've holed myself up in a
woodframe house
and let you watch me   15
burn up on the six o'clock news
should've run howling down the street
naked and assaulted you at breakfast
by AP wirephoto
should've screamed bloody murder   20
like Kitty Genovese[1]

Then
YOU would've
    come to my aid in shining armor
    laid yourself across the railroad track   25
    marched on Washington
    tatooed a Star of David on your arm
    written six million enraged
    letters to Congress

But we didn't draw the line   30
    anywhere
law and order Executive Order 9066[2]
social order moral order internal order

YOU let'm
I let'm   35
All are punished.

[1976]

✎ Topics for Critical Thinking and Writing

1. Has the lady's question (lines 2–4) ever crossed your mind? If so, what answers did you think of?
2. What, in effect, is the speaker really saying in lines 5–21? And in lines 22–29?
3. Explain the last line.

---

[1]**Kitty Genovese:** In 1964 Kitty Genovese of Kew Gardens, New York, was stabbed to death when she left her car and walked toward her home. Thirty-eight persons heard her screams, but no one came to her assistance.
[2]**Executive Order 9066:** An authorization, signed in 1941 by President Franklin D. Roosevelt, allowing military authorities to relocate Japanese and Japanese-Americans who resided on the Pacific Coast of the United States.

A Casebook on Crime

James Q. Wilson

James Q. Wilson, professor of management and public policy at the University of California, Los Angeles, is the author and co-editor of several books on crime. In 1994 Commentary *magazine invited him to write the following article. We print the article, along with a selection of the letters that it evoked.*

What to Do About Crime

When the United States experienced the great increase in crime that began in the early 1960's and continued through the 1970's, most Americans were inclined to attribute it to conditions unique to this country. Many conservatives blamed it on judicial restraints on the police, the abandonment of capital punishment, and the mollycoddling of offenders; many liberals blamed it on poverty, racism, and the rise of violent television programs. Europeans, to the extent they noticed at all, referred to it, sadly or patronizingly, as the "American" problem, a product of our disorderly society, weak state, corrupt police, or imperfect welfare system.

Now, 30 years later, any serious discussion of crime must begin with the fact that, except for homicide, most industrialized nations have crime rates that resemble those in the United States. All the world is coming to look like America. In 1981, the burglary rate in Great Britain was much less than that in the United States; within six years the two rates were the same; today, British homes are more likely to be burgled than American ones. In 1980, the rate at which automobiles were stolen was lower in France than in the United States; today, the reverse is true. By 1984, the burglary rate in the Netherlands was nearly twice that in the United States. In Australia and Sweden certain forms of theft are more common than they are here. While property-crime rates were declining during most of the 1980's in the United States, they were rising elsewhere.[1]

America, it is true, continues to lead the industrialized world in murders. There can be little doubt that part of this lead is to be explained by

---

[1]These comparisons depend on official police statistics. There are of course errors in such data. But essentially the same pattern emerges from comparing nations on the basis of victimization surveys.

the greater availability of handguns here. Arguments that once might have been settled with insults or punches are today more likely to be settled by shootings. But guns are not the whole story. Big American cities have had more homicides than comparable European ones for almost as long as anyone can find records. New York and Philadelphia have been more murderous than London since the early part of the 19th century. This country has had a violent history; with respect to murder, that seems likely to remain the case.

But except for homicide, things have been getting better in the United States for over a decade. Since 1980, robbery rates (as reported in victim surveys) have declined by 15 percent. And even with regard to homicide, there is relatively good news: in 1990, the rate at which adults killed one another was no higher than it was in 1980, and in many cities it was considerably lower.

This is as it was supposed to be. Starting around 1980, two things happened that ought to have reduced most forms of crime. The first was the passing into middle age of the postwar baby boom. By 1990, there were 1.5 million fewer boys between the ages of fifteen and nineteen than there had been in 1980, a drop that meant that this youthful fraction of the population fell from 9.3 percent to 7.2 percent of the total.

In addition, the great increase in the size of the prison population, caused in part by the growing willingness of judges to send offenders to jail, meant that the dramatic reductions in the costs of crime to the criminal that occurred in the 1960's and 1970's were slowly (and very partially) being reversed. Until around 1985, this reversal involved almost exclusively real criminals and parole violators; it was not until after 1985 that more than a small part of the growth in prison populations was made up of drug offenders.

Because of the combined effect of fewer young people on the street and more offenders in prison, many scholars, myself included, predicted a continuing drop in crime rates throughout the 1980's and into the early 1990's. We were almost right: crime rates did decline. But suddenly, starting around 1985, even as adult homicide rates were remaining stable or dropping, *youthful* homicide rates shot up.

Alfred Blumstein of Carnegie-Mellon University has estimated that the rate at which young males, ages fourteen to seventeen, kill people has gone up significantly for whites and incredibly for blacks. Between 1985 and 1992, the homicide rate for young white males went up by about 50 percent but for young black males it *tripled*.

The public perception that today's crime problem is different from and more serious than that of earlier decades is thus quite correct. Youngsters are shooting at people at a far higher rate than at any time in recent history. Since young people are more likely than adults to kill strangers (as opposed to lovers or spouses), the risk to innocent bystanders has gone

up. There may be some comfort to be had in the fact that youthful homicides are only a small fraction of all killings, but given their randomness,
it is not much solace.

The United States, then, does not have *a* crime problem, it has at least   10
two. Our high (though now slightly declining) rates of property crime
reflect a profound, worldwide cultural change: prosperity, freedom, and
mobility have emancipated people almost everywhere from those ancient
bonds of custom, family, and village that once held in check both some of
our better and many of our worst impulses. The power of the state has
been weakened, the status of children elevated, and the opportunity for
adventure expanded; as a consequence, we have experienced an explosion
of artistic creativity, entrepreneurial zeal, political experimentation—and
criminal activity. A global economy has integrated the markets for clothes,
music, automobiles—and drugs.

There are only two restraints on behavior—morality, enforced by individual conscience or social rebuke, and law, enforced by the police and the
courts. If society is to maintain a behavioral equilibrium, any decline in
the former must be matched by a rise in the latter (or vice versa). If familial and traditional restraints on wrongful behavior are eroded, it becomes
necessary to increase the legal restraints. But the enlarged spirit of freedom and the heightened suspicion of the state have made it difficult or
impossible to use the criminal-justice system to achieve what custom and
morality once produced.

This is the modern dilemma, and it may be an insoluble one, at least
for the West. The Islamic cultures of the Middle East and the Confucian
cultures of the Far East believe that they have a solution. It involves allowing enough liberty for economic progress (albeit under general state direction) while reserving to the state, and its allied religion, nearly unfettered
power over personal conduct. It is too soon to tell whether this formula—
best exemplified by the prosperous but puritanical city-state of Singapore—will, in the long run, be able to achieve both reproducible affluence
and intense social control.

Our other crime problem has to do with the kind of felonies we have:
high levels of violence, especially youthful violence, often occurring as
part of urban gang life, produced disproportionately by a large, alienated,
and self-destructive underclass. This part of the crime problem, though
not uniquely American, is more important here than in any other industrialized nation. Britons, Germans, and Swedes are upset about the insecurity of their property and uncertain about what response to make to its
theft, but if Americans only had to worry about their homes being burgled
and their autos stolen, I doubt that crime would be the national obsession
it has now become.

Crime, we should recall, was not a major issue in the 1984 presidential
election and had only begun to be one in the 1988 contest; by 1992, it was
challenging the economy as a popular concern and today it dominates all

other matters. The reason, I think, is that Americans believe something fundamental has changed in our patterns of crime. They are right. Though we were unhappy about having our property put at risk, we adapted with the aid of locks, alarms, and security guards. But we are terrified by the prospect of innocent people being gunned down at random, without warning and almost without motive, by youngsters who afterward show us the blank, unremorseful faces of seemingly feral, presocial beings.

Criminology has learned a great deal about who these people are. In studies both here and abroad it has been established that about 6 percent of the boys of a given age will commit half or more of all the serious crime produced by all boys of that age. Allowing for measurement errors, it is remarkable how consistent this formula is—6 percent causes 50 percent. It is roughly true in places as different as Philadelphia, London, Copenhagen, and Orange County, California.

We also have learned a lot about the characteristics of the 6 percent. They tend to have criminal parents, to live in cold or discordant families (or pseudo-families), to have a low verbal-intelligence quotient and to do poorly in school, to be emotionally cold and temperamentally impulsive, to abuse alcohol and drugs at the earliest opportunity, and to reside in poor, disorderly communities. They begin their misconduct at an early age, often by the time they are in the third grade.

These characteristics tend to be found not only among the criminals who get caught (and who might, owing to bad luck, be an unrepresentative sample of all high-rate offenders), but among those who do not get caught but reveal their behavior on questionnaires. And the same traits can be identified in advance among groups of randomly selected youngsters, long before they commit any serious crimes—not with enough precision to predict which individuals will commit crimes, but with enough accuracy to be a fair depiction of the group as a whole.[2]

Here a puzzle arises: if 6 percent of the males causes so large a fraction of our collective misery, and if young males are less numerous than once was the case, why are crime rates high and rising? The answer, I conjecture, is that the traits of the 6 percent put them at high risk for whatever criminogenic forces operate in society. As the costs of crime decline or the benefits increase; as drugs and guns become more available; as the glorification of violence becomes more commonplace; as families and neighborhoods lose some of their restraining power—as all these things happen, almost all of us will change our ways to some degree. For the most lawabiding among us, the change will be quite modest: a few more tools stolen from our employer, a few more traffic lights run when no police officer is watching, a few more experiments with fashionable drugs, and a few more business deals on which we cheat. But for the least law-abiding

15

[2]Female high-rate offenders are *much* less common than male ones. But to the extent they exist, they display most of these traits.

among us, the change will be dramatic: they will get drunk daily instead of just on Saturday night, try PCP or crack instead of marijuana, join gangs instead of marauding in pairs, and buy automatic weapons instead of making zip guns.

A metaphor: when children play the schoolyard game of crack-the-whip, the child at the head of the line scarcely moves but the child at the far end, racing to keep his footing, often stumbles and falls, hurled to the ground by the cumulative force of many smaller movements back along the line. When a changing culture escalates criminality, the at-risk boys are at the end of the line, and the conditions of American urban life—guns, drugs, automobiles, disorganized neighborhoods—make the line very long and the ground underfoot rough and treacherous.

Much is said these days about preventing or deterring crime, but it is important to understand exactly what we are up against when we try. Prevention, if it can be made to work at all, must start very early in life, perhaps as early as the first two or three years, and given the odds it faces—childhood impulsivity, low verbal facility, incompetent parenting, disorderly neighborhoods—it must also be massive in scope. Deterrence, if it can be made to work better (for surely it already works to some degree), must be applied close to the moment of the wrongful act or else the present-orientedness of the youthful would-be offender will discount the threat so much that the promise of even a small gain will outweigh its large but deferred costs. [20]

In this country, however, and in most Western nations, we have profound misgivings about doing anything that would give prevention or deterrence a chance to make a large difference. The family is sacrosanct; the family-preservation movement is strong; the state is a clumsy alternative. "Crime-prevention" programs, therefore, usually take the form of creating summer jobs for adolescents, worrying about the unemployment rate, or (as in the proposed 1994 crime bill) funding midnight basketball leagues. There may be something to be said for all these efforts, but crime prevention is not one of them. The typical high-rate offender is well launched on his career before he becomes a teenager or has ever encountered the labor market; he may like basketball, but who pays for the lights and the ball is a matter of supreme indifference to him.

Prompt deterrence has much to recommend it: the folk wisdom that swift and certain punishment is more effective than severe penalties is almost surely correct. But the greater the swiftness and certainty, the less attention paid to the procedural safeguards essential to establishing guilt. As a result, despite their good instincts for the right answers, most Americans, frustrated by the restraints (many wise, some foolish) on swiftness and certainty, vote for proposals to increase severity: if the penalty is 10 years, let us make it 20 or 30; if the penalty is life imprisonment, let us make it death; if the penalty is jail, let us make it caning.

Yet the more draconian the sentence, the less (on the average) the chance of its being imposed; plea bargains see to that. And the most draconian sentences will, of necessity, tend to fall on adult offenders nearing the end of their criminal careers and not on the young ones who are in their criminally most productive years. (The peak ages of criminality are between sixteen and eighteen; the average age of prison inmates is ten years older.) I say "of necessity" because almost every judge will give first-, second-, or even third-time offenders a break, reserving the heaviest sentences for those men who have finally exhausted judicial patience or optimism.

Laws that say "three strikes and you're out" are an effort to change this, but they suffer from an inherent contradiction. If they are carefully drawn so as to target only the most serious offenders, they will probably have a minimal impact on the crime rate; but if they are broadly drawn so as to make a big impact on the crime rate, they will catch many petty repeat offenders who few of us think really deserve life imprisonment.

Prevention and deterrence, albeit hard to augment, at least are plausible strategies. Not so with many of the other favorite nostrums, like reducing the amount of violence on television. Televised violence may have some impact on criminality, but I know of few scholars who think the effect is very large. And to achieve even a small difference we might have to turn the clock back to the kind of programming we had around 1945, because the few studies that correlate programming with the rise in violent crime find the biggest changes occurred between that year and 1974. Another favorite, boot camp, makes good copy, but so far no one has shown that it reduces the rate at which the former inmates commit crimes.

Then, of course, there is gun control. Guns are almost certainly contributors to the lethality of American violence, but there is no politically or legally feasible way to reduce the stock of guns now in private possession to the point where their availability to criminals would be much affected. And even if there were, law-abiding people would lose a means of protecting themselves long before criminals lost a means of attacking them.

As for rehabilitating juvenile offenders, it has some merit, but there are rather few success stories. Individually, the best (and best-evaluated) programs have minimal, if any, effects; collectively, the best estimate of the crime-reduction value of these programs is quite modest, something on the order of 5 or 10 percent.[3]

What, then, is to be done? Let us begin with policing, since law-enforcement officers are that part of the criminal-justice system which is closest to the situations where criminal activity is likely to occur.

---

[3]Many individual programs involve so few subjects that a good evaluation will reveal no positive effect even if one occurs. By a technique called meta-analysis, scores of individual studies can be pooled into one mega-evaluation; because there are now hundreds or thousands of subjects, even small gains can be identified. The best of these meta-analyses, such as the one by Mark Lipsey, suggest modest positive effects.

It is now widely accepted that, however important it is for officers to drive around waiting for 911 calls summoning their help, doing that is not enough. As a supplement to such a reactive strategy—comprised of random preventive patrol and the investigation of crimes that have already occurred—many leaders and students of law enforcement now urge the police to be "proactive": to identify, with the aid of citizen groups, problems that can be solved so as to prevent criminality, and not only to respond to it. This is often called community-based policing; it seems to entail something more than feel-good meetings with honest citizens, but something less than allowing neighborhoods to assume control of the police function.

The new strategy might better be called problem-oriented policing. It requires the police to engage in *directed,* not random, patrol. The goal of that direction should be to reduce, in a manner consistent with fundamental liberties, the opportunity for high-risk persons to do those things that increase the likelihood of their victimizing others.

For example, the police might stop and pat down persons whom they reasonably suspect may be carrying illegal guns.[4] The Supreme Court has upheld such frisks when an officer observes "unusual conduct" leading him to conclude that "criminal activity may be afoot" on the part of a person who may be "armed and dangerous." This is all rather vague, but it can be clarified in two ways.

First, statutes can be enacted that make certain persons, on the basis of their past conduct and present legal status, subject to pat-downs for weapons. The statutes can, as is now the case in several states, make all probationers and parolees subject to nonconsensual searches for weapons as a condition of their remaining on probation or parole. Since three-fourths of all convicted offenders (and a large fraction of all felons) are in the community rather than in prison, there are on any given day over three million criminals on the streets under correctional supervision. Many are likely to become recidivists. Keeping them from carrying weapons will materially reduce the chances that they will rob or kill. The courts might also declare certain dangerous street gangs to be continuing criminal enterprises, membership in which constitutes grounds for police frisks.

Second, since I first proposed such a strategy, I have learned that there are efforts under way in public and private research laboratories to develop technologies that will permit the police to detect from a distance persons who are carrying concealed weapons on the streets. Should these efforts bear fruit, they will provide the police with the grounds for stopping, questioning, and patting down even persons not on probation or parole or obviously in gangs.

Whether or not the technology works, the police can also offer immediate cash rewards to people who provide information about individuals illegally carrying weapons. Spending $100 on each good tip will

[4] I made a fuller argument along these lines in "Just Take Away Their Guns," in the *New York Times Magazine,* March 20, 1994.

have a bigger impact on dangerous gun use than will the same amount spent on another popular nostrum—buying back guns from law-abiding people.[5]

Getting illegal firearms off the streets will require that the police be   35
motivated to do all of these things. But if the legal, technological, and motivational issues can be resolved, our streets can be made safer even without sending many more people to prison.

The same directed-patrol strategy might help keep known offenders drug-free. Most persons jailed in big cities are found to have been using illegal drugs within the day or two preceding their arrest. When convicted, some are given probation on condition that they enter drug-treatment pro-grams; others are sent to prisons where (if they are lucky) drug-treatment programs operate. But in many cities the enforcement of such probation conditions is casual or nonexistent; in many states, parolees are released back into drug-infested communities with little effort to ensure that they participate in whatever treatment programs are to be found there.

Almost everyone agrees that more treatment programs should exist. But what many advocates overlook is that the key to success is steadfast participation and many, probably most, offenders have no incentive to be steadfast. To cope with this, patrol officers could enforce random drug tests on probationers and parolees on their beats; failing to take a test when ordered, or failing the test when taken, should be grounds for immediate revocation of probation or parole, at least for a brief period of confinement.

The goal of this tactic is not simply to keep offenders drug-free (and thereby lessen their incentive to steal the money needed to buy drugs and reduce their likelihood of committing crimes because they are on a drug high); it is also to diminish the demand for drugs generally and thus the size of the drug market.

Lest the reader embrace this idea too quickly, let me add that as yet we have no good reason to think that it will reduce the crime rate by very much. Something akin to this strategy, albeit one using probation instead of police officers, has been tried under the name of "intensive-supervision programs" (ISP), involving a panoply of drug tests, house arrests, frequent surveillance, and careful records. By means of a set of randomized experi-ments carried out in fourteen cities, Joan Petersilia and Susan Turner, both then at RAND, compared the rearrest rates of offenders assigned to ISP with those of offenders in ordinary probation. There was no difference.

Still, this study does not settle the matter. For one thing, since the ISP   40
participants were under much closer surveillance than the regular proba-tioners, the former were bound to be caught breaking the law more fre-quently than the latter. It is thus possible that a higher fraction of the

---

[5]In Charleston, South Carolina, the police pay a reward to anyone identifying a student car-rying a weapon to school or to some school event. Because many boys carry guns to school in order to display or brag about them, the motive to carry disappears once any display alerts a potential informer.

crimes committed by the ISP than of the control group were detected and resulted in a return to prison, which would mean, if true, a net gain in public safety. For another thing, "intensive" supervision was in many cases not all that intensive—in five cities, contacts with the probationers only took place about once a week, and for all cities drug tests occurred, on average, about once a month. Finally, there is some indication that participation in treatment programs was associated with lower recidivism rates.

Both anti-gun and anti-drug police patrols will, if performed systematically, require big changes in police and court procedures and a significant increase in the resources devoted to both, at least in the short run. (ISP is not cheap, and it will become even more expensive if it is done in a truly intensive fashion.) Most officers have at present no incentive to search for guns or enforce drug tests; many jurisdictions, owing to crowded dockets or overcrowded jails, are lax about enforcing the conditions of probation or parole. The result is that the one group of high-risk people over which society already has the legal right to exercise substantial control is often out of control, "supervised," if at all, by means of brief monthly interviews with overworked probation or parole officers.

Another promising tactic is to enforce truancy and curfew laws. This arises from the fact that much crime is opportunistic: idle boys, usually in small groups, sometimes find irresistible the opportunity to steal or the challenge to fight. Deterring present-oriented youngsters who want to appear fearless in the eyes of their comrades while indulging their thrill-seeking natures is a tall order. While it is possible to deter the crimes they commit by a credible threat of prompt sanctions, it is easier to reduce the chances for risky group idleness in the first place.

In Charleston, South Carolina, for example, Chief Reuben Greenberg instructed his officers to return all school-age children to the schools from which they were truant and to return all youngsters violating an evening-curfew agreement to their parents. As a result, groups of school-age children were no longer to be found hanging out in the shopping malls or wandering the streets late at night.

There has been no careful evaluation of these efforts in Charleston (or, so far as I am aware, in any other big city), but the rough figures are impressive—the Charleston crime rate in 1991 was about 25 percent lower than the rate in South Carolina's other principal cities and, for most offenses (including burglaries and larcenies), lower than what that city reported twenty years earlier.

All these tactics have in common putting the police, as the criminolo- 45 gist Lawrence Sherman of the University of Maryland phrases it, where the "hot spots" are. Most people need no police attention except for a response to their calls for help. A small fraction of people (and places) need constant attention. Thus, in Minneapolis, *all* of the robberies during one year occurred at just 2 percent of the city's addresses. To capitalize on this fact, the Minneapolis police began devoting extra patrol attention, in brief but frequent bursts of activity, to those locations known to be trouble spots. Robbery rates evidently fell by as much as 20 percent and public disturbances by even more.

Some of the worst hot spots are outdoor drug markets. Because of either limited resources, a fear of potential corruption, or a desire to catch only the drug kingpins, the police in some cities (including, from time to time, New York) neglect street-corner dealing. By doing so, they get the worst of all worlds.

The public, seeing the police ignore drug dealing that is in plain view, assumes that they are corrupt whether or not they are. The drug kingpins, who are hard to catch and are easily replaced by rival smugglers, find that their essential retail distribution system remains intact. Casual or first-time drug users, who might not use at all if access to supplies were difficult, find access to be effortless and so increase their consumption. People who might remain in treatment programs if drugs were hard to get drop out upon learning that they are easy to get. Interdicting without merely displacing drug markets is difficult but not impossible, though it requires motivation which some departments lack and resources which many do not have.

The sheer number of police on the streets of a city probably has only a weak, if any, relationship with the crime rate; what the police do is more important than how many there are, at least above some minimum level. Nevertheless, patrols directed at hot spots, loitering truants, late-night wanderers, probationers, parolees, and possible gun carriers, all in addition to routine investigative activities, will require more officers in many cities. Between 1977 and 1987, the number of police officers declined in a third of the 50 largest cities and fell relative to population in many more. Just how far behind police resources have lagged can be gauged from this fact: in 1950 there was one violent crime reported for every police officer; in 1980 there were three viclent crimes reported for every officer.

I have said little so far about penal policy, in part because I wish to focus attention on those things that are likely to have the largest and most immediate impact on the quality of urban life. But given the vast gulf between what the public believes and what many experts argue should be our penal policy, a few comments are essential.

The public wants more people sent away for longer sentences; many (probably most) criminologists think we use prison too much and at too great a cost and that this excessive use has had little beneficial effect on the crime rate. My views are much closer to those of the public, though I think the average person exaggerates the faults of the present system and the gains of some alternative (such as "three strikes and you're out"). 50

The expert view, as it is expressed in countless op-ed essays, often goes like this: "We have been arresting more and more people and giving them longer and longer sentences, producing no decrease in crime but huge increases in prison populations. As a result, we have become the most punitive nation on earth."

Scarcely a phrase in those sentences is accurate. The probability of being arrested for a given crime is lower today than it was in 1974. The amount of time served in state prison has been declining more or less steadily since the 1940's. Taking all crimes together, time served fell from 25 months in 1945 to 13 months in 1984. Only for rape are prisoners serving as much time today as they did in the 40's.

The net effect of lower arrest rates and shorter effective sentences is that the cost to the adult perpetrator of the average burglary fell from 50 days in 1960 to 15 days in 1980. That is to say, the chances of being caught and convicted, multiplied by the median time served if imprisoned, was in 1980 less than a third of what it had been in 1960.[6]

Beginning around 1980, the costs of crime to the criminal began to inch up again—the result, chiefly, of an increase in the proportion of convicted persons who were given prison terms. By 1986, the "price" of a given burglary had risen to 21 days. Also beginning around 1980, as I noted at the outset, the crime rate began to decline.

It would be foolhardy to explain this drop in crime by the rise in imprisonment rates; many other factors, such as the aging of the population and the self-protective measures of potential victims, were also at work. Only a controlled experiment (for example, randomly allocating prison terms for a given crime among the states) could hope to untangle the causal patterns, and happily the Constitution makes such experiments unlikely.

Yet it is worth noting that nations with different penal policies have experienced different crime rates. According to David Farrington of Cambridge University, property-crime rates rose in England and Sweden at a time when both the imprisonment rate and time served fell substantially, while property-crime rates declined in the United States at a time when the imprisonment rate (but not time served) was increasing.

Though one cannot measure the effect of prison on crime with any accuracy, it certainly has some effects. By 1986, there were 55,000 more robbers in prison than there had been in 1974. Assume that each imprisoned robber would commit five such offenses per year if free on the street. This means that in 1986 there were 275,000 fewer robberies in America than there would have been had these 55,000 men been left on the street.

Nor, finally, does America use prison to a degree that vastly exceeds what is found in any other civilized nation. Compare the chance of going to prison in England and the United States if one is convicted of a given crime. According to Farrington, your chances were higher in England if you were found guilty of a rape, higher in America if you were convicted of an assault or a burglary, and about the same if you were convicted of a

[6]I take these cost calculations from Mark Kleiman, *et al.*, "Imprisonment-to-Offense Ratios," Working Paper 89-06-02 of the Program in Criminal Justice Policy and Management at the Kennedy School of Government, Harvard University (August 5, 1988).

homicide or a robbery. Once in prison, you would serve a longer time in this country than in England for almost all offenses save murder.

James Lynch of American University has reached similar conclusions from his comparative study of criminal-justice policies. His data show that the chances of going to prison and the time served for homicide and robbery are roughly the same in the United States, Canada, and England.

Of late, drugs have changed American penal practice. In 1982, only about 8 percent of state-prison inmates were serving time on drug convictions. In 1987, that started to increase sharply; by 1994, over 60 percent of all federal and about 25 percent of all state prisoners were there on drug charges. In some states, such as New York, the percentage was even higher.

This change can be attributed largely to the advent of crack cocaine. Whereas snorted cocaine powder was expensive, crack was cheap; whereas the former was distributed through networks catering to elite tastes, the latter was mass-marketed on street corners. People were rightly fearful of what crack was doing to their children and demanded action; as a result, crack dealers started going to prison in record numbers.

Unfortunately, these penalties do not have the same incapacitative effect as sentences for robbery. A robber taken off the street is not replaced by a new robber who has suddenly found a market niche, but a drug dealer sent away is replaced by a new one because an opportunity has opened up.

We are left, then, with the problem of reducing the demand for drugs, and that in turn requires either prevention programs on a scale heretofore unimagined or treatment programs with a level of effectiveness heretofore unachieved. Any big gains in prevention and treatment will probably have to await further basic research into the biochemistry of addiction and the development of effective and attractive drug antagonists that reduce the appeal of cocaine and similar substances.[7]

In the meantime, it is necessary either to build much more prison space, find some other way of disciplining drug offenders, or both. There is very little to be gained, I think, from shortening the terms of existing non-drug inmates in order to free up more prison space. Except for a few elderly, nonviolent offenders serving very long terms, there are real risks associated with shortening the terms of the typical inmate.

Scholars disagree about the magnitude of those risks, but the best studies, such as the one of Wisconsin inmates done by John DiIulio of Princeton, suggest that the annual costs to society in crime committed by an offender on the street are probably twice the costs of putting him in a cell. That ratio will vary from state to state because states differ in what proportion of convicted persons is imprisoned—some states dip deeper

[7]I anticipate that at this point some readers will call for legalizing or decriminalizing drugs as the "solution" to the problem. Before telling me this, I hope they will read what I wrote on that subject in the February 1990 issue of *Commentary*. I have not changed my mind.

down into the pool of convictees, thereby imprisoning some with minor criminal habits.

But I caution the reader to understand that there are no easy prison solutions to crime, even if we build the additional space. The state-prison population more than doubled between 1980 and 1990, yet the victimization rate for robbery fell by only 23 percent. Even if we assign all of that gain to the increased deterrent and incapacitative effect of prison, which is implausible, the improvement is not vast. Of course, it is possible that the victimization rate would have risen, perhaps by a large amount, instead of falling if we had not increased the number of inmates. But we shall never know.

Recall my discussion of the decline in the costs of crime to the criminal, measured by the number of days in prison that result, on average, from the commission of a given crime. That cost is vastly lower today than in the 1950's. But much of the decline (and since 1974, nearly all of it) is the result of a drop in the probability of being arrested for a crime, not in the probability of being imprisoned once arrested.

Anyone who has followed my writings on crime knows that I have defended the use of prison both to deter crime and incapacitate criminals. I continue to defend it. But we must recognize two facts. First, even modest additional reductions in crime, comparable to the ones achieved in the early 1980's, will require vast increases in correctional costs and encounter bitter judicial resistance to mandatory sentencing laws. Second, America's most troubling crime problem—the increasingly violent behavior of disaffected and impulsive youth—may be especially hard to control by means of marginal and delayed increases in the probability of punishment.

Possibly one can make larger gains by turning our attention to the unexplored area of juvenile justice. Juvenile (or family) courts deal with young people just starting their criminal careers and with chronic offenders when they are often at their peak years of offending. We know rather little about how these courts work or with what effect. There are few, if any, careful studies of what happens, a result in part of scholarly neglect and in part of the practice in some states of shrouding juvenile records and proceedings in secrecy. Some studies, such as one by the *Los Angeles Times* of juvenile justice in California, suggest that young people found guilty of a serious crime are given sentences tougher than those meted out to adults.[8] This finding is so counter to popular beliefs and the testimony of many big-city juvenile-court judges that some caution is required in interpreting it.

There are two problems. The first lies in defining the universe of people to whom sanctions are applied. In some states, such as California, it may well be the case that a juvenile *found guilty of a serious offense* is punished with greater rigor than an adult, but many juveniles whose behav-

70

[8]"A Nation's Children in Lock-up," *Los Angeles Times,* August 22, 1993.

ior ought to be taken seriously (because they show signs of being part of the 6 percent) are released by the police or probation officers before ever seeing a judge. And in some states, such as New York, juveniles charged with having committed certain crimes, including serious ones like illegally carrying a loaded gun or committing an assault, may not be fingerprinted. Since persons with a prior record are usually given longer sentences than those without one, the failure to fingerprint can mean that the court has no way of knowing whether the John Smith standing before it is the same John Smith who was arrested four times for assault and so ought to be sent away, or a different John Smith whose clean record entitles him to probation.

The second problem arises from the definition of a "severe" penalty. In California, a juvenile found guilty of murder does indeed serve a longer sentence than an adult convicted of the same offense—60 months for the former, 41 months for the latter. Many people will be puzzled by a newspaper account that defines five years in prison for murder as a "severe" sentence, and angered to learn that an adult serves less than four years for such a crime.

The key, unanswered question is whether prompt and more effective early intervention would stop high-rate delinquents from becoming high-rate criminals at a time when their offenses were not yet too serious. Perhaps early and swift, though not necessarily severe, sanctions could deter some budding hoodlums, but we have no evidence of that as yet.

For as long as I can remember, the debate over crime has been between those who wished to rely on the criminal-justice system and those who wished to attack the root causes of crime. I have always been in the former group because what its opponents depicted as "root causes"—unemployment, racism, poor housing, too little schooling, a lack of self-esteem—turned out, on close examination, not to be major causes of crime at all.

Of late, however, there has been a shift in the debate. Increasingly those who want to attack root causes have begun to point to real ones—temperament, early family experiences, and neighborhood effects. The sketch I gave earlier of the typical high-rate young offender suggests that these factors are indeed at the root of crime. The problem now is to decide whether any can be changed by plan and at an acceptable price in money and personal freedom.

If we are to do this, we must confront the fact that the critical years of a child's life are ages one to ten, with perhaps the most important being the earliest years. During those years, some children are put gravely at risk by some combination of heritable traits, prenatal insults (maternal drug and alcohol abuse or poor diet), weak parent-child attachment, poor supervision, and disorderly family environment.

If we knew with reasonable confidence which children were most seriously at risk, we might intervene with some precision to supply either medical therapy or parent training or (in extreme cases) to remove the

75

child to a better home. But given our present knowledge, precision is impossible, and so we must proceed carefully, relying, except in the most extreme cases, on persuasion and incentives.

We do, however, know enough about the early causes of conduct disorder and later delinquency to know that the more risk factors exist (such as parental criminality and poor supervision), the greater the peril to the child. It follows that programs aimed at just one or a few factors are not likely to be successful; the children most at risk are those who require the most wide-ranging and fundamental changes in their life circumstances. The goal of these changes is, as Travis Hirschi of the University of Arizona has put it, to teach self-control.

Hirokazu Yoshikawa of New York University has recently summarized what we have learned about programs that attempt to make large and lasting changes in a child's prospects for improved conduct, better school behavior, and lessened delinquency. Four such programs in particular seemed valuable—the Perry Preschool Project in Ypsilanti, Michigan; the Parent-Child Development Center in Houston, Texas; the Family Development Research Project in Syracuse, New York; and the Yale Child Welfare Project in New Haven, Connecticut.

All these programs had certain features in common. They dealt with low-income, often minority, families; they intervened during the first five years of a child's life and continued for between two and five years; they combined parent training with preschool education for the child; and they involved extensive home visits. All were evaluated fairly carefully, with the follow-ups lasting for at least five years, in two cases for at least ten, and in one case for fourteen. The programs produced (depending on the project) less fighting, impulsivity, disobedience, restlessness, cheating, and delinquency. In short, they improved self-control.

They were experimental programs, which means that it is hard to be 80 confident that trying the same thing on a bigger scale in many places will produce the same effects. A large number of well-trained and highly motivated caseworkers dealt with a relatively small number of families, with the workers knowing that their efforts were being evaluated. Moreover, the programs operated in the late 1970's or early 1980's before the advent of crack cocaine or the rise of the more lethal neighborhood gangs. A national program mounted under current conditions might or might not have the same result as the experimental efforts.

Try telling that to lawmakers. What happens when politicians encounter experimental successes is amply revealed by the history of Head Start: they expanded the program quickly without assuring quality, and stripped it down to the part that was the most popular, least expensive, and easiest to run, namely, preschool education. Absent from much of Head Start are the high teacher-to-child case loads, the extensive home visits, and the elaborate parent training—the very things that probably account for much of the success of the four experimental programs.

In this country we tend to separate programs designed to help children from those that benefit their parents. The former are called "child development," the latter "welfare reform." This is a great mistake. Everything we know about long-term welfare recipients indicates that their children are at risk for the very problems that child-helping programs later try to correct.

The evidence from a variety of studies is quite clear: even if we hold income and ethnicity constant, children (and especially boys) raised by a single mother are more likely than those raised by two parents to have difficulty in school, get in trouble with the law, and experience emotional and physical problems.[9] Producing illegitimate children is not an "alternative life-style" or simply an imprudent action; it is a curse. Making mothers work will not end the curse; under current proposals, it will not even save money.

The absurdity of divorcing the welfare problem from the child-development problem becomes evident as soon as we think seriously about what we want to achieve. Smaller welfare expenditures? Well, yes, but not if it hurts children. More young mothers working? Probably not; young mothers ought to raise their young children, and work interferes with that unless *two* parents can solve some difficult and expensive problems.

What we really want is *fewer illegitimate children*, because such children, by being born out of wedlock are, except in unusual cases, being given early admission to the underclass. And failing that, we want the children born to single (and typically young and poor) mothers to have a chance at a decent life.

Letting teenage girls set up their own households at public expense neither discourages illegitimacy nor serves the child's best interests. If they do set up their own homes, then to reach those with the fewest parenting skills and the most difficult children will require the kind of expensive and intensive home visits and family-support programs characteristic of the four successful experiments mentioned earlier.

One alternative is to tell a girl who applies for welfare that she can only receive it on condition that she live either in the home of *two* competent parents (her own if she comes from an intact family) or in a group home where competent supervision and parent training will be provided by adults unrelated to her. Such homes would be privately managed but publicly funded by pooling welfare checks, food stamps, and housing allowances.

A model for such a group home (albeit one run without public funds) is the St. Martin de Porres House of Hope on the south side of Chicago, founded by two nuns for homeless young women, especially those with drug-abuse problems. The goals of the home are clear: accept personal

---

[9]I summarize this evidence in "The Family-Values Debate," *Commentary,* April 1993.

responsibility for your lives and learn to care for your children. And these goals, in turn, require the girls to follow rules, stay in school, obey a curfew, and avoid alcohol and drugs. Those are the rules that ought to govern a group home for young welfare mothers.

Group homes funded by pooled welfare benefits would make the task of parent training much easier and provide the kind of structured, consistent, and nurturant environment that children need. A few cases might be too difficult for these homes, and for such children, boarding schools—once common in American cities for disadvantaged children, but now almost extinct—might be revived.

Group homes also make it easier to supply quality medical care to young mothers and their children. Such care has taken on added importance in recent years with discovery of the lasting damage that can be done to a child's prospects from being born prematurely and with a very low birth weight, having a mother who has abused drugs or alcohol, or being exposed to certain dangerous metals. Lead poisoning is now widely acknowledged to be a source of cognitive and behavioral impairment; of late, elevated levels of manganese have been linked to high levels of violence.[10] These are all treatable conditions; in the case of a manganese imbalance, easily treatable.

My focus on changing behavior will annoy some readers. For them the problem is poverty and the worst feature of single-parent families is that they are inordinately poor. Even to refer to a behavioral or cultural problem is to "stigmatize" people.

Indeed it is. Wrong behavior—neglectful, immature, or incompetent parenting; the production of out-of-wedlock babies—*ought* to be stigmatized. There are many poor men of all races who do not abandon the women they have impregnated, and many poor women of all races who avoid drugs and do a good job of raising their children. If we fail to stigmatize those who give way to temptation, we withdraw the rewards from those who resist them. This becomes all the more important when entire communities, and not just isolated households, are dominated by a culture of fatherless boys preying on innocent persons and exploiting immature girls.

We need not merely stigmatize, however. We can try harder to move children out of those communities, either by drawing them into safe group homes or facilitating (through rent supplements and housing vouchers) the relocation of them and their parents to neighborhoods with intact social structures and an ethos of family values.

Much of our uniquely American crime problem (as opposed to the worldwide problem of general thievery) arises, not from the failings of individuals but from the concentration in disorderly neighborhoods of

---

[10]It is not clear why manganese has this effect, but we know that it diminishes the availability of a precursor of serotonin, a neurotransmitter, and low levels of serotonin are now strongly linked to violent and impulsive behavior.

people at risk of failing. That concentration is partly the result of prosperity and freedom (functioning families long ago seized the opportunity to move out to the periphery), partly the result of racism (it is harder for some groups to move than for others), and partly the result of politics (elected officials do not wish to see settled constituencies broken up).

I seriously doubt that this country has the will to address either of its 95 two crime problems, save by acts of individual self-protection. We could in theory make justice swifter and more certain, but we will not accept the restrictions on liberty and the weakening of procedural safeguards that this would entail. We could vastly improve the way in which our streets are policed, but some of us will not pay for it and the rest of us will not tolerate it. We could alter the way in which at-risk children experience the first few years of life, but the opponents of this—welfare-rights activists, family preservationists, budget cutters, and assorted ideologues—are numerous and the bureaucratic problems enormous.

Unable or unwilling to do such things, we take refuge in substitutes: we debate the death penalty, we wring our hands over television, we lobby to keep prisons from being built in our neighborhoods, and we fall briefly in love with trendy nostrums that seem to cost little and promise much.

Much of our ambivalence is on display in the 1994 federal crime bill. To satisfy the tough-minded, the list of federal offenses for which the death penalty can be imposed has been greatly enlarged, but there is little reason to think that executions, as they work in this country (which is to say, after much delay and only on a few offenders), have any effect on the crime rate and no reason to think that executing more federal prisoners (who account, at best, for a tiny fraction of all homicides) will reduce the murder rate. To satisfy the tender-minded, several billion dollars are earmarked for prevention programs, but there is as yet very little hard evidence that any of these will actually prevent crime.

In adding more police officers, the bill may make some difference—but only if the additional personnel are imaginatively deployed. And Washington will pay only part of the cost initially and none of it after six years, which means that any city getting new officers will either have to raise its own taxes to keep them on the force or accept the political heat that will arise from turning down "free" cops. Many states also desperately need additional prison space; the federal funds allocated by the bill for their construction will be welcomed, provided that states are willing to meet the conditions set for access to such funds.

Meanwhile, just beyond the horizon, there lurks a cloud that the winds will soon bring over us. The population will start getting younger again. By the end of this decade there will be a million more people between the ages of fourteen and seventeen than there are now. Half of this extra million will be male. Six percent of them will become high-rate, repeat offenders—30,000 more muggers, killers, and thieves than we have now.

Get ready.   100

A. N. Barnett, Chris Gersten, Max Winkler

Professor Wilson's essay generated a good deal of comment. We here offer a brief selection from the correspondence.

Letters Responding to James Q. Wilson

To the Editor of Commentary:

James Q. Wilson does not tell us "What To Do About Crime" but "What To Do About Some Kinds of Crime: Murder, Robbery, Rape, Etc." ... What he ignores is the larger encompassing culture of criminal behavior in which the crimes that interest him are only a part.

When we follow the news, say by reading the *New York Times* or Canada's *Globe and Mail*, it is difficult to avoid concluding that criminal behavior is so widespread that it is no great distortion to describe it as endemic. Yes, there are murders and robberies and rapes, but there are also other crimes that appear to be irrepressible. I list a handful of recent examples from a virtually inexhaustible supply:

• *New York Times*, June 28, 1994: National Medical Enterprises Inc., one of America's largest psychiatric-hospital chains, pleaded guilty to paying kickbacks and bribes for referrals. The firm agreed to pay $362.7 million in settlement. . . .

• *Globe and Mail*, April 7, 1994: C. R. Bard Inc. of New Jersey admitted making faulty heart catheters and then covering up the defects. The company was fined $61 million. Two deaths have been traced to the faulty catheters and at least seventeen patients needed emergency surgery. . . .

• *New York Times*, September 12, 1994: Headline: "In Immigration Labyrinth, Corruption Comes Easily." . . .

• *Globe and Mail*, March 15, 1994: Deloitte & Touche, one of the biggest North American accounting firms, paid the U.S. government $313 million (U.S.) to settle charges it was negligent in audits of more than twenty thrifts and banks.

• *New York Times*, August 10, 1994: KPMG Peat Marwick, one of the Big Six accounting firms, agreed to pay $186.5 million to settle federal charges that it failed to audit a number of failed and distressed banks and savings institutions properly.

• *New York Times*, July 7, 1994: The "most prevalent form [of police corruption] is not [New York City] police taking money to accommodate criminals by closing their eyes to illegal activities such as bookmaking, as was the case twenty years ago," said the Mollen report, "but police acting as criminals, especially in connection with the drug trade."

• *New York Times*, March 9, 1994: Headline: "Managers of Coops and Condos Are Accused of Payoff Scheme: New York Inquiry Finds Contractors are Extorted."

I would be very pleased if Mr. Wilson would draw on his knowledge   10
and wisdom about crime to tell us how the culture of crime arose and
embedded itself in national life.

A. N. Barnett
West Kingston, Ontario, Canada

To the Editor of Commentary:

In his article, James Q. Wilson has provided us with a host of interesting ideas for reducing America's crime rate, but he is out of step with most law-and-order legislators and former U.S. Attorney General William Barr who support stiffer sentences for violent and repeat offenders as the primary weapon in the war on crime. . . .

Mr. Wilson is correct that sentencing felons to life for their third conviction is misguided. . . . But there is no legal reason why the judicial system cannot be reformed to incarcerate felons at the stage of their criminal careers when they are most likely to engage in criminal behavior.

First, eliminate parole, and require felons to serve at least 85 percent of their actual sentences. . . . According to a Gallup poll, 92 percent of the American people believe that criminals should serve their full sentences. But violent felons serve an average of only 37 percent of their actual sentences. . . .

Second, require mandatory minimum sentences for first-time violent offenders. Do not wait until a person is convicted for the second or third time. Let every potential murderer know that if he is convicted of first-degree murder, he will serve a minimum 25-year sentence without any chance of parole. Mandatory sentences for rape should be ten years and for aggravated assault at least five years.

Second-offense violent offenders should face the first-offense mini-   5
mum plus five years. Third-time offenders should get ten years extra.

Third, reform the juvenile-justice system to treat anyone fourteen or over as an adult when he commits a violent crime. Since judges are loath to sentence juveniles to adult prisons, special juvenile prisons will have to be constructed to house violent juvenile felons until they reach eighteen years of age. Colorado has already begun this practice.

If these three reforms are enacted, . . . violent offenders will be put away and kept off the streets for many years, often until they graduate out of the active criminal years. It is also very likely to have a deterrent effect on young potential criminals.

All these reforms are attempts to tie the hands of judges and parole boards who have been responsible for so much crime by allowing repeat and violent felons to serve short terms or no terms at all. . . .

If we enact these reforms, we will have to build more prisons. . . . But if this is the price we must pay for a safer society, it is well worth it.

Chris Gersten
Anti-Crime Alliance
Bethesda, Maryland

To the Editor of Commentary:

James Q. Wilson's "What To Do About Crime" is a pragmatic and objective analysis of the leading concern in America today. . . .

I am a professional who has been involved in corrections and law-enforcement for the past sixteen years, so I am qualified to assure you that Mr. Wilson is right on target in reporting that 6 percent of the boys of any given age have a criminal orientation. In fact, FBI statistics, as well as information from other reliable sources, point to 5 percent of criminal felons committing approximately 80 percent of all offenses.

There is a consistent number of individuals in all societies throughout the world and throughout history whose personalities and psychological makeup are essentially criminal. . . . Other societies have dealt with this reality soberly and sensibly. In liberal democracies such as Holland, Denmark, Sweden, and other nations, "psychopath laws" are enforced with indeterminate sentencing based on considerations of public safety. . . . Classification and targeting of this criminal class would make a significant dent in U.S. crime rates.

Mr. Wilson is also on target about the futility of intrusive gun-control laws. . . . The problem is not the availability of guns, but rather the criminal use of guns. In states like Florida, Alabama, and Idaho, the concealed-gun permits now available to any qualified citizen have certainly not led to a rise in crime. In fact, in Florida, the enactment of the "carrying" statute immediately led to a significant drop in violent crimes. . . .

Effectively dealing with the criminal class . . . requires innovative concepts. I have worked with "intensive supervision programs" (ISP) for the past seven years, . . . but what is so promising now is that electronic monitoring is entering its second generation. Rather than home detention and curfew, the new technology (currently available) makes it possible for . . . adjudicated stalkers, released felons, pre-trial detainees, and others to be controlled . . . with cellular triangulation and tracking systems that will notify authorities of their location at all times. . . . An approach to an off-limits location would set off a programmed alarm. . . . The major benefit of this new system is that it would permit . . . inexpensive control over lower-risk offenders . . . .

Mr. Wilson is strongly opposed to the legalization or decriminalization of drugs. I can understand his view. I too am against the use of drugs. But my own long experience with criminal drug enforcement leads me to . . . the conviction that drug prohibition and enforcement simply do not work. As a veteran of the "war on drugs," with experience in arresting career-criminal parolees involved in the drug trade, I, along with growing numbers of my colleagues, have little illusion about the possibility of winning this particular war. . . . In fact, the "war on drugs" itself has become a major industry in America today, separate from the massive profits generated by the illegal drug cartels. . . .

In the course of this campaign, the drug offender has been denigrated and dehumanized. The criminal incarceration of drug users and abusers will certainly be recognized one day as a barbarism of our age similar to the imprisonment of the mentally ill in the 18th and 19th centuries. Substance abuse is a medical and behavioral pathology that requires rational professional treatment of the user, not criminal sanctions. The social politics of drug enforcement serve, probably unintentionally, to target certain groups unfairly. For example, black Americans comprise approximately 12 percent of the U.S. population and they account for approximately 11 percent of all cocaine use (powder and rock forms), but they account for more than 80 percent of all cocaine arrests, prosecutions, and incarcerations because of the differing enforcement standards for rock and powder cocaine. . . .

The view that drug (as well as alcohol) abuse contributes to criminality is simplistic and ultimately erroneous. There is a real difference between people who are compelled to commit crimes because of the artificially high price of drugs and those with real criminal orientation who commit wanton crimes under the influence of drugs. . . . Gratuitous crime, under the influence of either drugs or alcohol, should be a cause for aggravation, not mitigation, of the act. Possibly the real choice for public policy is that of the availability of treatment for substance abusers combined with the realization that as long as substance use and abuse do not infringe on others, they should be private matters.

Max Winkler
Denver, Colorado

14
THE MILLENNIUM

Short Views

Never let the future disturb you. You will meet it, if you have to, with the same weapons of reason which today arm you against the present.
Marcus Aurelius

Democratic nations care little for what has been, but are haunted by visions of what will be.
Alexis de Tocqueville

I have seen the future and it works.
Lincoln Steffens, returning in 1919 from the newly formed Soviet Union

The future is not what it used to be.
Paul Valéry

The future is made of the same stuff as the present.
Simone Weil

The future bears a great resemblance to the past, only more so.
Faith Popcorn

This war no longer bears the characteristics of former inter-European conflicts. It is one of those elemental conflicts which usher in a new millennium and which shake the world once in a thousand years.
Adolf Hitler, speech to the Reichstag, 26 April 1942

In the satirical revue *Beyond the Fringe,* a group of devout end-of-the-worlders (Jonathan Miller, Alan Bennett, Dudley Moore) are squatting on a mountain-top in sure expectation of a mighty wind and the thrilling punishment of the

nondevout. They check their supplies of tinned food, then joyfully count down the seconds to the wonderful catastrophe. Nothing happens. A moment of understandable flatness follows, which is dispelled by their leader (Peter Cook) with the cheery punch line, "Never mind, lads—same time tomorrow—we must get a winner soon."
     Julian Barnes

We already have the statistics for the future: the growth percentages of pollution, overpopulation, desertification. The future is already in place.
     Günter Grass

The ordinary "horseless carriage" is at present a luxury for the wealthy; and although its price will probably fall in the future, it will never, of course, come into as common use as the bicycle.
     The Literary Digest, **October 14, 1899**

Heavier-than-air flying machines are impossible.
     Lord Kelvin, British physicist, president of the British Royal Society, c. 1895

The submarine may be the cause of bringing battle to a stoppage altogether, for fleets will become useless, and as other war matériel continues to improve, war will become impossible.
     Jules Verne, "The Future of the Submarine" (1904)

Our faith in the present dies out long before our faith in the future.
     Ruth Benedict

John

The author of the last book of the New Testament, called Revelation to St. John the Divine and also called Apocalypse, says that his name is John—more strictly, John is the anglicized form of a common Hebrew name usually transliterated as Johanan—but little is known about him, other than that he writes from the island of Patmos, one of the Dodecanese Islands, in the Aegean Sea, between Turkey and Crete. He probably wrote the book (in Greek) around 80–90 A.D.; his Greek includes Semitic features, indicating to specialists that he was a Judeo-Christian whose native language was Aramaic (the Semitic language that Jesus probably spoke); Patmos was the site of a penal colony, to which the Romans probably exiled him because of his missionary activities.

The Greek word apocalypse *means uncovering or unveiling, as does the Latin word* revelation *(putting aside the veil). The idea is that the work discloses or uncovers or reveals the future; it tells the reader what will take place as determined by God. The part of John's Revelation that especially concerns us is the part dealing with the* millennium *(from the Latin* mille *[equals] thousand, and* annus *[equals] year), a period when the enemy of God, variously called Satan, the dragon, and the serpent, will be imprisoned, and "a new heaven and a new earth . . . , new Jerusalem" (21.1–2) will appear. It happens that this imprisonment, according to John, is only temporary, and that Satan will be released and will then suffer a permanent defeat by God, but the term* millennium *has come to mean a new and permanently joyous age, especially such a period after a long period of chaos.*

John's book, reporting visions that he says were granted to him by Christ, is by no means the only apocalyptic book; in fact, John drew on apocalyptic elements in the Hebrew writings, especially the Book of Daniel in the Hebrew Bible. Apocalyptic literature—essentially, visions of a terrible end to the world as we know it, and the creation of a better world—can be found in religions other than Judaism and Christianity, and in classical myths.

We give the passages (parts of Chapters 6, 20, and 21) chiefly concerned with the destruction of the present age and the introduction of the millennium, about one-twentieth of the entire book of Revelation.

Revelation, from Chapters 6, 20, and 21

6.9 . . . I saw under the altar the souls of them that were slain for the word of God, and for the testimony which they held. . . .

11 And white robes were given unto every one of them. . . .

12 And lo, there was a great earthquake; and the sun became black as sackcloth of hair, and the moon became as blood;

13 And the stars of heaven fell unto the earth, even as a fig tree casteth her untimely figs, when she is shaken of a mighty wind. . . .

15 And the kings of the earth, and the great men, and the rich men, and the chief captains, and the mighty men, and every bond man, and every free man, hid themselves in the dens and in the rocks of the mountain.

16 And said to the mountains and rocks. Fall on us, and hide us from the face of him that sitteth on the throne, and from the wrath of the Lamb.

• • •

20.1 And I saw an angel come down from heaven, having the key of the bottomless pit and a great chain in his hand.

2 And he laid hold on the dragon, that old serpent, which is the devil, and Satan, and bound him a thousand years.

3 And cast him into the bottomless pit, and shut him up, and set a seal upon him, that he should deceive the nations no more, till the thousand years should be fulfilled; and after that he must be loosed a little season.

4 And I saw thrones, and they sat upon them, and judgment was given upon them, and judgment was given unto them; and I saw the souls of them that were beheaded for the witness of Jesus, and for the word of God, and which had not worshiped the beast, neither his image, neither had received his mark upon their foreheads, or in their hands; and they lived and reigned with Christ a thousand years.

5 But the rest of the dead lived not again until the thousand years were finished. This is the first resurrection.

6 Blessed and holy is he that hath part in the first resurrection; on such the second death hath no power, but they shall be priests of God and of Christ, and shall reign with him a thousand years.

7 And when the thousand years are expired, Satan shall be loosed out of his prison.

8 And shall go out to deceive the nations which are in the four quarters of the earth, Gog and Magog, to gather them together to battle the number of whom is as the sand of the sea.

9 And they went up on the breadth of the earth, and compassed the camp of the saints about, and the beloved city; and fire came down from God out of heaven, and devoured them. . . .

•   •   •

21.1 And I saw a new heaven and a new earth; for the first heaven and the first earth were passed away and there was no more sea.

2 And I John saw the holy city, new Jerusalem, coming down from God out of heaven, prepared as a bride adorned for her husband.

3 And I heard a great voice out of heaven saying, "Behold, the tabernacle of God is with men, and he will dwell with them, and they shall be his people, and God himself shall be with them, and be their God.

4 And God shall wipe away all tears from their eyes; and there shall be no more death, neither sorrow, nor crying, neither shall there be any more pain; for the former things are passed away.

✎ Topics for Critical Thinking and Writing

The Bible that most of us read is a translation—Revelation was written in Greek—and of course translations differ. The King James Version has regularly been called "the noblest monument of English prose," but it has long been recognized that this version was based on a Greek text that included countless errors produced by fourteen centuries of copying and miscopying of manuscripts. Not surprisingly, by the late nineteenth century it was felt that a new version was overdue; the English Revised Version was published in 1881–85, and an Americanized version, the American Standard Version, was published in 1901. The idea of these revised versions was to take advantage of accumulated scholarship, but also to stay as close as possible to the beloved King James Version. But scholarship did not stop in 1901, and a few decades later a revision of the ASV was published, called the Revised Standard Version

(1946). The translators of the RSV sought to "embody the best results of modern scholarship as to the meaning of the scripture, and express this meaning in English diction which is designed for use in public and private worship and preserves those qualities which have given to the King James Version a supreme place in English literature."

Compare a sample of the King James Version with the corresponding passage in the Revised Standard Version.

Here again is the King James Version (1611) of the beginning of Chapter 21:

> 21.1 And I saw a new heaven and a new earth; for the first heaven and the first earth were passed away and there was no more sea.
>
> 2 And I John saw the holy city, new Jerusalem, coming down from God out of heaven, prepared as a bride adorned for her husband.
>
> 3 And I heard a great voice out of heaven saying, "Behold, the tabernacle of God is with men, and he will dwell with them, and they shall be his people, and God himself shall be with them, and be their God.
>
> 4 And God shall wipe away all tears from their eyes; and there shall be no more death, neither sorrow, nor crying, neither shall there be any more pain; for the former things are passed away.

The corresponding passage in the Revised Standard Version goes thus:

> 21.1 Then I saw a new heaven and a new earth; for the first heaven and the first earth had passed away, and the sea was no more.
>
> 2 And I saw the holy city, new Jerusalem, coming down out of heaven from God, prepared as a bride adorned for her husband;
>
> 3 and I heard a loud voice from the throne saying, "Behold, the dwelling of God is with men. He will dwell with them, and they shall be his people, and God himself will be with them;
>
> 4 he will wipe away every tear from their eyes, and death shall be no more, neither shall there be mourning nor crying nor pain any more, for the former things have passed away."

Putting aside questions of faithfulness to the original Greek, do you have a preference for one version or the other? You may want to concentrate on a sentence or two.

Here is a third version, from the New Jerusalem Bible (1973), a revision of the 1966 Jerusalem Bible, a Roman Catholic translation that was not committed to retaining as much as possible of the King James Version.

> 21.1 Then I saw a new heaven and a new earth; the first heaven and the first earth had disappeared now, and there was no longer any sea.
>
> 2 I saw a holy city, Jerusalem, coming down out of heaven from God, prepared as a bride dressed for her husband.
>
> 3 Then I heard a loud voice call from the throne, "Look, here God lives among human beings. He will make his home among them; they will be his people. And he will be their God, God-with-them.
>
> 4 He will wipe away all tears from their eyes; there will be no more death, and no more mourning or sadness or pain. The world of the past has gone.

Again, compare this passage or a portion of it with the King James Version, and if you find one version more memorable or more moving than the other, explain why.

Miriam Lindsey Levering

Miriam Lindsey Levering, a specialist in Asian religions, wrote the following article for an encyclopedic volume, The Perennial Dictionary of World Religions, *ed. Keith Crim. (The book was originally published as* Abingdon Dictionary of Living Religions.*) Within its articles* The Perennial Dictionary *uses a system of cross-references that we have preserved here: The first time that the title of another article is mentioned, it is printed in small capitals. In Levering's second paragraph, for instance, notice that "Satan" and "Apocalyptic" appear in small capitals, thereby suggesting that the reader who wishes more information on the topic can find it by turning to these articles.*

Millenarian Movements

Generally, any religious movement that hopes for a salvation that is a) *collective,* to be enjoyed by all the faithful as a group; b) *terrestrial,* to be realized on this earth; c) *imminent,* to come soon and suddenly; d) *total,* to transform life on earth completely; e) *miraculous,* to be brought about by, or with the help of, supernatural agencies.

The term "millenarian" first appears in the NT book of Revelation (ch. 20) in the context of the final struggle between God and Satan at the end of history. Millennial expectations are thus strictly speaking one variety of Christian Apocalyptic beliefs. However, the term "millenarian" is used by scholars typologically to describe a large number of apocalyptic religious movements in many periods in non-Western as well as Western societies, many of which have had no history of contact with Christianity. Often the term is used interchangeably with "messianism" or "messianic movement," i.e., movements that expect a redeemer who will inaugurate a utopian age (*see* Messiah).

1. The persistence of millenarianism. Although the predominant Christian view has been the allegorical interpretations offered by Augustine in his *City of God* and followed by Luther, Calvin, and the English reformers, an apocalyptic form of millenarianism has had its proponents (*see* Millenarianism).

In Africa, the Caribbean, South America, and Asia there are many millenarian movements whose major symbols reflect contact with Western millenarian ideas reinterpreted by indigenous concerns. Notable examples include the T'ai-p'ing movement in China in the mid-nineteenth century, whose leader Hung Hsiu-Ch'üan believed that he was the younger brother of Christ; the RASTIFARIAN movement in Jamaica, which sought a return to Ethiopia as the black Zion; numerous African movements that regarded their leaders as incarnations of Christ, or as a second Christ; African "Watch Tower" movements directly inspired by missionaries from the JEHOVAH'S WITNESSES; and thousands of ZIONIST movements in Africa that regard biblical prophecy regarding an end to suffering and restoration of Zion for the Jews as applying directly to Africans.

Among the millenarian beliefs and movements that owe nothing to Western traditions are the following: In China, Taoist movements in the first century B.C. and the first and fourth centuries A.D. (*see* TAOISM, RELIGIOUS), and Buddhist-influenced popular millenarian WHITE LOTUS movements from the twelfth through the nineteenth centuries A.D.; in Japan, the *yo-naoshi* movements of the Tokugawa and Meiji periods; in South America, the millennial movements among the Tupi-Guarani in the interior of Eastern Brazil; the "CARGO CULTS" in Melanesia and elsewhere; and in North America, the Ghost Dances that spread through the Plains tribes in the late 1880s, culminating in the defeat of the Sioux Indians at the Battle of Wounded Knee in 1890 (*see* NATIVE AMERICAN TRIBAL RELIGION).

2. Chief characteristics. The history of Western and non-Western millenarianism illustrates the need to distinguish between millenarian beliefs within a tradition or culture and millenarian movements which place a strong emphasis on immediate action. Some of the chief characteristics of the latter include: a) origin in intense revelatory religious experience, b) charismatic leadership, c) missionary zeal, d) emotional commitment, e) promise of a definite, terrestrial blessing, f) moral reform, g) new symbolic forms, h) new voluntaristic organizations with a new sense of community, i) selective but often radical rejection of traditional ways and adoption of new ones, and j) concern for personal and spiritual renewal.

Millenarian movements vary remarkably in the ways in which they conceive of the future paradise, react to traditional moral codes and values, and view their own role in bringing about the new age. These movements also differ in their sense of who will be included in the coming kingdom, as well as in the degree to which hostility toward a powerful group (e.g., colonial powers, whites, Christians) gives direction to their movement. Perhaps most importantly, they vary in their response to the perceived delay in the coming of the millennium that they await so anxiously. Although one would expect that the failure of a prophesied millennium to arrive would create a fatal crisis of credibility, many movements emerge from such crises even stronger than before.

3. Interpretations. There are various attempts to understand the origin and functions of millenarian movements.

a) Deprivation theories hold that such movements arise in groups that are experiencing "relative social deprivation," defined as a discrepancy between legitimate expectations and social realities. The coming utopia will correct current injustices.

b) Acculturation theories see millenarian movements as bearers and for- 10 mulators of responses to the interaction between a literate, technically powerful culture and nonliterate tribal people. In this respect, movements can be described as "nativistic" or "revitalizing" (i.e., seeking to preserve or restore elements of one's own culture) or "adoptive" (introducing elements of a foreign culture).

c) Political theories. It has been argued that millenarian rebellions are politically futile and arise out of the failure of their participants to understand social and political forces which make them deprived. Others argue, however, that millenarian movements are politically fruitful in that they mobilize and unite diverse groups into a single movement.

d) Psychological theories regard millenarian movements as "collective flights from reality" by those who have unresolved and deep frustrations or psychological stress. Others point out that millenarian movements offer structures of meaning that provide solutions to problems of cognitive dissonance.

e) Parsonian identity theories. Critical of deprivation and political theories, Parsonian identity theories stress the way in which millenarian movements offer their followers a transition to a new sacred identity.

f) Liminality theories. Since a chief characteristic of millenarian movements is their orientation toward time, some scholars argue that such movements are a liminal (boundary) community living between present and future.

While all these theoretical approaches are useful, most are reduction- 15 istic. It is important to remember that the creativity or destructiveness that millenarian movements display in shaping personalities and in solving religious or cultural problems depends on a great many factors, not all of which are necessarily linked to the structure of the messianic movement or its message as such.

Bibliography. Bibliographical guides: W. La Barre, "Materials for a History of Crisis Cults: A Bibliographical Essay," *Current Anthropology* XII (1971), 3–44; H. Schwartz. "The End of the Beginning: Millenarian Studies, 1969–1975," *Religious Studies Review* II (1976), 1–15. Theoretical approaches: A. Wallace, "Revitalization Movements," *American Anthropologist* LVIII (1956), 264–81; R. Linton, "Nativistic Movements," *American Anthropologist* XLV (1943), 230–40; N. Cohn, *The Pursuit of the Millennium,* 3rd ed. (1970); P. Worsley, *The Trumpet Shall Sound* (1957); V. Turner, *The Ritual Process* (1969); D. Aberle, "A Note on Relative Deprivation Theory as Applied to Millenarian and Other Cult Movements," in S. L. Thrupp, ed., *Millennial Dreams in Action* (1970); H. Mol, *The Identity of the Sacred* (1976); J. Zygmunt, "Movements and Motives: Some Unresolved Issues in the

Psychology of Social Movements," *Human Relations* XXV (1972), 449–67; Y. Talmon, "Millenarian Movements," *European Journal of Sociology* VII (1966), 159–200.

✎ Topics for Critical thinking and Writing

1. In her fourth and fifth paragraphs Levering specifies several millenarian movements, some in the Judeo-Christian tradition (e.g., the Rastifarian movement) and some not within this tradition (e.g., the Cargo Cults of Melanesia). Choose one such movement, and consult several sources, perhaps beginning with other entries in *The Perennial Dictionary*, and prepare a summary of its millenarian aspects. (Incidentally, if you choose the Ghost Dance—a belief of the Plains Tribes in the United States in the late nineteenth century—you will find that not all sources agree with Levering's assertion that the movement owed nothing to Western traditions.) In preparing a summary, be sure to cite all of your sources.

2. If you belong to a Millenarian movement, for instance Jehovah's Witnesses, ask yourself if Levering has adequately stated your view. (You may also want to read the relevant articles in *The Perennial Dictionary*.) If you are not a member of such a movement, interview someone who is, and then write up your interview, in a sympathetic manner, and if possible ask the person to review it for accuracy. (For suggestions about conducting an interview, see pages 57–60 in our book.) You may find that some of the theories seeking to explain millenarianism, offered in Section 3 of Levering's article, will help you to formulate questions.

Edward Bellamy

Edward Bellamy (1850–98) was born in Chicopee Falls, in western Massachusetts. His ancestors included many ministers, and for a while Bellamy thought he would follow their footsteps, but when he was unable to experience the requisite rebirth in Christ he abandoned the family profession, studied law and was admitted to the bar, and then turned to journalism and the writing of fiction. Three novels brought him modest success, but Looking Backward, 2000–1887 *(1888) made his name a household word.*

The book belongs to a genre called utopian fiction, *named for Sir Thomas More's* Utopia *(1516). Greek for "no place," Utopia is (on the whole) More's view of an ideal society. (For a selection from More's book, see pages 532–38.) More's story, narrated by a man who supposedly traveled to remote places with Amerigo Vespucci, reports the doings of people in a geographically remote society. Bellamy's* Looking Backward, 2000–1887, *though published in 1888, supposedly reports the doings of people remote in time, the year 2000. That is, Bellamy, writing in the late nineteenth century, purports to tell his readers what life will be like in the year 2000. The fictional device is this: A young Bostonian, Julian West, is hypnotized in 1887 (i.e., the time when Bellamy was writing the book), falls asleep, and wakes up 113 years later, in the year 2000. When West, a rather naive fellow, tells the people of this new society about what life was a century ago—the present for Bellamy's readers—Bellamy is of course able to present an unflattering view of the age; and when the people of the year 2000 tell West what life is now like, Bellamy is in effect able to suggest to his readers that it is* this *sort of life that we should strive for.*

We give about one-tenth of the book.

Looking Backward

Chapter I

I first saw the light in the city of Boston in the year 1857. "What!" you say, "eighteen fifty-seven? That is an odd slip. He means nineteen fifty-seven, of course." I beg pardon, but there is no mistake. It was about four in the afternoon of December the 26th, one day after Christmas, in the year 1857, not 1957, that I first breathed the east wind of Boston, which, I assure the reader, was at that remote period marked by the same penetrating quality characterizing it in the present year of grace, 2000.

These statements seem so absurd on their face, especially when I add that I am a young man apparently of about thirty years of age, that no person can be blamed for refusing to read another word of what promises to be a mere imposition upon his credulity. Nevertheless I earnestly assure the reader that no imposition is intended, and will undertake, if he shall follow me a few pages, to entirely convince him of this. If I may, then, provisionally assume, with the pledge of justifying the assumption, that I know better than the reader when I was born, I will go on with my narrative. As every schoolboy knows, in the latter part of the nineteenth century the civilization of to-day, or anything like it, did not exist, although the elements which were to develop it were already in ferment. Nothing had, however, occurred to modify the immemorial division of society into the four classes, or nations, as they may be more fitly called, since the differences between them were far greater than those between any nations nowadays, of the rich and the poor, the educated and the ignorant. I myself was rich and also educated, and possessed, therefore, all the elements of happiness enjoyed by the most fortunate in that age. Living in luxury, and occupied only with the pursuit of the pleasures and refinements of life, I derived the means of my support from the labor of others, rendering no sort of service in return. My parents and grand-parents had lived in the same way, and I expected that my descendants, if I had any, would enjoy a like easy existence.

But how could I live without service to the world? you ask. Why should the world have supported in utter idleness one who was able to render service? The answer is that my great-grandfather had accumulated a sum of money on which his descendants had ever since lived. The sum, you will naturally infer, must have been very large not to have been exhausted in supporting three generations in idleness. This, however, was not the fact. The sum had been originally by no means large. It was, in fact, much larger now that three generations had been supported upon it in idleness, than it was at first. This mystery of use without consumption, of warmth without combustion, seems like magic, but was merely an ingenious application of the art now happily lost but carried to great perfection by your ancestors, of shifting the burden of one's support on the shoulders of others. The man who had accomplished this, and it was the end all sought, was said to live on the income of his investments. To explain at this point how the ancient methods of industry made this possible would delay us too much. I shall only stop now to say that interest on investments was a species of tax in perpetuity upon the product of those engaged in industry which a person possessing or inheriting money was able to levy. It must not be supposed that an arrangement which seems so unnatural and preposterous according to modern notions was never criticised by your ancestors. It had been the effort of lawgivers and prophets from the earliest ages to abolish interest, or at least to limit it to the smallest possible rate. All these efforts had, however, failed, as they necessarily must so long as the ancient social organizations prevailed. At the time of which I write, the latter part of the nineteenth century, governments had generally given up trying to regulate the subject at all.

By way of attempting to give the reader some general impression of the way people lived together in those days, and especially of the relations of the rich and poor to one another, perhaps I cannot do better than to compare society as it then was to a prodigious coach which the masses of humanity were harnessed to and dragged toilsomely along a very hilly and sandy road. The driver was hunger, and permitted no lagging, though the pace was necessarily very slow. Despite the difficulty of drawing the coach at all along so hard a road, the top was covered with passengers who never got down, even at the steepest ascents. These seats on top were very breezy and comfortable. Well up out of the dust, their occupants could enjoy the scenery at their leisure, or critically discuss the merits of the straining team. Naturally such places were in great demand and the competition for them was keen, every one seeking as the first end in life to secure a seat on the coach for himself and to leave it to his child after him. By the rule of the coach a man could leave his seat to whom he wished, but on the other hand there were many accidents by which it might at any time be wholly lost. For all that they were so easy, the seats were very insecure, and at every sudden jolt of the coach persons were slipping out of them and falling to the ground, where they were instantly compelled to take hold of the rope and help to drag the coach on which they had before ridden so pleasantly. It was naturally regarded as a terrible misfortune to lose one's seat, and the apprehension that this might happen to them or their friends was a constant cloud upon the happiness of those who rode.

But did they think only of themselves? you ask. Was not their very luxury rendered intolerable to them by comparison with the lot of their

5

brothers and sisters in the harness, and the knowledge that their own weight added to their toil? Had they no compassion for fellow beings from whom fortune only distinguished them? Oh, yes; commiseration was frequently expressed by those who rode for those who had to pull the coach, especially when the vehicle came to a bad place in the road, as it was constantly doing, or to a particularly steep hill. At such times, the desperate straining of the team, their agonized leaping and plunging under the pitiless lashing of hunger, the many who fainted at the rope and were trampled in the mire, made a very distressing spectacle, which often called forth highly creditable displays of feeling on the top of the coach. At such times the passengers would call down encouragingly to the toilers of the rope, exhorting them to patience, and holding out hopes of possible compensation in another world for the hardness of their lot, while others contributed to buy salves and liniments for the crippled and injured. It was agreed that it was a great pity that the coach should be so hard to pull, and there was a sense of general relief when the specially bad piece of road was gotten over. This relief was not, indeed, wholly on account of the team, for there was always some danger at these bad places of a general overturn in which all would lose their seats.

It must in truth be admitted that the main effect of the spectacle of the misery of the toilers at the rope was to enhance the passengers' sense of the value of their seats upon the coach, and to cause them to hold on to them more desperately than before. If the passengers could only have felt assured that neither they nor their friends would ever fall from the top, it is probable that, beyond contributing to the funds for liniments and bandages, they would have troubled themselves extremely little about those who dragged the coach.

I am well aware that this will appear to the men and women of the twentieth century an incredible inhumanity, but there are two facts, both very curious, which partly explain it. In the first place, it was firmly and sincerely believed that there was no other way in which Society could get along, except the many pulled at the rope and the few rode, and not only this, but that no very radical improvement even was possible, either in the harness, the coach, the roadway, or the distribution of the toil. It had always been as it was, and it always would be so. It was a pity, but it could not be helped, and philosophy forbade wasting compassion on what was beyond remedy.

The other fact is yet more curious, consisting in a singular hallucination which those on the top of the coach generally shared, that they were not exactly like their brothers and sisters who pulled at the rope, but of finer clay, in some way belonging to a higher order of beings who might justly expect to be drawn. This seems unaccountable, but, as I once rode on this very coach and shared that very hallucination, I ought to be believed. The strangest thing about the hallucination was that those who had but just climbed up from the ground, before they had outgrown the marks of the rope upon their hands, began to fall under its influence. As for those whose parents and grand-parents before them had been so fortunate as to keep their seats on the top, the conviction they cherished of the essential difference between their sort of humanity and the common article was absolute. The effect of such a delusion in moderating fellow feeling for the sufferings of the mass of men into a distant and philosophical compassion is obvious. To it I refer as the only extenuation I can offer for the indifference which, at the period I write of, marked my own attitude toward the misery of my brothers.

In 1887 I came to my thirtieth year. Although still unmarried, I was engaged to wed Edith Bartlett. She, like myself, rode on the top of the coach. That is to say, not to encumber ourselves further with an illustration which has, I hope, served its purpose of giving the reader some general impression of how we lived then, her family was wealthy. In that age, when money alone commanded all that was agreeable and refined in life, it was enough for a woman to be rich to have suitors; but Edith Bartlett was beautiful and graceful also.

My lady readers, I am aware, will protest at this. "Handsome she   10
might have been," I hear them saying, "but graceful never, in the costumes which were the fashion at that period, when the head covering was a dizzy structure a foot tall, and the almost incredible extension of the skirt behind by means of artificial contrivances more thoroughly dehumanized the form than any former device of dressmakers. Fancy any one graceful in such a costume!" The point is certainly well taken, and I can only reply that while the ladies of the twentieth century are lovely demonstrations of the effect of appropriate drapery in accenting feminine graces, my recollection of their great-grandmothers enables me to maintain that no deformity of costume can wholly disguise them.

Our marriage only waited on the completion of the house which I was building for our occupancy in one of the most desirable parts of the city, that is to say, a part chiefly inhabited by the rich. For it must be understood that the comparative desirability of different parts of Boston for residence depended then, not on natural features, but on the character of the neighboring population. Each class or nation lived by itself, in quarters of its own. A rich man living among the poor, an educated man among the uneducated, was like one living in isolation among a jealous and alien race. When the house had been begun, its completion by the winter of 1886 had been expected. The spring of the following year found it, however, yet incomplete, and my marriage still a thing of the future. The cause of a delay calculated to be particularly exasperating to an ardent lover was a series of strikes, that is to say, concerted refusals to work on the part of the brick-layers, masons, carpenters, painters, plumbers, and other trades concerned in house building. What the specific causes of these strikes were I do not remember. Strikes had become so common at that period that people had ceased to inquire into their particular grounds. In one department of industry or another, they had been nearly incessant ever since the great business crisis of 1873. In fact it had come to be the exceptional thing to see any class of laborers pursue their avocation steadily for more than a few months at a time. . . .

Chapter V

When, in the course of the evening the ladies retired, leaving Dr. Leete and myself alone, he sounded me as to my disposition for sleep, saying that if I felt like it my bed was ready for me; but if I was inclined to wakefulness nothing would please him better than to bear me company. "I am a late bird, myself," he said, "and, without suspicion of flattery, I may say that a companion more interesting than yourself could scarcely be imagined. It is decidedly not often that one has a chance to converse with a man of the nineteenth century."

Now I had been looking forward all the evening with some dread to the time when I should be alone, on retiring for the night. Surrounded by these most friendly strangers, stimulated and supported by their sympathetic interest, I had been able to keep my mental balance. Even then, however, in pauses of the conversation I had had glimpses, vivid as lightning flashes, of the horror of strangeness that was waiting to be faced when I could no longer command diversion. I knew I could not sleep that night, and as for lying awake and thinking, it argues no cowardice, I am sure, to confess that I was afraid of it. When, in reply to my host's question, I frankly told him this, he replied that it would be strange if I did not feel just so, but that I need have no anxiety about sleeping; whenever I wanted to go to bed, he would give me a dose which would insure me a sound night's sleep without fail. Next morning, no doubt, I would awake with the feeling of an old citizen.

"Before I acquire that," I replied, "I must know a little more about the sort of Boston I have come back to. You told me when we were upon the house-top that though a century only had elapsed since I fell asleep, it had been marked by greater changes in the conditions of humanity than many a previous millennium. With the city before me I could well believe that, but I am very curious to know what some of the changes have been. To make a beginning somewhere, for the subject is doubtless a large one, what solution, if any, have you found for the labor question? It was the Sphinx's riddle[1] of the nineteenth century, and when I dropped out the Sphinx was threatening to devour society, because the answer was not forthcoming. It is well worth sleeping a hundred years to learn what the right answer was, if, indeed, you have found it yet."

[1]In Greek mythology, the sphinx, a winged monster with the head of a woman and the body of a lion, asked this riddle: "What goes on four legs in the morning, two at noon, and three in the evening?" Those who did not know the answer—man—were killed. [Editors' note]

"As no such thing as the labor question is known nowadays," replied Dr. Leete, "and there is no way in which it could arise, I suppose we may claim to have solved it. Society would indeed have fully deserved being devoured if it had failed to answer a riddle so entirely simple. In fact, to speak by the book, it was not necessary for society to solve the riddle at all. It may be said to have solved itself. The solution came as the result of a process of industrial evolution which could not have terminated otherwise. All that society had to do was to recognize and coöperate with that evolution, when its tendency had become unmistakable."

"I can only say," I answered, "that at the time I fell asleep no such evolution had been recognized."   5

"It was in 1887 that you fell into this sleep, I think you said."

"Yes, May 30th, 1887."

My companion regarded me musingly for some moments. Then he observed, "And you tell me that even then there was no general recognition of the nature of the crisis which society was nearing? Of course, I fully credit your statement. The singular blindness of your contemporaries to the signs of the times is a phenomenon commented on by many of our historians, but few facts of history are more difficult for us to realize, so obvious and unmistakable as we look back seem the indications, which must also have come under your eyes, of the transformation about to come to pass. I should be interested, Mr. West, if you would give me a little more definite idea of the view which you and men of your grade of intellect took of the state and prospects of society in 1887. You must, at least, have realized that the widespread industrial and social troubles, and the underlying dissatisfaction of all classes with the inequalities of society, and the general misery of mankind, were portents of great changes of some sort."

"We did, indeed, fully realize that," I replied. "We felt that society was dragging anchor and in danger of going adrift. Whither it would drift nobody could say, but all feared the rocks."

"Nevertheless," said Dr. Leete, "the set of the current was perfectly   10 perceptible if you had but taken pains to observe it, and it was not toward the rocks, but toward a deeper channel."

"We had a popular proverb," I replied, "that 'hindsight is better than foresight,' the force of which I shall now, no doubt, appreciate more fully than ever. All I can say is, that the prospect was such when I went into that long sleep that I should not have been surprised had I looked down from your house-top to-day on a heap of charred and moss-grown ruins instead of this glorious city."

Dr. Leete had listened to me with close attention and nodded thoughtfully as I finished speaking. "What you have said," he observed, "will be regarded as a most valuable vindication of Storiot, whose account of your era has been generally thought exaggerated in its picture of the gloom and confusion of men's minds. That a period of transition like that should be full of excitement and agitation was indeed to be looked for; but seeing how plain was the tendency of the forces in operation, it was natural to believe that hope rather than fear would have been the prevailing temper of the popular mind."

"You have not yet told me what was the answer to the riddle which you found," I said. "I am impatient to know by what contradiction of natural sequence the peace and prosperity which you now seem to enjoy could have been the outcome of an era like my own."

"Excuse me," replied my host, "but do you smoke?" It was not till our cigars were lighted and drawing well that he resumed. "Since you are in the humor to talk rather than to sleep, as I certainly am, perhaps I cannot do better than to try to give you enough idea of our modern industrial system to dissipate at least the impression that there is any mystery about the process of its evolution. The Bostonians of your day had the reputation of being great askers of questions, and I am going to show my descent by asking you one to begin with. What should you name as the most prominent feature of the labor troubles of your day?"

"Why, the strikes, of course," I replied.

"Exactly; but what made the strikes so formidable?"

"The great labor organizations."

"And what was the motive of these great organizations?"

"The workmen claimed they had to organize to get their rights from the big corporations," I replied.

"That is just it," said Dr. Leete; "the organization of labor and the strikes were an effect, merely, of the concentration of capital in greater masses than had ever been known before. Before this concentration began, while as yet commerce and industry were conducted by innumerable petty concerns with small capital, instead of a small number of great concerns with vast capital, the individual workman was relatively important and independent in his relations to the employer. Moreover, when a little capital or a new idea was enough to start a man in business for himself, workingmen were constantly becoming employers and there was no hard and fast line between the two classes. Labor unions were needless then, and general strikes out of the question. But when the era of small concerns with small capital was succeeded by that of the great aggregations of capital, all this was changed. The individual laborer, who had been relatively important to the small employer, was reduced to insignificance and powerlessness over against the great corporation, while at the same time the way upward to the grade of employer was closed to him. Self-defense drove him to union with his fellows.

"The records of the period show that the outcry against the concentration of capital was furious. Men believed that it threatened society with a form of tyranny more abhorrent than it had ever endured. They believed that the great corporations were preparing for them the yoke of a baser servitude than had ever been imposed on the race, servitude not to men but to soulless machines incapable of any motive but insatiable greed.

Looking back, we cannot wonder at their desperation, for certainly humanity was never confronted with a fate more sordid and hideous than would have been the era of corporate tyranny which they anticipated.

"Meanwhile, without being in the smallest degree checked by the clamor against it, the absorption of business by ever larger monopolies continued. In the United States there was not, after the beginning of the last quarter of the century, any opportunity whatever for individual enterprise in any important field of industry, unless backed by a great capital. During the last decade of the century, such small businesses as still remained were fast-failing survivals of a past epoch, or mere parasites on the great corporations, or else existed in fields too small to attract the great capitalists. Small businesses, as far as they still remained, were reduced to the condition of rats and mice, living in holes and corners, and counting on evading notice for the enjoyment of existence. The railroads had gone on combining till a few great syndicates controlled every rail in the land. In manufactories, every important staple was controlled by a syndicate. These syndicates, pools, trusts, or whatever their name, fixed prices and crushed all competition except when combinations as vast as themselves arose. Then a struggle, resulting in a still greater consolidation, ensued. The great city bazaar crushed its country rivals with branch stores, and in the city itself absorbed its smaller rivals till the business of a whole quarter was concentrated under one roof, with a hundred former proprietors of shops serving as clerks. Having no business of his own to put his money in, the small capitalist, at the same time that he took service under the corporation, found no other investment for his money but its stocks and bonds, thus becoming doubly dependent upon it.

"The fact that the desperate popular opposition to the consolidation of business in a few powerful hands had no effect to check it proves that there must have been a strong economical reason for it. The small capitalists, with their innumerable petty concerns, had in fact yielded the field to the great aggregations of capital, because they belonged to a day of small things and were totally incompetent to the demands of an age of steam and telegraphs and the gigantic scale of its enterprises. To restore the former order of things, even if possible, would have involved returning to the day of stage-coaches. Oppressive and intolerable as was the régime of the great consolidations of capital, even its victims, while they cursed it, were forced to admit the prodigious increase of efficiency which had been imparted to the national industries, the vast economies effected by concentration of management and unity of organization, and to confess that since the new system had taken the place of the old the wealth of the world had increased at a rate before undreamed of. To be sure this vast increase had gone chiefly to make the rich richer, increasing the gap between them and the poor; but the fact remained that, as a means merely of producing wealth, capital had been proved efficient in proportion to its consolidation. The restoration of the old system with the subdivision of capital, if it were possible, might indeed bring back a greater equality of conditions, with more individual dignity and freedom, but it would be at the price of general poverty and the arrest of material progress.

"Was there, then, no way of commanding the services of the mighty wealth-producing principle of consolidated capital without bowing down to a plutocracy like that of Carthage? As soon as men began to ask themselves these questions, they found the answer ready for them. The movement toward the conduct of business by larger and larger aggregations of capital, the tendency toward monopolies, which had been so desperately and vainly resisted, was recognized at last, in its true significance, as a process which only needed to complete its logical evolution to open a golden future to humanity.

"Early in the last century the evolution was completed by the final 25 consolidation of the entire capital of the nation. The industry and commerce of the country, ceasing to be conducted by a set of irresponsible corporations and syndicates of private persons at their caprice and for their profit, were intrusted to a single syndicate representing the people, to be conducted in the common interest for the common profit. The nation, that is to say, organized as the one great business corporation in which all other corporations were absorbed; it became the one capitalist in the place of all other capitalists, the sole employer, the final monopoly in which all previous and lesser monopolies were swallowed up, a monopoly in the profits and economies of which all citizens shared. The epoch of trusts had ended in The Great Trust. In a word, the people of the United States concluded to assume the conduct of their own business, just as one hundred odd years before they had assumed the conduct of their own government, organizing now for industrial purposes on precisely the same grounds that they had then organized for political purposes. At last, strangely late in the world's history, the obvious fact was perceived that no business is so essentially the public business as the industry and commerce on which the people's livelihood depends, and that to entrust it to private persons to be managed for private profit is a folly similar in kind, though vastly greater in magnitude, to that of surrendering the functions of political government to kings and nobles to be conducted for their personal glorification."

"Such a stupendous change as you describe," said I, "did not, of course, take place without great bloodshed and terrible convulsions."

"On the contrary," replied Dr. Leete, "there was absolutely no violence. The change had been long foreseen. Public opinion had become fully ripe for it, and the whole mass of the people was behind it. There was no more possibility of opposing it by force than by argument. On the other hand the popular sentiment toward the great corporations and those identified with them had ceased to be one of bitterness, as they came to realize their necessity as a link, a transition phase, in the evolution of the true industrial system. The most violent foes of the great private monopolies were now forced to recognize how invaluable and indispensable had been their office in educating the people up to the point of assuming control of their own business. Fifty years before, the consolidation of the industries of the country under national control would have seemed a very daring experiment to the most sanguine. But by a series of object lessons, seen and studied by all men, the great corporations had taught the people an entirely new set of ideas on this subject. They had seen for many years syndicates handling revenues greater than those of states, and directing the labors of hundreds of thousands of men with an efficiency and economy unattainable in smaller operations. It had come to be recognized as an axiom that the larger the business the simpler the principles that can be applied to it; that, as the machine is truer than the hand, so the system, which in a great concern does the work of the master's eye in a small business, turns out more accurate results. Thus it came about that, thanks to the corporations themselves, when it was proposed that the nation should assume their functions, the suggestion implied nothing which seemed impracticable even to the timid. To be sure it was a step beyond any yet taken, a broader generalization, but the very fact that the nation would be the sole corporation in the field would, it was seen, relieve the undertaking of many difficulties with which the partial monopolies had contended."

Chapter VI

Dr. Leete ceased speaking, and I remained silent, endeavoring to form some general conception of the changes in the arrangements of society implied in the tremendous revolution which he had described.

Finally I said, "The idea of such an extension of the functions of government is, to say the least, rather overwhelming."

"Extension!" he repeated, "where is the extension?"

"In my day," I replied, "it was considered that the proper functions of government, strictly speaking, were limited to keeping the peace and defending the people against the public enemy, that is, to the military and police powers."

"And, in heaven's name, who are the public enemies?" exclaimed Dr. Leete. "Are they France, England, Germany, or hunger, cold, and nakedness? In your day governments were accustomed, on the slightest international misunderstanding, to seize upon the bodies of citizens and deliver them over by hundreds of thousands to death and mutilation, wasting their treasures the while like water; and all this oftenest for no imaginable profit to the victims. We have no wars now, and our governments no war powers, but in order to protect every citizen against hunger, cold, and nakedness, and provide for all his physical and mental needs, the function is assumed of directing his industry for a term of years. No, Mr. West, I am sure on reflection you will perceive that it was in your age, not in ours, that the extension of the functions of governments was extraordinary. Not even for the best ends would men now allow their governments such powers as were then used for the most maleficent."

5

"Leaving comparisons aside," I said, "the demagoguery and corruption of our public men would have been considered, in my day, insuperable objections to any assumption by government of the charge of the national industries. We should have thought that no arrangement could be worse than to entrust the politicians with control of the wealth-producing machinery of the country. Its material interests were quite too much the football of parties as it was."

"No doubt you were right," rejoined Dr. Leete, "but all that is changed now. We have no parties or politicians, and as for demagoguery and corruption, they are words having only an historical significance."

"Human nature itself must have changed very much," I said.

"Not at all," was Dr. Leete's reply, "but the conditions of human life have changed, and with them the motives of human action. The organization of society with you was such that officials were under a constant temptation to misuse their power for the private profit of themselves or others. Under such circumstances it seems almost strange that you dared entrust them with any of your affairs. Nowadays, on the contrary, society is so constituted that there is absolutely no way in which an official, however ill-disposed, could possibly make any profit for himself or any one else by a misuse of his power. Let him be as bad an official as you please, he cannot be a corrupt one. There is no motive to be. The social system no longer offers a premium on dishonesty. But these are matters which you can only understand as you come, with time, to know us better."

"But you have not yet told me how you have settled the labor problem. It is the problem of capital which we have been discussing," I said. "After the nation had assumed conduct of the mills, machinery, railroads, farms, mines, and capital in general of the country, the labor question still remained. In assuming the responsibilities of capital the nation had assumed the difficulties of the capitalist's position."

10

"The moment the nation assumed the responsibilities of capital those difficulties vanished," replied Dr. Leete. "The national organization of labor under one direction was the complete solution of what was, in your day and under your system, justly regarded as the insoluble labor problem. When the nation became the sole employer, all the citizens, by virtue of their citizenship, became employees, to be distributed according to the needs of industry."

"That is," I suggested, "you have simply applied the principle of universal military service, as it was understood in our day, to the labor question."

"Yes," said Dr. Leete, "that was something which followed as a matter of course as soon as the nation had become the sole capitalist. The people were already accustomed to the idea that the obligation of every citizen, not physically disabled, to contribute his military services to the defense of the nation was equal and absolute. That it was equally the duty of every citizen to contribute his quota of industrial or intellectual services to the maintenance of the nation was equally evident, though it was not until the nation became the employer of labor that citizens were able to render this sort of service with any pretense either of universality or equity. No organization of labor was possible when the employing power was divided among hundreds or thousands of individuals and corporations, between which concert of any kind was neither desired, nor indeed feasible. It constantly happened then that vast numbers who desired to labor could find no opportunity, and on the other hand, those who desired to evade a part or all of their debt could easily do so."

"Service, now, I suppose, is compulsory upon all," I suggested.

"It is rather a matter of course than of compulsion," replied Dr. Leete. 15 "It is regarded as so absolutely natural and reasonable that the idea of its being compulsory has ceased to be thought of. He would be thought to be an incredibly contemptible person who should need compulsion in such a case. Nevertheless, to speak of service being compulsory would be a weak way to state its absolute inevitableness. Our entire social order is so wholly based upon and deduced from it that if it were conceivable that a man could escape it, he would be left with no possible way to provide for his existence. He would have excluded himself from the world, cut himself off from his kind, in a word, committed suicide."

"Is the term of service in this industrial army for life?"

"Oh, no; it both begins later and ends earlier than the average working period in your day. Your workshops were filled with children and old men, but we hold the period of youth sacred to education and the period of maturity, when the physical forces begin to flag, equally sacred to ease and agreeable relaxation. The period of industrial service is twenty-four years, beginning at the close of the course of education at twenty-one and terminating at forty-five. After forty-five, while discharged from labor, the citizen still remains liable to special calls, in case of emergencies causing a sudden great increase in the demand for labor, till he reaches the age of fifty-five, but such calls are rarely, in fact almost never, made. The fifteenth day of October of every year is what we call Muster Day, because those who have reached the age of twenty-one are then mustered into the industrial service, and at the same time those who, after twenty-four years' service, have reached the age of forty-five, are honorably mustered out. It is the great day of the year with us, whence we reckon all other events, our Olympiad, save that it is annual."

Chapter IX

Dr. and Mrs. Leete were evidently not a little startled to learn, when they presently appeared, that I had been all over the city alone that morning, and it was apparent that they were agreeably surprised to see that I seemed so little agitated after the experience.

"Your stroll could scarcely have failed to be a very interesting one," said Mrs. Leete, as we sat down to table soon after. "You must have seen a good many new things."

"I saw very little that was not new," I replied. "But I think what surprised me as much as anything was not to find any stores on Washington Street, or any banks on State. What have you done with the merchants and bankers? Hung them all, perhaps, as the anarchists wanted to do in my day?"

"Not so bad as that," replied Dr. Leete. "We have simply dispensed with them. Their functions are obsolete in the modern world."

"Who sells you things when you want to buy them?" I inquired.

"There is neither selling nor buying nowadays; the distribution of goods is effected in another way. As to the bankers, having no money we have no use for those gentry."

"Miss Leete," said I, turning to Edith, "I am afraid that your father is making sport of me. I don't blame him, for the temptation my innocence offers must be extraordinary. But, really, there are limits to my credulity as to possible alterations in the social system."

"Father has no idea of jesting, I am sure," she replied, with a reassuring smile.

The conversation took another turn then, the point of ladies' fashions in the nineteenth century being raised, if I remember rightly, by Mrs. Leete, and it was not till after breakfast, when the doctor had invited me up to the house-top, which appeared to be a favorite resort of his, that he recurred to the subject.

"You were surprised," he said, "at my saying that we got along without money or trade, but a moment's reflection will show that trade existed and money was needed in your day simply because the business of production was left in private hands, and that, consequently, they are superfluous now."

"I do not at once see how that follows," I replied.

"It is very simple," said Dr. Leete. "When innumerable different and independent persons produced the various things needful to life and comfort, endless exchanges between individuals were requisite in order that they might supply themselves with what they desired. These exchanges constituted trade, and money was essential as their medium. But as soon as the nation became the sole producer of all sorts of commodities, there was no need of exchanges between individuals that they might get what they required. Everything was procurable from one source, and nothing could be procured anywhere else. A system of direct distribution from the national storehouses took the place of trade, and for this money was unnecessary."

"How is this distribution managed?" I asked.

"On the simplest possible plan," replied Dr. Leete. "A credit corresponding to his share of the annual product of the nation is given to every citizen on the public books at the beginning of each year, and a credit card issued him with which he procures at the public storehouses, found in every community, whatever he desires whenever he desires it. This arrangement, you will see, totally obviates the necessity for business transactions of any sort between individuals and consumers. Perhaps you would like to see what our credit cards are like.

"You observe," he pursued as I was curiously examining the piece of pasteboard he gave me, "that this card is issued for a certain number of dollars. We have kept the old word, but not the substance. The term, as we use it, answers to no real thing, but merely serves as an algebraical symbol for comparing the values of products with one another. For this purpose they are all priced in dollars and cents, just as in your day. The value of what I procure on this card is checked off by the clerk, who pricks out of these tiers of squares the price of what I order."

"If you wanted to buy something of your neighbor, could you transfer part of your credit to him as consideration?" I inquired.

"In the first place," replied Dr. Leete, "our neighbors have nothing to sell us, but in any event our credit would not be transferable, being strictly personal. Before the nation could even think of honoring any such transfer as you speak of, it would be bound to inquire into all the circumstances of the transaction, so as to be able to guarantee its absolute equity. It would have been reason enough, had there been no other, for abolishing money, that its possession was no indication of rightful title to it. In the hands of the man who had stolen it or murdered for it, it was as good as in those which had earned it by industry. People nowadays interchange gifts and favors out of friendship, but buying and selling is considered absolutely inconsistent with the mutual benevolence and disinterestedness which should prevail between citizens and the sense of community of interest which supports our social system. According to our ideas, buying and selling is essentially anti-social in all its tendencies. It is an education in self-seeking at the expense of others, and no society whose citizens are trained in such a school can possibly rise above a very low grade of civilization."

"What if you have to spend more than your card in any one year?" I asked.

"The provision is so ample that we are more likely not to spend it all," replied Dr. Leete. "But if extraordinary expenses should exhaust it, we can obtain a limited advance on the next year's credit, though this practice is not encouraged, and a heavy discount is charged to check it. Of course if a man showed himself a reckless spendthrift he would receive his allowance monthly or weekly instead of yearly, or if necessary not be permitted to handle it all."

"If you don't spend your allowance, I suppose it accumulates?"

"That is also permitted to a certain extent when a special outlay is anticipated. But unless notice to the contrary is given, it is presumed that the citizen who does not fully expend his credit did not have occasion to do so, and the balance is turned into the general surplus."

"Such a system does not encourage saving habits on the part of citizens," I said.

"It is not intended to," was the reply. "The nation is rich, and does not wish the people to deprive themselves of any good thing. In your day, men were bound to lay up goods and money against coming failure of the means of support and for their children. This necessity made parsimony a virtue. But now it would have no such laudable object, and, having lost its utility, it has ceased to be regarded as a virtue. No man any more has any care for the morrow, either for himself or his children, for the nation guarantees the nurture, education, and comfortable maintenance of every citizen from the cradle to the grave."

"That is a sweeping guarantee!" I said. "What certainty can there be that the value of a man's labor will recompense the nation for its outlay on him? On the whole, society may be able to support all its members, but some must earn less than enough for their support, and others more; and that brings us back once more to the wages question, on which you have hitherto said nothing. It was at just this point, if you remember, that our talk ended last evening; and I say again, as I did then, that here I should suppose a national industrial system like yours would find its main difficulty. How, I ask once more, can you adjust satisfactorily the comparative wages or remuneration of the multitude of avocations, so unlike and so incommensurable, which are necessary for the service of society? In our day the market rate determined the price of labor of all sorts, as well as of goods. The employer paid as little as he could, and the worker got as much. It was not a pretty system ethically, I admit; but it did, at least, furnish us a rough and ready formula for settling a question which must be settled ten thousand times a day if the world was ever going to get forward. There seemed to us no other practicable way of doing it."

"Yes," replied Dr. Leete, "it was the only practicable way under a system which made the interests of every individual antagonistic to those of every other; but it would have been a pity if humanity could never have devised a better plan, for yours was simply the application to the mutual relations of men of the devil's maxim, "Your necessity is my opportunity." The reward of any service depended not upon its difficulty, danger, or hardship, for throughout the world it seems that the most perilous, severe, and repulsive labor was done by the worst paid classes; but solely upon the strait of those who needed the service."

"All that is conceded," I said. "But, with all its defects, the plan of settling prices by the market rate was a practical plan; and I cannot conceive what satisfactory substitute you can have devised for it. The government being the only possible employer, there is of course no labor market or market rate. Wages of all sorts must be arbitrarily fixed by the government. I cannot imagine a more complex and delicate function than that must be, or one, however performed, more certain to breed universal dissatisfaction."

"I beg your pardon," replied Dr. Leete, "but I think you exaggerate the difficulty. Suppose a board of fairly sensible men were charged with settling the wages for all sorts of trades under a system which, like ours, guaranteed employment to all, while permitting the choice of avocations. Don't you see that, however unsatisfactory the first adjustment might be, the mistakes would soon correct themselves? The favored trades would have too many volunteers, and those discriminated against would lack them till the errors were set right. But this is aside from the purpose, for, though this plan would, I fancy, be practicable enough, it is no part of our system."

"How, then, do you regulate wages?" I once more asked.

Dr. Leete did not reply till after several moments of meditative silence. "I know, of course," he finally said, "enough of the old order of things to understand just what you mean by that question; and yet the present order is so utterly different at this point that I am a little at loss how to answer you best. You ask me how we regulate wages; I can only reply that there is no idea in the modern social economy which at all corresponds with what was meant by wages in your day."

"I suppose you mean that you have no money to pay wages in," said   30
I. "But the credit given the worker at the government storehouse answers to his wages with us. How is the amount of the credit given respectively to the workers in different lines determined? By what title does the individual claim his particular share? What is the basis of allotment?"

"His title," replied Dr. Leete, "is his humanity. The basis of his claim is the fact that he is a man."

"The fact that he is a man!" I repeated, incredulously. "Do you possibly mean that all have the same share?"

"Most assuredly."

The readers of this book never having practically known any other arrangement, or perhaps very carefully considered the historical accounts of former epochs in which a very different system prevailed, cannot be expected to appreciate the stupor of amazement into which Dr. Leete's simple statement plunged me.

"You see," he said, smiling, "that it is not merely that we have no   35
money to pay wages in, but, as I said, we have nothing at all answering to your idea of wages."

By this time I had pulled myself together sufficiently to voice some of the criticisms which, man of the nineteenth century as I was, came uppermost in my mind, upon this to me astounding arrangement. "Some men do twice the work of others!" I exclaimed. "Are the clever workmen content with a plan that ranks them with the indifferent?"

"We leave no possible ground for any complaint of injustice," replied Dr. Leete, "by requiring precisely the same measure of service from all."

"How can you do that, I should like to know, when no two men's powers are the same?"

"Nothing could be simpler," was Dr. Leete's reply. "We require of each that he shall make the same effort; that is, we demand of him the best service it is in his power to give."

"And supposing all do the best they can," I answered, "the amount of   40
the product resulting is twice greater from one man than from another."

"Very true," replied Dr. Leete; "but the amount of the resulting product has nothing whatever to do with the question, which is one of desert. Desert is a moral question, and the amount of the product a material quantity. It would be an extraordinary sort of logic which should try to determine a moral question by a material standard. The amount of the effort alone is pertinent to the question of desert. All men who do their best, do the same. A man's endowments, however godlike, merely fix the measure of his duty. The man of great endowments who does not do all he might, though he may do more than a man of small endowments who does his best, is deemed a less deserving worker than the latter, and dies a debtor to his fellows. The Creator sets men's tasks for them by the faculties he gives them; we simply exact their fulfillment."

"No doubt that is very fine philosophy," I said; "nevertheless it seems hard that the man who produces twice as much as another, even if both do their best, should have only the same share."

"Does it, indeed, seem so to you?" responded Dr. Leete. "Now, do you know, that seems very curious to me? The way it strikes people nowadays is, that a man who can produce twice as much as another with the same effort, instead of being rewarded for doing so, ought to be punished if he does not do so. In the nineteenth century, when a horse pulled a heavier load than a goat, I suppose you rewarded him. Now, we should have whipped him soundly if he had not, on the ground that, being much stronger, he ought to. It is singular how ethical standards change." The doctor said this with such a twinkle in his eye that I was obliged to laugh.

"I suppose," I said, "that the real reason that we rewarded men for their endowments, while we considered those of horses and goats merely as fixing the service to be severally required of them, was that the animals, not being reasoning beings, naturally did the best they could, whereas men could only be induced to do so by rewarding them according to the amount of their product. That brings me to ask why, unless human nature has mightily changed in a hundred years, you are not under the same necessity."

"We are," replied Dr. Leete. "I don't think there has been any change   45 in human nature in that respect since your day. It is still so constituted that special incentives in the form of prizes, and advantages to be gained, are requisite to call out the best endeavors of the average man in any direction."

"But what inducement," I asked, "can a man have to put forth his best endeavors when, however much or little he accomplishes, his income remains the same? High characters may be moved by devotion to the common welfare under such a system, but does not the average man tend to rest back on his oar, reasoning that it is of no use to make a special effort, since the effort will not increase his income, nor its withholding diminish it?"

"Does it then really seem to you," answered my companion, "that human nature is insensible to any motives save fear of want and love of luxury, that you should expect security and equality of livelihood to leave them without possible incentives to effort? Your contemporaries did not really think so, though they might fancy they did. When it was a question of the grandest class of efforts, the most absolute self-devotion, they depended on quite other incentives. Not higher wages, but honor and the hope of men's gratitude, patriotism and the inspiration of duty, were the motives which they set before their soldiers when it was a question of dying for the nation, and never was there an age of the world when those motives did not call out what is best and noblest in men. And not only this, but when you come to analyze the love of money which was the general impulse to effort in your day, you find that the dread of want and desire of luxury was but one of several motives which the pursuit of money represented; the others, and with many the more influential, being desire of power, of social position, and reputation for ability and success. So you see that though we have abolished poverty and the fear of it, and inordinate luxury with the hope of it, we have not touched the greater part of the motives which underlay the love of money in former times, or any of those which prompted the supremer sorts of effort. The coarser motives, which no longer move us, have been replaced by higher motives wholly unknown to the mere wage earners of your age. Now that industry of whatever sort is no longer self-service, but service of the nation, patriotism, passion for humanity, impel the worker as in your day they did the soldier. The army of industry is an army, not alone by virtue of its perfect organization, but by reason also of the ardor of self-devotion which animates its members.

"But as you used to supplement the motives of patriotism with the love of glory, in order to stimulate the valor of your soldiers, so do we. Based as our industrial system is on the principle of requiring the same unit of effort from every man, that is, the best he can do, you will see that the means by which we spur the workers to do their best must be a very essential part of our scheme. With us, diligence in the national service is the sole and certain way to public repute, social distinction, and official power. The value of a man's services to society fixes his rank in it. Compared with the effect of our social arrangements in impelling men to be zealous in business, we deem the object-lessons of biting poverty and wanton luxury on which you depended a device as weak and uncertain as it was barbaric. The lust of honor even in your sordid day notoriously impelled men to more desperate effort than the love of money could." . . .

✎ Topics for Critical Thinking and Writing

1. Let's assume that, like Bellamy in 1887, you are writing a book in which the narrator chats with people who are living a hundred years from now. Write the opening paragraphs, using Bellamy's device of setting forth a view of life that you hope in the future will be regarded as barbaric. (The present, as Bellamy saw it, was ruthlessly capitalistic, and the future he envisioned was ideally socialistic, but of course your own view may be very different.) *Alternative topic:* You may want to envision a *dystopia,* horrific society (George Orwell's *1984* is a famous example), in which case your narrator, speaking

in 2100, will probably ironically see our time as wicked (though the reader should understand that what is being condemned is good), and the society of 2100 as good (though the reader should understand that what is being praised is evil).

2. The questions that are always asked about books such as *Looking Backward* are: (1) Is the writer's vision practical; that is, might this imagined world really come into existence, or has the writer misunderstood human nature?, and (2) Is the writer's vision desirable; that is, would we want to live in the world described in the book? In an essay of 500 to 750 words, give your response to both of these questions, as applied to *Looking Backward.*

Nicholas Negroponte

Nicholas Negroponte, born in 1943, was trained in architecture at the Massachusetts Institute of Technology, where he now teaches and serves as director of the Media Lab. The author of influential books including The Architecture Machine *and* Being Digital, *and a monthly columnist for* Wired *magazine, he says in the Introduction to* Being Digital *that "Computing is not about computers any more. It is about living." What he means is evident in the selection that we give from* Being Digital.

Being Digital

Bits and Mortar

Educated as an architect, I have found that many valuable concepts of architecture feed directly into computer design, but so far very little in the reverse, aside from populating our environment with smarter devices, in or behind the scenes. Thinking of buildings as enormous electromechanical devices has so far yielded few inspired applications. Even the Starship *Enterprise*'s architectural behavior is limited to sliding doors.

Buildings of the future will be like the backplanes of computers: "smart ready" (a term coined by the AMP Corporation for their Smart House program). Smart ready is a combination of prewiring and ubiquitous connectors for (future) signal sharing among appliances. You can later add processing of one kind or another, for example, to make the acoustic ambience of four walls in your living room sound like Carnegie Hall.

Most examples of "intelligent environments" I have seen are missing the ability to sense human presence. It is the problem of personal computers scaled up: the environment cannot see or sense you. Even the thermostat is reporting the temperature of the wall, not whether you feel hot or cold. Future rooms will know that you just sat down to eat, that you have gone to sleep, just stepped into the shower, took the dog for a walk. A phone would never ring. If you are not there, it won't ring because you are not there. If you are there and your digital butler decides to connect you, the nearest doorknob may say, "Excuse me, Madam," and make the connection.

Some people call this ubiquitous computing, which it is, and some of the same people present it as the opposite of using interface agents, which it is not. These two concepts are one and the same.

The ubiquity of each person's computer presence will be driven by the   5
various and disconnected computer processes in their current lives (air-line reservation systems, point-of-sales data, on-line service utilization, metering, messaging). These will be increasingly interconnected. If your early-morning flight to Dallas is delayed, your alarm clock can ring a bit later and the car service automatically notified in accordance with traffic predictions.

Currently absent from most renditions of the home of the future are household robots: a curious turn, because twenty years ago almost any image of the future included a robotic theme. C3PO[1] would make an excellent butler; even the accent is appropriate.

Interest in household robots will swing back, and we can anticipate digital domestics with legs to climb stairs, arms to dust, and hands to carry drinks. For security reasons, a household robot must also be able to bark like a ferocious dog. These concepts are not new. The technology is nearly available. There are probably a hundred thousand people world-wide who would be willing to pay $100,000 for such a robot. That $10 billion market will not go overlooked for long.

Good Morning, Toaster

If your refrigerator notices that you are out of milk, it can "ask" your car to remind you to pick some up on your way home. Appliances today have all too little computing.

A toaster should not be able to burn toast. It should be able to talk to other appliances. It would really be quite simple to brand your toast in the morning with the closing price of your favorite stock. But first, the toaster needs to be connected to the news.

Your home today probably has more than a hundred microprocessors   10
in it. But they are not unified. The most integrated home system is probably the alarm system and, in some cases, the remote control of lights and small appliances. Coffee makers can be programmed to grind and brew fresh coffee before you wake up. But if you reset your alarm to ring forty-five minutes later than usual, you will wake up to terrible coffee.

---

[1]**C3PO** a robot in the film *Star Wars*. (Editors' note)

The lack of electronic communication among appliances results in, among other things, very primitive and peculiar interfaces in each. For example, as speech becomes the dominant mode of interaction between people and machines, small accessories will also need to talk and listen. However, each one of them cannot be expected to have the full means of producing and understanding spoken language. They must communicate and share such resources.

A centralist model for such sharing is tempting, and some people have suggested information "furnaces" in our basements—a central computer in the home that manages all input and output. I suspect it will not go that way, and the function will be much more distributed among a network of appliances, including one that is a champion at speech recognition and production. If both your refrigerator and your cupboard keep track of your food by reading universal product codes, only one of them needs to know how to interpret them.

The terms "white goods" and "brown goods" are used to differentiate between kitchen-top appliances like toasters and blenders and larger, usually built-in, machines like dishwashers and refrigerators. The classic division between white and brown does not include information appliances, which must change, because white goods and brown goods will increasingly be both information consuming and producing.

The future of *any* appliance is likely to be a stripped-down or puffed-up PC. One reason to move in this direction is to make appliances more friendly, usable, and self-explicating. Just think for a moment about how many machines you have (microwave oven, fax machine, cellular telephone) that have a giant vocabulary of functions (some useless) about which you have not bothered to learn, just because it is too hard. Here is where built-in computing can help a great deal, beyond just making sure the microwave oven does not soften the Brie into a puddle. Appliances should be good instructors.

The notion of an instruction manual is obsolete. The fact that computer hardware and software manufacturers ship them with product is nothing short of perverse. The best instructor on how to use a machine is the machine itself. It knows what you are doing, what you have just done, and can even guess at what you are about to do. Folding that awareness into a knowledge of its own operations is a small step for computer science, but a giant step forward and away from a printed manual you can never find and rarely understand.

Add some familiarity with you (you are left-handed, hard of hearing, and have little patience with mechanical things), and that machine can be a far better aide (the *e* in *aide* is purposeful) to its own operations and maintenance than any document. Appliances of tomorrow should come with no printed instructions whatsoever (except This Side Up). The "warranty" should be sent electronically by the appliance itself, once it feels it has been satisfactorily installed.

15

Topics for Critical Thinking and Writing

1. In paragraph 3 Negroponte says, "Most examples of 'intelligent environments' I have seen are missing the ability to sense human presence." What examples can you give of "intelligent environments" that *do* sense human presence?
2. What do you take the term "ubiquitous computing" (paragraph 4) to mean?
3. In paragraph 15 Negroponte says that "the notion of an instruction manual is obsolete" because the machine itself should teach the owner. If you have had experience with the printed manual for a PC, and with the help-features built into the PC, report your experience and evaluate Negroponte's comment.
4. In his final paragraph Negroponte pauses for a moment to call attention (parenthetically) to the spelling of *aide.* Exactly what is his point here?
5. Basing your opinion on this selection, in an essay of 250 words characterize Negroponte. Support your view by pointing to specific passages in his writing. One suggestion: You may want to quote one paragraph, which you think is representative, and talk about the personality that the paragraph reveals. Consider choosing the final paragraph. (If you quote a paragraph, your essay should consist of about 250 words *not counting the quoted paragraph.)*

Robert B. Reich

Robert B. Reich was born in Scranton, Pennsylvania, in 1946, and educated at Dartmouth College, Oxford University (he was a Rhodes scholar), and Yale Law School. After working for the federal government he taught at Harvard University's John F. Kennedy School of Government, when President Clinton chose him as Secretary of Labor. (He describes his years in the Department of Labor in an engaging book, Locked in the Cabinet.*) After leaving Washington, Reich accepted a post at Brandeis University, in the Heller School, Graduate Studies in Social Welfare.*

This essay, originally a memorandum circulated to undergraduate students in 1989, has been slightly revised for wider publication.

The Future of Work

It's easy to predict what jobs you *shouldn't* prepare for. Thanks to the wonders of fluoride, America, in the future, will need fewer dentists. Nor is there much of a future in farming. The federal government probably won't provide long-term employment unless you aspire to work in the Pentagon or the Veterans Administration (the only two departments accounting for new federal jobs in the last decade). And think twice before plunging into higher education. The real wages of university professors have been declining for some time, the hours are bad, and all you get are complaints.

Moreover, as the American economy merges with the rest of the world's, anyone doing relatively unskilled work that could be done more cheaply elsewhere is unlikely to prosper for long. Imports and exports now constitute 26 percent of our gross national product (up from 9 percent in 1950), and barring a new round of protectionism, the portion will move steadily upward. Meanwhile, 10,000 people are added to the world's population every hour, most of whom, eventually, will happily work for a small fraction of today's average American wage.

This is good news for most of you, because it means that you'll be able to buy all sorts of things far more cheaply than you could if they were made here (provided, of course, that what your generation does instead produces even more value). The resulting benefits from trade will help off-set the drain on your income resulting from paying the interest on the nation's foreign debt and financing the retirement of aging baby boomers like me. The bad news, at least for some of you, is that most of America's traditional, routinized manufacturing jobs will disappear. So will rou-tinized service jobs that can be done from remote locations, like key-punching of data transmitted by satellite. Instead, you will be engaged in one of two broad categories of work: either complex services, some of which will be sold to the rest of the world to pay for whatever Americans want to buy from the rest of the world, or person-to-person services, which foreigners can't provide for us because (apart from new immigrants and illegal aliens) they aren't here to provide them.

Complex services involve the manipulation of data and abstract symbols. Included in this category are insurance, engineering, law, finance, computer programming, and advertising. Such activities now account for almost 25 percent of our GNP, up from 13 percent in 1950. They already have surpassed manufacturing (down to about 20 percent of GNP). Even *within* the manufacturing sector, executive, managerial, and engineering positions are increasing at a rate almost three times that of total manufac-turing employment. Most of these jobs, too, involve manipulating symbols.

Such endeavors will constitute America's major contribution to the   5
rest of the world in the decades ahead. You and your classmates will be exporting engineering designs, financial services, advertising and com-munications advice, statistical analyses, musical scores and film scripts, and other creative and problem-solving products. How many of you undertake these sorts of jobs, and how well you do at them, will determine what goods and services America can summon from the rest of the world in return, and thus—to some extent—your generation's standard of living.

You say you plan to become an investment banker? A lawyer? I grant you that these vocations have been among the fastest growing and most lucrative during the past decade. The securities industry in particular has burgeoned.

The crash of October 1987 temporarily stemmed the growth, but by mid-1988 happy days were here again. Nor have securities workers had particular difficulty making ends met. (But relatively few security workers have enjoyed majestic compensation. The high average is due to a few thousand high-rolling partners in Wall Street investment banks.)

Work involving securities and corporate law has been claiming one-quarter of all new private sector jobs in New York City and more than a third of all the new office space in that industrious town. Other major cities are not too far behind. A simple extrapolation of the present trend suggests that by 2020 one out of every three American college graduates will be an investment banker or a lawyer. Of course, this is unlikely. Long before that milestone could be achieved, the nation's economy will have dried up like a raisin, as financiers and lawyers squeeze out every ounce of creative, productive juice. Thus my advice: Even if you could bear spending your life in such meaningless but lucrative work, at least consider the fate of the nation before deciding to do so.

Person-to-person services will claim everyone else. Many of these jobs will not require much skill, as is true of their forerunners today. Among the fastest growing in recent years: custodians and security guards, restaurant and retail workers, day-care providers. Secretaries and clerical workers will be as numerous as now, but they'll spend more of their time behind and around electronic machines (imported from Asia) and have fancier titles, such as "paratechnical assistant" and "executive paralegal operations manager."

Teachers will be needed (we'll be losing more than a third of our entire corps of elementary- and high-school teachers through attrition over the next seven years), but don't expect their real pay to rise very much. Years of public breast-beating about the quality of American education notwithstanding, the average teacher today earns $28,000—only 3.4 percent more, in constant dollars, than he or she earned fifteen years ago.

Count on many jobs catering to Americans at play—hotel workers, recreation directors, television and film technicians, aerobics instructors (or whatever their twenty-first-century equivalents will call themselves). But note that Americans will have less leisure time to enjoy these pursuits. The average American's free time has been shrinking for more than fifteen years, as women move into the work force (and so spend more of their free time doing household chores) and as all wage earners are forced to work harder just to maintain their standard of living. Expect the trend to continue.

The most interesting and important person-to-person jobs will be in what is now unpretentiously dubbed "sales." Decades from now most salespeople won't be just filling orders. Salespeople will be helping customers define their needs, then working with design and production engineers to customize products and services in order to address those needs. This is because standardized (you can have it in any color as long

10

as it's black) products will be long gone. Flexible manufacturing and the new information technologies will allow a more tailored fit—whether it's a car, machine tool, insurance policy, or even a college education. Those of you who will be dealing directly with customers will thus play a pivotal role in the innovation process, and your wages and prestige will rise accordingly.

But the largest number of personal-service jobs will involve health care, which already consumes about 12 percent of our GNP, and that portion is rising. Because every new medical technology with the potential to extend life is infinitely valuable to those whose lives might be extended—even for a few months or weeks—society is paying huge sums to stave off death. By the second decade of the next century, when my generation of baby boomers will have begun to decay, the bill will be much higher. Millions of corroding bodies will need doctors, nurses, nursing-home operators, hospital administrators, technicians who operate and maintain all the fancy machines that will measure and temporarily halt the deterioration, hospice directors, home-care specialists, directors of outpatient clinics, and euthanasia specialists, among many others.

Most of these jobs won't pay very much because they don't require much skill. Right now the fastest growing job categories in the health sector are nurse's aides, orderlies, and attendants, which compose about 40 percent of the health-care work force. The majority are women; a large percentage are minorities. But even doctors' real earnings show signs of slipping. As malpractice insurance rates skyrocket, many doctors go on salary in investor-owned hospitals, and their duties are gradually taken over by physician "extenders" such as nurse-practitioners and midwives.

What's the best preparation for one of these careers?

Advice here is simple: You won't be embarking on a career, at least as we currently define the term, because few of the activities I've mentioned will proceed along well-defined paths to progressively higher levels of responsibility. As the economy evolves toward services tailored to the particular needs of clients and customers, hands-on experience will count for more than formal rank. As technologies and markets rapidly evolve, moreover, the best preparation will be through cumulative learning on the job rather than formal training completed years before.

This means that academic degrees and professional credentials will count for less; on-the-job training, for more. American students have it backwards. The courses to which you now gravitate—finance, law, accounting, management, and other practical arts—may be helpful to understand how a particular job is *now* done (or, more accurately, how your instructors did it years ago when they held such jobs or studied the people who held them), but irrelevant to how such a job *will* be done. The intellectual equipment needed for the job of the future is an ability to define problems, quickly assimilate relevant data, conceptualize and reorganize the information, make deductive and inductive leaps with it, ask hard questions about it, discuss findings with colleagues, work collaboratively to find solutions, and then convince others. And *these* sorts of skills can't be learned in career-training courses. To the extent they can be found in universities at all, they're more likely to be found in subjects such as history, literature, philosophy, and anthropology—in which students can witness how others have grappled for centuries with the challenge of living good and productive lives. Tolstoy and Thucydides are far more relevant to the management jobs of the future, for example, than are Hersey and Blanchard (*Management of Organizational Behavior,* Prentice-Hall, 5th Edition, 1988).

✎ Topics for Critical Thinking and Writing

1. Consider Reich's first three paragraphs. Has he taken account of his audience? What sort of personality does the writer reveal?
2. In paragraph 7 Reich suggests that one should think twice before spending one's "life in . . . meaningless but lucrative work." What makes any sort of work "meaningless"? For instance, is sorting or delivering mail meaningless work? Is working as a butcher in a supermarket? Being a criminal lawyer? Breeding or grooming dogs? Designing bathing suits? Explain.
3. Assuming that much of your career as a worker is in the future, how much of a role does prediction of the future play in your plans for a career?
4. In paragraph 11 Reich says that "Salespeople will be helping customers to define their needs, then working with design and production engineers to customize products and services in order to address those needs." If you are old enough to have seen some jobs change in this direction, in 500 words document Reich's point. Or interview an older person, to gain information about what Reich is saying. (On interviewing, see page 57–60 of this book.)
5. In his final paragraph Reich sets forth what he thinks is "the intellectual equipment needed for the job of the future." Read this paragraph carefully, and then ask yourself (1) if you think he is probably right about the skills that will be needed; (2) if you think his suggestion about how those skills may be developed in college is probably right; and (3) if you plan in any way to act on his suggestions. Set forth your answers in an essay of about 500 words.

Kurt Vonnegut, Jr.

Kurt Vonnegut, Jr., born in Indianapolis in 1922, studied biochemistry at Cornell University, was drafted into the army, and was captured by the Germans in the Battle of the Bulge in late 1944. A survivor of the Allied fire-bombing of Dresden in February 1945, along with other prisoners he was required to search for corpses hidden in the rubble. Two months later he was freed. After the war, he studied anthropology at the University of Chicago, then worked as a publicist for General Electric from 1947 until 1950, when he became a full-time writer.

Vonnegut has written stories, novels, and plays. His two most famous works probably are Cat's Cradle *(1963), which ends with the freezing of the world, and* Slaughterhouse Five *(1969), which draws on his experience in Dresden.*

Harrison Bergeron

The year was 2081, and everybody was finally equal. They weren't only equal before God and the law. They were equal every which way. Nobody was smarter than anybody else. Nobody was better looking than anybody else. Nobody was stronger or quicker than anybody else. All this equality was due to the 211th, 212th, and 213th Amendments to the Constitution, and to the unceasing vigilance of agents of the United States Handicapper General.

Some things about living still weren't quite right, though. April, for instance, still drove people crazy by not being springtime. And it was in that clammy month that the H-G men took George and Hazel Bergeron's fourteen-year-old son, Harrison, away.

It was tragic, all right, but George and Hazel couldn't think about it very hard. Hazel had a perfectly average intelligence, which meant she couldn't think about anything except in short bursts. And George, while his intelligence was way above normal, had a little mental handicap radio in his ear. He was required by law to wear it at all times. It was tuned to a government transmitter. Every twenty seconds or so, the transmitter would send out some sharp noise to keep people like George from taking unfair advantage of their brains.

George and Hazel were watching television. There were tears on Hazel's cheeks, but she'd forgotten for the moment what they were about.

On the television screen were ballerinas.   5

A buzzer sounded in George's head. His thoughts fled in panic, like bandits from a burglar alarm.

"That was a real pretty dance, that dance they just did," said Hazel.

"Huh?" said George.

"That dance—it was nice," said Hazel.

"Yup," said George. He tried to think a little about the ballerinas. They   10 weren't really very good—no better than anybody else would have been, anyway. They were burdened with sashweights and bags of birdshot, and their faces were masked, so that no one, seeing a free and graceful gesture or a pretty face, would feel like something the cat drug in. George was toying with the vague notion that maybe dancers shouldn't be handicapped. But he didn't get very far with it before another noise in his ear radio scattered his thoughts.

George winced. So did two out of the eight ballerinas.

Hazel saw him wince. Having no mental handicap herself, she had to ask George what the latest sound had been.

"Sounded like somebody hitting a milk bottle with a ball peen hammer," said George.

"I'd think it would be real interesting, hearing all the different sounds," said Hazel, a little envious. "All the things they think up."

"Um," said George.   15

"Only, if I was Handicapper General, you know what I would do?" said Hazel. Hazel, as a matter of fact, bore a strong resemblance to the Handicapper General, a woman named Diana Moon Glampers. "If I was Diana Moon Glampers," said Hazel, "I'd have chimes on Sunday—just chimes. Kind of in honor of religion."

"I could think, if it was just chimes," said George.

"Well—maybe make 'em real loud," said Hazel. "I think I'd make a good Handicapper General."

"Good as anybody else," said George.

"Who knows better'n I do what normal is?" said Hazel.   20

"Right," said George. He began to think glimmeringly about his abnormal son who was now in jail, about Harrison, but a twenty-one-gun salute in his head stopped that.

"Boy!" said Hazel, "that was a doozy, wasn't it?"

It was such a doozy that George was white and trembling, and tears stood on the rims of his red eyes. Two of the eight ballerinas had collapsed to the studio floor, [and] were holding their temples.

"All of a sudden you look so tired," said Hazel. "Why don't you stretch out on the sofa, so's you can rest your handicap bag on the pillows, honeybunch." She was referring to the forty-seven pounds of birdshot in a canvas bag, which was padlocked around George's neck. "Go on and rest the bag for a little while," she said. "I don't care if you're not equal to me for a while."

George weighed the bag with his hands. "I don't mind it," he said. "I   25
don't notice it any more. It's just a part of me."

"You been so tired lately—kind of wore out," said Hazel. "If there was just some way we could make a little hole in the bottom of the bag, and just take out a few of them lead balls. Just a few."

"Two years in prison and two thousand dollars fine for every ball I took out," said George. "I don't call that a bargain."

"If you could just take a few out when you came home from work," said Hazel. "I mean—you don't compete with anybody around here. You just set around."

"If I tried to get away with it," said George, "then other people'd get away with it—and pretty soon we'd be right back to the dark ages again, with everybody competing against everybody else. You wouldn't like that, would you?"

"I'd hate it," said Hazel.   30

"There you are," said George. "The minute people start cheating on laws, what do you think happens to society?"

If Hazel hadn't been able to come up with an answer to this question George couldn't have supplied one. A siren was going off in his head.

"Reckon it'd fall all apart," said Hazel.

"What would?" said George blankly.

"Society," said Hazel uncertainly. "Wasn't that what you just said?" 35

"Who knows?" said George.

The television program was suddenly interrupted for a news bulletin. It wasn't clear at first as to what the bulletin was about, since the announcer, like all announcers, had a serious speech impediment. For about half a minute, and in a state of high excitement, the announcer tried to say, "Ladies and gentlemen—"

He finally gave up, handed the bulletin to a ballerina to read.

"That's all right—" Hazel said of the announcer, "he tried. That's the big thing. He tried to do the best he could with what God gave him. He should get a nice raise for trying so hard."

"Ladies and gentlemen—" said the ballerina, reading the bulletin. She 40 must have been extraordinarily beautiful, because the mask she wore was hideous. And it was easy to see that she was the strongest and most graceful of all the dancers, for her handicap bags were as big as those worn by two-hundred-pound men.

And she had to apologize at once for her voice, which was a very unfair voice for a woman to use. Her voice was a warm, luminous, timeless melody. "Excuse me—" she said, and she began again, making her voice absolutely uncompetitive.

"Harrison Bergeron, age fourteen," she said in a grackle squawk, "has just escaped from jail, where he was held on suspicion of plotting to overthrow the government. He is a genius and an athlete, is under-handicapped, and should be regarded as extremely dangerous."

A police photograph of Harrison Bergeron was flashed on the screen upside down, then sideways, upside down again, then right side up. The picture showed the full length of Harrison against a background calibrated in feet and inches. He was exactly seven feet tall.

The rest of Harrison's appearance was Halloween and hardware. Nobody had ever borne heavier handicaps. He had outgrown hindrances faster than the H-G men could think them up. Instead of a little ear radio for a mental handicap, he wore a tremendous pair of earphones, and spectacles with thick wavy lenses. The spectacles were intended to make him not only half blind, but to give him whanging headaches besides.

Scrap metal was hung all over him. Ordinarily, there was a certain 45 symmetry, a military neatness to the handicaps issued to strong people, but Harrison looked like a walking junkyard. In the race of life, Harrison carried three hundred pounds.

And to offset his good looks, the H-G men required that he wear at all times a red rubber ball for a nose, keep his eyebrows shaved off, and cover his even white teeth with black caps at snaggle-tooth random.

"If you see this boy," said the ballerina, "do not—I repeat, do not—try to reason with him."

There was the shriek of a door being torn from its hinges.

Screams and barking cries of consternation came from the television set. The photograph of Harrison Bergeron on the screen jumped again and again, as though dancing to the tune of an earthquake.

George Bergeron correctly identified the earthquake, and well he might have—for many was the time his own home had danced to the same crashing tune. "My God—" said George, "that must be Harrison!"

The realization was blasted from his mind instantly by the sound of an automobile collision in his head.

When George could open his eyes again, the photograph of Harrison was gone. A living, breathing Harrison filled the screen.

Clanking, clownish, and huge, Harrison stood in the center of the studio. The knob of the uprooted studio door was still in his hand. Ballerinas, technicians, musicians, and announcers cowered on their knees before him, expecting to die.

"I am the Emperor!" cried Harrison. "Do you hear? I am the Emperor! Everybody must do what I say at once!" He stamped his foot and the studio shook.

"Even as I stand here—" he bellowed, "crippled, hobbled, sickened— I am a greater ruler than any man who ever lived! Now watch me become what I *can* become!"

Harrison tore the straps of his handicap harness like wet tissue paper, tore straps guaranteed to support five thousand pounds.

Harrison's scrap-iron handicaps crashed to the floor.

Harrison thrust his thumbs under the bar of the padlock that secured his head harness. The bar snapped like celery. Harrison smashed his headphones and spectacles against the wall.

He flung away his rubber-ball nose, revealed a man that would have awed Thor, the god of thunder.

"I shall now select my Empress!" he said, looking down on the cowering people. "Let the first woman who dares rise to her feet claim her mate and her throne!"

A moment passed, and then a ballerina arose, swaying like a willow.

Harrison plucked the mental handicap from her ear, snapped off her physical handicaps with marvelous delicacy. Last of all, he removed her mask.

She was blindingly beautiful.

"Now—" said Harrison, taking her hand, "shall we show the people the meaning of the word dance? Music!" he commanded.

The musicians scrambled back into their chairs, and Harrison stripped them of their handicaps, too. "Play your best," he told them, "and I'll make you barons and dukes and earls."

The music began. It was normal at first—cheap, silly, false. But Harrison snatched two musicians from their chairs, waved them like batons as he sang the music as he wanted it played. He slammed them back into their chairs.

The music began again and was much improved.

Harrison and his Empress merely listened to the music for a while—listened gravely, as though synchronizing their heartbeats with it.

They shifted their weights to their toes.

Harrison placed his big hands on the girl's tiny waist, letting her sense   70
the weightlessness that would soon be hers.

And then, in an explosion of joy and grace, into the air they sprang!

Not only were the laws of the land abandoned, but the law of gravity and the laws of motion as well.

They reeled, whirled, swiveled, flounced, capered, gamboled, and spun.

They leaped like deer on the moon.

The studio ceiling was thirty feet high, but each leap brought the   75
dancers nearer to it.

It became their obvious intention to kiss the ceiling.

They kissed it.

And then, neutralizing gravity with love and pure will, they remained suspended in air inches below the ceiling, and they kissed each other for a long, long time.

It was then that Diana Moon Glampers, the Handicapper General, came into the studio with a double-barreled ten-gauge shotgun. She fired twice, and the Emperor and the Empress were dead before they hit the floor.

Diana Moon Glampers loaded the gun again. She aimed it at the musi-   80
cians and told them they had ten seconds to get their handicaps back on.

It was then that the Bergerons' television tube burned out.

Hazel turned to comment about the blackout to George. But George had gone out into the kitchen for a can of beer.

George came back in with the beer, paused while a handicap signal shook him up. And then he sat down again. "You been crying?" he said to Hazel.

"Yup," she said.

"What about?" he said.   85

"I forget," she said. "Something real sad on television."

"What was it?" he said.

"It's all kind of mixed up in my mind," said Hazel.

"Forget sad things," said George.

"I always do," said Hazel.   90

"That's my girl," said George. He winced. There was the sound of a riveting gun in his head.

"Gee—I could tell that one was a doozy," said Hazel.

"You can say that again," said George.

"Gee—" said Hazel, "I could tell that one was a doozy."

✎ Topics for Critical Thinking and Writing

1. The Declaration of Independence, drafted by Thomas Jefferson, tells us that "all men are created equal." What does this statement mean? Does the society of Harrison Bergeron—a society in which, according to the first sentence

of the story, "everybody was finally equal"—show us a society in which Jefferson's words are at last fulfilled? Exactly what are the values of the world in 2081?

2. One sometimes hears that it is the duty of government to equalize society, hence, for instance, inheritance taxes are sometimes said to be a device employed in an effort to equalize wealth. What forces, if any, can you point to, for example in educational or political systems, that seek to equalize people? If there are such forces at work, do you think they represent unwise and perhaps unlawful government meddling, and are essentially at odds with a basic American idea of rugged individualism and of wholesome competition?

3. Speaking of competition, George says (paragraph 31) to Hazel, "The minute people start cheating on laws, what do you think happens to society?" Hazel replies, "Reckon it'd fall all apart" (33). What do you think that we, as readers, are supposed to make out of this statement? In your response—an essay of 500 words—consider the actions of Harrison Bergeron, who declares himself Emperor and who says (54), "Everybody must do what I say at once!" Is Vonnegut suggesting, in George's behavior, that only laws can keep talented individuals from tyrannizing over others?

Ray Bradbury

Ray Bradbury (b. 1920) was born in Waukegan, Illinois, and educated there and in Los Angeles. While a high school student he published his first science fiction in the school's magazine, and by 1941 he was publishing professionally.

The story printed here is from The Martian Chronicles *(1950), a collection of linked short stories. Among his other works are* Fahrenheit 451 *(1953),* Something Wicked This Way Comes *(1962), and* Death Is a Lonely Business *(1985).*

August 2026: There Will Come Soft Rains

In the living room the voice-clock sang. *Tick-Tock, seven o'clock, time to get up, time to get up, seven o'clock!* as if it were afraid that nobody would. The morning house lay empty. The clock ticked on, repeating and repeating its sounds into the emptiness. *Seven-nine, breakfast time, seven-nine!*

In the kitchen the breakfast stove gave a hissing sigh and ejected from its warm interior eight pieces of perfectly browned toast, eight eggs sunny-side up, sixteen slices of bacon, two coffees, and two cool glasses of milk.

"Today is August 4, 2026," said a second voice from the kitchen ceiling, "in the city of Allendale, California." It repeated the date three times for memory's sake. "Today is Mr. Featherstone's birthday. Today is the anniversary of Tilita's marriage. Insurance is payable, as are the water, gas, and light bills."

Somewhere in the walls, relays clicked, memory tapes glided under electric eyes.

Eight-one, tick-tock, eight-one o'clock, off to school, off to work, run, run,   5
eight-one! But no doors slammed, no carpets took the soft tread of rubber heels. It was raining outside. The weather box on the front door sang quietly: "Rain, rain, go away; rubbers, raincoats for today. . . ." And the rain tapped on the empty house, echoing.

Outside, the garage chimed and lifted its door to reveal the waiting car. After a long wait the door swung down again.

At eight-thirty the eggs were shriveled and toast was like stone. An aluminum wedge scraped them into the sink, where hot water whirled them down a metal throat which digested and flushed them away to the distant sea. The dirty dishes were dropped into a hot washer and emerged twinkling dry.

Nine-fifteen, sang the clock, *time to clean.*

Out of warrens in the wall, tiny robot mice darted. The rooms were acrawl with the small cleaning animals, all rubber and metal. They thudded against chairs, whirling their mustached runners, kneading the rug nap, sucking gently at hidden dust. Then, like mysterious invaders, they popped into their burrows. Their pink electric eyes faded. The house was clean.

Ten o'clock. The sun came out from behind the rain. The house stood   10
alone in a city of rubble and ashes. This was the one house left standing. At night the ruined city gave off a radioactive glow which could be seen for miles.

Ten-fifteen. The garden sprinklers whirled up in golden founts, filling the soft morning air with scatterings of brightness. The water pelted windowpanes, running down the charred west side where the house had been burned evenly free of its white paint. The entire west face of the house was black, save for five places. Here the silhouette in paint of a man mowing a lawn. Here, as in a photograph, a woman bent to pick flowers. Still farther over, their images burned on wood in one titanic instant, a small boy, hands flung into the air; higher up, the image of a thrown ball, and opposite him a girl, hands raised to catch a ball which never came down.

The five spots of paint—the man, the woman, the children, the ball—remained. The rest was a thin charcoaled layer.

The gentle sprinkler rain filled the garden with falling light.

Until this day, how well the house had kept its peace. How carefully it had inquired, "Who goes there? What's the password?" and, getting no answer from lonely foxes and whining cats, it had shut up its windows and drawn shades in an old-maidenly preoccupation with self-protection which bordered on a mechanical paranoia.

It quivered at each sound, the house did. If a sparrow brushed a window, the shade snapped up. The bird, startled, flew off! No, not even a bird must touch the house!

The house was an altar with ten thousand attendants, big, small, servicing, attending, in choirs. But the gods had gone away, and the ritual of the religion continued senselessly, uselessly.

Twelve noon.

A dog whined, shivering, on the front porch.

The front door recognized the dog voice and opened. The dog, once huge and fleshy, but now gone to bone and covered with sores, moved in and through the house, tracking mud. Behind it whirred angry mice, angry at having to pick up mud, angry at inconvenience.

For not a leaf fragment blew under the door but what the wall panels flipped open and the copper scrap rats flashed swiftly out. The offending dust, hair, or paper, seized in miniature steel jaws, was raced back to the burrows. There, down tubes which fed into the cellar, it was dropped into the sighing vent of an incinerator which sat like evil Baal in a dark corner.

The dog ran upstairs, hysterically yelping to each door, at last realizing, as the house realized, that only silence was here.

It sniffed the air and scratched the kitchen door. Behind the door, the stove was making pancakes which filled the house with a rich baked odor and the scent of maple syrup.

The dog frothed at the mouth, lying at the door, sniffing, its eyes turned to fire. It ran wildly in circles, biting at its tail, spun in a frenzy, and died. It lay in the parlor for an hour.

Two o'clock, sang a voice.

Delicately sensing decay at last, the regiments of mice hummed out as softly as blown gray leaves in an electrical wind.

Two-fifteen.

The dog was gone.

In the cellar, the incinerator glowed suddenly and a whirl of sparks leaped up the chimney.

Two thirty-five.

Bridge tables sprouted from patio walls. Playing cards fluttered onto pads in a shower of pips. Martinis manifested on an oaken bench with egg-salad sandwiches. Music played.

But the tables were silent and the cards untouched.

At four o'clock the tables folded like great butterflies back through the paneled walls.

Four-thirty.

The nursery walls glowed.

Animals took shape: yellow giraffes, blue lions, pink antelopes, lilac panthers cavorting in crystal substance. The walls were glass. They looked out upon color and fantasy. Hidden films clocked through well-oiled sprockets, and the walls lived. The nursery floor was woven to resemble a crisp, cereal meadow. Over this ran aluminum roaches and iron crickets, and in the hot still air butterflies of delicate red tissue wavered among the sharp aroma of animal spoors! There was the sound like a great matted yellow hive of bees within a dark bellows, the lazy bumble of a purring lion. And there was the patter of okapi feet and the murmur of a fresh jungle rain, like other hoofs, falling upon the summer-starched grass. Now the walls dissolved into distances of parched weed, mile on mile, and warm endless sky. The animals drew away into thorn brakes and water holes.

It was the children's hour.

Five o'clock. The bath filled with clear hot water.

Six, seven, eight o'clock. The dinner dishes manipulated like magic tricks, and in the study a *click.* In the metal stand opposite the hearth where a fire now blazed up warmly, a cigar popped out, half an inch of soft gray ash on it, smoking, waiting.

Nine o'clock. The beds warmed their hidden circuits, for nights were cool here.

Nine-five. A voice spoke from the study ceiling: 40

"Mrs. McClellan, which poem would you like this evening?"

The house was silent.

The voice said at last, "Since you express no preference, I shall select a poem at random." Quiet music rose to back the voice. "Sara Teasdale. As I recall, your favorite. . . ."

There will come soft rains and the smell of the ground,
And swallows circling with their shimmering sound;

And frogs in the pools singing at night,
And wild plum trees in tremulous white;

Robins will wear their feathery fire,
Whistling their whims on a low fence-wire;

And not one will know of the war, not one
Will care at last when it is done.

Not one would mind, neither bird nor tree,
If mankind perished utterly;

And Spring herself, when she woke at dawn
Would scarcely know that we were gone."

The fire burned on the stone hearth and the cigar fell away into a mound of quiet ash on its tray. The empty chairs faced each other between the silent walls, and the music played.

At ten o'clock the house began to die.   45

The wind blew. A falling tree bough crashed through the kitchen window. Cleaning solvent, bottled, shattered over the stove. The room was ablaze in an instant!

"Fire!" screamed a voice. The house lights flashed, water pumps shot water from the ceilings. But the solvent spread on the linoleum, licking, eating, under the kitchen door, while the voices took it up in chorus: "Fire, fire, fire!"

The house tried to save itself. Doors sprang tightly shut, but the windows were broken by the heat and the wind blew and sucked upon the fire.

The house gave ground as the fire in ten billion angry sparks moved with flaming ease from room to room and then up the stairs. While scurrying water rats squeaked from the walls, pistoled their water, and ran for more. And the wall sprays let down showers of mechanical rain.

But too late. Somewhere, sighing, a pump shrugged to a stop. The 50
quenching rain ceased. The reserve water supply which had filled baths and washed dishes for many quiet days was gone.

The fire crackled up the stairs. It fed upon Picassos and Matisses in the upper halls, like delicacies, baking off the oily flesh, tenderly crisping the canvases into black shavings.

Now the fire lay in beds, stood in windows, changed the colors of drapes!

And then, reinforcements.

From attic trapdoors, blind robot faces peered down with faucet mouths gushing green chemical.

The fire backed off, as even an elephant must at the sight of a dead 55
snake. Now there were twenty snakes whipping over the floor, killing the fire with a clear cold venom of green froth.

But the fire was clever. It had sent flames outside the house, up through the attic to the pumps there. An explosion! The attic brain which directed the pumps was shattered into bronze shrapnel on the beams.

The fire rushed back into every closet and felt of the clothes hung there.

The house shuddered, oak bone on bone, its bared skeleton cringing from the heat, its wire, its nerves revealed as if a surgeon had torn the skin off to let the red veins and capillaries quiver in the scalded air. Help, help! Fire! Run, run! Heat snapped mirrors like the brittle winter ice. And the voices wailed Fire, fire, run, run, like a tragic nursery rhyme, a dozen voices, high, low, like children dying in a forest, alone, alone. And the voices fading as the wires popped their sheathings like hot chestnuts. One, two, three, four, five voices died.

In the nursery the jungle burned. Blue lions roared, purple giraffes bounded off. The panthers ran in circles changing color, and ten million animals, running before the fire, vanished off toward a distant steaming river. . . .

Ten more voices died. In the last instant under the fire avalanche, 60
other choruses, oblivious, could be heard announcing the time, playing music, cutting the lawn by remote-control mower, or setting an umbrella

frantically out and in the slamming and opening front door, a thousand things happening, like a clock shop when each clock strikes the hour insanely before or after the other, a scene of maniac confusion, yet unity; singing, screaming, a few last cleaning mice darting bravely out to carry the horrid ashes away! And one voice, with sublime disregard for the situation, read poetry aloud in the fiery study, until all the film spools burned, until all the wires withered and the circuits cracked.

The fire burst the house and let it slam flat down, puffing out skirts of spark and smoke.

In the kitchen, an instant before the rain of fire and timber, the stove could be seen making breakfasts at a psychopathic rate, ten dozen eggs, six loaves of toast, twenty dozen bacon strips, which, eaten by fire, started the stove working again, hysterically hissing!

The crash. The attic smashing into kitchen and parlor. The parlor into cellar, cellar into sub-cellar. Deep freeze, armchair, film tapes, circuits, beds, and all like skeletons thrown in a cluttered mound deep under.

Smoke and silence. A great quantity of smoke.

Dawn showed faintly in the east. Among the ruins, one wall stood   65
alone. Within the wall, a last voice said, over and over again and again, even as the sun rose to shine upon the heaped rubble and steam:

"Today is August 5, 2026, today is August 5, 2026, today is . . ."

✎ Topics for Critical Thinking and Writing

1. What do you know about the family in the story? Does it seem to be a typical family?
2. What does the poem seem to say about the relationship between nature and human beings? In what way, if any, is the poem relevant to the rest of the story?
3. Do you take the story to be mere fantasy, or, on the other hand, do you take it to be a comment on our life? Or neither? Explain.
4. If possible, characterize your final response to the story. Did the story create uneasiness, a sense of your own involvement in a sadly deficient society? Or perhaps, on the other hand, the story created in you a sense of satisfaction, a sense that your own life is superior to the life depicted here. Answer in a well-developed paragraph.

William Butler Yeats

William Butler Yeats (1865–1939) was born in Dublin, Ireland, and established himself as Ireland's leading man of letters. (His contemporary, James Joyce, had left Ireland, in self-imposed exile.) In 1923 Yeats was awarded the Nobel Prize for poetry.

The early Yeats was much interested in highly lyrical, romantic poetry, often drawing on Irish mythology. The later poems, from about 1910, are often more colloquial, more down to earth—indignation, for instance, may replace romantic sighs—but Yeats always retained his visionary quality. "The Second Coming" was written in 1919, shortly after the first world war, and when British soldiers in Ireland were seeking to quell the republican movement.

"The Second Coming," written "twenty centuries" (line 19) after the birth of Jesus, alludes to two books in the New Testament. In Matthew 24, Jesus predicts his Second Coming; and in St. John's Revelation 13.1 John sees a beast ("And I stood upon the sand of the sea, and saw a beast rise up out of the sea, having seven heads and ten horns, and upon his horns ten crowns, and upon his heads the name of blasphemy"). There is a further allusion to Revelation 21, when John sees "a new heaven and a new earth."

In line 1, a gyre is a circular or spiral motion, and in line 12 Spiritus Mundi is the Soul of the Universe, a place that, for Yeats, was the source of images. In line 14, the lion-man is the Egyptian sphinx.

The Second Coming

Turning and turning in the widening gyre
The falcon cannot hear the falconer;
Things fall apart; the center cannot hold;
Mere anarchy is loosed upon the world,
The blood-dimmed tide is loosed, and everywhere   5
The ceremony of innocence is drowned;
The best lack all conviction, while the worst
Are full of passionate intensity.

Surely some revelation is at hand;
Surely the Second Coming is at hand;   10
The Second Coming! Hardly are those words out
When a vast image out of *Spiritus Mundi*
Troubles my sight: somewhere in sands of the desert
A shape with lion body and the head of a man,
A gaze blank and pitiless as the sun,   15
Is moving its slow thighs, while all about it
Reel shadows of the indignant desert birds.
The darkness drops again; but now I know
That twenty centuries of stony sleep
Were vexed to nightmare by a rocking cradle,   20
And what rough beast, its hour come round at last,
Slouches towards Bethlehem to be born?

✎ Topics for Critical Thinking and Writing

1. What is the connection between the first two lines, about the falcon and the falconer, and line 4, "Mere anarchy is loosed upon the world"?
2. Do you imagine that an educated pagan of, say, the second or third century A.D. might have said of the new creed and its adherents that "Things fall

apart" (3) and that "The best [of our age] lack all conviction, while the worst/Are full of passionate intensity"? Explain.

3. Do you think it may be generally true that in every age "The best lack all conviction, while the worst/Are full of passionate intensity"?
4. Why is it that the beast "Slouches towards Bethlehem" (22)? What does its way of going suggest? What line earlier in the poem connects with Bethlehem?
5. What is Yeats's view of the millennium?
6. In your view, is the "center" holding? Whether your answer is yes or no, in your view is it a good thing?
7. Consider some conflict with which you are familiar, perhaps in the Middle East, or racial conflict in America. What chance do you see for a harmonious conclusion?

A Casebook on Cloning

Robert Wachbroit

Robert Wachbroit is a Research Scholar at the Institute for Philosophy and Public Policy, at the School of Public Affairs, University of Maryland. The Institute conducts research cooperatively with philosophers, policymakers, and analysts, both within and outside the government.

Genetic Encores: The Ethics of Human Cloning

The successful cloning of an adult sheep, announced in Scotland this past February, is one of the most dramatic recent examples of a scientific discovery becoming a public issue. During the last few months, various commentators—scientists and theologians, physicians and legal experts, talk-radio hosts and editorial writers—have been busily responding to the news, some calming fears, other raising alarms about the prospect of cloning a human being. At the request of the President, the National Bioethics Advisory Commission (NBAC) held hearings and prepared a report on the religious, ethical, and legal issues surrounding human cloning. While declining to call for a permanent ban on the practice, the

Commission recommended a moratorium on efforts to clone human beings, and emphasized the importance of further public deliberation on the subject.

An interesting tension is at work in the NBAC report. Commission members were well aware of "the widespread public discomfort, even revulsion, about cloning human beings." Perhaps recalling the images of Dolly the ewe that were featured on the covers of national news magazines, they noted that "the impact of these most recent developments on our national psyche has been quite remarkable." Accordingly, they felt that one of their tasks was to articulate, as fully and sympathetically as possible, the range of concerns that the prospect of human cloning had elicited.

Yet it seems clear that some of these concerns, at least, are based on false beliefs about genetic influence and the nature of the individuals that would be produced through cloning. Consider, for instance, the fear that a clone would not be an "individual" but merely a "carbon copy" of someone else—an automaton of the sort familiar from science fiction. As many scientists have pointed out, a clone would not in fact be an identical *copy*, but more like a delayed identical *twin*. And just as identical twins are two separate people—biologically, psychologically, morally and legally, though not genetically—so, too, a clone would be a separate person from her non-contemporaneous twin. To think otherwise is to embrace a belief in genetic determinism—the view that genes determine everything about us, and that environmental factors or the random events in human development are insignificant.

The overwhelming scientific consensus is that genetic determinism is false. In coming to understand the ways in which genes operate, biologists have also become aware of the myriad ways in which the environment affects their "expression." The genetic contribution to the simplest physical traits, such as height and hair color, is significantly mediated by environmental factors (and possibly by stochastic events as well). And the genetic contribution to the traits we value most deeply, from intelligence to compassion, is conceded by even the most enthusiastic genetic researchers to be limited and indirect.

It is difficult to gauge the extent to which "repugnance" toward cloning generally rests on a belief in genetic determinism. Hoping to account for the fact that people "instinctively recoil" from the prospect of cloning, James Q. Wilson wrote, "There is a natural sentiment that is offended by the mental picture of identical babies being produced in some biological factory." Which raises the question: once people learn that this picture is mere science fiction, does the offense that cloning presents to "natural sentiment" attenuate, or even disappear? Jean Bethke Elshtain cited the nightmare scenarios of "the man and woman on the street," who imagine a future populated by "a veritable army of Hitlers, ruthless and remorseless bigots who kept reproducing themselves until they had finished what the historic Hitler failed to do: annihilate us." What happens,

5

though, to the "pity and terror" evoked by the topic of cloning when such scenarios are deprived (as they deserve to be) of all credibility?

Richard Lewontin has argued that the critics' fears—or at least, those fears that merit consideration in formulating public policy—dissolve once genetic determinism is refuted. He criticizes the NBAC report for excessive deference to opponents of human cloning, and calls for greater public education on the scientific issues. (The Commission in fact makes the same recommendation, but Lewontin seems unimpressed.) Yet even if a public education campaign succeeded in eliminating the most egregious misconceptions about genetic influence, that wouldn't settle the matter. People might continue to express concerns about the interests and rights of human clones, about the social and moral consequences of the cloning process, and about the possible motivations for creating children in this way.

Interests and Rights

One set of ethical concerns about human clones involves the risks and uncertainties associated with the current state of cloning technology. This technology has not yet been tested with human subjects, and scientists cannot rule out the possibility of mutation or other biological damage. Accordingly, the NBAC report concluded that "at this time, it is morally unacceptable for anyone in the public or private sector, whether in a research or clinical setting, to attempt to create a child using somatic cell nuclear transfer cloning." Such efforts, it said, would pose "unacceptable risks to the fetus and/or potential child."

The ethical issues of greatest importance in the cloning debate, however, do not involve possible failures of cloning technology, but rather the consequences of its success. Assuming that scientists were able to clone human beings without incurring the risks mentioned above, what concerns might there be about the welfare of clones?

Some opponents of cloning believe that such individuals would be wronged in morally significant ways. Many of these wrongs involve the denial of what Joel Feinberg has called "the right to an open future." For example, a child might be constantly compared to the adult from whom he was cloned, and thereby burdened with oppressive expectations. Even worse, the parents might actually limit the child's opportunities for growth and development: a child cloned from a basketball player, for instance, might be denied any educational opportunities that were not in line with a career in basketball. Finally, regardless of his parents' conduct or attitudes, a child might be burdened by the *thought* that he is a copy and not an "original." The child's sense of self-worth or individuality or dignity, so some have argued, would thus be difficult to sustain.

How should we respond to these concerns? On the one hand, the existence of a right to an open future has a strong intuitive appeal. We are   10 troubled by parents who radically constrict their children's possibilities for growth and development. Obviously, we would condemn a cloning parent for crushing a child with oppressive expectations, just as we might condemn fundamentalist parents for utterly isolating their children from the modern world, or the parents of twins for inflicting matching wardrobes and rhyming names. But this is not enough to sustain an objection to cloning itself. Unless the claim is that cloned parents cannot help but be oppressive, we would have cause to say they had wronged their children only because of their subsequent, and avoidable, sins of bad parenting—not because they had chosen to create the child in the first place. (The possible reasons for making this choice will be discussed below.)

We must also remember that children are often born in the midst of all sorts of hopes and expectations; the idea that there is a special burden associated with the thought "There is someone who is genetically just like me" is necessarily speculative. Moreover, given the falsity of genetic determinism, any conclusions a child might draw from observing the person from whom be was cloned would be uncertain at best. His knowledge of his future would differ only in degree from what many children already know once they begin to learn parts of their family's (medical) history. Some of us knew that we would be bald, or to what diseases we might be susceptible. To be sure, the cloned individual might know more about what he or she could become. But because our knowledge of the effect of environment on development is so incomplete, the clone would certainly be in for some surprises.

Finally, even if we were convinced that clones are likely to suffer particular burdens, that would not be enough to show that it is wrong to create them. The child of a poor family can be expected to suffer specific hardships and burdens, but we don't thereby conclude that such children shouldn't be born. Despite the hardships, poor children can experience parental love and many of the joys of being alive: the deprivations of poverty, however painful, are not decisive. More generally, no one's life is entirely free of some difficulties or burdens. In order for these considerations to have decisive weight, we have to be able to say that life doesn't offer any compensating benefits. Concerns expressed about the welfare of human clones do not appear to justify such a bleak assessment. Most such children can be expected to have lives well worth living; many of the imagined harms are no worse than those faced by children acceptably produced by more conventional means. If there is something deeply objectionable about cloning, it is more likely to be found by examining implications of the cloning process itself, or the reasons people might have for availing themselves of it.

Concerns about Process

Human cloning falls conceptually between two other technologies. At one end we have the assisted reproductive technologies, such as in vitro fertilization, whose primary purpose is to enable couples to produce a child with whom they have a biological connection. At the other end we have the emerging technologies of genetic engineering—specifically, gene transplantation technologies—whose primary purpose is to produce a child that has certain traits. Many proponents of cloning see it as part of the first technology: cloning is just another way of providing a couple with a biological child they might otherwise be unable to have. Since this goal and these other technologies are acceptable, cloning should be acceptable as well. On the other hand, many opponents of cloning see it as part of the second technology: even though cloning is a transplantation of an entire nucleus and not of specific genes, it is nevertheless an attempt to produce a child with certain traits. The deep misgivings we may have about the genetic manipulation of offspring should apply to cloning as well.

The debate cannot be resolved, however, simply by determining which technology to assimilate cloning to. For example, some opponents of human cloning see it as continuous with assisted reproductive technologies; but since they find those technologies objectionable as well, the assimilation does not indicate approval. Rather than argue for grouping cloning with one technology or another, I wish to suggest that we can best understand the significance of the cloning process by comparing it with these other technologies, and thus broadening the debate.

To see what can be learned from such a comparative approach, let us consider a central argument that has been made against cloning—that it undermines the structure of the family by making identities and lineages unclear. On the one hand, the relationship between an adult and the child cloned from her could be described as that between a parent and off-spring. Indeed, some commentators have called cloning "asexual reproduction," which clearly suggests that cloning is a way of generating *descendants*. The clone, on this view, has only one biological parent. On the other hand, from the point of view of genetics, the clone is a *sibling*, so that cloning is more accurately described as "delayed twinning" rather than as asexual reproduction. The clone, on this view, has two biological parents, not one—they are the same parents as those of the person from whom that individual was cloned.

Cloning thus results in ambiguities. Is the clone an offspring or a sibling? Does the clone have one biological parent or two? The moral significance of these ambiguities lies in the fact that in many societies, including our own, lineage identifies responsibilities. Typically, the parent, not the sibling, is responsible for the child. But if no one is unambiguously the parent, so the worry might go, who is responsible for the clone? Insofar as social identity is based on biological ties, won't this identity be blurred or confounded?

Some assisted reproductive technologies have raised similar questions about lineage and identity. An anonymous sperm donor is thought to have no parental obligations towards his biological child. A surrogate mother may be required to relinquish all parental claims to the child she bears. In these cases, the social and legal determination of "who is the parent" may appear to proceed in defiance of profound biological facts, and

15

to subvert attachments that we as a society are ordinarily committed to upholding. Thus, while the *aim* of assisted reproductive technologies is to allow people to produce or raise a child to whom they are biologically connected, such technologies may also involve the creation of social ties that are permitted to override biological ones.

In the case of cloning, however, ambiguous lineages would seem to be less problematic, precisely because no one is being asked to relinquish a claim on a child to whom he or she might otherwise acknowledge a biological connection. What, then, are the critics afraid of? It does not seem plausible that someone would have herself cloned and then hand the child over to her parents, saying, "You take care of her! She's *your* daughter!" Nor is it likely that, if the cloned individual did raise the child, she would suddenly refuse to pay for college on the grounds that this was not a sister's responsibility. Of course, policymakers should address any confusion in the social or legal assignment of responsibility resulting from cloning. But there are reasons to think that this would be *less* difficult than in the case of other reproductive technologies.

Similarly, when we compare cloning with genetic engineering, cloning may prove to be the less troubling of the two technologies. This is true even though the dark futures to which they are often alleged to lead are broadly alike. For example, a recent *Washington Post* article examined fears that the development of genetic enhancement technologies might "create a market in preferred physical traits." The reporter asked, "Might it lead to a society of DNA haves and have-nots, and the creation of a new underclass of people unable to keep up with the genetically fortified Joneses?" Similarly, a member of the National Bioethics Advisory Commission expressed concern that cloning might become "almost a preferred practice," taking its place "on the continuum of providing the best for your child." As a consequence, parents who chose to "play the lottery of old-fashioned reproduction would be considered irresponsible."

Such fears, however, seem more warranted with respect to genetic   20
engineering than to cloning. By offering some people—in all probability, members of the upper classes—the opportunity to acquire desired traits through genetic manipulation, genetic engineering could bring about a biological reinforcement (or accentuation) of existing social divisions. It is hard enough already for disadvantaged children to compete with their more affluent counterparts, given the material resources and intellectual opportunities that are often available only to children of privilege. This unfairness would almost certainly be compounded if genetic manipulation came into the picture. In contrast, cloning does not bring about "improvements" in the genome: it is, rather, a way of *duplicating* the genome—with all its imperfections. It wouldn't enable certain groups of people to keep getting better and better along some valued dimension.

To some critics, admittedly, this difference will not seem terribly important. Theologian Gilbert Meilaender, Jr., objects to cloning on the grounds that children created through this technology would be "designed as a product" rather than "welcomed as a gift." The fact that the design process would be more selective and nuanced in the case of genetic engineering would, from this perspective, have no moral significance. To the extent that this objection reflects a concern about the commodification of human life, we can address it in part when we consider people's reasons for engaging in cloning.

Reasons for Cloning

This final area of contention in the cloning debate is as much psychological as it is scientific or philosophical. If human cloning technology were safe and widely available, what use would people make of it? What reasons would they have to engage in cloning?

In its report to the President, the Commission imagined a few situations in which people might avail themselves of cloning. In one scenario, a husband and wife who wish to have children are both carriers of a lethal recessive gene:

> Rather than risk the one in four chance of conceiving a child who will suffer a short and painful existence, the couple considers the alternatives: to forgo rearing children; to adopt; to use prenatal diagnosis and selective abortion; to use donor gametes free of the recessive trait; or to use the cells of one of the adults and attempt to clone a child. To avoid donor gametes and selective abortion, while maintaining a genetic tie to their child, they opt for cloning.

In another scenario, the parents of a terminally ill child are told that only a bone marrow transplant can save the child's life. "With no other donor available, the parents attempt to clone a human being from the cells of the dying child. If successful, the new child will be a perfect match for bone marrow transplant, and can be used as a donor without significant risk or discomfort. The net result: two healthy children, loved by their parents, who happen [sic] to be identical twins of different ages."

The Commission was particularly impressed by the second example. That scenario, said the NBAC report, "makes what is probably the strongest possible case for cloning a human being, as it demonstrates how this technology could be used for lifesaving purposes." Indeed, the report suggests that it would be a "tragedy" to allow "the sick child to die because of a moral or political objection to such cloning." Nevertheless, we should note that many people would be morally uneasy about the use of a minor as a donor, regardless of whether the child were a result of cloning. Even if this unease is justifiably overridden by other concerns, the "transplant scenario" may not present a more compelling case for cloning than that of the infertile couple desperately seeking a biological child.

Most critics, in fact, decline to engage the specifics of such tragic (and presumably rare) situations. Instead, they bolster their case by imagining very different scenarios. Potential users of the technology, they suggest, are narcissists or control freaks—people who will regard their children not as free, original selves but as products intended to meet more or less rigid specifications. Even if such people are not genetic determinists, their recourse to cloning will indicate a desire to exert all possible influence over what "kind" of child they produce.

The critics' alarm at this prospect has in part to do, as we have seen, with concerns about the psychological burdens such a desire would impose on the clone. But it also reflects a broader concern about the values expressed, and promoted, by a society's reproductive policies. Critics argue that a society that enables people to clone themselves thereby endorses the most narcissistic reason for having children—to perpetuate oneself through a genetic encore. The demonstrable falsity of genetic determinism may detract little, if at all, from the strength of this motive. Whether or not clones will have a grievance against their parents for producing them with this motivation, the societal indulgence of that motivation is improper and harmful.

It can be argued, however, that the critics have simply misunderstood the social meaning of a policy that would permit people to clone themselves even in the absence of the heartrending exigencies described in the NBAC report. This country has developed a strong commitment to reproductive autonomy. (This commitment emerged in response to the dismal history of eugenics—the very history that is sometimes invoked to support restrictions on cloning.) With the exception of practices that risk coercion and exploitation—notably baby-selling and commercial surrogacy— we do not interfere with people's freedom to create and acquire children by almost any means, for almost any reason. This policy does not reflect a dogmatic libertarianism. Rather, it recognizes the extraordinary personal importance and private character of reproductive decisions, even those with significant social repercussions.

Our willingness to sustain such a policy also reflects a recognition of the moral complexities of parenting. For example, we know that the motives people have for bringing a child into the world do not necessarily determine the manner in which they raise him. Even when parents start out as narcissists, the experience of childrearing will sometimes transform their initial impulses, making them caring, respectful, and even self-sacrificing. Seeing their child grow and develop, they learn that she is not merely an extension of themselves. Of course, some parents never make this discovery; others, having done so, never forgive their children for it. The pace and extent of moral development among parents (no less than among children) is infinitely variable. Still, we are justified in saying that those who engage in cloning will not, by virtue of this fact, be immune to the transformative effects of parenthood—even if it is the case (and it won't always be) that they begin with more problematic motives than those of parents who engage in the "genetic lottery."

Moreover, the nature of parental motivation is itself more complex than   the critics often allow. Though we can agree that narcissism is a vice not to be encouraged, we lack a clear notion of where pride in one's children ends and narcissism begins. When, for example, is it unseemly to bask in the reflected glory of a child's achievements? Imagine a champion gymnast who takes delight in her daughter's athletic prowess. Now imagine that the child was actually cloned from one of the gymnast's somatic cells. Would we have to revise our moral assessment of her pleasure in her daughter's success? Or suppose a man wanted to be cloned and to give his child opportunities he himself had never enjoyed. And suppose that, rightly or wrongly, the man took the child's success as a measure of his own untapped potential—an indication of the flourishing life he might have had. Is *this* sentiment blamable? And is it all that different from what many natural parents feel?

Conclusion

Until recently, there were few ethical, social, or legal discussions about human cloning via nuclear transplantation, since the scientific consensus was that such a procedure was not biologically possible. With the appearance of Dolly, the situation has changed. But although it now seems more likely that human cloning will become feasible, we may doubt that the practice will come into widespread use.

I suspect it will not, but my reasons will not offer much comfort to the critics of cloning. While the technology for nuclear transplantation advances, other technologies—notably the technology of genetic engineering—will be progressing as well. Human genetic engineering will be applicable to a wide variety of traits; it will be more powerful than cloning, and hence more attractive to more people. It will also, as I have suggested, raise more troubling questions than the prospect of cloning has thus far.

Sources: National Bioethics Advisory Commission, "Cloning Human Beings: Report and Recommendations" (June 9, 1997); James Q. Wilson, "The Paradox of Cloning," *Weekly Standard* (May 26, 1997); Jean Bethke Elshtain, "Ewegenics," *New Republic* (March 31, 1997); R. C. Lewontin, "The Confusion over Cloning," *New York Review of Books* (October 23, 1997); Leon Kass, "The Wisdom of Repugnance," *New Republic* (June 2, 1997); Susan Cohen, "What is a Baby? Inside America's Unresolved Debate about the Ethics of Cloning," *Washington Post Magazine* (October 12, 1997); Rick Weiss, "Genetic Enhancements' Thorny Ethical Traits," *Washington Post* (October 12, 1997).

Charles Krauthammer

Charles Krauthammer (b. 1950) was educated at McGill, Oxford, and Harvard Universities. He is a medical doctor and is a licensed psychiatrist, but he is chiefly known as a writer. His essays appear regularly in Time *magazine and in* The New Republic.

Of Headless Mice . . . and Men

Last year Dolly the cloned sheep was received with wonder, titters and some vague apprehension. Last week the announcement by a Chicago physicist that he is assembling a team to produce the first human clone occasioned yet another wave of *Brave New World* anxiety. But the scariest news of all—and largely overlooked—comes from two obscure labs, at the University of Texas and at the University of Bath. During the past four years, one group created headless mice; the other, headless tadpoles.

For sheer Frankenstein wattage, the purposeful creation of these animal monsters has no equal. Take the mice. Researchers found the gene that tells the embryo to produce the head. They deleted it. They did this in a thousand mice embryos, four of which were born. I use the term loosely. Having no way to breathe, the mice died instantly.

Why then create them? The Texas researchers want to learn how genes determine embryo development. But you don't have to be a genius to see the true utility of manufacturing headless creatures: for their organs—fully formed, perfectly useful, ripe for plundering.

Why should you be panicked? Because humans are next. "It would almost certainly be possible to produce human bodies without a forebrain," Princeton biologist Lee Silver told the London *Sunday Times.* "These human bodies without any semblance of consciousness would not be considered persons, and thus it would be perfectly legal to keep them 'alive' as a future source of organs."

"Alive." Never have a pair of quotation marks loomed so ominously.   5
Take the mouse-frog technology, apply it to humans, combine it with cloning, and you are become a god: with a single cell taken from, say, your finger, you produce a headless replica of yourself, a mutant twin, arguably lifeless, that becomes your own personal, precisely tissue-matched organ farm.

There are, of course, technical hurdles along the way. Suppressing the equivalent "head" gene in man. Incubating tiny infant organs to grow into larger ones that adults could use. And creating artificial wombs (as per Aldous Huxley), given that it might be difficult to recruit sane women to carry headless fetuses to their birth/death.

It won't be long, however, before these technical barriers are breached. The ethical barriers are already cracking. Lewis Wolpert, professor of biology at University College, London, finds producing headless humans "personally distasteful" but, given the shortage of organs, does not think distaste is sufficient reason not to go ahead with something that would save lives. And Professor Silver not only sees "nothing wrong, philosophically or rationally," with producing headless humans for organ harvesting; he wants to convince a skeptical public that it is perfectly O.K.

When prominent scientists are prepared to acquiesce in—or indeed encourage—the deliberate creation of deformed and dying quasi-human life, you know we are facing a bioethical abyss. Human beings are ends, not means. There is no grosser corruption of biotechnology than creating a human mutant and disemboweling it at our pleasure for spare parts.

The prospect of headless human clones should put the whole debate about "normal" cloning in a new light. Normal cloning is less a treatment for infertility than a treatment for vanity. It is a way to produce an exact genetic replica of yourself that will walk the earth years after you're gone.

But there is a problem with a clone. It is not really you. It is but a twin, a perfect John Doe Jr., but still a junior. With its own independent consciousness, it is, alas, just a facsimile of you.   10

The headless clone solves the facsimile problem. It is a gateway to the ultimate vanity: immortality. If you create a real clone, you cannot transfer your consciousness into it to truly live on. But if you create a headless clone of just your body, you have created a ready source of replacement parts to keep you—your consciousness—going indefinitely.

Which is why one form of cloning will inevitably lead to the other. Cloning is the technology of narcissism, and nothing satisfies narcissism like immortality. Headlessness will be cloning's crowning achievement.

The time to put a stop to this is now. Dolly moved President Clinton to create a commission that recommended a temporary ban on human cloning. But with physicist Richard Seed threatening to clone humans, and with headless animals already here, we are past the time for toothless commissions and meaningless bans.

Clinton banned federal funding of human-cloning research, of which there is none anyway. He then proposed a five-year ban on cloning. This is not enough. Congress should ban human cloning now. Totally. And regarding one particular form, it should be draconian: the deliberate creation of headless humans must be made a crime, indeed a capital crime. If we flinch in the face of this high-tech barbarity, we'll deserve to live in the hell it heralds.

Laurence H. Tribe

Laurence H. Tribe (b. 1941), a graduate of Harvard College and of Harvard Law School, teaches constitutional law at Harvard. In addition to writing for the legal profession, Tribe writes for the general public. Among the books written for all of us are Constitutional Choices *(1985),* On Reading the Constitution *(1991), and* Abortion: The Clash of Absolutes *(1992). We reprint an op-ed piece that he published in* The New York Times *in 1997, and we follow it with a letter written in response.*

Second Thoughts on Cloning

Some years ago, long before human cloning became a near-term prospect, I was among those who urged that human cloning be assessed not simply in terms of concrete costs and benefits, but in terms of what the technology might do to the very meaning of human reproduction, child rearing and individuality. I leaned toward prohibition as the safest course.

Today, with the prospect of a renewed push for sweeping prohibition rather than mere regulation, I am inclined to say, "Not so fast."

When scientists announced in February that they had created a clone of an adult sheep—a genetically identical copy named Dolly, created in the laboratory from a single cell of the "parent"—ethicists, theologians and others passionately debated the pros and cons of trying to clone a human being.

People spoke of the plight of infertile couples; the grief of someone who has lost a child whose biological "rebirth" might offer solace; the prospect of using cloning to generate donors for tissues and organs; the possibility of creating genetically enhanced clones with a particular talent or a resistance to some dread disease.

But others saw a nightmarish and decidedly unnatural perversion of human reproduction. California enacted a ban on human cloning, and the President's National Bioethics Advisory Commission recommended making the ban nationwide.

That initial debate has cooled, however, and many in the scientific field now seem to be wondering what all the fuss was about.

They are asking whether human cloning isn't just an incremental step beyond what we are already doing with artificial insemination, in vitro fertilization, fertility enhancing drugs and genetic manipulation. That casual attitude is sure to give way before long to yet another wave of prohibitionist outrage—a wave that I no longer feel comfortable riding.

I certainly don't subscribe to the view that whatever technology permits us to do we ought to do. Nor do I subscribe to the view that the Constitution necessarily guarantees every individual the right to reproduce through whatever means become technically possible.

Rather, my concern is that the very decision to use the law to condemn, and then outlaw, patterns of human reproduction—especially by invoking vague notions of what is "natural"—is at least as dangerous as the technologies such a decision might be used to control.

Human cloning has been condemned by some of its most articulate detractors as the ultimate embodiment of the sexual revolution, severing sex from the creation of babies and treating gender and sexuality as socially constructed.

But to ban cloning as the technological apotheosis of what some see as culturally distressing trends may, in the end, lend credence to strikingly similar objections to surrogate motherhood or gay marriage and gay adoption.

Equally scary, when appeals to the natural, or to the divinely ordained, lead to the criminalization of some method for creating human babies, we must come to terms with the inevitable: the prohibition will not be airtight.

Just as was true of bans on abortion and on sex outside marriage, bans on human cloning are bound to be hard to enforce. And that, in turn, requires us to think in terms of a class of potential outcasts—people whose very existence society will have chosen to label as a misfortune and, in essence, to condemn.

One need only think of the long struggle to overcome the stigma of "illegitimacy" for the children of unmarried parents. How much worse might be the plight of being judged morally incomplete by virtue of one's man-made origin?

There are some black markets (in narcotic drugs, for instance) that may be worth risking when the evils of legalization would be even worse. But when the contraband we are talking of creating takes the form of human beings, the stakes become enormous.   15

There are few evils as grave as that of creating a caste system, one in which an entire category of persons, while perhaps not labeled untouchable, is marginalized as not fully human.

And even if one could enforce a ban on cloning, or at least insure that clones would not be a marginalized caste, the social costs of prohibition could still be high. For the arguments supporting an ironclad prohibition of cloning are most likely to rest on, and reinforce, the notion that it is unnatural and intrinsically wrong to sever the conventional links between heterosexual unions sanctified by tradition and the creation and upbringing of new life.

The entrenchment of that notion cannot be a welcome thing for lesbians, gay men and perhaps others with unconventional ways of linking erotic attachment, romantic commitment, genetic replication, gestational mothering and the joys and responsibilities of child rearing.

And, from the perspective of the wider community, straight no less than gay, a society that bans acts of human creation for no better reason than that their particular form defies nature and tradition is a society that risks cutting itself off from vital experimentation, thus losing a significant part of its capacity to grow. If human cloning is to be banned, then, the reasons had better be far more compelling than any thus far advanced.

Holly Finn

The following letter was published as a response to Laurence Tribe's op-ed piece (page 804). The title above the letter presumably was created by the editor of the "letters" page of The New York Times.

Letter Responding to Laurence H. Tribe
Romance of Childbirth

To the Editor:

Laurence H. Tribe's "Second Thoughts on Cloning" (Op-Ed, Dec. 5) was masterfully written, and sneaky. The emotional whammy was tucked in at the end, where he said, "A society that bans acts of human creation . . . is a society that risks cutting itself off from vital experimentation, thus losing a significant part of its capacity to grow." What a taunt. All good Americans want to grow, after all.

Mr. Tribe asks for better reasons to oppose human cloning. How about this? I have not yet had children, but I hope to have many. I don't want just to replicate mine and another's genes (that seems a bit perfunctory); I want to feel as my mother did after giving birth: "very clever," she says. There's romance, delight and mystery in that. Call me a Luddite, but I believe in the ancient means of production.

Holly Finn
New York, Dec. 5, 1997

15
CLASSIC ESSAYS

Plato

Plato (427–347 B.C.) in his dialogues often uses the Athenian philosopher Socrates as a mouth-piece for ideas that scholars believe are Platonic, but in the dialogue called Crito *he probably was fairly careful to represent Socrates' own ideas.*

In 399 B.C. Socrates was convicted of impiety and was sentenced to death. Behind the charge of impiety was another, that Socrates had "corrupted the young." It seems clear, however, that the trial was a way of getting rid of a man considered by some to be a troublesome questioner of conventional opinions.

About a month intervened between the trial and Socrates' death because the law prohibited execution until a sacred ship had returned to Athens. Socrates could easily have escaped from prison but made no effort to leave, as we see in this dialogue reporting his decision to abide by the unjust decision of a duly constituted group of jurors.

Crito

(*Scene: A room in the State prison at Athens in the year 399 B.C. The time is half an hour before dawn, and the room would be almost dark but for the light of a little oil lamp. There is a pallet bed against the back wall. At the head of it a small table supports the lamp; near the foot of it Crito is sitting patiently on a stool. He is an old man, kindly, practical, simple-minded; at present he is suffering from acute emotional strain. On the bed lies Socrates asleep. He stirs, yawns, opens his eyes and sees Crito.*)

Socrates: Here already, Crito? Surely it is still early?

Crito: Indeed it is.

Socrates: About what time?

Crito: Just before dawn.

Socrates: I wonder that the warder paid any attention to you.   5

Crito: He is used to me now, Socrates, because I come here so often; besides, he is under some small obligation to me.

Socrates: Have you only just come, or have you been here for long?

Crito: Fairly long.

Socrates: Then why didn't you wake me at once, instead of sitting by my bed so quietly?

Crito: I wouldn't dream of such a thing, Socrates. I only wish I were   10
not so sleepless and depressed myself. I have been wondering at you, because I saw how comfortably you were sleeping; and I deliberately didn't wake you because I wanted you to go on being as comfortable as you could. I have often felt before in the course of my life how fortunate you are in your disposition, but I feel it more than ever now in your present misfortune when I see how easily and placidly you put up with it.

Socrates: Well, really, Crito, it would be hardly suitable for a man of my age to resent having to die.

Crito: Other people just as old as you are get involved in these misfortunes, Socrates, but their age doesn't keep them from resenting it when they find themselves in your position.

Socrates: Quite true. But tell me, why have you come so early?

Crito: Because I bring bad news, Socrates; not so bad from your point of view, I suppose, but it will be very hard to bear for me and your other friends, and I think that I shall find it hardest of all.

Socrates: Why, what is this news? Has the boat come in from Delos— the boat which ends my reprieve when it arrives?[1]

Crito: It hasn't actually come in yet, but I expect that it will be here today, judging from the report of some people who have just arrived from Sunium and left it there. It's quite clear from their account that it will be here today; and so by tomorrow, Socrates, you will have to—to end your life.

Socrates: Well, Crito, I hope that it may be for the best; if the gods will it so, so be it. All the same, I don't think it will arrive today.

Crito: What makes you think that?

Socrates: I will try to explain. I think I am right in saying that I have to die on the day after the boat arrives?

Crito: That's what the authorities say, at any rate.

Socrates: Then I don't think it will arrive on this day that is just beginning, but on the day after. I am going by a dream that I had in the night, only a little while ago. It looks as though you were right not to wake me up.

Crito: Why, what was the dream about?

Socrates: I thought I saw a gloriously beautiful woman dressed in white robes, who came up to me and addressed me in these words: "Socrates, to the pleasant land of Phthia on the third day thou shalt come."

Crito: Your dream makes no sense, Socrates.

Socrates: To my mind, Crito, it is perfectly clear.

Crito: Too clear, apparently. But look here, Socrates, it is still not too late to take my advice and escape. Your death means a double calamity for me. I shall not only lose a friend whom I can never possibly replace, but besides a great many people who don't know you and me very well will be sure to think that I let you down, because I could have saved you if I had been willing to spend the money; and what could be more contemptible than to get a name for thinking more of money than of your friends? Most people will never believe that it was you who refused to leave this place although we tried our hardest to persuade you.

Socrates: But my dear Crito, why should we pay so much attention to what "most people" think? The really reasonable people, who have more claim to be considered, will believe that the facts are exactly as they are.

Crito: You can see for yourself, Socrates, that one has to think of popular opinion as well. Your present position is quite enough to show that the capacity of ordinary people for causing trouble is not confined to petty annoyances, but has hardly any limits if you once get a bad name with them.

---

[1]**Delos . . . arrives** Ordinarily execution was immediately carried out, but the day before Socrates' trial was the first day of an annual ceremony that involved sending a ship to Delos. When the ship was absent—in this case for about a month—executions could not be performed. As Crito goes on to say, Socrates could easily escape, and indeed he could have left the country before being tried. [All notes are the editors'.]

Socrates: I only wish that ordinary people *had* unlimited capacity for doing harm; then they might have an unlimited power for doing good; which would be a splendid thing, if it were so. Actually they have neither. They cannot make a man wise or stupid; they simply act at random.

Crito: Have it that way if you like; but tell me this, Socrates. I hope   30 that you aren't worrying about the possible effects on me and the rest of your friends, and thinking that if you escape we shall have trouble with informers for having helped you to get away, and have to forfeit all our property or pay an enormous fine, or even incur some further punishment? If any idea like that is troubling you, you can dismiss it altogether. We are quite entitled to run that risk in saving you, and even worse, if necessary. Take my advice, and be reasonable.

Socrates: All that you say is very much in my mind, Crito, and a great deal more besides.

Crito: Very well, then, don't let it distress you. I know some people who are willing to rescue you from here and get you out of the country for quite a moderate sum. And then surely you realize how cheap these informers are to buy off; we shan't need much money to settle them; and I think you've got enough of my money for yourself already. And then even supposing that in your anxiety for my safety you feel that you oughtn't to spend my money, there are these foreign gentlemen staying in Athens who are quite willing to spend theirs. One of them, Simmias of Thebes, has actually brought the money with him for this very purpose; and Cebes and a number of others are quite ready to do the same. So as I say, you mustn't let any fears on these grounds make you slacken your efforts to escape; and you mustn't feel any misgivings about what you said at your trial, that you wouldn't know what to do with yourself if you left this country. Wherever you go, there are plenty of places where you will find a welcome; and if you choose to go to Thessaly, I have friends there who will make much of you and give you complete protection, so that no one in Thessaly can interfere with you.

Besides, Socrates, I don't even feel that it is right for you to try to do what you are doing, throwing away your life when you might save it. You are doing your best to treat yourself in exactly the same way as your enemies would, or rather did, when they wanted to ruin you. What is more, it seems to me that you are letting your sons down too. You have it in your power to finish their bringing up and education, and instead of that you are proposing to go off and desert them, and so far as you are concerned they will have to take their chance. And what sort of chance are they likely to get? The sort of thing that usually happens to orphans when they lose their parents. Either one ought not to have children at all, or one ought to see their upbringing and education through to the end. It strikes me that you are taking the line of least resistance, whereas you ought to make the choice of a good man and a brave one, considering that you profess to have made goodness your object all through life. Really, I am ashamed, both on your account and on ours your friends'; it will look as though we had played something like a coward's part all through this affair of yours. First, there was the way you came into court when it was quite unnecessary—that was the first act; than there was the conduct of the defense—that was the second; and finally, to complete the farce, we get this situation, which makes it appear that we have let you slip out of our hands through some lack of courage and enterprise on our part, because we didn't save you, and you didn't save yourself, when it would have been quite possible and practicable, if we had been any use at all.

There, Socrates; if you aren't careful, besides the suffering there will be all this disgrace for you and us to bear. Come, make up your mind. Really it's too late for that now; you ought to have it made up already. There is no alternative; the whole thing must be carried through during this coming night. If we lose any more time, it can't be done, it will be too late. I appeal to you, Socrates, on every ground; take my advice and please don't be unreasonable!

Socrates: My dear Crito, I appreciate your warm feelings very much—   35 that is, assuming that they have some justification; if not, the stronger they are, the harder they will be to deal with. Very well, then; we must consider whether we ought to follow your advice or not. You know that this is not a new idea of mine; it has always been my nature never to accept advice from any of my friends unless reflection shows that it is the best course that reason offers. I cannot abandon the principles which I used to hold in the past simply because this accident has happened to me; they seem to me to be much as they were, and I respect and regard the same principles now as before. So unless we can find better principles on this occasion, you can be quite sure that I shall not agree with you; not even if the power of the people conjures up fresh hordes of bogies to terrify our childish minds, by subjecting us to chains and executions and confiscations of our property.

Well, then, how can we consider the question most reasonably? Suppose that we begin by reverting to this view which you hold about people's opinions. Was it always right to argue that some opinions should be taken seriously but not others? Or was it always wrong? Perhaps it was right before the question of my death arose, but now we can see clearly that it was a mistaken persistence in a point of view which was really irresponsible nonsense. I should like very much to inquire into this problem, Crito, with your help, and to see whether the argument will appear in any different light to me now that I am in this position, or whether it will remain the same; and whether we shall dismiss it or accept it.

Serious thinkers, I believe, have always held some such view as the one which I mentioned just now: that some of the opinions which people entertain should be respected, and others should not. Now I ask you, Crito, don't you think that this is a sound principle?—You are safe from the prospect of dying tomorrow, in all human probability; and you are not likely to have your judgment upset by this impending calamity. Consider, then; don't you think that this is a sound enough principle, that one should not regard all the opinions that people hold, but only some and not others? What do you say? Isn't that a fair statement?

Crito: Yes, it is.

Socrates: In other words, one should regard the good ones and not the bad?

Crito: Yes.   40

Socrates: The opinions of the wise being good, and the opinions of the foolish bad?

Crito: Naturally.

Socrates: To pass on, then: What do you think of the sort of illustration that I used to employ? When a man is in training, and taking it seriously, does he pay attention to all praise and criticism and opinion indiscriminately, or only when it comes from the one qualified person, the actual doctor or trainer?

Crito: Only when it comes from the one qualified person.

Socrates: Then he should be afraid of the criticism and welcome the   45
praise of the one qualified person, but not those of the general public.

Crito: Obviously.

Socrates: So he ought to regulate his actions and exercises and eating and drinking by the judgment of his instructor, who has expert knowledge, rather than by the opinions of the rest of the public.

Crito: Yes, that is so.

Socrates: Very well. Now if he disobeys the one man and disregards his opinion and commendations, and pays attention to the advice of the many who have no expert knowledge, surely he will suffer some bad effect?

Crito: Certainly.   50

Socrates: And what is this bad effect? Where is it produced?—I mean, in what part of the disobedient person?

Crito: His body, obviously; that is what suffers.

Socrates: Very good. Well now, tell me, Crito—we don't want to go through all the examples one by one—does this apply as a general rule, and above all to the sort of actions which we are trying to decide about: just and unjust, honorable and dishonorable, good and bad? Ought we to be guided and intimidated by the opinion of the many or by that of the one—assuming that there is someone with expert knowledge? Is it true that we ought to respect and fear this person more than all the rest put together; and that if we do not follow his guidance we shall spoil and mutilate that part of us which, as we used to say, is improved by right conduct and destroyed by wrong? Or is this all nonsense?

Crito: No, I think it is true, Socrates.

Socrates: Then consider the next step. There is a part of us which is   55
improved by healthy actions and ruined by unhealthy ones. If we spoil it by taking the advice of nonexperts, will life be worth living when this part is once ruined? The part I mean is the body; do you accept this?

Crito: Yes.

Socrates: Well, is life worth living with a body which is worn out and ruined by health?

Crito: Certainly not.

Socrates: What about the part of us which is mutilated by wrong actions and benefited by right ones? Is life worth living with this part ruined? Or do we believe that this part of us, whatever it may be, in which right and wrong operate, is of less importance than the body?

Crito: Certainly not.

Socrates: It is really more precious?

Crito: Much more.

Socrates: In that case, my dear fellow, what we ought to consider is not so much what people in general will say about us but how we stand with the expert in right and wrong, the one authority, who represents the actual truth. So in the first place your proposition is not correct when you say that we should consider popular opinion in questions of what is right and honorable and good, or the opposite. Of course one might object "All the same, the people have the power to put us to death."

Crito: No doubt about that! Quite true, Socrates; it is a possible objection.

Socrates: But so far as I can see, my dear fellow, the argument which we have just been through is quite unaffected by it. At the same time I should like you to consider whether we are still satisfied on this point: that the really important thing is not to live, but to live well.

Crito: Why, yes.

Socrates: And that to live well means the same thing as to live honorably or rightly?

Crito: Yes.

Socrates: Then in the light of this agreement we must consider whether or not it is right for me to try to get away without an official discharge. If it turns out to be right, we must make the attempt; if not, we must let it drop. As for the considerations you raise about expense and reputation and bringing up children, I am afraid, Crito, that they represent the reflections of the ordinary public, who put people to death, and would bring them back to life if they could, with equal indifference to reason. Our real duty, I fancy, since the argument leads that way, is to consider one question only, the one which we raised just now: Shall we be acting rightly in paying money and showing gratitude to these people who are going to rescue me, and in escaping or arranging the escape ourselves, or shall we really be acting wrongly in doing all this? If it becomes clear that such conduct is wrong, I cannot help thinking that the question whether we are sure to die, or to suffer any other ill effect for that matter, if we stand our ground and take no action, ought not to weigh with us at all in comparison with the risk of doing what is wrong.

Crito: I agree with what you say, Socrates; but I wish you would consider what we ought to *do.*

Socrates: Let us look at it together, my dear fellow; and if you can challenge any of my arguments, do so and I will listen to you; but if you can't, be a good fellow and stop telling me over and over again that I ought to leave this place without official permission. I am very anxious to obtain

60

65

70

your approval before I adopt the course which I have in mind; I don't want to act against your convictions. Now give your attention to the starting point of this inquiry—I hope that you will be satisfied with my way of stating it—and try to answer my questions to the best of your judgment.

Crito: Well, I will try.

Socrates: Do we say that one must never willingly do wrong, or does it depend upon circumstance? Is it true, as we have often agreed before, that there is no sense in which wrongdoing is good or honorable? Or have we jettisoned all our former convictions in these last few days? Can you and I at our age, Crito, have spent all these years in serious discussions without realizing that we were no better than a pair of children? Surely the truth is just what we have always said. Whatever the popular view is, and whether the alternative is pleasanter than the present one or even harder to bear, the fact remains that to do wrong is in every sense bad and dishonorable for the person who does it. Is that our view, or not?

Crito: Yes, it is.

Socrates: Then in no circumstances must one do wrong.   75

Crito: No.

Socrates: In that case one must not even do wrong when one is wronged, which most people regard as the natural course.

Crito: Apparently not.

Socrates: Tell me another thing, Crito: Ought one to do injuries or not?

Crito: Surely not, Socrates.   80

Socrates: And tell me: Is it right to do an injury in retaliation, as most people believe, or not?

Crito: No, never.

Socrates: Because, I suppose, there is no difference between injuring people and wronging them.

Crito: Exactly.

Socrates: So one ought not to return a wrong or an injury to any per-   85
son, whatever the provocation is. Now be careful, Crito, that in making these single admissions you do not end by admitting something contrary to your real beliefs. I know that there are and always will be few people who think like this; and consequently between those who do think so and those who do not there can be no agreement on principle; they must always feel contempt when they observe one another's decisions. I want even you to consider very carefully whether you share my views and agree with me, and whether we can proceed with our discussion from the established hypothesis that it is never right to do a wrong or return a wrong or defend one's self against injury by retaliation; or whether you dissociate yourself from any share in this view as a basis for discussion. I have held it for a long time, and still hold it; but if you have formed any other opinion, say so and tell me what it is. If, on the other hand, you stand by what we have said, listen to my next point.

Crito: Yes, I stand by it and agree with you. Go on.

Socrates: Well, here is my next point, or rather question. Ought one to fulfill all one's agreements, provided that they are right, or break them?

Crito: One ought to fulfill them.

Socrates: Then consider the logical consequence. If we leave this place without first persuading the State to let us go, are we or are we not doing an injury, and doing it in a quarter where it is least justifiable? Are we or are we not abiding by our just agreements?

Crito: I can't answer your question, Socrates; I am not clear in my mind. 90

Socrates: Look at it in this way. Suppose that while we were preparing to run away from here (or however one should describe it) the Laws and Constitution of Athens were to come and confront us and ask this question: "Now, Socrates, what are you proposing to do? Can you deny that by this act which you are contemplating you intend, so far as you have the power, to destroy us, the Laws, and the whole State as well? Do you imagine that a city can continue to exist and not be turned upside down, if the legal judgments which are pronounced in it have no force but are nullified and destroyed by private persons?"—how shall we answer this question, Crito, and others of the same kind? There is much that could be said, especially by a professional advocate, to protest against the invalidation of this law which enacts that judgments once pronounced shall be binding. Shall we say "Yes, I do intend to destroy the laws, because the State wronged me by passing a faulty judgment at my trial"? Is this to be our answer, or what?

Crito: What you have just said, by all means, Socrates.

Socrates: Then what supposing the Laws say, "Was there provision for this in the agreement between you and us, Socrates? Or did you undertake to abide by whatever judgments the State pronounced?" If we expressed surprise at such language, they would probably say: "Never mind our language, Socrates, but answer our questions; after all, you are accustomed to the method of question and answer. Come now, what charge do you bring against us and the State, that you are trying to destroy us? Did we not give you life in the first place? Was it not through us that your father married your mother and begot you? Tell us, have you any complaint against those of us Laws that deal with marriage?" "No, none," I should say. "Well, have you any against the laws which deal with children's upbringing and education, such as you had yourself? Are you not grateful to those of us Laws which were instituted for this end, for requiring your father to give you a cultural and physical education?" "Yes," I should say. "Very good. Then since you have been born and brought up and educated, can you deny, in the first place, that you were our child and servant, both you and your ancestors? And if this is so, do you imagine that what is right for us is equally right for you, and that whatever we try to do to you, you are justified in retaliating? You did not have equality of rights with your father, or your employer (supposing that you had had one), to enable you to retaliate; you were not allowed to answer back when you were scolded or to hit back when you were beaten, or to do a great many other things of the same kind. Do you expect to have such license against your country and its laws that if we try to put you to death in the belief that it is right to do so, you on your part will try your hardest to destroy your country and us its Laws in return? And will you, the true devotee of goodness, claim that you are justified in doing so? Are you so wise as to have forgotten that compared with your mother and father and all the rest of your ancestors your country is something far more precious, more venerable, more sacred, and held in greater honor both among gods and among all reasonable men? Do you not realize that you are even more bound to respect and placate the anger of your country than your father's anger? That if you cannot persuade your country you must do whatever it orders, and patiently submit to any punishment that it imposes, whether it be flogging or imprisonment? And if it leads you out to war, to be wounded or killed, you must comply, and it is right that you should do so; you must not give way or retreat or abandon your position. Both in war and in the law courts and everywhere else you must do whatever your city and your country commands, or else persuade it in accordance with universal justice; but violence is a sin even against your parents, and it is a far greater sin against your country"—What shall we say to this, Crito?—that what the Laws say is true, or not?

Crito: Yes, I think so.

Socrates: "Consider, then, Socrates," the Laws would probably continue, "whether it is also true for us to say that what you are now trying to do to us is not right. Although we have brought you into the world and reared you and educated you, and given you and all your fellow citizens a share in all the good things at our disposal, nevertheless by the very fact of granting our permission we openly proclaim this principle: that any Athenian, on attaining to manhood and seeing for himself the political organization of the State and us its Laws, is permitted, if he is not satisfied with us, to take his property and go away wherever he likes. If any of you chooses to go to one of our colonies, supposing that he should not be satisfied with us and the State, or to emigrate to any other country, not one of us Laws hinders or prevents him from going away wherever he likes, without any loss of property. On the other hand, if any one of you stands his ground when he can see how we administer justice and the rest of our public organization, we hold that by so doing he has in fact undertaken to do anything that we tell him; and we maintain that anyone who disobeys is guilty of doing wrong on three separate counts: first because we are his parents, and secondly because we are his guardians; and thirdly because, after promising obedience, he is neither obeying us nor persuading us to change our decision if we are at fault in any way; and although all our orders are in the form of proposals, not of savage commands, and we give him the choice of either persuading us or doing what we say, he is actually doing neither. These are the charges, Socrates, to which we say that you will be liable if you do what you are contemplating; and you will not be the least culpable of your fellow countrymen, but one of the most guilty." If I said "Why do you say that?" they would no doubt pounce upon me with perfect justice and point out that there are very few people in Athens who have entered into this agreement with them as explicitly as I have. They would say "Socrates, we have substantial evidence that you are sat-

95

isfied with us and with the State. You would not have been so exceptionally reluctant to cross the borders of your country if you had not been
exceptionally attached to it. You have never left the city to attend a festival
or for any other purpose, except on some military expedition; you have
never traveled abroad as other people do, and you have never felt the
impulse to acquaint yourself with another country or constitution; you
have been content with us and with our city. You have definitely chosen
us, and undertaken to observe us in all your activities as a citizen; and as
the crowning proof that you are satisfied with our city, you have begotten
children in it. Furthermore, even at the time of your trial you could have
proposed the penalty of banishment, if you had chosen to do so; that is,
you could have done then with the sanction of the State what you are now
trying to do without it. But whereas at that time you made a noble show
of indifference if you had to die, and in fact preferred death, as you said,
to banishment, now you show no respect for your earlier professions, and
no regard for us, the Laws, whom you are trying to destroy; you are
behaving like the lowest type of menial, trying to run away in spite of the
contracts and undertakings by which you agreed to live as a member of
our State. Now first answer this question: Are we or are we not speaking
the truth when we say that you have undertaken, in deed if not in word,
to live your life as a citizen in obedience to us?" What are we to say to that,
Crito? Are we not bound to admit it?

Crito: We cannot help it, Socrates.

Socrates: "It is a fact, then," they would say, "that you are breaking
covenants and undertakings made with us, although you made them under
no compulsion or misunderstanding, and were not compelled to decide in a
limited time; you had seventy years in which you could have left the country, if you were not satisfied with us or felt that the agreements were unfair.
You did not choose Sparta or Crete—your favorite models of good government—or any other Greek or foreign state; you could not have absented
yourself from the city less if you had been lame or blind or decrepit in some
other way. It is quite obvious that you stand by yourself above all other
Athenians in your affection for this city and for us its Laws;—who would
care for a city without laws? And now, after all this, are you not going to
stand by your agreement? Yes, you are, Socrates, if you will take our advice;
and then you will at least escape being laughed at for leaving the city.

"We invite you to consider what good you will do to yourself or your
friends if you commit this breach of faith and stain your conscience. It is
fairly obvious that the risk of being banished and either losing their citizenship or having their property confiscated will extend to your friends as
well. As for yourself, if you go to one of the neighboring states, such as
Thebes or Megara, which are both well governed, you will enter them as
an enemy to their constitution[2] and all good patriots will eye you with suspicion as a destroyer of law and order. Incidentally you will confirm the

---

[2]**as an enemy to their constitution** As a lawbreaker.

opinion of the jurors who tried you that they gave a correct verdict; a destroyer of laws might very well be supposed to have a destructive influence upon young and foolish human beings. Do you intend, then, to avoid well governed states and the higher forms of human society? And if you do, will life be worth living? Or will you approach these people and have the impudence to converse with them? What arguments will you use, Socrates? The same which you used here, that goodness and integrity, institutions and laws, are the most precious possessions of mankind? Do you not think that Socrates and everything about him will appear in a disreputable light? You certainly ought to think so. But perhaps you will retire from this part of the world and go to Crito's friends in Thessaly? That is the home of indiscipline and laxity, and no doubt they would enjoy hearing the amusing story of how you managed to run away from prison by arraying yourself in some costume or putting on a shepherd's smock or some other conventional runaway's disguise, and altering your personal appearance. And will no one comment on the fact that an old man of your age, probably with only a short time left to live, should dare to cling so greedily to life, at the price of violating the most stringent laws? Perhaps not, if you avoid irritating anyone. Otherwise, Socrates, you will hear a good many humiliating comments. So you will live as the toady and slave of all the populace, literally 'roistering in Thessaly,' as though you had left this country for Thessaly to attend a banquet there; and where will your discussions about goodness and uprightness be then, we should like to know? But of course you want to live for your children's sake, so that you may be able to bring them up and educate them. Indeed! by first taking them off to Thessaly and making foreigners of them, so that they may have that additional enjoyment? Or if that is not your intention, supposing that they are brought up here with you still alive, will they be better cared for and educated without you, because of course your friends will look after them? Will they look after your children if you go away to Thessaly, and not if you go away to the next world? Surely if those who profess to be your friends are worth anything, you must believe that they would care for them.

"No, Socrates; be advised by us your guardians, and do not think more of your children or of your life or of anything else than you think of what is right; so that when you enter the next world you may have all this to plead in your defense before the authorities there. It seems clear that if you do this thing, neither you nor any of your friends will be the better for it or be more upright or have a cleaner conscience here in this world, nor will it be better for you when you reach the next. As it is, you will leave this place, when you do, as the victim of a wrong done not by us, the Laws, but by your fellow men. But if you leave in that dishonorable way, returning wrong for wrong and evil for evil, breaking your agreements and covenants with us, and injuring those whom you least ought to injure—yourself, your friends, your country, and us—then you will have to face our anger in your lifetime, and in that place beyond when the laws of the other world know that you have tried, so far as you could, to destroy even us their brothers, they will not receive you with a kindly welcome. Do not take Crito's advice, but follow ours."

That, my dear friend Crito, I do assure you, is what I seem to hear them saying, just as a mystic seems to hear the strains of music; and the sound of their arguments rings so loudly in my head that I cannot hear the other side. I warn you that, as my opinion stands at present, it will be useless to urge a different view. However, if you think that you will do any good by it, say what you like.

Crito: No, Socrates, I have nothing to say.

Socrates: Then give it up, Crito, and let us follow this course, since God points out the way.

✎ Topics for Critical Thinking and Writing

1. Socrates argues that because throughout his life he lived in Athens, in effect he established a compact with the city to live by its laws and must therefore now accept the judgment—however mistaken—of a duly constituted court. How convincing is this argument? Suppose this argument were omitted. Would Socrates' conclusion be affected?
2. Socrates argues that just as in matters of caring for the body we heed only experts and not the multitude, so in moral matters we should heed the expert, not the multitude. How convincing is this analogy between bodily health and moral goodness? Socrates sometimes compared himself to an athletic coach, saying he trained people to think. Judging from the dialogue, how did he train a student to think?
3. The personified figure of the laws does not add much to the essential argument. Why, then, is the passage included?
4. The ancient Chinese teacher Confucius asked one of his pupils, "Do you think of me as a man who knows about things as the result of wide study?" When the pupil replied "Yes," Confucius disagreed: "I have one thing, and upon it all the rest is rooted." Exactly what did Confucius mean? In an essay of 500 words explain what Socrates would have said, if he had been asked the question.

Jonathan Swift

Jonathan Swift (1667–1745) was born in Ireland of an English family. He was ordained in the Church of Ireland in 1694, and in 1714 he became dean of St. Patrick's Cathedral, Dublin. He wrote abundantly on political and religious topics, often motivated (in his own words) by "savage indignation." It is ironic that Gulliver's Travels, *the masterpiece by this master of irony, is most widely thought of as a book for children.*

From the middle of the sixteenth century, the English regulated the Irish economy so that it would enrich England. Heavy taxes and other repressive legislation impoverished Ireland, and in 1728, the year before Swift wrote "A Modest Proposal," Ireland was further weakened by a severe famine. Swift, deeply moved by the injustice, the stupidity, and the suffering that he found in Ireland, adopts the disguise or persona of an economist and offers an ironic suggestion on how Irish families may improve their conditions.

A Modest Proposal
For Preventing the Children of Poor People in Ireland from Being a Burden to Their Parents or Country, and for Making Them Beneficial to the Public

It is a melancholy object to those who walk through this great town or travel in the country, when they see the streets, the roads, and cabin doors, crowded with beggars of the female sex, followed by three, four, or six children, all in rags and importuning every passenger for an alms. These mothers, instead of being able to work for their honest livelihood, are forced to employ all their time in strolling to beg sustenance for their helpless infants: who as they grow up either turn thieves for want of work, or leave their dear native country to fight for the pretender in Spain, or sell themselves to the Barbadoes.

I think it is agreed by all parties that this prodigious number of children in the arms, or on the backs, or at the heels of their mothers, and frequently of their fathers, is in the present deplorable state of the kingdom a very great additional grievance; and, therefore, whoever could find out a fair, cheap, and easy method of making these children sound, useful members of the commonwealth, would deserve so well of the public as to have his statue set up for a preserver of the nation.

But my intention is very far from being confined to provide only for the children of professed beggars; it is of a much greater extent, and shall take in the whole number of infants at a certain age who are born of parents in effect as little able to support them as those who demand our charity in the streets.

As to my own part, having turned my thoughts for many years upon this important subject, and maturely weighed the several schemes of our projectors, I have always found them grossly mistaken in their computation. It is true, a child just dropped from its dam may be supported by her milk for a solar year, with little other nourishment; at most not above the value of 2s.,[1] which the mother may certainly get, or the value in scraps, by her lawful occupation of begging; and it is exactly at one year old that I propose to provide for them in such a manner as instead of being a charge

---

[1]2s. = two shillings. Later in the essay, "£" and "l" stand for pounds and "d" for pence. (Editors' note)

upon their parents or the parish, or wanting food and raiment for the rest of their lives, they shall on the contrary contribute to the feeding, and partly to the clothing, of many thousands.

There is likewise another great advantage in my scheme, that it will prevent those voluntary abortions, and that horrid practice of women murdering their bastard children, alas! too frequent among us! sacrificing the poor innocent babes I doubt more to avoid the expense than the shame, which would move tears and pity in the most savage and inhuman breast.

The number of souls in this kingdom being usually reckoned one million and a half, of these I calculate there may be about 200,000 couple whose wives are breeders; from which number I subtract 30,000 couple who are able to maintain their own children (although I apprehend there cannot be so many, under the present distress of the kingdom); but this being granted, there will remain 170,000 breeders. I again subtract 50,000 for those women who miscarry, or whose children die by accident or disease within the year. There only remain 120,000 children of poor parents annually born. The question therefore is, how this number shall be reared and provided for? which, as I have already said, under the present situation of affairs, is utterly impossible by all the methods hitherto proposed. For we can neither employ them in handicraft or agriculture; we neither build houses (I mean in the country) nor cultivate land; they can very seldom pick up a livelihood by stealing, till they arrive at six years old, except where they are of towardly parts; although I confess they learn the rudiments much earlier; during which time they can, however, be properly looked upon only as probationers; as I have been informed by a principal gentleman in the county of Cavan, who protested to me that he never knew above one or two instances under the age of six, even in a part of the kingdom so renowned for the quickest proficiency in that art.

I am assured by our merchants, that a boy or a girl before twelve years old is no saleable commodity; and even when they come to this age they will not yield above 3l. or 3l. 2s. 6d. at most on the exchange; which cannot turn to account either to the parents or kingdom, the charge of nutriment and rags having been at least four times that value.

I shall now therefore humbly propose my own thoughts, which I hope will not be liable to the least objection.

I have been assured by a very knowing American of my acquaintance in London, that a young healthy child well nursed is at a year old a most delicious, nourishing, and wholesome food, whether stewed, roasted, baked, or broiled; and I make no doubt that it will equally serve in a fricassee or a ragout.

I do therefore humbly offer it to public consideration that of the 120,000 children already computed, 20,000 may be reserved for breed, whereof only one-fourth part to be males; which is more than we allow to sheep, black cattle, or swine; and my reason is, that these children are seldom the fruits of marriage, a circumstance not much regarded by our savages; therefore one male will be sufficient to serve four females. That the remaining 100,000 may, at a year old, be offered in sale to the persons of quality and fortune through the kingdom; always advising the mother to let them suck plentifully in the last month, so as to render them plump and fat for a good table. A child will make two dishes at an entertainment for friends; and when the family dines alone, the fore or hind quarter will make a reasonable dish, and seasoned with a little pepper or salt will be very good boiled on the fourth day, especially in winter.

I have reckoned upon a medium that a child just born will weigh 12 pounds, and in a solar year, if tolerably nursed, will increase to 28 pounds.

I grant this food will be somewhat dear, and therefore very proper for landlords, who, as they have already devoured most of the parents, seem to have the best title to the children.

Infant's flesh will be in season throughout the year, but more plentiful in March, and a little before and after: for we are told by a grave author, an eminent French physician, that fish being a prolific diet, there are more children born in Roman Catholic countries about nine months after Lent than at any other season; therefore, reckoning a year after Lent, the markets will be more glutted than usual, because the number of popish infants is at least three to one in this kingdom: and therefore it will have one other collateral advantage, by lessening the number of papists among us.

I have already computed the charge of nursing a beggar's child (in which list I reckon all cottagers, laborers, and four-fifths of the farmers) to be about 2s. per annum, rags included; and I believe no gentleman would repine to give 10s. for the carcass of a good fat child, which, as I have said, will make four dishes of excellent nutritive meat, when he has only some particular friend or his own family to dine with him. Thus the squire will learn to be a good landlord, and grow popular among the tenants; the mother will have 8s. net profit, and be fit for work till she produces another child.

Those who are more thrifty (as I must confess the times require) may flay the carcass; the skin of which artificially dressed will make admirable gloves for ladies, and summer boots for fine gentlemen.

As to our city of Dublin, shambles may be appointed for this purpose in the most convenient parts of it, and butchers we may be assured will not be wanting: although I rather recommend buying the children alive, and dressing them hot from the knife as we do roasting pigs.

A very worthy person, a true lover of his country, and whose virtues I highly esteem, was lately pleased in discoursing on this matter to offer a refinement upon my scheme. He said that many gentlemen of this kingdom, having of late destroyed their deer, he conceived that the want of venison might be well supplied by the bodies of young lads and maidens, not exceeding fourteen years of age nor under twelve; so great a number of both sexes in every country being now ready to starve for want of work and service; and these to be disposed of by their parents, if alive, or otherwise by their nearest relations. But with due deference to so excellent a friend and so deserving a patriot, I cannot be altogether in his sentiments;

for as to the males, my American acquaintance assured me from frequent experience that their flesh was generally tough and lean, like that of our schoolboys by continual exercise, and their taste disagreeable; and to fatten them would not answer the charge. Then as to the females, it would, I think, with humble submission be a loss to the public, because they soon would become breeders themselves: and besides, it is not improbable that some scrupulous people might be apt to censure such a practice (although indeed very unjustly), as a little bordering upon cruelty; which, I confess, has always been with me the strongest objection against any project, how well soever intended.

But in order to justify my friend, he confessed that this expedient was put into his head by the famous Psalmanazar, a native of the island Formosa, who came from thence to London about twenty years ago: and in conversation told my friend, that in his country when any young person happened to be put to death, the executioner sold the carcass to persons of quality as a prime dainty; and that in his time the body of a plump girl of fifteen, who was crucified for an attempt to poison the emperor, was sold to his imperial majesty's prime minister of state, and other great mandarins of the court, in joints from the gibbet, at 400 crowns. Neither indeed can I deny, that if the same use were made of several plump young girls in this town, who without one single groat to their fortunes cannot stir abroad without a chair, and appear at the playhouse and assemblies in foreign fineries which they never will pay for, the kingdom would not be the worse.

Some persons of a desponding spirit are in great concern about that vast number of poor people, who are aged, diseased, or maimed, and I have been desired to employ my thoughts what course may be taken to ease the nation of so grievous an encumbrance. But I am not in the least pain upon that matter, because it is very well known that they are every day dying and rotting by cold and famine, and filth and vermin, as fast as can be reasonably expected. And as to the young laborers, they are now in as hopeful a condition: they cannot get work, and consequently pine away for want of nourishment, to a degree that if at any time they are accidentally hired to common labor, they have not strength to perform it; and thus the country and themselves are happily delivered from the evils to come.

I have too long digressed, and therefore shall return to my subject. I think the advantages by the proposal which I have made are obvious and many, as well as of the highest importance. 20

For first, as I have already observed, it would greatly lessen the number of papists, with whom we are yearly overrun, being the principal breeders of the nation as well as our most dangerous enemies; and who stay at home on purpose to deliver the kingdom to the Pretender, hoping to take their advantage by the absence of so many good Protestants, who have chosen rather to leave their country than stay at home and pay tithes against their conscience to an Episcopal curate.

Secondly, The poor tenants will have something valuable of their own, which by law may be made liable to distress and help to pay their landlord's rent, their corn and cattle being already seized, and money a thing unknown.

Thirdly, Whereas the maintenance of 100,000 children from two years old and upward, cannot be computed at less than 10s. a-piece per annum, the nation's stock will be thereby increased £50,000 per annum, beside the profit of a new dish introduced to the tables of all gentlemen of fortune in the kingdom who have any refinement in taste. And the money will circulate among ourselves, the goods being entirely of our own growth and manufacture.

Fourthly, The constant breeders beside the gain of 8s. sterling per annum by the sale of their children, will be rid of the charge of maintaining them after the first year.

Fifthly, This food would likewise bring great custom to taverns, where   25
the vintners will certainly be so prudent as to procure the best receipts for dressing it to perfection, and consequently have their houses frequented by all the fine gentlemen, who justly value themselves upon their knowledge in good eating; and a skilful cook who understands how to oblige his guests, will contrive to make it as expensive as they please.

Sixthly, This would be a great inducement to marriage, which all wise nations have either encouraged by rewards or enforced by laws and penalties. It would increase the care and tenderness of mothers toward their children, when they were sure of a settlement for life to the poor babes, provided in some sort by the public, to their annual profit instead of expense. We should see an honest emulation among the married women, which of them would bring the fattest child to the market. Men would become as fond of their wives during the time of their pregnancy as they are now of their mares in foal, their cows in calf, their sows when they are ready to farrow; nor offer to beat or kick them (as is too frequent a practice) for fear of a miscarriage.

Many other advantages might be enumerated. For instance, the addition of some thousand carcasses in our exportation of barreled beef, the propagation of swine's flesh, and improvement in the art of making good bacon, so much wanted among us by the great destruction of pigs, too frequent at our table; which are no way comparable in taste or magnificence to a well-grown, fat, yearling child, which roasted whole will make a considerable figure at a lord mayor's feast or any other public entertainment. But this and many others I omit, being studious of brevity.

Supposing that 1,000 families in this city would be constant customers for infants' flesh, besides others who might have it at merry-meetings, particularly at weddings and christenings, I compute that Dublin would take off annually about 20,000 carcasses; and the rest of the kingdom (where probably they will be sold somewhat cheaper) the remaining 80,000.

I can think of no one objection that will possibly be raised against this proposal, unless it should be urged that the number of people will be thereby much lessened in the kingdom. This I freely own, and it was indeed one principal design in offering it to the world. I desire the reader will observe, that I calculate my remedy for this one individual kingdom of Ireland and for no other that ever was, is, or I think ever can be upon earth. Therefore let no man talk to me of other expedients: of taxing our absentees at 5s. a pound: of using neither clothes nor household furniture except what is of our own growth and manufacture: of utterly rejecting the materials and instruments that promote foreign luxury: of curing the expensiveness of pride, vanity, idleness, and gaming in our women: of introducing a vein of parsimony, prudence, and temperance: of learning to love our country, in the want of which we differ even from Laplanders and the inhabitants of Topinamboo: of quitting our animosities and factions, nor acting any longer like the Jews, who were murdering one another at the very moment their city was taken: of being a little cautious not to sell our country and conscience for nothing: of teaching landlords to have at least one degree of mercy toward their tenants: lastly, of putting a spirit of honesty, industry, and skill into our shopkeepers; who, if a resolution could now be taken to buy only our native goods, would immediately unite to cheat and exact upon us in the price, the measure, and the goodness, nor could ever yet be brought to make one fair proposal of just dealing, though often and earnestly invited to it.

Therefore, I repeat, let no man talk to me of these and the like expedients, till he has at least some glimpse of hope that there will be ever some hearty and sincere attempt to put them in practice. 30

But as to myself, having been wearied out for many years with offering vain, idle, visionary thoughts, and at length utterly despairing of success, I fortunately fell upon this proposal; which, as it is wholly new, so it has something solid and real, of no expense and little trouble, full in our own power, and whereby we can incur no danger in disobliging England. For this kind of commodity will not bear exportation, the flesh being of too tender a consistence to admit a long continuance in salt, although perhaps I could name a country which would be glad to eat up our whole nation without it.

After all, I am not so violently bent upon my own opinion as to reject any offer proposed by wise men, which shall be found equally innocent, cheap, easy, and effectual. But before something of that kind shall be advanced in contradiction to my scheme, and offering a better, I desire the author or authors will be pleased maturely to consider two points. First, as things now stand, how they will be able to find food and raiment for 100,000 useless mouths and backs. And secondly, there being a round million of creatures in human figure throughout this kingdom, whose subsistence put into a common stock would leave them in debt 200,000,000l. sterling, adding those who are beggars by profession to the bulk of farmers, cottagers, and laborers, with the wives and children who are beggars in effect; I desire those politicians who dislike my overture, and may perhaps be so bold as to attempt an answer, that they will first ask the parents of these mortals, whether they would not at this day think it a great happiness to have been sold for food at a year old in the manner I prescribe, and thereby have avoided such a perpetual scene of misfortunes as they have since gone through by the oppression of landlords, the impossibility of paying rent without money or trade, the want of common sustenance, with neither house nor clothes to cover them from the inclemencies of the weather, and the most inevitable prospect of entailing the like or greater miseries upon their breed for ever.

I profess, in the sincerity of my heart, that I have not the least personal interest in endeavoring to promote this necessary work, having no other motive than the public good of my country, by advancing our trade, providing for infants, relieving the poor, and giving some pleasure to the rich. I have no children by which I can propose to get a single penny; the youngest being nine years old, and my wife past child-bearing.

✎ Topics for Critical Thinking and Writing

1. Characterize the pamphleteer (not Swift but his persona) who offers his "modest proposal." What sort of man does he think he is? What sort of man do we regard him as? Support your assertions with evidence.
2. In the first paragraph, the speaker says that the sight of mothers begging is "melancholy." In this paragraph what assumption does the speaker make about women that in part gives rise to this melancholy? Now that you are familiar with the entire essay, explain Swift's strategy in his first paragraph.
3. Explain the function of the "other expedients" (listed in paragraph 29).
4. How might you argue that although this satire is primarily ferocious, it also contains some playful touches? What specific passages might support your argument?

Elizabeth Cady Stanton

Elizabeth Cady Stanton (1815–1902), born into a prosperous conservative family in Johnstone, New York, became one of the most radical advocates of women's rights in the nineteenth century. In 1840 she married Henry Brewster Stanton, an ardent abolitionist lecturer. In the same year, at the World Anti-Slavery Convention in England—which refused to seat the women delegates— she met Lucretia Mott, and the two women resolved to organize a convention to discuss women's rights. Not until 1848, however, did the convention materialize. Of the three hundred or so people who attended the Seneca Falls convention, sixty-eight women and thirty-two men signed the Declaration of Sentiments, but the press on the whole was unfavorable. Not until 1920, with the passage of the Nineteenth Amendment, did women gain the right to vote. (For further details about her life and times, see Stanton's Eighty Years & More: Reminiscences 1815–1897.)

Declaration of Sentiments and Resolutions

When, in the course of human events, it becomes necessary for one portion of the family of man to assume among the people of the earth a position different from that which they have hitherto occupied, but one to which the laws of nature and of nature's God entitle them, a decent respect to the opinions of mankind requires that they should declare the causes that impel them to such a course.

We hold these truths to be self-evident: that all men and women are created equal; that they are endowed by their Creator with certain inalienable rights; that among these are life, liberty, and the pursuit of happiness; that to secure these rights governments are instituted, deriving their just powers from the consent of the governed. Whenever any form of government becomes destructive of these ends, it is the right of those who suffer from it to refuse allegiance to it, and to insist upon the institution of a new government, laying its foundation on such principles, and organizing its powers in such form, as to them shall seem most likely to effect their safety and happiness. Prudence, indeed, will dictate that governments long established should not be changed for light and transient causes; and accordingly all experience hath shown that mankind are more disposed to suffer, while evils are sufferable, than to right themselves by abolishing the forms to which they were accustomed. But when a long train of abuses and usurpations, pursuing invariably the same object, evinces a design to reduce them under absolute despotism, it is their duty to throw off such government, and to provide new guards for their future security. Such has been the patient sufferance of the women under this government, and such is now the necessity which constrains them to demand the equal station to which they are entitled.

The history of mankind is a history of repeated injuries and usurpations on the part of man toward woman, having in direct object the establishment of an absolute tyranny over her. To prove this, let facts be submitted to a candid world.

He has never permitted her to exercise her inalienable right to the elective franchise.

He has compelled her to submit to laws, in the formation of which she had no voice.

He has withheld from her rights which are given to the most ignorant and degraded men—both natives and foreigners.

Having deprived her of this first right of a citizen, the elective franchise, thereby leaving her without representation in the halls of legislation, he has oppressed her on all sides.

He has made her, if married, in the eye of the law, civilly dead.

He has taken from her all right in property, even to the wages she earns.

He has made her, morally, an irresponsible being, as she can commit   10
many crimes with impunity, provided they be done in the presence of her
husband. In the covenant of marriage, she is compelled to promise obedience to her husband, he becoming to all intents and purposes, her master—the law giving him power to deprive her of her liberty, and to administer chastisement.

He has so framed the laws of divorce, as to what shall be the proper
causes, and in case of separation, to whom the guardianship of the children shall be given, as to be wholly regardless of the happiness of
women—the law, in all cases, going upon a false supposition of the
supremacy of man, and giving all power into his hands.

After depriving her of all rights as a married woman, if single, and the
owner of property, he has taxed her to support a government which recognizes her only when her property can be made profitable to it.

He has monopolized nearly all the profitable employments, and from
those she is permitted to follow, she receives but a scanty remuneration.
He closes against her all the avenues to wealth and distinction which he
considers most honorable to himself. As a teacher of theology, medicine,
or law, she is not known.

He has denied her the facilities for obtaining a thorough education, all
colleges being closed against her.

He allows her in Church, as well as State, but a subordinate position,   15
claiming Apostolic authority for her exclusion from the ministry, and, with
some exceptions, from any public participation in the affairs of the Church.

He has created a false public sentiment by giving to the world a different code of morals for men and women, by which moral delinquencies
which exclude women from society, are not only tolerated, but deemed of
little account in man.

He has usurped the prerogative of Jehovah himself, claiming it as his
right to assign for her a sphere of action, when that belongs to her conscience and to her God.

He has endeavored, in every way that he could, to destroy her confidence in her own powers, to lessen her self-respect, and to make her willing to lead a dependent and abject life.

Now, in view of this entire disfranchisement of one-half the people of
this country, their social and religious degradation—in view of the unjust
laws above mentioned, and because women do feel themselves aggrieved,
oppressed, and fraudulently deprived of their most sacred rights, we
insist that they have immediate admission to all the rights and privileges
which belong to them as citizens of the United States.

In entering upon the great work before us, we anticipate no small   20
amount of misconception, misrepresentation, and ridicule; but we shall
use every instrumentality within our power to effect our object. We shall
employ agents, circulate tracts, petition the State and National legislatures, and endeavor to enlist the pulpit and the press in our behalf. We

hope this Convention will be followed by a series of Conventions embracing every part of the country.

[The following resolutions were discussed by Lucretia Mott, Thomas and Mary Ann McClintock, Amy Post, Catharine A. F. Stebbins, and others, and were adopted:]

Whereas, The great precept of nature is conceded to be, that "man shall pursue his own true and substantial happiness." Blackstone in his Commentaries remarks, that this law of Nature being coeval with mankind, and dictated by God himself, is of course superior in obligation to any other. It is binding over all the globe, in all countries, and at all times; no human laws are of any validity if contrary to this, and such of them as are valid, derive all their force, and all their validity, and all their authority, mediately and immediately, from this original; therefore,

Resolved, That such laws as conflict, in any way, with the true and substantial happiness of woman, are contrary to the great precept of nature and of no validity, for this is "superior in obligation to any other."

Resolved, That all laws which prevent woman from occupying such a station in society as her conscience shall dictate, or which place her in a position inferior to that of man, are contrary to the great precept of nature, and therefore of no force or authority.

Resolved, That woman is man's equal—was intended to be so by the Creator, and the highest good of the race demands that she should be recognized as such.

Resolved, That the women of this country ought to be enlightened in regard to the laws under which they live, that they may no longer publish their degradation by declaring themselves satisfied with their present position, nor their ignorance, by asserting that they have all the rights they want.

Resolved, That inasmuch as man, while claiming for himself intellectual superiority, does accord to woman moral superiority, it is preeminently his duty to encourage her to speak and teach, as she has an opportunity, in all religious assemblies.

Resolved, That the same amount of virtue, delicacy, and refinement of behavior that is required of woman in the social state, should also be required of man, and the same transgressions should be visited with equal severity on both man and woman.

Resolved, That the objection of indelicacy and impropriety, which is so often brought against woman when she addresses a public audience, comes with a very ill-grace from those who encourage, by their attendance, her appearance on the stage, in the concert, or in feats of the circus.

Resolved, That woman has too long rested satisfied in the circumscribed limits which corrupt customs and a perverted application of the Scriptures have marked out for her, and that it is time she should move in the enlarged sphere which her great Creator has assigned her.

Resolved, That it is the duty of the women of this country to secure to themselves their sacred right to the elective franchise.

Resolved, That the equality of human rights results necessarily from the fact of the identity of the race in capabilities and responsibilities.

Resolved, therefore, That, being invested by the Creator with the same capabilities, and the same consciousness of responsibility for their exercise, it is demonstrably the right and duty of woman, equally with man, to promote every righteous cause by every righteous means; and especially in regard to the great subjects of morals and religion, it is self-evidently her right to participate with her brother in teaching them, both in private and in public, by writing and by speaking, by any instrumentalities proper to be used, and in any assemblies proper to be held; and this being a self-evident truth growing out of the divinely implanted principles of human nature, any custom or authorities adverse to it, whether modern or wearing the hoary sanction of antiquity, is to be regarded as a self-evident falsehood, and at war with mankind.

[At the last session Lucretia Mott offered and spoke to the following resolution:]

Resolved, That the speedy success of our cause depends upon the zealous and untiring efforts of both men and women, for the overthrow of the monopoly of the pulpit, and for the securing to woman an equal participation with men in the various trades, professions, and commerce.

✎ Topics for Critical Thinking and Writing

1. Stanton echoes the Declaration of Independence because she wishes to associate her ideas and the movement she supports with a document and a movement that her readers esteem. And of course she must have believed that if readers esteem the Declaration of Independence, they must grant the justice of her goals. Does her strategy work, or does it backfire by making her essay seem strained?
2. The Declaration claims that women have "the same capabilities" as men (paragraph 32). Yet in 1848 Stanton and the others at Seneca Falls knew, or should have known, that history recorded no example of an outstanding woman philosopher to compare with Plato or Kant, a great composer to compare with Beethoven or Chopin, a scientist to compare with Galileo or Newton, or a creative mathematician to compare with Euclid or Descartes. Do these facts contradict the Declaration's claim? If not, why not? How else but by different intellectual capabilities do you think such facts are to be explained?
3. Stanton's Declaration is almost 150 years old. Have all of the issues she raised been satisfactorily resolved? If not, which ones remain?
4. In our society, children have very few rights. For instance, a child cannot decide to drop out of elementary school or high school, and a child cannot decide to leave his or her parents in order to reside with some other family that he or she finds more compatible. Whatever your view of children's rights, compose the best Declaration of the Rights of Children that you can.

Virginia Woolf

Virginia Woolf (1882–1941) was born in London into an upper-middle-class literary family. In 1912 she married a writer, and with him she founded the Hogarth Press, whose important publications included not only books by T. S. Eliot but also her own novels.
This essay was originally a talk delivered in 1931 to The Women's Service League.

Professions for Women

When your secretary invited me to come here, she told me that your Society is concerned with the employment of women and she suggested that I might tell you something about my own professional experiences. It is true I am a woman; it is true I am employed, but what professional experiences have I had? It is difficult to say. My profession is literature; and in that profession there are fewer experiences for women than in any other, with the exception of the stage—fewer, I mean, that are peculiar to women. For the road was cut many years ago—by Fanny Burney, by Aphra Behn, by Harriet Martineau, by Jane Austen, by George Eliot— many famous women, and many more unknown and forgotten, have been before me, making the path smooth, and regulating my steps. Thus, when I came to write, there were very few material obstacles in my way. Writing was a reputable and harmless occupation. The family peace was not broken by the scratching of a pen. No demand was made upon the family purse. For ten and sixpence one can buy paper enough to write all the plays of Shakespeare—if one has a mind that way. Pianos and models, Paris, Vienna and Berlin, masters and mistresses, are not needed by a writer. The cheapness of writing paper is, of course, the reason why women have succeeded as writers before they have succeeded in the other professions.

But to tell you my story—it is a simple one. You have only got to figure to yourselves a girl in a bedroom with a pen in her hand. She had only to move that pen from left to right—from ten o'clock to one. Then it occurred to her to do what is simple and cheap enough after all—to slip a few of those pages into an envelope, fix a penny stamp in the corner, and drop the envelope in the red box at the corner. It was thus that I became a journalist; and my effort was rewarded on the first day of the following month—a very glorious day it was for me—by a letter from an editor containing a check for one pound ten shillings and sixpence. But to show you how little I deserve to be called a professional woman, how little I know of the struggles and difficulties of such lives, I have to admit that instead of spending that sum upon bread and butter, rent, shoes and stockings, or butcher's bills, I went out and bought a cat—a beautiful cat, a Persian cat, which very soon involved me in bitter disputes with my neighbors.

What could be easier than to write articles and to buy Persian cats with the profits? But wait a moment. Articles have to be about something.

Mine, I seem to remember, was about a novel by a famous man. And while I was writing this review, I discovered that if I were going to review books I should need to do battle with a certain phantom. And the phantom was a woman, and when I came to know her better I called her after the heroine of a famous poem, The Angel in the House. It was she who used to come between me and my paper when I was writing reviews. It was she who bothered me and wasted my time and so tormented me that at last I killed her. You who come of a younger and happier generation may not have heard of her—you may not know what I mean by the Angel in the House. I will describe her as shortly as I can. She was intensely sympathetic. She was immensely charming. She was utterly unselfish. She excelled in the difficult arts of family life. She sacrificed herself daily. If there was chicken, she took the leg; if there was a draught she sat in it—in short she was so constituted that she never had a mind or a wish of her own but preferred to sympathize always with the minds and wishes of others. Above all—I need not say it—she was pure. Her purity was supposed to be her chief beauty—her blushes, her great grace. In those days—the last of Queen Victoria—every house had its Angel. And when I came to write I encountered her with the very first words. The shadow of her wings fell on my page; I heard the rustling of her skirts in the room. Directly, that is to say, I took my pen in hand to review that novel by a famous man, she slipped behind me and whispered: "My dear, you are a young woman. You are writing about a book that has been written by a man. Be sympathetic; be tender; flatter; deceive; use all the arts and wiles of our sex. Never let anybody guess that you have a mind of your own. Above all, be pure." And she made as if to guide my pen. I now record the one act for which I take some credit to myself, though the credit rightly belongs to some excellent ancestors of mine who left me a certain sum of money—shall we say five hundred pounds a year?—so that it was not necessary for me to depend solely on charm for my living. I turned upon her and caught her by the throat. I did my best to kill her. My excuse, if I were to be had up in a court of law, would be that I acted in self-defense. Had I not killed her she would have killed me. She would have plucked the heart out of my writing. For, as I found, directly I put pen to paper, you cannot review even a novel without having a mind of your own, without expressing what you think to be the truth about human relations, morality, sex. And all these questions, according to the Angel in the House, cannot be dealt with freely and openly by women; they must charm, they must conciliate, they must—to put it bluntly—tell lies if they are to succeed. Thus, whenever I felt the shadow of her wing or the radiance of her halo upon my page, I took up the inkpot and flung it at her. She died hard. Her fictitious nature was of great assistance to her. It is far harder to kill a phantom than a reality. She was always creeping back when I thought I had despatched her. Though I flatter myself that I killed her in the end, the struggle was severe; it took much time that had better have been spent upon learning

Greek grammar; or in roaming the world in search of adventures. But it was a real experience; it was an experience that was bound to befall all women writers at that time. Killing the Angel in the House was part of the occupation of a woman writer.

But to continue my story. The Angel was dead; what then remained? You may say that what remained was a simple and common object—a young woman in a bedroom with an inkpot. In other words, now that she had rid herself of falsehood, that young woman had only to be herself. Ah, but what is "herself"? I mean, what is a woman? I assure you, I do not know. I do not believe that you know. I do not believe that anybody can know until she has expressed herself in all the arts and professions open to human skill. That indeed is one of the reasons why I have come here—out of respect for you, who are in process of showing us by your experiments what a woman is, who are in process of providing us, by your failures and successes, with that extremely important piece of information.

But to continue the story of my professional experiences. I made one pound ten and six by my first review; and I bought a Persian cat with the proceeds. Then I grew ambitious. A Persian cat is all very well, I said; but a Persian cat is not enough. I must have a motor car. And it was thus that I became a novelist—for it is a very strange thing that people will give you a motor car if you will tell them a story. It is a still stranger thing that there is nothing so delightful in the world as telling stories. It is far pleasanter than writing reviews of famous novels. And yet, if I am to obey your secretary and tell you my professional experiences as a novelist, I must tell you about a very strange experience that befell me as a novelist. And to understand it you must try first to imagine a novelist's state of mind. I hope I am not giving away professional secrets if I say that a novelist's chief desire is to be as unconscious as possible. He has to induce in himself a state of perpetual lethargy. He wants life to proceed with the utmost quiet and regularity. He wants to see the same faces, to read the same books, to do the same things day after day, month after month, while he is writing, so that nothing may break the illusion in which he is living—so that nothing may disturb or disquiet the mysterious nosings about, feelings round, darts, dashes and sudden discoveries of that very shy and illusive spirit, the imagination. I suspect that this state is the same both for men and women. Be that as it may, I want you to imagine me writing a novel in a state of trance. I want you to figure to yourselves a girl sitting with a pen in her hand, which for minutes, and indeed for hours, she never dips into the inkpot. The image that comes to my mind when I think of this girl is the image of a fisherman lying sunk in dreams on the verge of a deep lake with a rod held out over the water. She was letting her imagination sweep unchecked round every rock and cranny of the world that lies submerged in the depths of our unconscious being. Now came the experience, the experience that I believe to be far commoner with women writers than with men. The line raced through the girl's fingers. Her imagination had rushed away. It had sought the pools, the depths, the dark places where the largest fish slumber. And then there was a smash. There was an explosion. There was foam and confusion. The imagination had dashed itself against something hard. The girl was roused from her dream. She was indeed in a state of the most acute and difficult distress. To speak without figure she had thought of something, something about the body, about the passions which it was unfitting for her as a woman to say. Men, her reason told her, would be shocked. The consciousness of what men will say of a woman who speaks the truth about her passions had roused her from her artist's state of unconsciousness. She could write no more. The trance was over. Her imagination could work no longer. This I believe to be a very common experience with women writers—they are impeded by the extreme conventionality of the other sex. For though men sensibly allow themselves great freedom in these respects, I doubt that they realize or can control the extreme severity with which they condemn such freedom in women.

These then were two very genuine experiences of my own. These were two of the adventures of my professional life. The first—killing the Angel in the House—I think I solved. She died. But the second, telling the truth about my own experiences as a body, I do not think I solved. I doubt that any woman has solved it yet. The obstacles against her are still immensely powerful—and yet they are very difficult to define. Outwardly, what is simpler than to write books? Outwardly, what obstacles are there for a woman rather than for a man? Inwardly, I think the case is very different; she has still many ghosts to fight, many prejudices to overcome. Indeed it will be a long time still, I think, before a woman can sit down to write a book without finding a phantom to be slain, a rock to be dashed against. And if this is so in literature, the freest of all professions for women, how is it in the new professions which you are now for the first time entering?

Those are the questions that I should like, had I time, to ask you. And indeed, if I have laid stress upon these professional experiences of mine, it is because I believe that they are, though in different forms, yours also. Even when the path is nominally open—when there is nothing to prevent a woman from being a doctor, a lawyer, a civil servant—there are many phantoms and obstacles, as I believe, looming in her way. To discuss and define them is I think of great value and importance; for thus only can the labor be shared, the difficulties be solved. But besides this, it is necessary also to discuss the ends and the aims for which we are fighting, for which we are doing battle with these formidable obstacles. Those aims cannot be taken for granted; they must be perpetually questioned and examined. The whole position, as I see it—here in this hall surrounded by women practising for the first time in history I know not how many different professions—is one of extraordinary interest and importance. You have won rooms of your own in the house hitherto exclusively owned by men. You are able, though not without great labor and effort, to pay the rent. You are earning your five hundred pounds a year. But this freedom is only a beginning; the room is your own, but it is still bare. It has to be furnished; it has to be decorated; it has to be shared. How are you going to furnish it, how are you going to decorate it? With whom are you going to share it, and upon what terms? These, I think, are questions of the utmost importance and interest. For the first time in history you are able to ask them; for the first time you are able to decide for yourselves what the answers should be. Willingly would I stay and discuss those questions and answers—but not tonight. My time is up; and I must cease.

 ## Topics for Critical Thinking and Writing

1. How would you characterize Woolf's tone, especially her attitude toward her subject and herself, in the first paragraph?
2. What do you think Woolf means when she says (paragraph 3): "It is far harder to kill a phantom than a reality"?
3. Woolf conjectures (paragraph 6) that she has not solved the problem of "telling the truth about my own experiences as a body." Is there any reason to believe that today a woman has more difficulty than a man in telling the truth about the experiences of the body?
4. In paragraph 7, Woolf suggests that phantoms as well as obstacles impede women from becoming doctors and lawyers. What might some of these phantoms be?
5. This essay is highly metaphoric. Speaking roughly (or, rather, as precisely as possible), what is the meaning of the metaphor of "rooms" in the final paragraph? What does Woolf mean when she says: "The room is your own, but it is still bare. . . . With whom are you going to share it, and upon what terms?"
6. Evaluate the last two sentences. Are they too abrupt and mechanical? Or do they provide a fitting conclusion to the speech?

May Sarton

May Sarton (1912–95), born in Belgium, was brought to the United States in 1916 and in 1924 she became a citizen. A teacher of writing and a distinguished writer herself, she has received numerous awards for her fiction, poetry, and essays.

The Rewards of Living a Solitary Life

The other day an acquaintance of mine, a gregarious and charming man, told me he had found himself unexpectedly alone in New York for an hour or two between appointments. He went to the Whitney and spent the "empty" time looking at things in solitary bliss. For him it proved to be a shock nearly as great as falling in love to discover that he could enjoy himself so much alone.

What had he been afraid of, I asked myself? That, suddenly alone, he would discover that he bored himself, or that there was, quite simply, no self there to meet? But having taken the plunge, he is now on the brink of adventure; he is about to be launched into his own inner space, space as immense, unexplored, and sometimes frightening as outer space to the astronaut. His every perception will come to him with a new freshness and, for a time, seem startlingly original. For anyone who can see things for himself with a naked eye becomes, for a moment or two, something of a genius. With another human being present vision becomes double vision, inevitably. We are busy wondering, what does my companion see or think of this, and what do I think of it? The original impact gets lost, or diffused.

"Music I heard with you was more than music."[1] Exactly. And therefore music *itself* can only be heard alone. Solitude is the salt of personhood. It brings out the authentic flavor of every experience.

"Alone one is never lonely: the spirit adventures, walking/In a quiet garden, in a cool house, abiding single there."

Loneliness is most acutely felt with other people, for with others, even   5
with a lover sometimes, we suffer from our differences of taste, temperament, mood. Human intercourse often demands that we soften the edge of perception, or withdraw at the very instant of personal truth for fear of hurting, or of being inappropriately present, which is to say naked, in a social situation. Alone we can afford to be wholly whatever we are, and to feel whatever we feel absolutely. That is a great luxury!

For me the most interesting thing about a solitary life, and mine has been that for the last twenty years, is that it becomes increasingly rewarding. When I can wake up and watch the sun rise over the ocean, as I do most days, and know that I have an entire day ahead, uninterrupted, in which to write a few pages, take a walk with my dog, lie down in the afternoon for a long think (why does one think better in a horizontal position?), read and listen to music, I am flooded with happiness.

---

[1]**Music . . . music":** A line from Conrad Aiken's *Bread and Music* (1914).

I am lonely only when I am overtired, when I have worked too long without a break, when for the time being I feel empty and need filling up. And I am lonely sometimes when I come back home after a lecture trip, when I have seen a lot of people and talked a lot, and am full to the brim with experience that needs to be sorted out.

Then for a little while the house feels huge and empty, and I wonder where my self is hiding. It has to be recaptured slowly by watering the plants, perhaps, and looking again at each one as though it were a person, by feeding the two cats, by cooking a meal.

It takes a while, as I watch the surf blowing up in fountains at the end of the field, but the moment comes when the world falls away, and the self emerges again from the deep unconscious, bringing back all I have recently experienced to be explored and slowly understood, when I can converse again with my hidden powers, and so grow, and so be renewed, till death do us part.

✎ Topics for Critical Thinking and Writing

1. The essay opens with an anecdote about an acquaintance of the author's. Why are we told at the outset that he is "a gregarious and charming man"?

2. In paragraph 2 Sarton compares inner space with outer space. And in paragraph 3 she writes. "Solitude is the salt of personhood." How do you interpret these metaphors? How do they enrich her main point, that solitude is rewarding?

3. What does Sarton mean when in her first paragraph she says, "Anyone who can see things for himself with a naked eye becomes, for a moment or two, something of a genius"? Does your own experience confirm her comment? Explain.

4. What phrase in the last paragraph connects the ending with the first paragraph?

5. Drawing on Sarton's essay, in a paragraph explain the distinction between being "alone" and being "lonely."

6. In an essay of about five hundred words explain the difference between loving and being in love.

Martin Luther King, Jr.

Martin Luther King, Jr. (1929–68), clergyman and civil rights leader, achieved national fame in 1955–56 when he led the boycott against segregated bus lines in Montgomery, Alabama. His policy of passive resistance succeeded in Montgomery, and King then organized the Southern

Christian Leadership Conference in order to extend his efforts. In 1963 Dr. King was arrested in Birmingham, Alabama, for participating in a march for which no parade permit had been issued by the city officials. In jail he wrote a response to a letter that eight local clergymen had published in a newspaper. Their letter titled "A Call for Unity" is printed here, followed by King's response. In 1964 he was awarded the Nobel Peace Prize, but he continued to encounter strong opposition. On April 4, 1968, while in Memphis to support striking sanitation workers, he was shot and killed.

Letter from Birmingham Jail
In Response to "A Call for Unity"

A Call for Unity

April 12, 1963

We the undersigned clergymen are among those who, in January, issued "An Appeal for Law and Order and Common Sense," in dealing with racial problems in Alabama. We expressed understanding that honest convictions in racial matters could properly be pursued in the courts, but urged that decisions of those courts should in the meantime be peacefully obeyed.

Since that time there had been some evidence of increased forebearance and a willingness to face facts. Responsible citizens have undertaken to work on various problems which cause racial friction and unrest. In Birmingham, recent public events have given indication that we all have opportunity for a new constructive and realistic approach to racial problems.

However, we are now confronted by a series of demonstrations by some of our Negro citizens, directed and led in part by outsiders. We recognize the natural impatience of people who feel that their hopes are slow in being realized. But we are convinced that these demonstrations are unwise and untimely.

We agree rather with certain local Negro leadership which has called for honest and open negotiation of racial issues in our area. And we believe this kind of facing of issues can best be accomplished by citizens of our own metropolitan area, white and Negro, meeting with their knowledge and experience of the local situation. All of us need to face that responsibility and find proper channels for its accomplishment.

Just as we formerly pointed out that "hatred and violence have no sanction in our religious and political traditions," we also point out that such actions as incite to hatred and violence, however technically peaceful those actions may be, have not contributed to the resolution of our local problems. We do not believe that these days of new hope are days when extreme measures are justified in Birmingham.

We commend the community as a whole, and the local news media and law enforcement officials in particular, on the calm manner in which these demonstrations have been handled. We urge the public to continue to show restraint should be demonstrations continue, and the law enforcement officials to remain calm and continue to protect our city from violence.

We further strongly urge our own Negro community to withdraw support from these demonstrations, and to unite locally in working peacefully for a better

Birmingham. When rights are consistently denied, a cause should be pressed in the courts and in negotiations among local leaders, and not in the streets. We appeal to both our white and Negro citizenry to observe the principles of law and order and common sense.

C.C.J. Carpenter, D.D., L.L.D., Bishop of Alabama; Joseph A. Durick, D.D., Auxiliary Bishop, Diocese of Mobile-Birmingham; Rabbi Milton L. Grafman, Temple Emanu-El, Birmingham, Alabama; Bishop Paul Hardin, Bishop of the Alabama–West Florida Conference of the Methodist Church; Bishop Nolan B. Harmon, Bishop of the North Alabama Conference of the Methodist Church; George M. Murray, D.D., L.L.D., Bishop Coadjutor, Episcopal Diocese of Alabama; Edward V. Ramage, Moderator, Synod of the Alabama Presbyterian Church in the United States; Earl Stallings, Pastor, First Baptist Church, Birmingham, Alabama.

Letter from Birmingham Jail

April 16, 1963

My Dear Fellow Clergymen:

While confined here in the Birmingham city jail, I came across your recent statement calling my present activities "unwise and untimely."[1] Seldom do I pause to answer criticism of my work and ideas. If I sought to answer all the criticisms that cross my desk, my secretaries would have little time for anything other than such correspondence in the course of the day, and I would have no time for constructive work. But since I feel that you are men of genuine good will and that your criticisms are sincerely set forth, I want to try to answer your statement in what I hope will be patient and reasonable terms.

I think I should indicate why I am here in Birmingham, since you have been influenced by the view which argues against "outsiders coming in." I have the honor of serving as president of the Southern Christian Leadership Conference, an organization operating in every southern state, with headquarters in Atlanta, Georgia. We have some eighty-five affiliated organizations across the South, and one of them is the Alabama Christian Movement for Human Rights. Frequently we share staff, educational, and financial resources with our affiliates. Several months ago the affiliate here in Birmingham asked us to be on call to engage in a nonviolent direct-action program if such were deemed necessary. We readily consented, and

---

[1]This response to a published statement by eight fellow clergymen from Alabama (Bishop C.C.J. Carpenter, Bishop Joseph A. Durick, Rabbi Milton L. Grafman, Bishop Paul Hardin, Bishop Nolan B. Harmon, the Reverend George M. Murray, the Reverend Edward V. Ramage, and the Reverend Earl Stallings) was composed under somewhat constricting circumstances. Begun on the margins of the newspaper in which the statement appeared while I was in jail, the letter was continued on scraps of writing paper supplied by a friendly Negro trusty, and concluded on a pad my attorneys were eventually permitted to leave me. Although the text remains in substance unaltered, I have indulged in the author's prerogative of polishing it for publication. [King's note]

when the hour came we lived up to our promise. So I, along with several members of my staff, am here because I was invited here. I am here because I have organizational ties here.

But more basically, I am in Birmingham because injustice is here. Just as the prophets of the eighth century B.C. left their villages and carried their "thus saith the Lord" far beyond the boundaries of their home towns, and just as the Apostle Paul left his village of Tarsus and carried the gospel of Jesus Christ to the far corners of the Greco-Roman world, so am I compelled to carry the gospel of freedom beyond my own home town. Like Paul, I must constantly respond to the Macedonian call for aid.

Moreover, I am cognizant of the interrelatedness of all communities and states. I cannot sit idly by in Atlanta and not be concerned about what happens in Birmingham. Injustice anywhere is a threat to justice everywhere. We are caught in an inescapable network of mutuality; tied in a single garment of destiny. Whatever affects one directly, affects all indirectly. Never again can we afford to live with the narrow, provincial "outside agitator" idea. Anyone who lives inside the United States can never be considered an outsider anywhere within its bounds.

You deplore the demonstrations taking place in Birmingham. But your statement, I am sorry to say, fails to express a similar concern for the conditions that brought about the demonstrations. I am sure that none of you would want to rest content with the superficial kind of social analysis that deals merely with effects and does not grapple with underlying causes. It is unfortunate that demonstrations are taking place in Birmingham, but it is even more unfortunate that the city's white power structure left the Negro community with no alternative.

In any nonviolent campaign there are four basic steps: collection of the facts to determine whether injustices exist; negotiation; self-purification; and direct action. We have gone through all these steps in Birmingham. There can be no gainsaying the fact that racial injustice engulfs this community. Birmingham is probably the most thoroughly segregated city in the United States. Its ugly record of brutality is widely known. Negroes have experienced grossly unjust treatment in the courts. There have been more unsolved bombings of Negro homes and churches in Birmingham than in any other city in the nation. These are the hard, brutal facts of the case. On the basis of these conditions, Negro leaders sought to negotiate with the city fathers. But the latter consistently refused to engage in good-faith negotiation.

Then, last September, came the opportunity to talk with leaders of Birmingham's economic community. In the course of the negotiations, certain promises were made by the merchants—for example, to remove the stores' humiliating racial signs. On the basis of these promises, the Reverend Fred Shuttlesworth and the leaders of the Alabama Christian Movement for Human Rights agreed to a moratorium on all demonstrations. As the weeks and months went by, we realized that we were the victims of a broken promise. A few signs, briefly removed, returned; the others remained.

As in so many past experiences, our hopes had been blasted, and the shadow of deep disappointment settled upon us. We had no alternative except to prepare for direct action, whereby we would present our very bodies as a means of laying our case before the conscience of the local and the national community. Mindful of the difficulties involved, we decided to undertake a process of self-purification. We began a series of workshops on nonviolence, and we repeatedly asked ourselves: "Are you able to accept blows without retaliating?" "Are you able to endure the ordeal of jail?" We decided to schedule our direct-action program for the Easter season, realizing that except for Christmas, this is the main shopping period of the year. Knowing that a strong economic-withdrawal program would be the by-product of direct action, we felt that this would be the best time to bring pressure to bear on the merchants for the needed change.

Then it occurred to us that Birmingham's mayoralty election was coming up in March, and we speedily decided to postpone action until after election day. When we discovered that the Commissioner of Public Safety, Eugene "Bull" Connor, had piled up enough votes to be in the run-off, we decided again to postpone action until the day after the run-off so that the demonstrations could not be used to cloud the issues. Like many others, we waited to see Mr. Connor defeated, and to this end we endured postponement after postponement. Having aided in this community need, we felt that our direct-action program could be delayed no longer.

You may well ask: "Why direct action? Why sit-ins, marches, and so   10
forth? Isn't negotiation a better path?" You are quite right in calling for negotiation. Indeed, this is the very purpose of direct action. Nonviolent direct action seeks to create such a crisis and foster such a tension that a community which has constantly refused to negotiate is forced to confront the issue. It seeks so to dramatize the issue that it can no longer be ignored. My citing the creation of tension as part of the work of the nonviolent resister may sound rather shocking. But I must confess that I am not afraid of the word "tension." I have earnestly opposed violent tension, but there is a type of constructive, nonviolent tension which is necessary for growth. Just as Socrates felt that it was necessary to create a tension in the mind so that individuals could rise from the bondage of myths and half-truths to the unfettered realm of creative analysis and objective appraisal, so must we see the need for nonviolent gadflies to create the kind of tension in society that will help men rise from the dark depths of prejudice and racism to the majestic heights of understanding and brotherhood.

The purpose of our direct-action program is to create a situation so crisis-packed that it will inevitably open the door to negotiation. I therefore concur with you in your call for negotiation. Too long has our beloved Southland been bogged down in a tragic effort to live in monologue rather than dialogue.

One of the basic points in your statement is that the action that I and my associates have taken in Birmingham is untimely. Some have asked: "Why didn't you give the new city administration time to act?" The only answer that I can give to this query is that the new Birmingham administration must be prodded about as much as the outgoing one, before it will act. We are sadly mistaken if we feel that the election of Albert Boutwell as mayor will bring the millennium to Birmingham. While Mr. Boutwell is a much more gentle person than Mr. Connor, they are both segregationists, dedicated to maintenance of the status quo. I have hope that Mr. Boutwell will be reasonable enough to see the futility of massive resistance to desegregation. But he will not see this without pressure from devotees of civil rights. My friends, I must say to you that we have not made a single gain in civil rights without determined legal and nonviolent pressure. Lamentably, it is an historical fact that privileged groups seldom give up their privileges voluntarily. Individuals may see the moral light and voluntarily give up their unjust posture; but as Reinhold Niebuhr[2] has reminded us, groups tend to be more immoral than individuals.

We know through painful experience that freedom is never voluntarily given by the oppressor; it must be demanded by the oppressed. Frankly, I have yet to engage in a direct-action campaign that was "well timed" in the view of those who have not suffered unduly from the disease of segregation. For years now I have heard the word "Wait!" It rings in the ear of every Negro with piercing familiarity. This "Wait" has almost always meant "Never." We must come to see, with one of our distinguished jurists, that "justice too long delayed is justice denied."[3]

We have waited for more than 340 years for our constitutional and God-given rights. The nations of Asia and Africa are moving with jetlike speed toward gaining political independence, but we still creep at horse-and-buggy pace toward gaining a cup of coffee at a lunch counter. Perhaps it is easy for those who have never felt the stinging darts of segregation to say, "Wait." But when you have seen vicious mobs lynch your mothers and fathers at will and drown your sisters and brothers at whim; when you have seen hate-filled policemen curse, kick, and even kill your black brothers and sisters; when you see the vast majority of your twenty million Negro brothers smothering in an airtight cage of poverty in the midst of an affluent society; when you suddenly find your tongue twisted and your speech stammering as you seek to explain to your six-year-old daughter why she can't go to the public amusement park that has just been advertised on television, and see tears welling up in her eyes when she is told that Funtown is closed to colored children, and see ominous clouds of inferiority beginning to form in her little mental sky, and see her beginning to distort her personality by developing an unconscious bitterness toward white people; when you have to concoct an answer for a five-year-old son who is asking: "Daddy, why do white people treat colored

---

[2]**Reinhold Niebuhr** (1892–1971). Minister, political activist, author, and professor of applied Christianity at Union Theological Seminary. [This and the following notes are the editors'.]
[3]**Justice . . . denied:** A quotation attributed to William E. Gladstone (1809–98), British statesman and prime minister.

people so mean?"; when you take a cross-country drive and find it necessary to sleep night after night in the uncomfortable corners of your automobile because no motel will accept you; when you are humiliated day in and day out by nagging signs reading "white" and "colored"; when your first name becomes "nigger," your middle name becomes "boy" (however old you are) and your last name becomes "John," and your wife and mother are never given the respected title "Mrs."; when you are harried by day and haunted by night by the fact that you are a Negro, living constantly at tiptoe stance, never quite knowing what to expect next, and are plagued with inner fears and outer resentments; when you are forever fighting a degenerating sense of "nobodiness"—then you will understand why we find it difficult to wait. There comes a time when the cup of endurance runs over, and men are no longer willing to be plunged into the abyss of despair. I hope, sirs, you can understand our legitimate and unavoidable impatience.

You express a great deal of anxiety over our willingness to break laws.   15
This is certainly a legitimate concern. Since we so diligently urge people to obey the Supreme Court's decision of 1954 outlawing segregation in the public schools, at first glance it may seem rather paradoxical for us consciously to break laws. One may well ask: "How can you advocate breaking some laws and obeying others?" The answer lies in the fact that there are two types of laws: just and unjust. I would be the first to advocate obeying just laws. One has not only a legal but a moral responsibility to obey just laws. Conversely, one has a moral responsibility to disobey unjust laws. I would agree with St. Augustine that "an unjust law is no law at all."

Now, what is the difference between the two? How does one determine whether a law is just or unjust? A just law is a man-made code that squares with the moral law or the law of God. An unjust law is a code that is out of harmony with the moral law. To put it in the terms of St. Thomas Aquinas: An unjust law is a human law that is not rooted in eternal law and natural law. Any law that uplifts human personality is just. Any law that degrades human personality is unjust. All segregation statutes are unjust because segregation distorts the soul and damages the personality. It gives the segregator a false sense of superiority and the segregated a false sense of inferiority. Segregation, to use the terminology of the Jewish philosopher Martin Buber, substitutes an "I-it" relationship for an "I-thou" relationship and ends up relegating persons to the status of things. Hence segregation is not only politically, economically, and sociologically unsound, it is morally wrong and sinful. Paul Tillich[4] has said that sin is separation. Is not segregation an existential expression of man's tragic

---

[4]**Paul Tillich:** Tillich (1886–1965), born in Germany; taught theology at several German universities, but in 1933 he was dismissed from his post at the University of Frankfurt because of his opposition to the Nazi regime. At the invitation of Reinhold Niebuhr, he came to the United States and taught at Union Theological Seminary.

separation, his awful estrangement, his terrible sinfulness? Thus it is that I can urge men to obey the 1954 decision of the Supreme Court, for it is morally right; and I can urge them to disobey segregation ordinances, for they are morally wrong.

Let us consider a more concrete example of just and unjust laws. An unjust law is a code that a numerical or power majority group compels a minority group to obey but does not make binding on itself. This is *difference* made legal. By the same token, a just law is a code that a majority compels a minority to follow and that it is willing to follow itself. This is *sameness* made legal.

Let me give another explanation. A law is unjust if it is inflicted on a minority that, as a result of being denied the right to vote, had no part in enacting or devising the law. Who can say that the legislature of Alabama which set up that state's segregation laws was democratically elected? Throughout Alabama all sorts of devious methods are used to prevent Negroes from becoming registered voters, and there are some counties in which, even though Negroes constitute a majority of the population, not a single Negro is registered. Can any law enacted under such circumstances be considered democratically structured?

Sometimes a law is just on its face and unjust in its application. For instance, I have been arrested on a charge of parading without a permit. Now, there is nothing wrong in having an ordinance which requires a permit for a parade. But such an ordinance becomes unjust when it is used to maintain segregation and to deny citizens the First Amendment privilege of peaceful assembly and protest.

I hope you are able to see the distinction I am trying to point out. In no sense do I advocate evading or defying the law, as would the rabid segregationist. That would lead to anarchy. One who breaks an unjust law must do so openly, lovingly, and with a willingness to accept the penalty. I submit that an individual who breaks a law that conscience tells him is unjust, and who willingly accepts the penalty of imprisonment in order to arouse the conscience of the community over its injustice, is in reality expressing the highest respect for law.   20

Of course, there is nothing new about this kind of civil disobedience. It was evidenced sublimely in the refusal of Shadrach, Meshach, and Abednego to obey the laws of Nebuchadnezzar, on the ground that a higher moral law was at stake. It was practiced superbly by the early Christians, who were willing to face hungry lions and the excruciating pain of chopping blocks rather than submit to certain unjust laws of the Roman Empire. To a degree, academic freedom is a reality today because Socrates practiced civil disobedience. In our own nation, the Boston Tea Party represented a massive act of civil disobedience.

We should never forget that everything Adolf Hitler did in Germany was "legal" and everything the Hungarian freedom fighters did in Hungary was "illegal." It was "illegal" to aid and comfort a Jew in Hitler's Germany. Even so, I am sure that, had I lived in Germany at the time, I would have aided and comforted my Jewish brothers. If today I lived in a Communist country where certain principles dear to the Christian faith are suppressed, I would openly advocate disobeying that country's anti-religious laws.

I must make two honest confessions to you, my Christian and Jewish brothers. First, I must confess that over the past few years I have been gravely disappointed with the white moderate. I have almost reached the regrettable conclusion that the Negro's great stumbling block in his stride toward freedom is not the White Citizen's Counciler or the Ku Klux Klanner, but the white moderate, who is more devoted to "order" than to justice; who prefers a negative peace which is the absence of tension to a positive peace which is the presence of justice; who constantly says: "I agree with you in the goal you seek, but I cannot agree with your methods or direct action"; who paternalistically believes he can set the timetable for another man's freedom; who lives by a mythical concept of time and who constantly advises the Negro to wait for a "more convenient season." Shallow understanding from people of good will is more frustrating than absolute misunderstanding from people of ill will. Lukewarm acceptance is much more bewildering than outright rejection.

I had hoped that the white moderate would understand that law and order exist for the purpose of establishing justice and that when they fail in this purpose they become the dangerously structured dams that block the flow of social progress. I had hoped that the white moderate would understand that the present tension in the South is a necessary phase of the transition from an obnoxious negative peace, in which the Negro passively accepted his unjust plight, to a substantive and positive peace, in which all men will respect the dignity and worth of human personality. Actually, we who engage in nonviolent direct action are not the creators of tension. We merely bring to the surface the hidden tension that is already alive. We bring it out in the open, where it can be seen and dealt with. Like a boil that can never be cured so long as it is covered up but must be opened with all its ugliness to the natural medicines of air and light, injustice must be exposed, with all the tension its exposure creates, to the light of human conscience and the air of national opinion before it can be cured.

In your statement you assert that our actions, even though peaceful, must be condemned because they precipitate violence. But is this a logical assertion? Isn't this like condemning a robbed man because his possession of money precipitated the evil act of robbery? Isn't this like condemning Socrates because his unswerving commitment to truth and his philosophical inquiries precipitated the act by the misguided populace in which they made him drink hemlock? Isn't this like condemning Jesus because his unique God-consciousness and never-ceasing devotion to God's will precipitated the evil act of crucifixion? We must come to see that, as the federal courts have consistently affirmed, it is wrong to urge an individual to cease his efforts to gain his basic constitutional rights because the quest may precipitate violence. Society must protect the robbed and punish the robber.

I had also hoped that the white moderate would reject the myth concerning time in relation to the struggle for freedom. I have just received a letter from a white brother in Texas. He writes: "All Christians know that the colored people will receive equal rights eventually, but it is possible that you are in too great a religious hurry. It has taken Christianity almost two thousand years to accomplish what it has. The teachings of Christ take time to come to earth." Such an attitude stems from a tragic misconception of time, from the strangely irrational notion that there is something in the very flow of time that will inevitably cure all ills. Actually, time itself is neutral; it can be used either destructively or constructively. More and more I feel that the people of ill will have used time much more effectively than have the people of good will. We will have to repent in this generation not merely for the hateful words and actions of the bad people but for the appalling silence of the good people. Human progress never rolls in on wheels of inevitability; it comes through the tireless efforts of men willing to be co-workers with God, and without this hard work, time itself becomes an ally of the forces of social stagnation. We must use time creatively, in the knowledge that the time is always ripe to do right. Now is the time to make real the promise of democracy and transform our pending national elegy into a creative psalm of brotherhood. Now is the time to lift our national policy from the quicksand of racial injustice to the solid rock of human dignity.

You speak of our activity in Birmingham as extreme. At first I was rather disappointed that fellow clergymen would see my nonviolent efforts as those of an extremist. I began thinking about the fact that I stand in the middle of two opposing forces in the Negro community. One is a force of complacency, made up in part of Negroes who, as a result of long years of oppression, are so drained of self-respect and a sense of "somebodiness" that they have adjusted to segregation; and in part of a few middle-class Negroes who, because of a degree of academic and economic security and because in some ways they profit by segregation, have become insensitive to the problems of the masses. The other force is one of bitterness and hatred, and it comes perilously close to advocating violence. It is expressed in the various black nationalist groups that are springing up across the nation, the largest and best-known being Elijah Muhammad's Muslim movement. Nourished by the Negro's frustration over the continued existence of racial discrimination, this movement is made up of people who have lost faith in America, who have absolutely repudiated Christianity, and who have concluded that the white man is an incorrigible "devil."

I have tried to stand between these two forces, saying that we need emulate neither the "do-nothingism" of the complacent nor the hatred and despair of the black nationalist. For there is the more excellent way of love and nonviolent protest. I am grateful to God that, through the influence of the Negro church, the way of nonviolence became an integral part of our struggle.

If this philosophy had not emerged, by now many streets of the South should, I am convinced, be flowing with blood. And I am further convinced that if our white brothers dismiss as "rabble-rousers" and "outside agitators" those of us who employ nonviolent direct action, and if they refuse to support our nonviolent efforts, millions of Negroes will, out of frustration and despair, seek solace and security in black-nationalist ideologies—a development that would inevitably lead to a frightening racial nightmare.

Oppressed people cannot remain oppressed forever. The yearning for 30 freedom eventually manifests itself, and that is what has happened to the American Negro. Something within has reminded him of his birthright of freedom, and something without has reminded him that it can be gained. Consciously or unconsciously, he has been caught up by the *Zeitgeist*,[5] and with his black brothers of Africa and his brown and yellow brothers of Asia, South America, and the Caribbean, the United States Negro is moving with a sense of great urgency toward the promised land of racial justice. If one recognizes this vital urge that has engulfed the Negro community, one should readily understand why public demonstrations are taking place. The Negro has many pent-up resentments and latent frustrations, and he must release them. So let him march; let him make prayer pilgrimages to the city hall; let him go on freedom rides—and try to understand why he must do so. If his repressed emotions are not released in nonviolent ways, they will seek expression through violence; this is not a threat but a fact of history. So I have not said to my people: "Get rid of your discontent." Rather, I have tried to say that this normal and healthy discontent can be channeled into the creative outlet of nonviolent direct action. And now this approach is being termed extremist.

But though I was initially disappointed at being categorized as an extremist, as I continued to think about the matter I gradually gained a measure of satisfaction from the label. Was not Jesus an extremist for love: "Love your enemies, bless them that curse you, do good to them that hate you, and pray for them which despitefully use you, and persecute you." Was not Amos an extremist for justice: "Let justice roll down like waters and righteousness like an ever-flowing stream." Was not Paul an extremist for the Christian gospel: "I bear in my body the marks of the Lord Jesus." Was not Martin Luther an extremist: "Here I stand; I cannot do otherwise, so help me God." And John Bunyan: "I will stay in jail to the end of my days before I make a butchery of my conscience." And Abraham Lincoln: "This nation cannot survive half slave and half free." And Thomas Jefferson: "We hold these truths to be self-evident, that all men are created equal. . . ." So the question is not whether we will be extremists,

---

[5]*Zeitgeist:* German for "spirit of the age."

but what kind of extremists we will be. Will we be extremists for hate or for love? Will we be extremists for the preservation of injustice or for the extension of justice? In that dramatic scene on Calvary's hill three men were crucified. We must never forget that all three were crucified for the same crime—the crime of extremism. Two were extremists for immorality, and thus fell below their environment. The other, Jesus Christ, was an extremist for love, truth, and goodness, and thereby rose above his environment. Perhaps the South, the nation, and the world are in dire need of creative extremists.

I had hoped that the white moderate would see this need. Perhaps I was too optimistic; perhaps I expected too much. I suppose I should have realized that few members of the oppressor race can understand the deep groans and passionate yearnings of the oppressed race, and still fewer have the vision to see that injustice must be rooted out by strong, persistent, and determined action. I am thankful, however, that some of our white brothers in the South have grasped the meaning of this social revolution and committed themselves to it. They are still all too few in quantity, but they are big in quality. Some—such as Ralph McGill, Lillian Smith, Harry Golden, James McBride Dabbs, Ann Braden, and Sarah Patton Boyle—have written about our struggle in eloquent and prophetic terms. Others have marched with us down nameless streets of the South. They have languished in filthy, roach-infested jails, suffering the abuse and brutality of policemen who view them as "dirty nigger-lovers." Unlike so many of their moderate brothers and sisters, they have recognized the urgency of the moment and sensed the need for powerful "action" antidotes to combat the disease of segregation.

Let me take note of my other major disappointment. I have been so greatly disappointed with the white church and its leadership. Of course, there are some notable exceptions. I am not unmindful of the fact that each of you has taken some significant stands on this issue. I commend you, Reverend Stallings, for your Christian stand on this past Sunday, in welcoming Negroes to your worship service on a nonsegregated basis. I commend the Catholic leaders of this state for integrating Spring Hill College several years ago.

But despite these notable exceptions, I must honestly reiterate that I have been disappointed with the church. I do not say this as one of those negative critics who can always find something wrong with the church. I say this as a minister of the gospel, who loves the church; who was nurtured in its bosom; who has been sustained by its spiritual blessings and who will remain true to it as long as the cord of life shall lengthen.

When I was suddenly catapulted into the leadership of the bus protest 35 in Montgomery, Alabama, a few years ago, I felt we would be supported by the white church. I felt that the white ministers, priests, and rabbis of the South would be among our strongest allies. Instead, some have been outright opponents, refusing to understand the freedom movement and misrepresenting its leaders; all too many others have been more cautious than courageous and have remained silent behind the anesthetizing security of stained-glass windows.

In spite of my shattered dreams, I came to Birmingham with the hope that the white religious leadership of this community would see the justice of our cause and, with deep moral concern, would serve as the channel through which our just grievances could reach the power structure. I had hoped that each of you would understand. But again I have been disappointed.

I have heard numerous southern religious leaders admonish their worshipers to comply with a desegregation decision because it is the law, but I have longed to hear white ministers declare: "Follow this decree because integration is morally right and because the Negro is your brother." In the midst of blatant injustices inflicted upon the Negro, I have watched white churchmen stand on the sideline and mouth pious irrelevancies and sanctimonious trivialities. In the midst of a mighty struggle to rid our nation of racial and economic injustice, I have heard many ministers say: "Those are social issues, with which the gospel has no real concern." And I have watched many churches commit themselves to a completely otherworldly religion which makes a strange, unbiblical distinction between body and soul, between the sacred and the secular.

I have traveled the length and breadth of Alabama, Mississippi, and all the other southern states. On sweltering summer days and crisp autumn mornings I have looked at the South's beautiful churches with their lofty spires pointing heavenward. I have beheld the impressive outlines of her massive religious-education buildings. Over and over I have found myself saying: "What kind of people worship here? Who is their God? Where were their voices when the lips of Governor Barnett dripped with words of interposition and nullification? Where were they when Governor Wallace gave a clarion call for defiance and hatred? Where were their voices of support when bruised and weary Negro men and women decided to rise from the dark dungeons of complacency to the bright hills of creative protest?"

Yes, these questions are still in my mind. In deep disappointment I have wept over the laxity of the church. But be assured that my tears have been tears of love. There can be no deep disappointment where there is not deep love. Yes, I love the church. How could I do otherwise? I am in the rather unique position of being the son, the grandson, and the great-grandson of preachers. Yes, I see the church as the body of Christ. But, Oh! How we have blemished and scarred that body through social neglect and through fear of being nonconformists.

There was a time when the church was very powerful—in the time 40 when the early Christians rejoiced at being deemed worthy to suffer for what they believed. In those days the church was not merely a thermometer that recorded the ideas and principles of popular opinion; it was a thermostat that transformed the mores of society. Whenever the early Christians entered a town, the people in power became disturbed and immediately sought to convict the Christians for being "disturbers of the peace" and "outside agitators." But the Christians pressed on, in the conviction that they were "a colony of heaven," called to obey God rather than man. Small in number, they were big in commitment. They were too God-intoxicated to be "astronomically intimidated." By their effort and example they brought an end to such ancient evils as infanticide and gladiatorial contests.

Things are different now. So often the contemporary church is a weak, ineffectual voice with an uncertain sound. So often it is an archdefender of the status quo. Far from being disturbed by the presence of the church, the power structure of the average community is consoled by the church's silent—and often even vocal—sanction of things as they are.

But the judgment of God is upon the church as never before. If today's church does not recapture the sacrificial spirit of the early church, it will lose its authenticity, forfeit the loyalty of millions, and be dismissed as an irrelevant social club with no meaning for the twentieth century. Every day I meet young people whose disappointment with the church has turned into outright disgust.

Perhaps I have once again been too optimistic. Is organized religion too inextricably bound to the status quo to save our nation and the world? Perhaps I must turn my faith to the inner spiritual church, the church within the church, as the true *ekklesia* and the hope of the world. But again I am thankful to God that some noble souls from the ranks of organized religion have broken loose from the paralyzing chains of conformity and joined us as active partners in the struggle for freedom. They have left their secure congregations and walked the streets of Albany, Georgia, with us. They have gone down the highways of the South on tortuous rides for freedom. Yes, they have gone to jail with us. Some have been dismissed from their churches, have lost the support of their bishops and fellow ministers. But they have acted in the faith that right defeated is stronger than evil triumphant. Their witness has been the spiritual salt that has preserved the true meaning of the gospel in these troubled times. They have carved a tunnel of hope through the dark mountain of disappointment.

I hope the church as a whole will meet the challenge of this decisive hour. But even if the church does not come to the aid of justice, I have no despair about the future. I have no fear about the outcome of our struggle in Birmingham, even if our motives are at present misunderstood. We will reach the goal of freedom in Birmingham and all over the nation, because the goal of America is freedom. Abused and scorned though we may be, our destiny is tied up with America's destiny. Before the pilgrims landed at Plymouth, we were here. Before the pen of Jefferson etched the majestic words of the Declaration of Independence across the pages of history, we were here. For more than two centuries our forebears labored in this country without wages; they made cotton king; they built the homes of their masters while suffering gross injustice and shameful humiliation—and yet out of a bottomless vitality they continue to thrive and develop. If the inexpressible cruelties of slavery could not stop us, the opposition we now face will surely fail. We will win our freedom because the sacred heritage of our nation and the eternal will of God are embodied in our echoing demands.

Before closing I feel impelled to mention one other point in your state-   45
ment that has troubled me profoundly. You warmly commended the Birmingham police force for keeping "order" and "preventing violence." I doubt that you would have so warmly commended the police force if you had seen its dogs sinking their teeth into unarmed, nonviolent Negroes. I doubt that you would so quickly commend the policemen if you were to observe their ugly and inhumane treatment of Negroes here in the city jail; if you were to watch them push and curse old Negro women and young Negro girls; if you were to see them slap and kick old Negro men and young boys; if you were to observe them, as they did on two occasions, refuse to give us food because we wanted to sing our grace together. I cannot join you in your praise of the Birmingham police department.

It is true that the police have exercised a degree of discipline in handling the demonstrators. In this sense they have conducted themselves rather "nonviolently" in public. But for what purpose? To preserve the evil system of segregation. Over the past few years I have consistently preached that nonviolence demands that the means we use must be as pure as the ends we seek. I have tried to make clear that it is wrong to use immoral means to attain moral ends. But now I must affirm that it is just as wrong, or perhaps even more so, to use moral means to preserve immoral ends. Perhaps Mr. Connor and his policemen have been rather nonviolent in public, as was Chief Pritchett in Albany, Georgia, but they have used the moral means of nonviolence to maintain the immoral end of racial injustice. As T. S. Eliot has said: "The last temptation is the greatest treason: To do the right deed for the wrong reason."

I wish you had commended the Negro sit-inners and demonstrators of Birmingham for their sublime courage, their willingness to suffer, and their amazing discipline in the midst of great provocation. One day the South will recognize its real heroes. They will be the James Merediths, with the noble sense of purpose that enables them to face jeering and hostile mobs, and with the agonizing loneliness that characterizes the life of the pioneer. They will be old, oppressed, battered Negro women, symbolized in a seventy-two-year-old woman in Montgomery, Alabama, who rose up with a sense of dignity and with her people decided not to ride segregated buses, and who responded with ungrammatical profundity to one who inquired about her weariness: "My feets is tired, but my soul is at rest." They will be the young high school and college students, the young ministers of the gospel and a host of their elders, courageously and nonviolently sitting in at lunch counters and willingly going to jail for conscience' sake. One day the South will know that when these disinherited children of God sat down at lunch counters, they were in reality standing up for what is best in the American dream and for the most sacred values in our Judaeo-Christian heritage, thereby bringing our nation back to those great wells of democracy which were dug deep by the founding fathers in their formulation of the Constitution and the Declaration of Independence.

Never before have I written so long a letter. I'm afraid it is much too long to take your precious time. I can assure you that it would have been much shorter if I had been writing from a comfortable desk, but what else can one do when he is alone in a narrow jail cell, other than write long letters, think long thoughts, and pray long prayers?

If I have said anything in this letter that overstates the truth and indicates an unreasonable impatience, I beg you to forgive me. If I have said anything that understates the truth and indicates my having a patience that allows me to settle for anything less than brotherhood, I beg God to forgive me.

I hope this letter finds you strong in the faith. I also hope that circum-   50
stances will soon make it possible for me to meet each of you, not as an integrationist or a civil-rights leader but as a fellow clergyman and a Christian brother. Let us all hope that the dark clouds of racial prejudice will soon pass away and the deep fog of misunderstanding will be lifted from our fear-drenched communities, and in some not too distant tomorrow the radiant stars of love and brotherhood will shine over our great nation with all their scintillating beauty.

Yours for the cause of Peace and Brotherhood,
Martin Luther King, Jr.

✎ Topics for Critical Thinking and Writing

1. In his first five paragraphs how does King assure his audience that he is not a meddlesome intruder but a man of good will?
2. In paragraph 3 King refers to Hebrew prophets and to the Apostle Paul, and later (paragraph 10) to Socrates. What is the point of these references?
3. In paragraph 11 what does King mean when he says that "our beloved Southland" has long tried to "live in monologue rather than dialogue"?
4. King begins paragraph 23 with "I must make two honest confessions to you, my Christian and Jewish brothers." What would have been gained or lost if he had used this paragraph as his opening?
5. King's last three paragraphs do not advance his argument. What do they do?
6. Why does King advocate breaking unjust laws "openly, lovingly" (paragraph 20)? What does he mean by these words? What other motives or attitudes do these words rule out?
7. Construct two definitions of *civil disobedience,* and explain whether and to what extent it is easier (or harder) to justify civil disobedience, depending on how you have defined the expression.

8. If you feel that you wish to respond to King's letter on some point, write a letter nominally addressed to King. You may, if you wish, adopt the persona of one of the eight clergymen whom King initially addressed.
9. King writes (paragraph 46) that "nonviolence demands that the means we use must be as pure as the ends we seek." How do you think King would evaluate the following acts of civil disobedience: (a) occupying a college administration building in order to protest the administration's unsatisfactory response to a racial incident on campus, or in order to protest the failure of the administration to hire minority persons as staff and faculty; (b) sailing on a collision course with a whaling ship to protest against whaling; (c) trespassing on an abortion clinic to protest abortion? Set down your answer in an essay of five hundred words.

Peter Singer

Peter Singer teaches philosophy at Monash University in Melbourne, Australia. This essay originally appeared in 1973 as a review of Animals, Men and Morals, *edited by Stanley and Roslind Godlovitch and John Harris.*

Animal Liberation

I

We are familiar with Black Liberation, Gay Liberation, and a variety of other movements. With Women's Liberation some thought we had come to the end of the road. Discrimination on the basis of sex, it has been said, is the last form of discrimination that is universally accepted and practiced without pretense, even in those liberal circles which have long prided themselves on their freedom from racial discrimination. But one should always be wary of talking of "the last remaining form of discrimination." If we have learned anything from the liberation movements, we should have learned how difficult it is to be aware of the ways in which we discriminate until they are forcefully pointed out to us. A liberation movement demands an expansion of our moral horizons, so that practices that were previously regarded as natural and inevitable are now seen as intolerable.

Animals, Men and Morals is a manifesto for an Animal Liberation movement. The contributors to the book may not all see the issue this way. They are a varied group. Philosophers, ranging from professors to graduate students, make up the largest contingent. There are five of them, including the three editors, and there is also an extract from the unjustly neglected German philosopher with an English name, Leonard Nelson, who died in 1927. There are essays by two novelist/critics, Brigid Brophy and Maureen Duffy, and another by Muriel the Lady Dowding, widow of Dowding of Battle of Britain fame and the founder of "Beauty Without Cruelty," a movement that campaigns against the use of animals for furs and cosmetics. The other pieces are by a psychologist, a botanist, a sociologist, and Ruth Harrison, who is probably best described as a professional campaigner for animal welfare.

Whether or not these people, as individuals, would all agree that they are launching a liberation movement for animals, the book as a whole amounts to no less. It is a demand for a complete change in our attitudes to nonhumans. It is a demand that we cease to regard the exploitation of other species as natural and inevitable, and that, instead, we see it as a continuing moral outrage. Patrick Corbett, Professor of Philosophy at Sussex University, captures the spirit of the book in his closing words:

> . . . We require now to extend the great principles of liberty, equality and fraternity over the lives of animals. Let animal slavery join human slavery in the graveyard of the past.

The reader is likely to be skeptical. "Animal Liberation" sounds more like a parody of liberation movements than a serious objective. The reader may think: We support the claims of blacks and women for equality because blacks and women really are equal to whites and males—equal in intelligence and in abilities, capacity for leadership, rationality, and so on. Humans and nonhumans obviously are not equal in these respects. Since justice demands only that we treat equals equally, unequal treatment of humans and nonhumans cannot be an injustice.

This is a tempting reply, but a dangerous one. It commits the non-racist and non-sexist to a dogmatic belief that blacks and women really are just as intelligent, able, etc., as whites and males—and no more. Quite possibly this happens to be the case. Certainly attempts to prove that racial or sexual differences in these respects have a genetic origin have not been conclusive. But do we really want to stake our demand for equality on the assumption that there are no genetic differences of this kind between the different races or sexes? Surely the appropriate response to those who claim to have found evidence for such genetic differences is not to stick to the belief that there are no differences, whatever the evidence to the contrary; rather one should be clear that the claim to equality does not depend on IQ. Moral equality is distinct from factual equality. Otherwise it would be nonsense to talk of the equality of human beings, since humans, as individuals, obviously differ in intelligence and almost any ability one cares to name. If possessing greater intelligence does not entitle one human to exploit another, why should it entitle humans to exploit nonhumans?

Jeremy Bentham expressed the essential basis of equality in his famous formula: "Each to count for one and none for more than one." In other words, the interests of every being that has interests are to be taken into account and treated equally with the like interests of any other being. Other moral philosophers, before and after Bentham, have made the same point in different ways. Our concern for others must not depend on whether they possess certain characteristics, though just what that concern involves may, of course, vary, according to such characteristics.

Bentham, incidentally, was well aware that the logic of the demand for racial equality did not stop at the equality of humans. He wrote:

> The day *may* come when the rest of the animal creation may acquire those rights which never could have been withholden from them but by the hand of tyranny. The French have already discovered that the blackness of the skin is no reason why a human being should be abandoned without redress to the caprice of a tormentor. It may one day come to be recognized that the number of the legs, the villosity of the skin, or the termination of the *os sacrum*, are reasons equally insufficient for abandoning a sensitive being to the same fate. What else is it that should trace the insuperable line? Is it the faculty of reason, or perhaps the faculty of discourse? But a full-grown horse or dog is beyond comparison a more rational, as well as a more conversable animal, than an infant of a day, or a week, or even a month, old. But suppose they were otherwise, what would it avail? The question is not, Can they *reason?* nor Can they *talk?* but, Can they *suffer?*[1]

Surely Bentham was right. If a being suffers, there can be no moral justification for refusing to take that suffering into consideration, and, indeed, to count it equally with the like suffering (if rough comparisons can be made) of any other being.

So the only question is: Do animals other than man suffer? Most people agree unhesitatingly that animals like cats and dogs can and do suffer, and this seems also to be assumed by those laws that prohibit wanton cruelty to such animals. Personally, I have no doubt at all about this and find it hard to take seriously the doubts that a few people apparently do have. The editors and contributors of *Animals, Men and Morals* seem to feel the same way, for although the question is raised more than once, doubts are quickly dismissed each time. Nevertheless, because this is such a fundamental point, it is worth asking what grounds we have for attributing suffering to other animals.

It is best to begin by asking what grounds any individual human has for supposing that other humans feel pain. Since pain is a state of consciousness, a "mental event," it can never be directly observed. No observations, whether behavioral signs such as writhing or screaming or physiological or neurological recordings, are observations of pain itself. Pain is something one feels, and one can only infer that others are feeling it from various external indications. The fact that only philosophers are ever

---

[1]*The Principles of Morals and Legislation*, ch. XVII, sec. 1, footnote to paragraph 4.

skeptical about whether other humans feel pain shows that we regard such inference as justifiable in the case of humans.

Is there any reason why the same inference should be unjustifiable for other animals? Nearly all the external signs which lead us to infer pain in other humans can be seen in other species, especially "higher" animals such as mammals and birds. Behavioral signs—writhing, yelping, or other forms of calling, attempts to avoid the source of pain, and many others— are present. We know, too, that these animals are biologically similar in the relevant respects, having nervous systems like ours which can be observed to function as ours do.

So the grounds for inferring that these animals can feel pain are near- ly as good as the grounds for inferring other humans do. Only nearly, for there is one behavioral sign that humans have but nonhumans, with the exception of one or two specially raised chimpanzees, do not have. This, of course, is a developed language. As the quotation from Bentham indi- cates, this has long been regarded as an important distinction between man and other animals. Other animals may communicate with each other, but not in the way we do. Following Chomsky, many people now mark this distinction by saying that only humans communicate in a form that is governed by rules of syntax. (For the purposes of this argument, linguists allow those chimpanzees who have learned a syntactic sign language to rank as honorary humans.) Nevertheless, as Bentham pointed out, this distinction is not relevant to the question of how animals ought to be treat- ed, unless it can be linked to the issue of whether animals suffer.

This link may be attempted in two ways. First, there is a hazy line of philosophical thought, stemming perhaps from some doctrines associated with Wittgenstein, which maintains that we cannot meaningfully attribute states of consciousness to beings without language. I have not seen this argument made explicit in print, though I have come across it in conver- sation. This position seems to me very implausible, and I doubt that it would be held at all if it were not thought to be a consequence of a broad- er view of the significance of language. It may be that the use of a public, rule-governed language is a precondition of conceptual thought. It may even be, although personally I doubt it, that we cannot meaningfully speak of a creature having an intention unless that creature can use a lan- guage. But states like pain, surely, are more primitive than either of these, and seem to have nothing to do with language.

Indeed, as Jane Goodall points out in her study of chimpanzees, when it comes to the expression of feelings and emotions, humans tend to fall back on non-linguistic modes of communication which are often found among apes, such as a cheering pat on the back, an exuberant embrace, a clasp of hands, and so on.[2] Michael Peters makes a similar point in his con- tribution to *Animals, Men and Morals* when he notes that the basic signals

10

---

[2]Jane van Lawick-Goodall, *In the Shadow of Man* (Boston: Houghton Mifflin, 1971), p. 225.

we use to convey pain, fear, sexual arousal, and so on are not specific to our species. So there seems to be no reason at all to believe that a creature without language cannot suffer.

The second, and more easily appreciated way of linking language and the existence of pain is to say that the best evidence that we can have that another creature is in pain is when he tells us that he is. This is a distinct line of argument, for it is not being denied that a non-language-user conceivably could suffer, but only that we could know that he is suffering. Still, this line of argument seems to me to fail, and for reasons similar to those just given. "I am in pain" is not the best possible evidence that the speaker is in pain (he might be lying) and it is certainly not the only possible evidence. Behavioral signs and knowledge of the animal's biological similarity to ourselves together provide adequate evidence that animals do suffer. After all, we would not accept linguistic evidence if it contradicted the rest of the evidence. If a man was severely burned, and behaved as if he were in pain, writhing, groaning, being very careful not to let his burned skin touch anything, and so on, but later said he had not been in pain at all, we would be more likely to conclude that he was lying or suffering from amnesia than that he had not been in pain.

Even if there were stronger grounds for refusing to attribute pain to those who do not have a language, the consequences of this refusal might lead us to examine these grounds unusually critically. Human infants, as well as some adults, are unable to use language. Are we to deny that a year-old infant can suffer? If not, how can language be crucial? Of course, most parents can understand the responses of even very young infants better than they understand the responses of other animals, and sometimes infant responses can be understood in the light of later development.

This, however, is just a fact about the relative knowledge we have of our own species and other species, and most of this knowledge is simply derived from closer contact. Those who have studied the behavior of other animals soon learn to understand their responses at least as well as we understand those of an infant. (I am not referring to Jane Goodall's and other well-known studies of apes.) Consider, for example, the degree of understanding achieved by Tinbergen from watching herring gulls.[3] Just as we can understand infant human behavior in the light of adult human behavior, so we can understand the behavior of other species in the light of our own behavior (and sometimes we can understand our own behavior better in the light of the behavior of other species).

The grounds we have for believing that other mammals and birds suffer are, then, closely analogous to the grounds we have for believing that other humans suffer. It remains to consider how far down the evolutionary scale this analogy holds. Obviously it becomes poorer when we get further away from man. To be more precise would require a detailed

[3]N. Tinbergen, *The Herring Gull's World* (New York: Basic Books, 1961).

examination of all that we know about other forms of life. With fish, rep-
tiles, and other vertebrates the analogy still seems strong, with molluscs
like oysters it is much weaker. Insects are more difficult, and it may be that
in our present state of knowledge we must be agnostic about whether they
are capable of suffering.

If there is no moral justification for ignoring suffering when it occurs,
and it does occur in other species, what are we to say of our attitudes
toward these other species? Richard Ryder, one of the contributors to *Animals, Men and Morals,* uses the term "speciesism" to describe the belief that
we are entitled to treat members of other species in a way in which it
would be wrong to treat members of our own species. The term is not
euphonious, but it neatly makes the analogy with racism. The non-racist
would do well to bear the analogy in mind when he is inclined to defend
human behavior toward nonhumans. "Shouldn't we worry about improving the lot of our own species before we concern ourselves with other
species?" he may ask. If we substitute "race" for "species" we shall see
that the question is better not asked. "Is a vegetarian diet nutritionally
adequate?" resembles the slave-owner's claim that he and the whole economy of the South would be ruined without slave labor. There is even a
parallel with skeptical doubts about whether animals suffer, for some
defenders of slavery professed to doubt whether blacks really suffer in the
way whites do.

I do not want to give the impression, however, that the case for Animal Liberation is based on the analogy with racism and no more. On the
contrary, *Animals, Men and Morals* describes the various ways in which
humans exploit nonhumans, and several contributors consider the
defenses that have been offered, including the defense of meat-eating
mentioned in the last paragraph. Sometimes the rebuttals are scornfully
dismissive, rather than carefully designed to convince the detached critic.
This may be a fault, but it is a fault that is inevitable, given the kind of
book this is. The issue is not one on which one can remain detached. As the
editors state in their Introduction:

> Once the full force of moral assessment has been made explicit there can be
> no rational excuse left for killing animals, be they killed for food, science, or
> sheer personal indulgence. We have not assembled this book to provide the
> reader with yet another manual on how to make brutalities less brutal.
> Compromise, in the traditional sense of the term, is simple unthinking weak-
> ness when one considers the actual reasons for our crude relationships with
> the other animals.

The point is that on this issue there are few critics who are genuinely   20
detached. People who eat pieces of slaughtered nonhumans every day
find it hard to believe that they are doing wrong; and they also find it hard
to imagine what else they could eat. So for those who do not place nonhumans beyond the pale of morality, there comes a stage when further argument seems pointless, a stage at which one can only accuse one's oppo-

nent of hypocrisy and reach for the sort of sociological account of our practices and the way we defend them that is attempted by David Wood in his contribution to this book. On the other hand, to those unconvinced by the arguments, and unable to accept that they are merely rationalizing their dietary preferences and their fear of being thought peculiar, such sociological explanations can only seem insultingly arrogant.

II

The logic of speciesism is most apparent in the practice of experimenting on nonhumans in order to benefit humans. This is because the issue is rarely obscured by allegations that nonhumans are so different from humans that we cannot know anything about whether they suffer. The defender of vivisection cannot use this argument because he needs to stress the similarities between man and other animals in order to justify the usefulness to the former of experiments on the latter. The researcher who makes rats choose between starvation and electric shocks to see if they develop ulcers (they do) does so because he knows that the rat has a nervous system very similar to man's, and presumably feels an electric shock in a similar way.

Richard Ryder's restrained account of experiments on animals made me angrier with my fellow men than anything else in this book. Ryder, a clinical psychologist by profession, himself experimented on animals before he came to hold the view he puts forward in his essay. Experimenting on animals is now a large industry, both academic and commercial. In 1969, more than 5 million experiments were performed in Britain, the vast majority without anesthetic (though how many of these involved pain is not known). There are no accurate U.S. figures, since there is no federal law on the subject, and in many cases no state law either. Estimates vary from 20 million to 200 million. Ryder suggests that 80 million may be the best guess. We tend to think that this is all for vital medical research, but of course it is not. Huge numbers of animals are used in university departments from Forestry to Psychology, and even more are used for commercial purposes, to test whether cosmetics can cause skin damage, or shampoos eye damage, or to test food additives or laxatives or sleeping pills or anything else.

A standard test for foodstuffs is the "LD50." The object of this test is to find the dosage level at which 50 percent of the test animals will die. This means that nearly all of them will become very sick before finally succumbing or surviving. When the substance is a harmless one, it may be necessary to force huge doses down the animals, until in some cases sheer volume or concentration causes death.

Ryder gives a selection of experiments, taken from recent scientific journals. I will quote two, not for the sake of indulging in gory details, but in order to give an idea of what normal researchers think they may legitimately do to other species. The point is not that the individual researchers are cruel men, but that they are behaving in a way that is allowed by our speciesist attitudes. As Ryder points out, even if only 1 percent of the experiments involve severe pain, that is 50,000 experiments in Britain each year, or nearly 150 every day (and about fifteen times as many in the United States, if Ryder's guess is right). Here then are two experiments:

> O. S. Ray and R. J. Barrett of Pittsburgh gave electric shocks to the feet of 1,042 mice. They then caused convulsions by giving more intense shocks through cup-shaped electrodes applied to the animals' eyes or through pressure spring clips attached to their ears. Unfortunately some of the mice who "successfully completed Day One training were found sick or dead prior to testing on Day Two." [*Journal of Comparative and Physiological Psychology,* 1969, vol. 67, pp. 110–116]

> At the National Institute for Medical Research, Mill Hill, London, W. Feldberg and S. L. Sherwood injected chemicals into the brains of cats—"with a number of widely different substances, recurrent patterns of reaction were obtained. Retching, vomiting, defaecation, increased salivation and greatly accelerated respiration leading to panting were common features." . . . The injection into the brain of a large dose of Tubocuraine caused the cat to jump "from the table to the floor and then straight into its cage, where it started calling more and more noisily whilst moving about restlessly and jerkily . . . finally the cat fell with legs and neck flexed, jerking in rapid clonic movements, the condition being that of a major [epileptic] convulsion . . . within a few seconds the cat got up, ran for a few yards at high speed and fell in another fit. The whole process was repeated several times within the next ten minutes, during which the cat lost faeces and foamed at the mouth." This animal finally died thirty-five minutes after the brain injection. [*Journal of Physiology,* 1954, vol. 123, pp. 148–167]

There is nothing secret about these experiments. One has only to   25
open any recent volume of a learned journal, such as the *Journal of Comparative and Physiological Psychology,* to find full descriptions of experiments of this sort, together with the results obtained—results that are frequently trivial and obvious. The experiments are often supported by public funds.

It is a significant indication of the level of acceptability of these practices that, although these experiments are taking place at this moment on university campuses throughout the country, there has, so far as I know, not been the slightest protest from the student movement. Students have been rightly concerned that their universities should not discriminate on grounds of race or sex, and that they should not serve the purposes of the military or big business. Speciesism continues undisturbed, and many students participate in it. There may be a few qualms at first, but since everyone regards it as normal, and it may even be a required part of a course, the student soon becomes hardened and, dismissing his earlier feelings as "mere sentiment," comes to regard animals as statistics rather than sentient beings with interests that warrant consideration.

Argument about vivisection has often missed the point because it has been put in absolutist terms: Would the abolitionist be prepared to let thousands die if they could be saved by experimenting on a single animal? The way to reply to this purely hypothetical question is to pose another: Would the experimenter be prepared to experiment on a human orphan under six months old, if it were the only way to save many lives? (I say "orphan" to avoid the complication of parental feelings, although in doing so I am being overfair to the experimenter, since the nonhuman subjects of experiments are not orphans.) A negative answer to this question indicates that the experimenter's readiness to use nonhumans is simple discrimination, for adult apes, cats, mice, and other mammals are more conscious of what is happening to them, more self-directing, and, so far as we can tell, just as sensitive to pain as a human infant. There is no characteristic that human infants possess that adult mammals do not have to the same or a higher degree.

(It might be possible to hold that what makes it wrong to experiment on a human infant is that the infant will in time develop into more than the nonhuman, but one would then, to be consistent, have to oppose abortion, and perhaps contraception, too, for the fetus and the egg and sperm have the same potential as the infant. Moreover, one would still have no reason for experimenting on a nonhuman rather than a human with brain damage severe enough to make it impossible for him to rise above infant level.)

The experimenter, then, shows a bias for his own species whenever he carries out an experiment on a nonhuman for a purpose that he would not think justified him in using a human being at an equal or lower level of sentience, awareness, ability to be self-directing, etc. No one familiar with the kind of results yielded by these experiments can have the slightest doubt that if this bias were eliminated the number of experiments performed would be zero or very close to it.

III

If it is vivisection that shows the logic of speciesism most clearly, it is the use of other species for food that is at the heart of our attitudes toward them. Most of *Animals, Men and Morals* is an attack on meat-eating—an attack which is based solely on concern for nonhumans, without reference to arguments derived from considerations of ecology, macrobiotics, health, or religion.

The idea that nonhumans are utilities, means to our ends, pervades our thought. Even conservationists who are concerned about the slaughter of wild fowl but not about the vastly greater slaughter of chickens for our tables are thinking in this way—they are worried about what we would lose if there were less wildlife. Stanley Godlovitch, pursuing the Marxist idea that our thinking is formed by the activities we undertake in satisfying our needs, suggests that man's first classification of his environment was into Edibles and Inedibles. Most animals came into the first category, and there they have remained.

Man may always have killed other species for food, but he has never exploited them so ruthlessly as he does today. Farming has succumbed to business methods, the objective being to get the highest possible ratio of output (meat, eggs, milk) to input (fodder, labor costs, etc.). Ruth Harrison's essay "On Factory Farming" gives an account of some aspects of modern methods, and of the unsuccessful British campaign for effective controls, a campaign which was sparked off by her *Animal Machines* (Stuart: London, 1964).

Her article is in no way a substitute for her earlier book. This is a pity since, as she says, "Farm produce is still associated with mental pictures of animals browsing in the fields . . . of hens having a last forage before going to roost. . . ." Yet neither in her article nor elsewhere in *Animals, Men and Morals* is this false image replaced by a clear idea of the nature and extent of factory farming. We learn of this only indirectly, when we hear of the code of reform proposed by an advisory committee set up by the British government.

Among the proposals, which the government refused to implement on the grounds that they were too idealistic, were: *"Any animals should at least have room to turn around freely."*

Factory farm animals need liberation in the most literal sense. Veal   35
calves are kept in stalls five feet by two feet. They are usually slaughtered when about four months old, and have been too big to turn in their stalls for at least a month. Intensive beef herds, kept in stalls only proportionately larger for much longer periods, account for a growing percentage of beef production. Sows are often similarly confined when pregnant, which, because of artificial methods of increasing fertility, can be most of the time. Animals confined in this way do not waste food by exercising, nor do they develop unpalatable muscle.

"A dry bedded area should be provided for all stock." Intensively kept animals usually have to stand and sleep on slatted floors without straw, because this makes cleaning easier.

"Palatable roughage must be readily available to all calves after one week of age." In order to produce the pale veal housewives are said to prefer, calves are fed on an all-liquid diet until slaughter, even though they are long past the age at which they would normally eat grass. They develop a craving for roughage, evidenced by attempts to gnaw wood from their stalls. (For the same reason, their diet is deficient in iron.)

"Battery cages for poultry should be large enough for a bird to be able to stretch one wing at a time." Under current British practice, a cage for four or five laying hens has a floor area of twenty inches by eighteen inches, scarcely larger than a double page of the *New York Review of Books*. In this space, on a sloping wire floor (sloping so the eggs roll down, wire so the dung drops through) the birds live for a year or eighteen months while

artificial lighting and temperature conditions combine with drugs in their food to squeeze the maximum number of eggs out of them. Table birds are also sometimes kept in cages. More often they are reared in sheds, no less crowded. Under these conditions all the birds' natural activities are frustrated, and they develop "vices" such as pecking each other to death. To prevent this, beaks are often cut off, and the sheds kept dark.

How many of those who support factory farming by buying its produce know anything about the way it is produced? How many have heard something about it, but are reluctant to check up for fear that it will make them uncomfortable? To non-speciesists, the typical consumer's mixture of ignorance, reluctance to find out the truth, and vague belief that nothing really bad could be allowed seems analogous to the attitudes of "decent Germans" to the death camps.

There are, of course, some defenders of factory farming. Their arguments are considered, though again rather sketchily, by John Harris. Among the most common: "Since they have never known anything else, they don't suffer." This argument will not be put by anyone who knows anything about animal behavior, since he will know that not all behavior has to be learned. Chickens attempt to stretch wings, walk around, scratch, and even dustbathe or build a nest, even though they have never lived under conditions that allowed these activities. Calves can suffer from maternal deprivation no matter at what age they were taken from their mothers. "We need these intensive methods to provide protein for a growing population." As ecologists and famine relief organizations know, we can produce far more protein per acre if we grow the right vegetable crop, soy beans for instance, than if we use the land to grow crops to be converted into protein by animals who use nearly 90 percent of the protein themselves, even when unable to exercise.

There will be many readers of this book who will agree that factory farming involves an unjustifiable degree of exploitation of sentient creatures, and yet will want to say that there is nothing wrong with rearing animals for food, provided it is done "humanely." These people are saying, in effect, that although we should not cause animals to suffer, there is nothing wrong with killing them.

There are two possible replies to this view. One is to attempt to show that this combination of attitudes is absurd. Roslind Godlovitch takes this course in her essay, which is an examination of some common attitudes to animals. She argues that from the combination of "animal suffering is to be avoided" and "there is nothing wrong with killing animals" it follows that all animal life ought to be exterminated (since all sentient creatures will suffer to some degree at some point in their lives). Euthanasia is a contentious issue only because we place some value on living. If we did not, the least amount of suffering would justify it. Accordingly, if we deny that we have a duty to exterminate all animal life, we must concede that we are placing some value on animal life.

This argument seems to me valid, although one could still reply that the value of animal life is to be derived from the pleasures that life can

40

have for them, so that, provided their lives have a balance of pleasure over pain, we are justified in rearing them. But this would imply that we ought to produce animals and let them live as pleasantly as possible, without suffering.

At this point, one can make the second of the two possible replies to the view that rearing and killing animals for food is all right so long as it is done humanely. This second reply is that so long as we think that a nonhuman may be killed simply so that a human can satisfy his taste for meat, we are still thinking of nonhumans as means rather than as ends in themselves. The factory farm is nothing more than the application of technology to this concept. Even traditional methods involve castration, the separation of mothers and their young, the breaking up of herds, branding or ear-punching, and of course transportation to the abattoirs and the final moments of terror when the animal smells blood and senses danger. If we were to try rearing animals so that they lived and died without suffering, we should find that to do so on anything like the scale of today's meat industry would be a sheer impossibility. Meat would become the prerogative of the rich.

I have been able to discuss only some of the contributions to this book, saying nothing about, for instance, the essays on killing for furs and for sport. Nor have I considered all the detailed questions that need to be asked once we start thinking about other species in the radically different way presented by this book. What, for instance, are we to do about genuine conflicts of interest like rats biting slum children? I am not sure of the answer, but the essential point is just that we do see this as a conflict of interests, that we recognize that rats have interests too. Then we may begin to think about other ways of resolving the conflict—perhaps by leaving out rat baits that sterilize the rats instead of killing them.   45

I have not discussed such problems because they are side issues compared with the exploitation of other species for food and for experimental purposes. On these central matters, I hope that I have said enough to show that this book, despite its flaws, is a challenge to every human to recognize his attitudes to nonhumans as a form of prejudice no less objectionable than racism or sexism. It is a challenge that demands not just a change of attitudes, but a change in our way of life, for it requires us to become vegetarians.

Can a purely moral demand of this kind succeed? The odds are certainly against it. The book holds out no inducements. It does not tell us that we will become healthier, or enjoy life more, if we cease exploiting animals. Animal Liberation will require greater altruism on the part of mankind than any other liberation movement, since animals are incapable of demanding it for themselves, or of protesting against their exploitation by votes, demonstrations, or bombs. Is man capable of such genuine altruism? Who knows? If this book does have a significant effect, however, it will be a vindication of all those who have believed that man has within himself the potential for more than cruelty and selfishness.

✎ Topics for Critical Thinking and Writing

1. Reread Singer's first seven paragraphs carefully, observing how he leads us to see that "animal liberation" is not a joke. It will help you to understand his strategy if for each of his paragraphs you write one sentence either summarizing the paragraph or commenting on what it accomplishes in his argument.

2. What grounds does Singer find for attributing suffering to nonhumans? List the arguments he offers to dismiss the relevance of a developed language. Why does he find it necessary to offer these arguments?

3. Does Singer attribute the capacity to feel pain to all species? Explain.

4. How does Singer define *speciesism?* To what extent does he use the analogy of speciesism to racism?

5. What is vivisection? Why, according to Singer, *must* defenders of vivisection also defend speciesism? Why do many of us who would not be willing to defend speciesism tolerate or even participate in experiments on animals?

6. What use of animals does Singer analyze beginning with paragraph 30? Why does he reserve this discussion for the last part of his essay? Why does he offer more detailed and more concrete examples in this section than in the second part, beginning with paragraph 21?

7. When Singer wrote "Animal Liberation," more than 20 years ago, he used language that would now be described as sexist. In paragraph 8, for example, he wrote "Do animals other than man suffer?" where he might today write "Do animals other than human beings suffer?" How would you revise his concluding paragraph to avoid sexist language?

Appendix
A WRITER'S GLOSSARY

analogy. An analogy (from the Greek *analogos,* proportionate, resembling) is a kind of comparison. Normally an analogy compares substantially different kinds of things and reports several points of resemblance. A comparison of one city with another ("New York is like Chicago in several ways") does not involve an analogy because the two things are not substantially different. And a comparison giving only one resemblance is usually not considered an analogy ("Some people, like olives, are an acquired taste"). But if we claim that a state is like a human body, and we find in the state equivalents for the brain, heart, and limbs, we are offering an analogy. Similarly, one might construct an analogy between feeding the body with food and supplying the mind with ideas: the diet must be balanced, taken at approximately regular intervals, in proper amounts, and digested. An analogy may be useful in explaining the unfamiliar by comparing it to the familiar ("The heart is like a pump . . ."), but of course the things compared are different, and the points of resemblance can go only so far. For this reason, analogies cannot prove anything, though they are sometimes offered as proof.

analysis. Examination of the parts and their relation to the whole.

argument. Discourse in which some statements are offered as reasons for other statements. Argument, then, like emotional appeal and wit, is a form of persuasion, but argument seeks to persuade by appealing to reason. (See Chapter 4, and *deduction,* page 869.)

audience. The writer's imagined readers. An essay on inflation written for the general public—say, for readers of *Newsweek*—will assume less specialized knowledge than will an essay written for professional economists—say, the readers of *Journal of Economic History.* In general, the imagined audience in a composition course is *not* the instructor (though in fact the instructor may be the only reader of the essay); the imagined audience usually is the class, or, to put it a little differently, someone rather like the writer but without the writer's specialized knowledge of the topic.

cliché. Literally, a *cliché* was originally (in French) a stereotype or an electrotype plate for printing; in English the word has come to mean an oft-repeated expression such as "a sight for sore eyes," "a heartwarming experience," "the acid test," "a meaningful relationship," "last but not least." Because these expressions implicitly claim to be impressive or forceful, they can be distinguished from such unpretentious common expressions as "good morning," "thank you," and "see you tomorrow." Clichés in fact are not impressive or forceful; they strike the hearer as tired, vague, and unimaginative.

compare/contrast. Strictly speaking, to compare is to examine in order to show similarities. (It comes from the Latin *comparare,* "to pair," "to match.")

To contrast is to set into opposition in order to show differences. (It comes from the Latin *contra,* "against," and *stare,* "to stand.") But in ordinary usage a comparison may include not only similarities but also differences. (For a particular kind of comparison, emphasizing similarities, see *analogy.*) In comparing and contrasting, a writer usually means not simply to list similarities or differences but to reveal something clearly, by calling attention either to its resemblances to something we might not think it resembles, or to its differences from something we might think it does resemble.

connotation. The associations that cluster around a word. *Mother* has connotations that *female parent* does not have, yet both words have the same denotation or explicit meaning.

convention. An agreed-on usage. Beginning each sentence with a capital letter is a convention.

deduction. Deduction is the process of reasoning from premises to a logical conclusion. Here is the classic example: "All men are mortal" (the major premise); "Socrates is a man" (the minor premise); "therefore Socrates is mortal" (the conclusion). Such an argument, which takes two truths and joins them to produce a third truth, is called a *syllogism* (from Greek for "a reckoning together"). Deduction (from the Latin for "lead down from") moves from a general statement to a specific application; it is, therefore, the opposite of *induction* (page 872), which moves from specific instances to a general conclusion.

Notice that if a premise of a syllogism is not true, one can reason logically and still come to a false conclusion. Example: "All teachers are members of a union"; "Jones is a teacher"; "therefore Jones is a member of a union." Although the process of reasoning is correct here, the major premise is false—all teachers are *not* members of a union—and so the conclusion is worthless. Jones may or may not be a member of the union.

Another point: some arguments superficially appear logical but are not. Let's take this attempt at a syllogism: "All teachers of Spanish know that in Spanish *hoy* means *today*" (major premise); "John knows that in Spanish *hoy* means *today*" (minor premise); "therefore John is a teacher of Spanish" (conclusion). Both of the premises are correct, but the conclusion does not follow. What's wrong? Valid deduction requires that the subject or condition of the major premise (in this case, teachers of Spanish) appear also in the minor premise, but here it does not. The minor premise should be "John is a teacher of Spanish," and the valid conclusion, of course, would be "therefore John knows that *hoy* means *today*."

denotation. The explicit meaning of a word, as given in a dictionary, without its associations. *Daytime serial* and *soap opera* have the same denotation, though *daytime serial* probably has a more favorable connotation (see *connotation*).

description. Discourse that aims chiefly at producing a sensory response (usually a mental image) to, for example, a person, object, scene, taste, smell, and so on. A descriptive essay, or passage in an essay, uses concrete words (words that denote observable qualities such as *hair* and *stickiness*) and it uses specific language (words such as *basketball* rather than *game*, and *steak, potatoes, and salad* rather than *hearty meal*).

diction. Choice of words. Examples: between *car, auto,* and *automobile,* between *lie* and *falsehood,* between *can't* and *cannot.*

euphemism. An expression such as *passed away* for *died,* used to avoid realities that the writer finds unpleasant. Thus, oppressive governments "relocate people" (instead of putting them in concentration camps).

evaluation. Whereas an interpretation seeks to explain the meaning, an evaluation judges worth. After we interpret a difficult piece of writing we may evaluate it as not worth the effort.

explication. An attempt to reveal the meaning by calling attention to implications, such as the connotations of words and the tone conveyed by the brevity or length of a sentence. Unlike a paraphrase, which is a rewording or rephrasing in order to set forth the gist of the meaning, an explication is a commentary that makes explicit what is implicit. If we paraphrased the beginning of the Gettysburg Address (page 556), we might turn "Four score and seven years ago our fathers brought forth" into "Eighty-seven years ago our ancestors established," or some such statement. In an explication, however, we would mention that *four score* evokes the language of the Bible, and that the biblical echo helps to establish the solemnity and holiness of the occasion. In an explication we would also mention that *fathers* initiates a chain of images of birth, continued in *conceived in liberty, any nation so conceived,* and *a new birth.* (See Highet's explication of the Gettysburg Address, page 557.)

exposition. An expository essay is chiefly concerned with giving information—how to register for classes, the causes of the French Revolution, or the tenets of Zen Buddhism. The writer of exposition must, of course, have a point of view (an attitude or a thesis), but because exposition—unlike persuasion—does not assume that the reader's opinion differs from the writer's, the point of view in exposition often is implicit rather than explicit.

general and **specific** (or **particular**). A general word refers to a class or group; a specific (particular) word refers to a member of the class or group. Example: *vehicle* is general compared with *automobile* or with *motorcycle.* But *general* and *specific* are relative. *Vehicle* is general when compared to *automobile,* but *vehicle* is specific when compared to *machine,* for *machine* refers to a class or group that includes not only vehicles but clocks, typewriters, and dynamos. Similarly, although *automobile* is specific in comparison with *vehicle, automobile* is general in comparison with *Volkswagen* or *sportscar.*

generalization. A statement relating to every member of a class or category, or, more loosely, to most members of a class or category. Example: "Students from Medford High are well prepared." Compare: (1) "Janet Kuo is well prepared" (a report of a specific condition); (2) "Students from Medford High are well prepared" (a low-level generalization, because it is limited to one school); (3) "Students today are well prepared" (a high-level generalization, covering many people in many places).

imagery and **symbolism.** When we read *rose,* we may more or less call to mind a picture of a rose, or perhaps we are reminded of the odor or texture of a rose. Whatever in a piece of writing appeals to any of our senses (including sensations of heat and pressure as well as of sight, smell, taste, touch, sound) is an image. In short, images are the sensory content of a work, whether literal (the roses discussed in an essay on rose-growing) or figurative (a comparison, in a poem, of a girl to a rose). It is usually easy to notice images in literature, particularly in poems, which often include comparisons such as "I wandered lonely as a cloud," "a fiery eye," and "seems he a dove? His feathers are but borrowed." In literature, imagery (again, literal as well as figurative) plays a large part in communicating the meaning of the work. For instance, in *Romeo and Juliet* abundant imagery of light and dark reenforces the conflict between life and death. Juliet especially is associated with light (Romeo says, "What light through yonder window breaks? It is the east and Juliet is the sun"), and at the end of the play, when the lovers have died, we are told that the morning is dark: "The sun for sorrow will not show his head."

If we turn from imaginative literature to the essay, we find, of course, that descriptive essays are rich in images. But other kinds of essays, too, may make use of imagery—and not only by literal references to real people or things. Such essays may use figures of speech, as Thoreau does when he says that the imagination as well as the body should "both sit down at the same table." The imagination, after all, does not literally sit down at a table—but Thoreau personifies the imagination, seeing it as no less concrete than the body.

The distinction between an image and a symbol is partly a matter of emphasis and partly a matter of a view of reality. If an image is so insisted on that we feel that the writer sees it as highly significant in itself and also as a way of representing something else, we can call it a symbol. A symbol is what it is, and yet it is also much more. We may feel that a passage about the railroad, emphasizing its steel tracks and its steel cars, its speed and its noise, may be not only about the railroad but also about industrialism and, even further, about an entire way of life—a way of thinking and feeling—that came into being in the nineteenth century.

A symbol, then, is an image so loaded with significance that it is not simply literal, and it does not simply stand as a figure for something else; it is both itself *and* something else that it richly suggests, a kind of manifestation of something too complex or too elusive to be otherwise revealed. Still, having said all of this, one must add that the distinction between *image* and *symbol* is not sharp, and usage allows us even to say such things as, "The imagery of light symbolizes love," meaning that the imagery stands for or represents or is in part about love.

induction. Reasoning from the particular to the general, or drawing a conclusion about all members of a class from a study of some members of the class. Every elephant I have seen is grayish, so by induction (from Latin, "lead into," "lead up to") I conclude that all elephants are grayish. Another example: I have met ten graduates of Vassar College and all are females, so I conclude that all Vassar graduates are females. This conclusion, however, happens to be incorrect; a few years ago Vassar began to admit males, and so although male graduates are relatively few they do exist. Induction is valid only if the sample is representative.

Because one can rarely be certain that it is representative, induced conclusions are usually open to doubt. Still, we live our lives largely by induction; we have dinner with a friend, we walk the dog, we write home for money—all because these actions have produced certain results in the past and we assume that actions of the same sort will produce results consistent with our earlier findings. Nelson Algren's excellent advice must have been arrived at inductively: "Never eat at a place called Mom's, and never play cards with a man called Doc."

interpretation. An explanation of the meaning. If we see someone clench his fist and tighten his mouth, we may interpret these signs as revealing anger. When we say that in the New Testament the passage alluding to the separation of sheep from goats is to be understood as referring to the saved and the damned, we are offering an interpretation.

irony. In *verbal irony*, the meaning of the words intentionally contradicts the literal meaning, as in "that's not a very good idea," where the intended meaning is "that's a terrible idea."

Irony, in distinction from sarcasm, employs at least some degree of wit or wryness. Sarcasm reveals contempt obviously and heavily, usually by asserting the opposite of what is meant: "You're a great guy" (if said sarcastically) means "It's awful of you to do this to me." Notice that the example of irony we began with was at least a trifle more ingenious than this sarcastic remark, for the sarcasm here simply is the opposite of what is meant, whereas our example of verbal irony is not quite the opposite. The opposite of "that's not a very good idea" is "that is a very good idea," but clearly (in our example) the speaker's meaning is something else. Put it this way: sarcasm is irony at its crudest, and finer irony commonly uses overstatement or especially understatement, rather than a simple opposite. (For a brief discussion of the use of irony in satire, see *satire,* page 875.)

If the speaker's words have an unintentional double meaning, the irony may be called *dramatic irony:* a character, about to go to bed, says, "I think I'll have a sound sleep," and dies in her sleep. Similarly, an action can turn dramatically ironic: a character seeks to help a friend and unintentionally harms her. Finally, a situation can be ironic: thirsty sailors are surrounded by water that cannot be drunk.

All these meanings of irony are held together, then, by the sense of a somewhat bitter contrast.

jargon. Technical language used inappropriately or inexactly. *Viable* means *able to survive.* To speak of a *viable building* is to use jargon. "A primary factor in my participation in the dance" is jargon if what is meant is "I dance because. . . ."

metaphor. Words have literal meanings: a lemon is a yellow, egg-shaped citrus fruit; to drown is to suffocate in water or other fluid. But words can also have metaphoric meanings: we can call an unsatisfactory automobile a *lemon,* and we can say that we are *drowning* in paperwork. Metaphoric language is literally absurd; if we heed only the denotation it is clearly untrue, for an automobile cannot be a kind of citrus fruit, and we cannot drown in paperwork. (Even if the paper literally suffocated someone, the death could not be called a drowning.) Metaphor, then, uses not the denotation of the word but the associations, the connotations. Because we know that the speaker is not crazy, we turn from the literal meaning (which is clearly untrue) to the association.

myth. (1) A traditional story dealing with supernatural beings or with heroes, often accounting for why things are as they are. Myths tell of the creation of the world, the creation of man, the changes of the season, the achievements of heroes. A Zulu myth, for example, explains that rain is the tears of a god weeping for a beloved slain bird. *Mythology* is a system or group of such stories, and so we speak of Zulu mythology, Greek mythology, or Norse mythology. (2) Mark Schorer, in *William Blake,* defines myth as "a large controlling image that gives philosophic meaning to the facts of ordinary life. . . . All real convictions involve a mythology. . . . Wars may be described as the clash of mythologies." In this sense, then, a myth is not a traditional story we do not believe, but any idea, true or false, to which people subscribe. Thus, one can speak of the "myth" of democracy or of communism.

narration. Discourse that recounts a real or a fictional happening. An anecdote is a narrative, and so is a history of the decline and fall of the

Roman Empire. Narration may, of course, include substantial exposition ("four possible motives must be considered") and description ("the horse was an old gray mare"), but the emphasis is on a sequence of happenings ("and then she says to me, . . .").

parable. A parable is a short narrative from which a moral or a lesson can be drawn. A parable may, but need not, be an allegory wherein, say, each character stands for an abstraction that otherwise would be hard to grasp. Usually the parable lacks the *detailed* correspondence of an allegory.

paradox. An apparent self-contradiction, such as "He was happiest when miserable."

paraphrase. A rewording of a passage, usually in order to clarify the meaning. A paraphrase is a sort of translating within the same language; it can help to make clear the gist of the passage. But one must recognize the truth of Robert Frost's charge that when one paraphrases a line of good writing one puts it "in other and worse English." Paraphrase should not be confused with *explication,* page 870.

parody. A parody (from the Greek *counter song*) seeks to amuse by imitating the style—the diction, the sentence structure—of another work, but normally the parody substitutes a very different subject. Thus, it might use tough-guy Hemingway talk to describe not a bullfighter but a butterfly catcher. Often a parody of a writer's style is a good-natured criticism of it.

persona. The writer or speaker in a role adopted for a specific audience. When Abraham Lincoln wrote or spoke, he sometimes did so in the persona of commander in chief of the Union army, but at other times he did so in the persona of the simple man from Springfield, Illinois. The persona is a mask put on for a performance (*persona* is the Latin word for *mask*). If *mask* suggests insincerity, we should remember that whenever we speak or write we do so in a specific role—as friend, or parent, or teacher, or applicant for a job, or whatever. Although Lincoln was a husband, a father, a politician, a president, and many other things, when he wrote a letter or speech he might write solely as one of these; in a letter to his son, the persona (or, we might say, personality) is that of father, not that of commander in chief. The distinction between the writer (who necessarily fills many roles) and the persona who writes or speaks a work is especially useful in talking about satire, because the satirist often invents a mouthpiece very different from himself. The satirist—say, Jonathan Swift—may be strongly opposed to a view, but his persona (his invented essayist) may favor the view; the reader must perceive that the real writer is ridiculing the invented essayist.

persuasion. Discourse that seeks to change a reader's mind. Persuasion usually assumes that the writer and the reader do not agree, or do not fully agree, at the outset. Persuasion may use logical argument (appeal to reason), but it may also try to win the reader over by other means—by appeal to the emotions, by wit, by geniality.

rhetoric. Although in much contemporary usage the word's meaning has sadly decayed to "inflated talk or writing," it can still mean "the study of elements such as content, structure, and cadence in writing or in speech." In short, in the best sense rhetoric is the study of the art of communicating with words.

satire. A work ridiculing identifiable objects in real life, meant to arouse in the reader contempt for its object. Satire is sometimes distinguished from comedy in that comedy aims simply to evoke amusement, whereas satire aims to bring about moral reform by ridicule. According to Alexander Pope, satire "heals with morals what it hurts with wit." Satire sometimes uses invective (direct abuse), but if the invective is to entertain the reader it must be witty, as in a piling up of ingenious accusations. Invective, however, is probably less common in satire than is irony, a device in which the tone somehow contradicts the words. For instance, a speaker may seem to praise ("well, that's certainly an original idea that you have"), but we perceive that she is ridiculing a crackpot idea. Or the satirist may invent a naive speaker (a persona) who praises, but the praise is really dispraise because a simpleton offers it; the persona is sincere, but the writer is ironic and satiric. Or, adopting another strategy, the writer may use an apparently naive persona to represent the voice of reason; the persona dispassionately describes actions that we take for granted (a political campaign), and through this simple, accurate, rational description we see the irrationality of our behavior. (For further comments on *irony*, see pages 872–73.)

style. A distinctive way of expression. If we see a picture of a man sitting on a chair, we may say that it looks like a drawing for a comic book, or we may say that it looks like a drawing by Rembrandt, Van Gogh, or Andrew Wyeth. We have come to recognize certain manners of expression—independent of the content—as characteristic of certain minds. The content, it can be said, is the same—a man sitting in a chair—but the creator's way of expressing the content is individual.

   Similarly, "Four score and seven years ago" and "Eighty-seven years ago" are the same in content; but the styles differ, because "Four score and seven years ago" distinctively reflects a mind familiar with the Bible and an orator speaking solemnly. Many people (we include ourselves) believe that the content is not the same if the expression is not the same. The "content" of "Four score and seven years ago" includes suggestions of the Bible and of God-fearing people not present in "eighty-seven years ago."

In this view, a difference in style is a difference in content and therefore a difference in meaning. Surely it is true that in the work of the most competent writers, those who make every word count, one cannot separate style and content.

Let C. S. Lewis have the next-to-last word: "The way for a person to develop a style is (a) to know exactly what he wants to say, and (b) to be sure he is saying exactly that. The reader, we must remember, does not start by knowing what we mean. If our words are ambiguous, our meaning will escape him. I sometimes think that writing is like driving sheep down a road. If there is any gate open to the left or the right the readers will most certainly go into it." And let the Austrian writer Karl Kraus have the last word: "There are two kinds of writers, those who are and those who aren't. With the first, content and form belong together like soul and body; with the second, they match each other like body and clothes."

summary. The word *summary* is related to *sum,* to the total something adds up to. (The Greeks and Romans counted upward, and wrote the total at the top.) A summary is a condensation or abridgment briefly giving the reader the gist of a longer work. Here are a few principles that govern summaries:

1. A summary is much briefer than the original. It is not a paraphrase—a word-by-word translation of someone's words into your own—for a paraphrase is usually at least as long as the original, whereas a summary is rarely longer than one-fourth the original, and may even be much briefer, perhaps giving in a sentence or two an entire essay.
2. A summary usually achieves its brevity by omitting almost all the concrete details of the original, presenting only the sum that the details add up to.
3. A summary is accurate; it has no value if it misrepresents the point of the original.
4. The writer of a summary need not make the points in the same order as that of the original. In fact, a reader is occasionally driven to write a summary because the original author does not present the argument in an orderly sequence; the summary is an attempt to disengage the author's argument from the confusing presentation.
5. A summary normally is written in the present tense, because the writer assumes that although the author wrote the piece last year or a hundred years ago, the piece speaks to us today. (In other words, the summary is explicitly or implicitly prefaced by "He says," and all that follows is in the present tense.)
6. Because a summary is openly based on someone else's views, not your own, you need not use quotation marks around any words that you take from the original.

Here is a summary of this entry on *summary:*

A summary is a condensation or abridgment. These are some characteristics: 1) it is rarely more than one-fourth as long as the original; 2) its brevity is usually achieved by leaving out most of the concrete details of the original; 3) it is accurate; 4) it may rearrange the organization of the original, especially if a rearrangement will make things clearer; 5) it normally is in the present tense; 6) quoted words need not be enclosed in quotation marks.

thesis. The writer's position or attitude; the proposition advanced.

thesis statement. A sentence or two summarizing the writer's position or attitude. An essay may or may not have an explicit thesis statement.

tone. The prevailing spirit of an utterance. The tone may be angry, bitter, joyful, solemn, or expressive of any similar mood or emotion. Tone usually reflects the writer's attitude toward the subject, the audience, and the self. (For further comments on tone, see pages 16–17.)

ACKNOWLEDGMENTS

Literary Acknowledgments

Dennis Altman, "Why Are Gay Men So Feared?" from *The New Internationalist,* November 1989. Reprinted with permission.

Maya Angelou, "Graduation" from *I Know Why the Caged Bird Sings* by Maya Angelou. Copyright © 1969 by Maya Angelou. Reprinted by permission of Random House, Inc.

Anonymous. "Confessions of an Erstwhile Child" from *The New Republic,* June 15, 1974. Reprinted by permission of *The New Republic.* © 1974, The New Republic, Inc.

W. H. Auden, "The Unknown Citizen" from *Collected Poems* by W. H. Auden, edited by Edward Mendelson. Copyright © 1940, renewed 1968 by W. H. Auden. By permission of Random House, Inc. and Faber and Faber Limited.

W. H. Auden, "Work, Labor, and Play" from *A Certain World.* Copyright © 1970 by W. H. Auden. Reprinted by permission of Curtis Brown, Ltd.

Jere L. Bacharach, Richard Cummins, Sharon Stoerger, and Kenneth Zanca, "Letters Responding to David Rothenberg," *Chronicle of Higher Education,* October 10, 1997. Copyright © 1998 by The Chronicle of Higher Education. Reprinted with permission of the publisher.

Toni Cade Bambara, "The Lesson" from *Gorilla, My Love* by Toni Cade Bambara. Copyright © 1972 by Toni Cade Bambara. Reprinted by permission of Random House, Inc.

A. N. Barnett, "Letter To The Editor of *Commentary,*" *Commentary,* January 1995. Reprinted by permission of the publisher and Abraham Barnett.

Stephen Bates, "The Next Front in the Book Wars," *The New York Times,* November 6, 1994.

Copyright © 1994 by The New York Times Company. Reprinted by permission.

Mary Beard, "Culturally Variable Ways of Seeing: Art and Literature," *Issues in World Literature,* Mary Ann Caws, Patricia Wright, and Sarah Bird Wright, eds. Copyright © 1994 by HarperCollins. By permission of Addison-Wesley Educational Publishers.

Sharon Begley, from "Three Is Not Enough" in *Newsweek,* February 13, 1995. Copyright © 1995 by Newsweek, Inc. All rights reserved. Reprinted by permission.

Mary Field Belenky et al., "Reminiscences of College." From "How Women Learn" from *Women's Ways of Knowing* by Mary Field Belenky et al. Copyright © 1986 by Basic Books, Inc. Reprinted by permission of BasicBooks, a division of HarperCollins Publishers, Inc.

William J. Bennett and C. Delores Tucker, "Smut-Free Stores," *The New York Times,* December 9, 1996 (op-ed). Copyright © 1996 by The New York Times Company. Reprinted by permission.

Richard Benson and John Szarkowski, from *A Maritime Album: 100 Photographs and Their Stories,* © 1997 by Yale University Press. By permission of the publisher, Yale University Press.

Robert M. Berkman, "Letter To The Editor," *The New York Times,* May 21, 1996. By permission of Robert M. Berkman.

Black Elk, "War Games" and "High Horse's Courting" from John G. Neihart, *Black Elk Speaks.* Copyright © 1932, 1959, 1972 by John G. Neihart. Reprinted by permission of the John G. Neihart Trust.

Derek Bok, "Protecting Freedom of Expression on the Campus" from *The Boston*

Globe, March 25, 1991. Reprinted by permission of the author.

Ray Bradbury, "There Will Come Soft Rains," first published in *Collier's Magazine,* May 6, 1950. Copyright © 1950 by the Crowell Collier Publishing Co., renewed 1977 by Ray Bradbury. Reprinted by permission of Don Congdon Associates, Inc.

Judith Bruk, "Letter To The Editor," *The New York Times,* May 21, 1996. By permission of Judith Bruk.

Barbara S. Cain, "Older Children and Divorce," *The New York Times Magazine,* February 1, 1990. Copyright © 1990 by The New York Times Company. Reprinted by permission.

Scott Cargle, "Letter To The Editor" titled "Music vs. Money" appearing in *The New York Times,* December 11, 1996. By permission of Scott Cargle.

Robert Coles, from *The Moral Intelligence of Children.* Copyright © 1997 by Robert Coles. Reprinted by permission of Random House, Inc.

Ronald K. L. Collins, "Letter To The Editor," *The New York Times,* December 11, 1996.

Frank Conroy, "A Yo-Yo Going Down, A Mad Squirrel Coming Up" from *Stop-Time* by Frank Conroy. Copyright © 1965, 1966, 1967 by Frank Conroy. Used by permission of Viking Penguin, a division of Penguin Putnam Inc.

Lewis Coser, "The Family" from Lewis Coser, *Sociology Through Literature.* Copyright © 1963, pp. 250–251. Reprinted by permission of Prentice-Hall, Inc. Englewood Cliffs, New Jersey.

Stanley Crouch, "Race is Over," *The New York Times Magazine,* September 29, 1996. Copyright © 1996 by The New York Times Company. Reprinted by permission.

Countee Cullen, "Incident" from *Color* by Countee Cullen. Copyright © 1925 by Harper & Brothers; copyright 1953 by Ida M. Cullen. Reprinted by permission of GRM Associates, Inc., Agents for the Estate of Ida M. Cullen.

Natalie Zemon Davis, "A Life of Learning" in the *1997 Charles Homer Haskins Lecture,* Occasional Paper No. 39. Copyright © 1997 by Natalie Zemon Davis. By permission of the author.

Robert P. DeSieno, "Letter To The Editor," *The New York Times,* May 21, 1996. By permission of Robert P. DeSieno.

William J. Doherty, from *The Intentional Family.* Copyright © 1997 by Addison-Wesley Publishing Company. Reprinted by permission of Perseus Books Publishers, a member of Perseus Books, L.L.C.

Melvin Dubnick, "Letter To The Editor," *The New York Times,* May 21, 1996. By permission of Melvin Dubnick.

Barbara Ehrenreich and Annette Fuentes, "Life on the Global Assembly Line" from *Ms.,* June 1981. Reprinted by permission of the author.

Fan Shen, "The Classroom and the Wider Culture: Identity as a Key to Learning English Composition" from *College Composition and Communication,* 40, December 1989. Copyright © 1989 by the National Council of Teachers of English. Reprinted with permission.

John S. Fielden, "What Do You Mean You Don't Like My Style" in *Harvard Business Review,* May/June 1982. Copyright © 1982 by the President and Fellows of Harvard College; all rights reserved. Reprinted by permission of *Harvard Business Review.*

Holly Finn, "Letter To The Editor," *The New York Times,* December 7, 1997.

Milton Friedman, "The Social Responsibility of Business is to Increase Its Profits," *The New York Times,* September 13, 1970. Copyright © 1970 by The New York Times Company. Reprinted by permission.

Henry Louis Gates, Jr., "Delusions of Grandeur." First appeared in *Sports Illustrated.* Copyright © 1991 by Henry Louis Gates, Jr. Reprinted by permission of Brandt & Brandt Literary Agents, Inc.

Roger C. Geissler, "Letter To The Editor," *The New York Times,* December 11, 1996. Reprinted by permission of Robert C. Geissler.

David Gelernter, "Unplugged," *The New Republic,* September 1994. Reprinted by permission of *The New Republic.* © 1994, The New Republic, Inc.

Chris Gersten, "Letter To The Editor of Commentary," *Commentary,* January 1995. Reprinted by permission of the publisher and Chris Gersten.

Malcolm Gladwell, "Chip Thrills" from *The New Yorker,* January 27, 1997. Reprinted with permission from *The New Yorker.*

Malcolm Gladwell, "The Sports Taboo" from *The New Yorker,* May 19, 1997. Reprinted with permission from *The New Yorker.*

Gabrielle Glaser, "Faith is a Gamble; Scenes from an Intermarriage" published in *The New York Times Magazine,* December 7, 1997. By permission of Gabrielle Glaser.

Paul Goodman, "A Proposal to Abolish Grading." Reprinted from *Compulsory Mis-Education* by Paul Goodman. Copyright 1964. By permission of the publisher, Horizon Press, New York.

Doris Kearns Goodwin, "Fan" from *Baseball* by Geoffrey Ward and Ken Burns. Copyright © 1994 by Doris Kearns Goodwin. By permission of the author.

Stephen Jay Gould, "Women's Brains" from *the Panda's Thumb: More Reflections in Nat-*

ural History by Stephen Jay Gould. Copyright © 1980 by Stephen Jay Gould. Reprinted by permission of W. W. Norton & Company, Inc.

Edward T. Hall, "Proxemics in the Arab World" from *The Hidden Dimension* by Edward T. Hall. Copyright 1966, 1982 by Edward T. Hall. Used by permission of Doubleday, a division of Bantam Doubleday Dell Publishing Group, Inc.

Linda Hasselstrom, "Why One Peaceful Woman Carries a Pistol." Reprinted with permission from *Land Circle, Writings Collected from the Land*, by Linda Hasselstrom. © 1991 Fulcrum Publishing, Inc., Golden, Colorado. All rights reserved.

Richard Hawley, "Television and Adolescents: A Teacher's View" from *American Film*, Vol. 4, No. 1 (October 1978). Reprinted by permission of the author.

Liliana Heker, "The Stolen Party" from *Other Fires: Short Fiction by Latin American Women* translated and edited by Alberto Manguel. Copyright © 1982 by Liliana Heker. Translation Copyright © 1985, 1986 by Alberto Manguel. Reprinted by permission of Clarkson N. Potter, Inc., a division of Crown Publishers, Inc. and by permission of Westwood Creative Artists.

Gilbert Highet, "The Gettysburg Address" from *The Clerk of Oxenford*. Copyright © 1954 by Gilbert Highet. Reprinted by permission of Curtis Brown, Ltd.

Arlie Hochschild and Ann Machung, a selection appearing in *The Utne Reader*, March/April 1990, from *The Second Shift* by Arlie Hochschild and Ann Machung. Copyright © 1989 by Arlie Hochschild. Used by permission of Viking Penguin, a division of Penguin Putnam Inc.

Jeanne Wakatsuki Houston, "Double Identity." Originally published as "Beyond Manzanar" in *Ethnic Lifestyles* (University of Oklahoma Press, 1978). Copyright © 1978 by Jeanne Wakatsuki Houston. By permission of the author.

Lou Jacobs, Jr., "What Qualities Does a Good Photograph Have?" *The New York Times*, February 8, 1981. Copyright © 1981 by The New York Times Company. Reprinted by permission.

Margo Jefferson, "Sinatra, Not a Myth But a Man, and One Among Many," *The New York Times*, June 1, 1998. Copyright © 1998 by The New York Times Company. Reprinted by permission.

LeAlan Jones and Lloyd Newman, "Interview at Donoghue Elementary School." Reprinted with the permission of Scribner, a division of Simon & Schuster from *Our America: Life and Death on the South Side of Chicago* by LeAlan Jones and Lloyd Newman with David Isay. Text copyright © 1997 by LeAlan Jones, Lloyd Newman, and David Isay.

Mary Karr, from *The Liar's Club*. Copyright © 1995 by Mary Karr. Used by permission of Viking Penguin, a division of Penguin Putnam Inc.

Don B. Kates, Jr., "Shot Down" from *National Review*, March 6, 1995. Copyright © 1995 by National Review, Inc., 215 Lexington Avenue, New York, NY 10016. Reprinted by permission.

Barbara L. Keller, from "My Turn: Frontiersmen Are History," in *Newsweek*, August 16, 1993. Copyright © 1993 by Newsweek, Inc. All rights reserved. Reprinted by permission.

Jamaica Kincaid. Reprinted by permission of Farrar, Straus & Giroux, Inc.: "Girl" from *At the Bottom of the River* by Jamaica Kincaid. Copyright © 1983 by Jamaica Kincaid.

Martin Luther King, Jr., "Non-Violent Resistance" from *Stride Toward Freedom*. Copyright © 1958 by Martin Luther King, Jr., copyright renewed 1986 by Coretta Scott King. Reprinted by arrangement with The Heirs to the Estate of Martin Luther King, Jr., c/o Writers House, Inc. as agent for the proprietor.

Martin Luther King, Jr., "Letter from Birmingham Jail" from *Why We Can't Wait*. Copyright © 1963 by Martin Luther King, Jr., copyright renewed 1991 by Coretta Scott King. Reprinted by arrangement with The Heirs to the Estate of Martin Luther King, Jr., c/o Writers House, Inc. as agent for the proprietor.

Perri Klass, "King of the Jungle." First published as "Lions and Shadows" in *The New York Times*. Copyright © 1994 by Perri Klass. Reprinted by permission of the author.

Peter D. Kramer, "Divorce and Our National Values," *The New York Times*, August 29, 1997. Copyright © 1997 by The New York Times Company. Reprinted by permission.

Charles Krauthammer, "Of Headless Mice . . . and Men," *Time*, January 19, 1998. Copyright © 1998 Time Inc. Reprinted by permission.

Robin Lakoff, "You Are What You Say" from *Ms.*, July 1974. Reprinted by permission of the author.

Andrew Lam, "Goodbye Saigon, Finally," *The New York Times*, April 30, 1993 (op-ed). Copyright © 1993 by The New York Times Company. Reprinted by permission.

Barbara Lawrence, "Four Letter Words Can Hurt You," *The New York Times*, October 27, 1973. Copyright © 1973 by The New York Times Company. Reprinted by permission.

Miriam Lindsey Levering, "Millenarian Movements" from *Abingdon Dictionary of Living*

Religions, 1981. Copyright © 1981 by Abingdon Press. Reprinted by permission of Abingdon Press.

C. S. Lewis, "We Have No Right to Happiness," from *God in the Dock* by C. S. Lewis. Copyright © 1970 by C. S. Lewis Pte. Ltd. Reproduced by permission of Curtis Brown, London, and HarperCollins Ltd.

Patricia Nelson Limerick, "The Phenomenon of Phantom Students: Diagnosis and Treatment" from *The Harvard Gazette,* November 11, 1983. Reprinted by permission of the author.

Eric Liu, from *The Accidental Asian: Notes of Native Speaker.* Copyright © 1998 by Eric Liu. Reprinted by permission of Random House, Inc.

Julie Matthaei, "Political Economy and Family Policy." Reprinted from Union for Radical Political Economics, *The Imperiled Economy, Book II: Through the Safety Net.* Copyright 1988. By permission of the author.

Frank McCourt. Reprinted with the permission of Scribner, a division of Simon & Schuster from *Angela's Ashes: A Memoir* by Frank McCourt. Copyright © 1996 by Frank McCourt.

Terry McDonnell, "Hunters Are Not Gun Nuts," *The New York Times,* June 3, 1995. Copyright © 1995 by The New York Times Company. Reprinted by permission.

Yona Zeldis McDonough, "Lives: What Barbie Taught Me" as reprinted in January 25, 1998 issue of *The New York Times Magazine.* Reprinted with the permission of Touchstone, a Registered Trademark of Simon & Schuster, Inc. from *The Barbie Chronicles: A Real Doll Turns 40* by Yona Zeldis McDonough. Copyright © 1999 by Yona Zeldis McDonough.

Diane Medved, from *The Case Against Divorce.* Copyright © 1989 by Diane Medved. Used by permission of Donald I. Fine, an imprint of Penguin Putnam Inc.

Pat Mora. "Immigrants" is reprinted with permission from the publisher of *Borders* by Pat Mora (Houston: Arte Publico Press-University of Houston, 1986). Copyright © 1986 by Pat Mora.

Sir Thomas More, from *Utopia: A Norton Critical Edition,* Second Edition by Sir Thomas More, translated by Robert M. Adams. Translation copyright © 1992, 1975 by W. W. Norton & Company, Inc. Reprinted by permission of W. W. Norton & Company, Inc.

Barbara Mujica, "No Comprendo," *The New York Times,* January 3, 1995. Copyright © 1995 by The New York Times Company. Reprinted by permission.

Bharati Mukherjee, "Two Ways to Belong in America," *The New York Times,* September 22, 1996 (op-ed). Copyright © 1996 by The New York Times Company. Reprinted by permission.

David Mura, "How America Unsexes the Asian Male," *The New York Times,* August 22, 1996. Copyright © 1996 by The New York Times Company. Reprinted by permission.

Vladimir Nabokov, from *Speak, Memory.* Copyright © 1989 by the Estate of Vladimir Nabokov. Reprinted by permission of Vintage Books, a division of Random House, Inc.

Gloria Naylor, "A Question of Language," first appearing in *The New York Times Magazine.* Copyright © 1986 by Gloria Naylor. Reprinted by permission of Sterling Lord Literistic, Inc.

Nicholas Negroponte, "Being Asynchronous;" "Bits and Mortar;" and "Good Morning Toaster" from *Being Digital* by Nicholas Negroponte. Copyright © 1995 by Nicholas Negroponte. Reprinted by permission of Alfred A. Knopf, Inc.

The NewsHour with Jim Lehrer. Transcript, "Death Do Us Part" from *The NewsHour with Jim Lehrer,* August 20, 1997. Copyright © 1997 by MacNeil-Lehrer Productions. By permission of MacNeil-Lehrer Productions.

Sharon Olds, "I Go Back to May 1937" from *The Gold Cell* by Sharon Olds. Copyright © 1987 by Sharon Olds. Reprinted by permission of Alfred A. Knopf, Inc.

George Orwell, "Politics and the English Language." Copyright 1946 by Sonia Brownell Orwell and renewed 1974 by Sonia Orwell, reprinted from George Orwell's volume *Shooting an Elephant and Other Essays.* By permission of Harcourt Brace & Company and A.M. Heath & Company Ltd.

Steven Pinker, "The Game of the Name," *The New York Times,* April 5, 1994 (op-ed). Copyright © 1994 by The New York Times Company. Reprinted by permission.

J. H. Plumb, "The Dying Family" from *In the Light of History* by J. H. Plumb. Published by Houghton Mifflin Company and Penguin Books Ltd. Reprinted by permission of Sir John Plumb.

Katha Pollitt, "Why Boys Don't Play With Dolls," *The New York Times Magazine,* October 8, 1995. Copyright © 1995 by The New York Times Company. Reprinted by permission.

Neil Postman, "Order in the Classroom" from *Teaching as a Conserving Activity* by Neil Postman. Copyright © 1979 by Neil Postman. Used by permission of Delacorte Press, a division of Bantam Doubleday Dell Publishing Group, Inc.

"Race," from *The Columbia Encyclopedia,* 5th Edition, edited by Barbara Ann Chernow. Copyright © 1993 by Columbia University Press. Reprinted with the permission of the publisher.

Robert B. Reich, "The Future of Work," *Harper's Magazine,* April 1989. By permission of the author, Robert B. Reich.

Richard Rodriguez, from "Aria" in *Hunger of Memory* by Richard Rodriguez. Reprinted by permission of David R. Godine, Publisher, Inc. Copyright © 1982 by Richard Rodriguez.

Celia E. Rothenberg, "Child of Divorce." By permission of the author, Celia E. Rothenberg.

David Rothenberg, "How the Web Destroys the Quality of Students' Research Papers," *The Chronicle of Higher Education,* August 15, 1997. Reprinted by permission of the author, David Rothenberg.

Edward Rothstein, "Cultural View; Ethnicity and Disney: It's a Whole New Myth," *The New York Times,* December 14, 1997. Copyright © 1997 by The New York Times Company. Reprinted by permission.

Bertrand Russell, "Work" from *The Conquest of Happiness* by Bertrand Russell. Copyright © 1930 by Horace Liveright, Inc., renewed © 1958 by Bertrand Russell. Reprinted by permission of Liveright Publishing Corporation.

Scott Russell Sanders, "The Men We Carry in Our Minds . . . and How They Differ From the Real Lives of Most Men." Copyright © 1984 by Scott Russell Sanders. First appeared in *Milkweed Chronicle,* Spring/Summer 1994; from *The Paradise of Bombs.* Reprinted by permission of the author and the Virginia Kidd Agency, Inc.

May Sarton, "The Rewards of Living a Solitary Life," *The New York Times,* April 6, 1974. Copyright © 1974 by The New York Times Company. Reprinted by permission.

Felice Schwartz, "The 'Mommy Track' Isn't Anti Woman," *The New York Times,* March 22, 1989. Copyright © 1989 by The New York Times Company. Reprinted by permission.

John Simon, "Triumph Over Death," *New York* Magazine, May 17, 1976. Copyright © 1976 PRIMEDIA Magazine Corporation. All rights reserved. Reprinted with the permission of *New York* Magazine.

Peter Singer, "Animal Liberation" from *The New York Review of Books,* April 5, 1973. Copyright © 1973 by Peter Singer. Reprinted by permission of the author.

Stevie Smith, "Not Waving But Drowning" from *Collected Poems of Stevie Smith.* Copyright © 1972 by Stevie Smith. Reprinted by permission of New Directions Publishing Corporation.

Brent Staples, "Editorial Notebook; The Scientific War on the Poor," *The New York Times,* October 28, 1994 (op-ed). Copyright © 1994 by The New York Times Company. Reprinted by permission.

Gloria Steinem, "The Importance of Work" from *Outrageous Acts and Everyday Rebellions* by Gloria Steinem. Copyright © 1983 by Gloria Steinem. © 1984 by East Toledo Productions, Inc. Reprinted by permission of Henry Holt and Company, Inc.

Clifford Stoll, "Invest in Humanware," *The New York Times,* May 19, 1996 (op-ed). Copyright © 1996 by The New York Times Company. Reprinted by permission.

Andrew Sullivan, "Here Comes the Groom: A (Conservative) Case for Gay Marriage," *The New Republic,* August 28, 1989. Reprinted by permission of *The New Republic.* © 1989, The New Republic, Inc.

Amy Tan, "Required Reading." Originally appeared in *The Threepenny Review,* Fall 1996. Copyright © 1996 by Amy Tan. Used by permission of Amy Tan and the Sandra Dijkstra Literary Agency.

Amy Tan, "Snapshot: Lost Lives of Women." Originally appeared in *Life Magazine,* April 1991. Copyright © 1991 by Amy Tan. Text and photo used by permission of Amy Tan and the Sandra Dijkstra Literary Agency.

Deborah Tannen, "The Workings of Conversational Style" from *That's Not What I Meant* by Deborah Tannen. Copyright © 1986 by Deborah Tannen. By permission of William Morrow & Company, Inc.

Carol Tavris, "How Friendship was 'Feminized,'" *The New York Times,* May 28, 1997. Copyright © 1997 by The New York Times Company. Reprinted by permission.

Paul Theroux, "The Male Myth," *The New York Times,* November 27, 1983. Copyright © 1983 by The New York Times Company. Reprinted by permission.

Florence Trefethen, "Points of a Lifelong Triangle: Reflections of an Adoptive Mother" from *The Washington Post,* January 29, 1991. Copyright © 1991 by Florence Trefethen. Reprinted by permission of the author.

Lawrence H. Tribe, "Second Thoughts on Cloning," *The New York Times,* December 5, 1997 (op-ed). Copyright © 1997 by The New York Times Company. Reprinted by permission.

Emily Tsao, "Thoughts of an Oriental Girl," first published in *Newsday,* 1991. Copyright © 1991 by Newsday, Inc. Reprinted with permission.

John Updike, "The Bliss of Golf" from *Golf Dreams* by John Updike. Copyright © 1996 by John Updike. Reprinted by permission of Alfred A. Knopf, Inc.

Ernest van den Haag, "Why Do American Kids Learn So Little?" from *National Review,* August 3, 1992. © 1992 by National Review, Inc., 150 East 35th Street, New York, NY 10016. Reprinted by permission.

Thomas Vinciguerra, "Yes, Virginia, a Thousand Times Yes," *The New York Times,* September 21, 1997. Copyright © 1997 by The New York Times Company. Reprinted by permission.

Kurt Vonnegut, Jr., "Harrison Bergeron," from *Welcome to the Monkey House* by Kurt Vonnegut, Jr. Copyright © 1961 by Kurt Vonnegut, Jr. Used by permission of Delacorte Press/Seymour Lawrence, a division of Random House, Inc.

Robert Wachbroit, "Genetic Encores: The Ethics of Human Cloning," *Report from the Institute for Philosophy and Public Policy,* 17:4 (Fall 1997). By permission of Robert Wachbroit.

Mary P. Walker, "Letter To The Editor" titled "Wal-Mart's Rights" appearing in *The New York Times,* December 11, 1996. By permission of Mary P. Walker.

Eudora Welty, "A Worn Path" from *A Curtain of Green and Other Stories.* Copyright © 1941 and renewed 1969 by Eudora Welty. Reprinted by permission of Harcourt Brace & Company.

Eudora Welty. Reprinted by permission of the publisher from *One Writer's Beginnings* by Eudora Welty. Cambridge, Mass.: Harvard University Press. Copyright © 1983, 1984 by Eudora Welty.

Eudora Welty, "Is Phoenix Jackson's Grandson Really Dead?" from *The Eye of the Story* by Eudora Welty. Copyright © 1978 by Eudora Welty. Reprinted by permission of Random House, Inc.

E. B. White, "Education" from *One Man's Meat* by E. B. White. Copyright 1939 by E. B. White. Copyright renewed. Reprinted by permission of HarperCollins Publishers, Inc.

Merry White, "Japanese Education: How Do They Do It," *The Public Interest,* No. 76, Summer 1984. Copyright © 1984 by National Affairs, Inc. By permission of the author and the publisher.

Margaret A. Whitney, "Playing to Win," *The New York Times Magazine,* July 1, 1998. Copyright © 1998 by The New York Times Company. Reprinted by permission.

James Q. Wilson, "What To Do About Crime," reprinted from *Commentary,* September 1994. Copyright © 1994 by James Q. Wilson. By permission of the publisher and author; all rights reserved.

Max Winkler, "Letter To The Editor of *Commentary,*" *Commentary,* January 1995. Reprinted by permission of the publisher and Max Winkler-Wang.

Marie Winn, "The End of Play" from *Children Without Childhood* by Marie Winn. Copyright © 1981, 1983 by Marie Winn. Reprinted by permission of Pantheon Books, a division of Random House, Inc.

Tobias Wolff, from *This Boy's Life.* Copyright © 1989 by Tobias Wolff. Used by permission of Grove/Atlantic, Inc.

Virginia Woolf, "Professions for Women" from *The Death of the Moth and Other Essays* by Virginia Woolf. Copyright © 1942 by Harcourt Brace & Company and renewed 1970 by Marjorie T. Parsons, Executrix. Reprinted by permission of Harcourt Brace & Company and The Society of Authors as the Literary Representative of the Estate of Virginia Woolf.

Richard Wright, excerpt from *Black Boy.* Copyright © 1937, 1942, 1944, 1945 by Richard Wright. Copyright renewed 1973 by Ellen Wright. Reprinted by permission of HarperCollins Publishers, Inc.

Wu-tsu Fa-Yen, "Zen and the Art of Burglary" from Suzuki, Daisetz, T., ed., *Zen and Japanese Culture,* Bollingen Series 44. Copyright © 1959, renewed 1987, by Princeton University Press. Reprinted by permission of Princeton University Press.

Mitsuye Yamada, "To the Lady" from *Camp Notes and Other Poems.* Copyright © 1992 by Mitsuye Yamada. Reprinted by permission of Rutgers University Press and the author.

Photo Acknowledgments
47 Buffalo Bill Historical Center, Cody, WY.
95 Dorothea Lange/FSA Photo/Library of Congress.
98 (top) Dorothea Lange/© The Dorothea Lange Collection, The Oakland Museum of California, City of Oakland. Gift of Paul S. Taylor.
98 (bottom) Dorothea Lange/FSA Photo/ Library of Congress.
99 (top) © The Dorothea Lange Collection, The Oakland Museum of California. Gift of Paul S. Taylor.
99 (bottom) Dorothea Lange/FSA Photo/ Library of Congress.
100 Dorothea Lange/FSA Photo/Library of Congress.
106 Mariners' Museum, Newport News, Virginia. Gift of George Tucker. Photo by Clifton Guthrie.
112 Marc Chagall. "I and the Village," 1911. Oil on canvas, 63-5/8 X 59-5/8 in. The Museum of Modern Art, New York. Mrs. Simon Guggenheim Fund. Photograph © 2000 The Museum of Modern Art, New York. © 2000 Artists Rights Society (ARS), New York/ADAGP, Paris.
113 J. Scott Applewhite/AP/Wide World Photos.
114 © Robert Doisneau/Rapho/Liaison International.
115 © Robert Doisneau/Rapho/Liaison International.
174 (top) Joanne Leonard/Woodfin Camp.

174 (bottom) R. Chast/© The New Yorker Collection 1990 Roz Chast from cartoonbank.com. All Rights Reserved.

175 Faith Ringgold. "Mrs. Brown and Catherine," 1973. Tapestry, pieced fabric and painted on canvas. 1973 © Faith Ringgold.

176 Acrobat's Family with a Monkey, 1905. By Pablo Picasso. Goteborgs Kunstmuseum.© 2000 Estate of Pablo Picasso/ Artists Rights Society (ARS), New York

260 Dorothea Lange/War Relocation Authority/The National Archives.

261 Marion Post Wolcott/FSA Photo/Library of Congress.

262 Grant Wood. "American Gothic," 1930. Oil on beaverboard, 74.3 X 62.4 cm. Friends of American Art Collection. All rights reserved by The Art Institute of Chicago and VAGA, New York, NY (1930.934).

263 © Gordon Parks.

354 Catherine Wagner/Museum of Fine Arts, Houston. Target Collection of American Photography. © Catherine Wagner.

355 Ron James.

356 "St. Jerome Studying in His Cell," c. 1640. By Georges de la Tour. Photo: Bulloz.

357 Gary Trudeau/Doonesbury © 1985 G. B. Trudeau. Reprinted with permission of Universal Press Syndicate. All rights reserved.

466 Dorothea Lange/FSA Photo/Library of Congress.

467 W. Eugene Smith/Life Magazine © Time, Inc.

468 Florida State Archives.

468 © Helen Levitt.

483 Mariners' Museum, Newport News, Virginia.

550 "Born Kicking," Graffiti on Billboard, London 1983 © Jill Posener.

551 Mary Cassatt. "The Letter," c. 1890. Drypoint and aquatint on cream laid paper, 34.5 X 21.1 cm. The Metropolitan Museum of Art, New York. All rights reserved.

552 Fair Street Pictures.

553 "Just what is it that makes today's homes so different and appealing?," 1956. Photograph by Richard Hamilton. Collection G. F. Zundel, Kunsthalle Tübingen.

622 (top) "The Checkered House." 1943. By Grandma Moses © 1982, Grandma Moses Properties Co., New York. Courtesy Collection IBM Corporation, Armonk, New York.

622 (bottom) "The Checkered House is old. . . ." Hand-written note from "Grandma Moses: American Primitive" (1946) edited by Otto Kallir.

623 Arnold Newman.

624 Henri Cartier-Bresson/Magnum Photos.

625 Jack Vartoogian.

632 Ansel Adams Publishing RightsTrust.

678 "The Third of May, 1808." 1814. By Francisco de Goya. Museo del Prado, Madrid/Erich Lessing/Art Resource, NY.

679 Bernie Boston.

680 Henri Cartier-Bresson/Magnum Photos.

681 "The Problem We all Live With," 1964. By Norman Rockwell. Norman Rockwell Family Trust.

742 National Maritime Museum, Greenwich, London.

743 "Day of Wrath." Albrecht Durer. New York Public Library, General Research Division. Astor, Lenox and Tilden Foundations.

744 "Visionary City," 1908. By William Robinson Leigh. Culver Pictures.

745 © Remi Benali and Stephen Ferry/ Liaison Agency.

INDEX